P9-BZX-471

PATROLOGY

BERTHOLD ALTANER

PATROLOGY

Translated by

HILDA C. GRAEF
One-Time Senior Assistant
Oxford Lexicon of Patristic Greek

HERDER AND HERDER

HERDER AND HERDER NEW YORK
232 Madison Avenue, New York, N. Y. 10016

Original edition "Patrologie", Herder, Freiburg

2nd Edition, 1961

Translations in French, Spanish, Hungarian, and Italian have already appeared

Nihil Obstat: Joannes M. T. Barton, S.T.D., L.S.S.
Censor deputatus
Imprimatur: E. Morrogh Bernard, Vic. Gen.
Westmonasterii, die 9a Novembris, 1959

The Nihil Obstat and the Imprimatur are a declaration that a book or pamphlet is considered to be free from doctrinal or moral error.
It is not implied that those who have granted the Nihil Obstat and Imprimatur agree with the contents, opinions or statements expressed.

Library of Congress Catalog Card Number: 58-5869

Made and printed in West Germany by Herder

Contents

Introduction

Part One

Christian Literature from the End of the First to the Beginning of the Fourth Century

CHAPTER ONE

BETWEEN BIBLE AND PATRISTIC WRITINGS, BOOKS OF THE CHRISTIAN COMMUNITY, POPULAR BOOKS, ETC.

CHAPTER TWO

The Apostolic Fathers

CHAPTER THREE

The Greek Apologists of the Second Century

CHAPTER FOUR

The Anti-Heretical Literature of the Second Century

CHAPTER FIVE

The Christian Literature of the Third Century (to the Council of Nicaea)

A. The Western Authors of the Third Century

CHAPTER ONE

Eastern Authors

A. Alexandrians and Egyptians

B. Theologians of Asia Minor

C. Antiochenes and Syrians

D. The Syriac and Armenian Literature

CHAPTER TWO

The Great Fathers and Ecclesiastical Authors of the West

Part Three

The End of the Patristic Period of Literature

CHAPTER ONE

Latin Authors

CHAPTER TWO

Greek Authors

Abbreviations

I. Periodicals, Academy Publications, Lexica and Individual Terms

The books of the Bible are cited by the customary abbreviations. If these are combined with the name of an ecclesiastical author they denote either homilies or commentaries on the relevant books, e.g. Bas. Ps. 14: St. Basil, homily on Psalm 14. Other patristic writings are cited by abbreviated titles.

AB	Analecta Bollandiana, Brussels.
AbhB	Abhandlungen der Preussischen Akademie der Wissenschaften, Phil.-hist. Klasse, Berlin.
AbhMn	Bayerische Akademie der Wissenschaften, Abhandlungen der philos.-philol.-hist. Klasse, Munich.
AC	Doelger, F. J., Antike und Christentum, 6 vols., 1929 ff.
ACl	Antiquité classique, Louvain.
Aeg	Aegyptus, Rivista italiana di Egittologia, Milan.
Aev	Aevum, Rassegna di scienze storiche-linguistiche-filologiche, Milan.
AGP	Archiv fuer Geschichte der Philosophie, Berlin.
AHD	Archives d'histoire doctrinale et littéraire, Paris.
AIP	Annuaire de l'Institut de philologie et d'histoire orientales et slaves, Paris.
AJP	American Journal of Philology, Baltimore.
AKK	Archiv fuer katholisches Kirchenrecht.
AL	Archivum latinitatis medii aevi (Bulletin Du Cange), Paris.
Al-M	Al-Machriq, Beirut.
ALW	Archiv fuer Liturgiewissenschaft, Regensburg.
Ang	Angelicum, Rome.
Ant	Antonianum, Rome.
AnT	L'Année théologique augustinienne, Lormy-Paris.
AP	Archives de Philosophie, Paris.
AR	Archivum Romanicum, Florence.
ARW	Archiv fuer Religionswissenschaft, Berlin and Leipzig.
ASS	Acta Sanctorum, ed. Bollandists.
AST	Analecta sacra Tarraconensia, Ba.
ATR	Anglican Theological Review, New York.
Aug	Augustiniana, Louvain 1951 f.

B	Bishop.
b.	born.
Baz	Bazmavep, Venezia (Mechitharists).
BBI	Bulletin of the Byzantine Institute, Boston.
BBR	Bulletin de l'Institut historique belge de Rome.
Bess	Bessarione, Rome.
BFC	Bolletino di Filologia classica, Turin.
BGDS	Beitraege zur Geschichte der deutschen Sprache.
Bi	Biblica, Rome.
BiNJ	Bijdragen van de Philosophische en Theologische Faculteiten der Nederlandsche Jezuiten, 1938 ff.
BiZ	Biblische Zeitschrift, Paderborn.
BJ	Bursians Jahresbericht ueber die Fortschritte der klassischen Altertums-Wissenschaft, Leipzig.
BJR	Bulletin of John Ryland's Library, Manchester.
BLE	Bulletin de littérature ecclésiastique, Toulouse.
BM	Benediktinische Monatschrift, Beuron.
BNJ	Byzantinisch-neugriechische Jahrbuecher, Athens.
BoS	Bogoslovska Smotra, Zagreb.
BoZ	Bonner Zeitschrift fuer Theologie und Seelsorge, Duesseldorf.
BTAM	Bulletin de théologie ancienne et médiévale (suppl. de RTA), Louvain.
BullAcad-BelgClLett	Académie Royale de Belgique. Bulletin de la Classe des lettres et des sciences morales et politiques.
BV	Bogoslovni Vestnik, Ljubljana.
Byz	Byzantion, P-Liège.
BZ	Byzantinische Zeitschrift, Munich.
CBQ	Catholic Biblical Quarterly, W 1939 ff.
CC	Civiltà Cattolica, Rome.
CD	La Ciudad de Dios, Madrid.
cent.	century.
CH	Church History, Chicago.
CHR	Catholic Historical Review, Washington.
CJ	Classical Journal, Chicago.
CP	Classical Philology.
CQ	Classical Quarterly, London-Oxford.
CQR	Church Quarterly Review, London.
CR	Classical Review, London.
CRI	Comptes rendus de l'Académie des Inscriptions et Belles-Lettres, Paris.
CT	Collectanea Theologica, Lvov.
d.	died.
DA	Dictionnaire d'Apologétique, Paris.
DAL	Dictionnaire d'Archéologie chrétienne et de Liturgie, Paris.

DB	Dictionnaire de la Bible, Paris.
DBSuppl I	Devreesse, R., Chaînes exégétiques grecques.
DH	History of Dogma.
DHG	Dictionnaire d'Histoire et de Géographie ecclésiastiques, Paris.
Did	Didaskaleion, Turin.
Diss.	thesis (dissertation); Diss. typ. = thesis only in typescript.
DLZ	Deutsche Literaturzeitung, Leipzig.
DOP	Dumbarton Oaks Papers, Cambridge (Mass.).
DR	Downside Review.
DS	Dictionnaire de Spiritualité, Paris.
DSO	Dominican Studies, Oxford.
DT	Divus Thomas, Fribourg.
DTC	Dictionnaire de théologie catholique, Paris.
DTP	Divus Thomas, Piacenza.
E	'Ελπίς, Warsaw.
EB	Études Byzantines, 1943–5.
ed.	edited.
EE	Estudios eclesiásticos, Madrid.
EEBS	'Επετηρὶς τῆς 'Εταιρείας Βυζαντινῶν Σπουδῶν, At.
EH	Ecclesiastical history.
EL	Ephemerides liturgicae, Rome.
EO	Échos d'Orient, Paris.
Eos	Eos. Commentarii societatis philologicae Polonorum, Leopoli.
EPH	'Εκκλησιαστικὸς, φάρος, Alexandria.
Er	Eranos, Gotenburg.
ET	Expository Times, Edinburgh.
ETL	Ephemerides theologicae Lovanienses, Louvain.
F	Fascicule.
Folia	Folia, Studies in the Christian Perpetuation of the Classics.
FS	Franciscan Studies, St. Bonaventura, New York.
GA	Goettingische Gelehrte Anzeigen, Goettingen.
GAb	Abhandlungen der Gesellschaft der Wissenschaften zu Goettingen.
Gn	Gnomon, Berlin-Wiesbaden.
GN	Nachrichten von der Gesellschaft der Wissenschaften zu Goettingen. Phil.-hist.-Klasse.
Gr	Gregorianum, Rome.
GTT	Gereformeerd Theologisch Tijdschrift, Aalten.
HA	Handes Amsorya, Monatsschrift fuer die armenische Philologie, Washington.
Ha	Harmathena. A Series of Papers on Literature, Science, and Philosophy, Dublin-London.
Hel	Helmántica, Salamanca.

Her	Hermes, Berlin.
HJ	Hibbert Journal, London.
HJB	Historisches Jahrbuch der Goerresgesellschaft, Munich-Cologne.
Ho	Hochland, Munich.
HTR	Harvard Theological Review, Cambridge (Mass.).
HVS	Historische Vierteljahrschrift, Dresden.
HZ	Historische Zeitschrift.
Id.	Idem.
IER	Irish Ecclesiastical Record, Dublin.
IKZ	Internationale kirchliche Zeitschrift, Bern.
Ir	Irénikon, Amay.
ITQ	Irish Theological Quarterly, Maynooth.
JA	Journal Asiatique, Paris.
Jb	Yearbook.
JBL	Journal of Biblical Literature, Boston-New-Haven.
JDAI	Jahrbuch des Deutschen Archaeologischen Instituts, Berlin.
JEH	Journal of Ecclesiastical History, London.
JL	Jahrbuch fuer Liturgiewissenschaft, Muenster.
JQR	Jewish Quarterly Review, Philadelphia.
JR	Journal of Religion, Chicago.
JSOR	Journal of the Society of Oriental Research, Chicago.
JTS	Journal of Theological Studies, London.
KA	Kyrkohistorisk Aarskrift, Stockholm.
Lat	Latomus, Revue d'études latines, Brussels.
Lit.	Literature.
LJ	Liturgisches Jahrbuch, Regensburg.
LTK	Lexikon fuer Theologie und Kirche, Freiburg.
MA	Middle Ages.
MAH	Mélanges d'Archéologie et d'Histoire, Paris.
Mar	Marianum, Rome.
MC	Mondo classico.
med.	medieval.
Mg.	Monograph.
MGWJ	Monatsschrift fuer Geschichte und Wissenschaft des Judentums, Breslau.
MiscSLCA	Miscellanea di studi di litteratura cristiana antica, Catania.
Mn	Mnemosyne, Bibliotheca philologica Batavorum, Leipzig.
MS	Manuscript; MSS = Manuscripts.
MSR	Mélanges de science religieuse, Lille, 1944ff.
MTZ	Muenchener Theologische Zeitschrift, Munich 1950ff.
Mu	Le Muséon, Louvain.

NA	Neues Archiv der Gesellschaft fuer aeltere deutsche Geschichtskunde, Berlin.
NAKG	Nederlandsch Archief voor Kerkgeschiedenis, Haag.
NClio	La Nouvelle Clio, Brussels.
NDid	Nuovo Didaskaleion, Catania.
NewSch	New Scholasticism.
NKZ	Neue kirchliche Zeitschrift, L.
NRT	Nouvelle Revue Théologique, Tournai.
NS	Νέα Σιών, Jerusalem.
NT	New Testament.
NTT	Nieuw Theologisch Tijdschrift, Haarlem.
OC	Oriens Christianus, Wiesbaden.
OCP	Orientalia christiana periodica, Rome.
OCR	Orientalia christiana, Rome.
OLZ	Orientalische Literaturzeitung, Leipzig.
Or	Orientalia, Rome.
Orph	Orpheus. Rivista di umanità classica e cristiana, Catania.
OrSyr	L'Orient syrien, 1956 ff.
OstkSt	Ostkirchliche Studien, Würzburg 1952 ff.
OT	Old Testament.
ParPass	La Parola del Passato. Rivista di studi classici, Naples 1946 ff.
PC	Paraula Christiana, Barcelona.
Phil	Philologus, Leipzig.
PJB	Philosophisches Jahrbuch der Goerresgesellschaft, Fulda.
POC	Proche-Orient chrétien, 1951 ff.
PW	Philologische Wochenschrift, Leipzig.
PWK	Pauly-Wissowa-Krill, Realencyklopaedie der klassischen Altertumswissenschaft, Stuttgart.
QLP	Questions liturgiques et paroissiales, Louvain.
RAC	Rivista di Archeologia Cristiana, Rome.
RACh	Reallexikon fuer Antike und Christentum, ed. T. Klauser, Stuttgart.
RAL	Rendiconti della Reale Accademia nazionale dei Lincei, Classe di scienze mor., stor. e filol., Rome.
RAM	Revue d'ascétique et de mystique, Toulouse.
RB	Revue biblique, Paris.
RBn	Revue Bénédictine (Bulletin), Maredsous.
RBP	Revue belge de philologie et d'histoire, Brussels.
RC	Religión y Cultura, Madrid.
RCC	Revue des cours et conférences, Paris.
RDC	Revue de droit canonique, Strasbourg 1951 ff.
RE	Realencyklopaedie fuer protestantische Theologie und Kirche,[3] ed. A. Hauck, Leipzig.
REA	Revue des études arméniennes, Paris.

REAug	Revue des études Augustiniennes, Paris.
REB	Revue des études Byzantines, 1946ff.
REG	Revue des études grecques, Paris.
REL	Revue des études latines, Paris.
Rel	Religio, ed E. Buonaiuti, Rome.
RET	Revista Española de Teología, Madrid 1941ff.
RevEA	Revue des études anciennes, Bordeaux.
RevR	Review of Religion, New York.
RevSR	Revue des sciences religieuses, Paris.
RF	Razón y Fe, Madrid.
RFC	Rivista di filologia e d'istruzione classica, Turin.
RFE	Revista de filología española, Madrid.
RFN	Rivista di filosofia neoscolastica, Milan.
RGG	Religion in Geschichte und Gegenwart, ed. Gunkel-Zscharnack, T [2]1927ff.
RH	Revue historique, Paris.
RHE	Revue d'histoire ecclésiastique, Louvain.
RHEF	Revue d'histoire de l'Église de France, Paris.
RHL	Revue d'histoire et de littérature religieuses, Paris.
RHPR	Revue d'histoire et de philosophie religieuses, Strasbourg.
RHR	Revue de l'histoire des religions, Paris.
RLM	Revue liturgique et monastique, Maredsous-Mont César-St. André.
RM	Rheinisches Museum fuer Philologie, Frankfurt a. M.
RML	Revue du moyen âge latin, 1945ff.
ROC	Revue de l'Orient chrétien, Paris.
RP	Revue de philologie, Paris.
RPA	Revue pratique d'apologétique, Paris.
RQ	Roemische Quartalschrift, Freiburg.
RR	Ricerche religiose, Rome.
RSCI	Rivista di storia della Chiesa in Italia, Rome 1947ff.
RSPT	Revue des sciences philosophiques et théologiques, Paris.
RSR	Recherches de science religieuse, Paris.
RStR	Ricerche di storia religiosa, Rome 1954ff.
RT	Revue Thomiste, Paris.
RTA	Recherches de théologie ancienne et médiévale, Abbaye de Mont César, Louvain.
RTr	Riv. Trimestr. di Studi filosof. e relig., Perugia.
RUO	Revue de l'Université d'Ottawa.

SbB	Sitzungsberichte der Preussischen Akademie der Wissenschaften, Phil.-hist. Klasse, Berlin.
SbHei	Sitzungsberichte der Heidelberger Akademie der Wissenschaften, Phil.-hist. Klasse.
SbMn	Sitzungsberichte der Bayerischen Akademie der Wissenschaften, Philos.-philol.-hist. Klasse, Munich.

SbW	Sitzungsberichte der Wiener Akademie der Wissenschaften, Phil.-hist. Klasse.
SC	Scuola Cattolica, Milan.
Sc	Scriptorium, Brussels 1946ff.
SCh	Sources Chrétiennes, Paris.
Sch	Scholastik, Freiburg.
SE	Sacris Erudiri, Steenbrugge 1948ff.
SIF	Studi italiani di filologia classica, Florence.
SM	Studien und Mitteilungen zur Geschichte des Benediktinerordens und seiner Zweige, Munich.
SO	Symbolae, Osloenses, Oslo.
So	Sophia, Padua.
Sp	Speculum, Cambridge (Mass.).
ST	Studi e Testi, Rome.
StAns	Studia Anselmiana, Philosophica et Theologica, Rome.
StBNeoell	Studi Bizantini a Neoellenici, 1947ff.
StC	Studia Catholica, Naples.
StPat	Studia Patavina, 1954ff.
Θ	Θεολογία, Athens.
TB	Theologische Blaetter, Leipzig.
TG	Theologie und Glaube, Paris.
Th	Theology, Journal of Historic Christianity, London.
TheolV	Theologia Viatorum.
TJB	Theologische Jahrbuecher, ed. Barnikol.
TLB	Theologisches Literaturblatt, Leipzig.
TLZ	Theologische Literaturzeitung, Leipzig.
TP	Transactions and Proceedings of the American Philolog. Association, Boston (Mass.).
TQ	Theologische Quartalschrift, Stuttgart.
TR	Theologische Revue, Muenster.
tr.	translated, translation(s).
Trad	Traditio, NY 1943ff.
TrTZ	Trierer Theologische Zeitschrift.
TS	Texts and Studies.
TSK	Theologische Studien und Kritiken, Gotha.
TSW	Theological Studies, Woodstock (Madison), 1940ff.
TU	Texte und Untersuchungen, ed. Gebhardt-Harnack-Schmidt, Leipzig-Berlin.
TZ	Theologische Zeitschrift, Basle 1945ff.
VC	Vigiliae Christianae, Amsterdam 1947ff.
VD	Verbum Domini, Rome.
VizVrem	Vizantijskij Vremennik, 1947ff.
VS	Vie spirituelle, Paris.

WJB	Wuerzburger Jahrbuch fuer klassische Altertumswissenschaft, 1947 ff.
WS	Woodbrooke Studies, Manchester.
WSt	Wiener Studien, Zeitschrift fuer klassische Philologie, Vienna.
ZAM	Zeitschrift fuer Aszese und Mystik, Innsbruck.
ZAW	Zeitschrift fuer alttestamentliche Wissenschaft, Giessen.
ZBW	Zentralblatt fuer Bibliothekswissenschaft, Leipzig.
ZDADL	Zeitschrift fuer deutsches Altertum und deutsche Literatur, Wiesbaden.
ZKG	Zeitschrift fuer Kirchengeschichte, Stuttgart.
ZKT	Zeitschrift fuer katholische Theologie, Innsbruck.
ZMW	Zeitschrift fuer Missionswissenschaft, Muenster.
ZMR	Zeitschrift fuer Missions- und Religionswissenschaft, Muenster.
ZNTW	Zeitschrift fuer neutestamentliche Wissenschaft und die Kunde der aelteren Kirche, Giessen-Berlin.
ZRGG	Zeitschrift fuer Religions- und Geistesgeschichte, Marburg, 1948 ff.
ZS	Zeitschrift fuer Semitistik und verwandte Gebiete, Leipzig.
ZSG	Zeitschrift der Savigny-Stiftung für Rechtsgeschichte, Germanistische Abteilung, Weimar.
ZSK	Zeitschrift der Savigny-Stiftung fuer Rechtsgeschichte, Kanonistische Abteilung, Weimar.
ZSR	Zeitschrift der Savigny-Stiftung fuer Rechtsgeschichte, Romanistische Abteilung, Weimar.
ZTK	Zeitschrift fuer Theologie und Kirche, Tuebingen.

II. Collected and Individual Works

ACW	*Ancient Christian Writers,* ed. Quasten-Plumpe, Westminster (Md), 1946ff.
Amand, Fatalisme 1945	D. Amand de Mendieta, *Fatalisme et liberté dans l'antiquité grecque. Recherches sur la survivance de l'argumentation morale antifataliste de Carnéade chez les philosophes grecs et les théologiens chrét. des 4 premiers siècles,* Lou 1945.
AugMag	Augustinus Magister, *Congrès international Augustinien, Paris 21–24 septembre 1954.* Vols. 1 and 2 Communications, vol. 3 Actes, P 1954–5.
Bardy, G.,	*La vie spirituelle d'après les Pères des trois premiers siècles,* 1935.
Bauer, W.,	*Rechtglaeubigkeit und Ketzerei im aeltesten Christentum,* 1934.
Baumstark, A.,	*Geschichte der syrischen Literatur,* 1922.
BKV	*Bibliothek der Kirchenvaeter,* ed. Reithmayr-Thalhofer, 1860ff.
BKV^2	*Bibliothek der Kirchenvaeter,* ed. Bardenhewer-Wyman-Schermann-Martin-Zellinger, 1911ff.
CCL	*Corpus Christianorum, series Latina,* Turnholti (Belgium) 1935ff.
ClavisPL	E. Dekkers-A. Gaar, *Clavis Patrum Latinorum* = SE 3, 1951.
Courcelle, P.,	*Les lettres grecques en Occident. De Macrobe à Cassiodore,* P 1948.
CSCO	*Corpus scriptorum christianorum orientalium,* P.
CSEL	*Corpus scriptorum ecclesiasticorum latinorum,* V.
De Ghellinck, J.,	*Le mouvement théologique du XIIme siècle,* Bru-P ^{2}1948.
De Labriolle, P.	*La réaction païenne. Étude sur la polémique antichrétienne du Ier au VIme siècle,* 1934.
Diekamp, AP	F. Diekamp, *Analecta Patristica,* R 1938.
DP	Pisciculi, *Festschrift F. J. Doelger,* 1939.
EA	*Enchiridion asceticum,* coll. Rouet de Journel et Dutilleul, ^{2}1947.
Edsman, C.-M.,	*Le baptême de feu,* L-Mp 1940.
Égl	*L'Église et les Églises, 1054–1954,* Chevetogne, 1954.
EH	*Enchiridion fontium historiae ecclesiasticae antiquae,* coll. C. Kirch, 1941.
Ehrhard, A.,	*Die Kirche der Maertyrer,* 1932.
Ellspermann 1949	G. L. Ellspermann, *The Attitude of the Early Christian Writers toward Pagan Literature and Learning,* W 1949.
Emonds 1941	N. Emonds, Zweite Auflage im Altertum, 1941.
EP	*Enchiridion Patristicum,* coll. M. J. Rouët de Journel, ^{18}1953.
ES	*Enchiridion Symbolorum,* coll. Denzinger-C. Rahner, ^{30}1955.
FathCh	*Fathers of the Church,* ed. Roy J. Deferrari and others, NY 1947.
Festschr. Dold	*Colligere Fragmenta, Festschrift A. Dold,* Beuron 1952.
Fischer 1947	J. Fischer, *Die Voelkerwanderung im Urteil der zeitgenoessischen*

	kirchlichen Schriftsteller Galliens unter Einbeziehung des heiligen Augustinus, Hei 1947.
FP	*Florilegium Patristicum,* ed. Geyer-Zellinger.
García Villada	García Villada, Z., *Historia ecclesiástica de España,* 2 vols., Ma 1929–3.
GCS	*Griechische christliche Schriftsteller,* ed. by the Kirchenvaeter-Kommission der Preussischen Akademie, Berlin.
Gedaechtnisschr. Casel	*Vom christlichen Mysterium.* Casel Gedaechtnisschrift, Duesseldorf 1951.
Giesecke, H. E.,	*Die Ostgermanen und der Arianismus,* Mn 1939.
Graf	G. Graf, *Geschichte der christlichen arabischen Literatur,* Rome 1, 1944.
Grillmeier-Bacht	A. Grillmeier and H. Bacht, *Das Konzil von Chalkedon, Geschichte und Gegenwart,* 3 vols., Wuerzburg 1951-4.
Haase, F.,	*Altchristliche Kirchengeschichte nach orientalischen Quellen,* 1925.
Hennecke, E.,	*Neutestamentliche Apokryphen,* [2]1924.
Hoh, J.,	*Die kirchliche Busse im 2. Jahrhundert,* 1932.
Honigmann	E. Honigmann, *Patristic Studies,* (ST 173), 1953.
KGAbh	*Kirchengeschichtliche Abhandlungen,* ed. M. Sdralek, Br.
KlT	*Kleine Texte fuer Vorlesungen und Uebungen,* ed. H. Lietzmann, Berlin.
Krapp 1950	H. Krapp, *Probleme altchristlicher Anthropologie,* G 1950.
Kroll, J.,	*Gott und Hoelle. Der Mythos vom Descensuskampfe,* 1932.
Krueger 1933	G. Krueger, *A Decade of Research in Early Christian Literature 1921–30,* in HTR 1933, 173/321.
Krueger, G.,	*Die christliche Literatur,* in M. Schanz, *Geschichte der roemischen Literatur,* 3. pt. 1922 and 4. pt. 2. half Mn 1920.
Laurentin 1953	R. Laurentin, *Court traité de théologie mariale,* P 1953.
Loofs, F.,	*Theophilus von Antiochien Adv. Marcionem und die anderen theol. Quellen bei Irenaeus,* 1930.
Loewenich, W. v.,	*Das Johannesverstaendnis des 2. Jahrhunderts,* 1932.
Ludwig 1952	J. Ludwig, *Die Primatsworte Mt. 16, 18. 19 in der altkirchlichen Exegese,* 1952.
Madoz 1951	J. Madoz, *Segundo decenio de estudios sobre patrística Española 1941–1950,* Madrid 1951.
Mansi, J. D.	*Sacrorum Conciliorum nova et amplissima collectio,* 1759 ff.
Mél. Cavallera	*Mélanges offerts au R. P. F. Cavallera,* Toulouse 1948.
Mél. De Ghellinck	*Mélanges J. de Ghellinck* (Museum Lessianum sect. hist. No. 13), 1951.
Mem. E. Loh.	*In memoriam E. Lohmeyer,* 1951.
Mercati, OM	G. Mercati, *Opere minore,* 4 vols. (ST 76–79), 1937.
Mersch, E.,	*Le corps mystique du Christ. Études de théologie historique,* 2 vols., Louvain [2]1936.
MG	Migne, *Patrologia series graeca.*
MGSS	*Monumenta Germaniae historica, Scriptores.*
Misc.A.	*Miscellanea Agostiniana,* 2 vols., Rome 1930 f.

Misc.Isid.	*Miscellanea Isidoriana,* Rome 1936.
Misc.Mercati	*Miscellanea Giovanni Mercati,* 6 vols. (ST 121–126), 1946.
Misc.Mohlberg	*Miscellanea liturgica L. C. Mohlberg I,* Rome 1948.
Misc.Ubach	*Miscellanea Biblica B. Ubach,* Montserat 1953 (1954).
ML	Migne, *Patrologia series latina.*
Oliger, L.,	*De expositione regulae Fr. Minorum auctore Angelo Clareno,* Quarracchi 1912.
Opitz, H. G.,	*Untersuchungen zur Ueberlieferung der Schriften des Athanasius,* 1935.
Opitz, AW	H. G. Opitz, *Athanasius' Werke,* 1934 ff.
Plumpe 1946	J. C. Plumpe, *Mater Ecclesia, an Inquiry into the Concept of the Church as Mother in Early Christianity,* Washington 1946.
PO	*Patrologia Orientalis,* ed. Graffin-Nau, Paris.
Poschmann, Poenit.	B. Poschmann, *Poenitentia secunda,* Bonn 1940.
Preuschen, E.,	*Antilegomena,* [2]1905.
Quasten	J. Quasten, *Patrology,* vols. 1 and 2, Utrecht 1950–3.
RAl	Rauschen-Altaner, *Patrologie,* 1931.
Reuß, J.,	*Matthaeus-, Markus- und Johannes-Katenen,* Mr 1941.
Reuss, J. (TU 61)	*Matthaeus-Kommentare aus der griech. Kirche,* B 1956.
Riedinger, 1956	*Die Heilige Schrift im Kampfe der griech. Kirche gegen die Astrologie v. Origenes bis Joh. Damaskos,* J 1956.
Rivière, J.,	*Le dogme de la rédemption. Études critiques et doctrinales,* Lou 1931.
Routh, M. J.,	*Reliquiae sacrae,* Oxford [2]1846 ff.
Rucker, I.,	*Florilegium Edessenum anonymum,* 1933 (SbMn 1933 5th part).
SACO	Schwartz, E., *Acta Conciliorum oecumenicorum,* B.
SCh	*Sources chrétiennes,* dir. par H. de Lubac et J. Daniélou, 1947 ff.
Schiwietz, St.,	*Das morgenlaendische Moenchtum III,* 1938.
Severus	Severus Antiochenus, *Liber contra impium Grammaticum,* ed. J. Lebon, 3 vols., 1929–38 (CSCO, SS Syri 4–6), Versio latina.
Siegmund 1948	A. Siegmund, *Die Ueberlieferung der griechischen christlichen Literatur in der lateinischen Kirche bis zum 12. Jahrhundert,* Munich 1949.
Souter, A.,	*The Earliest Latin Commentaries on the Epistles of St. Paul,* 1927.
SPCK	*Society for Promoting Christian Knowledge,* London.
Staab, K.,	*Pauluskommentare aus der griechischen Kirche,* 1933.
Staehlin, O.,	*Die altchristliche griechische Literatur,* 1924.
Stelzenberger, J.,	*Die Beziehungen der fruehchristlichen Sittenlehre zur Ethik der Stoa,* 1933.
StFriend	*Studies in Honor of M. A. Friend,* Pr 1955.
Streeter, H.,	*The Primitive Church Studied with Special Reference to the Origins of the Christian Ministry,* 1930.
StU	*Studi dedicati alla memoria di Paolo Ubaldi,* Milan 1937.
Vaccari	A. Vaccari, *Scritti di erudizione e di filologia I. Filologia biblica e patristica,* Rome 1952.
Viller, M. and Rahner, K.	*Aszese und Mystik in der Vaeterzeit,* Freiburg 1939.

III. Place Names

A	Amsterdam	Mn	Munich
At	Athens	Mr	Muenster
B	Berlin	Mund	Mundelein (Ill.)
Ba	Barcelona	N	Nijmegen
Br	Breslau	Na	Naples
Bru	Brussels	NY	New York
C	Cambridge	O	Oxford
Ca	Catania	P	Paris
Ch	Chicago	Pa	Paderborn
E	Escorial	Ph	Philadelphia
Fl	Florence	Pi	Pinneberg
Fr	Freiburg (Germany)	Pr	Princeton
Frib	Fribourg (Switzerland)	R	Rome
G	Guetersloh	Rb	Regensburg
Gie	Giessen	St	Stuttgart
Go	Goettingen	Str	Strasbourg
H	Hamburg	T	Tuebingen
Hei	Heidelberg	Th	Thessalonica
Hel	Helsingfors	Tr	Treves
I	Innsbruck	Tu	Turin
K	Kempten	Up	Upsala
L	Leipzig	Ut	Utrecht
Ley	Leyden	V	Vienna
Lo	London	W	Washington
Lou	Louvain	War	Warsaw
Ma	Madrid	Wu	Wuerzburg
Mi	Milan	Zu	Zurich

Preface

The present English translation of my *Patrologie* is based on the completely revised fifth German edition published in 1958. Since my last revision in 1949 of a work originally published in German in 1938, I have noted, on the basis of the literature accessible to me and the bibliographies published in the standard periodicals concerned with patrology, approximately four thousand new publications. The total number of relevant contributions is likely to be much higher and provides impressive evidence for the growing and universal interest in the Fathers and their writings. Confronted by such a rich harvest, I naturally had to limit my selection rigorously and to omit a large number of bibliographical references given in earlier German editions so as to be able to include some three thousand new items. In making these changes I was anxious that the work should not become a mere bibliography of patrology. Conscious as I am of many omissions, I trust that the extensive bibliographical notes will nonetheless be considered useful aids by scholars and students.

I have tried to assemble the bibliographical references according to their subject matter, a method which has also typographical advantages. As far as this was possible I have indicated the results of researches and the authors' points of view. The latest results of international researches have been included in so far as the framework of this one-volume work, and consideration for the different interests of those likely to use it, allowed.

Lack of space has prevented me from following the method of citation normally adopted in works of scholarship, but I trust that readers will be able to trace with ease those independent works and essays published in periodical literature which they may be looking for, despite the brevity and irregularity of their citation. The bibliographical notes beginning on page 17 offer a survey of the large number of general works, arranged according to subject matter. This literature has been divided into twenty-eight sections. I have refrained from citing again the books mentioned here under the various authors and their works.

Berthold Altaner, Wuerzburg

Preface to the Second Edition

I was asked early in 1959 by Professor Altaner to continue his *Patrology*. For the purpose of this edition, certain corrections have been made in the text and the most recent titles have been added to the bibliographies as far as this was possible without radical rearrangement of the text. A more extensive revision of the book did not seem necessary only a year after publication of the first English edition.

Meanwhile, there has been encouraging progress in the publication of the papyri of Chenoboskion and of the Christian texts of the Bodmer Papyri. However, only when these editorial labours will have been brought to some conclusion and evaluated by scholars, will it be possible to revise the relevant chapters of the *Patrology* so as not to be liable to be superceded at once. While thus confining ourselves to the most important emendations, we have at least the advantage of being able to produce this new edition without delay and at the same price.

Alfred Stuiber, Bonn

INTRODUCTION

§ 1. CONCEPT AND VALUE OF PATROLOGY

PATROLOGY is a science that serves the knowledge of God arising from faith; hence it is a branch of theology. It apprehends as a unity all those writers of Christian antiquity whom the Catholic Church calls to bear witness to her doctrine, treating them according to the methodical principles of the science of history. Even though the notion of "Fathers-witnesses" contained in it is determined by the tradition of the Church, that is, by theological and dogmatic reasons, not by literary considerations, in actual fact patrology is identical with the history of ancient Christian literature as regards both subject matter and time.

The term patrology was first used by the Lutheran theologian Johannes Gerhard (d. 1637), whose *Patrologia* appeared in 1653. Until approximately the nineteenth century this meant the history of ecclesiastical and theological literature down to the Middle Ages and even to the Reformation. But ever since the era following the Christianization of the Greco-Roman world had come to be regarded as a separate period, the sphere of patrology was gradually restricted to this time.

Following the practice of St. Jerome, patrology must include in its scope not only the old Christian literary history but also the works of writers outside the Church. This is necessary, because there is a close relationship between the writings of the Fathers and those of the heretical authors which is illuminating from the cultural and literary points of view, but more especially because, within the framework of the history of theology and dogmatics, the Fathers were often greatly stimulated by their opponents, whose influence played a considerable part in solving their problems.

The less personal old Christian documents such as liturgical texts, Acts of Councils and Martyrs, Lives of the Saints, Monastic Rules, Creeds, Inscriptions and non-literary papyri belong only indirectly to the sphere of patrology. The sources methodically investigated by the patrologist furnish the Catholic dogmatic theologian with the necessary material for building up the proof from tradition.

The term patrology is sometimes equated with, or further enlarged by, that of patristics. This term originated from the title *theologia patristica,* under which from the seventeenth century dogmatists treated the doctrine of the Fathers as distinct from the *theologia biblica, scholastica, symbolica,* and *speculativa.* From the *theologia patristica* developed the history of dogma, which extends much farther than the teaching of the Fathers as cultivated by patrology, since it draws on the sources offered by the history of the liturgy and the councils as much as on the writings of the Fathers. Despite its close relationship and intimate connexion with these two sciences, patrology can be neither history of doctrine nor of the councils, though it must combine the presentation of the lives and writings of the Fathers with an appreciation of their importance for the synodal life of the Church and for the progress of the knowledge of the faith.

The term "Father" is of purely ecclesiastical origin. It is the name which the reverent love of the congregation gave to their bishop and teacher.

Even the man of antiquity had the idea that his spiritual personality was generated by his teacher, hence he might call the latter his father and himself the teacher's son. See the term "sons of the prophets" 3 Kings 20, 35; further 1 Pet. 5 : 13; Iren., *Haer.* 4, 41, 2 ("qui enim ab aliquo doctus est, verbo filius docentis dicitur et ille eius pater") and Clem. Al., *Strom.* 1, 1, 1. Thus St. Paul writes to the Corinthians (1 Cor. 4 : 15): "For if you have ten thousand instructors in Christ, yet not many fathers. For in Christ Jesus, by the gospel, I have begotten you." In A.D. 155 Bishop Polycarp of Smyrna was called, though spitefully, "the Teacher of Asia, the Father of the Christians" (*Mart. Polyc.* 12, 2), by pagans and Jews. In the Letter of the Martyrs of Lyons (A.D. 177–8) to the Bishop of Rome the latter is addressed as Πάτερ 'Ελεύθερε (Eus., *Hist.* 5, 4, 2). In his letter to Origen, Bishop Alexander of Jerusalem praises his teachers and friends, Pantaenus and Clement of Alexandria, adding· πατέρας γὰρ ἴσμεν τοὺς μακαρίους ἐκείνους (Eus., *Hist.* 6, 14, 9). About 251 Bishop Cyprian received letters addressed "Cypriano papae" (Cypr., *Ep.* 30, 31, 36). From that time this use of the name Father is abundantly attested; even deceased bishops were not deprived of it (Eus., *Hist.* 7, 7, 4) and it was given especially to those bishops of the past who were adduced as witnesses for the doctrine of the Church (Bas., *Ep.* 140, 2; Greg. Naz., *Or.* 33, 15; Cyr. Al., *Ep.* 39). As witnesses of the tradition of the Church the bishops of bygone ages become a definite body, the Fathers. As late as the fifth century only bishops were generally called thus, though St. Augustine broke this rule by so naming an ecclesiastical writer who was not a bishop, viz. St. Jerome, in view of his learning and sanctity as a witness to the Church's teaching on original sin (*Contra Iul.* 1, 7 n. 31 and 34). The proof from the Fathers plays an important role in the great councils of the fifth century.

The term that had been extended by Augustine was taken over by Vincent of Lerins in his *Commonitorium* of 434; but he defined it more exactly as referring to those writers, "qui suis quisque temporibus et locis in unitate communionis et fidei permanentes magistri probabiles exstitissent" (41). Vincent, too, was the first to propound, as it were, a theory of proof from the Fathers, basing it on the Council of Ephesus (431). The earliest list of Christian authors, recognized as Fathers or rejected as such, is offered by the so-called Gelasian *Decretum de libris recipiendis et non recipiendis,* which strongly emphasizes communion with the Roman Church (ES 165):

"Qui in nullo a sanctae ecclesiae Romanae consortio deviarunt nec ab eius fide vel praedicatione seiuncti sunt, sed ipsius communicationis per gratiam Dei usque in ultimum diem vitae suae fuere participes" (4. 3).

Since the circle of doctrinal witnesses has been extended also to those writers who were not bishops, the marks of the Fathers can be summed up as: 1. *doctrina orthodoxa* (not, however, in the sense of complete absence of error, but of faithful doctrinal adherence to the orthodox Church), 2. *sanctitas vitae* (in the sense of the old Christian veneration of saints), 3. *approbatio ecclesiae* (as deduced from ecclesiastical discussions and documents, not necessarily *approbatio expressa*), 4. *antiquitas* (in the sense of ecclesiastical antiquity).

All theological writers of antiquity, including those without the marks of *doctrina orthodoxa* and *sanctitas,* can be called "ecclesiastical authors" a term coined by Jerome (*Vir. ill.,* Prol.; *Ep.* 112, 3). These men are called ecclesiastical authors as such, to distinguish them from the Fathers.

The circle of the Fathers of the Church is partly identical with that of the Doctors of the Church, who do not all possess the mark of antiquity, but instead have the further characteristics of *eminens eruditio* and *expressa ecclesiae declaratio.*

Vincent of Lerins was the first to call the Fathers of the Church *magistri probabiles* (EH 818); John of Antioch asks Nestorius to follow τοῖς ἐν τῇ 'Εκκλησίᾳ τοῦ Θεοῦ εὐδοκιμήσασι διδασκάλοις (SACO I 1, 1, 96 l 3f.); in a letter of B. Licinianus of Cartagena addressed to Gregory the Great, the Fathers Hilary, Ambrose, Augustine and Gregory of Nazianzus are called *doctores defensoresque ecclesiae* (Gregory, *Ep.* I 41a). In a synodal letter addressed to the emperor the Milanese B. Mansuetus (680) mentions as witnesses to the faith besides four Greek (Athanasius, Basil, Chrysostom and Cyril of Alexandria), also four Latin Fathers (Hilary, Ambrose, Jerome and Augustine) (Mansi II, 296f.), and about the year 800 a monk John praises Ambrose, Augustine, Jerome and Gregory, who are even now called the four great Western Fathers of the Church, as *doctissimi in utraque scientia* and "the four rivers of paradise" (HJB 1894, 95). These four Fathers were officially mentioned for the first time by Pope Boniface VIII as *egregii doctores ecclesiae* after the apostles and evangelists (*Corp. jur. can.* Lib. sext. lib. 3, tit. 22, cap. un.), as Gregory I had already called the apostles *doctores ecclesiae* and the Church Fathers *expositores sequentes* (*Hom. Ev.* 30, 7; *Mor.* 27, 8).

Since then the title of the great Western Doctors of the Church has remained restricted to these four Fathers, whereas the simple title of *Doctores ecclesiae* was officially given also to the Western saints Hilary of Poitiers, Peter Chrysologus, Leo the Great, Isidore of Seville and to the Easterns Athanasius, Ephraem (only since Benedict XV), Basil, Cyril of Jerusalem, Chrysostom and Cyril of Alexandria, later also to medieval and modern authors, for example, to SS. Anthony of Padua, Albert the Great, Thomas Aquinas, Bonaventure, Peter Canisius, Bellarmine, John of the Cross, Francis of Sales and Alphonsus of Liguori.

A similar development took place in the Eastern Church, in whose liturgical books three Fathers are venerated as οἰκουμενικοὶ μεγάλοι διδάσκαλοι: Basil, Gregory of Nazianzus and Chrysostom. Probably on grounds of symmetry and because of the close relations of St. Athanasius with the West (Rome and Treves) the Western Church, and especially ecclesiastical art, has added St. Athanasius to these three doctors, and Pope Pius V, influenced by the humanists' interest in Greek literature, honoured these four Eastern Fathers for the first time with the title Doctor of the Church in his Breviary of 1568.

The Doctors of the Church were honoured by a special office on their feast days and the recitation of the Creed in the Mass, as well as by ecclesiastical recommendation of their doctrine.

The authority of the Fathers in the Catholic Church rests not only on their literary importance, but especially on the teaching of the Church on tradition as a source of the faith. No single Father of the Church is infallible by himself, except if as Pope he was teaching *ex cathedra,* or if and in so far as individual propositions of his writings were approved by a general council.

All other concepts and sayings of the Fathers are taken as fallible statements of doctrine, not as its final formulation. Sometimes the Fathers corrected themselves and, after some serious intellectual struggle, attained a greater clarity and a deeper grasp of the traditional teaching. Hence their extensive writings furnish the historian of dogma with abundant material for his task of presenting the gradual emergence of the Church's teaching, which has often aroused heated controversies. The authority of the individual Father depends on his scholarship and sanctity, his relation to other Fathers, and his position in the hierarchy. The votes of the Fathers should not be counted, but weighed (August., *Contra Iul.* 2, 10 n. 35).

On questions of Scriptural exegesis the Church accepts the unanimous teaching of the Fathers, the *unanimis consensus patrum,* as infallible faith (Vatic. sess. 3, c. 2; ES 1788). Theologians are divided on the question of the foundation of the *consensus patrum,* which need not be a numerical but only a moral one. In which sense one can speak of an inspiration of the Fathers (EH 812/8) is a question which has not yet been clarified.

A. Deneffe, *Der Traditionsbegriff,* 1931. J. Ranft, *Der Ursprung des kathol. Traditionsprinzips,* 1931. D. van den Eynde, *Les normes de l'enseignement chrét. dans la littérature patristique des trois premiers siècles,* 1933. Amann, DTC 12, 1192/1215. Du Manoir, RSR 1935, 441/61, 531/59 ("Father"). J. Ranft, *Die Traditionsmethode als aelteste Methode des Christentums,* 1934. B. Simovic, *France francisc.,* 1938, 193/222, 245/64 (*Pater* in Tert. and Cypr.). De Lubac, RSR 39/40, 1951/52, 27/40 (Harmonizing the statements of the Fathers). Bardy, RSR 1952, 7/26 (Inspiration of the Fathers). Smulders, RSR 1952, 41/62 (concept of tradition in the Greek Fathers). W. Schneemelcher, TheolV 5, 1950/51, 207/22 (Essence and task of patristics).

Apart from their ecclesiastical importance, the Fathers of the Church occupy a prominent position also in the general, and especially in the Greco-Roman history of literature. They are the last representatives of antiquity, whose literary art frequently shines forth in their works, and they have influenced all later literatures. Trained by the best teachers of classical antiquity, they placed their oral and written work at the service of the Christian idea. It is true, apart from individual rhetorical achievements in apologetics, sermons and epistles, they did not, in the first place, want to be literary men, but exponents of Christian doctrine and morals. Yet an inborn and acquired art became for them a means to this end. However, if exciting thoughts and literary wit be sought in these works, they will be found wanting. In the early Middle Ages to speak as a Christian meant to speak the language of the Fathers. The reader must bring to them an open, willing heart that is attuned to the Christian truth. Then they will become for him a source of light, joy and spiritual edification.

Until *c.* 180 A.D. the language of the Fathers was Greek, which was understood at least in educated circles throughout the East, but also in Rome, the rest of Italy, Africa and Southern Gaul. Its advanced development, wealth of words and inflexions, made it the fitting organ for conveying the richness of Christian ideas. In the East its place was later taken partly by the individual native languages, particularly by Syriac and Armenian. Even if the Acts of the Scilitan Martyrs is to be considered the oldest Latin document that can be dated exactly (A.D. 180), the Latin translation of the First Letter of Clement probably originated in Rome several decades earlier. It did not take long for the language of Latium to become the universal language of the Western Fathers from the third century. Under the influence of the creative power of Christianity the Latin language underwent a certain change. Already Tertullian had, together with Cyprian, inaugurated the development of an early Christian language; he enriched Latin and increased its power of expression by additions from the Greek vocabulary, popular speech and legal terms as well as new formations. Apart from differences in the vocabulary, early Christian Latin also uses certain peculiarities of syntax and style.

The early Fathers, like the contemporaries of the apostles, did not speak the Attic dialect but the κοινὴ διάλεκτος which had developed in the empire of Alexander the Great. Moreover, these first Christian writers did not want to compose literary works in the narrower sense. They meant to offer and present a new meaning of life. Since many of them were not in touch with Greek culture and literature, they attached no importance to literary form. But with the growth of Christianity, Hellenistic influences increased in proportion; hence the works of the later Fathers reflect the contemporary rhetorical and also philosophical schools. Thus certain Fathers like Gregory of Nazianzus and John Chrysostom who had absorbed the culture of their time are among the most brilliant representatives of late Hellenistic literature.

G. Koffmane, *Geschichte des Kirchenlateins,* 2 vols., 1879/81. J. Stiglmayr, *Kirchenvaeter und Klassizismus,* 1913. E. Norden, *Die antike Kunstprosa* II, 1918. H. P. V. Nunn, *An Introduction to Ecclesiastical Latin,* NY 1928. J. Schrijnen, *Charakteristik des altchristlichen Latein,* N 1932. W. Matzkow, *De vocabulis quibusdam Italae et Vulgatae christianis quaestiones lexicographae,* 1933. Schrijnen, REL 1934, 96/116. Marrou, AL 1934, 5/24. G. B. Pighi, *Latinità crist. negli scritt. pagani del sec. IV,* 1936 and StU 41/72 (Ammian. Marcell.). H. Janssen, *Kultur u. Sprache,* N 1938. M. A. Sainio, *Semasiologische Untersuch. ueber die Entstehung der christl. Latinitaet,* Helsinki 1940. Hoogterp, AL 15, 39/112 (African popular language, 4th cent.). The important works on Christian Latin including those on liturgical and biblical Latin by C. Mohrmann which appeared until 1948 are listed in De Ghellinck, RHE 1949, 402/44. For the latest studies by the same author I would list the following sources: VC 1949, 67/106, 163/83; 1950, 1/19, 193/211; 1952, 1/19; 1953, 1/15; RSCI 1950, 153/63; 1951, 1/6; Aev 1950, 133/61; Ir 1950, 5/30; 1952, 3/19; *Mél. F. de Vischer,* 1950, 4, 225/34; *Conférences de l'Institut de linguistique de l'Univ. de Paris* 10, 1950/51, 125/40; *Mél. J. de Ghellinck* 1, 1951, 278/85; EL 1952, 37/52; 274/81; *Latin vulgaire latin des Chrétiens,* P 1952; *Festschrift Alph. Mulders,* N 1953, 241/56; *Paideia* 8, 1953, 241/56; TR 1956, 1/18. Duerig, LJ 1951 32/47 (bibliograph. account). SE 1952, 245/77 (*disciplina*). Baus, TrTZ 1952, 192/205. C. Battisti, *Avviamento allo studio del latino volgare,* 1950. Memoli, Aev 1954, 419/44 (Rhythm and Bibl. texts in literary Lat. Christian prose). C. Becker, *Tert.'s Apologeticum,* Mn 1954, 335/45. Cf. also bibliographies in § 29,1 and § 86 (Vulgate). Ch. Mohrmann, *Études sur le latin des chrét.,* R 1958.

The time of the Fathers, which is the first age of the Church, is best divided into three periods:

1. The time of foundation (till the Council of Nicaea, 325).

2. The peak period (from 325 to the Council of Chalcedon, 451).

3. The decline (in the West till the death of Isidore of Seville, 636, in the East till the death of John of Damascus, 749).

In general, the plan of the present book follows this division. In certain cases, however, it has been found advisable to disregard these time limits so as to be able to present larger groups of writings, for example, the apocrypha, the Church Orders, the historical works and legends, as a unity.

§ 2. HISTORY OF PATROLOGY

BETHLEHEM is the birthplace of Christian patrology. There St. Jerome, at the suggestion of his friend Dexter, produced in 392 the first *Catalogus scriptorum ecclesiasticorum* under the title *De viris illustribus,* in order to counter the proud argument of the pagans vaunting the high literary culture of paganism (EH 634/6).

His model was Suetonius' work of the same title (first half of second century), his source especially the Church History of Eusebius. His accounts of fourth century authors are mostly based on personal knowledge. The work gives a survey of the lives and writings of 135 Christian authors including the heretical ones as well as the Jews Philo and Josephus, and the pagan Seneca, and enumerates in the last chapter (135) the author's own writings, down to 392. It has sometimes been criticized, first by Augustine (*Ep*. 40: for its incomplete enumerations and lack of distinction between heretical and orthodox authors), and, after being unanimously admired in the Middle Ages, again by modern critics (for hasty judgements, partiality and many inaccuracies). Nevertheless, it is a great achievement, of permanent value as a source, and remained the pattern of patristic history down to the eighteenth century.

Edd.: ML 23, 601ff. C. A. Bernoulli 1895. E. C. Richardson, L 1896. G. Herding, L 1924. Mgs.: A. Feder, *Studien z. Schriftstellerkatalog des hl. H.*, 1927.

Continuations of this work were written under the same title by 1. the semi-Pelagian priest Gennadius at Massilia, *c*. 480;

Edd.: Bernoulli, Richardson, Herding (v. supra). Feder, Sch 1933, 380/99.

2. St. Isidore of Seville, between 615 and 618 (with special reference to Spain);

ML 83, 1081/1106. Koeppler, JTS 1936, 16–34. Villada and De Aldama, *Misc. Isid*. 1936, 37 f, 86/8.

3. St. Ildefonsus of Toledo (d. 667), who gives an account of fourteen Churchmen, among them eight authors (ML 96, 195–206).

J. Madoz, *S. Ildefonso de T.*, Ma 1943. A. Braegelmann, *The Life and Writings of St. I. of T.*, W 1942. Rivera, RET 1946, 573/88 (spurious sermon ?). Madoz, EE 1952, 467/505. V. Blanco García, *S. Ildef., Tratado de perpetua virginitad de S. María*, Saragossa 1954 (with tr.).

In the ninth century Photius wrote the *Myriobiblon* (or *Bibliotheca*), an account of 280 pagan and Christian books with biographical notes and extracts, especially from less well-known works, the knowledge of which we owe in part exclusively to him.

Edd.: I. Becker, 2 vols., B 1824. MG 103 (= Codd. 1–249); 104 (= Codd. 250–280).

There are no further patrological accounts for nearly five hundred years. Towards the end of the eleventh century they were resumed by Sigebert of Gembloux (d. 1112) and continued *c.* 1122 by Honorius of Augustodunum, *c.* 1135 by the Anonymus Mellicensis and in 1494 by Trithemius, but as regards antiquity these writers were content to reproduce notices from Jerome and Gennadius.

Complete edition of the literary historians: J. A. Fabricius, *Bibliotheca ecclesiastica,* 1718.

Among the earlier post-Reformation works those by Cardinal Bellarmine and the Benedictine Ceillier were the most distinguished. They paved the way for the scholarly treatment of patrology, to which the discussions of the Council of Trent had given a powerful impulse.

R. Bellarmine, *De scriptoribus eccl. liber unus,* 1613 (till 1500). R. Ceillier, *Histoire générale des auteurs sacrés et ecclésiastiques,* 23 vols., 1729/63 (till 1250).

In the sixteenth and seventeenth centuries appeared the first great collections of the Fathers (v. § 4) as well as excellent individual editions, with prolegomena and critical apparatus that raised patrology from the level of simple accounts to the heights of scholarly investigation. Beside the aforementioned 23 volume work of Ceillier there were many others, particularly Tillemont's 16 volume collection of scholarly biographies of the Fathers, *Mémoires pour servir à l'histoire eccl. des six premiers siècles,* 1693–1712, which has remained indispensable even down to our own time.

Patrology received a new impetus in the nineteenth century, owing to the many discoveries of lost works, particularly from the earliest period and from the Syriac, Armenian, Georgian and Coptic languages. Special chairs for patrology were founded in many universities, while academies undertook the edition of large groups of works by the Fathers. The many volumes of patristic histories were replaced by innumerable individual treatises, monographs and concise manuals. At the beginning of the twentieth century the Fathers were studied even more profoundly and thoroughly; scholars strove to present comprehensively the doctrinal contents of the works of individual Fathers and to investigate the history of particular thoughts, ideas and words. In most recent times the number of new texts of both known and unknown authors or lost pieces of the old Christian literature has been greatly increased through the assiduous exploration of libraries, especially in the now more accessible East and by discoveries of papyri in Egypt.

D. Gorce, *Petite introduction à l'étude des Pères,* [2]1951. J. de Ghellinck, *Patristique et Moyen Age,* t. II: *Études d'hist. litt. et doctrinale,* 1947 (hist. of patrist. research in the first five cents. and the dissemination and transmission of patrist. writings in antiquity); t. III: *Compléments à l'étude de la patristique,* 1948. Altaner, *Misc. Mercati* I 483/520 (State of patrology and the problem of a new early Christian lit. hist.); cf. De Ghellinck: *Mél. Cavallera,* 1948, 65/85.

§ 3. RECENT LITERATURE ON THE HISTORY AND TEACHING OF THE FATHERS

MODERN comprehensive works by Catholic authors: J. A. Moehler, *Patrologie,* ed. Reithmayr, 1840 (treats 1st to 3rd cents.). J. Fessler, *Institutiones Patrologiae,* 2 vols., ed. B. Jungmann, [2]1890–96 (good treatment of doctrinal questions). H. Kihn, *Patrologie* I–II, 1904 and 1908. The two works by O. Bardenhewer: (a) *Patrologie,* [3]1910; (b) *Geschichte der altkirchlichen Literatur* I (1st – 2nd cents.) [2]1913; II (3rd cent.) [2]1914; III (4th cent.) 1912 [new impression with supplements, 1923]; IV (5th cent. and syr. lit. of 4th cent.) 1924; V (last period and oldest Armenian literature) 1932 [the leading work of international authority]. B. Steidle, *Patrologia,* Fr 1937. Of my own *Patrologie,* Fr [5]1958, there are three different Italian editions or adaptations, Tu 1940, 1944 and 1952 (the last by A. Ferrua and E. Della Zuanna); one French translation by M. Grandclaudon, Mulhouse 1941; Spanish editions,

Ma 1945, 1949 and 1953 (a 4th revised ed. in 1956 by E. Cuevas and U. Domínguez-Del Val); a Hungarian translation by H. I. Lászlo, Budapest 1947; this English translation by H. C. Graef, Lo 1960. J. Tixeront, *Précis de Patrologie,* 1923. F. Mourret, *Histoire générale de l'Église,* 2: *Les Pères de l'Église,* 1919. F. Cayré, *Patrologie et Hist. de la Théologie,* 3 vols., [3]1945–55 (to the present time). P. de Labriolle, *Histoire de la littérature latine chrétienne,* 2 vols., ed. G. Bardy 1947. P. Monceaux, *Histoire de la littérature latine chrétienne,* 1924. A. Puech, *Histoire de la littérature grecque chrétienne jusqu'à la fin du 4e siècle,* 3 vols., 1928–30.

U. Mannucci - A. Casamassa, *Istituzioni di Patrologia,* 2 vols., [6]1948–50. U. Moricca, *Storia della letteratura latina cristiana* I, II 1–2, III 1–2 1924–34. A. G. Amatucci, *Storia della letteratura latina cristiana,* [2]1955. L. Salvatorelli, *Storia della lett. lat. crist.,* Mi 1936 (till 550). M. Pellegrino, *Disegno stor. della lett. greca crist.,* Tu 1955 and R 1956.

J. M. Campbell, *The Greek Fathers,* Lo 1929. E. J. Goodspeed, *A Hist. of Early Christ. Literature,* Ch 1942. J. Quasten, *Patrology,* so far vols. 1–2 have been published, Ut 1950–53 (until 3rd cent., French trans. by J. Laporte, 1955–57, with latest literature).

A Polish Patrology by J. Czuj, Poznań (without knowledge of, and out of touch with international research).

Works of German Protestant authors valuable for research: A. Harnack, *Geschichte der altchristl. Literatur bis Eusebius,* First Part: Ueberlieferung und Bestand, 1893; Second Part: Chronologie, 1 (to Irenaeus) 1897, 2 (to Eusebius) 1904. G. Krueger, *Geschichte der altchristlichen Literatur in den ersten 3 Jh.,* 1895, Appendix 1897. H. Jordan, *Geschichte der altchristlichen Literatur,* 1911, attempt to give the history of the individual literary forms. H. v. Campenhausen, *Griech. Kirchenvaeter,* St 1955.

Important sections of patrology are treated also in the literary histories of individual countries and languages, mostly written by philologists:

W. S. Teuffel, *Geschichte der roem. Literatur,* III [6]1913, ed. W. Kroll and F. Skutsch (Christian authors, by E. Klostermann). M. Schanz, C. Hosius and G. Krueger, *Gesch. der roem. Lit.,* part 3 (till Constantine) [3]1922, part 4, 1 (4th cent.) 1914, 4, 2 (5th–6th cents.) 1920. E. Bickel, *Lehrbuch der Gesch. der roem. Literatur,* 1937. M. Manitius, *Gesch. der latein. Lit. des MA* 1, 1911 (6th cent. ff.). A. Gudeman, *Gesch. der altchristl. latein. Lit.,* 1925 (Goeschen). A. Kappelmacher and M. Schuster, *Die Lit. der Roemer bis zur Karolingerzeit,* 1935. W. Christ - W. Schmid, *Gesch. der griech. Lit.* 2, 2 (100–530 A.D.), [6]1924 (old Chr. lit. ed. by O. Staehlin). M. Dibelius, *Gesch. der urchristl. Lit.,* 1926 (Goeschen). K. Krumbacher, *Gesch. der byzant. Lit.,* [2]1897 (theol. lit. by A. Ehrhard). A. Ehrhard - J. M. Hoeck, *Ueberlieferung und Bestand der hagiograph. und homiletischen Lit. der griech. Kirche. Die Ueberlieferung* (till end of 16th cent.), 3 vols., 1936–52 (TU 50–52). P. Monceaux, *Hist. littéraire de l'Afrique chrét.,* 7 vols., 1901–23. N. Terzaghi, *Storia della letteratura latina da Tiberio a Giustiniano,* Mi 1934. E. S. Duckett, *Latin Writers of the Fifth Century,* NY 1930. A. Sizoo, *Geschiedenis der oud-christelijke latijnse griekse Letterkunde,* 2 vols., Haarlem 1951 f. K. Brockelmann, F. N. Finck, J. Leipoldt, E. Littmann, *Gesch. der christl. Literaturen des Orients* (Syr., Armen., Copt., Arab.), 1907. R. Duval, *La littérature syriaque,* 1907. A. Baumstark, *Die christl. Literaturen des Orients,* 2 vols., 1911 (Goeschen), the same, *Geschichte der syrischen Literatur,* 1922. J. B. Chabot, *Littérature syriaque,* 1935. Leclercq, DAL 9, 1576–99 *(Litt. armén.).* O'Leary, DAL 9, 1599–1635 *(Copt. lit.).* J. Karst, *Litt. géorgienne chrét.,* 1934. G. Peradze, *Die altchristl. Lit. in der georg. Ueberlieferung:* OC 3–8, 1930–3. M. Tarchnisvili - J. Assfalg, *Gesch. der kirchl. Georgischen Lit.* (ST 185), 1955. J. M. Harden, *An Introduction to Ethiopic Christ. Lit.,* 1926. I. Guidi, *Storia della letteratura etiopica,* 1932. G. Graf, *Gesch. der christl. arab. Literatur,* 1–5, R 1944–53 (ST 118, 133, 146/47 171).

In this connexion we would draw attention to important

works of reference containing many contributions, written from various points of view, which are of value to the patrologist. For reasons of space we must refrain from indicating *suo loco* all relevant titles and questions that are treated there. We would mention the following: DAL: *Dictionnaire d'Archéologie chrétienne et de Liturgie,* P; DB: *Dictionnaire de la Bible,* with several suppl. vols., P; DHG: *Dictionnaire d'Histoire et de Géographie ecclésiastiques,* P; DS: *Dictionnaire de la Spiritualité,* P; DTC: *Dictionnaire de Théologie catholique,* P; PWK: Pauly-Wissowa-Kroll: *Realenzyklopaedie der klassischen Altertumswissenschaft, Str.*; RACh: *Reallexikon fuer Antike und Christentum,* ed. T. Klauser, St; RE: *Realenzyklopaedie fuer protestantische Theologie und Kirche,* ed. A. Hauck, L; TWNT: *Theolog. Woerterbuch zum Neuen Testament,* ed. G. Kittel - G. Friedrich, 1933ff. (treats also the oldest patristic texts).

A general presentation of the teaching of the Fathers, more or less comprehensively treated also in some of the works mentioned above, is given in works on the history of dogma.

The Jesuit, Dionysius Petavius (d. 1652), may be regarded as the father of the history of dogma. In his great work *De theologicis dogmatibus* (1–4, 1643–50) he first established Catholic doctrine by the proof from tradition and, in contrast with scholasticism, pre-eminently from the historical point of view. In the following century there is the work by the Protestant scholar Walch, *Entwurf einer vollstaendigen Historie der Ketzereien* (1–11, 1762–85). The first *Handbuch der christlichen Dogmengeschichte* (Manual of the Christian history of dogma) was published by the Protestant, W. Muenster, in 1797ff. (1–4, takes account only of the first six centuries); in 1811 he published a textbook of the Christian history of dogma. The study of doctrinal history was furthered by the idea of development which penetrated also into theology. At that time J. H. Newman wrote his *Essay on the Development of Christian Doctrine.* Following the line of Petavius, J. Schwane wrote his four volumes *Dogmengeschichte* (1862 to 1890, ^{2}1892ff.), followed by the smaller work by Zobl, *Dogmengeschichte der katholischen Kirche* (1865). Since then an immense number of treatises on individual questions of doctrinal history have appeared. Scholars realized that much preliminary research was still needed, which explains why J. Tixeront did not risk publishing a comprehensive *Histoire des dogmes* in 3 vols. till 1905 ff. (^{11}1930 ff.; up to 800; first volume to 300). He was followed by B. J. Otten, *A Manual of the History of Dogmas,* 1 and 2, 1917. Fundamental questions are treated by R. M. Schultes, *Introductio in historiam dogmatum,* 1924, and especially by F. Marin-Sola, *L'évolution homogène du dogme catholique,* 2 vols., ^{2}1924; Spanish ed., Ma 1952 (neglecting the historical development). J. Creusen and F. van Eyen, *Tabulae fontium traditionis christ. ad annum 1926,* Lou 1926. J. F. de Groot, *Conspectus historiae dogmatum ab aetate PP. apostolicorum usque ad saeculum XIII,* 2 vols., R 1931. R. Draguet, *L'évolution des dogmes,* P ^{2}1948. *Handbuch der Dogmengeschichte* ed. Schmaus - Geiselmann - H. Rahner 1950 ff. (2 parts have so far appeared).

Of general presentations of dogmatic history by non-Catholic scholars we would name the following: A. Harnack, *Lehrbuch der Dogmengesch.,* 3 vols., ^{4}1909–10, new impression 1931–2, and *Grundriss der Dogmengeschichte,* ^{6}1922. R. Seeberg, *Lehrbuch der Dogmengeschichte,* 1 ^{3}1922, 2 ^{3}1923, 3 ^{4}1930, 4 $^{2-3}$1917–20. Also the outlines of the history of dogma by F. Loofs, 5th ed. ed. K. Aland, 3 parts, 1951 ff., R. Seeberg ^{7}1936, N. Bonwetsch ^{2}1919. F. Wiegand, *Dogmengeschichte,* 1 1928, 2 1919. De Balanos, Εἰσαγωγὴ εἰς τὴν ἱστορίαν τῶν δογμάτων, 1919. A. Cuchman-McGiffert, *Hist. of Christ. Thought,* 2 vols., 1931 f. J. Turmel, *Hist. des dogmes,* 6 vols., 1931–6. M. Werner, *Die Entstehung des christl. Dogmas,* Berne ^{2}1954. W. Koehler, *Dogmengeschichte als Geschichte des christl. Selbstbewusstseins,* 2 vols., Zu 1950 f. Schneemelcher (*Das Problem der Dogmengeschichte*) ZKT 1951, 63/89.

Apart from the works on general Church history, which need not be mentioned more fully, the general history of philosophy deals with the doctrine of the Fathers. The following should be mentioned in the first place: Ueberweg-Geyer, *Die patristische und scholastische Philosophie,* [11]1928. H. Eibl, *Augustin und die Patristik,* 1923, and *Die Grundlegung der abendlaendischen Philosophie,* 1934. C. J. Logothetis, Ἡ φιλοσοφία τῶν πατέρων καὶ τοῦ μέσου αἰῶνος, 1930. F. Sassen, *Geschiedenis der patrist. en middeleeuwsche Wijsbegeerte,* [4]1950. B. Romeyer, *La philosophie chrét.,* 2 vols., 1936 (to Augustine). É. Gilson and P. Boehner, *Gesch. der christl. Philosophie,* Pa [2]1952ff. Hans Meyer, *Geschichte der abendlaendischen Weltanschauung,* 2nd vol., 1953. A. Rivaud, *Histoire de la philosophie* I, P 1948. J. Hirschberger, *Geschichte der Philosophie* I, [4]1960. O. Perler, *Patristische Philosophie,* Berne 1950 (a bibliography).

Works on Church History: A. Ehrhard, *Die Kirche der Maertyrer,* 1932, and *Urkirche und Fruehkatholizismus,* 1935. K. Bihlmeyer-H. Tuechle, *Kirchengeschichte* I, [14]1955. H. Lietzmann, *Geschichte der Alten Kirche,* 4 vols., 1932–44. *Histoire de l'Église* published under the direction of A. Fliche et V. Martin, vols. 1–5, 1934ff (till 757).

Most of the works published between 1925 to 1931 are listed in Rauschen-Altaner, *Patrologie,* 1931. For the following years I would refer the reader to the various translations of my Patrology, especially to the German editions of 1950, 1951, 1955 and 1958.

Études Augustiniennes: Mémorial G. Bardy, 4 parts, 1956 (24 contributions). *Studia Patristica,* Proceedings of the Second International Conference on Patristic Studies, O 19th–21st Sept. 1955; 2 vols. in TU 1957f.

1. History of Patristic MSS

G. Pasquali, *Storia della tradizione e critica del testo,* Fl 1934, [2]1952. M. Manitius, *Handschriften antiker Autoren in mtl. Bibliothekskatalogen,* 1935. Bardy, *Vivre et*

Penser, 1944, 242/67 (bilingual works and MSS). Bardy, RevSR 1949, 38/52 (Apoll. Sidon. Sulp. Sev. Ruricius). M. Richard, *Répertoire des bibliothèques et des catalogues de MSS grecs,* 1948; cf. Laurent, REB 9, 1951–52, 252/95. Richard, *Actes du VIe Congrès internat. d'Ét. byz.* I, 1950, 308/18 (doctrinal anthologies of the 5th and 6th cents.); cf. Nautin, RHE 1951, 681/83. Richard, Byz. 20, 1950, 191/222 (Importance of the MS 'Ἀπὸ φωνῆς). Richard, *Bull. Informat. Instit. Rech. et d'Hist. Textes* I, 1952, 48/80 *(mission d'études en Grèce).* Richard, *Invent. MSS Grecs du British Mus.,* 1952. A. Siegmund, *Die Ueberlieferung der griech. christl. Lit. in der latein. Kirche bis z. 12. Jh.,* Mn 1948. Courcelle, *Mél. Grat.,* P 1949, 145/57 (hitherto unused fragm. of Rufinus, Orig., *In Lev.,* Jerome, *In Ez.,* and Gregory, *Moral.*). Olivar, AST 1949, 75/92 (patrist. and liturg. MSS of the Univ. of Salamanca). Peebles, RB 1951, 261/64 (*Homiliarium* with sermons by Caesarius, Jerome and Augustine). Dekkers, *Festschr. Dold,* 1952, 128/39 (autographs of Lat. Fathers). Garitte, *Script.* 1952, 114/46 (Bibliography of Greek MSS, 1940/50). E. A. Parsons, *The Alexandrian Library...,* Houston (Tex.), 1952. K. W. Clark, *Checklist of MSS in the Libraries of the Greek and Armenian Patriarchates in Jerusalem.* W 1953. Wendel, *Handbuch der Bibliothekswissenschaft* III, [2]1953, 51/143 and RACh 2, 231/74 (Libraries). Koep-Morenz-Leipoldt, RACh 2, 664/731 (The book). Hagendahl, Er 1947, 114/28 (Methods of Citation in Min. Felix, Lactant. and Salvian). Brugnoli, *Benedictina* 6, 1952, 287/303; 1953, 85/120, 287/94 (some patristica among the MSS of Farfa). R. Devreesse, *L'introduction à l'et. des MSS grecs,* P 1954. Casey, Mu 1955, 55/59 (Armen. ined. MSS of Tuebingen). C. Baur, *Initia Patrum,* 2 vols. (ST 180/81), 1955.

2. *Style and Text Criticism*

K. Pohlheim, *Die latein. Reimprosa,* 1925, 210/324. A. Sizoo, *Eloquentia divina. Het stijlproblem der oude christenen,* 1939 (20 pp.). Kleberg, Er 1940, 47/54 *('Weinfaelschung'* as cliché of style). Ehrhardt, HTR 1945, 177/93 *(Vir bonus quadrato lapidi comparatur).* Mohrmann, REL 1947, 280/97 (Language and style of Christ. poetry). H. Zilliacus, *Untersuchungen zu den abstrakten Anredeformen u. Hoeflichkeitstiteln im Griechischen,* Hel 1949. Boismard, RB 1950, 388/408 (Patristic Scriptural citations and textual criticism). Bulhart, RB 1951, 259/61 (Textual criticism on Augustine, Basil's homilies and African anonymous writers). Madoz, *Publicaciones de la Facultad de Filosof. y Lit.,* Ser. 1, 4, Zaragoza 1950, 1/39 *(Literat. patríst. españ. y estética de los clásicos).* S. Lundstroem, *Uebersetzungstechnische Untersuchungen auf dem Gebiete der christl. Latinitaet,* Lund 1955. Den Boer, VC 1947, 150/67 (Hermeneutic problems till Origen). Chatillon, RML 1953, 267/342 (*etiam* . . . [Animadversiones Augustinianae]). Mohrmann, VC 1955, 222/46 *(Problèmes stylistiques* [from Tertull. to August.]). Bartelink, VC 1956, 1/13 *(Ellipse u. Bedeutungsverdichtung b. griech. Vaetern).* Courcelle, REL 1955, 231/40 ("Cliché virgilien des cent bouches"). Mueller, Mu 1956, 53/72 (Coptic and Greek rhetoric).

3. *History of Terms and Ideas*

A. van Herten, θρησκεία, εὐλάβεια, ἱκέτης, A 1934. C. Zijderveld jr., Τελετή, thesis Ut 1934. H. Willms, Εἰκών I: Philon v. Alexandria, 1935; cf. JL 15, 1941,

355/9. J. C. Bolkestein, "Οσιος *en* εὐσεβής, thesis Ut 1936. H. Oppel, Κανών, L 1937. Pruemm, ZKT 1937, 391/425 (mysterion from St. Paul to Origen); ibid. 1939, 207/25 (mysterion in Hippolytus); ibid. 1939, 350/9 (myst. in Athanasius); cf. Casel, JL 15, 1941, 269/305. Botte, AL 1938, 43/5 (*consummare*). Segovia, Gr 1938, 3/36 (ἀπάτωρ ἀπαράλλακτος). Garin, *La Rinascita* I, 1939, 102/46, 191/226 (*dignitas hominum*). De Lubac, RSR 1939, 257/302, 429/40; 1940, 40/80, 191/226 (*corpus mysticum*). De Labriolle, AL 1939, 23/36 (*salvator*). Altaner, ZKG 1939, 132/41 (*paganus*). Against this: Zeiller, CRI 1940, 526/43; further Mohrmann, VC 1952, 109/21 and W. Schmid, RM 1953, 160/65. Further: Grégoire-Orgels, *Mél. G. Smets*, 1952, 363/400; Grégoire, Byz 22, 1952–53, 333/35, 539; Roblin, *Annales-Économies-Sociétés-Civilisations* 8, 1953, 173/83. Bickel, RM 1954, 1/47. F. Erdin, *Das Wort Hypostasis*, 1939; cf. TR 1941, 60/4. De Ghellinck, AL 1939, 95/105 (*originale et originalia*). Jungmann, ZKT 1940, 26/37 (*Missa*). De Mayol de Lupé, REL 1940, 29/31 (*sacramentum*). De Ghellinck, AL 1941, 151/9 (*imitari, imitatio*); 16, 1942, 77/112 (*essentia, substantia*). Doelger, AC 6, 1941, 161/95 (*Kirche:* cult-edifice). E. Guenther, Μάρτυς, *Die Geschichte eines Wortes*, 1941. W. J. Terstegen, Εὐσεβής *en* ὅσιος *en het grieksch taal gebruik na de IV*[e] *eeuw*, 1941. O. Mauch, *Der latein. Begriff "disciplina"*, Frib 1941. De Urbina, OCP 1942, 194/209 (ὁμοούσιος *preniceno*). De Labriolle, *Salvator*, Mél. F. Martroye, 1941, 59/72, A.-J. Festugière, *La sainteté*, P 1942. Peterson, *Christianus*, Misc. Mercati I, 355/72. Bardy, RSR 1946, 211/35 (*tractare, tractatus*). Auerbach, *Arch. Romanic.* 22, 436/89 (*figura*). Skard, SO 1947, 26/30 (*vexillum*). De Ghellinck, Mél. A. Pelzer 1947, 23/59 (*"Pagina" et "sacra pagina"*). Waszink, VC 1947, 13/41 (*pompa diaboli*). Spicq, Rb 1947, 321/39 (*Bénignité, mansuétude*). Smothers, Tr 1947 (Καλός *in Acclamation*). Tailliez, OCP 1947, 299/354 (βασιλικὴ ὁδός). Lampe, JTS 1948, 58/73 (βασιλεία τοῦ θεοῦ). De Ghellinck, *Stud. Mediev.* R. J. Martin 1948, 39/59 (*iuventus, gravitas, senectus*). Dekkers, *Horae monasticae* I, Thielt 1948, 67/80 (*humilitas*). H. Pétré, *Caritas*, Lou 1948. Garitte, Miscell. J. Gessler 1948, 522/25 (*dominicum*). Bardy, RAM 1949, 97/108 (*philosophie et philosophe*). Rheinfelder, *Die Sprache* I, 1949, 56/67 (*confiteri, confessio, confessor*). Bolleli, RFIC 1950, 117/41 (*caritas*). Doelger, AC 6, 1950, 241/72 (*Heiland* in Justin, Lact., Constantine, Origen). Schmeck, VC 1951, 129/47 (*infidelis*). Hiltbrunner, VC 1951, 55/60 (*exterior homo*). Duerig, SE 1952, 245/79 (*disciplina*). Mohrmann, VC 1953, 221/45 (*statio*). VC 1954, 154/173 (*tropaeum – nomen*); EL 1952, 37 ff. (*pascha, passio, transitus*). Bernardi, VC 1954, 174f. (τρόπαιον). Adam, ZKG 65, 1953–54, 209/39 (Monasticism from Plato to Suidas). Olivar, AST 1952, 209/20 (*Sol intaminatus*). Mohrmann, HTR 1954, 141/52 (*sacramentum*); Maison-Dieu 39, 1954, 97/107 (*Praedicare, tractare, sermo*); *Festg. A. Debrunner*, Bern 1954, 211/28 (*Note sur doxa*). Doerrie, GN 3, 1955, 35/92 (ὑπόστασις). Downey, *Historia* 4, 1955, 199/208 (Philanthropia in the 4th cent.). Mendizábal, EE 1956, 147/96 (*El homoousios preniceno extraecles.*). A. J. Vermeulen, *The Semantic of Gloria in Early Christ. Latin*, N 1956. Theiler, RAC 3, 694/711 (*Demiurgos*). S. Riccobono Jr., Atti Congresso Dir-Rom, Verona 1948, Mi 1951, 209/30 (*humanitas*). F. Beckmann, *Humanitas*, Mr 1952; cf. W. Schmid, Gn 1956, 589/601.

4. Literary History

Leclercq, DAL 8, 2683/885 (*Lettres chrét.* till 9th cent.). Nelson, *Univ. of Michigan Publications* 10, 1933, 59ff. (Cicero, *De offic.* in Christ. Thought 300–1300). P. de Labriolle, *La réaction païenne,* 1934 (anti-Christian polemics till the 6th cent.). A. L. Williams, *Adv. Judaeos. A Bird's-eye View of Christ. Apologiae until the Renaissance,* 1935. Bardy, RB 1935, 356/80 *(éd. et rééditions d'œuvres patrist.);* RHE 1936, 5/23, 275/302 *(Faux et fraudes litt.).* C. Favez, *La consolation lat. chrét.,* 1937. H. Emonds, *Zweite Auflage im Altertum,* 1941. P. Courcelle, *Les lettres grecques en Occident: De Macrobe à Cassiodore,* 1948. Hagendahl, Er 35, 41/67 (Lucretius in the Lat. apologists). Madoz, *Rev. Principe de Viana,* No. 24, 3/12; the same also in Folia 1, 1952, 40/52 (Lucretius). G. Bardy, RHE 1948, 179/91 (Flavius Josephus). Carlson, CP 1948, 93/104 (Pagan examples of the fortitude in the Lat. Fathers). Madoz, RET 1950, 275/87 (Fathers as mediators of the culture of antiquity). Brok, VC 1951, 101/110 (festal letters among friends, Theodoret, Avitus of Vienne). Lio, Ant 1952, 349/66 (the source for the formula: *pasce fame morientem*). P. Courcelle, *Hist. littéraire des grandes invasions germaniques,* 1948; id., RBP 1953, 23/37 (Addenda to the work of 1948). A. W. Ziegler, *Stimmen aus der Voelkerwanderung* (select patristic texts), 1950. Cf. the 3 vols. by De Ghellinck, cited supra p. 12. Hermann-Bardy, RAC 3, 928/55 (Dialogue in Antiquity and Christendom). Buscheit, RAC 3, 712/35 (Demosthenes). Vischer, TZ 1956, 320/36 (justification of literary work). Courcelle, RP 1957, 23/51 (pre-Augustinian autobiogr.).

5. Ecclesiastical and Cultural History

Talamo, *La schiavitù sec. i Padri della Chiesa,* [2]1927. T. Gérold, *Les Pères de l'église et la musique,* 1931. P. Oppenheim, *Das Moenchskleid im christl. Altertum,* 1931; *Symbolik u. religioese Wertung des Moenchskleides im christl. Altertum,* 1932. G. Bardy has investigated the question of ecclesiastical and cultural relations between the Greek East and the Latin West in numerous treatises. Here I will note only where these essays are to be found: RevSR 1932, 1/28; 1934, 525/49; 1935, 1/27; Ir 1937, 5/39, 313/38; RSR 1939, 5/58; DBSuppl. 2, 1442/82; La France Franciscaine 1939, 101/30, 380/430; RSR 1940, 257/306; L'année théol. 4, 1943, 457/503; Mél. Cavallera 1948, 191/214; RHE 1950, 5/24 *(Le patriotisme égyptien);* Mél. De Ghellinck I, 1951, 293/309 *(Écoles monastiques en Orient);* SE 1953, 86/104 *(Écoles monastiques en Occident).* Independent works by the same author: *La question des langues dans l'Église anc.* I, 1948 (here several older essays have been reprinted); *L'Église et les derniers Romains,* 1948; *La conversion au christianisme durant les premiers siècles,* 1949. A. Visser, *Die Entwicklung des Christusbildes . . .,* 1934. H. C. Weiland, *Het oordeel der Kerkvaders over het orakel,* 1935. C. J. Henning, *De eerste Schoolstrijd tusschen Kerk en Staat onder Jul. den Afv.,* 1937. E. M. Pickman, *The Mind of Latin Christendom,* 1937. P. Vielhauer, *Oikodome. Das Bild vom Bau i. d. christl. Lit., vom N.T. bis Clemens Alex.,* 1939. J.-R. Palanque, H. Davenson (and others), *Le christianisme et la fin du monde ant.,* Lyons 1943. Jungmann, ZKT 1947, 36/99 (Repudiation of Germanic Arianism). A. T. Geoghegan, *The Attitude towards Labor in Early Christianity and Ancient Culture,* W 1945. Ch. N. Cochrane, *Christianity and Classical Culture,* NY 1940 (till Augustine). Delaruelle, *Mél. de la société Toulousaine d'ét.*

class., 1946, 209/26 *(Le grec en Occid. du 5e au 9e s.)*. M. Hirschberg, *Studien zur Geschichte der "simplices" in der Alten Kirche,* thesis (typed), Hei 1944. L. Griffe, *La Gaule chrét. à l'époque romaine* I, 1947. H.-I. Marrou, *Hist. de l'éducation dans l'antiquité,* 1948, 416/61 (Christianity and Christian school). VC 1949, 208/36 (Patristic writings very rarely disseminated through booksellers). H. J. Schoeps, *Theologie und Geschichte des Judenchristentums,* 1949. G. L. Ellsperman, *The Attitude of the Early Christ. Latin Writers toward Pagan Literature and Learning,* W 1949 (Tertullian to Augustine). R. Wilde, *The Treatment of the Jews in Greek Christ. Writers of the First Three Cents.,* W 1949. E. Stein, *Hist. du Bas Empire* II (476–565), 1949. R. Stob, *Christianity and Classical Civilization,* Grand Rapids (Michigan) 1950. W. Laistner, *Festschrift P. Lehmann,* 1950, 47/61 (Pagan schools and Christian teachers); id., *Christianity and Pagan Culture in the Later Roman Empire,* Ithaca (N.Y.) 1951. G. Lapeyre–A. Pellegrin, *Carthage latine et chrét.,* 1950. E. Staehlin, *Die Verkuendigung des Reiches Gottes in der Kirche Jesu Christi*, vol. 1. (Testimonies from Christian antiquity) 1951. W. Jentsch, *Urchristliches Erziehungsdenken. Die Paideia Kyriou im Rahmen der jued.-christl. Umwelt,* 1951. Peterson, TZ 1951, 2 (Problem of nationalism). M. Maeder, *La liberté et l'esclavage dans l'Église primitive,* thesis, Neuchâtel 1951. E. Demougeot, *De l'unité à la division de l'Empire rom.* (395–410), 1951. Madoz, Folia 5, 1951, 5/25 (Arianism and Priscillianism in Galicia). Pellegrino, *Umanesimo e mondo crist.,* R 1951, 3/29 *(Umanità della prima letteratura crist.)*. E. R. Hardy, *Christian Egypt. Church and People,* O 1952. Dekkers, SE 1953, 193/233 (Greek translations of Lat. Patristic Writings). Killy-Hoepfner-Kollwitz, RAC 2, 287/320ff. (the image). Koepp-Stommel-Kollwitz, RAC 2, 194/219 (funeral). C. Schneider, *Geistesgesch. des antiken Christentums,* 2 vols., 1954 (follows completely the views of radical historians of religion: Christianity is mainly a product of Hellenism). Pellegrino, *Convivium* 1954, 257/70 *(Cultura crist.)*. Steinacker, *Mitteil. Instit. Oesterreich. Gesch.* 62, 1954, 28/66 (Rom. Church and the knowledge of Greek in the early Middle Ages). Mohrmann, ZMR 1954, 103/11 (Language problem of early Christian Missions). C. Becker, RAC 3, 104/25 (Cicero). J. Leipoldt, *Die Frau in der antiken Welt und im Urchristentum,* L 1954. J.-R. Laurin, *Orientations maîtresses des Apologistes chrét. de 270 à 361,* R 1954 (Euseb., Athanas., Method., Firm. Maternus). Van den Vyver, RHE 1957, 5/25 (Development of *computus*). R. Schmidt, ZKG 1957, 288/317 (*Aetates mundi* and the division of history).

6. *History of Philosophy*

L. Stefanini, *Il problema morale nello Stoicismo e nel Cristianesimo,* 1926. F. Rüsche, *Blut, Leben und Seele . . .,* 1930; *Das Seelenpneuma,* 1933. A. J. Festugière, *L'idéal relig. des Grecs et l'Évangile,* 1932, 221/63: *Aristote . . . jusqu'à Théodoret*. F. J. v. Rintelen, *Der Wertgedanke in der europaeischen Geistesentwicklung* I, 1932 (Greg. of Nyssa, Aug., Ps.-Dionys.). L. Ventura, *La pedagogia del Cristianesimo* I, [2]1943; II, 1936. J. Stelzenberger, *Die Beziehungen der fruehchristl. Ethik zur Ethik der Stoa,* 1933. F. Billicsich, *Das Problem der Theodizee im philosoph. Denken des Abendlandes* I 1, 1935. H. Emonds, *Hl. Ueberlieferung, Festschr. I. Herwegen,* 1938, 21/50 (*militia spirit.* in antique philos.). E. Bignone, RFC 1936, 225/37 *(Framm. del Protrettico di*

Aristot.). G. Lazzati, *L'Aristotele perduto e gli Scrittori crist.*, 1939. E. Seeburg, ZKG 1941, 390/431 (early Christian conceptions of history). R. Arnou, *Platonisme des Pères*, DTC 12, 2258/392. R. Arnou, *De "Platonismo" Patrum (Textus)*, R 1935. G. Verbeke, *L'évolution de la doctrine du pneuma, du Stoïcisme à S. Augustin*, Lou 1945. De Ghellinck, *Patristique et Moyen-âge* III, 1948, 245/310 (Dialectics in the Arian controversies). E. Ivánka, *Hellenisches u. Christl. im fruehbyz. Geistesleben*, V 1948. C. Moeller, *Sagesse grecque et paradoxe chrét.*, 1948. P. Giochetta, *La teologia della storia e i Padri della Chiesa*, R 1953 (Ignat., Justin, Iren., Clem. Al., John Chrysost.). P. Milburn, *Early Christ. Interpretations of History*, 1954. A. Quaquarelli, *La concezione della storia nei Padri prima da s. Agost.* I, R 1955.

7. *History of Religion*

Antiquity and Christianity: T. Klauser, *Die Cathedra im Totenkult der heidn. u. christl. Antike*, 1927. F. J. Doelger, *Antike und Christentum. Kultur- u. religionsgeschichtl. Studien* I–VI 1929/50; ΙΧΘΥΣ I–V 1910/41 (I [2]1928); *Sol Salutis*, [2]1925. *Reallexikon fuer Antike und Christentum*, ed. T. Klauser, L 1941 ff. F. Suehling, *Die Taube als religioeses Symbol im christl. Altertum*, 1930. G. Staehlin, *Skandalon*, 1930. H. Rahner, ZKT 1932, 231/53 (The willow as a symbol of chastity). F. Wiesehoefer, *Das Weihwasser in der Fruehzeit des Christentums und bei den klass. Voelkern des Altertums*, 1933. A. D. Nock, *Conversion. The Old and the New in Religion from Alexander the Great to Augustine of Hippo*, 1933 (Justin, Arnobius, Augustine). K. Pruemm, Sch 1932, 239/57 (Virgil's 4th Ecloge, cf. Kurfess, *Pastor bonus*, 1930, 262/71; PW 1938, 812/16); id., *Der christl. Glaube und die altheidnische Welt*, 2 vols., 1935. *Christentum als Neuheitserlebnis*, 1939. *Religionsgeschichtliches Handbuch f. d. Raum der altchristl. Umwelt*, [2]1954. W. Voelker, *Fortschritt u. Vollendung bei Philo v. Alex.*, 1938. Von der Leeuw, Mn 3, 1935–6, 125/48 *(refrig.)*. Parrot, RHR 113, 1936, 149/87; 114, 1936, 69/92, 158/96; 115, 1937, 53/89 *(refrig.)*. Cecchelli, StU 199/204, 481/3 *(refrig.)*. C. Marot, *Refrigerium*, Szeged 1937. The older literature on *refrigerium* is listed in J. Zellinger, *Augustinus u. die Volksfroemmigkeit*, 1933, 76 A. 54. L. Bieler, θεῖος Ἀνήρ, 2 fascs., V 1935–6. M.-J. Lagrange, *Critique hist.* I: *Les mystères: L'Orphisme*, 1937. W. Staerk, *Die Erloesererwartung in den oestl. Religionen*, 1938. W. Wittmann, *Das Isisbuch des Apuleius*, 1938, 163/86 (on the African Fathers from Tertullian to Augustine). H. Bergema, *De Boom des levens in Schrift en Hist.*, 1938. O. Kern, *Die Religion der Griechen* III: *Von Platon bis Kaiser Julian*, 1938. H. Leisegang, *Das Mysterium der Schlange*, *Eranos-Jahrbuch* 1939, 151/250. H. Hanse, *"Gott haben" in der Antike und im fruehen Christentum*, 1939. K. Baus, *Der Kranz in Antike u. Christentum*, 1940. H. W. Ruessel, *Antike Welt u. Christentum*, A 1941. Plumpe, *Vivum saxum, vivi lapides*, Tr 1, 1943, 1/14. H. Rahner, *Griech. Mythen in christl. Deutung*, 1945, and *Eranos-Jahrb.* 1943, Zu 1944, 305/404 (Mystery of sun and moon). D. Amand, *Fatalisme et liberté dans l'antiquité grecque*, Lou 1945 (also on the polemics of the Greek Fathers against the belief in fate widespread until the end of the 4th cent.). H. A. Wolfson, *Philo*, C (Mass.), 2 vols., 1947.

H. Rahner, *Eranos-Jb.* 1948–49, 11/87 (playing man). Blumenkranz, TZ 1948, 119/47 (Jewish proofs against the Latin-Christian arguments of the 5th–11th cents.). Bietenhard, TZ 1948, 174/92 (Church and Synagogue). M. Simon, *Verus Israel,* 1948 (relations betw. Christians and Jews; 135/425); cf. Blumenkranz, RÉt Juives 9, 1948–49, 3/67 (contd. till Gregory the Gt.). J. Giblet, *L'homme image de Dieu* (in Philo), Lou 1949. Quispel, TZ 1949, 429/36 (Philo and the old Christian heresies); id., Eranos-Jb. 1952, 109/68 (Man and energy in ancient Christianity). E. Bréhier, *Les idées philos. et relig. de Philon d'Al.,* 1950. H. J. Schoeps, *Aus fruehchristl. Zeit. Religionsgeschichtl. Untersuchungen,* 1950. E. Benz, *Der gekreuzigte Gerechte bei Plato . . . u. in der alten Kirche,* Mainz 1950; id., ZNTW 43, 1950 f., 194/224 (Socrates and the ancient Church); id., *Indische Einfluesse auf die fruehchristl. Theologie,* AkWiss, Mainz 1951, No 3. Arbesmann, Tr 7, 1949–51, 1/71 (Fasting and prophecy in antiquity and Christianity). P. Le Cour, *Hellénisme et christianisme,* 1951 (influence on Western Christianity). De Lubac, *Aspects du Bouddhisme,* 1951, pp. 93/141 and 172/91 (relations to the religion of the patristic period). K. Schubert, ZKT 1952, 1/62 (Jewish and Judaeo-Christian sects in the light of the MSS of 'En Fešcha). Nock, Mn 1952, 177/213 (Hellen. mysteries and Christian Sacraments). R. M. Grant, *Miracle and Natural Law in Greco-Roman and Early Christian Thought,* A 1952. L. Koep, *Das Himmelsbuch in Antike u. Christentum,* 1952. E. L. Backman, *Religious Dances in the Christian Church and in Popular Medicine,* Lo 1952. K. H. Rengstorf, *Die Anfaenge der Auseinandersetzung zw. Christusglaube u. Asklepiusfroemmigkeit,* 1953. C. Becker, RACh 3, 104/25 (Cicero). Pepin, RevSR 1955, 105/22 (contest from Homer to Moses). Dihle, SIF 1952, 169/90 (Antique politeness and Chr. humility). Theiler, *Festschr. A. Debrunner,* 1954, 431/40 (Language of the spirit: also Greg. of Nyssa). K. Pruemm, *Religionsgeschichtliches Handbuch,* R 1954. Riedinger, 1956. E. Pax, *Epiphaneia,* Mn 1955. M. Simon, *Hercule et le christianisme,* P 1955. J. Hessen, *Griech. oder bibl. Theologie? Probleme der Hellenisierung des Christentums,* L 1956. A. Stuiber, *Refrigerium interim. Die Vorstellungen vom Zwischenzustand und d. fruehchristl. Grabeskunst,* Bonn 1957.

8. Papyrological and non-literary texts

Bibliographical list of Christian elements in the papyri in K. Preisendanz, *Papyrusfunde u. Papyrusforschung,* 1933, 330 f. Christian papyrus texts in L. Mitteis and U. Wilcken, *Grundzuege u. Chrestomathie der Papyruskunde* I 2, 1912, 151/61; cf. also W. Schubart, *Einfuehrung in die Papyruskunde,* 1918, 174/83. Largest publication of texts by C. Wessely, PO 4, 1907, 95/210; 18, 1924, 343/509. G. Ghedini, *Lettere crist. dai Papiri greci del III e IV sec.,* 1923; SC 1935, 500/12 *(Nuovi framm.); Atti del IV Congresso Internaz. di Papirologia* 1936, 333/50 (list of all Christ. letters); Aeg 1937, 98/100, 334/7 *(Echi di eresie).* Leclercq, DAL 8, 2778/94; 13, 70/112, 1370/1520 *(Lettres chrét.).* C. del Grande, *Liturgiae preces (e papyris collecti),* Na 1934. Derouaux, NRT 1935, 810/43 *(Littérature chrétienne et papyrologie).* Modena, *Bull. Soc. d'Archéol. Alexandrie* 1937, 254/69; 1939, 293/310 *(il cristianesimo ad Osirinco).* Stegmüller, Aeg 1937, 452/62 (Christian texts from the Berlin collection). G. Bjoerk, *Der Fluch des Christen Sabinus,* Pap. Ups., Up 1938. Ausenda, Aeg 1940, 43/7 *(omiletica crist.).* P. Sanz, *Griech. liter. Pap. christl. Inhalts,* V 1946 (esp. Origen). Cavassini, Aeg 1954, 266/82 *(Lettere crist. nei papiri greci).* Pedretti, Aeg 1955, 292/98 (for the study of the liturg. papyri). J. O. Tjaeder, *Die nichtliterar. latein. Papyri in Italien . . .,* Lund 1955.

9. Archeology and Christian Art

W. Ellinger, *Die Stellung der alten Christen zu den Bildern . . .,* 1930; *Zur Entstehung der fruehen Entwicklung der altchristlichen Bildkunst,* 1934. G. Wilpert, *La fede della Chiesa nasc. secondo i monum. dell'arte funer. ant.,* 1937. Eltester, ZNTW 1937, 251/86 (The Churches of Antioch in the 4th cent.). F. Gerke, ZKG 1940 (History of ideas of the earliest Chr. art). T. K. Kempf, *Christus der Hirt,* R 1942. *Misc. G. de Jerphanion* (= OCP 1947, 586/696). C. Leonardi, *Ampelos,* R 1947. Kollwitz, TG 1947, 95/117 (Christ-King). Stuhlfauth, RAC 1942, 111/41 (The ship as a symbol of early Christian art). Norwood, *Journ. Hist. Ideas* 1947, 431/48 (Pre-Nicene Fathers and Greek art). L. H. Grondijs, *L'Iconographie Byzant. du Crucifié mort sur la croix,* Bru, 2nd ed. 1947; cf. Grillmeier, *Bibl. Orient.* 10, 1953, 66/70. De Bruyne-A. Ferrua, RAC 1949, 215/84 (literary account). A. Richmond, *Archeology and the After-Life in Pagan and Christ. Imagery,* O 1950. L. Hertling-E. Kirschbaum, *Die roem. Katakomben u. ihre Maertyrer,* V 1950. J. Kollwitz, *Das Christusbild des 3. Jh.,* 1953. RQ 1953, 1/20 (On the early hist. of the veneration of images). H. v. Campenhausen, ZTK 1952, 33/60 (Question of images). Ladner, DOP 1953, 3/34, *The Concept of Image and the Byzant. Iconoclastic Controversy.* R. Canova, *Iscrizioni e monumenti protocristiani del paese di Moab,* Città del Vat. 1954. Wessel, *Archaeol. Anz.* 68, 1953, 118/36 (Emperor cult and image of Christ). A. Grillmeier, *Der Logos am Kreuz. Z. christolog. Symbolik des aelteren Kreuzigungsbildes,* Mn 1956. J. Carcopino, *Le mystère d'un symbole chrét.,* L'Ascia 1955. U. Fabricius, *Die Legende im Bild des 1. Jahrtausends der Kirche,* 1956.

On the Sator-Arepo problem: Dornseiff, ZNTW 36, 1937, 222/38. De Jerphanion, RSR 1937, 326/35 and OCP 1941, 5/35. Wendel, ZNTW 40, 1941, 139/51. Focke, WuerzbJB 3, 2. fasc. 1948. Henke, TZ 1949, 4. fasc. Eitrem, Er 1950, 73 f. Fuchs, TZ 1949, 6. fasc. and *Archiv f. Volkskunde* 1951, 28/54. Dirichs, TG 1950, 529/34 and 1951, 339 f. Atkinson, JEH 1951, 1/18. Euringer, HJB 1952, 334/53. Hommel, *Jahrb. der kirchl. Hochschule Berlin* 1952, 108/180. Last, JTS 1952, 92/7. Orzibal, RHR 146, 1954, 51/66 *(Sator Arepo, sa valeur et son origine).*

10. History of the Canon. Tradition. Patristic Exegesis

Leclercq, DAL 9, 1791/1835 (Hist. of the Canon to the Decret. Gelas.). M.-J. Lagrange, *Hist. ancienne du Canon du Nouv. Test.,* 1933. H. Opel, Κανών, L 1937 (History of the concept). L. Wenger, WSt 220, 2, 1942 (Canon in the Roman legal sources). A. Souter, *The Earliest Commentaries on the Epistles of Paul,* O 1927 (Victorinus of Pettau, Ambrosiaster, Jerome, August., Pelag.). G. Wuttke, *Melchisedech, der Priesterkoenig von Salem,* 1927. N. B. Stonehouse, *The Apocalypse in the Ancient Church,* 1929. E. Stein, *Die allegorische Exegese des Philo aus Alexandrien,* 1929 and CT 1935 (OT Bibl. criticism in the late Hellenistic period). K. Staehle, *Die Zahlenmystik b. Philo v. Alex.,* 1932. M. Pohlenz, *Philo v. Alex.,* GN 1942, 409/87. K. T. Schaefer, *Untersuchungen zur Gesch. der lat. Uebersetzung des Hebraeerbriefes,* 1929. G. Bardy, *Commentaires patrist. de la Bible,* DBSuppl. fasc. 6, 1931, 73/103. W. v. Loewenich, *Das Johannes-Verstaendnis im 2. Jh.,* 1932. K. Schluetz, *Isaias 11,2* (The seven gifts of the Holy Ghost) *in den ersten 4 christl. Jh.,* 1932. Bardy, *La litt. patristique des "Quaestiones et Responsiones" sur l'Écriture S.,* RB 1932, 210/36,

341/69, 515/37; 1933, 14/30, 211/29, 328/52 (offprint P 1933). H. Schlingensiepen, *Die Wunder des NT. Wege und Abwege ihrer Deutung in der alten Kirche bis zur Mitte des 5. Jh.,* 1933. K. Staab, *Pauluskommentare aus der griech. Kirche, aus Katenenhandschriften gesammelt u. hg.,* 1933. R. Devreesse, *Anciens commentateurs grecs de l'Octateuque,* RB 1935, 166/91; 1936, 201/20, 364/84. J. Schmid, *Untersuchungen zur Gesch. d. griech. Apocalypsetextes. Der K-Text,* Bi 1936, 11/44, 167/201. N. Y. Homes, *Het Testimoniaboek, Studien over O. T. Citaten in het N. T. en bij de Patres,* 1935. E. Aleith, *Das Paulusverstaendnis in der alten Kirche,* 1937. Wikenhauser, RQ 45, 1937, 1/24; TQ 1947, 399/417 (Millennium in Apoc. of John). J. L. Koole, *De overname van het O.T. door de christ. Kerk,* 1938. Skrinjar, Bi 1935, 1/24,113/40 (Apoc. 1, 4 etc.: *spiritus septiformis*). Simon, RHP 1936, 58/93 (Melchisedech). K. Burdach, *Der Gral,* 1938, 49/105 (Jo. 19, 33–37: piercing by the lance). E. A. Cerney, *Firstborn of every Creature: Col. 1, 15,* Baltimore 1938. G. Mitosiuka, *Patrum Graec. interpretationes Ex. 3, 14,* Prague 1939. F. Anizan, *La clef patrist. des paraboles,* Laudun 1939. C.-M. Edsman, *Le baptême de feu,* L-Up 1940 (Mt. 3, 11). H. Rahner, Bi 1941, 269/302, 367/403 (Jo. 7, 37f.). H. W. Wolff, *Jesaja 53 im Urchristentum* (till Justin), thesis Halle 1942. Plumpe, TS 6, 1945, 509/23 (Tit. 1, 25). Sickenberger, TQ 1946, 361/74 (Apoc. 12). Cerfaux, *Misc. Mercati* I, 107/26 (Acts 15). Galdós, EE 1945, 221/46 (Melchizedech). Wallach, RevRel 1944, 130/6 *(Testimonia bibl.)*. Pettirsch, ZKT 1947, 257/327, 417/44 (prohibition of *opera servilia*). Grant, HTR 1947, 1/17 (The Decalogue). Saunders, TSW 1948, 536/53 (Devil and Divinity of Christ). Gewiess, TQ 1948, 463/87 (Phil. 2, 5–11). Bonsirven, Mél. Cavallera 1948, 47/63 (Mt. 19, 9). Mercati, ST 142, 1948 *(Proemi del Salterio di Origene, Ippolito, Eusebio, Cirillo Aless. e alteri)*. Leclercq, DAL 170 f, 1951, 1778/1811 (Symbolism). De Lubac, RSR 1947, 180/226 (Typology and allegory). Mél. Cavallera 1948, 347/66 (fourfold sense of Scripture); RSR 1949, 542/76 (spiritual sense). Daniélou, ETL 1948, 119/26 (different senses of Scripture); Bi 1947, 363/93 *(Typologie d'Isaac)*; RSR 1948, 382/411 *(Typologie de la semaine)*; RSR 1946, 402/30 (Passage through the Red Sea and Baptism); Dieu Vivant 8, 1947, 97/112 *(déluge—baptême)*; Ir 1949, 26/45 (Rahab type of the Church); Maison-Dieu 18, 1949, 7–33 (Types of Eucharist); id., *Sacramentum futuri, Études sur les origines de la typologie biblique,* 1950. H. Schneider, Bi 1949, 28/65 and contd. (Bibl. codes in Chr. antiquity). Zeller, ZKT 1949, 385/465 (Study on Mt. 27, 52f.). Puzo, *Estud. Bíblicos* 1950, 407/39 (literary forms and authority of Fathers). Munoz Iglesias, *Estud. Bíblicos* 1949, 213/37 (History and Patristic exegesis). Turrado, *ibid.* 1949, 287/308 (Authority of the Fathers in questions of authorship of Bibl. books). Asensio, Gr 1950, 490/520, with 3 continuations (tradition of the sin in paradise as a sexual offence). E. Massaux, *Influence de l'Év. de S. Matth. sur la littérature chrét. avant S. Irénée,* Lou 1950. Boismard, RB 1950, 388/408 (Bibl. textual criticism and Patristic citations). D. Lerch, *Isaaks Opfer christlich gedeutet,* T 1950 (from Origen to modern times). L. E. Froom, *The Prophetic Faith of our Fathers,* vol. 1, W 1950. Schelkle, TQ 1951, 17/31, 189/207 (Election and freedom in Rom. in the Greek Fathers); TQ 1952, 129/51 (Exegesis as understanding of symbols); ZNTW 44, 1952–53, 223/36 (Rom. 13, 1–7). Plumpe, *Mél. De Ghellinck* I, 1951, 387/403 (Apoc. 2, 11). Burleigh, *Austral. Bibl. Rev.* 1, 1951, 75/85 (OT Wisdom lit. and early Chr. doctrine). Grant, *Interpreter* 5, 1951, 186/202 (The OT and the early Christians). C. Menchini, *Il discorso di S. Stefano protomart. nella letteratura e nella predicazione crist. primitiva,* R 1951. R. Balducelli, *Il concetto teolog. di carità . . . di 1 Cor. 13,* W 1951 (Patristic period and MA). Blumenkranz, *Mél. L. Halphen,* P 1951, 11/17 (Lc. 15, 16). G. T. Kennedy, *St. Paul's Conception of the Priesthood of Melchisedech,* W 1951 (incl. the Fathers).

F. H. Keienburg, *Die Geschichte der Auslegg. von Roem. 13, 1–7,* thesis Basle 1952. J. Gennaro, *Exegetica in Prologum S. Joannis sec. maximos Ecclesiae doctores antiquitatis latinae,* R 1952. Michl, Bi 1952, 371/401, 476/505 (Gen. 3, 15). Vaccari, *Dold-Festschr.,* 1952, 34/39 (Gen. 3, 15). Pétré, RSR 1952, 63/79 (readings of the 4th Lat. petition of the Our Father). Riesenfeld, *Svensk Exegetik Arsbok* 1952, 106/18 (Jo. 7, 53–8, 11). Voelker, ZKG 1952–53, 1/33 (Wisdom literature in the Alexandrines). V. E. Hasler, *Gesetz und Evangelium in der alten Kirche bis auf Origenes,* Zu 1953. B. Schneider, CBQ 1953, 163/207 (St. Paul's antithesis "The Letter and the Spirit" also in the Fathers). Crehan, CBQ 1953, 418/26 (St. Peter's Journey to Emmaus). Rivera, *EstMarianos* 1953, 62/72 (symbolic significance of the miracle of Cana). Bardy, *Bible et Vie chrét.* 1953, 25/39; 1954, 40/52 (Reading of Bible and dissemination of Bible). Van Unnik, VC 1949, 1/36 (immutability of Canon). J. Leipoldt, ZNTW 44, 1952–53, 118/45 (Early hist. of doctrine of inspiration). E. Flesseman-van Leer, *Tradition and Scripture in the Early Church,* A 1954. Fernes Ros, *Misc. B. Ubach,* 1953 (1954), 31/48 (Creation of Eve in the Greek Fathers till Chrysost.). Daniélou, Th 1954, 83/89 (The Fathers and the Scriptures). Menard, RUO 1954, 5/25 (Patristic exegesis of Jo. 7, 38). L. Vischer, *Die Auslegungsgesch. v. 1 Kor. 6, 1–11,* T 1955. Lyonnet, Bi 1955, 436/56 (Rom. 5, 15 in the Greek Fathers). Somers, *Folia 9,* 1955, No. 2, 63/101 (The Riddle of a Plural: Gen. 1, 21 till Augustine). Schelkle, TQ 1954, 290/318 (Church and Synagogue in the exegesis of Rom.). J. Gnilka, *Ist 1 Kor 3, 10–15 ein Schriftzeugnis f. d. Fegefeuer?* Thesis Wu 1955. Bacht, Sch 1955, 1/32 (Tradition and Sacrament; Cullmann, *Die Tradition,* Zu 1954). K. H. Schelkle, *Paulus, Lehrer der Vaeter. Die altkirchl. Auslegung v. Roem. 1–11,* Duesseld. 1956. J. Kremer, *Was an den Leiden Christi noch mangelt. Eine interpretationsgeschichtl. und exeg. Untersuchung,* Bonn 1956.

On Individual Questions of the Patristic History of Dogma

11. God

N. Weber, *Das Wunder als Glaubenskriterium in der Werdezeit des Christentums,* thesis Bonn 1942. Pera, Ang. 1942, 39/95 (Concept of theology, Clem. Al., Porphyry, Eusebius Caes., Basil, Dionys. Areop.). A. Welykyj, *Die Lehre der Vaeter des 3. Jh. von der Gotteslehre u. Gottesfurcht,* thesis R 1948 (excerpt). G. L. Prestige, *God in Patristic Thought,* Lo [2]1952 (French tr. P 1955).

12. Doctrine of the Trinity

J. Lebreton, *Hist. du dogme de la Trinité* I: *Origenes,* [6]1927; II: *De S. Clément à S. Irénée,* 1928. M. Jugie, *De processione Spiritus S. ex fonte revelationis et sec. Orientales dissidentes,* R 1936. Quasten, *Festschr. f. Ild. Herwegen,* 1938, 51/8 (The Good Shepherd in the Logos theol.). Segovia, Gr 1938, 3/36 (trinit. terminology in the 4th cent.); EE 1947, 435/78 (Greek and Lat. trinit. formulae); RET 1948, 385/407 (eternal generation of the Son); *Mél. De Ghellinck* I, 1951, 375/86 (*sine differentia discretionis sentimus* and the Fathers). Gómez, EE 1946, 347/98 (unity and trinity). Camelot, *Russie et Chrétienté,* 1950, 179/92 (the *filioque* in M. Vict., Hil., Ambr., August.). T. Ruesch, *Die Entstehung der Lehre vom Hl. Geist bei Ign. u. Ant., Theoph. von Ant. und Iren.,* Zu 1952. Simonetti, *Aevum* 1952, 33/41 (*process. Spiritus S.* in Orig., Athan., Basil, Didym., Cyril Al.); *Maia* 1954, 201/17 (*process. Spir. S.* in Hil., Ambr., M. Vict., Gregory of Elv., August.). Ortiz de Urbina, OCP 8, 194/209 *(ὁμοούσιος preniceno).* Hommel, Theol V 5, 1953–54, 322/78 (Pantocrator, concept of the Father God). G. Kretzschmar, *Stud. z. fruehchristl. Trinitaetstheologie,* 1955. Armstrong, VC 1954, 234/38 (Plotinus' doctrine of the *Nous* in the Fathers). Kraft, ZKG 66, 1954–55, 1/24 *(Homoousios).* Meinhold, PWK 21, 1066/1101 *(Pneumatomachi).* Hammerschmidt, TR 1955, 145/54 (development of theol. concepts betw. 325 and 381). H. Wolfson, *The Philosophy of the Church Fathers: Faith, Trinity, Incarnation,* C (Mass.) 1956. Camelot, RSPT 1956, 443/71 *(Théologie de l'image de Dieu).*

13. Doctrine of Creation

Simonin, DTC 13, 914/60 (Providence in the Greek Fathers). F. Sanc, *Providnost Bozja,* Zagreb 1939, 39/139 (Providence in the Greek Fathers). G. Borgenstierna, *Foersyntanken i gammalgrakisk teologi,* Up 1948 (Belief in Providence in ancient Greek theology: Nemesius of Emesa, John Chrys., Theodoret, John of Damascus). E. Peterson, *Das Buch von den Engeln,* 1935. Mattingly, HTR 1937, 103/17 (angels). J. Daniélou, *Les anges et leur mission d'après les Pères de l'Église,* 1952. G. Karpp, *Probleme altchristl. Anthropologie,* 1950 (Teaching on the soul in Tert., Clement Al., Arnob., Lact., Orig.). Quispel, *Nd. Arch. KG* 1949, 1/15 (Concept of man in Chr. antiquity); *Eranos-Jb* 21, 1952, 109/168 (Man and energy in ancient Christianity). Daniélou, *Eranos-Jb* 22, 1953, 433/72 *(Terre et paradis).* B. Krivoshein in *The Angels of Light and the Powers of Darkness,* ed. by E. L. Mascall, Lo 1954, 22/46 (in *Vita s. Antonii,* Evagr. Pont., Ps.-Macar., Diadochus of Phot. and Isaac of Nin.).

14. Christology and Doctrine of Redemption

J. Rivière, *Le dogme de la rédemption après S. Augustin,* 1930; *Le dogme de la rédemption. Études critiques et documents,* Lou 1931, 59/240; *Le dogme de la rédemption au début du moyen âge,* 1934. F. Loofs, *Theophilus von Antiochien (Adv. Marcionem) und die anderen theol. Quellen des Irenaeus,* 1930, 101/210 (*Geistchristologie* before Irenaeus). A. Wintersig, *Die Heilsbedeutung der Menschheit Jesu in der vornizaen. griech. Theologie,* 1932. I. Rucker, *Das Dogma von der Persoenlichkeit Christi und das Problem der Haeresie des Nestorius,* 1934 (publ. by author at Oxenbronn nr. Guenzburg a. D.). A. d'Alès, *Le dogme d'Ephèse,* 1931. Favre, RHE 1937, 687/724 (Christ's rest in the tomb). J. de J. Pérez, *La Cristología en los Símbolos Toledanos* IV, VI y XI, R 1939. R. V. Sellers, *Two Ancient Christologies,* 1940 (School of Alex. and Antioch). J. Barbel, *Christos Angelos,* Bonn 1941. L. Capéran, *Le problème du salut des infidèles* 2, 1934, 33/168 (teaching of the Fathers). Kollwitz, TG 34, 182/93

(*Salus infidel.* in the Roman Missal). T. Tschipke, *Die Menschheit Christi als Heilsorgan der Gottheit . . .,* 1940. Gaudel, RevSR 1937, 186/234; 1938, 45/71, 201/17 *(assumptus homo)*. A. Spindeler, *Cur verbum caro factum?* (4th/5th cent.), R 1938. Richard, MSR 1945, 5/32, 243/70 *(hypostasis* from Apollinaris of L. to Chalcedon). Xiberta, *Misc. Mercati* I, 327/54 *(Christological controversies)*. Rivière, RevSR 1947, 53/89 *(Le mérite du Christ)*. P. Brezzi, *Accad. Lincei. Rend. ser.* 8, 2, 1947, 222/58 *(La teopoiesi nel pensiero crist. dei primi sec.)*. Lamme, JTS 1948, 58/73 (βασιλεία of God and βασιλεία of Christ in the Greek Fathers). Nédoncelle, RevSR 1948, 277/99 (*Prosopon* and *persona* in class. antiquity). Grillmeier, ZKT 1949, 1/53, 184/203 (Doctrine of *descensus* and hypostatic union). E. Amann, DTC 15, 1946, 505/12 *(Theopaschit.)*. Lépez Oreja, Hel 1951, 129/60 (Terminology of Incarnation to Cyril). H. J. Schoeps, *Vom himmlischen Fleisch Christi,* 1951, 5/24 (patrist. period). E. W. Turner, *The Patristic Doctrine of Redemption,* Lo 1952. Delaruelle, BLE 1952, 161/72 (human person in 3rd cent.). A. Grillmeier-H. Bacht, ed. *Das Konzil von Chalkedon* I, 1952; II, 1953. All contributions treating Christological or soteriological questions are cited suo loco. Here I would only mention three summarizing works: Grillmeier I, 5/202 (the linguistic and theol. preparation of the Christolog. formula of Chalcedon); II, 791/839 (relation of Chalcedonism and Neo-Chalcedonism in the Latins from Boethius to Gregory the Gt.); C. Moeller, I, 637/720 *(Chalcédonisme et néo-chalcédonisme en Orient de 451 à la fin du VIe siècle)*. R. Hardy and C. Richardson, *Christology of the Later Fathers,* Ph 1954 (Translation of texts from 4th to 7th cents.). Elert, ZSystT 1954, 1/15 *(Christusbild u. Christusdogma)*. Casey-Thomson, JTS 1955, 49/65 (Dialogue betw. Christ and Devil; 4th/5th cent.). A. Gilg, *Weg u. Bedeutung der altchristl. Christologie,* Mn 1955. Crehan, JTS 1955, 87/90 *(Verbum Dei incarn.* and *Verb. Dei script.)*. Simonetti, *Maia* N. S. 7, 1955, 308/24 (*processio Spir. S.* in Latin Fathers). M. Feitsma, *Het Theopaschitisme. Een dogma-hist. Studie . . .,* Thesis A, Kampen, 1956.

15. Mariology

O. Bardenhewer, *Marienpredigten aus der Vaeterzeit uebersetzt,* 1934. F. Drewniak, *Die mariologische Deutung von Gn. 3, 15 in der Vaeterzeit,* 1934; cf. Lennerz, Gr 1946, 300/18. F. S. Mueller, OCR 35, 1934, 157/92 (Immacul. in the Copts and Aethiopians); Sch 1934, 161/201 (Immacul. in the Syrians and Armenians); Gr 1935, 74/96, 225/50; 1936, 82/115 (Immacul. in the Greek Church). P. Botz, *Die Jungfrauschaft Mariens im NT u. der nachapostol. Zeit,* 1935. H. Koch, *Virgo Eva — Virgo Maria,* B 1937; cf. K. Adam, TQ 1938, 171/89. Barré, RSR 1939, 129/62, 303/34 *(la royauté de Marie)*. De Urbina, OCP 1940, 40/82 *(Mariologia nella Patrologia orient.)*. D. Franses, *Mariavereering in de eerste eeuven der Kerk,* 1941. L. Carli, *La morte e l'assunzione di S. Maria nelle omelie grecche dei secoli VII e VIII,* R 1941. De Orbiso, *Estudios bíbl.* I, 1941, 187/207, 273/89 *(La Mujer del protoevang.)*. Capelle, Mu 1943, 1/39 (Marian feast in Jerusalem). O. Faller, *De priorum saeculorum silentio circa Assumpt. B. M. V.,* R 1946; cf. Altaner, TR 1948, 129/40. M. Jugie, *La Mort et l'Assomption de la S. Vierge,* R 1944. Cf. Altaner, TR 1949, 129/42 and 1950, 5/20. A. Dufourcq, *Comment s'éveilla la foi à l'Immaculée Concept. et à l'Assomp. aux Ve et VIe s.,* 1946. Rush, AmEcclRev 116, 3/31 *(Assumption in the Apocrypha)*. Plumpe, TSW 1948, 567/77 *(virginitas in partu)*. Bover,

Estud. Marianos 7, 1948, 91/104; 8, 1949, 185/256 (Mary's spiritual motherhood in the Greek Fathers). Garreta, *ibid.* 1948, 105/20 (in the Latin Fathers). *BullSociétéFrançÉtMariales: Assomption de Marie,* parts 6–8, 1948–50; *Marie et l'Église,* parts 9–10, 1951–52. Madoz, EE 1949, 291/306 (beginning of Marian exegesis of Gen. 3, 15); EE 1951, 361/74 (Mary's death in the Spanish Fathers). Botte, SE 1949, 111/22 (Feast of Theotokos in Armen. lectionary). Rivera, *Estud. Marianos* 9, 1950 (Mary's death in tradition till the 8th cent.). Mohrmann, RSCI 1951, 1/6 *(Ave gratificata).* Alois Mueller, *Ecclesia-Maria,* Frib 1951. H. Frévin, *Le mariage de la S. Vierge dans l'hist. de la théologie,* thesis Lille 1951 (not printed); cf. on this Didier in MSR 1952, 135/38. Soell, TQ 1951, 163/88, 288/319 (Mariology of Cappadocians). Leal, EE 1951, 475/508 (Mary's external appearance in ancient Chr. lit.). S. C. Estopañan, *Estud. Josefinos* 1951, 176/87 (St. Joseph's paternity in the Greek Fathers). H. Rahner, *Maria u. die Kirche,* I 1951 (texts). Capelle, EL 1952, 241/51 (Mary's death and assumption into heaven in the Oratio *Veneranda*); *Marianum* 15, 1953, 241/76 (Assumption into heaven and liturgy). M. Jugie, *L'Immaculée Conception dans l'Écriture S. et la tradition orientale,* R 1952; R. Laurentin, *Court traité de théologie mariale,* 1953 (p. 121/73: important survey on the state of research, in so far as it is a question of spurious or dubious Mariological texts printed in ML and MG). Congar, RSPT 1954, 3/38 (Mary and the Church). A. Wenger, *L'assomption de la S. Vierge dans la tradition byzant. du 6e au 10e s.,* 1954 (4 new Greek and several Lat. texts). H. Frévin, *Le mariage de la Vierge dans l'hist. de la théologie* (till the 13th cent.), Wardin (Nord), chez l'auteur (1954?). M. Gordillo, *Mariologia Orientalis,* R 1954. H. Caothalem, *Le parallélisme entre la S. Vierge et l'église lat.* (till 12th cent.), R 1954. Gianelli, REB 1953, 106/19 (patrist. testimonies for the appearance of the risen Christ before Mary). Dold, MTZ 1953, 232/35 (Sap. 3, 1 and the *Assumpta*). Bardy, *Bible et Vie Chrét.* 7, 1954, 32/41 (Mary in the Canticle). Sibum, *Christ. Oosten en Hereeniging* 8, 1955, 56/76 (Immaculata in the Greek tradition). *BullSociétéFrançÉtMariales,* part 12: *La nouvelle Ève,* I 1954 (with contributions by Jouassard, Capelle and Laurentin). Spedalini, Mar 1955, 153/82 (Mariology in the African Church). G. Schueckler, *Maria im Geheimnis der Kirche,* Cologne 1955 (Patristic texts in trans.). C. Dillenschneider, *Le sens de la foi et le progrès dogmat. du myst. marial,* R 1954. W. Delius, *Texte zur Marienverehrung . . .,* 1956 (KlT 178).

16. Grace, Justification, Predestination

Gaudel, DTC 12, 275/606 *(Péché originel).* Simonin - Saint-Martin - Garrigou-Lagrange, DTC 12, 2832/901 *(Prédestination).* A. Michel, DTC 12, 1261/9 *(Persévérance).* J. Schnitzer, *Die Erbsuende im Lichte der Religionsgeschichte,* Bologna 1931. A. Slomkowski, *L'état primitif de l'homme dans la tradition de l'Église avant S. Augustin,* 1928. Lot-Borodine, RHR 1932–33, 105/07 *(déification dans l'Église grecque).* S. Tromp, *De Spiritu S., anima corporis mystici (Testimonia),* 2 fascs., R 1932. K. Rahner, ZKT 1935, 333/418 *(Gottesgeburt im Herzen der Glaeubigen);* id., ZKT 1936, 471/510 *(Todsuendenbegriff bis Tertullian).* E. Mersch, *Le corps mystique du Christ,* 2 vols., Lou 1936; id., NRT 1938, 681/702 *(Filii in Filio); La théologie du Corps mystique,* 2 vols., Bru 1944. P. Galtier, *Le S.*

Esprit en nous d'après les pères grecs, R 1946. H. Rondet, *Gratia Christi. Essai d'hist. du dogme et de théologie dogmatique,* 1948.

17. Baptism and Confirmation

A. Michel, DTC 14, 585/627 *(Les sacrements en général).* B. Welte, *Die postbaptismale Salbung,* 1938. F. C. Macdonald, *A Hist. of Confirmation,* 1938. Van den Eynde, RTA 1939, 97/109 (2nd Council of Orange 441); Ant 1939, 257/76 *(Rites postbaptismaux).* Dick, ZKT 1939, 1/49 (Godfathers). Elfers, TG 1942, 334/41 (anointing with chrism). P. Lundberg, *La typologie baptismale dans l'anc. Église,* Up 1942. J. Schuett, *Die sakramentale Materie der hl. Firmung in der Zeit vom 1. bis 7. Jh.,* thesis Mr 1943. Chavasse, *Mél. E. Podéchart,* 1945, 103/20 (2. Council of Orange 441). Retcliff, *Theology* 49, 1946, 258/65, 290/95 (Relation of Confirmation to Bap.). Quasten, TSW 1946, 309/13 (Consecration of the bapt. water in the Syr. rite of the 4th cent.). P.-H. Menoud, *Verbum Caro* 2, 1948, 15/26 (infant baptism in the ancient Church). Chavasse, RSR 1948, 325/81 *(scrutins prébaptismaux avant le 9e s.).* J. H. Crehan, *Early Christ. Bapt. and the Creed,* Lo 1950. W. H. Lampe, *The Seal of the Spirit,* Lo 1951 (Doctrine of Bapt. and Confirm. in NT and the Fathers). W. M. Bedard, *The Symbolism of the Bapt. Font in Early Christ. Thought,* W 1951. Didier, MSR 1949, 233/46 and 1952, 191/220 (Infant baptism in Asterius Soph., Greg. Naz., Constit. Apost., John Chrys.). A. Benoît, *Le baptême chrét. au 2e s.,* P 1953. H. Kraft, KIT 174 *(Geschichte der Taufe bis Augustin).* O. Heggelbacher, *Die christliche Taufe als Rechtsakt,* Fri 1953. A. Mostaza-Rodríguez, *Il problema del ministro extraordinario de la confirmación,* Ma 1952. Peterson, VC 1955, 1/20 (Baptism in the Acherusian Lake). B. Neunheuser, *Taufe u. Firmung,* Fr 1956.

18. Eucharist and Mass

Ruch-Gaudel, DTC 10, 864/85 *(La messe).* Leclercq, DAL 11, 513/774 *(La messe);* 14, 2385/89 *(Réserve eucharistique).* J. Coppens, DBSuppl. 2, 1146/1215 *(L'Eucharistie).* Perler, RACh 1, 667/76 *(Disciplina arcani).* P. Batiffol, *Études d'hist. et de théol. positive* II: *L'Eucharistie,* 91930. W. Goossens, *Les origines de l'eucharistie, sacrement et sacrifice,* 1931. P. Browe, *De frequenti communione in eccles. occidentali . . .* (till A.D. 1000) *documenta . . .,* R 1932. J. H. Rohling, *The Blood of Christ in Christ. Lat. Literature before the Year 1000,* W 1932. J. Quasten, *Monumenta euch. et liturg. vetustissima, 7 partes* (FP 7), 1935. A. Astori, *L'eucharistia nei primi tre secoli della Chiesa,* Mi 1935. Casel, *Neue Zeugnisse fuer das Kultmysterium,* JL 1936, 99/150. J. Lacchello, *L'eucar. nei primi tre Concili di Toledo,* Tu 1939. W. de Vries, *Sakramententheologie bei den syr. Monophysiten,* R 1940; *Sakramententheologie bei den Nestorianern,* R 1947. G. A. Michell, *Euch. Consecration in the Primitive Church,* Lo 1948. Baus, *Festschr. J. A. Jungmann,* 1950, 55/70 *(eucharist. Glaubensverkuendigung).* Dekkers, *Festschr. G. v. d. Leeuw,* 1950, 141/56 (Reservation of the Euch.). B. Reicke, *Diakonie, Festfreude u. Zelus in Verbindung mit der altchristl. Agapefeier,* Up 1951. Diaz de Cerio, RF 145, 1952, 454/67 (euchar. theology in the poets of the first 4 cents.). Betz, *K. Adam-Festschrift,* 1952, 109/37 (eucharistic Cup in Judaeo-Christianity). Brinktrine, TG 1953, 411/25 (sacrament.

form of Euch. in the Fathers). W. Elert, *Abendmahl u. Kirchengemeinschaft in der Alten Kirche, hauptsaechlich des Ostens,* 1954. J. Solano, *Textos eucarísticos,* 2 vols., Ma 1952 and 1954 (4th to 8th cents.). J. Betz, *Die Euch. in der Zeit der griech. Vaeter,* 1955. N. Maurice-Denis et R. Boulet, *Euch. ou la messe dans ses variétés, son histoire et ses origines,* 1953.

19. Penance and Extreme Unction

J. A. Jungmann, *Die lat. Bussriten,* I 1932. P. Galtier, *L'Église et la rémission des péchés aux premiers siècles,* 1932. Amann, DTC 12, 748/845 *(Pénitence—sacrement).* Leclercq, DAL 14, 186/215. Galtier, DTC 14, 1137/95 (satisfaction). R. C. Mortimer, *The Origins of Private Penance,* O 1939. B. Poschmann, *Paenitentia secunda,* 1940 (till Origen). F. de S.-Palais d'Aussac, *La réconciliation des hérétiques dans l'Église lat.,* 1943. Janini Cuesta, RET 1947, 337/63 (*penitencia medicinal,* sec. 3/4). Galtier, Gr 1948, 288/94 (penitential canons of Nicaea); *Aux origines du sacrement de pénitence,* R 1951. Gaudemet, RevSR 1949, 64/77 (kinds of excommunication). S. Gonzales Rivas, *La penitencia en la primitiva Iglesia española,* 1950. Emonds-Poschmann, RACh 2, 802/14 (Penance, penitential dress, grades of penance). B. Poschmann, *Busse u. Letzte Oelung,* 1951. J. Fernández Alonso, *Hispania sacra* 4, 1951, 243/311 (Penitential discipline in Rom. Visigoth Spain). C. Vogel, *La discipline pénitentielle en Gaule,* 1952 (till 7th cent.). H. Braun, ZTK 1953, 243/58 (Conversion—*Umkehr*—in late Jewish, heretical and early Christian view).

D'Alès, DB Suppl. I, 261/72 (Extreme Unction). F. Lehr, *Die sakramentale Krankenoelung im ausgehenden Altertum u. im FruehMA,* 1934. Aramean, Baz 1939, 8/13, 202/13; 1940, 33/8 (Extreme unction in the Armen. Church). A. Chavasse, *L'Étude sur l'onction des infirmes dans l'Église latine,* Lyons 1942. Paladini, EL 1949, 208/11 *(De unctione infirm.).*

J. Grotz, *Die Entwicklung des Bußstufenwesens in der vornizaen. Kirche,* 1955. Galtier, RSR 1954, 58/85 (Penance in Ireland). Vogel, RevSR 1956, 1/26, 157/86 *(Discipline pénit. en Gaule des origines au 9*[e] *s. Le dossier hagiographique).*

20. Ordination and Matrimony

A. Schebler, *Die Reordinationen in der "altkatholischen" Kirche,* 1936. J. Mayer, *Monumenta de viduis diaconissis virginibusque tractancia* (FP 42), 1938. Botte, RTA 1939, 223/41 (Ordination rite acc. to the *Statuta ecclesiae antiquae*). Jonkers, Mn 1942, 286/302 (slaves and freedmen as priests). González, *Miscell. Comillas* 1943, 273/93 (Education of clergy in Visigoth time). Croce, ZKT 1948, 257/314 (minor orders). F. de B. Vizmanos, *Las vírgenes crist. en la Iglesia. Estud. hist. y Antología patrística,* Ma 1949. M. A. Siotis, *Die klassische u. christl. Cheirotonia,* thesis, typed Marburg; printed in Θ 20–22 (1949–51). P. Dabin, *Le sacerdoce royal des fidèles dans la tradition ancienne et moderne,* Bru 1950. R. Loeher, *Priestertum im Zeugnis der Vaeter,* Lucerne 1951. R. Metz, *La consécration des vierges dans l'Égl. romaine,* 1954.

J. Koehne, *Die Ehen zwischen Christen u. Heiden in den ersten christl. Jhh.,* 1931. L. Anné, *La conclusion du mariage dans la tradition et le droit de l'Église lat. jusqu'au 6*[e] *siècle,* Lou 1935 and ETL 1935, 513/50. G. d'Ercole, *Stud. et Documenta hist. et iuris* 6, 1939, 18/75 (Consent to marriage in Rom. law and in the Fathers).

A. L. Ballini, *Il valore giuridico della celebrazione nuziale crist. dal primo sec. all'età guistiniana,* Mi 1939. A. de Manaricua, *El matrimonio de los esclavos,* R 1940. B. Koetting, *Die Beurteilung der 2. Ehe im heidn. u. christl. Altertum,* thesis Bonn 1943. L. Bopp, *Das Witwentum als organische Gliedschaft im Gemeinschaftsleben der alten Kirche,* 1950. K. Ritzer, *Eheschließung, Formen, Riten und religioeses Brauchtum der Eheschliessung in den christl. Kirchen des 1. Jahrtausends,* 2 vols., thesis, typed Mn. 1951/52. D'Izarny, VS, Suppl. 6, 1953, 92/118 *(Mariage et consécrat. virgin. au 4e s.).*

21. Church. Ecclesiastical Ministry. Ecclesiastical Law

L. Marchal, DBSuppl. 2, 1297/1333 *(Origine de l'épiscopat).* A. Michel, DTC 15, 2000/15 *(Unité de l'Église: Les Pères grecs).* O. Linton, *Das Problem der Urkirche in der neueren Forschung,* Up 1932. E. Altendorf, *Einheit und Heiligkeit der Kirche,* 1932 (Tertull. to Augustine). D. van den Eynde, *Les normes de l'enseignement chrét. dans la litt. patrist. des trois premiers s.,* 1933. Reynders, *Paradosis,* RTA 1933, 155/91 (to Irenaeus). W. Bauer, *Rechtglaeubigkeit und Ketzerei im aeltesten Christentum,* 1934. Steinwenter, *Der antike kirchl. Rechtsgang und seine Quellen,* ZRK 23, 1934, 1/116 (to Justinian). E. Roesser, *Goettliches und menschliches, unveraenderliches und veraenderliches Kirchenrecht von der Entstehung der Kirche bis zur Mitte des 9. Jh.,* 1934. J. Boeni, *Der Kampf um die Kirche. Studien zum Kirchenbegriff des christl. Altertums,* 1934. Tromp, Gr 1937, 3/29 *(Ecclesia sponsa, virgo, mater).* Madoz, EE 1942, 433/52 *(Mater Ecclesia).* H. Rahner, ZKT 1939, 311/49, 428/42; 1940, 61/80, 121/31 *(Mysterium lunae. Ein Beitrag zur Kirchentheologie der Vaeterzeit);* 1941, 123/52; 1942, 89/118; 1943, 1/21 *(Antenna crucis);* 1953, 129/73, 385/410. De Lubac, *Corpus mysticum.* Goldammer, ZNTW 40, 76/86 *(navis ecclesia).* Beumer, *Wiss. Weish.* 9, 13/22 (the pre-existing Church). J. C. Plumpe, *Mater Ecclesia,* W 1943 (1st–3rd cents.). A. van Hove, *De bronnen van het kerk. recht* (till 6th cent.). *Mededeel. Vlaam. Acad. Wetensch.* III 7, 1941. W. Bieder, *Ekklesia u. Polis im NT u. in d. Alt. Kirche,* Zu 1941. G. Bardy, *La théol. de l'Égl. de S. Clém. de Rome à S. Irénée,* 1945. Id., *La théol. de l'Égl. de S. Irénée au Concile de Nicée,* 1947. Greenslade, JTS 1943, 162/75 (eccl. office). H. Rahner, *Abendl. Kirchenfreiheit* (Documents), 1943 and *Mater Eccl. Lobpreis der Kirche* (1st millennium), 1944. Welsersheimb, ZKT 1948, 393/449 (Church in Greek commentaries on Canticle). K. E. Kirk, *The Apostolic Ministry,* 1946. Daniélou, Ir 1949, 26/45 *(Rahab, figure de l'Église).* Gil Atrio, RET 1949, 59/103; 1950, 227/73 (The Church in the old liturg. texts of the East). Gaudemet, RevSR 1949, 64/77 (Excommunication in 4th/5th cent.). Peterson, TZ 1950, 77/79 (ship as symbol of Church). De Zwaan, *Mél. M. Goguel* 1950, 270ff. (Idea of Church in 2nd cent.). De Vries, OCP 1951, 95/132 (Concept of Church of Nestorian theologians). J. Colson, *L'évêque dans les communautés primitives,* 1951 (to Iren.). G. F. Hollinghurst, *The Ministry of Teaching in the Christ. Church,* O 1951 (to Augustine). Stommel, MTZ 1952, 17/32 (Growth of importance of episcopal office for Church policy). Kohlmeyer, ZSK 1952, 1/36 (Charisma and law). Seumois, *Euntes Docete* 5, 1952, 126/53 (lay apostolate in antiquity). H. v. Campenhausen, *Kirchl. Amt u. geistl. Vollmacht in den ersten 3 Jhh.,* 1953. Schneemelcher, *Studium* 1953, 60/101 (Service and office of deacons in the Church).

A. Ehrhardt, *The Apostolic Succession in the First Two Cents.*, 1953. A. García Diego, *Katholike ecclesia,* Mexiko 1953 (from Ignatius of Ant. to Origen). Molland, RHPR 1954, 1/29 (Idea of apostolic succession). H. Rahner, ZKT 1953, 129/73, 385/410 and contd. (patristic symbolism of cross). R. Honig, *Beitraege zur Entwicklung des Kirchenrechts,* Go 1954 (4th/8th cents.). W. M. Ploechl, *Gesch. des Kirchenrechts* I, V 1953. G. Dix, *Le ministère dans l'Égl. anc.,* Neuchâtel 1955 (tr. from the Engl., 1946). E. W. Turner, *The Pattern of Christ. Truth,* 1954 (Orthodoxy and heresy in the ancient Church). Botte, Ir 1956, 5/28 *(Presbyterium* and *ordo episcoporum).*

22. Papal Primacy

E. Caspar, *Geschichte des Papsttums,* I 1930, II 1933. F. X. Seppelt, *Der Aufstieg des Papsttums* I [2]1939. Id., *Das Papsttum im Frueh-MA,* 1934. J. Haller, *Das Papsttum* I [2]1950. Glez, *Primauté du pape,* DTC 13, 247/94 (to Gregory the Gt.). M. Jugie, *Primauté dans les Églises séparées,* DTC 12, 344/91. C. Papadopulos, Τὸ πρωτεῖον τοῦ ἐπισκόπου Ῥώμης, At 1930. Guggisberg, ZKG 1935, 276/300 (Mt. 16, 18f. in Church hist.). K. Heussi, *War Petrus in Rom?* 1936; Chr. Welt 4, 1937; cf. Lietzmann, SbB 1936, 29. H.; Altaner, TR 1937, 177/88; Molland, TLZ 1937, 439/44. B. J. Kidd, *The Roman Primacy to* A.D. *461,* 1936. U. Holzmeister, *Vita s. Petri,* P 1937. H. Vogels (FP 9) 1937. E. Metzner, *Die Petrustradition u. ihre neuesten Gegner,* 1937. K. Heussi, Christl. Welt 4, 1937 and *Neues zur Petrusfrage;* cf. TR 1939, 365f and TLZ 1940, 24/6. U. Gmelin, *Auctoritas, Roem. Princeps u. paepstl. Primat,* 1937; *Deutsch. Arch. Gesch. MA* 1938, 509/31. J. A. Eisele, *Die Rechtsstellung des Papstes im Verhaeltnis z. d. Allg. Konzilien,* 1938. P. Batiffol, *Cathedra Petri. Ét. d'hist. anc. de l'Égl.,* 1938. H. A. Moreton, *Rome et l'Égl. primitive,* 1938. E. Fascher, PWK 19, 1335/61 (Peter). H. E. Symonds, *The Church Universal and the See of Rome,* Lo 1939. E. Dinkler, *Die ersten Petrusdarstellungen,* 1939. F. Heiler, *Altkirchl. Autonomie u. paepstl. Zentralismus,* 1941. Madoz, RET 1942, 229/55 (Papal primacy in Spain in the 7th cent.). Vega, CD 154, 1942, 23/56 cont.; RET 2, 63/99 (Rom. Primacy in Spain till the 7th cent.). E. Stauffer, ZKG 62, 3/34 (On the early hist. of the *Primatus Petri*). L. Hertling, *Misc. hist. pontif.* 9, R 1943, 1/48 (Communion and primacy). T. G. Jalland, *The Church and the Papacy,* 1946. H. Rahner, ZKT 1947, 1/35 *(navicula Petri).* Rush, TSW 1950, 570/76 (Primacy of Peter in NT apocrypha). Colson, VS, Suppl. 4, 1950, 181/205 (Rome and the bishops of the 1st and 2nd cents.). Wuyts, OCP 1951, 265/82 (Can. 28 of Chalcedon and Rome). B. Schultze, OCP 1951, 203/17 (Peter and John and the primacy). H. v. Campenhausen, ZKG 63, 1950–51, 133/44 (James and the early Christ. caliphate). Ribera de Santana, *The Thought of the Fathers on St. Peter's Denial,* R 1951 (thesis Gregor.). Griffe, BLE 1951, 193/209 (The legend of the translation of the bodies of the apostles *Ad Catacumbas*). C. Moeller, RSPT 1951, 413/23 (The 5th Council 553 and the *magisterium ordinarium*). J. Ludwig, *Die Primatworte Mt 16, 18 19 in der altkirchl. Exegese,* 1952. Staufer, ZRGG 1952, 193/214 (On the caliphate of James). De Vries, OCP 1952, 52/88 (Primacy, communion and Church in the Syr. Monophysites). Mohlberg, *Festschrift A. Dold,* 1952, 52/74 (On the so-called *Memoria Apostolorum*). Wessel, *Archaeol.*

Anzeiger 1950/51 (Berlin 1952), 298/323 (The *head* of the Church). O. Cullmann, *Petrus, Juenger—Apostel—Maertyrer,* Zu 1952. E. Giles, *Documents Illustrating Papal Authority* (96–454), 1952. T. O. Martin-E. Herman-A. Michel in: *Grillmeier-Bacht* II, 1953, 433/58; 459/490; 491/562 (Chalcedon-Byzantium and the primacy). M. Maccarone, *Vicarius Christi, Storia del titolo papale,* 1953. V. Seumois, *La papauté et les missions au cours des six premiers siècles,* 1953 (Peter, Leo the Gt., Gregory the Gt.). O. Karrer, *Um die Einheit der Christen. Die Petrusfrage,* 1953 (A colloquy with E. Brunner, O. Cullmann and v. Campenhausen). S. Bettini, *Jahrb. oesterreich. byzant. Gesellsch.* 1, 1951, 67/87 *(Tusco et Basso consulibus; tomba di s. Pietro).* K. Heussi, *Die roemische Petrustradition in krit. Sicht,* T 1955. C. Journet, *Primauté de Pierre dans la perspective protestante et dans la perspective cath.,* P 1953 (against Cullmann). Molland, NorTTidskr 54, 1953, 63/69 (apostolic succession). H. Marot, *Église et les Églises* I, Chevetogne 1955, 209/40 *(Les conciles romains du 4e et 5e s.).* Carcopino, CRI 1952, 424/34 *(2 textes controversés de la trad. apost. romaine).* Voegtle, MTZ 1954, 1/47 (on the book on Peter by O. Cullmann). Aland, NewTStud 2, 1956, 267/75 (against Heussi, 1955). Gilg, TZ 1955, 185/206 (on the Petrine question). Kathenmayer, IKZ 1956, 28/40 *(Peter in Rome?).*T. Klauser, *Die roem. Petrustradition im Lichte der neuen Ausgrabungen unter der Petruskirche,* 1956. E. Dinkler, *Th. Rundschau* 1959, 189/230.

23. *Eschatology*

A. Michel, *Purgatoire,* DTC 13, 1191/1237. J. A. MacCullogh, *The Harrowing of Hell,* 1930. Martínez Gómez, EE 1935, 505/39 (Indwelling of the H. Ghost and resurrection). Leclercq, DAL 11, 1181/95 *(Millénarisme).* F. Acaniz, *Ecclesia patrist. et millenarismus,* Granada 1934 (to 5th cent.) On *Refrigerium* v. supra No. 7. DTC 13, 2520/44 (Resurrection). Staerk, ZNTW 1936, 83/95 (Eschatology in the 2nd cent. till Iren.). Cullmann, RHP 1938, 174/86 (2nd cent. till 150). A. C. Rush, *Death and Burial in Christian Antiquity,* W 1941. Goguel, RHR 132, 1946, 124/69 *(Pneumatisme et eschatologie).* Philips, ETL 1947, 521/56 *(Les justes de l'Anc. Test.).* Daniélou, VC 1948, 1/16 *(La typologie millénariste de la semaine).* Botte, RTA 1948, 5/17 *(Prima resurrectio* in the Western Liturgies). F. Cumont, *Lux perpetua,* 1949 (Hist. of belief in the beyond; hist. of religions). J. A. Fischer, *Studien zum Todesgedanken in der alten Kirche* I, 1954 (in the first 3 cents.). W. Bauer, RACh 2, 1073/78 (Chiliasm). Pedicini, *Rend. Acad. di Arch. Napoli* 28, 1953, 13/57 (demonology). Cabaniss, VC 1953, 65/74 (Ps. 24 and Pliny jun., Ep. 10, 69; on descent into Hades). R. Franco, *El final del reino de Cristo en algunos autores antenic.,* thesis Greg., Granada 1955 (partial print).

24. *History of Morals*

F. Wagner, *Der Sittlichkeitsbegriff in der Hl. Schrift und i. d. altchristl. Ethik,* 1931. Mich. Müller, *Ethik u. Recht i. d. Lehre von der Verantwortlichkeit,* 1932. J. Stelzenberger, *Die Beziehungen der fruehchristl. Sittenlehre zur Ethik der Stoa,* 1933. W. S. Mackowiak, *Die ethische Beurteilung der Notluege in der altheidn., patrist., scholast. u. neueren Zeit,* Gniezno 1933. E. H. Perreau, *Mém. Acad. Sc., Inscr. et Belles-lettres de Toulouse, sér. XII* 14, 1936, 239/57 *(Coquettes et Pères de l'Égl.).* H. Frhr. v. Campenhausen, *Die Idee des Martyriums i. d. alten Kirche,* 1936. A. Nygren, *Eros u. Agape,* 2nd pt. 1937. Marty, RHP 1939, 288/97 *(hospitalité aux 3 premiers siècles).* A. Heitmann, *Imitatio Dei. Die ethische Nachahmung Gottes* (1st/2nd cents.), R 1940. Voegtle, TQ 1941, 217/37 (schema of capital sins). H. Holzapfel, *Die sittl. Wertung der koerperl. Arbeit im christl. Altertum,* 1941. Cherel, RHEF 1941, 129/64 (*à suivre;* history of toleration). G. della Volpe, *La morale religiosa nell'età patristica e medievale,* Messina 1941. C. Chavasse, *The Bride of Christ. An Enquiry into the Nuptial Element in Early Christianity,* Lo 1940. A. T. Geoghegan, *The Attitude towards Labor in Early Christianity and Ancient Culture,* W 1945. A. Ispanki, *De impotentia morali hominis Ecclesiae doctrina in saec. V,* Budapest 1946. Keseling, PJB 1948, 283/88 (4 cardinal virtues from Plato to Thomas). Giet, RSR 1948, 55/91 *(La doctrine de l'approbation des biens).* T. Ruether, *Die sittl. Forderung der Apatheia i. d. beiden ersten christl. Jhh. u. bei Klem. v. Alex.,* 1949. D. Lang, *Geist u. Leben* 1951, 209/22, 284/99 (Teaching on patience in Tert., Cypr., August., Thomas Aquin.). C. H. Dodd, *Gospel and Law . . . in Early Christ.,* C 1951. R. Balducelli, *Il concetto teologico di carità attraverso le maggiori interpretazioni patrist. e medievali di 1 Cor. 13,* R 1951. J. Leipoldt, *Der soziale Gedanke i. d. alten Kirche,* L 1952. Ryan, TSW 1952, 1/32 (rejection of military service). v. Campenhausen, *Festschr. K. Jaspers,* Mn 1953, 255/64 (Military service in the early Church). Barrosse, TSW 1954, 355/88 (Unity of love of God and love of neighbour in Orig., Didym., Cyr. Alex., John Chrys.).

25. Spirituality—Asceticism—Mysticism—Preaching—Pastoral Care

Dictionnaire de spiritualité ascétique et mystique, doctrine et histoire, publ. par les PP. M. Viller, F. Cavallera et J. de Guibert, 1935 ff. The 3rd vol. has begun to appear. All ascet. and myst. questions and notions are treated in separate articles also acc. to their hist. development, as well as all the more important Fathers; e. g. Bardy, 1, 727/46 *(Apatheia);* Viller-Olphe-Galliard, I, 938/77 *(Ascèse);* II, 1265/1520 *(connaissance de soi);* Arnou-Daniélou-Lemaître-Roques-Viller-Olphe-Galliard, II, 1521/2288 (Contemplation). — Strathmann-Keseling, RACh 1, 749/95 (Asceticism). Wilpert, RACh 1, 844/54 *(Ataraxia).* Survey of recent literature on patristic-Greek piety in J. Loosen, *Logos und Pneuma . . . bei Maximus Confessor,* 1941, XII–XXII. M. Viller und K. Rahner, *Aszese und Mystik i. d. Vaeterzeit,* 1939. Hopfner, PWK Suppl. 7, 50/64 (Asceticism). P. Pourrat, *La spiritualité chrét.* I, 1947. F. Arnaldi, *Dopo Costantino. Saggio sulla vita spirituale del 4 e 5 sec.,* Pisa 1927. H. Stadler, *Die Einschaetzung der Jungfraeulichkeit in altchristl. Zeit,* thesis, typed Wu 1930. H. Koch, *Quellen zur Gesch. der Askese u. des Moenchtums i. d. alten Kirche,* 1933. I. Hausherr, *De doctrina spirituali Christianorum orientalium quaestiones et scripta,* OC 30, 3, 1933; *Les grands courants de la spiritualité orientale,* OCP 1935, 114/38. G. Bardy, *La vie spirituelle d'après les Pères des trois premiers s.,* 1935. Hausherr, *Ignorance infinie,* OCP 1936, 351/62. J. Ziegler, *Dulcedo Dei* 1937, 58/104. H. Kerr, *The Preaching in the Early Church,* NY 1942. I. Hausherr, *Penthos. La doctr. de la componction dans l'Or. chrét.,* R 1944. R. Nugent, *Portrait of the Consecrated Woman in Greek Christ. Lit. of the First Four Cents.,* W 1941. T. Camelot, *Virgines Christi,* P 1944. A. Segovia, *Espiritualidad patrística,* Cadix 1944. H. Dressler, *The Usage of ἀσκέω . . .*

(till 100 B.C.), W 1947. Hausherr, RAM 1947, 3/7 *(Dogme et spiritualité orient.)*; *Mél. Cavallera* 1948, 231/59 *(L'imitation de Jés.- Chr.)*; OCP 1947, 195/218 *(Opus Dei)*.Y. Brilioth, *Predikans-historia*, Lund 1946. T. Illiez, OCP 1947, 299/354 (The royal Way). M. Marx, *Incessant Prayer in Ancient Monastic Literature*, Città del Vaticano 1947. A.J.Phytrakis, Ὁ κλαυθμὸς τῶν μοναχῶν, At 1946; Μαρτύριον καὶ μοναχικὸς βίος, At 1948. Dumon, SE 1, 1948 (Devotion to the humanity of Christ in antiquity). B. Fischer, *Die Psalmenfroemmigkeit der Maertyrerzeit*, 1949. Peterson, ZRGG 2, 1949/50, 197/205 (Origin of Christ, asceticism). v. Campenhausen, *Die Askese im Urchristentum*, 1948. Lemaître, RAM 1950, 121/72 (Contemplation among the Greeks and other Eastern Christians). G. J. Beck, *The Pastoral Care of Souls in Southeast France during the Sixth Cent.*, R 1950. E. E. Malone, *The Monk and the Martyr*, W 1950. O. Casel, *Gedaechtnisschr.*, 1951 (Martyrdom and monastic profession as second baptism). A. Hamann, *Le Pater expliqué par les Pères*, 1951; id., *Prières des premiers chrétiens*, 1952 (texts). F. Schultze, OCP 1952, 319/43 (The Jesus Prayer). D'Izarny, VS, Suppl. 6, 1953, 92/118 (Marriage and consecration of virgins in the 4th cent.). V. Monachino, *La cura pastorale a Milano, Cartagine e Roma nel sec. IV*, R 1947. J. E. Stewart, *The Influence of the Idea of Martyrdom in the Early Church*, thesis St. Andrews 1951. Peterson, ZRGG 1949/50, 192/205 (Origin of Chr. asceticism). Camelot in: *Mystique et Continence*, Bruges 1952, 273/92 (The 4th cent. treatises *De virginitate*). I. Hausherr, *Direction spirit. en Orient autrefois* (Or. Chr. Anal. 144), R 1955; DS, F. 20/21, 1955, 1008/60 *(Direct. spirit. en Orient)*; RAM 1956, 33/56 and contd. *(Comment prièrent les Pères?)*. Diehle, RACh 3, 735/78 (humility). Wenger, REB 1955, 140/95 (review of more than 100 writings on the spirituality and theol. of the East). Camelot, RSPT 1956, 443/71 *(Théologie de l'image de Dieu)*. J. Fernández Alonso, *La cura pastoral en la España romanovisigoda*, R 1955.

26. History of the Liturgy

Casel, JL 14, 1938, 1/78 (Celebration of Easter in earliest times). Severus, *Liturg. Leben* 5, 1938, 18/30 (Church Fathers and liturg. life). Dohmes, *ibid.* 5, 1938, 48/71 (People's chant of Pss. at celebration of sacrifice). K. Burdach, *Der Gral*, 1938, 151/80 (Piercing with the lance and burial in orient. mystag.). Callewaert, RHE 1942, 20/45 (hist. of *Kyrie*). Quasten, *Misc. Mercati* I, 373/406 (The Good Shepherd, early Chr. lit. of the dead and sepulchr. art). Klauser, *Misc. Mercati* I, 467/82 (introduction of Lat. Lit. in Rome). Michels, Tr 1944, 486/91 (Roman canon: 359); on this Capelle, RHE 1946, 417/21. M. Pellegrino, *Vox Patrum. Pensieri dei SS. Padri sulle feste lit.*, Tu 1944. Quasten, CHR 1941, 3/19 (Liturg. Singing of Women). Jungmann, *Missarum sollemnia* [4]1958. Leclercq, DAL F. 164/69, 242/85 *(Sacramentaires)*. E. Bourque, *Ét. sur les sacramentaires Romains*, 1949. Dekkers, *Misc. Mohlberg* I, 1948, 231/57 (Evening Mass in the Old Church?). Duerig, TQ 1949, 385/98 (*pignus* in the Rom. liturgy); id., LJ 1, 1951, 32/47 (Bibliography on the Lat. Chr. sacred language). Voelkl, RAC 1949, 155/70 (orientation). Stadlhuber, ZKT 1949, 129/83 (Hours of the laity). Pax, *Die Sprache. Zeitschr. f. Sprachwissenschaft* 1, 1949, 87/100 *(missa)*. *Vom christl. Mysterium, Gedaechtnisschr. f. O. Casel*, 1951; in Dohmes, 35/53 (pneumatic character of liturg. chant). *ibid.*, Quasten, 66/75

(Eucharist. piety in 4th cent.). *ibid.,* Dekkers, 97/114 (Old Monasticism and Liturgy). M. P. Nilsson, *Opuscula selecta* I, Lund 1951, 214/311 (Pre-history of feast of Christmas). A. S. Todd, *The Theolog. Understanding of Music in the Eschatology and Liturgy* (1st/6th cents.), thesis Edinburgh 1951. M. Steinheimer, *Die δόξα τοῦ θεοῦ in der roem. Liturgie,* 1951. J. Daniélou, *Bible et Liturgie. La théologie biblique des sacrements et des fêtes d'après les Pères de l'égl.,* 1951. Segovia, *Mél. De Ghellinck,* 375 ff. *(sine differentia discretionis; Praef. Trinit.).* H. Frank, SE 1952, 193/225 (Patristic sources of Christmas texts). Harrison, EL 1952, 252/73, 352/66 (The formulae *Ad virgines sacras*). H. Urner, *Die ausserbiblische Lesung im Gottesdienst* (till Augustine), Go 1952. Stommel, MTZ 1952, 17/32 (the episcopal cathedra). C. Mohrmann, *Epiphania,* RSPT 1953, 644/70. Engberding, OC 37, 1953, 56/88 (Style in the liturg. piety of the Chr. East). Capelle, RTA 1954, 5/22 *(Autorité de la liturgie chez les Pères).* Bellis, RSR 1, 1954, 9/39 *(Levantes puras manus nell'antica lett. crist.).* Dekkers, SE 1955, 99/130 *(La messe à la fin de l'antiquité et au moyen-âge).* J. Magne, *Argument d'un travail à paraître sur les origines de la messe,* I: *Des liturgies actuelles à leurs textes ou à leur teneur primitive,* 1955 (69 pp.) *(Chez l'auteur, Fontaine-Chaâlis par Senlis, Oise).* J. Beckmann. *Quellen zur Gesch. des christl. Gottesdienstes,* G 1956.

27. *Veneration of Saints and Relics, Pilgrimages*

P. Séjourné, DTC 13, 2318/51 (Cult of relics); DTC 14, 886/939 (veneration of saints). F. Ruetten, *Die Victorverehrung im christl. Altertum,* 1936, 16/32. Cecchelli, *Rend. Pont. Acc. Rom. Arch.* 1939, 97/106 *(Culto delle reliquie nell'Afr. Rom.).* Grappi, *Riv. liturg.* 1939, 206 ff., 227 ff., 249 ff. (cult of relics in 6th cent.). A. Grabar, *Martyrium,* 3 vols., P 1946 (Cult of relics and Chr. art). Bardy, AB 1949, 224/35 (Pilgrimages to Rome towards the end of the 4th cent.). B. Koetting, *Peregrinatio religiosa,* Mr 1950 (Pilgrimages in antiquity and Christianity). Simon, RHP 1954, 98/127 *(Les saints d'Israel dans la dévotion de l'Égl. anc.).*

28. *Law, State and Society*

K. Voigt, *Staat u. Kirche von Konstantin d. Gr. bis zum Ende der Karolingerzeit,* 1936. G. Krueger, *Die Rechtsstellung der vorkonstantinischen Kirche,* 1935. M. Roberti, E. Bussi e G. Vismara, *Cristianesimo e diritto romano,* Mi 1935. E. Peterson, *Der Monotheismus als polit. Problem,* 1935. P. Charanis, *Church and State in the Later Roman Empire* (491–518), Madison 1939. V. H. Rutgers, *De invloed van het Christ. op het Rom. recht,* 1940. Wenger, *Misc. Mercati* I, 596/607 (Christianity and Rom. Law). Bruck, Tr 1944, 97/121 (The *cheerful giver* in the Fathers and in Roman Law). K. M. Setton, *The Chr. Attitude towards the Emperor* (4th cent.), NY 1941. H. Berkhof, *De Kerk en de Keizer,* A 1946. I. Giordani, *Il messaggio sociale di Gesù* III and IV: *I Padri,* Mi 1947. Cerutti, RR 1949, 20/34 *(Pensiero politico del cristianesimo antico).* P. Brezzi, *Le dottrine politiche dell' età patristica,* Mi 1949. G. Bovini, *La proprietà eccl. e la condizione giuridica della Chiesa in età precostantiana,* Mi 1949. Jonkers, *RevInternatDroitsAnt.* 2, 1949, 493/509 (Fathers and Councils as sources for the relations betw. Church and state). R. Orestano, *La struttura giuridica del matrimonio rom. dal diritto classico al diritto giustiniano* I, Mi 1951. F. M.

Stratmann, *Die Heiligen u. der Staat,* 5 vols., 1949/50 (I: Christ, II: Peter and Paul, Martyrs, Helena; III: Athan., Ambr., Chrys., Aug.). Brasiello, *Scritti Ferrini* 2, Mi 1947, 1/29 (Infl. of Christianity on Roman Law). Further literature in § 3 n. 20 and § 50 n. 21. A. Bruch, *Kirchenvaeter u. soziales Erbrecht. Wanderungen rel. Ideen durch d. Rechte d. oestl. u. westl. Welt,* Hei 1956; extract from this in: ZSR 1955, 191/210; other relevant studies are cited on p. v. Bakhuizen van den Brink, *Episcopalis audientia,* A 1956.

§ 4. EDITIONS, COLLECTIONS AND TRANSLATIONS

1. The best older printed editions of works of the Fathers were produced by the philologists Robert and Henry Stephanus (Étienne) at Paris in the sixteenth century; those of the two brothers Frobenius at Basle, for whom Erasmus of Rotterdam did much work, were of a lesser standard. On the other hand, the folio editions of the Maurists are in part unsurpassed even today; these Benedictines of the French congregation of St. Maur (founded at Paris in 1618) counted important scholars like Mabillon, Maran, Montfaucon and Ruinart among their members. During the seventeenth and eighteenth centuries these produced masterly editions of many patristic writings. Beside the original text of the Greek Fathers these contain also the Latin translation as well as excellent indices.

The largest collection of patristic writings was made in Paris by Abbé J. P. Migne (d. 1875): *Patrologiae cursus completus.*

It is divided into a *Series Latina* (to Innocent II, d. 1216) in 221 quarto vols. (218–221: *Indices*) and a *Series Graeca* (to 1439) in 161 quarto vols. (with Lat. trans.). The plates of vol. 162 were burned in 1868, shortly before the printing; parts of the contents of this vol. were given a place in the *Patrologia graeca latine tantum edita.* The whole edition is an often faulty reprint of the best editions that had appeared till then. Frequently only the older editions used by Migne or those patristic texts that have in the meantime appeared in modern editions are of value for scholarly research.

F. Cavallera, Migne, *Patrologiae cursus completus, Series graeca. Indices digessit,* P 1921. T. Hopfner, Migne, *Patrologiae cursus completus, Series graeca. Index locupletissimus,* P 1928/45 (2 vols.). M. Vattasso, *Initia Patrum,* 2 vols., R 1906/08 (for Lat. texts). Chr. Baur, *Initia Patrum Graecorum,* 2 vols., St 1955, 180/181. Leclercq, DAL 11, 941/57 (Migne). Cotter, TSW 1946, 46/71 (Migne). P. Glorieux, *Pour revaloriser Migne* (MSR 9, 1952, Cahiers supplém.). A. Hamman, *Patrologiae lat. supplementum* I P 1958/59.

2. While the older collections, especially as regards their annotations and indices, were wholly devoted to the service of theology, in the latter ones the philological point of view is prevalent.

a. *Corpus scriptorum ecclesiasticorum latinorum,* ed. by the Wiener Akademie der Wissenschaften 1866ff. (so far 73 vols.).

b. St. Peter's Abbey, Steenbrugge (Belgium) intends to produce a new edition of all ancient Christian literary texts in three series *(latina, graeca, orientalis)* under the direction of E. Dekkers, with the help of an international staff of collaborators. Several volumes of the *Series latina* have already been brought out.

On the programme cf. Dekkers, SE 1948,405/14; TLZ 1949,162f. E. Dekkers - A. Gaar, *Clavis Patrum latinorum,* [2]1957 (SE 3), gives a survey of all Lat. writings, letters, documents etc. down to the 8th cent.

c. *Monumenta Germaniae historica, Auctores antiquissimi,* 13 vols., 1877–98 (important also for later Latin Fathers).

d. Individual works of the Fathers were included in the Leipzig *Bibliotheca Teubneriana.*

e. *Die griechischen christlichen Schriftsteller der ersten drei Jahrhunderte* with German introductions and indices have been edited since 1897 by the *Preussische Akademie der Wissenschaften (Kirchenvaeterkommission,* now *Kommission fuer spaetantike Religionsgeschichte der Deutschen Akademie der Wissenschaften zu Berlin);* so far 48 vols. have appeared.

f. Formerly the old Christian Syriac literature, as far as it was then known, had been published in extracts by the Maronite J. S. Assemani in the *Bibliotheca orientalis,* 4 vols., 1719–28; now two collections are appearing simultaneously (1903ff.), viz. a *Patrologia orientalis* (26 vols.) under the direction of R. Graffin and

F. Nau, and a *Corpus scriptorum christianorum orientalium* ed. by J. B. Chabot, J. Guidi, H. Hyvernat, B. Carra de Vaux, J. Forget (present director R. Draguet); this Corpus has six series: Syriac, Coptic, Arabic, Armenian, Georgian and Ethiopic texts (over 170 vols.). — *Patrologia syriaca* ed. R. Graffin, P 1894–1926 (3 vols.).

3. Minor collections for use in schools and universities

SS. patrum opuscula selecta by H. Hurter, 1st ser. 48 vols. 1868–85, 2nd ser. 6 vols., 1884–92: the Greek works only in Lat. trans. — *Florilegium patristicum,* recently ed. by J. Zellinger and B. Geyer and extended to medieval texts, 1904ff. (so far 44 numbers, partly with new critical text, the Greek texts with Lat. tr.). — *Textes et documents pour l'étude hist. du christianisme,* ed. H. Hemmer and P. Lejay, P 1904–12, 20 vols. (texts and tr.). — *Cambridge Patristic Texts,* ed. A. J. Mason, C 1899. — *Sammlung ausgewaehlter kirchen- und dogmengeschichtlicher Quellenschriften,* ed. G. Krueger, 1891ff. (1st series 12 numbers; 2nd series 9 numbers, New Series 6 numbers). — *Kleine Texte,* ed. H. Lietzmann, 1902ff. (so far 167 numbers, of these *c.* 35 patristic). — *Corona Patrum Salesiana* (so far *c.* 30 vols., with ital. tr.), Tu 1936ff. — *Textus et documenta in usum exercitationum et praelectionum academicarum,* Ser. theol., ed. Universitas Gregoriana, R 1932ff. — *Corpus Scriptorum latin. Paravianum,* Tu. — *The Loeb Classical Library,* Lo-NY, also contains many patristic texts. — *Sources Chrétiennes,* ed. H. de Lubac and J. Daniélou, 1941ff. (so far *c.* 40 vols., but not all of them contain the original text, freq. only a French translation); cf. Mondésert, Byz 22, 1952–53, 313/21. — *Stromata patristica et mediaevalia,* ed. C. Mohrmann et J. Quasten, Ut-Bru 1950ff. — *Monumenta Christiana,* Ut-Bru 1948ff. *Verba Seniorum* till 1956 6 vols. Patristic and medieval texts and trans., ed. Franceschini, Lazzati, Bussi, Pellegrino; till 1955 4 vols.

4. *Translations*

a. English: *Edinburgh Collection:* The Ante-Nicene Christian Library, 1866–72, 24 vols. and 1 suppl. vol. by A. Menzies, 1897. — *Buffalo Collection:* Reprint of the Edinburgh one 1884–86, 10 vols., suppl. by *A Select Library of Nicene and Post-Nicene Fathers,* 1886–1900, 28 vols. — *Translations of Christian Literature,* ed. by the Society for Promoting Christian Knowledge (SPCK), Lo 1917 (4 series, Greek, Lat., liturg. and oriental texts). — *Ancient Christian Writers,* ed. J. Quasten and J. C. Plumpe, Westminster, Maryland and London 1946 ff. (so far 23 vols.). — *The Fathers of the Church,* ed. L. Schopp, G. W. Walsh, R. J. Deferrari, 1947 ff. (18 vols. till 1956).

b. French: v. supra No. 3: Hemmer-Lejay and De Lubac-Daniélou. *Bibliothèque patristique de spiritualité,* P 1932 ff. — *Moralistes chrétiens. Textes et commentaires,* 1924–32, 12 vols.

c. German: Reithmayr-Thalhofer, *Bibliothek der Kirchenvaeter,* Kempten 1869–88, 80 vols. — O. Bardenhewer, T. Schermann, C. Weyman, J. Zellinger, J. Martin, *Bibliothek der Kirchenvaeter,* Kempten, 1911–30, 61 vols. and 2 index vols., 1931. The second series comprises 20 vols. ed. by Bardenhewer, J. Zellinger, J. Martin, 1932–39.

d. Italian: *Testi cristiani con versione* ed. G. Manacorda, Fl 1930 ff. — *I classici cristiani* ed. P. Misciatelli, Siena 1928 ff. — Vide supra No. 3 (p. 40): *Corona Patrum,* Salesiana.

e. Spanish and Catalan: *Biblioteca de autores griegos y latinos* ed. L. Segala and C. Parpal, Ba 1916 ff. — *Collección Excelsa,* Ma 1940 ff. — *Biblioteca de Sant Pacia,* Ba 1931 ff. — *Biblioteca de La Paraula cristiana,* Ba 1933 ff. Cf. Madoz, RET 1951, 437/72 (survey of all Spanish translations).

f. Dutch: H. U. Meyboom, ed. Lei 1906 ff. (*c.* 50 vols.).

g. Polish: *Biblioteka Ojców Kosciola* ed. J. Sajdak, Poznan 1924 ff. (c. 25 vols.).

h. Russian: Kern, Ir 1955, 57/70 (on hist. of trans. into Russian).

5. Enchiridia and Anthologies

M.-J. Rouët de Journel, *Enchiridion Patristicum,* Fr [18]1953. — H. Denzinger, *Enchiridion Symbolorum* ed. K. Rahner, [30]1955. — C. Kirch, *Enchiridion fontium historiae ecclesiasticae,* [6]1947. — M.-J. Rouët de Journel et J. Dutilleul, *Enchiridion asceticum,* 1947 (to John of Damasc.). — F. Cavallera, *Thesaurus doctrinae catholicae ex documentis magisterii ecclesiastici ordine methodico dispositus,* P [2]1937. J. de Guibert, *Documenta ecclesiastica christianae perfectionis studium spectantia,* R 1931. — E. Amann, *Le dogme catholique dans les Pères de l'Église,* P 1922. — C. Mirbt, *Quellen zur Geschichte des Papsttums und des roem. Katholizismus,* [5]1934. — J. Madoz, *La Iglesia de Jesucristo. Fuentes y documentos para el estudio de su constitución e historia,* Ma 1935; *El Primado romano. Fuentes y documentos para el estudio de su constitución e historia,* Ma 1936 (texts in Spanish tr.). — A. Heilmann, *Gottestraeger. Das Schoenste aus den Kirchenvaetern,* 1922.—L. v. Rudloff, *Das Zeugnis der Vaeter. Ein Quellenbuch zur Dogmatik,* 1937. — G. Bardy, *En lisant les Pères,* [2]1933. — Suggestions and instructions for reading selected Patr. texts in J. de Ghellinck, *Un programme de lectures patristiques,* Gr 1933, 303/36 414/47; *Lectures spirituelles dans les écrits des Pères,* NRT 1934, 5/29, 140/57, reprinted in *Patristique et Moyen âge* III, 1948.

6. Reference Works and Lexica

Du Cange, *Glossarium ad scriptores mediae et infimae graecitatis,* 1688 and 1890ff. — Du Cange-Henschel-Favre, *Glossarium mediae et infimae latinitatis,* 1678; lastly 1882–87. — H. Stephanus, *Thesaurus graecae linguae,* 1831–65. — E. Forcellini, *Lexicon totius latinitatis,* 1858–79. — W. Smith and H. Wace, *Dictionary of Christian Biography, Literature, Sects and Doctrine,* 1877–87. — E. A. Sophocles, *Greek Lexicon of the Roman and Byzantine Periods* (146 B.C. to 1100 A.D.), NY 1888. — Pauly-Wissowa-Kroll, *Realenzyklo-*

paedie der klass. Altertumswissenschaft, 1893ff. — A. Hauck, *Realenzyklopaedie der protestantischen Theologie u. Kirche,* 1896 to 1913. — *Thesaurus linguae latinae,* ed. by 5 German Academies, 1900ff. — Vacant-Mangenot-Amann, *Dictionnaire de Théologie catholique* (DTC), 1903ff. — U. Chevalier, *Répertoire des sources hist. du moyen âge,* Bio-Bibliographie, 1905–7. — Cabrol-Leclercq, *Dictionnaire d'archéologie chrétienne et de liturgie* (= DAL), 1907ff. — J. Brun, *Dictionarium Syriacum-Latinum,* Beyruth ^{2}1912. — Baudrillart-De Meyer-Van Cauwenbergh, *Dictionnaire d'histoire et de géographie ecclésiastiques,* 1912ff. — A. d'Alès, *Dictionnaire d'apologétique de la foi catholique,* 1914–22. — J. Hastings, *Dictionary of the Apostolic Church,* 1915–18. — C. Brockelmann, *Lexicon Syriacum,* B 1923ff. — Villien-Magnin-Naz, *Dictionnaire de droit canonique,* 1924ff. — Preisigke-Kiessling, *Woerterbuch der griechischen Papyrusurkunden,* 1–4, 1, 1925–44. — Gunkel-Zscharnack, *Die Religion in Geschichte und Gegenwart,* ^{2}1927–31. — M. Buchberger, *Lexikon fuer Theologie und Kirche,* ^{2}1957ff. — Viller, *Dictionnaire de spiritualité ascétique et mystique,* 1932ff. — W. Bauer, *Griechisch-deutsches Woerterbuch zu den Schriften des NT u. der uebrigen urchristlichen Literatur,* ^{4}1949ff. — Liddell-Scott, *A Greek-English Lexicon,* 2 vols., O 1925–40. — G. Kittel, *Theologisches Woerterbuch zum Neuen Testament,* 1932ff. — T. Klauser, *Reallexikon fuer Antike u. Christentum,* 1941ff. — F. Arnaldi-M. Turriani, *Latinitatis italicae . . . lexicon imperfectum* (from 476–1022) in *Archivum latinitatis medii aevi* 1935, 5/240; 1937, 65/152; 20, 1947–48, 65/206; 21, 1949–50, 193/360. — A. Souter, *A Glossary of Later Latin to 600* A.D., Lo 1949. AL 25, 1955, 101/41 (on Souter's Lexicon). H. Siegert, *Griechisches in der Kirchensprache. Ein sprach- u. kulturgeschichtl. Woerterbuch,* 1950. — *The Lexicon of Patristic Greek* (Oxford) is in preparation. A. Blaise-H. Chirat, *Dictionn. Latin-Français des auteurs chrét.,* Str-P 1955.

7. *Bibliographies*

A. Ehrhard, *Die altchristl. Literatur u. ihre Erforschung seit 1880,* 1894, and *Die altchristl. Literatur u. ihre Erforschung von 1884–1900.* First part: *Die vornizaenische Literatur,* 1900. H. Hurter-F. Pangerl, *Nomenclator literarius Theologiae cath.* I, [4]1926. — F. Drexl, *Zehn Jahre griech. Patristik* (1916–25), 1st part: 2nd and 3rd cent. in BJ 220, 1929, 131/263; 2nd part: The 4th and 5th cents., ibid. 230, 1931, 163/273. —J. Martin, *Christl.-latein. Dichter* (1900–27), ibid. 221, 1929, 65/140. — W. Wilbrand, *Die altchristl.-latein. Literatur* (1921–24), ibid. 226, 1930, 157/206. — G. Krueger, *A Decade of Research in Early Christian Literature* (1921–30), HTR 1933, 173/321. — J. Madoz, RET 1941, 919/62 (patrist. studies in Spain from 1931 to 1940); id., *Segundo decenio de estudios sobre patríst. Española,* 1941–50, Ma 1951; id., SE 1952, 355/71 (on the period from 1930–51). — O. Perler, *Patristische Philosophie,* Bern 1950. — K. Buechner, *Latein. Literatur in der Forschung seit 1937,* Bern 1951, 172ff. — F. Doelger- A. M. Schneider, *Byzanz,* Bern 1952. — M. Pellegrino, SC 1952, 424/52 (20 years of patristic studies in Italy).

The following give reliable information on current new publications: J. Marouzeau, *L'année philologique,* 1927ff. t. 24, 1955. — *Bibliographisches Beiblatt der TLZ.* — The bibliography of RHE. — The *Bulletin d'ancienne littér.* of the *RevBénéd.* — The Bulletin of the *Recherches de théologie ancienne et médiévale* (RTA). Excellent information on Greek patristics in *Byzantinische Zeitschrift* (BZ). — The *Elenchus bibliographicus of the Biblica* of the Papal *Biblical Institute* (Bi) is also valuable. — B. M. Metzger, Index of *Articles on the NT and the Early Church* publ. in *Festschriften,* Philadelphia 1951. B. Altaner, List of my Publications 1907–53, Wu 1953. A. G. de Veer, REAug 1956, 2, 9/37 (bibliography by G. Bardy). T. Klauser, F. J. Doelger, Mr 1956 (bibliography).

PART ONE

CHRISTIAN LITERATURE FROM THE END OF THE FIRST TO THE BEGINNING OF THE FOURTH CENTURY

CHAPTER ONE

Between Bible and Patristic Writings.
Books of the Christian Community, Popular Books, etc.

§ 5. THE APOSTLES' CREED

THE name Apostles' Creed is given to a creed which was used with minor variants in the instruction of catechumens in Gaul and Spain from the sixth century, and soon also in Ireland and Germany. As early as the end of the fourth century (Ambrose, Rufinus), when it had not yet been cast in its later form of twelve parts, it was attributed to the apostles themselves; hence its name. In the sixth century it was thought that each of the twelve articles was to be attributed to one apostle (ML 39, 2189f.). The Fathers of the Council of Ferrara (1438) were greatly surprised when the Greek Archbishop of Ephesus, Marcus Eugenicus, declared that the Eastern Church knew nothing about the existence of a Creed of the Apostles. Shortly afterwards, the humanist Laurentius Valla (d. 1457) denied the apostolic origin of the symbol.

The *Symbolum Apostolicum* has slowly developed from the inner needs of the Christian community itself, especially from its liturgical activities. Since the developing credal formulae also served, whether consciously or unconsciously, as the foundation of polemical and apologetical documents (cf. Justin's Dialogue with Trypho and the Epideixis of Irenaeus), the opposition to heretics (Ebionites, Gnostics), sometimes caused some idea to be added or to be more strongly emphasized. Philip baptized the eunuch from Ethiopia according to his confession: "I believe that Jesus Christ is the Son of God." (Acts 8: 37.) The mysterious acrostich ΙΧΘΥΣ = Ἰησοῦς Χριστὸς Θεοῦ Υἱὸς Σωτήρ may be regarded as a further development of the simplest confession of Christ. Apart from this, more developed formulae expressing the most important facts of salvation were known even in the apostolic age (1 Cor. 15 : 3; 1 Pet. 3 : 18–22); cf. also Ignatius of Antioch, *Eph.* 18, 2; *Smyrn.* 1, 1f. Beside the confession of one single affirmation we find from the earliest times also a twofold confession of God the Father and Jesus Christ (1 Cor. 8 : 6; 2 Tim. 4 : 1; Iren., *Haer.* 3, 1, 2; 3, 4, 1f.). Finally the liturgical act of baptism suggested a threefold (Trinitarian) confession of faith in the Father, the Son and the Holy Ghost, in connexion with the command to baptize in this form, given in Matt. 28 : 19; cf. Justin, *1 Apol.* 61 (*c.* 150). We find an already slightly enlarged Trinitarian confession in the *Epistola Apostolorum,* composed about the same time (v. 11, 3), ch. 5: "[We believe] in the Father, the ruler of the whole world, and in Jesus Christ, our Saviour, and in the Holy Ghost, the Paraclete, and in the holy Church and the forgiveness of sins." Similar confessions are found also in Iren., *Haer.* 1, 10.

A further development took place perhaps as early as the middle of the second century in the form of a more elaborate confession of Christ. This development was aided by the fact that at a very early age the thanksgiving prayer (Preface) of the eucharistic liturgy contained a rather explicit confession of Christ; cf. Justin, *1 Apol.* 61, 3, 10, 13 and Iren., *Haer.* 1, 10 (EH 102f.) and *Epid.* 3.

Thus the balance of the symmetrically constructed primitive creed was disturbed by the type of creed that enlarged the affirmations concerning Christ and soon developed into a formula of eight or nine parts. This is already to be found in the Roman baptismal liturgy about A.D. 200 and is attested by Tertullian and Hippolytus of Rome *(Traditio Apostolica).* This old Roman creed shows largely the same form in which it is later attested in Greek by the Letter of Marcellus of Ancyra to Pope Julius I (*c.* 340) and in Latin by Rufinus and Nicetas of Remesiana (both *c.* 400), except that the article on the forgiveness of sins may have been missing. This older Roman form of the Creed has certainly been the basis of all other Western baptismal creeds. But it cannot be proved that this is the case also for the Eastern creeds (ES 8/14), all of which contain anti-heretical additions. Even in the Roman Creed of nine parts the following pieces are still missing in the fourth and fifth centuries: in the article one: *creatorem caeli et terrae;* in article three: *conceptus;* in article four: *passus, mortuus, descendit ad inferos;* in article nine: *catholicam;* in article ten; *sanctorum communionem;* in article twelve: *vitam aeternam.* In the Eastern Church, for which we have the testimony of Eusebius of Caesarea, Cyril of Jerusalem and Epiphanius, the christological confession was particularly developed, following the Roman example. The text of the present complete form appears first in the sixth century, in Caesarius of Arles and in the liturgical books of Rome and Gaul.

Edd.: ES 1–14. A. Hahn, *Bibliothek der Symbole,* ³1897. H. Lietzmann (KlT 17/8) ²1931. Hennecke ²1924, 587f. De Ghellinck, *Patristique et Moyen âge,* I: *Les recherches sur les origines du symbole des Apôtres,* Bru-P ²1949. Camelot, RSR 39, 1951, 323/37 (account of research). F. Kattenbusch, *Das Apostol. Symbolum,* 2 vols., 1894/1900. B. Doerholt, *Das Taufsymbol der Alten Kirche,* 1891. P. Feine, *Die Gestalt des apostol. Glaubensbekenntnisses in der Zeit des NT,* 1925. O. Smital, *Symbolum Apostolicum,* NY 1929. A. Jeremias, *Die Bedeutung des Mythos fuer das apostol. Glaubensbekenntnis,* 1930. J. Burr, *Studies on the Apostles' Creed,* 1931. E. v. Dobschuetz, *Das Apostolicum in bibl. theolog. Beleuchtung,* 1932. J. Kroll, *Gott u. Hoelle,* 1932. K. Pruemm, *Der christl. Glaube u. die altheidn. Welt,* 2 vols., 1935. F. J. Badcock, *The History of the Creeds,* ²1938. H. Elfers, *Die Kirchenordnung Hippolyts von Rom,* 1938, 305/29. Carpenter, JTS 1942, 1/11 (*Symbolum,* hist. of the concept); id. ibid. 1943, 1/11 (creeds and baptismal rites). P. Nautin, *Je crois à l'Esprit S. dans la Sainte Église pour la résurrection de la chair,* 1947. O. Cullmann, *Die ersten christl. Glaubensbekenntnisse,* ²1948. G. Hedley, *The Symbol of the Apostles' Creed,* 1948. W. Bieder, *Die Vorstellung von der Hoellenfahrt Jesu Christi,* Zu 1949. J. Crehan, *Early Christian Baptism and Creed. A Study in Ante-Nicene Theology,* 1950. J.N.D. Kelly, *Early Christian Creeds,* 1950 (to Chalcedon and *Quicumque*). Lichtenstein, ZKG 63, 1950/51, 1/74 (The oldest Christian formula of faith). Benoît, *Lumière et Vie* 1, 1952,

39/60 (beginnings of the Apostol. Creed in the NT). Camelot, *ibid.* 1, 1952, 61/80 (origin of the Apostol. Creed).—Further works on the history of the Creed I see under "Symbolum Athanasianum", § 54, 20.

§ 6. THE DIDACHE OR THE TEACHING OF THE TWELVE APOSTLES

In 1873 the Metropolitan Bryennius of Nicomedia discovered in Constantinople a Greek MS, written in 1056 (now in the library of the Greek Patriarchate in Jerusalem), which contained, as well as the complete texts of the Letter of Barnabas and the two Letters of Clement, the Διδαχὴ τῶν δώδεκα ἀποστόλων. In antiquity this small treatise served as a model for later writings on matters of the liturgy and of ecclesiastical law (*Didascalia, Apostolic Church Order,* Book VII of the *Apost. Constitutions*). Eusebius however, classed it among the apocrypha (*Hist.* 3, 25, 4). Elsewhere in patristic literature it was used just as little as the original work *(Grundschrift)* which it contains; cf. e.g. Clement of Alex. *(Strom.* I 20, 100, 4 [3, 5]); Athanasius (39th *Festal Letter* and *De virginitate* 13 [9, 3–4]) in the East and Ps.-Cyprian, *Adv. aleat.* 4 (14, 2); *Gesta apud Zenophilum* (CSEL 26, 192 line 6 to 2, 7); Optatus of Mileve I 21 (4, 3); Augustine, *Enarrat. in Ps. 103,* ser. 3, 10 et saepe (1, 6); *Epist. Titi,* SbB 1925, 195 (3, 1) in the West.

The *Didache* is one of the most valuable literary finds of recent decades. In 1900 the first six chapters became known in an Old Latin translation made before 300, and, besides Greek papyrus fragments, a larger piece (10, 3b–12, 2a) has recently been found in a Coptic translation. Minor Syriac, Arabic and Georgian fragments are also extant.

Apart from the title just mentioned, the Greek MS gives a longer one which is probably original: "Teaching of the Lord through the Twelve Apostles to the Pagans (or Gentile Christians)" — Διδαχὴ κυρίου διὰ τῶν δώδεκα ἀποστόλων τοῖς ἔθνεσιν; this

MS does not contain the actual preaching of the Christian faith, but is content with inculcating the most important moral duties, liturgical prescriptions and legal ordinances in force in the community.

Syria is to be considered the home of the *Didache;* it belongs to the first half of the second century, probably before the appearance of Montanism (160). This early date is suggested especially by the ecclesiastical conditions the work presupposes (position of prophets, teachers, apostles or bishops, and deacons, the form of the prayers given in chapters nine and ten, the designation of Jesus as "servant of God" etc.). Hence it is scarcely to be dated as late as the second half of the second century. Recent research attempts to prove that *Did.* 1–6 depends on Barnabas 19–20 (v. § 11, 2). It cannot be said with certainty that the *Shepherd of Hermas* (Robinson, Connolly, Muilenberg, Voskes, Peterson) or even Tatian's *Diatessaron* (Dix) has been used. The hypothesis that the *Didache* is contained in the original form of the *Didascalia* (Athenagoras) is to be rejected even more decisively. According to A. Adam the *Didascalia* (i.e. chs. 7–16) was written between 90 and 100, perhaps at Pella. It was intended as a directive for the development of new East Syrian communities (ZKG 1957, 1/47).

The opinion recently put forward by Goodspeed is far more probable. According to him the Latin translation of *Did.* 1–6 first publ. by H. Schlecht (1900 and 1901) is not a translation of the Greek *Did.* 1–6, but one of the original *Grundschrift* of the *Didache,* which had long been postulated by other scholars, and which was a short moral catechism for Jewish proselytes. This Jewish teaching on the "Two Ways" was given the title *De doctrina apostolorum* and a trinitarian doxology at the end, and thus found entrance also in Christian circles. The *Didache* was unknown to the *Letter of Barnabas* and other Christian writings (the *Apostolic Church Order,* two pseudo-Athanasian treatises: the *Syntagma* and the *Fides Nicaena,* and the *Vita of Schenute of Atripe* extant in an Arabic trans.) which knew only this moral catechism which circulated as an independent work. The author of the *Didache* (*Did.* 7–16) added the so-called "Christian insertion" (ch. 1, 3–2, 1) and placed the "Christianized" teaching on the Two Ways at the beginning of his work, which thus became the *Didache* as we have it today. We are probably justified in considering the so-called *Grundschrift* (*Did.* 1–6) as the oldest "Christian work" of post-apostolic times.

Contents (EP 1/10, EH 1/6, EA 1/3). Part I (1–6): a summary of Christian moral teaching under the image of the two ways of life and death. Part II (7–10), liturgical: on baptism (7), fasting and prayer (8), prayers at ritual meals (9 and 10). Part III (11–15), disciplinary: behaviour towards members of the Church, especially the ordinary ecclesiastical superiors and the wandering apostles or evangelists, prophets and teachers; Conclusion (16), exhortation to vigilance, with reference to the approaching end of the world.

Details. a. It is doubtful whether 6, 3 refers to the Jewish food laws; only abstinence from meat sacrificed to idols is demanded.

b. Baptism by infusion is permitted in an emergency (7); this is the only witness for this kind of baptism in the first two centuries, for the third century see Cyprian, *Ep.* 69, 12ff.

c. Station fasts on Wednesday and Friday (8).

d. The Our Father to be said three times every day (8).

e. It is very improbable that 9 and 10 should contain the oldest extant eucharistic prayers which the congregation said at the celebration of the eucharist. Even 10, 3 is no proof of this. Cf. once again Perler, DT 1950, 444/46; Jungmann, *Missarum sollemnia* I, ²1949, 17f., and Peterson, RAC 1952, 58 and formerly EL 1944, 3/13. — The eucharistic celebration is called "sacrifice" (θυσία) with reference to Mal. 1, 10f. (14).

f. Lefort, CSCO 136, 26A. 13 and A. Adam, ZKG 1957, 8/11 how that the important supplement of ch. 10 in the Coptic fragment does not refer to the prayers of consecration for the μύρον (chrism). The Coptic term should be translated not as "chrism" or "holy oils", but as "refreshment" (with reference to the preceding celebration of the Agape, which is concluded by this prayer). This new interpretation is undoubtedly the most decisive corroboration of the frequently held view that chs. 9 and 10 do not refer to the eucharist but to the Agape. A prayer of the consecration of the μύρον (myron) would interrupt the sequence at this point.

g. A confession of sins is prescribed before prayer in church (4) and the Sunday celebration (14). Thus the faithful are probably exhorted to make a general confession of sins before receiving the eucharist; cf. the Confiteor.

h. Prophets play an important part in the churches. They are men who speak in the spirit and either wander from place to place or reside in the individual communities. They hold a very high rank, are esteemed as "high priests" and receive tithes of all income. To criticize them is considered a sin against the Holy Ghost.

i. In the epistles of St. Paul and in Clement of Rome's Letter to the Corinthians, the permanent superiors of the churches are called ἐπίσκοποι καὶ διάκονοι.

Edd.: Coll. editions of the Apost. Fathers 14. J. Rendel-Harris (with facsimile), Lo 1887. T. Klauser (FP 1), 1940. H. Lietzmann (KlT 6) 1936. — Trans.: F. Zeller (BKV² 35) 1918. R. Knopf in *Handb. zum NT,* suppl. 1920, 1/40 (with commentary). Hennecke 1924, 555/65. H. Lilje, *Die Lehre der 12 Apostel,* ²1956. G. Bosio, *I Padri Apostolici,* Tu 1940, 1/59. J. A. Kleist, ACW 6, 1948, 3/25. A. Winterswyl, ²1954. — Treatises: A. Robinson, *Barnabas, Hermas and the Didache,* 1920. C. Schmidt, ZNTW 1925, 81/99 (Coptic fragm. with Myron Prayer). J. Muilenburg, *The Literary Relations of the Epistle of Barnabas and the Teaching of the Twelve Apostles,* 1929; cf. Connolly, JTS 33, 1931–32, 237/53; Robinson-Connolly, JTS 1934, 113/46, 225/48. Cadbury, JQR 1936, 403/6. Streeter, JTS 1936, 369/74; cf. 1937, 165/7. Dix, *Did. and Diatessaron,* JTS 1933, 242/50; on this Connolly, ibid. 1933, 346 f. Athenagoras, EPh 1933 (67 pp.). Middleton, JTS 1935, 259/67 (eucharist. prayers). Gibbins, JTS 1935, 373/86 (the liturg. section of the *Did.*). Broek-Utne, ZKG 1935, 576/81 (*Did.* 11, 11). Staerk, ZNTW 1936, 83 ff. (eschatology). Connolly, JTS 1937, 364/79 (1, 3b–2, 1 not interpolated); DR 1937, 339/49 (*Did.*

presupposes appearance of Montanism); DR 1937, 477/89 (*Did.* 9/10; *Agape,* not eucharist). Creed, JTS 1938, 370/87 (composed considerably later than 130). Dibelius, ZNTW 1938, 32/41 (*Did.* 9/10: Christianized prayers of Hellenistic Jews). Dix, Th 1938, 261/83 (Primitive Consecration Prayers). Telfer, JTS 1939, 133/46, 258/71 (composed as *Epistola encyclica* at Antioch c. 180); 1944, 141/51. Knox, JTS 1939, 146/9 (*Did.* 3, 4). F. E. Vokes, *The Riddle of the Didache,* 1938. Klauser, DP 157/64 (*Did.* 7, 1–3). Poschmann 1940, 88/97 (penance). Oulton, JTS 1940, 177/9 (Clem. Alex.). Philbin, IER 1941, 19/39 (crit. report). Schuster, SC 1942, 265/70 (*Did.* in Benedict). Telfer, JTS 1944, 141/51 (The "Plot" of the *Did.*). Peterson, EL 1944, 3/13 (c. 10/11: christolog. hymn). Goodspeed, ATR 1945, 228/47 (Did., Barnab. and the Doctrina). Johnson, Munera studiosa 1946, 107/22 (Subsidiary motive for the writing of the *Did.:* expansion of Mt. 28, 19f.). E. Besson, *Une Étude sur l'Église primitive,* 1948 (text and commentary). E. Ladd, *The Eschatology of the Did.,* Harvard thesis 1948. M. Milanovich, *The Teachings of the Did. Compared with Teachings of the NT,* thesis Southern Bapt. Theol. Sem., 1948. Massaux, ETL 1949, 5/41 (Mt. in the *Did.*). Sass, *Mem. E. Loh.* 1951, 233/39 (The apostles in the *Did.*). Peterson, RAC 1952, 39/68 (Problems of transmission). Audet, RB 1952, 219/38 (*Did.* 1–6 depend. on "Manual of Discipline" recently found in Jordan district, both works utilize common source). Altaner, VC 1952, 160/67 (On the problem of the Lat. *Doctrina Apostolorum*). Stommel, RQ 48, 1953, 21/42 (*Did.* 16, 6). Ruiz Bueno, Hel 3, 1952, 135/73 (La paz en la iglesia: *Did.* y la I[a] Clementis). Moule, JTS 1955, 240/43 (on 9, 4). J.-P. Audet, *La Didachè,* P 1958 (Introd., text, comm.); also Botte, RHE 1959, 515/23; Bligh, VD 1958, 350/6.

§ 7. THE DIDASCALIA AND OTHER CHURCH ORDERS

THE *Didache,* being the first manual of Church customs, liturgy and constitution, became the model of a number of writings on the liturgy and ecclesiastical legislation. Though their redaction belongs to the following centuries, their precepts give in part the impression of a most venerable age. Following the example of the *Didache,* they purport to have been written by the apostles or at least claim apostolic authority for their precepts.

Edd.: F. X. Funk, *Didascalia et Constitutiones Apostolorum* I–II, 1905. E. Hauler, *Didascaliae Apostolorum fragmenta Veronensia lat.,* 1900. W. Riedel, *Die Kirchenrechtsquellen des Patriarchats Alexandrien,* 1900. — Treatises: E. Schwartz, *Ueber die pseudoapost. Kirchenordnungen,* 1910. T. Schermann: 1. *Die Allgem. Kirchenordnung,* 1914; 2. *Fruehchristl. Liturgien,* 1915; 3. *Die kirchl. Ueberlieferung,* 1916. V. J. Bartlet, *Church-Life and Church-Order during the First Four Cents.,* O 1943. A. Ehrhardt, ZSR 67, 1950, 403/39 (Interpolations in the Apostolic Church Orders).

1. The *Apostolic Tradition* of Hippolytus (Ἀποστολικὴ παράδοσις). In 1916 Connolly proved that what E. Schwartz had already asserted in 1910 was all but certain: the so-called *Egyptian Church Order* — it first became known in its Ethiopic and Coptic versions — may in the main be regarded as a genuine work of Hippolytus of Rome (though Lorentz and Engberding reject its authenticity), viz. as his Ἀποστολικὴ παράδοσις, *traditio apostolica* (*c.* 215), the title of which is to be seen already on the famous statue of Hippolytus. This conclusion is of the greatest importance and gives us valuable information about the life of the Christian congregation in Rome at the beginning of the third century; it has actually provided a new foundation for the history of the liturgy. The work of Hippolytus, which has been preserved only in Coptic, Arabic, Ethiopic and, in part, in Latin translations, is the oldest Church Order and a source of the later ones, i.e. of Book Eight of the *Apostolic Constitutions,* of the so-called epitome of this eighth book, of the *Testamentum Domini,* of the so-called *Canones Hippolyti* also called *Constitutiones per Hippolytum.*

The first part treats of the consecration of bishops, the liturgy of the eucharist, the blessing of oil, cheese and olives, the ordination of priests and deacons, the confessors, widows, lectors, virgins, subdeacons and those who possess the gift of healing. The second part enumerates the laws and regulations concerning the laity: those for neophytes and for the professions, mentioning those that are forbidden to Christians, for catechumens, for the administration of baptism, confirmation and communion. The third part deals with ecclesiastical practices and customs; distribution of Holy Communion on Sundays, fasts and the celebration of the Agape. These are followed, inter alia, by directions on oblations for the bishop, Lenten fasts, reception of Holy Communion, administration of the cemetery, attendance at catechetical instructions, times of prayer and the sign of the cross.

Edd.: in Funk (v. supra) II, 97/119. Hennecke [2]1924, 569/83. R. H. Connolly *The so-called Egyptian Church Order and Derived Documents,* 1916. B. S. Easton, C 1924. G. Dix, *The Treatise on the Apostolic Tradition of St. Hippolytus of Rome,* Lo 1937 (crit. ed.). B. Botte (SCh 11), 1946 (with the Lat. fragments). H. Duensing, GAh, 3. F. No. 32, 1946 (Ethiop. text). W. Till-Leipoldt, TU 58, 1954 (Copt. text). Quasten, FP 7, 26/33 (selection). — Studies: R. Lorentz, *De Egyptische Kerkordening en Hipp. v. Rome,* Ley 1929 (for spuriousness). Hamel, ZNTW 36, 1937, 238/50 (for genuineness). Charvet, Stud. et Docum. Hist. Jur. 2, 1937, 336/47 (matrimony). H. Elfers, *Die Konst. Hipp.s von Rom,* 1938 (against Lorentz). Connolly, JTS 1938, 359/69 (eucharist. prayers). Richardson, HTR 1947, 101/08 (question of epiclesis against Dix, 1937, 75/79); also Botte, RTA 1947, 241/51 (Hippol.'s epiclesis does not effect consecration). Richardson, ATR 1948, 38/44 (on date); RTA 1948, 357/59 (question of epiclesis). Van Unnik, VC 1947, 77/100 (Les cheveux défaits des femmes). Engberding, *Misc. Mohlberg* I, 1948, 47/71 (Spuriousness of the Consts. of Hipp.); against this Botte, RTA 1949, 177/85 and Elfers, *Festschrift f. K. Adam,* 1952, 169/211. Van den Eynde, *Misc. Mohlberg* I, 1948, 407/11 (Const. in Rom. liturgy). Callewaert, SE 1949, 95/110 (on question of epiclesis). Grillmeier, ZKT 1949, 14/23 (doctrine of *descensus*). Botte, *Mél. De Ghellinck* I, 1951, 189/200 (baptismal creed, against Nautin). J. B. Bauer, ZKT 1952, 71/75 (blessing of fruit). Casel, ALW 2, 1952, 115/30 (Const. Hipp.). Sales, RHR 148, 1955, 181/213 (no proof of the Roman liturgy). Botte, RTA 1955, 161/72 (on the text). Blanc, RTA 1955, 173/92 (Lexique comparé des versions de la Trad. apost.). J. M. Hanssens, *La liturgie d'Hipp.,* R 1959.

2. The *Didascalia,* that is, "the Catholic Teaching of the Twelve Apostles and Holy Disciples of our Saviour", called Διατάξεις τῶν ἀποστόλων in Epiphanius. The author is a bishop with considerable medical knowledge, probably a Jew by birth. He wrote his work for a Jewish-Christian church in N. Syria most probably in the first half, perhaps even in the first decades of the third century. He sharply rebukes those Christians who still accept the Jewish ceremonial Law as binding. In contrast with his Western contemporaries (Tertullian, Hippolytus, Cyprian) he shows himself more indulgent towards sinners. All sins can be remitted, including adultery and apostasy, not, however, the sin against the Holy Spirit. A fairly long period of penance is presupposed after excommunication. But before the bishop decides on reconciliation, he should demand a fast lasting from two to seven weeks after examining the penitential zeal of the sinner. The effect of reconciliation is placed almost on a par with the effect of bap-

tism. Apart from the canonical writings the author has used the *Didache,* the *Gospel of St. Peter,* the *Acts of Paul,* Ignatius, Hermas and Irenaeus.

Apart from minor fragments, the original Greek text of the *Didascalia* is lost, but it is preserved complete in Syriac, partly (approximately three eighths of the whole) also in a Latin translation. Apart from these we have a Coptic, Ethiopic and Arabic translation. It contains a Church Order giving special attention to married couples, the bishop, the administration of property, the order of widows, further to baptism, church services and penance; it demands a six days' fast before Easter.

Edd.: Funk (v. supra) I, 3 ff. (Lat.). R. H. Connolly, *Didascalia Apostolorum. The Syriac Version translated and accompanied by the Verona Fragments,* 1929. Germ. by H. Achelis and J. Flemming (TU 25, 2), 1904. J. M. Harden, *The Ethiopic Didascalia translated,* 1920 (SPCK). Graf I, 564/69 (Arabic transmission). W. Till-J. Leipoldt, *Hippol. Romanus. Kopt. Texte der Didask. u. Constit. Apostolorum,* 1954 (TU 58). Treatises: E. Tidner, *Sprachl. Kommentar zur lat. Didaskalia,* Stockholm 1938. Van Unnik, NAKG 1939, 65/100 (Mosaic Law). Galtier, RHE 1947, 315/51 (Date: 1st half of 3rd cent., reprinted in: Aux origines du Sacrement de pénitence, R 1951). Poschmann, *Paenitentia,* 1940, 476/78. Cuesta, RET 1947, 337/62 (Penitencia medicinal desde la Didascalia a S. Gregorio di Nysa). Beaucamp, BLE 1949, 26/47 (penance). K. Rahner, ZKT 1950, 257/81 (doctrine and practice of penance). Colson, VS Suppl. 4, 1951, 271/90 (L'évêque dans la Didascalie).

3. The *Apostolic Church Order,* known since 1843, is a short Greek treatise which probably originated in Egypt at the beginning of the fourth century and was intended to take the place of the *Didache* which it used in the first half (4–14, moral precepts). It indicates a more advanced situation than that presupposed in the *Didache.* In its second half (15–29) it gives precepts concerning the election of bishops, presbyters, lectors, deacons and widows. It exists in Latin, Syriac, Coptic, Arabic and Ethiopic versions.

Text in Schermann, *Die allgemeine Kirchenordnung,* 1914, 12 ff.

4. The *Apostolic Constitutions* (Διαταγαὶ τῶν ἁγίων ἀποστόλων), eight books, the largest collection of legislative and liturgical material of earlier antiquity. The apostolic origin of the work is

asserted according to 6, 18, 11, with the addition that it was sent to the bishops and priests "by our colleague Clement" (of Rome). The work was first printed in Venice in 1563. The first six books are identical with the *Didascalia* except for some alterations and additions due to the changed conditions; e.g. infant baptism is recommended (6, 15, 3f.), baptism by heretics and atheists is declared invalid (6, 15, 1f.) and a forty days fast is demanded before Easter (5, 13); the *Didascalia* knows only a fast in Holy Week. The reading of pagan writings is altogether forbidden (1, 6). Whereas the *Didascalia* knows only the lectorate as an inferior ecclesiastical office, the *Constitutions* mention also the subdeacon, the door keeper and the psaltes. The apse of the church is to be oriented and to have pastophoria, i. e. sacristies at either side of it. 6, 30 contains a burial order. The first half of the seventh book is an enlargement of the *Didache;* its second half contains forms of prayers and instructions on the teaching of catechumens and on baptism. Among the prayers there is a morning offering (7, 47), the μεγάλη δοξολογία, which from early times has played a part in all oriental rites, even though in slightly varying forms. We also find this morning prayer as the *Gloria* in the Roman Mass; according to the *Liber Pontificalis* it is said to have been introduced already by Pope Telesphorus (d. *c.* 136). We find the almost identical version of the Byzantine Liturgy already in the Cod. Alex. of the Bible.

The eighth book is the most valuable part of the whole work; its source (chs. 4ff.) is the above-mentioned *Apostolic Tradition* of Hippolytus. It deals first with the charismatic gifts (1–2) and then presents formularies of individual consecrations and blessings (3–22); here the whole liturgy of the Mass (6–15), the so-called Clementine Liturgy (EH 679/91), was inserted among the prayers and ceremonies for the consecration of a bishop; it is the oldest complete Mass existing. This section is followed by regulations concerning the confessors, virgins, widows and exorcists (23–26), proselytes, feast days etc. (27–46). The last (47th) chapter contains the *Eighty-Five Apostolic Canons* (see below 5).

All eight books are probably by the same author and originated *c*. 380 in Syria or Constantinople. The author, Pseudo-Clement, was an Arian and is presumably to be identified with the author of the spurious longer recension of the Ignatian Letters. Except for the *Apostolic Canons* (ch. 47), the *Apostolic Constitutions* were rejected by the Council *in Trullo*, 692, as "falsified by the heretics" (EH 1089). They did not have much influence on the life and practice of the Greek Church. Only excerpts from them found their way into the Eastern collections of Canon Law. The eighth book of the *Apostolic Constitutions* has also come down to us in a slightly different form which is called *Epitome* or *Constitutiones per Hippolytum.*

Text: Funk I (v. supra); II, 72–96. J. Quasten, FP 7, 180/233.—Trans.: F. Boxler, BKV 1874. 8th bk. (without ch. 47): R. Storf (BKV²5), 1912. On the Arianism of the compiler cf. Turner, JTS 15, 1913/14, 53/65; 16, 1914/15, 54/61; 31, 1929/30, 128/41; Lebreton, RHE 1924, 27/30; Capelle, RHE 1949, 439/57 (original Arianized text of the *Gloria* in Cod. Alex.). Van den Eynden, RSR 1937, 196/212 (on VII, 44, 3). Spanier, MGWJ 1937, 71/5. Galtier, RSR 1937, 464/6 (VII, 42f.). E. R. Goodenough, *By Light, Light; the Mystic Gospel of Hellenistic Judaism,* 1935 (on liturg. texts from lib. VII and VIII). Mercati, OM 3, 338f. (MSS of the Ed. princeps); 4, 143/8 (medieval euchologia). Peterson, *Misc. C. Mohlberg,* R 1948, 413/7 (VII, 33 ff.). W. Stapelmann, *Der Hymnus angelicus, Gesch. u. Erklaerung des Gloria,* Hei 1948. J. A. Jungmann, *Missarum sollemnia* I, ²1949, 429/45 (on the *Gloria*). Alvarez, *Rev. de Espiritualidad* 8, 1949 and 1950 (Pss. in the *Apost. Constit.*). Kastner, TG 1952, 18/22 (on *Gloria*). Pitt, JEH 1958, 1/7 (Institution Account). Treu, VC 1957, 208/11 (Fragm.).

5. The *Eighty-Five Apostolic Canons* (EH 692/706) contained in the *Apostolic Constitutions* 8, 47 and apparently compiled by the redactor of the work, deal almost exclusively with the election, ordination and duties of the clergy and are entirely in the form of the canons of councils. They are also largely similar to the decisions of Antioch 341 (EH 490/99) and Laodicea (between 343 and 381; EH 520/25). Canon 85 enumerates the canonical books, among them three Books of the Maccabees, two Letters

and the Constitutions of Clement, but the Apocalypse is missing. The first fifty canons were translated into Latin by the Roman monk Dionysius Exiguus (d. *c.* 545), who added them to his larger collection of Canons. Thus these fifty canons came to be known in the West.

Turner, JTS 16, 1914/15, 523/38. Graf I, 572/77. Tr.: F. Boxler, BKV1874.

6. *The Testament of Our Lord Jesus Christ,* two books, originally written in Greek, but extant only in Syriac, Coptic, Ethiopic and Arabic. They are an enlarged version of the Church Order of Hippolytus, preceded by an introduction which is taken from an otherwise unknown Apocalypse (*Epistola Apostolorum?* v. 11, 3); Syriac version with a Latin translation first edited at Mainz 1899. Book One contains instructions our Lord gave to his disciples before his ascension. Jesus speaks of the signs of the end of the world, of the qualifications of a superior of a church and of the way in which he should furnish the house of God. Book Two gives rules for the life of the Christian from the catechumenate (not yet divided into degrees) and baptism to his burial. The communion service, the love feast and the burial are minutely described. The authors of the *Testament* call themselves the apostles John, Peter and Matthew; actually the book originated in the second half of the fifth century probably in Monophysite circles in Syria.

Text: J. E. Rahmani, *Test. Domini nostri Jesu Christi,* 1899. J. Quasten (FP 7 235/73) 1936 (selection). — Treatises: F. X. Funk, *Das Test. unseres Herrn u. verwandte Schriften,* 1901. Burmeister, Mu 1933, 203/35. Ruecker, CO 31, 1934, 114f. Graf I, 569/72. Amann, DTC 15, 194/200.

7. The *Canones Hippolyti, c.* 500, are also based on the Church Order of Hippolytus; they are extant in Arabic and Ethiopic versions.

Trans. in W. Riedel (supra before No. 1) 1900, 193/230. H. Achelis, *Die Canones Hippolyti,* 1891. C. J. Oehlander, *Canones H.i och beslaekta de skrifter,* 1911. Graf I, 602/05. K. Mueller, ZNTW 1924, 226/31. Botte, *Mél. Andrieu,* Str 1956, 53/63 (Canon originated 341/60).

In this connexion we would mention two other sources which are important for the history of the liturgy, even though they have no literary connexion with the preceding "Church Orders".

8. The Papyrus *Dêr Balyzeh.* Parts of a Greek Euchologium found in a Coptic monastery in 1907. According to Capelle it should be dated not in the third but in the fifth/sixth centuries.

Text: C. Wessely, PO 18, 1924, 425/29. J. Quasten, FP 7, 37/44. The ed. by C. H. Roberts and B. Capelle, *An Early Euchologium: The Dêr Balyzeh Pap.,* Lou 1949, contains *c.* 40 fragments newly discovered by Rob.; comm. by Capelle, Bugnini, EL 1951, 157/70 (bib. and Lat. trans. based on the new ed.). K. Gamber, OstkSt. 1958, 48/65.

9. The *Euchologium of Bishop Serapion* of Thmuis (4th cent.), v. § 55 n. 1.

§ 8. THE APOCRYPHA OF THE NEW TESTAMENT. GENERAL REMARKS

Edd.: J. A. Fabricius, *Codex apocryphus NT,* 2 vols., 1703/19; ²1719 and 1743. A. Birch, *Auctuarium codicis apocryphi NT Fabriciani* I, 1804. J. C. Thilo, *Codex apocryphus NT* I, 1832. A. Hilgenfeld, *NT extra canonem receptum,* ²1884. M. R. James, *Apocrypha anecdota,* 1893/7. E. Klostermann and A. Harnack, *Apocrypha,* 1–4 (KlT 3, 8, 11, 12). F. Stegmueller, *Repertorium biblicum medii aevi,* I: *Initia biblica, apocrypha, prologi,* Ma 1950. — Syriac texts: W. Wright, *Contributions to the Apocr. Literature of the NT,* 1865. Armen. texts: *Collection of the Mechitarists of S. Lazzaro,* 2 vols., 1898/1904. Coptic texts: E. Revillout, *Apocryphes coptes du NT,* 1876 and PO 2, 2, 1907; 9, 2, 1913. E. A. W. Budge, *Coptic Apocrypha in the Dialect of Upper Egypt,* 1913. Among the well over 50 Gnostic writings (all Coptic) found in the sands of Egypt in recent years there are not a few apocryphal gospels, letters of apostles and esp. apocalypses. See § 24 on these Ethiopic texts: Guerrier and S. Grébaut in PO 9, 3, 1913; 12, 4, 1919; CSCO 1, 7–8. Ruthenian texts: J. Franko, *Codex apocryph.,* 1–5, Lemberg 1896–1910. — Trans.: E. Hennecke, *Ntl. Apokryphen,* ²1924; *Handb. zu den ntl. Apokr.,* 1914. M. R. James, *The Apocr. NT,* ²1950. R. Basset, *Les Apocryphes éthiopiens,* 1893. — Treatises: J. Geffcken, *Christl. Apokryphen,* 1908. J. A. Robinson, *Excluded Books of the NT,* 1927. E. Amann, *Apocryphes du NT:* Suppl. du DB L. 1928, 460/533. The following on *Copt.* apocrypha: Hallock, JBL 1933, 163/74. McCulloch, Laudate 12, 1934, 11/30. W. Grossouw, StC 1933, 10/36; 1934, 434/46; 1935, 19/36. Aescoly, JA 1932, 87/137 (Ethiopic Apocr.). E. J. Goodspeed, *The Apocrypha:* An American Trans., Ch 1938; *The Story of the Apocr.,* Ch 1939. Burmester, Or 7, 1938, 355/67 (Egypt. mythology in Copt. apocrypha). Lefort, Mu 1939, 1/10 (fragments of

Copt. apocrypha). Turdeanu, RHR 138/39, 1950, 22/52, 176/218 (Apocrypha and the Bogumils).

THE ancients called *apocrypha* those writings whose origin was unknown or wrongly attributed and those that were not included in the Canon of Scripture though, from their titles, they might claim to be so, and also a few that had been considered canonical for some time (Jerome, *Ep.* 107, 12; August., *De civ.* 15, 23, 4; Jerome, *Prol. gal. in Samuel et Mal.*). Eusebius calls such writings νόθα (*Hist.* 3, 25, 4). Protestant authors call the O.T. apocrypha pseudepigrapha, the N.T. ones frequently antilegomena, since they call apocrypha the deuterocanonical books of the O.T.

Even in the second century B.C. writers had begun to imitate Biblical books or to give their own inventions the names of Scriptural authors. Thus originated the *Third Book of Esdras* and the first part of the *Book of Henoch*. Both were continued in Christian times. Throughout the first century A.D. such Jewish apocrypha made their appearance, e.g. the *Book of Jubilees* and the *Apocalypse of Baruch*.

On the Jewish apocrypha: E. Kautzsch, *Die Apokryphen und Pseudepigraphen des A.T.*, 1900. P. Riessler, *Altjued. Schrifttum ausserhalb der Bibel*, 1928.

Some of the Jewish O.T. apocrypha were enlarged by Christian writers, e.g. the *Book of Henoch* and the *Testament of the Twelve Patriarchs*, some were even included in the Canon, e.g. the *Fourth Book of Esdras*, the *Third Book of Maccabees* and the *Eighteen Psalms of Solomon*.

W. Bousset - H. Gressmann, *Religion des Judentums*, [3]1926. A. v. Gall, *Βασιλεία τοῦ θεοῦ*, Hei 1926. C. Bonner, *The Last Chapt. of Enoch in Greek*, 1937. Gry, Mu 1939, 337/78 (Paraboles d'Hénoch); Rb 1940, 195/204 (Les noms d'anges en II Hénoch). Jeremias, ZNTW 38, 1939, 115/24 (NT passages in the light of the newly found text of Henoch). Di S. Marco, Bi 1937, 383/417 ("giustizia" nell' Enoc etiopico). McColley, HTR 1938, 21/39 (The Book of Henoch and *Paradise Lost*). Gry, *Mémorial Lagrange*, 1940, 133/9 (La "mort du Messie" en 4 Esdras VII 29). E. Sjoeberg, *Der Menschensohn im aethiop. Henochbuch*, Lund 1946. Black, JTS 3, 1952, 1/10 (Eschatol. in the Ethiopic Bk. of Henoch). M. Hadas, *The Third and Fourth Books of Maccabees*, NY 1953 (ed. and transl.). M. de

Jonge, *The Testaments of the Twelve Patriarchs,* Gorcum 1953 (written by a Christian towards the end of the 2nd cent.).

The following are written entirely by Christian authors:

1. The second part (6–11) of the *Ascension of Isaias* (prophecies about Christ and his Church) in the second century. The first part which gives an account of the Jewish legend of the martyrdom of the prophet also contains Christian interpolations. The whole work is extant only in the Ethiopic version, parts also in Greek, Latin and Old Slavonic.

Trans.: Hennecke [2]1924, 303/14. E. Tisserant, *Ascens. d'Isaie,* 1909 (French trans.). E. Schuerer, *Gesch. des jued. Volkes im Zeitalter Christi* III, [4]1909, 386/93. Lefort, Mu 1938, 24/32; 1939, 1/10. Lacau, Mu 1946, 453/67 (*Asc. Is.,* Copt.). Flusser, Bull. of the Israel Exploration Society 17, 28/46 (*Ascensio Isaiae* and the Dead Sea Scrolls).

2. The *Odes of Solomon,* formerly known only from a citation in Lactantius (*Inst.* 4, 12, 3) and from the Coptic *Pistis Sophia* (v. § 24) which gives the complete text of five odes. In 1909 J. R. Harris discovered them in a Syrian MS, the beginning of which was mutilated, and edited them from this. Only the second hymn is missing from these forty-two odes which are a beautiful document of primitive mystical piety influenced by John. They date from the second century and were originally written in Greek. It is still a matter of controversy whether they are of direct Gnostic origin or whether their undeniably syncretistic flavour (esp. in 19 and 35) is still compatible with the piety of the great Church. Bardesanes is certainly not the author.

Ode 12 is a hymn to the Logos, Ode 17 on Christ's descent into Hades, Ode 19 on the conception of the Virgin by the Father with the co-operation of the Holy Spirit. As had been stated already in the *Ascension of Isaias,* here, too, it is said that the Virgin gave birth without a midwife: "Without feeling pain . . . and like a man she gave birth with a (firm) will." Ode 29 treats of the Passion, Ode 42 of the Resurrection of Christ.

An Encratite attitude hostile to marriage shows itself in several passages (e.g. 21, 5; 33, 5–7).

Text, trans. and comment. by R. Harris and A. Mingana, 2 vols., 1916/20, W. Bauer (KlT 64) 1933. Hennecke [2]1924, 437/72.—Treatises: Leclercq, DAL 12, 1903/21. H. Lewy, *Sobria ebrietas,* Gie 1929, 85 ff. J. Kroll 1932, 34/44. Van Unnik, JTS 1936, 172/5 (34, 4). Abramowski, ZNTW 1936, 44/69 (Christ). J. Ziegler, *Dulcedo Dei* 1937, 98/104. De Zwaan, *Quantulacunque*. Stud. present. to K. Lake 1937, 285/302 (Edessene origin). L. G. Rylands, *The Beginnings of Gnostic Christianity,* Lo 1940, 23/118. Grant, JBL 1944, 363/77 (The *Odes* and the Church of Antioch). Omodeo, ParPass 1, 1946, 84/118 (Le ode di Sal.). M. Baumgartner, *Festschr. Bertholet,* 1950, 50/7 (on 28, 4). A. Vööbus, *Celibacy, a Requirement for Admission to Baptism in the Early Syrian Church,* Stockh. 1951 (Or. lang. Syriac; hostile to marriage). Braun, RTh 1957, 597/625. *Pap. Bodmer,* X – XII (ed. M. Testuz), Cologny-Genève 1959 (*Pap. Bodmer,* XI prints for the first time Gk. text of Ode 11).

3. The *Testament of Solomon* belongs to the third or fourth century and is written in Greek. In the framework of a novel based on a Jewish Solomonic book it gives an account of the mysteries of the other world (angelology and demonology): it is a monument of Judaeo-Christian ways of thought.

Text: C. C. McCown, *The Testament of Solomon,* Lo 1922.

The remaining Christian apocrypha belong to the New Testament. They imitate the four literary forms of the New Testament and pretend to be works of N. T. personages. There are apocryphal Gospels, Acts, Epistles and Apocalypses. They are partly writings with an heretical (mostly Gnostic) tendency, partly Catholic redactions of such writings, and partly originally Catholic devotional books. According to Irenaeus (*Haer.* 1, 20) they were extremely numerous. The Church's attitude was sometimes opposed to them (Tert., *Bapt.* 17).

Their contents and form will lead even the most superficial reader to appreciate the great distance and difference between them and the canonical N.T. writings. The exaggerated, sometimes actually absurd miraculous element makes a particularly unpleasant impression. Nevertheless, these old Christian documents are of great value for the history of the Church, because they reflect the religious ideas, customs and tendencies prevalent among simple people. We have here the oldest Christian legends and romances.

Their influence on ancient Christian art was already considerable; it affected even more medieval, and through them also modern, artistic conceptions. Sculpture, painting and poetry were influenced by these apocrypha. The frescoes in Santa Maria Maggiore, reliefs on sarcophagi, miniatures in liturgical books, stained glass in medieval cathedrals, presentations of the Crib, Dante's Divine Comedy and many a recent literary work bear witness to them.

§ 9. APOCRYPHAL GOSPELS

Edd.: C. Tischendorf, *Evangelia apocr.*, [2]1876. E. Preuschen, *Antilegomena* (with German trans.), [2]1905. F. Robinson, *Coptic Apocryphal Gospels,* 1896. E. Klostermann (KlT 3, 8). C. Michel and P. Peeters 1–2, P 1911/14. G. Bonaccorsi, *I Vangeli apocrifi* I, 1948 (Greek and Lat. texts with trans.). F. Amiot, *La Bible apocryphe: Evv. apocr.*, 1952. — Treatises: W. Bauer, *Das Leben Jesu im Zeitalter der ntl. Apokryphen,* 1909. L. Couard, *Altchristl. Sagen ueber das Leben Jesu u. der Apostel,* 1909. A. F. Findlay, *Byways in Early Chr. Literature. Studies in the Uncanonical Gospels and Acts,* Edinb. 1923. P. Saintyves, RHR 106, 1932, 435/57 (valeur hagiographique). H. J. Bardsley, *Reconstructions of Early Christ. Documents* I, 1935 (apocr. Gospels and Acts). Ghedini, StU 443/80 (language of the apocr. Gospels). M. Goguel, *La foi à la résurr. de Jésus dans le Christianisme primitif,* 1933. H. J. Schonfield, *Readings from the Apocr. Gospels,* 1940. K. L. Schmidt, *Kanon. u. apokryphe Evv. u. Apostelgeschichten,* Basle 1944. See also § 8. De Santos Otero, *Los Evang. Apócrifos,* Ma 1956 (trans.). Hennecke-Schneemelcher, [3]1959.

THE apocryphal Gospels, which are mostly of Gnostic origin, deal chiefly with those years of the life of Jesus that are omitted by the canonical records, that is, with his youth and his teaching after his resurrection, which is extended to many (18) months.

1. *Extra-canonical fragments of the Gospels*

a. The *Fragment of Fajjum,* a parallel text of Mc. 14, 26–30, omitting 28.

E. Preuschen, *Antilegomena,* [2]1905, 21 f.

b. The *Logia of Jesus of Oxyrhynchos,* publ. by Grenfell and Hunt in 1897 and 1904. The two fragments are probably taken from two different apocryphal Gospels.

E. Preuschen, *Antilegomena,* ²1905, 22ff. FP 3², 44ff.

c. The *Fragments of an Unknown Gospel and Other Early Christian Papyri,* ed. by H. I. Bell and T.-C. Skeat.

Here we have also to do with an apocryphal Gospel which is dependent on Jo. Cf. Vogels, Ho 32, 1934/35, 12. F., 558/62; RSR 1935, 358/62; ETL 1935, 579/81; ZNTW 1935, 285/91; DLZ 1936, 3/11; RB 1935, 318ff.; Mu 1936, 55/77; K. F. W. Schmidt and J. Jeremias, TB 1936, 34/45. Bell, TB 1936, 72/4. Galbiati, Accademie e Biblioteche d'Italia 59, 1940, 471/78. G. Majeda, *Das Leben-Jesu-Fragm. Pap. Egerton,* Bern 1946. Bell, HTR 1949, 53/63. Leaney, VC 1955, 212/17 (author prob. Heracleon or Origen). Hennecke ³1959, 56/74.

2. The *Gospel according to the Hebrews,* known from the accounts of St. Jerome (*Vir. ill.* 2), who translated it from the original into Greek and Latin. He says that this Gospel was written in Chaldaic (i.e. Aramaic), but with Hebrew letters and that it was in use among the Nazarenes; further, that most people thought it was the original Hebrew (Aramaic) text of St. Matthew's Gospel. This opinion seems sometimes to have been shared by Jerome himself.

The small fragments show that it is, indeed, very close to the Gospel of St. Matthew. Hence it is usually supposed that the *Gospel of the Hebrews* is an edited and enlarged version of the Aramaic original of the Gospel of St. Matthew. It was certainly written before the year 150 and was probably already in the hands of St. Ignatius of Antioch; it owes its name to the fact that it was used by the Hebrew—or rather Aramaic—speaking Jews in Palestine and Syria, whom Jerome usually called Nazarenes.

Bauer 1934, 55/7. J. T. Dodd, Lo 1933. Lagrange, RB 1922, 161/81, 321/49. Schmidtke, ZNTW 1936, 24/43. Leaney, VC 1955, 212/17 (author prob. Heracleon or Orig.). Bardy, MSR 1946, 5/36 (against the credibility of Jerome).

3. The *Gospel of the Ebionites,* attested by Epiphanius, *Haer.* 30,

13ff., is apparently identical with the *Gospel of the Twelve* attested by Origen (*Hom. Lc.* 1); only small fragments are extant.

A. Hilgenfeld, *NT extra canonem*, ^{2}1884, 33f. Hennecke ^{2}1924, 39/48. A. Schmidtke, ZNTW 1936, 24/44 seeks again to prove his earlier thesis (TU 37, 1) that the *Gospel of the Hebrews* was originally written in Greek and is identical with the *Gospel of the Ebionites;* Waitz, ZNTW 1937, 60/81 (against Schmidtke). H. J. Schoeps, *Theol. u. Gesch. des Judenchristentums,* 1949, 25/33. Teicher, ZRGG 1951, 193/209 (The Dead Sea Scrolls and the Ebionites). L. Goppelt, *Christentum u. Judentum im 1. u. 2. Jh.,* G 1954.

4. The *Gospel of the Egyptians,* written probably after 150, accepted as canonical in Egypt. It was used to prove the doctrines of the Encratites (rejection of marriage), Naassenes (theories on body and soul) and Sabellians (modalist teaching on the Trinity) (Clem. Alex., *Strom.* 3, 9, 63f.; 13, 92f.; Hippol., *Philos.* 5, 7; Epiph., *Haer.* 62, 2). Certain fragment: a Dialogue of Jesus with Salome in Clem. Alex., *Strom.* 3, 9, 66; 13, 92.

E. Klostermann (KlT 8) 12f. W. Bauer 1934, 54f. Quispel, TZ 1949, 2. pt. (The repentance of the Creator acc. to the Egypt. Gospel). A. P. Schwab, *Studien zur Kosmologie der Naassener,* thesis I 1949.

5. The *Gospel of Peter,* known through Eus., *Hist.* 6, 12, 3–6 and a fragment on parchment which, together with fragments of the *Apocalypse of Peter* and the Greek *Henoch* was found by H. Bouriant in a Christian tomb at Akhmim in Upper Egypt in the winter of 1886–7. The piece gives an account of the Passion and Resurrection of the Lord, the latter embellished with miracles. The responsibility for Christ's death is laid exclusively on the Jews. Herod orders the crucifixion. It is a very free redaction of the four canonical Gospels. Though there are traces of Docetism this does not prove that it was written by a heretic (perhaps even before 150 in Syria).

E. Klostermann (KlT 3) 3/8; FP 3^{2}, 47/58. Hennecke ^{2}1924, 59/63. L. Vaganay, *L'Évangile de Pierre,* 1930. Fascher, PWK 19, 1373/81 (apocrypha of St. Peter).

6. The *Protoevangelium of James* was used perhaps already by Justin; it was certainly written before A.D. 200. It tells, freely inventing, the life of the Blessed Virgin Mary until the massacre of the

Innocents, betraying great ignorance of Jewish conditions. It gives for the first time the names of Joachim and Anna as the parents of Mary, and asserts that they had received her from God as their only child in their old age, had consecrated her to the service of God when she was three years old and describes her betrothal. As in the *Gospel of Peter*, the "brethren of Jesus" are described as sons of Joseph by a former marriage. The perpetual virginity of Mary (also the *virginitas in partu*) is especially emphasized. The author calls himself James. The work is extant in more than thirty Greek MSS. Besides, we have the work in old Syriac, Armenian, Coptic and Old Slavonic translations. An Old Latin version has not so far come to light. The work has exercised a far-reaching influence on the development of later Marian legends. Cf. the Feast of the *Presentation BMV* (21st Nov.).

Greek in Tischendorf, *Ev. apocr.*[2], 1/50; FP 3, 59/68; complete in C. Michel, *Évangiles apocr.* I, [2]1924. P. Bonaccorsi, *I Vangeli apocr.* I, 1948, 58/109 (text and trans.). Daniel-Rops, *Les évangiles de la Vierge*, 1948 (trans.). E. Amann, *Le protévangile de Jacques et ses remaniements latins*, 1910. P. Vannutelli, Synoptica 4, 1939, 1/64; 5, 1940, 65/96. Mingana, BJR 1927, 329 ff. (Vita syr. Joh. Baptistae). M. R. James, *Latin Infancy Gospels*, 1927. Hennecke [2]1924, 84 ff. On papyrus fragments cf. A. Ehrhard, TU 50, 57 and 69. A. Janssens, *De H. Maagd en Moeder Gods Maria: het Dogma en de Apocriefen*, A [2]1930. Kindred later apocrypha in E. A. W. Budge, *Legends of our Lady Mary the Perpetual Virgin and her Mother Hanna*, 1933; *One Hundred and Ten Miracles of our Lady Mary, trans. from Ethiopic MSS*, 1933. Klawek, CT 1936, 327/37 (motive of immovability of nature). L. M. Peretto, *La mariologia del Protoev. di Giacomo*, R 1955; partially printed in Marianum 16, 1954, 228/65. M. Testuz, *Nativité de Marie*, Cologny-Genève 1958 (*Pap. Bodmer* V); Hennecke [3]1959, 277/90. Perler, *Freib. Z. f. Phil. u. Theol.* 1959, 23/35.

7. *The History of Joseph the Carpenter* was evidently inspired by the *Protoevangelium of James* of which it is a counterpart; it is the oldest document of a veneration of St. Joseph. It was very probably written in Greek in Egypt towards the end of the fourth century, but is extant only in Coptic and in an Arabic translation based on the Coptic version. It contains additions dating from the fifth century or an even later date. Chs. 1–11 describe antecedents, the birth and early childhood of Jesus; chs. 11–12 the illness,

death and burial of Joseph. In the description of the latter, two old Egyptian myths and rites of the cult of Osiris are interpreted in a Christian sense.

Text: P. de Lagarde, *Aegyptiaca,* Go 1883, 1–37; on this Lefort, Mu 1953, 201/23 (new fragms.). Arabic: G. Wallin, L 1722. — Klameth, *Angelos* 3, 1930, 6/31. S. Morenz, *Die Geschichte von Joseph dem Zimmermann* (TU 56), 1951 (with trans.); on this Boehlig, BZ 1953, 142/45 and Engberding, OC 37, 1953, 56/88 (against the hist. derivation of the feast of St. Joseph from the festival of the Nile). Further lit. in Graf I, 234/36.

8. A *Gospel of Thomas* which, according to Hippolytus (*Philos.* 5, 7) originated in the circles of the Gnostic Naassenes is lost. Cyril of Jerusalem (*Cat.* 4, 36; 6, 31) mentions a Gospel of Thomas which he says was of Manichean origin. But under the name of the apostle Thomas we possess a Gospel in various Greek, Latin, Syriac, Armenian and Slavonic recensions which gives many legends of the childhood of Jesus until his twelfth year. The longer Greek recension (2) tells, for example, that Jesus, playing with other children, had made twelve birds of clay on the Sabbath; a Jew complained about this to St. Joseph. When the latter reproached the child for it, Jesus clapped his hands and the birds flew away. All these recensions were probably based on the rather sizable originally Gnostic work.

In later times many other Gospels of the Infancy were produced, all of which are somehow connected with the two preceding ones (*Protoev. of James* and the *Gospel of Thomas*). According to P. Peeters all these stories including the Gospel of Thomas go back to a Syriac source which originated before 400 and utilized, among other things, also Buddhist legends.

Greek text in Tischendorf, *Ev. apocr.,*[2] 140ff. P. Peeters, *Ev. apocr.,* II: *L'év. de l'enfance, rédactions syriaques, arabes et armén., trad. et annotées,* 1914. — Trans.: Hennecke [2]1924, 93ff. and E. Bock, *Die Kindheit Jesu, Zwei apokr. Evv. uebers.,* 1924. L. Richard, *Mémorial J. Chaine,* 1950, 297/308 (L'év. de l'enfance et le décret impérial de recensement). Ferri, *Studi Medioev. e Volgari* 1, 1953, 119/21 (Lat. text).

9. The *Gospel of Bartholomew,* mentioned by Jerome (*Mt., Prol.*) and in the *Decretum Gelasianum,* is preserved in some Coptic, Greek,

Slavonic and Latin fragments. It contains revelations of the Lord after his resurrection called forth by question of Bartholomew. The descent into hell is treated in great detail. The Greek original was written in Gnostic circles in Egypt in the third century.

Bonwetsch, GN 1897, 1/42 (Greek and Slav. texts). E. Revillout, PO 2, 185/98 (Copt. text). A. Wilmart et E. Tisserant, RB 1913, 161/90, 321/68 (Gr. and Lat. fragms.); cf. Moricca, RBn 1921, 481/516, 1922, 20/30 and Haase, ZNTW 1915, 93/112. Vitti, VD 1927, 138/44, 171/81 *(descensus Christi)*. J. Kroll, 71/82. Hennecke, [3]1959, 359/76.

10. The *Acts of Pilate (Gospel of Nicodemus),* like the *Protoevangelium of James* of great influence in the Middle Ages, were probably inspired by suggestions and statements of Justin (1 *Apol.* 35, 48) and Tertullian (*Apoc.* 5, 21) and by the spurious *Acts of Pilate* officially publ. under Maximus Daza in 311 or 312 for use against the Christians (Eus., *Hist.* 9, 5, 1).

In the first part (chs. 1–11) they give an account of the trial, crucifixion and burial of Christ, in the second part (chs. 12–14) of the discussions of the sanhedrin on the fact of the resurrection; chs. 1–16 are also extant separately under the title of *Acta Pilati.* The third part (chs. 17–27), with the special title *Descensus Christi ad inferos* (cf. supra no. 9) gives an account of the statements of two witnesses of the descent of Christ into hell who have themselves risen from the dead. The work originated as late as the beginning of the fifth century. It uses older material and, like the *Gospel of Peter* and a fictitious letter of Pilate in the *Acta Petri et Pauli,* it wants to play off Pilate as a witness to Christianity against the Jews. The Coptic Church venerates Pilate as a saint and martyr. The work is extant in Greek as well as in Latin, Syriac, Armenian, Coptic and Arabic translations.

Other Acts of Pilate, like the *Anaphora Pilati* (report to the Emperor) and *Paradosis Pilati* (condemnation of Pilate by the Emperor), a letter of Pilate to Tiberius, a correspondence between Herod and Pilate and others belong to the Middle Ages.

Greek text in Tischendorf, *Ev. apocr.*,[2] 210ff. Revillout, PO 2, 61ff. (Copt. text); on this Barns in: *Copt. Studies in Honour of W. E. Crum,* 1950, 245/50 and *Bull. of the Byzantine Inst.* (Boston) 2, 1950, 245/50 (fragm. of another Copt. version). A. Westcott, *The Gospels of Nicodemus and Kindred Documents,* 1915. — Vitti, VD 1927 (supra no. 9). J. Kroll 1932, 83/95. P. Vannutelli, *Actorum Pilati textus synoptici,* R 1938. Mingana, BJR 12, 1928, 41ff. *(Lament. Virginis).* 491ff. *(Martyrium Pilati).* Hennecke, [3]1959 330/58.

11. The *Gospel of Matthias,* stated by Eusebius (*Hist.* 3, 25, 6) to be heretical (cf. Origen, *Hom. 1 Lk.*), perhaps to be identified with the "traditions of Matthias" mentioned by Clement of Al. (*Strom.* 2, 9, 45 et saepe). It contained secret teachings used by the Gnostics following Basilides; it originated probably in Egypt, perhaps in Alexandria, in the first half of the second century, but is now lost.

A. Hilgenfeld, *NT extra canonem,* [2]1884, 49f. Hennecke [2]1924, 139f.

12. The *Gospel of Philip,* mentioned probably already in the *Pistis Sophia,* certainly by Epiphanius (*Haer.* 26, 13) as Gnostic.

Hennecke [2]1924, 69.

13. The *Gospel of Barnabas,* mentioned in the so-called *Decretum Gelasianum* and in a Greek list of canonical books (eighth/ninth centuries), is completely lost. The so-called *Italian Gospel of Barnabas* which considered Mohammed to have been the Messias was written by a fourteenth century Christian who had apostatized to Islam.

Lo and La Ragg, *The Gospel of B.,* O 1907. J. Schmid, RACh 1, 1209/12.

14. The *Gospel of Andrew* is mentioned in the so-called *Decretum Gelasianum* and probably to be identified with the *Acta Andreae* known to Pope Innocent I, *Ep.* 6, 7. Perhaps Augustine, *C. adversarios leg. et prophet.* I, 20, 39, also refers to this apocryphon. Further information in Quasten I, 128.

15. Other Gnostic Gospels, known mostly only by their titles, are: *Gospel of Thomas* (not identical with no. 8), *of Judas, of Eve, of Mary* (Kapsomenos, Ἀθηνᾶ 49, 1939, 177/86; texts from Greek papyri), *of Basilides, of Truth* and others. Cf. also Quasten I, 128.

On an apocr. Gospel of Jo. cf. Bi 143, 194f. O. Loefgren, *Fakta och dokument angaende det apokr. Jo.-Ev.*, Up 1942.

§ 10. APOCRYPHAL ACTS OF THE APOSTLES

Edd. and trans.: Greek texts: R. A. Lipsius and M. Bonnet, *Acta apostolorum apocrypha,* 2 vols., 1891/1903. Syr. texts: W. Wright, *Apocr. Acts* 1–2, 1871. Armen. texts: P. Vetter, OC 1901, 217ff.; 1903, 16ff., 324ff.; TQ 1906, 161ff. Arab. text: A. Smith Lewis in *Horae semit.* 3/4, 1904. Ethiop. texts: E. A. W. Budge, *The Contendings of the Apostles* 1–2, 1899/1901. Copt. texts: I. Guidi and O. v. Lemm 1887/90. — Treatises: R. A. Lipsius, *Die apokr. Apostelgesch.* 1–2 and suppl. vol. 1883/90. F. Haase, *Apostel u. Evangelisten in den oriental. Ueberlieferungen,* 1922. DB Suppl. 1, 488/514. R. Soeder, *Die apokr. Apostelgesch. u. die romanhafte Lit. der Antike,* 1932. M. Blumenthal, *Formen u. Motive i. den apokr. Apostelgesch.,* 1933. Bardy, DS 1, 752/65 (encrat. tendencies). R. Helm, *Der antike Roman,* 1948, 53/61. Hatch, *Bull. of Byz. Institute* (Boston) 2, 1950, 305/17 (three hitherto unknown pieces from Copt. Acts of Apostles). See also § 8.

Like the apocryphal Gospels, the apocryphal Acts belong to the mass of popular legendary literature, though they sometimes contain an historical core. In a certain sense they may be considered parallels of the novels of antiquity.

They originated in part as heretical propaganda writings and were later revised by Catholic authors in order to fill the noticeable gaps in the canonical account of the missionary activities of the apostles. It is not always easy to distinguish with certainty earlier and later, heretical and orthodox forms. This group of writings contains much interesting information on the history of religious services as they were celebrated in private houses in the second and third centuries. Here we meet with prayers and hymns, witnesses of the oldest extra-Biblical poetry, and become acquainted with the ascetical ideals of the heretical communities and the syncretism and superstition rife in the Gnostic sects. Only from the fifth century a certain Leucius (in Photius, *Cod.* 114: L. Charinus) is mentioned as the author; this is perhaps the name or pseudonym of the author of the Gnostic *Acts of John*. In any case the authors of all these Acts remain completely obscure.

On the feasts of the apostles the accounts of their martyrdoms were read in church from their Acts; even now they are the basis of certain lessons of the Breviary.

Leclercq, DAL 8, 2982/6 (Leucius).

1. The *Acts of Paul* (Πράξεις Παύλου, *Acta Pauli*) is a romance which makes arbitrary use of the canonical Acts and the Pauline Epistles. Tertullian (*Bapt.* 17) calls it the work of a priest who wrote this romance for love of St. Paul but who was dismissed from his office because he had falsified historical facts (EH 196). This must have happened in Asia Minor in the last quarter of the second century. Only the discovery of the fragments of the Coptic translation (1904) made it possible more accurately to determine the contents and scope of the work. C. Schmidt proved that the following three pieces, that had long been known, belong to these Acts:

a. The *Reply of the Corinthians* to the Second Epistle of St. Paul and a third Epistle of the latter to the Corinthians. V. infra § 11, 1 c.

b. *Acta Pauli et Theclae,* Greek, called by Jerome (*Vir. ill.* 7) *Periodi Pauli et Theclae*. They recount, quite in the manner of a novel and probably without any historical foundation, the story of Thecla, a noble virgin from Iconium and an enthusiastic follower of St. Paul, who preached like a missionary and administered baptism to herself. Chapter Three describes the physical appearance of St. Paul.

It is very doubtful whether there is an historical nucleus to the legend, viz. that a virgin Thecla who lived at Iconium and later at Seleucia (Isauria) was converted by Paul, suffered for the faith, baptized and preached and had connexions with the historically attested Queen Tryphaena at Antioch (Pisidia).

c. *Martyrium* or *Passio S. Pauli,* Greek, quite legendary (tells e.g., that when the apostle was beheaded, milk spurted on to the clothes of the hangman).

C. Schmidt's view of the original form of the *Acta Pauli* has been brilliantly confirmed by the discovery of a larger portion of the Greek original which is preserved for us in a Hamburg papyrus. The new texts contain mostly new subject matter, including the fable of the baptized lion mentioned by Jerome (*Vir. ill.* 7).

Greek text of *Acta Pauli et Theclae:* Lipsius-Bonnet I, 235/72. Apart from five Lat. transs. many Oriental ones have also been preserved. The *Martyrium Pauli* ibid. I, 104 ff. with two Latin versions. The Copt. fragments in C. Schmidt, *Acta Pauli,* [2]1905. The new Greek parts: C. Schmidt, Πράξεις Παύλου, 1936; on this SbB 1929, 176/83; 1931, 37/41; cf. Baumstark, OC 1937, 122/6; Halkin, AB 1937, 354/7 and Kurfess, ZNTW 38, 1939, 164/70. L. Vouaux, *Les Actes de Paul et ses lettres apocr.,* 1913. Sanders, HTR 1938, 73/90 (fragm. belonging to the Berlin Pap. ed. by Schmidt [SbB 1931, 37/41]). Kilpatrick-Roberts, JTS 1946, 196/9 (new fragm.). Peterson, AB 1947, 57/60 (*Acta Xanthippae* and *Acts of Paul*). Most recent publications on the Hamburg Papyrus: Metzger, *Princeton Seminary Bull.* 39, 2, 1945, 11/21 (Paul and the baptized lion); Peterson, VC 1949, 142/62 (esp. on the dependance of the *Acta Pauli* on the *Acts of Thomas*); against this Devos, AB 1951, 119/30; Alfonsi, Aeg 1950, 67/71 (*Echi protettici* in this text). — Roberts, *The Antiopolis Papyri* I, Lo 1950, 27 (fragm. from the *Acta Pauli et Theclae*).

2. *Acts of Peter:* a. The Πέτρου κήρυγμα (= Missionary Preaching of Peter) originated in Catholic circles probably in Egypt as early as the first third of the second century and was destined to give general directions to missionaries working among the heathen. Fragments are preserved in Clement of Alex.

Hennecke [2]1924, 143 ff. E. Klostermann (KlT 3) 13 ff. Quispel-Grant, VC 1952, 31f.

b. The *Acts of Peter* (Πράξεις Πέτρου) have not been preserved as a whole. According to C. Schmidt the work was written by a Catholic (?) author not in Rome, but in Syria-Palestine between 180 and 190.

α. The *Actus Vercellenses* (so called after the place where they were found) = *Actus Petri cum Simone* are extant in a Latin translation. They give an account of Peter's fight against the marvellous feats of Simon Magus, who is fatally injured in an attempted flight (ascension) on the Roman forum.

β. *Martyrium Petri,* Greek, an account of the *Domine, quo vadis?* and the crucifixion of Peter with a speech on the symbolic significance of the Cross which has a strongly Gnostic flavour.

γ. The *Martyrium b. Petri apostoli a Lino conscriptum* is a late Latin legend, belonging probably to the sixth century and independent of the *Actus Vercellenses.*

Texts: Lipsius-Bonnet I, 1/22, 45/103. L. Vouaux, *Les Actes de Pierre,* 1922. A. H. Salonius ed. Helsingfors 1926 the writings mentioned under γ. — Trans.: Hennecke [2]1924, 226/49. G. Stuhlfauth, *Die apokr. Petrusgeschichten in der altchristl. Kunst,* 1925. C. Schmidt, *Stud. zu den Pseudo-Klementinen,* 1929. D. de Bruyne, JTS 1933, 395 f. (two apocr. sayings of Peter not so far identified).

3. The *Acts of Peter and Paul,* Greek and Latin, to be distinguished from the two Acts named under 1 and 2, perhaps written in the third century to replace heretical Acts and to describe the close relations between the two princes of the Apostles. The following pieces have been preserved: a. St. Paul's journey to Rome, b. the martyrdom of the two apostles. Another, later combination of the stories of Peter and Paul is found in Syria.

Texts: Lipsius-Bonnet I, 178/234. L. Vouaux, *Les Actes de Pierre,* 1922. On the question of Peter's sojourn in Rome cf. here the literature that has appeared since 1936: L. Herrmann, *RevUnivBruxelles* 1936, 189/99 (year of death 58!) and Lat 5, 1946, 303/10. K. Heussi, *War Petrus in Rom?* 1936; id., *Petrus, wirklich roem. Maertyrer?,* Christl. Welt, 4. H., 1937; on this H. Lietzmann, SbB 1936, 29; Altaner, TR 1937, 167/88. Dannenbauer, HZ 1938, 80/87. Katzenmayer, IKZ 1938, 85/93, 129/40. W. Lowrie, *SS. Peter and Paul in Rome,* O 1940. Schuler, TrTZ 1941, 94/116. M. Dibelius, SbHei 1941, 2, 18/29. Heussi, TLZ 1952, 67/72. Compiche, RUC 1952, 249/73. Fascher, PWK 19, 1377/81. P. Schindler, *Petrus.* Trans. from Danish into Italian by A. Zucconi, Vicenza 1951; cf. OCP 1952, 222/24. But cf. also 15, 1 and § 3, 22. — Rimoldi, SC 1955, 196/224 (Peter in the apocr. lit. of the first 6 cents.). van Lantschoot, Mu 1955, 17/46, 219/33 (new pieces of the Acts of Peter and Paul in Ethiop. trans.).

4. The *Acts of Andrew,* mentioned by Eusebius (*Hist.* 3, 25, 6) as used by the heretics, written perhaps *c.* 200 by Leucius (Charinus). Only very little of these has been preserved. It is difficult to ascertain what in the diverse later Acts of Andrew goes back to the old Acts. The following fragments are extant:

a. *Acts of Andrew and Matthias in the City of Man-Eaters,* in a Catholic recension, Latin, Coptic, Syriac, Ethiopic and Anglo-saxon;

b. *Acts of the Holy Apostles Peter and Andrew* (continuation of a.);

c. *Martyrdom of St. Andrew,* allegedly written by the priests and deacons of Achaja, extant in Greek and Latin, probably an independent narrative of the time after 400, without certain connexion with the old Gnostic Acts of Andrew;

d. *Discourses of the Apostle* in the prison of Patrae;

e. *Martyrdom of the Apostles,* preserved in several recensions.

Texts: Lipsius-Bonnet II, 1, 1/127. Hennecke² 249/56. F. Blatt, *Die lat. Bearbeitungen der Acta Andreae et Matthiae apud antropophagos,* 1930. Morenz, TLZ 1947, 295/7 (Copt. text). Quispel, VC 1956, 129/48 (Copt. fragm.).

5. The *Acts of John,* mentioned by Eusebius together with the Acts of Andrew, alleged to be a work of Leucius. Extant are among others:

a. three short pieces in the Acts of the second Council of Nicaea (787) with a Hymn of the Lord which, according to Augustine (*Ep.* 237) was used by the Priscillians. The last two pieces are found in the following work published by James in 1897:

b. *Marvellous History of the Deeds and Visions which St. John the Theologian saw of Our Lord Jesus Christ,* an alleged sermon of St. John of docetic tendency. The first piece from those Acts of the Council (on the portrait of St. John by the painter Lycomedes) is found again in the work published by Bonnet in 1893;

c. *Miracles of St. John* from a Codex Patmiacus, which also contains

d. the *Acts of Drusiana,* published by Zahn in 1880 from a Cod. Marcianus;

e. an *Account of the Passing* (μετάστασις) *of John.*

Later recensions are: 1. *Virtutes Joannis,* 2. *Passio Joannis* by Mellitus of Laodicea (?), 3. *The Deeds of John by Prochorus, his Disciple* (of Cath. origin), 4. The Syriac *Acts of John.*

Texts: T. Zahn, *Acta Joannis,* 1880. Lipsius-Bonnet II, 1, 151/216. Musikides, NS 1947, 245f.; 1948, 51/53, 21/22 (*Acta Jo.* of Prochorus acc. to Cod. 35 of the Greek Patriarchate of Jerus.). — Hennecke² 171/91. P. Bonaccorsi, *I Vangeli apocrifi* I, 1948, 260/88 (on the death of Mary). M. Pulver, *Eranos-Jb* 1942, Zu 1943, 141/77 (*Acts of Jo.* on the Passion). Ehrhard, TU 50, 57f. Loewenich 1932, 102/9. M. Jugie, *La mort et l'assomption de la S. Vierge,* 1944, 710/26 (death and ascension of apostle). Till, JEH 1952, 14/22 (Gnostic Apocryphon of John).

6. The *Acts of Thomas* dates from the first half of the third century and may have originated in the circles of Bardesanes in Edessa. It was written in Syriac and was soon revised by a Catholic Syrian and a Catholic Greek. Apart from the Greek and Syriac versions it is extant in an Ethiopic, an Armenian and two different Latin versions. It tells that the apostle Thomas went to India where he converted, among others, King Gundaphorus (a Parthian-Indian king of this name is historically attested on coins). Having worked many miracles he at last died a martyr's death, pierced by many spears. Though repeated efforts have been made to prove the historicity of the apostle's missionary activities in India (the Thomas Christians on the coast of Malabar), these cannot be considered successful. The Acts contain several fine liturgical hymns. The best-known is the "Hymn of the Soul" (i.e. of the redemption).

Greek text: Lipsius-Bonnet II, 2, 99/291. Hennecke² 256/89. A. Vaeth, *Der hl. Thomas, der Apostel Indiens,* ²1925. Kirylowicz, 'Eλ. 1931, 118/47. T. K. Joseph, *Bull. of the Internat. Committee of Hist. Science* 1933, 560/9. G. Bornkamm, *Mythos und Legende in den apokr. Thomasakten,* 1933. Connolly, JTS 1935, 353/7. J. Kroll, 1932, 30/4. Bornkamm, PWK II, 6, 316/23. On the hymns of the Acts of Thomas cf. G. Hoffmann, ZNTW 1903, 273/309; Bousset, ibid. 18, 1917/18, 1/39; Reitzenstein, ibid. 21, 1922, 35/7 and Pantelakis, Θ 15/16, 1937; 16, 1938, 5/31 (BZ 1938, 220f,. 507). Omodeo, ParPass 1, 1946, 323/37 (I miti gnostici). Devos, AB 1948, 231/75 (medieval legends). Peterson, VC 1949, 12/62;against this Devos, AB 1951, 119/30 (v. under no. 1). Quasten, *Medieval Studies* 9, 1947, 1/18. A. Adam, *Die Psalmen des Thomas und das Perlenlied,* B 1959.

7. The *Acts of Thaddaeus,* in two recensions:

a. The *Document from the Archives of Edessa,* in Eusebius (*Hist.* 1, 13), translated from Syriac into Greek, an exchange of letters between Christ and King Abgar (Abgar V. Ukkama, i.e. the

Black One, reigned from 4 B.C. to A.D. 7, and again from A.D. 13 to 50). Abgar asks the Lord to come to him to Edessa to heal his disease: the latter replies that he must accomplish his destiny in Palestine, but would send the king one of his disciples after his ascension. Later, Eusebius continues, the apostle Thomas sent Thaddaeus, one of the seventy-two disciples (also called Addaeus) who cured Abgar and preached to his subjects. It is out of the question that the letter should be genuine. Already Augustine (*Faust.* 28, 4; *Cons. Ev.* 1, 7, 11) rejects the existence of authentic letters of Jesus. The so-called *Decr. Gelasianum* calls the letter of Jesus apocryphal.

b. The *Doctrina Addaei,* Syriac, published in 1876. It is largely identical with the report of Eusebius, but the reply of the Lord is given by word of mouth, which shows that the Syriac redactor doubted the authenticity of the letter but did not want to make his presentation appear untrustworthy. Instead, he inserted a mention of the portrait of the Lord which had been painted by Abgar's messenger. The *Doctrina Addaei* is a development of the old legend; it originated *c.* 400. As the reply of Jesus was here embellished by a promise of safety for the city of Edessa, the Letter of Jesus was used as a talisman in the form of inscriptions on city gates (e.g. at Edessa, Ephesus, Philippi), sepulchres and door posts.

Lipsius-Bonnet I, 273/83. J. Tixeront, *Les origines de l'Église d'Édesse,* 1888. E. v. Dobschütz, *Christusbilder,* 1899, 102ff. Joutie, HTR 1930, 299/302; 1931, 61/5. A. M. Kropp, *Ausgewaehlte kopt. Zaubertexte* II, Bru 1930/31, no. 15ff. Perdrizet, *Seminarium Kondakov.* 1932, 1/15 (portraits of Christ). Runciman, *Cambr. Hist. Journ.* 3, 1929/31, 238/52 (Picture of Edessa). W. Bauer 1934, 7/10, 15/17, 40/5. Further lit. in Halkin, AB 1951, 402.

8. Of the many other legendary Acts of Apostles we would name those of Philip, Matthew, Bartholomew, Mark, Timothy and Barnabas, which are all of later date (4th/5th cent. and later).

Peterson, ZNTW 1932, 97/111; OC 1932, 172/9; TQ 1932, 289/98 (Acts of Philip). Kurfess, ZNTW 44, 1952/3, 145/51 (Acts of Philip prob. originally in Lat.). J. Keil, *Jahresh. Oesterr. Arch. Inst.* 29, 1934, 82/92 (Acta Timothei).

Delehaye, *Anatolian Stud. presented to W. H. Buckler,* ed. by M. Calder and J. Keil 1939, 77/84 (Acts of Timothy, untrustworthy).

§ 11. APOCRYPHAL EPISTLES OF THE APOSTLES[1]

THE Epistles of the apostles have been imitated in legends and forgeries much more rarely than the Gospels and the Acts. Some of the apocryphal epistles have for a time been regarded as canonical.

1. *Apocryphal Pauline Letters.*

a. The *Epistle to the Laodiceans* originated at the latest in the fourth century. Its Latin text is extant in many Biblical MSS of the sixth to the fifteenth centuries, but it has survived also in other languages. It consists of words and sentences taken from genuine Pauline Epistles (esp. Phil.). Harnack's thesis that the present Letter is a Marcionite forgery of the second century has not gained acceptance.

A. Harnack (KlT 12) 1931. Hennecke² 150 f. Harnack, *Marcion,* ²1924, 172 f., 64* ff. SbB 1923, 235/45. Against this Capelle, RB 1924, Bull. I, n. 283. MacKnight, Bibl. Rev. 1932, 519/39. Quispel, NTT 1950, 43/6 (new arguments for Harnack's thesis).

b. The *Epistle to the Alexandrines,* mentioned as Marcionite by the Muratorian Fragment (EP 268, 64 f.) has left no other trace.

c. The *Third Epistle to the Corinthians,* with an introductory note written to Paul by the priests at Corinth, was thought authentic for some time by the Syrian and Armenian Churches. It was translated into Latin as early as the third century. It is part of the *Acts of Paul* (supra § 10, 1a) and deals with important doctrinal issues: the position of the old Christian prophets, the creation of the world and of man, the birth of the Lord from the Virgin Mary, the human nature of Christ and the resurrection of the body.

[1] For editions, translations and treatises see § 8.

A. Harnack (KlT 12) 1931. Pink, Bi 1925, 68/91. W. Bauer 1934, 45/8. De Bruyne, RB 1933, 189/95. Rist, JR 1942, 39/62. Boese, ZNTW 44, 1952/53, 66/76 (ed. of new Latin witness of text).

d. The Latin *Exchange of Letters between Paul and Seneca,* eight letters of the philosopher who has become a Christian and six of the apostle about the conversion of the apostle, the style of his letters, the persecution of Christians under Nero and the nomination of Seneca as preacher of the Gospel at the Imperial Court. Such a correspondence is unknown till Jerome (*Vir. ill.* 12). It is quite probable that it may have been written by a student at the Roman school of rhetoric at the suggestion of a master (perhaps *c.* 380). It would fit this idea e.g. that Seneca asks the apostle to give a better linguistic form to his profound thoughts. There are over 300 MSS of this correspondence.

Edd.: C. W. Barlow, *Epp. Senecae ad Paulum et Pauli ad Senecam,* R 1938. F. Haase, *Senecae Opera,* Supplem. 1902, 74/9. — Liénard, RBP 1932, 5/23 (originated in the circle of Symmachus, end of 4th cent.). Kurfess, TG 1937, 317/22; ZNTW 1936, 307; Mn 1938, 265/9 (Ep. 12); 1939f.; TQ 1938, 318/31. Liénard, RBP 1941, 589/98 (Alcuin and the correspondence). Labriolle 1934, 25/8. Benoît, RB 1946, 7/35 (Sen. and P.). Kurfess, ZRGG 2, 1949/50, 67/70; *Aevum* 1952, 42/8. Franceschini, *Mél. De Ghellinck* I, 149/70 (new MS). Leclercq, DAL 15, 1, 1193/8.

2. The *Epistle of Barnabas,* attributed to the apostle by Clement of Alexandria and Origen as well as in the MS tradition. Eusebius (*Hist.* 3, 25, 4), however, and Jerome (*Vir. ill.* 6) count it among the apocrypha. Written in Greek, it is preserved in the Cod. Sinaiticus (discovered by Tischendorf in 1859) and (together with the *Didache*) in Cod. Hieros. of 1056. Till 1859 the first chapters to 5, 7 were known only from an old Latin translation (third cent.?), in which, however, chs. 18–21 are missing.

Contents. Part 1 (doctrinal), chs. 1–17: Value and importance of the O.T. God's directives on sacrifice, circumcision and food were meant in a higher, spiritual sense; instead of external sacrifices God has demanded a contrite heart, instead of the circumcision of the flesh rather that of the heart and the ears. The Jews, however, seduced by a bad angel, had perverted the will of God and understood and fulfilled the Law in the literal sense. Accordingly, the author finds "the glory of Jesus" suggested in all the facts and institutions of the O.T.; e.g. the 318 servants whom Abraham circumcised signified Jesus (ιη = 18) on the cross (τ = 300). — Part 2 (moral), chs. 18–21, describes, just like the *Didache* (chs. 1–6) the two ways, which are here called the ways of light and of darkness.

Today it is certain that the Apostle Barnabas cannot have been the author of this letter. For St. Paul, whose companion he was, saw in the institutions of the Old Covenant, especially in the circumcision, a work of God, while the author sees in the O.T. a work of the devil (ch. 9, 4). He was probably a Christian teacher of Gentile origin, who wrote his letter—in fact a didactic devotional treatise—after the fall of Jerusalem (ch. 16). The radically anti-Jewish tendency of the work is unique in primitive Christian literature. The allegorical exegesis of Scripture which betrays the influence of Philo probably points to Alexandria as its place of origin.

Date: 4, 4, which reproduces a prophecy of Daniel (7, 24) about the end of the world can hardly supply a certain historical interpretation which might offer a support for dating it (96–8). If 16, 3ff. should contain an allusion to Hadrian's building of the temple in Jerusalem (130) rather than to the building of the spiritual temple of the Church, the Epistle would have to be dated shortly after 130. If 11, 9 cites the Greek *Apocalypse of Baruch* (6, 10, 7) written *c.* 115-16, this would be the *terminus post quem* (B. Violet, *Die Apokalypsen des Esra u. des Baruch,* 1924, p. XCII, 297; id., *Die Esra-Apokalypse,* 1910, p. XLVIII). 140 is certainly the *terminus ante quem*. On the relation to the *Didache* v. supra § 6.

Edd. and trans. v. § 14. The Epistle of Barn. is generally included among the Apost. Fathers. Lit. supra § 6. Ed. T. Klauser (FP 1) 1940. J. M. Heer, *Die Versio latina des Barnabasbriefes . . .*, 1908. P. Haeuser, *Der Barnabasbrief,* 1912. Meinhold,

ZKG 1940, 255/303 (history and exegesis). K. Thieme, *Kirche u. Synagoge,* Olten 1945 (author: Jewish Christian). On this Thieme and Oesterreicher, ZKT 1952, 63/70. Dahl, *Mél. off. à M. Goguel,* 1950, 62/70 (on c. 6, 8–19). C. F. Andry, *Introduction to the Ep. of Barn.,* thesis Harvard Univ., 1950. J. Schmid, RACh I 1207/17. F. M. Braun, *N.T. Studies* 1957/58, 119/24. Barnard, CQR 1958, 211/30; AThR 1959, 177/90. Schille, ZntW 1958, 31/52.

3. The *Epistola Apostolorum* or *Dialogues of Jesus with his Disciples after the Resurrection,* originally Greek, is extant completely only in Ethiopic; there is also a badly mutilated Coptic translation and the fragment of a Latin version. After a few pages the work changes from the form of a letter into that of an apocalypse.

Contents: The Eleven begin with a confession of Christ and an account of the miracles Jesus performed on earth. This is followed by an account of the resurrection compiled from the canonical gospels. To these are added revelations of the risen Christ in response to questions of the disciples on the second coming, the resurrection of the body (particularly stressed, anti-Gnostic), the Last Judgement, the signs of the end of the world (not chiliastic), the fate of the damned, but also on the incarnation (Gabriel as an apparition of the Logos), the redemption (not through the passion and death, but through the restoration of the corrupted doctrine of the pre-existent Logos), descent into hell, missionary work of the apostles, mission of Paul, threats against false teachers (Simon and Cerinthus). The conclusion describes the ascension according to Acts 1: 9.

Doctrinal Contents: An early, short Creed (v. § 5). — God as the creator of light and darkness is a contributory cause of evil. Sin is not a free act, though the sinner can resist. — Baptism is so much a condition of salvation that Christ also baptized his disciples and the just in limbo. Nevertheless, the baptized person must achieve salvation by his actions. — The celebration of the eucharist is called the Pasch. The work takes a rigorist view in the matter of penance.

C. Schmidt supposes the author to be a Catholic, though there are clear traces of Gnostic views. The "Letter" was written *c.* 140 or 170 in Asia Minor or Egypt. Its contents are similar to those of the *Testament of Our Lord* (v. supra § 7, 6). Apart from the N.T. the author uses the *Apocalypse of Peter,* the *Epistle of Barnabas* and the *Shepherd of Hermas.*

Text: L. Guerrier, PO 9, 3 (Ethiop.). C. Schmidt, *Gespraeche Jesu mit seinen Juengern nach der Auferstehung* (Ethiop. text by I. Wajnberg, TU 43, 1919). German trans. by H. Duensing (KlT 152) 1925. Hennecke[2] 146/50. Bardy, RB 1921, 110/34 (Gnost. milieu). Delazer, Ant 1928, 369/406; 1929, 257/92, 387/430 (written in Syria before 150). De Zwaan, *Amicitiae Corolla* (for R. Harris), Lo 1933, 344/55 (Syr. orig. lang.). Poschmann 1940, 104/12. Gry, RB 1940, 86/97 (date of parousia).

4. The *Epistula Titi discipuli Pauli, De dispositione sanctimonii,* discovered by De Bruyne, treats of virginity and opposes the custom of having *virgines subintroductae.* The apocryphal work originated very probably in Priscillianist circles.

De Bruyne, RBn 1925, 47/72. On this Harnack, SbB 1925, 180/213; H. Koch, ZNTW 1933, 131/44 (Cyprian and the treatise *De singularitate clericorum* have been used). Bulhart, RBn 1952, 297/99 (text. criticism). Cf. Morin, RBn 1935, 101/13, which points to an unedited pseudonymous treatise of the same tendency.

§ 12. APOCRYPHAL APOCALYPSES

Edd. and treatises: C. Tischendorf, *Apocalypses apocr.,* 1866. F. C. Burkitt, *Jewish and Christian Apocalypses,* 1914. Weinel, *Festgabe Gunkel* II, 1923, 141/73. — See also § 8.

THE border line between apocryphal letters and apocryphal apocalypses cannot always be defined with certainty, cf. the *Epistola Apostolorum.* Here imagination and fiction are even farther from the canonical writings than in the other apocrypha.

1. The *Apocalypse of Peter,* which the Muratorian Canon places beside the *Apocalypse of John,* was commented on by Clement of Alexandria (Eus., *Hist.* 6, 14, 1), but was considered uncanonical by Eusebius (*Hist.* 3, 3, 2) and Jerome (*Vir. ill.* 1), though it continued for a long time to be read in some churches of Palestine

on Good Friday (Soz., *Hist.* 7, 19). A fragment, found at Akhmim in 1886–7, which comprises about half of it (cf. supra § 9, 5) describes in visions the sunny splendour of heaven and of the departed brethren, then the place of punishment and the penalties of individual sinners. The description of hell is the most important part of the text from the point of view of the history of religion. It calls to mind Dante's *Divine Comedy*. The author takes his conception of hell from Jewish, oriental-pagan and Orphic-Pythagorean traditions. The complete text came to light only in 1910, in an Ethiopic translation which, however, is a frequently divergent version. The work was written as late as the first half of the second century.

Text: E. Klostermann (KlT 3) 8/12. E. Preuschen, *Antilegomena*[2], 84ff. Grébaut, ROC 1910, 198ff., 307ff., 425ff. (Ethiop. text). Hennecke[2], 314/27. On fragm. in PO 18, 1924, 482f.; cf. Pruemm, Bi 1929, 62/80 and James, JTS 32, 1930/1, 270/8. A late, medieval Arab. version in Syr. script was publ. by Mingana, WS III, 2, 1931 (= BJR 1929, 382/474; 1930, 182/297, 423/562; 1931, 179/279). Edsman 1940, 57/66. Peterson, *Misc. G. Belvederi,* R 1955, 181/85 (martyrdom of Peter acc. to *Apocal. of Peter*).

2. The apocalyptic *Address of Jesus to his Disciples in Galilee.* In the Ethiopic MSS of the *Epistola Apostolorum* (2–11) it precedes the Epistola, which itself turns into an apocalypse. Its description of the apocalyptic sufferings is inserted from the Epistola.

C. Schmidt, *Gespraeche,* 358/61; German trans. of the Ethiop. text publ. by Guerrier (PO 9, 3) in C. Schmidt, 48*/66*.

3. The *Second Coming of Christ and the Resurrection of the Dead,* a more recent Ethiopic text, dependent on the *Apocalypse of Peter.*

Ed. and trans. by Grébaut in ROC 1910.

4. The *"Shepherd" of Hermas,* so called after the figure of the Shepherd under which appears the angel of the revelation. Though usually classed with the writings of the Apostolic Fathers, it is in fact an apocryphal apocalypse. According to the trust-

worthy evidence of the *Fragmentum Muratorianum,* Hermas is the brother of the Roman Bishop Pius I, in whose reign he is supposed to have written the work *nuperrime temporibus nostris.* The later frequently repeated opinion of Origen that he is identical with the Hermas of Rom. 16:4 is unfounded. If the author seems to claim to be a contemporary of Clement of Rome (*Vis.* 2, 4, 3), this may be explained by the theory that the first part goes back as far as the time of Clement, since it is admitted that the individual parts of the work date from different periods. It will then have been finally edited only under Pius. That Hermas was held in very high esteem can be seen from the fact that Irenaeus (*Haer.* 4, 20, 2), Tertullian (only in his pre-Montanist period: *Or.* 16; but *Pud.* 10), and Origen (*Mt.* 14:21; *Princ.* 4, 11) regard his work as Scripture, though according to Origen it was not generally read in church. According to the *Fragm. Mur.* it might be read, but not proclaimed as Scripture in church (EP 268, 73ff.).

Apart from some sixteen small, recently discovered papyrus fragments (PO 4, 195/9; 18, 4, 68/81; C. Wessely) the text is extant in three incomplete MSS. In the relatively complete MS of a monastery on Mt. Athos the conclusion is missing (Sim. 9, 30, 3 – 10, 4, 5). The famous Biblical Cod. Sinait. has only the first quarter to Mand. 4, 3, 6. The lately ed. papyri of the University of Michigan (end of third century) contain Sim. 2, 8 to 9, 5, 1 (also almost a quarter of the whole). Besides, the complete work is extant in two old Latin (second and fourth/fifth centuries respectively) and one Ethiopic translation. There are, moreover, fragments of a Coptic and a middle-Persian version.

Contents: Hermas is a simple man of narrow outlook, but genuinely pious and conscientious, who has proved his perseverance in persecution. As a freedman he has acquired a fortune, but had again been reduced to poverty by ill luck. This has brought about a melancholy mood enhanced by a fresh persecution inaugurating the end of the world. At this stage he receives revelations from the "Church" which appears to him and from the angel of penance. There is no reason to think the personal data supplied by Hermas to be fictitious.

The book is divided into five visions, twelve mandates and ten similitudes. In the first four visions Hermas sees the Church as a matron in a white dress, who becomes increasingly younger. She orders him to exhort his family, but also all other Christians, to do penance at once, because now is the last opportunity to do so. In the third vision he sees the building of a great tower that represents the Church. Those stones that are built into the tower are the good Christians, whereas those that cannot be used and are thrown aside are the great sinners who must first be cut into shape by penance if they are still to be fitted into the building. From the fifth vision that forms a transition to the second part, the teaching is given by the angel of penance in the form of a shepherd. The mandates as well as the first five similitudes contain a summary of Christian moral teaching, a Christian adaptation and extension of the O.T. decalogue; the last four similitudes concern the description of penance. The ninth similitude, which was added only later, repeats and supplements the vision of the building of the tower. A new feature is that the building has been interrupted before being completed so as further to extend the time for penance that had at first been strictly limited. This correction was necessary because the expected parousia had not taken place.

Doctrinal Contents

1. Hermas teaches unequivocally that penance is a remedy for sin parallel to baptism, not, indeed, as if this were something new and an opportunity offered only exceptionally, but as a normal institution. What is new in his teaching is not that there is a first, but that there is a last opportunity for penance offered to sinners. The effect of penance extends to all sinners without regard to the

objective gravity of their guilt. But normally Christians can avail themselves of penance only once. If anyone falls a second time, he can hardly be saved (Mand. 4, 3, 6; EP 87 90). Penance consists in a mental change and in making atonement. God will forgive, if he considers the penance sufficient. Membership of the Church is the indispensable condition for the forgiveness of sins. Very great sinners are excluded from the Church. A reconciliation is not expressly mentioned, but must be considered as certain for important internal and external reasons.

2. Hermas calls the Holy Spirit who has appeared in the flesh, Son of God. As regards his human nature it seems that he holds Christ to be the adopted Son of God (Sim. 5, 6, 5; 9, 1, 1). Sim. 9, 16, 5 teaches a *Descensus ad inferos* of the apostles and teachers.

3. With regard to the moral doctrine of the *Shepherd* it is noteworthy that it clearly represents the Catholic teaching on the *opera supererogatoria* (difference between commandment and counsel) (EP 88f.). He mentions three counsels: fasting, celibacy and martyrdom. On adultery he writes (Mand. 4, 1): If the adulterous wife does not do penance the husband must dismiss her and may not marry another, since it is possible that the wife may repent later. If she does so, the husband must receive her again, but only once: "for there is only one penance for the servants of God" (EP 86; EH 50). In contrast to some authors of the primitive age Hermas permits a second marriage (Mand. 4, 4, 1–2).

Edd. and trans. in § 14; also C. Bonner, *A Papyrus Codex of the Shepherd of Hermas* (Sim. 2–9) with a Fragm. of the Mandates, Ann Arbor (Mich.) 1934. Cf. TQ 1934, 278/80; RSR 1936, 464/7. M. Whittaker, crit. ed. in GCS 48, 1956. — Treatises: Bareille, DTC 6, 2268/88. Leclercq, DAL 6, 2265/90. A. Baumeister, *Die Ethik des Pastor H.*, 1912. R. van Deemter, *Der Hirt des H., Apokalypse od. Allegorie?* A 1929. Wilson, HTR 1927, 21/62. Svennung, ZNTW 1933, 294/308 (Station-*fast;* hist. of concept). Bardy, 1935, 73/8. Puech, *Mél. Navarre,* 1935, 361/63. Ake V. Stroem, *Der Hirt des H., Allegorie od. Wirklichkeit?* L 1936. Puech, StU 83/5 (text crit.). On Greek papyri fragments cf. Stegmueller, Aeg 1937, 457f. Lefort, Mu 1938, 239/76 (coll.of all Copt. fragms. so far known incl.

new ones); Mu 1939, 223/8 (a new Copt. fragm.). G. Mercati, ST 95, 1941, 81f. (stichometry of the *Shepherd*). Poschmann 1940, 134/205. Alberte, *Miscell. Comillas* II, 1943, 235/58 (penance). Seitz, JBL 1944, 131/40 (relations to Ep. of James) and 1947, 211/19 (δίψυχος). Prete, *Convivium N. S.* 1, 1946, 114/28 (Cristianesimo antico e riforma ortodossa). F. W. Young, *The Sheph. of Hermas. A Study of his Concept of Repentance,* thesis Duke Univ., 1946, Kilpatrick, JTS 1947, 204f. (A New Pap.). Peterson, OCP 1947, 624/35 (on explanation of visions) and VC 1954, 52/71 (on vis. 4). Musurillo, TSW 1951, 382/87 (necessity of a new crit. ed.). Grobel, *Vanderbilt Studies in the Humanities* 1, 1951, 50/55 (on Sim. 2). W. Schmid, *Convivium,* Festschr. K. Ziegler, 1954, 121/30 (on concept of Arcadia; sim. 9, 1, 4). Audet, RB 1953, 41/82 (relation to the Manual of Discipline from the Dead Sea Scrolls). Van Unnik, ZNTW 44, 1952/53, 250/55 (ταπεινοῦν τὴν ψυχήν). Joly, NClio 5, 1953, 394/406 (Judaism, Christianity and Hellenism in the *Pastor Herm.*); RHR 149, 1955, 32/49 (on doctrine of penance). K. Rahner, ZKT 1955, 385/431 (doct. of penance). Joly, SCh 53, 1958.

5. The Gnostic *Ascension of Paul* (᾿Αναβατικὸν Παύλου) mentioned by Epiphanius (*Haer.* 38, 2) is no longer extant. But the *Apocalypse of Paul* (in Lat. MSS mostly *Visio S. Pauli*) has been preserved.

The Greek original of the work, written probably in Egypt *c.* 240–50 and mentioned already by Origen is no longer extant. The Greek version known to us is a new recension, written between 380 and 388; the introduction gives an account of the marvellous discovery of the work under the house of St. Paul at Tarsus (cf. Sozom., *Hist.* 7, 19). The Latin translation, made at the latest *c.* 500, is, like the Syriac and Coptic ones, more reliable than the Greek text. The Latin *Visio S. Pauli* is preserved in more than twelve recensions, most of which abbreviate it.

Contents: The work is closely related to the *Apocalypse of Peter.* Christ commands the apostle to preach penance to sinful mankind. Sun, moon and stars, sea and waters cry out for vengeance upon men. One of the angels who at sunset report to God on the deeds of men leads the apostle past the dying to the place of the just, then to the radiant land of the meek and to the Acherusian Lake from which rises the city of God. After this blissful journey the angel shows him by the rivers of fire the sufferings of the damned, to whom the Lord, at the request of the apostle and his companion, grants Sunday as their time of respite (ch. 44). Chapter 14 refers to the angel Michael as the protector and guide of the souls who ascend from earth to heaven (ψυχοπόμπος); cf. the offertory in the Mass for the Dead of the Roman Missal. Paul is also allowed to see paradise. The author is a true poet of great creative power. Dante knew the work and referred to it *Inf.* 2, 28.

Greek text: C. Tischendorf, *Apocalypses apocr.*, 1866, 34/69. Ehrhard, TU 50, 69. Lat.: M. R. James, *Apocr. anecdota*, 1893, 11/42. T. Silverstein, *Visio s. Pauli*, Lo 1935, 131/218. G. Ricciotti, *L'apocalisse di Paolo siriaca*, I: *Introduzione, testo e commento*, II: *La cosmologia della Bibbia e la sua trasmissione fino a Dante*, Brescia 1932; *Apocalypsis Pauli syriace*, Orientalia 2, 1933, 1/25, 120/49. Kraeling, HTR 1931, 209/44. Casey, JTS 1933, 1/32. Silverstein, *Visio s. Pauli*, 219/29 (good bibliography). On the question of *Mitigatio poenarum* on Sunday cf. Merkle, *Deutsches Dante-Jahrb.* 1929, 24ff. L. G. A. Getino, *Del gran número de los que se salvan y de la mitigación de las penas eternas*, Ma 1934. Landgraf, ZKT 1936, 299/370. Silverstein, *Harvard Studies and Notes in Philology* 1937, 231/47 (Dante and the *Visio s. Pauli*). Caminal, Sc 1946/7, 240/2 (Cod. Lat. 28 Barcelona). B. Fischer, VC 1951, 84/7 (used by Caesarius of Arles).

6. The *Apocalypse of Thomas*, mentioned in the *Decretum Gelasianum*, was written *c.* 400, probably in Latin, and first edited in 1907 under the title *Epistola Domini nostri Jesu Christi ad Thomam discipulum;* it contains revelations of the Lord on the end of the world. The portents of the Last Day are spread over seven days. The work originated probably in Gnostic-Manichean circles and was used by the Priscillians.

Text: P. Bihlmeyer, RB 1911, 270/82. M. Foerster, *Stud. z. engl. Philologie* 1913, 116ff. (Der Vercelli-Cod. CXVII).

7. The *Apocalypse of Stephen* owes its name to the misunderstood opening words of an account of the finding (= ἀποκάλυψις) of the relics of St. Stephen; it was written in Greek by the presbyter Lucianus in 415. This *Revelatio* is probably also rejected in the *Decretum Gelasianum*.

Two different Latin transs. of this *Revelatio* in ML 41, 805/18. The Spanish presbyter Avitus of Braga translated the recension A. A critical text with the accompanying letter of Avitus now ed. by Vanderlinden, REB 1946, 178/217 with information on two further forms of the text. An Armen. trans. ed. B. Mercier, ROC 30, **1946**. On MSS of the Gr. text and the ed. by Papadopoulos-Kerameus, 1898, cf. Altaner, ZKG 1941, 456/68 (Avitus of Braga). Vogels, *Heiliges Land* 79, 1935, 65/72. G. Segur Vidal, *La Carta-enciclica del obispo Severo,* 1938; cf. TR 1939, 64f. Devreesse, RB 1938, 556f. P. Peeters, *Orient et Byzance. Le tréfonds oriental de l'hagiographie byzantine,* Bru 1950, 49/58. Leclercq, DAL 5, 632/47.

8. From the number of apocalypses that have come to light mostly in very recent times we would list the following: Two *Apocalypses of John* (the Baptist), several forms of *Apocalypses of Mary,* one *Apocalypse of Bartholomew* and one *of Zacharias.* To this must be added several texts found in the Gnostic-Coptic writings that have come to light in such great number in the last years. (Cf. § 24.)

A. Berendts, *Die handschriftl. Ueberlieferung der Zacharias- u. Johannesapokryphen,* 1904. J. H. Schoenfield, *The Lost Book of the Nativity of John,* 1929. A. Delatte, *Anecdota Atheniensia* I, 1927, 272/88 (two new versions of the Apocalypse of the Bl. Virgin). Harris, BJR 1927, 385/412 (a new Syr. Vita of John the Bapt.). — A. M. Kropp, *Ausgewaehlte Zaubertexte* 2, 1930/1, No. 76 (Apocalypse of Bartholomew). Dawkins, BZ 1929/30, 300/4 (Apocalypse of Mary).

§ 13. COMPOSITIONS IN VERSE

1. *Beginnings of Hymnography*

According to modern ecclesiastical usage the hymn is normally a metrical composition capable of being sung; in primitive times, however, the metrical composition did not belong to its essential characteristics; on the contrary, prose hymns were more numerous, especially in Hellenism. Besides these there were other kinds, particularly Jewish and Gnostic hymns, in definitely stylized, solemnly hieratic diction. The Christian hymn developed under their influence. When the contact between Christianity and Greek culture became closer, the Greek poetic forms, too, exercised a stronger influence on Christian poetry.

As the oldest hymns we would mention the *Magnificat* (Luke 1:45ff.), *Benedictus* (ibid. 1:68ff.), *Gloria in excelsis* (2:14), and *Nunc dimittis* (2:29ff.), further the beginning of Eph., 1 Tim. 3:16, and the *new song* (Apoc. 5:9f.; cf. also 1:4–7; 4:8–11; 15:3 f. etc.). Hymnodic style is evident in Ign., *Eph.* 7, 2 (Christ the physician) and in the thirteenth and fourteenth fragments of Melito (ed. Otto). Some apocryphal Acts contain hymnodic pieces, e. g. the dance hymns on Christ in the *Acts of John* 94f., the nuptial song in the *Acts of Thomas* 6f. Such poetry found a home in Gnosticism; cf. the hymn of the Naassenes in Hippolytus, *Phil.* 5, 10, 2 (supra § 8, 2 and § 24). After their example Clement of Alexandria composed his *Hymn to Christ* (EH 145/9) and Hippolytus his no longer extant odes. According to his accusers (Eus., *Hist.* 7, 30, 10) Paul of Samosata suppressed more recent hymns to Christ. A morning and an evening hymn are to be found in the *Apost. Const.* (7, 47f.), an evening hymn in Routh (2nd ed., 3, 515, EP 108). Old Christian prayers and hymns have also come to light in recently discovered papyri in Egypt. A small papyrus fragment of a Christian hymn with musical notation was found in 1922 (Oxyrh. Pap. XV n. 1786, 21–25).

C. del Grande, *Liturgiae, preces et hymni Christianorum e papyris coll.*, Na ²1933. Kroll in Hennecke ²1924, 435f., 596/601; id., *Die christl. Hymnodik bis Klemens von Alex.* in *Verzeichnis der Vorles. zu Braunsberg* 1921 and 1921/2. On the hymn φῶς ἱλ. (EP 108) cf. Smothers, RSR 1929, 266/83 and Doelger, AC 5, 11/26. Mercenier, Mu 1939, 229/33 (Marian antiphone; 3rd cent.?). Pighi, Aeg 1941, 189/220 *(Notazione ritmica greca)*. Wellesz, CQ 1945, 34/45 (oldest Chr. hymns). Dohmes, *Gedaechtnisschr. f. Casel,* 1951, 35/53 (pneumatic character of ritual chant). M. Pellegrino, *La poesia greca crist. dei primi secoli,* F. 2, Tu 1952. M. Simonetti, *AttiAccadNazLincei,* Memorie Ser. 8, vol. 4, 1952, 342/58 (oldest Gr. hymns). Further lit. in Quasten I, 159f. T. Michels, *Mysterien Christi. Fruehchristl. Hymnen* (trans. from Greg. Naz., Clem. Alex., Method., Synesius), Mr 1952.

2. *The Christian Sibyllines*

The Jewish-Christian Sibylline sayings are in Greek hexameters; they treat partly historico-political, partly religious subjects in frequently unintelligible terms. Yet some sections reach truly poetic heights; but the contents are not uniform and the structure of the whole is often confused and far from clear. Many times the sequence of thought is interrupted by alien insertions or lacunae. Historical narratives, threats and warnings of impending catastrophes alternate with prophecies on the destinies of the nations. The Oracles frequently admonish, warn and call for penance.

Since the Sibyl introduces herself as God's messenger and her statements agree with the facts known from the Bible as well as with much data of secular history, these were fully accepted and gave comfort and hope in troubled times to both Jews and Christians; they were used for apologetical purposes even centuries later. The Sybil is mentioned or cited already in the *Shepherd of Hermas* (Vis. 2, 4), in Justin (*Apol.* I, 20, 1; 44, 12) and Athenagoras (*Suppl.* 30, 1). The adversaries of Christianity soon came to know about such prophecies; cf. Orig., *C. Celsum* 7, 53. Augustine, (*Civ. Dei* 18, 23) already knows a Latin translation of 8, 217–243. The influence of the work extends to the beginning of modern times (*Dies irae,* Thomas Aquinas, Dante, Calderón, Niccolò and Giovanni Pisano, Giotto, Van Eyck, Raffael, Michelangelo).

Until the new discovery of Card. A. Mai (1817) only eight books of the *Oracula Sibyllina* were known, which originated in the time from the second century B.C. to the second century A.D. Since in the relatively best group of MSS Book 8 is divided into three parts, hence counted as Books 8–10, the books discovered by A. Mai were numbered 11–14. No books are lost between 8 and 11 (cf. Aev 1952, 228f.). Books 1–5 contain mainly poems composed by Hellenistic Jews between the second century B.C. and the first century A.D., though many Christian interpolations have been inserted. The oldest Jewish poem (3, 97ff.) was composed in the time of Antiochus III Epiphanes soon after 165 B.C. and then enlarged by probably genuine oracles of the *Erythrean*

Sibyl (first century B.C.). The mainly Christian Books 6–8 date from the second half of the second century. Book 6 (only 28 lines) contains a fine hymn of praise on Christ and the wood of the cross. Book 8 is the most important (500 lines, Lactantius cites it no less than 30 times). Its first part (1–216) which may also have been written by a Jew, announces the judgement of God and describes the destruction of depraved and godless Rome. The second part begins with the famous acrostich (217–250), an eschatological song of triumph to Christ the Lord and Judge of the world, the initials of which make up the words Ἰησοῦς Χρειστὸς (sic!) θεοῦ Υἱὸς σωτὴρ σταυρός. These verses are referred to in the speech of Constantine *Ad coetum sanctorum* (18) (§ 48, 2c) and by Augustine (*Civ. Dei* 18, 23) in Latin translation (without the σταυρός verse). The following lines 251ff. treat of the Person of Christ, of God's omnipotence, his goverment of the world and his avenging justice at the end of time. The third part (429ff.) contains a hymn to God the Creator and the Logos his Son, who became Man. The Book ends with some moral rules of life. Apart from interpolations, Books 11–14 which were discovered by Mai are probably of Jewish origin; they date from the first or third–fourth centuries A.D. Since their contents are purely historical and political they are never cited by the Fathers.

Edd.: J. Geffcken, *Oracula Sibyllina* (GCS 8), 1902. A. Kurfess, *Sibyll. Weissagungen,* Mn 1951 (Bks. 1–8 and 11; also pp. 204/279 texts on later infl.; all texts are also trans. and commented). — Trans.: E. Kautzsch (supra § 8) 2, 1900, 177ff., and Hennecke[2] 399/422. A. Pincherle, R 1922 (Bks. 3–5). — Treatises: J. Geffcken, TU 23, 1, 1902. W. Bousset, RE 18, 265/80. A. Rzach, PWK II 2, 2117/83. Pruemm, Sch 1929, 54ff. and contd. K. Holzinger, SbW 216, 1936, F. 3. The following works by A. Kurfess, the last editor of the Sib., omitting the contributions on text. crit. that have been cited before: Pastor Bonus 1934, 414/25; TQ 1936, 351/66, 532/42; ZNTW 38, 1939, 171/81 (II 34/153: poem of Phocylides); ibid. 40, 1941, 151/65; WJB 1948, 402/5; SO 1950, 95/104 (text crit.); ZRGG 1951, 353/57 (Virgil and the Sib.); TQ 1951, 458/63; ZRGG 1952, 42/57; SO 1952, 54/77 (text. crit.); Festschr. A. Dold, 1951, 75/83; Mn 4. ser. 5, 1952; Aev 1952, 228/35 (order of fragments); TQ 1953, 80/96 and ZRGG 1953,

70/73 (on the new Lat. texts discovered by B. Bischoff); RM 1954 No. 2; HJB 1954, 120/27 (Virgil's 4th Eclogue). — H. Jeanmaire, AIP 4, 1936, 297/304 (on 8, 190/212); *La Sib. et le retour de l'âge d'or,* 1939. Mariès, RP 1936, 5/19 (Strophes et poèmes). Kerenyi, Klio 11, 1936, 1/35 (the Persian millennium in the Mahabharata, the Sib. and Virgil). H. Fuchs, *Der geistige Widerstand gegen Rom . . .,* 1938. H. Erbse, *Fragmente griech. Theosophien,* 1941. A. Peretti, *Sib. Babilonese nella propaganda ellenistica,* Fl 1943. Stocks, BNJ 15, 1939, 29/57. Bulst, ZDADL 1938, 105ff. (Anglo-Lat. trans.). Mercati, *Mél. Grégoire* 1949, 473/81 (Greek source of Sibyll. Tiburt.). Altaner, AB 1949, 244/47 (Augustine and the Sibyll.). Bischoff, *Mél. De Ghellinck,* 1951, 121/47 (Lat. trans.). Applebaum, *Jew. Stud.* 2, 1950, 26/39 (5, 26/38 and the Jewish insurr. under Trajan). Dornseiff, SbLeipz. 1951, 44/63 (Vergil—Horace and the Sibyll.). Thomson, RevR 16, 1952, 115/36 (Sibyll. in the Fathers). Demougeot, RevEA 1952, 83/92 (Jerome and the Sibyll.). P. Dalbert, *Die Theologie der hellenist.-jued. Missionsliteratur . . .,* H. 1954 (106/23 on the Sibyll.). Kurfess, *Gymnasium* 62, 1955, 110/12 (Virgil's 4th Eclogue); ZRGG 1955, 270/72; ibid. 1956, 253/56 (Horace and the Sibyll.); Phil 1956, 147/53 (Homer and Hesiod in the Sibyll.). Bauer, Marialia 18, 118/24, R 1956 (Mother of Messias in Sibyll.). Kurfess, RM 1956, 225/42 (text. crit. of Bk. 5).

3. The Proverbs of Sextus

A large collection of pagan sayings circulating under the name of (the Pythagorean philosopher?) Sextus was given a Christian form about the turn of the second century and translated from Greek into Latin (451 sayings) by Rufinus (d. 410). The tradition reported by Rufinus, according to which the Roman bishop and martyr Sixtus II (257–58) was the translator, was rejected already by Jerome (*Ep.* 132, 2).

The sayings reflect the wisdom of Clement of Alexandria; they propound the Platonic teaching on purification, illumination and deification, praising continence in food and drink, sleep and marriage (which is esteemed very little; Prov. 13, 273: advice to practise self-castration?). The conception of God is also Platonic.

A. Elter, *Gnomica* I, 1892 (610 proverbs, Greek). E. F. de Paola, Mi 1937 (text and trans.). Ed. of Syr. trans. by Ryssel in Z. f. wiss. Theol. 1895, 67/730 and contd. Hermann, ZKG 1938, 217/26 (Armen. text). De Paola, *Osservaz. alle sent. di Sesto,* R 1938. — Trans.: J. Kroll, Hennecke[2] 625/43; F. X. Murphy, Rufinus of Aquileja, Wa 1945, 119/23. — On other hitherto unknown collections of proverbs cf. Premerstein in: *Festschr. der Nationalbibl. in Wien,* 1926, 647/66 and BNJ 9, 1932, 338/74; Festschr. Lampros, At 1935, 177/89. New edition: H. Chadwick, *The Sentences of Sextus,* C 1959.

4. *Epitaphs of the second and third centuries*

Since the inscriptions on the monuments of Christian antiquity belong to the sphere of ancient Christian epigraphy only those are a subject of patrology which are important products of ancient Christian literature contributing to the understanding of the Fathers. Such are the Epitaphs of Abercius and Pectorius, or those composed by individual Fathers, e.g., Ambrose, Jerome or Damasus.

Of collections of Christian Inscriptions we would mention the following: E. Diehl, *Inscriptiones lat. christ. veteres,* 3 vols., 1925/31; KlT 26/28, [2]1913. K. M. Kaufmann, *Gebete auf Stein nach Denkmaelern der Urchristenheit,* 1921; *Handbuch der altchristl. Epigraphik,* 1917. Jalabert et Mouterde, DAL 7, 623/94 (Gr. inscriptions). Leclercq, DAL 7, 694/850 (Lat. inscrs.); 850/1089 (collections of inscrs.). A. Grossi Gondi, *Trattato di Epigrafia crist.,* 1920. J. Vives, *Inscripc. crist. de la España rom. y visigoda,* Ba 1942. Creaghan-Raubitschek, *Early Christ. Epitaphs from Athens,* 1947. P. V. Nunn, *Christian Inscriptions,* NY 1952 (selection). Knott, VC 1956, 65/79 (language of inscrs.). A. Stuiber, *Refrigerium interim. Vorstellungen zum Zwischenzustand u. d. fruehchristl. Grabeskunst,* 1957.

Two epitaphs are akin both in thought and language to the writings treated in this chapter, hence they are here included.

1. The *Epitaph of Abercius* of Hierapolis near Synnada in Phrygia Salutaris, found there by Ramsay, in 1883, on the torso of a marble stone which is now in the Lateran museum. It was restored according to the stele of Alexander of the year A.D. 216 and the fourth century legendary Greek *Vita Abercii,* published by Boissonade in 1838, which elaborated the statements on the inscription into a story. It was thoroughly investigated during a long controversy about its Christian character, which should now be finally established, and has been found to be a poem in a secret language, composed at the end of the second century.

According to the statement of the *Vita,* Abercius (EH 155; EP 187) was Bishop of Hierapolis, perhaps the Avircius Marcellus to whom, according to Eusebius (*Hist.* 5, 16, 3) an anonymous author dedicated three anti-Montanist books. The epitaph which he had carved in his lifetime says that, guided by the "Shepherd", he had travelled to Rome, Syria and across the Euphrates, and had everywhere seen the Church and the Christian people, baptism and the eucharist, the sphragis and the ΙΧΘΥΣ, and that he had the inscription made when he was 72 years old.

Leclercq, DAL 1, 66/87. T. Nissen, *S. Abercii vita,* 1912. F. J. Doelger, *Ichthys* II, 1922, 454/507. Abel, Byz 3, 1926, 321/411 (here a good bibliogr.). Orth, PW 1928, 1149/52. Smialek, Eos 32, 1929, 701/3. Quasten, FP 7, 21/24. Strathmann and Klauser, RACh 1, 12/17. Calder, *Journ. Roman Stud.* 1939, 1/4. Grabka, Americ. Eccl. Rev. 131, 1954, 145/55 (Eucharist in Abercius and Pectorius). Ferrua, RAC 1943, 279/305.

2. The *Epitaph of Pectorius* (EH 236), found in 1839 in seven fragments on a marble slab in an old cemetery near Autun, contains eleven lines, three Greek distichs and five hexameters; epigraphically it is to be assigned to the time between 350 and 400, but is entirely composed in the language of the second or third centuries, in the secret language of Abercius.

K. M. Kaufmann, *Handbuch der altchristl. Epigraphik,* 1917, 178/80. F. J. Doelger, *Ichthys* I, 1910, 12/5, 177/83; II, 1922, 507/15. Quasten, FP 7, 24/6. Leclercq, DAL I, 2, 3213/16. Perler, Miscell. G. Belvederi, 1955, 199/208.

The first five lines, an acrostich of ΙΧΘΥΣ, call Christendom "the divine race of the heavenly Fish" that refreshes itself in the "immortal fountain of divine water" (baptism) and exhort it to receive "the Saviour's honey-sweet food of the saints" (eucharist). These lines are clearly distinguished from the loosely added following ones, so that they can be recognized as an older model. In lines 7–11 Pectorius, the son of Aschandius, asks his departed parents to remember him "in the peace of the Fish". The name Aschandius calls to mind the Syrian Christian colonies at Lyons and Vienne (see § 45)..

CHAPTER TWO

The Apostolic Fathers

§ 14. GENERAL REMARKS

THE Apostolic Fathers is a name given to a circle of authors who had actually or allegedly still been in touch with the apostles themselves.

Originally, these were five authors, whose works the patrologist J. B. Cotelier edited together under the title *Patres aevi apostolici,* viz. Barnabas, Clement of Rome, Ignatius, Polycarp and Hermas. Later it became the custom to add Papias and the *Epistle to Diognetus,* which brought their number up to seven. In most recent times the *Didache,* too, came to be included in the editions. The *martyria* of St. Ignatius and St. Polycarp had already been added to the oldest editions of their writings; nowadays the former is no longer printed with the other works because of its later origin. The *Didache,* the apocryphal *Letter of Barnabas,* the *Shepherd* of Hermas and the *Letter to Diognetus* belong to other groups of writings on account of their form, contents and reputation.

If we count among the Apostolic Fathers only those authors who were actually or probably still in contact with the men of the apostolic age, or whose teaching, even without such personal acquaintance, was nearest to the spirit of the N.T. both in language and content, then the writings of this group will be confined to the *Letter of Clement,* the seven *Epistles of Ignatius,* the *Letter of Polycarp* and the *Quadratus fragment* (§ 20, 1). This justified distinction and limitation was first introduced in the edition of J. A. Fischer, 1956.

The writings of the Apostolic Fathers are both in contents and form closely connected with the Holy Scriptures, especially with the epistles of the apostles. Like these they are written in Greek, have a practical paraeneic tendency and mostly also the form of letters; hence they may be called the pastoral literature of the primitive Church.

In simple words the authors seek to impress on the faithful the grandeur of the salvation revealed in Christ, they demand obedience to the ecclesiastical superiors and warn against heresies and schisms. They are still far from attempting to provide a scientific foundation for Christianity or for individual doctrines, as did the apologists of the second century, but as monuments of the primitive Christian spirit and as the oldest witnesses to the tradition of the faith, these writings are of exceptional value. Some of them were at one time even put forward for inclusion in the canon.

Edd.: O. Gebhardt, A. Harnack and T. Zahn, *Patrum apost. Op.* 1–3, 1875/7; 1, ²1876/8; Ed. minor, ²1920. F. X. Funk, *Patres apostolici* 1–2, 1901; 2, ³1913, ed. F. Diekamp; minor ed., ²1906 and 1, 1924 ed. K. Bihlmeyer. J. B. Lightfoot, *The Apost. Fathers* (Clem., Ign., Polyc.), 5 vols., 1886/90 (3–5, ²1890). H. Hemmer, G. Oger, A. Laurent, A. Lelong, *Les Pères apost.,* 4 vols., 1907/12 (1–2, ²1926). K. Lake, *The Apostolic Fathers,* Lo and NY 1930. S. Colombo, Tu 1934. B. Mustaki, At 1953. — L.-T. Lefort, CSCO, SS Copt. 17/18, 1952. J. A. Fischer (crit. text and trans. of *1 Clem., Letter of Ignat., Letter of Polyc.* and *Quadratus fragm.*), Mn 1956. E. J. Goodspeed, *Index patrist. sive clavis Patr. apost.,* 1907. — Trans.: F. Zeller (BKV² 35) 1918. H. Lietzmann, *Handb. zum NT,* suppl. vols., 1920/3 (with comment.). Hennecke ²1924, 480/540, 588/95. G. Bosio, *I Padri Apostolici,* Tu 1940. Glimm-Walsh-Marique, NY 1947 (FathCh). J. A. Kleist (ACW 1) 1946 and (ACW 6) 1948. E. J. Goodspeed, NY 1950. C. Ricci, *Los padres apostól.,* Buenos-Aires 1929. D. Franses, *De Apostol. Vaders,* Hilversum 1941. Ruiz Bueno, *Padres Apostólicos,* Ma 1950 (text and trans.). — Treatises: A. Casamassa, *I Padri Apostolici,* 1938. W. Roslan, *Istotne cechy laski wedlug pism Ojców apost.,* War 1934. G. Bardy, *La vie spirituelle d'après les Pères des trois premiers siècles,* 1935; VS 1937 (Le sacerdoce chrét.); *La théologie de l'église de S. Clément à S. Irénée,* 1945. J. Brosch, *Das Wesen der Haeresie,* 1936 (NT and Ap. Fathers). K. Rahner, ZKT 1936, 471/91 (sin as loss of grace). W. Roslan in Miscell. Theologica, War 1936 (ζωή). TQ 1938, 200/25, 275/317, 470/503 (grace). Simonin, VS 1937, 165/78 (διψυχία). A. Heitmann, *Imitatio Dei. Die ethische Nachahmung Gottes nach der Vaeterlehre der 2 ersten Jh.,* R 1940. E. Scharl, *Recapitulatio mundi bei*

Irenaeus, 1941, 110/19. P. Palazzini, *Il monoteismo nei padri apost. e negli apologisti del II s.,* 1946. J. Klevinghaus, *Die theol. Stellung der Apostol. Vaeter zur alttest. Offenbarung,* 1948. T. Torrance, *The Doctrine of Grace in the Apost. Fathers,* 1948. W. S. Miller, *An Anthology of the Theology of the Apostol. Fathers,* thesis S. W. Bapt. Theol. Sem., 1948. E. Massaux, *Influence de l'Év. de S. Matth. sur la littér. chrét. avant S. Irénée,* Lou 1950. Walke, ATR 1950, 39/53 (The Use of *ecclesia* in the Apost. Fathers). Kittel, ZNTW 43, 1950/51, 54/112 (*Ep. of James* and the Apost. Fathers). W. Jentsch, *Urchristl. Erziehungsdenken,* 1951 (also on the Apost. Fathers and Clement Alex.). K. Hoermann, *Leben in Christus. Zusammenhaenge zw. Dogma u. Sitte b. d. Apost. Vaetern,* 1952. J. M. Bartelink, *Lexicologisch-semantische studie over de taal van de Apost. Vaders,* N 1952. A. Benoît, *Le baptême au 2e siècle,* 1953 (from *Didache* to Irenaeus). Starck, *La foi à la résurrection de J.-Chr. d'après les écrits des Pères Apost.,* NRT 1953, 337/64. Flesseman-van Leer, NTT 1955, 230/44 (OT in the Apostol. Fathers and Apologists).

§ 15. ST. CLEMENT OF ROME

Clement of Rome enjoyed a very high reputation in Christian antiquity, though only one work from his pen has been preserved: the Letter to the Corinthians, which the Syrian Church counted among the Scriptures and which is also contained in the Biblical *Codex Alexandrinus.*

Origen (*Jo.* 6, 54) and Eusebius (*Hist.* 3, 15) identified him with the collaborator of Paul mentioned in Phil. 4:3. According to Irenaeus (*Haer.* 3, 3, 3) he was the third successor of Peter in Rome (Peter, Linus, Anacletus, Clement; EH 126), according to Tertullian, however (*Praescr.* 32), he was consecrated by Peter himself (EH 192). Already Epiphanius (*Haer.* 27, 6) harmonized both accounts by stating that Clement had indeed been consecrated by Peter, but had given up the episcopate to Linus for the sake of peace. The *Pseudo-Clementines* wrongly make him a member of the Flavian imperial family; on the strength of this false statement he has also been thought to have been the consul Titus Flavius Clement, the cousin of Domitian. The accounts of his exile to the Taurian Chersonesus and his martyr's death in the Black Sea are legendary (4th cent.). Feast day: November 23.

The basilica of San Clemente in Rome is alleged to stand on the foundations of his house.

1. *Letter to the Christian Church at Corinth (c. 96)*

This so-called *First Epistle of Clement* was used already in the letter of St. Polycarp and was obviously written in the last years of the Emperor Domitian or shortly afterwards. The complete text of this and the *Second Letter to the Corinthians* has become known to us only through the *Codex Hierosol.* of the year 1056 (supra § 6); until then scholars had to rely only on the Biblical *Cod. Alex.,* in which chs. 58–63 of the First and nearly half of the Second Letter (12–20) are missing. In most recent times a probably second century Latin translation as well as one Syriac and two different incompletely preserved Coptic translations of the Letter have been discovered.

The *First Letter to the Corinthians* was occasioned by the troubles in the Christian church at Corinth. Several younger members had risen against the presbyters and ousted them from their position; when this became known to the Roman Church it addressed this letter to Corinth. Clement's authorship is attested by Dionysius of Corinth (Eus., *Hist.* 4, 23, 11; EH 62).

Contents: Part I (1–37): general exhortations (EA 4/9); part II (37–61): discusses the dissensions of the Corinthians and demands submission to the ecclesiastical superiors appointed by the apostles or their successors, with reference to the organization of an army and of the human body as well as to the O.T. hierarchy. The conclusion (62–65) expresses the hope that the bearer of the letter will soon return with the news that peace has been restored (EP 11/29).

Points of Doctrine

1. The Roman Church sought to reconcile the parties in Corinth without having been asked to do so (47, 6–7). It is true, we cannot

read into the whole letter a precise and directly authoritative intervention which would place the sister church under a juridical obligation. This proceeding of the Roman Church—Clement himself plays nowhere an immediately active part—may partly be explained by the primitive Christian vigilance and the concern of the Churches for one another, also by the particularly close political and cultural relations that existed between Corinth and Rome, since the former had been re-founded as a Roman colony (44 B.C.). Yet, this may already foreshadow the spirit, the power and the claim of Rome to a special position among all other communities of the καθολικὴ ἐκκλησία (Ign., *Smyrn.* 8, 2); cf. 59. 1f.; 63, 2. The particular esteem in which the epistle was held as early as the second century points in the same direction.

2. The superiors are called ἐπίσκοποι καὶ διάκονοι in this letter; in other passages (e. g. 44, 5 and 57, 1) they are comprised under the one name πρεσβύτεροι. It is explicitly stated that they may not be deposed by the community, because they do not derive their authority from it. They have received their powers directly from the apostles, who in their turn have acted on the orders of Jesus Christ, the "ambassador of God" (42–44; EH 12f.). The "offering of the sacrificial gifts" is called their most important office.

3. A magnificent communal prayer of thanksgiving (59,4–61, 3) which was probably used in the liturgy attests faith in the divinity of Jesus, who is called "supreme priest and guide of our soul" (61, 3) and in the providence and mercy of God (EH 14). In ch. 20 we read an attractive description of the purposeful order and beauty of the world, which betrays Stoic influences. Ch. 24f. treats of the resurrection of the dead, utilizing the legend of the phoenix (v. § 37, 6).

4. In ch. 5–6, 4 (EH 10f.) we have the oldest witness to Nero's persecution and the martyrdom of the princes of the apostles Peter and Paul and many other Christians in Rome (ἐν ἡμῖν). At the same time we are told that Paul had gone ἐπὶ τὸ τέρμα τῆς

δύσεως, i.e. to Spain. To understand this account correctly it should be remembered that it is influenced by the Stoic Diatribe. Cf. ch. 20.

Edd.: v. supra 14. L. Clarke (SPCK) 1937. C. T. Schäfer, FP 44, 1941 (with old Lat. trans.). The Gr. legendary *Passio S. Clementis* (4th/5th cent.) in Funk-Diekamp 2, 3rd ed., 50/80. — Treatises: H. Bruders, *Die Verfassung der Kirche,* 1904. A. Harnack, *Einfuehrung i. d. alte Kirchengesch.,* 1929. F. Gerke, *Die Stellung des 1. Klemensbriefes innerhalb der Entwicklung der altchristl. Gemeindeverfassung u. des Kirchenrechts,* 1931. W. Brandt, *Jahrb. der theol. Schule Bethel,* 1930, 145/76 (λειτουργεῖν). Bardy 1935, 44/59. Barnikol, *Theol. Jahrb.* 1936, 61/80 (Christol., baptism, eucharist). Loesch, StU 1937, 177/88 (concept of Church). Lemarchand, RevSR 1938, 448/57 (composition). Meinhold, ZKG 1939, 82/129 (event and interpretation). Poschmann 1940, 112/24. Hertling, Bi 1939, 276/83 (I, 42: ἀπαρχία) M. Giraudo, *L'ecclesiol. di S. Cl. Rom.,* Bol 1943. L. Sanders, *L'hellénisme de S. Cl. de Rome et le Paulinisme,* Lou 1943. G. Bardy, *La théol. de l'Égl. de S. Cl. à S. Irénée,* 1945. Mohrmann, VC 1949, 67/106 (hist. of language of old Lat. trans.). Boismard, RB 1948, 376/87 (Gospel of John in Clement). Peterson, *Festschr. van d. Leeuw,* 1950, 351/57 (The *praescriptum* proves that the letter is ἐπιστολὴ καθολική). Van Unnik, VC 1950, 181/89 (ch. 20 depends on OT apocrypha); VC 1951, 204/48 (c. 34, 6f. does not refer to the Eucharist. celebration of the *Sanctus*); ZNTW 44, 250/55 (ταπεινοῦν τὴν ψυχήν). C. Eggenberger, *Die Quellen der politischen Ethik des 1. Klemensbriefes,* Zu 1951; on this Campenhausen, TLZ 1952, 38f. and Sch 1953, 598f. Kwa Joe Liang, *Het begrip Deemoend in I Klemens,* thesis Ut 1951. Tailliez, Neophilol. 35, 1951, 46/50 (on Lat. Ep. of Clement). Gewiess, HJB 1953, 20/22 (on eccl. constitution). Bardy, DHGE F. 81, 1090/3. Stuiber, RACh 3, 188/97. Javierre, RET 1953, 483/519 (Apostol. succession and 1 Clem.: criticism of work by H. v. Campenhausen, 1953; v. supra § 3, 21). — On the primacy: Van Cauwelaert, RHE 1935, 267/306, 765f.; cf. Zeiller, ibid. 762/4; Altaner, TR 1936, 41/5; Segarra, EE 1936, 380/9. W. Bauer 1934, 99/109. Katzenmayer, IKZ 1942, 28/37.—Peter and Paul in Rome (ch. 5f.): O. Marrucchi, *Pietro e Paolo a Roma,* Tu [4]1934. A. S. Barnes, *The Martyrdom of St. Peter and St. Paul,* NY 1933. Zakrzewski, *Kwartalnik historyczny,* 1934, 1/46. E. Barnikol, *Spanienreise und Roemerbrief,* 1934. Against this E. Dubowy, *Cl. v. R. ueber die Reise Pauli nach Spanien,* 1914. Friedrichsen, Er 24, 1946, 161/47 (*propter invidiam* in ch. 5). Altaner, HJB 62/69, 1950, 25/30 (on 5, 1ff.). Schuler, *Festschr. Bornewasser,* 1950, 94/116. Dain, RSR 39, 1951, 353/61 (text. crit. on 6). Mohlberg, *Festschr. A. Dold,* 1952, 52/74 (on *Memoria Apostolorum*). Davis, *JournBiblRel* (Baltimore) 1952, 167/71 (Peter buried in Rome?). Cf. further lit. § 3, 22. Giet, RevSR 1955, 123/36 (Clement's witness on Peter in Rome; RevSR 1955, 333/45 (Clement's witness on persecutions of Chrs.). *Passio s. Clem.:* Franchi de' Cavalieri, ST 27, 1915, 1/40. H. Delehaye, *Ét. sur le légendrier rom.,* Bru 1936, 96/115. C. Amati, *La nazionalità di S. Clem. . . . e l'invenzione delle sue reliquie in Chersona,* Velletri 1941. Vasica, *ActaAcadVelehrad* 19, 1948, 38/80 (Clement's relics in Cherson). Griffe, BLE 1955, 3/22 (Beginnings of Christianity in Gaul and Clem. legends). Ziegler, *Neue Studien zum 1. Klemensbrief,* M 1958. Ponthot, EThL 1959, 339/61 ("Name").

2. The So-called Second Epistle of Clement

Eusebius (*Hist.* 3, 38, 4) writes: "There is supposed to be a second Letter of Clement, but which, as far as we know, the ancients did not use." In the two MSS mentioned above, the *First Epistle of Clement* is, indeed, followed by a second which is also addressed Πρὸς Κορινθίους. It is a sermon of quite general contents, in fact the oldest extant Christian sermon. This work, too, was counted as Holy Scripture in the Syrian Church and is included in the *Codex Alexandrinus,* though at the end (EA 10/11). Clement cannot be its author, as is evident from the difference of style in the two Epistles. The document, which is very valuable for our knowledge of the old Christian church service, seems to have originated at Corinth, most probably before 150 (Funk, G. Krueger). Others (Harnack) think it was written in Rome (Pope Soter, *c.* 170) or Alexandria (R. Harris, Streeter). Brief statements on Christ, who is called e.g. (20, 5) "Redeemer and guide of immortality", on the ecclesiastical community (14, 1–4), on baptism and penance and the importance of good works (16, 4) are important for the history of dogma.

Edd.: v. supra § 14; also the separate edd. by T. W. Crafer, Lo 1921. H. Hemmer, P 1926.—Trans.: R. Knopf in *Handb. zum NT,* suppl. vol., 1920, 151/84 and Hennecke[2] 588/95.—Treatises: Streeter, 238/47. Harris, ZNTW 1924, 193/200. Krueger, ZNTW 1932, 204f. (on 14, 2). Poschmann 1940, 124/33. J. C. Plumpe, *Mater Ecclesia,* W 1943, 22f.

3. The two pseudo-Clementine Letters "Ad virgines"

These two epistles form one single circular letter to ascetics of either sex and were written probably as late as the third century by an experienced spiritual guide. They oppose the practice of having subintroductae, i.e. the extra-matrimonial living together of religious men and women. Of the Greek original only sizable fragments are extant as citations of the monk Antiochus in the

Sabas monastery near Jerusalem (v. § 105, 3). The complete text has been preserved in a Syriac translation.

Text: Funk-Diekamp, *Patres Apostolici,* 2, [3]1913, 1/49 (here the fragms. and a Lat. trans. of the Syr. text made by T. Beelen). German: S. Wenzlowsky, *Briefe der Paepste,* 1, 1875, 55/97 (BKV). — Lefort, Mu 1927, 249/64; 1929, 197/274, and *Bull. de l'Institut franç. d'archéol. orient. au Caire,* 1931, 509/11 Rothenhaeusler, BM 1948, 148/51. Duensing, ZKG 63, 1950/51, 166/88.

4. *The Pseudo-Clementines*

This is the title of a long apostolic romance which tells in two different versions (*Homiliae* and *Recognitiones*) of the journeys of Peter, his controversies with Simon Magus and the conversion of Clement of Rome, the disciple of the apostle, by Peter. Clement gives an account of his experiences as Peter's companion.

a. The twenty *Homilies* contain what purports to be Peter's sermons during his journeys; they are preceded by two letters of Peter and Clement addressed to James the Less, Bishop of Jerusalem. The romance is but the frame for theological discussions of Judaistic-Gnostic character. Christ is a divine aeon who had revealed himself earlier in Adam and Moses. Christianity is nothing but a form of Judaism purified from distortions. The church of Jerusalem is given a special place of honour, and James the Less is called "bishop of bishops" *(Ep. Clementis).*

b. Ten books of *Recognitiones* (ἀναγνωρισμοί), a romance of recognition whose motif is derived from pagan antiquity; it is preserved only in the Latin translation of Rufinus. The whole family of Clement of Rome (parents and three sons) who through strange circumstances had been scattered throughout the world, meet again through the intervention of Peter and recognize each other; hence the name. Though the subject matter is largely the same, the doctrine is less Judaic and more Christian.

Many highly ingenious attempts have been made to solve the extremely intricate problems of literary criticism which the origin of the *Pseudo-Clementines* presents to scholars, yet so far none of the diverse theses has gained universal assent. In contrast with older views, it is generally assumed today that one and the same original has been used in both versions *(Hom.* and *Recogn.)*. Yet the very next question—if there are connexions between *Hom.* and *Recogn.*, and what they are—as well as the problem of dating these writings, is solved very differently. Opinions differ even more with regard to the various sources for the postulated original work. We need not here discuss details. The original, which is supposed to have originated in the East (Syria — East Jordan) in the first decades of the third century, is frequently considered to have derived from circles belonging to the Great Church, i.e. Catholic; but it will probably be more correct to look for the author in heretical Judaeo-Christian (Ebionite) circles. The Ebionite original, postulated by Schoeps, and believed to be dated between 160 and 190, is supposed to be the most important witness for the theology of Jewish Christianity. According to Rehm, the version of the *Homilies* as we have it today is to be dated between 325 and 381 and that of the *Recognitions* before 360–80.

c. Two *Greek Epitomae* from the *Homilies* and other well-known writings, e.g. the *Martyrium S. Clementis,* in Symeon Metaphrastes.

d. Two *Arabic Epitomae* from the *Homilies* and the *Recognitions* On the pseudo-Clementine *Apostolic Constitutions* v. supra § 7, 4.

Edd.: *Homilies:* PG 2; ed. P. de Lagarde 1865. B. Rehm, *Die Pseudoklementinen,* I: *Homilien,* 1953 (GCS 42). B. Rehm - F. Paschke, *Recognitionen,* 1958 (GCS). French trans. with comm. by A. Siouville, P 1934. *Recogn.:* MG 1; German by G. Arnold, B 1702. Hennecke[2] 151/63, 212/26. Greek Epit.: A. M. R. Dressel, L [2]1873. W. Frankenberg, TU 48, 3, 1937 (Syr. texts). On the Arab. extracts and Ethiop. Ps. Clem. cf. Staehlin 1213 and the ed. of an apoc. of Peter in Karschuni noted in § 12, 1, the last books of which go back to the Ps.-Clem. — Treatises: H. Waitz, TU 25, 4 (1904). W. Heintze, TU 40, 2 (1914). C. Schmidt, TU 46, 1 (1929). O. Cullmann, *Le problème littér. et hist. du roman Ps.-Clémentin,* 1930; E. Schwartz, ZNTW 1932, 151/99; cf. ZKG 1933, 305/18. J. Thomas,

RHE 1934, 275/96 (a new attempt at solving the probl.); *Le mouvement baptiste en Palestine et Syrie,* Lou 1935. Cadiou, RSR 1930, 506/28 (attempt to date Recogn.). James, JTS 33, 1931/2, 262/5. Rose, ibid. 382f. Svennung, Phil. 1933, 473/6. Donckel, EL 1933, 101/12 (accounts of meals). Pieper, TG 1936, 164/8. Frankenberg, ZDMorgenlGes. 1937, 577/604. Rehm, Phil 1938, 218/47 (Bardesanes and the Ps.-Clem.); ZNTW 1938, 77/184 (origin). Waitz, ZKG 1940, 304/41. Graf I, 283/92, 302/4, 580/4. H. J. Schoeps, *Theologie u. Geschichte des Judenchristentums,* 1949, 37/61 (Ebionite source); 381/456 *(Ebionite Acta Apostolorum);* 457/79 (Epiphanius and Ps.-Clement); id., *Aus fruehchristl. Zeit,* 1950, 38/81 (demonology of *Ps.-Clem.;* on Hom. 8–9). Id., VC 1951, 88/100 (astrolog. matters). Cullmann, Beiheft z. ZNTW 21, 1954, 35/51 (Qumrân texts and the Jewish Christianity of the *Ps.-Clem.*). Rehm, RACh 3, 197/206. H. J. Schoeps, *Urgemeinde, Judentum, Gnosis,* Tu 1956 (reply to his critics). G. Strecker, *Das Judenchristentum i. d. Ps.-Klementinen,* TU 70, 1957.

§ 16. IGNATIUS OF ANTIOCH (d. *c.* 110)

In the reign of the Emperor Trajan, Ignatius, Bishop of Antioch, was taken from Syria to Rome where he was thrown to the beasts in the arena (Eus., *Hist.* 3, 22; Jerome, *Vir. ill.* 16). On this journey the saint wrote seven letters, four from Smyrna and three from Troas. At Smyrna he wrote to the churches of Ephesus, Magnesia and Tralles in Asia Minor to thank them for having sent legates to salute him on his way of suffering; in the fourth letter, addressed to the Romans, he asks them not to intervene with the Emperor to obtain his deliverance (EA 18/21). At Troas he received news that the persecution at Antioch had ceased; hence he wrote from there to the churches of Philadelphia and Smyrna as well as to Polycarp, the Bishop of Smyrna, asking them to send legates to congratulate the brethren at Antioch on the restoration of peace.

About 380 the seven Letters of Ignatius were worked over and enlarged; besides, six further letters were added to them at the same time; on the interpolator of the Letters v. supra § 7, 4. In the Middle Ages four short letters in Latin were tacked on to them. The longer recension was printed in Latin in 1498, in Greek in 1557. It was generally taken to be genuine until, in 1646, six letters were published in their original, shorter form, followed by the Letter to the Romans in 1689. Then scholars were soon agreed that the longer recension was spurious. An even shorter, Syriac recension of three letters, published by Cureton in 1845, proved to be extracts from the authentic Letters. From the Protestant side the authenticity of the seven Letters was almost unanimously rejected, because they clearly proved the monarchical episcopate and the division of the hierarchy into bishop, presbyters and deacons. Today, after the brilliant defence of T. Zahn, F. X. Funk, J. B. Lightfoot and A. Harnack, the Letters are almost universally recognized as authentic.

The authenticity of the Letters is well attested. St. Polycarp already mentions the Epistles of Ignatius in his own Letter in these terms: "They contain faith and patience and all edification that pertains to our Lord." This description well fits the Letters that have come down to us, which are also attested by Irenaeus, Origen and Eusebius. Their style is of inimitable originality, a strange mixture of powerful, bold formlessness and elaborate rhetoric. Here speaks a deeply religious personality, filled with passionate mystical love of Christ and ardent longing for martyrdom.

Points of Doctrine

1. Christ is called γεννητὸς καὶ ἀγέννητος, καὶ ἐκ Μαρίας καὶ ἐκ θεοῦ (*Eph.* 7, 2) and ἄχρονος, ἀόρατος (*Ad Polyc.* 3, 2).

2. The expectation of the prophets has really been fulfilled: Christ became to them (in the *descensus ad inferos*) παρών (*Philad.* 5, 2; 9, 1; *Magn.* 9, 2).

3. The Eucharist is for him σάρξ Ἰησοῦ Χριστοῦ παθοῦσα (*Smyrn.* 7, 1), φάρμακον ἀθανασίας and ἀντίδοτος τοῦ μὴ ἀποθανεῖν (*Eph.* 20, 2).

4. The Church is called θυσιαστήριον (*Eph.* 5, 2; *Trall.* 7, 2), thus recalling the term θυσία in the *Didache*.

5. The Letters presuppose that individual bishops are at the head of the communities and treat the monarchical episcopate as a normal institution. In *Eph.* 3, 2 Ignatius speaks of "bishops that are appointed even in the farthest countries".

6. In all Letters except that to the Romans the author exhorts to unity within the Church, which he finds in the close connexion with the hierarchy consisting, according to all the Letters, in bishops, priests and deacons. Christ, the bishop, and the Church are closely connected (*Smyrn.* 8).

7. The term "Catholic Church" for all the faithful is used here for the first time (*Smyrn.* 8, 2).

8. The Roman Church is distinguished before all others by an especially solemn address that contains an extraordinary number of *epitheta ornantia* (EH 25, EP 52). Ignatius praises the Roman church, influenced probably by Rom. 1:8 and 1 Clem. 5f. as leading in faith and charity, emphasizing its faith even more than its charity; it is said of it, inter alia: ἥτις καὶ προκάθηται ἐν τόπῳ χωρίου Ῥωμαίων and it is called προκαθημένη τῆς ἀγάπης. A "doctrinal activity" of the Roman community in regard to other churches is mentioned in Rom. 3, 1 (ἄλλους ἐδιδάξατε), probably alluding to the *First Epistle of Clement.* The special authority and a factual pre-eminence of the position of the Roman community is already clearly noticeable. Nevertheless, the frequently used translation of προκαθημένη τῆς ἀγάπης as "president of the union of love" (= universal Church) is not correct, considering the context and the general thought of Ignatius. It would be more accurate to translate: "who holds the pre-eminence also in charity", understanding by ἀγάπη all the new things "that came into the world with the love of Christ and constitute the essence of Christianity" (J. Thiele). The first mentioned translation is opposed also by the Old Latin, Syriac and Armenian versions and especially by Rom. 9:3.

9. In Rom. 4:3 Peter and Paul are mentioned in their authori-

tative position with regard to the Romans, and thus their sojourn in Rome, too, is indirectly attested (EH 26).

10. Virginity is recommended in the sense of St. Paul; marriage is to be contracted μετὰ γνώμης τοῦ ἐπισκόπου (*Ad Polyc.* 5, 2; EP 67; EH 27).

Ed. and trans.: v. § 14 and P. G. Crone, Mr 1936. *Pseudo-Ignatiana* and *Martyria* in Funk-Diekamp, *Patres apost.* 2, 1913, 83/396. T. Camelot, SCh 10, 1951 (Letters of Ig., Polyc. and Mart. Polyc.). A. Winterswyl, *Briefe,* Fr [4]1954. — Mg.: T. Zahn 1873. F. X. Funk, *Die Echtheit der Ig.-Br.,* 1883. M. Rackl, *Die Christologie des hl. Ig. v. A.,* 1914. Bareille, DTC 7, 685/713. H. Schlier, *Religionsgeschichtl. Untersuchungen zu den Ig.-Br.,* 1929. Streeter 1930; cf. Michell, CQR 1931, 219, 32. Loofs 1930, 194/205 (spirit Christology). Doelger, AC 4, 1933, 73/80 (title of Christophorus). W. Bauer 1934, 65/73, 81/5, 112/4. C. C. Richardson, *The Christianity of Ig. of A.,* NY 1935. D'Alès, RSR 1935, 489/91 (Polyc. 5, 2). Bardy 1935, 19/33. Moffat, HTR 1936, 1/38 (Trall.). Staerk, ZNTW 1936, 83ff. (eschatology). Doelger, AC 5, 218/23 (Phil. 7, 1). Campenhausen 1936, 67/78. Richardson, JR 1937, 428/43 (Church). Preiss, RHP 1938, 197/241 (imitation of Christ). G. Cloin, *De Spiritualit. van de Ig. Bischofs-Idee,* N 1938. On this, Id. StC 1938, 19/42 (Bishop and Pneuma), and ib. 231/54 (Bishop and Agape). Villain, RPA 1938, 257/71 (l'unité du Corps mystique: Ig. et Irénée). H. W. Bartsch, *Gnost. Gut u. Gemeindetradition by Ig. v. A.,* 1940. Burghardt, TSW 1940, 1/26 (Ig. and John's Gosp.). H. v. Torre, *Het vocabularium v. Ig. v. Ant.,* thesis Lou 1942. C. Mauerer, *Ig. u. d. Jo.-Ev.,* Zu 1949. Cristiani, RAM 1949, 109/116 (Life with Christ). Perler, RAC 1949, 3/26 (Macc. 4 and Ig.); 35. Congresso Eucarist. Intern., Ba 1952, Sess. de Estud. 2, 424/29 (Eucharist and Church). Chadwick, HTR 1950, 169/72 (silence of bishops in Ig.). Jouassard, *Mémorial Chaine,* 1950, 213/21 (date of 3 letters from Troas); RSR 1951, 362/67 (on Rom. 2, 2: culte des martyrs?). Lusk, ScotJournTheol. 3, 1950, 255/77 (on the hist. of the episcopate). Stradre, Hel 1, 1950, 310/18 (on Rom. 5, 1 and 6, 1). Chrestos, Θ 1950, 618/37; 1951, 82/107 (Ζωὴ ἀληθινή). Katzenmayer, IKZ 1951, 104/7 (position of bishop). T. Ruesch, *Die Entstehung der Lehre v. Hl. Geist bei Ig., Theophil v. Antioch. u. Iren.,* Zu 1952. Cecchini, Mar 14, 1952, 373/83 (Mary). Bolhuis, VC 1953, 143/53 (*Acta Romana* of the *Martyrium* of Ig., parallel to Old Chr. apologetics). Bultmann, *Studia Paulina in hon. de Zwaan,* 1953, 37/51 (Ig. and Paul). Riesenfeld, Relig. och Bibel 12, 1953, 5/18 (Ig. sasom hellenist.). Molland, JEH 1954, 1/6 (heretics in Ig.). Bieder, TZ 1956, 28/43 (eccl. silence in Ig.).

On the question: Ig. and the Rom. community: Thiele, TG 1927, 701/9. F. Haase, 1925, 178f. Ehrhard 1932, 275f. Perler, DT 1944, 413/51. Schuster, SC 1949, 130/2. Katzenmeyer, IKZ 1953, 65/72 (on Rom. 4, 3). Authenticity of Letters disputed by M. Simon, RevHist 1948, 51. H. Grégoire, Mémoires de l'Acad. Royale de Belgique 46, 1, 1951, 102/4.

§ 17. ST. POLYCARP (d. 156)

In his youth Polycarp still saw and listened to the apostle John, who appointed him Bishop of Smyrna (Tert., *Praescr.* 32, 2; Eus., *Hist.* 5, 20, 5f.; EH 96 100 192). About 155 he discussed the date and object of the celebration of Easter with Pope Anicetus, but could not come to an agreement with him. When Marcion, who had been excommunicated by his bishop, asked Polycarp whether he knew him, he answered: "Certainly I know you, the firstborn of Satan" (Iren., *Haer.* 3, 3, 4). According to the statement of Irenaeus reproduced by Eus., *Hist.* 5, 20, 8 he wrote several letters to churches and individual Christians. Only his letter to the Philippians is still extant. Four documents, which are witnesses of his life and death, bear his name.

1. *The Epistle of St. Ignatius to Polycarp*

Ignatius instructs Polycarp (EP 66/68) on his pastoral duties, exhorts him to be an "athlete" and to stand firm like an anvil under the blows of the hammer. He is to send a "courier of God" to Antioch and to write to the other churches to do the same (ecclesiastical organization by means of messengers).

2. *The Epistle of Polycarp to the Philippians* (EP 71/76)

The church at Philippi had asked Polycarp for a copy of the Letters which St. Ignatius had written to him and to several churches of Asia Minor. These epistles he now sent "as many as he had", adding a covering letter of his own. This epistle, which uses the *First Letter of Clement,* gives various exhortations on the true faith and a Christian way of life, occasionally stressing obedience to "the presbyters and deacons" (5, 3); he does not mention a bishop at Philippi (presbyterial constitution of the church of Philippi?).

The view represented by Harrison is very probable, according to which two separate letters of Polycarp would have been worked together in the Epistle as we have it. Chapter 13 is the first short letter written during Ignatius' journey to his death (*c.* 110), which accompanied the Ignatian epistles. The second letter (chs. 1–12), which in chapter 9 already presupposes Ignatius' death, was written considerably later (*c.* 135), when the Philippians, apparently disquieted by the appearance of Marcion (ch. 7), asked the advice of Polycarp, who had achieved a great reputation in the meantime. Chapter 14, being a postscript, fits the first as well as the second letter.

Objections have been raised against the thesis advanced by Harrison concerning Polycarp's *Two Epistles to the Philippians,* 1936; cf. the six authors named in ACW 6, 1948, 184 A, esp. A. Puech, RHR 119, 1939, 96/102; on the other hand, Meinhold, PWK 21, 1683/87, supports Harrison with new reasons. Lately H. v. Campenhausen has tried to prove, though not altogether convincingly, that Polycarp or a cleric acting on his instructions is the author of the canonical *Pastorals* (SbHei 1951, 2. mg.). Cf. against this, Meinhold, PWK 21, 1691 f.

The Epistle is preserved in full only in Lat.; the Gr. MSS give 1–9, 2; in Eus. 3, 36, 13–15; also 9 and 13.

3. *The Martyrdom of Polycarp*

This oldest extant, essentially authentic and reliable account of the passion and death of a martyr has the form of a letter of the community at Smyrna to the church of Philomelium in Phrygia. It was written by a certain Marcion (ch. 20) soon after Polycarp's death. Later the end of the Letter received several additions. Reminiscent of the Passion of Christ, it describes the martyrdom of the bishop who, ordered by the proconsul Statius Quadratus to curse Christ, replied: "Eighty-six years I have served him and he has never done me wrong; how then can I blaspheme the King who saved me?" The author puts into the mouth of the martyr bound to the stake a prayer (ch. 14) which is also important for the history of primitive Christian prayer. Since the flame only made a vault like a sail over him without killing him, the executioner stabbed him with a dagger. This happened probably on February 22, 156 (E. Schwartz); in the Latin Church Polycarp has always been venerated on January 26. His companions collected his bones, "more valuable than jewels and more precious than gold, and laid them in a suitable place, to gather together there every year on the anniversary of his death" (ch. 18).

4. The *Vita Polycarpi* by *Pionius* (in Funk-Diekamp 2, 1913, 402/50) is an unimportant, completely legendary piece of work, written probably *c.* 400 to supplement the old Martyrdom. The Presbyter Pionius of Smyrna, martyred under Decius, is certainly not the author. C. Schmidt, *Gespraeche Jesu mit seinen Juengern,* 1919, 705/25. Funk-Bihlmeyer, *Die Apost. Vaeter,* 1924, p. XLI. Streeter 1929, 265/72.

Edd. and trans. v. § 14, also the *Martyrdom of Polyc.* in FP 1, 1914, 40/60 and in R. Knopf-G. Krueger, *Ausgewaehlte Maertyrerakten,* [3]1929, 1/7.—Treatises: W. Bauer 1934, 73/8 and freq. Bardy 1935, 34/43. Meinhold, PWK 21, 1952, 1662/93 (fundamental). A. C., CQR 1945, 1/25 (Letter to the Phil.). H. Caroll, *Polycarp of Sm.,* thesis Duke Univ. 1946. Katzenmayer, IKZ 1951, 146/56. — On date of death and Martyrdom of Polycarp: W. Reuning, *Zur Erklaerung des Polykarpmartyriums,* 1917. H. Delehaye, *Les passions des martyrs,* 1921, 11/59. Ramsay, Jahresh. des oesterr. Arch. Inst. 1932, 245/8 (year of death: 155). H. W. Surkau, *Martyrien in jued. u. fruehchristl. Zeit,* 1938, 126/34. The thesis, defended by H. Grégoire-P. Orgels, AB 1951, 1/38, that Polyc. did not die until Feb. 23, 177, is untenable. Cf. against it Griffe, BLE 1951, 170/77, and Meinhold, PWK 21, 1673/80; further Camelot, SCh 10, 1951, 227/9 and RSPT 1952, 492/4; Bardy, nAT 1953, 175. Telfer, JTS 1952, 79/83 date 168. Marrou, AB 1953, 5/20 dates between 161 and 168/9; cf. Griffe, BLE 1953, 178/81. On the *Pseudo-Polycarpiana:* Harnack, SbB 1921, 266/84, 834f. Bover, EE 1935, 5/19; fragm. n. 3 in Funk-Diekamp, 2, 1913, 398f. is supposed to be genuine; against it Meinhold, PWK 21, 1690f. H. v. Campenhausen, *Bearbeitungen und Interpolationen des Polykarpmartyriums,* SbHei 1957, 3; also Marrou, ThLZ 1959, 361/63.

§ 18. PAPIAS OF HIERAPOLIS

PAPIAS was Bishop of Hierapolis in Phrygia Minor (Eus., *Hist.* 3, 36, 2), a pupil of the Apostle John and a companion of Polycarp (Iren., *Haer.* 5, 33, 4). Eusebius (*Hist.* 3, 39, 13) calls him σφόδρα γάρ τοι σμικρὸς ὢν τὸν νοῦν, probably because he was a confirmed chiliast and uttered many fabulous (μυθικώτερα) sayings.

About 130 Papias wrote five books of Λογίων κυριακῶν ἐξηγήσεις *(Explanations of Sayings of the Lord),* chiefly according to oral communications from disciples of the apostles; but he also used other sources, e. g. the daughters of the "evangelist" Philip (Acts 21:8). Only small fragments of this work are extant, among them one on the origin of the first two gospels and on his authorities, where John is cited twice (Eus., *Hist.* 3, 39; EP 94f.; EH 45/9). Other fragments contain legends, e.g. of Joseph Barsabas (Acts 1:23) who drank poison without being harmed, and of the end of the traitor Judas.

Fragms.: in Funk-Bihlmeyer 1924, 133/40. M. Bucclato, *P. di H. Frammenti e testimonianze nel testo greco,* Mi 1936. — Trans.: Hennecke ²1924, 129f. Kleist, ACW 6, 1948, 105/24. — Treatises: Bardy, DTC 11, 1944/7. Lawlor, Ha 1922, 167/222. Lambot, RB 1931, 116/23. F. Loofs 1930, 328/38 (P. in Iren.). Froevig, NKZ 1931, 344/76. Dix, Th 1932, 8/20. P. Vannutelli, *De Presbytero Ioanne ap. Papiam,* R 1933; SC 1935, 202/9. W. Bauer 1934, 187/91 and freq. Bartlet, *Amicitiae Corolla* ed. H. G. Wood, Lo 1933, 15/44 (date: c. 110). P. Vannutelli, *Synoptica* 1, 1936, 12ff. N. J. Hommes, *Het Testimonialboek,* 1935, 230/55. Vaccari, Bi 1939, 413f. (un preteso scritto perduto di P.). Perrella, DTP 1940, 47/56 *(Giovanni l'anziano).* Grant, ATR 1943, 218/22. Kleist, St. Louis Univ. Stud. Series A, vol. 1, No. 1, 1945, 1/17 (Pap. and Mk). Brown, Quarterly and Holborn Rev., 1945, 440/5 (P. and the Elder John). Gry, RB 1946, 197/206 (Henoch 10, 9 in P.). Gutwenger, ZKT 1947, 385/416 (chronol.). Bligh, TSW 1952, 234/40 (prologue of P.). Kürzinger, BiZ 1960, 19/38 (Revolutionary new interpretation of accounts of the Gospels of St. Mark and St. Matthew).

CHAPTER THREE

The Greek Apologists of the Second Century

§ 19. GENERAL REMARKS

Complete Edd.: MG 6. J. C. T. de Otto, *Corpus apologetarum,* 1–9, Jena 1847/72, (1–5 Justin), [3]1876/81. E. J. Goodspeed, *Die aeltesten Apologeten,* 1914 (without Theophilus). — Aids: E. J. Goodspeed, *Index apologeticus sive clavis Iustini martyris operum et aliorum apologetarum christianorum,* 1912.

Treatises: Bareille, DTC 1, 1580/1602. J. Geffcken, *Zwei christl. Apologeten,* 1907 (Aristides and Athenagoras). A. Puech, *Les apologistes grecs du 2e s.,* 1912. A. Hauck, *Apologetik i. d. alten Kirche,* 1918. J. Lortz, *Tertullian als Apologet* I, 1927. J. Giordani, *La prima polemica crist.,* Brescia [2]1943. Rivière, BLE 1930, 5/20. Mersch 1, [2]1936, 309/14. Doelger, AC 4, 188/288: *Sacramentum infanticidii.* W. van Es, *De grond van het Schriftgeloof bij de Apologeten,* GTT 1934, 113/42, 282/310; 1937, 305/30, 385/96. V. A. S. Little, *The Christology of the Apologists,* 1934. Losacco, ArchStorFilosIt 1935, 85/108 (dialectics). H. Rossbacher, *Die Apologeten als politisch-wissenschaftl. Schriftsteller,* 1937. Shepherd, JR 1938, 60/79 (Christ. worship). E. Scharl, *Recapitulatio mundi bei Irenaeus,* 1941, 120/31. A. Casamassa, *Gli apologisti greci,* 1944. P. Palazzini, 1946 (supra § 14). M. Pellegrino, *Gli apologetici greci,* R 1947, and *Studi su l'antica apologetica,* R 1947 (107/207, also on Cyprian and Lactantius). E. Massaux, *Influence de l'év. de Matth. sur la littér. chrét. avant s. Irénée,* Lou 1950. Monachino, Gr 1951, 5/49, 187/222 (Intento practico e propagandistico). A. Benoît, *Le baptême au 2e siècle,* 1953. Grant, VC 1955, 25/33 (The Chronology of the Greek Apologists). M. Pellegrino, *Il cristianesimo del 2 sec. di fronte alla cultura class.,* Tu 1954.

In the course of the second century the new conditions caused Christian writers to adopt scholarly reasoning in the form of apologetic discussions, a form that had been foreshadowed by Stephan's speech in Acts 7. Educated men and scholars joined the Church in greater numbers. The newly found truth compelled them quite naturally to enter the discussion with pagan philosophy. With the literary activities of the Apologists Christianity left quite consciously its former narrow sphere in which it had developed shut off from the world, and, skilfully adapting itself to the philosophical trends of the time, made its first definite effort to present its new ideas to the educated world as the crowning perfection of its highest cultural ideals.

If so far only the pagan populace had indulged in wicked stories about the Christians (Thyestean meals and Oedipean unions), now, in the second century, pagan philosophers began to attack Christianity. Only some of their writings are known:

1. The speech of the famous rhetor Fronto of Cirta, the teacher of Marcus Aurelius, against the Christians (Min. Fel., *Oct.* 9, 6; 31, 2).

2. In a satire *De morte Peregrini* (*c.* 170) Lucian of Samosata, who had been a member of the Christian community for some time (chs. 11–16), mocks the Christians for their love of the brethren and their contempt of death (chs. 12f.).

Text in E. Chernberg, *L. de Samosata, Oeuvres complètes,* 1934. J. Schwartz, *L. de S., Philopseudès et De morte Peregrini* (with commentary), 1951. German trans. W. Nestle, 1925. — Riessler, TQ 1933, 64/72 (L. v. S. and Holy Scripture). M. Caster, *Lucien et la pensée rel. de son temps,* 1938. Curti, MiscStLCA 1954, 86/109 *(Luciano e i cristiani).* Bagnani, Historia 4, 1955, 107/12 (Peregr. and the Christians).

3. The attack of the Platonist Celsus Ἀληθὴς λόγος (*c.* 178), preserved for the greater part in Origen's work against him (cf. § 40).

The tradition of hostility against the Christians on the part of the philosophers was continued in the later centuries, especially among the neo-Platonists, e.g. Porphyry (v. infra § 48, 4 d; 70, 5), Hierocles and the Emperor Julian.

O. Gloeckner, *Celsus,* Ἀληθὴς λόγος (KlT 151) 1924. W. den Boer, *Scripta paganorum I–IV saec. de Christ. testimonia,* Ley 1948. — Merlan, RACh 2, 954/65 (with good bibliogr.). A. Miura-Stange, *Celsus u. Origenes,* 1926. W. Voelker, *Das Bild vom nichtgnostischen Christentum bei Celsus,* 1928. H. O. Schroeder, *Der* Ἀληθὴς λόγος *des Celsus,* 1939 (only part printed). R. Bader, *Der* Ἀληθὴς λόγος *des Kelsos,* 1940 (restoration of the text of Celsus). A. Wifstrand, *Die wahre Lehre des Kelsos:* K. Human. vetenskapessamfundets i Lund, 1941/2, V, 391/431. J. Geffcken, *Der Ausgang des griech.-roem. Heidentums,* [2]1929. P. de Labriolle, *La réaction païenne. Étude sur la polémique antichrét. du 1er au 6e s.,* 1934. Lods, RHP 1941, 1/33 (Jewish sources of Celsus). Cataudella, NDid 1, 1947, 28/34 (Celsus and the Christ. Apologists). W. den Boer, *De eerste bestrijder van het Christendom,* Groningen 1950. On *Porphyry* cf. also A. Harnack, AbhB 1916, 1 and SbB 1921, 266/84, 834f. Vaganay, DTC 12, 2555/90. Moffat, ET 1931, 72/8. A. B. Hulen, *Porphyry's Work against the Christians,* Scottdale 1933. Nestle, ARW 1941, 51/100 (principal arguments of the philosophers against Christianity). Benoît, RB 1947, 543/72. Nautin, RB 1950, 409/16 (3 new fragments of Porphyry's *Contra Christ.*). Frasinetti, RendIstLombClLett 86, 1953, 194/210 (Porfirio esegeta del Profeta Daniele). Den Boer, Varia hist. aangeb. van Prof. Byvanck, 1954, 83/96 (Porphyry as an historian). C. Andresen, *Logos u. Nomos. Polemik des Kelsos wider das Christentum,* B 1955.

It is true, the first emperors of the second century were anxious to restrain the fury of the enraged people; but they accepted proper accusations and confirmed convictions for the *nomen christianum*. In 176 the Emperor Marcus Aurelius issued a rescript which forbade the setting up of new religions and which could easily be applied to the Christians. Besides, Judaism was still hostile. Its doctrines and customs continued to penetrate into Christian circles, so that in this direction too, refutations and clarifications were necessary.

The apologetic writings of the second century are mostly in the form of the speech or the dialogue, composed according to the rules of Greek rhetoric and frequently destined to be presented to the emperor. They refute the pagan slanders, reveal the absurdities and immorality of the myths of the gods, and defend particularly monotheism and the doctrine of the resurrection. They show that pagan philosophy, resting only on human reason obscured by the activities of the demons, knew only part of the truth, itself mixed with error, whereas Christianity offers the whole truth, because in Christ, the Logos, that is divine Reason itself, appeared on earth.

Since the apologists wanted to gain influence also with the educated pagan readers, their writings already use technical philosophical terms and considerations, a practice which later increased considerably. This, however, did not transform or paganize the religious and theological content of the Christian faith in any essential points. The well-worn and often abused slogan that Christianity was Hellenized when the philosophy of antiquity invaded Christian speculation, fails to hit the mark; we would rather speak of a gradual Christianization of Hellenism.

Individual proofs of the truth of Christianity:

1. The proof from the moral effects of Christianity, especially neighbourly love;

2. the proof from the predictions of Christ and the prophets; the second century authors were probably already provided with a written collection of the O.T. prophecies;

3. the proof from antiquity: the inner unity and the connexion between the Old and the New Testament were emphasized; the teaching of the prophetical books of the O.T. is fulfilled in the N.T., and Christianity is not a new religion, because Moses had lived before the Greek poets and sages;

4. the proof from the miracles of Christ, only rarely applied, since, according to Tertullian (*Marc.* 3, 3), Origen (*Cels.* 3, 26/38) and Lactantius (*Inst.* 5, 3), pseudo-Christs and magicians helped by demons also wielded miraculous powers.

The best and oldest manuscript of the Greek apologists of the second century is the *Codex of Arethas* in Paris, written in 914 for Archbishop Arethas of Cappadocian Caesarea, originally a *corpus apologetarum* of the first three centuries including Eusebius. Most MSS of the Greek apologists go back to this codex (except Justin, Theophilus, the *Letter to Diognetus* and Hermias).

§ 20. QUADRATUS AND ARISTIDES

1. Quadratus, who was a disciple of the apostles probably living in Asia Minor, whom Jerome (*Vir. ill.* 19; *Ep.* 70, 4) erroneously identified with the later Bishop Quadratus of Athens, presented an apology to the Emperor Hadrian during the latter's stay in

Asia Minor (Eus., *Hist.* 4, 23, 3) on the occasion of a persecution of the Christians.

A fragment is preserved in Eusebius' *History*. It treats of the witnesses of the works of Christ, especially of those still alive who had been cured or raised from the dead (EP 109). R. Harris has tried to trace the use of a lost second century apology which may perhaps have been that of Quadratus in the romance *Barlaam and Joasaph* (§ 107, 3 h), in the Apology of St. Catherine (MG 116, 267ff.) and other documents; but this attempt was not successful. P. Andriessen is collecting noteworthy arguments for his thesis that the Apology of Quadratus is identical with the *Letter to Diognetus*.

Harris, ET 1921, 147/60; BJR 1923, 355/82; 1924, 384/92; against it E. Klostermann and E. Seeberg, *Die Apologie der hl. Katharina,* 1924. Amann, DTC 13, 1429/31. P. Andriessen, RTA 1946, 5/39, 125/49; 1947, 121/56; VC 1947, 129/36; SE 1949, 44/54 and BiNJ 1950, 140/50. Bardy, AIP 9, 1949, 75/86.

2. The Athenian philosopher Aristides whom Eusebius (*Hist.* 4, 3, 3) names together with Quadratus as the author of an Apology addressed to Hadrian.

The Apology as a whole remained lost until in 1889 the American scholar Rendel Harris found it in a faithful Syriac translation in a MS of the monastery of St. Catherine on Mount Sinai, and then J. A. Robinson made the surprising discovery that the greater part of the Greek text, though in a free redaction, had already been contained in chs. 26 and 27 of the *Vita Barlaam et Joasaph,* preserved among the writings of St. John of Damascus (§ 107, 2). Moreover, it appeared that the Mechitarists of St. Lazzaro had published an Armenian fragment of the Apology as early as 1878. Recently two considerable papyrus fragments (chs. 5, 4; 6, 1 2 and 15, 6 – 16, 1) have been published from the collection of the British Museum. The address of the Syriac translation, it is true, runs: *To Adrianus Antoninus,* but inner reasons favour the address attested by Eusebius (to Ael. Hadrianus).

Points of Doctrine

The Apology is divided into two unequal parts: chapters 1–14 contain the polemics against the religion of the three "races" of Barbarians, Greeks, and Jews. Chapters 15–17 treat of the teaching and life of the fourth "race" of Christians. Through reflexions from the sphere of natural philosophy (consideration of the motion and harmony of the cosmos) Aristides arrives in chapter 1 at the notion of an eternal and uncreated God. The notion he has thus gained is his standard by which he judges all other religions. The barbarians (Chaldeans) worship transitory elements such as earth, water, fire, sun and winds as gods, and offer divine honours also to men (chs. 3–7). The Greeks have furnished their gods with human weaknesses and passions (chs. 8–11 and 13; ch. 12 against the animal cult of the Egyptians). The Jews, it is true, worship the angels rather than God and observe new moons, food laws and other externals, but they deserve respect on account of their active philanthropy (ch. 14). The Christians have the true conception of God and are distinguished by the purity of their morals which is here (15–17) enthusiastically described (EP 110/2) in a way similar to the *Letter to Diognetus,* which some scholars would therefore like to ascribe to Aristides.

Syr. and Gr. text ed. R. Harris and J. A. Robinson, C [2]1893.—Trans.: K. Julius (BKV[2] 12), 1913. C. Vona, R 1950 (Lateranum, N. S. 16: trans. based on Syr. text; incl. all known Gr. texts and trans. of Armen. fragms.). So far four attempts have been made to reconstruct the text: R. Seeberg, *Die Apologie des A. untersucht u. wiederhergestellt,* 1893, and *Der Apologet A.,* 1894; E. Hennecke, *Die Apologie des A.* (TU 4, 3), 1893. J. Geffcken, *Zwei griech. Apologeten,* 1907, 1/96; E. J. Goodspeed, *Die aeltesten Apologeten,* 1914, 2/23. The new Gr. fragms. in Milne, JTS 25, 1923/4, 73/7 and G. Krueger, TLZ 1924, 47f.; J. de Zwaan, HTR 1925, 109/11. An Armen. homily on Lk. 23, 42f. is certainly spurious, also an Armen. fragm. *ex epistula Aristidis,* cf. P. Pape, TU 12, 2, 1894. M. Fermi, RR 1925, 541/5 (relation to *Letter to Diogn.*). I. P. Bock, BoS 1931, 1/16 (Ar. author of *Letter to Diogn.*). Altaner, RACh 1, 652/4. Friedrich, ZKT 1919, 31/77 (doctrinal content). Lazzati, SC 1938, 35/51 (ch. 1). v. d. Boer, VC 1947, 155f. Hunger, Sch 20/24, 1949, 390/400 (The Apology, a treatise of conversion). O'Ceallaigh, HThR 1958, 227/54 (Apology originally Jewish).

§ 21. ARISTON OF PELLA AND JUSTIN MARTYR

1. Ariston of Pella, the author of a lost *Dialogue between Jason and Papiscus concerning Christ,* is probably the earliest literary apologist of Christianity in its struggle with Judaism. He wrote about 140; in any case the work was known already to Celsus (Origen, *Cels.* 4, 52). The Latin translation which is also lost is attested by a prologue (CSEL 3, 3, 119/32) falsely ascribed to Cyprian. Jerome (*In Gal.* ad 3, 13f. and *Quaest. hebr. in Gen. 1, 1*) too, knew this work. The proof from O.T. prophecy adduced by the Jewish Christian Jason results in the Jew Papiscus' request to be baptized.

A. M. Williams 1935, 28/30 (supra § 3 n. 4).

2. Justin (d. *c.* 165), philosopher and martyr, first called thus by Tertullian (*Val.* 5), is considered the most important apologist of the second century. He belonged to a pagan Greek family at Flavia Neapolis (ancient Sichem, modern Nablus) in Palestine.

He himself tells (*Dial.* 2/8) how, as a youth avid for knowledge, he established contact with teachers of Stoic, Peripatetic and finally Pythagorean philosophy. But he was repelled partly by the doctrines of these philosophical schools, partly by the personalities of their representatives. A teacher of Platonic philosophy introduced him to a more profound knowledge of Plato. But the failure of all philosophical efforts to throw light on the nature and the immortality of the soul was proved to him by an old man he met accidentally, probably near Ephesus, who at the same time drew his attention to the "prophets" and thus to Christianity, telling him that only incessant prayer could finally open the way to God and Christ. From that time his life was exclusively devoted to the defence of the faith, the "only reliable and profitable philosophy" (*Dial.* 8). Clothed in the pallium, the cloak of the Greek philosophers, he went as an itinerant teacher from place to place and founded a school in Rome. Here Tatian was among his disciples, but he met a vehement adversary in the Cynic philosopher Crescens (Tatian, *Or.* 19, 4). His death is reliably recorded in an ancient account, *Martyrium S. Justini et sociorum* (§ 45, n. 4. Lazzati, Aev 1953, 473/97: on the crit. text of the *Mart. of St. Just.*). According to this he was beheaded as a Christian with six companions in Rome, under the prefect of the city Junius Rusticus, in 165. Leo XIII honoured him, after the example of the Greek Church, by giving him a place in the Breviary and the Missal (14th April).

Of his eight treatises known to Eusebius (*Hist.* 4, 18, 1 ff.) we possess only three, the two *Apologies against the Gentiles* and the *Dialogue with the Jew Trypho*. They have been preserved in a single bad MS of 1364, together with nine spurious works. Justin is not a particularly skilful writer. He often digresses from his subject and the sequence of thought is interrupted by incoherence and repetitions. His sentences are awkwardly constructed and his manner of expression is devoid of force, though he can sometimes be full of enthusiasm; nevertheless, he is always frank and honest.

1. Justin's Apologies

Eusebius (*Hist.* 4, 18) reports that Justin wrote two Apologies and presented one to the Emperor Antoninus Pius, the other to his successors Marcus Aurelius and Lucius Verus. We possess indeed, two Apologies written by Justin, of which the longer (68 chs.) is addressed in the MS to Antoninus Pius, the shorter (15 chs.) to the Roman senate. The majority of the most recent critics, however, seek to prove that both Apologies were actually addressed to Antoninus Pius (138–61).

a. In the first Apology (written *c.* 150/55, cf. *1st Apol.* 146) two parts can be distinguished (EP 113/29), the first of which (1–12) is mainly negative, refuting the accusations raised against the Christians. The second is more positive and more broadly based, presenting and justifying the contents of the Christian religion. Most of it is taken up with the proof of the divinity of Christ from the O.T. prophecies (30–53). The first Apology also carries an appended letter of the Emperor Hadrian to Minucius Fundanus, the proconsul of Asia (EH 57), which demands orderly trials for the Christians (*c.* 68).

b. The second Apology (EP 130 f.) is usually considered an appendix or postscript to the longer one. According to E. Schwartz it originally formed the conclusion of the first Apology and was arbitrarily placed before it as an independent treatise by the MSS, probably owing to Eusebius' statement that Justin had written two Apologies. K. Hubik thinks it is an independent reply to the attack of the rhetor Fronto of the year 164–5. G. Bardy is of a similar opinion; he thinks it was written after 161 (RSR 1923, 491 ff.; 1924, 33 ff.). A. Ehrhardt, JEH 4, 1953, 1/12 thinks they are two independent Apologies, dating the first in the year 150.

2. The Dialogue with Trypho

This long dialogue, from which the introduction and a large part of ch. 74 are missing, gives an account of Justin's two days' conversation with a learned Jew, who is probably to be identified with the well-known rabbi Tarpho, a contemporary of Justin. The introduction (2–8) describes Justin's spiritual development. Part I (9–47) shows that the Jewish ceremonial law had only temporary validity, part II (58–108) that the worship of Jesus is not contrary to monotheism, part III (109–142) that the gentiles, too, are called to become members of the Church of Christ (EP 132/46).

The *Dialogue* was written after the first Apology, since the latter is cited in it (120). The *Dialogue* is in literary form; it is, however, possible that it was preceded by a real disputation, which in that case would have taken place at Ephesus during the revolt of

Bar-Cochba (132–5; chs. 1 and 9). Recently, as also in former times, the genuineness of the *Dialogue* has been disputed, though without compelling reasons.

Edd. and trans.: v. § 19. *The Apologies,* ed. by G. Krueger, [4]1915; G. Rauschen (FP 2) [2]1911; J. M. Pfaettisch, 2 vols., 1912 (with commentary). *The Dialogue* ed. G. Archambault, 2 vols., 1909. Engl. by A. L. Williams (SPCK), Lo 1930. S. Frasca, S. Giustino M.: *Apologie. S. Teofilio Antiocheno,* Tu 1938 (with trans.). — Mg.: K. Semisch, 2 vols., 1840/2. M. J. Lagrange, P 1914. G. Bardy, DTC 8, 2228/77. — Treatises: K. Hubik, *Die Apologien des hl. Just.,* 1912. A. Harnack, *Judentum u. Judenchristentum in Justins Dialog mit Tryphon,* 1913. W. Jehne, *Die Apologie Justins,* 1914. Keseling, RM 1926, 223/6 (*Dial.* 1–10 and Plato's *Protagoras*). On the question of the genuineness of the *Dialogue* cf. Preuschen, ZNTW 1919/20, 102/27 (spurious); against this Fonck, Bi 1921, 342/7 (genuine). Schlaeger, NTT 1924, 117/43 (spurious). Huentemann, TG 1933, 410/28 (technique of composition). Hulen, JBL 1932, 58/70 (*Dial.* as a source of Jewish antichr. polemics). W. v. Loewenich 1932, 39/50. Richardson, HTR 1936, 89/91 (Apol. 65, 1). Barnikol, TJB 6, 1938, 17/9 (against Marcion). Simon, RHP 1938, 54/8 (J. sur deux hérés. juives). W. Schmid, ZNTW 40, 87/138 (transmission of Apol.). Vysoki, Listy Filologicke, 1938, 435/40 (Un prétendu souvenir autobiographique de S. J.). G. Mercati, Bi 1941, 339/66 (frammento nuovo del *Dialogo*). Enslin, JQR 1943, 179/205 (An appreciation). Weis, JTS 1944, 199/205 (Samaritanism). Sagnard, *Mél. De Ghell.* I, 1951, 171/82 (Disposition of the *Dial.*). V. Schmid, *Festschr. O. Regenbogen,* 1952, 163/82 (Justin's Platonism. *Dial.* 2ff.). Andresen, ZNTW 44, 1952/3, 157/95 (Just. and mid-Platonism). Massaux, ETL 1952, 411/28 (Mt. text of the Serm. on the Mount in J.). H. Braun, ZTK 50, 1953, 39/43 (Accounts of the bapt. of Jesus from Mc. to J.). W. Schmid, Maia 7, 1954, 1/10 (on *1 Apol.* 68; earlier date of the fictitious rescripts of Antoninus). Heard, NTStud. 1, 1954, 122/34 (*Apomnemoneumata* in Papias, Justin and Iren.). Hyldahl, *Stud. theol.,* 1956, 77/90 (Tarpho).

3. *Lost, dubious and spurious writings*

Of Justin's other writings mostly only the titles or minor fragments have been preserved.

a. More extensive fragments are extant only of the treatise *On the Resurrection,* though their genuineness has been disputed. They have been preserved mostly in the *Sacra Parallela* of John of Damascus.

Cf. F. Loofs 1930, 211/57, 281/99 (in favour of genuineness; against it Hitchcock, ZNTW 36, 1937/8, 35/60). Delius, *Theologia viatorum,* B 4, 1952, 181/204, (author perh. Melito of Sardes).

b. *Against Marcion,* used by Irenaeus and attested by Eusebius (*Hist.* 4, 11, 8 f.).

Cf. F. Loofs 1930, 225 f. Robinson, JTS 31, 1929/30, 374/8. Marta Mueller, *Unters. z. Carmen adv. Marcionitas,* thesis Wu 1936, 74/87 (depend. on Just., *Adv. Marc.*). Barnikol, TJB 6, 1938, 17/19.

c. Among the spurious writings there are three whose titles are identical with those of genuine, but lost works. The longest (38 chs.) is the *Cohortatio ad gentiles;* it points out especially the many contradictions of the Greek philosophers who make true statements only when they draw on Moses or the prophets. — The short *Oratio ad Graecos* (5 chs.) introduces itself as an apologia of a Greek converted to Christianity. — The third treatise, *De monarchia* (On the unity of God), sets out to prove the truth of monotheism from partly forged citations from Greek poets.

On other pseudo-Justin writings v. infra § 67 and 73. Ed. of the spurious works in De Otto 3 and 4 (§ 19).—Trans.: (Germ.) of the *Coh. ad gent.* by P. Heuser (BKV[2] 33) 1917. Goodenough, HTR 1925, 187/200 *(Or. ad Graec.);* cf. Harnack, TLZ 1925, 441/3. J. Geffcken, *Zwei griech. Apologeten,* 1907, 267/72 *(Cohort. ad gent.)*. Alfonsi, VC 1948, 65/88 (Aristotle in the *Cohort. ad gent.*).

Points of Doctrine

1. According to Justin and other Apologists God is without origin and name. His substantial omnipresence in the world is denied; He inhabits the regions above the heavens, which he cannot leave, hence cannot appear in the world (*Dial.* 60 and 127). He is called Father especially because he is πατὴρ τῶν πάντων (*2 Ap.* 6).

2. Justin's theory of the λόγος σπερματικός is a link between the old philosophy and Christianity. In Christ the divine Logos appeared in its fullness; nevertheless, every man possesses a germ (σπέρμα) of the Logos in his reason. Now this share in the Logos, and hence the capacity for truth, was particularly great in some men, as in the Jewish prophets and among the Greeks in Heraclitus and Socrates. Justin thinks that the Greek poets and

philosophers derived some elements of truth from the Old Jewish literature; for Moses was the oldest of all writers. Hence, in so far as the philosophers taught and lived according to reason, they were in a certain sense Christians before Christ; but after Christ had come, the Christians have the whole and undiluted truth (*1 Ap.* 46; *2 Ap.* 8, 13). In his theological thought Justin is greatly influenced by Platonic and also by Stoic philosophy.

3. On the question of the relation of the Logos to the Father Justin's thought is subordinatianist. The Logos-Son became externally independent, that is a divine Person, but subordinate to the Father, only for the purpose of the creation and government of the world (*2 Ap.* 6; *Dial.* 61; EP 130 and 137).

4. The angels have an ethereal body and take real food, the manna (*Dial.* 57). The evil spirits have almost crudely material bodies; Satan, their head, fell when he tempted Eve in the form of a serpent (*Dial.* 100 and 124); other angels sinned with women, with whom they produced the demons (*2 Ap.* 5). The devils are condemned to the fire of hell, but will enter it only after the Last Judgement, together with wicked men (*1 Ap.* 28); until then the devils inhabit the lower regions of the air and seek to tempt men to evil and to prevent the spread of Christianity in every way (*1 Ap.* 26 54 57f. 62).

5. The human soul too, has a certain bodily being; it lives not because it is itself life (like God), but because it participates in life (*Dial.* 6; EP 133). After death the souls, except those of the martyrs, first enter Hades, where they remain to the end of the world; even there the good are separated from the bad, and both are happy or unhappy in anticipation of their future destiny (*Dial.* 5). Justin explicitly identifies (*Dial.* 80) the belief that the souls enter heaven immediately after death with the denial of the resurrection of the dead. After his death Christ descended into Hades, to the dead just of the Old Covenant (*Dial.* 45 72, 4 99). Justin, like Papias, was a chiliast; though he says that even some orthodox

Christians did not hold this doctrine; but those he considers "not in all respects perfect Christians" (*Dial.* 80f.).

6. *1 Ap.* 66 and *Dial.* 100 (EP 128 and 141) attest the existence of the *Memoirs of the apostles* (ἀπομνημονεύματα), i.e. of the canonical gospels. In the *Dialogue* (100) Mary is opposed to Eve for the first time in ancient Christian literature.

7. The information Justin gives on baptism (*1 Ap.* 61; EP 126) and the divine service (*1 Ap.* 65–67; EH 54ff.) which he calls "the eucharistic sacrifice of bread and chalice" (*Dial.* 117) is invaluable. Belief in the real presence of Christ in the eucharist is clearly attested, and *1 Ap.* 66 is the first attempt to formulate the doctrine of transsubstantiation. The food by which our flesh and blood are nourished and transformed is not ordinary bread and ordinary drink; it is the flesh and blood of the incarnate Jesus, which we owe to a prayer that came from him. This liturgical logos of prayer, which comes from Christ the incarnate Logos, participates in his divine power and in his creative and transforming action.

8. Whether Justin had recognized the sacrificial character of the Eucharist is a controversial question. He says (*Dial.* 117) in reply to a word of Trypho that prayer and thanksgiving are the only perfect sacrifices pleasing to God. But he mentions explicitly (*Dial.* 41; EP 135; EH 58) that the sacrifice of wheat-flour is a type of the eucharistic bread; God had predicated through Malachias the sacrifices (θυσίαι) which the Gentiles would offer to him everywhere, i.e. the eucharistic bread and the eucharistic chalice. In *1 Ap.* 66 he clearly attests the words of consecration. The food is blessed δι' εὐχῆς λόγου τοῦ παρ' αὐτοῦ. This λόγος is named a few lines further on: "Do this in memory of me. This is my body."

Mg.: L. Feder, *J.s Lehre von Jesus Chr.,* 1906. J. M. Pfaettisch, *Der Einfluss Platos auf d. Theologie J.s,* 1910. F. Andres, *Die Engellehre der griech. Apologeten,* 1914, 1/35. E. R. Goodenough, *The Theol. of J. Martyr,* Jena 1923. J. Lebreton, *Hist. du dogme de la Trinité,* 2, 1928. Loofs 1930, 339/74 (influence on Iren.). Rivière 1931, 79/86. Bardy 1935, 103/16. Staerk, ZNTW 1934, 97/104 (Eve-

Mary). Beran, DTP 1936, 46/55 (*1 Ap.* 67). Buckley, JTS 1935, 173/6 (extra-canon. gospels). Pantaleo, Rel 1935, 231/8 (dogma and discipline in J. and Diogn.). B. Seeberg, ZKG 1939, 1/81 (theol. of hist.). Perler, DT 1940, 296/316 (Logos and euch. *1 Ap.* 66). J. Barbel, Christos Angelos, 1941, 50/63. Pellegrino, SC 1942, 130/40 (topicality of his apologetics). Gervais, RUO 1943, 129/46, 193/208 (messian. prophecy). Otilio del N. Jesus, RET 1944, 3/58 (doctr. of euch.). K. Thieme, *Kirche u. Synagoge,* Olten 1945. Amand, *Fatalisme,* 1945, 195/207). Leclercq, AnT 1946, 83/95 (La royauté du Christ). B. Kominiak, *The Theophanies of the O.T. in the Writings of St. J.,* W 1948. Ratcliff, Th 1948, 133/9 (confirmation). Carrington, Th 1949, 448/52 (confirmation). Tihen (Chan), L., *Apologetica s. Justini c. paganos et judaeos,* thesis Univ. De Propag. Fide, 1949. Bacht, Sch 1951, 481/95; 1952, 12/33 (prophetic inspiration). Hofmans, ETL 1954, 416/39 (Moses in the Apologists). Jouassard, BibleVieChrét. 7, 1954, 19/31 (parallel betw. Eve and Mary in oldest patristics). Andresen (v. supra § 19, 3), 1955, 312/72 (*Logos* and *nomos* in the theol. of hist.). Holte, *Stud. theol.* 1958, 109/68 (Christendom and philosophy).

§ 22. APOLOGISTS OF THE LAST DECADES OF THE SECOND CENTURY

1. TATIAN the Syrian was the son of pagan parents. He studied philosophy, and his extensive travels also took him to Rome, where he became a Christian and a disciple of Justin. He returned to the East probably in 172; there he founded the Gnostic-Encratite sect which rejected all (not only the second) marriage as well as the use of meat and wine and replaced the latter by water (Aquarii) when administering Holy Communion. His activities covered Syria (Antioch), Cilicia and Pisidia (Epiph., *Haer.* 46, 1).

a. *Oration to the Greeks* (λόγος πρὸς Ἕλληνας), preserved in the codex of Arethas.

The oration (42 chs.) is less an apology for Christianity than a passionate, quite unmeasured polemical treatise rejecting and disparaging the entire Greek civilization and combating especially its mythology, philosophy, poetry, rhetoric and art. Everything good in Greek culture it owes to the barbarians; however, most of it is worthless and silly or conducive to immorality. In chs.

33–5 Tatian devastatingly criticizes works of Greek sculpture which, he says, principally serves lasciviousness. His list of artists is of special value to the art historian. The work was very probably written after the death of Justin, presumably not in Rome, but after the author's defection from the Church. Even if it should have been delivered as a speech inaugurating a school (διδασκαλεῖον), it was meant from the beginning to reach a wider public.

b. The *Diatessaron* (τὸ διὰ τεσσάρων εὐαγγέλιον), a harmony of the gospels which gave a uniform presentation of the four gospels, though using the originals rather freely. Tatian almost certainly compiled the work, probably in Syriac, only after his return to the East, making use of an Old Syriac translation of the gospels already in existence. A fragment of the Greek *Diatessaron* containing fourteen lines was found in 1933 in Dura-Europos, dating from before 254. The Greek translation was probably made already before 223 (P. Kahle). In the Syrian Church the *Diatessaron* was used in the services till the fifth century. Evidently it also greatly influenced the gospel text of the rest of Christendom (cf. *Codex Bezae*). The very early Latin translation (Old Lat. *Diatessaron*) is presumably the first effort to give the gospel a Roman dress. The whole work can be reconstructed in its essential features from Arabic (11th cent.), Latin and Middle Dutch versions as well as from the sixth century Armenian translation of Ephrem's Syriac commentary on it. The *Diatessaron* takes the Gospel of St. John as the chronological framework into which the Synoptic accounts are fitted. All other writings of Tatian are lost; only five or six are known by their titles.

Text of the *Oration* v. § 19 and E. Schwartz 1888. Botti, StU 87/97 (the *Logos* not a school speech). Alfonsi, *Convivium* 1942, 273/81 (on the *Logos*). Bardy, DTC 15, 59/66. G. Blond, *Science Rel.* 1944, 157/210 (the encratite heresy towards the end of the 4th cent.). Grant, HTR 1953, 99/101 (date of the *Oratio*) and JTS 1954, 62/8 (The Heresy of Tat.). — Treatises on the *Diatess.*: T. Zahn, *T.s Diatess.,* 1881. Leclercq, DAL 4, 747/70. H. J. Vogels, *Die altsyr. Evv. in ihrem Verhaeltnis zu T.s Diatess.,* 1911; *Beitr. z. Gesch. des Diat. im Abendland,* 1919.

E. Preuschen - A. Pott, *T.s Diat. aus dem Arab. uebers.*, 1926. A. Ciasca, *T.i Evangeliorum harmoniae arabice*, R 1934 (Manual-print). D. Plooij - C. A. Phillips - A. J. Barnouw, *The Liège Diat.*, ed. with a Textual Apparatus and Engl. Trans., A 1929/35. Baumstark, OC 1930, 165/74; *Islam* 20, 1932, 308/13; OC 1933, 1/12; 1934, 165/88, 226/39, 278f. Vaccari, Bi 1931, 326/54 (*Diat.* in West). A. Ruecker, BiZ 20, 1932, 342/54. Dix, JTS 1933, 242/9 (*Didache* and *Diat.*); on this Connolly, ibid. 346 f.; 1934, 351/7 (Mt. 7:12 in *Diat.*). Heffening-Peters, OC 1935, 225/38; 1936, 96f. — C. H. Kraeling, *Greek Fragm. of T. Diat. from Dura,* 1935. Cf. Burkitt, JTS 1935, 255/9; Lagrange, RB 1935, 321ff.; Menoud, RevThéolPhilos. Lausanne 1935, 379/82; Cerfaux, ETL 1936, 98/100; Merk, Bi 1936, 234/41; Baumstark, OC 1935, 244/51; Plooij, ET 1935, 471/6. — A.-S. Marmardii, *Diat. de Tatien.* Texte arabe (with French trans.), Beyrouth 1935; cf. RSR 1937, 91/7; Baumstark, OC 1936, 235/52; id. Bi 16, 1935, 257/99 (The Syr. Titus of Bostra and the *Diat.;* Hebr. Gosp. in *Diat.*); OC 1936, 80/96 (Lower German *Diat.*); OC 36, 1, 1939, 19/37 (Lk. 24:13 in Tat.); OC 34, 1937, 169/91 (Tatian's text in the Manich. *Kephalaia*). P. Essabalian, *Le Diat. de T. et la Ie trad. des évang. armén.,* W 1937. Lyonnet, Bi 1938, 121/50 (*Diat.* armeno). V. Todesco and A. Vaccari, *Il Diat. in volgare ital. Testi ined.,* ST 81, 1938; cf. Bi 1939, 294/305; OC 36, 2, 1941, 225/42. Casey, JBL 1938, 185/94 (Marcionites and the *Diat.*). Stegmueller, ZNTW 1938, 223/9 (new Gr. fragm.); cf. OC 36, 1, 1939, 111/15; Bi 1940, 51/5. C. Peters, *Das Diat. Ts. Seine Ueberlieferung ...,* R 1939. Black, OC 36, 1, 1939, 101/11 and cont. (*Diat.* and Syr. gospels). Beston, Journ. Royal Asiatic. Soc. 1939, 608/10 (Arabic version). Peters, Bi 1942, 68/77 (state of research); Bi 1942, 323/32 (Mt. 2, 9); OCP 1942, 468/76 (in Byzantine Church poetry). Messina, Bi 1942, 268/305; 1943, 59/106 (*Diat.* Persiano tradotto dal Siriaco); also separately R 1943. Williams, JTS 1942, 37/42 (Mc. and Mt.). Higgins, JTS 1944, 187/99 (Arabic version). P. Kahle, *The Cairo Geniza,* Lo 1947 (3rd ch.). van Boer, VC 1947, 156f. G. Baesecke, *Die Ueberlieferung des althochdeutschen Tat.,* 1948. Higgins, JourManchesterUniv. 1947, 28/32 and JTS 1952, 83/7 (Persian Harmony of Gospels and Tat.). Metzger, JBL 1950, 261/80 (Pers. Harm. of Gospels). S. Lyonnet, *Les origines de la version de la Bible et le Diat.,* R 1950. G. Messina, Bi 1949, 10/27 (apocryphal variants in the Pers. *Diat.*) and Bi 1949, 356/76 (Semitisms in Pers. *Diat.*). Id., *Diatessaro persiano,* 2 vols., R 1951 (The trans. based on the Syriac [of the 13th cent.] is more important than the Middle Dutch *Diat.*). Leloir, OrSyr 1, 1956, 208/31.

2. The rhetor Miltiades from Asia Minor wrote an anti-Montanist and an anti-Valentinian treatise (Eus., *Hist.* 5, 28, 4; Tert., *Val.* 5) as well as three Apologies, which are all lost, but are attested by Eusebius (*Hist.* 5, 17, 5): two books against the Greeks, two books against the Jews, and one defence of the "Christian philosophy" addressed to "the secular authorities", i.e. probably the Emp. Marcus Aurelius (161–180) and his co-regent Lucius Verus (161-169).

3. Apollinaris, Bishop of Hierapolis, the city of Papias, wrote four Apologies (Eus., *Hist.* 4, 26, 1; 27, 1): one defence of the Christian faith addressed to Marcus Aurelius (172), five books against the Greeks, two books on truth and two books against the Jews; besides, an epistle against the Montanists (together with other bishops) and a treatise on Easter. All writings are lost.

C. Schmidt, *Gespraeche Jesu* . . . (TU), 1919, 623 (on the fragm. Περὶ τοῦ Πάσχα). W. Bauer 1934, 146f.

4. Athenagoras, a Christian philosopher from Athens, perhaps the same to whom the Alexandrian Boethus dedicated his treatise *On Difficult Expressions in Plato* (Photius, *Cod.* 154f.). He is more skilful than Justin in language, style and rhythm as well as in the arrangement of his material; he differs from Tatian in his friendlier attitude to Greek philosophy and culture, even though we must admit that he, like the other ancient Christian authors, owes his literary and philosophical knowledge almost exclusively to *florilegia* containing τόποι and δόξαι. Nevertheless, there is an unmistakable progress in philosophical and theological thought.

a. *Supplication for the Christians* (Πρεσβεία περὶ χριστιανῶν). The treatise (37 chs.), addressed to Marcus Aurelius and his son Commodus about 177, refutes one by one three accusations levelled against the Christians, viz. atheism (chs. 4–30), Thyestean meals and Oedipean incest (chs. 31–6; EP 161/7).

b. *On the Resurrection of the Dead* (Περὶ ἀναστάσεως τῶν νεκρῶν). The work (25 chs.), promised at the end of the Apology, is probably the best early Christian treatise on the subject. Firstly, the possibility of the resurrection is proved from God's omnipotence (1–10). It is fitting or even necessary i. because man, as a rational being, is destined for eternal survival. Now the body belongs to man's nature, hence the soul cannot achieve its destiny without it (11–17; EP 168ff.); ii. because of the necessity of a retribution in the next world in which the body, too, must share (18–23); iii. because man is destined to eternal bliss, which cannot be found on earth (24–5).

Points of Doctrine

i. Athenagoras is an eminent witness of the pre-Nicene Trinitarian faith. Like Justin, he proves that Christians are not atheists by their worship of the Father, Son and Spirit and their veneration of the angels (Suppl. 10; EP 164f.; cf. Just., *1 Ap.* 6). With Justin, and like Theophilus, Tertullian and Hippolytus, he says of the Son that he was νοῦς and λόγος in God from eternity and came forth from him to create the world, but without being himself a creature. Athenagoras is the first to attempt to prove the unity of God from reason (8).

ii. Many Christians grow old in the virginal state; Christians hold a second marriage to be "decent adultery" (33; EP 167).

iii. In the magnificent description of the Christian life (31–3; EP 166f.; cf. Aristides and *Letter to Diognetus*) there is a confession of faith in the presence of God (31).

Edd.: v. § 19; also E. Schwartz (TU 4, 2) 1891 and P. Ubaldi and M. Pellegrino, Tu 1947 (with trans.). Edd. of Suppl. in Geffcken, *Zwei griech. Apologeten,* 1907, 120/54. — Transs.: A. Eberhard in BKV[2] 12, 1913. G. Bardy, SCh 3, 1943 (suppl.). J. H. Crehan, ACW 23, 1956. — Studies: J. Geffcken (v. supra), 155/238. Preysing, TQ 1929, 85/100 (purpose of marriage and second marriage). Roasenda, Aevum 1934, 522f. (suppl.). G. Lazzati, *L'Aristotele perduto . . .,* 1938, 69/72. H. A. Lucks, *The Philosophy of Athenag.,* W 1936. Festugière, REG 1943, 367ff. and VC 1952, 209ff. (florilegia in Athenag., Arnobius and others). Pellegrino (v. supra § 19), 146/71 and 67/105 (2nd contribution also in Atti R. Accad. Scien. To. 77, II, 189/220). Alfonsi, VC 1953, 129/42 (the young Aristotle in Clem. Alex. and Athenag.). Grant, HTR 1954, 121/9 (Athenag. or Pseudo-Athenag.). Keseling, RAC 1, 881/8.

5. St. Theophilus of Antioch, born near the Euphrates, received a Hellenistic education; he became a Christian only as an adult (I 14) and later Bishop of Antioch.

a. The three books addressed *To Autolycus,* written shortly after

180 (III 72f.), may be taken as three treatises loosely strung together. In the first book Theophilus refutes the attacks of his friends by treating of the nature of God, of providence, of the meaning of the name of Christian, of faith in the resurrection and the folly of believing in the gods. The second book—a supplement of the first—opposes pagan mythology and the contradictory teachings of the Greek poets and philosophers to the doctrine of the prophets and the Genesis account of Biblical pre-history (EP 172/84). In the third book he refutes the accusations of the pagans, which throw doubt on the morality of the Christians, and describes the immoral pagan view of life. Moreover, Christianity and its sacred scriptures (O.T.) are defended by the proof from antiquity; Moses must have lived 900 to 1000 years before the Trojan War (3, 21).

b. The following writings are lost: *Against the Heresy of Hermogenes* and *Oration against Marcion;* besides, he wrote an historical work (Περὶ ἱστοριῶν; 2, 30), catechetical writings and commentaries on Prov. and the gospels (Eus., *Hist.* 4, 24; Jerome, *Vir. ill.* 25) and finally a harmony of the gospels (Jerome, *Ep.* 121, 6, 15).

Points of Doctrine

i. Theophilus is the first witness of the Church to use the word τριάς *(trinitas)* of the Godhead. He consistently calls the Divine Persons: God, Logos and Wisdom (2, 15; EP 180). In fact the Valentinian Theodotus cited in Clem. Alex., *Exc. ex Theod.* 80, 3 used the term in the same sense; cf. R. P. Casey, *The Excerpta ex Theod. of Clem. Alex.,* 1934, 5, 7, 88; G. L. Prestige, *God in Patristic Thought,* 1936, 93f. The passages on Trias occurring in Theophilus in Loofs, 1930, 48 A. 5.

ii. God generated the *Logos* he contained within himself (λόγος ἐνδιάθετος) before the creation of the world; this Logos spoke to Adam in paradise (λόγος προφορικός: 2, 10 22; EP 182).

iii. The human soul is created neither mortal nor immortal, but capable of mortality and immortality, according to the decision of the free will (2, 27; EP 184; cf. Just., *Dial.* 5, and Iren., *Haer.* 4, 4, 3).

iv. Whereas Justin calls the gospels only "memoirs" of the apostles (supra § 21, 6), Theophilus calls the evangelists, just like the prophets, bearers of the spirit, and the gospels and the epistles of Paul a "holy, divine word"; he is the first to have clearly stated the inspiration of the N.T. (2, 22; 3, 13f.; EP 182).

Text: v. § 19 and E. Rapisarda, Tu 1935. S. Frasca, *S. Giustino M., Apologie. S. Teofilo Antiocheno,* Tu 1938 (Testo e tra.). G. Bardy et J. Sender (SCh 20), 1948 (text and trans.). — Transs.: A. di Pauli (BKV² 14) 1913; E. Rapisarda, Tu 1937. — Bardy, DTC. F. Loofs 1930, 10/100, 397/431 attempted to prove that the treatise against Marcion could be partly reconstructed from Irenaeus (*Haer.*) who was supposed to have used it; but this attempt must be considered to have failed; cf. RSR 1931, 596/601; RHE 1930, 675/9; PWK II 5, 2149; v. also infra § 27, 1. J. Lebreton, *Hist. du dogme de la Trinité* II, 1928, 508/13. E. Rapisarda, StU, 381/400 (life and work). Aguado, *Estud. Bíbl.* 1932, 176ff., 281ff.; 1933, 3ff. (NT canon). Richard, RB 1938, 389f., 397 (fragments from *catenae*). Ogara, Gr 1944, 74/102 (relations to Aristides and *Ep. ad Diogn.*). Grant, HTR 1947, 227/56; ibid. 1950, 179/96 (The Problem of T. of Ant.) and VC 1952, 146/59 (textual trad.). Alfonsi, NDid 1948, 71/73. T. Ruesch, *Die Entstehung der Lehre vom Heiligen Geist,* Zu 1952. Grant, VC 1958, 133/44 (Text).

6. Melito, Bishop of Sardes in Lydia, venerated as a prophet and counted among the "great stars" of Asia Minor that have passed away, by Bishop Polycrates of Ephesus *c.* 190 (Eus., *Hist.* 5, 24, 5), was a versatile writer. Until recently we had few fragments and knew the exact titles of his works only through Eusebius (*Hist.* 4, 26, 1–44) and Anastasius Sinaita (*Viae Dux* 12 and 13). Only in 1940 an American scholar (C. Bonner) edited a fourth century papyrus containing a paschal homily, *De passione,* attributed to Melito. The paschal meal and the following exodus from Egypt are a type of the redemptive work of Christ. The statements on original sin, Christology, redemption and Christ's descent into hell are important for the history of dogma. His *Apology,* addressed to Marcus Aurelius (*c.* 172), expresses perhaps for the first

time the idea that a peaceful relationship between state and Church is normal and fruitful for both parties (Eus., *Hist.* 5, 24, 7–11); cf. also Athenag., Suppl. 37.

The titles of the other writings are: two books *On the Feast of Easter* (166/7). Melito here defends the Quartodeciman practice; one book on each of the following subjects: *On Baptism, On Right Conduct and the Prophets* (probably anti-Montanist), *On the Church, On Sunday Observance, On Creation, On Soul and Body, On Hospitality, On the Devil, Whether God has a Body,* six books of *Excerpts from the Law and the Prophets* (with oldest list of O.T. books), *On Faith and the Birth of Christ,* three books *On the Incarnation of Christ* (against Marcion), and others.

Fragm. in Otto (supra § 19) 9, 1872, 374/8, 494/512; in Harnack, *Marcion,* [2]1924 422f. Amann, DTC 10, 540/7. W. Bauer 1934, 155/7.— On the newly discovered homily cf. Bonner, AJP 1936, 107/19; HTR 1938, 175/90; 1939, 140f. (Copt. fragm.). Rist, HTR 1938, 249f. Casel, JL 14, 1938, 6f. — Text and trans.: C. Bonner, *Mel. of Sardes, The Homily on the Passion. With some Fragms. of Ezekiel,* Lo 1940. Syr. fragm. in Rucker 1933, 12/16, 67/73. Kahle, JTS 1943, 52/6 (perhaps written in Syr.); Bonner, HTR 1943, 316/9. Zuntz, HTR 1943, 299/315. Wellesz, JTS 1943, 41/52 (Source of Byzantine Hymnography). Nautin, RHE 1949, 429/38 (*De passione* spurious, 4th cent.). Id., *Le dossier d'Hippolyte et de Méliton dans les florilèges dogmatiques . . .,* 1953 (with new arguments for its being spurious). Wifstrand, VC 1948, 201/23 (style criticism favours genuineness). Peterson, VC 1951, 33/43 (relations to Ps.-Cyprian, *Adv. Jud.;* points favouring genuineness). Bonner, VC 1949, 184f. (text. crit.). Delius, TheolV 4, 1952, 181/204 (Ps.-Justin, *On the Resurrection,* perhaps by Melito). Zuntz, VC 1952, 193/201 (*De passione* not Syriac; against Kahle). Schneemelcher, *Festschr. f. G. Dehn,* 1957, 141f. (defends genuineness of *Hom. de passione*).—Grillmeier, ZKT 1949, 5/14 (*Descensus Christi*). Id., Sch 1949, 20/4; 481/502 (*The inheritance of the sons of Adam*). Grant, VC 1950, 33/6 (on baptism). *Passionshom.,* ed. Lohse, Lei 1958.

Spurious writings: 1. An *Apology,* presumably written in Syriac, probably dating from the time of Caracalla; cf. Haase 1925, 133f. 2. The *Clavis scripturae,* a Latin compilation, especially from Augustine and Gregory the Gt. (Pitra, Anal. sacra 2, 1884). 3. *De transitu B. Mariae Virg.* This is the title (ἡ κοίμησις τῆς θεοτόκου) of an apocryphal account of the death and assumption of Mary, which circulated in the most diverse Eastern and Western versions and adaptations. In one of the Latin versions which perhaps belongs to the fifth century, the work is wrongly ascribed to Melito.

Text: C. Tischendorf, *Apocal. apocr.*, 1866, 124/36. A. Wilmart, *L'ancien récit lat. de l'Assomption* (ST 59, 1933, 323/62); an old Engl. trans. of this text ed. R. Willard, Rev. of Engl. Studies 1936, 1/17. RTA 1937, 341/64 (an Irish trans.); EO 1939, 346/54 (The city Agathe in *Transitus C*). Rivière, RTA 1936, 5/23 (Le plus vieux *Transitus* lat. et son dérivé grec). Capelle, RTA 1940, 209/35 (anc. récits de l'Assomption et Jean de Thessal.). Graf I, 249/51. M. Jugie, *La mort et assomption de la S. Vierge* (ST 114), 1944, 106/16; 150/4. Bover, EE 1946, 415/33 (*Transitus* and John of Thess.). Capelle, AB 1949, 21/48 (Edd. and research on an old *Transitus*). Rush, CBQ 1950, 367/78 (Script. citations in the *Transitus*); id., Americ. Eccl. Review 1950, 93/110 (doctrine of the Assumption in the *Transitus*). García Castro, CienTom 1950, 145/75 (Apócrifos asuncionistas). Lausberg, JHB 1953, 25/49 (lit. formation of *Transitus*). A. Wenger, *L'assomption de la S. Vierge dans la tradition byz. du 6e au 10e s.*, 1954. Further lit.: Altaner, TR 1948, 134 A. 6.

§ 23. APPENDIX. THE LETTER TO DIOGNETUS AND THE SATIRE OF HERMIAS

1. The *Letter to Diognetus,* never mentioned in antiquity or in the Middle Ages and preserved among the works of Justin Martyr only in a single MS which was burned at Strasbourg in 1870, is addressed to a highly placed, otherwise unknown pagan personality called Diognetus. In the form of an epistle it attractively presents in brilliant style a not very profound apology of Christianity. In content it is akin to the treatise of Aristides (supra § 20, 2), though we cannot assume a direct dependence. Recently Andriessen has attempted to prove that the *Letter to Diognetus* is identical with the lost Apology of Quadratus (§ 20, 1). Though he gives impressive reasons, it is clear that such a bold thesis cannot easily be proved conclusively. Today the second half of the second century, not the third, is once more generally supposed to be the date (e.g. Meecham and Marrou). Marrou, who wants to attribute the work to Pantaenus, the teacher of Clement of Alex., defends the

genuineness of the final chs. 11 and 12 which have long been considered spurious and assigned to Hippolytus of Rome, but his reasons are not decisive.

Contents (EP 96/100): Diognetus had put three questions to his Christian friend: 1. What worship do Christians offer to God and why do they reject that of the Jews and pagans? 2. What is their so highly praised neighbourly love? 3. Why has this religion appeared so late? The author answers by giving (2–4) a criticism of paganism and Judaism, followed (5–6) by his famous description of the unearthly life of the Christians "who are in the world, what the soul is in the body". In chs. 7–8 he shows that the Christian religion comes from God, who has sent us his Son to make his nature known to us. The third question is answered by the statement (9) that God wanted to make men realize that they were unable to help themselves. He concludes (10): If Diognetus accepted the Christian teaching, he too, would be led by God's benefits to the true love of God and men.

Edd. and transs.: v. supra § 14; in Otto (supra § 19) 3, 1879, 158/211. Separate edd.: E. Buonaiuti, R 1921. J. Geffcken, Hei 1928. E. H. Blakeney (SPCK), 1943. H. C. Meecham, Manchester 1949 (with trans. and commentary). H. I. Marrou (SCh 33), 1952 (with trans. and comm.). — Transs.: in Hennecke ²1924, 619/23. G. Rauschen: BKV² 12, 155ff. Kleist, ACW 6, 1948, 125ff. — Treatises: Altaner, HJB 1927, 730/2 (on the hist. of the MS). Fermi, RR 1925, 541/7 (Aristides not the author). Geffcken, ZKG 1926, 348/50 (date: 3rd cent.). Molland, ZNTW 1934, 289/312 (Diognetus, teacher of Marcus Aurelius). Bardy 1935, 88/93. Roasenda, Aevum 1934, 522f. (ad 2, 1; 2, 3); 1935, 248/53 (ad. c. 11/12; spurious); 468/73 (Pauline ideas). Connolly, JTS 1935, 347/53; 1936, 2/15 (c. 11/12, end of Refut. of Hippolytus). E. Schwartz, *Zwei Predigten Hippolyts,* 1936, 33 A. 1, 47 A. 1 (chs. 11/12 belong to one of the two treatises of Hippol. on Easter). Blakeney, JTS 1941, 193/5 (on 10, 1). Meecham, ET 1943, 97/101 (on the theol. of the Epistle). Ogara, Gr 1944, 74/102 (Aristides and Diogn. in their relation to Theoph. of Ant.). Andriessen, RTA 1946, 5/39; 125/49 and VC 1947, 129/36 (identical with Quadratus); against this Meecham 1949; for it Telfer, JTS 1949, 223f. C. La Vespa, *La lett. a Diog.,* Ca 1947. G. Mercati in *Da incunaboli a codici (Festschr. T. Accurti),* 1947 (hist. of MS). Skard, SO 1952, 92 (on 1, 1). O'Neill, IER 1956, 92/106.

2. The *Satire of Hermias* (Διασυρμὸς τῶν ἔξω φιλοσόφων) characterizes in ten brief chapters the various mutually contradictory

efforts of pagan philosophers to know the nature of God, the soul and the world, with keen, sometimes even drastic humour, and without pursuing didactic ends. The unknown author whose treatise is not mentioned anywhere in ancient Christian literature does not owe his philosophical knowledge to a deeper study of the old philosophers, but to the popular philosophical manuals current at the time. He seems to have belonged to the second half of the second or to the third century. He does not yet mention neo-Platonism. See the criticism of the philosophers in Tatian, *Orat.* 25f.

MG 6, 1169/80. H. Diels, *Doxographi graeci,* [2]1929, 651ff. — Transs.: A. di Pauli (BKV[2] 14), 1913. E. A. Rizzo, Siena 1929. — Treatises: A. di Pauli, *Die Irrisio des Hermias,* 1907. E. A. Rizzo, *Ermia,* Livorno 1931 (trans. and comment.). L. Alfonsi, *Ermia filosofo,* Brescia 1947. S. Gennaro, *Sull "Scherno" di Ermia filosofo,* Ca 1950. Alfonsi, VC 1951, 80/3 (Plato's Theaetetus in H.).

CHAPTER FOUR

The Anti-heretical Literature of the Second Century

§ 24. GENERAL REMARKS. THE GNOSTIC LITERATURE

THE apologetic literature was called forth by the opposition of Christianity to paganism and Judaism. In the second century Montanism, Monarchianism and Gnosticism became just as dangerous adversaries of the Church.

Montanism, it is true, wanted to lead Christianity from its childhood to the adult age of the Paraclete; in fact, however, it was an attempt to turn it back to its former charismatic state from its development in the world, where it was already beginning to use the means of profane scholarship and to enter into discussion with contemporary civilization. Montanism was opposed by the apologists Apollinaris of Hierapolis, Miltiades (supra § 22, 2) and Melito of Sardes (supra § 22, 6), by the Patripassian Praxeas (infra § 30, 13), by an unnamed bishop from Asia Minor who dedicated three books against Montanism to his friend Avircius Marcellus (probably identical with Abercius of Hierapolis, § 13, 4), and who served Eusebius as a source (*Hist.*, 5, 16 with fragments), further, by Apollonius who wrote probably *c.* 196–7 (Eus., *Hist.* 5, 18), and a little later by the Roman writer Gaius who wrote a *Dialogue with Proclus the Montanist* under Pope Zephyrinus (198–217; Eus., *Hist.* 2, 25, 6f.; 3, 28, 1f.; 3, 31, 4 with three fragments, including the witness to the tombs of the Princes of the Apostles on the Vatican and in the Via Ostiensis; EH 138).

One of these anti-Montanists, Praxeas (EH 218[bis]), prevented Montanus from receiving the letter of communion from the Roman Church and was responsible for his condemnation. But he spread the Monarchian doctrine of the Logos (Father and Son only names for different ways *[modi]* of God's self-revelation: *pater passus est,* Patripassianism) which had already been taught by Noetus (of Smyrna) in Italy and Africa. He was opposed by Tertullian (cf. infra § 30) who was also a vigorous adversary of Gnosticism.

P. de Labriolle, *Les sources de l'hist. du Montanisme,* 1913, and *La crise Montaniste,* 1913. N. Bonwetsch (KlT 129) 1914. Bardy, DTC 10, 2355/70. A. Faggiotto, *L'eresia dei Frigi,* R 1924; *La diaspora catafrigia,* R 1924. W. Schepelern, *Der Montanismus u. die phryg. Kulte,* 1929. Bacht, TQ 1944 and Sch 19, 1/18 (prophetic inspiration in pre-Montanist time). W. Bauer 1934, 136/40. Peterson, RQ 1934, 173/6 and Grégoire, Byz 1935, 247/50 (2 Montanist inscriptions?). A. Hollard, *Deux hérétiques: Marcion et Montan,* 1935. Kuehnert, TLZ 1949, 436/46 (The anon. author in Euseb., *Hist.* 5, 16). Freeman, DSO 1950, 297/316 (Montanism and the Phryg. cults). Freeman-Grenville, JEH 5, 1954, 7/15 (The date of the outbreak of Montanism). Aland, ZNTW 46, 1955, 109/16 (Montanism and the theol. of Asia Minor). Kraft, TZ 1955, 249/71 (prophecy and Montanism).

The followers of Gnosticism, intent on the philosophical knowledge of religion (γνῶσις as opposed to πίστις), discarded revelation as the basis of all theological knowledge, watering down its contents by allegorical exegesis, and mixed up what was left with pagan philosophical tenets and elements of Oriental cults. Thus, helped by a vivid imagination, the Gnostics fashioned new systems of thought that allowed for manifold nuances. The false gnosis is concerned especially with the questions of the origin of the world and of evil, and of the nature of salvation. The answers it gave envisaged mostly a dualism of God and the world, the good God and the evil Creator-Demiurge, of spirit and matter, of the Saviour Jesus and the heavenly Aeon Christ. Gnosticism was very widespread both in the East and in the West, especially among the educated. Its literature was the first Christian theological literature in existence and in the second century much larger than the orthodox one. As far as we know the Gnostics were also the first to cultivate Christian poetry and a widespread popular religious literature comprising the apocryphal Acts of Christ and the Apostles as well as Apocalypses (cf. § 9, 10, 12). The intellectual and spiritual culture of Gnosticism, whose monuments have perished in its struggle with the Church except for relatively few remains, was so vigorous and elevated that its conquest by the Church and her small army is celebrated as a convincing proof of her divine origin. The Hellenization of the East, initiated by Alexander the Gt. (336–23 B.C.), produced in the religious sphere the fusion of the Eastern religions with Greek philosophy and mysticism (syncretism) which had far-reaching results when its encounter with Christianity transformed it into Gnosticism.

Some works of the voluminous Gnostic literature were discovered in the sands of Egypt and only published in the nineteenth century. In most recent times, after the second World War, the number of original Gnostic documents has unexpectedly been greatly increased by further happy finds in Egypt. In most cases we have probably to do with Coptic translations of Greek texts. Unfortunately the publication of the papyri which are mostly preserved in Cairo will probably be delayed for a long time.

W. Voelker, *Quellen zur Gesch. der christl. Gnosis,* 1932. Bousset, PWK 7, 1503/47. Bareille, DTC 6, 1434/67. Leclercq, DAL 6, 1327/67. Cerfaux, DBSuppl II, 659/701. A. Hilgenfeld, *Die Ketzergesch. des Urchristentums,* 1884. J. P. Steffes, *Das Wesen des Gnostizismus,* 1922. H. Leisegang, *Die Gnosis,* [3]1955. E. de Faye, *Gnostiques et Gnosticisme,* [2]1925. F. C. Burkitt, *Church and Gnosis,* 1932. A. Ehrhard 1932, 122/227. H. Jonas, *Gnosis u. spaetantiker Geist,* 1934. Casey, JTS 1935, 45/60 (The Study of G.). v. Loewenich, 1932, 60/115. Torm, ZNTW 1936, 70/5 (γνωστικός). Bergh von Eysinga, NTT 1939, 301/31 (The Epistle to the Hebrews in Gnosticism). S. Pétrement, *Le dualisme chez Platon, les Gnostiques et les Manichéens,* 1947. Stuermer, TLZ 1948, 581/92. Amand, *Fatalisme,* 1945, 228/57, Till, ParPass 1949, 230/49 (Gnosticism in Egypt). H. Soederberg, *La religion des Cathares,* 1949 (survival of Gnost. ideas). L. Tondelli, *Gnostici,* Tu 1950. H. Kraft, *Gnost. Gemeinschaftsleben (im 2. Jh.),* thesis Hei 1950. G. Quispel, *Gnosis als Weltreligion,* Zu 1951. Widengren, ZRGG 1952, 97/114 (Iran. background of Gnosticism). Haenchen, ZTK 1952, 316/49 (pre-Christian Gnost.?);

id., ZTK 1953, 123/58 (Book of Baruch and Christ. Gnost.). Grant, CH 22, 1953, 81/98 (Earliest Christ. Gnost.). Orbe, Gr 1954, 18/55 (wings of soul in Gnost.; on Plot. II 9, 3, 18ff.). Frend, JEH 1953, 13/26 (Gnost.-Manich. tradition in N. Africa); id., ibid. 1954, 25/37 (Gnost. sects and the Roman Empire). Bouyer, JTS 1953, 188/203 (Gnosis. Le sens orthodoxe de l'expression jusqu'aux Pères Alexandrins). Quispel, EvTheol 14, 1954, 474/84 (Christ. Gnost. and Jewish heterodoxy). H. Jonas, *Gnosis u. spaetantiker Geist,* I: *Die mythol. Gnosis,* [2]1954; II: *Von der Mythologie zur myst. Philosophie,* 1954. W. Kingsland, *The Gnosis or Ancient Wisdom in the Christian Scriptures or the Wisdom in a Mystery,* Lo 1954. Wilson, VC 1955, 193/211 (Gnost. originated in Christ. sphere). Id., VC 1957, 93/100 (origin of Gnosticism). R. M. Grant, *Gnosticism and Early Christianity,* NY 1959.

The original Gnostic literature, so much of which has been discovered especially in most recent times, is almost always anonymous. Only few genuine works of the heads of schools and sects have been preserved.

1. Simon Magus appeared in Samaria (cf. Acts 8: 9–24) and in Rome under the Emperor Claudius (Just., *1 Apol.* 26, 56). The *Great Revelation* used by Hippolytus, *Philos.* 6, 7–20 can hardly be considered genuine.

Texts partly in Voelker, *Quellen* (v. supra) 1–11. Quispel, NTT 1951, 338/45 (Simon and Helena).

2. Basilides, 120–145 in Alexandria, wrote a *Gospel* and a *Commentary* on it (Exegetica in 24 books) and *Psalms* or *Odes* (EH 109/13).

Texts in Voelker, 1932, 38/57. — Mg. by P. Hendrix, thesis Dordrecht 1926. Quispel, EranosJb 16, 1948, 89/139 (the doctrine of B.). Waszink, RACh 1, 1217/25. Quispel, VC 1948, 114f.

3. Isidore, the son and disciple of Basilides (Hipp., *Philos.* 7, 20), wrote an *Ethics,* also *An Explanation of the Prophet Parchor* and *On the In-grown Soul.*

Fragm. in Voelker, 1932, 38f. — Hendrix 1926, 85/92.

4. Epiphanes, who died aged seventeen, the son of the heresiarch Carpocrates, whose existence cannot be doubted, advocated community of property and wives in his treatise *On Justice.*

Texts in Voelker, 1932, 33/38. — H. Liboron, *Die karpokrat. Gnosis,* 1938. Kraft, TLZ 1952, 434/43 (Was there a Gnostic Carpocrates?).

5. Valentinus came from Alexandria and lived in Rome about 135–60. He taught a richly developed doctrine of Aeons. His dualism was mitigated by the influence of Platonism. He composed *Letters, Homilies* and *Psalms*. The *Gospel of Truth* contained in the recently discovered Coptic *Jung Codex* is probably a genuine work of Valentinus, written in Rome 140–5 (cf. Iren., *Haer.* 3, 11, 9). It has also been preserved among the MSS of Chenoboskion (v. infra).

Texts in Voelker, 1932, 57/136. — Quispel, VC 1947, 43/73 and EranosJb 15' 1947, 249/86 (Man in Valentinian Gnost.). F.-M. Sagnard, *La gnose valent. et le témoignage de S. Irénée,* 1947. Festugière, VC 1949, 193/207 (on the fragm. of Valent. in Clement Alex.). F. L. Cross, *The Jung Codex,* Lo 1955 (with contributions of Puech-Quispel-van Unnik). Puech-Quispel, *Opzoek naar het Ev. der Waarheid,* Nijkerk 1954. Quispel, ZRGG 6, 1954, 289/305 (on *Cod. Jung*). van Unnik, MeldKonNederlAkWetenschLetterk 17, 3, 1954, 71/101 (on Gospel of Truth). Orbe, *En los albores de la exegesis joh.* (Jo. 1, 3). *Est. valentinianos* II, R 1955 (Anal. Greg. 65). Id., *Los primeros herejes ante la persecución,* 1956 (AnalGreg. 83). *Evangelium veritatis,* ed. Malinine-Puech-Quispel, Zu 1956. Hennecke, ^{3}1959, 160/66. W. Till, ZntW 1959, 165/85 (new trans. of complete text). H. M. Schenke, *Die Herkunft des sog. Ev. veritatis,* Go 1959.

6. Disciples of Valentinus in the West (Italy): Ptolemy, whose *Letter to Flora* is preserved in Epiphanius, *Haer.* 33, 3–7 (criticism of the Mosaic Law), Secundus, Heracleon and Florinus (Euseb., *Hist.* 5, 20, 4), in the East: Theodotus and Marcus.

Texts: *Ep. ad Floram* in KlT 9, 1912 (ed. Harnack) and in SCh 1949 (ed. G. Quispel). F. Sagnard, *Extraits de Théodote* in SCh 1948. Cesarini, *Boll. di stud. storico-relig.* 1, 1922, 155/71 (Marcus). W. Foerster, *Von Valentin zu Herakleon,* 1928. R. P. Casey, *The Excerpta ex Theodoto of Clem. Alex.,* 1934. Edsman 1940, 15/9 (on Theodot.). Hering, HistPhilRel 21, 1941, 192/206 (on *Ep. ad Floram*). F. Fliedner, *Die ketzergeschichtl. Angaben des Agapius u. das System des Florinus,* thesis Mr 1942. Quispel, NTT 8, 1953/4 (Mandaeans and Valentinians); id., ZRGG 1954, 289/305 *(Cod. Jung)*. Puech-Quispel, VC 1954, 1/54 (*Cod. Jung:* three of the works it contains come from the school of Valentinus). F. L. Cross, *The Jung Codex, A Primary Source for the Study of Gnosticism* (with contributions of Puech, Quispel and van Unnik), Lo 1954. Collantes, EE 1953, 65/83, 339/45 (Heracleon on Jo. 1, 3 and 4, 35). Moussaon, ETL 1954, 301/22 (Jo. Bapt. in Heracleon). Puech-Quispel, VC 1955, 65/102 (the 4th treatise in *Cod. Jung On the Three Natures;* author perh. Heracleon). Orbe, EE 1956, 5/36 (on Heracleon).

7. Bardesanes (Bar Daisan) of Edessa (d. 222). Together with his son Harmonius he gave his teaching in the form of 150 hymns which are partly known from Ephrem Syrus. It has recently been denied that he was a representative of authentic Gnostic dualism. His *Dialogue on Fate or the Book of the Laws of the Countries* is extant in the Syriac original; it shows him to have been an adherent of an astrological form of belief in fate. Bardesanes was essentially an astrologer and philosopher of a practical Christian attitude. V. supra § 8, 2 *(Odes of Sol.)* and § 10, 6.

Text: F. Nau, *Bardesane, Le livre des lois des pays,* 1931. German by H. Wiesmann in: *75 Jahre Stella Matutina* I, 1931, 553/72. — Treatises: Nau, DTC 2, 391/401. Cerfaux, RACh 1, 1180/6. Schaeder, ZKG 1932, 21/73. G. v. Wesendonk, *B. u. Mani: Acta Orientalia* 10, 1932, 336/63. W. Bauer 1934, 33/8. L. Tondelli, *Mani Rapporti con Bardesane . . .,* Mi 1932, Rehm, Phil. 1938, 218/47 (B. and the Pseudo-Clement. lit.). Furlani, *Arch. Orientalni* 1937, 347/52 (B.'s Stoicism). Amand, *Fatalisme,* 1945, 228/57.

8. Marcion is a Gnostic who exhibits special characteristics. He emphasized practical religious aims and was not encumbered by the fantastic doctrines of the Aeons and an exaggerated allegorical exegesis of Scripture. He was excommunicated by his own father (Bishop of Sinope), but at first given a friendly reception by the Roman community *c.* 139, though here, too, he was excommunicated as early as 144. The main characteristics of his teaching are his opposition to Judaism and a radical rejection of the O.T. To the irate just Creator God of the Jews (Demiurge) he opposes the hitherto unknown God of love who revealed himself in Christ, and whose body was but a phantom. Marcion produced his own N.T. (Gospel acc. to St. Luke omitting chs. 1–2 and ten Pauline Epistles without Heb. and the Pastorals) and sought to give his teaching a better basis in his *Antitheses* (oppositions between O.T. and N.T.). The separate church which he established was the most important heretical foundation of the time and the one that was most dangerous to the Catholic Church; it survived for centuries.

One of Marcion's disciples, Apelles, wrote *Syllogisms* (critique of O.T.) and *Revelations* (of the alleged prophetess Philumene).

A. Harnack, *Marcion*, [2]1924. E. Barnikol, *Die Entstehung der Kirche im 2. Jh. u. die Zeit Marcions*, [2]1933; *Philipper 2. Der marcionit. Ursprung des Mythos-Satzes Phil. 2, 6f.*, 1932. Lagrange, RB 1932, 5/30. R. S. Wilson, *Marcion*, Lo 1933. W. Bauer 1934, 135f., 224/7. A. Hollard, *Deux hérétiques: Marcion et Montan*, 1935. Couchoud, HJ 1936, 265/77; cf. Loisy, HJ 1936, 378/87. Kayser, TSK 1938, 370/86 (ritual of bapt.). Knox, JBL 1939, 193/201 (Did Marcion use a primitive Gospel of Luke, *Ur-Lukas?*). Rist, JR 1942, 39/62 (Pseudoepigr. Refutations of M.). J. Knox, *M. and the NT*, C 1942. Enslin, ATR 27, 1945, 1/16. E. C. Blackman, *Marcion and his Infl.*, Lo 1949. P. W. Evans, *Some Lessons from Marcion*, Birmingham 1950 (?) (16 pp.). Scherer, JJurPapyr. 4, 1950, 229/33 (on 2 Cor. 12: 19 in Marc.). Vogels in: *Festschr. A. W. Wikenhauser*, 1954, 278/89 (Marcion's and Tatian's infl. on the NT). Bardy, DBSuppl 5, 1954, 862/77.

9. Gnostic Writings preserved in Coptic translation

Till 1850 the Gnostic literature was known only from the fragments found in the refutations of ecclesiastical authors, especially of Irenaeus, Tertullian, Hippolytus and Epiphanius (but see § 9ff.). Since then there have been edited two Coptic MSS belonging to the second half of the fourth and to the fifth–sixth centuries respectively and containing four major treatises.

a. The *Cod. Askewianus* in London (former owner A. Askew) contains three books of the *Pistis Sophia*, conversations of the risen Christ with his men and women disciples, especially with John and Mary Magdalene; they concern the fall and redemption of *Pistis Sophia*, a being belonging to the world of aeons (date: second half of third cent.). The fourth book of the same MS is an independent work containing the revelations of Jesus to his disciples on the subject of penance (from the first half of the third century).

b. The *Cod. Brucianus* (formerly property of J. Bruce) in Oxford contains two books of the *Mystery of the Great Logos* which, according to Carl Schmidt, is identical with the *Books of Jeû* cited in the *Pistis Sophia*. The second treatise of this MS, extant only in a mutilated form, probably originated in the circles of the Sethians (written between 170 and 200), while the first three treatises mentioned here are apparently to be assigned to the sect of the Barbelo-Gnostics.

c. A third *Pap. Copt. Berolin. 8502,* shortly to be publ. in TU by W. Till, contains the following pieces: 1. *Gospel of Mary;* 2. *Apocryphon of John;* 3. *Sophia of Jesus Christ.*

Texts: C. Schmidt-W. Till, *Kopt.-gnost. Schriften* (GCS), ²1954; *Pistis Sophia* (only Copt.), Copenhagen 1925; L 1925 (trans.). G. Horner, Lo 1924 (Engl.). C. Baynes, C 1933 (second work of *Cod. Brucianus*). H. R. Mead, *Pistis Sophia*, Lo 1947 (Engl.). C. H. Roberts, *Catalogue of Greek and Lat. Papyri* . . . III, Manchester 1938, No. 463 (Gr. fragms. from the *Gospel of Mary*). Till, ParPass 1, 1946, 260/5 *(Gospel of Mary).* — Amann, DTC 11, 1063/75 (Ophites). Puech, AIP 1936, 935/62 (L'apocalypse d'Allogène). Ghedini, Aeg 1936, 334/7 (Gnost. influences). Roché, Cahiers d'Ét. Cathares 1950, 6. F. *(Pistis Sophia).* Hennecke, 1³, 168/73; 229/43; 251/55.

d. *The Library of Chenoboskion, found in 1946*

In 1946 an incredibly rich find of MSS came to light near the former Monastery of Pachomius Chenoboskion, not far from the present town of Nag-Hammadi, *c.* 30 miles north of Luxor. This contains about twelve papyrus MSS written in the third and at the beginning of the fourth century, which will be of the greatest importance for further research on Gnosticism. Today these MSS are preserved for the greater part in the Coptic Museum at Cairo.

Approximately one thousand pages contain about fifty different, mostly unknown works which originated in the circles of the Sethians and the Barbelo-Gnostics (Ophites). The documents belong to the most ancient Coptic witnesses. They are written in various dialects including treatises in a hitherto unknown idiom. Further research will have to clarify whether and in how far these are Coptic originals or translations from the Greek.

The titles of not a few of the newly discovered works are known from Irenaeus, Hippolytus, Plotinus and Epiphanius. Five different treatises are ascribed to Hermes Trismegistos. They will also furnish new evidence on Hermetic teaching. A number of writings have titles the same or akin to those of Christian apocrypha, but their contents are totally different. The new find contains, inter alia, a Gospel of the Egyptians, a Gospel of Philip, a Gospel of Thomas, Traditions of Matthias, Acts of Peter, a Letter of Peter to Philip, a Prayer of Peter, further Apocalypses of Peter, John, Paul, three different Apocalypses of James and one of Seth. There are, further, writings of Gnostic teachers: a *Letter of the blessed Eugnostes* and *Instructions of Silvanus*. The titles of other treatises only mention the subject, e.g., *Explanation of the Gnosis, Explanation of the Essence of the Soul, On the Nature of the Cosmos,* etc. On further writings contained in the *Cod. Jung* (now in Zurich) cf. § 24, nos. 5 and 6.

As far as we know the titles of the books of the Sethians from Hippolytus and Epiphanius, the literature of this Gnostic group seems to have been preserved almost completely. All the writings had evidently been the property of a Gnostic community. As Coptic scholars are hard at work on these MSS we shall probably soon receive much new information on the subject.

Treatises: Puech-Doresse, ComptR 1948, 87/95 *(Ép. d'Eugnoste, Dialogue du Sauveur, Év. des Égypt.)*. Doresse, VC 1948, 137/60 *(Év. des Égypt., Ép. d'Eugnoste, Sagesse de Jésus-Christ)*; id., BullInstit.d'Égypte 31, 1949, 409/19 (= *Ophites et Séthiens)*; ibid., NClio 1, 1949, 59/70; Doresse-Togo-Mina, VC 1949, 129/41. Doresse, BullByzantInst. 2, Boston 1950, 91/154; id., AcadBelgique 36, 1950, 432/9; CoptStudHonor of E. Crum, W 1950, 255/63 *(Apocalypses de Zoroastre, de Zostrien, de Nicothée)*. Puech, CoptStudHonor of E. Crum, 1950, 91/154 *(Essai d'identification)*. Graf, MTZ 1950, 91/5. Altaner, TR 1950, 41f. Till, JEH 9, 1952, 14/22 (Apocryphon of John). Foerster, TLZ 1954, 377/84 (bibliogr. report on the MSS of Chenoboskion). Pericoli-Ridolfini, RivStudOrient 30, 1955, 269/96 (on the latest Coptic-Gnostic finds). Hennecke, 1[3], *Gnost. Ev. nach Thomas,* ed. Guillanmont *et al.,* Lei 1959. H. M. Schenke, ThLZ 1958, 661/70; 1959, 1/26; 243/56 (Trans.: "Das Wesen der Archonten", "Das Ev. nach Philippus", "Vom Ursprung der Welt").

The anti-Gnostic literature of the second century is for the greater part lost; but some important pieces have been preserved, especially in the anti-Gnostic writings of Tertullian, Irenaeus and Clement of Alex. These were especially intended to safeguard faith in the one God, the Creator of the world and the Lawgiver of the Old Covenant, to establish the sources from which the

Christian revelation is derived (determining the Canon) and to prove the teaching authority of the Church (apostolic succession of bishops, tradition). Her struggle against the false gnosis even more than the activities of the Apologists forced the Church into the way of learning (Christian gnosis).

§ 25. SECOND CENTURY PAPAL AND EPISCOPAL WRITINGS AGAINST MONTANISM, GNOSTICISM AND OTHER HERESIES

1. Soter (*c.* 166–74) sent, together with a charitable gift, a letter to Corinth, an account of which is given in the fragments of the reply of Dionysius of Corinth (Eus., *Hist.* 4, 23, 9f.; EH 61). According to the untrustworthy statement of the *Praedestinatus* (v. § 91, 4) he is supposed to have written a treatise against the Montanists. It seems, however, that the Pope wrote against them in an encyclical (cf. Tertull., *Prax.* 1). On Soter and the *Second Letter of Clement* v. supra § 15, 2.

2. Eleutherus (*c.* 174–89) who, like Soter, seems to have opposed Montanism in a Letter, received in this connexion the priest Irenaeus as a delegate of the Martyrs of Lyons (177–8) who advocated a more lenient attitude (Eus., *Hist.* 5, 3, 4 – 4, 2; EH 65).

3. Victor I (*c.* 189–98) wrote in the course of the Easter controversy several letters which are important for the history of the Papal primacy. If Jerome (*Vir. ill.* 34) tells us that he had written *super quaestione paschae et alia quaedam opuscula* he presumably means his epistles (Eus., *Hist.* 5, 23–25). One of Victor's letters condemned the teaching of the Monarchian Theodotus, the tanner of Byzantium (Eus., *Hist.* 5, 28, 6 and 9). It remains doubtful if Victor wrote this in Latin (Jerome, *Vir. ill.* 53).

4. According to a none too reliable account (Optatus, *Contra Parm.* 1, 9), Zephyrinus (*c.* 198–217) defended the Catholic faith

against heretics in several treatises. A declaration which he made during the struggle with Sabellius gave rise to much controversy; it concerned the unity of the essence in God and the divinity of Christ (Hippol., *Ref.* 9, 11, 3; ES 3036), but is certainly not to be understood in a modalistic way.

Text: P. Coustant-Schoenemann, *Pontificum Rom. Epistolae,* 1796, 78ff. — Trans.: S. Wenzlowsky, *Die Briefe der Paepste* 1 (BKV) 1875. Cf. supra § 3 the works of E. Caspar and F. X. Seppelt. E. Lacoste, *Les Papes à travers les âges,* II: *De S. Pie à S. Fabien,* 1929. G. Buonocore, *Da S. Pio I a S. Vittore I,* Siena 1932. C. Schmidt, *Gespraeche Jesu,* 1919, 577/725 (Paschal controversy). Zernov, CQR 116, 1933, 24/41 (Paschal contr.). Butler, DR 1951, 393/410 (against Zernov). B. Lohse, *Das Passahfest der Quartodezimaner,* G 1953. — La Piana, HTR 1925, 201/77. — On the declaration of Zephyrinus: Harnack, SbB 1923, 51/7. Capelle, RBn 1926, 321/30. H. Koch, RR 1929, 50/9.

5. Dionysius of Corinth, the contemporary of Soter of Rome, is outstanding among non-Roman bishops. Eus., *Hist.* 4, 23, 8 gives some information on seven encyclicals and a private letter; a reply from Bishop Pinytus of Cnossus is also mentioned here. Mention should also be made of Bishop Serapion of Antioch (*c.* 190–211). His Letter to the church of Rhossus forbidding the reading of the *Gospel of Peter* is of special importance (supra § 9, 5; Eus., *Hist.* 6, 12).

A. Harnack, *Die Briefsammlung des Apostels Paulus . . .,* 1926, 36/40. W. Bauer 1934, 128/31 and freq. (Dionysius of Corinth). J. Hoh 1932, 87/9 (Dionysius).

§ 26. HEGESIPPUS

THE names of a number of anti-Gnostic defenders of the faith, all of whose writings are lost, are known to us especially through Eusebius. Agrippa Castor (Eus., *Hist.* 4, 7, 6–8) wrote against Basilides. Philip of Gortyna, Modestus (ibid. 4, 25) and Rhodon from Asia Minor, a disciple of Tatian (ibid. 5, 13), wrote against Marcion. Musanus opposed the Encratites (ibid. 4, 28). Candidus, Apion, Sextus and Heraclitus published works probably also directed against the Gnostics (ibid. 5, 27). Larger fragments are extant only of the *Memoirs* of Hegesippus, MSS of which were probably still extant in Greek monasteries in the sixteenth and seventeenth centuries.

Hegesippus came from the East; he was probably a Jew by birth, since he knew Aramaic. Under Pope Anicetus (*c.* 154–66) he came to Rome via Corinth, in order to learn the true faith, as the Gnostic sects were spreading far and wide. Having returned home he wrote his five books of *Memoirs* (Ὑπομνήματα) *c.* 180. They contained much information on Church history, but in the main they were anti-Gnostic polemical treatises.

Here he wanted to gather the fruits of his journey, namely "the sound doctrine, such as it has been handed down from the apostles". Like later Irenaeus, he too, saw the best guarantee of the truth of the Church's doctrine in the uninterrupted succession of the bishops from the apostles. Eusebius (*Hist.* 4, 22, 3) reproduced from this work, inter alia, the much discussed passage γενόμενος δὲ ἐν Ῥώμῃ διαδοχὴν ἐποιήσαμεν μέχρις Ἀνικήτου (EP 188; EH 69f.). According to the investigations of C. H. Turner and E. Caspar, in the time of Eusebius διαδοχή meant not a succession of persons of the same kind, but had approximately the same sense as παράδοσις, i.e. handing on, or better "continuing to receive from hand to hand". The pure doctrine is the object of the διαδοχή. What Hegesippus means to say is, in paraphrase: "On the occasion of my stay in Rome I convinced myself that there has been an uninterrupted diadoche of the pure doctrine from the apostles to the present, i.e. to Anicetus." The exponents and guarantors of the pure teaching were evidently the bishops, whose list of succession Hegesippus certainly found already in Rome *c.* 160, just as later Irenaeus (*Haer.* 3, 3, 3), without having to make investigations of his own. Only in and after Eusebius is there a change of meaning: διαδοχή no longer = παράδοσις, but κατάλογος.

Fragm. in Routh I, 207/19; T. Zahn, Forsch. zur Gesch. des ntl. Kanons 6, 243/6, and E. Preuschen, *Antileg.*[2] 107/13. On *Diadoche* and lists of Popes: C. H. Turner in H. B. Swete, *Essays on the Early Hist. of the Church*, 1918, 207ff. E. Caspar, *Die aelteste roem. Bischofsliste*, 1926, 233ff., 443ff. Leclercq, DAL 9, 1207/36. Klauser, BoZ 1931, 193/213. Kohlmeyer, TSK 1931, 230/43. J. Ranft, *Der Ursprung des kath. Traditionsprinzips*, 1931. W. Bauer 1934, 199f., 216f. H. J. Bardsley 1935 (supra § 9). Buonaiuti, Rel 1936, 401/13 (Marcion and H.); see also infra § 27f.; Hermann, RevUnivBrux 1937, 387/94 *(La famille du Christ)*. Koepp, RACh 2, 407/15 (list of bishops). v. Campenhausen, Mem. E. Loh. 1951, 240/9; id., *Kirchliches Amt . . .*, 1953 (v. supra § 3, 21). Stauffer, ZRGG 1952, 193/214 (caliphate of James).

§ 27. IRENAEUS OF LYONS

IRENAEUS is the most important of the second century theologians and in a certain sense the Father of Catholic dogmatics. He came from Asia Minor and had been a disciple of Polycarp in his youth (Eus., *Hist.* 5, 20, 5ff.). In the time of Marcus Aurelius he was a priest at Lyons and as legate of the martyrs in Lyon, went to Rome on account of the Montanist controversy (supra § 25, 2). In 177–8 he became the successor of the martyr bishop Photinus of Lyons.

As a bishop he interested himself especially in the struggle against the false gnosis. After Victor I had placed the Christians of Asia Minor under the ban because of the Easter controversy he exhorted the Pope to make peace with them. Nothing certain is known about his later life. The report that he died a martyr (*c.* 202) appears very late, in Gregory of Tours (*Hist. Franc.* 1, 27; *In glor. mart.* 50).

Irenaeus wrote several works in his native Greek, only two of which have been preserved.

1. *Unmasking and Refutation of the False Gnosis,* usually called *Adversus haereses* (Ἔλεγχος καὶ ἀνατροπὴ τῆς ψευδωνύμου γνώσεως).

We possess this work in full only in a quite literal Latin translation which, however, cannot yet be dated with certainty (Sanday: *c.* 200; H. Koch: before 250; Souter: 370–420; Altaner:

before 396). But there are many fragments of the Greek text (e.g. almost the whole first book and others) in later ecclesiastical authors (Hippolytus, Eusebius, especially Epiphanius, also in *catenae*). To this must be added an Armenian translation of the fourth and fifth books which faithfully reproduces the original, as well as twenty-three pieces preserved in Syriac.

The book was written at the request of a friend who wanted to know the Gnostic system of Valentinus (EP 191/262; EH 102/36). Irenaeus develops this system in the first book, opposes to it a résumé of the doctrine of the Church, and then gives a survey of the history of Gnosticism from Simon Magus onwards. This unmasking of the Gnostic doctrines is followed by their refutation in Books Two to Five, which is based in Book Two on reason, in Book Three on tradition and the teaching of the apostles, and in Book Four on sayings of our Lord (also passages from the prophets of the Old Covenant); the fifth book deals with the Last Things, especially the resurrection of the body; here the author represents Chiliasm.

These five books are no more a homogeneous work than the apologies of Justin; the individual parts grow gradually by way of enlargements and additions. Irenaeus' knowledge of Gnostic theology is partly based on his own reading of Gnostic writings; but he is also familiar with the older ecclesiastical literature (Clement of Rome, Ignatius, Polycarp, Papias, Pastor Hermae, Justin, Ps.-Justin *[De resurrectione]*, Hegesippus). Whether Theophilus of Antioch's treatise *Against Marcion* (supra § 22, 5) was of such profound importance for his knowledge and theology as F. Loofs attempts to show is very questionable. All later writers against heresy, beginning with Tertullian, have taken their material for the earlier period from Irenaeus.

Ed.: R. Massuet, P 1710 in MG 7. A. Stieren, 2 vols., 1948/53. W. Harvey, 2 vols., C 1857; new impression C 1949. F. Sagnard, SCh 34, 1952 (crit. ed. of 3rd bk.), cf. RhE 1953, 141/50 and RTA 1953, 185/201. B. Reynders, *Lexique comparé du texte grec et des versions lat., armén. et syriaque*, 2 vols., Lou 1954. —

Armen. text: H. Jordan in TU 35, 2, 1910, and 36, 3, 1913. PO 12, 1919, 732/44. — Transs. E. Klebba (BKV² 3/4), 1912. Engl. M. Hitchcock (SPCK), 2 vols., 1916. Bayan-Froidevaux, ROC 29, 315/77; 30, 1946, 285/340 (trans. of Armen. text). — Mgs. and treatises: Vernet, DTC 7, 2394/533. Leclercq, DAL 10, 127/43. On Lat. text: A. Sanday and Turner, edd. Nov. Test. S. Irenaei, O 1923. H. Koch, TSK 1929, 462/69 (Lat. trans. before 250). Klostermann, ZNTW 1937, 1/34 (MSS). Hitchcock, Ha 1939, 93/100 (St. Patrick and the Lat. Ir.). S. Lundstroem, *Studien zur lat. Ir.-Uebers.*, Lund 1943; Er 1945, 285/300; *Neue Stud. z. lat. Ir.-Uebers.*, Lund 1948. R. Forni, *Problemi della tradizione. Ir. di L.*, 1939. Olivar, Sc 1949, 11–25 (new MSS). Altaner, TQ 1949, 167f. (Lat. trans. before 396). — On source criticism and textual exegesis: F. Loofs, *Theophilus v. Antiochien u. die anderen theol. Quellen bei Ir.*, 1930; against this Hitchcock, JTS 1937, 130/9 255/66; ZNTW, 1937, 35/60; v. also supra § 22, 5. Audet, Tr 1943, 15/54. Reynders, RTA 1935, 5/27 (method of polemics). Enslin, HTR 1947, 137/65 (prolegomena). Grant, HTR 1949, 41/51 (Hellenistic culture). Nautin, RTA 1953, 185/202 (on 3rd book); VC 1955, 34/6 (on ed. of Sagnard). Schlier, BeihZNTW 21, 1954, 67/82 (on Ir., *Haer.* 1, 23f.). Daniélou, RSR 1954, 193/203 (on Ir., *Haer.* 4, 34, 4). Botte, RTA 1954, 165/78 (text. crit. of *Haer.*). Perrat et Austin, Cahiers d'hist. 1956, 227/51 *(St. Ir. L'hist. et la légende)*.

2. *Presentation of the Apostolic Preaching* (Ἐπίδειξις τοῦ ἀποστολικοῦ κηρύγματος), mentioned by Eus., *Hist.* 5, 26, ed. in Armenian translation in 1907.

The treatise, which presupposes earlier preliminary studies on which it is based, is divided into a theological part (monarchy, Trinity, baptism) and a Christological part (Jesus, the Lord, the Son of David, the Christ, the Son of God; the glory of the Cross and the kingdom of God). It is catechetical, edifying, and at the same time apologetic, but avoids any direct polemics and proves the truth of the gospel from O.T. passages (EP 263).

Edd.: TU 31, 1, 1907. PO 12, 1919, 655/731 (with Engl. trans.); S. Weber in BKV² 4, 1912 (German trans.); 1917 (Lat. trans.). Engl. trans. and commentary (ACW 16) by J. P. Smith, 1952. — Froidevaux, RSR 1951, 368/80 (on § 31, 33, 89). On No. 1 Strobel, ZKG 1957, 139/43 (Greek fragm.). Le Froideraux, SCh 62, 1959 (epid.). Reynders, *Vocabulaire de la "Démonstration" et les fragments de St Ir.*, Chevetogne 1958.

3. Of the other writings of Irenaeus we have fragments, some of them important, especially those from his letters (cf. e. g. Eus., *Hist.* 5, 20 24; EP 264/6; EH 96). The so-called *Pfaff Fragments* which were published by the Tuebingen professor C. M. Pfaff,

allegedly from Turin MSS, in 1715, have been proved to be forgeries (A. Harnack in TU 20, 3, 1900). On fragments from other writings cf. H. I. Bell and T. S. Skeat 1935 (supra § 9, 1c); Martin, RHE 1942, 143/52.

Points of Doctrine

1. In the third book of *Adv. haereses* Irenaeus treats extensively of the principle of tradition that had already been formulated by Hegesippus. In his view the doctrinal tradition of the apostles continued in the Church is the source and norm of the faith. The true tradition of the faith is particularly the concern of those churches that were founded by the apostles; for the uninterrupted succession of the bishops of these churches from the apostles guarantees the truth of their teaching. But since it would be too difficult to give the lists of the bishops of all the churches founded by the apostles, he will prove (3, 3, 1–2) only "of the greatest and very old Church in Rome which is known to all and was founded by the glorious apostles Peter and Paul" that the succession of its bishops goes back to the apostles and hence its teaching too, is apostolic.

Then follows the well-known sentence which unfortunately is not extant in the original text: *Ad hanc enim ecclesiam propter potentiorem (potiorem) principalitatem necesse est omnem convenire ecclesiam, hoc est eos, qui sunt undique fideles, in qua semper ab his qui sunt undique, conservata est ea quae est ab apostolis traditio* and the list of succession of the Roman bishops (3, 3, 3; EH 124/6; EP 209/11). The relative clause *in qua semper* is referred by some scholars to the Roman Church *(ad hanc)*, by others to *omnem ecclesiam*. In the first case, which is more probable, we may translate thus with A. Ehrhard: "For all (other) churches everywhere must agree with this Church because of its more effective leadership, since in it Christians everywhere have preserved intact the apostolic tradition." It is clear from the general context that

Irenaeus does not here speak of the legal obligation of the other churches to agree with the Roman Church in matters of faith; he rather means to say that the statement of the faith of the Roman Church at the same time guarantees the existence of the same faith of all other apostolic churches. In order to prove that the freely invented Gnostic speculations are untenable, it would in fact be sufficient for Irenaeus to show the totally different tradition of the faith of any apostolic church. But so as to refute more effectively the Gnostic theories which utterly defy all apostolic tradition, he emphasizes the unique position of the Roman Church among the other communities founded by the apostles. Thus he stresses the more effective leadership *(potentior principalitas)* of this Church, which for him evidently results from the double apostolicity (Peter and Paul) that distinguishes it; besides, he emphasizes the co-operation of members of many churches who gather there and who help to keep pure the apostolic tradition.

It is true, the passage does not attest and establish the Roman primacy directly and immediately, especially as Irenaeus concentrates his thought not on the question of ecclesiastical constitution, but on the proof of the faith which is common to all individual churches and which is diametrically opposed to Gnosticism. Nevertheless, the fact remains that we have here the first, though theologically very imperfect, foundation of the pre-eminence of Rome. Since for Irenaeus everything depends on the apostolicity of doctrine, this form of argumentation was the most obvious, and also the most effective one in view of the Gnostics. Already Tertullian and the anonymous author in Euseb., *Hist.* 5, 28, 3 went a step further in that they were the first, as far as we know from our sources, to declare that Peter alone is the source and starting point of the series of Roman bishops (Tert., *Praescr.* 32).

From the number of recent attempts to make the *crux inter-*

pretum (3, 3, 2) more intelligible, we would here only refer to the fundamental idea of two authors who complement each other (Jacquin, AnT 1948, 95/8; RevSR 1950, 72/87 and Mohrmann, VC 1949, 57/61). According to these authors *ab his qui sunt undique* is supposed to describe a comparative (*ab* = *prae;* Greek probably = παρά). Miss Mohrmann is able to prove this use from vulgar Latin. The meaning would then be this: "In the Church of Rome the apostolic tradition has always been preserved, and better than in other churches formed by the faithful living in all parts of the world." This new hypothesis would have to be examined in the light of Greek linguistics, i.e. it would have to be shown that the Greek text, unfortunately still unknown, would warrant such a translation. In the wake of older authors (cf. RB 1908, 515/20 and TR 1909, 94 f.) — though these are unknown to him — Díaz y Díaz (RET 1954, 397/9) proposes to read *ubique* instead of the first *undique* and to eliminate the second *qui sunt undique* as an interpolation or a gloss. — The work of D. J. Unger, TSW 1952, 359/418, presents the example of an interpretation inspired by post-Vatican dogmatics.

L. Spikowski, *La doctrine de l'église dans S. Ir.,* Str 1926. A. Ehrhard 1932, 277. Wolf Schmidt, *Die Kirche bei Ir.,* Helsingfors 1934. Madoz, EE 1936, 360/6. Doyle, IER 1939, 298/306 (the Popes and the Heretics). Knox, JTS 1946, 180/4 (*Haer.* 3, 3, 2). Molland, *Festschr. J. Norregaard,* 1947, 157/76 (*successio apostolica*). G. Bardy, *La théol. de l'église de S. Ir. au concile de Nicée,* 1947. Holstein, RSR 1947, 454/61 (creeds); RSR 1949, 229/70 (apostol. tradition in Ir.); ibid. 1949, 122/35 (on 3, 3, 2); ibid. 1953, 410/20 (witnesses of revelation in Ir.). Katzenmeyer, IKZ 1948, 12/28 (Peter, Primacy, Church). Jacquin, AnT 1948, 95ff.; RevSR 1950, 72/87 (on 3, 3, 2). Mohrmann, VC 1949, 57/61 (3, 3, 1 f.); against this Galtier, RHE 1949, 411/28 (3, 3, 2). Molland, JEH 1950, 12/28 (apost. succession). Lanne, Ir 1952, 113/41 (apostol. office). Unger, TSW 1952, 359/418 (3, 3, 2). Díaz y Díaz, RET 1954, 393/99 (Lat. trans.: second half of 4th cent.; on 3, 3, 2). W. Leuthold, *Das Wesen der Haeresie nach Ir.,* thesis (typed), Zu 1954.

2. Doctrine of God. Irenaeus is not a speculative theologian, intent on acquiring new theological knowledge. In the main he is content to establish the Church's preaching of the faith on a Scriptural basis. His thoroughly practical religious point of view

is characterized by the following famous sentence (2, 26, 1): "It is better and more useful for a man to know little or nothing, while coming near to God through love, than to imagine that he knows much and has gained many experiences, and yet to be found a blasphemer and an enemy of God." He fights especially what he calls that fundamental teaching of the false gnosis, namely that the Maker of the world is one other than God. He clearly states the *circumincessio* (in late Scholasticism *circuminsessio)* of the divine Persons: "The Son is in the Father and bears the Father in him" (3, 6, 2).

3. Irenaeus has summed up and deepened the Christology of his predecessors. The redemption must be real and not only mediate gnosis. Now for a real redemption we need a God–man. Christ has become man so that mankind should be "deified"; this is the recapitulation, restoration and perfection of mankind and of the universe in Christ (*recapitulatio*, ἀνακεφαλαίωσις. Cf. Eph. 1, 10; Iren., *Haer*. 3, 18, 7). Because Christ did not surrender to the devils temptings he has become the counterpart of Adam (5, 21, 2); whereas the Virgin Mary has by her obedience made amends for the disobedience of the "virginal" Eve (v. supra § 21, 2. 6). Because of her obedience she is "advocata Evae" and "causa salutis" for the whole human race (5, 19, 1; 3, 22, 4).

F. Loofs 1930, 343/57 (doctrine of God, of the Logos, and Christology). G. N. Bonwetsch, *Die Theologie des Ir.,* 1925. Theory of recapitulation: Loofs 1930, 357/74. E. Mersch 1936, I², 315/48 and Staerk, ZNTW 1936, 90/5. N. F. Moholy, *The Doctrine of Recapitulation in St. Ir.,* thesis Laval Univ. 1948. Potter, DSO 1951, 192/200. — J. N. Bakhuizen van den Brink, *Incarnatie en Verlossing bij Ir.,* 1934. Rynders, RTA 1936, 225/52 (optimisme et théocentrisme). Pruemm, Sch 1938, 206/24, 342/66 (divine plan); DP 1939, 192/219 (terminology and essence of Christian newness). E. Scharl, *Recapitulatio mundi. Der Rekapitulationsbegriff des hl. Ir.,* 1941; partly in OCP 1940, 376/416 (= 6–39). Hunger, Sch 1942, 161/77 (unity of world plan and of Adam). Escuela, NRT 1939, 385/400, 551/67 *(Le verbe sauveur);* RSR 1940, 252/70 (natural knowledge of God). Peterson, SC 1941, 46/55 (conception of God). Audet, Tr 1943, 15/54 (orientat. théolog.). C. M. Ramsey, *The Concept of God and Salvation (in Ir.),* thesis Duke Univ. 1944. Amand, *Fatalisme,* 1945, 212/23. Unger, FS 1945, 3/20 (Christ's role in the universe). G. Wingren, *Maenniskan och Incarnat. enligt Ir.,* 1947; Svensk Theol.

Kvartalschr. 1946, 133/55 *(creatio, lex, incarnatio)*. Daniélou, RSR 1947, 227/31 (theology of history). T. Ruesch, *Die Entstehung der Lehre vom hl. Geist bei I., Theoph. v. Ant. u. Ir.*, Zu 1951. R. A. Markus, VC 1954, 193/224 (Pleroma and Fulfilment). W. Leuthold, *Das Wesen der Haeresie nach Iren.*, thesis Tu 1954. A. Houssiau, *La christologie de S. Ir.*, Lou 1955. — On Mariology: H. Koch, *Adhuc virgo*, 1929; cf. Jouassard, RevSR 1932, 509/32; 1933, 25/37. J. Garçon, *La Mariologie de S. Ir., 1932.* Génévois, RT 1936/51 *(Maternité universelle)*. B. Przybylski, *De Mariologia s. Ir.*, R 1937. H. Koch, *Virgo Eva-Maria*, 1937, 17/60; cf. K. Adam, TQ 1938, 171/89. Jouassard, *La théologie mariale de S. Ir.*, Lyons 1954 (14 pp.). Moholy, *First Franciscan Nation*. Marian Congress, Burlington (Wisc.) 1952, 129/87 (Ir., father of Mariology). Wingren, *Maenniskan*, tr. by Mackenzie: *Man and Incarnation*, Edinburgh 1959.

4. Irenaeus clearly attests the Catholic doctrine of original sin. The first men, created according to the *imago* and *similitudo Dei*, lost their *similitudo* through their sin, and Christ restored this (5, 2, 1; 5, 6, 1; 5, 16, 3). Infant baptism is here attested for the first time (2, 22, 4).

E. Klebba, *Die Anthropologie des hl. Ir.*, 1894. H. Koch, TSK 1925, 183/214. Gaudel, DTC 12, 322/9.

5. In Irenaeus the term γραφή for the O.T. is also applied to the writings of the N.T., which already form a complete collection. They share the character of inspiration with the books of the O.T. and are used as proof texts. What gives these writings their canonicity is not only their apostolic origin but also the tradition of the Church. Irenaeus adduces two groups of N.T. writings as Scripture, the gospels and the apostolic writings in which he seems to include the *Shepherd of Hermas*, but not the Epistle to Hebrews. *Haer.* 3, 11, 8 speaks of an εὐαγγέλιον τετράμορφον and derives the number four from the four cherubs, assigning the lion to John the Evangelist and the eagle to Mark, as well as from God's fourfold covenant with man: with Adam, Noe, Moses and Christ (EH 127/34).

J. Hoh, *Die Lehre des hl. Ir. ueber das NT*, 1919. B. Kraft, *Die Evv.-Zitate des hl. Ir.*, 1924. Loewenich 1932, 115/41. Curran, CBQ 1943, 34/46, 160/78, 301/10 (Dates of the Synoptics). J. Lawson, *The Biblical Theology of St. Ir.*, Lo 1948. K. T. Schaefer, *Festschr. M. Meinertz*, 1951, 50/9 (Ir.-citations and their value for the hist. of the NT text). Stenzel, TZ 1953, 88/90 (Lat. Dodecapropheton). Luckhart, RUO 1953, 65/79 (Mt. 11, 27). Houssiau, ETL 1953, 328/54 (Mt. 11, 27). Dulière, NClio 1954, 73/90 (Ir. does not know Mt. 16, 18 f.). Dulière, ibid. 199/224 (NT Canon and the Chr. writings recognized by Ir.). P. Ciani, *S. Ir. e il IV Vangelo,* Aversa 1955.

6. Irenaeus, following Paul, calls the eucharist a participation in the body and blood of the Lord. This, he says, would have no meaning if there were no resurrection of the dead (5, 2, 2); how could the Gnostics admit the bread over which the thanksgiving is spoken, to be the body of the Lord and the chalice to be the chalice of his blood if they do not hold him to be the Son of the Creator of the world? The eucharist "consists of two elements, one earthly and one heavenly" (4, 18, 4 f.). He sees in it the new sacrifice (*Haer.* 4, 17, 5 f.) that had been announced by Malachias (1, 10 f.): this consists essentially in this, that God the Father is offered representatives of his creation, viz. bread that has been changed into the flesh of Jesus and wine that has been changed into his blood.

7. Like Justin (supra § 21, 2) and Tertullian, Irenaeus, too, considers Hades to be the sojourn of souls, and like them he is a Chiliast (5, 32, 1; EP 259 f.).

J. Brinktrine, *Der Messopferbegriff in den ersten 2 Jhh.,* 1918, 127 ff. Simonin, RSPT 1934, 281/92 (on 4, 18, 4). Koole, GTT 1936, 295/303; 1938, 412/7 (Euch.). J. Hoh 1932, 89/103. G. Bardy 1935, 119/48. V. Cremers, BiNJ 1938, 28/80 *(Millénarisme).* Poschmann 1940, 211/29. On *Haer.* 4, 18, 4 f. cf. also v. d. Eynde, Ant 1940, 13/28 and Perler, DT 1940, 310/4. Hochban, TSW 1946, 525/57 (penance). K. Rahner, ZKT 1948, 450/5 and Holstein, RSR 1948, 282/8 (penance). Jugie, *Mémorial J. Chaine,* Lyons 1950, 223/44 *(La forme du sacrement de l'Eucharistie).* A. Benoît, *Le baptême au 2e siècle,* 1953. Sagnard, *35o Congr. Eucar. Intern. Sesiones de Est.* I, Ba 1954, 383/86 (on Jo 2). Jouassard, RSR 1954, 528/39 (on Ir.'s sacramental doctrine).

§ 28. THE MURATORIAN FRAGMENT AND THE ANCIENT PROLOGUES TO THE GOSPELS AND THE PAULINE EPISTLES

1. The *Muratorian Fragment.* The old lists of canonical books which came into being during the struggle against the Gnostic

apocryphal literature are of great importance for our knowledge of the history of the Canon. The oldest list of N.T. books known to us was published at Milan by L. A. Muratori from an eighth century MS in the Ambrosian Library in 1780. Four small fragments of the same text were found also in MSS of Monte Cassino belonging to the eleventh and twelfth centuries. The fragment of eighty-five lines is written in barbaric Latin and shocking orthography; it is mutilated at the beginning and end (supra § 24, 6 on the *Canon of Marcion*).

The enumeration of the sacred Scriptures which also takes into account their origin begins in the middle of its account of Mark; Heb., Jas. and 1 and 2 Pet. are missing. Apart from the Apoc. of John the *Sapientia Salomonis* is mentioned and also, though with reservations, the Apoc. of Peter. Paul's Epistles to the Alexandrians and the Laodiceans (supra § 12, 4) are rejected as Marcionite forgeries, as well as several other heretical writings. The *Pastor Hermae* (supra § 12, 4) is recognized only as commendable reading.

The pun *fel enim cum melle misceri non congruit* (67) can scarcely be accepted as a convincing argument against the theory of a Greek original. The remark (73ff.) that the *Pastor of Hermas* was written *nuperrime temporibus nostris* at Rome by the brother of Pope Pius I (*c.* 142–55) certainly does not allow us to date the Fragment later than 200. If a definite author may be suggested the most likely candidate would be the young Hippolytus (infra § 31, 7) (so Lightfoot, T. Robinson, T. Zahn, N. Bonwetsch, M. J. Lagrange). Harnack's view that it is an official document of the Roman Church is, as H. Koch has shown, untenable.

Text: FP 3, [2]1914. H. Lietzmann (KlT 1) [2]1933. M. Meinertz, *Einleitung in das NT,* [5]1949, 410/14. — Treatises: Zahn, NKZ 1922, 417/36; Bonwetsch, GN 1923, 27ff., 63f.; Harnack, ZNTW 1925, 1/16 (official list of Rom. Church); cf. against this H. Koch, ZNTW 1926, 154/60; Lagrange, RB 1926, 83/8. G. Roethe, *Zur Gesch. der roem. Synoden im 3. u. 4. Jh.*, 1937, 112/4. Faure, Z. syst. Th. 19, 143/9 (4th Gospel). Leclercq, DAL 12, 543/60. Lagrange, RB 1933, 161/86;

Hist. anc. du Canon du NT, 1933, 66/84. J. Schmid, LTK 7, 382f. Ehrhard, OstkSt 2, 1953, 121/38 (The Gospels).

2. The ancient prologues to the Gospels and the Pauline Epistles. Many MSS of the Vulgate contain introductions or prologues to individual books of holy Scripture. The prologues belong mostly to later centuries. Three groups of such prologues which were written early have engaged the particular attention of most recent scholars: a. The anti-Marcionite prologues of Mk., Lk., Jo. (the prologue to Mt. is lost) originated, according to De Bruyne and Harnack in the second half of the second century (160–80). The three prologues are extant in a Latin translation; only the prologue to Lk. has also been preserved in the Greek original. b. The Latin prologues to the Pauline Epistles are probably of partly Marcionite origin. c. The so-called *Monarchian prologues* to the gospels are nowadays generally no longer considered as dating from the first decades of the third century, but from the late fourth or beginning of the fifth century and as emanating from Priscillian circles.

On a.: De Bruyne, RBn 1928, 193/214; cf. Lagrange, RB 1929, 115/21; against this, De Bruyne, RBn 1929, Bull. 2 n. 22; Harnack, SbB 1928, 322/41; against it Bacon, JBL 1930, 43/54 (Jo.-Prol. of 3rd cent.) and Eisler, RP 1930, 350/71. Howard, ET 1936, 534/8. Gutwenger, TSW 1946, 393/409. Heard, JTS 1954, 1/16 (Mk.-Prol.: end of 2nd cent.; Lk.-Prol.: 3rd/4th cent.; Jo.-Prol.: 5th or 6th cent. On b.: De Bruyne, RBn 1907, 1/16. Harnack, ZNTW 1925, 204/18; against this, Mundle, ZNTW 1925, 56/77. Lagrange, RB 1935, 161/73. Bardy, DBSuppl. 5, 1954, 877/81. — On c.: H. Lietzmann (KlT 1) [4]1933. F. Loofs 1930, 158[1], 161[2]. Baumstark, JL 12, 1932, 194/7 (3rd cent.; Rom. origin). Dold, ZBW 1935, 125ff. (MS of Lk.-Prol.). Taeschner, OC 1935, 80/99 (Prol. in Isaac Velásquez). F. Stegmueller, *Repertorium biblicum Medii Aevi,* I: *Initia bibl., apocrypha, prologi,* Ma 1949.

CHAPTER FIVE

The Christian Literature of the Third Century
(To the Council of Nicaea)

A. The Western Authors of the Third Century

§ 29. THE BEGINNINGS OF THE LATIN CHRISTIAN LITERATURE. MINUCIUS FELIX

1. The gradual adoption of Latin as the language of Christians living in the West of the Roman Empire can, up to a point, be best pursued in Rome and Africa. In the early period (1st cent.) the faithful in Rome were mainly Greek-speaking Christians who had immigrated from the East; hence Greek was also the official language of the Roman Church which was used for preaching, catechesis and the liturgy. As may be gathered however, inter alia from the Latinisms of the *Shepherd of Hermas* written *c.* 150, about this time the Mass of the faithful in Rome must have spoken Latin. This is supported especially by the Latin translation of the First Epistle of Clement which is to be dated about 150. Perhaps the Bible too, or at least parts of it, had been translated into Latin about this time. Towards the end of the second century the Popes used Latin for their official correspondence (Victor I). Two letters written in Latin by Pope Cornelius (251–3) to Cyprian of Carthage have been preserved. The gradual Latinization of the Roman Church, however, was completed only very late when Latin was introduced also as the language of the Mass under Pope Damasus (366–84). The theolo-

gical authors writing in Rome during the second and in the first decade of the third century generally still used Greek (Clement, Hermas, Justin, Gaius, Hippolytus). By about 250, on the other hand, Latin had already gained the ascendancy (Letters of Popes Cornelius and Stephen, Novatian's *De Trinitate*).

Probably as early as the middle of the second century, at least substantial parts of the Bible were translated into Latin also in N. Africa. The oldest Latin Christian document which can be dated with certainty originated in N. Africa: the *Passio Martyrum Scilitanorum* of A.D. 180 (v. infra § 45 n. 6). To the Africans falls the honour of having exercised the greatest influence on the formation and development of the so-called Christian Latin; for instance Tertullian (though he still found it necessary to write also in Greek), Minucius Felix and Cyprian. As the language of the liturgy, too, Latin gained ground in Africa much earlier than in the other parts of the Latin West.

G. la Piana, *Il problema della Chiesa latina in Roma,* 1922. A. Harnack, *Die Mission u. Ausbreitung d. Christentums,* [4]1924, 817/32. Suess, HVS 1932, 1/39 (Bible Latin). G. J. D. Aalders, *Tertullianus' citaten uit dem Evangelien en de oudlatijnsche Bibelvertalingen,* A 1932. M. Mueller, *Der Uebergang von der griech. zur latein. Sprache der abendlaendischen Kirche von Hermas bis Novatian,* R 1943. Klauser, Misc. Mercati I, 1946, 467/82 (introduction of Latin into the liturgy in Rome). G. Bardy, *La question des langues dans l'Église anc.,* 1948, 81/121. Mohrmann, VC 1949, 67/106, 163/83 *(Latinité chrét. à Rome):* cf. the works cited supra p. 7f. — On the history of the Old Lat. Bible cf. F. Stummer, *Einfuehrung i. d. lat. Bibel,* 1928. Botte, DBSuppl fasc. 21, 1948, 777/82; 5, 1952, 334/47. Stenzel, TR 1953, 97/103; id., SE 1953, 71/84. Stummer, ALW 1954, 233/83 (rhythm in the Bible and the Liturgy). Kusch, Forsch. u. Fortschritte 1955, 46/57 (on the importance of the new *Beuron Vetus Latina*). B. Fischer, *Vetus latina. Die Reste der altlatein. Bibel nach P. Sabatier gesammelt u. hg. von der Erzabtei Beuron* I, 1949/54. The best information on research on the hist. of the Lat. Bible is in the bulletin of RBn. Further literature v. supra § 1 and § 86. T. Ayuso Marazuela, *Vetus Latina Hispana* I, Ma 1953. A. Juelicher, *Itala,* III: *Lucas-Ev.,* B 1954. M. Stenzel, ZNTW 1955, 31/66 (Old Lat. texts of the Canticles in the Dodecapropheton). Rost, *Die Bibel i. d. ersten Jhh.,* Westheim b. Augsb., 1946, 81/105 (bibliography and language of Lat. Bible).

2. Minucius Felix. The *Dialogue Octavius* has been preserved only in a single MS, the *Paris Arnobius Cod.* (9th cent.), as the eighth

book of the work *Adversus nationes* (§ 46). This Latin apology has the form of a philosophical dialogue and is superior to all apologies of the second and third centuries both in literary design and grace of presentation. The author, the lawyer Marcus Minucius Felix (2, 3) who resides in Rome, and his two friends, the Christian Octavius and the pagan Caecilius take part in the probably fictitious religious discussion. Octavius, a friend of Minucius' student days, is like him a lawyer, but in a province beyond the sea (Africa?) and is in Rome on a visit. Caecilius calls Fronto of Cirta his countryman, so he is a Numidian.

The book was written in memory of Octavius who had died in the meantime. Though it is also addressed to the Christian relatives of Octavius for their consolation, it intends primarily to influence pagan readers. Hence it is understandable that it says nothing of the doctrinal contents of the Christian faith and does not cite Scripture. Tertullian's *Apologeticum* and Arnobius (§ 46) also rightly refrain from using the argument from Scripture. Cyprian, on the contrary, when arguing with the pagan Demetrianus, constantly used scriptural texts, for which he is blamed already by Lactantius (DivInst 5, 4, 4–7). Christianity is considered from the purely philosophical point of view: its essence is monotheism, the belief in immortality and moral perfection. The treatise is modelled on Cicero's dialogue *De natura deorum*. Stoic ideas such as had been developed by Posidonius, Cicero and Seneca can be traced in many passages. Minucius Felix is not, indeed, particularly original, but he is distinguished by an objectivity such as is hardly to be met elsewhere. In his polemics he treats the opposite point of view with a noble reserve and avoids offensive invective almost entirely.

Contents: The three friends make an excursion from Rome to Ostia. When they meet a statue of Serapis on their way the pagan Caecilius kisses his hand to it. This is the occasion for a religious disputation in which the three engage shortly afterwards, while sitting on a dam by the sea. Minucius, called Mark in the dialogue, is to be umpire (1–4).

Caecilius: The greatest sages have been unable to find out anything certain about the gods and the beyond, and Socrates, the prince of philosophers, has declared: *Quod supra nos, nihil ad nos.* In this uncertainty it is best to remain loyal to the traditional cult of the gods to which Rome owes its greatness. The invisible God of the Christians is a phantom. The Christians themselves are uneducated men and credulous women who practise horrible fornication at their meetings (5–13).

Octavius (EP 269/73) follows his opponent step by step: Man is called to the knowledge of the truth and cannot pass it by indifferently. It is true, we cannot see God, but neither can the human eye look into the sun. The gods of the pagans were mere men to whom divine honours were paid later. Rome became the mistress of the world not through her religion but by robbery and violence. The accusations against the Christians are caused by slanders (EH 222ff.) circulated by the demons (14–38).

Caecilius declares himself defeated, and the author concludes: "After this we departed rejoicing, Caecilius because he had become a believer, Octavius because he had gained a victory, I in the faith of the one and the victory of the other."

Date: Both in thought and expressions *Octavius* is so similar to Tertullian's *Apologeticum* and also to his treatise *Ad nationes* that a dependence of one on the other can be taken as certain. If we could trust Jerome's chronology (*Vir. ill.* 53; Ep. 70, 5) Tertullian would be given priority. The question of the relation between them has been discussed time and again with the greatest zeal and the most penetrating acumen during the last 90 years or so (A. Ebert, 1868). Nevertheless, no generally accepted decision has been reached so far. Owing to the great number of relevant studies we can not even indicate a critical appreciation of the mutually opposed points of view. It seems to me that Tertullian's priority is better established, if not certain.

On the oldest research cf. G. Krueger 1922, 268f. and 1933, 279: RAl 87; Quasten II, 161f. The priority of Min. Fel. is defended by: P. Borleffs, *De Tertulliano et Minucio Felice,* Groningen 1925. J. Schmidt, *Min. Fel. oder Tert.,* L 1932. R. Beutler, *Philosophie u. Apologie bei Min. Fel.,* 1936, 48, 54. Quispel, VC 1949, 113/22 (Jewish Source of Min. Fel.) and Eranos Jb 1950, 173ff.; also in his ed. of the text, Ley 1949. Helm, Wissenschaftliche Z. der Univ. Rostock 2, 1953, 88/91. — P. Ferrarino, *Il problema critico e cronologico dell'Octavio,* Bologna 1947 (not accessible to me). For the priority of Tertullian: Opitz, PWK 15, 1816/20. Colombo, Did 1914, 79/121 (fonti); 1915, 215/44 (Min. Fel. e Cipriano). Schuster, WSt 1934, 163/7. Diller, Phil. 1935, 98/114; 216/39. Visoky, Listy Filol. 1938, 110/23. B. Axelson, *Das Prioritaetsproblem Tert. - Min. Fel.,* Lund 1941. C. Becker, *Tertullians Apologeticum,* 1954, 313 A. 314 lists a number of adverse criticisms of Axelson; it does not mention Borleffs, *Museum* 50, 1943, 216f. For Tert. also: Paratore, RR 1947, 132/59. M. Pellegrino, ed. of text Tu 1947, 7/23. Klotz, WJB 4, 1949/50, 379/81. Büchner, Her 1954, 231/45. C. Becker, *Tertullians Apologeticum,* 1954, 309/32. Kurfess, *Orpheus* 1, 1954, 125/29. Frassinetti, In mem. A. Beltrami, Varese 1954, 83/96 (Min. Fel. and Tert., Apol.).

Edd.: C. Halm (CSEL 2, 1/71) 1867. J. P. Waltzing, Lou 1903, Bruges 1909 (with commentary), L ^{2}1926 and a Lexicon Minucianum, 1910. A. Schöne, L. 1913. J. van Wageningen, 2 vols., Ut 1923 (philol. comment.). J. Martin (FP 8) 1930. E. U. Moricca, R 1933. E. P. H. Damsté, A 1936. A. Simpson, NY 1938. G. Quispel, Ley 1949. M. Pellegrino, Tu 1947 and Tu 1950. — Transs.: A. Müller (BKV^2 14) 1913. J. H. Freese (SPCK) Lo 1919. J. P. Waltzing, Lou 1914. D. Bassi, Mi 1929. S. De Domingo, Ma 1946. — Treatises: Leclercq, DAL 11, 1388/412. H. J. Baylis, *M. Fel. and his Place Among the Early Fathers of the Lat. Church,* 1928. B. Berge, *Exeget. Bemerkungen zur Daemonenauffassung des Min. Fel.,* 1929. J. J. de Jong, *Apologetiek en christendom in den Oct. van Min. F.,* 1935. Van Haeringen, Mn 3, 1935/6, 29/32 (on 9, 6). Wotke, WSt 1935, 110/28. G. Lazzati, *L'Aristotele perduto . . .,* 1938. 62/6. Kurfess, TG 1938, 546/52; WSt 1938, 121/4. WJB 1947, 1. 4 (text. crit.). Prinz, WSt 57, 1939, 138/47 (text. crit.). Axelson, Er 1941, 64/81 (on 29, 6: Tert. Apol. 9, 18 on Arnob. maior 2, 67 et alia). Alfonsi, SC 1942, 70/3. Boor, Mn 11, 1943, 161/90 (Min. and Clem. Alex.). Axelson, *Textkritisches zu Florus, Min. Fel. und Arnobius,* Lund 1944. Lavallée, Mél. Saumier, Lyons 1944, 121/38 (on apologetic of Min. Fel.). Tomaselli-Nicolosi, MiscStLCA 1, 1947, 67/78 (Lucretius in Min. Fel.). Quispel, VC 1949, 113/22 (Jewish source); Lat 10, 1951, 163/9 *(Anima naturaliter christ.).* Kuijper, VC 1952, 207 (text. crit.). Van Winden, VC 1954, 72/7 (on 19, 9). Waszink, VC 1954, 129/33 (text. crit.). Scheidweiler, Her 1954, 487/94 (text. crit.). Buechner, Her 1954, 231/45. Préaux, Lat 1955, 262/70.

The treatise *De fato* announced in the *Dialogue* (36, 2) has either not been written or is lost. Jerome knew a treatise *De fato vel contra mathematicos* circulating under the name of Min. Fel., but doubts its authenticity (*Vir. ill.* 58).

See Préaux, Latomus 9, 1950, 395/413.

§ 30. TERTULLIAN (d. after 220)

QUINTUS Septimius Florens Tertullianus was born at Carthage *c.* 160; he was the son of a pagan Roman captain. He received a very good education, including especially, legal and rhetorical training (Eus., *Hist.* 2, 2, 4). He was also thoroughly familiar with Greek. He is very probably identical with the jurist of the same name quoted in the pandects. About 195 he returned as a Christian from Rome, where he had been a lawyer, to his native town, having drained, as he writes himself (*Res. carn.* 59), the cup of lust to its dregs. He soon embarked on a lively literary career in the service of the Church. It is very improbable that he was a priest, as Jerome asserts (*Vir. ill.* 53). In 207 at the latest, he broke with the Church. His austere and gloomy cast of mind which abhorred neutrality and compromise led him to the Montanist sect where he soon became the head of a party of his own, the Tertullianists. He died an old man at Carthage, after 220.

Tertullian is one of the most original, and until Augustine the most individual of all Latin ecclesiastical authors. He combined Punic fervour with Roman practical sense. A religious enthusiast, he had a penetrating intelligence, passionate eloquence, ever-ready wit and was extraordinarily well-versed in all departments of knowledge. Moreover, he mastered Latin like no one else and freely moulded it into quite new forms. As H. Hoppe (1932) states, Tertullian formed 509 new nouns, 284 adjectives, 28 adverbs and 161 verbs, i. e. together 982 new words. Apart from the *Vetus Latina* and the *Vulgate* his writings have exercised the greatest influence on old Christian Latin. It is, however, an exaggeration to call him the author of Christian Latinity. He writes a concise, vigorous, but for this reason also often obscure style; Vincent of Lerins says rightly of him: *Quot paene verba, tot sententiae* (c. 18). But continuing: *Quot sensus tot victoriae* Vincent is wrong; for Tertullian's dialectic is dazzling rather than convincing, and this is due to his nature. He is excitable, inclined to extremes, and he himself must confess that he is wholly lacking in the virtue (patience) in whose praise he wrote a special treatise (*Pat.* 1). In his rhetoric he plays the whole register of impassioned wrath, mocking wit and legal volubility. In controversy he gives no quarter, and all his writings are controversial. As a Catholic he branded the procedure of the pagan governors and attacked and ridiculed the pagan religion in general, and later, when he had become a Montanist, he attacked the supposed laxity of the Catholic Church with equal bitterness, not even refraining from casting suspicion on the celebration of the *Agape* by dark allusions (*Ieiun.* 17). However, on account of his difficult language, but even more because of his defection to Montanism, he was soon no longer read or at least not named, as is the case already in Cyprian.

It is hardly possible to give an exact chronological order for Tertullian's writings; one can normally only say with a fair degree of certainty whether they belong to the Catholic or to the Montanist period of the author. The frequent cross references in his works as well as internal reasons make it possible to establish a relative sequence of many of his writings. The textual tradition, too, is rather defective. Not a few treatises are lost; of others, *(Pud., Ieiun.)* the MSS from which the oldest editions were printed have perished; others are extant only in the single *Codex Agobardinus* (at Paris), which dates from Archbishop Agobardus of Lyons (814–40). Only the *Apologeticum* exists in numerous MSS. Thirty-one treatises have survived in all. Tertullian was the most fertile Latin author of the time before Constantine.

The most important modern literature on Tertullian is assembled and classified, apart from Quasten's *Patrology* (II, 248ff.), in J. H. Waszink, *Tertulliani De anima,* 1947, 597/620 as well as in the first facsimile of Tertullian in the CCL II, 1953, X–XXV.

Edd.: ML 1–2. F. Oehler 1–3, 1851/4 and ed. minor 1854. In CSEL so far 4 vols.: 20, 1890 by A. Reifferscheid and G. Wissowa 47, 1906 by A. Kroymann, 69, 1939 by H. Hoppe *(Apolog.)* and 70, 1942 (Kroymann). A new complete ed. appeared in 2 vols. in the CCL in 1935/4.—Transs.: by H. Kellner, 2 vols., 1882 and selection by H. Kellner and G. Esser (BKV ²7 and 24) 1912/5. S. Thelwall, P. Holmes and others (ANCL 7, 11, 15, 18, 1869/70). H. U. Meyboom, Ley 1931. —Mg.: Bardy, DTC. S. F. Sajdak, *Tert. Czast-zycie-dziela,* Poznan, 1949. A. Hauck 1878. E. Noeldechen 1890. P. Monceaux (supra § 3) 1, 1901. C. Guignebert, P. 1091. F. Ramorino, Mi 1923. H. Koch, PWK II 5, 822/44. On individual questions: G. Esser, *Die Seelenlehre T.s,* 1893. H. Hoppe, *Syntax u. Stil des T.,* 1903; *Beitraege zur Sprache u. Kritik T.s,* Lund 1932. A. d'Alès, *La théol. de T.,* 1905. G. Thoernell, *Studia Tertullianea* 1–4, Up 1917/26. E. R. Roberts, *The Theology of T.,* 1924. P. Vitton, *I concetti giuridici nelle opere di T.,* 1924. A. Beck, *Roem. Recht bei T. u. Cyprian,* 1930; S. W. J. Teeuwen, *Sprachl. Bedeutungswandel bei T.,* 1926. J. Lortz, *T. als Apologet,* 2 vols., 1927/8. J. Berton, *T. le schismatique,* 1928. J. Morgan, *The Importance of T. in the Development of Christ. Dogma,* 1928. T. Brandt, *T.s Ethik,* 1929. L. Bayard, *T. et Cyprien,* 1930 *(Moralistes chrét.).* R. Hoeslinger, *Die alte afrik. Kirche im Lichte der Kirchenrechtsforschung nach der kulturhist. Methode,* W 1935. G. Krueger 1933, 261, 280f. V. Nemes, *Tert. goeroeg mueveltsége* (= Greek education of T.). Pannonhalme 1935. D'Alès, REG 1937, 320/62 *(T. helléniste).* H. Janssen, *Kultur u. Sprache,* N 1938 (development of language in T. and Cyprian). K. Vysoky, *Remarques sur les sources des œuvres de T.,* Prague 1937. F. A. Demmel, *Die Neubildungen auf -anita und -entia b. T.,* thesis Zurich 1944. A. Roelli, *T.s Stellung z. roem. Staat,* thesis Tub 1944. M. M. Baney, *Some Reflections of Life in North Africa in the Writings of Tert.,* W 1948. S. Oswiecimski, *De scriptorum Rom. vestigiis ap. Tert. obviis quaest. selectae,* Kraków 1951. B. Nisters, *Tert., seine Persoenlichkeit u. sein Schicksal,* Mr 1950.

Treatises: Borleffs, Mn 1935, 299/308 (MS). Restrepo-Jaramillo, Gr 1934, 3/58 (symbol). H. Koch, *Gelasius* (BAS 1935, 6) 1935, 77/82 (T.'s language in Gelasius). Waszink, Mn 3, 1935/6, 165/74. D'Alès, RSR 1936, 468; 1937, 620. Aalders, Mn 1937, 241/82 (Lk.-citations). Waszink, Mn 9, 1940, 129/37 and 11, 1942, 68ff. (text. crit.). Brou, EL 1938, 237/57 (Tert. in the *Officium Joannis Bapt.*). — View that Tert. was not a priest defended by: H. Koch, TSK 1931, 108/14; J. Schrijnen, *Charakteristik des altchristl. Latein,* N 1932, 30 A. 1; J. Klein, *Tert. Christl. Bewusstsein u. sittl. Forderungen,* 1940, 268/73. G. Smitz, Th 1943, 127/39 (Tert. and Montanism). Casamassa, Ang 1943, 184/94 *(L' acusa di hesterni).* Evans, CQR 1944/5, 56/77 (Theological terminology). Waszink, VC 1948, 224/42 (Roman dramatic art). Borleffs-Diercks, SE 1949, 383/6 *(Lexikon Tertullianeum).* Basanoff, ACl 1950, 463/5 (pagan concepts contd. in Tert. and August.). Mohrmann, VC 1951, 111f. (Tert. in Jerome and August.). Borleffs, VC 1951, 65/79 (new MS frag.); cf. also Dekkers, SE 1952, 372/83. CSEL 76, 1957 (Bulhard - Borleffs).

I. Apologetic writings

1. *Ad nationes,* two books (197), a defence against pagan attacks and an attack on paganism which, Tertullian asserts, is in a state of moral and religious dissolution (EH 186f.). This treatise should be considered as a provisional draft dealing with paganism, which was more fully elaborated in the *Apologeticum* written in the same year.

Text: J. G. Borleffs 1953 (CCL 1, 1). — Text. criticism in Castiglioni in StU 1937, 257ff.; Waszink, Mn 3, 1943, 71f. Kuijper, VC 1954, 78/82; Evans, VC 1955, 37/44. — M. Heidenthaller, *T.s 2. Buch Ad nat. u. De test. animae,* Pa 1942 (Trans. and commentary).

2. The *Apologeticum* (end of 197) is addressed to the provincial governors of the Roman Empire. In contrast with all other ancient apologies it considers almost exclusively the political accusations directed against the Christians, i. e. scorn of the state gods and *lèse majesté,* thus transferring apologetics from the philosophical to the juridical sphere (EH 164/75; EP 274/85).

He cleverly blames the peculiar procedure used by the secular pagan authorities against the Christians: the only crime for which they are condemned is the *nomen Christianum.* All other criminals are allowed a defence, but not the Christians; to others torture is applied to force a confession, to Christians to obtain a denial. He refutes the vile suspicions circulated against the Christians and gives information on the most important points of the Christian faith and the life of the community. Christianity, he concludes, is a philosophy, but the pagan philosophers are not forced to sacrifice like the Christians, they may even deny the gods without incurring punishment. Yet the pagan cruelties will not harm the Christians, on the contrary: *Plures efficimur, quoties metimur a vobis, semen est sanguis christianorum* (50).

The text of the *Apologeticum* has raised much controversy. The treatise was preserved in the *Codex Fuldensis,* now lost, in a version frequently differing from that in the normal tradition (*Vulgata,* more than 30 MSS). The view has often been voiced (H. Schroers, G. Thoernell) that we are faced with two different versions made by Tertullian himself. This has also guided the most recent editors (H. Hoppe, C. Becker, E. Dekkers) in shaping the text of the book. This view is opposed by another one, according to which the two traditions, as is proved by common errors, go back to one and the same archetype which early split into two branches, owing to the intervention of unenlightened copyists. In the *Codex Fuldensis* the original text is less corrupt than in the *Vulgata* (J. P. Waltzing, J. Martin, Loefstedt, Mohrmann). — The *Apologeticum* was translated into Greek as early as the beginning of the third century.

Text, Trans., Commentary: B. Mayor-A. Souter, C 1917 (with trans.). S. Colombo, Tu 1918 (with commentary) and Tu 1926. G. Rauschen, 1919 (FP 12). J. P. Waltzing-A. Severyns, P 1929, and Waltzing, P 1931 (with trans. and commentary). A. Souter, Aberdeen 1926. J. Martin, 1933 (FP 6). C. Ijsseling, A 1947 (trans.). J. Sajdak, Poznan 1947 (trans.). F. Guarino, R 1950 (trans.). O. Tescari, Tu 1951 (with trans.). Mohrmann, Ut-Bru 1951 (trans. also of 7 other pre-Montanist treatises). C. Becker, Mn 1952 (with trans.).

Mgs.: Doelger, AC 5, 188/200 (on 6, 4, 6). Emonds, RM 1937, 180/91 (on 46, 16); id., 2nd ed., 1941, 137/87. Bourgery, Lat. 1938, 106/11 *(Institutum Neronianum)*. Bickel, DP 54/61 (on 18). Doelger, AC 6, 157/9 (on 40, 2). Tescari, RAC 1947/8, 349/52 (on 46, 14). Volterra, *Scritti in onore di C. Ferrini,* 1947, 471/88 (on 5, 1–2). Griffe, BLE 1949, 129/45 (persecutions of Chrs.). Zeiller, AB 1949, 49/54 (persecutions of Chrs.). Alfonsi, Lat 2, 1949, 5/11 (on 46, 15). Oswiecimski, Eos 44, 1950, 111/22 (on 15). Grant, VC 1951, 113 (on 47, 6f.). Borleffs, VC 1952, 129/45 *(Institutum Neronianum)*. C. Becker, *Tertullians Apologeticum, Werden u. Leistung,* Mn 1954 (383 pp.). Beran, Misc. Mohlberg 2, 7/32 *(De ordine Missae)*. Quacquarelli, Gr 1950, 145/74, 562/89 (persecution of Chrs.). Zeiller, RHE 1955, 393/99 *(Instit. Neronianum)*.

3. *De testimonio animae* elaborates a sentence from the *Apologeticum* (17): *O testimonium animae naturaliter christianae* (EP 286). In their spontaneous exclamations the pagans show that they believe, in the depth of their soul, in the unity of God, the survival of the soul and the existence of evil spirits, e.g. when they say: God sees it, or: May the departed rest in peace.

Text: G. Quispel, Ley 1952; id., Ley 1952 (trans.). J. C. Scholte, A 1934 (with trans.). — Treatises: Lazzati, *Atene e Roma,* 1939, 153/66 (fonti). Quispel, Lat 1951, 163/9. Tibiletti, AttiAccadSc, Tu 88, 1953/4, II 84/117.

4. *Ad Scapulam* (212), an open letter threatening Scapula, proconsul in Africa and an enraged enemy of the Christians, with the punishment of God, referring to an eclipse of the sun (EH 217f.; EP 369).

Mgs.: Doelger, AC 6, 1940, 70f. (on 4). Quacquarelli, Gr 1950, 562/89 (persecution of Chrs.). A. Quacquarelli, *Tertull. Ad Scapulam,* R 1957.

5. *Adversus Iudaeos* (EH 207f.). The old law of retaliation must cede to a new law of love. The pagans too, share in the grace of God (1–8). The second part (9–14) is spurious, an excerpt from the third book of the treatise *Adv. Marcionem.*

Mgs.: A. L. Williams, *Adversus Iudaeos,* C 1935, 43/52. Brou, EL 1938, 237/57 (on 9). Capelle, RTABull 4, 1943, 8f. G. Quispel, *De Bronnen v. Tert.' Adv. Marc.,* Ley 1943, 61/79; cf. Borleffs, VC 1947, 195f. M. Simon, *Versus Israel,* P 1948.

II. Dogmatic-polemical writings

6. *De praescriptione haereticorum* (*c.* 200). This work shows most clearly Tertullian's juridical training and his knowledge of the Roman law. The title of this work means, in free translation, that in dealing with heretics the law of *praescriptio* may be applied. In the language of the legal experts of Imperial Rome *praescriptio* meant that the defendant invoked a *praescriptio* which rejected the claim of the plaintiff *a limine* so that there could be no trial at all. Tertullian's "theological *praescriptio*" was suggested by this legal procedure.

Two statements *(praescriptiones)* are at the centre of his not always very clear exposition: i. Christ has commissioned no one except the apostles to propagate his teaching; ii. The apostles have entrusted this teaching to no one except the communities founded by them. This proves the greater age not only of the apostolic communities but also of their doctrine in comparison with all heresies. This statement alone convicts the heresies of error, because they came later. From this point of view Tertullian has no need at all to examine the Gnostic doctrines in detail and to refute them as false. Every doctrine that agrees with the doctrine of the apostolic Churches is to be regarded as true, because these Churches have received their doctrine from the apostles, the apostles have received it from Christ, and Christ from God (21).

The Church is the rightful owner of the faith; it also possesses the Scriptures (19). The heretics have no right to judge the sense of Scripture. The scope and content of the faith is decided by the rule of faith, i. e. by the teaching of the apostolic Churches. Private exegesis of Scripture and disputes about the sense of Biblical passages lead nowhere (16). The apostolic tradition also guarantees the correct exegesis of Scripture (15–19). To know nothing against the rule of faith means to know everything (*Adversus regulam nihil scire omnia scire est;* 14, 5).

Edd.: E. Preuschen, ²1910. P. de Labriolle, P 1907. J. Martin (FP 4), 1930. J. N. Bakhuizen van den Brink, Haag 1946. — Transs.: C. Mohrmann, 1951 (v. supra no. 2). J. Giordani, Brescia 1935. C. F. Savio, Varallo 1944. — Studies: P. U. Huentemann, *De praescr. haeret. libri analysis,* 1924. A. Vellico, *La rivelazione e le sue fonti, nel De praescr. haeret. di Teret.,* R 1935. G. Zimmermann, *Die hermeneutischen Prinzipien T.s,* thesis, L 1937. Allie, RUO 1937, 211/25; 1938, 16/28. J. Stirnimann, *Die Praescr. T.s im Lichte des roem. Rechts und der Theologie,* Fri 1949. Czuj, CT 1954, 194/247 (on *Praescr. haeret.*).—Refoulé-De Labriolle 1957 (SCh 46).

The *Collection of Thirty-Two Heresies* added to the book *De praescriptione* (chs. 46–53; text: CSEL 47, 213/26) is, according to E. Schwartz (SbMn 1936, 3), a Greek treatise written by Pope Zephyrinus or one of his clerics, translated and modified in an anti-Origenist sense by Victorinus of Pettau (v. infra § 31, 2).

7. The five books *Adversus Marcionem* (v. § 24, 8) are by far the most voluminous work. Tertullian wrote it in three different recensions, of which however, only the last and longest version is extant. The first book in its present form was written in the

fifteenth year of the reign of the Emperor Severus, i.e. in 207 (cf. 1, 15). In 5, 10 the author refers to his treatise *De carnis resurrectione*. The work belongs to his Montanist period (cf. 1, 19; 3, 24; 4, 22).

In Books 1–2 he proves that the creator of the world cannot be different from the good God, in Book 3 that Christ was the Messias prophesied in the Old Covenant, not a higher aeon in an unreal body. In Books 4 and 5 Tertullian criticizes Marcion's New Testament and shows that there are no contradictions between the Old and the New Testaments (EP 331/45; EH 210; EA 64/66).

Studies: E. Bosshardt, *Essai sur l'originalité et la probité de Tert. dans son traité contre Marcion,* thesis Fri 1921. A. Harnack, *Marcion* (TU 45), ²1924. Neumann, ZKT 1934, 311/63; 533/51 (problem of evil in *Marc.* 2). D'Alès, RSR 1936, 99f., 585f.; 1937, 228/30 (on *Marc.* 3, 18; 4, 21). Aalders, Mn 1937, 241/82 (citations from Lk.). G. Fligersdorfer, *De Tert. adv. Marc. lib. tertii argumento sententiarumque connexu,* thesis W 1939. Rist, JR 1942, 39/62 (Pseudographic Refutations of Marcionism). M. C. Tenney, *The quotations from Luke in Tert.,* thesis Harvard Univ. 1944 (unpubl.). Waszink, Mn 1935/6, 172; 1943, 72/4; 1947, 127/9 (text. crit.). G. Quispel, *De bronnen van Tert.' Adv. Marc.,* Ley 1943, and VC 1947, 47. Grant, VC 1951, 114f. (on 1, 13). Higgins, VC 1951, 1/42 (Text of Luke in Marc. and Tert.).

8. *Adversus Hermogenem* (EP 321/8), a defence of the Christian doctrine of creation against the Gnostic painter H. at Carthage.

Text: J. H. Waszink, Ut 1956 (Strom. patrist.). Ibid., ACW 24, 1956; id., VC 1955, 129/47 (text. crit.). Hiltbrunner, VC 1956, 215/28 (text. crit.).

9. *Adversus Valentinianos,* directed against the Gnostic V. and his followers; makes extensive use of Irenaeus, *Haer.* 1.

AC 5, 1936, 272/4 (on *Valent.* 8). Quispel, NTT 2, 1948, 280/90 (Tert.'s satire in *Adv. Valent.*). D'Alès, RSR 1935, 496 (on *Valent.* 12).

10. *Scorpiace,* a "remedy for the sting of the scorpion" of the Gnostic heresy, defends the moral value of martyrdom (213).

Waszink, Mn 3, 1935/6, 165ff. (text. crit.). Castiglioni, StU 256ff.

11. *De carne Christi* (EP 353/9; EH 209) refutes the docetism of the Gnostics; here (9) it is alleged that Christ was ugly (*c.* 210/12).

12. *De carnis resurrectione* (EP 360/5) defends the resurrection of the flesh against the Gnostics.

Trans. by A. Souter (SPCK), Lo 1922. Gewiess, TQ 1948, 474ff. (on 6). Davies, JTS 1955, 90/4 (on *resurr. carnis* 63).

13. *Adversus Praxean,* the clearest ante-Nicene presentation of the Church's doctrine of the Trinity, directed against the Patripassian Praxeas; first use (3) of the term *trinitas.*

Edd. of text: A. Kroymann, Tu 1907. E. Evans (SPCK), Lo 1948 (with trans. and commentary), cf. Wascink, VC 1953, 246/53.—Studies: J. Barbel, *Christos Angelos,* Bonn 1941, 70/9. T. L. Verhoeven, *Studien over Tert., Adv. Praxean,* A 1948 (thesis Ut); VC 1951, 43/48. Camelot, RSPT 1949, 31/3 (on 8). Quacquarelli, RassScFilos 3, 1950 (Tert. against the Monarchians).

14. *De baptismo,* a presentation of the Church's doctrine of Baptism, its necessity and its effects. Heretical baptism is invalid (15).

Edd. of text: G. Rauschen, FP 11, 1916. J. W. P. Borleffs, Mn 1931, 1/102; Ley 1831. A. d'Alès, R 1933. Borleffs, Haag 1948 (together with *De Patientia* and *De paenitentia*). R. F. Refoulé-M. Drouzy (SCh 35), 1952 (with trans. and comm.); cf. Borleffs, VC 1948, 185/200 (value of MS of Troyes). ibid. 1954, 188/92. Schepens, RSR 1948, 112f. (on 5). Mohrmann, VC 1951, 49 (on 2, 2). W. Bedard, *The Symbolism of the Baptismal Font in Early Christ. Thought,* W 1951.

15. *De anima* (210–13), apart from the work against Marcion his largest treatise, belongs to the series of anti-Gnostic writings and is akin to the lost treatise *De censu animae* directed against Hermogenes (v. supra No. 8). It is not a systematic treatise on the doctrine of the soul but has polemical tendencies; Tertullian is concerned to refute philosophical and Gnostic errors. Beside other authors he uses especially the physician Soranus of Ephesus.

Edd. of text: J. H. Waszink, A 1933 (with trans. and comm.); id., *Index verborum et locutionum quae Tertulliani de anima libro continentur,* Bonn 1935; id., *Tert., De anima ed. with commentary,* A 1947 (large ed.); cf. C. Becker, Gn 1953, 47/56.

Studies: F. Seyr, Commentationes Vindobonenses 3, 1937, 51/74 (doctrine of soul and knowledge of Tert. and the Stoa). Waszink, *Pisciculi,* Mr 1939, 276/78; id., VC 1947, 137/49 (Aristotle in Tert.); id., VC 1949, 107/12; VC 1950, 212/45 (technique of clauses). Festugière, RSPT 1949, 129/61 *(Composition et l'esprit)*; id., Jahresber. des Goerres-Ges. 1951, Cologne 1952, 53/68 (philosophy and Gnosis). Nock, VC 1950, 129/247 (Ahori in T.). H. Karpp, *Probleme altchristl. Anthropologie,* 1951, 40/91.

III. Practical-ascetical writings

a. From the Catholic period.

16. *Ad martyres* (EA 40f.) intended to console and strengthen Christians languishing in prison (197 or 202/03).

H. v. Campenhausen, *Die Idee des Martyriums,* 1936, 17/28. Schlegel, DR 1945, 125/28 (Circumstance of the Composition). Vysoky, Listy Filologicke 1948, 156/66 (the sources). E. E. Malone, *The Monk and the Martyr,* W 1950, 30/4. C. Becker, *Tert.s Apologeticum,* 1954, 350/4 (on the date: before *Ad nat.* and *Apol.*). Alfonsi, In mem. A. Beltrami, Varese 1954, 39/49.

17. *De spectaculis* (197–200) forbids Christians to visit any kind of pagan plays because of their immorality and their close connexion with idolatry.

Edd. of text: T. R. Glover, *Tert., Apology and De spect., with trans.,* Lo-NY 1931. A. Boulanger, P 1933. G. Marra, Tu 1954 (with *De fug.* and *De pall.*).— Treatises: J. Koehne, *Die Schrift Tert.s ueber die Schauspiele in kultur- u. religionsgeschichtl. Beleuchtung,* thesis Br 1929. J. Buechner, *Tert., De spect., Kommentar,* Wu 1935. P. de Labriolle, 2 vols. (trans. and comm.), P 1936. E. Witters, *Tert., De spect. Index verborum omnium,* Lou 1943. Waszink, VC 1948, 224/42 (Varro, Livy and Tert. on Roman drama). Couratin, JEH 1951, 19/23 (on 25). Lieftinck, VC 1951, 193/203 (new MS fragm.). C. Becker, *Tert.s Apologeticum,* 1954, 348f. (on date: before *Ad nat.*).

18. *De oratione* (EA 44/8) gives instructions for catechumens on prayer in general and expounds the Our Father (198–204).

Edd. of text: R. W. Muncey, Lo 1926. G. F. Diercks, Bussum 1947 (with trans. and comm.). E. Evans (SPCK), 1953 (with trans. and comm.). — Studies: Doelger, AC 5, 1936, 116/37 (on 16). Simovic, France Francisc. 1938, 193/222, 145/64 (Our Father). O. Schaefer, TG 1943, 1/6 (Our Father). Higgins, JTS 1945, 179/83 (Sixth petition of the Our Father). Pétré, RSR 1951, 63/79 (Fourth petition of the Our Father). G. F. Diercks, *Tert., De or. et De virg. vel. (Strom. patrist.* 4), Ut 1956.

19. *De patientia* (EA 49/52). Tertullian wants to speak about this virtue which he does not possess, in the same way as the sick

man likes to praise health; its greatest enemy is the thirst for revenge (200–203).

Edd. of text: Borleffs, Haag 1948 (v. supra No. 14). — Carlson, CP 43, 1948, 93/104 (Pagan Examples of Fortitude in Latin Christ. Apologists).

20. *De paenitentia* (EH 199/203; EP 311/7) (prob. 203) treats of the mind and practice of penance before Baptism (1–6) and the single ecclesiastical penance a baptized person must undergo after committing a "grave sin" (7–12).

Edd. of text: P. de Labriolle, P 1906 (*Paen.* and *Pud.* with trans.). E. Preuschen, Fr 1910. G. Rauschen (FP 10), 1915. Borleffs, Haag 1948 (v. supra No. 14). — Lukman, BV 1939, 263/66; id., *Festschr. R. Egger,* Klagenfurt 1952, 343/46 (on 7, 7/9). Le Saint, ACW 28, 1959, (*Paenit.* and *Pud.*).

21. *De cultu feminarum* (two books; EA 57/62) attacks the various forms of feminine adornments (197–201).

Edd.: J. Marra, Tu [2]1951. W. Kok, Dokkum 1934 (with trans. and com.). Braun, SE 1955, 35/48 (text. crit.). A. Ducheyn, *Proeve van vertaling en commentaar* (of the first book), thesis Gand 1941. Seliga, *Munera philologia L. Cwiklinski oblata,* Poznan 1936, 262/9 *(Tert. et Cyprianus: De feminarum moribus pravis).*

22. *Ad uxorem* (two books; EH 204/6; EA 53/6) asks his wife either to remain a widow or to marry only a Christian after his death (*c.* 203).

Trans. with comm. P. Le Saint (ACW 13), 1951; cf. Waszink, VC 1952, 183/90 (text. crit.). Kuijper, VC 1955, 247f. (text. crit.).

b. From the Montanist period.

23. *De exhortatione castitatis* (EP 366; EA 68f.) exhorts a friend who is a widower not to contract a second marriage, which he actually calls a "kind of fornication" (9) (before 207).

Trans. with comm.: P. Le Saint (ACW 13), 1951.

24. *De monogamia* (EP 380/2) a violent attack on the lawfulness of the second marriage (c. 217).

Trans. with comm.: P. Le Saint (ACW 13), 1951; on this Plumpe, TSW 1951, 557/9 (text. crit.).

25. *De virginibus velandis* (EP 329f.) demands that all virgins

should be veiled, not only in church, but also in public (before 207).

26. *De corona* (211) rejects the crowning of soldiers as a specifically pagan custom and forbids military service as incompatible with the Christian faith.

Edd. of text: J. Marra, Tu ²1951. — Studies: Franchi de' Cavalieri, ST 65, 1935, 357/86. K. Baus, *Der Kranz in Antike u. Christentum,* 1940. Doelger, AC 6, 1941, 77 (on 12). Minn, *Ev. Quarterly* 1941, 202/13 (Tert. and war). Bainton, HTR 1946, 190f. (T. and war). De Plinval, *Mél. De Ghellinck,* 1951, 183/8. Ryan, TSW 1952, 17ff. (T. and military service).

27. *De idololatria* demands the strictest rejection of idolatry and of all professions in any way connected with it (artists, teachers, state and military officials).

Studies: J. L. Schulte, *Het Heidendom bij T.,* thesis Ley 1923. Waszink, Mn 3, 1935/6, 171ff. (text. crit.). G. L. Ellspermann, *The Attitude of Early Christian Writers Toward Pagan Literat. and Learning,* W 1949, 23/42. C. Becker, *Tert.'s Apologeticum,* 1954, 349f. (on the date). Quacquarelli, RassScFilos 3, 1951 (Tert. on paganism).

28. *De fuga in persecutione* (EP 370): Flight in persecution is not permitted and opposed to the will of God (*c.* 212).

Edd. of text: J. J. Thierry, Hilversum 1941 (with trans.). J. Marra, Tu 1932 (with *De pallio*). — Castiglione, STU 1937, 260ff. Waszink, *Museum* 1, 1943, 168/70.

29. *De ieiunio adversus psychicos,* a defence of the Montanist fasting practice with violent attacks on the *psychici,* i.e. the Catholics who indulge their lusts (16f.); important for the history and practice of fasting.

J. Schuemmer, *Die altchristl. Fastenpraxis . . .,* Mr 1933.

30. *De pudicitia* EP 383/7; EH 219/21) denies the Church the right to forgive sins, in contrast with his earlier views (supra No. 20). This power is not the privilege of the juridically organized "church of the bishops" but only of the *homines spiritales,* the spiritual men (apostles and prophets). Tertullian passionately opposes an *edictum peremptorium* of a not clearly identified bishop *(pontifex maximus quod est episcopus episcoporum)* who had

declared: *Ego et moechiae et fornicationis delicta paenitentia functis dimitto* (1). The frequently held view that the opponent here indicated is Pope Callistus (217–22) should be rejected. *De pudicitia* does not offer a satisfactory argument for assuming that Tertullian opposes a bishop living outside Africa, and besides, the account of Hippolytus (*Philos.* 9, 12), which attacks Callistus and his "lax" practice, is based on an entirely different situation from that which is to be deduced from the treatise of Tertullian. Tertullian evidently attacked Bishop Agrippinus of Carthage (Cypr., *Ep.* 71, 4).

Edd. of text: E. Preuschen, T 1910. P. de Labriolle, P 1906 (with *De paen.* and trans.). G. Rauschen, FP 10, 1915. — Treatises: On the more recent literature on the bishop opposed by Tert. see Altaner, TR 1939, 129/38. Stoekkius, AKK 1937, 24/126. W. Koehler, *Omnis ecclesia Petri propinqua* (SbHei 1938) and ZKG 1942, 124/35. Poschmann 1940, 348/67. Nock, HTR 1939, 83/96 *(edictum peremptorium)*. Keseling, PJB 1947 (Aristotle in 1, 1). Cf. 20.

31. *De pallio,* the shortest of all Tertullian's writings, is a personal apology. With bitter sarcasm he justifies himself before his fellow citizens for having exchanged the toga for the philosopher's cloak (c. 210). On the *Passio ss. Perpetuae et Felicitatis* v. § 45 n. 8.

Edd.: J. Marra, Tu 1933 (with trans.) and Tu 1954 (with *De spect.* and *De fuga*). A. Gerlo, *Wetteren,* 2 vols. (with trans. and comm.). Q. Cataudella, Genoa 1947 (with trans.). — Studies: Castiglioni, StU 261f. Gerlo, RBP 1939, 393/408 (text. crit.). Albizatti, Athenaeum 1939, 138/49. J. Klein, *Tert. Christl. Bewusstsein,* 1940, 252/68 (on date: 193). Waszink, Mn 1941, 131/7. Van Berchem, Museum Helveticum 1, 1944, 100/19. J. M. Vis, *Tert.'s De pallio,* thesis N 1949. C. Becker, *Tert.'s Apologeticum,* 1954, 354f. (on date: 209/11). G. Saeflund, *De pallio und d. stilist. Entwicklung T.s,* Lund 1955.

32. Lost and spurious writings. From the imposing number of lost writings we would mention especially the seven books *De ecstasi,* a defence of the ecstatic speech of the Montanist prophets. *Quaestio* 115 of the work *Quaestiones Vet. et Novi Test.* (318/49, ed. A. Souter 1908) which belongs to the Ambrosiaster uses perhaps the treatise *De fato*. The treatise *De exsecrandis gentium diis* is spurious.

Bickel, RM 1927, 394/417 (6th cent.).

IV. Points of Doctrine

1. In view of the contradictory results of pagan philosophizing, Tertullian's attitude to philosophy is sceptical, if not altogether negative, though he remains in favour of a naïve exercise of reason, even though he proceeds rather summarily. He accepts philosophy in so far as it agrees with the Christian truth *(Credo, ut intelligam)*. He clearly affirms that the existence of God and the immortality of the soul can be known by rational reflexion (*Resurr.* 3); also that God's absolute perfection results from the fact that he is without origin: *Imperfectum non potest esse, nisi quod factum est* (*Herm.* 28).

C. de L. Shortt, *The Influence of Philosophy on the Mind of Tert.*, 1933. Labhardt, MusHelvet 7, 1950, 159/80 *(Tert. et la philosophie)*. Refoulé, RevSR 1956, 42/5 *(Tert. et la philos.)*.

2. Everything that exists is a *corpus,* though a *corpus sui generis* (*Carn.* 11), hence God too, is a *corpus, etsi spiritus est* (*Prax.* 7). It is not impossible that *corpus* here means actually *substance,* so that Tertullian ascribes only substantiality to God; but then he attributes to the spiritual substance qualities such as are also possessed by the body; for he says of the soul that it has *corpus* or *corporalitas,* but also possesses lineage and colour, the colour of luminous air (*An.* 7 9; EP 346f.). Cf. Justin n. 4 and n. 5.

3. Tertullian's Trinitarian doctrine (EP 371/9) is expressed in the treatise *Adv. Praxean* in terms surprisingly definite for his time: *Connexus Patris in Filio et Filii in Paracleto tres efficit cohaerentes, alterum e altero. Qui tres unum sunt, non unus* (25); *tres unius substantiae et unius status et unius potestatis* (2). Cf. *Pud.* 21: *Trinitas unius Divinitatis, Pater et Filius et Spiritus Sanctus.* The technical term *persona* occurs for the first time in his writings: *Alium . . . personae, non substantiae nomine, ad distinctionem, non ad divisionem* (*Prax.* 12). The Logos was a *res et persona* already before the creation of the world, and that *per substantiae proprietatem,* but only with the

creation of the world did his coming forth from the Father become a *nativitas perfecta* (*Prax.* 7), and the *Wisdom* became the *Son*. Hence the Son as such is not eternal (*Herm.* 3; EP 321); it is true, his *diversitas* from the Father is denied (*Prax.* 9), but he differs from him *gradu* (order of origin). The Father possesses the fullness of the Godhead *(tota substantia est)*, the Son only a part *(derivatio totius et portio)*, hence he said: The Father is greater than I (9). The Son proceeds from the Father as the ray from the sun (13).

B. B. Warfield, *Studies in Tert. and Augustine,* O 1930, 1–109. M. Kriebel, *Studien zur aelteren Entwicklung der abendlaend. Trinitaetslehre bei Tert. u. Novatian,* thesis Marburg 1932. Hanson, Ha 45, 1945, 67/73 (theophanies in the OT and the Second Person). Morel, StC 1940, 194/206 (on Jo. 16, 13).

4. Tertullian affirms unequivocally the duality of natures in the one Person of Christ; in this doctrine he became the guide of the West. We find the following expressions in his works: *Proprietas utriusque substantiae (in una persona), duplicem statum, non confusum sed coniunctum in una persona, deum et hominem Iesum* (*Prax.* 27, EO 379). The miracles of Jesus show forth his true divinity, the affections and sufferings his true humanity (*Carn.* 5; EP 353).

Favre, BLE 1936, 130/45 *(communicatio idiomatum)*.

5. Tertullian is against the *virginity of Mary in partu* and *post partum* (*Carn.* 7 23; *Marc.* 4, 19; EP 359) which we meet in tradition for the first time in the apocryphal *Gospel of James* and in the *Odes of Solomon*. Later Helvidius claimed the authority of Tertullian for his opinions (Jerome, *Adv. Helv.* 17).

H. Koch, *Virgo Eva — Virgo Maria,* 1937, 8/17; against this K. Adam, TQ 1938, 171 ff. Motherway, TSW 1, 1940, 97 ff. (creation of Eve). Madoz, EE 1944, 187/200 (Influence of Tert.'s Mariology).

6. The soul of the child is a shoot *(tradux,* Traducianism) from the soul of the parent; this explains the similarity of the psychological endowment of parents and children (*An.* 36 f.). V. supra n. 2.

7. Original sin is taught to be *vitium originis* in *De anima* 41: The poison of evil desire has invaded human nature through the sin of Adam; this is the *vitium originis* which has become a *naturale quodammodo* through the devil. Nevertheless, infant baptism is not advisable except in cases of necessity (*Bapt.* 18).

8. The conception of the Church in *Fug.* 14, *Pud.* 21, 17 is purely Montanist: *Ubi tres, ecclesia est, licet laici* (*Esch.* 7).

9. According to *Pud.* 21, 9–11 the primacy and the power to bind and loose were given to St. Peter personally, not also to other bishops. Peter and Paul died in Rome (*Scorp.* 15; *Marc.* 4, 5; EH 215; EP 341). On the term *pontifex maximus* supra III 30.

K. Adam, *Der Kirchenbegriff Tert.s,* 1907. H. Koch, *Callist. u. Tert.,* 1920. U. Gmelin, *Auctoritas. Roem. Princeps u. paepstl. Primat,* 1937, 83/91. Bardy, VS 1939, 109/24 (Le sacerdoce chrét.). J. C. Plumpe, *Mater Ecclesia,* W 1943, 45/62. Morel, RHE 1939, 243/65; 1944/5, 5/46 (*disciplina*). De Pauw, ETL 1942, 5/46 (traditions non écrites). Quasten, Tr 1944, 481/4 (*traditio*). V. Morel, *De ontwikkeling van de christ. Overlevering folgens Tert.,* Bruges 1946. J. Ludwig 1952, 11/20.

10. *The Doctrine of Penance.* In his Catholic treatise *De paenitentia* Tertullian urges all sinners to submit to the one single, unrepeatable ecclesiastical penance. The question whether he also envisages an ecclesiastical forgiveness (reconciliation) in this work is probably to be answered in the affirmative; cf. *an melius est damnatum latere quam palam absolvi?* (10). In *Paen.* 9f. Tertullian treats extensively of public confession (*exhomologesis*). Later, as a Montanist, he distinguishes *peccata remissibilia* and *peccata irremissibilia* (*Pud.* 2) and restricts the ecclesiastical penance to the *peccata leviora.* Among the unforgiveable sins the so-called trias of sins stands out particularly, viz. adultery, murder and apostasy or idolatry. According to Tertullian the power of forgiving sins exercised by Christ was purely personal and was not fully transmitted to the Church (*Pud.* 11). The power of forgiveness belongs to the *spiritalis homo,* not to the episcopal office; the *pneumatici* are organs of the Holy Spirit (*Pud.* 21; EP 387).

11. Tertullian calls the eucharistic service *gloriae relatio et benedictio et laus et hymni* and sees in it the fulfilment of the prophecy of Mal. 1, 10f. (*Marc.* 22; *Jud.* 5). In other places he speaks of *orationes sacrificiorum, munditiae sacrificiorum;* those present receive "the body of the Lord", "the sacrament of the eucharist" (*Orat.* 19; *Marc.* 3, 22; *Pud.* 9, 16; *Cor.* 3). For the consecrated bread we find (Marc. 4, 40) the expression *figura corporis mei* which means as much as: the body under the symbol of bread. The reality of the body that is to be consumed is for him so certain that he wants to prove from it the reality of the crucified body against Marcion (3, 19; EP 337). *Caro corpore et sanguine Christi vescitur, ut et anima de Deo saginetur* (*Resurr.* 8).

J. Hoh 1932, 43/58 = TG 1931, 625/38. Chartier, Ant 1935, 301/44, 499/536. K. Rahner, ZKT 1936, 491/507. Poschmann 1940, 283/348. Joyce, JTS 1941, 18/42. Daly, IER 1947, 693/707, 815/21; 1948, 731/46; 1950, 156/69. Quacquarelli, RassScFilos 1949, 16/37. K. Rahner, *Festschr. K. Adam,* 1952, 139/67. Doelger, AC 6, 1940, 108/17 (on *dominica sollemnis*). Hitchcock, CQR 1942, 21/36. E. Dekkers, *Tert. en de geschiedenis der Liturgie,* Bru-A 1947, 49/67. A. Kolping, *Sacramentum Tertullianeum,* Mr 1948.

12. Tertullian knows a state of expiatory suffering after death. The dead, with the exception of the martyrs, remain in Hades until the Day of the Lord. There they suffer *supplicia* out of which the intercessions of the living lead them to the *refrigerium* (*An.* 55 58; *Resurr.* 43; *Monog.* 10; EP 352, 382). Tertullian was a Chiliast (*Marc.* 3, 24; *Spect.* 30).

Daniélou, VC 1948, 1/16 (chiliast. interpretation of the week in ancient Christianity). Quacquarelli, RassScFilos 1949, 14/47 (anthropology and eschatology). Tescari, Misc. G. Galbiati, Mi 1951, 13/18 (on angelology). Pelikan, CH 21, 1952, 108/22 (eschatology).

Further studies on dogmatic and philos. history: J. Koehne, *Die Ehen zw. Christen u. Heiden in den ersten christl. Jhh.,* 1931. Delazer, Ant 1932, 441/61 (indissolubility of marriage). Doelger, AC 5, 262/71 (*misericordia*). J. Klein, *Tertullians christliches Bewusstsein u. sittl. Forderungen,* 1940. Gonella, RivIntern-Filos Dir 1937, 23/37 (*Le leggi sec. Tert. e Lattanzio*). H. Pétré, *L'exemplum chez Tert.,* Dijob 1945. Skard, NorskTTidskr 40, 145/81 (catechumenate). Sevenster, NTT 9, 1954/5, 364/73 (resurrection of the body in Tert. and N.T.). H. Karpp, *Schrift u. Geist b. Tert.,* G 1955. Da Lio, StPat 1955, 358/95; 1956, 185/212 (proof from miracles in T.). H. Finé, *Die Terminologie d. Jenseitsvorstellung bei Tert.,* Bonn 1958.

31. § HIPPOLYTUS OF ROME (d. 235)

HIPPOLYTUS, who lived and worked in Rome as a presbyter from the beginning of the third century, wrote in Greek. In the variety of his interests and the number of his writings he may be compared with his outstanding contemporary Origen. As an independent theological thinker, however, Hippolytus is far inferior to the Alexandrian; he is principally a learned and industrious compiler interested not so much in abstract problems as in practical questions. Many problems which the person and work of Hippolytus had raised in the minds of scholars were solved only after his principal work, the *Philosophoumena,* had become known (1851). Its authenticity as well as that of other writings of his has recently been disputed, though without convincing reasons.

Hippolytus (a pupil of Irenaeus?) was probably neither Roman nor Latin by birth, but a native of the Greek East. Being himself a passionate opponent of the Trinitarian Modalists and Patripassians (Noetus, Cleomenes, Sabellius), he subscribed to a subordinatianist Logos doctrine. The ambitious, rigorist presbyter came into conflict with Pope Callistus (217–22) on questions of penance and ecclesiastical discipline, and accused the Pope of Sabellianism and excessive leniency towards sinners. Having been elected antipope, Hippolytus, who was supported by a small circle of followers influential by birth and education, remained in schism also under the Popes Urban and Pontianus. In the persecution under Maximinus Thrax, both heads of the Church, Pontianus and Hippolytus, were exiled to Sardinia. Since Hippolytus was reconciled to the Church during his lifetime and died in exile (235), he was buried on the same day as Pontianus (13th August) in the *Via Tiburtina* in Rome and venerated as a martyr. (Cf. the epitaph of Pope Damasus which is dedicated to *the Presbyter Hippolytus;* EH 590; see EH 544, 7; 547, 19.)

His followers erected, probably in his burial vault, the famous marble statue to him which was rediscovered in 1551 (today in the Lateran museum), on which is engraved his table of Easter and an incomplete list of his writings. Interest in him vanished surprisingly quickly. Eusebius and Jerome call him bishop, but do not know his see. In Pope Damasus' inscription he is connected with the Novatianist schism.

Edd. of text: MG 10 and 16, 3. G. N. Bonwetsch - H. Achelis, GCS 1, 1937 (exegetic. and homilet. writings). P. Wendland, GCS 26, 1916 *(Philosoph.)*. A. Bauer - R. Helm, GCS 46, 1955 (chronicles). Bonwetsch, TU 26, 1a, 1904 (texts preserved in Georg.). E. Schwartz, SbMn 1936, 3 (fragms. *Contra Noet.* and *Contra Jud.*). P. Nautin, *Hipp., Contre les hérésies,* P 1949 (fragms. of *Syntagma*). M. Brière - L. Mariès - B. C. Mercier, *Hippolyte de Rome, sur les Bénédictions d'Isaac, de Jacob et de Moïse* (Bénédict. d'Isaac et de Jacob: Greek text and Armen. and Georg. transs.; *Bénédict. de Moïse:* Armen. and Georg. transs.) in PO 27, 1954 (with French trans.).

Trans.: K. Preysing (BKV² 40), 1922 *(Philosoph.)*. A. Siouville, 2 vols., P 1928 *(Philosoph.)*. V. Groene, BKV 1873 (On the Antichrist). Bonwetsch in GCS 1 (Daniel). G. Bardy - M. Lefèvre, *Comment. sur Daniel* (SCh 14) 1947 (trans. and comm.). J. Legge (SPCK) 1921.

Studies: Amann, DTC 6, 2487/2511. K. J. Neumann, *Hipp. in seiner Stellung zu Staat u. Welt,* 1902. A. Donini, *Ipp. di Roma,* 1925. M. da Leonissa, *S. Ipp. della Via Tiburtina,* 1935. Josi, RAC 1936, 231/6 (fragm. of the *Titulus* of Damasus). G. Bovini, RAC 1942, 35/85; *S. Ipp., Dott. e Martire,* 1943. G. Da Bra, *Studio su S. Ipp.,* 1944. R. Reuterer, *Der hl. Hipp.,* Klagenfurt 1947. — On the Hipp. statue: Wendel, TSK 1938, 362/9. Bovini, *Bollet. della Commissione Archeol. Communale di Roma,* 1940, 109/28. — De Gaiffier, RAM 1949, 219/24 (Hipp.-Office in the *Libellus Orationum* of Verona). Amore, RAC 1954, 63/97 *(Note su S. Ippol.)*.

1. Ten books of *Philosophoumena,* called by the author Κατὰ πασῶν αἱρέσεων ἔλεγχος, in most editions *Refutatio omnium haeresium* (EH 228/33; EP 397/9).

Strangely enough this work is not mentioned under his name either on the statue or in the old authors. The first book has been known since 1701, but circulated under Origen's name; books 2 and 3 are still lost; 4–10 were discovered by Minoïdes Mynas in a Greek MS of Mount Athos, now in Paris, and edited as a work of Origen for the first time by E. Miller. Chapters 11 and

12 of the *Letter to Diognetus* are sometimes regarded as the conclusion of the work (§ 23, 1).

Contents: The first part (1–4) for which alone the title *Philosophoumena* is suitable, wants to show that the heretics have drawn their teachings not from the Christian revelation, but "from the wisdom of the pagans". The first book gives a précis of Greek philosophy from inferior sources; the fourth deals with astrology and magic, and these together with the mysteries must have been the subject of the lost books 2 and 3.

The second part (5–9) is a description of the heresies, by which are here meant thirty-three Gnostic systems. Apart from Irenaeus' *Adversus haereses,* other writings are used as sources, especially heretical works which have partly been preserved in the most recent papyrus finds which have given us Gnostic original writings in Coptic translation (v. supra § 24, 9d). Since Callistus was already dead (cf. 9, 11–13), the work was written after 222.

Treatises: Reinhardt, Her 1942, 1/27 (Heraclitus' doctrine of fire). G. Da Bra, *I filosofumeni sono di Hipp.?,* 1942. Filliozat, RHR 130, 1945, 59/91 (teaching of the Brahmans acc. to Hipp.). Peterson, RSR 34, 1947, 232/8 (Elkesites). Quispel, VC 1948, 115f. (Basilides). H. J. Schoeps, *Theol. u. Gesch. des Judenchristentums,* 1949. Haenchen, ZTK 1952, 316/49 (pre-Christ. Gnosis). P. Nautin, *Hipp. et Josipe,* 1947. Nautin wants to divide the works of Hipp. between two authors. Josipe, an author unknown to the history of literature is supposed to be represented by the Lateran statue and to have written the *Philosophoumena, De Universo* and the *Chronicle.* The *Commentary on Daniel, De Antichristo, Contra Noëtum,* the *Apostolic Tradition,* the *Blessings of Jacob* etc. belong to the other, an Hippolytus of unknown nationality, probably a native of the East. Nautin's sensational assertions have been opposed by the following: Bardy, MSR 1948, 63/88; Richard, ibid. 1948, 294/308; 1950, 237/68; 1951, 19/51; 1953, 13/52 and 145/180; RSR 1955, 379/94; also Capelle, RTA 1950, 145/74; 1952, 193/202; Botte, RTA 1949, 177/85; 1951, 5/18; Giet, RevSR 1950, 315/22; 1951, 75/85; Oggioni, SC 1950, 126/43; 315/22; 1951, 75/85; 1952, 513/25; Elfers, *Festschr. K. Adam,* 1952, 181/98. But Nautin defends his opinion against all objections; cf. Nautin, RSR 1947, 100/07; 347/59; RHE 1952, 5/43; RSR 1954, 226/57; MSR 1954, 215/18.

2. The *Syntagma* or Πρὸς ἁπάσας τὰς αἱρέσεις, written considerably earlier than the *Philosophoumena,* is lost in the original;

according to Lipsius, however, it can be reconstructed from other writings (Pseudo-Tertullian, *De praescr.* 46–53 [supra § 30 II 6], Epiphanius and Philastrius); it discussed thirty-two heresies, the last of which was that of Noëtus.

E. Schwartz, SbMn 1936, 3 (text) 5/18 *(Contra Noetum)*; 37f. P. Nautin, *Hipp., Contre les hérésies,* Ét. et éd. critique, 1949, R. A. Lipsius, *Zur Quellenkritik des Epiphanius,* 1865. V. Machioro, *L'eresia Noetiana,* Na 1921. Martin, RHE 1941, 1/23 (*Contra Noëtum* belongs to the *Syntagma*). Giet, RevSR 1950, 315/22 (text of fragm. *Contra Noët.*).

3. Only little is preserved of Hippolytus' exegetical writings, which bear honourable witness to his scholarship and exegetical skill. Even these small remains, like the fragments of other writings, are to be found only in out-of-the-way places and in the most varied languages (Latin, Syriac, Coptic, Ethiopic, Armenian, Georgian, Old Slavonic).

a. Four books of a *Commentary on Daniel* (EP 390). The work was written *c.* 204, and its author is still under the impression of the recent persecution of the Christians by Septimius Severus. The whole is preserved in Old Slavonic and the greater part also in Greek. The author uses the Greek translation of Theodotion and has also given an exegesis of the deutero-canonical parts of the book. The commentary of Hippolytus on Daniel is the oldest exegetical work of the Church that has come down to us. Book 4, 23 is the first patristic reference to give an exact date for the day of Christ's birth and that of his death. According to him, Jesus was born on Wednesday, December 25th in the 42nd year of the reign of the Emperor Augustus and died on Friday, March 25th, in the 18th year of the reign of the Emperor Tiberius. The passage is, however, certainly an interpolation, though a very early one.

b. The *Commentary on the Canticle* (only to 3, 7) has been edited by Bonwetsch from a Georgian translation.

c. Treatises on the *Blessing of Jacob* (Gn. 49), the *Blessing of*

Moses (Dt. 33) and a homily on the *Narrative of David and Goliath* (1 Sam. 17) are all three preserved in Armenian and Georgian, the first also in Greek.

On the *Commentary on Daniel:* Ogg, JTS 1942, 187f. (year of Christ's death). Andriessen, VC 1928, 248f. (on 4, 60). R. Wilde, *The Treatment of the Jews in Greek Christ. Writers,* W 1949, 159/68. J. Ziegler, GN 1952, No. 8, 163/99 (text of Bible in *Comm. on Dan.*). — On other exeget. works: G. Mercati, ST 142, 1948 (Proemi del Salterio di Origene, Ippolito . . . e altri). Jouassard, RevSR 1937, 2/17 (Comm. on Sam.) and 290/305. Belet, Sefarad 6, 1946, 355/61 (on Mt. 24, 15–34; Copt. fragm.). L. Mariès, *Hipp. de Rome, Sur les bénédict. d'Isaac, de Jacob et de Moïse,* 1935; RSR 39, 1951, 381/96 *(Le Messie issu de Lévi).* Welsersheimb, ZKT 1948, 400/4 (idea of Church in comm. on Cant.).

4. Of the dogmatic writings only the monograph *De antichristo* (EP 388f.) has been completely preserved in Greek. It was written *c.* 200. Depending partly on Irenaeus, it discusses the person and marks of Antichrist and of the events of the last times.

5. The *Chronicle* begins with the creation of the world and ends with the year A.D. 234. Only a small part is extant in Greek, the whole is preserved in three Latin versions that are independent of each other, the so-called *Excerpta latina Barbari* and the two *Libri generationis;* there is also an Armenian translation.

Hippolytus wrote his chronicle of the world in order to show that the hope of the advent of the millennium, still widespread among the Christians, was futile.

Of his Ἀπόδειξις χρόνων τοῦ πάσχα the most important remains is the Easter table for the years 222–33 engraved on the statue.

6. Major Greek fragments preserved under the name of Hippolytus: *Contra gentes* (Πρὸς Ἕλληνας καὶ πρὸς Πλάτωνα ἢ καὶ περὶ τοῦ παντός); a fragment is extant in the *Sacra Parallela* of John of Damascus; this shows contradictions in Plato.

Cf. Vergote, OCP 1938, 47/64 (new Copt. fragm.?).

Against the Heresy of Artemon, called by Theodoret of Cyrus *The Little Labyrinth,* opposes the Monarchians; a fragment in Euseb., *Hist.* 5, 28; today its authenticity is mostly denied.

For it being spurious: E. Schwartz, SbMn 1936, 49/51; Vergote, OCP 1938, 60; Schoene, DP 1939, 252/65; P. Nautin, *Le dossier d'Hipp. et de Méliton . . .*, P 1953. For it being genuine: Connolly, JTS 1948, 73/9.

The homily *Against the Jews* lately ed. by E. Schwartz (SbMn 1936, 19/23) is proved to be spurious by Nautin, *Le dossier d'Hippolyte et de Méliton . . .*, 1953. On the homily against the heresy of Noëtus v. supra n. 2. Nautin also denies that Hippolytus is the author of chapters 11 and 12 of the *Letter to Diognetus*, as has frequently been asserted (v. supra § 23, 1).

C. Martin attempts to prove that an *Easter sermon* of Pseudo-Chrysostom (MG 59, 735/46) which has also been used by Proclus of Constantinople belongs to Hippolytus. Even though this is untenable, it may be taken for certain that the lost treatise of Hippolytus *De S. Pascha* was used in this homily. We see from this that the Exodus account (12, 14 43–9) was used already by Hippolytus to interpret the events of Easter.

Martin, AIP 1936, 321/63 and RHE 1937, 255/76; against this Connolly, JTS 1945, 195/8. Trans. by Casel, JL 1938, 25/8. Crit. text by P. Nautin, *Homélies pascales*, I: *Une homélie inspirée du traité sur la Pâque d'Hipp.* (SCh 27), 1950; cf. Richard, RHE 1951, 727/9. Daniélou, *Dieu Vivant* 18, 1951, 45/56 (symbolism of Easter).

From the *catenae* MSS P. Nautin edits an almost complete *Homily on a Psalm:* P. Nautin, *Le dossier d'Hippolyte et de Méliton dans les florilèges dogmatiques et chez les historiens modernes*, 1953, 166/83. Hulshoff, Sc 6, 1952, 33/8 (Hipp. fragments in Anast. Sinaita).

7. On the liturgical and canonical, Ἀποστολικὴ παράδοσις, today largely recognized as genuine, § 7, 1; on the *Canones Hippolyti* v. supra § 7, 7. The treatise Περὶ χαρισμάτων *(De donationibus)* is lost. On Hippolytus and the *Muratorian Fragment* v. supra § 28, 1.

8. Ὑπὲρ τοῦ κατὰ Ἰωάννην εὐαγγελίου καὶ ἀποκαλύψεως defends the Johannine authorship of the Gospel and the Apocalypse against the Alogi and the Roman presbyter and anti-Montanist Gaius (supra § 24); this lost treatise is perhaps identical with the Κεφάλαια κατὰ Γαΐου, of which Syriac fragments are extant.

Points of Doctrine

Hippolytus is a witness for the Church's teaching on 1. the inspiration of Scripture (fragm. in Eus., *Hist.* 5, 28; EP 400);

2. the resurrection of the body and the eternity of the punishments in hell (fragm. *Contra gentes;* EP 395f.);

3. the Eucharist as a sacrifice: the prophecy of Malachias (1, 10f.) referred to the Eucharist as in the *Didache* (*Dan.* 4, 35, 3).

4. Like earlier Apologists (Justin, Athenagoras, Theophilus, Tertullian) Hippolytus too, interprets the relation of the Logos to the Father in a subordinatianist sense. Like Theophilus he distinguishes a λόγος ἐνδιάθετος and προφορικός and thinks that the Logos became a Person only later, "at the time and in the way the Father willed"; he even thinks if God had so willed it he could also have made a man into God (*Philos.* 10, 33). Hence his opponent, Pope Callistus, rightly calls him a ditheist (EP 398; EH 231).

5. As regards the treatment of grave sin, Hippolytus subscribed to rigorist principles. Pope Callistus, so he relates, had granted fornicators re-admission to the Church. Hippolytus opposed him in this and demanded also greater severity in the treatment of bishops who had incurred punishment and in the admission of bigamists to offices in the Church; he also denied the ecclesiastical validity of marriages between free women and slaves (*Philos.* 9, 12; EH 228ff.). It is true, he recognized the hierarchical offices in the Church (cf. his *Trad. Apost.*), yet in his ethical rigorism he eventually not only strove for a Church of the pure and of saints, as did Novatian (§ 33) soon after him, but he made the functions of the representatives of the hierarchy dependent on their personal holiness (*Philos.* 9, 12; *Dan.* 1, 17; 2, 5; *Antichr.* 59).

A. d'Alès, *La théologie de S. Hipp.*, [2]1929. A. Hamel, *Der Kirchenbegriff Hipp.s*, thesis Bonn 1929. Hoh 1932, 58/63. Jouassard, RevSR 1933, 25/37 (virginity of Mary). H. Rahner, ZKT 1936, 73/81; 1936, 577/90 (theotokos); against this Doelger, AC 5, 152 and RSR 1936, 204 A 25. G. Bardy 1935, 149/59. Cullmann,

RHP 1936, 1 ff. *(La sainte Cène)*. Capelle, RTA 1937, 109/24 (Logos doctrine). Pruemm, ZKT 1939, 207/25 *(mysterion)*. Poschmann 1940, 348/67. H. Rahner, Bi 1941, 368 ff. (on Jo. 7, 37). E. Lengling, *Die Heilstat des Logos-Christos bei Hipp.*, R 1947. Grillmeier, ZKT 1949, 32/4, 187/97 (descent into Hades). A. Hamel, *Die Kirche bei Hipp. v. Rom*, 1951. Lecuyer, RSR 1953, 30/50 (episcopate and presbyterate). Gaudemet, *Studi in onore de U.E. Paoli* (Fi 1956) 333/44 (Concubinage).

§ 32. PAPAL LETTERS OF THE THIRD CENTURY

1. THE legislation of Callistus (217–22), a former slave, and the excommunication of Sabellius are recorded by his opponent Hippolytus (*Philos.* 9, 12; EH 231) in an exaggeratedly polemical spirit. On his alleged edict on penance v. supra § 30, III 30; EH 228/33; ES 43.

2. Pontianus (230–5) probably communicated to Bishop Demetrius of Alexandria in a letter that is now lost the decisions of a Roman synod of 231 or 232 (Jerome, *Ep.* 33, 5) which opposed Origen.

3. Cornelius (251–53) wrote seven letters to Cyprian of Carthage, of which only two are found among the Letters of Cyprian (*Ep.* 49 f.). He also wrote three Greek letters to Bishop Fabius of Antioch, the third of which is extant in sizable extracts in Eusebius (*Hist.* 6, 43; EH 254/6). Here the Pope describes the disgraceful behaviour of Novatian especially when he founded his schismatic community and gives important information on the organization of the Roman Church (ES 45).

4. Lucius I (253–4) wrote letters to Cyprian (*Ep.* 68, 5) on the question of the lapsed.

5. Stephen I (254–7) wrote to the churches of Syria and Arabia (Eus., *Hist.* 7, 5, 2), to the bishops of Asia Minor on heretical baptism (Cypr., *Ep.* 75, 25) and to Cyprian (EH 308/9). From the latter epistle a passage that is important for the teaching on tradition has been preserved; it concerns the preservation of the traditional practice in the matter of heretical baptism (Cypr., *Ep.* 74, 1; ES 46).

6. Sixtus II (257–8) is probably the author of a treatise on heretical baptism. V. supra § 13, 3, *Sayings of Sextus.*

7. Dionysius (259–68) wrote a letter of consolation to the church of Caesarea in Cappadocia (Basil, *Ep.* 70) and two letters to Bishop Dionysius of Alexandria on Sabellianism and Subordinatianism. A lengthy passage of the former on the Trinity and the Incarnation is preserved in Athanasius (*Ep. de decr. Nic. syn.* 26; ES 48/51).

8. Felix I (269–74). On a letter falsely ascribed to the Pope by the Apollinarians at the beginning of the fifth century cf. H. Lietzmann, *Apollinaris von Laodicea und seine Schule,* 1904, 162, 318/21. I. Rucker 1933, 3*.

Sources and Lit. supra § 25. Turner, JTS 17, 1915/6, 338/53 (chronol. of the Popes). Sybel, ZKG 1926, 316f. (Church painting introduced by Callistus). Mercati, OM 2, 1937, 226/40 (*Ep. Cornelii;* text. crit.). Styger, ZKT 1932, 67/81 (catacomb of Callistus). On Cornelius and Stephen cf. § 34. G. Roethe, *Zur Gesch. der roem. Synoden im 3. u. 4. Jh.,* 1937.

§ 33. NOVATIAN

THOUGH only a "clinic", i.e. baptized during a grave illness and not confirmed, Novatian had become a priest "against the opposition of all the clergy as well as of many laymen" (Eus., *Hist.* 6, 43; EH 254/6). About 250 he held a position of high repute among the Roman clergy, as is shown by the two letters which he addressed in their name to St. Cyprian during the vacancy of the see (Cypr., *Ep.* 30 and 36). His writings show him to have been a man highly trained in rhetoric, (Stoic) philosophy and theology. He was the first theologian in Rome to write in Latin. On the question of how to treat the lapsed *(lapsi)* he at first shared Cyprian's point of view against Felicissimus (§ 34). But when, in March 251, Cornelius was elected Bishop of Rome and showed himself lenient towards the lapsed, Novatian set himself up as anti-Pope at the head of a party of rigorists and had himself consecrated by three bishops from Southern Italy. His schism gained adherents even in the East and survived for centuries.

Nothing is known of Novatian's later life and his end; according to Socr., *Hist.* 4, 28, he was said to have died a martyr under Valerian. This information is probably confirmed by an inscription found in a Donatist catacomb in Rome: *Novatiano beatissimo martyri Gaudentius diaconus.* It is surprising that Novatian is not called a bishop.

The Novatianists excluded from their Church ever those who had lapsed from the faith, and later also all others who had committed mortal sin. They called themselves the pure ones (καθαροί), and considered invalid even the baptism of Catholics and re-baptized their converts.

1. The two letters to Cyprian (v. supra).

2. Four treatises preserved under another name (while others, mentioned by Jerome, *Vir. ill.* 70, have been lost): a. *De trinitate,* b. *De cibis Iudaicis* (both among Tertullian's writings), c. *De spectaculis,* d. *De bono pudicitiae* (both among Cyprian's writings).

De Trinitate, written probably before 250 in rhythmic prose, the most important and the largest of these four treatises, was attributed to Novatian already by Jerome, and is a work excellent in form. The doctrine of the Trinity is treated comprehensively, while use is made of Theophilus of Antioch, Irenaeus, Hippolytus and Tertullian. The Monarchians are heavily attacked. In Novatian, too, the Logos is subordinated to the Father and the Holy Spirit to the Son (EP 603/8).

De cibis Iudaicis proves that Christians are not bound by Jewish dietary laws and need only avoid meat sacrificed to idols. The author addresses this work, which has the form of a pastoral letter, to the Novatianist community in Rome from which he was absent at that time. A warning against the morning drink seems to be borrowed from Seneca (*Ep.* 122, 6), as are other matters.

De spectaculis forbids attendance at pagan plays just like Tertullian's treatise of the same title. *De bono pudicitiae* is an excellent study of the various degrees of chastity (virginity, continence in marriage, conjugal faithfulness).

Edd.: ML 3. CSEL 3, 2, 549/56, 572/5 (Letters). W. Y. Fausset, C 1909 *(De Trin.)*. H. Moore (SPCK), Lo 1919 (trans. of *De Trin.*). Landgraf u. Weyman, *Arch. fuer Lexikographie* 11, 1898–1900, 221/49 *(De cib. Iud.)*. CSEL 3, 3, 3/25 *(De spect.; De bono pud.)*. A. Boulenger, *Tertullien, De spect.;* id., *Pseudo-Cyprien, De spect.,* P 1933. — Mg.: A. d'Alès, *Novatien,* P 1924. Amann, DTC 11, 816/49. H. Koch, PWK 17, 1138/56. M. Kriebel 1932 (supra § 30 IV 3).

Treatises: Doelger, AC 2, 258/67 (Baptism of N.). Keilbach, BoS 1933, 193/224 (Logos doctr.). H. Koch, Rel 1935, 320/32 (N., Cyprian and Pliny the Younger); ZNTW 1935, 303/06 (genuineness of N.'s letter [Cypr., *Ep.* 30]); Rel 1936, 245/65 (genuineness of *De spect.*); 1937, 278/94 (language and style). Favre, BLE 1936, 139ff. (Communic. idiomat.). Stelzenberger 1933, 262/4, 465/7 and freq. Doelger, AC 6, 1940, 61/4 (on Eus., *Hist.* 6, 43, 16). B. Melin, *Studia in Corpus Cyprianeum,* Up 1946, 67/122. Gewiess, TQ 1948, 463ff. (on Phil. 2, 5–11). Daly, ITQ 1952, 33/43 (Nov. and Tertullian). Scheidweiler, ZKG 66, 1955, 126/39 (angels and Christol.). On the inscription of the martyr N. cf. Josi, RAC 1933, 21f.; J. P. Kirsch, *Le catacombe rom.,* 1933, 132/5; P. Styger, *Die roem. Katakomben,* 1933, 189ff.; Van den Eynde, RHE 1937, 792/4. Mohlberg, EL 1937, 242/9. H. Koch, Rel 1938, 192/8. Ferrua, CC 1944, 4, 232/9. J. Barbel, TrThZ 1958, 96/105 (Angels — Christology, against Scheidweiler).

§ 34. CYPRIAN (d. 258)

His *Vita,* alleged to have been written after his death by his deacon Pontius, gives an account of the very agitated life of Thascius Caecilius Cyprianus. Its value as a source is much disputed and it has proved historically very unreliable. It is in the main a panegyric or *martyrium.* The so-called *Acta proconsularia Cypriani,* on the other hand, which give an account of the trial and martyrdom of Cyprian, are based on records of the minutes. The most important source is his writings, especially his letters, for his conversion the treatise *Ad Donatum.*

Cyprian was born between 200 and 210, probably at Carthage. The son of wealthy pagan parents, he first became a rhetor, then *c.* 246 he was converted to Christianity by the priest Caecilianus at Carthage and baptized. He became bishop of his native city in 248–9. His zealous pastoral work was soon interrupted by the Decian persecution (250), during which he hid himself in the vicinity of the city, but remained in constant touch with his church. A schism was caused by the question of re-admitting the many lapsed who had denied their faith in the persecution.

Cyprian refused to submit to the arrogance of the confessors who demanded the immediate reconciliation of the lapsed; hence the discontented formed themselves into a party under the deacon Felicissimus. This was also joined by five priests who had opposed Cyprian's consecration; one of them, Novatus, went to Rome soon afterwards and supported the schism of Novatian. Cyprian was able to return to Carthage in the spring of 251. He now held a synod there and excommunicated the heads of the opposing party; he decided that the *sacrificati* and *thurificati* would have to submit to a severe penance even if they mended their ways. If, however, a new persecution should break out, they might be strengthened for the fight by the reception of the eucharist even before their time of penance had expired. Though in 252 an anti-bishop was put up in the person of Fortunatus, the schism remained without great importance.

The terrible plague which visited the Roman Empire (252–54) brought the Christians in Africa new sufferings and persecutions. Cyprian heroically organized the service of the sick in his Church and also exercised a favourable influence on his pagan fellow-citizens. His last years (from 255) were saddened by the controversy about heretical baptism.

Like Tertullian before him and like the bishops of Asia Minor, Cyprian thought heretical baptism invalid. Three synods at Carthage over which he presided in 255 and 256 declared themselves in favour of the invalidity of heretical baptism. Though Pope Stephen rejected the opinion of the African Church, Cyprian persisted in his view (EH 257/307). This did not later prevent St. Augustine from emphatically defending and excusing him as a *catholicus episcopus* and *catholicus martyr* when the Donatists appealed to his authority.

In the persecution under Valerian, Cyprian was beheaded in a place near Carthage on September 14, 258. Later he was confused with the legendary magician and martyr, Cyprian of Antioch.

Edd.: G. Hartel (CSEL 3, 1–3), 1868/71. S. Colombo, *Corona Patrum Salesiana,* Ser. lat. 2, Tu 1935 (Tractatus, with trans.). — Trans.: J. Baer (BKV 34 60) 1918 and 1928. — Mg.: J. Peters 1877. B. Fechtrup 1878. E. W. Benson, Lo 1897. P. Monceaux (supra § 3) 2, 1902 and shorter P 1914. J. Boutet 1923. S. Colombo, Did 1928, 1, 1/80 (C. as a person and a writer). A. Beck and L. Bayard (supra § 30). J. Ludwig, *Der hl. Maertyrerbischof Cypr. v. Carthago,* 1951. J. H. Fichter, *Cyprian, Defender of the Faith,* St. Louis 1942. — J. Voegtle, *Die Schriften des hl. Cypr. als Erkenntnisquelle des roem. Rechts,* thesis B 1920. H. Koch, *Cyprianische Untersuchungen,* 1926. P. C. Knook, *De overgang van metrisch tot rhythmisch Proza bij Cypr. en Hieronymus,* A 1932. D. D. Sullivan, *The Life of North Africa as Revealed in the Works of St. Cypr.,* W 1933. J. Grasmueller, *Koordin., subord. u. fragende Partikel bei Cypr.,* thesis Erlangen 1933. R. Hoeslinger 1935 (v. supra § 30). H. Janssen, *Kultur u. Sprache i. d. alten Kirche,* N 1938 (from Tert. to Cypr.). J. Merkx, *Zur Syntax der Kasus u. Tempora i. d. Traktaten Cyprians,* N 1939. Mohrmann, *Tijdschr. v. taal en lett.,* 1939, 163/75 (puns). Favez, REL 1941, 191/201 (C.'s flight). Ehrhardt, CQR 133, 1941/2, 178/96 (C. the Father of Western Christianity). M. T. Ball, *Nature and the Vocabulary of Nature in the Works of St. C.,* W 1946. B. Melin, *Studia in Corpus Cyprianeum,* Up 1946.

On the *Vita of Pontius* and the *Acta Proconsularia:* Reitzenstein, SbHei 1913, 46/69 and GN 1919, 177/219. Martin, HJB 1919, 674/712. H. Delehaye, *Les passions des martyrs,* 1921, 82/104. Franchi de' Cavalieri in ST 49, 1928, 243 f. M. Pellegrino, *Vita des Pontius* (Text and trans.), Alba 1955.

A. Cyprian's literary work

In accordance with his character Cyprian aimed neither at novelty and depth of ideas nor at originality of form in his writings. For he was above all a man of action, and his literary activities, too, were intimately connected with this. In his thought he is frequently influenced by Tertullian, his "master" (Jerome., *Vir. ill.* 53), but he keeps himself free from the one-sided exaggerations of the latter. He also differs from him in that he writes an easily intelligible style which is nevertheless perfect in form. His treatise *De ecclesiae unitate* is his most independent work. He remained the authoritative Latin writer down to Augustine. His writings were much read both in antiquity and in the Middle Ages and have come down to us in numerous MSS (his Letters, e.g., are preserved in more than 150 MSS, though these are not complete). Three lists belonging to antiquity give their titles.

1. The small treatise *Ad Donatum* (EP 548), written soon after his baptism in the form of a monologue addressed to his friend D. with an apologetic tendency, gives an enthusiastic description of the joyous inner transformation of the rhetor by the sacrament of rebirth. It foreshadows the *Confessions* of St. Augustine.

2. The treatise *Quod idola dii non sint* is insignificant in content and does not deserve Jerome's praise, *Ep*. 70, 5; its genuineness has often been doubted. It is, like the treatise *Ad Demetrianum*, a discussion about paganism; the Christians are not responsible for the catastrophes that have befallen the world, such as plague, famine and war. Since in the latter, apologetically a valuable work, Cyprian frequently uses Scriptural citations, we may perhaps assume that it was also destined to encourage Christian readers who were weak in the faith.

3. *Testimoniorum libri III ad Quirinum* (249–50) contains a collection of Scriptural passages (1. polemics against the Jews, 2. Christology, 3. mirror of Christian virtues). The treatise *Ad Fortunatum de exhortatione martyrii* (253 or 257) gathers Scriptural passages suitable for strengthening Christians also in time of persecution. Both treatises are important for our knowledge of the Old Latin text of the Bible.

4. In *De ecclesiae unitate* (EH 266; EP 555/7) Cyprian attacks, probably at the time of the synod of Carthage in May 251, first of all the schism of Novatian in Rome, and also the party led by Felicissimus at Carthage (supra § 34). He emphasizes and

proves that for the salvation of his soul every Christian has the duty to remain in the Catholic Church, i. e. in communion with a legitimate Catholic bishop: *Habere non potest Deum patrem qui ecclesiam non habet matrem* (6). Like Tertullian, Cyprian is convinced that the *cathedra Petri* is present not only in the Roman, but in every other Church presided over by a lawful Catholic bishop. Mt. 16:18 is the charter of the monarchic episcopate (*Ep.* 33, 1). In the interest of countering the Novatianist schism he quickly sent his treatise to Rome (*Ep.* 54 f.).

The fourth chapter of this work is extant in a double recension. The recent researches of van den Eynde, O. Perler and Bévenot have made it more than probable that both recensions derive from Cyprian himself. The text formerly considered interpolated is the original one, while the version taken as the *textus receptus* is a recension made by Cyprian himself during the controversy on heretical baptism. The former version, considered more favourable to the primacy, was thought a forgery mainly because the statements *primatus Petro datur* and *qui cathedram Petri super quem fundata ecclesia est deserit, in ecclesia se esse confidit?* were wrongly supposed to be proof texts for the papal primacy. In fact, however, we should read into the term *primatus* no more than the thought of a vocation earlier in time (*quem Deus primum elegit et super quem aedificavit ecclesiam suam; Ep.* 71, 3). The sentence cited in the second place *(Qui cathedram ... confidit?)* contains no reference to the Roman Church.

New Cyprian-MSS: Bévenot, RBn 1937, 191/5 (MS de Morimond) and BJR 1944, 76/87 (fragm. of a letter). Lawson, JTS 1943, 56/8 (MS of Cypr. and Bachiarius). — Bakhuizen van den Brink ed. *Ad Donatum,* Den Haag 1946. — Diller, Phil 1935, 98/114, 216/39 *(Quod idola).* Axelson, Er 1941, 67/74 (*Quod idola:* spurious). Simonetti, *Maia* 3, 1950, 1/24 (*Quod idola:* genuine). — M. Lavarenne ed. *Contre Démétrien,* Clermont-Ferrand 1940. M. Pellegrino, *Su l'antica apologetica,* 1947, 107/49. N. J. Hommes, *Het Testimonialboek,* A 1935 (ch. 6: *Ad Quirinum*). A. L. Williams, *Adv. Judaeos,* C 1935, 56/64 (*Ad. Quir.* 1st book). Daniélou, RSR 39, 1951, 335/52 (citation from Lament. Jer. in *Ad Quir.*). Lukman, *Slovenska AK. Filozofsko-Filolosko-Hist. Razred* II 9, 1944, 197/209 (on date of *De zelo et livore:* 256f.; *Ad Fortunatum:* 257; against H. Koch; pp. 209/11 a German summary). — *De ecclesiae unitate* ed. E. H. Blakeney, Lo 1929 and P. de Labriolle, P 1942 (both edd. with transs.). Bakhuizen van den Brink, Den Haag 1946. — Essays esp. on ch. 4f.: Van den Eynde, RHE 1933, 5/24; against this Lebreton, RSR 1934, 456/67; in favour, Franses, StC 1934, 214/9. Perler, RQ 1936, 1/44, 151/68; Z. f. Schweiz. Kirchengesch. 1936, 49/57; AugMag 2, 1954, 835/58; here 836f., against Le Moyne. M. Bévenot, *St. Cypr.'s De unit. cap. 4 in the Light of the MSS,* R 1937. Butler, DR 1939, 452/68. Schepens, RSR 1948, 288f. J. Ludwig, *Primatworte,* 1952, 20/36. Le Moyne, RBn 1953, 70/115 (the text allegedly favourable to the primacy is post-Cyprian; v. supra Perler). Bévenot, JTS 1954, 19/35 *(Primatus Petro datur);* ibid. 68/72; ibid. 1955, 244/8 *(In solidum);* id., *The Lapsed and the Unity of the Cath. Church,* ACW 25, 1957. MLS 1, 41 (=BJR 1944, 76/87).

5. In *De lapsis* (EH 257/65; EP 551/4), which was sent to the Roman confessors together with *De ecclesiae unitate* in 251, he laments the apostasy of so many brethren during the persecution; he also declares that they can be re-admitted, but only after a serious penance which must correspond to the seriousness of their fault.

6. *De habitu virginum* (249) warns the consecrated virgins, the "flowers of the garden of the Church" (3) against vanity and worldliness; his enthusiasm for the virginal state is very noticeable (EA 149/57). Here, as in *De dominica oratione* (EP 558f.; EA 159/62) and in *De bono patientiae* (256, a sermon occasioned by his own situation in the dispute on heretical baptism) we frequently meet ideas and occasionally also expressions from Tertullian's works on the same subjects. The small treatise *De zelo et livore* (On envy and jealousy; 251–2 or 256–7), written in the style of a sermon, is a companion to that *On Patience.*

7. *De mortalitate* (252 or later), a pastoral letter which is meant to console and strengthen the Christians during the terrible time of the plague (EA 163/7). *De opere et eleemosynis,* an ardent exhortation to good works, dates from the same time.

J. Martin ed. *De lapsis* (FP 21), 1930 and M. Lavarenne, Clermont-Ferrand 1940 (with trans.). *De hab. virg.* ed. Bakhuizen van den Brink, Den Haag 1946 and A. E. Keenan, W 1932 (with trans. and comm.). *De mortalitate* ed. M. L. Hannan, W 1933 (with trans. and comm.). A. M. Schneider, *Stimmen aus der Fruehzeit der Kirche,* 1948, 141/60 (trans. of *De mortal.*). — Treatises: Donna, Tr 1946, 399/407

(Hab. virg.). Simovic, *La France franc.*, 1938, 245/64 *(Domin. Or.)*. Janssen, StC 1940, 273/86 (lit. value of *Dom. Or.*). Higgins, JTS 1945, 179/83 (variation of the sixth question in *Dom. Or.)*. Blakeney, ET 47, 1945/6 *(De dom. or. 7)*. Lang-Hinrichsen, *Geist u. Leben*, 1951, 209/22; 284/99 (On patience in Tert., Cypr., August., and Thom. Aquinas). C. Favez, *La consolation lat. chrét.*, 1937 (also on *De mortal.*).

B. The Letters

The collection of letters (EP 568/99; EH 267/300; EA 177/81), highly esteemed by Jerome and Augustine, and extremely valuable for the history of the time, comprises eighty-one pieces, sixty-five of which are from the pen of Cyprian, and sixteen addressed to him or to the clergy, among them two of the Roman clergy, written by Novatian (*Ep.* 30 and 36) and of Pope Cornelius from the years 250–3.

In the Decian persecution Cyprian addressed twenty-seven letters to his clergy and people from his hiding place. Twelve contain the correspondence with Rome during the same time (January 250 to March 251). Twelve letters (44–5) deal with the Novatianist schism. Nine letters (67–75) date from the time of the controversy on heretical baptism. Ep. 4 combats the disorders connected with the *subintroductae*. Ep. 63 is directed against the abuse prevailing in some communities of celebrating the Eucharist with water instead of wine.

L. Bayard, *S. Cypr., Correspondance*. Texte et trad., 2 vols., [2]1945. — Studies: L. Nelke, *Die Chronologie der Korrespondenz C.s*, 1902. H. v. Soden, *Die Cypr. Briefsammlung*, 1904; *Das lat. NT in Afrika zur Zeit Cypr.s*, 1909. J. Schrijnen - C. Mohrmann, *Studien zur Syntax der Briefe Cypr.s*, 2 vols., N 1936f. Mercati, OM 2, 226/40 (*Ep.* 49 and 50). Ferrua, CC 1939, 436/45 *(S. Saturino martire)*.

C. Spurious writings

1. *Ad Novatianum,* a polemical treatise against Novatian on the question of the lapsed. The author seems to be an African bishop who shared Cyprian's point of view on the matter of heretical baptism. Date: 253–7.

2. *De rebaptismate,* written in Africa probably still in Cyprians' lifetime, after 256, defends, not very satisfactorily, the validity of heretical baptism against Cyprian. It distinguishes baptism with water, from the spiritual baptism effected by the imposition of hands by the bishop (EP 601).

3. *De singularitate clericorum,* i.e. on the celibacy of the clergy, is saturated with Cyprian's ideas and was written by a Catholic bishop not later than the third century.

4. *Adversus aleatores,* a sermon written in late Latin against dice-playing, which is supposed to excite the wildest passions: a man who gambles commits idolatry and is no longer a Christian but a pagan. The author is perhaps a Catholic bishop in Africa, writing about 300.

5. *De pascha computus* (243) intends to correct the faulty Easter cycle of Hippolytus by means of Scriptural passages.

6. On the treatises *De spectaculis* and *De bono pudicitiae* which are to be assigned to Novatian v. supra § 33. Further pseudo-Cyprian writings: *De montibus Sina et Sion* (before 240), *De laude martyrii* (3rd cent.), *Adversus Iudaeos* (3rd cent.), *Ad Vigilium Episcopum de iudaica incredulitate* is the preface of the lost Latin translation of the dialogue of Ariston of Pella (supra § 21, 1; probably still 3rd cent.); besides, several letters, poems, and prayers. *De duodecim abusivis saeculi* originated in Ireland in the seventh century.

7. *Exhortatio de paenitentia* (4th–5th cent.), *Caena Cypriani* (5th cent.), *De centesima, sexagesima, tricesima,* i.e. *On the threefold reward of martyrs, ascetics and just Christians,* originated probably in N. Africa in the fourth century; it is greatly influenced by Cyprian's thought and language.

Edd.: G. Hartel (CSEL 3, 3) 1871; the writings named under No. 7 are not in Hartel's ed. *De rebapt.* ed. G. Rauschen (FP 11) 1916, *De centesima . . .* ed. R. Reitzenstein, ZNTW 1914, 60/90. — Treatises: H. Koch, *Cypr. Unters.*, 1926, 358/420 *(Ad Novat.)*, 426/72 *(sing. cler.)*; IKZ 1924, 134/64 *(De rebapt.)*; Festg. K. Müller 1922, 58/67 *(Adv. aleat.)*; ZNTW 1932, 248/72 *(De centesima . . .)*. S. Hellmann, TU 34, 1, 1909 *(De duod. abus. saec.)*. Esposito, Ha 1933, 221/49

(MSS of the *De duod. abus. saec.*). Leclercq, DAL 12, 2324/45 *(Oratio Cypriani)*. Schepens, RSR 1922, 178/210, 297/327; 1923, 47/65 *(De rebapt.)*. Edsman 1940, 142/7 *(De rebapt.)*. B. Melin, *Studia in Corpus Cyprianeum,* Up 1946, 215/32 (*De sing. cler.* and the pseudo-Cypr. Ep. 4 [CSEL 3, 3, 274/82] are by the same author; against this Duhr, RHE 1952, 274/82: Bachiarius is the author of Ep. 4; cf. § 81, No. 12). — Ogg, JTS 1947, 206f. and VC 1954, 134/44 (on *De pascha computus*). — Peterson, VC 1952, 33/43 (*Adv. Iud.* uses Melito of Sardes). — Lapôtre, RSR 1912, 497/596 *(Caena Cypriani)*; on this Wilmart, RBn 1923, 255/63 (on a medieval comment. on this treatise). — On *De centesima . . .*: E. Seeberg, NKZ 1914, 472/94 and Heer, RQ 1914, 87/186. G. Ogg, The Ps.-Cyprianic *De pascha computus* (SPCK), 1955. MLS 1, 53 ff. *(De centes.)*.

Points of Doctrine

Until the time of Augustine and Gregory the Great, Cyprian was the theological authority of the Western Church. Somewhat like Ambrose, he was a man of action rather than of ideas; despite his hasty and incomplete theological training he became a particularly highly esteemed witness to the doctrine of the Church. By independent argument he established especially the old idea of the unity of the Catholic Church according to the development it had then reached, and he generally exercised a decisive influence on the doctrine of the Church. He firmly kept ecclesiastical discipline midway between laxity and rigorism.

1. According to Cyprian the unity of the Church is achieved by adhering to one's bishop; if a man is not united to his bishop, he is not in the Church (*Ep*. 43, 5; 69, 3). The bishops, for their part, are united to each other, apart from being connected with their common origin (v.n. 2), through the *lex individuae caritatis et concordiae* (*Ep*. 54, 1; 68, 5). Christ first gave to one, Peter, and first to him alone, the power to bind and to loose; and so he has shown it for ever to be his will that his Church should be and remain one. Cyprian further compares the Church with the one undivided garment of Christ (*Eccl. un.* 7). His conviction that the Church is necessary for salvation is expressed in the classic formula *Salus extra ecclesiam non est* (*Ep*. 73, 21) and in *Ep*.

55, 24 he writes: *Christianus non est qui in Christi ecclesia non est.* Cf. also supra treatise n. 4.

2. Cyprian and the Roman Primacy. Since the authority of governing the Church was first given to Peter (Mt. 16 : 18), this apostle became not only the symbol or type of unity, but also, and principally, the real foundation of this unity which is internally established through and from him. For the appointment of Peter is also the juridical basis of all episcopal authority, i.e. each bishop is really and directly connected with Peter. The authorization of the other apostles (John 20: 21f.; *Eccl. un.* 4), which took place later, means, in Cyprian's view, that according to the will of Christ all apostles received a share in the *unus episcopatus* which had already been established in the person of Peter (*episcopatus unus est, cuius a singulis in solidum pars tenetur, Eccl. un.* 5). From this position of Peter, Cyprian did not yet draw further conclusions, i.e. he did not recognize an active power of jurisdiction given to Peter over the other apostles: *Hoc erant utique et ceteri apostoli quod fuit Petrus, pari consortio praediti et honoris et potestatis* (*Eccl. un.* 4); the primacy that belongs to Peter (*Ep.* 71, 3) is a position of honour in the sense of a *primus inter pares.*

With Peter the "original Church" *(ecclesia principalis)* established itself in Rome; from here, too, derived (*exorta est, Ep.* 59, 14) the *unitas sacerdotalis* at the time when Peter was bishop in Rome. This, however, does not mean that Cyprian attributed to the Roman Church of his time a special importance for the preservation of unity in the sense of a primacy of jurisdiction, as is clear from the immediately following discussions, where he writes, e. g., with regard to Rome: *Cum singulis pastoribus portio gregis sit adscripta, quam regat unusquisque et gubernet rationem sui actus Domino redditurus;* precisely for this reason he also expects Rome not to interfere in the disputes of his diocese. His conduct in the controversy on heretical baptism agrees completely with this view. On September 1, 256, he presided over an African synod which, in accordance with his teaching (*Ep.* 69ff.), affirmed that the baptism of heretics was invalid, though Pope Stephen had already given a contrary decision. Here he made the following sharp statement with an obvious thrust at Rome: *neque enim quisquam nostrum episcopum se episcoporum constituit aut tyrannico terrore ad obsequendi necessitatem collegas suos adigit . . . sed expectemus universi iudicium Domini nostri Iesu Christi, qui unus et solus habet potestatem et praeponendi nos in ecclesiae suae gubernatione et de actu nostro iudicandi* (Hartel I, 436).

In Cyprian's theory, the unity was principally to be preserved by the fraternal love and concord of the bishops among themselves established by the Holy Spirit. In the stark reality of the Church's life, this conception, however, proved to be incapable of preventing a schism within the Church; and the clearer this became, the more energetically did Pope Stephen, conscious of his primacy, fight for the acceptance of the Roman claims; cf. the severance of ecclesiastical relations with Cyprian and the African Church and his energetic demand that the bishops of Cappadocia, Galatia and Asia should submit to the Roman view (*Ep.* 75, 17 and 25).

3. Cyprian considers tradition divine only in so far as it does not go beyond the Scriptures (*Ep.* 71, 31; 74, 2). Nevertheless, he greatly esteems private revelations and visions (*Ep.* 11, 3 f. 16, 4).

4. He made infant baptism a law. There was no reason to leave the children, who from Adam were under the *contagium mortis antiquae,* for eight days without divine grace (*Ep.* 64, 2 5; EH 296).

5. The sacrifice of the priest is the repetition of the sacrifice of Christ at the Last Supper, both being the representation of the unique sacrifice on the cross. The celebration of the eucharist consists in *oblatio* and *sacrificium* (*Ep.* 37, 1; 63, 9; 66, 2); the *oblatio* is bread and wine and becomes *sacrificium Christi* through the Holy Spirit (*Eccl. un.* 17): *Jesus Christus . . . sacrificium patri se ipsum obtulit* (*Ep.* 63, 14). Cyprian is the first to enunciate with all

clarity the belief, so far known only *implicite,* that the body and blood of Christ are sacrificial gifts (*Ep.* 63, 14). The sacrifice is offered also for the martyrs (*Ep.* 39, 3). Outside the Catholic Church the eucharist is invalid (*Ep.* 72, 2).

6. Penance consists in the exomologesis, i.e. in the confession of sins and the public rite of penance, through the satisfaction proportionate to the measure of the sin and by the reconciliation which is granted after the time of penance has expired (*Ep.* 16, 2). The actual effacing of the sin takes place in the performance of penance (*De laps.* 17; *Ep.* 59, 13 and freq.); the reconciliation is *pignus vitae* (*Ep.* 55, 13) in so far as the loosing on earth is the presupposition of the loosing in heaven (*Ep.* 57, 1; *De laps.* 28–30; EH 262/5).

7. Cyprian believed with the ancient Church in general that the martyrs are immediately admitted to the vision of God, whereas the others have to wait after death till "the day of judgement for the decisions of the Lord" (*Eccl. un.* 14; *Ep.* 55, 17 20; 58, 3).

A. d'Alès, *La théologie de S. Cyprien,* 1922. — On the concept of the Church and the question of the primacy: Caspar, ZSK 1927, 253/331. Adam, TQ 1928, 203/56. H. Koch, *Cathedra Petri,* 1930. E. Altendorf 1932, 44/116 (v. supra § 3, 21). B. Poschmann, *Ecclesia principalis,* Br 1933; cf. TR 1933, 425/32. Zapelena Gr 1934, 500/23; 1935, 196/224. J. C. Plumpe, *Mater Ecclesia,* W 1943, 81/108. G. Bardy, *La théologie de l'église de S. Irénée au concile de Nicée,* 1947, 171/251. Bévenot, RSR 1951, 379/415. J. Ludwig, *Primatworte,* 1952, 20/36. Butler, DR 1953, 1/13, 119/34, 258/72. G. Klein, ZKG 1957, 48/68 (doctrine of Church).— On the doctrine of the Sacraments: J. C. Navickas, *The Doctrine of St. C. on the Sacraments,* Wu 1924. Capelle, RTA 1935, 221/34 (priestly absolution). Bardy, VS 1939, Suppl. 87/119 (Christian priesthood). Nicotra, SC 1940, 380/7 (*De cent.* 4, 12); 1940, 496/504 and 583/7. — On the doctrine of the Eucharist: P. Batiffol, *Eucharistie,* 91930, 266/47. Salaville, EO 39, 1941/2, 268/82 *(L'épiclèse africaine).*—On the question of penance: Koehne, TG 1937, 245/56 (duration of penance). Charlier, Ant 1939, 17/42, 135/56. Poschmann 1940, 368/424. Joyce, JTS 1941, 18/42 (private penance). Taylor, TSW 1942, 27/46 (reconciliation of apostates). K. Rahner, ZKT 1952, 252/76, 381/438. —A. G. Welykyi, *Die Lehre der Vaeter des 3. Jh. von der Gottesliebe u. Gottesfurcht,* R 1948. Bardy, DS 2, 1952, 2661/9. S. Barbalato, *La dottrina della gracia in S. Cypr.,* thesis R Gregor. 1953. Busch, *Nova et Vetera,* Festschr. Metten 1939, 64/80 (martyrdom).

E. L. Hummel, *The Concept of Martyrdom acc. to St. Cypr.*, W 1946. Nilsson, HTR 1947, 167/76 (Greek mysteries). Bévenot, TSW 1955, 175/213 (sacrament of penance in *De lapsis*). A. Stenzel, Sch 1955, 372/87 (Baptism in the name of Jesus). J. Capmany, *"Miles Christi" en la espiritualidad de S. Cypr.*, Ba 1956.

§ 35. VICTORINUS OF PETTAU (d. 304)

VICTORINUS, Bishop of Poetovio, the modern Pettau in the Jugoslav part of Steiermark, was the first exegete to write in Latin. He was probably a Greek by birth and was martyred in the persecution of Diocletian (d. 304; Jerome, *Vir. ill.* 74).

In none too fluent Latin he wrote especially *commentaries on the Bible* (Gn., Ex., Lv., Is., Ez., Hab., Eccl., Cant., Mt., Apc.) of which only the one on the Apocalypse is extant. The original text which was not edited until 1916 clearly shows the chiliastic mood. Before it was known only in Jerome's version. Apart from this we have a short treatise of his, *De fabrica mundi* (On the Week of Creation), also of chiliastic leanings. Victorinus is perhaps the translator and redactor of the originally Greek treatise *Adversum omnes haereses* which is preserved as an appendix of Tertullian's *De praescriptione* (46 to 53; v. supra § 30 II 6c). In his exegesis he depends on Papias, Irenaeus, Hippolytus and especially on Origen.

Edd.: ML 5, 281/344 (incomplete). J. Haussleiter (CSEL 49) 1916. — Treatises: Haussleiter, RE 20, 614/9. Bardy, DTC 15, 2882/7. Two minor writings ed. by J. Woehrer the editor would assign to Victor, without sufficient reasons: J. Woehrer, *Eine kleine Schrift, die vielleicht dem hl. Maertyrerbischof Vikt. v. P. angehoert*, in Jahresber. des Privatgymnasiums Wilhering 1927, 3/8 and *Victorini ep. Petav. (?) ad Justinum Manichaeum*; ibid. 1928, 3/7; cf. RBn Bull. 2, n. 44f., 1929; on the second treatise cf. § 81, 10. — E. Benz, *Marius Victorinus*, 1932, 23/30 (Vict. as translator of Origen). N. J. Hommes, *Het Testimonialboek*, 1935, 225/30 (Vict. and Papias). E. Schwartz, SbM 1936, 3.

§ 36. ARNOBIUS THE ELDER

LIKE all important ante-Nicene authors of the Latin Church, Arnobius, too, hailed from Africa. He was a distinguished teacher of rhetoric in his native city of Sicca in Numidia. Having been an opponent of Christianity, he embraced the religion of Jesus after having a vision in a dream. In order to overcome the misgivings of the Bishop of Sicca who doubted the sincerity of his conversion he wrote his seven books *Adversus nationes* during the time of the persecution of Diocletian or soon afterwards (304–10). This account of Jerome (*Chron.* ad 2343) is, however, not very trustworthy. For it can hardly be assumed that a Catholic bishop should have regarded the views of Arnobius as a valid confession of faith, since they differ from the orthodox teaching in many points and are influenced by conceptions of pagan religious thought and philosophy as well as by heterodox (Marcionite?) Christian teachings.

The work is extant only in a single MS (Paris, 1661, saec. 9), the *Octavius* of Minucius Felix being appended to it as an eighth book (supra § 29, 2). Arnobius wrote it purely as a rhetor; his argumentation is nowhere thorough, his expression is artificial and verbose. When he cites fifty-one different philosophers and authors he owes his knowledge almost exclusively to the contemporary *florilegia* and manuals in which τόποι and δόξαι were brought together. Since the author does not yet possess an inner relationship to Christianity he lacks warmth of feeling for which he seeks to compensate by declamatory rhetoric. The so-called *Decretum Gelasianum* counts the work among the *apocrypha*.

The first book defends Christianity against the accusation that it is responsible for the present miseries. Actually the new religion seeks to diminish them; for if Christian principles were put into practice, wars, e.g., would be impossible (1, 6). In the second book he points out, among other things, that certain Christian doctrines that are mocked by the pagans are also to be found in the great philosophers, i.e. the doctrine of immortality in Plato (2, 13 ff.). Books two–five reveal the nonsense and immorality of the myths of the gods, the allegorical interpretation of which cannot be admitted; they are a rich source of our knowledge of mythology.

Book six rejects the worship of the gods by the erection of temples and statues; Book seven, which has not yet been examined in its entirety combats the sacrificial service.

Points of Doctrine

1. The treatise betrays clearly that the author, though approaching Christianity, has not even properly understood its basic doctrines. God the Father is the real God *(Deus princeps);* he does not think it proved that the pagan gods do not exist but they can only be regarded as inferior gods and receive their existence and power from the God of the Christians. Christ, too, is a god of the second rank (1, 28; 3, 2).

2. The human soul does not come from God, but from another higher being (2, 36). Like Justin and Theophilus of Antioch, Arnobius assumes that it is not immortal by nature, but that it can be made immortal by the grace of the Christian God (2, 32 61). This view was one of his main reasons for embracing Christianity.

Edd.: ML 5. A. Reifferscheid (CSEL 4) 1875. G. Marchesi, Tu 1934. — Trans.: F. A. v. Besnard 1842 and J. Alleker 1858. McCracken (ACW 7 and 8) 1949. — Treatises: P. Monceaux (supra § 3) 3, 1905, 241/86. F. Gabarrou, *Arn., son œuvre,* 1921; *Le Latin d'Arn.,* 1921. P. de Labriolle, DHGE 4, 542/7. S. Colombo, Did. 1930, 3, 1/124. F. Tullius, *Die Quellen des A. im 4., 5. u. 6. Buch seiner Schrift Adv. nat.,* 1934. G. Wiman, *Textkritiska Studier till Ar.,* Goeteborg 1931. G. Brunner, JL 13, 1936, 172/81 (7, 32: A., not a witness against the feast of Christmas). H. Hagendahl, Er 1937, 36/40 (Ovid); *La prose métrique d'A.,* Goeteborg 1937. Guinagh, Class. Weekly 1936, 69f., 152. E. Rapisarda, *Clemente (Aless.) fonte di Ar.,* Tu 1939. Festugière, Mémorial Lagrange 1940, 97/132 (doctrine of the soul [2, 11/66]). E. F. Micka, *The Problem of Divine Anger in Ar. and Lactant.,* W 1943. B. Axelson, *Textkritik. zu Florus, Min. Fel. u. Arn.,* Lund 1944. E. Rapisarda, *Arnobio,* 1945. McCracken, CJ 1947, 474/76 and VC 1949, 37/47 (text. crit.). Wiman, Er 1947, 129/52 (text. crit.). Plumpe, VC 1949, 230/6 (text. crit.). G. L. Ellspermann, W 1949, 54/66. H. Karpp, *Probleme altchristl. Anthropologie,* 1950, 171/85. Festugière, VC 1952, 208/54 (text. crit. on trans. by McCracken). Courcelle, REL 1953, 257/71 (on 2, 15: *viri novi!*). Scheidweiler, ZNTW 1954, 42/67 (Ar. influenced by Marcion).

§ 37. L. CAECILIUS FIRMIANUS LACTANTIUS

THE two African rhetors Cyprian and Arnobius were soon joined by a third, L. Caecilius Firmianus Lactantius, who, according to Jerome, was a disciple of Arnobius (*Vir. ill.* 80). The Emperor Diocletian called him to his new capital Nicomedia as a teacher of Latin rhetoric. At the beginning of the persecution Lactantius was compelled to resign his office, as he had since become a Christian. He remained in Nicomedia in strained circumstances until, in his old age, the Emperor Constantine called him to his court at Treves *c.* 317 to act as tutor to his son Crispus. Nothing is known of his later life.

Lactantius was a master of form. His language is pleasantly fluent and akin to that of Cicero whom he had read assiduously and whom he resembled also in his gentle character; hence the humanists called him the Christian Cicero. He was less familiar with Greek literature. As in the case of Arnobius, his knowledge of Christian doctrine and literature was defective. Jerome writes (*Ep.* 58, 10): *Utinam tam nostra adfirmare potuisset, quam facile aliena destruxit.*

1. *Divinae institutiones* in seven books, the principal work of Lactantius (EP 624/47), was written 304–13.

It was occasioned by the attacks of contemporary pagan writers (one of them probably Hierocles of Bithynia) and is an apology of Christianity and at the same time an introduction to its principal doctrines. It is the first attempt to give a comprehensive presentation of the Christian faith in Latin, though a rather defective one.

Books one and two show up the absurdity of the pagan religion. Belief in the gods originated in the deification of departed men (euhemerism); actually the gods are to be identified with the demons led by the devil. Book three exposes the contradictions of pagan philosophy. Book four shows that only Christ has brought true wisdom down from heaven. The fifth book deplores the disappearance of justice from this earth; it will return only when all men acknowledge the true God and are united by the bond of being children of God (5, 8, 6). After this the right manner of worshipping God practised by the Christians is described in the sixth book. These two books are written with enthusiasm and are the best part of the whole work. Book seven treats of the Last Things. In some MSS the work has dualistic and panegyrical additions; the former contain the teaching that God had willed and created evil; the latter are addressed to the Emperor Constantine. All additions are probably by Lactantius himself and were later removed as being either superfluous or objectionable.

2. *Epitome,* an extract from the principal work made by Lactantius himself; its many corrections and alterations give it a value of its own (after 314).

3. In *De opificio Dei* (*c.* 303–4) the beauty and purposefulness of man's organism and the advantages of his reason are discussed, quite in contrast with his teacher Arnobius (2, 29, 37, 52), in order to prove man a "work of God", but without any Christian features.

4. *De ira Dei* (not before 313) shows against the Epicureans and Stoics that God is not only goodness, but that there must also be a punitive justice of God.

5. *De mortibus persecutorum,* preserved only in one Parisian MS (11th cent.).

The small book deals briefly with the sorry end of the various persecutors of the Christians, treating more explicitly of the present, i.e. of the persecution under Diocletian and its continuations. It gives an account of the death of Maximinus Daza (313) and Diocletian (prob. 316), but not of the persecution of Licinius which began in 321 at the latest; hence it must have been written before 321, probably between 314 and 317. It differs from Lactantius' other writings in that it was written in a mood of irritation;

the author is passionately excited and likes to exaggerate and to enlarge on gruesome events.

Though the genuineness of the work has frequently been attacked in the past, it should be accepted despite some recent doubts.

6. The poem *De ave Phoenice* which relates the legend of the marvellous bird Phoenix, a motif used already by Herodotus (11, 37) and in the *Epistle of Clement* (ch. 25). Every thousand years the bird comes from the far East to Phoenicia where it dies on a palm tree (φοίνιξ). The corpse burns itself and the ashes produce a worm which in its turn develops into a butterfly. The latter carries the remains of the bones to the temple of the sun in the Egyptian city of Heliopolis and then returns to the East. Gregory of Tours (*De cursu stell.* 12) already names Lactantius as the author of the legend which he interprets in a Christian sense.

From early times it has been a matter of controversy whether the poem is of pagan or Christian inspiration, whether it was written by Lactantius himself (before or after his conversion?) or by a pagan or by a later Christian author. These are questions which have not yet been decided. Certain internal evidence favours the genuineness of the work.

7. Various writings mentioned by Jerome (*Vir. ill.* 80), e.g. several collections of letters and *De motibus animi* are lost. The poems *De Pascha* and *De passione Domini* are spurious.

Points of Doctrine

1. Lactantius knows no Holy Spirit different from the Son of God; it is true, in the beginning God generated a third being beside the Son, but the latter grew envious of the Son, fell into sin and is henceforth called the devil (*Inst.* 2, 8). On his dualism cf. supra n. 1.

2. In the seventh book of the *Div. Instit.* Lactantius professes a chialistic doctrine. Only about two hundred years are lacking to

the six thousand years the world is destined to last; then, after the brief reign of Antichrist has been abolished the happiness of the millennium will begin, in which Christ will reign with the risen just. At the end of these thousand years the godless will rise once more, and the Last Judgement will bring about the final separation of heaven and hell.

3. In the doctrine of the soul Lactantius represents the teaching of Creatianism (*Opif.* 19).

Edd.: ML 6–7. S. Brandt u. G. Laubmann (CSEL 19, 27) 1890/7. — Special edd. of individual works: W. T. Radius, *Selections from Lact. Div. Inst.*, 1951. E. H. Blakeney, *Epitome,* 1950 (SPCK); cf. Borleffs, VC 1953, 253/6 (negative criticism). G. Crone, Mr 1953 (selections from *Epit., Ira* and *De mort.*). *De mort.* ed. S. Brandt, W 1897; also I. B. Pesenti, Tu 1922 and 1934; G. Mazzoni, Siena 1930; *L. De Regibus,* Tu 1931; U. Moricca, Mi 1933; J. Moreau, 2 vols. (SCh 39; crit. text and comm.), 1954/5. Nautin, RHE 1955, 892/9 (on Moreau's ed.). M. C. Fitz-Patrick, Ph 1933 (*De ave Phoen.;* trans. with comm.). — Transs.: A. Hartl (BKV² 36), 1919. G. Mazzoni, Siena 1930 *(De mort.)* and 1937 *(Div. instit.)*. D. Franses, A 1941 *(De mort.)*. E. Faessler, Lucerne 1946 *(De mort.)*.G. Sánchez Aliseda, Ma 1947 *(De mort.)*. — Studies: R. Pichon, *Lactance,* 1901. P. Monceaux (supra § 3) 3, 287/359. Amann, DTC 8, 2425/44. Leclercq, DAL 8, 1018/41. Lietzmann, PWK 12, 351/6. H. Jagielski, *De F. Lactantii fontibus quaestiones sel.*, 1912. K. Roller, *Die Kaisergesch. in L.s De mort. pers.*, 1927. Borleffs, Mn 1930, 223/92 (*De mort.*: spurious). B. Bianoy, *Il carme De ave Phoenice di Latt.*, 1931. G. Kutsch, *In Lact.i De ira Dei librum quaest. philologicae,* L 1933. Stelzenberger 1933, 83/6, 125/8 et saepe. Schuster, WSt 54, 1936, 55ff., 118/28 (*De ave Phoen.*: genuine), 303f. Billiet, *Philolog. Studien* 5, 1933/4, 117/21, 198/214 (*De mort.*: genuine). Maddalena, *Atti Ist. Veneto* 94, 1934/5, 557/88 (*De mort.*: genuine). Blochet, Mu 1937, 123/44 *(De ave Phoen.)*. J. Martin, *Wuerzburger Festschr. H. Bulle,* 1938, 151/68 *(De pass. Domini)*. Gonella, RivInternFilosDiritto 1937, 23/37 *(Le leggi sec. Tert. e Latt.)*. Bolkestein, DP 1939, 62/5 *(humanitas in L.)*. J. Hubeaux et M. Leroy, *Le mythe du Phénix dans les littératures grecques et lat.*, 1939. K. Vilhelmson, *Lact. u. die Kosmogonie des spaetantiken Synkretismus,* Tartu 1940. Wuillenmier, Mél. Ernout, 1940, 383/88 (Cato Maior in L.). Emonds 1941, 55/72. G. Richard, RevEA 1940, 498/507 (freedom of conscience). Micka, W 1943 (v. supra § 36). E. Schneweis, *Angels and Demons acc. to L.,* W 1943. J. Nicolosi, *L'influsso di Lucrezio su L.*, 1945. E. Rapisarda, *Il carme De ave Phoen.*, 1946 (genuine). MiscSLCA I, 1947, 5/20 *(L. contro Epicuro)*. Pellegrino 1947 (supra § 19), 151/207 (dependent on Min. Fel.). P. J. Couvee, *Vita beata en vita aeterna . . . bij L., Ambros. en Augustinus,* Baarn 1947. Corlson, CP 1948, 93/104 (Pagan Examples of Fortitude). Edsman, *Ignis divinus,* 1949, 178/203 *(Phoenix)*. Ellspermann 1949, 67/101. F. di Capua, *Il cursus e le clausole nei prosatori latini e in Latt.,* Bari 1949. Alfonsi, IstLombardScLett 82, 1949, 19/27 (Lact. depends on Justin). Karpp

1950, 132/71 (anthropology). E. v. Ivánka, Anzeiger der Philos. hist. Kl., W 1950, No. 10, 187/91 (Stoic anthropology in L. and Ambrose). J. Fischer, MTZ 1950, 96/101 (Victorinus of Pettau and L. on Apc. 5:2). Prete, *Gymnasium* 63, 1956, 365/82, 486/509 (historical background of Lactantius' works). Kraft-Wlosok, *De ira dei,* Darmstadt 1957.

Appendix

1. Reticius of Autun is prominent among the bishops of the Constantinian period. According to Jerome (*Vir. ill.* 82) he wrote two works now lost: a *Commentary on the Canticle* which Jerome judged very adversely (*Ep.* 37, 3) and a treatise *Adversus Novatianum* (cf. § 87, 1).

2. An anonymous collection of Biblical prophecies which originated in Africa in the first quarter of the fourth century was published by A. M. Amelli, *Miscellanea Cassin.* 1897 under the title *Prophetiae ex omnibus libris collectae;* it is important for our knowledge of the Old Latin African text of the Bible.

T. Zahn in *A. Hauck-Festschr.* 1916, 52/63; cf. Wohlenberg, TLB 1916, 65/9. Bardy, DTC 13, 2571 f. (Reticius). Lokin, DHG 8, 379 (*Prophetiae*).

B. The Authors of the Greek East

§ 38. THE OLD CHRISTIAN THEOLOGICAL SCHOOLS

THE apologetical and anti-heretical literature of the second century constituted the first stage in the formation of the science of theology. The law of intellectual life and growth demanded that theology should be developed as systematically and comprehensively as possible and thus be raised to the rank of a science. It is part of this development that gradually there arose schools of learning which may be regarded as the birthplace of the science of theology. The oldest and most famous of them was the Catechetical School of Alexandria.

From the foundation of Alexandria in 331 B.C., Egyptian, Oriental, Greek and soon also Jewish influences met in this city, the result of this mixture being the Hellenistic civilization. Since the first Ptolemaeans it boasted two great libraries of learning, the *Museion* and the *Serapeion*. Judaism adopted the Greek language and culture; cf. the Biblical books of Wisdom and Ecclesiasticus and the writings of Philo. The theological school of Alexandria first appears in history *c.* 180, when it was directed by Pantaenus, native of Sicily (Eus., *Hist.* 5, 10). Clement, his pupil and successor, made the first attempt to build up a system of theology.

When bishop Demetrius entrusted the direction of the school to the young Origen it was officially recognized by the ecclesiastical authorities and achieved under him its highest reputation. Such important men as Dionysius, Pierius, Peter, Athanasius, Didymus and Cyril were either trained in it or directed it. More detailed information on the activities of this catechetical school after Origen's departure and on its influence are not, unfortunately, at our disposal.

After his enforced departure from Alexandria, Origen founded a new school at Caesarea in Palestine (232). Here a remarkable Christian library was soon established; it owed its growth especially to the efforts of the later director of the school, the priest Pamphilus. Here Gregory Thaumaturgus and Eusebius of Caesarea received their theological training. Through Caesarea the Alexandrian tradition influenced the leading theologians of Cappadocia, especially Basil the Great and the two Gregorys, who sought to reconcile the spirit of Alexandria with that of Antioch (*Neo-Alexandrian School;* infra § 51).

Under the influence of Clement and Origen the Alexandrian School interpreted the Scriptures according to the allegorical method of exegesis, which had long been used by the Greek philosophers for interpreting the myths and the poets (e.g. Homer). Jewish scholars such as Aristobulus of Alexandria and the religious philosopher Philo also adopted it for the interpretation of the Biblical books. The Alexandrian theologians were convinced that a literal or historico-grammatical exegesis would produce results unworthy of God or contrary to faith; hence they sought to find a so-called deeper, mysterious meaning in the individual Biblical sayings and facts, thus frequently turning the Bible into a book of riddles and Scriptural exegesis into a puzzle game. This unbelievably one-sided method became necessary because the notion of inspiration was given too narrow a meaning.

The allegorizing and speculative philosophical tendencies of this school were explicitly opposed by another group, which appeared towards the end of the third century. This was the *Antiochene School,* also called the "exegetical school", because its followers worked mainly in the field of Scriptural exegesis. It excelled in sober reasoning and a strictly scholarly mentality; it explained the Scriptures mainly according to their historical and grammatical sense.

Lucian of Samosata is held to be the founder of this school; he taught at Antioch, the second great city of the Greek East famous for its fine pagan schools, from the sixties of the third century (d. 312). The greatest period of this school was introduced by Diodore of Tarsus; but this belongs to the following period (infra § 51). Antioch influenced the school of Edessa which dated from the first half of the third century. Ephraem the Syrian (d. 373) was its greatest teacher.

W. Bousset, *Jued.-christl. Schulbetrieb in Alexandrien u. Rom,* 1915. H. R. Nelz, *Die theol. Schulen der morgenlaend. Kirchen,* 1916. Schemmel, PW 1925, 1277/80 (on Caesarea). Bardy, RHE 1932, 501/32 (Rom. schools in the 2nd cent.); RevSR 1932, 1/28 (eccl. teaching in the first three cents.); RevSR 1934, 525/49 (4th cent.); RSR 1937, 65/90 (Alexandria); *Vivre et Penser* 2, 1942, 80/109 (on the hist. of the school of Alex.). J. Munck, *Unters. ueber Klemens v. Alex.,* 1933, 180/5, 224/9. L. Allevi, *Ellenismo e Cristianesimo,* Mi 1934 (ch. 2). E. Molland, *The Conception of the Gospel in the Alexandrian Theology,* Oslo 1938. R. Cadiou, *La jeunesse d'Origène,* 1936 and RevSR 1936, 474/83 (Caesarea). G. H. Ranson, *The Anthropology of the Catechetical School of Alex.,* thesis S. Bapt. Theol. Sem. 1944. Guillet, RSR 1947, 247/302 (exegesis of Alexandrians and Antiochenes). De Lubac, RSR 1947, 180/226 (typology and allegory). D. J. Harris, *A Study of the Antioch. School in the Interpret. of the N.T.,* thesis S. Bapt. Theol. Sem. 1948. B. Tiplea,

Scholae Alex. exegesis et doctrina in Mt. 16:13. 19, thesis Univ. de Propaganda Fide 1949. Hoffmann-Aleith, *Pantainos:* PWK 36, 3, 1949, 684f. P. Brezzi, *La gnosi crist. di Aless. e le antiche scuole crist.,* R 1950. W. Jentsch, *Urchristl. Erziehungsdenken,* G 1951. Knauber, TTZ 1951, 243/66 (Catechetical school or school catechumenate?). Vaccari, *Scritti* 1952, 101/42 = Bi 1920, 4/36 and 1934, 94/101 (The *theoria* of the Antioch. exegetes). Alvarez Seisdedos, EstBibl 1952, 31/67 *(La teoria antiochena).* H. I. Marrou, *Diognète* (SCh 33), 1952, 266ff. (Pantaenus is supposed to be the author!). Ternant, Bi 1953, 135/58, 354/83 and 456/86 (the exeget. *theoria* of the Antiochenes). Bouyer, JTS 1953, 188/203 (The meaning of *gnosis* down to the Alexandrians). P. Nautin, *Tome commémoratif du Millénaire de la Bibliothèque d'Alexandrie,* Alexandria 1953, 145/52 (Pantaenus).

§ 39. CLEMENT OF ALEXANDRIA (d. before 215)

TITUS Flavius Clemens was probably born at Athens, of pagan parents. As a Christian he travelled far, to S. Italy, Syria and Palestine, and later joined Pantaenus, who was probably a native of Sicily, in Alexandria. After the latter's death (prob. before 200) he continued his teaching at a kind of private catechetical school (Eus., *Hist.* 5, 11; Clem., *Strom.* 1, 1, 11). Whether he was a priest cannot be deduced with certainty either from the corrupt passage in *Paed.* 1, 37, 3 nor from the letter of Alexander of Jerusalem (Eus., *Hist.* 6, 11, 6). Owing to the persecution under Septimius Severus he emigrated again in 202 or 203 and went to Asia Minor, where he died before 215.

Clement may be called the first Christian scholar. He was not only familiar with Holy Scripture and almost the whole Christian literature before him; his citations, taken from more than 360 profane authors, prove that he also had an extensive knowledge of the philosophical and classical literature based on independent study, though much of his material was taken from learned manuals and *florilegia.* Clement taught his readers to see revelation in relation to all true knowledge, especially pre-Christian philosophy. He gathered from the latter its elements of truth in order to show that they received their unity in the Christian faith, in which they are transfigured and glorified; and he did this with a holy enthusiasm that raised even his language to poetic heights. It is true that he fell into many errors while thus attempting to harmonize the content of faith with current philosophy. He was a good observer and critic of life.

Apart from one homily, of the many writings of the learned Alexandrian only one group of three inter-related works has been preserved in full, the Προτρεπτικός, the Παιδαγωγός, and the Στρωματεῖς.

1. *The Exhortation to the Gentiles* (Προτρεπτικὸς πρὸς Ἕλληνας) in twelve chapters, first celebrates Christ as the teacher of the new world; then, following the example of the Jewish and old Christian apologists, it paints a frightening picture of the stupidity and immorality of the pagan myths and mystery cults. Here Clement often uses the same arguments that Hellenistic philosophy had also adduced against the popular pagan religion with its unworthy conceptions of God and forms of worship. If he opposes (chs. 5–7) the teaching of the Greek philosophers on the nature of God he does not forget that the philosophers, especially Plato, and certain poets have made many true statements about God. In the last chapters he describes in glowing terms the sublime revelation of the Logos and the marvellous riches of divine grace in which all human longing for light, truth and life is fulfilled. Since the Logos has brought salvation to the Christians, his hearers must decide for judgement or grace, for death or for life (EP 401/05).

2. *The Pedagogue* (Παιδαγωγός), in three books, is the continuation of the former work. The converted pagan is to be instructed how to arrange the practice of his daily life. Christ is the teacher of all the redeemed. The second and third books contain a loosely arranged series of detailed instructions, e.g., on eating and drinking, rest and recreation, physical culture, clothes, housing, social life, marriage and so forth. The background of all these exhortations is the life in the opulent city of Alexandria, the home of

all kinds of luxury and debauchery. In his instructions on the behaviour of the true Christian Clement does not preach an ascetical ideal; he does not demand that Christians should give up all worldly pleasures and enjoyments, but that they should not be completely absorbed by them and should be temperate in all things. The Christian is to preserve his interior independence of the good things of this world and to be content with a simple and natural life. The work concludes with a magnificent *Hymn to Christ* in which we perhaps possess the prayer of praise of the Alexandrian School (EH 139/49; EP 406/14; EA 73/81).

3. *Stromata* (Στρωματεῖς), eight books. The title chosen by Clement was meant to indicate that the book belongs to a species of literature frequent in antiquity, which allowed an author to treat various questions in loose sequence without a definite arrangement or fixed plan. Since, in *Paed.* 1, 1f., Clement outlines his plan to write a trilogy, the second part of which, represented by the *Pedagogue,* was to be followed by the Διδάσκαλος as the conclusion and crown of the whole, it has often wrongly been assumed that the *Stromata* is to be identified with the proposed *Didaskalos.* In fact Clement seems already to have given up his original plan while composing the *Stromata,* which contains much of what the *Didaskalos* was meant to offer.

In the *Stromata* Clement addresses a wider public of pagans interested in philosophy, his aim being to prove that the Christian gnosis is superior to any other gnosis. He discusses above all the question of the relation between Christianity and secular culture, especially Greek philosophy. In connexion with this he embarks on extensive historical dissertations designed to prove that Greek philosophy had borrowed much from the "barbaric" philosophy that had been expounded by the O.T. prophets. In other parts he attacks the religious and moral teachings of the false gnosis, to which he opposes the ideal of the Christian Gnostic (EP 415/35; EA 82/94). The work remained unfinished (cf. *Stom.* 7, 111, 4).

The eighth book contains only outlines and preliminary material that had already been used in the preceding books and were probably not meant for publication.

4. *What rich man shall be saved?* (Τίς ὁ σωζόμενος πλούσιος; *Quis dives salvetur?*), a homily on Mk. 10:17–31. This treatise proposes to show that a rich man too, can go to heaven, for not the rich man, but the sinner is excluded from heaven. To prove this Clement tells the legend of John the apostle and the young man who had become a savage robber, but was eventually converted by the apostle and brought back into the Church (EP 436/8; EA 95/7).

5. The *Excerpta ex Theodoto* (a Valentinian Gnostic, § 24, 6) and the *Eclogae propheticae* are, like the eighth book of the *Stromata*, notes and excerpts from the writings of others for his own works.

6. *Lost works and fragments:*

a. The most important is the Ὑποτυπώσεις (in eight books), i.e. outlines, notes commenting on selected passages from all the Scriptures (EP 439/42). Apart from a few citations in later writers, e.g., in Eus., *Hist.* 6, 14, the exegetical texts on 1 Pet., Jude and 1 and 2 John (*Adumbrationes*) are preserved in a Latin translation that goes back to Cassiodorus (*c.* 540). b. Unimportant fragments are known of the following: *On the Pasch, Ecclesiastical Canon or Against the Judaizers, On Providence, Exhortation to Patience or Address to the newly baptized, Letters.* Apart from these Eusebius mentions in his list (*Hist.* 6, 13) also sermons on fasting and on calumny. Palladius, *Hist. Laus.* ch. 139 mentions a treatise on the prophet Amos.

Edd.: MG 8–9. O. Staehlin, 3 vols., 1905/9, 1 [2]1936, 2 [2]1939; 4th vol. Reg., 1934/6; cf. PW 1935, 1189/92 (fragm. 59). Edd. of individual works: Strom. 7, ed. J. A. Hort and J. B. Mayor, Lo 1902 (with trans. and comment.) *Quis div.* ed. O. Staehlin 1908. *Protr., Quis div.* and Fragm. *On Patience* ed. G. W. Butterworth, Lo 1919 (with trans.). *Exc. ex Theodot.* ed. R. P. Casey, Lo 1934 (with trans. and comm.). A. Boatti, *Il pedagogo,* Tu 1937 *(testo e trad.).* Q. Cataudella, *Protrept.,* Tu 1941 *(testo e trad.).* F. Sagnard, *Extrait de Théodote* (SCh 23, text and trans.), 1949; cf. Festugière, VC 1949, 193, 207. C. Mondésert - A. Plassart, *Le Protreptique* (SCh 2, text and study), [2]1949. C. Mondésert - M. Caster, *Stromata*

I (SCh 30, text and trans.) 1951; cf. Nautin, RHE 1952, 618/31. Oulton-Chadwick, *Alexandr. Christianity* (trans. of texts from Clem. and Orig.), Lo 1954. T. Camelot-C. Mondésert, *Stromata* II (SCh 38, text and trans.); cf. Nautin, RHE 1954, 835/41. — Transs.: O. Staehlin (BKV² II, 7, 8, 17, 19) 1934/7. F. Overbeck, *Die Teppiche,* ed. C. A. Bernoulli u. L. Fruechtel, 1936; cf. JTS 1936, 418/22.

Mgg.: E. de Faye ²1926. J. Patrick, Lo 1914. R. B. Tollinton, 2 vols., Lo 1914. G. Bardy, P 1926. O. Staehlin in BKV² II 7, 7/67. De la Barre, DTC 3, 137/99. H. Mossbacher, *Praepositionen u. Praepositionsadverbien . . . bei Kl. v. A.,* 1931. E. Tengblad, *Syntaktisch-stilist. Beitraege zur Kritik u. Exegese des Kl. v. A.,* 1932. J. Munck, *Untersuchungen ueber Kl. v. Al.,* 1933. J. Tsermoulas, *Die Bilderspr. des Kl. v. A.* (thesis Wuerzburg 1933), Cairo 1934. G. Lazzati, *Introd. allo studio di Cl. Al.,* 1939. M. G. Murphy, *Nature Allusions in the Works of C. of Al.,* W 1941. M. Pugliese, *L'Apologetica greca e C. Aless.,* thesis Ca 1947. G. Catalfamo, *C. Aless.,* Brescia 1951. Fruechtel, RACh 3, 182/88.

Studies: Lewy, RevEA 1935, 5/8 (*Strom.* 1, 21, 105). Munck, ZKG 1937, 343/8 (*Indices* vol. of Staehlin's ed.). Fruechtel, ZNTW 1937, 81/90 and PW 1939, 765f. (citations from C. in the Church Fathers); ibid. 1937, 591f. (Clem. and Albinus). Festugière, RSPT 1931, 476/82 and 1937, 41f. (*Protr.* 9, 83, 2). Vergote, Mu 1939, 199/222; *Chronique d'Égypte* 1941, 21/38 (*Strom.* 5, 4, 20f.: *l'écriture égypt.).* Windhorst, RSR 1939, 496f. (*Protr.* 1, text. crit.). Van Unnik, NAKG 1941, 49/61 (his treatise *Canon eccles.*). Oulton, JTS 1940, 177/9 (C. and the *Didache*). Cataudella, SIF 1940, 271/81 (Minucius Fel. and C.). Mariotti, *Atene e Roma,* 1940, 48ff. (C. and Aristotle). Alfonsi, Aev 1942, 83/6 (text. crit. on *Protr.*); SC 1945, 209/16 (art form of *Protr.*); Aev 1946, 100/8 (C. and the *Letter to Diogn.*). Den Boer, Mn 11, 1943, 161/90 (C. and Minucius Fel.). Hermaniuk, ETL 1945, 5/60 (parable in C.). Echle, Tr 1945, 365/8 (fragm. of the *Hypotyp.* in J. Moschus). Ogg, JTS 1945, 59/63 (*Strom.* 1, 144, 1ff.). Fleisch, MélUniv-Beyrouth 27, 1947, 67/71 (Arab. fragms. on Mt. 5:7 28; 10:39; 19:3–15; Jo. 1: 8 11). Fruechtel, WJB 1947, 148/51. Mondésert, RSR 1949, 580/4 (on GCS, Staehlin 3 n. 36). Oreja, Hel 1950, 402/52 (C. and the School of Alex.). Colunga, Hel 1950, 453/71 (C. as an author). Fantini, Hel 1950, 472/507 (Sintaxis participal in: *Quis div.*). Festugière, REG 1952, 221f. (on *Protr.* 2, 14, 2). Voelker, ZKG 64, 1952/3, 1/33 (Wisdom lit. in C.). Alfonsi, VC 1953, 129/38 (dependence on Aristotle, *Protr.*). Recheis, Tr 1953, 419f. (fragm. *De paen.* belongs to *Quis div.*). K. Ziegler, PWK 40, 1948, 91 (plagiarism = κλοπή). Mondésert, RSR 1954, 258/65 (Le mot Λογικός). Enslin, HTR 1954, 213/41 (Gentleman among the Fathers [C. of Alex].).

Points of Doctrine

1. In a certain sense Clement attributes a supernatural character to Greek philosophy, though its contents were for the greater part "stolen" from the O.T. revelation. As the Law educated the Jews, so philosophy trained the pagans for Christ; indeed it had a

certain power of justification similar to the Law (*Strom.* 1, 28ff.; 1, 99).

2. Whilst the Gnostics alleged that faith and knowledge are absolutely opposed to each other, Clement wanted to bring both into a proper, harmonious relationship. Faith is for him the foundation (θεμέλιος) and starting point of all philosophizing. Nevertheless, philosophy can render important service to the Christian who wants to examine the contents of faith with the help of reason. It does not make the Christian truth any more true, but it reveals the futility of the attacks of its opponents; through it every believer can gain knowledge and thus become a "Christian Gnostic" (*Strom.* 1, 99, 1ff.). Knowing is more than believing (6, 18, 114). It is true, all the faithful can obtain salvation (4, 114, 1), but gnosis is a sort of perfection of man as man (7, 55, 1f.). Not everyone can reach the goal of the true Gnostic, for the road that leads to it is neither easy nor comfortable. The labours of the Gnostic are not in the first place of an intellectual kind, however necessary the mental training by which he ascends from the world of sense to the grasp of spiritual reality. He can attain to his goal only by striving for moral perfection. His soul must be free from all evil impulses; for only the pure of heart can see God (5, 7, 7; 6, 102, 1ff.; 7, 13ff.; 7, 56, 5; 7, 68, 4). The way to this peace of soul is the way of love of one's neighbour and of God. As the shadow follows the body, so the good works follow knowledge (7, 82, 7). Even though the true home of the Gnostic is in heaven, he also regards the earthly life as a God-given task (7, 70, 6–8; 7, 82, 7).

3. It is true, according to the testimony of Photius, Clement held in the *Hypotyposeis,* like some representatives of Greek philosophy, the doctrine of the eternity of matter; however, he later called God the cause of the being of all things (*Paed.* 1, 62; EP 409).

4. His notion of sin was formed in the controversy with Gnosticism, hence it had to exclude above all materialization of evil;

man can be defiled only by his personal act (*Strom.* 2, 62–66; 4, 93). Adam's sin consisted in his escape from God's education. This sin, which had bad consequences for men, was perpetuated not by generation but by bad example (*Adumbr. in Iud.* 11; *Strom.* 3, 100–4; *Protr.* 111).

5. In *Strom.* 7, 14 Clement stresses against the pagan concept of sacrifice that Christians do not offer sacrifices to "God, who needs nothing"; but this does not exclude his belief in the sacrificial meal of the Eucharist. Cf. *Strom.* 4, 161, 3 (The sacrifice of Melchisedech as a type of the eucharistic offerings). In *Paed.* 2, 19 he writes: "The blood of the Lord is twofold; the one is of the flesh, by which we are redeemed from perdition, the other is spiritual; this is that by which we are anointed. And to drink the blood of Jesus means sharing in the incorruptibility of the Lord." The Eucharistic drink is a union with the Logos, a praiseworthy and glorious gift of grace; if a man has part in it in faith, he is sanctified in body and soul. Cf. also *Paed.* 1, 42f. (EP 410).

6. "There is only one virginal Mother; I will call her Church" (*Paed.* 7, 42; EP 408). The threefold ecclesiastical hierarchy (bishops, priests, deacons) is fashioned on the angelic hierarchy (*Strom.* 6, 107; EP 427).

7. Clement assumes with Plato that God's punishments serve only to purify men. Plato said: "He who suffers punishment receives a benefit" (*Paed.* 1, 67). Clement, however, does not explicitly apply this word to the punishment in hell. He also teaches the Platonic trichotomy of man (σῶμα, ψυχή, νοῦς).

Mgg.: W. Scherer, *K. v. A. u. seine Erkenntnisprinzipien,* 1907. T. Ruether, *Die Lehre v. d. Erbsuende bei K. v. A.,* 1922. J. Héring, *Étude sur la doctrine de la chute et de la préexistence des âmes chez C. d'A.,* 1923. J. Meifort, *Der Platonismus bei K. v. A.,* 1928. R. B. Tollinton, *Alexandrine Teaching on the Universe,* NY 1932. N. S. Georgescu, *Doctrina moralà dupa C. A.,* Bucharest 1933. J. Pascher, *Studien zur Gesch. der aegypt. Mystik:* no. 2, *Klem. v. Alex.,* 1934. A. I. Phytraki, Αἱ κοινωνικαὶ ἰδέαι Κλ. 'Αλ., At 1935. J. Frangoulis, *Begriff des Geistes bei K. v. A.,* 1936. A. Dekker, *Kenntnis u. Pflege des Koerpers bei K. v. A.* I, 1936. E. Molland, *The Conception of the Gospel in the Alex. Theology,* Oslo 1938. S. Simon, *C. Alex. es a mysteriumok* (mysteries), Budapest 1938 (pp. 54/64 German summary). F. Buri, *C. Al. u. der paulinische Freiheitsbegriff,* Zu 1939. P. Vielhauer, *Oikodome. Das Bild vom Bau i. d. christl. Literatur vom N.T. bis C. Alex.,* 1939. P. J. Schmidt, *C. Alex. in seinem Verhaeltnis zur griech. Religion u. Philosophie,* thesis W 1939. W. den Boer, *De Allegor. in het werk van Cl. Al.,* thesis Ley 1940. G. Békés, *De continua oratione C. Al. doctrina,* R 1941; StAns 18/9, 1947, 157/72 *(Oratio pura).* A. Mayer, *Nova et Vetera. Festschr. Metten,* 1939, 44/64 (similarity to God); *Das Gottesbild im Menschen nach C. v. Al.,* R 1952. Polenz, GN 1943, 3, 103/80 (C.'s Hellenistic Christianity). C. Mondésert, C. d'Al., P 1944 (his theology). T. Camelot, *Foi et gnose . . . chez C. d'Al.,* 1945. F. Quatember, *Die christl. Lebenshaltung des K. v. Al.,* W 1946; cf. TLZ 1951, 296f. T. Ruether, *Die sittl. Forderung der Apatheia i. d. beiden ersten christl. Jhh. u. bei C. Al.,* 1949. H. E. Echle, *The Terminology of the Sacrament of Regeneration acc. to C. Al.,* thesis W 1949; *Sacramental Initiation as Christ. Mystery-Initiation acc. to C. Al.,* in *Gedaechtnisschrift Casel,* 1951, 54/65. F. van der Grinten, *Die natuerl. u. uebernatuerl. Begruendung des Tugendlebens bei C. Al.,* Bonn 1949. G. Kretschmer, *Jesus Christus i. d. Theologie des C. Al.,* thesis typed Hei 1950. W. Voelker, *Der wahre Gnostiker nach K. v. Al.* 1952 (fundamental). Orbe, Gr 1955, 410/48 (on *Paed.* I 26, 3 to 27, 2: baptismal theol.). Bierbaum, MTZ 1954, 246/72 (Hist. as *Paidagogia* of God). I. G. Gussen, *Het leven in Alex. volgens de cultuurhist. gegevens in de Paed.* (lib. 2 and 3), Assen 1955. Lichtenstein, VJWissPaed 1956, 20/39.

Studies: Gaudel, DTC 12, 329/32 (original sin). Camelot, RSR 1931, 38/66 541/69 (learning and philosophy). J. Hoh 1932, 115/29. Stelzenberger 1933 166/70, 226/31 and freq. Bardy 1935, 183/214. Doelger, AC 5, 87/94 (baptismal symbol). Mondésert, RSR 1936, 155/80 (symbolism). Marsh, JTS 1936, 64/80 (mystery). Seesemann, TSK 1936, 312/46 (interpretation of Paul); ZNTW 1937, 90/7 (Pauline text). Molland, SO 1936, 57/85 (origin of Greek philos.). J. Ziegler *Dulcedo Dei,* 1937, 62f., 70/2. Pruemm, Sch 1937, 17/57 (faith and knowledge in *Strom.* 2). K. Rahner, Gr 1937, 426/31 (super-nature). Pire, RSPT 1938, 427/31 (*apatheia*). B. Pade, *Logos Theos bei K.,* R 1939. Poschmann 1940, 229/60. Hitchcock, CQR 1939, 57/70 (Holy Comm. and Creed). Doelger, AC 6, 147/51 (Jesus, Holy Light). Oustler, JR 1940, 217/40 (Platonism). Alfonsi, RFN 1942, 238/41 *(Protr.).* Amand, *Fatalisme,* 1945, 258/74. Voelker, TZ 1947, 15/40 (doctrine of perfection). Lebreton, RSR 1947, 55/76, 142/79 (doctrine of Trinity). Ruvet, Bi 1948, 77/99, 240/68, 391/308 (Canon of Scripture and apocrypha); 1949, 133/60 *(Agrapha).* Moingt, RSR 1950, 195/251, 381/421, 537/64; 1951, 82/118 (relation of gnosis to faith and philosophy). Karpp, ZNTW 43, 1950/1, 224/42 (doctrine of penance). Wolfson, CH 1951, 72/81 (The generation of the Logos). Stelzenberger, MTZ 1953, 27/33 *(syneidesis).* Dumortier, MSR 1954, 63/70 *(Idées morales).* Méhat, VC 1954, 225/33 (on doctrine of penance). Wytzes, VC 1955, 146/58 *(paideia* and *pronoia).* F. Hofmann, *Festg. f. K. Adam* 1956, 11/57 (the Church in Cl. A.). E. F. Osborn, *The Philosophy of C. of A.,* 1957.

§ 40. ORIGEN (d. 253–4).

ORIGEN, probably the greatest scholar of Christian antiquity, is the first ecclesiastical author on whose life we have more detailed information: through Eusebius *(Hist.* 6), through the first book of the apology of the priest Pamphilus, which is preserved in Latin (§ 41, 8) through the panegyric that Gregory Thaumaturgus preached on him (§ 41, 4), through Jerome (*Vir. ill.* 54 62; *Ep.* 33 44, 1) and Photius (*Bibl. cod.* 118).

He was born *c.* 185, probably at Alexandria. When his father Leonidas was martyred in 201–2 Origen and his family found themselves in very straitened circumstances which he sought to improve by giving lessons. In 202–3, after the departure of Clement, his bishop, Demetrius, appointed him, despite his youth, the first ecclesiastically authorized head of the catechetical school which under him reached the summit of its fame.

He chose his friend Heraclas as his assistant for teaching grammar, while he himself taught the more advanced philosophy, speculative theology and finally Holy Scripture. At first he also attended the lectures of the famous Neo-Platonist Ammonius Saccas, whose method and philosophy were to exercise a great influence on his theology. Origen probably also acquired some knowledge of Hebrew. He led a very ascetical life; a wrong interpretation of Mt. 19 : 12 induced him to castrate himself, probably soon after 202–3. About 212 he travelled to Rome, "to see the ancient Church of the Romans" (Eus., *Hist.* 6, 14, 10). At that time he probably became acquainted with the presbyter Hippolytus. Origen left Alexandria probably because of the massacres ordered by the Emperor Caracalla in 215 and went to Caesarea in Palestine, where he lectured to the congregation on Scripture at the request of Bishop Theoctistus as well as of Alexander, the Bishop of Jerusalem. His bishop, Demetrius, however, demanded his early return. When he came to Caesarea on a journey to Greece fifteen years later, his two episcopal friends ordained him priest despite his self-mutilation. Bishop Demetrius, enraged by this event, caused two synods held at Alexandria in 230–1 to depose him from his teaching office and his priesthood and to excommunicate him from the Alexandrian Church on the grounds of unlawful ordination and probably also unorthodox doctrine. Now he definitely moved to Caesarea where he remained until the reign of Decius and founded a school similar to that at Alexandria. Gregory Thaumaturgus was his pupil at that time. Origen had long been known also in pagan circles for his scholarly achievements. Julia Mammaea, the mother of the Emperor Alexander Severus, called him to Antioch (218–22) to hear his lectures. In 244 he went to Arabia and converted Bishop Beryllus of Bostra from his Patripassian errors. He was imprisoned and cruelly tortured under Decius, probably at Caesarea. As a result of his sufferings he died in his 70th year, probably 253–4, at Tyre, where his tomb was shown for a long time (EH 439f.).

Origen was considered the greatest theologian of the Greek Church even in his lifetime; neither friend nor enemy could escape his influence. No other author excited so much controversy in Christian antiquity, no other name was mentioned with so much enthusiasm or so much indignation. Noble scholars followed in his footsteps, some heretics appealed to him; but orthodox teachers, too, learned from him. Origen wanted to be an orthodox Christian, which can be seen from the fact that he attaches such importance to the doctrinal teaching of the Church and considers an error of doctrine worse than a moral fault.

Nevertheless, his addiction to the allegorical exegesis of Scripture and the influence of Platonic philosophy caused him to fall into grave doctrinal errors. Controversies on his orthodoxy arose soon after his death; they flared up with particular violence *c.* 400, when Epiphanius and the patriarch Theophilus of Alexandria were his chief opponents. They came to an end in the sixth century when the Emperor Justinian I condemned nine theses of Origen in an edict (543). Soon all the bishops of the Empire agreed to this verdict, especially Patriarch Mennas of Constantinople and Pope Vigilius (537–55) (ES 203/11).

Origen's literary output surpasses in volume that of all other writers of Christian antiquity. According to Jerome, Eusebius' list of his writings which has unfortunately not been preserved counted no less than 2000 "books" (*Adv. Ruf.* 2, 22). An incomplete list in Jerome, *Ep.* 33, gives scarcely 800 *(libri.)* Eusebius (*Hist.* 6, 14, 10) calls him 'Αδαμάντιος (man of steel) and reports that his wealthy disciple Ambrose, whom he had converted from Valentinian Gnosticism to Catholic Christianity, paid for his seven stenographers and as many copyists as well as several woman calligraphers (Eus., *Hist.* 6, 23).

Many of his writings, however, are but products of the moment, i.e. sermons and lectures taken down by stenographers; only this explains the enormous bulk of his output as well as certain peculiarities of language and style. Origen did not possess great literary talent.

Only a small number of his works, dealing mostly with Biblical subjects (textual criticism and exegesis) have come down to us, and these too, mostly not in the Greek original but in Latin translations. Besides, we possess the *Philocalia,* an anthology from his writings compiled by Basil the Great and Gregory of Nazianzus.

1. *The Hexapla*

This enterprise, which was conceived on a grand scale and could be realized only through the generous contribution of his wealthy convert Ambrose, was intended to produce an exact text of the LXX, which was then considered verbally inspired, and to make clear its relation to the Hebrew original.

Hence the following were put side by side in six columns: the Hebrew text in Hebrew characters, the Hebrew text in Greek script, the Greek translations of Aquila, Symmachus, the LXX and Theodotion. In the LXX text all words and paragraphs missing in the Hebrew were marked with an obelus (÷), all *lacunae,* on the other hand, inserted from one of the other translations, mostly from Theodotion, are marked with an asterisk (*). If something had been wrongly translated in the LXX, the right reading was inserted either by itself or behind the one marked with an obelus. These six columns earned the work the name *Hexapla,* i.e. the sixfold Bible. In the Psalter further columns were added for a fifth, sixth, and sometimes even a seventh translation.

Of this gigantic work of Origen only the LXX text in its *Hexapla* revision was frequently copied. Extracts from Aquila, Symmachus, LXX and Theodotion *(Tetrapla)* were circulated less often. The whole work was preserved at Caesarea and consulted by interested scholars such as Pamphilus and Jerome. Jerome's translations of the Bible are a still almost untouched mine of *Hexapla* readings in Latin.

2. Scholia, Homilies and Commentaries

Origen wrote commentaries on almost all the books of the Bible, on many of them in two, on some even in three different literary forms. These are either *scholia* (σχόλια), i.e. brief notes on difficult passages or words after the example of the Alexandrian grammarians; or *homilies (ὁμιλίαι, tractatus),* i.e. popular and edifying lectures or sermons often delivered without preparation, which were taken down by stenographers and later revised and published, sometimes only after Origen's death; or learned *commentaries* in the modern sense *(τόμοι, volumina),* the interpretations of which sometimes amounted to long theological treatises.

a. Complete *scholia* commentaries are no longer extant. Some sentences are hidden in the *Philocalia* and in *catenae*. The *Scholienkommentar zur Apokalypse Johannis* published by Harnack (TU 38, 3) 1911 (better text in Turner, JTS 13, 191–2, 386/97) is very probably part of a *catena* containing Origenist matter.

b. The following homilies are extant in the Greek original: twenty on Jer., one on 1 Sam. 28, 3–25 (witch of Endor); in the Latin translation of Rufinus (§ 85): sixteen on Gen., thirteen on Ex., sixteen on Lev., twenty-eight on Num., twenty-six on Jos., nine on Judges, nine on Ps.; in the translation of Jerome: two on Cant., eight (nine?) on Isa., fourteen on Jer., thirty-nine on Lk.; in the translation of Hilary of Poitiers: fragments of the twenty-two homilies on Jb.; in an anonymous Latin translation one on 1 Sam. 1–2 (prob. translated by Rufinus). Besides, fragments of homilies on the following have been edited: Jb., 1–2 Sam.; 1–2 Kings, 1 Cor., Hebr. and others (EP 474/7, 486/97; EA 111/27; cf. also § 85, 1a).

Only twenty-one of Origen's approximately 574 homilies are today extant in the Greek original, and 388 of those translated into Latin are lost. See the lists in the *Dictionary of Christian Biography* 4, 104/18. These sermons which are devoted to pastoral and spiritual ends have exercised a great influence on later spiritual and mystical theology.

c. Of the mostly very voluminous commentaries none has been preserved in full. Of the twenty-five books of the *Commentary on Matthew* we have eight books, and a still greater part in an anonymous Latin translation (cited as *Commentariorum in Mt. series*) on Mt. 16:13 to 27:63; eight of the thirty-two books of the *Commentary on John* in Greek; in the Latin translation of Rufinus books 1–4 of the *Commentary on the Canticle* and a revision of the *Commentary on Romans* (ten instead of the fifteen books of the original). Moreover, a great number of fragments have been preserved in the *Philocalia* and especially in *catenae* (EP 498/509). — A Latin commentary on Job in three books is spurious (Lommatzsch 16, 3/24), cf. § 53, 2.

3. *Against Celsus* (eight books), the most important, though not always thorough ante-Nicene apology (EP 510/36; EA 146/8).

Origen wrote this at the age of over sixty at the request of his friend Ambrose to refute the Ἀληθὴς λόγος of the Platonist philosopher Celsus (supra § 19, 3). The latter had represented Christ as a common impostor; he explained everything extraordinary in his life as inventions of his first followers and the quick spread of Christianity as due to the impression made on the ignorant crowds by the terrifying pictures of the Last Judgement and the fire of hell.

Origen's refutation follows the work of Celsus sentence by sentence. The argumentation is sometimes weak, but it impresses by its quiet, dignified tone and its superior scholarship. As proof of the truth of Christianity Origen adduces the cures of the possessed and the sick which are still constantly worked by Christ, and the moral purity of the faithful who are in the world like lights from heaven (φωστῆρες).

4. *On the Principal Doctrines* (of Christianity, Περὶ ἀρχῶν, *De principiis*) is the first manual of dogmatics; in this treatise the erroneous doctrines of the great Alexandrian are most evident; date 220–30.

The first book treats of the Triune God, the angels and their fall, the second of the creation of the world, of man as a fallen spirit imprisoned in the body, of his fall and his redemption by Jesus Christ and of the Last Things. The third gives the fundamentals of a moral theology: it discusses the freedom of the will, sin and the restoration of all things in God; the fourth presents Scripture as the source of faith and its threefold sense. In view of the difficulty of the undertaking, this work must be acknowledged as an outstanding achievement despite its defects. It is not a purely dogmatic presentation of the doctrine of the Church but makes frequent use of the speculations of Platonic philosophy

The work is preserved in full only in the translation of Rufinus, from which its errors have as far as possible been extirpated; Greek fragments survive in the *Philocalia* and in two letters of the Emperor Justinian I. Jerome's translation, made during his controversy with Rufinus, is no longer extant.

5. *On Prayer* (Περὶ εὐχῆς, *De oratione*): gives instructions on prayer in general and explains the *Our Father;* it is a beautiful witness to the deep piety of its author (EH 243/6; EA 103/7).

6. The *Exhortation to Martyrdom,* written at Caesarea in 235 at the beginning of the persecution under Maximinus Thrax is addressed to two friends, the deacon Ambrose and the priest Protectus who had both suffered. It exhorts to steadfast perseverance.

7. Only two have survived of his many Letters which were preserved in four different collections, one of which counted more than a hundred items. The first is addressed to Gregory Thaumaturgus, the second to Julius Africanus (§ 41, 1).

8. The papyrus find at Tura (1941), which has so far been published only in part, brought to light two hitherto unknown writings: the *Disputation with Heraclides* (important for the doctrine of the Trinity) and a treatise on the *Pascha.* There are also large parts of *Contra Celsum* (lib. I and II) and fragments from the commentaries on Romans 3:5 to 5:7, and on1 Kings 28. Cf. § 55, 2a.

J. Scherer, *Entretien d'O. avec Héraclide et les évêques ses collègues sur le Père, le Fils et l'âme,* Cairo 1949. Capelle, JEH 1951, 143/57; id., RHE 1952, 163/71. Puech, RHPR 1951, 293/329 (the MSS of Tura). Camelot, RSPT 1950, 4 *(The Disputation with Heraclides).* J. Fischer, MTZ 1952, 256/71 (disput. with Heracl.). Crehan, TSW 1950, 368/73 (O. in Dialektos on Jo. 21 : 17). Puech, Mél. M. Goguel 1950, 180/94 (Trinit. exegesis of Ps. 50, 12/14). RHP 1951, 293/329 (O. and Didymus-texts). Kretschmar, ZTK 1953, 258/79 (O. and the Arabs; Beryllus of Bostra prob. opponent). Doutreleau, RSR 1955, 161/76 (Pap. of Tura). J. Scherer, *Extraits des livres I et II du "Contre Celse" d'O.,* Cairo 1956; id., *Le Comment d'O. sur Rom. 3:5 – 5:7,* Cairo 1955.

Complete edd.: C. de la Rue, 4 vols., 1733/59 = MG 11/17. C. H. E. Lommatzsch, 25 vols., 1831/48. In GCS so far 12 vols., 1899/55, ed. P. Koetschau (3 vols.), E. Klostermann (4 vols.); Klostermann-Fruechtel XII 3 (fragms. and

Indices to Mt.-comm.), 1955. E. Preuschen (1 vol.), W. A. Baehrens (3 vols.), M. Rauer (1 vol.). Fragms. of *Hexapla:* F. Field, 2 vols., 1871/5. G. Mercati (ST 5). — Individual works: *C. Cels.,* 1899, *De orat. and Exhort.,* 1899, *De princ.,* 1913 by Koetschau. *Philocalia:* J. A. Robinson, 1893. E. Klostermann (KlT 4) [3]1914 (3 homs.); (KlT 83) 1912 (Witch of Endor). R. Cadiou, *Commentaires inédits des Psaumes,* 1935; cf. RevSR 1936, 474/83. — Transs.: F. Crombie, 2 vols., Edinburgh 1869/72. *Ausgew. Schriften* by P. Koetschau (BKV[2] 48 52f.) 1926f. G. Bardy, 1932 *(Orat. Exhort.).* G. W. Butterworth 1936 (Eng. trans. of *De princ.*). U. v. Balthasar, *Geist und Feuer,* [2]1951 (selected texts). L. Doutreleau, P 1944 (HomGen.). Fortier-De Lubac, *Hom. sur l'Ex.,* P 1947 (SCh 16). A. Méhat, *Hom. sur les Nombres,* 1951 (SCh 29). P. Nautin, *Hom. pascales II: 3 hom. dans la tradition d'O.,* 1953 (SCh 36). O. Rousseau, *O., Hom. sur le Cantique des Cant.,* 1954 (SCh 37). O. Chadwick, *O., Contra Celsum,* Lo 1953. E. E. Jay, *O., Treatise on Prayer* (SPCK), 1954. J. J. O'Meara, *O., Prayer, Exhort. to martyrd.,* 1954 (ACW 19). L. Oulton-H. Chadwick, *Alexandrian Christianity* (selected texts from Clem. Al. and O.), Lo 1954. E. Kadloubovsky - H. Palmer, *Early Fathers from the Philokalia* (selected and trans. from the Russian), Lo 1954. — Mgg.: E. R. Redepenning, 2 vols., 1841/6. E. de Faye, 3 vols., 1923/8 (cf. D'Alès, RSR 1930, 224/68); *Esquisse de la pensée d'O.,* 1925. G. Bardy, P 1931; DTC 11, 1489/1565. A. d'Alès, *Origénisme,* DA 3, 1228/58. G. Fritz, *Origénisme,* DTC 11, 1565/88. DB 4, 1870/89 and DBSuppl 2, 80/94. Hal Koch, PWK 18, 1, 1036/56. R. Cadiou, *La jeunesse d'Origène,* 1936. Krueger 1933, 217 and 241f. A. Harnack, *Der kirchengeschichtl. Ertrag der exeget. Arbeiten des* O. (TU 42, 3/4,1918f.) E. Klostermann u. E. Benz (TU 47, 2, 1931; 47, 4, 1932; tradition of Mt. exegesis); on this TLZ 1932, 323/8 and RB 1932, 261/3. M. Rauer, TU 47, 3, 1932 (trad. of Luke-homs.); on this TLZ 1934, 8/10. J. Daniélou, *Origène,* P 1948; Engl. trans., Lo 1955.

Mgg. and Treatises: Devreesse, DBSuppl 2, 1106f., 1120/2, 1215/7 and freq. Tasker, JTS 1935, 60/5 (citations from Synoptics in *Exhort.*); 1936, 146/55 (text of Jo.); 1937, 60/4 (text of Mt.). Orlinsky, JQR 1936, 137/50 *(Hexapla).* Procksch, ZATW 1935, 240ff.; 1936, 66ff. (Studies on *Tetrapla*). Richard, RHE 1937, 794/6 (citations in *florilegia* from *Princ.* 2, 6, 2 3). Skard, *Symb.* Osl. fasc. 16/7, 204/8 (scholia comment. on Apoc.). G. Krueger, *Die Rechtsstellung der vorkonst. Kirche,* 1935, 69/83 (*C. Cels.* 1, 1). Richard, RHE 1937, 44/6 (Schol. in Iac. 1, 13 = MG 12, 288f.). Staples, *J. Amer. Or. Sc.* 1939, 71/80 (2nd column of *Hexapla*). v. Balthasar, ZKT 1939, 86/106, 181/206 (Sel. in Pss. et in Prov.; belongs to Evagrius). Reuss, Bi 1939, 401/4 (fragm. of Mt. comm.). Vogliano, BNJ 15, 1939, 130/6 (fragm. of Hom. 2). Colon, RevSR 1940, 1/27 *(Philocalia).* Mercati, Nuove note (ST 95) 1941, 85/91 *(Onomast. delle Siroesaplare);* 139/50 *(testo esapl.);* 1/48 *(sottoscriz. a cod. esaplari e siroesapl.).* Mercati, OM 4, 1937, 89/97 *(Georg. Scholarios e i libri c. Celso).* Ruwet, Bi 1942, 18/42; 1943, 15/58 (*Antilegomena* in Origen); 1944, 143/66, 311/34 *(Apocrypha).* Steidle, ZNTW 1942, 236/43 (*De princ.* only 3 parts; anti-Marcionite tendency). Bardy, RMA 1945, 420f. (O. in Bernard of Clairv.?). Klostermann, TLZ 1947, 203/8 (forms of exegetical works). J. Daniélou, RAM 1947, 126/41 *(sources bibl. de la mystique);* RSR 1947, 359/61 (Maximus of Tyre). P. Sanz, *Griech. liter. Papyri,* W 1946,87/104 (Gen. comment.). Chadwick, JTS 1947, 34/49 (O., Celsus, Stoa). Elorduy,

Pensamiento 3, 1947, 5/27 (legend of the apostasy of A. Saccas). Grant-Pighi, VC 1948, 109/12, 161f., 243/7 (new hom. fragms.). Stenzel, ZATW 61, 1945/48, 30/43 (on Hom. on 1 Sam. 1–2). K. W. Kim, *The Mt.-Text of O. in his Comm. on Mt.,* thesis Chicago Univ. 1946. F. Pack, *The Methodology of O. as a Textual Critic in Arriving at the Text of the NT,* thesis S. Calif. Univ. 1948. Chadwick, HTR 1948, 83/102 (O., Celsus and the resurr. of the body); JTS 1953, 215/9 (text. crit. on O. *C. Celsum*). Caramella, NDid 1948, 62/70 *(Cristianesimo di Amm. Sacca).* Jonas, TZ 1948, 101/19 (*De princ.,* a system of patristic gnosis). G. Mercati, *Proemi del Salterio di O., Ippol., Eusebio, Cirillo Aless. e altri,* 1948 (ST 142). Leclercq, RB 1949, 183/95 (O. and St. Bernard); Ir 1951, 425/38 *(O. au 12^e^ s.).* Brouwer, RB 1949, 202f. (on *Comm. in Ct.* 1, 19). Ruwet, Bi 1949, 517ff. (on 1 Cor. 2, 9). Den Boer, VC 1950, 61/4 (on *C. Celsum* 3, 44ff.). Kim, JTS 1950, 78/84 (text. crit.); JBL 1950, 167/75 (Codd. 1582, 1739 and O.); JTS 1953, 42/9 (Mt.-text in *C. Celsum*). Klijn, NTT 1953, 296/302 (De Kerk op O. *Hexapla*). Laeuchli, TZ 1950, 151 (on Jo. 8, 1–11). Furlani, AttiAccadNaz-Lincei 1952, 7, 7/14 *(O. e i Yezidi).* Guéraud, JournEgyptArch 1954, 63/7 (O. in Proc. of Gaza). Hanson, VC 1956, 103/23 (Hebr. names). G. Frankowski, *O. ueber die Urgemeinde,* thesis, typed, Hei 1955. Lawson, ACW 26, 1957 (Comm. and Hom. on the Song of Songs). G. Mercati, *Psalterii Hexapli reliquiae,* Part I, Bibl. Vaticana 1958.

Points of Doctrine

1. Following the Platonic trichotomy, Origen distinguishes a threefold sense of Scripture: the somatic (= literal, historico-grammatical), the psychic (= moral) and the pneumatic (= allegorical-mystical). His notion of inspiration—he subscribes to a strict verbal inspiration—compelled him to have recourse to the allegorical method of exegesis, in order thus to explore the higher and spiritual sense of Scripture. For it seemed to him that the historical explanation of the text would often result in scandalous and impossible, even blasphemous statements. This explains how it was that he considered everything in Holy Scripture to have a "spiritual" sense but not everything an historical sense. This doctrine of the spiritual sense applies not only to the O.T., but also to the N.T., which is too, in a certain sense only the "letter" (*Princ.* 4, 16ff.). That in his scholarly anxiety, Origen should have been urged to such a one-sided search for the "spiritual sense" of the Biblical books is all the more understandable as this method was already practised by the classical as well as the Jew-

ish-Hellenistic (Philo) exegesis of texts. On the other hand, he could not be aware of the historical and cultural limitations governing the Scriptural narratives. Subsequently his practice came to be directly or indirectly an example responsible for the many excesses of the later typological and allegorical exegesis down to our own time, which is unable to recognize that just the "literal sense" is primarily the "spiritual" sense intended by the inspiring divine Spirit.

2. Creation is conceived as an eternal act. The divine omnipotence and goodness can never be without an object of their activity. The Son proceeds from God in an eternal radiation, and the Holy Spirit from the Son (EP 454; in Jo. 2:6). The present visible world was preceded by a world of spirits which were all equally perfect. Part of this fell away from God—the pre-existent human souls belonged to it— and was therefore banished into matter, which was created only then. The differences of men on earth and the measure of the graces God gives to each one of them is in proportion to their pre-cosmic guilt (*Cels.* 1, 32 33; *Princ.* 2, 8 f.).

3. Origen defined the relation of the three Persons in God in the subordinatianist sense. Though he emphasizes the eternity of the Son of God, whom he calls ὁμοούσιος (EP 540), only the Father is αὐτόθεος, the Logos is δεύτερος θεός. He is not, like the Father, ἁπλῶς ἀγαθός, but εἰκὼν ἀγαθότητος (*Cels.* 5, 39; *Princ.* 1, 2, 13). The Holy Spirit is inferior to the Son (*Princ.*, praef. 4).

4. The Logos assumed a true body and is God-Man (θεάνθρωπος). Origen is the first to use this term (*Hom. Ez.* 3, 3). The union of the two natures in Christ is extremely close (*Cels.* 2, 9), hence he teaches the *communicatio idiomatum* (*Princ.* 2, 6, 3; EP 460). According to Socrates (*Hist.* 7, 32, 17; EH 866) Origen called Mary, *Theotokos;* cf. *Hom. Lc.* 6, 7 (Rauer 44, 10; 50, 9). The term θεοτόκος certainly originated in the Alexandrian school and is for instance quite familiar to St. Athanasius.

5. Origen attests original sin; the filth of sin clings to every

soul that is born in the flesh (EP 496 and 501); hence it is an apostolic tradition to baptize infants.

6. Origen thinks that the Eucharistic Flesh and Blood comes into existence through the influence exercised on the natural elements by the Logos and through the *epiklesis* of men. He calls the Eucharistic Body *munus consecratum,* of which nothing may be lost (*Hom. Ex.* 13, 3; EP 490). In some passages he interprets the "Body and Blood of Christ" allegorically. Thus he once says (*Hom. Num.* 16, 9) that one can drink the Blood of Christ in a twofold way, viz. "sacramentally" *(sacramentorum ritu)* and "when we accept his words, in which is life". He describes the belief in the real presence of Christ as "generally Christian" (κοινοτέρα), but as the faith of the *parvuli,* whereas the symbolic conception is held by the *prudentiores* (*In Mt. ser.* 86; *In Mt.* 11:4). Origen clearly attests the sacrificial and expiatory character of the celebration of the Eucharist (*In Jes. Nave* 2, 1; *In Lev.* 13, 3).

7. The capital sins or "sins unto death" which Origen terms "incurable" are nevertheless, in his view, not absolutely incurable. They are not wholly withdrawn from the Church's power of forgiveness, but, unlike the less grave sins, they cannot be forgiven by an act of grace but have rather to be expiated in the long drawn-out public penance of excommunication (*Cels.* 3, 51; EH 253). Private ecclesiastical penance is not attested by Origen.

8. A principal point of his doctrine was the ἀποκατάστασις πάντων: after death the souls of those who have sinned on earth enter a purifying fire, but gradualy all, even the devils, ascend from step to step and will finally, completely purified, rise again in ethereal bodies when God will once more be all in all. This restoration (ἀποκατάστασις), however, does not mean the end of the world, but only a preliminary conclusion. Other worlds existed before this world, and others will come after it. He taught with Plato that one world follows the other in endless succession. Hence Origen denied the eternity of hell (EP 456f. 468).

9. Origen was the most influential teacher of the ascetic life for the following centuries and thus also the forerunner of monasticism. Self-knowledge is the first requirement for the imitation of Christ and the striving for perfection. The Christian must know what to do and what to avoid in order to progress on the way of union with God and Christ (*In Cant.* 2, 143/5). The first condition of union with God is the constant struggle against the passions (πάθη) and the spirit of this world which leads to sin. Eventually all passions will be suppressed (ἀπάθεια) by the mortification of the flesh. Hence he recommends the renunciation of marriage and praises the celibate life and the vow of virginity which Christ had taught (*Hom. in Num.* 24, 2). Ambition and earthly possessions do not permit the *vacare Deo* (*Hom. in Ex.* 8, 4). He greatly esteems all ascetical practices such as frequent vigils, meditation, strict fasts (*Hom. in Ex.* 13, 5; Ps. 34, 13) as well as the daily reading of Scripture (*Hom. in Gen.* 10, 3).

Mgg.: A. Zoellig, *Die Inspirationslehre des O.*, 1902. F. Prat, *O., le théologien et l'exégète*, 1907. Kyrillos II, *Reconstitution de la synthèse scientifique d'O.*, 2 vols., Alexandria 1907/9. A. Miura-Stange, *Celsus u. O.*, 1926. C. Verfaillie, *La doctrine de la justification dans O.*, 1926. G. Rossi, *Saggi sulla metafisica di O.*, Mi 1929. W. Voelker, *Das Vollkommenheitsideal des O.*, 1931. R. B. Tollinton, *Alexandrine Teaching on the Universe*, NY 1932. Hal Koch, *Pronoia und Paideusis, Studien ueber O. und sein Verhaeltnis zum Platonismus*, 1932. G. Massart, *Società e Stato nel cristianesimo primitivo. La concezione di O.*, Padua 1932. R. Cadiou, *Introduction au système d'O.*, 1932. A. Lieske, *Theol. der Logosmystik bei O.*, 1938. L. Grimmelt, *Die Eucharistiefeier . . .* (in O.), thesis Mr 1942. C. Vagaggini, *Maria nelle op. di O.*, R 1942. E. F. Latko, *O.'s Concept of Penance*, thesis Laval-Quebec Univ. 1949. S. Laeuchli, *Probleme des Geschichtlichen bei O.*, thesis Union Theol. Sem., NY 1950. J. Daniélou, *Sacramentum futuri. Ét. sur les origines de la typologie bibl.*, 1950. F. Bertrand, *Mystique de Jésus chez O.*, 1951. H. de Lubac, *Hist. et Esprit. L'intelligence de l'Écriture d'après O.*, 1950. C. V. Harris, *O.'s Interpretation of the Teacher's Function in the Early Christ. Hierarchy and Community*, thesis Duke Univ. 1952. H. J. Mumm, *A Critical Appreciation of O. as an Exegete of the Fourth Gospel*, thesis Hartford Seminary 1952. V. E. Hasler, *Gesetz u. Evangelium i. d. Alten Kirche bis O.*, Zu 1953. C. Hanson, *O.'s Doctrine of Tradition*, 1954 (SPCK). Riedinger 1956 (O., the source of the later polemics against astrology, passim). Treatises: Simonin, DTC 12, 282/8 (predestination). Gaudel, DTC 12, 332/9 (original sin). Mersch I, 1933, 282/305. F. Ruesche, *Das Seelen-*

pneuma. Seine Entwicklung v. d. Hauchseele zur Geistseele, 1933. Doelger, AC 4, 95/109 (epilepsy). F. Billicsich, *Das Problem der Theodizee im philos. Denken des Abendlandes* I, 1935. C. Bardy 1935, 215/71. Lowry, JTS 1936, 225/40; 1938, 39/42 (doctrine of Trinity). H. U. von Balthasar, RSR 1936, 513/62; 1937, 38/64 (mysterion). Hodžega, TG 1937, 431/40 (Primacy of Peter and the orthodox). E. Molland 1938 (supra § 39) 85/164. Knox, JTS 1938, 247f. (resurrection). Klostermann, ZNTW 37, 1938, 52/61 (definitions). Poschmann 1940, 425/80. Edsman 1940, 1/15. Casel, JL 15, 1941, 164/95 (faith and gnosis; 184/91: doct. of Eucharist). Hitchcock, CQR 1941, 216/39 (Eucharist). Rivière, BLE 1944, 3/12 (soteriology). Cavallera, BLE 1943, 61/75 (O. as an educationist). T. Bettencourt, *Doctrina ascet. O.is,* R 1945. H. Rahner, Eranos-Jb 1947, 1948, 197/248 (concept of man). Boer, VC 1947, 150/67 (hermeneut. problems). Hanson, JTS 1948, 17/27 (doctrine of tradition). Bonnefoy, Mél. Cavallera 1948, 87/145 (theol. method). Amand, *Fatalisme,* 1945, 275/325. Daniélou, RevSR 1948, 27/56 *(L'unité des deux Testaments).* Jonas, TZ 1949, 24/45 (speculation and mysticism). Javierre, RET 1949, 359/411 *(Espiritualidad en O.).* Lebreton, AB 1949, 35/69 *(Source et caractère de la mystique;* against Jonas 1949). De Lubac, RSR 1949, 542/76 *(De sensu spirituali);* Mémorial J. Chaîne, Lyons 1950, 255/80 *(Commentaire sur Jér. 20, 7);* On further contributions by De L. cf. TSW 1951, 365/81. Buerke, ZKT 1950, 1/39 (doctrine of man's original state). K. Rahner, RSR 1950, 47/97, 252/86, 422/56 (O. on penance). Doelger, AC 6, 1950, 273/5 (Christ as the heavenly Eros). Daniélou, RSR 1951, 132/7 *(Doctrine des Anges des Nations).* Ivánka, BZ 1951, 291/303 (philosophical classification of Origenism). Ludwig 1952, 31/44. Laeuchli, ATR 1952, 152, 102/16 (Conception of Symbolon); CH 1953, 253/68 (Interpretation of Judas Iscar.). TZ 1954, 175/97 (objectivity of O.'s exegesis). C. Schneider, TLZ 1953, 741/8 (on the Hellenist. religions). Weltin, Studies presented to D. M. Robinson 2, 1015/22 (O.'s "Church"), St. Louis 1953. Banner, DOP 1954, 49/82 (O. in the history of the concept of natural law). Barosse, TSW 1954, 355/88 (unity of love of God and of neighbour in O., Didym., Cyr. Al., Jo. Chrys.). Vagaggini, SC 1954, 169/200 (on the orthodoxy of O.'s dogmatics). Temple, ITQ 1954, 367/75 (O. and the Ellipsis in Lk. 2, 49). Pétré, RSR 1954, 40/57 *(ordinata caritas).* C. V. Harris, *The Interpretation of the Teacher's Function in the Early Christ. Hierarchy and Community,* thesis Dubuque Univ. 1952. Orbe, EstBibl 1955, 191/221 *(La excelencia de las profetas).* H. Crouzel, RAM 1955, 354/85 *(L'anthropologie d'O.); Théologie de l'image de Dieu chez O.,* P 1956. Méhat, VC 1956, 196/214 (apocatastasis). Teichtweier, *Die Suendenlehre des O.,* Rb 1958. Faessler, *Der Hagios-Begriff bei O.,* FrSch 1958. Harl, *O. et la fonction révélatr. du verbe incarné,* P 1958. R. P. C. Hanson, *Allegory and Event,* Lo 1959.

§ 41. ALEXANDRIANS AND FRIENDS OF ORIGEN

1. Sextus Julius Africanus (d. after 240) was born in Jerusalem and later lived at Emmaus-Nicopolis (but not as its bishop). In Alexan-

dria he attended the lectures of Heraclas (supra § 40), was a friend of Origen and had contact with the princely house of Edessa and with the Emperor Alexander Severus, in whose service he organized the public library which was housed in the Pantheon.

a. The first Christian chronicle of the world (Χρονογραφίαι, till 21 [221?]) in five books, of which only fragments have been preserved. It is a history of the world in the form of a synchronizing collection of the dates recorded by profane, O.T. and Christian history. The world has been in existence for 6000 years. Christ was born in the year 5500. The seventh thousand coincides with the millennium. The work has long served as a model for similar ones.

b. *Embroideries* (Κεστοί, a title which, like Στρωματεῖς [supra § 39, 3] is meant to emphasize the variety of the contents), in twenty-four books of which fairly large fragments are extant, dedicated to the Emperor Alexander Severus. It is a compilation containing excerpts on questions of natural science, medicine, magic, agriculture and military science. The Christianity of the author who believes in magic and sorcery here appears in a strange light (syncretism).

c. Two letters, one addressed to Origen (contests the authenticity of the story of Susanna), the second, extant only in fragments, addressed to an otherwise unknown Aristides (on the differences in the genealogies of Christ in Matthew and Luke).

Fragments: MG 10, 63/94. Routh 2, 238/309. Grenfell and Hunt, *The Oxyrhynchus Papyri* 3, 1903, n. 412. The Letters ed. W. Reichardt (TU 34, 3) 1909. J. R. Vieillefond, *Jules Africain, Fragm. des Cestes,* 1932; cf. BZ 1935, 145/9. — Treatises: H. Gelzer, *S. J. A. und die byzant. Chronographie,* 2 vols., 1880/98. Amann, DTC 8, 1921/5. W. Kroll-J. Sickenberger, PWK 10, 116/25. Vieillefond, REG 1933, 197/203 (new fragm.). W. Bauer 1934, 11 f., 162/7 (Lack of criticism). Lammert, BZ 1951, 362/9 (on the *Kestoi*).

2. Ammonius, the author of a treatise *On the Agreement between Moses and Jesus,* was probably a contemporary of Origen. Euse-

bius (*Hist.* 6, 19, 10) mistook him for the neo-Platonist Ammonius Saccas. He is probably to be identified with the author of a synopsis of the four gospels based on Matthew. See T. Zahn, ZKG 1920, 1 ff.

3. Dionysius of Alexandria, the Great (d. 264–5), disciple of Origen. In 231–2 he succeeded Heraclas as head of the catechetical school and in 247–8 also as Bishop of Alexandria. Because of his unflinching courage in many struggles and troubles he was surnamed the Great. He avoided the Decian persecution by flight, but was exiled to Libya under Valerian. He was involved as a leader in the internal-ecclesiastical disputes (Novatian, controversy on heretical baptism, chiliastic troubles, Trinitarian controversies) (EH 311/22).

Little remains of his numerous writings; cf. Eus., *Hist.* 7. We would mention here: a treatise *On Nature* dedicated to his son Timothy, which combats the atomistic theories of the Epicureans (fragments in Eus., *Praep. Ev.* 14, 23/7); his four books *Refutations and Defence* addressed to Bishop Dionysius of Rome (259–68) were written to expound the orthodoxy of his Trinitarian doctrine (fragms. in Eus., *Praep. Ev.* 7, 19, and in Athanasius, *De sententia Dionysii episc. Alex.*); in the two books *On the Promises* Dionysius denied that the Apocalypse had been written by John the Apostle in opposition to the chiliastically-minded Bishop Nepos of Arsinoe (Eus., *Hist.* 7, 24 f.). Only two of his Letters have been preserved in full (to Novatian in Eus., *Hist.* 6, 45; to Bishop Basilides on the duration of the lenten fast). Of his Paschal Epistles only fragments survive.

Edd.: MG 10. Best ed. by C. L. Feltoe, C 1904. Trans. by the same, Lo 1918. — Mgg.: F. Dittrich 1867. J. Burel, P 1910. C. Papadopulos, Ὁ ἅγ. Δ. ὁ Μ., Alex. 1918. P. S. Miller, *Studies in D. the Great of A.*, thesis Erlangen 1933. — Treatises: E. Schwartz, BAS 1927, 3 (2 spurious letters). Richard, RHE 1937, 44/6 (Scholion). Cf. § 100 the studies of Athenagoras. W. Till, *Osterbrief und Predigt in achmim. Dialekt*, 1931 (unknown 3rd cent. author). H. G. Opitz, Studies presented to K. Lake 1937, 41/53 (D. and the Libyans). Richard, RHE 1937, 44/6 (Schol. in Jac. 1, 13). Del Ton, SC 1942, 37/47 (on Eus., *Hist.* 6, 44).

4. Gregory Thaumaturgus (Θαυματουργός; d. *c.* 270). Gregory, the Apostle of Cappadocia, in whose ecclesiastical tradition he still held the highest place in the time of Basil the Great, came from a noble pagan family of Neocaesarea in Pontus. With his brother Athenodorus he was for five years a disciple of Origen at Caesarea. Here both brothers embraced Christianity. At his departure from Caesarea (238) he delivered a panegyric on his teacher which has been preserved (Εἰς Ὠριγένην προσφωνητικὸς καὶ πανηγυρικὸς λόγος), and which supplies welcome information on the master's teaching method. Soon afterwards he became bishop of his native city, working successfully for the spread of Christianity in Pontus.

Writings: a. The above-mentioned *Panegyric* attests belief in the guardian angel in 4, 40f. b. A trinitarian *Symbol* (ἔκθεσις τῆς πίστεως), incorporated by Gregory of Nyssa in his *Vita* of Gregory Thaum. (EP 611). c. The so-called *Canonical Epistle,* addressed to an unknown bishop, is important for our knowledge of the contemporary penitential practice of the Church. d. *The Metaphrase of the Preacher,* a short paraphrase of the Biblical book which the MSS usually ascribe to Gregory of Nazianzus. e. *Ad Theopompum on the Impassibility and Passibility of God,* a philosophic-apologetic dialogue extant only in Syriac. f. The treatise *Ad Philagrium on the Equality of Essence,* a brief exposition of the doctrine of the Trinity, preserved under his name in Syriac, and under those of Gregory of Nazianzus and Gregory of Nyssa in Greek, may be regarded as genuine. A Disputation with a certain Aelianus mentions Basil the Great, Ep. 210 n. 5. g. The *Short Treatise on the Soul, to Tatian,* also attributed to Maximus Confessor, is dubious, as are six Homilies extant in Armenian.

Four legendary biographies give accounts of his life, among them a *Vita* written by Gregory of Nyssa.

Edd.: MG 10, 963/1232. *Panegyric* ed. P. Koetschau 1894. — Trans.: H. Bourier (BKV²) 1911. — Mgg.: V. Ryssel, 1880 (73/99; trans. of *Ad Theopomp.*). Telfer,

JTS 31, 1929/30, 142/55, 354/63 (the Lat. *Vita* of Gregory dependent on the *Vita* of G. of Nyssa). Peradze, OC 1930, 90f. (Georg. trans.). Telfer, HTR 1936, 225/344 (hist. of cult). SACO I 6, 146/51; ed. of the spurious work Περὶ τῆς τοῦ Θεοῦ λόγου σαρκώσεως. Doelger, AC 6, 74f. (Logos doctr.). The New Year's sermon MG 10, 1197/1204. Belonging to Proclus of Cons.? cf. B. Marx, *Procliana,* 1940, 62f. Simonetti, IstLombScLett 86, 1953, 101/17 (*Ad Philagrium* genuine).

5. Firmilian, Bishop of Caesarea in Cappodocia (d. *c.* 268) was like Gregory a pupil of Origen. Of his works only one Letter to Cyprian is extant in a Latin translation (Cypr., *Ep.* 75) in which he violently attacks Pope Stephen in the controversy on heretical baptism.

Michell, JTS 1954, 215/20 (Firmilian and Eucharistic Consecration: cf. Cypr., *Ep.* 75, 10).

6. Of other third century heads of the Alexandrian catechetical school Theognostus and Pierius were also engaged in literary work. The former wrote between 250 and 280 seven books of *Hypotyposes,* a dogmatic treatise of Origenist leanings which is now lost. Pierius (*c.* 281—300) was an eminent exegete and preacher; he died after 309, probably in Rome. Photius still read twelve λόγοι (probably sermons) by him.

Fragms.: MG 10, 235/46. Routh 3, 405/35. C. de Boor (TU 5, 2) 1888, 165/84. L. B. Radford, *Three Teachers of Alex.: T., P. and Peter,* 1908. G. Fritz, DTC 12, 1744/6 (Pierius).

7. Peter of Alexandria, since 300 bishop of Alexandria, before that probably head of the catechetical school, fled during the persecution of Diocletian (303). During his absence Bishop Melitius of Lycopolis usurped the right of governing the Egyptian church (holding ordinations). This encroachment and Peter's leniency towards the lapsed caused the Melitian schism which lasted for centuries. Peter died a martyr in 311. The Acts of his martyrdom which are extant in Latin, Greek, Syriac and Coptic were written much later and are legendary.

Only fragments survive of his writings (Letters and Treatises).

The most important are the 14 *Penitential Canons,* probably excerpts from a Paschal Epistle *On Penance* (306) which was later incorporated in collections of canon law. Other writings were: *On the Pasch, On the Divinity (of Jesus Christ)* which is probably identical with the work *On the Advent of Our Saviour, On the Resurrection, On the Soul* — the last three directed against Origenist errors — and a Letter to the Alexandrians on Melitius.

Fragms.: Routh 4, 21/82. J. B. Pitra, Anal. sacra 4, 187ff., 425ff. MG 18, 467/522. PO 1, 383/400; 3, 353/61 (biographical items). C. Schmidt (TU, N. S. 5, 4b) 1901. — Treatises: Radford (supra n. 6) 1908. Fritz, DTC 12, 1802/4. A. Zikri, *Annales du service des antiquités d'Égypte* 29, 1930, 71/5 (Copt. fragms.). E. Schwartz, Cod. Vat. gr. 1431, 1927, 98 n. 4 and 5 (new fragments in Timothy Aelurus). Lefort, Mu 1933, 31 (ined. Copt. homily). Burmester, Mu 1932, 50f., 68f. (part of a Copt. hom. ed.). Kettler, PWK 19, 2, 1281/88. Richard, MSR 1946, 357f. (Christol.). Telfer, AB 1949, 117/30 (Peter of Al. and Arius); JEH 1952, 1/13 (Episcopal Succession in Egypt); HTR 1955, 227/37 (Melit. of Lycopolis and Episc. Succession). Kemp, JEH 1955, 125/42 (Bishop and Presbyters at Alex.). On the Melit. Schism: Amann, DTC 10, 531/6. E. Schwartz, GN 1905, 164/87. H. I. Bell, *Jews and Christians in Egypt,* 1924, 38/99. Crum, Journ. Aegypt. Archeol. 13, 1/6. Doelger, AC 4, 245/65 (divine service of the Melit.). Kettler, ZNTW 1936, 155/93.

8. The learned presbyter Pamphilus, a pupil of Pierius (supra no. 6), who had done much for the theological school and library of Caesarea (supra § 38), was put in prison under Maximinus Daza (307) and there wrote an *Apology for Origen* in five books; his pupil Eusebius later added a sixth; only the first book is preserved in the Latin translation of Rufinus. His efforts to produce a correct text of the Bible are very important. A biography of Pamphilus (three books) written by Eusebius is lost. He died a martyr in 309 (310?).

Book One of the Apol. in Lommatzsch, *Orig. Opera* 24, 293/412 and MG 17, 521/616. Bardy, DTC 11, 1839/41. Mercati, Nuove note (ST 95) 1941, 91 (spurious fragm.).

9. The Biblical critic Hesychius, probably an Alexandrian, revised the LXX and also the text of the N.T., as reported by Jerome, who criticizes his work. The so-called *Decretum Gelasia-*

num calls his text of the gospel apocryphal. It remains doubtful whether he is identical with the bishop and martyr who died under Diocletian (Eus., *Hist.* 8, 13, 7).

H. v. Soden, *Die Schriften des NT,* 1902ff. Lietzmann, PWK 8, 1327f. H. J. Vogels, *Handbuch der ntl. Textkritik,* 1923. J. Goettsberger, *Einleitung in das AT,* 1928. Kenyon, *Mémorial Lagrange,* 1940, 245/50 (text of N.T.).

§ 42. ANTIOCHENES AND OPPONENTS OF ORIGEN

1. Paul of Samosata, so called after his native town, governor of Queen Zenobia of Palmyra and since *c.* 260 also Bishop of Antioch. A synod held at Antioch in 268 condemned him for his trinitarian (dynamist Monarchianism) and Christological (predecessor of Nestorius) errors. We are informed about his life and doctrine mainly through fragments: a. from the disputation between him and the presbyter Malchion which was taken down in shorthand; b. from the synodal letter written in connexion with the synod (Eus., *Hist.* 7, 30); c. through the so-called *Hymenaeus-Letter.* The five fragments from Paul's *Logoi ad Sabinum* are spurious, as well as the *Symbol of Antioch* and the *Letter to Felix.* The fragments of the acts of the trial (now in the crit. ed. of Riedmatten, 135/58) are mainly transmitted in collections of doctrinal *testimonia* of the fifth and sixth centuries and have not so far been generally accepted as a sure source by which to establish the true teaching of Paul of Samosata. Supposing the fragments to be genuine, the heretic Paul of Samosata would be considerably exonerated; for in this case he would have been condemned by opponents who taught the so-called Logos-Sarx schema in their Christology, while he himself should probably be counted among those theologians who subscribed to the Logos-Man concept in Christ. On the Christology before 451 see Grillmeier in: Grillmeier-Bacht I, 5/202.

Fragms.: Routh 3², 287/367. F. Diekamp, *Doctrina patrum,* 1907, 303f. Lawlor, JTS 19, 1917/8, 20/45, 115/20. — Mgg.: F. Loors, 1924. G. Bardy, ²1929; DTC 12, 46/51. A. Harnack, SbB 1924, 129/51. Dumoutet, RAP 1930, 192/200 (P. de S.). E. Schwartz, SbMn 1927, 3: *Eine fingierte Korrespondenz mit P. v. S.;* AbhMn 32, 6, 1927, 102ff. (4 new fragms.?). Milburn, JTS 1945, 65/8. H. de Riedmatten, *Les Actes du Procès de P. de S. Ét. sur la Christologie du 3ᵉ au 4ᵉ s.,* Fri 1952. Scheidweiler, ZNTW 46, 1955, 116/29.

2. Lucian of Antioch, the founder of the Antiochene exegetical school (supra § 38) held a strongly subordinatianist doctrine of the Logos and thus became the father of Arianism; Arius was his pupil. He remained outside the orthodox community for a long time; but before his death (d. a martyr in 312) he seems to have been reconciled to the Church. He did valuable work as a text critic of the LXX and the N.T. The authenticity of his apology before the pagan judge is very doubtful.

G. Bardy, DTC 9, 1024/31; RSR 1932, 437/62; *Recherches sur L. d'A. et son école,* 1936 (2 different persons of this name); against this D'Alès, *Mél. Univ. Beyrouth* 21, 1937/8, 185/202 (for one L.). D. S. Balanos, *Actes de l'Acad. d'Athènes* 7, 1932, 306/11 (two different L.s). A. Ehrhard 1932, 304f. (for the identification). Doerrie, ZNTW 39, 1940, 57/110 (LXX); against this Mercati, Bi 1943, 1/17. Mercati, *Nuove note* (ST 95) 1941, 137. B. Fischer, StAns 27/8, 169/77 (readings of Lucian in the *Vetus Latina*).

3. Methodius. Nothing certain is known of his life. The oldest available information in Jerome, *Vir. ill.* 83, and Socrates, HE 6, 13 asserting that he was Bishop of Olympus in Lycia and later in Tyre and died a martyr in Chalcis cannot be admitted as reliable. Other testimonies mention the towns of Patara, Myra, Side and Philippi as his episcopal sees. If we would judge by his writings, we have no reliable evidence that he was a bishop at all. There are many indications that he lived as a free-lance teacher and ascetic in Lycia and perhaps also in Pamphylia, teaching philosophy to private circles of hearers and expounding Holy Scripture. The fact and place of his martyrdom are not reliably attested either.

He is important principally as a successful opponent of Origenism. Only one of his many works, most of which are quite skilfully cast in the form of Platonic dialogues, is preserved in full in its Greek original:

a. The *Symposium or on Virginity* (Συμπόσιον ἢ περὶ ἁγνείας). Its plan and many details are modelled on Plato's *Symposium.* Virginal chastity is praised by ten virgins in turn; at the end one of them, Thecla, intones an enthusiastic hymn (24 verses) on Christ the Bridegroom and the Church his Bride (EP 612f.).

The more or less complete text of his other writings is extant only in Old Slavonic translations.

b. *Aglaophon or on the Resurrection* (extant in Greek only in fragments) opposes Origen's teaching on the pre-existence of the soul and defends the identity of the resurrection body with the earthly body against the spiritualism of the Alexandrian (EP 616).

c. *On the Freedom of the Will* (Περὶ τοῦ αὐτεξουσίου) is directed against the dualism and determinism of the Valentinian gnosis (EP 614); fairly large Greek fragments have been preserved.

d. An exhortation to frugality, *On Life and Reasonable Action* is extant only in Old Slavonic, as well as several short exegetical writings with allegorical explanations of Num. 19, 2f.; Lev. 13; Prov. 30, 15ff.; Ps. 18, 2 and 5. A treatise directed against the polemical work of the neo-Platonist Porphyry is lost.

Edd.: MG 18. N. Bonwetsch (GCS 27; Slavonic texts in German) 1917. *De Autexusio* ed. A. Vaillant (PO 22, 5; with re-trans. into Greek and French trans.), 1930.—Transs.: L. Fendt, BKV² 2, 1911 *(Symposium),* 1911. French trans. by J. Farges *(Autex.)* 1929 and *(Sympos.)* 1932. — Mgg.: N. Bonwetsch, *Die Theol. des M.,* 1903. J. Farges, *Les idées morales et relig. de M.,* 1929. F. Bostroem, *Studier till den grekiska theologins fraelsingslaera med saerskild haensyn till M. av O. och Athanasius av Alex.,* Lund 1932. Amann, DTC 10, 1606/14. — Treatises: J. Martin, *Symposion, Die Gesch. einer liter. Form,* 1931, 285ff. Kmosko, Byz 6, 1931, 273/96 (Revelations of Pseudo-Meth.). G. Bardy 1935, 301/16. Lazzati, StU 117/24 (technique of dial. in *Symp.*). Margheritis, StU 401/12 (infl. of Plato). E. Badurina, *Doctrina S. Meth. de O. de peccato originali . . .,* R 1942. Devreesse, Rb 1935, 179 (fragm. of comm. Gen. 6). Stocks, BNJ 15, 1939, 29/57 (Pseudo-Meth. and the Babyl. Sibyl). Amand 1945, 326/41. V. Buchheit, *Studien z. M. v. Ol.,* thesis Mn 1952: OstkSt 1954, 51/9 (fragm. of *De resurr.* [in GCS Bonwetsch] spurious) id., RM 1956,

17/36 (Homer in Meth.). K. Quensell, *Die wahre Stellung u. Taetigkeit des faelschlich sog. Bischofs M. v. O.,* thesis Hei 1952. A. Zeoli, *Ital. trans. of Sympo. (Testi crist.).* Fl 1952. Musurillo, ACW 27, 1958 (Banquet). Pellegrino, *L'inno del simposio di S. Metodio,* To 1958 (Text, trans. and comm.).

4. The dialogue *De recta in Deum fide* is preserved in Greek and Latin under the name of Origen. The anonymous author is a contemporary of St. Methodius and, like him, an opponent of Origen. He wrote in Syria *c.* 300 and already used the writings of Methodius (*On the Resurrection* and *On Free Will*). The erroneous tradition is explained by the fact that the principal speaker of the dialogue is called Adamantius, a name also given to Origen. Adamantius as the spokesman of orthodoxy defeats the followers of Marcion, Bardesanes and Valentinus (EP 541/4).

Edd.: MG 11. W. H. van de Sande Bakhuyzen (GCS 4) 1911. — A. Harnack, Marcion, [2]1924, 56*/67* 181* 344*/8*. Brandhuber, Bi 1937, 303ff. (*Dial.* 5, 23). Buchheit, BZ 1958, 314/28 Dial. originated after 325, was back-dated by Rufin to the time of Origen.).

CHAPTER SIX

Hagiographers, Historians and Chroniclers of Christian Antiquity

THE historical sense, which was relatively well developed when the gospel and Acts presented the completed work of Christ and the apostles, remained almost dormant while the Church was growing out of the revelation of Christ, and, through struggle and persecution, became an historical force. The legendary Acts of Christ and the apostles produced by the apocryphal literature are almost the only manifestations of the historical sense in this period of the growth of the Church. To these may be added some historical and legendary information offered by the apologists and controversialists, for example, Hegesippus and Irenaeus, in the course of their arguments, and the *World Chronicles* of Julius Africanus and Hippolytus. But when, at the beginning of the fourth century, the growing period of the young Church came to an end, the historical sense awoke to a more vigorous life. True, it was still fettered by apologetic needs, but it already aimed high and created a working method. It meant to describe the organic development of the Church, but as it was not equal to the task, it supplied at least important collections of material. The archives now deliver their secrets, and the documents are studied with sound judgement and mostly with pleasing honesty. Jurists place their experience, gained in the examination of witnesses and in the law courts, at the disposal of Church history. The discussions of the sixth General Council of Constantinople (680–1) still show that the Fathers possessed remarkable palaeographical knowledge which enabled them to distinguish historical truth from forgery. Taken as a whole, however, ecclesiastical historiography did not long remain on the level it had reached with the achievement of Eusebius of Caesarea. Men became increasingly fond of legendary material and this interest obscured the historical sense more and more.

§ 43. THE ACTS AND LEGENDS OF THE MARTYRS OF CHRISTIAN ANTIQUITY (GENERAL REMARKS)

THE accounts of the old Christian martyrdoms may be divided into three groups. The first contains the Acts of Martyrs properly so called. Here the *Acta* or *Gesta,* for which the official minutes of the trial and condemnation of the martyrs were sometimes used, are presented in a framework suitable for spiritual reading (cf. § 45 n. 4 and 6). In the second group are descriptions given by eye witnesses or trustworthy contemporaries which are called *Passiones* or *Martyria* (cf. § 45 nos. 1, 5, 8). The third group consists of the *martyrs' legends;* they are historically almost wholly worthless products of a later or very late period. Sometimes, however, they are valuable for our knowledge of religious customs and folklore and for the cultural and social conditions of their time; occasionally they also contain welcome information on matters of geography and natural science. The Acts were usually read at the liturgical celebrations which took place by the tombs of the martyrs on the anniversary of their death (*natalicia*).

Edd.: J. Bollandus et socii, *Acta Sanctorum,* 1643ff. (acc. to the order of the saints in the Roman calendar); the latest, 65th vol. (1925) is devoted to the saints of 9th and 10th Nov. *Propylaeum ad ASS Dec. Martyrol. Rom.... scholiis hist. instructum,* 1940. Supplements are contained in the periodical *Analecta Bollandiana,* 1882ff. Reference works on the sources of the history of all the saints are given by the Bollandists in: *Bibliotheca hagiographica lat.,* 2 vols., 1898/1900 and Suppl. 1911; *Bibl. hag. graeca,* [2]1909; *Bibl. hag. orientalis,* 1910. T. Ruinart, *Acta primorum Mar-*

tyrum sincera, P 1689, Rb 1859. S. E. Assemani, *Acta Sanct. Mart. orient. et. occid.,* 2 vols., R 1748. P. Bedjan, *Acta martyrum et sanctorum,* 7 vols., P 1890/7 (Syriac). I. Balestri et H. Hyvernat, *Acta martyrum* (CSCO, SS copt.) 43 44 86 125 (Coptic). *Ausgewaehlte Martyrerakten,* ed. O. v. Gebhardt, 1902, Knopf ([3]1929 Krueger, best ed.). E. Le Blant, *Les Actes des martyrs. Suppl. aux "Acta sincera"* de D. Ruinart, P 1882. — Transs.: G. Rauschen (BKV[2] 14) 1913. O. Braun, (BKV[2] 22) 1915. P. Hanozin, *La geste des martyres,* 1936. — Mgg.: H. Leclercq, DAL I, 373/446. H. Delehaye, *Les légendes hagiographiques,* [3]1927 (German by E. A. Stueckelberg, 1907). *Les origines du culte des martyrs,* [2]1933; *Les légendes grecques des saints militaires,* 1909; *Les passions des martyrs et les genres littéraires,* 1921; *Sanctus. Essai sur le culte des saints dans l'antiquité,* 1927. *Cinq leçons sur la méthode hagiographique,* 1934. H. v. Campenhausen, *Die Idee des Martyriums i. d. Alten Kirche,* 1936. Krueger 1933, 191. H. W. Surkau, *Martyrien in jued. u. fruehchristl. Zeit,* 1938. C. Gallina, *I martiri dei primi secoli,* Fl 1939. E. Guenther, Μάρτυς. *Die Gesch. eines Wortes* 1941. C.-M. Edsman, *Ignis divinus,* 1949, 166/78. Lazzati, *Gli sviluppi della lett. sui martiri nei primi quattro secoli,* Tu 1956.

§ 44. LISTS OF MARTYRS AND CALENDARS

THE oldest list of martyrs is given by the *Depositio episcoporum* and the *Depositio martyrum* in the Roman chronographer of the year 354 (§ 49 II, 1, § 50, 5; EH 543 f.). The *Martyrologium Carthaginiense* discovered by Mabillon at Cluny belongs to approximately the same time. A third, very much longer list of saints is the so-called *Martyrologium syriacum* which was compiled by an Arian in Nicomedia before 400, probably in Greek, but is extant only in a Syriac MS of the year 411–12. The best known and largest old Christian calendar of saints is the one wrongly called *Martyrologium Hieronymianum.* Its oldest version, which has not been preserved, originated in Northern Italy, probably as early as the middle of the fifth century. In it were merged the two last-named calendars as well as the already enlarged list of the city of Rome and several other calendars of Italian cities. According to Duchesne and Quentin the martyrologium received its present form at Auxerre, *c.* 592–600, according to Krusch at Luxeuil in 627–8. A counterpart to the Latin martyrologies in the Greek Church are the *Synaxaria* and *Menaea,* liturgical books containing abridged texts of the martyrdoms and saints' lessons. The best known is the *Synaxarium ecclesiae Constantinopolitanae.* Our knowledge of the extraordinarily extensive hagiographical-liturgical material of the Greek Church has been very much enlarged by the great work of A. Ehrhard (TU 50 ff.), which also made it available for research.

Edd.: H. Lietzmann (KlT 2) [2]1911 (the three oldest martyrologies). *Mart. Hieron.* ed. G. B. de Rossi et L. Duchesne, Acta SS Nov. 2, 1, 1894; new ed. by H. Quentin, Acta SS Nov. 2, 2, 1931 (with comm. by H. Delehaye). H. Delehaye, *Synax. eccles. Constant.* in: *Propylaeum ad Acta SS Nov.,* 1902. H. Achelis, *Der Marmorkalender in Neapel,* 1929; cf. A. Ehrhard, RAC 1934, 119/50. F. Nau, PO 10, 2 (Syr. Menol.). H. Hyvernat et I. Balestri in CSCO 43 44 86 125 (Copt. Acts of martyrs). R. Basset, PO 3, 16 and 17 (Jacob. Copt.-Arab. *Synax.).* Forget, CSCO 47/49 67 78 90 (Jacob. *Synax.).* G. Bayan 5, 1; 6, 2; 15, 3; 16, 1; 18, 1; 19, 1; 21 (Armen. *Synaxar.* of the Ter Israel); cf. AB 1910, 5/26. N. Marr, PO 19, 5 (Georg. *Synaxar.*). I. Guidi, PO 1, 5; 7, 3; 9, 4; 15, 5; 26, 1 (Ethiop. *Synaxar.*) and C. A. W. Budge, *The Book of the Saints of the Ethiopian Church,* 4 vols., 1928. — Treatises: H. Achelis, *Die Martyrologien, ihre Geschichte u. ihr Wert,* 1900. H. Leclercq, DAL 8, 627/67 *(calendaria);* 10, 2523 2619 (martyrol.s); 11, 419/30 *(Ménologe).* J. P. Kirsch, *Der stadtroem. christl. Festkalender im Altertum,* 1924. H. Lietzmann, *Petrus u. Paulus in Rom,* [2]1927. On the *Mart. Hieron.* and *Romanum:* Morin, RevSR 1936, 138 f. H. Delehaye, *Étude sur le légendrier romain. Les Saints de novembre et décembre,* 1936. Laporte, Rev. Mabillon 1939, 1/16 *(Mart. Hieron.).* Delehaye, AB 1939, 5/64 *(Cal. marm. de Napl.).* Hertling, Gr 1944, 103/29 (number of martyrs). D. Mallardo, *Il cal. marmoreo di Nap.,* R 1947. Grosjean, AB 1947, 139/56 *(additions au Martyr. Hieron.).* Marrou, Mémorial J. Chaîne, 1950, 281/90 (O.T. saints in the martyr. Rom.). Dold, AB 1954, 35/8 (fragm. of the martyr. Hieron.). Marcon, Studi Gorziani 17, 1955, 77/93 (*Mart. Hieron.* originated in Aquileja). De Gaiffier, AB 1956, 5/49 (Martyrs under Jul. Apostata in the Mart. Rom.).

§ 45. THE OLDEST ACTS OF MARTYRS

1. The *Martyrium Polycarpi* (supra § 17, 3). 2. The *Martyrdom of Ptolemy and Lucius,* preserved in the Second Apology of Justin (supra § 21, 2). 3. The *Acts of Justin and His Seven Companions* (supra § 21). 4. The *Acts of SS. Carpus, Papylus and Agathonice* (EH 78/90). The death of these martyrs is very probably to be dated in the time of Marcus Aurelius, not in that of the Decian persecution.

The two first-named martyrs were condemned to be burned. Agathonice cast herself into the flames. The stirring account of it comes from eye-witnesses from Pergamon.

5. *The Letter of the Churches at Lyons and Vienne* to the Churches in Asia and Phrygia on the persecution of the Christians at Lyons (177–8), preserved in Eus., *Hist.* 5, 1, 1 to 2, 8. The Letter describes the spirit of fraternal charity in the churches, rejoicing in the courage of the martyrs, sorrowing at the defection of some; it also gives an account of the care of the Church and the martyrs for the lapsed.

6. The *Acts of the Scilitan Martyrs*. Six Christians from Scili in Numidia were the first African martyrs; they were condemned to death by the sword by the proconsul Saturninus and executed at Carthage in 180. The simple account movingly expresses the heroic steadfastness of their faith.

The Latin text is the oldest dated Latin Christian document we possess. The *Acts* are also preserved in a Greek translation.

7. The *Acts of Apollonius,* already included in Eusebius' collection of ancient acts of martyrs (*Hist.* 5, 21, 2–5) gives an account of the trial of the cultured Roman aristocrat Apollonius (183–5) that took place before the *Praef. praet.* Perennis.

The Armenian text of this Martyrdom became known in 1893, the Greek in 1895. It contains speeches in which Apollonius eloquently defends his faith before the judges; they are reminiscent of the ideas found in the apologetic literature. It is obviously a literary adaptation of the original record.

8. *Passio ss. Perpetuae et Felicitatis* (202–3), very probably written by Tertullian and translated into Greek by himself. It makes use of Perpetua's notes on her visions and experiences.

The touchingly simple account of the last days of the noble widow Perpetua, her slave Felicitas — both young mothers — and three catechumens is important for our knowledge of the ideas about the next world current in Christian antiquity.

9. *Martyrdom of the virgin Potamiana and the soldier Basilides* (202–3) in Alexandria, text in Eus., *Hist.* 6, 5.

10. The *Martyrdom of Pionius* in its extant form is not authentic, but a redaction based on the genuine Acts; the Greek original has been known only since 1896. Pionius, an educated, far-travelled priest suffered at Smyrna under Decius, not, as Eus., *Hist.* 4, 15, 46 has it, under Marcus Aurelius.

11. The *Proconsular Acts of Cyprian* (supra § 34). From the time of the persecutions under Diocletian we would mention the following accounts:

12. *Acta S. Maximiliani,* a young Christian in Numidia who refused to become a soldier (295).

13. *Acta S. Marcelli,* a centurion at Tangier who refused to attend the festivities and sacrifices in honour of the Emperor's birthday.

14. *Acta S. Felicis,* an African bishop who was condemned because he refused to give up the sacred books (303).

15. The *Acta S. Dasii,* a soldier, important for the history of religion because they describe the feast of the Saturnalia celebrated in the army (303 or 304).

16. The *Acts and Testament of the Forty Martyrs* who *c.* 320 suffered martyrdom together at Sebaste in Armenia under Licinius. The *Acts* in their present form are spurious and untrustworthy. The *Testament,* on the other hand, in which the martyrs demand to be buried together, is authentic.

17. *De martyribus Palestinae,* a work of Eusebius of Caesarea on the martyrdoms of the years 303–11. The *Collection of ancient martyrs' acts* made by Eusebius is lost, but he used a large part of it in his Church History (*Hist.* 4, 15, 47; 5 *Proem.*).

18. *Acts of Persian Martyrs* from the time of the persecution under Sapor II (339–79) were written in Syriac and collected by an unknown hand.

19. The Syriac *Acts of the Martyrs of Edessa,* on martyrs of the

Roman persecutions of Christians, are to be counted among martyrs' legends.

Edd. supra § 43: Those named under nos. 1-16 easiest to use in Knopf-Krueger 1929. Ruiz Bueno, Ma 1951 (text and trans.). Text of n. 17 in E. Schwartz (GCS 9, 2) 907/50. German in BKV[2] 9, 273/313. Text of n. 18 in Bedjan 2, 57/396, of n. 19 in F. C. Burkitt, *Euphemia and the Goths with the Acts of Martyrdom of the Confessors of Edessa,* 1913.—Transs. partly in BKV[2] 14, 1913, 291/369. A. Hamman, *La Geste du Sang,* P 1951 (trans. of 57 Acts of Martyrs). H. Rahner, *Maertyr.-Akten d. 2. Jh.,* Fr [2]1954.—Treatises: Vergote, ZNTW 37, 1938, 239/50; BBR 1939, 141/63 (kinds of torture). Poschmann 1940, 270/83 (penit. privilege of martyrs). H. I. Kotsones, At 1952 (enthusiasm of martyrs); cf. BZ 1954, 215. A. Hamann, TG 1955, 35/43 (dogmat. importance of Martyrs' Acts). Simonetti, REAug 1956, 39/57 (on the origin of the Martyrs' Acts; not dependent on pagan Acts).—On n. 3: Leclercq, DAL 8, 680/5. A. M. Schneider, JDAI 1934, 416/8. Delehaye, AB 1940, 142/76 (ed. of all Gr. and Lat. texts).—On nos. 4 and 10: Lietzmann, Festg. K. Mueller 1922, 46ff. M. Simonetti, *Studi agiographici,* R 1955 (on *Mart. Pionii:* under Marcus Aurelius; on *Acts of Carpus* etc., *of Phileas and Philor.,* on Irenaeus of Sirmium and others). On n. 5: Leclercq, DAL 10, 72/115; Bardy 1935, 160/73. A. Chagny, *Les Martyrs de Lyon de 177,* Lyons 1936. Zeiller, AB 1949, 49/54. G. Jouassard, trans., Lyons 1949.—On n. 7: AB 1895, 284/94. E. T. Klette (TU 15, 2) 1897. Max Prince of Saxony, *Der hl. Maert. Ap. v. R.,* 1903. Text also in FP 3, [2]1914. Zeiller, RSR 1951, Griffe, BLE 1952, 65/76 (legal basis of trial).—On n. 8: W. H. Shewring, *The Passion of SS. Perp. and Fel.,* Lo 1931 (Lat. text with trans. also of the four Augustinian *Sermons*). Dölger, AC 2, 1/40 (on the vision of Dinocrates, c. 7). Id., AC 3, 177/91 (martyrdom as fight with the devil, c. 10). Bardy 1935, 173/80. J. van Beek, *Passio SS. Perp. et Fel. I,* N 1936 (Lat and Gr. text ed.). Id., Ed. minor in FP 43, 1938. D'Alès, RSR 1937, 98f. J. Klein, Tertullian 1940, 274/313 (ethics of martyrdom). Rupprecht, RM 1941, 177/92 (against Tertull. as author and translator). Quasten, Byz 1940/1, 1/9 (Coptic parallel to vision); *The Jurist* 1941, 1/6 (Roman Law of Egypt. origin). Id., HJB 1953, 50/5 (mother and child in the *Passio*). J. van Beek, *Passio SS. Perp. et Fel. I,* N 1956 (large crit. ed.). Amatucci., StudOnareAr. Calderini e R. Paribeni 1, 1956, 363/67.—On n. 10: Wohleb, RQ 1929, 173/7 (Lat. Acts secondary).—On n. 12: L. Doelger, AC 2, 268/80 (*Sacram. militiae*). M. de Lupé, REL 1939, 90/104 (on hist. of language and culture).—On n. 13: Delehaye, AB 1923, 257/87 (ed. of text). De Sanctis, RFC 1924, 64/79. G. Villada, *Hist. Eccl. de Esp.* I 1, 1929, 377/9 (text). Boniauri, Did 1930, 1, 1/27.—On n. 14: Delehaye, AB 1921, 241/76 (text). Seston, *Mél. off. à M. Goguel,* Neuchâtel 1950, 239/46.—On n. 15: Mercati, OM 4, 1937, 318/36 *(storia dell'urna).*—On n. 16: P. Franchi de' Cavalieri, ST 49, 1928, 155/84; J. Simon, Orientalia 1934, 174/6 (cult in Egypt). Peeters, AB 1938, 118/43 *(Syméon de Séleucie).* Amand, Sc 3, 52/8 (ed. a poem).—On n. 18: Devos, AB 1946, 87/131 *(Sainte Sirin).* H. Delehaye, PO 2, 4 (1905): Gr. trans. of Acts of Pers. martyrs. Propyl. ad ASS Dec., Mart. Rom., 1940. Vööbus, Bi 1952, 222/34 (Gospel citations).—*Treatises* on Acts not mentioned here: *Acts of Phileas and Philoromus:* Knipfing, HTR 1923,

198/203 (written in 307). *Acts of Euplius:* P. Franchi de' Cavalieri, ST 49, 1928, 1/54 (Gr. text). C. Jullian, RevEA 1921, 305/23 *(Passio Victoris);* ibid., 1923, 367/78 (Prefect Rictiovar.). P. F. de' Cavalieri, ST 27, 1915; 33, 1920; 49, 1928; 65, 1935 (numerous *Passiones;* 65, 307/32 e. g. one Gr. *Pass. Marcelli trib. et Petri militis*). Delehaye, AB 1937, 201/25 (*La S. Théodote de Nicée:* text). F. de' Cavalieri, AB 1946, 132/75 *(martirio dei s. notari)*. Grégoire-Orgels, BZ 1951, 165/84 *(La Passion de S. Théodote, œuvre du Ps.-Nil.)*. Halkin, AB 1952, 249/61 *(Légende grecque inéd. de S. Zosime)*. Simonetti, RAC 1955, 223/52 (Romanus Antioch., Quirinus, Peter Balsamus). Id., GiornItFilol 10, 1957, 147/55 *(Luoghi communi negli Atti dei Mart.)*.

§ 46. LEGENDS OF MARTYRS AND SAINTS

Just as the canonical gospels and apostolic writings were followed by the apocryphal literature, so the oldest, on the whole historically reliable Martyrs' Acts were succeeded by the martyrs' legends. Later, besides historically valuable lives of monks there appeared legends of monks, so that the edifying and entertaining popular literature of the first centuries soon increased remarkably in volume. This literature does not belong to patrology in the strict sense of the word, but to hagiography.

The literary form increases in importance. The account of a short trial before the judge develops into a voluminous narrative of a long religious discussion in which the martyr expounds and defends his faith in speeches adorned with rhetorical devices, attacks and ridicules belief in the gods, expresses his contempt of the tortures in store for him, announces divine punishments and still attempts to convert his opponents. Dreams and visions play an important part in these legends, as do also accounts of large quantities of preferably substantial miracles. The authors give their special attention to the description of the most frightful tortures possible and of the miraculous powers of the sufferers displayed in these conditions. The original intention of these *Passions* to edify is frequently replaced by the desire to entertain readers avid for sensation.

Since we cannot here discuss individual legends of the martyrs, we would only point out that even the Acts of the best-known Roman martyrs, with the exception of those of St. Justin, are preserved only in embellished versions (cf. supra § 45, 7, Apollonius) which were soon replaced by free poetical inventions. We would give as examples the accounts of St. Hippolytus, St. Lawrence and St. Sixtus, SS. Caecilia, Agnes and Felicitas, St. Sebastian, the "Four Crowned Ones", SS. Cosmas and Damian, SS. John and Paul. Several similar "martyrdoms", viz. those of St. Clement, St. Ignatius, St. Irenaeus and St. Cyprian have been discussed above.

Ancient Christian hagiography came into being when the ideal of sanctity represented by monks and bishops was added to that of the martyrs. Like the legends of the martyrs, this produced an immense literature. The legends of saints and monks took over all the previously named motives and artistic devices. Some works stand out to advantage among the great mass of these literary products, and some hagiographical writings must rank as important historical and biographical sources.

The *Vita S. Antonii* of St. Athanasius became the type and pattern of this kind of literature. It soon became known throughout Christendom and was given to the West in the translation of the Antiochene author Evagrius. Basil the Great, Chrysostom, Ambrose and other Fathers contributed to this literature by their popular homilies on martyrs. Jerome wrote a whole series of lives of monks. Some of the later historians among the Fathers (v. § 49) wrote and collected several lives of the saints or included them in their Church histories. See the *Historia Lausiaca* (with the *Historia monachorum*) and Palladius' *Vita Chrysostomi,* the books on St. Martin by Sulpicius Severus and the *Chronicle of Arbela,* but also the legends of monks and miracles in the Church histories of Sozomen and Theodoret.

Apart from the literature mentioned above, § 43, we would here name the following important works: E. Lucius, *Die Anfaenge des Heiligenkults in der christl. Kirche,* 1904. H. Guenter, *Legendenstudien,* 1906; *Die christl. Legende des Abendlandes,* 1910. A. Dufourcq, *Étude sur les Gesta martyrum roman.,* 4 vols., 1900/10. P. Doerfler, *Die Anfaenge der Heiligenverehrung nach den roem. Inschriften u. Bildwerken,* 1913. J. P. Kirsch, *Die roem. Titelkirchen im Altertum,* 1918. H. Priessnig, *Die biograph. Formen der griech. Heiligenlegenden,* thesis Mn 1924. F. Lanzoni, *Genesi, Svolgimento e tramonto delle legende storiche* (ST 43) 1925. K. Kuenstle, *Ikonographie der christl. Kunst,* 2 vols., 1926/8. Bardy, DS 1, 1624/34. A complete survey of all current hagiographical publications in the *Analecta Bollandiana,* 1882ff. Zilliacus, BZ 1937, 302/44 (Lat. words in Gr. hagiography). E. E. Malone, *The Monk and the Martyr,* W 1950; *Gedaechtnisschr. Casel,* 1951, 115/34 (Martyrdom and Monastic Professions). Phytrakes, Θ 19, 1941/8 (offprint 31 pp.) (Martyrdom and Monasticism). H. Guenter, *Die Psychologie der Heiligenlegende,* 1949. Chirat, RevSR 1953, 134/46 *(patristique et hagiographie).* R. Aigrain, *L'hagiographie. Ses sources, ses méthodes, son histoire,* 1953.

I. Hagiographers of the East

1. Palladius, a disciple of Evagrius Ponticus, lived as a monk in Egypt and Palestine *c.* 388–99, and was later bishop of Helenopolis in Bithynia, d. before 431. In 419–20 he published his *Historia Lausiaca,* an extremely important source for the older monasticism; it derived its name from its dedication to the chamberlain Lausus (EH 784/8; EA 769/74). It is not certain whether Palladius also used written sources. Athanasius' *Vita S. Antonii* was his literary model. The work was early translated into Latin and several Oriental languages, and was also soon combined with the *Historia monachorum in Aegypto,* supposed to have been written by the archdeacon Timothy of Alexandria *c.* 400. Rufinus (§ 85) translated the latter into Latin (ML 21, 387/462; EA 710/25. According to Diekamp, AP 1938, 23/7, Rufinus is its author).

As a faithful friend of St. Chrysostom, Palladius wrote his *Dialogue de vita S. Ioannis* probably as soon as 408 during his stay at Syene. It has the form of a fictitious dialogue modelled on Plato's *Phaido.* The *Dialogue* is an important source. Of the treatise Περὶ τῶν τῆς 'Ινδίας ἔθνων καὶ τῶν Βραχμάνων which bears his name, probably only the first part belongs to Palladius.

Edd.: C. Butler, *The Lausiac Hist. of P.*, 2 vols., 1898/1904. A. Lucot, P 1912 (with French trans.). Chaîne, ROC 5, 1925/6, 232/75 (Copt. fragm.). German by S. Krottenthaler (BKV[2] 5) 1912. The interpolated text in MG 34, 997/1262. The *Dialogus* in MG 47, 5/82 and ed. by P. R. C. Norton, C 1928. The work on India ed. C. Mueller in F. Duebner, *Op. Arriani,* P 1846, 102ff. Trans. of *Hist. monach.*: T. Rufinus, *Moenchsgesch.,* W 1927, 1930. — Treatises: Amann, DTC 11, 1823/30. Leclercq, DAL 13, 912/30. Nagl, PWK Suppl. 7, 365f. (Lausus). Heussi-Kurfess, PWK 1943, 203/7. Ubaldi, *Mem. Acad. Torino* Ser. 2, 56, 1906, 217/96 *(Il Dialogo e Platone)*. R. Reitzenstein, *Hist. monachorum u. Hist. Laus.,* Go 1916. W. Bousset, *Apophthegmata-Studien,* 1923. Hergt, *Bayer. Bl. Gymn. Schulw.* 1935, 64/71 (*Hist. Laus.* 29). Wilmart, RB 1933, 29/42 (Lat. text of work on India). L. Fruechtel, thesis Erl. 1920 (work on India). Peeters, AB 1936, 366ff. (*Hist. Laus.* 35). Telfer, JTS 1937, 379/83 (*Hist. Laus.* 35). Schwartz, ZNTW 1937, 161/204 *(Palladiana)*. Tappert, TP 1937, 264/76 (Ms. *Hist. Laus.* and *Apophtheg.*). Morenz, *Z. für aegypt. Sprache u. Altertumsk.* 77, 1941, 52/4 (*Hist. Laus.* 35). Hausherr, OCP 1938, 497/520 (*Hist. Laus.* 35). S. Linnér, *Syntakt. u. lexik. Stud. z. Hist. L. des P.,* Up 1943. Draguet, Mu 1944, 53/145; 1945, 15/95 (c. 32: Copt. source; not historical); RHE 1946, 321/64; 1947, 5/49 (*Hist. Laus.* written in the spirit of Evagrius P.). Fruechtel, PW 1942, 621/3 *(Dialogue)*. Calvi, Salesianum 1936, 269/79; 1940, 204/23; 1941, 129/56 (cont.) *(Hist. Laus.)*. Draguet, Mu 1947, 227/55 (*Hist. Laus.* 8). Murphy, Tr 1947, 59/77 (Melan. Sen.). C. Baur, ZKT 1949, 466/8 (place of writing of *Dialogue*). Draguet, AB 1949, 300/8 (new MS of text G of *Hist. Laus.*); Mu 1950, 205/30 (on text of *Hist. Laus.*); against this: Chitty, JTS 1955, 102/10. Draguet, RSR 1952, 107/15 (MS of *Hist. Laus.*) Honigmann, BullAcadBelgClLett 46, 2, 3/43 (Menander citations in *Dialogus*); id., 1953, 104/22 (Heraclidas of Nyssa in *Hist. Laus.*). Dumortier, MSR 1951, 51/6 (on chronology in *Dialogus*). Draguet, Mu 1955, 239/58 (against Chitty's defence of Butler's text of the *Hist. Laus.,* 1955). Muyldermans, RSR 1955, 395/401 (on *Hist. Laus.* 35: John of Lycopolis). Festugière, Her 1955, 257/84 *(Le problème litt. de l'Hist. monach.)*.

2. The *Vita S. Melaniae Iunioris* (d. 430), a biography important for the history of culture, written probably by the priest Gerontius, the administrator of the Melania convents on the Mount of Olives, extant in Latin and Greek; the Greek version seems to be the original.

Edd.: Card. Rampolla, R 1905. German by S. Krottenthaler (BKV[2] 5) 1912. —Mg.: E. da Persico, German by R. Bang 1912. Leclercq, DAL 11, 209/30.

3. The *Vita S. Hypatii* (d. 446) is an important source for Church history. Hypatius was abbot of a monastery near Chalcedon; his disciple Callinicus was the author of the work.

Ed.: *Seminarii philologorum Bonnensis sodales,* L 1895. Bartelink, VC 1956, 124/6 (text. crit. and Bibl. citations).

4. Chrysippus of Cappadocia, later priest in Jerusalem (d. 479), a preacher trained in rhetoric. Of his works only four panegyrics *(encomia)* have been preserved, on St. Theodor Teron, the Archangel Michael, the Mother of God and John the Baptist.

Edd.: *Encomium on T. Teron* ed. A. Sigalas, ByzArch 7, 1921 and L 1927; ASS Nov 4, 55/72. *Enc. on Mich.* ed. Sigalas, EEBS 1926, 85/93. *Enc. on BMV* ed. M. Jugie, PO 9, 1926, 336/43; on this Sigalas, BNJ 11, 1934/5, 145/50. *Enc. on John* ed. Sigalas, At 1937. Cf. AB 1937, 337/9 and BZ 1937, 408/11. Martin, RHE 1939, 54/60 (Chrysipp. dependent on Hesychius). Sigalas, LTK 2, 949. Ehrhard, TU 50, 74f. Bardy, DHG 12, 1951, 784f.

5. The *Apophthegmata Patrum* are similar in content to the *Hist. Lausiaca* of Palladius. The former is an anonymous collection of didactic proverbs and examples of virtue from the lives of famous monks; they contain a wealth of important information on the cultural life of the times (MG 65, 71/440). They were written perhaps at the end of the fifth century and are preserved in various redactions and translations. Closely related to this collection is also the Greek work which was translated into Latin under the title *Verba seniorum* probably by the Roman deacon, later Pope Pelagius I (556–61), the subdeacon, later Pope John III (561–74) (= ML 73, 855/1024), and the monk Paschasius of Dumio (= ML 73, 1025/62). The *Verba seniorum* are (as books 5–7) part of the large Latin collection of saints' legends of the sixth century (ML 73/4) which is called *Vitae Patrum.*

Studies: W. Bousset, *Apophthegmata-Studien,* 1923. G. Gemoll, *Das Apophthegma. Literarhist. Studien,* 1924. A. H. Salonius, *Vitae patrum,* L 1920 (philolog. studies). Gorce, RLM 1929, 338/99 (infl. on Rule of St. Benedict). E. A. W. Budge, *The Wit and Wisdom of the Christian Fathers of Egypt,* O 1934 (Apophth. syr.). *Stories of the Holy Fathers,* O 1934 (Engl. trans.). Cavallera, DS 1, 765/70. Morin, SM 1937, 15/18 (MS of the *Vitae Patr.).* K. Heussi, *Der Ursprung des Moenchtums,* 1936, 132/280. Wilmart, RBn 1922, 185/98 (on 5/6 of *Vit. Patr.*); 1938, 222/45 (Lat. vita Abrahae: ML 73, 651/90). Tappert, TP 1937, 264/76 (MS *Hist. Laus.* and MS *Verba sen.;* partim ined.). N. Schedl, *Jesus Chr. Sein Bild b. d. Moenchen der Sketis,* thesis W 1942. Doerries, TLZ 1947, 215/22 (The Bible and the monks). Doresse, RHR 128, 1944, 84/93 (Copt. *Apophthegmata*). Duensing, GN 1944, 215/27 (Ed. of fragms. of an Aramaic trans. of the *Geronticon* and of *Apophthegmata*). Garitte, Misc. Mercati, 3, 16/40 *(Apophthegm. Patrum)*. Jugie, *Mém. L. Petit*, 1948, 245/53 (an uned. *Apophthegma* on purgatory). Draguet, Mu 1950, 25/46 *(Le Paterikon de l'Add. 22508 du British Mus)*. Mioni, Aev 1950, 319/31 (*Vitae Patrum* in the trans. of A. Traversari). Guiy, RSR 1955, 252/8 (on text of *Apophthegm. Patr.*).

6. The Vita of Bishop Porphyry of Gaza (395–420), supposed to have been written by his deacon Mark, is a strongly rhetorical recension of genuine notes of Mark which was probably made in the sixth century. The work, which is of interest for the history of culture and religion, deals chiefly with the battle against the paganism of Gaza which was partly conducted with military force.

Edd.: L. (Teubner) 1895. H. Grégoire et M. A. Kugener (with trans. and comm.), P 1930. German by G. Rohde 1927. Peeters, AB 1941, 65/216 (ed. Georg. trans.). — Treatises: Priessnig (supra § 46), 50/3. Leclercq, DAL 40, 1464/1504.

7. Cyril of Scythopolis, b. *c.* 523; 544 monk in the monastery of Euthymius, 555 hermit in the "New Laura" of St. Sabas where he died *c.* 558. He wrote several biographies of monks which are historically valuable, though they contain many legendary features: *Vita Euthymii* (d. 473) (ed. Montfaucon, *Anal. Graeca,* 1688, 1/99), *Vita Sabae* (d. 532) (ed. Cotelier, *Eccles. Graec. Monum.* 3, 1686, 220/376), *Vita Ioannis Silentiarii* (d. 558) (AAS Maii, 3, 16*/21*), *Vita Cyriaci* (d. 556) (AAS Sept. 8, 147/59), *Vita Theodosii* (d. 529) (ed. H. Usener, 1890), *Vita Theognii* (d. 522) (ed. J. van den Gheyn, AB 1891, 73/118) and *Vita Abramii* (d. 557) (ed. H. Grégoire, Rev. Instruct. publ. en Belgique 1906, 281/96). All the *Vitae* of Cyril have now been publ. in the standard ed. of E. Schwartz.

T. Hermann, ZKG 1926, 318/39 (chronology). Text ed. E. Schwartz, *K. v. S.* (TU 49, 2) 1939; cf. BZ 1940, 474/84. Alt, ZDtschPalVer 1940, 111/3 (place names). Gill, OCP 1940, 114/39 (*Vita S. Euthymii* in the 9th cent.). Stein, AB 1944, 169/86 (on Ed. of Schwartz). Graf I, 407f. Hausherr, DS **2**, 1953, 2687/90.

Draguet, RAM 1949, 213/8 (Palladius in *C. of S.*). Garitte, AB 1954, 75/84 (*Vita of John Silent.* enlarged in Georg. trans.).

Influenced by Cyril of Scythopolis, an anonymous author wrote, probably still in the sixth century, a legendary *Vita of St. Chariton* (d. *c.* 350), the founder of Palestinian monasticism.

First ed. of *Vita* by G. Garitte, BBR 1941, 5/50. The version of St. Metaphrastes in MG 115, 899/918. Garitte, DHG 12, 421/3.

8. John of Ephesus, b. *c.* 507, d. 586, a zealous Monophysite and finally Monophysite Bishop of Constantinople under Justinian. In 572, however, he was imprisoned by Justin II and later led an unsettled nomadic life. Apart from a history of the Church (§ 49 I 14) he wrote in exile a Syriac *History of the Eastern Saints* (566–8), fifty-eight sketches from monastic life in Mesopotamia which are of value for the history of culture.

Edd.: E. W. Brooks, PO 17, 1; 18, 4; 19, 2, 1923/5. Tisserant, DTC 8, 752f.

9. John Moschus, b. about the middle of the sixth century, monk at Jerusalem, in Egypt, on Mt. Sinai and at Antioch. After the conquest of Jerusalem by the Persians he went to Rome in 614, together with his friend Sophronius (n. 10); there he died in 619. His chief work is the *Pratum spirituale* (Λειμών; MG 87, 3, 2851/3112; Lat. ML 74, 119/240). It contains more than 300 edifying stories and miracles from the lives of mostly contemporary ascetics (EA 1286/95). Together with Sophronius he wrote a biography of the Alexandrian Patriarch John Eleemosynarius (d. 619); extant fragment published in H. Gelzer, *Leontios v. Neapolis,* 1893, 108/12.

Leclercq, DAL 7, 2190/6; Amann, DTC 10, 2510/13; selection in Lietzmann, *Byzant. Legenden,* 1911, 82/99. French selection by D. C. Hesseling, P 1931. N. von Wijk, *Das gegenseit. Verhaeltnis einiger Redaktionen der* Ἀνδρῶν ἁγίων βίβλος *u. der Entwickl.-Gesch. des* Μέγα Λειμωνάριον, A 1933; ZSlavPhil 1933, 60/6 (Slav. trans.). Delehaye, AB 1927, 5/74 (uned. *Vita* of John Eleem.). Nissen, BZ 1938, 351/76 (unknown texts). Z. franz. Spr. u. Lit. 1939, 393/403 (on n. 8 of the text ed. in BZ 1938, 361/5). Wijk, ZSlavPhil 1938, 1/17; Byz 1938, 233/41

(Slav. trans.). L. della Vida, AIP 1943, 83/126 (on Arab. trans. of *Pratum*) and Misc. Mercati III 104/15 (Arab. trans.). Rouët de Journel, P 1946 (trans.). Baynes, OCP 1947, 404/14 *(Pratum)*. Dawes-Baynes, *Three Byz. Saints,* O 1948; here trans. of *Vita Jo. Eleem.* by Moschus-Sophronius and by Leontius of Neapolis. Mioni, Aev 1950, 83/94 (uned. Texts in the *Cod. graec. Marc.* II 21); id., OCP 1951, 61/94 (survey of MSS of *Pratum*); StBNeoell 1953, 27/36 (*Paterika* del Ps.-Mosco). Kriaras, Ἑλληνικά 1953, 376/9 (text. crit.).

10. Sophronius, later Patriarch of Jerusalem (§ 106, 1) also wrote a panegyric on the Alexandrian martyrs Cyrus and John (under Diocletian; MG 87, 3, 3379/676), a work of great literary perfection. The *Vita Mariae Aegyptiacae* (ibid. 3697/726; Lat. ML 37, 671/90) is spurious.

Nissen, BZ 1937, 66/85 (text. crit. of the panegyric on Anastasius). AB 1939, 65/71 (Cyrus and John). Riedinger, 1956, 81/6 (on the miracles of the *Vita of Cyrus and John*).

11. Leontius of Neapolis on Cyprus (d. *c.* 650) also wrote a biography of John Eleemosynarius designed to complement that of his two friends (supra n. 9); (ed. by H. Gelzer 1893); besides a *Vita S. Simeonis Sali,* a saintly "odd" monk who lived in the Syrian desert in the time of Justinian (d. 565).

(MG 93, 1669/1748; German trans. partly in H. Lietzmann, supra n. 9, 63/81). Grégoire, AIP 1953, 653 (on *Vita Sim. Sali*).

12. A *Vita S. Spyridonis* of Trimithus on Cyprus (d. after 343) is lost; it was written in iambic verse probably towards the end of the fifth century. A panegyric, read by Bishop Theodore of Paphus before the assembled bishops in 655 is extant.

P. van den Ven, *La légende de S. Spyrid., év. de Trimith.,* Lou 1953; containing also the ed. of three further, later legends. Supplements to this in Garitte, RHE 1955, 125/40. On text. crit. censures by Scheidweiler, BZ 1955, 154/64, cf. Van den Ven, Byz 1956, 19/45.

13. Saints' lives by unknown authors.

a. *Syriac Biography of Bishop Eusebius of Samosata* (d. 380), a champion of the Nicene faith, perhaps modelled on the Greek works of a contemporary.

Text in Bedjan (supra § 43) 6, 335/77.

b. The *Life of St. Rabulas* (Bishop of Edessa 412–36), written in Syriac by a cleric of Edessa *c.* 450.

Text in Bedjan 4, 396/450. Germam by G. Bickell (BKV) 1874, 166/211; Swedish by K. v. Zettersteen, KA 1915, 1/41.—Treatises: Peeters, RSR 1928, 170/204; cf. RB 1931, 120/9. Schiwietz, 3, 348/60; cf. § 76, 3.

c. A *Greek Life of St. Simeon Stylites* (d. 459), written by one of his disciples named Anthony who used the account given by Theodoret in *Hist. rel.* c. 26 (§ 49, 1 h). A second biography, written in Syriac by two otherwise unknown authors, Simeon Bar Apollon and Bar Chatar, contains more material and is more reliable than the Greek *Vita.*

Greek text in H. Lietzmann, TU 32, 4, 1908. Syr. in Bedjan 4, 507/648; German in Lietzmann 79/188. H. Delehaye, *Les Saints Stylites,* 1928. Crum, ZNTW 1927, 119/28 (German trans. of Copt. *Vita*). Schiwietz 3, 315/47. Benz, *Kyrios* 3, 1938, 1/55 (Symeon and Andr. Salos). Peeters, AB 1943, 29/71 (biographies); on this Richard, MSR 1946, 147/56. M. Chaine, *La vie et les miracles de S. Sym. Styl. l'Anc.,* Cairo 1948. B. Koetting, ZMR 1953, 187/97 (missionary and edifying sermons of Sim. Styl.). Honigmann 1953, 92/100. Riedinger (v. supra n. 10), 1955, 84/8 (astrological matters). Leclercq, DAL 15, 1697/1718 (Stylites).

d. A *Life of Peter the Iberian* (411–91, monophysite-minded Bishop of Majuma near Gaza) very probably written by John Rufus, his successor as Bishop of Majuma, is extant in a Syriac translation and a shorter Greek recension.

Edd.: R. Raabe, L 1895; cf. E. Schwartz, SbHei 1912, Abh. 16. E. Honigmann, *Pierre l'Ibérien et les écrits du Ps.-Denys l'Aréop.* in MémAcadBelgClLett 47, 3, 1952. Russian trans. of Honigmann's work, Tiflis 1955; cf. BZ 1956, 179. A second work by John Rufus, *The Plerophoria,* ed. F. Nau and M. Brière: PO 8, F. 1. Lang, JEH 1951, 158/86 (Peter the Ib. and his biographers); cf. Devos, AB 1952, 385/88.

e. The *Life of St. Alexius;* in the oldest Syriac version of the legend (5th cent.) he is an unnamed *man of God,* d. at Edessa.

Edd.: A. Amiaud, P 1889. Lat. in ASS Jul 4, 251/3; cf. also AB 1941, 301 A. 2. De Gaiffier, AB 1945, 48/55; 1947, 157/95 (on the Lat. *Vita*). Herrmann, ACl 1942, 235/41 (Alexius = Commodian, v. § 87, 14).

II. Hagiographers of the West

Compared with the literary output of the East, the West has produced far fewer lives of saints that are historically useful. Practically all Latin authors who have left hagiographical works have also other, usually far more important, literary achievements to their credit, so that it is unnecessary to enumerate and discuss them here. But we would mention even here the following authors who have also distinguished themselves as hagiographers: Paulinus of Nola, Jerome, Eucherius of Lyons, Eugippius, Gregory of Tours, Venantius Fortunatus and Gregory the Great.

§ 47. PILGRIMS' ACCOUNTS OF PALESTINE

Since the pilgrims' books of Christian antiquity frequently also bear witness to the special characteristics of the ancient Christian veneration of saints, a discussion of this literature may be inserted at this stage. At a very early time not only holy persons, but also holy places were objects of Christian piety and longing.

Melito of Sardes (Eus., *Hist.* 4, 26, 14) and Origen may be regarded as the earliest pilgrims to Palestine known to us. The primitive Christian idea that the Christian is a pilgrim and without a home on this earth found a partial expression in the reality of the pilgrimages, which increased in popularity especially from the fourth century onwards. Several descriptions of such pilgrimages *(Itineraria)* have been preserved.

1. *Itinerarium a Burdigala Hierusalem usque* of the year 333, a dry survey of the stations of a pilgrimage from Bordeaux to Jerusalem and back via Rome to Milan.

Ed.: P. Geyer (CSEL 39) 1898, 1/33. O. Cuntz, *Itineraria Romana* I, 1929. Kubitschek, PWK 9, 2352/9.

2. *Peregrinatio ad loca sancta,* written towards the end of the fourth century by Aetheria (Eucheria or Egeria), a nun probably from the south of France; known only since 1887. The pilgrimage is

very probably to be dated 393–4. The account is a unique source for the history of the liturgy. It gives information especially on the liturgy of Holy Week and Easter Week at Jerusalem and contains many notes on the tombs and churches of Eastern martyrs.

Edd.: P. Geyer (CSEL 39) 35/101. W. Heraeus, Hei [3]1929. German by H. Richter 1919 and H. Dausend 1933. E. Franceschini ed. *Aether. Peregr.,* Padua 1940. H. Pétré, *Éthérie,* 1948 (SCh 19 with trans.). — Mgg. and Treatises: E. Loefstede, *Philol. Kommentar z. Peregr. Aeth.* (new impression), Up 1936 W. van Oordt, *Lexicon Aetherianum,* P 1929. Leclercq-Férotin, DAL 5, 552/84. Leclercq, DAL 7, 2374/92; 14, 1, 65/175 (Pilgrims' accounts). Wotke, PWK Suppl. 7, 875/85. J.-B. Thibaut, *Ordre des Offices de la Semaine Sainte à Jérusalem du 4e au 10e s.,* 1926. A. Bludau, *Die Pilgerreise der Aeth.,* 1927, Heiming, JL 3, 1926, 236f. (Pentecostal fast). Jarecki, Eos 31, 1928, 453/73; 32, 1929, 43/70; 33, 1930/1, 241/88 (*Silvaniae It.;* journey: 393/4). Ziegler, Bi 1931, 70/84 (*Onomast.* of Eus. used in trans. of Jerome, i. e. after 390), 162/98. Burger, Palästinae-Jb. 1931, 85/111 (beginnings of pilgrimages). A. Lambert, RevMabillon 1936, 71/94 (question of name); 1937, 1/42 *(Eg., sœur de Galla);* 1938, 49/69 (journey 414/6). Buescu, Rev. class., Bucharest 1934/5, 160/7 *(Aetheriana).* D. Brocke, *Pilgrims Were They All,* 1937 (ch. 2). Vaccari, Bi 1943, 388/97 *(Itinerarium).* Dekkers, SE 1948, 181/205 (journey 514/8. B. Koetting, *Peregrin. relig.,* Mr 1950. Chirat, RML 1949, 151/6 (text. crit.). L. Spitzer, *Comparative Literature,* 1949, 225/58 (epic style). R. Weber, VC 1952, 178/82 (Note sur le texte). Ernout, Emerita 20, 1952, 289/307 *(mots grecs).* Davies, VC 1954, 93/100 (on date against Dekkers). Ambrosini, AnnalScuola-NormSupPisa 1955, 97/109 (on syntax). E. Wistrand, *Textkr. zur Peregr. Aeth.,* Goeteborg 1955. New Ed. by Franceschini-Weber, Turnhout 1958.

3. *De situ terrae sanctae,* written by an otherwise unknown Theodosius Archidiaconus who probably hailed from N. Africa, *c.* 520–30.

Text in P. Geyer (CSEL 39, 135/50).

4. *Breviarius de Hierosolyma,* an enumeration of the sanctuaries of the city dating from the fifth or sixth centuries.

In P. Geyer 151/5. — RBn 1928, 101/6.

5. *Itinerarium Antonii Placentini,* written between about 560 and 570, gives an account of pilgrimage of several citizens of Piacenza to Palestine.

In P. Geyer, 157/218. De Izarra, *Bol. de la Comisión de monum. de Burgos* 18, 1939, 232/9; cf. RHE 1939, 896f. — González, *Archivos Leon.,* 1, 1947, 65/79 (Jachintus, a Spanish chronicler of the 5th/6th cent., pilgrim to Jerusalem).

§ 48. EUSEBIUS OF CAESAREA (d. 339)

EUSEBIUS lived between two eras. As regards his education, interests and works in which he summarized the achievements of the past, he belonged to the pre-Nicene period; as a bishop and church politician he was a representative of the new, turbulent Constantinian epoch. Born in Palestine, perhaps at Caesarea, in 263, he received his scholarly education from Pamphilus, whose slave he at first probably was, at the school and the famous library which had been founded by Origen. His early literary activity was interrupted by the great persecution of Christians that began in 303. After the death of his master, in whose memory he wrote a biography (supra § 41, 8), he fled to Tyre and to Egypt, where he was imprisoned. Perhaps as early as 313 he became Bishop of Caesarea. He gained great influence with the Emperor Constantine on account of his learning, but also because, as a follower of Origenist subordinatianism, he held an intermediary position in the Arian controversy.

He was excommunicated at the synod of Antioch (325) because he rejected the Creed directed against Arius. At the Council of Nicaea (325) he proposed a compromising creed, signed the decrees of the council with a mental reservation, but soon took part in the activities against the Nicene party, as also in the synod of Tyre (335), which deposed Athanasius. On the occasion of the dedication of the Church of the Holy Sepulchre at Jerusalem (335) which had been built by the Emperor, he dedicated to the latter an apologetical introduction to Christianity. In the same year he delivered the official panegyric in Constantinople, on the thirtieth anniversary of the Emperor's accession. Eusebius, who lived in the court atmosphere, may be regarded as the prototype of weak-kneed political bishops.

Despite his outstanding scholarship Eusebius is not one of the great theologians; his lasting fame is due to his work as *the* great historian of Christian antiquity; he was also an eminent apologist. In his exegetical writings he follows Origen's allegorical method.

1. *Historical works*

a. The *Chronicles* (Χρονικοὶ κανόνες καὶ ἐπιτομὴ παντοδαπῆς ἱστορίας Ἑλλήνων τε καὶ βαρβάρων). The introduction or first part gives short surveys of the history of the ancient peoples (Chaldeans, Assyrians, Hebrews, Egyptians, Greeks, Romans) in excerpts from their oldest writings accessible to him. The principal part consists in synchronistic tables placed in columns side by side, beginning with the year of the birth of Abraham (2016–5 B.C.). They are accompanied by notes on the most important historical events.

The work, which was published *c.* 303, is extant in Greek only in fragments, but is preserved complete in an Armenian translation dating from the sixth century. We also possess the second part, continued till the year 378, in the free Latin version of Jerome. In this form the work has dominated the chronology of the Middle Ages and saved much valuable historical material from destruction. Like Julius Africanus (supra § 41, 1), Eusebius wants to prove that the Jewish-Christian tradition is older than that of any other nation.

b. Ten books of *Church History* (Ἐκκλησιαστικὴ ἱστορία), from the foundation of the Church to the victory of Constantine over Licinius (324).

The work is governed by a fundamental apologetic idea: the history of Christianity and especially its victory over the hostile power of the state is the best proof of its divine origin and its justification. Eusebius is not yet capable of tracing a genetically developed picture of history; he gives in the main a collection of materials in which facts, excerpts from ancient Christian literature and historical documents are loosely strung together, though mostly in chronological order (EH 422/56; EP 652/60).

The work was published in seven books even before the beginning of the persecution under Diocletian (303). The quickly moving contemporary events, however, which were so decisive for the history of the world, compelled him to enlarge and add to it. The last supplement was added soon after 324, after the fall of Licinius. The *Church History* was translated into Syriac in the fourth century, and later into Armenian. Rufinus made a Latin translation in 403, continuing it till 395.

c. The treatise *On the Palestinian Martyrs* is extant in two different editions; only the older, shorter one has been preserved in Greek as an addition to the eighth book of the *Church History* (supra § 45, 17; EH 468/70).

2. *The Panegyrical Writings in honour of Constantine* do not belong to the properly historical works. a. The so-called *Vita Constantini* in four books is an extravagantly exaggerating panegyric on the Emperor, the "friend of almighty God" and "new Moses". The authenticity of the documents incorporated in the *Vita* must be considered as proved. b. Two pieces are comprised under the misleading title *Laus Constantini;* they are: chs. 1–10 of the panegyric Eusebius delivered on the occasion of the thirtieth anniversary of the Emperor's accession (335); chs. 11–18, an apologetic introduction to Christianity, dedicated to the Emperor and destined for pagan readers. c. As an appendix to the *Vita Constantini* Eusebius added a Good Friday sermon *Ad coetum sanctorum* (address to the assembly of the saints) as a specimen of the Emperor's eloquence. This almost certainly authentic speech was originally written in Latin with the help of secretaries, probably about 323.

Edd.: PG 19–24. *Chronicle* ed. A. Schoene, 2 vols., 1866/75. Trans. from the Armen. by J. Karst (GCS 20) 1911. Eusebius-Jerome Chronicle ed. R. Helm, 2 vols. (GCS 24 34) 1913/26 in 1 vol. 1956 (GCS 47). Ed J. K. Fotheringham, O 1905,

L 1923; cf. R. Helm, SbB 1929, 371/408 and Phil. Suppl. 21, 2, 1929. *Church Hist.* ed. E. Schwartz, 3 vols. (GCS 9; also contains Lat. version of Rufinus ed. by T. Mommsen), 1903/9. Small ed. [5]1952. French trans. ed. E. Grapin, 3 vols., P 1905/13 and G. Bardy, 1952ff. (SCh 31 41). German by P. Haeuser (BKV[2] II 1) 1932. Engl. by Lawlor and Oulton, 2 vols., 1952/3 with Greek text. Ital. by G. del Ton, Siena 1931 ff. *Panegyr. writings* ed. I. A. Heikel (GCS 7) 1902; cf. Heikel (TU 36, 4) 1911. German BKV[2] 9, 1913. — Transs.: *Eccl. hist.,* trans. A. C. McGiffert, O 1890. *Life of Const. etc.,* trans. E. C. Richardson, O 1890. *Dem. ev.,* trans. W. J. Ferrar, Lo 1920. — Mgg.: A. Bigelmair, BKV[2] 9, 1913, V/LXI. E. Schwartz, PWK 6, 1370/1439, Leclercq, DAL 5, 747/75. Palanque, DHG 13, 593/608. J. Vogt, *Const. d. Gr. u. sein Jh.,* 1949; RACh 3, 306/76. H. Doerries, *Das Selbstzeugnis Kaiser Konstantins,* 1954 (GAb 3, 34). H. Kraft, *Kaiser Konstantins religioese Entwicklung,* T 1955. H. Berkhof, *Kirche u. Kaiser ...,* Zu 1947. — On the hist. Works: R. Laqueur, *E. als Historiker seiner Zeit,* 1929. E. Caspar, *Die aelteste roem. Bischofsliste,* 1926. Delehaye, AB 1932, 241/83 (Mart. Pal.). F. J. Foakes-Jackson, *E., Bishop of C. and First Chr. Historian,* C 1933. W. Nigg, *Die Kirchengeschichtsschreibung,* 1934. W. Bauer 1934, 13/6, 151/61, 193/5 and freq. (against his reliability). A. Ehrhard, TU 50, 1936, 1/18 (Acts of martyrs). Santifaller, HJB 1939, 412/31 (uncial MS of the chronicle of Jerome). Schoene, DP 1939, 252/65 (on *Hist. E.* 5, 28, 13–19). Grégoire, Byz. 13, 1938, 557/60 (on *Hist. E.* 8, 14, 10). Carcopino, Mél. Fr. Martroye 1941, 73/9 (on Chron. ad 1932). Tailliez, OCP 1943, 431/49 *(un passage fameux).* Edmonds, 1941, 25/45 (EH), 45/55 (chronicle). Heichelheim-Schwarzenberger, SO 1947, 1/19 (An Edict of Const. ... Study of Interpolations). Kuehnert, TZ 1949, 436/46 (the anti-Montanist anonymous author in Eus.). Voelker, VC 1950, 157/80 (tendencies in the *Hist. E.*). Zuntz, VC 1951, 50/4 (text. crit. on *Hist. E.* VI 41, 15). Honigmann, 1953, 59/70 (erasure of the name from the diptychs; 431). W. Schmid, RM 1954, 190f. (text. crit. on *Hist. E.* 4, 13, 5). Garitte, Mu 1953, 245/66 (on De Mart. Pal. c. 1; Georg. trans.). Wallace-Hadrill, JTS 1955, 248/53 (date of *Chronicle*). — On the panegyr. writings: J. M. Pfaettisch, *Die Rede Konstantins d. Gr. an die Versammlung der Heiligen,* 1908; *Die 4. Ekloge Vergils i. d. Rede Konstantins ...,* Programm des Kgl. Gymnasiums im Benediktinerkloster Ettal, 1912/3 (betw. 313/25). N. H. Baynes, *Constantine the Great and the Chr. Church,* 1930, 50ff. (*Ad coet.* spurious). — Kurfess, TQ 1936, 11/26; ZNTW 1936, 97/100; PW 1936, 364/7; *Glotta* 25, 1936, 274/6 (for authenticity; 313!); Mn 1937, 282/8 (4th Ecl. of Vergil). Piganiol, RHP 1932, 370/2 (delivered on 7. 4. 323; genuine; revised by Lactantius). Kurfess, TG 1949, 167/74; TQ 1950, 145/65; ZRGG 1948/9, 4; 1952, 42/57 (Constantine and the Erythrean Sibyl). A. Bolhuis, *Vergils 4. Ecloga in de Orat. Const. ad sanct. coet.,* 1950 (thesis A) (Gr. original); VC 1956 (relation to Lactantius). Doerries, *Selbstzeugnis ...,* 1954, 129/61 (for authenticity). Vogt, RACh 3, 367 (with A. Heikel [TU 36, 4, 1911] for spuriousness). The speech is an important document for the history of Christian apologetics. Baynes, Mél. Bidez 1, 1934, 13/8 (*Laus Const.* 1/10). E. Peterson, *Der Monotheismus als polit. Problem,* 1935. J. Daniele, *I Documenti Costant. della "Vita Const." di Eus.,* R 1938. Grégoire, Byz 1938, 561/83 (*Vita Const.* spurious); against this: Baynes, BZ 1939, 466/9 and Zeiller, Byz 14, 1935, 329/39; reply by Grégoire, ibid. 341/51. Wendel, ZBW 1939, 165/75 (*Vita Const.* 4, 36). Berkhof, Nederl-

ArchKerkGesch 1943, 24/8 *(Vita Const.* 4, 24). Further studies on the *Vita Const.*, esp. on the question of authenticity: Staehlin, ZSchwG 1939, 396/403. Picard, OCP 1947, 266/81 (on *Vita Const.* 3, 49). Vogt, AIP 1949, 593/606; Historia 2, 1954, 463/71; the conversion of Const. in: Relazioni 10. *Congresso internaz. Scienze stor.* 6, 1955, 733/79 (for authenticity). Petit, *Historia* 1, 1950, 562/82 (Libanius et la *Vita Const.*); Byz 1951, 285/310 (Libanius' *Pro templis*). Piganiol, *Historia* 1, 1950, 82/95; AIP 10, 1950, 513/18 (against Grégoire). Downey, DOP 1951, 53/80 (*Vita* interpolated). P. Franchi de' Cavalieri, *Constantiana* (ST 171), 1951 (genuine). Orgels, AIP 12, 1952 (publ. 1953), 575/611 (against Vogt and Cavalieri; spurious). Scheidweiler, BZ 1953, 293/301 (*Vita* written *c.* 430). Grégoire, BullAcadBelgClLett 1953, 39, 462/79 (spurious). Vittinghoff, RM 1953, 330/73 (*Vita* genuine). Moreau, RevEa 1953, 307/33 (vision of Const.). Aland, *Forsch. u. Fortschr.* 1954, 213/7 and Jones-Skat, JEH 1954, 196/200 (papyrus citation from *Vita* 2, 27f.). Morreau, *Historia* 4, 1955, 334/45 and *Anales Univ. Sarav* 4, 1955, 89/97 (*Vita* prob. genuine). Scheidweiler, BZ 1956, 1/23 (*Vita* for the most part genuine; 24/32 text. crit.). Petersen, DanskTeolTidsskrift 19, 1956, 25/64 (agrees with Grégoire).

Testimonies on Constantine's building activities: E. Wistrand, *Konst.s Kirche am hl. Grab* (ActaUnivGotoburg 58, 1) 1952. Vogt, Her 1953, 111/17 (Church of the Apostles in Constant.). Voelkl, RAC 1953, 49/66 (church buildings). H. U. Instinsky, *Bischofsstuhl u. Kaiserthron*, 1955.—Supplement: Aland, *Stud. Patrist.*, B I 1957, 549/90 (Constantine's religious attitude). Id., *Aus d. Byz. Arbeit der Dtsch. Demokrat. Republik*, 1957, 188/212 (crit. of H. Berkhof's work, Zu 1947 [v. supra]).

3. *The apologetical writings* bear witness to the wide reading of the learned author and are important because they contain numerous extracts from literary works of antiquity that are otherwise lost.

a. The *Praeparatio evangelica* (Εὐαγγελικὴ προπαρασκευή) in fifteen books, written between 312 and 322, wants to show that the Christians rightly preferred Judaism to paganism. The "philosophy of the Hebrews" is superior to the cosmogony and mythology of the pagans. Moreover, the pagan sages, especially Plato, used the O.T. as a source (EP 661/3).

b. The *Demonstratio evangelica* (Εὐαγγελικὴ ἀπόδειξις) in twenty books—only books one to ten and part of book fifteen are still extant—continues the preceding work. It shows that the Mosaic Law had only preparatory character and that the prophecies have been fulfilled in Christ (EP 664/73).

c. The treatise *On the Theophany,* i.e. on the appearance of God in the flesh, preserved only in Syriac, is a popular, highly rhetorical apologetic work (five books) that draws on the *Praeparatio* and *Demonstratio.*

d. Of his first apologetic treatise, the *General Elementary Introduction* (at least ten books) only books six to nine are extant. They explain the Messianic prophecies of the O.T. under the title Περὶ τοῦ Χριστοῦ προφητικαὶ ἐκλογαί.

e. The twenty-five polemical books against the neo-Platonist Porphyry are lost, except for a few unimportant fragments; also the treatise *Refutation and Defence* (two books), a reply to pagan objections.

f. *Against Hierocles* is directed against the governor of Bithynia, because he had written a pamphlet placing Apollonius of Tyana above Christ.

Praep. ev. ed. E. H. Gifford, 4 vols., O 1903 (with trans.). K. Mras, *Praep. Ev.,* 2 vols. (GCS 43, 1. 2), 1954/6. *Demonstr. ev.* ed. I. A. Heikel (GCS 23) 1913. *Theoph.* ed. H. Gressmann (GCS 11, 2) 1904. *Eclogae proph.* ed. T. Gaisford, O 1842. *Adv. Hierocl.* ed. T. Gaisford, together with *Contra Marcell.* and *De eccl. theol.,* O 1852. — Treatises: H. Doergens, *Eusebius v. C. als Darsteller der phoeniz. Religion,* 1915; *Eus. v. C. als Darsteller der griech. Rel.,* 1922. J. Wieneke, *Ezechielis Iudaei poetae Alexandrini fabulae quae inscribitur* Ἐξαγωγή *fragmenta rec.,* Mr 1931 (*Praep. ev.* 9, 28f.). P. Henry, *Rech. sur la Prép. év. d'Eusèbe et l'ét. perdue des œuvres de Plotin publ. par Eustochius,* 1935. P. Kraus, RHR 113, 1936, 207/18. Tasker, HTR 1935, 61/7 (Gospel text in *Demonstr.*) Peters, OC 33, 1936, 1/25 (Mt. citations in the Syr. text of the Theoph.). P. Henry, *Les États du texte de Plotin,* 1938, 77/124 (*Praep. ev.* 15, 10 22). Mras, RM 1944, 217/36 (on the new ed. of the *Praep. ev.*); AnzAkadWissW 84, 1947, 115/20 (on ed. of *Praep. ev.*); WSt 66, 1953, 92f. (on conclusion of *Praep. ev.*). G. Mercati, *Mémorial L. Petit* 1948, 1/3 (on *Eclog. proph.*). Wallace-Hadrill, JTS 1950, 168/75 (Mt. citations in the *Demonstr. ev.*); JTS 1953, 41f. (on *Demonstr. ev.* 7, 1, 28). Des Places, *Aegyptus* 32, 1952, 223/31 (Plato's *Laws* in the *Praep. ev.*). Murphy, JBL 1954, 162/8 (N.T. in *Demonstr. ev.*). J. B. Laurin, *Orientations maîtresses des apologistes chrét. de 270 à 361,* R 1954.

4. Biblical works

a. Large fragments have been preserved of the learned *Commentary on the Psalms,* which Hilary of Poitiers and Eusebius of

Vercelli translated into Latin. It is hoped that with the help of *catenae* the work may be completely reconstructed (MG 23 24, 9/76). b. Research on the *catenae* and a lucky MS find have also given us almost the whole *Commentary on Isaias* (MG 24, 89/526). c. Of a rather large work *On Problems and Solutions in the Gospels* (Περὶ τῶν ἐν εὐαγγελίοις ζητημάτων καὶ λύσεων) only an excerpt made at a later date has been preserved (MG 22, 879/1006). d. Of a treatise *On the Passover* we only have one large fragment (MG 24, 693/706) containing a fine testimony to the sacrifice of the Mass. e. The *Evangelical Canons* (MG 22, 1275/92), dedicated to a certain Carpianus, contain ten tables which facilitate a quick synopsis of the parallel passages of the four Gospels. f. The *Onomasticon* (Περὶ τῶν τοπικῶν ὀνομάτων) is the fourth and most important part of a Biblical geographical work in four sections, and the only one that has survived. It is an alphabetical list of all the place names that occur in the Scriptures, accompanied by notes on the situation and history of these localities. Jerome edited the work in an emended Latin version.

Onomasticon ed. E. Klostermann (GCS 11, 1) 1904 (and Lat. text). — Treatises: Devreesse, DBSuppl 1, 1928, 1122/4 (Comm. on Pss.); RB 1933, 540/55 (Comm. on Is.). Moehle, ZNTW 1934, 87/9 (Comm. on Is.). Bardy, RB 1932, 228/36 (on c., above). Hebbelynck, Mu 1928, 81/120 (*Letter to Carp.*, Copt.). — On *Onom.* G. Beyer, ZDtschPalVer 1933, 218/53. C. Nordenfalk, *Die spaetantiken Kanontafeln* (Art-hist. studies on the Euseb. concordance of the Gospels), Goeteborg 1938. G. Mercati, *Proemi di Salterio* . . . (ST 142), 1948. — Supplement: J. Ziegler's crit. text of Isaias comment. appears in GCS.

5. Eusebius attacks (336 and later) Bishop Marcellus of Ancyra, a champion of the Nicene faith, in two dogmatic treatises *(Contra Marcellum* and *De ecclesiastica theologia)*, seeking to prove his Origenist teaching on the Logos as the "ecclesiastical theology". Ed. E. Klostermann (GCS 14) 1906.

6. Little has been preserved of his Letters and Sermons. We would mention the following: His *Letter to his church* (325) on his conception of the ὁμοούσιος (in Athanasius, *De decr. Nic. syn.*);

fragments of a *Letter* in the Acts of the 2nd Council of Nicaea (Acts 5 and 6 creed of Arius); fragments of a *Letter to Constantia,* the sister of the Emperor (against the veneration of images; *Conc. Nicaen.* 2). A sermon for the consecration of the basilica at Tyre (314–5) preserved in *Hist.* 10, 4.

Points of Doctrine

1. His Trinitarian doctrine is essentially Origenistic. In describing the divinity of the Son, Eusebius wanted theologians to confine themselves to Biblical terms; hence he rejected the ὁμοούσιος throughout his life. He regarded the doctrine of St. Athanasius as Sabellianism. The Father is the supreme God and unbegotten, the Son came into being only according to the will of the Father; he is the second God, subordinated to the Father. He rejected the ἐξ οὐκ ὄντων of the Arians. He regarded the Holy Spirit as a creature of the Father; he is active only in the saints.

2. The Eucharist. "We, the sons of the New Covenant, celebrate our Passover every Sunday, we always feed on the Body of the Saviour, we always share in the Blood of the Lamb... Every Sunday we are vivified by the consecrated Body of the same redeeming Paschal Lamb, and our soul is sealed by his precious Blood" (*De solemn. pasch.* 7, 12). God desires "smokeless, unbloody sacrifices, which the Saviour of the universe has commanded to be offered in the whole world in his memory through certain mystical words" (*Theoph.* 3, 71).

3. Veneration of images. As a follower of Origenist spiritualism he rejects, in his *Letter to Constantia,* any veneration of images as well as the making of images of Christ "so that we may not carry about our God in an image, like the pagans" (EH 471/5; cf. *Hist.* 7, 18).

M. Weis, *Die Stellung des Eusebius v. C. im arian. Streit,* 1920. J. Stevenson, *Studies in E.,* C 1929. Salaverri, Gr 1932, 211/40; 1933, 219/47; 1935, 349/73 (teaching on tradition and apost. succession). Opitz, ZNTW 1935, 1/19 (E. as a theologican). Balanos, TQ 1935, 309/22 (Logos doct.); Festschr. S. Lambros, At 1935, 515/22 (character of Eus.). Eger, ZNTW 38, 1939, 97/115 (emperor and Church). H. Berkhof, *Die Theol. des E. v. C.,* A 1939. J. Straub, *Vom Herrscherideal in der Spaetantike,* 1939, 113/29. Katzenmayer, IKZ 1948, 153/71 (Papal primacy). Amand, 1945, 344/81. Cranz, HTR 1952, 47/66 (Kingdom and polity). *Pallas,* Θ 1954, 470/83 (The *exedrae* in the Palest. Churches). Bardy, RHE 1955, 5/20 (the theol. of the *Hist. E.*).

Disciples and successors of Eusebius

1. Acacius of Caesarea, disciple and successor of Eusebius as bishop (d. 366), leader of the Homoeans in the East. His numerous writings have been lost except for a few remains. Works are mentioned by Jerome *Vir. ill.* 98 and Socrat. *Hist.* 2, 4; a fragment from a pamphlet against Marcellus of Ancyra in Epiph., *Haer.* 72, 6/10; fragments from *catenae* in K. Staab 1933, 53/6. Devreesse, RB 1935, 186/9 (Octateuch).

2. Bishop Eusebius of Emesa, also a disciple of Eusebius of Caesarea, Semi-Arian (d. *c.* 359); of the large volume of his writings only a small part has survived. The most important are the only recently discovered seventeen sermons which have been established as genuine.

Fragments in MG 86, 1, 535/62. Esposito, HA 1932, 253ff. (E. perh. author of the *Lib. de trib. habit.* in PL 40, 991/8 which Delius, TSK 1937, 28/39 assigns to the 12th cent.). Bardy, RB 1932, 344f. K. Staab, 1933, 46/52. Zanolli, Baz 1934, 186/92 (E. and Ps.-Cyril). Devreesse, RB 1936, 201/11 (O.T. comm.). Godet, DTC 5, 1537/9. Morin, ZNTW 1935, 92/115; v. § 95, 1. Baz 93, 1935, 345/52 (Gen. comm.). Buytaert, RHE 1948, 5/89 (genuineness of the 17 *opuscula*). E. M. Buytaert, *L'héritage litt. d'Eus. d'Emèse,* Lou 1949; *Hom. De Paenit.,* printed MG 31, 1476/88 under the name of Basil (now pp. 89*/96*) belongs to Eus. of Em.; on this, Richard, MSR 1951, 116/9. Buytaert, *Eus. d'Emèse. Discours conservés en latin,* I: *La collection de Troyes Discours* I–XVIII, 1953 (15 or 16 homilies are genuine); inter alia, Buytaert also ed. many Gr. fragms. collected from *catenae,* from the commentaries on Gen. and Gal.; p. 95*/159* fragms. on Gen. Texts preserved in Syr. and Armen. are also ed. The Vol. 2 will bring 12 further Opuscula which had been publ. as works of Eus. of Em. already by Surmond, in 1643. Buytaert, *Franciscan Stud.* 14, 1954, 34/48 (doct. of Trinity). Grillmeier in: Grillmeier-Bacht I, 130/5 (Christology). Amand de Mendieta, RHE 1955, 177/92 *(La virginité chez Eus. d'E.)*. Clavis PL n. 966ff.

3. One of the successors of this Eusebius, Nemesius of Emesa, wrote *c.* 400 a work of mainly neo-Platonist leanings which was much used in the Middle Ages called Περὶ φύσεως ἀνθρώπου.

Edd.: MG 40, 508/818. The Lat. trans. of Alfanus ed. C. Burkhard, L 1917. Germ. trans. E. Orth 1925. Skard, PWK Suppl. 7, 562/6. Amann, DTC 11, 60/7. W. Jaeger, *Nemesius von E.,* 1914. H. A. Koch, *Quellenunters. zu Nemesius von E.,* 1921. Arnou, Gr 1936, 116ff. (Nestorianism and neo-Platonism). Skard, SO 1936, 23/43; 1937, 9/25; 1939, 46/56; 1942, 40/8 (N. and Galenus). Lammert, Phil 1940, 125/41 (medicine in Ptolemy and N.). Klinge, ZKG 1939, 363/73 (Psychology of N. in Mose bar Kepha). Amand, 1945, 549/69. Brady, Francisc. Stud. 1948, 275/84 (Remigius and Nemesius). E. Dobler, *N. v. E. u. d. Psychologie d. menschl. Aktes bei Thomas v. Aquin,* Fri 1950. Lammert, Her 1953, 488/91 (on ch. 5). W. Telfer, *Cyr. of Jer. and N. of E.,* Lo 1955 (trans.).

§ 49. POST-EUSEBIAN CHURCH HISTORIES AND CHRONICLES

PART of the historical literature, viz. that of the history of literature, has already been considered above, § 2; all else will be discussed here in connexion with the "first Church History" in a comprehensive survey extending to the end of the patristic period.

Complete ed. of the Gr. Church historians from Eusebius to Evagrius by H. Valesius (de Valois), 3 fols., P 1659/73, emended by W. Reading, 3 fols., C 1720. On the hist. of the subject: F. C. Baur, *Die Epochen der kirchl. Geschichtsschreibung,* 1852. F. Oberbeck, *Ueber die Anfaenge der Kirchengeschichtsschreibg.,* 1892. G. Loeschcke, *Zwei kirchengeschichtl. Entwuerfe,* 1913. Leclercq, DAL 6, 2533/753. W. Nigg, *Die Kirchengeschichtsschreibung,* 1934. Gentz-Aland, ZNTW 42, 1949, 104/41 (Sources of the EH of Nicephorus and the oldest Church historians). Scheidweiler, BZ 1957, 74/98 (on source criticism of Greek Church historians).

1. *Church Histories*

1. *Gelasius of Caesarea* (d. 395), Eusebius' second successor in his see, wrote among other works a continuation of the *Hist. E.* of Eusebius, which served as a model for the last two books of the *Hist. E.* of Rufinus. The late P. Heseler wanted to supply a re-

construction of certain parts of the lost work. Diekamp and Van den Ven, however, defend the traditional view, according to which books nine and ten of the *Hist. E.* are the original work of Rufinus.

In a dogmatic work of which only few fragments are known, Gelasius treated of the fundamental doctrines of the Church probably in the same way as his uncle Cyril of Jerusalem in his twenty-three catecheses.

A. Glas, *Die KG des Gel. v. Kais.,* 1914. P. Heseler, *Hagiographica,* BNJ 9, 1932/3, 113/28, 320/37 (supports the thesis of the dependence of Rufinus with new material); Heseler u. Bidez, Byz 10, 1935, 438/42; BNJ 12, 1936, 347/51. Against Glas P. van den Ven, Mu 1915, 92/115; 1946, 281/94. Diekamp, AP 1938, 16/49 (17 partly uned. fragments). Scheidweiler, BZ 1953, 277/301 (against Rufinus as author of bks. 9 and 10); against this Van den Ven, *La légende de S. Spyridon,* Lou 1953, 195/200. As is shown by E. Honigmann, BullAcadBelgClLett 40, 1954, 122/61, Gelasius was already dead (cf. Jerome, Ep. 92/3 = synodal letter of Theophilus of Alex. of Sept. 400) when Rufinus began the trans. of the *Hist. E.* of Eusebius after 401. Scheidweiler, BZ 1955, 162/4 (against Honigmann 1954, who asserts the existence of a Gr. author of the name of Rufinus).

2. The oldest work on Church history produced in the West comes from the pen of Rufinus of Aquileia (§ 85). In 403 he translated the *Ecclesiastical History* of Eusebius into Latin; in his version, which was partly abridged and adorned with rhetorical additions, the work comprised nine books, to which he added two more (to 395); these are mainly a translation and redaction of the *Ecclesiastical History* of the above-mentioned Gelasius.

Edd.: T. Mommsen in the ed. of the *Hist. E.* of Eusebius (GCS 9) 1903/9. P. Peeters, Acad. roy. de Belg. Bull. de classe des lettres 17, 1931, 10/45 (on 10, 11); cf. Byz 7, 1932, 635/9. Villain, RSR 1946, 164/210 (R. and the *Hist. E.*).

3. Between 434 and 439 Philip of Side (in Pamphylia), a priest in Constantinople and a friend of Chrysostom, published a Χριστιανικὴ ἱστορία comprising thirty-six books, only fragments of which have survived. Photius was the last author still to have known about two-thirds of the bulky work.

Fragms.: C. de Boor, TU 5, 2, 1888, 165/84. E. Bratke, TU 19, 3, 1899, 153 ff. Heseler, Byz 10, 1935, 440. Honigmann 1953, 82/91.

4. The Eunomian Philostorgius, a resident of Constantinople, completed his *Church History* (twelve books), which extends to 425, between 425 and 433. It is mainly preserved in extracts of Photius. He gave particular attention to secular history and strongly emphasized the Arian standpoint (*Hist. E.* 789).

Ed.: J. Bidez (GCS 21) 1913. G. Fritz, DTC 12, 1495/8. Opitz, Byz 9, 1934, 535/93 (ed. of *Vita Constantini* of Cod. Ang. 22 with fragms. of Philost.). On further fragms. cf. Heseler, Byz 10, 1935, 399/402 and Bidez, ibid. 403/37.

5. The best of all the continuations of Eusebius' work is the *Church History* of the lawyer (scholasticus) *Socrates* (b. *c.* 380, d. after 439) at Constantinople, which treats of the time between 305 and 439. It comprises seven books; original documents such as decrees of councils and letters from emperors and bishops are frequently reproduced verbatim. The author aims at an objective presentation and expressly names most of his sources. He is particularly sympathetic toward the Novatianists (*Hist. E.* 843/67).

Edd.: MG 67, 29/872. R. Hussey, 3 vols., O 1853. — Treatises: Eltester, PWK II 3, 893/1901. F. Geppert, *Die Quellen des K.-Historikers S.,* 1898. Peeters, Mél. Bidez 2, 647/75 (Armen. trans.). H. G. Opitz, Unters. 1935, 155/7 (text. crit.). Heseler, Byz 10, 1935, 438ff. (Socr. has taken directly from Gelas. of Caes.). Baynes, JTS 1948, 165/8 (on Socr. 1, 15); against this Telfer, ibid. 1949, 187/91. Stephanides, EEBS 1956, 57/129 (Amendments).

6. The *Church History* (nine books) by the lawyer Sozomen in Constantinople, which gives an account of the years 324 to 425 (written between 439 and 450) depends very much on the *Hist. E.* of Socrates, but besides, Sozomen has also made use of much new documentary material. His literary style is superior to that of Socrates, but he is less critical than the latter and has included many decidedly legendary accounts.

Edd.: MG 67, 844/1630. R. Hussey, 3 vols., O 1860. — Treatises: Eltester, PWK II 3, 1240/8. G. Schoo, *Die Quellen des K.-Hist. Soz.,* 1911. Bidez, SbB 1935, no. 18 (ed. prologue and VI 28/34). Bardy, DTC 14, 2465/71.

7. The five books of a *Church History* written by Theodoret of Cyrus (cf. § 73) in 449–50 comprising the time from 325 to

428 are dominated by an apologetic anti-heretical tendency. According to Parmentier, the frequent agreement with Socrates and Sozomen is due to the use of common sources. His presentation is often superficial and chronologically inaccurate (*Hist. E.* 930/9).

Theodoret wrote two other historical works: a *History of the Monks (historia religiosa)*, similar to the *Hist. Lausiaca* of Palladius (supra § 46, 1; MG 82, 1283/1496) and a *History of Heresies* (as far as Eutyches) in five books (MG 83, 335/556); the fifth book is a systematic exposition of doctrine valuable for the history of dogma.

Ed. of the *Hist. E.* by L. Parmentier-Scheidweiler (GCS 19) ²1954. Germ. by A. Seider (BKV² 51) 1926. K. Gutberlet (BKV² 50) 1926 (hist. rel.). Opitz, PWK II 5, 1800 n. 30 (on Syn. of Chalc.). Honigmann 1953, 92/100.

8. Of the *Church History* of Hesychius of Jerusalem (d. after 450) only the chapter on Theodore of Mopsuestia which was read at the Council of 553, is preserved (MG 92, 948; 86, 1031; v. infra § 71, 3).

9. Gelasius of Cyzicus wrote his *Church History* (three books) in Bithynia, shortly after 475. The work is a history of the Eastern Church under Constantine the Great. It is largely a compilation from other sources known to us. The authenticity of documents reproduced only by him is controversial.

Edd.: G. Loeschcke and M. Heinemann (GCS 28) 1918. BNJ 10, 1933/4, 137. Opitz, Unters. 1935, 74. Mercati, OM 4, 1937, 56f. (new MS).

10. Between 512 and 518 the Syrian Monophysite (?) John Diacrinomenus wrote a *Church History* in ten books, treating of the time between 439 and the Emperor Anastasius I (491–518). Fragments are extant in Byzantine historians (cf. PWK 9, 1805). Honigmann 1953, 178.

11. The Monophysite Basilius Cilix (i.e. from Cilicia) wrote inter alia a no longer extant *Church History* in three books considering the time from *c.* 450 to 540. (Cf. PWK 3, 54f. and Baumstark 1922, 118.)

12. The *Church History* of Zacharias Rhetor, a convert from Monophysitism to neo-Chalcedonism (d. before 553 as Bishop of Mytilene), is lost in its Greek original, but preserved as books three to six of an anonymous Syriac *Chronicle of the World* (twelve books to 568/9). It gives an account of the history of the years 450–91. He also wrote an anti-Manichean work (a Gr. fragm. ed. Pita, *Anal. Sacr.* 5, 1, 1888, 67/70, Lat. in MG 85, 1143f.) and a *Dialogue "Amonius"* also extant in Greek, which proves, against pagan philosophy, that the world has been created (MG 85, 1011/44), as well as several biographies (of Severus of Antioch [§ 101, 1], Peter the Iberian [§ 47, 13d], the ascetic Isaias, d. 488, of whom twenty conferences are printed in MG 40, 1105/1206 in a Latin translation of the sixteenth century; besides Copt. fragments of an *Asceticon* ed. by Guillaumont in Copt. Stud. for W. E. Crum, 1950, 49/60 and S. Mercati, Aeg 1953, 464/73 [Greek fragm. of Orat. 21]).

Edd.: E. W. Brooks (CSCO, 83/4, 1919–21; French trans. ibid. 87/88, 1924. German K. Ahrens and G. Krueger, L 1899. Nissen, BZ 1940, 15/22 *(Amonius)*. Bardy DTC 15, 3676/80. Honigmann 1953, 194/204. New impression of the ed. of Brooks, l. c. 38 and 41, 1953. On Isaias cf. Petit, DTC 8, 79/81. On biography cf. also MG 65, 179/84 and Guillaumont, Ab 1949, 350/60 (new Syr. text). *L' ascéticon copte de l'abbé Isaie,* Cairo 1956.

13. About 530 Theodore Lector amalgamated the *Church Histories* of Socrates, Sozomen and Theodoret in a *Historia tripartita* (four books), the first two books of which are preserved in the Cod. Marc. 344. His independently written *Church History* (four books), preserved only in fragments, is more valuable; it continues the *Hist. trip.* to 527. An *Epitome of Church History* dating from the seventh to eighth centuries is a kind of substitute for the lost *Church History;* considerable extracts of it are preserved in the Byzantine chronographers.

J. V. Sarrazin, Commentat. philol. Jenenses, 1, 1881, 163/238. De Boor, ZKG 6, 1883/4, 487/91, 573/7. Opitz, PWK II 5, 1869/81 (fundamental).

14. The above-mentioned (§ 46, 8) John of Ephesus (d. 586) wrote a *Church History* in three parts of six books each, from Julius Caesar to 585. Only the third part (571–85) is preserved in Syriac in direct transmission. Cf. also § 49 II 18.

Edd.: E. W. Brooks, CSCO 105, 1935; ibid. 106, 1936 (Lat. trans.); cf. Honigmann, Byz 14, 1939, 615/25. German J. M. Schoenfelder 1862. Baz 1934, 52/9 (Armen. fragm.). Monogr. by Diakonow, St. Petersburg 1908. New impress. of the ed. Brooks in 2 vols., 1952.

15. Evagrius Scholasticus, a lawyer in Constantinople, later imperial quaestor and honorary prefect, d. *c.* 600, strictly orthodox, wrote a *Church History* in six books on the time between 431 and 594, which is important for the Nestorian and Monophysite controversies. He is truthful and impartial in his reports, but credulous and addicted to miracles.

MG 86, 2, 2415/2886. Ed. J. Bidez and L. Parmentier, Lo 1898. DTC 5, 1612f. Peeters, AB 1947, 35/40. DThC 5, 1612f.

16. The work of Rufinus (supra n. 2) was resumed in the West by Cassiodorus (d. *c.* 583; § 96, 6), the author of a *Chronicle of the World* and a *History of the Goths* preserved only in the extract of Jordanes. He caused the monk Epiphanius to translate the Church Histories of Socrates, Sozomen and Theodoret into Latin and then to amalgamate them after the example of Theodore Lector (supra n. 13) into a *Historia tripartita* in twelve books. The work became one of the most important aids to Church history of the Latin Middle Ages.

Edd.: ML 69, 879/1296. Mommsen, MGAuctAnt 5, 1 and 11 (*Hist. of Goths* and *World Chronicles*). W. Jacob - R. Hanslik, *Hist. Eccl. Trip.* (CSEL 71), 1952. — Treatises: F. A. Bieter, *The Syntax of the Cases and Propos. in Cass.'s H. eccl. trip.*, W 1938; cf. Gn 1939, 376/82 and ZNTW 38, 1939, 191/6. Laistner, HTR 1948, 51/67 *(Hist. trip.)*. W. Jacob, *Die handschrift. Ueberlieferung der sog. Hist. Trip. des Epiphanius-Cassiodor* (TU 59), 1954. S. Lundstroem, *Sprachliche Bemerkungen zur Hist. Trip. des Cass.:* AL 23, 1953, 19/34; Lunds Univers. Arsskrift, 49, 1, 1953 (on *Hist. Trip.*). Hanslik, VC 1954, 176/81 (on *Hist. Trip.* 7, 40, 4ff. and 7, 40, 43ff.). Bulhart, AL 1954, 5/17 (text. crit. on *Hist. Trip.*).

2. *Chronicles*

The chroniclers, as distinct from the historians, do not give a coherent presentation of the most important happenings, nor do they strive to grasp and elucidate the inner connexion of events. They aim almost exclusively at simply stringing together the greatest possible number of historical details of interest to a wide circle of readers, enumerating them in chronological order. The world chronicles of Julius Africanus, Hippolytus and Eusebius roused the interest in an—at first naïve—understanding of the development of mankind in the sense of Christianity.

Edd.: T. Mommsen, *Chronica minora saec. IV–VII,* 2 vols. (MG AuctAnt 9 and 11) 1891/4. C. Frick, *Chronica minora,* L 1892. — Treatises: H. Gelzer, *S. Jul. Africanus u. d. byzant. Chronographie,* 2 vols., 1880/98. A. Bauer, *Beitr. zu Euseb. u. den byzantin. Chronographen,* 1909.

1. *The Chronographer of the year 354* (infra § 50, 5) included in his compilation among other things also a chronicle of the world, the *Chronica Horosii,* which is nothing other than a Latin version and continuation (to 334) of the chronicle of Hippolytus.

2. On Jerome's version and continuation of the chronicle of Eusebius, v. supra § 48, 1.

3. The short chronographical survey *De cursu temporum,* written in 397 by the chiliastically minded African (?) Bishop Quintus Julius Hilarianus, is an original attempt to view the course of the history of the world.

Ed.: C. Frick (supra) 153/74. H. Gelzer (supra) 2, 1, 1885, 121/9. P. Monceaux, (supra § 3) 6, 249ff.

4. Sulpicius Severus, d. *c.* 420, came from a noble Aquitanian family. The early death of his wife and the exhortations of his friend, St. Martin of Tours, induced him to give up his post as a lawyer and retire into solitude. He probably also became a priest.

His not very long *Chronicle of the World* in two books gives the history of the world from its creation down to A.D. 400. It has value as an independent work only for the last decades of the author's lifetime. The history of Priscillianism which roused excitement in his own time and country is given special attention. The work is written with critical sense and in the concise classical style influenced by Sallustius and Tacitus (*Hist. E.* 717f.). It was published not before 403.

In contrast with the *Chronicle of the World* his two works on St. Martin (*Vita S. Martini* [d. 397] plus three letters and the two books of *Dialogi* which supplement the *Vita*) which treat of the great apostle of Gaul and the first father of the monks of the West were much read in the Middle Ages. In them his gift of stimulating and popular talk appears in the best light. Even here the historical sense that distinguishes the author of the *Chronicle* is not altogether absent, though Severus tried to prove by his legendary presentation that his hero surpassed even the Egyptian ascetics in holiness and miraculous powers.

Edd.: C. Halm (CSEL 1) 1866. A. Lavertujon, 2 vols., 1896/9 (*Chron.* with comm.). German by P. Bihlmeyer (BKV² 20) 1914 (writings on Martin). P. Monceaux, *Dialogi,* 1926/7 (French, 2 vols.). F. R. Hoare, *Western Fathers,* Lo 1954 (translates among others the work on Martin). — Treatises: J. Bernays, *Ges. Abh.* ed. H. Usener 2, 1885, 81/200. E. C. Babut, *St. Martin de T.,* 1912; against this Delehaye, AB 1920, 5/136 and Jullian, RevEA 1922/3. Peebles, *Memoirs of the American Acad. in Rome,* 1936 (MS of the Girol. da Prato of Sulp. Sev.). *Class. and Mediev. Stud. in Honour of E. K. Rand,* NY 1938, 231/44. Delehaye, AB 1937, 29/48 and Grosjean, AB 1937, 300/48 (Miracles of Martin in later times). P. Hyltén, *Studien zu Sulp. S.,* Lund 1940. Bardy, DTC 14, 2760/2. Ganshof, AB 1949, 203/23 (on *Dial.* 3, 4f.). Del Monte, GiorStorLettItal 1951, 81/7 (Il ritmo cassinese). Grosjean, AL 1954, 117/26 (on *Dial.* 1, 27, 1–6). De Wit, VC 1955, 45/9 (text. crit.). S. Prete, *I Cronica di Sulp. Sev.,* R 1955 (hist. crit. commentary).

5. In the meantime Augustine had summarized in classic form the events of the history of mankind as they were then known in his work *De civitate Dei* (§ 88, 2) under the one idea of the "State of God" as it had been present in Christian thought from the beginning, of its struggle against the *Civitas terrena* and its final

glorification at the end of time. Augustine distinguishes six periods of the world's history (*C. Faust.* 12, 8).

R. Schmidt, ZKG 67, 1957, 288/317 (periods of history).

6. Paulus Orosius, a priest born at Braga (Northern Portugal), fleeing from the Vandals, presented his *Commonitorium de errore Priscillianistarum et Origenistarum* to St. Augustine at Hippo in 414. Later, during his stay in Palestine (415; visit to Jerome at Bethlehem), he wrote his *Liber apologeticus contra Pelagianos*. In 417–18 he wrote his seven books of *Historiae adversus paganos* in Africa, at the suggestion of Augustine.

These are meant to supplement Augustine's work *De civitate Dei* by proving in detail that the pre-Christian world suffered even more from wars and misery than contemporary mankind, hence that Christianity was innocent of the troubles of the time. With this in mind Orosius gives a summary of the history of the world from Adam to the year A.D. 417. Following Dan. 7, he divides history into four periods, and this division survived till the eighteenth century.

For about the last forty years the work is of independent value, and even though it is written hastily, labouring the above-mentioned points of view and full of rhetorical exaggerations, it is nevertheless a respectable achievement. In the Middle Ages it was much used as a manual of universal history.

Edd.: C. Zangemeister (CSEL 5) 1882 (*Hist.* and *Lib. apol.*), minor ed. of *Hist.* 1889. I.-W. Raymond, NY 1936 (text and Engl. trans.). *Commonit.* ed. G. Schepss (CSEL 18) 1889, 149/57. — Treatises: Amann, DTC 11, 1602/11. J. Svennung, *Orosiana,* 1922. J. A. Davids, *De Orosio et S. Augustino Priscill. adversariis comment. hist. et phil.,* Haag 1930. Schnitzer, Rel 1937, 336/43 (O. and Pelagius). Coffin, CJ 31, 1935/6, 235/48 (Vergil and Or.). E. Karg-Gasterstaedt, *Beitr. Gesch. Dtsch. Spr. u. Lit.* 1940, 263/71 (old High German Or. glosses). H. Hagendahl, *O. u. Justinus,* Goeteborg 1941. Altaner, ZKG 1941, 458 (home of O.: Braga). C. Torres Rodríguez, *Cuad. de Est. Gallegos* 1948, n. 9, 23/48 (life and view of hist.). B. Schryer, *Die althochdeutschen Glossen zu Or.,* thesis Halle 1949. M. Martins, *Correntes da Filosofia relig. em Braga dos 4 a 7,* Porto 1950. S. Prieto, *Paulo Oros. e o Lib. apol.,* thesis Lisbon, Braga 1951. G. Fink, *P. Orose et sa conception de l'hist.*, thesis Aix-en-Provence 1951; id., RevArchBiblMus 1952, 271/322 (Rech. bibliograph. sur Or.). K. A. Schoendorf, *Die Geschichtstheol. des Or.*, thesis Mn 1952. G. Levi della Vida, Al-Andalus 1954, 257/93 (Arab. trans. of *Hist.*). De Carvalho, RevPortFilosof 1955, 11, 142/53 (Augustine dependent on Oros.?). De Castro, CuadEstGallegos 9, 1954, 193/250 *(El hispanismo de Or.)*.

7. Tiro Prosper of Aquitania (§ 89, 4) wrote a chronicle of the world from the creation to A.D. 455. For the time down to 412 it is a superficial excerpt from the chronicle of Jerome and other known historical writings. From this date, however, Prosper gives valuable fresh information based on his own experience (*Hist. E.* 945 f.).

Ed.: Mommsen 1, 341/485.

8. The *Chronicon* of the Spanish Bishop Hydatius (Idacius) continues Jerome's *Chronicle of the World* till 468, being of independent value for the years after 428.

Ed.: Mommsen 2, 13/36. Seeck, PWK 40/3. Courtois, Byz 1951, 23/54.

9. The Illyrian Marcellinus Comes describes in his *Chronicle*, written in Latin in Constantinople, the years 379–534 with almost exclusive regard to East Rome.

Ed.: Mommsen 2, 37/108.

10. The above-mentioned *Chronicle of the World* by Cassiodorus (§ 96, 7) goes as far as 519. The first book of the *History of the Franks* by Gregory of Tours (d. 594) also gives a summary of world history (§ 95, 6).

11. Of the African Bishop Victor of Tunnuna's (d. after 566) *Chronicle of the World*, only the second part (on the years 444–566) has been preserved. Ed. Mommsen 2, 163/206. An equally dry enumeration of unconnected dates is given in the continuations written by Abbot John of Biclaro (d. *c.* 621) for the years 567–90 and by Bishop Marius of Avenches (Lausanne; d. 594) for the years 455–81, beginning at the end of Prosper's chronicle.

Edd.: Mommsen, *Chron. min.* 2, 207/20, 225/39. — Treatises: Lambert, Rev. Zurita 1933, 65/80 (*reg. monast.* John Bicl.); cf. AB 1933, 416. Kirwan, Journ-

EgyptArch 1943, 201/3 *(Garamantes)*; cf. BZ 1935, 222. Morera, AST 1936, 59/84 (Juan Bicl.). De Urbel, *Hispania* 1, 1940, 7/12; 2, 1941, 3/52 (*Regula* John Bicl.). Eltester, PWK 14, 1822f. (Marius). Rubiano, AST 1943, 7/44 (trans. of Chron. of Bicl. and comm.). Arias, *Cuad. hist. Esp.*, 10, 1948, 129/41 (*Chron.* Bicl.).

12. St. Isidore of Seville (§ 98, 3) is the last Latin historian of the patristic period. He wrote a brief *Chronicle of the World (Chronicon)* which extends to 615 (ed. Mommsen 2, 391/488) and an *Historia Gothorum*, a chronicle of the Visigoths till 625 with two short appendices on the Vandals and Suevians. The author, though a Roman, shows great sympathy for the people of the Visigoths.

Ed.: Mommsen 2, 241/303. German by D. Coste, L 1909. Steidle, BM 1936, 425/34 (Visigoths). On *De viris illustribus* supra § 2, 2.

From Eastern chronography we would mention the following works:

13. At the beginning of the fifth century two Alexandrian monks, Panodorus (between 395 and 408) and Anianus (412), wrote chronicles of the world; both are known only through later Byzantine chronicles. An anonymous chronography, the so-called *Excerpta latina Barbari* (supra § 31, 5) was written about the same time, also in Alexandria. It extends to 387 and is preserved only in a Latin translation of the seventh to eighth centuries.

Ed.: Frick, 183/371. Jacoby, PWK 6, 1566/76. Honigmann, AIP 12, 1953, 178/82 (Anianus).

14. Only fragments are extant of the *World History* by Hesychius of Miletus (*c.* 550) and the *Chronicle* of John of Antioch (between 610 and 631).

H. Schultz, PWK 8, 1322/7.

15. John Malalas (i.e. Rhetor or Scholasticus), probably identical with John Scholasticus (d. 577) who was appointed Patriarch of Constantinople in 565, wrote his Χρονογραφία in seventeen books from a Monophysite, later an eighteenth book from an orthodox point of view. The extant text extends only as far as 563 (originally 574). The work, written in popular Greek, ministers to the taste of a

wider public also in its contents. It exercised a far-reaching influence on the annalistic literature both of East and West.

Edd.: L. Dindorf, 1831. MG 97, 9/790. A. Schenk Graf v. Stauffenberg, *Die roem. Kaisergesch. bei Mal.*, 1931 (ed. books 9–12). — Treatises: K. Wolf, PWK 9, 1795/9. M. Weingart, *Byzant. Chroniken i. d. kirchenslav. Lit.*, 1. Teil, Schr. d. philos. Fak. Univ. Pressburg no. 2, 1922. Krappe, RevEA 1933, 146/52. Downey, TP 1935, 55/72 (inscrs. in M.). TP 1937, 141/56 (hist. of Antioch); AmJourArch 1938, 106/60 (Seleucid. era); BZ 1938, 1/15 (buildings). M. Spinka-G. Downey, *Chron. of J. Mal. VIII–XVIII.* Trans. from the Church Slavonic, Ch 1940. Bikerman, Byz 1951, 63/83 *(Les Maccabées de Mal.)*.

16. The *Edessene Chronicle* was written in Syriac shortly after 540 by an orthodox anonymous author who nevertheless sympathizes with Nestorianism. Using material from the archives of his home town, he gives an account of the time from 133–2 B.C. to A.D. 540.

Ed.: I. Giudi (CSCO, 3 p. 4) 1903, and L. Hallier (TU 9, 1) 1893 (with German trans.). Baumstark 1922, 99.

17. The *Chronicle of Arbela,* written by the Syrian Mesihazek [h]a between 540 (or 551) and 569, contains a series of biographies on the lines of the Acts of Martyrs, dating from between 100 and 550. The historicity of the accounts of the earlier periods is open to serious doubt.

Edd.: A. Mingana, *Sources syriaques* L. 1, 1907. E. Sachau, AbhB 1915 n. 6 (trans.). F. Zorell, OC 8, 4, 1927, 142/204 (Lat. trans.). I. Ortiz de Urbina, *Die Gotth. Christi b. Afrahat,* R 1933, 28/30; OCP 1936, 5/32 (hist. value). Messina, Or 6, 1937, 234/44 (The feast *sahr-ab-agan-vad* in Abiadene).

18. The *Chronicle of Pseudo-Dionysius of Tell-Mahre*—perhaps compiled by Joshua Stylites from the Zuqnin monastery near Amida—is a universal history extending to 754–5 and written *c.* 775. The following have been preserved through being included in this compilation: part of the *Edessan Chronicle* (supra n. 16), also an excellent *Monophysite Chronicle* for the years 495–507 and extracts from the second part of the *Hist. E.* of John of Ephesus (supra I 14).

Edd.: J. B. Chabot (CSCO, ser. 3, 1. 2) 1927/33; new imp. 1949 and 1952. Baumstark 1922, 274. Haase 1925, 18f. R. Abramowski, *D. v. Tell., jak. Patr. von 814–45,* 1940. N. Pigulevskaja, *Mesopotamien an der Grenze des 5. u. 6. Jh.* (acc. to Joshua Styl.), Moscow 1940 (Russian).

19. The so-called *Chronicon Paschale,* the Easter chronicle, is a voluminous chronological-historical work on the time from Adam to A.D. 629, written probably in Constantinople in the first half of the seventh century. It is of independent value only for the last decades. It owes its name to Du Cange, because the author is greatly interested in the calculation of the date of Easter.

Edd.: L. Dindorf, 2 vols., 1832. MG 92, 67/1028. Schwartz, PWK 3, 2460/77. Schissel, Byz 9, 1934, 269/95 (MSS). Mercati, OM 2, 1937, 462/79 (MS tradition); 3, 1937, 46/9 (*Hexapla* fragms.).

20. The *World chronicle of the Monophysite B. John of Nikiu* (a city on an island in the Nile) was written probably in Coptic, not in Greek, about 700. It is extant only in an Ethiopic translation and is important for the history of the seventh century.

Edd.: H. Zotenberg, P [2]1935. R. H. Charles, Lo 1916 (trans.). Graf I, 470/2.

§ 50. COLLECTIONS RELATING TO CHURCH HISTORY AND CANON LAW

1. As early as the first three centuries several *Collections of Letters* were circulating which, in view of the dearth of such material, are of special value as historical sources. These were the *corpora* of the letters of Ignatius of Antioch, Dionysius of Corinth, Origen, Cyprian and Dionysius of Alexandria. Later collections of letters are numerous and need no special mention here.

A. Harnack, *Die Briefsammlung des Apostels Paulus und die andern vorkonstantinischen christlichen Briefsammlungen,* 1926.

2. The otherwise unknown *Book of the Documents of the Council of Nicaea* (= Book of the Archbishop Dalmatius of Cyzicus) used by Gelasius of Cyzicus (supra § 49 I 9) is of doubtful authenticity. A

corpus of documents on the history of the same Council which was compiled probably towards the end of the fourth century and is extant only in Coptic, contains mainly spurious material.

J. Lammeyer, *Die sog. Gnomen des Concils v. Nicaea,* Beirut 1912. F. Haase, *Die kopt. Quellen zum Konz. von N.,* 1920. M. a Leonissa, *Rass. Stud. Etiop.* 1942, 3/18 (Ethiopic trans. of the apocr. Canons of the Council of Nic.). Graf I, 586/93. Honigmann, Byz 1939, 17/76; 16, 1942/3, 20/80 (bishops' lists of the Councils of 325, 449, 451). Lebon, Mu 1938, 89/132 (Syn. of Caesarea c. 319). Jubany, AST 1942, 237/56 (can. 10 of Ancyra: celibacy). Richardson, *Church Hist.* 16, 1947, 32/6 (can. 13 of Ancyra). Honigmann, Byz 1950, 63/71 (ined. list of members of Nicaea); ST 173, 1/5 (Syn. of Ancyra 314 and Caesarea in Capp.). — Griffe, BLE 1953, 75/83 (on can. 3 of Arles 314).

3. The Macedonian Bishop Sabinus of Heraclea in Thracia edited a collection of synodal acts and speeches with connecting text (373–8), beginning with the Nicaenum. It was used by Socrates and Sozomen but is now lost.

Batiffol, BZ 1898, 265/84. G. Schoo, *Die Quellen des Kirchenhistor. Sozomenus,* 1911, 95ff.

4. The *Historia acephala* (= *Historia Athanasii*) has been preserved through the collection of Theodosius Diaconus (Cod. Veron. LX). The former contains official documentary material of Alexandria which was collected in 367–8 (Schwartz, GN 1904, 357ff.) or *c.* 385 (Batiffol, BZ 1901, 143).

H. Fromen, *Athanasii hist. acephala,* 1914. Schwartz, ZNTW 1936, 1/23 (Cod. Veron. LX). See also the Athanasian writings *Apologia contra Arianos* (MG 25, 247/410), *Epistola de decretis Nicaenae synodi* (Opitz, AW II 1935) and the *Epistola de synodis* (MG 26, 681/794) which contain a large number of documents. Telfer, HTR 1943, 169/246 (Cod. Veron. LX). De' Cavalieri, AB 54, 1946, 132/75 (excerpt from the Gr. text of *Hist. aceph.*).

5. The so-called *Roman Chronographer of the year 354* is a valuable state directory of varied contents. It was written perhaps *c.* 354 by Dionysius Philocalus, the later calligrapher of Pope Damasus I. Apart from a state calendar (with illustrations), consular fasts, Easter tables, a list of prefects of the city and a description of the fourteen districts of the city, it contains also a chronicle of the world

(supra § 49 II 1), a chronicle of the city of Rome, as well as a list of the anniversaries of the Roman bishops and martyrs (supra § 44) and finally a list of Popes down to Liberius (352–66) with exact statements on the duration of their reigns *(Catalogus Liberianus)*.

Edd.: Mommsen 1, 13/196. Seeck, PWK 3, 2477/81. C. Nordenfalk, *Der Kalender vom Jahre 354 u. d. lat. Buchmalerei des 4. Jh.*, Goeteborg 1936. Leclercq, DAL 9, 527/30 *(Cat. Liber.)*. F. Winkler, JbPreussKunst 1936, 141/55. Ferrua, CC 1939, genn. 7, 35/47; *Epigrammata Damasiana*, R 1942, 21/45 (Filocalus). Bijvanck, Mn 8, 1939/40, 177/98 (calendar of 354 and *Notitia dignit.*). H. Stern, *Le calendrier de 354. Ét. sur son texte et sur les illustrations*, 1953.

6. A *Collection of Documents relating to the Donatist controversy* compiled between 330 and 347 was added by Optatus of Mileve at the end of his anti-Donatist work (§ 82, 13).

Turner, JTS 27, 1925/6, 283/96. G. Roethe, *Z. Gesch. der roem. Synoden des 3. u. 4. Jh.*, 1937, 118/23 (against Duchesne).

7. *Breviculus collationis cum Donatistis* is an extract from the acts of the religious discussion held at Carthage in 411 produced by Augustine (EP 1714).

ML 43, 631/50 (v. § 88, 2).

8. *De gestis Pelagii,* a documentary account of St. Augustine on the beginnings of the Pelagian controversy, dating from the year 417 (ML 44, 319/60; CSEL 42, 49/122).

9. *Collectio Avellana,* a collection of 243 letters of popes and emperors dating from 367 to 553, among them many from Hormisdas (514–23), so called after a MS formerly belonging to the Umbrian monastery S. Croce di Fonte Avellana (now Vat. lat. 4616). It was compiled in Rome in the second half of the sixth century, probably only for private purposes.

Edd.: O. Guenther (CSEL 35) 1895/8. W. M. Peitz, *Das Register Gregors I,* 1917, 110ff. Schwartz, AbhMn N. F. 10, 1934, 280/7.

10. The *Synodal Canons,* laws enacted at various synods of the Greek East since the beginning of the fourth century, were collected in a code before 378, probably at Antioch, to which

several pieces were added before 400. The Council of Chalcedon (451) had before it this collection with a continuous enumeration of the canons. The no longer extant Greek *Corpus canonum* can be reconstructed on the basis of a Syriac translation made in 500–1 containing 193 synodal canons, and the Latin translation which is extant in the so-called *Collectio Isidoriana* of the older recension (*Cod. Monacensis* 6243 and *Cod. Wuerzburg*. Mp. theol. fol. 146). The oldest Greek collection preserved in direct tradition is the Συναγωγὴ κανόνων of John Scholasticus which was compiled *c.* 550 (v. supra § 49 II n. 15). This comprises the canons systematically arranged under fifty titles, to which is added as an appendix a *Collectio 87 capitulorum* from Justinian's *Novellae* (MG 104).

F. Schulthess, *Die syrischen Kanones der Synoden von Nizaea bis Chalcedon,* GAG 10, 2, 1908. V. N. Benesevic, *Ioannis Schol. Synagoga 50 titulorum . . .,* Mn 1937. E. Schwartz, SbMn 1933, 3 (Jo. Schol.); ZSK 1936, 1/43.

11. In Rome the Latin translation of the Nicene Canons was combined with the original Latin canons of Sardica to form an inseparable whole perhaps as early as the reign of Julius I (337–52). Thus the oldest Latin collection of canons came into being. The first larger Latin collection was produced shortly before 430 either in Rome (Turner, formerly also Schwartz) or in N. Africa (so now Schwartz); it comprised all the canons that had been united in the Greek Corpus (till 381) in Latin translation, to which original Latin documents were added (Acts on the quarrel on jurisdiction between Rome and N. Africa 419).

Schwartz, ZSK 1936, 48/83. Leclercq, DAL 9, 159/78 *(Lib. can. African. eccl.).* Hess, *The can. of Sardica,* O 1958.

12. The *Prisca canonum editio latina* (ed. Voel-Justellus, 1661; the second recension in ML 56, 747/816) was produced in Rome, probably under Gelasius I (492–6). About 500 a canonist from Southern Gaul or Rome compiled the *Collectio Quesnelliana* (ML 56, 359/746), so called after its first editor P. Quesnel (d. 1719).

Cf. Schwartz, ZSK 1936, 96/108 (Prisca).

13. The collection of Dionysius Exiguus, compiled in Rome *c.* 500, is of the greatest importance for the legal development of the West. It is extant in two recensions, a third being lost, and contains also the first fifty *Apostol. Canones* (§ 7 n. 5). The collection of papal letters (*Decretalia*) from Siricius (384–99) to Anastasius II (496–8) is an appendix or the second volume of this work.

ML 67, 139/316 (2nd ed.). The 1st ed. by A. Strewe, B 1931. Numerous extracts also in C. H. Turner, *Ecclesiae occid. Monumenta iuris antiq. Canones et conciliorum graec. Interpretationes latinae,* 2 vols., 1899/1930. Schwartz, ZSK 1936, 108/14. H. Wurm, *Stud. u. Texte z. Dekretalensammlg. des D. Ex.,* 1939; id. in *Apollinaris* 12, 1939, 40/93 (ed. 2 decretals).

14. The *Collectio Isidoriana (Hispana)* stands out from among the large number of later collections; it gives special attention to Spanish synods. It originated about 666, not in the south of France (Arles) but probably in Spain (ML 84, 25/846).

P. Séjourné, *Le dernier Père de l'Église, S. Isidore de Séville,* 1929. E. Anspach, *Taionis et Isidori nova fragmenta et opera,* Ma 1930, 108/17 and A. Ariño Alafont, *Coll. canon. hispana,* Avila 1942; cf. RHE 1943, 250f. consider Isidore to be the chief collaborator of the *Coll. Hisp.;* against this Le Bras, RevSR 1930, 230/42, and J. Tarré, Mél. P. Fournier 1929, 705/24; cf. EE 1936, 119/36. — de Lamadrid, EE 1943, 183/200 ("equidad" en los concilios de Toledo). Botte, RTA 1939, 222/41 (Ordination dans les *Statuta eccles. ant.*). Alafont, RevEspDerechoCan 1, 1946, 195/201 (prolegomena for ed. of *Coll. Hisp.*); AnalUnivMurcia 1948/9, 380/453 (Cod. 15/17 Toled. for *Coll. Hisp.*).

15. Information on many other Latin collections of Canon Law is contained in the following:

P. et G. Ballerini, ML 1956, 11/354 *(De antiquis collectionibus et collectoribus canonum).* F. Maassen, *Gesch. der Quellen u. d. Literatur des kanon. Rechts im Abendlande* I, 1870, and P. Fournier et G. Le Bras, *Hist. des collections can. en Occident,* 2 vols., 1931/2. Lietzmann, PWK 11, 488/501. Leclercq, DAL 9, 85/178. Schwartz, ZSK 1936, 1/114. H. Wurm, *Stud. . . .,* 1939 (supra n. 13). — Edd.: J. B. F. Pietra, *Iur. eccles. Graecorum historia et monumenta,* 1864ff. H. T. Bruns, *Canones Apostolorum et conciliorum,* 2 vols., 1839. — F. Lauchert, *Die Kanones der wichtigsten altkirchl. Konzilien,* 1896. Turner (supra n. 13). F. Schulthess, *Die syr. Kanones der Synoden von Nizaea bis Chalcedon,* GAG 10, 2, 1908. E. J. Junkers, *Acta et Symbola conciliorum quae saec. IV habita sunt,* Ley 1954. Further items n. 16.

16. Nearly all editions of *Acts of Early Christian Councils* print the individual collections only exceptionally in their original form;

generally the documents, taken out of the order in which they appeared in the MSS, are co-ordinated in a sequence which makes the historical development as clear as possible and thus reproduced in print.

Edd.: 4 vols., R 1608/12. P. Labbe et G. Cossart, 17 vols., 1674. S. Baluzius, *Nova Coll. Conciliorum,* P 1683. N. Coleti, 23 vols., 1728/34. J. Hardouin, 12 vols., 1715. J. D. Mansi, 31 vols., 1757/98; new impression and cont. by L. Petit and J. B. Martin in 53 vols., 1901/27.

A new line is followed only in the *Acta Conciliorum oecumenicorum,* edited by E. Schwartz since 1914, which affords a clear view of the contents, volume, history and tendency of the individual collections of Acts.

17. The first council of which the actual Acts are extant is the Synod of Ephesus (431). The Acts of this Council are preserved in the following collections: Apart from two minor collections, original Greek texts are contained in: 1. the *Collectio Vaticana* (cod. 830) with 172 pieces (SACO I, vol. 1, pars 1–6), 2. *Collectio Segueriana* with 146 pieces; all contained in the *Coll. Vat.,* 3. *Collectio Atheniensis* with 177 pieces; of these, fifty-eight pieces are missing in the other two collections (SACO I, vol. 1, pars 7). The original form preceding these collections was compiled by a follower of Cyril and later (7th cent.) enlarged and altered in various ways. Vat. Nos. 140–64 is for the most part taken from the *Collection of Comes Irenaeus* (d. *c.* 450 as archbishop of Tyre; DTC 7, 2533/6) which was favourable to Nestorius.

All the collections preserved in Latin translations apparently originated in the sixth century in connexion with the Three Chapters Controversy (Council of 553). The largest and most important of these is the *Collectio Casinensis* (1st part: SACO I, vol. 3; 2nd part: ibid. vol. 4). The documents united here were collected and translated by the Roman deacon Rusticus at Constantinople in 564–5, in order to prove that the Three Chapters had been wrongly condemned in 553. His principal source was the *Tragedy of Irenaeus,* which contained many Acts; 216 out of 236 pieces were taken from this. The first part of this collection mainly reproduces a Latin translation of Ephesine Acts that had been made shortly before at Constantinople (= *Coll. Turonensis*).

The compiler of the *Collectio Veronensis* (SACO I, vol. 2) is probably to be sought in Rome. He emphasizes the influence of the Pope by making more extensive use of the letters of Celestine I. — The *Collectio Palatina* (Vat. Pal. 234; SACO I, vol. 5, pars 1) containing the writings of Marius Mercator and many other documents (e.g. writings of Cyril, excerpts from Diodore, Theodore, Theodoret) is perhaps the work of a Scythian monk of "neo-Chalcedonian" tendencies in Constantinople or Thracia, written probably only after 553. See Amann, RevSR 1949, 8/17. Bark, HTR 1943, 93/107 identifies the collator of the *Palatina* with John Maxentius and Bishop John of Tomi; against this Altaner, TQ 1947, 152f. and Amann l. c. R. Devreesse, *Essai sur Théod. de Mopsueste,* 1948, 162, 195 n. 7. The *Collectio Sichardiana* (after 553; SACO I, vol. 5, 245/318) is not very large; neither is the *Collectio Winteriana* (ibid. 341/81) which cannot be dated with certainty.

I. Rucker, *Ephes. Konzilsakten in armen.-georg. Ueberl.* (SbMn 1930, 3) 1930; *Ephes. Konzilsakten in lat. Ueberl.,* Selbstverlag, Oxenbronn 1931; *Ephes. Konzilsakten in syr. Ueberl.,* 1935. E. Gerland et V. Laurent, *Les listes conciliaires: Constant. 394 and Ephes. 431* (*Corp. notitiarum episc. Eccl. Orient. graecae* I), 1936. On the hist. and DH of the Ephesinum: AST 7, 1931, 3/55 (Quera, Hist. of the Council); 57/9 (Segarra, Pope and Council); 81/93 (Puig de la Bellacasa, Humanity of Christ without personality); 139/69 (Bover, Mother of God); 215/33 (Vives, Cod. Barcinon; supplements *Coll. Veron.*). Neyeut, DTP 1931, 531/40 (Pelagianism). Disdier, EO 1931, 314/33 (Pelagianism). StC 7, 1931, 369/98 (Franses, Cyril); 399/419 (Féron, Nestorius); 420/45 (Cremers, The dogma of E.); 446/56 (Smits, Pelagianism). Jugie, EO 1931, 257/70 (decree on the formula of faith). Gerland, EO 1931, 334/8 (number of Fathers of Council). Lebon, ETL 1931, 393/412 (definition of faith). A. d'Alès, *Le dogme d'Ephèse,* 1931. Madoz, RF 1932, 168/78 (Creed). On papal primacy and council: Grumel, EO 1931, 293/313; Galtier, RSR 1931, 186/99, 269/98; Segarra, RSR 1932, 477f. (on SACO I, vol. 3, p. 58). M. de Mieres, *Est. franciscans* 1932, 257/320; C. Papadopulos, At 1932 and Lo 1933; against this Stephanou, EO 1933, 57/78, 203/17. Diamantopulos, Θ 9/11, 1931/3. Phokylides, NS 1933/4. Papadopulos, Θ 1932, 267/82 (Lit. trans.). G. del Monte, *Il concilio di Efeso,* Parma 1932. J. Flemming - G. Hofmann. *Akten der ephes. Synode vom Jahre 449* (Syr. and German): GAb N. S. 15, 1917,

Paciorkowski, *Prymat papieza na soboru efeskiego,* War 1931. Further lit. (§§ 56 72, 1). Schwartz, Phil 1933, 245/53 (Acts of Councils bilingual). Spanish works in Madoz, RET 1941, 927. Salaverri, EE 1945, 381/6 (alleged sentence of Council). O. de Urbina, REB 11, 1953, 233/40 (Il dogma di Efeso). Diepen, RT 1955, 300/88 (the 12 anathematisms of the Counc. of Eph. to 519).

18. Acts of the Council of Chalcedon (451). The following are extant in the Greek original: a. *Three collections of letters* which complement each other, compiled *c.* 451, the first two of which may be regarded as the preliminary Acts of the Council (SACO II, vol. 1, pars 1–2). The first collection was made in the interest of Patriarch Anatolius of Constantinople. The Greek translation of the *Tomus Leonis* (*Ep.* 28) belongs to the second collection. b. The *Accounts of the seventeen sessions of the Council (Actiones)* with 14 further documents contained in an appendix (SACO II, vol. 1, pars 1–3), which were all published soon after the Council.

The following are extant in Latin translation or as original Latin Acts: a. The *Collectio Novariensis de re Eutychis* which contains twelve documents published in 450 perhaps at the suggestion of Leo the Gr. (SACO II, vol. 2, pars 1; here and n. 5 the crit. ed. of the Tome of Leo); cf. RBnBull II, n. 596; BZ 1935, 421/3. b. The *Collectio Vaticana* (received its final form in Rome under Hormisdas [514–23]), *Canones et symbolum* (SACO II, vol. 2, pars 2). c. The Latin translation of the above-mentioned three collections of letters and of the accounts of the seventeen sessions of the Council which is preserved in three different recensions dating from the time of the Three Chapters controversy; the most important is the translation of the Deacon Rusticus (supra n. 17; SACO II, vol. 3, pars 1–3). d. *Leonis papae I epistularum collectiones* (15 in all) contain 114 letters which belong here; they go back partly to a collection produced by Leo himself in 458. The *Collectio Grimanica* (made *c.* 553) contains 104 items. e. *Codex encyclicus. Collectiones epistularum et libellorum de schismate Acaciano* (*Collectio Sangermanensis;* SACO II, vol. 5); the second part of the collection contains the *Breviarium* of Liberatus (§ 97, 6).

19. *Collectio Sabbaitica contra Acephalos et Origenistas destinata;* to this belong also the Acts of the Synods of Constantinople (536) and Jerusalem (536) (SACO III).

Schwartz, AC, vol. 6: *Prosopographia et topographia actorum Chalced. et encyclicorum.* Indices, 1938.

Treatises: Hatch, HTR 1926, 377/81 (fragm. of a Vita of Dioscurus). E. Schwartz, *Der Prozess des Eutyches* (SbMn 1929, 7), 1929; on this Draguet, Byz 6, 1931, 441/57. I. Rucker, *Florilegium Edessenum anonymum* (syriace ante 562; SbMn 1933, 5) 1933. E. Schwartz, *Publizist. Samml. zum acacian. Schisma,* 1934. A. Steinwenter, Μνημόσυνα Παπποῦλια 1934, 245/51 (Acts of Councils as source of profane law). Papadopulos, Θ 1934, 193/217 (Flavian to Leo I). Segarra, EE 1936, 407/13 (on SACO II 1, pars 2, 61, ll. 20/4: primacy). E. Schwartz, AbhMn 1937, 1 (lists of bishops); cf. Honigmann, Byz 1936, 429/49; 1937, 323/47. Diamantopulos, Θ 1936/9 (Hist. of Council). T. Schnitzler, *Im Kampf um Chalcedon* (Cod. encycl.), R 1938. Bittermann, Sp 1938, 198/203 (can. 4 of Chalc.). Mouterde, Mél. de l'Univ. S. Joseph, Beyrouth 15, 1930/1, 35/50 (Fragm. Syn. of Const. 450). Laurent, *Bull.Sect.hist.Acad.Roumaine,* 25, 1944, 152/73 (African bishops at the Counc. of Chalc.); ibid. 26, 1945, 33/46 (number of Fathers of Council). Du Manoir, NRT 1951, 785/803 *(15e centen. du Conc.);* Ant 1951, 291/304 (Leo the Gr. and the dogmat. defin. of Counc.). F. X. Murphy, TSW 1951, 505/19 (dogmat. defin.); AmerEcclRev 125, 1951, 241/54 (Chalcedon, October 451); *Peter speaks through Leo. The Council of Chalc.,* W 1952. Camelot, RSPT 1951, 505/19 (Gr. and Lat. theology at Chalc.). Brinktrine, TG 1951, 449/56 (Papal primacy). Wuyts, OCP 1951, 265/82 (can. 28). Steidle, BM 1951, 471/9 (Chalc. and monasticism). Monachino, Gr 1952, 261/91 (can. 28); Gr 1952, 321/65 (can. 28 and Leo the Gr.). Petru, Ang 1952, 130/4 (can. 14). Walz, Ang 1952, 110/29 (Pope and Emperor at Chalc.). Oliver, Regnum Dei 8, 1952, 89/109; 163/76 *(Las actas del Conc.).* McArthur, CQR 1952, 201/9 (the Papacy at Chalc.). R. V. Sellers, *The Council of Chalc.,* 1953 (SPCK). H. M. Diepen, *Les trois Chapitres au Conc. de Chalc.,* Oosterhout 1953; cf. Richard, MSR 1954, 89/92 and Moeller, RHE 1954, 907/10. Diepen, RT 1953, 573/608 (L'*assumptus homo* à Chalc.). Crosignani, DTP 1953, 99/149 (jubilee contribution). Chadwick, JTS 1955, 17/34 (exile and death of Flavian of Constant.).

A. Grillmeier-H. Bacht, ed. *Das Konzil von Chalkedon. Geschichte u. Gegenwart,* 3 vols., 1952/4 (important for the hist. and theol. of the Council down to present times). The first vol. contains fifteen contributions on eccl. and dogmatic hist. important for the theology before and after the Council down to the 6th cent. Vol. 2 contains twenty-one treatises dealing with the Church-polit. struggles and the effects on the inner life of the Church (monasticism, liturgy), the doctrines of the anti-Chalced. denominations and Western theology down to 13th cent. Scholasticism. The seventeen contributions of the third vol. treat of the Chalcedon. motif in the Cath. theology of the 19th and 20th cents. and in the contemporary discussions between the denominations and religions. Ibid. Grillmeier 2, 765/9 (hist. of Lat. trans. of Acts of Counc.); ibid. Schoenmetzer, 3, 826/65 (a valuable bibliography).

20. Acts on the History of the Council of Constantinople 553. *Johannis Maxentii libelli. Collectio cod. Novariensis* 30. *Coll. cod. Parisini* 1682. *Procli tomus ad Armenos. Iohannis papae II ep. ad viros ill.* (SACO IV, vol. 2).

21. State Collections of Laws which are frequently concerned with ecclesiastical matters: a. The *Codex Theodosianus*, publ. by the Emperor Theodosius II in 438, was accepted also by the West Roman Emperor Valentinian III; it contains the laws of Constantine the Gr. and his successors down to 438 (EH 820/42).

Edd.: T. Mommsen and P. M. Meyer, 2 vols., 1905; [2]1954. P. Krueger 1923/6. O. Gradenwitz, *Heidelberger Index zum Theodosianus,* suppl. vol., 1929. C. Pharr, *The Theodosian Cod.:* Trans. with Comment., Glossary and Bibliography, Princeton 1952. J. Vogt, *Festschr. f. Wenger*, 2, 1945, 118/48 (Christian infl. on the legislation of Constantine). Martin, AmerEcclRev 123, 117/36 (Theodosius' laws on heretics). Ensslin, SbMn 1953, 2 (religious policy of Theodosius the Gr.).

b. The *Codex Justinianus* was published as a legal code by the Emperor Justinian I in 534; it also comprises the time of the emperors before Constantine and extends to 534 (EH 1011/36).

Edd.: *Corpus iuris civilis* ed. P. Krueger [15]1928. M. Roberti, E. Bussi e G. Vismara, *Cristianesimo e diritto romano,* Mi 1935. B. Biondi, *Giustiniano I principe e legislatore cattolico,* Mi 1936. Leclercq, DAL 9, 2229/73 *(Lois Romaines)*. C. Hohenlohe, *Einfluss des Christentums auf das Corpus iuris civilis,* W 1937. G. Vismara, *Episcopalis audientia,* Mi 1937; against this Bucek, ZSK 1939, 453/92 and Masi, Arch. Giurid. 112, 1939, F. 1/2. Against Hohenlohe cf. Leifer, ZSR 1938, 185/201. Ensslin, ZSR 1937, 367/78 (Novellae 17 and 18). V. Bandini, *Etica e diritto nel mondo lat.,* Parma 1937. J. E. Jonkers, *Invloed v. h. Christend. op de rom. wetgeving betreff het concubinat en de echtscheiding,* A 1938. Castello, *Rend. R. Ist. Lomb.* 71, 1938, 201/21 *(diritto matrimon.)*. Roberti, Stud. . . . in on di E. Besta 3, 1939, 37/82 *(corpus myst. nella stor. della persona giurid.)*. Several contributions dealing with the relation betw. eccl. and Rom. law in the *Atti del Congresso Internaz. di Diritto Rom. I e II* 1934/35. Further lit. cf. § 3 n. 20 and n. 28.

PART TWO

THE PEAK PERIOD OF PATRISTIC LITERATURE

FROM THE COUNCIL OF NICAEA 325

TO THE COUNCIL OF CHALCEDON 451

§ 51. GENERAL CHARACTERISTICS

THE victory of Christianity over the pagan Roman Empire made evident by the edict of toleration (313) issued at Milan, soon produced favourable conditions for the flowering of Church literature and scholarship. We enter the period of the great Fathers of the Church.

Having first been tolerated, Christianity soon came to be openly favoured under Constantine and finally to be the only recognized religion, a development brought about by a series of legislative measures of the Emperors Constantius, Gratian and Theodosius I. The attempts of Licinius (324) and Julian (d. 363) to restore paganism were shortlived. From the time of Constantine the emperors exercised a protectorate over the Imperial Church thus established; this, however, actually meant the foundation of a State Church (Caesaropapism).

Being free from external pressure, the Church could now develop and spread its ideas and powers for the good of the world, especially by reforming the laws and caring for the poor and suffering. Moreover, magnificent churches were being built and the liturgy was celebrated with far greater solemnity; missionary enterprises were carried on also in countries outside the Roman Empire.

But the mass conversions, especially the admission of religiously indifferent elements to the privileged Church, resulted also in the relaxation of discipline and the decline of the religious life. The desire to work out the contents of the faith more clearly called forth violent controversies which were considerably embittered and drawn out when the state interfered in the inner concerns of the Church.

Church scholarship and literary production were greatly stimulated by the new freedom and the many theological controversies. Eminent exponents of contemporary learning appeared in many places which had till then remained unknown, in order to make their contribution to the most burning theological problems. Since they had mostly attended the rhetorical schools, they were not only capable of expressing themselves fluently and of utilizing the literary forms sometimes in masterly fashion, but they also had at their disposal a sound knowledge of antique literature, history and philosophy. They were at pains to give the traditional faith a Biblical foundation as well as a speculative basis, and thus became its champions against the manifold forms of heresy. Both the Emperor and the Church utilized at this time the hitherto unknown instrument of general councils in order to save the endangered unity of the Church; from then onwards their decisions became the unshakeable foundation of later theology.

The most varied literary forms were eagerly cultivated. The views of pagan and other opponents (Porphyry, Julian, Manicheism) were discussed in apologetical works. New problems had been raised by Arianism, Macedonianism, Apollinarianism, Nestorianism and Monophysitism in the East, by Donatism, Pelagianism and Semi-Pelagianism in the West, for which solutions were sought in dogmatic-polemical treatises. Many later historians took as their unattained example the writing of Church history that had begun with Eusebius, which spurred them on to new research. Apart from works on Church history and chronicles this period abounds in biographies, almost exclusively devoted to eminent monks (v. §§ 47/51). The growing epistolary literature is an important source for our knowledge of great personalities; its products, which were mostly destined for publication, followed exactly the rules of this literary form. Poetry, too, began once more to flourish especially within the

Latin civilization. The homiletic literature of this period is especially rich and important; this too, bears witness to the fact that the greatest preachers of that time usually knew how to apply the rules of the old rhetoric also to the spoken word.

Scripture was studied particularly at that time; and the effects of this study on the history of doctrine and theology went deeper than any other influence. The two exegetical schools of Alexandria and Antioch, whose fundamental characteristics have already been discussed (§ 38), became the principal sources that nourished contemporary theological tensions and controversies. The *Catechetical School of Alexandria* which had its greatest time under Origen experienced a second spring in the fourth century. Its principal exponents at that time were Eusebius of Caesarea, Athanasius, the three Cappadocians, Didymus the Blind, Cyril of Alexandria and Hesychius of Jerusalem. However, under the influence of the Antiochene Exegetical School the later Alexandrians differed from their predecessors in that they used the allegorical exegesis of Scripture almost exclusively for purposes of edification, whereas in their scholarly and polemical discussions they preferred the historical and grammatical sense (Neo-Alexandrian School).

The Antiochene Exegetical School which was particularly active during this time entered on its greatest period with Diodore of Tarsus. His disciples were Meletius of Antioch, John Chrysostom and Theodore of Mopsuestia. Nestorius and Theodoret of Cyrus also belong to this theological school. A one-sided use of the historico-grammatical method led some of its representatives into errors that are partly to be explained by a rationalistic attitude (the desire to rid Christian doctrine as far as possible from all elements of mystery): into Arianism, Macedonianism, Apollinarianism, Pelagianism and Nestorianism; whereas the pseudo-mystical heresies of Monophysitism and Monotheletism were fostered in a sense by the allegorical exegesis of the Alexandrians.

The national Syrian School of Edessa in Mesopotamia flourished in the fourth century; its greatest master was Ephrem Syrus. The Nestorian School of Nisibis, founded by Bishop Barsumas (450–95) produced its first famous teacher in Narses (§ 77).

T. Hermann, ZNTW 1926, 89/122 (Nisibis). E. R. Hayes, *L'école d'Édesse,* 1930. D'Alès, RSR 1931, 257/68 and supra § 38.

The earliest representatives of monasticism opposed the reconciliation and integration of the Christianized world with Western culture, and this reaction can readily be understood. Yet, despite this opposition, the influence and example of eminent bishops soon produced an attitude more favourable to literature and learning. Gradually the hermits and monks themselves joined the ranks of the early Christian writers not only as authors of monastic rules, letters, sermons, ascetical treatises and spiritual and hagiographical writings, but also of learned theological and historical works. Many monasteries became nurseries of theology, and many a Church Father received there not only his ascetical formation but also encouragement and help in his scholarly studies.

C. de Montalembert, *Précis d'hist. monastique,* nouv. éd. 1934. S. Schiwietz, *Das morgenlaendische Moenchtum,* 3 vols., 1904/38. M. Heimbucher, *Die Orden u. Kongregationen der kath. Kirche* 1, ^{3}1932. P. Pourrat, *La spiritualité chrét.,* 1, ^{9}1926. U. Berlière, *L'ordre monastique des origines au 12e s.,* ^{3}1924. Leclercq, DAL 2, 3047/248 *(Cénobitisme)*; 11, 1774/947 *(Monachisme)*. A. L. Schmitz, RQ 1929, 189/243 (The world [topogr.] of the hermits). H. G. E. White, *The Monasteries of the Wadi 'nNatrûn,* 3 vols., NY 1926/33. P. Resch, *La doctrine ascét. des premiers maîtres égypt. du 4e s.,* 1931. H. Koch, *Quellen zur Gesch. der Askese u. des Moenchtums i. d. alten Kirche,* 1933. F. Kozman, *Textes législatifs touchant le cénobitisme égypt.,* R 1935. K. Heussi, *Der Ursprung des Moenchtums,* 1936. Barison, Aeg 1938, 29/148 *(monasterii dell'Egitto bizant. ed. arabo)*. Bardy, Mél. De Ghellinck 1951, 293/309 (monastic schools in the East). Cf. supra § 46.

CHAPTER ONE

EASTERN AUTHORS

A. Alexandrians and Egyptians

§ 52. EGYPTIAN MONKS

1. ANTHONY (d. 356 aged 105) lived in the last years of his life near the Red Sea on Mount Kolzim, at the foot of which a considerable colony of hermits took up their abode. He was a man without education, but full of religious and ascetical wisdom. He wrote or dictated his letters in Coptic, which were then translated into Greek. According to the researches of F. Klejna the seven letters (MG 40, 972/1000) mentioned already by Jerome (*Vir. ill.* 88), which are preserved complete only in a Latin translation, may probably be considered genuine. They bear witness to the sound, sturdy asceticism of its author, which does not yet show mystical traits. The first letter gives introductory instructions for novices who would become monks. A second collection of twenty letters (including the seven letters) is extant in a more recent Latin translation from the Arabic (MG 40, 999/1066); it contains no further genuine items. A short Letter *On Proper Repentance* (MG 40, 1065) addressed to Abbot Theodore and his monks may be considered as certainly authentic. The twenty *Sermones ad filios suos* (ibid. 40, 961/78)and the so-called *Rule of St. Anthony* (ibid. 1065/74) as well as other works are apocryphal.

Ammonas, his disciple, and successor as superior of the colony of monks at Pispir, has left letters, seven of which are extant in a Greek version (PO 11, 1916, 432/54 ed. F. Nau) and 15 in the better and more complete Syriac tradition; letter 15 is spurious (Klejna) (PO 10, 1915, 555/639 ed. M. Kmosko). Here we meet a form of mysticism, clearly distinguished from the later one of Evagrius, in which the idea of the "soul's journey to heaven" plays an important part.

G. Garitte, *Georg. text of the Letters and Copt. fragms.* (CSCO 148 149) 1955; on this Mu 1951, 267/78. — David, DHG 3, 726/34. Bardy, DS I, 702/8. L. v. Hertling, *A. der Einsiedler,* 1929. D. Brooke, *Pilgrims Were They All,* Lo 1937 (ch. 1). Klejna, ZKT 1938, 309/48 (Letters of Ant. and Ammonas). Garitte, Mu 1939, 11/31 and Hertling 1929, 58/65 defend the authenticity of both collections of Anthony's Letters. Garitte, BBR 1939, 165/70 (edits an unknown Gr. fragm. of a letter); Mu 1942, 97/123 (ed. apocr. Gr. letter); Kraus, *Festschr. z. 50jaehr. Bestandsjubilaeum d. Missionshauses St. Gabriel,* 1939, 117/34 (The Holy Spirit in the Letters). Bardy, *Mémorial Lagrange,* 1940, 203/16 (beginnings of Copt. Christianity). K. Heussi, *Ursprung des Moenchtums,* 1936, 78/108. Graf I, 456/9. Garitte, OCP 1943, 100/31, 330/65 (ed. Copt. panegyric on Ant. by John of Hermopolis). I. Hausherr, OC 30, 3, 1933 (on a spurious work). L. Bouyer, *La vie de S. Ant.,* S.-Wandrille 1950. H. Queffébe, *S. Ant. du désert,* 1950. Baynes, JournEgypt-Archeol 1954, 7/10 (A. and the demons). On the *Vita S. Antonii* by St. Athanasius v. § 54 n. 18. Garitte, BBR 22, 1942/43, 5/29 (on Gr. text of *Vita Antonii*). B. Steidle, *Ant. Magnus Eremita,* ed. by StAns 38, 1956 (14 contributions).

2. Pachomius, the founder of cenobitic monasticism, established a monastery at Tabennisi in the Thebaid *c.* 320, followed later by eight religious houses for men and two for women, which he directed as abbot general. He wrote the first monastic rule in Coptic (d. 346). It is extant in full only in the Latin translation Jerome made from the Greek in 404; there are also fairly large fragments of the Coptic and Greek texts. The Rule has an appendix containing sayings and exhortations of the saint to his brethren as well as eleven letters, two of which are in a secret language. Pachomius created a type of monastic life to which belonged the future, and gave it a solid economic foundation from the beginning. Directly or indirectly the Rule of Pachomius has influenced the Rules of Basil, Cassian, Caesarius of Arles and Benedict of Nursia.

Edd.: ML 23, 61/88. P. B. Albers (FP 16) 1923. Best ed. A. Boon, *Pachomiana latina,* Lou 1932 (Copt. and Gr. fragms. ed. L. T. Lefort). Lefort, Mu 1935, 76/80; 1941, 111/38 (new Copt. fragms.). The longer recension of the Rule is the original.

Several biographies extant in diverse languages give accounts of P.'s life; their mutual relationship has not yet been completely clarified. — Edd.: F. Halkin, *S. Pachomii vitae graecae,* Bru 1932; AB 1930, 257/301. Copt. texts: L. T. Lefort (CSCO, SS copt. 7/8) 1925/34 and Lou 1936 (trans.). Lefort, *Vita S. Pachom. bohairice scripta* (CSCO 89 107), 1953; *Vitae s. Pachom. sahidice scriptae* (CSCO 99 100), 1952 (new impress.). Cf. Mu 1931, 115/35; 1936, 219/30 and AB 1934, 286/320. Lefort, Mu 1933, 1/33 (P. depends on Athanas.). German by H. Mertel (BKV² 31) 1917. Lefort, Mu 1939, 379/408 (topography of monasteries). Id., *Les vies coptes de S. P. et ses premiers successeurs* (French trans.), Lou 1943 (The Copt. Vitae are the original ones); on this Peeters, AB 1946, 258/77; Mu 1946, 17/34; 41/62; 1947, 269/83; 1946, 399/412 (fragms. of an Arab. *Vita*). Graf I, 459/61. Chitty, JEH 5, 1954, 38/77 (Gr. *vita prima* the most important); against this Lefort, Mu 1954, 217/29 (for Copt. sources). — Treatises: O. Gruetzmacher, *P. u. das aelteste Klosterleben.* 1896. P. Ladeuze, *Ét. sur le cénobitisme pakhômien,* 1898. Cf. supra § 51 and Leclercq, DAL 13, 499/510. Heussi 1936, 115/31. Loefgren, KyrkHistArsskr 48, 1948, 163/84 (Ethiop. trans. of Rule). Gnolfo, Salesianum 1948, 569/96 (pedagogies of Rule). H. Bacht, ZKT 1950, 350/9; RAM 1950, 308/26 (infl. of Rule). Id., *Vom gemeinsamen Leben. Die Bedeutung des pachomian. Moenchsideals ...: Moenchtum in der Entscheidung,* 1925, 91/110. K. Lehmann, ZSK 1951, 1/94 (imprisonment in the Pach.-monasteries). De Clercq, *Mél. L. Halphen,* 1951, 169/76 (infl. of the Rule in the West). Bacht, *Geist u. Leben,* 1955, 360/73 (*Meditatio i. d. aeltesten Moenchsquellen, bes. b. Pachomius);* StAns 1956, 66/107 (Anthony and Pachomius. From hermits to cenobites). Lefort, CSCO 159/60, 1956 (*Oeuvres de S. Pachôme et de ses disciples* [Theodore, Orsisius Carour]).

3. Of *Orsisius* (d. *c.* 380), the second successor of Pachomius, we possess *Doctrina de institutione monachorum* in the translation of Jerome (PL 103, 453/76 = PG 40, 869/94; also in Albers and Boon [v. supra]). A letter on the feast of Easter by his deputy Theodore (d. 368) has been preserved by Jerome (ML 23, 99 f. and in Boon). A dialogue with two Alexandrian deacons extant in Coptic in W. E. Crum, *Der Papyruscodex saec. 6/7 der Philippsbibliothek in Cheltenham,* 1915, 59 ff., 132 ff.; cf. W. Hengstenberg, *Festschr. f. A. Ehrhard* 1922, 228/52.

4. Macarius of Egypt (d. *c.* 390) also called the Elder or the Great, lived for sixty years in the desert of Scete. Neither Palladius, *Hist. Laus.* 17, nor Rufinus, *Hist. monach.* 28, mention his literary activity. On the grounds of later MS evidence he is credited with *apophthegmata,* eight letters (Syr., n. 1 also Latin), two short prayers and several collections of homilies. A collection of fifty Ὁμιλίαι

πνευματικαί (spiritual homilies) was printed under his name as early as 1559. Two MSS of this collection contain seven others in an appendix, which were edited only in 1918. But not even the first letter *Ad filios Dei,* extant in Latin and Syriac, can be regarded as genuine (MG 34, 406/10; Lat. now ed. Wilmart, RAM 1, 1920, 58ff.; the Gr. text now in W. Jaeger). The long second letter (MG 34, 409/41) has been established to be a compilation from a work of Gregory of Nyssa, *De instituto christiano* (§ 60) first ed. by W. Jaeger, and the homily 40 of the so-called Macarius. (W. Jaeger, *Two rediscovered Works of Ancient Christian Lit.: Greg. of Nyssa, De instituto christiano, and Macarius,* 'Επιστολὴ πρώτη πρὸς μονάχους, with text, Ley 1954.

The fifty homilies which have roused great interest since the sixteenth century, place Macarius in the forefront of the early Christian mystics. We find in them profound considerations of the means by which the Holy Spirit leads the soul to union with Christ. L. Villecourt was the first to recognize that certain particular ideas of the homilies are identical with the propositions of the Messalians condemned by the Church, which are known through Timothy of Constantinople (§ 103) and John of Damascus. The investigations of H. Doerries have supplied essentially new information on the origin and tradition of these documents of mystical piety that originated in Messalian circles. An examination of the MS material which is partly extant also in Syriac and Arabic translations brought to light, apart from the already known fifty or fifty-eight homilies, several other collections containing sixty-four, fifty-seven and twenty-four λόγοι; to these, shorter orations and questions are sometimes added. The material is amalgamated and grouped quite differently in the individual pieces of these collections.

By examining the "questions" contained in the various branches of the tradition, Doerries was able to reconstruct the probable original form and two enlargements of the *Catechism of the*

Messalians, the so-called *Asceticon* which was condemned by the Council of Ephesus in 431. The specifically Messalian ideas were gradually corrected, and certain passages opposed to the teaching of the Church were left out. Thus it became possible that readers who were unaware of this, greatly esteemed these documents of a modified and refined Messalianism, considering them innocuous spiritual reading. Certain indications favour the view that the works of Macarius were written by Simeon, whom Theodoret (*Hist. E.* IV 11, 2) mentions as one of the founders of the Messalian heresy and whose home is given by other sources as Mesopotamia. The mention of Macarius as the author of these writings carried by most MSS may perhaps be due to a confusion. Probably the anonymously circulating pieces were meant to be attributed to one who was "blessed" (μακάριος).

Edd.: MG 34, 235/62, 405/822. G. L. Marriott, *Macarii anecdota,* C (Mass.) 1918 (7 homilies). German by D. Stiefenhofer (BKV² 10) 1913. — Treatises: J. Stoffels, *Die myst. Theologie Mak. des Aegypters,* 1908. C. Flemming, *De Macarii Aeg. scriptis quaest.,* 1911. J. Stiglmayr, *Sachliches u. Sprachliches bei M. v. Ae.,* 1912. L. Villecourt, *Comptes rendus de l'Acad. d'Inscript.* 1920, 250/8 and Wilmart, RAM 1920, 361/77. Amann, DTC 9, 1452/5; 10, 792/5. H. G. E. White (supra § 51), 2nd vol. 1932. Mersch 2, 1933, 362/8. W. Strothmann, *Die arab. Makarius-tradition,* 1934; BJ 230, 1931, 175/80. H. Doerries, *Symeon von Mesopotamien. Die Ueberlieferung der messalianischen "Makarius"-Schriften,* 1941. E. Klostermann, *Symeon und Makarius* (AbhB 1943, 11); TLZ 1948, 687/90. Graf I, 389/95. Graef, VS 4, 1948, 455/68 *(Doctrine des Homélies).* R. A. Klostermann, *Die slav. Ueber-lieferung der Mak.-Schriften,* Goeteborg 1950. Stapelmann, TG 1954, 26/39 (Holy Scripture in Symeon of Mesop.). Darrouzès, Mu 1954, 297/309 (two MSS of Ps.-Mac.). — Lit. on the Messalians: *Liber graduum* ed. M. Kmosko (Patrol. Syriaca 3) 1926. Hausherr, OCP 1935, 495/502 (date), 328/60 (chief error of Mess.). Cf. works on Acts of Phil. noted above § 10, 8. J. Ziegler, *Dulcedo Dei* 1937, 85/8. Rahner, ZKT 1937, 258/71 (MG 40, 847ff.). Peterson, ZNTW 1932, 273/88 (Marcus Erem. and the Messal.). F. Doerr, *Diadochus von Phot. und die Messal.,* 1938. A. Kemmer, *Charisma maximum,* Lou 1938. Viller-Rahner 216/8. Edsman 1940, 147/54. A. M. Burg, *Messal. Schriften u. Lehren um d. Jahr 400,* thesis Fr 1943. A. Vööbus, *Les Messaliens et les réformes de Barcauma de Nisibe dans l'église perse,* Pinneberg 1947. Kemmer, StAns 38, 1956, 268/306 (pseudo-Mac. ad Greg. of Nyssa).

5. Macarius the Younger of Alexandria, d. *c.* 394 aged 100, was, like Macarius of Egypt, a hermit in the Scetian and Nitrian deserts.

The writings published under his name (MG 34, 261/3, 385/92, 967/78) are spurious. Amann, DTC 9, 1440f.

6. Evagrius Ponticus (346–99), a native of Pontus, ordained deacon by Gregory of Nazianzus, was a greatly esteemed preacher in Constantinople. For the sake of his salvation, however, he left the capital in 382 and henceforth lived with the monks of the Nitrian mountains. He became a disciple and friend of Macarius of Egypt. He earned his living by copying books (Pallad., *Hist. Laus.* 38).

Together with Origen and Didymus the Blind he was anathematized in 553 and again by the following councils. Hence his original Greek works are for the greater part lost; some have been preserved in Latin (Rufinus and Gennadius [§§ 85 and 95]), Syriac and Armenian translations or under another name. Further investigations of Eastern MSS should furnish a good many other works. Living in the spiritual atmosphere of Origen, he sought to introduce the monks to the ascetical and mystical teaching based on the works of the great Alexandrian. The writings that have so far come to light do not permit us to state with certainty to what extent he took over the Origenistic errors. Evagrius is the first monk to have developed a comprehensive literary activity; he has great achievements to his credit, especially as a representative of Christian gnomic wisdom. His influence on the history of spirituality is considerable. Most recent research has clearly shown that, among others, Palladius, John Cassian, Maximus Confessor and Peter of Damascus (12th cent.) depend on him.

a. Ἀντιρρητικός, a collection of Scriptural passages "against the tempting demons", divided into eight books according to the eight capital sins; preserved in Syriac and Armenian. The Greek excerpt published in MG 40, 1272/6 belongs to the longer recension of the work which comprises one hundred maxims. He is one of the first witnesses to the eight vices theory, which was later changed into the doctrine of the seven capital sins.

b. Of a collection of maxims with the title Μοναχικός the first part (Πρακτικός, i.e. destined for the uneducated hermit) is preserved in Greek in two recensions (71 and 100 chs. respectively), the second part (Γνωστικός, i.e. meant for the educated monk) in Syriac in fifty chapters.

c. The 600 Προβλήματα γνωστικά, divided into six groups of one hundred maxims each *(centuria)* are extant in Syriac and Armenian. They contain dogmatic and ascetical teaching without any recognizable order.

d. A *Mirror of Monks* and one of *Nuns,* books of maxims preserved in Greek, translated into Latin by Rufinus (MG 40, 1277 ff.).

e. In addition to sixty-seven Letters extant in Syriac, Ep. 8 of St. Basil also belongs to Evagrius.

f. In recent times two treatises hitherto regarded as belonging to Nilus of Ancyra, *De oratione* (MG 79, 1165/1200) and *De malignis cogitationibus* (ibid. 1199/1228), have also been assigned to him.

g. As has been proved by U. v. Balthasar, Evagrius may also be regarded as the author of commentaries on Pss. and Prov.; considerable fragments of these are preserved among Origen's *Selecta in Pss.* and the remains of his *Commentary on Proverbs.* Very probably Evagrius wrote several other commentaries on books of the O.T. (certainly on Job) and on Luke.

Edd.: MG 40, 1213/86. Wilmart, RBn 199, 143/54 (Lat. Rule of Nuns). W. Frankenberg, GAG 1912 (Syr. with Gr. re-translation: Gnost. Probl., Antirrh., Gnost., Letters). P. B. Sarghisean, Venice 1907 (Armen. writings). H. Gressmann, TU 39, 4b 1913 (Monks' and Nuns' Mirrors, Gr.). J. Muyldermans, *Evagr., Syriaca. Textes inéd.,* Lou 1952. — Studies: W. Bousset, *Apophthegmata,* 1923, 281/341. R. Melcher, *Der 8. Brief des hl. Basilius ein Werk des Ev. P.,* 1923. BJ 230, 1931, 180/2. Muyldermans, *A travers la tradition manuscrite d'Év. le P.,* 1932 (and the most complete text of *De mal. cog.*). I. Hausherr, OC 22, 2, 1931, 75/118 (value of Syr. and Arm. trans.); RAM 1934, 34/93, 113/70 (trans. of *De orat.*). OCP 1936, 351/62 (ἀπέραντος ἀγνωσία). Rahner, ZAM 1933, 21/38 (spirit. doctrine). S. Marsili, *G. Cassiano ed. Ev. P. Dottrina sulla carità e contemplazione,* R 1936. Muyldermans, Mu 1938, 191/226 (*Vat. Barb. gr.* 515). J. Moisescu, *Ev. P. in Biserica ort. rom.* 56, 1938, 230/74; this is an extract from a thesis At 1937 (153 pp.).

U. v. Balthasar, ZKT 1939, 86/106, 181/206 (on the *Hiera,* i. e. Script. commentaries). Hausherr, OCP 1939, 229/33 (new Gr. fragms.); 7/71 (*De oratione* Syr. and Arab.). Muyldermans, Mu 1940, 77/88 (Armen. fragm. of *Ad virg.*); 1941, 1/15 *(Evagriana de la Vaticane).* Mercati, OM 3, 1937, 393/401 (scholion on Prov.). Hausherr, OCP 1936, 351/62 (infl. on Maxim. Conf.). Gouillard, EO 1939, 257/78 (infl. on Peter of Damascus, 12th cent.). Graf I, 397/99. Draguet, RHE 1946, 321/64; 1947, 5/49 (infl. on *Hist. L.* of Palladius). Muyldermans, Mu 1946, 367/79 (Syr. and Armen. on Seraphim). Leclercq, RML 1948, 444 and Sc 1951, 195/213 (Lat. MS of *Mirror of Monks*). Lefort, BullAcadBelgClLett 36, 1950, 70/9 (Evagr. depend. on Pachom.). Muyldermans, Mu 1952, 11/6 (Armen. fragm. of *Mirror of Monks*). A. et C. Guillaumont, RHR 142, 1952, 156/205 (Syr. text of *Gnostica* in Brit. Mus. Add. 17 167 much better). Muehmelt, VC 1954, 101/3 (lexical matters on Lat. trans. of *Mirror of Monks*). Further bibliogr. ref. in De Ghellinck, *Patristique et Moyen Age* 3, 1948, 216 f. *Gnostica,* ed. Guillaumont, PO 28,1.

7. Isidore of Pelusium (d. *c.* 435), had received a classical and theological education. He lived in a monastery, though this is not expressly stated, probably as superior; for it is highly improbable that a hermit (μόναχος) living in the desert could have conducted his voluminous correspondence comprising several thousand items (at least *c.* 3000). About 2000 mostly short letters are extant. He was a master of the polished epistolary style. In his letters he discussed mostly ascetic, moral and exegetical questions, but in his correspondence with not a few educated men of his time he also touched on many events in the world and the Church. His letters contain much information on ecclesiastical and cultural matters of which only little use has so far been made.

In discussing Christological problems he is chiefly interested in defending the Divinity of Christ against Arianism by a careful exegesis of Scripture (III 31 166 334; IV 99 142 166). He teaches the separation of the two natures as definitely as he rejects their confusion even against Cyril of Alexandria (of the time before 433) (I 310 323; IV 99 419 496). He himself does not seem to have had a clear conception of the manner of the union of the two natures, though he occasionally comes near to the later formula of Chalcedon (I 199 201 236). For the rest, the Incarnation is for him "the great mystery of piety" (II 192).

MG 78; among the Letters of this ed. 19 duplicates; cf. Baur, TQ 100, 1919, 252/4. 49 Letters in Lat. ed. R. Aigrain 1911 and SACO I vol. 4, 9/25. — Treatises: Bareille, DTC 8, 84/98. D. S. Balanos, At 1922. L. Bayer, *I.s v. P. klass. Bildung,* 1915. Diamantopulos, NS 1925/6. Phytrakes 1936; cf. BZ 1937, 522. Fruechtel, PW 1938, 61/4, 764/8 (Is. and Clem. Alex.). Redl, ZKG 1928, 325/32 (Is., formerly a sophist). Severus of Antioch. III 39 (6. versio) 1933, 182 and freq. (spurious letters). Cava, DTP 1936, 529/33 (I. in Is. 6, 10). Altaner, BZ 1942, 91/100 (Ep. 3, 253 = Λόγ. περὶ τοῦ μὴ εἶναι εἱμαρμένην; a Λόγος πρὸς Ἕλλ. is lost). A. Schmid, *Die Christologie I.s v. P.,* Fri 1948. M. Smith, HTR 1954, 205/10 (The MS tradition).

8. Shenute of Atripe (d. 466), superior of a monastery since 385, was the most powerful organizer of Egyptian monasticism beside Pachomius, and the most important author of national Coptic Christianity. In 431 he accompanied Cyril of Alexandria to the Council of Ephesus. He left many ascetical Letters, Sermons and several Apocalypses or Visions in Coptic. The authenticity of his writings is difficult to ascertain; they are partly extant also in Syriac, Ethiopian and Arabic translations.

Edd.: J. Leipoldt (CSCO, SSCopt 2, 1; 4, 3; 5, 4) 1906ff. H. Wiesmann (ibid. 4) 1931/6. New texts or new impressions in CSCO 41 43 96 108 129 ed. by H. Wiesmann, J. Leipoldt and E. W. Crum, 1951/5. A. Amélineau, P 1907. Burmester, Mu 1932, 24/34, 53ff. (10 sermons). Treatises: J. Leipoldt (TU 25, 1) 1903. Lefort, Mu 1935, 55/73 (depend. on Athanas.); Orientalia 4, R 1935, 411/5. Buckle, BJR 1936, 383f. Graf I, 461/4. Lantschoot, Copt. Stud. W. E. Crum 1950, 339/63 (Shenute's knowledge of *Physiologus* doubtful). Morenz, MitteilInstitOrientforsch 1, 1953, 250/5 (belief in after-life). D. G. Mueller, Mu 1954, 231/70 (on *ars praedicandi* in the Old Copt. Church); *Die alte kopt. Predigt,* thesis Hei 1955. Lefort, NClio 1954, 225/50 (martyrs' relics in Egypt in 4th cent.). K. H. Kuhn, CSCO 157/58, 1956 (Letters and Sermons of Besa, a disciple of Shenute).

§ 53. ALEXANDER OF ALEXANDRIA. ARIUS AND HIS FRIENDS

1. The great Arian controversy broke out under Bishop Alexander (313–28). At a synod at Alexandria (318) summoned by him, Arius and his followers were excommunicated. A synod held at Antioch at the beginning of 325 concurred with this judgement.

At the imperial synod held at Nicaea in the same year Alexander and Athanasius obtained a further condemnation of Arius.

a. Three encyclicals are extant of a collection containing seventy letters, which are very important for the earliest history of the Arian controversy; one is in Theodoret, *Hist.* 1, 4, the other in Socrates, *Hist.* 1, 6 and Gelasius Cyz., *Hist.* 2, 3.

b. Fragments of Sermons have also been preserved; among them one complete homily in Syriac and Coptic translations, *De anima et corpore deque Passione Domini* (MG 18, 585/604). A panegyric on his predecessor Peter, preserved in Coptic (supra § 41, 7), is spurious.

Edd.: Opitz, AW 3, 1 (5 letters). Rucker 1933, 74/8. E. A. W. Budge, *Coptic Homilies in the Dialect of Upper Egypt,* 1910, 407/24. H. Hyvernat, *Les actes des martyrs de l'Égypte,* 1, 1886, 247/62. Lefort, Mu 1929, 256/9 (Copt. fragm. of a sermon attributed to A. Schneemelcher, *Festschr. f. G. Dehn,* 1957, 119/43 (Copt. *Sermo de anima et corpore* possibly genuine).

2. Arius (d. 336), a disciple of the famous Lucian of Antioch (supra § 42, 2), priest in Alexandria, is of small literary importance. His known writings are: a letter asking Eusebius of Nicomedia for help, in Epiphanius, *Haer.* 69, 7, and Theodoret, *Hist.* 1, 4; a creed sent to Alexander of Alexandria in the form of a letter (Athan., *De syn.* 16; Epiph., *Haer.* 69, 7; Hilar., *Trin.* 4, 12f.; 6, 5f.; EH 400f.); a creed presented to the Emperor Constantine (330/1), on the basis of which he was to have been received into the Church in 336 (Socr. 1, 26; Sozom. 2, 27). Of his treatise Θάλεια (Banquet), partly written in verse, only small fragments have been preserved.

Ed.: Opitz, AW 3, 1.—Treatises: Bardy, RP 1927, 211/33 *(Thalia);* RHE 1930, 253/68 (fragm.); *Recherches sur S. Lucien d'Antioche et son école,* 1936. Arnou, Gr 1933, 269/72 (Trinit. relations). Barnes, ET 1934, 18/24 (A. and Arianism). Telfer, JTS 1936, 60/3 (A. in Nicomedia). Bardy, RevSR 1940, 28/63 (L'Occident et les docum. de la controv. arienne). DeGhellinck, Misc. Mercati I, 127/44 (on Letter of Ar.); *Misc. hist. A. de Meyer* 1946, 159/80 (En marge des controv. ariennes). On the chronology of the Arian Controversy: Opitz, ZNTW 1934, 131/59 and Schneemelcher, TLZ 1954, 393/400 (beginning of 318ff.); against this Telfer, JTS 1946, 129/42, 323; 1949, 187/91; AB 1949, 117/30 (Peter of Alex. and Arius). Baynes, JTS 1948,

165/8 (on Sozomen I 15); against this Telfer, JTS 1949, 187/91 (Sozom. I 15). Moennich, NedTT 1949, 378/412 (Arian Christol.). Nautin, AB 1949, 131/41 (interpolation in a Letter of Arius).

Latest research has discovered or identified several works written by unknown Arians: 1. A Latin *Commentary on Job* transmitted under the name of Julian of Halicarnassus, v. § 40, 2c; Amand, *Fatalisme,* 1945, 533/48. Draguet, RHE 1924, 38/65. 2. *A homily on the devil* circulating under the name of Athanasius (v. § 54, 17); publ. by Casey, JTS 1935, 1/10 and examined by Tetz, ZKG 1952/3, 299/307; 1956, 5f. 3. Amand-Moons ed. and examined RBn 1953, 18/69 and 211/38 a treatise *De virginitate* of encratite tendency, which is perhaps to be dated before325. 4. Richard, BullInstRech. et d'Hist. of text 1, 1952 (1953), 76, indicates a Cod. of the Bibl. nat. Athens n. 212, which contains two Sermons of a hitherto unknown Arian. Scheidweiler, ZKG 67, 1955/56, 132/40, (examin. and ed. of hom. on devil).

3. Eusebius of Nicomedia (d. 341–2), the influential friend of Arius at the imperial court, wrote numerous letters in the course of the Arian controversy; an epistle addressed to Bishop Paulinus of Tyre in Theodoret, *Hist.* 1, 5, and Marius Victor, *Adv. Arium,* prol. The petition addressed to the Fathers of the Council of Nicaea attributed to him and B. Theognis of Nicaea (d. *c.* 342) by Socr. 1, 14 and Sozom. 2, 16 is probably to be regarded as genuine.

Opitz, AW 3, 1 (3 letters). A. Lichtenstein, *Eus. v. Nik.,* 1903. K. Mueller, ZNTW 1925, 290ff. (petition). De Bruyne, ZNTW 1928, 106/10 (two letters of Theogn.). Ensslin, PWK II 5, 1948f. (Theogn.). G. Bardy, *Recherches sur S. Lucien* (v. supra) 1936; id., RSR 1933, 340ff. (petition spurious).

4. Asterius Sophista (rhetor) (d. after 341), a disciple of Lucian of Antioch (§ 42, 2) defended his Arian theology in his *Syntagmation,* which is known only from fragments in Athanasius and Marcellus of Ancyra (§ 57, 1), written probably before the Council of Nicaea. The Arian Philostorgius (*Hist. Eccl.* 2, 15; 4, 4) accuses him of having falsified true Arianism as represented by Lucian. Evidently Asterius later belonged to a moderate Arian party as is also plain from some of his homilies. His homiletic remains collected chiefly from *catenae* have been clarified through the research of E. Skard and M. Richard. Richard was able to produce thirty-one homilies and twenty-seven partly considerable fragments for the first time in a critical edition. Many of these homilies have not

been preserved in their entirety and several of these texts (nos. 10, 14, 24, 27) are not certainly genuine. Apart from homilies 30 and 31 there are items belonging to a commentary on the Psalms. Nine of these homilies were sermons delivered during the octave of Easter. Asterius also probably left homilies on texts from the Gospels and Rom. Parts of them will probably one day be discovered among the Pseudo-Chrysostom texts. Research on the texts we now have will probably throw new light on the exegesis of the school of Lucian and on the pastoral use of Scriptural passages.

Texts: M. Richard, *Asterii Soph. Commentariorum in Pss quae supersunt,* Oslo 1956. Some already in MG 40, 389/478; 55, 35/9, 539/44, 549/58 transmitted under the name of Chrysostom. G. Bardy, *Recherches sur S. Lucien,* 1936, 316/57 (fragms.). E. W. Brooks, *The Sixth Book of the Select Letters of Severus* I 2, 1902, 321/22.—Treatises: Richard, RB 1935, 548/51; SO 1947, 54/73. Skard, SO 1940, 86/132; 1947, 80/2; 1949, 54/69; 1955, 138/70 (on legal hist.). Richard, SO 1952, 24/33 (new MSS); 93/8 (2 homs. ed.). Didier, MSR 1949, 233/46 (testimony on infant bapt.). Supplementary to ed. by Richard, SO 1958, 54/57, 58/66.

§ 54. ATHANASIUS (295–373)

Athanasius, the most famous of Alexandrian bishops, is one of the most remarkable personalities of ancient Church history. He is the great protagonist of the Nicene faith, in whose defence he went through the crucible of suffering. He had to fight hard against his Arian opponents and the ruthless secular power which so often backed them up; but he was utterly convinced that he was fighting in the service of truth. Five times he had to leave his episcopal see to become a fugitive, and for more than seventeen years he had to endure the hardships of exile. It is scarcely surprising that he, too, should have sought to defend himself energetically against his many powerful adversaries and that he should sometimes have used all the means of force at his disposal.

He was born in Alexandria in 295 and at an early age received a classical education. He assisted at the Council of Nicaea (325) as a deacon and secretary of his Bishop Alexander, and there gained fame by his disputes with the Arians (Socr. 1, 8). He succeeded Alexander as early as 328.

When he refused to re-admit Arius into the Church, he was deposed by the Synod of Tyre (335) owing to false accusations levelled against him by the Melitians, and exiled to Treves by the Emperor Constantine (1st exile). After the latter's death he could return to Alexandria in 337. Shortly afterwards he was again deposed by a Council of Antioch (339). In 340 Athanasius fled to Rome to Pope Julius I (2nd exile). The Synod of Sardica (343) appealed for his return, which the Emperor Constantius permitted only in 346, after his anti-bishop Gregory had died (345).

When the Synod of Milan (355), under pressure from the personally present Emperor Constantius, once more decreed his deposition, he fled (356) to the monks in the Egyptian desert (3rd exile); George the Cappadocian became his successor (murdered in 361). After Athanasius had been recalled by the Emperor Julian together with the other exiled bishops, he eagerly promoted the reconciliation between the Semi-Arians and the adherents of the Nicene Creed, especially through the decrees of a Synod held at Alexandria in 362. In the same year he was therefore expelled as "a disturber of the peace and enemy of the gods" (4th exile), but was able to return after Julian's death (363). He was exiled a fifth time under Valens (365), but was recalled only four months later (366) because of the threatening attitude of the people. From that time he was allowed to govern his diocese in peace until his death in 373.

His extensive literary activity was mainly devoted to his theological convictions, for which he had to suffer throughout his long life. On the whole Athanasius is little concerned with literary form; he certainly shows everywhere clarity and precision of thought, but his writings suffer from defective arrangement of his material as well as from frequent repetitions and diffusiveness. Feast day May 2.

Complete edd.: MG 25/8. Of the new Berlin crit. ed. in 3 vols. (1934ff.), the following have so far appeared: II 1 (The apologies) 1–280 and III 1 (documents on the hist. of the Arian controv.) 1–76 ed. H.-G. Opitz; on this Chadwick, JTS 1949, 168f. and Scheidweiler, BZ 1954, 73/94 (text. crit.). — Transs.: J. Fisch (BKV) 1875. A. Stegmann, J. Lippl and H. Mertel (BKV² 13. 31) 1913/7. — Mgg.: J. A. Moehler ²1844. F. Lauchert, Cologne 1911. Bardy, P ³1925; DHG 4, 1313/40. Le Bachelet, DTC 1, 2143/78. M. Constantinides, Ὁ Μέγας Ἀθ., At 1937. Gentz, RACh 860/6. — Biogr.: E. Schwartz, GN 1904/5, 1908, 1911. B. Beck, *Die griech. Lebensbeschr. des Ath.*, 1912. Fromen 1915 (supra § 50, 4). Basten, *Ath., Wirtschaftliches aus s. Schr.*, 1928. Eustratiades (date of death); cf. BZ 1933, 424. K. F. Hagel, *Kirche u. Kaisertum in Lehre u. Leben des Ath.*, 1933. Seel, Klio 32, 1939, 175/88 (A. and Jul. Apost.). Peeters, Acad. Roy. Belg. Bull. 30, 944, 131/77 (flight from Tyre 335); AB 1945, 131/44 (Syn. of Tyre 335). Chatillon, RML 3, 1947, 376 (a citation from Plato). Schneemelcher, ZNTW 43, 1950/1, 242/56 (Ath. as a theologian and eccl. politician). — Transmission of writings: Casey, HTR 1931, 43/59 (Armen. MSS); ZNTW 1931, 49/70 (Gr. MSS); JTS 1934, 66f. (Syr. MSS). Opitz, ZNTW 1934, 18/31 (Syr. corpus); *Unters. zur Ueberl. der Schr. des Ath.*, 1935. Lorimer, JTS 1939, 37/46 (crit. notes). Altaner, BZ 1941, 45/59 (Old Lat. trans. of writings of Ath.); cf. Bardy, RSR 1947, 239/42. F. L. Cross, *The Study of St. A.*, O 1945, 22 pp. Graf I, 310/16. G. Mueller, *Lexikon Athanasianum*, B 1944/52.

1. *Apologetic and dogmatic writings*

1. The *Oratio contra gentes* and the *Oratio de incarnatione Verbi* form a coherent whole (*c.* 318). The first part expounds the stupidity of polytheism and the truth of monotheism, the second part gives reasons for belief in the incarnation of Christ in answer to Jews and pagans.

So far it has been impossible to determine the relation of the longer recension of this work to the shorter one which became known only recently. Opitz, *Unters.* 190ff.; against this RHE 1935, 786f. Richard, MSR 1949, 125f. It may perhaps be assumed with R. P. Casey, *The Short Recension of Orat. De Incarn. Verbi*, 1946, that the shorter version is to be regarded as a later recension by Athanasius himself or by one of his inner circle of collaborators.

Or. de incarnat. ed. A. Robertson, Lo [2]1893 and F. C. Cross (SPCK), 1939. C. J. Ryan, *De incarnat.*, I: *The Long Recens. MSS,* 1945. T. Camelot, *Oratio and De incarnat.* (SCh 18), 1947. H. Berkhof, *Orat. de incarnat.* (Dutch), A 1949. Tetz, VC 1955, 159/75 (text. crit.).

2. The most important dogmatic work is the *Tres Orationes contra Arianos* (*c.* 335 or 356ff.). The first book defends the Nicene doctrine of the eternal origin of the Son from the Father and the unity of essence of the Father and the Son; the second and third books discuss the Scriptural passages adduced by the Arians, e.g. Prov. 8, 22. A fourth *oratio* by an anonymous author was added later.

Gaudel, RevSR 1929, 524/39 (*Tres Orationes* written c. 339); cf. RHE 1935, 324/9. J. de Vogel, *3 Orat. c. Arian.* (Dutch), Ut 1949. A. Vaillant, *Discours contre les Ariens de S. Ath., version slave* (only text of 1st oration), Sofia 1954.

3. The work *De incarnatione et contra Arianos,* the authenticity of which has been doubted, is probably to be assigned to Athanasius. The suspected εἷς θεὸς ἐν τρισὶν ὑποστάσεσιν is probably a later interpolation.

Cf. RHE 1925, 528f.; J. Rucker, *Dogma v. d. Persoenlichkeit Christi,* 1934, 108/10 Simonetti, NDid 1952, 5/19 (spurious).

4. A number of other dogmatic writings circulated under his name are to be considered spurious. To these belong, among others, two books *De incarnatione contra Apollinarem* (EP 796/800); Dimitropulos, Θ 1953, 442/61 (for genuineness). Twelve books, printed also under the name of Vigilius of Thapsus (§ 97, 2), ed. crit. M. Simonetti, *Ps.-Athanasius, De Trinitate,* X–XII, Bonn, 1956; NDid 1949, 57/72 (books 1–8 in 3 layers from the end of the 4th cent.; 5–12 from 5th and 6th cents.); *Maia* 1951, 9f. (Ambrose dependent on Ps.-Athanas. 12); *Maia* 6, 1953, 301/23. E. Schwartz, SbMn 1924, 6, assigned an *Expositio fidei* and *Sermo maior de fide* to Eustathius of Antioch. Scheidweiler, ZNTW 44, 1952/3, 237/49 (for Eustathius); BZ 1954, 333/57 for Marcellus of Ancyra (cf. § 57, 1). R. P. Casey, *The Armen. Version of the Ps.-Athan. Letter to*

the Antiochenes (= Sermo maior de fide) and the *Expositio Fidei,* Lo 1947; cf. MSR 1949, 130/3.

On Three Sermons of Ps.-Athanas. cf. Capelle, EL 1949, 5/26 (§ 104, 11). Jugie, EO 39, 1940/1, 283/9 (2 Sermons: MG 28, 917/48). M. Markovic; cf. BZ 1954, 208 (MS of the spurious treatise *De definitionibus*). P. C. Dimitropulos, *The Anthropology of Athan.* (Greek), At 1954. Tetz, ZKG 1956, 1/28 (faults of the editions of Casey). *Interpretatio in symbolum,* 2 *Dialogi contra Macedonianos* and 5 *Dialogi de sancta Trinitate.* Cf. also RAL 204; A. v. Premerstein, *Festschr. S. Lampros,* At 1935, 177/89 (apocryph. philosopher's sayings). M. Simon, RHP 1937, 58/93 (tract. De Melchisedek). Moss, OCP 1938, 65/84 (*Contra Apoll.* I, siriace). Segovia, Gr 1938, 87/107 (Dial. MSS); RET I, 603/9 (id., Dial.: Jo. 14, 28). Bardy, RB 1933, 328/32 (ps.-Athan. Quaest.). Mercati, OM 3, 1937, 49f. (MG 26, 1338/42. *De azymis*). A. Guenthoer, *Die 7 ps.-athan. Dialoge, ein Werk des Didymus,* R 1941. Segovia, EE 1943, 303/17 (on the *Dial. c. Maced.*). Meinhold, PWK 21, 1066/1101 (Pneumatomachi).

2. *Polemical, historical and dogmatical treatises and epistles.*

These were written to refute attacks of his opponents or to make attacks himself:

5. *Epistola ad episcopos encyclica* protests against his deposition (340).

6. *Apologia contra Arianos* (containing much documentary material) gives an account (*c.* 357) of the negotiations and decrees of the preceding councils.

7. *Epistola de decretis Nicaenae synodi* defends (350–1) the Nicene terms ἐκ τῆς οὐσίας and ὁμοούσιος; documents are appended. The *Epistola de sententia Dionysii episcopi Alexandrini* whom the Arians claimed as a supporter of their own opinions is perhaps an appendix to it.

8. *Ep. encyclica ad episcopos Aegyptii et Libyae* (356).

9. *Apologia ad Constantium imperatorem* (357) refutes in brilliant rhetoric the insinuation that he had stirred up the emperor's brother Constans against the emperor.

10. In the *Apologia de fuga* he defends himself against the reproach of cowardice (357).

11. *Historia Arianorum ad monachos* (*c.* 358); the fragment that

has been preserved gives an account of the years 335–57. To this belongs a *Letter to Bishop Serapion of Thmuis* on the death of Arius (EH 418/20).

12. *Epistola de synodis Arimini in Italia et Seleuciae in Isauria celebratis* (359).

13. Three Epistles were written at the demand of Councils: *Tomus ad Antiochenos* (362), *Ep. ad Iovianum imperatorem* (363). *Ep. ad Afros,* i.e. to the bishops of W. Africa (369).

14. Four *Letters to Bishop Serapion* (§ 55, 1); important for the doctrine of the divinity of the Holy Spirit (358–62) (EP 477/84).

15. Three letters, also dogmatic, treat of the Christological dogma: *Ep. ad Epictetum episcopum Corinthi, Ep. ad Adelphium episcopum, Ep. ad Maximum philosophum.* Later the Letter to Epictetus gained great authority (Council of Chalcedon).

R. Seiler, *Ath.' Apologia c. Arianos, ihre Entst. u. Datierung,* 1932; to this Opitz, *Unters.* 158 A. 3. Separate ed. of. *Ep. de decretis Nic. syn.* by H. G. Opitz, B 1935. *Ep. ad Epict.* ed. G. Ludwig, Jena 1911. Casey, HTR 1933, 127/50 (Arm. trans. of *Ep. ad Epict.*). Lebon, RHR 1935, 713/61 (Syr. trans. of *Ep. ad Epict.* falsified by Apollinarians). Jerphanion, RSR 1930, 529/44 (text of *Ep. ad monachos;* MG 26, 1185/8). R. B. Shapland, *Letters concerning the Holy Spirit* (trans.), Lo and NY 1951. J. Lebon, *Lettres à Sérapion* (SCh 15), 1947. Jones, JTS 1954, 224/7 (*Apol. c. Arian.* written between 367 and 370). Szymusiak, SCh 56, 1958 (Apologies),

3. *Exegetical and practical ascetical writings*

16. Fragments of exegetical works have become known through *catenae.*

On larger fragments of an allegorical *Exegesis of the Psalms* cf. Devreesse, DBSuppl 1, 1109 1125 1187 1200 and freq.; RB 1935, 180 (Gen., Ex.). Smythe, JTS 1950, 158/68 (Amons 4, 13 in Athanas. and Didymus). Recheis, Ant 1953, 219/60 (comment. on Gen. 1–3).

17. New finds and researches confirm the information handed on by Jerome (*Vir. ill.* 87) that Athanasius has frequently written on virginity. The authenticity of the writings or fragments we are about to mention could not so far be proved with certainty; but there is good reason to believe that at least in some cases we have

to deal with genuine material. E. v. d. Goltz, Λόγος σωτηρίας πρὸς τὴν παρθένον (TU 29, 2 a) 1905; cf. Lefort, Mu 1929, 197/274 (Copt. fragm. of a letter Πρὸς τὰς παρθένους which was used also by St. Ambrose and Shenonte and has much in common with the first-named work [Mu 1935, 55/73]). Two other texts extant in Syriac were ed. by Lebon, Mu 1927, 205/48; 1928, 169/216. The treatise *On Virginity* of which a large Syriac fragment has been published (Mu 1927, 205/48) is preserved complete in Armenian translation (Casey, SbB 1935, 1022/45). Cf. also Van Lantschoot, Mu 1927, 265/92, who published a Coptic letter *On Love and Self-control* ascribed to Athanasius; according to Lefort, Mu 1933, 1/33, the letter is genuine and Coptic the language of the original. The find which gives almost two thirds of the apocryphal First Letter of Clement *Ad virgines* (cf. § 15, 3) in a Coptic translation, naming Athanasius as its author, deserves special attention (Lefort, Mu 1927, 249/64; 1929, 265/9). Diekamp, AP 1938, 5/8 published fragments of an ascetical treatise *On Illness and Health* that had remained unknown until then; cf. ZKT 1938, 259. A further unpublished Coptic work is indicated by Lefort, Mu 1929, 204.

Lefort, AB 67, 1949, 142/52 and Mél. De Ghellinck I, 1951, 215/21 (Copt. fragm. of a new treatise *De virginitate*). Bardy, DS 1, 1049f. Lantschoot, Ang 1943, 249/53 (Allocution à des moines en visite chez S. Ath.). Aubineau, RAM 1955, 140/73 (Les écrits sur la virginité). 3 Copt. Sermons ascribed to Ath. in Burmester, Mu 1932, 44/8. Bernardin, JTS 1937, 113/29 (Copt. hom.). A closer examination of the diverse Sermons ascribed to Ath. and to be found in A. Ehrhard (TU 50/2) will certainly also bring to light genuine material among them.

18. About 357 he wrote the legendary *Vita S. Antonii* (supra § 52, 1), whom he had known personally in his youth. Through this work he greatly contributed to the spread of the monastic ideal especially in the West (Augustine). Evagrius of Antioch, the friend of St. Jerome, soon translated the work into Latin.

Reitzenstein, SbHei 1914, 8. Abh. J. List, *Das Antoniusleben des hl. A.,* At 1930; supra § 52, 1. K. Heussi, *Der Ursprung des Moenchtums,* 1936, 78/108. Festugière, REG 1937, 470/502 (La *Vita* dépend d'un modèle païen). M. Marx, *Incessant Prayer in Anc. Monast. Literat.,* R 1946. Garitte, BBR 22, 1942/3, 5/29 (hist. of the printed Gr. text). — Transs. of Evagrius: MG 26, 835/976 and ML 73, 125/70. A second, even later Lat. trans. ed. G. Garitte, *Un témoin important du texte de la Vie de S. Antoine par S. Ath.*, R 1939. Doerries, GAG 1949, 359/410 (*Vita Ant.* as a hist. source). R. T. Meyer (ACW 10) 1950. Garitte, CSCO 117 118 (Copt. text), 1949. L. T. Lorié, *Spirit. Terminology in Lat. Translations of the Vita Ant.*, N 1955. Baynes, JournEgyptArchaeol 1954, 7/10 (on demonology).

19. Following an ancient custom (supra § 41, 3) Athanasius wrote, if possible, every year soon after Epiphany a so-called festal letter (Ἐπιστολὴ ἑορταστική) to the Egyptian churches under his authority, in which he informed them of the date of Easter and the beginning of the Lenten fast, and also discussed other matters (Lenten pastoral). Apart from Greek fragments, the full text of thirteen such festal letters from the years 329–48 is extant in a Syriac translation.

The *Thirty-ninth Festal Letter* of 367 is particularly valuable. It has been almost completely reconstructed from Greek, Syriac and Coptic fragments and contains a list of the canonical books (EP 791). Athanasius excludes the deuterocanonical books of the O.T. from the canon, admitting them only as devotional reading; on the other hand, the twenty-seven books of the present N.T. are stated to be the only canonical ones for the first time.

The fourth century *Cod. Vaticanus* of the Bible agrees in contents and order with this canon. The former is perhaps the MS which was made by Alexandrian scribes for the Emperor Constans, during Athanasius' stay in Rome in 340.

Citations from 3 festal letters (27 29 44) in Severus Antioch. III 41 (6. versio) 1933, 216f. Mercati, ST 95, 1941, 78/80 (Canon bibl.). Schwartz, ZNTW 1935, 129/37 (chronol. of Letters). Pieper, ibid. 1938 (Fest. Letter of 364). Lefort, BullAcadBelgClLett 39, 1953, 643/56; 41, 1955, 183/5; Mu 67, 1954, 43/50 (new Festal Letters in Copt. trans.: E. Schwartz's chronology is untenable). Copt. text in CSCO 150 151, 1955.

20. The *Symbolum Athanasianum* (ES 39f.), also called *Quicunque* after its opening word, is not by St. Athanasius, but gained great authority on account of its lucid exposition, in forty rhythmic clauses, of the doctrine of the Three Persons in God and the

two natures in Christ. It is still in use in the Church's liturgy (Prime of Trinity Sunday).

From the seventh century it came gradually to be attributed to Athanasius. In the seventeenth century it was realized that it was certainly later and originally written in Latin. The question of its date and authorship is still under discussion, though the thesis of H. Brewers (1909) that Ambrose (392–3) was its author has received relatively considerable support.

F. J. Badcock, *The Hist. of the Creeds,* 1930; J. R. Palanque, S. *Ambroise,* 1933, 508; Schepens, RHE 1936, 548/69. Against this: Capelle, RTA Bull II n. 930; F. H. Dudden, *The Life and Times of St. Ambrose,* 1935, 676f.; Palanque, RHE 1936, 941 A. 2; B. Fischer, TLZ 1952, 288. Various other Church Fathers have been suggested as authors in recent times, e. g. Vincentius of Lerinum (d. *c.* 450), Hilary of Arles (d. 449), Fulgentius of Ruspe (d. 533), Caesarius of Arles (d. 542), Martin of Bracara (d. *c.* 580) and others. Pasté, SC 1932, 142/7 (for Eusebius of Vercelli [d. 362]). Morin, RBn 1932, 207/19 (Caesarius of Arles already knew the *Symb.,* which was probably composed in S. Gaul about this time). M. J. Ryan, *The Eccl. Review* (Philadelphia) 88, 1933, 625/7 (written before 451). Laurent, EO 1936, 385/404 (*Quicunque* in the Byz. Church). On terminological parallels to the Creed in Vincentius of Lerins cf. J. Madoz, *Excerpta Vinc.i Ler.,* 1940, 65/90. Hughes, ET 57, 1945/6, 184f. (5th cent. in France or Spain). Schiltz, ETL 1948, 440/54 (La comparaison du *Quicumque*). De Aldama, EE 1950, 237/9.

Lit. on the Hist. of other Creeds: Creed of Nicaea and Constantinople cf. Lietzmann, ZNTW 1925, 193/202. Harnack, ibid. 202. A. E. Burn, *The Council of Nicaea,* 1925. Schwartz, ZNTW 1926, 38/88; on this Lebon, RHE 1936, 537/47 809/76; Ortiz de Urbina, OCP 1936, 330/50 and D'Alès, RSR 1936, 85/92 579/84. Abramowski, ZNTW 1930, 129/35 (Creed of Amphil.). Du Manoir, Gr 1931, 104/37 *(Symb. Nic. au concile d'Éphèse).* Cavallera, BLE 1938, 94/7 (Symb. Tolet. I). J. A. de Aldama, *El simbolo Toledano* I, R 1934; here 148/50 an uned. *Fides Hieronymi;* RHE 1933, 74/81 (B. Pastor); Gr 1933, 485/500 *(Clemens trinitas).* Morin, RBn 1934, 178/89 (Caesarius of Arles); RBn 1923, 233/45 (Afric. Creeds 5th/6th cent.). G. Villada, Hist. 2, 2, 274/80 (Span. Creeds 7th/8th cent.). Akinian-Casey, HTR 1931, 143/51 (2 Arm. creeds). Madoz, RHE 1938, 5/20 (Toledo 633); Gr 1938, 161/93 (Toledo 638); *Le Symb. du XIe Conc. de Tolède,* Lou 1938; cf. TR 1938, 189/91. González, Gr 1938, 130/4 (Greg. of Nyssa). J. de J. Pérez, *La Cristología en los Símbolos Toledanos IV, VI y XI,* R 1939; cf. TR 1940, 112f. C. Maly, *De verbis symb. Nicaeno-Constant. "Cuius regni n. e. finis",* Mn 1939. Madoz, RET 1944, 457/77 (Trinity in the Creed *of Toledo*); *El Símb. del Concil. XVI de Toledo,* 1946; RET 1947, 363/72 (Holy Spirit in *Creed of Toledo*). J. Ortiz de Urbina, *El Símb. Niceno,* Ma 1947; cf. TLZ 1949, 42f. De Urbina, OCP 1946, 275/85 *(Symb. Constantinop.);* De Urbina in: Grillmeier-Bacht I, 398/418 *(Creed of Chalcedon). Camelot,* OCP 1947,

425/33 *(Creed of Nicaea).* Nautin, *Je crois à l'Esprit Saint . . .,* 1947 (in Hippolytus). A. Van Selms, *Licht uit Licht. Het christ. geloof naar de belijdenis van Nicea,* A 1948. J. De Ghellinck, *Patristique et Moyen Age* I, [2]1949 (hist. of research on symbols). Karmiris, Θ 1951, 617/33 *(Symb. Nic.-Constantinop.)* Davies, VC 1955, 218/21 (on Creed of Jerusal.).

Points of Doctrine

1. Athanasius' doctrinal importance is due mainly to his scientific presentation and explanation of the Church's doctrine of the Trinity, and particularly of the Logos doctrine. He effectively defended not only the identity of nature *(homoousia)* of the Father and the Son, but also expounded the nature and generation of the Logos more clearly than previous theologians.

His opponent Arius taught, like Philo and Origen (supra § 40), that God needed the Logos as an intermediary being for the creation of the world. Athanasius replies to this that God is neither so powerless that he could not create without an intermediary being, nor so proud that he would not create without one (*Or. Ar.* 2, 24 25). Arius called the Son a creature of the Father, a product of the will of the Father. Athanasius answers that the term "Son" includes the notion of "being generated"; but to be generated means to come forth not from the will, but from the Being of the Father. Hence the Son of God could not be called a creature of the Father, but shares with him the fullness of the Godhead (1, 16; 3, 6). But in God generation is not the same as in men; for God, being spirit, is indivisible. Hence his generation has to be conceived in the manner of the light radiating from the sun, and of the thought proceeding from the soul; hence the Son of God is eternal like the Father (3, 62 66f.). Father and Son, therefore, are two, but the same (ταὐτόν), i.e. they have the same nature (φύσις). When the Son says: "The Father is greater than I", this means: the Father is the origin, the Son the derivation (3, 3; 4; EP 760/76).

Lebon, RHE 1952, 485/529 (*consubstantialis* in Ath. also after 362 = of the same nature = doctrine of Nicaea).

2. The Logos doctrine of Athanasius is rooted above all in the concept of redemption, i.e. in the thesis: We should not have been redeemed, if God himself had not entered into humanity, hence, if Christ were not God. The Logos, as God, has deified humanity itself by uniting to himself a human nature, and by conquering death in himself, has conquered it for all of us. But if he had had the privilege of being God not by nature but by communication, he could not have transmitted it (*Or. Ar.* 1, 39; *Ep. de syn.* 52; EP 787).

3. Athanasius asserted the Divinity and *homoousia* of the Holy Spirit in his letters to Serapion and at the synod of Alexandria in 362. Like the three great Cappadocians he regards the Son as the immediate source of the Holy Spirit; their formula is this: The Holy Spirit proceeds from the Father through the Son (ἐκ πατρὸς διὰ υἱοῦ. *Ep. Ser.* 3, 1 and *Inc. Ar.* 9).

4. About 362 Athanasius also turned to Christological questions. According to him Christ is one, i.e. one Person. What he did, did not belong separately to the human nature or to the divinity, but to both together (*Ep. Ser.* 4, 14f.; *Nic.* 14); what his body suffered the indwelling Logos took upon himself, so that he too suffered; yet he did not suffer himself (*Epict.* 5f.). Hence Mary is *Theotokos* (*Or. Ar.* 3, 14 29), and Christ is to be adored also in his humanity (*Adelph.* 3). There are also two wills in Christ (*Inc. Ar.* 21). Nevertheless, he did not yet go so far as to recognize and emphasize consistently that the Logos assumed the whole human nature, i.e. also the human soul.

Richard, MSR 1947, 5/54 and Grillmeier in Grillmeier-Bacht I, 81/91.

5. He considers the baptism administered by Arians invalid, because they do not baptize in the name of the true and real Trinity (*Or. Ar.* 2, 42; *Ep. Ser.* 1, 30). The same has been taught

by Basil, Cyril of Jerusalem, the *Apost. Canons* (46 and 47) and the *Apost. Constitutions* (6, 15), in a certain sense even by the Council of Nicaea (can. 19), which demanded that the Paulianists, i.e. the followers of Paul of Samosata, should be rebaptized.

6. It has wrongly been alleged that Athanasius held the symbolic view of the eucharist in the sense of Zwingli (esp. *Ep. Ser.* 4, 19). He says unequivocally: "Before the petitions and prayers this bread and this wine are of the ordinary kind; but when the great and glorious prayers have been sent up, the bread becomes the body and the drink the blood of our Lord Jesus Christ" (EP 802).

E. Weigl, *Unters. zur Christologie des hl. A.,* 1914. V. Cremers, *De Verlossigsidee bij A.,* Turnhout 1921. Gaudel, RevSR 1931, 1/26 (Logos doctr.). Bostroem 1932 (supra § 42, 3; doctr. of redemption). Mersch 1, [2]1936, 374/409. Prestige, JTS 1933, 258/65 (Ἀγέν[ν]ητος). Berchem, EO 1934, 316/30 (Incarnation). Lebon, RHE 1935, 307/29 (ὁ κυριακὸς ἄνθρωπος); cf. Loofs 1930, 138 A. 11. Bardy, DS 1, 1047/52. C. Hauret, *Comment le "Défenseur de Nicée" a-t-il compris le dogme de Nicée?* Bruges 1936. Berchem, Ang 1938, 201/32, 515/58 *(Créat. et sanctif. par le Verbe).* Pruemm, ZKT 1939, 350/9 *(Mysterion).* T. M., SC 1939, 728/37 *(Redenz. e figliaz. adottiva in S. At. e S. Cir. Aless.).* Schoemann, Sch 1941, 335/50 (Eikon). L. Bouyer, *L'incarn. et l'Égl.-Corps du Christ dans la théol. de S. Ath.,* 1943. Unger, *Franciscan Studies* 6, 1946, 30/53, 171/94 (soteriology). Prestige, *Fathers and Heretics* (SPCK), Lo 1948 (Athan., Apollin., Nestor., Cyril Al.). Ruwet, Bi 1952, 1/29 (Can. of Script.). R. Bernard, *L'image de Dieu d'après S. Ath.,* 1952. J. R. Laurin, *Orientations maîtresses des apologistes chrét. de 270 à 361,* R 1954. De Urbina, OCP 1954, 27/43 (soul of Christ). P. Dimitropulos, *The Anthropology of the Gr. Ath.,* At 1954. Galtier, Gr 1955, 553/89 (soul of Christ).

§ 55. OTHER EGYPTIANS OF THE FOURTH AND FIFTH CENTURIES (TILL 451)

1. SERAPION of Thmuis, superior of a monastery and from 339 Bishop of Thmuis in Lower Egypt (d. after 362). Athanasius addressed several letters to him (supra § 54). Among his extant works are, apart from two letters (MG 40, 923/42), a controversial work against the Manicheans which has only recently come to be known in full, and a collection of thirty liturgical prayers composed by him *(Euchologium).*

R. P. Casey, *S. of T. against the Manichees,* C (Mass.) 1931 (first crit. ed.). *Euchol.,* ed. G. Wobbermin (TU 17, 3b) 1898; F. X. Funk, *Didasc. et Const. Apost.* 2, 1905, 158/95; J. Quasten (FP 7) 1935, 48/67 (18 Euch. prayers). German by R. Storf (BKV² 5) 1912. Devreesse, RB 1935, 181 (fragm. in Gen.). Wilcken, AbhB 1933 no. 6, 31/6 (prayers). Bardy, DTC 14, 1908/12. Capelle, Mu 1946, 425/43 *(Anaphora).* Peters, SE 1949, 55/94 (treatise against Manicheans). Draguet, Mu 1950, 1/25 (a letter [Armen. and Syr.] to disciples of St. Anthony: 356). Rodopoulos, Θ 1957, 252/75, 420/39, 578/91; 1958, 45/54, 208/17.

2. Didymus the Blind of Alexandria (d. *c.* 398) was the celebrated teacher and head of the Alexandrian catechetical school for over half a century, though he was a layman and had become blind at the age of four.

As regards the doctrine of the Trinity he was a correct Nicene theologian. But he followed Origen in the doctrine of the pre-existence and *apocatastasis* of human souls; hence he was anathematized with him and Evagrius Ponticus at the general Council of 553. This accounts for the fact that most of his very considerable literary output is lost.

a. Many not yet critically sifted fragments of his numerous Scriptural commentaries have survived in *catenae.* The largest of these is the commentary on the Psalms (MG 39, 1155/1616). He always prefers the allegorical exegesis. The *Brevis enarratio in Epistolas canonicas (= catholicas)* preserved in a Latin translation made at the suggestion of Cassiodorus may now be regarded as genuine (Staab, Bi 1924, 314/8). The papyrus find of Tura contains, inter alia, also texts from the commentaries of Gen., Zach. (almost complete) and Job; cf. supra § 40, 8 and Bardy, *Science rel.* 1944, 247/50; Puech, RHP 1951, 293/329 (Tura find).

b. Of dogmatic treatises we possess his principal work, three books *De Trinitate* (written betw. 381 and 392) which is directed against Arianism and Macedonianism (EP 1068/76), three books *De Spiritu Sancto* in the Latin translation of Jerome (EP 1066 f.) and a short work *Contra Manichaeos* (EP 1077). Several other writings seem to be preserved under other names; thus two books *De dogmatibus et contra Arianos,* which are appended to St. Basil's *Adv. Eunomium.*

Edd.: MG 39 (incomplete). F. Zoepfl, *Didymi Alex. in epist. canonicas brevis enarratio,* 1914. K. Staab, 1933, 1/45. — Mgg. by J. Leipoldt (TU 29, 3) 1905. G. Bardy, P 1910. W. J. Gauche, *D. the Blind, an Educator of the Fourth Cent.,* W 1934. Lebon, Mu 1937, 61/83 (*De dogm. et c. Arianos* genuine). Devreesse, DBSuppl I, 1125 f. and freq.; RB 1935, 181/6 (fragms. in Gen. and Ex.). E. L. Heston, *The Spiritual Life ... as Described in the Works of D. of A.,* R 1938. G. Crone, *Did. Der hl. Geist,* erlaeutert, Steyl 1939. A. Guenthoer, *Die 7 ps.-athanas. Dialoge, ein Werk des Did.,* R 1941; against this H. Rahner, ZKT 1941, 111 f.; for it, Dietzsche, ScPT 2, 1941/2, 380/414; W. Dietzsche, *Did. v. A. als Verf. der Schrift ueber d. Seraphimvision,* Fr 1941 (= Morin, *Anecdota Maredsol.* III 3, 103/22); against it Altaner, TR 1943, 147/51 (author perh. Theophilus of Alex.). Smythe, JTS 1950, 158/68 (Amos 4, 13 in Athanas. and Didym.). Quattrone, Regnum Dei 8, 1952, 82/8, 140/52; 1953, 81/8 (doctr. of Holy Spirit). Bardy, DS F. 20 f., 668/71. Doutrelean, RSR 1957, 514/57 (*De trin.* false).

3. The voluminous literary work of the autocratic Bishop Theophilus of Alexandria (385–412) notorious especially for his violent opposition to Chrysostom has perished almost entirely. Among the few remains are several letters (in the Corpus of Jerome's Letters nos. 87, 92, 96, 98, 100), homilies (partly only in fragments) and a fragment of an Easter Table (380–479) presented to the Emperor Theodosius (*c.* 388). The genuineness of the so-called *Vision of the Flight of the Holy Family to Egypt* is dubious.

MG 65, 33/68. Mingana, BJR 1929, 383–474 (Syr. text of *Visio*); on this Doelger, AC 3, 189/91. Mingana, WS 3, 1; 4, 14 (ed. apocrypha). G. Lazzati, *Teofilo d'A.,* Mi 1934; SC 1935, 513/7. H. de Vis, *Homélies coptes,* 1929; cf. OLZ 1930, 871/81. BJ 230, 170 f. Richard, RHE 1937, 46/56 (Hom. on the Euch. in MG 77, 1017/29); RB 1938, 387/97 (exeg. fragms.). A list of writings and extant fragms. in Opitz, PWK II 5, 2149/65; even more complete in Richard, Mu 1939, 33/50. Lefort, Mu 1933, 31 (on an uned. exeget.-dogmat. [Copt.] treatise; author prob. Theoph.). Altaner, TR 1943, 150 f. on T. as probable author of the anti-Origenist treatise *In Is. VI 1–7* (v. supra § 55, 2). Richard, DTC 1946, 523/30. Graf I, 229/32. Astruc, Sc 1, 1946/7, 162/4 (MSS). Fleisch, ROC 10, 1946, 371/419 (Arab. hom. on Pet. and Paul). Reuss, TU 61, 1956, 151 f. (fragm. of Mt. comm.). A. Favale, *Teofilo d'A.,* To 1958.

4. We would mention here for the first time the monk Marcianus, of whom noteworthy texts on the Logos doctrine and the Christology of the fourth century are extant in the Syriac *Flori*-

legium Edessenum (ed. I. Rucker, SbMn 1933, 5, 60/4. Further information in J. Lebon, *Miscell. de Meyer,* Lou 1946, 1, 181/93.

5. Synesius of Cyrene (370–5—413–4) came from a noble pagan family of Cyrene in Libya. He studied at Alexandria, where he was a pupil of the neo-Platonist woman philosopher Hypatia. As an ambassador at Constantinople (399–402) he was able to obtain tax relief for his impoverished home city, and later took the lead in its successful defence (begun in 405) against invading Berber tribes. In 410 his grateful countrymen elected him Bishop of Ptolemais and Metropolitan of the Pentapolis, though he was probably not yet baptized and inwardly opposed to Christianity. After considerable hesitation he suffered himself to be consecrated by Bishop Theophilus of Alexandria on condition that he should be allowed to continue in his marriage also as a bishop and to retain his philosophical views on the pre-existence of the soul, the eternity of the world and the resurrection of the flesh, which he interpreted allegorically (*Ep.* 105). Though he took his episcopal office seriously and tried to come nearer to the Christian faith, he never attained to an integral Christianity, especially as he died very early.

a. His treatises, which were all composed before his consecration, reflect a philosophy formed by Neo-Platonism. We would mention the following: *Egyptian Tales or On Providence,* which describes conditions and controversies at the Imperial Court in Constantinople in philosophical and mythological disguise. *Dion (Chrysostom) or On his Way of Life* expresses his attitude to sophistic thought and monasticism. The *Praise of Baldness* is a sophistic jest. The treatise *On Dreams* attempts to prove dreams to be revelations of God.

b. Orations and Sermons; among them is his courageous address *On Kingship* which presents the young Emperor Arcadius with the ideal image of a king.

c. His ten (nine) Hymns in the Doric dialect show a strange mixture of neo-Platonist and Christian ideas.

d. His 156 Letters are not only a valuable source for contemporary history but also evidence of his excellent education and noble mind.

Edd.: MG 66, 1021/1578. Hymns ed. J. Flach, T 1875 and N. Terzaghi, Atti Accad. r. Napoli 4, 1915. Letters ed. R. Hercher, *Epistolographi graeci,* P 1873, 638/739. Hymnus ed. N. Terzaghi, R 1939; II 1944; cf. BZ 1941, 176/88. Engl. A. Fitzgerald, 1 vol. Letters 1926, 2 vols. Treatises and Hymns 1930. Hymns (French) by M. Meunier, P 1947. — Mgg.: G. Gruetzmacher 1913. v. Campenhausen, PWK II 4, 1362/5. W. Lang, *Das Traumbuch des S. v. K.,* 1926. X. H. Simeon, *Unters. zu den Briefen d. Bischofs S. v. K.,* 1933. J. Hermelin, *Zu den Briefen d. Bischofs S.,* Up 1934. Souter, JTS 1935, 176/8 (lexical matters). P. Henry, *Les États du Texte de Plotin,* 1938, 202/5. G. Lazzati, *L'Aristotele perdutto,* 1938, 55/8, 74. M. M. Hawkins, *Der 1. Hymnus des S. v. K. Text und Kommentar,* thesis Mn 1939. Pepzopulos, EEBS 1937, 305/52 (hymns); 1939, 288/351 (the ps.-Plutarchian treatise on Homer a work of S.). J. C. Pando, *The Life and Times of S. of C. as Revealed in His Work,* W 1940. W. Theiler, *Die chaldaeischen Orakel u. die Hymnen des S.,* 1942. Bizocchi, Gr 1942, 91/115 202/37 (chronology of Hymns against Terzaghi); 1944, 130/70; 1946, 261/99 (episc. consecr.). G. Bettini, *L'attività pubblica di S.,* Udine 1938. Terzaghi, BZ 1938, 289/98 (10. hymn). Keydell, BJ 272, 1941. Kurfess, PW 1943, 288 (hymn 9, 32f.). Coster, Byz 15, 1940/1, 10/38 (Syn. *curialis*). Festugière, REG 1945, 208/77 (Les Hymnes). Lacombrade, RevEA 48, 1946, 260/6 *(L'énigme du loup).* Cocco, So 1948, 199/202, 351/6 (on first hymn). C. Lacombrade, *S. de C. hellène et chrétien,* 1951; on this Theiler, Gn 1953. 195/7; Bizocchi, Gr 1951, 347/87 *(S. analyste du rêve et inventeur du densimètre).* Karlsson, Er 1952, 144f. (Ep. n. 158 of Hercher ed. spurious). Marrou, REG 1952, 474/84 *(La conversion de S.).* Bonadies-Nani, Aev 1952, 385/409 (relation of Proclus to S.). Visser, NedArchKerkGesch 1952, 67/80 (comprehensive appreciation). K. Treu, TU 71, 1958 (Dion.).

6. Nonnus of Panopolis in the Thebaid, famous for his epic poem *Dionysiaca* which reproduces the myth of the journey of the god Dionysus to India is also the author of a *Paraphrase of St. John's Gospel* in hexameters. Since, despite Christian allusions, the first-named work is definitely pagan, it seems more probable to assume a conversion of the poet, about the dates and circumstances of whose life nothing definite is known. The paraphrase was evidently written after 431.

Edd.: A. Scheindler, L 1881. A. Ludwich, *Dionysiaca,* 1909. R. Janssen, *Paraphrase* (TU 23, 4) 1903. T. v. Scheffer, *Dion.* (Germ.), 2 vols., 1929/33. — Treatises: Amann, DTC 11, 793/5. Keydell, PWK 17, 904/21. J. Golega, *Stud. ueber d. Ev.-Dichtung des N. v. P.,* 1930. Costa, *Bilychnis* 1931, 143/50 (date *c.* 431). Keydell,

BZ 1933, 243/54 (Apollinaris and N.). Bogner, Phil 1934, 320/33 (conversion). Cataudella, SIF 1934, 15/32 (depends on Greg. of Nazianzus). Keydell, BJ 272, 1941. Dostálová-Jenistova, *Z. Verbreitung des Namens Nonnus;* cf. BZ 1956, 156. The most recent lit. exclusively referring to the *Dion.* is not listed here.

7. The priest Ammonius of Alexandria wrote commentaries on Daniel, John and Acts of which considerable fragments (especially on John) are preserved in *catenae* (MG 85, 1361/1610, 1823/6). The fragments on Matthew printed in MG 85, 1381/92 are all spurious; Ammonius did not write a commentary on Matthew. The scholia on John (l. c. 1392/1254) contain very many spurious pieces. Almost the whole commentary on John can be reconstructed from the fragments already known and many others that have not yet been edited. The author is generally identified with the Ammonius who opposed Timothy Aelurus in 457 (Bardenhewer 4, 83/6). According to T. Zahn, ZKG 1920, 1/22 311/36 he is to be identified with the monk of the Nitrian desert mentioned by Palladius, *Hist. Laus.* 10f. 24 and freq., whereas Devreesse, DBSuppl I, 1174 1204 assigns the author to the sixth century.

M. Faulhaber, *Propheten-Catenen,* 1899, 185/7. J. Reuss, Bi 1941, 13/20. J. Reuss, *Matth.-, Mark.- u. Joh.-Katenen,* 1941 (cf. Index).

§ 56. CYRIL OF ALEXANDRIA (d. 444)

Cyril of Alexandria, the nephew of the Patriarch Theophilus (supra § 55, 3) succeeded the latter in 412. His vehement and ruthless measures against the Novatianists and the Jews of Alexandria brought him into opposition to the governor Orestes. He cannot, however, be held guilty of the murder of the woman philosopher Hypatia (415).

In the history of the Church and of dogma he is famous above all as the great defender of orthodoxy in the struggle against the heresy of Nestorius; though his conduct often lacked the caution, tact and delicate psychological understanding so necessary in this controversy.

As early as 429 Cyril opposed the bishop of the capital of the East in his paschal letter and soon after asked Pope Celestine I for a decision, as did also Nestorius. A Roman synod decided against the latter (430). At the behest of the Pope, Cyril demanded that his opponent should revoke his errors within ten days, at the same time threatening him with excommunication and sending him twelve anathematisms (ES 113/24).

At the synod which assembled with Cyril as its president at Ephesus and which ranks as the third Oecumenical Council (431), Nestorius was declared deposed in the very first session (22nd June); he was excommunicated and his Christology (refusal of the title θεοτόκος) was condemned.

The Patriarch John of Antioch who had arrived with his suffragans only four days later held a counter-synod which deposed Cyril. The Emperor Theodosius II confirmed the decrees of both synods and had both Cyril and Nestorius put in prison. After lengthy negotiations Cyril was eventually freed, while Nestorius was exiled to a monastery at Antioch. The Council of Ephesus was dissolved.

The schism which had arisen in 431 was healed in 433, when both sides accepted the symbol which the Antiochenes had already proposed at Ephesus, and which was probably drawn up by Theodoret of Cyrus. Throughout his life Cyril had to defend his Christology and the symbol of union against many attacks and misinterpretations.

Cyril's writings, though very important for the history of the Church and her doctrine, do not rank high as literary products. Their language and presentation are not very attractive, often formless and boringly diffuse; but they are the products of a born dogmatist, excelling in clarity of thought and cogency of argumentation. The following works may be mentioned as the most important:

a. The exegetical writings are the most voluminous. The exegesis, especially of the O.T. books, is strongly allegorical, whereas in the N.T. writings the literal sense receives more attention.

i. The following deal with the exegesis of the O.T. (EP 2091 ff.): seventeen books *De adoratione et cultu in spiritu et veritate* and the complementary thirteen books of *Glaphyra* (= polished explanations), which give an allegorical-typological exegesis of selected passages of the Pentateuch. We possess further a commentary on Isaias and one on the Minor Prophets. Large fragments of other O.T. books are partly preserved in *catenae* (e.g. on Pss. 1–119).

ii. Of N.T. commentaries we still possess the greater part of the *Commentary on John* (written before 429), a cycle of 156 *Homilies on Luke* (after 429) preserved in a Syriac translation, and fragments on Matthew, Romans, 1 and 2 Corinthians and Hebrews (EP 2101/23).

b. Dogmatic-polemical works:

i. Two long treatises are directed against Arianism: *Thesaurus de sancta et consubstantiali Trinitate;* and *De sancta et consubstantiali Trinitate* in seven dialogues, which attempts a more positive presentation of the doctrine (EP 2081/90), both written probably between 423 and 425. Cyril's Christology, like that of Athanasius, here follows the so-called *Logos-Sarx-schema,* in which the human soul is completely disregarded. The following formula, taken over from Athanasius, *C. Arian.* 3, 30, is characteristic: The Logos has become flesh, but did not enter into a man (*Dialog.* 1; MG 75, 681C).

ii. The anti-Nestorian controversial writings are numerous: three memoirs *De recta fide:* one addressed to the Emperor Theodosius II, the other two, which supplement each other, addressed *Ad reginas* (the theologically interested three sisters and the consort of the Emperor) (EP 2126 f.); twelve *Anathemata* and three *Apologies* for these (430/1); five books *Adv. Nestorii blasphemias* (430) directed against a collection of Nestorius' Sermons publ. in 429; *Apologeticus ad imperatorem,* a justification of his attitude at Ephesus (431); *Scholia de incarnatione Unigeniti* (EP 2124f.); the dialogue *Quod unus sit Christus* (EP 2134), famous already in antiquity; a treatise *Adv. nolentes confiteri s. Virginem esse Deiparam;* large fragments are extant of a treatise *Contra Diodorum* (of Tarsus) *et Theodorum* (of Mopsuestia).

c. The great apologetical work *Adv. libros athei Iuliani* refutes the three books of the Emperor Julian's treatise *Against the Galileans.* Of the thirty books of Cyril only the first ten are completely extant, from which the first book of Julian can be almost entirely reconstructed.

d. Apart from twenty-nine Paschal Letters of moral and practical contents (for the years 414–42) there are extant also about ninety mostly dogmatically important Letters (EP 2058/62); some of them are also of historical and canonical significance. A *Table of Easter* for 403–512 destined for the Emperor Theodosius II is lost; only the accompanying letter is extant in Armenian.

e. Of his many Sermons we possess only about twenty (partly only as fragments), among them some homilies delivered at the Council of Ephesus, among which is the *Praises of the Theotokos* the most famous Marian homily of antiquity (Hom. 4).

Edd.: J. Aubert, 6 vols., P 1638. MG 68/77. E. Schwartz, AC I, vols. 1/5 (here many anti-Nestorian writings, especially memoranda, letters and homilies have been ed.). P. E. Pusey, 7 vols., O 1868/77. J. B. Chabot in CSCO 70, 1912 (Lk.). R. M. Tonneau, CSCO 140, 1953 (trans. of the Comm. on Lk.). — Transs.: H. Hayd (BKV) 1879 and O. Bardenhewer (BKV² II 12) 1935. — Mgg.: J. Kopallik, 1881. J. Mahé, DTC 3, 2476/257. P. Baphides, Thessalonich 1932. C. Papadopulos, Alexandria 1933. E. Schwartz, *C. u. d. Moench Victor* (SbW 208, 4), 1928. Rucker, HA 1927, 699/714 (C. in the Armen. Church). Pericoli-Ridolfini, RivStudOrient 29, 1954, 187/217 (Cyr. of Al. and Jo. of Ant. in the Letters of Andrew of Samosata). — On the individual works: P. Mariès, *Hippolyte de Rome* (supra § 31), 33 (Armen. MS of an Ez.-comm.). Devreesse, DBSuppl 1, 1134 (Ps.). A. Ruecker, *Die Lukashom. des hl. Cyr.,* 1911. Lebon, Mu 1931, 69/114; 1933, 237/46 (Arm. fragm. on Hebr.). Mingana, WS 4, 47 (Hebr.). Papadopulos, *Festschr. S. Lampros,* At 1935, 35/41 (Ascension sermon); against this C. Martin, RHE 1936, 345/50. Vaccari, StU 27/39 (Greek lang. of C.). Devreesse, RevSR 1931, 543/63 (C. against Theod. and

Ibas). Fruechtel, ZNTW 1937, 88/90 (citations from *C. Jul.*). Abel, Vivre et Penser 1, 1941, 94/119, 212/30 (C. depends on Jerome). Euringer, Or 1943, 113/27 (Germ. trans. of 2 Ethiop. Homs. *De Melchisedech*). P. Henry, *Les États du Texte de Plotin,* 1938, 125/40 (*C. Jul.* 8). Reuss, Bi 1944, 207/9 (Jo.-comm.). Van Roey, Mu 1942, 87/92 (B. Succensus to C.). Richard, *Mél. Fel. Grat* I, 1946, 99/116 (C. against Diodore and Theod.). A. Cordoliani, *Bibl. de l'Éc. des Chartres,* 1945, 5/34 (Easter table). Jouassard, *Mél. E. Podechard,* 1945, 159/74 (chronol. of writings till 428). Graf I, 358/65. Many new fragms. in Severus Antioch. ed. Lebon 1929/38. *Kyrilliana (444-1944)* Cairo 1947 (10 contributions on biogr. and hist. of dogma); cf. RHE 1948, 205/7. P. Sanz, *Griech. lit. Papyri,* W 1946, 111/24 (9th book *De adorat.*). Quasten, AJP 63, 1942, 207/15 (wool and linen in the allegor. interpretation of C.). G. Mercati, ST 142, 1948 (Proemi del Salterio . . .). Charlier, RHE 1950, 25/81 (on *Thes. de Trin.*). Richard, RSR 1952, 116/28 (On *Scholia de incarn. unig.*). Honigmann, ST 173, 52f. (on Letter to the monks of Fua). Liébart, MSR 1955, 5/26 (S. Cyr. d'Alex. et la culture antique). Reuss, TU 61, 1957, 103/269 (Matt. Comm.). Bardy, DHG 13, 1169/77. Hintze-Morenz, Z. Aegypt. Spr. 79, 1954, 125/40 (Dialogue in MG 76, 249/56 not genuine).

Cyril's Christology and Mariology

Cyril calls the union of the two natures in Christ ἕνωσις φυσική or also ἕνωσις καθ' ὑπόστασιν or κατὰ φύσιν, whereas the Nestorians used ἕνωσις σχετική, συνάφεια or ἐνοίκησις for it.

In this way Cyril wanted to describe the union of both natures as a very close, true and real one. This idea, which he emphasized even more strongly in speaking of the *one nature of the Logos become flesh* (μία φύσις τοῦ λόγου σεσαρκωμένη) (EP 46, 2; EP 2061) was bound to cause all the more scandal to his opponents, the Antiochene theologians, as it had not been coined, as Cyril believed (*Rect. Fid. ad Reg.* 1, 9) by Athanasius, but by Apollinaris (infra § 65) (MG 28, 25/30). The misgivings were not lessened by the fact that Cyril not infrequently spoke of δύο φύσεις before the union and μία φύσις after it (*Ep.* 40). At the same time, however, Cyril rejected Apollinarianism and taught not only the integrity of the human nature, to which belongs the ψυχὴ λογική, but also a union which does not result in a mixture of the two natures (ἀσύγχυτος ἕνωσις) (*Ep.* 39; EP 2060). In his view the most exact analogy to the union of the two natures in Christ is to be found in the union of the flesh with the reasonable soul in man (EP 2061); he also adduces by way of comparison the burning coal (cf. Is. 6, 6), the burning wood and the dyed wool.

The fact that Greek theology had no definite term for the two natures in the one Person of Christ was a source of misunderstandings and the reason why Cyril was accused of Apollinarianism and Monophysitism. This was aggravated by a lack of sensitiveness on his part, which prevented him from recognizing the inadequacy of the terms he used. Among the Latins, Tertullian had already spoken of *proprietas utriusque substantiae in una persona* (supra § 30). Cyril, however, used φύσις and ὑπόστασις without distinction for designating the nature as well as the person. It is true, Basil had coined the formula: τρεῖς ὑποστάσεις, μία φύσις for the Holy Trinity, and Cyril at first also spoke of τρία πρόσωπα in God; but one dared not quite speak of μία ὑπόστασις in Christ, because in the Trinity ὑπόστασις was the individualized nature, whereas the two natures in Christ preserved their properties unchanged. It was the Council of Chalcedon which finally clarified the technical terms by speaking of δύο φύσεις which are united εἰς ἓν πρόσωπον καὶ μίαν ὑπόστασιν (ES 148).

For Cyril the applicability of the *communicatio idiomatum* follows immediately from the ἕνωσις φυσική: The Son of God was born and died (*Nest.* 1, 2; 5, 5, 7). Hence Mary must be called θεοτόκος; he even says: θεοτόκον λέγειν καὶ ὁμολογεῖν τὴν ἁγίαν παρθένον suffices for a correct and blameless confession of our faith (*Ep.* 1; *Hom.* 15 *Incarn.;* EP 2058).

Mgg.: A. Rehrmann, *Die Christologie des hl. Cyrill von A.*, 1902. E. Weigl, *Die Heilslehre des hl. Cyrill von A.*, 1905; *Die Christologie vom Tode des Athanasius bis zum Ausbruch des nestor. Streites*, 1925, 121 ff. A. Struckmann, *Die Eucharistielehre des hl. C. von A.*, 1910. A. Eberle, *Die Mariologie des hl. C. v. A.*, 1921. J. N. Hebensperger, *Die Denkwelt des hl. C. v. A.*, 1927. J. B. Wolf, *Commentat. in S. Cyr. Alex. de Spiritu S. doctrinam*, R 1934. I. Rucker, *Das Dogma v. d. Persoenlichkeit Christi*, 1934 (supra § 3, 14); *Cyrill u. Nestorius im Lichte der Ephesus-Enzyklika*, 1934. — Treatises: Mersch I, [2]1936, 487/536. Malevez, RSR 1935, 280/91 (The

Church in Christ). Du Manoir, RSR 1935, 531/59 (proof from Fathers). P. Renaudin, *La théol. de S. C. d'A. d'après S. Thomas d'A.,* 1937 (from RT 1934ff.). Du Manoir, RSR 1937, 385/407, 549/96 (Le problème de Dieu chez C.); Gr 1938 573/603; 1939, 83/100 (L'Église, Corps du Christ). Janssens, ETL 1938, 233/78 (being a child of God). Dubarle, ETL 1939, 111/20 (Ignorance of Christ). J. van der Dries, *The Formula of St. C. of A.: mia physis tou Theou sesarkomene,* Lo 1939. L. Turrado, *Δόξα en el Ev. de S. Juan seg. S. C. de Al.,* R 1939. Du Manoir de Juaye, *Dogme et spiritualité chez s. C. d'A.,* 1944. Richard, MSR 1945, 243/52 (hypostasis). Nilus a. S. B., *De maternitate div. B. M. V. Nestorii et Cyr. sent.,* R 1944. Sagué, EE 1947, 35/83 (Holy Spirit and soul). Monsgú, RET 1947, 161/220 (Holy Spirit); 1948, 1/57 275/328 (doct. of Trin.). G. L. Prestige, *Fathers and Heretics,* Lo 1948. P. Polakes, *Orthodoxia,* Constantinople 1948 (unity of Church and relation to Papacy); cf. BZ 1953, 240f. Dubarle RSPT 1948, 359/62 (*Salus gentium* before Christ). Hulsbosch, StC 1949, 65/94 (hypostat. union). G. Giudici, *La dottrina della grazia nel Commento ai Rom. di S. C. d'A.,* thesis Greg., R 195. Lyonnet, Bi 1951, 25/31 (on 2 Cor. 3, 17). J. Liébart, *La doctrine christol. de S. C. d'A. avant la querelle nestorienne,* Lille 1951. Galtier in Grillmeier-Bacht I, 345/87 (Cyril's Christol. and Leo the Gr.); Gr 1952, 351/98 (hypost. union). A. Kerrigan, *S. Cyr. Interpreter of the OT,* R 1952. Jouassard, REB 1953, 175/86 (on C.'s early Christol.). Manoir, DS 2, 2672/83. Stead, DSO 1953, 12/20 (*perichoresis* in *De Trin.* of *Ps.-Cyr.*). Jouassard, RSR 1955, 361/78 (on anthropol. and Christol.). Diepen, RT 1955/300/38 (The 12 anathemat. at the Conc. of Eph. till 519). Fraigneau-Julien, RevSR 1956, 135/56 *(L'inhabitation de la S. Trin. dans l'âme).* W. J. Burghardt, *God in Man acc. to St. C. of A.,* W 1957. Jouassard, RSR 1956, 234/42 *(le schéma Verbe-chair).* H. M. Diepen, *Aux origines de l'anthropologie de S. Cyrille d'A.,* P 1957.

B. Theologians of Asia Minor

§ 57. MARCELLUS OF ANCYRA AND BASIL OF ANCYRA

1. Marcellus, Bishop of Ancyra (d. *c.* 374) was a prominent ally of St. Athanasius at Nicaea (325) and later. After the publication (*c.* 334) of his controversial work against the Arian Asterius (supra § 53, 4) he was deposed on account of his near-Sabellian doctrine of the Trinity (336). He was condemned as a heretic by can. 1 of the Second General Council of 381. 129 fragments of his work, edited by E. Klostermann (GCS 14) 1906, 185/215 are contained in Eusebius' reply (supra § 48, 5) to him; later works which he wrote in his defence have perished completely.

Mgg.: T. Zahn 1867. Chénu, DTC 9, 1993/8. W. Gericke, *M. v. A. Der Logos-Christologe u. Biblizist,* 1940. Richard, MSR 1949, 5/28 (The small treatise *De s. ecclesia* publ. under the name of Anthimus of Nicomedia belongs to M. of A.). Lampe, JTS 1948, 169/75 (Ps. 96). J. M. Fondevila, *Ideas cristológ. de M. de A.,* thesis Greg., Excerpta Ma 1953 and EE 1953, 21/64. Scheidweiler, BZ 1954, 33/57 (M. of A. prob. the author of the so-called *Sermo maior de fide* and of the *Expositio fidei*). Her 1955, 220/57 (philological research on *Sermo maior*); supra § 54, 4. Id., ZNTW 1956, 202/14.

2. Basil, Bishop of Ancyra, originally a physician, succeeded Marcellus of A. after the latter had been deposed in 336. In 358 (Synod of Ancyra) he became the leader of the homoiousian party together with George of Laodicea; the synod of Constantinople which was under the influence of Acacius (Homoian) exiled him to Illyria in 360 (d. *c.* 364). A *Memoir on the Doctrine of the Trinity* which he wrote together with George of L. is extant (MG 42, 425/44). The treatise *De virginitate* (MG 30, 669/810), which has been preserved under the name of Basil the Gr., is perhaps also to be attributed to him (EA 291/4).

Mgg.: J. Schladebach 1898. J. Gummerus, *Die homoeousianische Partei,* 1900, 121 ff. Cavallera, RHE 1905, 5/14 *(De virg.).* Janin, DHG 6, 1104/7. Olphe-Galliard, DS 1, 1283 f. A. Vaillant, *De virg. de S. B. Texte vieux slave,* 1943. Jan. Cuesta, *Misc. Comillas* 14, 1950, 187/97 (*Dieta y virginidad:* Bas. of A. author of *De virg.,* and Greg. of Nyssa).

§ 58. BASIL THE GREAT (b. *c.* 330, d. 379)

THE three great Cappadocians also belong to the neo-Alexandrian school of theology so brilliantly represented by Athanasius. Basil, his younger brother Gregory of Nyssa and his friend Gregory of Nazianzus were united not only by common intellectual and spiritual interests, but also by an intimate friendship. Their influence on the development of the Church and especially on its attitude to secular culture can hardly be exaggerated.

Basil came from a family distinguished by its traditional zeal for the faith as well as by its piety. His mother Emmelia, his grandmother Macrina the Elder, and besides Gregory his third brother, Peter, Bishop of Sebaste, as well as their sister Macrina the Younger, are all venerated as saints. He was the son of the distinguished rhetor, Basil of Caesarea in Cappadocia. He was educated at the rhetorical schools of Caesarea (Capp.), Constantinople and lastly at Athens, where he became the lifelong friend of Gregory of Nazianzus.

After his return home (*c.* 356) Basil taught rhetoric for a time, but soon resolved to renounce the world. He was baptized and visited the most famous ascetics of Syria, Palestine, Egypt and Mesopotamia in order to acquaint himself with the spirit of monasticism. Afterwards he lived with like-minded companions in a desert near Neocaesarea in Pontus. Here Gregory of Nazianzus visited him (*c.* 358), and together they compiled the *Philocalia* (supra § 40) and wrote two monastic rules which have been of decisive importance for the development and spread of the cenobitic life in the East (cf. Basilians).

Bishop Eusebius caused him to move to Caesarea and persuaded him to let himself be ordained priest and work in the cure of souls (*c.* 364). In 370 he became Bishop of Caesarea and thus not only metropolitan of Cappadocia, but also exarch of the political diocese of Pontus. His extensive work as a father of souls, apostle of charity and prince of the Church gained him the epithet "the Great" even during his lifetime.

His successful struggle against Arianism, which was very powerful under the Emperor Valens, was especially important. The Emperor succeeded only in diminishing Basil's external position by dividing Cappadocia into two provinces, whereby his metropolitan see (*c.* 50 suffragans) was also divided (371). In order to safeguard orthodoxy which was threatened in the East, he worked for better relations and a unanimous policy of the Western and Eastern bishops and sought the mediation of Athanasius and direct contact with Pope Damasus. The main obstacle to the longed-for union between East and West was the so-called Meletian schism at Antioch (since 362). Basil's efforts to obtain the recognition of Melitius in the West remained without result; Pope Damasus would not disown Bishop Paulinus (Synod of Antioch 379). Nevertheless, the harmonizing mediation of St. Basil contributed largely to the collapse of Arianism which soon (381) became manifest. If Basil can be called a "Roman among the Greeks" this is due to the fact that he was mainly concerned with the practical pastoral and moral consequences of the truths of the faith, whereas most Greek Fathers were chiefly interested in theological speculation. This is also evident from his writings. Feast day: June 14th.

Edd.: J. Garnier and P. Maran, 3 vols., P 1721/30. MG 29/32. Amand, RBn 1940, 141/61; 1941, 119/51; 1942, 145/50; 56, 1945/6, 126/73 *(Hist. crit. des éditions grecques)*. Mercati, OM 4, 1937, 372/6 (Cod. Vat. gr. 428: *Ascetica*). — Individual edd.: *S. Basil, Letters* ed. R. J. Deferrari and McGuire, 4 vols., Lo 1926/34. *De Spir. S.* ed. C. F. H. Johnston, O 1892. L. Oliger 1921, 36/40 (I ep. 22 = MG 32, 287 ed. complete in Lat. trans. for the first time), p. XL (Lat. trans. of other works). P. Trevisan, *S. Bas., Commento al prof. Isaia,* 2 vols., Tu 1939 (text and trans.). — Trans.: A. Stegmann (BKV[2] 46 47) 1925. W. K. L. Clarke, *Ascet. Works,* 1925. E. Leggio, *L'ascetica,* Tu 1934. H. de Vis (supra § 55, 3) 1929 (Copt. hom.). E. Neri e G. Balponi, *S. Bas. Le omelie* (5), Siena 1938. B. Pruche, trans. *De Spiritu S.* (SCh 17), 1947; S. Giet, *Homélies sur l'Hex.* (SCh 26), 1950. R. J. Deferrari, trans. of Letters (FathCh 13), 1951. A. C. Way, Letters 1–185 (FathCh 13), 1951. — Altaner, HJB 61, 1941, 208/12 (Lat. trans. of Rufinus). Graf I, 319/29. Amand, RBn 1947, 12/81 (first ed. of an Old Lat. trans. of 2 homs.; MG 31, 217 ff., 237 ff.). Huglo, RBn 1954, 129/32 (MSS of 13 homs. trans. into Lat.).

On biography and various works: Bardy, RACh 1, 1261/5. Theiler, BZ 1941, 171/4 (Porphyry in B.). Richard, AB 1949, 178/202 (Bas. and the Roman deacon Sabinus). W. M. Roggisch, *Platons Spuren bei Bas. d. Gr.,* thesis typescr. Bonn 1949. L. Vischer, *Bas. d. Gr. Untersuchungen zu einem Kirchenvater des 4. Jh.,* Basle 1953. Giet, RevSR 1953, 131/3 (Danses liturgiques?); JTS 1955, 94/9 (B. and the Council of Const. 360). Driessen, Mu 1953, 65/95 (Armen. MSS). for the older lit. see infra 341.

1. *Dogmatic writings*

a. Three books *Against Eunomius* (infra § 62), the spokesman of the strict Arians (Anomoeans), written *c.* 364; two further books, belonging very probably to Didymus (4 and 5) are appended to this. b. *De Spiritu Sancto* (EP 943/54), dedicated to Bishop Amphilochius in 375, treats of the homoousia of the Holy Spirit. Basil shows inter alia that beside the doxology διὰ τοῦ υἱοῦ ἐν τῷ ἁγίῳ πνεύματι the other formula he uses in the liturgy, μετὰ τοῦ υἱοῦ σὺν τῷ πνεύματι ἁγίῳ, has also a sound Scriptural and traditional foundation. On the *Philocalia* v. supra.

2. *Ascetical writings* (MG 31, 620/1428)

Several works, some of them of very doubtful authenticity, are collected under the title *Ascetica.* The most important genuine pieces are the following: a. *Moralia,* eighty moral precepts *(regulae)* proved by N.T. sayings. b. The two monastic Rules (supra): the longer rules *(reg. fusius tractatae)* with fifty-five items, and the shorter rules *(reg. brevius tractatae)* with 313 items, are mainly a catechism on duties and virtues in the form of questions and answers (EP 974/8; EA 267/84). The rules are partly the spiritual property of Eustathius of Sebaste, which had so far been preserved only in oral tradition; he was an older friend of Basil who had contributed to the spread of monasticism. Both collections received their final form only gradually through repeated redactions. St. Benedict, too, used and recommended these rules. On *De virginitate* v. supra, § 57, 2.

On dogmatic and ascet. works: List of genuine *ascetica* in D. Amand, *L'ascèse monast. de S. Bas.,* 1949, XXVI. *Guétet, Mél. bénédictines . . .,* Fontenelle 1947 (Une récension stoudite des Règles bas.). Pruche, RSPT 1948, 207/21 (On *De Spiritu S.*). J. Gribomont, *Hist. du texte des Ascétiques de s. Bas.,* Lou 1953; cf. RHE 1954, 507/13. On the older lit. v. infra 341.

3. *Homilies and Orations*

a. The nine long *Homilies on the Hexaemeron* are concerned only with the literal sense of the Scriptural account; they contain magnificent descriptions of God's creative power and the beauty of nature. Basil here shows himself in full possession of the philosophic and scientific knowledge of his time. Ambrose adapted this commentary on the creation account in his *Sermons on the Hexaemeron*.

Shortly before 400 the *Homilies on the Hexaemeron* were translated into Latin by an otherwise little known Eustathius who lived in Italy (Rome?) (MG 30, 869/968); cf. Altaner, ZNTW 39, 161/70. Crit. ed. by Amand-Rudberg in TU 1957.

b. Thirteen of the eighteen rather devotional *Homilies on the Psalms* may well be genuine. They are strongly dependent on Eusebius (supra § 48, 4). The *Commentary on Isaias* 1–16 which also draws on Eusebius is probably spurious.

c. About twenty-three orations, sermons on special themes and panegyrics on martyrs (MG 31, 163/618, 1429/1514) can also be considered genuine. They contain much information on the cultural and moral history of the time, e.g. those on fasting (no. 1), against the rich (no. 7) and against drunkards (no. 14) (EP 966/73; EA 255/60).

In addition to the lit. cited below: S. J. Rudberg, *Ét. sur la tradition manuscrite de s. B.,* Lund 1953, and Er 1952, 60/70 (R. investigates the tradition of the homilies except those on the *Hexaem.* and the *Letters*); cf. on this Amand, RHE 1954, 514/21; Gribomont, Mu 1954, 51/69 and Sc 1954, 298/304. Rudberg, RBn 1952, 189/200 (text. crit. of the Ps.-Bas. hom. ed. Amand, RBn 1948, 223/63); cf. further Amand, ibid. 1952, 300 f. The two homilies *(De hominis structura)* which were formerly attributed to Bas. (MG 30, 10/62) or Greg. of Nyssa (MG 44, 257/97) have been proved to be spurious by most recent scholars, though no definite author has been suggested. Cf. Stéphanu, EO 1932, 385/98 (for Bas.); v. Ivánka, BZ 1936, 47/57, and R. Leys, *L'image de Dieu chez s. Gr. de Nysse,* 1951, 130/8 (f. Greg. Nyss.); against this Giet, RSR 1946, 317/58; Amand, RBn 1949, 3/54; RHE 1953, 824. H. Merki, Ὁμοίωσις Θεῷ ... *bei Gregor v. Nyssa,* Fri 1952, 165/73. Gribomont, OCP 1955, 375/98 (*Exhortatio de renunt.*: MG 31, 625/48 spurious).

4. The treatise *Admonitions to Young Men on the Profitable Use of Pagan Literature* (Πρὸς τοὺς νέους) instructs his nephews who are students to train their intellect on pagan classical literature till they are able to grasp the deeper sense of Holy Scripture. Those

pieces should be selected for study which may be of value for one's moral education. In this matter man must imitate the bees which seek only honey and avoid poison; they offer many instructive examples. With this educational aim in view, many illustrations are given from Greek literature, especially from the poets, which prove that the pagans, too, bear witness to goodness and give the palm to virtue. These, for those days very broadminded expositions, exercised a decisive influence on the attitude of the Church to the cultural achievements of antiquity.

On Πρὸς νέους (MG 31, 563/90). Separate ed.: A. Dirking, Mr 1934. F. Boulanger, P [2]1952. A. Nardi, Tu 1931. — Treatises: Amatucci, RFC 1949, 191/7. P. Kukules, At 1951 (Bas., Greg. Naz., Jo. Chrys. as educationists); cf. BZ 1952, 450. — P. Lehmann, SbMn 1955, 7 (ed. of *Admonitio s. Bas. ad filium spiritualem in Benedict of N.* prob. genuine, cf. A. Adam, DLZ 1957, 579/82).

5. The 365 Letters (partly addressed to Basil) collected by the Maurists give a vivid picture of the many-sided activities and the exquisite culture of their author and contain precious material for the political and cultural history of the time. One can distinguish historical, dogmatic-polemical, moral-ascetical and canonical letters (including inter alia the three *Canonical Epistles* 188 199 217 which are important for the penitential discipline) as well as letters of comfort, recommendation and friendship. The correspondence with Apollinaris (*Epp.* 361/4), among others, is to be discarded as spurious. Several pieces of the correspondence between Basil and Libanius (*Epp.* 335/59) are also spurious or dubious. On *Ep.* 8 v. supra § 52, 6, 4 (EP 911/29; EA 287/90).

Apart from the lit. listed infra: G. Pasquali, *Greg. Nyss. Opera. Epp.*, 1925, p. LIX/LXI, 70f. (*Ep.* 10 spurious). C. Cavallin, *Stud. z. d. Briefen des hl. B.*, Lund 1944 (*Ep.* 38 belongs to Greg. of Nyssa; *Ep.* 44 spurious; so also Rudberg, *Étud.* 1953, 136/8, who gives a crit. ed. of epp. 2, 150, and 173). Tadin, RSR 1950, 457/68 (recipient of *Ep.* 91). Bonis, BZ 1951, 62/78 (on the three canonical Epistles). Voelker, VC 1953, 23/6 (*Ep.* 366 spurious, mosaic from Clem. of Alex.). V. d. Muehll, MusHelv 11, 1955, 47/9 (on *Ep.* 11; reminiscence from Epicure). G. L. Prestige, *St. Bas. the Gr. and Apollinaris of Laod.*, 1956 (SPCK) (correspondence genuine). Y. Courtonne, *S. Basile, Lettres* 1 (Text, tr.). P 1957; also Gn 1959, 123/8.

6. Basil did much to renew the order of the liturgy, as is already attested by Gregory of Nazianzus (*Or.* 43, 34). It is no longer possible to reconstruct the authentic original form of the so-called *Liturgy of Basil* which is still in use in the Orthodox Church on ten days of the year; like the so-called *Liturgy of Chrysostom* (infra § 69, 5) it underwent far-reaching changes in the course of time. It is extant in Greek as well as in several Oriental languages.

Mgg.: P. Allard, P [4]1903. R. Janin, P 1929. Allard and Besse, DTC 2, 441/59. Bardy, DHG 6, 1111/26. J. Schaefer, *B.' d. Gr. Beziehungen zum Abendlande,* 1909. J. Wittig, *Die Friedenspolitik des Papstes Damasus I,* 1912. W. K. L. Clarke, *B. the Gr. A Study in Monasticism,* 1913. M. G. Murphy, *St. B. and Monasticism,* W 1930. F. Laun, ZKG 1925, 1/61 (monastic Rules). J. M. Campbell, *The Influence of the Second Sophistic on the Style of the Sermons of St. B.,* W 1922. L. V. Jacks, *B. and Greek Literature,* W 1922. A. C. Way, *The Language and Style of the Letters of St. B.,* W 1927. J. Wittig, *Des hl. B. d. Gr. geistl. Uebungen,* 1922. M. M. Fox, *The Life and Times of St. B. the Gr. as Revealed in His Works,* W 1939. P. Calasanctius (J. Joosen), *De beeldspraak bij den hl. B. d. Gr.,* N 1941. M. Goemans, *Het tract. v. B. d. Gr. over de klass. studie,* N 1945. For the genuineness of the Comm. on Is.: P. Humbertclaude, RevSR 1930, 47/68, and *La doctrine ascét. de s. B.,* 1932, 4/27; against this Devreesse, RB 1933, 145 f.; Stephanu, EO 1934, 238/40. Amand, *L'ascèse monast. de s. Bas.,* 1949, 30 A. 1. O. Ring, *Drei Homilien aus d. Fruehzeit B.' d. Gr.,* 1930; id., ZKG 1932, 365/83. Y. Courtonne, *S. B. et l'Hellénisme,* 1934 (comment. on Hexaem.-homs.); *S. B. Homélies sur la richesse.* Ed. crit. et exégét. 1935. K. Gronau, *Poseidonius u. d. jued.-christl. Genesis-Exegese,* 1914, 7/112 *(Hexaem.);* 281/93 (*Or.* 2). Bidez, ACl 1938, 19/31 (*Hex.* 6, 6). — Treatises: Ruge, PWK 16, 2409/13 (Neocaesarea). De Jerphanion, OCP 1936, 260/72; 491/6 and Grégoire, Byz 1935, 760/3 (geogr. situation of Dazimon; cf. *Ep.* 212). S. Giet, *Sasimes. Une méprise de s. B.,* 1941. E. Schwartz, ZNTW 1935, 158/213 (Melit. schism). Stauronikita, Γρηγόριος ὁ Παλαμᾶς, 1933, 281/5 (ed. *Orat. in Barlaam*). G. Lazzati, *L'Aristotele perduto . . .* 1938, 34/43 (*Ep.* 22). P. Henry, *Les États du Texte de Plotin,* 1938, 159/96 (Bas. and Plot.); 162/70 (*De Spiritu S.* genuine; written already *c.* 360). H. Doerries, *Symeon v. Mesopotamien,* 1941, 451/65 (Rules). P. J. Bratsiotes, At 1939; cf. BZ 1941, 523 (hist. of the veneration of Bas., Greg. Naz. and Jo. Chrys. in the MA). Schwartz, ZSK 1936, 22/7 (sources of canon. Epistles). Cavallin, Erani 43, 1945, 136/49 (second part of *Ep.* 197 spurious). On Basil.-Liturgy: Text in MG 31, 1629/56 and F. E. Brightman, *Liturg. Eastern and Western* I, 1896, 309/44, 400/11; Germ. R. Storf (BKV[2] 5) 1912, 263/78. Meester, DAL 6, 1596/1604. J. Moreau, *Les anaphores des liturgies de s. J. Chr. et de s. B.,* 1927. H. Engberding, *Das euch. Hochgebet der B.-Liturgie,* 1931. S. Salaville, *Lit. orientales,* 1932. S. Euringer, *Die aethiop. Anaphora des hl. B.,* R 1934. S. Antoniadis, *Place de la liturgie dans la trad. des lettres grecques,* Ley 1939. Lubatschiwskyj, ZKT 1942, 20/38 (the liturg. struggle ag. Arianism). Strittmatter, Tr 1943, 79/137 (oldest Lat. trans.). Gelsinger, East Church Quart. 10, 1954, 243/48 (The Epiklesis of St. B.). Raes, REB 1958, 158/61.

Points of Doctrine

1. The natural knowledge of God. Eunomius had pretended to find the essence of God solely in his *agennesia,* and hence asserted that we are able to comprehend it; against him Basil argued thus: We can know God only from his works, hence we can know about him only as much as he has shown in them; but even if he had used his whole power in his works, we could nevertheless grasp from them only his power, not an adequate conception of his essence. We derive the various properties of God from the things of sense by means of our reason; thus they are in a certain sense subjective. Yet they are not empty words, for they correspond to a reality in God. We shall not be able to understand God even in eternity, else he would be finite. The *agennesia* is only one of God's properties, and a negative one at that; it by no means expresses the whole of the divine Being (*Eun.* 1, 5 11; *Epp.* 233/5; EP 923f. 930/2).

2. On the doctrine of the Trinity. St. Athanasius, like the older Fathers, had nearly always used the terms οὐσία and ὑπόστασις for God in the same sense; even the synod of Alexandria (362) still permitted to speak of one and three hypostases in God. Basil was the first to admit only the formula μία οὐσία and τρεῖς ὑποστάσεις in God; for he understands ὑπόστασις in the sense of the being that subsists by itself and is circumscribed by certain special properties (εἰδιότητες), that is, in the sense of individual or person, according to the legal terminology of the Latins *(persona).* The occasion for this more exact definition was the Meletian Schism (supra 337), where Paulinus as a representative of the old Nicene school spoke of one divine hypostasis (= οὐσία), while the neo-Nicene Meletius confessed three hypostases (not = οὐσία). Basil designates as personal properties in God the Fatherhood, the Sonship and the Sanctification (*Ep.* 38, 3; 236, 6; EP 926 952 970f.).

3. The doctrine of the Holy Spirit. Athanasius *(Epp. ad Serap.)* and Basil created a theology of the Holy Spirit and paved the way for the definition of the Council of Constantinople (381). a. In essence Basil definitely taught in his writings the divinity and homoousia of the Holy Spirit, though he did not actually use the term ὁμοούσιος τῷ πατρί. Cf. *Eun.* 3, 4: τὸ Θεῖον τῆς φύσεως; 3, 5: Θεότης αὐτοῦ. Since he did not express himself equally clearly in his sermons, he was, as Gregory of Nazianzus tells us (*Ep.* 48), vehemently rebuked by certain over-zealous bishops. Gregory rejects these attacks on his friend by pointing out, among other things, that Basil rightly used such caution so as not to irritate the then very powerful Arians. Otherwise Basil would have been expelled, and his metropolis, which was so important to the Church, would have been lost to orthodoxy; for "salvation lies not in terms, but in the thing they express" (*Or.* 43 n. 68). "Those who call the Holy Spirit God before the low-minded do not act with pastoral prudence ('oeconomically'); they cast the pearl into the mud and give solid food instead of milk" (*Or.* 41 n. 6). The N.T. only hinted at the divinity of the Holy Spirit, and it would have been a great risk to burden men, as it were, with the divinity of the Holy Spirit while that of the Son had not yet been generally acknowledged (*Or.* 31 n. 27).

b. Like most Greek Fathers Basil, too, says that the Holy Spirit proceeds "from the Father through the Son". But he distinctly disapproves of Eunomius' teaching which called the Son his only source; on the contrary, the Son has everything in common with the Father, and in Scripture the Holy Spirit is not only called Spirit of the Father but also of the Son (*Eun.* 2, 34; 3, 1; *Spir.* 18 n. 45). It can be deduced from *Eun.* 2, 32 that the Holy Spirit also proceeds from the Son, even though it is not directly asserted (cf. also supra 337 f.).

4. Penance and Confession. Basil attests that there are four classes of public penitents in his church (*Ep.* 217; EH 593/6). In his

Rule for Religious Basil prescribes for his monks the confession of all, including interior, sins. It is to be made before an experienced spiritual guide, in the first place before the superior (προεστώς). The confession can also be received by a chosen representative of the superior. But it is nowhere mentioned that the superior or his representative must be a priest, or that there is an absolution (*Reg. fus. tract.* 26 and 45). The confession practised here was not so much a *confessio sacramentalis* as a *directio spiritualis.*

5. Papal Primacy. Basil does not yet consider the Bishop of Rome the jurisdictional head of the universal Church, even though he assigns to him an authoritative position in all questions of dogma. The unity and agreement is to consist in a community of like-minded bishops who are in contact with each other through constant communication by letter and messengers; the Bishop of Rome is one of these bishops, but one among others and the leader of the Western bishops.

6. Principal ascetical theories. Basil rejected the ideal of the anchorites (MG 31, 928/33); he was after Pachomius the founder of Eastern monasticism. He equates man with his soul; the body is united to the soul only accidentally and the soul is fettered to it. If it is to remain faithful to its spiritual nature it must free itself from the bond of the body. The soul frees itself and subjects the body through asceticism, i. e. through renouncing the satisfaction of the dormant passions and struggling against them. In his Rules and other writings Basil proves all his rigoristic precepts destined to form the perfect Christian, that is, the monk, by an enormous number of Scriptural texts. The human person, the image of God, is equipped with the power of knowledge and the capacity for love (In Ps. 48, 8; MG 29, 37/40). Reason and free will are its characteristic marks. "Know thyself and Watch thyself" are the most important rules in the struggle for perfection (MG 31, 197 ff.). The Christian and *a fortiori* the monk must fulfil all God's commandments; he may not disregard a single one; for he is indeed

capable of observing them all. Transgressing a single one of the commandments of God means transgressing all others and merits eternal death (MG 31, 661/76). In his view especially of the relation between body and soul Basil is strongly influenced by neo-Platonism (Porphyry). Cf. D. Amand, *L'ascèse . . .*, 1949, 351/64.

Mgg. and treatises: T. Schermann, *Die Gottheit des Hl. Geistes nach d. griech. Vaetern des 4. Jh.*, 1901. K. Weiss, *Die Erziehungslehre der 3 Kappadozier*, 1903. K. Unterstein, *Die natuerl. Gotteserkenntnis nach der Lehre der kappadoz. Kirchenvaeter B., Gregor v. Nazianz u. Gregor v. Nyssa*, 2 Progr., Straubing 1902/3. F. Nager, *Die Trinitaetslehre des hl. B.*, 1912. J. Maier, *Die Eucharistielehre der 3 grossen Kappadozier*, 1915. K. Gronau, *Das Theodizeeproblem in altchristl. Auffassung*, 1922. J. Rivière, *S. B.*, P 1925 *(Moralistes chrét.)*. T. Papakonstantinu, Ὁ Μέγας Β., ἡ δογματικὴ αὐτοῦ διδασκαλία, At [3]1931. P. Humbertclaude, *La doctrine ascétique de s. B.*, 1932. B. K. Exarchos, At 1938; cf. BZ 1940, 261 (pedagogics). B. Kostits, Τὸ πρόβλημα τῆς σωτηρίας (in B.), At 1936. J. K. Zonevsky, Sofia 1940 (doctrine of Trin.); cf. BZ 1942, 308. Batiffol, EO 1922, 9/30 (doctrine of the Church); against this Diamantopulos, 'Εναίσιμα (papers publ. in honour of C. Papadopulos), At 1931, 38/51. Arnou, Gr 1934, 242/54 (Trin. doct. of neo-Nicenes). De Ghellinck, *Patristique et Moyen Age* III, 1948, 311/38 (H. Spirit). Bardy, DS 1, 1273/83. F. Delpiano, Anales FacultadTeol, Santiago 1940, 15/29 *(Unitas in Trinitate)*. Pera, Ang 1942, 39/95 (inter alia on Eunomius and Basil). Giet, *Science rel.* 1944, 95/128 (prohibition of interest in B. and Ambrose). Cuesta, RET 1947, 337/63 (penitence in *Didascalia*, B. and Gr. of Nyssa). F. Reilly, *Imperium and Sacerdotium acc. to St. B.*, W 1945. S. Giet, *Les idées et l'action sociales de s. B.*, P 1941. B. Schewe, *B. d. Gr. als Theologe*, N 1943 (on theol. theory of knowl.). Amand 1945, 383/400; *L'ascèse monastique de s. B.*, 1949; on this Giet, RevSR 1949, 333/42. Coman, *Festschr. f. d. Patriarch. Nicodim*, Bucharest 1946, 255/72 (envy in Plutarch, Cyprian and Bas.); cf. BZ 1950, 97. Daniélou, RSR 1948, 382/411 *(La typologie de la semaine au 4e s.)*. Soell, TQ 1951, 161/88, 288/319, 426/57 (Mariology of Cappadocians). Gribomont, VS Suppl 1952, 192/250 *(Obéissance et l'Évang.)*. W. A. Tieck, *Bas. of Caes. and the Bible*, thesis Columbia Univ. NY 1953. Lebon, RHE 1953, 632/82 (*Consubstantialis* in Bas.). Dirking, TQ 1954, 202/12 *(Apatheia)*. Nothomb, POC 1954, 309/21 *(Sur la charité)*. T. Pichler, *Das Fasten b. Bas. d. Gr. u. im antik. Heidentum* I, 1955. E. Bruck (v. supra § 3), 1/75 (social right of inheritance in the 3 Cappadocians and John Chrys.). H. Doerries, *De Spiritu S. Der Beitrag des Bas. z. Abschluss des trinitarischen Dogmas*, GAb 39, 1956; also Jaeger, ThLZ 1958, 255/8.

§ 59. GREGORY OF NAZIANZUS (b. 329–30, d. *c.* 390)

Gregory was born on the estate of Arianzus near Nazianzus in Cappadocia. He was the son of Bishop Gregory the Elder of Nazianzus (329–30); his pious mother Nonna, who had been responsible for her husband's conversion to Christianity (325) exercised a powerful influence on the young Gregory. He was educated at first at the school of rhetoric in Caesarea (Cappadocia); he then spent a short time at the Christian schools at Caesarea in Palestine and at Alexandria, and finally went to the pagan university at Athens where he remained till *c.* 356–7 and became Basil's lifelong friend (supra § 58). He was probably baptized only after his return home. At that time he intended to become a monk.

About 362 his father, the bishop, ordained him priest against his will, at the insistence of the people. Angry at the "violence" inflicted on him he fled into the desert and there wrote his *Apologeticus de fuga* to justify himself (on the dignity and burden of the priest; infra 1b). Soon, however, he returned to Nazianzus and there assisted his father in the administration and the cure of souls. When Basil founded new episcopal sees to consolidate his influence as metropolitan which had been diminished by the partition of Cappadocia, he consecrated his friend Gregory, who once more resisted, Bishop of the small city of Sasima, but the latter never entered upon his new office in that "bewitched and miserable little place". After the death of his father (374) he administered for a time the fatherless diocese of Nazianzus, but he soon devoted himself once more to the contemplative life at Seleucia (Isauria).

In 379 he accepted a call to undertake the direction and reorganization of the Nicene community at Constantinople, which had at that time shrunk considerably. For a short time he thus entered the stage of ecclesiastical policy. In 380 the Emperor Theodosius solemnly inducted him into the Church of the Apostles of the city; in 381 he was confirmed as bishop by the second General Council then being held in Constantinople. Many worries and intrigues — the legality of his episcopal office being disputed among other things — caused him so much disgust with his new position that, in order to end all disputes, he decided to resign after a few days. Before his departure he delivered his famous *Parting Speech* (*Or.* 42) to the bishops and the people. For two years he administered the still vacant diocese of his home town; after that he devoted himself entirely to literary works and the practice of asceticism, spending the remaining time of his life quietly on his country estate at Arianzus (d. *c.* 390). Feast day: May 9th.

Gregory of Nazianzus had a sensitive, contemplative nature, and, in contrast to Basil, possessed only little gift and inclination for practical activities. He liked best to devote himself to a life of scholarly and contemplative leisure; though from time to time he allowed himself to be drawn into public life and activities, since he realized his own intellectual powers and wanted to follow the noble desire to be useful to the troubled Church or to his friends. As a result of his poor health he could be nervous and irritable, and, especially towards the end of his life, also bitter against others, though these defects were mitigated by a conciliatory disposition. Rhetorics was the element of his life, and he used its rules and artifices both in prose and poetry with consummate skill; none of the great preachers of the fourth century equalled him in eloquence and breadth of literary knowledge. The Byzantine scholars called him the Christian Demosthenes and placed him above the pagan one. His *Orations* continued to be commented down to the sixteenth century.

Gregory had as little inclination as Basil for independent speculative thought and strictly followed Scripture and tradition in his theological expositions, hence he can be regarded as a reliable witness to the doctrinal state of the Greek Church of his time.

His writings

1. Gregory's greatest achievement is the forty-five *Orations,* which are only a selection from his rhetorical and literary work (EP 979/1016; EA 295/315).

a. 5 *Theological Orations* stand out from the number of his doctrinal sermons (27–31). These were delivered at Constantinople in 380 and defend the orthodox doctrine of the Trinity against Eunomians and Macedonians. They have earned him the honourable title "The Theologian".

b. His *Panegyrical Orations* are the most numerous: sermons for ecclesiastical feasts, panegyrics on the Maccabeans, Cyprian and Athanasius, funeral orations on the death of his father, his brother (Caesarius) and sister (Gorgonia) and his friend Basil (43).

c. Controversial speeches and invectives against Julian the Apostate (EH 580/2); several speeches are concerned with events of his own life; *Apologeticus de fuga,* the farewell sermon of Constantinople. On the works written in collaboration with Basil v. supra § 58.

2. His 245 *Letters* nearly all written at the time of his later retirement at Arianzus, are for the greater part concerned with his own personal affairs or those of his friends, some are only cards of recommendation. As a rule they are carefully worked out, rich in maxims, and often witty. *Epp.* 101 and 102 *ad Cledonium* and *Ep.* 207 are directed against Apollinarianism.

3. His *Poems* were also composed in his last years to help to refute the reproach that Christians were backward. His *Poemata dogmatica* and *moralia* which have didactic aims are mostly nothing but versified prose. In the *Poemata historica,* however, which tell of the seeking and erring, the love and hope of his own soul, we meet many truly poetic passages full of tender, mostly elegiac feeling. The longest of his poems, *De vita sua* (1949 iambic trimeters) is valuable not only as a source of his life but also as an autobiographical document. This and similar poems may be compared with the *Confessions* of St. Augustine. The tragedy *Christus patiens* which is printed among his works is very late; it was written probably in the eleventh or twelfth century.

Edd.: C. Clémencet and A. B. Caillau, 2 vols., 1778 and 1840. MG 35/38. *Orat. theol.* ed. A. J. Mason, C 1899. *Orat. 7 et 43* ed. F. Boulenger, P 1908. G. Mercati (ST 11) 1903, 53/6 (1 letter). H. Gerstinger (SbW 208, 3) 1928 (*Epp.* 80 and 90). Baz 1933, 444/8 (oration on the holy cross, Armen.). — I. Hausherr, *Anaphora Gregorii Naz.* (syriace) R 1940. — Transs.: *Select Orations,* trans. C. G. Browne and J. E. Swallow, O and NY 1894. P. Haeuser (BKV[2] 59) 1928 and J. Roehm (BKV) 1874 1877 (orations). J. Stahr, *Letters* (Polish), Poznan 1933. Q. Cataudella, *Selected Orations,* Tu 1935. P. Gallay, *G. de Naz.,* I: *Poèmes et lettres,* II: *Discours théol.,* 1941. — Mgg.: A. Donders, *G. von N. als Homilet,* 1909. M. Guignet, *S. G. de N. Orateur et épistolier,* 1911. P. Gallay, *La vie de s. G. de Naz.,* 1943. J. Sajdak, *Hist. crit. Scholiastarum et Commentariorum Gregorii Naz.,* Cracow 1914; *De Gregorio Naz. poetarum christ. fonte,* Cracow 1917. T. Sinko, *De traditione orationum G. N.,* 2 parts, Cracow 1917/23; *De Cypriano mart. a Gregorio Naz. laudato,* Cracow 1916. F. Martroye, *Le testament de S. G. de N.,* 1924. H. Pinault, *Le Platonisme de G. de N.,* 1925. E. Fleury, *Hellénisme et Christianisme. S. Grég. et son temps,* 1930. A. N. Malin, Οἱ ἐπιτάφιοι λόγοι Γ. Ν., At 1929. M. Pellegrino, *La poesia di S. G. N.,* Mi 1932. P. Gallay, *Langue et style de s. G. de N. dans sa correspond.,* 1943. G. Misch, *Gesch. der Autobiographie* I, 1931, 383/402. 4 brief works written in Roumanian by J. Coman (1937/8) are listed in BZ 1939, 239: (a) *The Genius of G. v. N.;* (b) *G. and the Emp. Julian* (*Or.* 4. 5); (c) *The Causes of Julian's anti-Christian Policy acc. to the Testimony of the Fathers;* (d) *The Melancholy in the Lyric Poetry of Gregory.* H. L. Davids, *De Gnomologieen van S. G. v. N.,* N 1940 (*Poem. moral.* 30/4). R. de Lima Henoy, *The Late Greek Optative and its Use in the Writings of G. of Naz.,* W 1943. — Treatises: On the hist. of the city of Nazianzus cf. Ruge, PWK 16, 2099/101; Leclercq, DAL 6, 1667/1711; 12, 1054/65. Keydell, BJ 272, 1941. Graf I, 330/2. S. Skimina (rhythmic prose); cf. BZ 1935, 186. Doelger, AC 5, 44/75 (*Or.* 18, 9f. etc.). Mersch 1 [2]1936, 438/50. Byz 6, 1931, 343 A. 2 (older lit.). Disdier, EO 1931, 485/97 (lit. 1918/31). Bignone, RFC 1936, 225ff. (*Or.* 40: *Protrett. di Aristotele*). Gallay, Mél. Desrousseaux 1937, 165/9 (MSS of the letters). Wyss, Her 1938, 360 (Or. 28, 8: text. crit.). Gallay, REG 1944, 106/24 (MSS of letters). P. Galley, *Mél. J. Saunier,* Lyons 1944, 81/93 (MSS of letters). Keenan, *Bull. Hist. of Medicine* 9, 8/30 (G. of Naz. and Early Byz. Medicine). Davids, VC 1947, 244/6; 1948, 113f. (*Epp.* 65 and 199). Brou, EL 1944, 14/22 (Laudes-antiphone *Mirabile mysterium*). P. Gallay, *Catalogue des MSS parisiens des lettres de s. G. de Naz.,* Mâcon 1945. C. Przychocki, *Hist. Listow. Sw. G. N.,* Cracow 1946. J. Lercher, *Die Persoenlichkeit des hl. G. v. Naz.* (attitude to class. education), thesis I 1949; cf. BZ 1953, 381/3. Wyss, MusHelvet 6, 1949, 177/210 (G. of N. as a poet). Doubouniotis, Θ 1950, 354/84 (Nicetas of Heracleia, introduction to the orations of G.). Tailler, Actes CongrInternatEtByz (1948) I 1950, 403/9 (*Christus patiens* written in 4th cent.); against this Doelger, BZ 1952, 159. Keydell, BZ 1950, 334/7 (*Exhortatio ad virgines* spurious); BZ 1951, 315/21 (a dogmatic didactic poem; MG 38, 397/456); StudBizNeoell 7, 1953, 134/43 (position of poems in hist. of lit.). E. Rapisarda, MiscStLettChristAnt 3, 1951, 136/61 and StudBizNeoell 1953, 189/201 (G.'s pessimism). Meehan, ITQ 1951, 203/19 (editions of G.). H. M. Werhahn, *Ed. Gregorii Naz.* Σύνκρισις βίων, Wiesbaden 1953. On the treatise by K. G. Bones on G. of Naz.'s genealogical tree, At 1953, cf. Werhahn, BZ 1954,

414/18; against this Bones, ibid. 1955, 211f. M. Simonetti, RendIstLombClLett, Mi 86, 1953, 101/17 *(G. Naz. o Gregorio Taumaturgo?)*. Agathangelos of Cyd., Γρηγόριος ὁ Παλαμᾶς 36, 1953, 20/4 (Aristophanes in G.). On G.'s brother Caesarius of Naz. cf. PWK 3, 1298/1300. V. Casoli, *Cesario medico del sec. 4*, Modena 1931. — On the spurious dialogues of Caesar. (MG 38, 851/1190) cf. BZ 1953, 221 (written in 5th cent.). Barisic, *Sbornik radowa* 1, 1952, 29/51 (Belgrade) (date of Dialogues). Dujcev, Slavia antiqua 4, 1953, 193/209 (Ps.-Caes. on the Slavs). Bones, EEBS 1953, 261/79 (author perh. Severus of Ant.). Duprey, POC 5, 1955, 14/30, 297/315 (date 1st half of 6th cent.). Riedinger 1956, 45, 47; on anti-astrolog. texts in Ps.-Caes. ibid. freq.

Points of Doctrine

1. Doctrine of the Trinity. Gregory of Nazianzus was the first to give the differences between the three divine Persons themselves the names ἀγεννησία and ἐκπόρευσις (ἔκπεμψις) (*Or*. 25, 16; EP 983). He differed from Basil in that he clearly and formally stated the divinity of the Holy Spirit (τὸ πνεῦμα ἅγιον καὶ Θεός) and asked: "How long shall we still place the light under the bushel and withhold the perfect Divinity (of the Holy Spirit) from others?" (*Or*. 12, 6) (v. supra § 58, 3).

2. Christology: He clearly attests the unity of the Person in Christ: "Christ is One out of two, two natures unite in him to the One, there are not two Sons" (*Or*. 37, 2; EP 1001). In opposition to the Apollinarians he teaches the completeness of the human nature of Christ, in which the νοῦς may not be absent. In defining the manner of the union of the two natures he coins the following formula which is important for later developments: Κατ' οὐσίαν συνῆφθαί τε καὶ συνάπτεσθαι. "If a man does not call St. Mary Θεοτόκος he is far from the Godhead" (*Ep*. 101, 4f.; EP 1017). He writes of St. Justina that she had invoked the Bl. Virgin for help (*Or*. 24, 10f.).

3. Original Sin and Baptism. Gregory states clearly the evil consequences of Adam's sin: "I have altogether fallen and am condemned because of the disobedience of the first man and the

deceitful guile of the devil (*Or.* 22, 13). We do not, however, find original sin clearly attested by him, even though he says: "Woe be to my weakness, for that of the first man is mine also" (*Or.* 38, 12). Hence he calls the small children guiltless (ἀπόνηρος). If anyone cannot receive baptism because he is too young or dies suddenly, he does not, indeed, go to hell, but neither does he go to heaven (*Or.* 40, 23; EP 1012). If there is no danger, Gregory advises to have infants baptized only after three years (*Or.* 40, 28).

4. Eucharist and Holy Sacrifice. He says in his Easter sermon (*Or.* 45, 19): "If you long for life, eat the Body and drink the Blood without fear and doubt." On his recovery from an illness he writes to his friend Bishop Amphilochius: "Do not cease, pious man, to pray and intercede for me, when you draw down the Logos through the word, when you sacrifice the body and blood of the Lord with unbloody cut through the sharpness of your word" (*Ep.* 171; EP 1019).

Mg.: K. Holl, *Amphilochius von Ikon.*, 1904, 158/96. E. Weigl, *Christologie vom Tode des Athanas. bis zum Ausbruch des nestor. Streites*, 1925, 53/79. H. Fuchs, *Augustin u. der antike Friedensgedanke*, 1926, 96/125 (Or. 6). J. Sajdak, *The Educational Views of G. of N.*, Poznan 1933 (Polish). L. Stephan, *Die Soteriologie des hl. G. v. Naz.*, W 1938. F. X. Portmann, *Die goettliche Paedagogie bei G. v. Naz.*, St. Ottilien 1954. J. Plagnieux, *S. G. de Naz. Théologien*, P 1951 (cf. 453f.: G. author of a Mt. commentary?). Serra, OCP 1955, 337/74 (*Carità pastorale* in S. G. Naz.).

§ 60. GREGORY OF NYSSA (d. 394)

GREGORY, the younger brother of St. Basil, was at first a rhetor, but later, influenced by his friend Gregory of Nazianzus, he retired into the solitude of the monastic life. He accepted the episcopal dignity only at the insistence of his brother Basil; he became Bishop of Nyssa in Cappadocia in 371.

Gregory sometimes failed before the difficulties of the practical ecclesiastical activities. In 376 he was deposed at a synod at Nyssa which had been called by the vicar of the political diocese of

Pontus, where he was slanderously accused of wasting Church property. After the death of the Emperor Valens (378) he returned to his diocese. The synod of Antioch (379) entrusted him with the visitation of the diocese of Pontus; at this time he was elected metropolitan of Sebaste, where he had to reside several months "in Babylonian captivity". At the Council of Constantinople (381) he was one of the pillars of orthodoxy. He died in 394, soon after the Synod of Constantinople which he had attended.

Gregory was of an introspective nature and possessed eminent speculative gifts. He surpassed the other Cappadocians as a philosopher and a theologian, and contributed much to the philosophical penetration of the doctrines of the faith. He was held in great esteem at the Imperial Court because of his eloquence. On the deaths of the Empress Flaccilla and her daughter Pulcheria in 386 he delivered the funeral orations.

1. *Dogmatic writings*

a. The so-called twelve books *Against Eunomius* (infra § 62) of the older editions actually combine four different treatises directed against Eunomius. The first work (book 1) is written against the first book of a treatise by Eunomius (Ὑπὲρ τῆς ἀπολογίας ἀπολογία) attacking Basil (supra § 58), a second treatise (book 12b or 13) against the second book of Eunomius. A third work in ten books (3–12a) attacks a new work by Eunomius which was also directed against Basil. The fourth work (book 2) is the refutation of an *Expositio fidei* of Eunomius. The edition by W. Jaeger now gives the right order (EP 1040/51); cf. infra § 62, 2.

b. Three further writings are also directed against heretics: *Antirrheticus adv. Apollinarem,* the most important of the extant anti-Apollinarian works (EP 1052/5); it had been preceded by a short treatise *Adversus Apollinarem* addressed to Theophilus of Alexandria: *Against Macedonians and Pneumatomachi.*

c. Four minor treatises are important for the doctrine of the Trinity: *Ad Eustathium de Trinitate* (in F. Oehler, BKV I, 2, 1858); *Ad Ablabium; Contra Gentes; Ad Simplicium.*

d. The *Oratio catechetica magna* is perhaps the most important dogmatic work; it establishes and defends the principal Christian doctrines against heretics, Jews and pagans; it is not so much polemical as destined for the "ecclesiastical superiors".

Part I (1–4) treats of the one God in three Persons, Part II (5–32) of sin, the incarnation and redemption by Christ, Part III (33–40) of baptism and the eucharist (EP 1028/36).

e. The *Dialogus de anima et resurrectione,* a companion piece to Plato's *Phaedo,* is dedicated to the memory of his sister Macrina whom he saw again on her deathbed, when he was returning from the synod of Antioch (379). Gregory lets his dying sister state the Christian views on the soul, death, immortality, resurrection and the restoration of all things (ch. 13). A second short dialogue *Contra fatum* opposes astrological fatalism.

2. *Exegetical Treatises and Homilies*

a. The creation story is the subject of two works *De opificio hominis* and *In Hexaëmeron.* Both are intended to supplement Basil's homilies on the *Hexaëmeron* (supra § 58) and to prevent them from being misunderstood. Here Gregory still does justice to the historical and grammatical sense of Scripture. In his other exegetical works he shows himself a representative of uninhibited allegorical interpretation. These are:

b. *De vita Moysis.* The life of Moses represents the gradual mystical ascent of the soul to God (EA 340/5). *In psalmorum inscriptiones;* here Gregory wants to show that the division and the titles of the Psalms if interpreted allegorically can furnish instruction on the life of virtue and perfection. In his fifteen homilies *On the*

Canticle God is represented as the bridegroom of the human soul (bride) (EA 330/6). Also: a treatise *On the Witch of Endor* (1 Sam. 28, 12ff.), eight homilies *On Ecclesiastes* (1:1–3:13), eight homilies *On the Beatitudes* (Mt. 5:1–10) (EA 337f.) and five homilies *On the Lord's Prayer*.

3. The ascetical writings include four minor works on Christian perfection, the divinely willed final goal, the monastic life and monastic penances, as well as the treatise *De virginitate*, an attractive instruction on the celibate life and the "espousal of Christ with the soul" (EA 322f.) and the *Vita S. Macrinae*, a devotional biography of his sister.

4. The *Orations* and *Sermons* are written in the pompous style of contemporary rhetoric; they are not so vigorous and lively as those of the other two Cappadocians (EP 1061/5). He treats moral and dogmatic subjects (e.g. against deferring baptism, against usury, on the divinity of the Son and the Holy Spirit). There are also sermons for the feasts of the Church, on saints (Gregory Thaumaturgus, the 40 martyrs) and funeral orations.

5. Thirty *Letters* (in Pasquali) are mostly occasional writings of purely personal content. Ep. 2 has attracted much attention; it castigates the abuses during pilgrimages to Jerusalem and warns against over-estimating pilgrimages.

Edd.: MG 44/46. W. Jaeger, *Contra Eunom.*, 2 vols., 1921f. G. Pasquali, *Epistulae*, 1925. W. Jaeger aliique, *Gregorii Nyss. Op. VIII pars I. Op. ascetica* ed., Ley 1952 *(De instituto christ., De profectione christ., De perfectione, De virginitate, Vita S. Macrinae)*. W. Jaeger, *Two Rediscovered Works of Anc. Christ. Literature: Greg. of Nyssa* (*De instituto Christ.* and *Macarius*) Ley 1954 (ed. 'Επιστολὴ πρώτη of Macarius); cf. Doerries in: TLZ 1954, 643/56. Separate edd.: *De or. dom.* ed. J. G. Krabinger, 1840; *Or. catech.* ed. J. H. Srawley, C 1903. L. Méridier, P 1908. *De an. et resurr.* ed. Krabinger, 1837. E. Klostermann (KlT 83) 1912 (Witch of Endor). C. van den Eynde, *La version syr. du comment. de G. de N. sur le cantique des cant.*, Lou 1939 (cf. § 104, 1). G. Mercati (ST 75) 1938, 191/9 (ined. *ep. ad Philippum* in vers. lat.). Diekamp, AP 1938, 13/5 (fragm. ined.). — Transs.: H. Hayd and J. Fisch (BKV) 1874, 1880; K. Weiss and E. Stolz (BKV² 56) 1927. U. v. Balthasar, *Der versiegelte Quell* (= comm. on Cant.), 1939. J. Daniélou, *G. Nyss., Vie de Moïse*, ²1956 (Gr. text and trans.). J. Laplace, *La créat. de l'homme*, 1944. H. C.

Graef, *The Lord's Prayer - The Beatitudes* (ACW 18), 1954. — Mgg.: Godet, DTC 6, 1847/52. J. A. Stein, *Encomium of St. G. Bishop of N. on his Brother Bas.*, W 1928. H. F. Cherniss, *The Platonism of G. of N.*, Berkeley 1930. Doelger, AC 3, 81/116 *(Vita Macr.)*. v. Ivánka, *Arch. Philologicum* 59, 1935, 10/2: *Poseidonis bei G. v. N.* Pellegrino, RFN 1938, 437/74 (Platonismo nel *De an. et resurr.*). F. Mueller, Her 1939, 66/91 (*Ep.* 20). Graf I, 332/5. Jaeger, Tr 1947, 79/102 (MS *de opif.* hom.). T. Goggin, *The Time of St. G. of N....*, W 1947. Keenan, BullHist of Medic. 15, 1944, 150/61 (medical profession in G.). J. J. Cuesta, *La antropología y la medicina pastoral de G. de N.*, Ma 1946 (*De opif. hom.* and Galenus). W. Jaeger, Festg. f. K. Reinhardt, Cologne 1952, 161/8 (on *Ep. ad Harmonium*). On question of genuineness of *Vita Greg. Thaum.* (MG 46, 893/957) cf. R. Laurentin, *Court traité de théologie mariale,* 1953, 161. Halkin, NClio 1954, 70/2 (MS of *Vita Greg. Thaumat.*). J. Daniélou, RevSR 1955, 346/72 (on chronology of sermons). On question of genuineness of second hom. *De struct. hom.* (MG 44, 257/97) v. § 58, 3. *Greg. Nyss. op. ed. Jaeger:* III, 1, ed. Mueller 1958 (lesser dogmatic writings); VI ed. Langerbeck 1960 (comm. on Ct.).

Points of Doctrine

1. The knowledge of God. Under the influence of Philo and Plotinus Gregory teaches not only a natural knowledge of God ascending from the sense world to supra-sensual realities, but states that the summit of the knowledge of God is the elevation of the human mind to an immediate vision of God, an anticipation of the beatitude of heaven, "a divine and sober inebriation" (*Beat.* 6; *Cant.* 10). The fundamental traits of a "negative theology" found in his works, his doctrine of the divine names and his conception of ecstasy make him a fore-runner of the Areopagite (§ 100). Directly or indirectly (Evagrius [52, 6] or Dionysius Areop.) he also influenced Maximus Confessor (§ 160, 2).

2. Doctrine of the Trinity. Influenced by Plato's doctrine of ideas, Gregory assigns reality to the universals when he says that the term "man" designates the nature, not the individual, and that one must call Peter, Paul and Barnabas together only one, not three men (MG 45, 177 and 180). Gregory, who energetically repudiates the reproach of tritheism, uses this example only to make the divine Trinity more intelligible.

He finds the difference between the divine Persons only in their relations; therefore every external activity of God is common to all three Persons. In the Deity "the one is the cause, the other from the cause, and in that which is from the cause we assume a difference; for the one is immediately from the first, whereas the other is through that which is immediately from the first" (EP 1037f.). Hence Gregory, like other Greek Fathers, takes the Holy Spirit to proceed from the Father through the Son, that is immediately only from the Father.

3. Christology. Gregory clearly teaches the mutual exchange of the attributes of the two natures in Christ which remain unconfused *(Communicatio idiomatum)* (*Eun.* 5; ed. Jaeger 2, 1921, 123f. n. 63 and 66; MG 45, 705). The Logos has fashioned for himself from the flesh of the Virgin "a receptacle of God not made by human hands" (MG 46, 616). Hence the Virgin is Θεοτόκος and not, as the innovators dare to say, ἀνθρωποτόκος (*Ep.* 3).

4. Though Gregory definitely rejects Origen's doctrine of the pre-existence of souls he has taken over from him the idea of the restoration of all things (supra § 40, 8). The non-baptized as well as the baptized person who has not expiated his later sins "by prayers and philosophy" must be purified by fire after death, "more or less quickly"; after evil has thus been purged from nature, all creation will give thanks to the Creator, and "the origin of evil" (the devil), too, will be cured of evil (*Cat.* 26).

5. Eucharist. "Hence we believe very rightly that even now the bread at the moment when it is sanctified by the Word of God, is changed [μεταποιεῖσθαι] into the body of the divine Logos" (*Cat.* 37, 3; EP 1035).

F. Diekamp, *Die Gotteslehre des hl. G. von N.,* 1896. W. Vollert, *Die Lehre G.s v. N. vom Guten u. Boesen,* 1897. K. Holl, *Amphilochius v. I.,* 1904, 196/235. J. B. Aufhauser, *Die Heilslehre des hl. G. v. N.,* 1910. J. Lenz, *Jesus Christus nach d. Lehre des hl. G. v. N.,* 1925. M. G. de Castro, *Die Trinitaetslehre des hl. G. v. N.,* Fr 1938. S. González, *La fórmula* μία φύσις τρεῖς ὑποστάσεις *en S. G. d. N.,* R 1939. H. O. Knackstedt, *Die Theologie der Jungfraeulichkeit beim hl. G. v. N.,* R 1940. J. Daniélou, *Platonisme et théologie mystique* (bei Greg. v. Nyssa), ²1954. — J. Rivière, 1931,

222/8. Mersch I, [2]1936, 450/63. J. Bayer, *Greg.s v. Nyssa Gottesbegriff,* 1935. Vollert, TB 1935, 106/12 (Eschatol.). Malevez, RSR 1935, 260/80 *(l'égl. dans le Christ).* See Ivánka, StC 11, 1934/5, 45/7 (Gotteslehre). Id., Sch 1936, 163/95 (Theory of mysticism). V. Koperski, *Doctr. Gregorii Nyss. de process. filii Dei,* R 1936. Isaye, RSR 1937, 422/39 *(l'unité de l'opération divine).* Lieske, Sch 1939, 485/514 (Christusmystik). See Balthasar, RSR 1939, 513/49 *(la philos. relig.).* Daniélou, RSR 1940, 328/55 *(l'apocatastase).* S. González, Gr 1938, 130/4 (Symbolum), 280/301 (Trinity); 1939, 189/206 *(realismo Platonico).* Schoemann, Sch 1943, 31/53 175/200 (Anthropology). U. v. Balthasar, *Présence et pensée. Philos. relig. de Grég. de Nyssa,* 1942. J. Muckle, MedievalStud 7, 1945, 55/84 (the doctrine on man as the image of God). Cuesta, RET 1947, 337ff. (Penance). Lieske, ZKT 1948, 1/45 129/68 315/40 (Christusmystik). McClear, TSW 1948, 175/212 (the Fall and Original Sin). Amand, *Fatalisme,* 1945, 405/39. Armstrong, DSO 1, 1948, 113/26 (platonic elements in the doctrine of man). Id., East. Churches Quart. 8, 1949, 3rd Suppl. Issue 2/9 (nature of man). Keenan, DOP 1950, 167/207 (ascetical doctrine). R. Leys, *L'Image de Dieu chez s. Grég. de Nyssa,* Bru 1951. Trinick, EastCathQuart 9, 1951/2, 175/84 (doctrine of the image). A. A. Weiswurm, *The Nature of Human Knowledge according to St. Grég. of Nyssa,* W 1952. Soell, TQ 1951, 178/88 (Mariology. Christmas sermon [MG 46, 1127/50]: genuine). Daniélou, *Gedaechtnisschr. Casel,* 1951, 79/93 (Cult mystery). Id., VC 1953, 154/70 (Resurrection of the body). Id., RevSR 1953, 219/49 *(Akolouthia).* Id., DS, fasc. 14/15, 1952, 1872/85 *(mystique de la ténèbre).* H. Merki, *Ὁμοίωσις Θεῷ bei Greg. v. Nyssa,* FrSch 1952; also Jaeger, Gn 1955, 573/80. W. Voelker, *Festschr. G. Biundo* 4, 1952, 9/16 (Ontology). Id., VC 1955, 103/28 (theology). Id., *Greg. v. Nyssa als Mystiker,* Wiesbaden 1955. Floeri, Rev SR 1953, 105/11 *(la division des sexes).* J. Gaith, *La conception de la liberté chez Grég. de Nysse,* P 1953. Ladner, StHon Friend, 88/95 (Greg. of Nyssa and St. Augustine on the symbolism of the cross). Zonewski, *Annuaire de Théol.,* Sofia 2, 1951/52, 287/314 (the social teaching of Greg. Naz. and Greg. of Nyssa). W. Voelker, *Gregor v. Nyssa als Mystiker,* 1955.

§ 61. AMPHILOCHIUS OF ICONIUM (d. after 394)

AMPHILOCHIUS, a friend of the three great Cappadocians and a cousin of Gregory of Nazianzus, was educated at Antioch under Libanius. He was a lawyer at Constantinople for about six years, and became Bishop of Iconium at the instigation of St. Basil (373). He vigorously opposed Arianism as well as various sects that were under the influence of Manicheism and devoted to exaggerated asceticism (Apotactites, Gemellites, Messalians).

Little has remained of his large literary output. The thirty-three *Iambi ad Seleucum* are intended to give instructions on a devout life and successful study (MG 37, 1577/1600): 251–319 contain a list of Biblical books important for the history of the canon (EP 1078). Apart from eight sermons on Church feasts and texts of Scripture we possess a treatise directed against the sectarian Apotactites and Gemellites extant in Coptic.

Edd.: MG 39, 9/130. On the authenticity of the eight sermons cf. K. Holl, *Amphil. von I.*, 1904, 58/83 and the lit. listed by R. Laurentin, *Court traité de Théol. mariale*, 1953, 160. G. Ficker, *Amphilochiana*, 1906. Moss, Mu 1930, 317/64 (Syr. hom.). Zetterstéen, OC 1934, 67/98 (German trans. of prob. apocryphal hom. on Basil, formerly [*Festschr. E. Sachau* 1915, 223/47] ed. in Syr.). Bardy, DS 1, 544. Rucker 1933, 87/91 (symb.). — Notes on individual homs.: B. Marx, *Procliana*, Mr 1940, 50, 96; OCP 1941, 355 A. 1. Severus of Antioch. III 34, CSCO 102, 1933, 143f. (new fragms.). Richard, *Mél. E. Podechard* 1945, 199/210 (fragm. 22 spurious). Rivière, BLE 1945, 129/38 (doct. of redemption). Bones, StudBizNoell 1953, 3/10 (on date of *Iamb. ad Sel.* not before 396). Ortiz de Urbina, OCP 1957, 186/91 (Mariology).

Asterius, b. of Amasea in Pontus was a younger contemporary of Amphilochius (d. *c.* 410). He left sixteen stirring homilies and panegyrics on martyrs (fourteen in MG 40, 163/390 and two in Bretz 1914, 107/21). Photius (Cod. 217) has reproduced extracts from other sermons. The fourth homily attacks the pagan feast of the Calendae (1. Jan.). Homily eleven which describes a picture with scenes from the martyrdom of St. Euphemia was read at the second Council of Nicaea (787) as a witness to the veneration of images. On spurious homilies v. § 53, 4.

M. Schmid, *Beitr. zur Lebensgesch. des A. v. A.*, 1911. Mg. by M. Bauer, 1911; A. Bretz, (TU 40, 1) 1914. Fecioru, *Biserica ortod. rum.* 55, 1937, 624/94; cf. BZ 1939, 241.

C. Antiochenes and Syrians

§ 62. EUSTATHIUS OF ANTIOCH

1. Eustathius, Bishop of Antioch, was an ardent opponent of Arianism at Nicaea (325) and later. In 330 the Emperor Constantine banished him to Thracia, where he died before 337. Most of his writings are lost. Only his treatise on the witch of Endor

(1 Sam. 28) *(De engastrimytho)* has been preserved in full. It is directed against Origen, whose allegorical exegesis is severely criticized, though Eustathius is not in principle opposed to this method.

There are fragments of *Adv. Arianos* (eight books), *Adv. Photinum, De anima,* also exegetical writings on the Psalms and Prov. 8, 22. A *Letter to Bishop Alexander,* recently reconstructed from fragments of *catenae* treats the question of Melchisedech. The *Homilia christologica* (ed. F. Cavallera, P 1905) and the *Commentary on the Hexaemeron* (MG 18, 707 ff.) are spurious.

Edd.: MG 18, 613/704. E. Klostermann (KlT 83) 1912 (witch of Endor). F. Cavallera, *S. Eust. In Lazarum, Mariam et Martham Hom. Christol.,* P 1905 (here also the fragms.). Altaner, BZ 1940, 30/47 (reconstruction of letter on Melchisedech). — Mgg. and Treatises: Salaville, DTC 5, 1547/6. P. Krause, thesis Br 1921. F. Zoepfl, *Der Kommentar des Ps.-Eust. zum Hexaemeron,* 1927. R. V. Sellers, *E. of A. and his Place in the Early Hist. of Christ. Doctrine,* 1928. W. Brockmeier, *De S. Eustathii ep. Ant. dicendi ratione,* thesis Mr 1932. Schwartz, ZNTW 1935, 126/213 (Antioch. schism). Devreesse, RB 1935, 189/91 (fragm. in Gen.). Severus Antioch. III, 26, CSCO 102, 47 (new fragm.).—On the question of the ps.-Athan. *Sermo maior de fide* and *Expositio fidei* cf. Schwartz, SbMn 1924 n. (6); Lebon, RHE 1935, 309 311 317. and supra § 54 I 4; § 57, 1. — Chadwick, JTS 1948, 27/35 (deposed 326, not 330). M. Spanneut, *Rech. sur les écrits d'E. d'A.* 1948 (complete collection of fragms.). Richard, MSR 1950, 305/7 and 1951, 113 (deposed 331). Schneemelcher, TLZ 1954, 398 (deposed 326). Grillmeier in Grillmeier-Bacht I, 124/30 (Christology: opponent of *Logos-sarx-schema*). Spanneut, MSR 1952, 215/20 (Hippol. fragm. belongs to Eust.); ed. Spanneut, Recherches 1948, 102 n. 23. Scheidweiler, RM 1953, 319/208 (text. crit. on witch of Endor); BZ 1955, 73/85 (text. crit. of fragms.). Spanneut, JTS 1954, 215/20 *(position théol.)*.

2. After the fall of Eustathius Antioch became a centre of Arianism. Of Arians known for their literary activities we would mention: Aëtius of Antioch (d. 366) and his disciple Eunomius, Bishop of Cyzicus (d. *c.* 394), leader of the neo-Arians. Only few remnants of their writings have been preserved.

A work of A. in Epiph. *Haer.* 76, 11. An Apology of E. in MG 30, 835/68. M. Albertz, *Unters. ueber die Schr. des E.,* 1908. Bardy, RHE 1928, 809/27 (writings of A.). Grumel, EO 1929, 159/66 *(textes monothélites d'A.)*. De Ghellinck, RHE 1930, 5/42 (Aristotelianism). Vandenbussche, RHE 1944/5, 47/72 (dialectic of Eun.). Slomkowski, CT 1935, 95/103 (Trin. doct. of Semi-Arians).

§ 63. HEGEMONIUS AND TITUS OF BOSTRA

1. HEGEMONIUS, otherwise unknown, probably a native of Syria. According to reliable sources he wrote an anti-Manichean work, the *Acta Archelai*, before 350. In his probably fictitious dialogues the Catholic Bishop Archelaus defeats Turbo, a disciple of Mani, and especially Mani himself. This important source for the history of Manicheism is preserved in full only in a fourth century Latin translation of the Greek original.

Edd.: MG 10, 1405/1528: Routh 5², 1/206; C. H. Beeson (GCS 16) 1906. Polotzky, Mu 1932, 18/20 (Copt. citations).

2. Titus of Bostra (d. before 378), Bishop of the capital of the Roman province Arabia, wrote soon after 363 four books *Against the Manicheans* extant in Greek as far as 3, 7, complete in a Syriac translation. In books one and two he seeks to refute the Manichean views from the purely philosophical point of view. Books three and Four defend the O.T. and N.T. by a careful exegesis of wrongly interpreted passages. Titus is a rhetorically trained controversialist.

Of his *Homilies on Luke* many *catenae* fragments have been preserved, as well as Syriac fragments of a *Sermon for the Epiphany*.

Edd.: MG 18, 1069/1264. P. A. de Lagarde, B 1859 (Syr.). New impression Hanover 1924. J. Sickenberger (TU 21, 1) 1901 (Lk. homs.). — Baumstark, OC 1931, 23/42 (Mani-citations in Syr. trans.); Bi 1935, 257/99 (Syr. text and *Diatessaron*). Rucker 1933, 82/7 (Epiph. sermon). Casey, PWK II 6, 1586/91; HTR 1928, 97/111. C. H. Roberts, *Catalogue of the Greek and Lat. Papyri in the John Rylands Libr.* 3, 1938; n. 469 contains the second half of a 3rd cent. pastoral letter against the Manicheans.

Since the discovery of new original Manichean sources in Chinese Turkestan and Egypt the latest literature has greatly increased and we must refer the reader to the relevant works on Church history and the history of religion. On the Manichean lit. cf. P. Alfaric, *Écritures manichéennes,* 2 vols., 1918/9. On the newly found sources see: Nyberg, ZNTW 1935, 70/91; Alberry, JTS 1938, 337/49. E. Rose, *Christologie des Manichaeismus*, thesis Marburg 1942. A survey of anti-Manichean writings of the Fathers in Alfaric, l. c. I, 1918, 112/9, and Bardy, DTC 9, 1954/57. A. Boehlig, *D. Bibel bei d. Manichaeern,* thesis typed Mr 1947; *Probleme des manich. Lehrvortrags,* Mn 1953 (19 pp.). Puech, *Le Manichéisme, son fondateur, sa doctrine,* P 1949. Klima, *Archiv Orientalni,* Prague 19, 1951, 393/403 (on chronol. of Mani's life). Maricq, AIP 1951, 245/68 (on the beginnings of Mani's preaching). Frend, JEH 1953, 13/26 (Gnost.-Manich. tradition in N. Africa). T. Saeve-Soederbergh, *Studies in the Coptic Manichean Psalmbook,* Up 1953; cf. VC 1954, 252f. A. Adam, *Texte zum Manichaeismus* (KlT 175), 1954. O. Stegmueller, ZKT 1952, 450/63 (Manich. *Fundamentum* in a sacramentary of Carolingian time). Boehlig, WissZUnivHalle-Wittenberg 5, 1956, 1066/85 (trans. of *Kephalaia of the Teacher*).

§ 64. CYRIL OF JERUSALEM (d. 386)

In 348 Cyril was consecrated Bishop of Jerusalem by the Arian-minded metropolitan Acacius of Caesarea, but being himself faithful to the Nicene Creed he soon came into conflict with him. He was twice deposed and exiled by a synodal decree (357, 360) and a third time by the Emperor Valens (367). His last exile lasted eleven years (till 378). After his return in 362 the Emperor Julian attempted to rebuild the Temple at Jerusalem (EH 580/2). In 381 Cyril attended the Council of Constantinople. (He was proclaimed *Doctor Ecclesiae* in 1883.)

His most famous works are the twenty-four *Catecheses* (Addresses) which he delivered mostly in the Church of the Sepulchre, built by Constantine, in 348 (or 350); they were published from the shorthand notes of a member of the congregation.

Apart from an introductory address the first eighteen catecheses, delivered during Lent, were destined for the catechumens (φωτιζόμενοι), the last five, given in Easter Week, for the newly baptized (νεοφώτιστοι) (EP 807/53; EH 526/42; EA 228/44). The first five orations treat of sin, penance and faith. Numbers 6–18 are a running commentary on the baptismal creed of Jerusalem, which is very similar to the Creed of the Synod of Constantinople 381 (ES 9) (supra § 54, 20). The most important are the last five, fairly short addresses on the sacraments received at Easter: 19 and 20 on baptism, 21 on confirmation, 22 on the eucharist and 23 on the liturgy of the faithful. These five catecheses are called mystagogical (Κατηχήσεις μυσταγωγικαί). The serious difficulties of the history of their transmission, recently once more emphasized by Swaans, are not sufficient definitely to deny Cyril's authorship and to assign them to his successor, Bishop John of Jerusalem (386–417).

We also possess a Homily of Cyril on the paralytic (Jo. 5), a Letter to the Emperor Constantius on a miraculous apparition of the Cross in Jerusalem, and four small fragments from homilies.

Edd.: A. A. Touttée, P 1720. MG 33. W. K. Reischl u. J. Rupp, 2 vols., Mn 1848/60. J. Quasten (FP 7) 1935, 69/111 (myst. cat.). F. L. Cross (SPCK 51) Lo 1951 (procat. and 5 myst. cat.: text and trans.). German by P. Haeuser (BKV² 41) 1922, and A. Winterswyl, Fr ²1954. W. Telfer, *Cyr. of Jer. and Nemesius of Emesa,* Lo 1955 (trans.). — Treatises: J. Mader, 1891. Le Bachelet, DTC 3, 2527/77. Bardy, DS 16/7, 1953, 2683/7. A. Heisenberg, *Grabeskirche u. Apostelkirche,* 1908, 47/89. Leclercq, DAL 7, 2390/2 (Lit. of Jerus.). Doelger, AC 3, 100/16 (on Cat. 10, 19: particle of the Cross). Further information TR 1936, 141. Spurious Copt. and Arab. texts: E. A. W. Budge, *Miscellaneous Coptic Texts,* 1915, 49/73, 183/230. P. Carali, Al-M 1933/4 (Arab. hom. on Cross); cf. Graf, OC 1935, 274/6. Diekamp, AP 10/2 (new fragm.). Swaans, Mu 1942, 1/43 (the 5 *Mystag. catecheses* a work of John of Jerus.); against this Peeters, AB 1943, 270f., F. L. Cross in SPCK 51, 1951 (v. supra), and Fruytier, StC 1951, 282/8. Graf I, 335/7. *Anaphorae Syriacae* I 3 (A. Raes, *Anaph. Cyrilli Hierus.*), R 1944. Bulacu, *Studii Theol.* 7, 1939, 141/78 (Christ. conscience acc. to C. of J.). Moraitis in: Γρηγόριος ὁ Παλαμᾶς 30, 1948, 57/9, 122/30 and cont. (Cyr. as catechist and educationist). A. W. Ziegler, *Klerusblatt* 1949 (on Breviary text of 4th *Myst. cat.*). Vogt, AIP 1949, 593/606 (apparition of Cross in 4th cent.). Touton, POC 1, 1951, 265/85 (catechet. method in Cyr. and Theod. Mops.). Stephenson, TSW 1954, 103/16 (fasting regulations in Jerus.); 573/93 (infl. of Clem. Al. and Orig.). J. H. Greenlee, *The Gospel Text* of Cyr. of J.), Copenhagen 1955; cf. TR 1956, 20f. Bardy, DHG 13, 1181/85.

Points of Doctrine

1. Logos Doctrine. Cyril avoided the ὁμοούσιος consciously and on principle, because this term was not attested by Holy Scripture and seemed rather to favour Sabellianism; nevertheless he decisively opposed all the main tenets of Arianism and confessed Christ as Θεὸν ἀληθινόν, Θεὸν ἐκ Θεοῦ (*Cat.* 11, 14 and 18).

2. Eucharist and Mass. Cyril expressed more clearly than all the Fathers before him the real presence of Christ in the eucharist

and transubstantiation (μεταβάλλεσθαι). We also find mentioned in his works the *Epiclesis* and the *Commemoration of the dead* in the Mass (*Cat*. 22, 2f. 9; 23, 7 9f.; EP 844f., 848, 850, 852f.).

B. Niederberger, *Die Logoslehre des hl. C. v. J.*, 1923. Lebon, RHE 1924, 181/210 357/86 (Logos doct.). Rios, Pax 25, 1935, 77/81 (Eucharist). C. M. Fruytier, *Het woord* μυστήριον *in de Cat. v. C. v. J.*, N 1950.

§ 65. APOLLINARIS OF LAODICEA (d. *c.* 390)

APOLLINARIS, b. *c.* 310 at Laodicea in Syria, was the son of a presbyter of the same name; *c.* 361 he became Bishop of the Nicene community of his native city. He was a man of exceptional learning and an able and versatile writer. He was a friend of Athanasius and rendered great service to the orthodox in their battle against Arianism; but in doing so he defeated only its Trinitarian, not its Christological error. As an exegete he followed the principles of the Antiochene school.

Under the influence of Arianism Apollinaris denied the full human nature of Christ and, guided by the Platonic trichotomy, he denied the Saviour, not, indeed, the ψυχὴ ἄλογος but the rational soul (νοῦς, ψυχὴ λογική). Christ is neither a complete man nor only God, but a mixture of God and Man. According to him the divine Logos took the place of the νοῦς; two complete beings (God and Man) could not become one, and besides, the existence of the νοῦς would make impossible the sinlessness of Christ, because the νοῦς includes free will and hence sin. This would rule out the redemption. Since Apollinaris further identified nature and person and could not accept two persons, he logically taught only one nature in Christ (μία φύσις τοῦ Θεοῦ λόγου σεσαρκωμένη): (cf. H. Lietzmann, *Apoll. v. Laod. u. s. Schule,* 1904, 251 lin. 1f.) supra § 56. The heresy was condemned by the Synod of Alexandria (362), by Pope Damasus (377 and 382) and by the Council of Constantinople (381).

1. Almost the only writings of Apollinaris that have been preserved are those that were foisted on orthodox Fathers. His many commentaries on books of the O.T. and N.T. are lost, except for mostly unimportant fragments, as are also his apologetical works against Porphyry (thirty books) and the Emperor Julian, and his dogmatic-polemical writings against Origen, Dionysius of Alexandria, Eunomius of Cyzicus, Marcellus of Ancyra, Diodore of Tarsus and Flavian of Antioch. The remains of his commentary on Romans recently gleaned from *catenae* are important (especially on chs. 9–16; in Staab 1933). He is equally far removed from the linguistic researches of the Antiochenes and from the allegorical explanations of the Alexandrians. Being a dogmatist, he seeks first of all to make clear the doctrinal contents of the Letter.

2. Only a Paraphrase of the Psalms has been preserved of his poetical works (hymns and metrical versions of O.T. subjects), which were designed to replace the classical authors who had been banned from the education of Christian youth by Julian's school law; but the genuineness of this work has recently been doubted.

3. The following dogmatic writings of his have been preserved under other names: a. among the writings of Gregory Thaumaturgus (supra § 41, 4) a detailed creed (ἡ κατὰ μέρος πίστις) b. Three pseudo-Athanasian writings: a sermon *Quod unus sit Christus; De incarnatione Dei Verbi,* and a Creed addressed to the Emperor Jovian. c. Three treatises under the name of Pope Julius I (337–52): *De unione corporis et divinitatis in Christo; De fide et incarnatione,* and a Letter to a Presbyter Dionysius.

4. His principal dogmatic work Ἀπόδειξις περὶ τῆς θείας σαρκώσεως can largely be reconstructed from Gregory of Nyssa's *Antirrheticus.* — A further short treatise *(Recapitulatio)* can be reconstructed from the fifth pseudo-Athanasian dialogue *De s. Trinitate.*

Text in H. Lietzmann, *A. v. L. u. seine Schule,* 1, 1904. F. Flemming u. H. Lietzmann, GAG 7, 4 (1904) (Syr. texts). A. Ludwich, L 1912 (Metaphr. Psalm.). Staab 1933, 57/82. Rucker 1933, 25f. 47/50. — Mgg.: G. Voisin, *L'Apollinarisme,* 1901. Aigrain, DHG 3, 962/82. C. E. Raven, *Apollinarianism,* C 1923. — Treatises: E. Weigl, *Christologie vom Tode des Athanasius* (supra § 56) 6/18. Devreesse, RB 1936, 213/6 (Octateuch comm.). Bardy, *Paul de Samosate,* [2]1929, 139/44. P. S. Miller, TP 65, 1934 (Greek Psalter). Jugie, EO 1936, 257ff. (Holy Spirit). Gentz, RACh 1, 520/2. Gitschel, *Munera philol. L. Cwiklinski . . ., oblata,* Poznan 1936, 104/10 (the author of the Ps. paraphrase was not physically blind; against Ganszíniec, BNJ 1920, 375f.). Golega, BZ 1939, 1/22 (Ps. paraphrase spurious; suggested perh. by a Presbyter Marcianus, d. after 471 at Constant.). Reuss, 1941 (fragm.), cf. Index. De Riedmatten, DSO 1, 1948, 239/60 (on the Christology of A.); RT 1951, 553/72 (opponents of A.: Athanasius, the author of *Contra A.* and Epiphanius). Grillmeier in Grillmeier-Bacht I, 102/17 (Christology). Reuss, TU 61, 1/54 (Mt. comm.). De Riedmatten, *Studia Patrist.* 2, 1937, 208/34 (Christology). — *Anti-apollinarist. Fragm.* ed. A. Souter, Misc. Ehrle I, 1924, 46/49.

§ 66. EPIPHANIUS OF SALAMIS (d. 403)

He was born *c.* 315 in a village near Eleutheropolis in Judaea; after a short stay with the Egyptian monks he founded a monastery at Eleutheropolis which he governed for about 30 years. In 367 the bishops of Cyprus elected him Bishop of Constantia (Salamis) and thus metropolitan of the island. According to Jerome (*Adv. Ruf.* 2, 22; 3, 6) he understood Greek, Syriac, Hebrew, Coptic and also some Latin.

Despite his scholarship and his austere asceticism he lacked prudence and serenity. His ardent but unenlightened zeal for orthodoxy involved him in disputes which darken the impression of his character. His lack of moderation showed itself not only in his iconoclasm, but also in his violent fight against Origenism which he considered the most dangerous heresy.

In 392 (390?) he preached against Origen in Jerusalem, and from this followed the so-called first Origenist Controversy, in which he fought on the side of Jerome against Bishop John of Jerusalem and Rufinus. What was worse, he suffered himself to be used by Theophilus of Alexandria (supra § 55, 3) in the latter's deceitful action against the Origenist monks of the Nitrian desert and against St. Chrysostom (400). He realized the ignoble motives of Theophilus too late; he left Constantinople even before the decree of the Synod of the Oaks and died on the return journey to Salamis.

Epiphanius represented a one-sidedly traditionalist party; in contrast to the three great Cappadocians and other contemporaries he denied Greek learning any right in the Church and rejected theological speculation as well as historical criticism. In his writings he is often inaccurate, superficial and verbose and, as was already observed by Photius (Cod. 122) is generally lacking in cultivated form as well as in the Attic spirit. Despite these shortcomings his works are very important because he copied many sources which are now lost.

1. The *Ancoratus* is a compendium of the doctrines of the Church containing many polemical anti-heretical digressions. Two Creeds are appended at the end. The first (ch. 119) is the baptismal creed of the Church of Salamis (Constantia); it was taken over almost without change by the Council of Constantinople (381) and soon became the baptismal creed of the East; the other (ch. 120) was composed by Epiphanius himself (EP 1081/9; ES 13f.). (Cf. supra § 54, 20.)

2. The *Medicine Box* (Πανάριον), generally cited as *Haereses* (written 374–77). It is his most voluminous and most valuable work on account of the many verbatim extracts from lost sources. It is destined to heal those bitten by poisonous snakes, that is, the heretics, by presenting them with an antidote.

Among the eighty heresies with which he deals there are also pagan philosophers' schools and Jewish sects (*Haer.* 9–20). Irenaeus and the *Syntagma* of Hippolytus were his sources for the earlier times. At the end there is a summary, the *Expositio fidei* (chs. 1–24).

A concise extract from the large work, the *Recapitulatio* ('Ανακεφαλαίωσις) was very probably not made by Epiphanius himself but by a later writer; it is a rather unskilful composition. This work was the main source of Augustine's treatise *De haeresibus* (ML 42, 21/50).

3. A work composed in 392 with the not very precise title *De mensuris et ponderibus* is a Biblical encyclopedia. It treats of the books and versions of the O.T., of the measures and weights occurring in the Bible, and finally of the geography of Palestine. Only the first part is extant in Greek; the whole in a Syriac translation.

4. In *De duodecim gemmis* the twelve jewels in the breastplate of the High Priest are explained allegorically and their *medial* effects are enumerated. The whole of the treatise is extant only in a Georgian translation. The greater part is preserved also in Latin (in the *Collectio Avellana;* supra § 50, 9) and Armenian; there are also Greek, Coptic and Ethiopic fragments.

5. Lately fragments have come to light from three works against images to which the Iconoclasts appealed (a treatise, a letter to the Emperor Theodosius I and a Testament addressed to his diocese).

6. Two Letters have been preserved in Latin. A considerable number of works have falsely been attributed to him; they include homilies on Genesis and Luke, a commentary on the Canticle, legends about prophets, apostles and the seventy-two disciples, feast day sermons and much else, e.g. the Greek version of the so-called *Physiologus,* a manual of Christian nature symbolism.

Edd.: MG 41/3. W. Dindorf, 5 vols., 1859/62. F. Oehler, *Corp. haereseolog.* 2 *(Haer.* and *Anac.),* 1859/61. K. Holl (GCS 25, 31, 37) 1915/33 *(Anc., Haer.)*; Ges. Aufs. zur KG 2, 1928, 204/24 (fragm. of letter). J. E. Dean, Ch 1935 (*mens. et pond.;* Syr.). R. P. Blake and H. de Vis, Lo 1934 (*De gemmis;* Georg.); cf. TR 1935, 329/35 and ZMorgenlGes 1936, 209/20; BZ 1937, 400/8. R. Bleichsteiner, *Jahrb. Oesterr. Leoges.* 1930, 232/70 (trans. of Georg. text of *De gemmis*). Severus Antioch. III 41 (6 versio), 1933, 235f. (citations from 3 unknown letters). An unknown λόγος on the Holy Spirit is mentioned in Andrew of Caes. (MG 106, 224); German by J. Hoermann (BKV² 38) 1919. — Treatises: K. Holl (TU 36, 2) 1910 (MS trad.); SbB 1916, 828/68 (iconocl. writings) = Ges. Aufs. zur KG 2, 1928,

351/87. G. Ostrogorsky, *Stud. zur Gesch. des byz. Bilderstreites,* 1929 (against Holl); against this F. Doelger, GA 1929, 353/72. C. Martin, RHE 1935, 356/9 (Hom. MS). Villain, RSR 1937/5/18 (1. Origenist controv.). Mercati, OM 1, 1937, 20/92 (on *De mens. et pond.*). Graf I, 356/8, 548f. Lebon, Misc. Mercati I, 145/74 (8 hitherto unknown fragms. from letters). Amand, *Fatalisme,* 1945, 440/60. H. J. Schoeps, *Theologie u. Gesch. des Judenchristentums,* 1949, 457/79 (Epiph. and Ps.-Clement). Smothers, AmerEcclRev 125, 1951, 355/72 *(Assumptio BMV).* Spuria: *Physiologus,* in MG 43, 517/34. F. Sbordone, *Phys.,* Mi 1936 (crit. ed.). Perry, PWK 20, 1, 1074/1129 *(Phys.).* Garmady, Sp 1938, 153/9 (Lat. *Physiol.*). F. Lauchert, *Gesch. des Physiologus,* 1889. E. Peters, *Der griech. Physiologus u. s. orient. Uebers.,* 1898. M. Wellmann, *Der Phys.,* 1930. — Devreesse, RB 1936, 216f. *(Hom. in Gen.).* E. A. W. Budge, *Miscell. Coptic Text,* 1915, 120/46, 699/724 (Marian Sermon). E. Franceschini, *Studi e note di filol. lat. medioev.,* 1938, n. 2: *Vita B. Mar. Virg. lat. Aethiop. Anaph. of St. E.,* trans. S. Euringer, OC 1927, 98/142. Van Lantschoot, BBI 2, 1950, 339/63 *(Physiologus).* P. Nautin, *Le dossier d'Hippol. et de Méliton . . .,* P 1953, 154/9 (ed. unknown hom. of ps.-Epiph.). Peterson, BZ 1954, 60/72 (ascet.-encratite tendency of *Physiol.*)

Points of Doctrine

1. On the Procession of the Holy Spirit Epiphanius, like Basil (supra § 58, 3), teaches clearly that the Holy Spirit proceeds also from the Son (*Haer.* 74, 4; *Anc.* 7, 5: ἐκ τῆς αὐτῆς οὐσίας πατρὸς καὶ υἱοῦ); cf. also *Anc.* 8, 6; 67, 1; 75, 3. Besides, he also uses (*Haer.* 62, 4; *Anc.* 7, 1) the formula παρὰ πατρὸς ἐκπορευόμενον καὶ ἐκ τοῦ υἱοῦ λαμβάνον (EP 1081f., 1099).

2. Apart from the three works mentioned above his hostile attitude to images is revealed also in a letter to Bishop John of Jerusalem (printed as EP 51 among the Letters of Jerome, EH 677). Art and images are for him a new "idolatry, thought out and brought into the world by the devil" (Letter to Theodos.). In his *Testament* he anathematizes anyone "who, appealing to the Incarnation, undertakes to look upon the divine image of the God-Logos in earthly colours".

3. Epiphanius attests as the universal belief of the Church that Mary is ever-Virgin (ἡ ἁγία ἀειπαρθένος) (*Haer.* 78, 6 23; *Anc.* 120; EP 1111).

§ 67. DIODORE OF TARSUS (d. before 394)

Diodore received a thorough secular and theological education in his native city of Antioch and at Athens; later he was for a long time teacher and monastic superior at Antioch, where he established the fame of its Exegetical School. St. John Chrysostom and Theodore of Mopsuestia were his most renowned disciples. He was banished from Antioch by the Emperor Valens, after whose death in 378 he became Bishop of Tarsus.

During his life Diodore was highly esteemed as a pillar of orthodoxy, who fought paganism as well as diverse heresies. Later, however, he was condemned as the author of Nestorianism at a synod of Antioch (499). Thus his many works were doomed to destruction.

Diodore's literary activities were extraordinarily varied. Ebedjesu (d. 1318) gives the number of his writings as sixty. Apart from cosmological scientific works he left numerous doctrinal monographs as well as polemical-apologetic works (against the Manicheans, Porphyry, the Jews and various heresies [Eunomians, Apollinarians, Melchizedechites]) and especially Scriptural commentaries of a historical-grammatical exegetical bent that were distinctly opposed to the allegorical exegesis of the Alexandrians. According to the testimony of Theodore Lector in Suidas he commented on all the books of the O.T. as well as the Gospels, Acts, Rom. and 1 John of the N.T.

Apart from his treatise *De fato* (in Photius, Cod. 223), large fragments are extant in a *catena* on the Octateuch and in one on Romans. L. Mariès assigns to him an as yet unedited *Commentary on Psalms* which has been preserved complete under the name of Bishop Anastasius III of Nicaea.

Harnack and Fetissof have assigned to him four pseudo-Justin treatises *(Quaestiones et responsiones ad orthodoxos, Quaestiones christianorum ad gentiles, Quaestiones gentilium ad christianos,*

Confutatio dogmatum Aristotelis), but apparently without justification (v. infra § 73).

Fragms. in MG 33, 1561/1628. P. de Lagarde, *Anal. Syriaca,* 1858, 91/100. J. Deconinck, *Essai sur la chaîne de l'Octateuch,* 1912, 85ff. K. Staab 1933, 83/112 (Rom.). SACO I, vol. 5, 177/9. A. Sanda, *Severi Philalethes,* 1928. The ps.-Justin treatises: MG 6 and in Otto 3 (supra § 19). *Quaest. et respons.* ed. A. Papadopulos-Kerameus (36th vol. of Studies of St. Petersburg Univ.) 1895. Severus Antioch, CSCO 111/12, 1938; cf. Index. — Mgg.: A. Harnack (TU 21, 4) 1901; against this F. X. Funk, KGAbh 3, 1907, 323/50. N. Fetissof, Kiev 1915; cf. Bess 1916, 188/97. Godet, DTC 4, 1363/6. — Treatises: Abramowski, ZNTW 1931, 234/62 (ed. inter alia a Syr. Vita of D. from the EH of Barhadbesabba, *c.* 600). L. Mariès, *Ét. préliminaires à l'éd. de D. de T. sur les Psaumes,* 1933 (partly also in RSR 1932, 385/408, 513/40). Bardy, RB 1933, 211/29 *(Quaest. et resp.).* Vaccari, Bi 1920, 3/36; 1934, 94/101 *(La teoria eseget. antiochena).* Devreesse, Rb 1936, 217/20 (Octateuch cat.). P. Doll, thesis Bonn 1923 (Κατὰ εἱμαρμένης). Schweizer, ZNTW 40, 1942, 33/75 (D. as an exegete). Amand, *Fatalisme,* 1945, 461/79. Brière, ROC 30, 231/83 (new ed. of 33 texts from a work *Adv. Synousiastas* partly falsified by Apollinarians, which had been ed. by P. de Lagarde from a Syr. florileg. in 1858). Abramowsky, ZNTW 42, 1949, 16/69 (list of writings incl. all fragms. and citations). Jugie, *Euntes docete,* R 2, 1949, 171/90 (Christol. based on fragms.). On Mariès, *Ét. prélim.* (v. supra), 1933, cf. Richard, Byz 1950, 219/22 (Ps. comm. spurious). Bardy, DS, F. 20f., 1955, 986/94. L. Abramowski, DHG 14, 1958, 495/504.

§ 68. THEODORE OF MOPSUESTIA (d. 428)

THEODORE, Bishop of Mopsuestia in Cilicia, was a native of Antioch. Together with John Chrysostom he was a disciple of the pagan rhetor Libanius and of Diodore. He lived for some time as a monk in the surroundings of Antioch in company with his friend John. When he suddenly left the monastery to devote himself to the study of law the reproachful letters of his friend soon brought him back to the silence of the monastic life. After having been a priest at Antioch, he became Bishop of Mopsuestia in 392 (d. 428).

This greatest exegete of the Antiochene school wrote commentaries on almost the whole Bible with a critical acumen quite extraordinary in the ancient Church. The Nestorian Church appeals to his authority as "the exegete" par excellence. But he also treated in his writings many theological questions of his time in a thoroughly independent way. Like his master Diodore, he was considered orthodox during his life; only after his death, during the Nestorian controversy, was he attacked as holding heretical Christological views, Nestorius having been his pupil. Cyril of Alexandria (supra § 56) wrote against him. In the "Three Chapters" the fifth General Council of Constantinople condemned also him and his writings as Nestorian. Consequently almost all his works have been lost. M. Richard, E. Amann, R. Devreesse and A. Grillmeier have shown that Theodore had done well in the struggle against Apollinarianism; the clear statement of the doctrine of the natures (Christ = Logos-Man; not only Logos-Sarx) formulated at the Council of Chalcedon is due to him. Moreover, Richard and Devreesse have proved that the texts which were the cause of his condemnation as the father of Nestorianism in 553 are mostly spurious. His writings which have recently become known in a Syriac translation show that he taught a largely orthodox Christology, even though his terminology was still partly inadequate and liable to be misinterpreted. Theodore has been largely exonerated by his recently discovered writings, but his notions cannot be expected to be so clearly defined as they were later at Chalcedon.

1. The following Scriptural Commentaries are extant either whole or for the greater part: A *Commentary on the Psalms* written at the age of 20, which R. Devreesse was able to reconstruct in the Greek original from *catenae* almost completely for Pss. 32–80. Only small fragments are extant for Pss. 1–31. In an Old Latin translation the commentary on Pss. 1–16:11 is preserved completely, that on 16:12 to 40:13 in large fragments. Approximately half of the fragments printed in MG 66, 448/696 are spurious. His *Commentary on the Minor Prophets* is his only work to be preserved completely in its Greek original. The *Commentary on St. John's Gospel* is extant in Syriac; many Greek fragments have been

collected from *catenae* (in Devreesse 1948, 289/419). The *Commentary on the ten shorter Pauline Letters* is preserved in a fifth century Latin translation. Considerable fragments on Romans, 1 and 2 Cor. and Hebrews have also been preserved in *catenae.*

2. His main dogmatic work *De incarnatione,* which had been discovered by Seert in 1905, perished in the First World War. His *Disputatio cum Macedonianis,* held at Anazarbus in 392, is extant in Syriac. His sixteen *Catechetical sermons* (1–10 on the creed, 11 on the Our Father, 12–14 on the baptismal liturgy, 15–16 on the eucharist) form a companion work to the principal treatise of Cyril of Jerusalem. They were published by A. Mingana in a Syriac translation as late as 1932–3. Theodore delivered these catecheses probably at Antioch, between 388 and 392, before he became a bishop.

Texts: MG 66, H. B. Swete, 2 vols., C 1880/2 (minor Pauline Letters). K. Staab 1933, 113/212 (greater Pauline Letters). J. B. Chabot, P 1897 (Jo.). F. Nau (PO 9) 1913 (Disput.). A. Mingana, WS 5–6, 1932/3 (Catech.). A. Rücker, Mr 1933 *(Ritus bapt. et missae).* R. Tonneau et R. Devreesse, *Homél. catéch. Reproduction phototypique* (ST 145), 1949. Reuss, TU 61, 96/150 (Mt. comm.). Fragms. in A. Sanda, *Severi Philalethes,* 1928. R. Devreesse, *Le commentaire de T. de M. sur les Psaumes (I–LXXX),* (ST 93) 1939. I.-M. Vosté, *Ti. M.i commentarius in Ev. Joh. Ap.* (CSCO, 115/16) 1940. SACO I 5, 23/5, 173/7 (various texts). — Mgg.: H. Kihn, *T. v. M. u. Julius Africanus als Exegeten,* 1880. L. Pirot, *L'œuvre exégét. de T. de M.,* R 1913. L. Patterson, *T. of M.* and *Modern Thought,* 1926. Opitz, PWK II 5, 1881/90. — Treatises: Devreesse, RB 1936, 364/83 (Octateuch). De Bruyne, RBn 1935, 305 (MS fragms. on 2 Tim.).

On the Contents of the Catecheses: Devreesse, RevSR 1933, 425/36: Lietzmann, SbB 1933, 915/36 (Liturgy). Doelger, AC 4, 230/2 (Liturgy). Abramowski, ZNTW 1934, 66/84; Amann, RevSR 1934, 161/90 (Christol. almost orthodox). Jugie, EO 1935, 257/71. Casel, JL 13, 1936, 96/126 (mystery of cult). Quasten, ZKT 1934, 253f. (acclamat. liturg.). F. J. Reine, *The Euch. Doctrine and Liturgy of the Myst. Cat. of T. of M.,* W 1942. Vosté, OCP 1943, 211/28. Touton, POC 1, 1951, 265/85 (catech. method). — Arnou, Gr 1936, 116/31 (Christol. dependent on neo-Platonism). Mingana, WS 7, 1934, 85 and 109 (fragms. of *De sacerdotio* and *De perfectione*). M. Jugie, *Theolog. dogmatica Christ. orient.* 5, 1935, 16ff. and freq. De Vries, OCP 1941, 91/148 (Nestorianism in its sacrament. teaching; against Amann 1934). Reuss 1941 (v. Index). — On Ps. Comm.: Mercati, OM 2, 66/72; Bulhart, WSt 54, 1941, 134/45 (text. crit.). Vosté, Ang 1942, 179/98; Vaccari, Bi 1942, 1/17 (text. crit.); Misc. Mercati I, 175/98. — Vosté, OCP 1942,

477/81 (Syr. trans. of his works). Richard, Mu 1943, 55/75 (fragm. of Περὶ τῆς ἐνανθρωπήσεως); MSR 1945, 21/9 (concept of hypostasis). Devreesse, RB 1946, 207/41 (exeget. method). Quasten, HTR 1942, 209/19 (exorcism). R. Devreesse, *Essai sur Théod. de M.* (ST 141) 1948; on this Sullivan, TSW 1951, 179/207. Vosté, Bi 1944, 210/35 (titles of Pss. in the Peshitta); Bi 1944, 261/96 (Mar Iso' dad de Merv on the Pss.). J. Rivière, *Le dogme de la Rédemption ...*, Albi 1948, 181/223 (in Theod., Nestorius, Theodoret and Amphilochius). Ducros, *Actes du 21e Congrès Internat. des Orientalistes,* P 1948, P 1949, 366f. (Eucharist in Theod.'s comm. Jo.). Lécuyer, RSR 1949, 481/516 (priesthood and Eucharist). Grillmeier in: Grillmeier-Bacht I, 120/59 (Christol.). McNamara, ITQ 1952, 254/78 and cont. (T. and the Nestorian heresy). Altaner, BZ 1952, 64/6 on Devreesse, 1939 (ST 93). McKensie, TSW 1953, 73/84 (on comm. Jo.). Tonneau, Mu 1953, 45/64 (on comm. Gen.). Gross, ZKG 65, 1953/4, 1/15 (T., an opponent of the doctr. of original sin). Dekkers, SE 1954, 429/33 (MS of Comm. on Pauline letters). Ontibia, Scriptorium Victoriense 1, 1954, 100/33 *(La vid. crist. tipo de las realidades celestes)*. Quasten, TSW 1954, 431/9 (Liturg. Mayst.). Amann, DTC 15, 235/79. F. A. Sullivan, *The Christology of T. of M.,* R 1956. Abramowski, ZKG 67, 1955/56, 252/87 (controversy about Diodore and Theodore 431/49). De Vries, OCP 1958, 309/38 (eschatolog. salvation). Wickert, *Studien zu den Pauluskommentaren,* Diss. T 1957, cf. ThLZ 1958, 728/30.

Theodore's brother, Polychronius, Bishop of Apamea in Syria (d. *c.* 430), an important exegete of the Antiochene school, wrote commentaries on O.T. books. Fragments on Jer. (?), Ezech., Dan. and Job are extant in *catenae.*

MG 93, 13/470. Mg. by O. Bardenhewer 1879. L. Dieu, RHE 1913, 685/701 (Jr.). Bertini, Bi 1923, 129/42 (Job *catenae*).

§ 69. JOHN CHRYSOSTOM (344 – 54 — 407)

The year of John's birth, like other dates of his life before 381, cannot be stated with certainty. He came from a noble family at Antioch and has been called Chrysostom (golden mouth) from the sixth century. He was brought up by his devout mother Anthusa, who had become a widow at the early age of 20. The philosopher Andragathius and the famous pagan rhetor Libanius (365) were his masters.

Like the other great fourth century Church Fathers, Chrysostom too, was not baptized until later (372), probably by the Bishop of Antioch. At first he led a strictly ascetical life in the house of his mother, then he was for four years under the direction of an old hermit, and at last he lived alone as a monk for two years in the mountain solitude near the city. From the time of his baptism he was instructed in theology, together with Theodore, later Bishop of Mopsuestia, through his contact with Diodore of Tarsus. His weak health compelled him to return to the city, where he was ordained deacon by Meletius in 381 and priest by Bishop Flavian in 386. He preached for twelve years (till 397) in the principal church and thus established his fame as an orator. The most famous of his exegetical homilies were delivered during this time.

His brilliant eloquence showed itself most forcefully in the twenty-one homilies which he delivered in 387 after the outbreak of a rebellion caused by an increase in taxation. As on this occasion the imperial statues had been smashed, these sermons were called *De statuis*. At the last sermon at Easter he was able to announce that Bishop Flavian, who had gone to Constantinople, had secured a complete amnesty for the city.

When, in 397, the Patriarch Nectarius of Constantinople died, John became his successor. At the command of the Emperor Arcadius, the great preacher, who resisted, was lured by a ruse to the capital where Bishop Theophilus of Alexandria had to consecrate him bishop (Feb. 26th, 398).

The new bishop set an example of the greatest simplicity and plain living and used his rich revenues to establish hospitals and help the poor. He was anxious to abolish various abuses in the life of the Church, but his reforming zeal soon made him unpopular in certain circles. At a synod of Ephesus he had several simoniacal bishops deposed, and he also incurred the hatred of the Empress Eudoxia during the intrigues and political confusion that followed the fall of the powerful minister Eutropius (399). Hence dissatisfied elements began to intrigue against him. Besides the Bishops Severian of Gabala, Acacius of Beroea and Antiochus of Ptolemais, his principal enemy was Theophilus of Alexandria. Avid of power, this latter sought to save the pre-eminent position of his own Church which had been threatened by the bishop of the imperial city since 381.

When Theophilus had to face several accusations brought against him in Constantinople by the monks of the Nitria desert (402), he put the blame on Chrysostom and prepared his counter-blow. In August 403 he sat in judgement on his opponent, who had three times refused to appear, at the Oak Synod—so called after the country estate Δρῦς near Chalcedon—which was attended by thirty-six bishops. Because Chrysostom had refused to appear he was declared deposed and exiled by order of the Emperor.

On the following day, however, he was already recalled, since an accident in the palace had frightened the Empress, and the exile returned in triumph. The peace, however, lasted only two months. When a statue of the Empress was unveiled near the church of the bishop, the games and dances were very noisy, and Chrysostom complained in the church that one could hardly hear the words of the preacher. This annoyed the Empress. She felt even more offended by a sermon on the feast of John the Baptist beginning with the words: "Once more Herodias rages in fury, once more she dances, demanding the head of John in a dish" (Socrat. 6, 18; Sozomen 8, 20). Even if the sermon beginning with these words, which is extant in more than seventy MSS, should be spurious and Chrysostom should only have delivered a homily on the saint beginning with these words but otherwise quite innocuous, it was risky to start a sermon with these words, which could quite easily be thought to contain an allusion to the Empress (cf. Ehrhard, BZ 1934, 98f.; TU 50, 65).

The tension between the opponents and the followers of the bishop continued to increase. On the Vigil of Easter, when those priests who had remained faithful to the bishop were about to administer baptism to more than 3000 catechumens, they were prevented by force of arms, and an attempt was made to murder Chrysostom himself. The attempt to have the bishop deposed by another synod miscarried, but his episcopal opponents at last succeeded in obtaining another decree of banishment from the Emperor, which Chrysostom soon obeyed (June 9th, 404) in order to prevent disturbances.

He was first brought to Kukusus in Armenia, and three years later to distant Pityus, a city on the Eastern shore of the Black Sea, since his enemies found it intolerable that Chrysostom should be in constant contact with his old friends in Constantinople and especially at Antioch which was even closer. He died on his way there on September 14th, 407, at Comana in Pontus. The Emperor Theodosius II, the son of Eudoxia, who had died in 404, had the remains of the saint solemnly buried in the Church of the Apostles in Constantinople on January 27th, 438. About 1204 his relics were brought to Rome (St. Peter's).

At Constantinople his followers were persecuted; they were called Johannites, because they refused communion with the new Patriarch Arsacius (d. 405) who had been appointed in his place, and later with Atticus (d. 425). Pope Innocent I, as well as the whole of the West were on the side of Chrysostom and for a time broke off communion with Constantinople.

Chrysostom was above all a practical guide of souls and more particularly a preacher. His contemporaries as well as later generations never tire of proclaiming him the greatest preacher of the Greek Church. Pius X made him the patron of Christian preachers. The volume of his literary production is greater than that of any of the other Eastern authors as far as their writings are still extant. In the West only Augustine can be compared with him. As regards contents, his works are an inexhaustible mine of information not only for the theologian, but also for the archaeologist and the cultural historian.

Chrysostom's speeches fascinate both by their contents and their effective eloquent presentation. His style combines the Christian spirit with Greek beauty of form. His sermons, which must often have lasted for two hours, are not fatiguing, for they are skilfully enlivened by imagery and parables; at the beginning and end they refer to contemporary events and often digress to interesting outside subjects. Feast day: Jan. 27th.

Biogr. sources: Palladius (supra § 46, 1); Socrates, HE 6, 2/23; 7, 25 and 45; Sozomen, HE 8, 2/28; Theodoret, HE 5, 27/36. Dyobuniotes, EPh 1932, 80/91 (encomium on Chr., Basil and Greg. Naz.); cf. AB 1935, 366; Θ 1934, 51/68 (encomium of Nicetas Paphlagonius). — Edd.: B. de Montfaucon, 13 vols., 1718/38. MG 47/64. Separate edd.: F. Field, 3 vols. (Mt.), C 1839; 7 vols. (Pauline Letters), O 1845/62. *De sacerd.* ed. J. A. Nairn, C 1906; J. Stiglmayr, Mr 1930 (selection). *De inani glor.* ed. F. Schulte 1914 (Germ. by S. Haidacher, 1907). S. Colombo, *De sacerd.,* Tu 1934. C. Piazzino, *S. Paolo ai Colossei,* Tu 1939. J. F. d'Alton, *Selections from S. J. Chr.,* Gr. Text with Introd. and Comm., Lo 1940. B. K. Exarchos, *Ueber Hoffart u. Kindererziehung* (Gr. text), At 1948 and 1954 (in the collection *Wert der Antike* 4). J. Dumortier, *S. J. Chr., Les cohabitations suspectes. Comment observer la virginité,* 1955 (crit. text). — Transs.: C. Baur, J. Jatsch, A. Naegle and V. Stoderl in BKV² (23, 25/7, 39, 42, II 15) 1915/36; further works in BKV 1869/83. Max v. Sachsen (Gen.) 2 vols., Pa 1913/14; (Mt.) 2 vols., RB 1910/11. E. Negrin (*De sacerd.,* Ital.), Vicenza 1931; P. E. Legrand (*Adv. oppug. vit. monast., Ad Theod.,* 4 letters to Olympias), 2 vols., P 1933. F. Martin (*De sacerd., De non iter. coniug.; Ad vid. iun.*), P 1933. G. Zandonella, Tu 1933 (letters). M. Pellegrino, *G. Cris. Ricchezza e povertà,* Siena 1938 (8 homs.). B. M. Bejarano, *Letters to Olympias,* Ma 1944; J. Oteo Uruñella, *De statuis,* Ma 1945. A.-M. Malingrey, *Lettres à Olympias,* P 1947 (SCh 13; with Gr. text). T. Sinko, Cracow 1947 (trans. of 20 sermons). R. Flacelière-F. Cavallera-J. Daniélou, *Sur l'incompréhensibilité de Dieu* (SCh 28), 1951. M. Heidenthaler, *J. Chrys., Nachweis der Gottheit Christi u. 8 Pred. ueber atl. Gesetz u. Evang.* (trans.), Linz 1951. A. Juergens, trans. of *De sacerd.,* NY 1954. — Mgg.: A. Neander, 2 vols., ⁴1858. A. Puech, P ⁵1905. P. E. Legrand, P 1924 *(Moralistes chrét.)*. C. Bauer, 2 vols., Mn 1929/30; *S. J. Chr. et ses œuvres dans l'hist. litt.,* Lou 1907. Bardy, DTC 8, 660/90. Lietzmann, PWK 9, 1811/28. J. Giordani, R 1929. A. Moulard, *J. Chr., sa vie, son œuvre,* P 1949. M. Constanza, *De Heil. Joh. Chr.,* Haarlem 1952. — Biogr.: BJ 230, 234/47. V. Schultze, *Altchristl. Staedte u. Landschaften,* 3rd vol., 1930. D'Alton, IER 1935, 225/38 (Chr. in exile). Balducci, *Atti IV. Congr. naz. di studi rom.* 1, 1938, 303/10 (J. Chrys. and Eudoxia). Schwartz, ZNTW 1937, 168/81 (Theophilus and J. Chrys.). Schiwietz 3, 1938, 254/73, 290/3 (Chrys. as a monk). P. Tzortzatos, *J. Chr.* (in his letters), At 1952. Demougeot, StBizNeoell 1953, 44/54 (declarations of sympathy with the exile). Jones, HTR 1953, 171/3 (descent and education). Visser, NAKG 1954, 193/206 (anti-Jewish polemics). Cataudella, ParPass 1954, 25/40 (Jo. Chr. in the novel of Achilleus Tatios). Dumortier, MSR 1953, 53/62 *(la culture profane de J. Chr.)*. Gruninger, POC 1956, 3/10 (his last years; no sources given). — On rhetorics and style: Peterson, RM 1929, 221/3; cf. Her 1931, 112. RAL 250. Kukules, At 1939, 355/68 (proverbs); cf. BZ 1940, 264. M. Sofray, *Rech. sur la syntaxe de S. J. Chr. d'après les Hom. sur les statues,* 1939. W. A. Maat, *A Rhetor. Study of . . . De sacerd.,* W 1944. Simonetti, RendIstLombScLett 86, 1953, 159/80 *(struttura dei Panegirici)*. A. J. Festugière, *Antioche païenne et chrét.,* P 1959.

The vast majority of the speeches and the works in general are homilies which were often taken down by stenographers and published afterwards. In part they are probably only written sermons which have never been delivered.

1. *The Exegetical Homilies*

Chrysostom seeks to elucidate the historical sense of the Scriptural texts according to the principles of the Antiochene school. No other Father has explained the sacred text so thoroughly and at the same time in such a practical manner as he; even today his homilies may not only be enjoyed with profit, but can often be fully approved from the exegetical point of view, which is not always the case with the homilies of the other Fathers, including St. Augustine.

Chrysostom has explained a large number of Biblical books.

a. Two series of homilies on Genesis (nine of the year 386; sixty-seven probably delivered in 388); a series of homilies on fifty-eight selected Psalms; six on Isaias 6; the commentary on Is. 8–64 preserved in Armenian is probably also genuine. Other series of homilies on O.T. books are not certainly genuine (EP 1147/55, 1208).

b. Of N.T. homilies we would mention: ninety homilies on Matthew, seven homilies on Lk. 16, 19–31; eighty-eight homilies on John; three series of homilies on Acts (fifty-five, four, and four homilies respectively) (EP 1158/80; 1214/6). Chysostom was an enthusiastic admirer of St. Paul to whom he was akin in spirit.

He has explained all Pauline Letters in truly magnificent homilies, although the prize will probably be given to the homilies on Romans (EP 1181/1207, 1217/24). Isidore of Pelusium writes (*Ep*. 5,32): "If the divine Paul had interpreted himself, he would not have done it differently from that famous master of the Attic language."

2. Numerous homilies also served special purposes. We would mention the following: from the group of speeches for special occasions the famous *Homiliae 21 de statuis* (v. supra § 69); two sermons on the transitoriness and vanity of all earthly happiness, on the occasion of the fall of the minister Eutropius (399); the sermon on the invincibility of the Church, preached in 403, shortly before his exile. In his panegyrics on O.T. saints, martyrs and bishops of the Antiochene Church he praises among others Job, Eleazar, the Maccabean Brothers, St. Paul (in seven homilies), the martyrs Romanus, Barlaam, Pelagia, the Bishops Ignatius, Babylas, Eustathius, Meletius, and his teacher Diodore of Tarsus. His twelve homilies against the Anomoeans on the incomprehensibility of God and the unity of essence of the Father and the Son serve dogmatic and polemical purposes. Eight sermons *Adv. Iudaeos* warn against participating in the Jewish feasts and the superstitious practices of the Jews. Moral-ascetical sermons: two catecheses addressed to catechumens; three on the devil; nine on penitence; one against the New Year superstition; one against theatres and circus. Of his sermons for feasts of the Church we would mention:

On the Feast of Christmas (386), of which he says that it came from Rome to Antioch scarcely ten years ago; on the Epiphany, Easter and the Ascension.

Homs. on Matthew, trans. G. Prevost, 3 vols., O 1843/51. Homs. on John, trans. G. F. Stupart, 2 vols., O 1848/52. Homs. on Acts, 2 vols., O 1851/2. Homs. on Rom., trans. J. B. Morris, O 1841. Homs. on 1 Cor., trans. H. K. Cornish and J. Medley,

2 vols., O 1839. Homs. on 2 Cor., trans. J. Ashworth, O 1848. Comm. on Gal. and Homs. on Eph., trans. W. J. Copeland, O 1840. Homs. on Phil., Eph., and Thess., trans. J. Ashworth and J. Tweed, O 1843. Homs. on Tim., Tit., and Philem., trans. J. Tweed, O 1843. Homs. on Hebr., Trans., O 1877. Hom. stat., trans. E. Budge, O 1942.

3. Treatises

a. The work *De sacerdotio* (Περὶ ἱερωσύνης) in six books was destined to meet with an extraordinary success. The introductory remarks on the reason why it was written (1 to 2, 6) cannot be regarded as historical. Chrysostom wants to justify himself before his otherwise unknown fellow student Basil and explains why he caused the other to accept the episcopal office by keeping secret his own intention, while he himself avoided the same dignity by flight. The work was written *c.* 386 in the form of a fictitious dialogue between him and Basil, making use of a similar work by Gregory of Nazianzus (supra § 59). Because of its unique description of the dignity of the priesthood it has always been very popular reading with priests and ordinands (EP 1118/20).

b. In his treatise *On Arrogance and the Education of Children* he first shows the bad consequences of arrogance which had caused the sad Church troubles at Antioch, and in the second part proceeds to expound the principles of the education of children.

c. Several treatises commend and defend monasticism: *Duae Paraeneses ad Theodorum lapsum* are probably addressed to his friend, the later Bishop Theodore of Mopsuestia, who had succumbed to the charms of a certain Hermione and turned his back on the religious life. Chrysostom's admonition bore fruit, and his friend returned to the monastery. The two books *On Penitence* are dedicated to two monk friends; three books are written *Adversus oppugnatores vitae monasticae*.

d. The following praise and recommend virginity: *De virginitate, Ad viduam iuniorem, De non iterando coniugio*. Two treatises oppose the bad custom of having *subintroductae,* which was rife in certain clerical circles of Constantinople (MG 47, 495/532; EA 346/9, 357/8, 363/8).

e. Three treatises of consolation are devoted to the meaning and importance of suffering: *Ad Stagirium a daemone vexatum; Quod nemo laeditur nisi a se ipso; Ad eos, qui scandalizati sunt ob adversitates.*

f. Two not certainly genuine works have apologetic purposes: *In s. Babylam contra Iulianum et Gentiles,* and *Contra Iudaeos et Gentiles, quod Christus est Deus.*

4. His 236 letters are mostly very short. They all date from the time of his second exile and are addressed to more than a hundred different recipients. They aim principally at consoling his persecuted adherents and friends and giving them news of his health. The most important are the seventeen letters addressed to his most faithful follower in Constantinople, the widow and deaconess Olympias; two letters to Pope Innocent I (EH 728/37).

5. The so-called Liturgy of Chrysostom is spurious (BKV[2] 5, 1912, 198/262); it is still in use in the Greek Catholic Church on most days of the year. The same holds good for the *Synopsis Veteris et Novi Testamenti,* a manual of introduction to the Scriptures. Besides, several hundred printed sermons are spurious, and about 500–600 spurious sermons have so far remained unedited.

Treatises: Wilmart, JTS 19, 1917/8, 305/27 (La collect. des 38 hom. lat.). Peradze, OC 1931, 97/107 (Georg. trans.). Ehrhard, TU 50, 130ff. and freq. (on ined. homs.). A. C. de Albornoz, *J. Crisóstomo y su influencia social en el imperio bizantino,* Ma 1934 (on 52 MSS). Bartolozzi, STU 125/32 (2 homs. on Romans). Auetisean, Sion 9, 1935, 21/4 (Prol. and 1 to 2, 2 of the comm. on Is. Armen.); cf. OC 1937, 152. Powell, JTS 1938, 132/40 (palimpsest of hom. *Adv. Jud.*). Eltester, ZNTW 37, 1938, 286/8 (on Hom. in MG 56, 172: Macedon. calendar). Altaner, HJB 61, 1941, 212/26 (old Lat. transs.). Siegmund, 1948, 91/101. Brunner, ZKT 1941, 32/5 (date of *Ad. vid. iun.* May 392). Martin, Mu

1941, 30/3, 48/52: MG 56, 385/94: genuine. Graf I 337/54. Bardy, MSR 1945, 271/84 (chronol. of letters to Olymp.). Ogara, Gr 1946, 145/55 (*Hom. de sacerd.* VII). Costanza, StC 1952, 145/54 (date of homs. on Eph.). Dumortier, MSR 1952, 63/72 *(Principes d'ecdotique concern. les traités de J. Chr.)*. G. Mercati, *Alla ricerca dei nomi degli "alteri" traduttori nelle omelie sui Salmi di S. Giov. Cris....* (ST 158), 1952. Flecchia, Aev 1952, 113/30 (on hom. trans. of Burgundio). M. Costanza, *De heil. J. Chr...*, Haarlem 1952. Honigmann, ST 173, 54/8 (on the translator Anianus of Celeda). P. Hamelian, *Tome commémorative de la Bibl. Patriarchale d'Alex.*, 1953, 225/30 (here also on MSS of J. Chr. and Basil). Bickersteth, StBizNeoell 1953, 401/4 (J. Chr. on the feast of the Hypapante). Wenger, REB 10, 1953, 47/59 (ed. part. of an uned. sermon). Vandeberghe, ZRGG 1955, 34/46 (on the spectacles). Dumortier, JTS 1955, 99/102 (on authorship of the Corpus ascet. of J. Chr.).

Text, source and literary criticism: M. v. Bonsdorf, *Zur Predigttaetigkeit des J. Chr.*, Helsingf. 1922 (date of NT homs.). A. Méan, *Ét. des hom. que J. C. a prononcées sur le 1. chap. de l'ép. aux Rom.*, Neuchâtel 1930. Merzagora, Did 1931, 1/73 (C. as commentator of Paul). S. New, HTR 1931, 121/42 (text of Mk.). A. Naegle, TQ 1935, 117/42 (date of Tim. homs.). Karnthaler, BNJ 9, 1932/3, 36/8 (*De sac.: a comparatio*). Coleman-Norton, CP 1930, 305/17 (Gr. philosophers); 1931, 85/9 (Flav. Josephus); 1932, 213/21 (Gr. poets). Cataudella, Athenaeum 1940, 236/43 (Aristophanes in Chr.). Smothers, RSR 1937, 513/48 (text of homs. on Acts). Exarchos, Θ 19, 1941/8, 153/70 (genuineness of *Education of Children*). Dumortier, RevScHumaines 1947, 222/38 (Education). G. J. Theocharidis, *Beitraege z. Gesch. des Profantheaters im 4. u. 5. Jh. hauptsaechl. auf Grund der Pred. des J. Chr.* (thesis Mn), Th 1940. Bezdecki, Rev. Teol. (Rouman.) 34, 1944, 407/17 and 6 conts. (Plato in J. Chr.). Sinko, AIP 1, 1949, 531/45 (date of *De sacerd.* 404[?]). Dumortier, MSR 1949, 247/52 (date of treatises to Monks and Virgins 381/3). L. M. Laistner, *Christianity and Pagan Culture in the Later Roman Empire,* Ithaca, NY 1951 (here also trans. of *De inani gloria*); VC 1951, 179/85 (MS of *De inani gloria*). Brunner, Aev 1955, 272/4 (Chr. on *Quod regulares feminae* ... ch. 8). — Exegetical points: L. J. Ohleyer, *The Pauline Formula Induere Christum with Special Ref. to the Works of J. Chr.,* W 1921. Merzagora, StU 205/46 *(Cris. comment. di S. Paolo)*. Hoffmann-Aleith, ZNTW 38, 1939, 181/8 (St. Paul). Lyonnet, RSR 1939, 335/51 *(J. Chr. et s. Jérôme sur Jacques le Frère du Seigneur)*. Kaupel, TG 1938, 17/24 (O.T. on homs. on Rom.). F. Ogara, *El Apost. s. Pablo* (in J. Chr.), R 1944. I. Moisescu, *Candela* (Rouman.), 50/1, 1939/41, 116/238 (exeg. of Scripture). C. D. Dicks, *The Mt.-Text of Chr. in his Homs. on Mt.,* thesis Ch 1946/7. P. W. Harkins, *Text-Trad. of Chr.'s Comm. on John,* thesis Michigan 1948. Pruemm, Bi 1949, 161/96, 377/400 (on 2 Cor. 3, 1 to 4, 6). N. M. Robertson, *St. J. Chr. as NT Commentator,* thesis St. Andrews 1951. Smothers, RSR 1951, 416/27 (on Acts 20, 13); HTR 1953, 203/15 (on Acts 15, 4). J. Foerster, *Die Exegese des 4. Ev. in den Joh.-Hom. des Chr.,* thesis B 1951.— On spurious works: Franchi de' Cavalieri, ST 65, 1935, 281/303 (2nd Pelagia hom.). Holloway, ET 1935, 238. J. Simon, *Orientalia* 3, 1934, 217/42; 4, 1935, 222/34 (Copt. Michael hom.). Van Wijk, Byzantinoslavica 7, 1937/8, 108/23 (hom. *In Annuntiat.,* Old Slavonic). On ps.— Chr. homs. which B. Marx assigns to Proclus and Basil of Sel. cf. § 72, 3 and 71, 6. On MG 61, 715/20 cf. Byz 12, 1937, 361. On MG 61, 763/8 cf. Mercati, OM 4, 1937, 46/8. Lampe, JTS 1948, 169/75 (Ps.-Chr. on Ps. 96). G. Mercati, Misc. Ubach, 22/30 (excerpt from Jerem. comm. of Ps.-Chr.). J. Weyer, *De homiliis, quae Ioanni Chrys. falso attribuuntur,* thesis typescript Bonn (2 homs. on prayer). — On Chr.-Liturgy: ed. P. de Meester, Lo [2]1930; Gr. and Germ., Mn 1932. De Meester, DAL 6, 1596/1604. Engl. F. E. Brightman, Lo 1931, French V. Ghiga, P 1934. H. G. Codrington, *Anaphora S. J. Chr.,* R 1940 (Syriac). Tarchnisvili, JL 14, 1938, 79/94 (Georg. Lit.). Engberding, OC 1937, 213/47 (on pre-hist. of Chr.-Lit.). Strittmatter, EL 1941, 2/73; Tr 1943, 79/137 (text of oldest Lat. trans.). Engberding, OC 39, 1955, 33/47 (W. Syr. Anaphora of J. Chr.).

Points of Doctrine

1. Christology. He clearly attests belief in the two separate natures in Christ. "If I say one (Christ) I mean to assert by this a union, not a mixture; the one nature was not changed into the other, but only united to it" (7 Heb. 3). Man should not ask how this union (ἕνωσις, συνάφεια, not σύγχυσις) was effected, Christ alone knows this (11 Jo. 2). Like other Antiochenes he occasionally uses the rhetorical metaphor that the Logos dwelt in the Man Jesus as in a temple (Ps. 44, 3; 4 Mt. 3; 11 Jo. 2). But he often emphasizes that Christ was only one; thus he says (1 Mt. 2): "The (essential thing) is e.g., the fact that God became man, that he worked miracles . . . that he is the Son . . . of the same essence as the Father." (Cf. 7 Phil. 2–4.)

He does not use Mary's name of honour Θεοτόκος, which the Antiochenes opposed, but he does not use the term Χριστοτόκος either. His words about Mary, which were already censured by Thomas Aquinas (S. Th. 3 q. 27 a. 4 ad 3), are probably influenced by the sharp distinction he makes between the divinity and the humanity in Christ; they are wholly lacking in the tender devotion and loving praise of the other Fathers; cf. 4 Mt. 4f.; 44 Mt. 1; 21 John 2.

2. Original Sin. On Chrysostom's view on original sin a dispute arose between St. Augustine and the Pelagian Julian of

Eclanum. Julian cited the following passage from the homily *Ad neophytos:* "We baptize infants, though they do not have sins" (ἁμαρτήματα) thinking that he found in it a denial of the guilt inherited from our first parents. Augustine replied (*Jul.* 1, 22) that the plural "sins" proved that here it was a question of personal sins; he adduced other passages (eight in all) from the works of Chrysostom as proving original sin. Now Augustine was quite right in realizing that Chrysostom could not be claimed for the Pelagian error. But it would also be wrong to assert that the passages adduced by Augustine clearly attest the insight and more accurate terminology which Augustine himself achieved only during the controversy, and according to which not only the punishment, but also the guilt was transmitted by Adam to all men; cf. 28 Mt. 3; 11 Rom. 1 and 3. Chrysostom, like the other Greek Fathers of the fourth century, is here lagging behind the more advanced doctrinal development of the West. He saw and preached the inherited punishment, though he certainly did not mean intentionally to exclude the inherited guilt from the notion of original sin.

3. The Eucharist. Chrysostom is the classical witness of Christian antiquity for the Catholic doctrine of the eucharist and is therefore called *Doctor eucharistiae.* He mentions the eucharist in very many passages and in the most definite terms. Thus he says that in the eucharist we hold in our hands the body that walked on earth, and that Christ drank his own blood at the Last Supper (24 1 Cor. 4; 82 Mt. 1). Christ becomes present through the change; He effects it himself and is the real priest at the altar: Christ's words "This is my Body" change the offerings (μεταρρυθμίζει τὰ προκεῖμενα) (1 Prod. Iudae 6). He often calls the eucharist a sacrifice and says it is identical with the sacrifice on the Cross (17 Heb. 3) (EP 1180, 1195, 1222).

4. Penance. Chrysostom cannot be cited as a witness to private penance under the direction of the Church. How different was

the penitential practice of his time from that of a later age emerges from this fact alone that he discusses seventeen tasks and spheres of duties in his treatise *De sacerdotio,* but hearing confessions is not one of them. This statement is not surprising in view of the fact that in Christian antiquity the man who had committed a mortal sin was admitted only once to ecclesiastical penance, which was then public (*De sacerd.* 3, 17), even though at the beginning of the procedure a secret confession made directly or indirectly before the bishop took place. Since, therefore, in the lives of many Christians ecclesiastical penance (sacrament of penance) scarcely became a reality, the great preacher speaks all the more frequently of the forgiveness of sins to be obtained by a humble confession before God; cf. e.g. MG 50, 658 (*Non esse ad gratiam concionandum* 3): "God alone is to see you in your confession, God, who does not blame you for your sins, but frees you from them because of your confession. Before this tribunal there are no witnesses, and you, the sinner, judge yourself."

5. Extreme Unction. In *De sacerd.* 3, 6 he derives the dignity of the priesthood not only from the priests' power to baptize, but also from their authority, given in Jas. 5: 14f. to anoint the sick which brings about the remission of sin; cf. also 32 Mt. 6.

6. Papal Primacy. A clear, unequivocal recognition of the Roman Primacy cannot be found anywhere in Chrysostom. This may partly be explained by the fact that such a recognition would have put himself and his bishops in the wrong, since he was an adherent of Meletius and Flavian, who were not recognized by Rome for some time. It is certain that Chrysostom taught a primacy of St. Peter (cf. *Hom. in illud "Hoc scitote"* 4); but he has nowhere in his writings drawn the conclusion from this that the Bishop of Rome has a right to the same position in the universal Church. The idea that he recognized the Pope as the supreme court of appeal cannot be deduced even from his first letter (EP 728/37) to Pope Innocent I (404), since he also sent identical ones at the same time

to the Bishops of Milan and Aquileja. Chrysostom asks the three bishops on no account to recognize his illegal deposition and above all not to exclude him from their communion. It is true, however, that the confusion created by the opposition to Chrysostom and the behaviour of the two quarrelling parties, who both communicated with Rome, contributed to strengthening the idea of the primacy.

7. The Oath. Like Justin (1 Ap. 16, 5), Chrysostom interpreted the passage Mt. 5: 34 in the sense of definitely forbidding Christians to swear an oath: "Let no one say: I am taking an oath in a just cause; it is not permitted to swear one, whether in a just or in an unjust cause" (15 Gen. 5); cf. also 5 Stat. 7; 7 Stat. 5; 9 Stat. 5.

Mgg.: A. Naegle, *Die Eucharistielehre des hl. J. Chr.*, 1900. G. Kopp, *Die Stellung des hl. J. Chr. zum weltlichen Leben,* 1905. J. H. Juzek, *Die Christologie des hl. J. Chr.,* 1912. A. Moulard, *S. J. Chr. le défenseur du mariage et l'apôtre de la virginité,* 1923. P. E. Legrand, *S. J. Chr.,* 1924 *(Moralistes chrét.).* L. Meyer, *S. J. Chr. maître de la perfection chrét.,* 1934; some items also in RSR 1933, 283/305 and RAM 1933, 332/62. N. Marini, *Il primato di s. Pietro e de' suoi successori in S. G. Cr.,* ²1922; against this C. Baur, *J. Chr. und seine Zeit,* I, 383/91; II, 254/8. H. Hlebbowicz, *Jednosc Kosciola Chryst. wedlug sw. J. Chr.,* Wilno 1932. D. N. Jaksic, *Zivot i ucenie sv. I. Zlatousta,* Karlovci 1934; cf. Spacil, Gr 1936, 176/194, 335/76; 1937, 70/87. J. Seidlmayer, *Die Paedagogik des J. Chr.,* 1926. A. C. de Albornoz, *S. J. Chr. y su influencia social en el imperio bizantino del siglo IV,* Ma 1934; some items also in RF 1932 and 1933; 110, 1936, 80/98. P. Andres, *Der Missionsgedanke in den Schriften des hl. J. Chr.,* 1935. C. N. Stratiotes, Ἡ ποιμαντικὴ τοῦ ἁγίου Ἰω. τοῦ Χρυσ., Salonica 1935. F. Fromm, *Das Bild des verklaerten Christus beim hl. Paulus nach d. Kommentaren des hl. J. Chr.,* R 1938. E. Boularand, *La venue de l'homme à la foi d'après S. J. Chr.,* R 1939; partly in Gr 1938, 515/42. B. Giorgiatis, *Die Lehre des J. Chr. ueber d. hl. Schrift,* At 1947; cf. Bi 1951, n. 756. M. S. Wasylyk, *De servitute apud J. Chr.,* thesis Propag. R 1948 f. M. Striedl, *Antiker Volksglaube bei J. Chr.,* thesis Wu 1948. D. Chatziioannu, Αἱ κοσμοθεωρικαὶ ἀπόψεις *des J. Chr.,* At 1949; cf. BZ 1952, 154. L. Morins, *Eucharistiae promissio sec. J. Chr. in Hom. ad Jo. 6,* thesis Propag. R 1949. J. a Jesus Macias, *La doctr. de la justificación en el coment. de J. Cris. a los Rom.,* thesis Greg. R 1951. G. Fittkau, *Der Begriff des Mysteriums bei J. Chr.,* Bonn 1953.—Treatises: Mersch 1², 1936, 464/86. Fabbi, Bi 1933, 330/47 (doctr. of inspiration). E. F. Bruck, Studi in onore di S. Riccobono 3, 1933, 377/423 (eccl. right of inheritance); Μνημόσυνα Παππούλια 1934, 65/83 (intention of donor). Gorce, Ét. Carmélit. 21, 1936, 245/85 (marriage and perfection). Kyriakides, Λαογραφία, 1936, 634/41 (folklorist. matters). M. Simon, AIP 1936, 403/21 (anti-Jewish polemics). Groehl, TG 1942, 301/7 (family education). Lampen, Ant 1943, 3/16 *(doctr. de Christo se offerente in Missa)*. Konewski 1941 (on social ethics); cf. BZ 1942, 309. Lukatos 1940 (popular usage at death and funeral acc. to J. Chr.); cf. BZ 1942, 309; cf. also Kukules 1940 in BZ 1941, 231. Solano, Misc. Comillas 1941/1942, 2, 1943, 91/138 (re-birth). Ogara, Gr 1943, 62/77 *(prophetia typica)*. Amand, *Fatalisme,* 1945, 480/532. Daniélou, RSR 1950, 176/94 (*L'incompréhensibilité de Dieu;* against Eunomius). Lécuyer, NRT 1950, 561/79 *(Le sacerdoce céleste du Christ)*. Dumortier, MSR 1955, 27/36 *(Les idées morales)*.

§ 70. OPPONENTS OF JOHN CHRYSOSTOM

1. Theophilus of Alexandria v. supra § 55, 3.

2. Acacius, Bishop of Beroea (= Aleppo), died after 437; of his voluminous correspondence only five letters have been preserved (MG 77, 99/102; 84, 647f., 658/60; SACO I 1, 1, 99f.). The five panegyrics composed on him by the Syrian poet Balaeus in BKV[2] 6, 1913, 71/89. Ermoni, DHG 1, 241f., Bardy, RevSR 1938, 20/40 *(Son rôle dans la controverse nestor.)*. In Severus Antioch. III 2 (ed. Lebon) 2 citations. Schiwietz 3, 1938, 182/90.

3. Antiochus, Bishop of Ptolemais (Acco in Phoenicia), died at the latest in 408. Two treatises mentioned by Gennadius (*Vir. ill.* 20) are lost. J. Zellinger, *Die Genesishomilien des Bischofs Severian v. Gabala,* 1916, 44/7 (spurious sermon). Aigrain, DHG 3, 709f. Martin, Mu 54, 1941, 34/8, 53/7 (two Christmas homilies which probably belong to him). Severus Antioch., III 41 (ed. Lebon): three citations from sermons.

4. Severian, Bishop of Gabala (d. after 408) was appreciated as a preacher in the court circles of Constantinople; he defended the Nicene faith and violently opposed heretics and Jews. Of his literary remains the following have so far been recognized as genuine: fourteen Greek homilies, eight in Armenian and one in Ethiopic. Two further Greek sermons are not certainly genuine; one of them is the *Sermo in dedicatione pretiosae et vivificae crucis* which does not mention the legend of the finding of the Cross. Other homilies, extant in Syriac, Coptic and Arabic are also

dubious. Severian prefers Genesis as a source of material. He wrote a commentary on all the Pauline Epistles which was published in a double recension, large parts of which, especially on 1 and 2 Corinthians, are extant in *catenae* (ed. Staab). Recently B. Marx has sought to prove that twelve in part incompletely preserved homilies of Chrysostom are the property of Severian. The preacher possessed an extraordinarily good knowledge of the Bible.

MG 56, 429/500 (6 homs. in Gen.). Staab 1933, 213/351 (texts from Pauline commentaries). — J. Zellinger, *Die Genesishom. des Bisch. S. v. G.*, 1916. *Studien zu S. v. G.*, 1926; LTK 9, 503f. Lietzmann, PWK II 2, 1930/2. G. Duerks, *De Sev. G.*, 1917. C. Martin, Mu 1935, 311/21 (ed. hom. *In illud: Pater, transeat*). Torossian, Baz 1937, 4/11 (9. hom.). B. Marx, OCP 1939, 281/367 (12 homs. among the spuria of Chrysost.). Severus Antioch. III 39, 41 (ed. Lebon), (5 citations from 5 unknown sermons); cf. also Martin, Byz 12, 1937, 361. Bardy, DTC 14, 2000/6. Moss, BullSchoolOrAfricSt 1948, 555/66 (Christmas serm.). Wenger, REB 10, 1953, 47/59; AugMag 1, 175/85 (a Ps.-Chrys. homily belonging to Severian). Garitte, Mu 1953, 97/102 (hom. 9, Georg. fragm.). Soares, Marianum 15, 1953, 401/11 (protev.). Laurentin 1953, 162f. (on Mariolog. sermons). H. D. Altendorf, *Unters. zu Severian v. G.*, (Diss.) T 1957 (ThLZ 1958, 583f.).

5. Macarius Magnes, probably identical with the Bishop of Magnesia (in Caria or Lydia), who accused Bishop Heraclides of Ephesus, a friend of Chrysostom, at the Oak Synod (403). About 400 he wrote an apologia in five books in the form of a dispute (Ἀποκριτικὸς ἢ Μονογενὴς πρὸς Ἕλληνας), about half of which is extant. It is very valuable, since it probably contains the objections from the lost books of the neo-Platonist Porphyry (not of Hierocles). Macarius probably worked only on an edited extract from Porphyry (EP 2166). All except one of the fragments of homilies on Genesis published under his name are spurious.

Ed.: C. Blondel, P 1876. — Transs.: T. W. Crafer, Lo 1920. G. Schalkhausser (TU 31, 4) 1907. A. Harnack (TU 37, 4) 1911 (supra § 19, 3). Bardy, DTC 9, 1456/9. G. Mercati, ST 95, 1941, 49/74 (chapter headings of lib. 1–3).

§ 71. EXEGETES AND ASCETICS

1. Probably in the first half of the fifth century Hadrian, perhaps both priest and monk, wrote a Biblical hermeneutics for which he used for the first time the title, *Introduction to Holy Scripture*.

MG 98, 1273/1312; ed. F. Goessling, B 1887. Mercati, RB 1914, 246/55. Schweizer, ZNTW 40, 73f.

2. Hesychius of Jerusalem (v. supra § 49, 8), first a monk, since *c.* 412 presbyter in Jerusalem (d. after 450). He was important as an exegete of the allegorizing Alexandrian school and is said to have explained the whole of Scripture. His theology is altogether Biblical; he mistrusted philosophy. His Christology is based on Cyril of Alexandria without accepting his terminology; he comes dangerously near to holding monophysite views. He is an important witness to the Church's teaching on original sin.

Among the extant works from his rich literary output are the following: A Commentary on Leviticus in the Latin translation of a certain Jerome (6th cent.; MG 93, 787/1180); twenty-four homilies on Job 1–20 (Arm.; ed. C. Tscherakian, Venice 1913); Glosses on Is. (ed. M. Faulhaber 1900); Glosses on the Pss., printed under the name of Athanasius (MG 27, 649/1344); large fragments of a sizable commentary on the Psalms (MG 93, 1179/1340; 55, 711/84). A third explanation of the Psalms of medium length seems also to belong to him; ed. V. Jagic, *Suppl. Psalterii Bononiensis,* W 1917, where his exegetical glosses to thirteen hymns of the O.T. and N.T. are also edited. Several sermons are printed in MG 93, 1449/80. Several items have not yet been edited or are doubtful, some are certainly spurious. A reliable survey of genuine and spurious writings is to be found in K. Juessen 1, 10/47. Two *centuria* of a collection of ascetical maxims, printed among the works of Hesychius of Jerusalem (MG 93, 1479/1544), belong to an Abbot Hesychius of a Sinaite monastery who lived in the sixth and seventh centuries.

A. Vaccari, Bess 22, 1918, 8/46 (comm. in Lev.) = Vaccari, Scritti 1, 165/206; AL 11, 1937, 35 (*gilberosus* in MG 93, 1063). Devreesse, RB 1924, 498/521 (commentaries on Pss.). K. Juessen, *Die dogmat. Anschauungen des H. v. J.,* 1st part 1931, 2. part 1934. Bardy, RB 1933, 226/9 (Coll. difficult.). C. Martin, RHE 1935, 356/9 (Marian homs.). Martin, RHE 1939, 54/60 (Chrysippus dependent on Hes.). Santifaller, ZBW 1943, 241/66 (uncial fragm. of Lev. comm.). Graf I 367/9 (H = Theodulus?). G. Mercati, OCP 10, 1944, 7/22 (prob. author of Ps. Ath. treatise *De titulis psalmorum*); Misc. P. Paschini, 1951, 205/11 (Salterio greco e una *catena* greca del salterio: belong to Hes.). Wenger, REAug 2, 1956, 457/70 (on trad. of Gr. comment. *In Lv.*).

3. Nilus of Ancyra (d. *c.* 430), formerly falsely called N. Sinaita. He was a monastic superior at Ancyra, of theological and literary education, and a follower of St. John Chrysostom. He wrote a number of moral and ascetical treatises destined for monks. Besides he left many letters to mostly unknown recipients which sometimes contain but a few sentences. They are frequently only reproductions of what he had read and extracts from the writings of various authors; their epistolary character is sometimes only fictitious (EA 851/76). Spurious works are among others: *Narrationes de caede monachorum in monte Sinai,* a romance of an unknown author. On two works belonging to Evagrius v. supra § 52, 6.

MG 79. F. Degenhart, *Der hl. N. Sinaita,* 1915; *Neue Beitraege zur N.-Forschung.* K. Heussi, *Unters. zu N. dem Asketen,* 1917; *Das Nilusproblem,* 1921; PWK 16, 2186f. Disdier, DTC 11, 661/74. C. Martin, RHE 1936, 929/32 (2 spurious homs.). V. Fradinski, *Nilus. His life and his Literary Activity,* Belgrade 1938 (Serbian). Muyldermans, Mu 1938, 191f. (24 new maxims of the spurious [Evagrian] *Institut. ad monachos:* MG 79, 1235/40); Mu 1939, 235/74 *(Nouv. recension de De 8 spirit. mal.);* 1942, 93/6 *(De magistris et discip.);* Mu 1943, 77/114 (Armen. trans.). On an uned. comm. on the Cant. cf. A. Sovic, Bi 1921, 45/52; BOS 1925, 1/22 and without new material once more Zagreb 1932. On the so-called *Christ. Epictetus* cf. Schissel, BNJ 7, 1930, 444/7; Liguori, SC 1930, 297/303. Stelzenberger 1933, 478/87 and freq. Warnach, *Gedaechtnisschr. Casel* 1951, 135/51 (pneumat. philos. in the Letters). Astruc, Sc 1954, 293/96 (MS for MG 79, 589/712). Henninger, *Anthropos* 50, 1955, 81/148 (*Narrationes de caede worthless* for ethnography and hist. of religion).

4. Marcus Eremita (d. after 430), probably abbot at Ancyra and later a hermit in the Judaean desert. We have of his, seven

short practical ascetical treatises and two dogmatic polemical ones, *De Melchisedek* and *Contra Nestorianos* (EA 877/92).

MG 65, 905/1140. Mg. by J. Kunze 1895 (ed. c. Nest.). Amann, DTC 9, 1964/8 Doerries, PWK 14, 1867/9 and Opitz, ibid. Suppl. 6, 281 f. Peterson, ZNTW 1932, 273/88 (*De bapt.* and Messalians). Hausherr, OCP 1935, 340 ff. (M. and Messalians). K. Rahner, ZKT 1937, 258/71 (Messalian fragm. on bapt.). Juessen, ZKT 1938, 76/91 (original sin). Khalifé, MélUnivSt Jos. Beyrouth 28, 1949/50, 61/6 (*De temperantia* spurious); ibid. 28, 115/224 (Arab. trans. of works).

5. Diadochus, Bishop of Photice in Epirus, wrote about the middle of the fifth century his *Capita centum de perfectione spirituali* which are important for the history of mysticism and asceticism.

MG 65, 1167/1212 (Lat.). J. E. Weis-Liebersdorf, L 1912 (Gr. and Lat.). E. des Places, Crit. text and trans. also of *De ascensione* (SCh 5bis) 1955; RevEA 1943, 61/80 (extracts from introd. of trans.). P. Chrestos, *Mg. on Diadochus,* Th 1952. Des Places, RSR 1952, 129/38 (the catechesis printed in ML 120, 709/11 is supposed to belong to D., not to Simeon the "New Theologian"); against this BZ 1952, 453; 1956, 178. Des Places, DS F. 20/1, 817/34. — Treatises: Horn, RAM 1927, 402/19 *(Sens de l'esprit).* Peterson, BNJ 5, 1927, 412/8 (text. crit.). Rothenhaeusler, Ir 1937, 536/53; *Hl. Ueberlieferung.* Festschrift fuer I. Herwegen 1938, 86/95. F. Doerr, *D. v. P. u. die Messalianer,* 1938. Viller-Rahner 1939, 216/28. Oberhummer, PWK 20, 1, 660/2 (geogr. situation of Photice). Marrou, RevEA 1943, 225/32 (D. and Victor de Vita). Honigmann, ST 173, 174/84 (d. c. 468).

6. The Metropolitan Basil of Seleucia (Isauria, d. *c.* 468) adopted a wavering attitude at the beginning of the Monophysite troubles; from the time of Chalcedon (451), however, he was a faithful follower of orthodoxy (cf. his letter in SACO II 5, 46/9). Of the forty-one sermons on Scriptural personages and texts in Migne, nos. 38 and 39 should be rejected as spurious, according to the investigations of B. Marx (the latter sermon is assigned to Proclus of Const.). Besides, six ps.-Athanasian (MG 28, 1074/61 and 1073/1108) and one ps.- Chrysostom (MG 64, 417/24) homilies belong to him, as well as one *In Lazarum* ed. by P. Camelot and two further unedited homilies. The intellectual content of these sermons is swamped by bombastic rhetorical phrases. Hence the homilies are without importance for contemporary history and their exegetical value is equally negligible.

His verbose work *De vita et miraculis s. Theclae libri II* (mutilated at the end) has no historical value. In the second book the miracle worker Thecla is almost more like a pagan goddess than a Christian saint. A versified version by him of the same subject has not been preserved.

MG 85, 27/668; P. Camelot, *Une homélie inédite de B. de S.* (Vat. Ottob. gr. 14): Mél. A. M. Desrousseaux 1937, 35/48 *(In Lazarum)*. — F. Fenner, *De B. Seleuc. quaestiones selectae,* thesis Marburg 1912. B. Marx, *Procliana,* Mr 1940, 84/9 (hom. 39); the homiletic remains of B. of S. in OCP 1941, 329/69. On the *Miracula s. Theclae* cf. E. Lucius, *Die Anfaenge des Heiligenkults in der christl. Kirche,* 1904, 205/14; L. Radermacher, SbW 182, 3, 1916, 121/6, and H. Delehaye, AB 1925, 49/57. Honigmann, ST 173, 174/84.

7. Gennadius I, Patriarch of Constantinople (458–71) wrote many Scriptural commentaries, among others on all the Pauline Letters. Only little has remained of most of these commentaries. Important fragments of the commentary on Genesis and Romans have survived; of the latter we have almost three quarters of the text. Some considerable fragments of several dogmatic treatises are extant, thus of an extraordinarily violent controversial work against Cyril's twelve anathemata (431–2), and of a treatise Πρὸς Παρθένιον in at least two books, addressed to a partisan of Nestorius, which also very probably pursued an anti-Cyrillian line. His point of view was orthodox, i.e. in harmony with the Council of Chalcedon, as is proved by a fragment from an *encomium* on Leo the Great's *Tomus ad Flavianum*. A synodal letter belonging to the year 458 or 459 is extant in two versions. The many homilies which Gennadius mentions in *Vir. ill.* 89 do not seem to have been preserved.

MG 85, 1613/1734. K. Staab 1933, 352/422. Partly unknown texts in F. Diekamp, AP 54/108. R. Devreesse, RB 1936, 384 (7 fragms. on Gen. and 1 on Ex.).

§ 72. NESTORIUS, HIS FRIEND EUTHERIUS AND HIS OPPONENT PROCLUS

1. Nestorius, born after 381 of Persian parents, was a priest-monk at Antioch and probably a pupil of Theodore of Mopsuestia. Because of his great fame as a preacher, Theodosius II elevated him to the patriarchal See of Constantinople (428). He violently attacked Jews and heretics, treating only the Pelagians with leniency.

When he preached the Antiochene Christology in the pulpit (controversy about the title *Theotokos*) he came to be regarded as a heretic. The Council of Ephesus (431) condemned his doctrine and declared him deposed as a "godless teacher"; the Emperor exiled him to a monastery and in 436 to Oasis in Egypt, where he died at the earliest in 451.

The writings of Nestorius have been preserved only in fragments. The texts collected by F. Loofs contain fifteen letters and thirty sermons, part of them only fragments. The doctrinally most important letters are the three epistles to Pope Celestine I and the second letter to Cyril of Alexandria.

His apology, the *Liber Heraclidis,* which came to light in a Syriac translation as late as 1910, was published under a pseudonym and is not absolutely certain to be genuine. It criticizes the decrees of Ephesus and sharply opposes the doctrines of Cyril of Alexandria and Dioscorus, at the same time it attacks Manicheism. Further fragments in a Syriac translation have come to light in writings of Severus of Antioch (§ 101, 1); these have recently been published for the first time. The so-called *Twelve Counter-anathemata* against Cyril were composed not by Nestorius himself but by one of his followers.

On the heresy of Nestorius. According to the traditional view (Cyril, Council of Ephesus) he denied the hypostatic union and taught two only morally united hypostases in Christ. Nestorius rejected the accusation of holding the doctrine of the "two Sons" which the Church had condemned before, and of splitting the unity of Christ. According to his philosophical (neo-Platonist) view on the union of the physical and the intelligible, the unity in Christ did not seem to be impaired. In fact, however, his teaching on the ἓν πρόσωπον in Christ in which the two "nature prosopa" of the humanity and the divinity are united κατ' εὐδοκίαν is incapable of excluding the thought of a merely moral union of the natures. Thus Nestorius explicitly rejected the idea of a physical or hypostatic union and was prepared only to acknowledge Christ, but not the Logos, as the subject of all divine and human attributes and actions. Hence no decisive importance can be attached to the fact that he recognized the *communicatio idiomatum* as referring to Christ, which later allowed him even to admit the "rightly understood" title of *Theotokos,* nor to his silence on the dangerous Antiochene *Bewaehrungslehre* (doctrine of proving). Nevertheless, Nestorius believed to the end of his life that he was orthodox and that Leo I, too, had taught his dualist Christology (EP 2057 a/g).

Edd.: F. Loofs, *Nestoriana,* 1905. P. Bedjan, *Nestorius. Le livre d'Héraclide de Damas,* 1910; French by F. Nau 1910; Engl. by G. R. Driver and L. Hodgson 1925. Letters etc. in SACO I (supra § 50, 17). *The new Syr. fragms. in Lebon,* Mu 1923, 47/65; cf. on this Severus Antioch., 3 vols., 1929/38, Index, and Martin, RHE 1936, 929/32. A. Sanda, *Severi Philalethes,* 1928, and Lebon in CSCO, 93/4 101/2, 1929/33. — Mgg.: Amann, DTC 11, 76/157. Rucker, PWK 17, 126/37. J. F. Bethune-Baker, *N. and his Teaching,* 1908. L. Fendt, *Die Christologie des N.,* 1910. J. P. Junglas, *Die Irrl. des N.,* 1912. F. Loofs, *N.,* C 1914. C. Pesch, *N. als Irrl.,* 1921. E. Schwartz, SbMn 1922, 1 (counter-anathem.). I. Rucker, *Stud. zum Concil. Ephesinum* (1, 2, 3, 4 and 4d), Oxenbronn ueber Guenzburg a. D. (publ. by himself) 1930/5; cf. Sch 1935, 548/60. M. Jugie, EO 1935, 5/25 (Ecclesiology); Theol. dogm. Christianorum orient. 5, 1935. Opitz, Unters. 1935, 210/2 (Symbol?). Arnou, Gr 1936, 116/31 (neo-Platon. infl.). Lohn, CT 1933, 1/37 *(Doctrina Nestorii).* R. V. Sellers, *Two Ancient Christologies,* 1940. Chabot, CRI 1947, 152/5 *(à propos du Nestorianisme).* Amann, RevSR 1949, 5/37, 207/44; 1950, 28/52, 235/65 (Nest. as judged from Rome); cf. Ciccone, DTP 1951, 33/50. Laignol-Lavestine, *Actes du VIe Congr. Internat. des Sciences,* A 1950, 334/43 *(L'hérésie de N. dans les relations médicales entre l'Or. et l'Occid.).* Camelot in Grillmeier-Bacht 1, 213/42 (Christol. of N. and Eutyches). Chadwick, JTS 1951, 145/64 (Eucharist and Christol. in Nest. controversy). C. Baur, Tr 9, 1953, 101/26 (3 ined. ps.-Chrys. Sermons with Nestor. tendency; n. 2 perh. by Nest.). Galtier, Gr 1953, 427/33 *(N. mal compris et mal traduit)*. L. J. Scipioni, *Ricerche sulla Cristologia del "Libro di Eraclide" di N.*, Fri 1956. Further lit. supra § 50, 17 and § 56.

2. Eutherius, archbishop of Tyana, a zealous supporter of Nestorius, was excommunicated at Ephesus in 431 and exiled in 434. Five letters of his are extant as well as a treatise *Confutationes quarumdam propositionum* which was preserved under the names of St. Athanasius and of Theodoret of Cyrus and which clearly shows the rationalizing tendency of Nestorianism.

MG 28, 1337/94; SACO 1, 4, 109/12, 144/8, 213/31 (letters), 5, 179/81 (Conf.). — Mgg.: G. Ficker 1908. Opitz, Unters. 210/2 (Creed?). Severus Antioch II 17, CSCO 94, 207 (new fragm.).

3. Proclus of Constantinople (d. 446). He was consecrated Bishop of Cyzicus in 426, but not recognized by his city; in 434 he became Patriarch of Constantinople, the second successor of Nestorius, whose heresy he was one of the first to refute in his famous sermon on the Blessed Virgin (429) (EP 2141a).

He worked successfully for the firm establishment of the union concluded in 433, for the reconciliation of the Johannites (supra § 69) and for the settlement of the quarrel about the recently deceased Theodore of Mopsuestia (d. 428) which was then troubling the Armenian Church. He introduced the great *Trisagion* into the Liturgy. It is true that Proclus differed from Theodoret in that he did not publicly denounce the Theopaschite heresy; it is, however, hardly correct that he coined its formula, "One of the Trinity was crucified" which aroused violent controversy in the sixth century. As a preacher he was among the best successors of Chrysostom.

Twenty-seven sermons are extant under his name, some of which are spurious; further there are seven letters, among them the important *Tomus ad Armenios* on the two natures in Christ. Recently B. Marx has assigned to him more than eighty other sermons, two of them *inedita*, from the great number of the *spuria* of Chrysostom, on the grounds of internal evidence which, however, is often hardly convincing. The fragment *De traditione divinae missae* published under his name is spurious.

MG 65, 679/888. SACO I 1, 1, 103/7 (sermons BMV); IV 2, 65/8, 187/205 (tom. Armen.). — Mgg.: F. X. Bauer, Mn 1919. Fritz, DTC 13, 662/70. E. Schwartz, *Konzilsstudien,* 1914, 18/53. Devreesse, RevSR 1931, 543/65 (tom. Armen.). Ehrhard, TU 50, 132, 133 and freq. (Hom. MSS). Lebon, Mu 1933, 170ff. Proclus also has a part in the Marian sermon printed in MG 65, 716/21 = MG 59, 707/10 which belongs to Atticus of Constant. The Syr. trans. of this serm. ed. by Lebon 1933 was also ed. by M. Brière, ROC 29, 1933/34, 160/87. Martin, RHE 1937, 255/76 (the Easter homily in MG 65, 796/800 depends on Hippolytus); Mu 1941, 20/30, 40/8 (Gr. text of sermons hitherto known only in Syr.). B. Marx, *Procliana. Untersuchungen ueber d. homilet. Nachlass des Patriarchen P. v. K.,* 1940. Richard, RHE 1942, 303/31 *(P. et le théopaschisme);* Mémorial L. Petit 1947, 393/412 (P. and Greater Armenia). R. Devreesse, *Essai sur Théod. de Mops.,* 1948, 125/52 (Tomus). Amand, RBn 1948, 223/63 (Proc. perh. author of a Ps. Basil. Christmas hom. ed. here). Against Richard, RHE 1942, 303/31 cf. E. Stein, *Hist. du Bas Empire,* 2, 1949, 229 A. 1. Elert, TLZ 1950, 195/206 (on hist. of Theopaschite formula). On question of genuineness of sermons cf. Laurentin 1953, 161, 163, 164f.

§ 73. THEODORET OF CYRUS (d. *c.* 466)

THEODORET was born at Antioch *c.* 393 and received his education in the monastic schools of that city. It is unlikely that Theodore of Mopsuestia was his teacher and Nestorius and John of Antioch his fellow pupils. As early as 423 he was—against his will—consecrated Bishop of the small town of Cyrus, east of Antioch. He worked with the greatest zeal for the spiritual and material wellbeing of his flock.

In 431 he intervened in the Christological controversy on the side of Nestorius with a treatise *(Refutation of the twelve anathemata of Cyril of Alexandria)* which is now lost. This was followed in the same year by a second treatise in five books directed against Cyril and the Council of Ephesus. He joined the union concluded in 433, the formula of which he had probably composed himself, only in 434, without, however, by this act abandoning Nestorius. Naturally he was a determined opponent of the heresy of Eutyches, which was contrary to that of Nestorius. Hence he was deposed at the "Robber Synod of Ephesus" (499). Thereupon he appealed to Pope Leo I (ep. 113). After having agreed to a declaration against the teaching of Nestorius, he was allowed to attend the Council of Chalcedon (451) as an "orthodox teacher". Later the fifth General Council (553) condemned his writings against Cyril and the Council of Ephesus, as well as some of his letters and sermons under the *Three Chapters*. It should, however, be noted that Theodoret's writings were condemned by Pope Vigilius *secundum subiectos intelligentiae sensus* (*Constit.* 1; ML 69, 102C) and that their author had meant them in a different way from that in which they were interpreted. Since Theodoret never completely approved of the Nestorian teaching, he ought not to be accused of having sacrificed his theological conviction for opportunist reasons (cf. RSPT 1936, 459/81). He is one of the most fertile authors of the Greek Church.

1. Dogmatic-polemical writings. a. Apart from the two works against Cyril extant only in fragments, he wrote, still before 431, a treatise Περὶ θεολογίας καὶ τῆς θείας ἐνανθρωπήσεως which is preserved under the name of Cyril of Alexandria; it is extant as a work in two parts with independent titles (MG 75, 1147/90, 1419/78).

b. *Eranistes seu polymorphus* ("The Beggar or the Multiform One"), a dialogue between a beggar and an orthodox person (*c.* 447). The beggar is supposed to represent Monophysitism (or Eutyches), which had as it were collected its views from previous heresies (EP 2150f.). This work is particularly valuable because it contains 239 testimonies of the Fathers taken from eighty-eight different works.

c. Two treatises preserved under the name of Justin: *Expositio rectae fidei* and *Quaestiones et responsiones ad orthodoxos* (ed. de Otto IV; supra § 19; Lebon, RHE 523/50; RB 1934, 9). An anonymous work in MG 83, 1433/41 should also be assigned to him. Further writings against Arians and Eunomians, Macedonians, Apollinarians, Marcionites and Origen are lost, as well as a *Liber mysticus* and *Libri de virginitate*.

2. The following belong to the apologetical writings: His twelve books *Graecorum affectionum curatio* (Cure of the Pagan Diseases), the last and perhaps the most beautiful of the Old Christian apologies directed against paganism. It opposes to each other the pagan and the Christian answers to the main questions of philosophy and theology. He cites more than a hundred pagan authors (EP 2143/8; EA 915f.). His *Orations on Providence*, in a very carefully worked-out style, were delivered before an educated audience at Antioch (between 435 and 437).

3. His numerous exegetical writings are excellent in content as well as in form. Next to Theodore of Mopsuestia, Theodoret may be considered the leading exegete of the Antiochene School and the greatest Greek interpreter of Scripture in Christian antiquity. Despite its fundamental grammatical-historical attitude his exegesis is frequently typological and allegorical.

He wrote complete commentaries on the Psalms, the Canticle, all the Prophets and the fourteen Epistles of Paul; besides treatises *(quaestiones)* on difficult passages of the historical books of the O.T. (Gen. to Par.) in the form of questions and answers.

4. Of his sermons only small remnants have survived. His large collection of letters (209 Greek, 27 Latin ones) is one of the most important sources for the history of the fifth century. On his historical writings v. supra § 49, 7.

Edd.: J. L. Schultze and J. A. Noesselt, 5 vols., 1769/74. MG 80/84. Separate edd.: *Graec. aff. cur.* ed. J. Raeder, L 1904; N. Festa, Fi 1931 (1–6 with Ital. trans.). Is. Comment. ed. A. Moehle, B 1932. J. Sakkelion, Τοῦ μακαριωτάτου Θεοδωρήτου ἐπιστολαί, At 1885 (first ed. of 48 letters). SACO I, 1, 4 (27 Lat. epp.); other vols. of SACO also contain letters, sermons etc.; cf. e. g. SACO II, 1, 3 n. 20; on this AB 1936, 146/9. Y. Azéma, trans. of *Discours sur la Providence*, P 1954 (with comm.) and *Correspondence* I, 1955, with Gr. text (SCh 40). — Trans.: *The*

Eccl. Hist., Dialogues and Letters, trans. with notes by B. Jackson, O 1892. — Mgg. and treatises: A. Seider (BKV² 51) 1926, pp. IX–IC. Opitz, PWK II, 5, 1791/1801. J. Schulte, *T. als Apologet,* 1904. E. Schwartz, *Zur Schriftstellerei T.s,* SbMn 1922, 1. P. C. da Mazzarino, *La dottrina di T. di C. sull'unione ipost...,* R 1941. Lebon, RHE 1930, 523/50 *(Restitutions à T.).* Devreesse, RB 1935, 167/70 *(Quaest. in Octat.).* M. Richard, RevSR 1934, 34/61 (MG 83, 1433/41): RB 1934, 88/96 (fragms. of the 5 books against Cyril); RSPT 1935, 83/106 (chronol. of works); ibid. 1936, 459/81 *(Évolut. doctrinale).* Juessen, TG 1935, 438/52 (Christol. of Is. comm.). D. C. Fives, *The Use of the Optative Mood in the Works of T., B. of C.,* W 1937. Cullmann, RHP 1936, 216ff. (2 Thess. 2, 6f.). P. Henry, *États du Texte de Plotin,* 1938, 141/54 (excerpts from Plotinus in *Graec. aff. cur.*). Schiwietz 3, 1938, 238/53 (Hist. relig.). Fruechtel, PW 1939, 765f. (Clem. Alex. in T.). Severus Antioch. III 18, 29 (new fragms.: *Ep. adv. Joh. ex Aegaeis Ciciliae*). Richard, MSR 1946, 147/56 (T. et les moines d'Orient); *Les Sciences Phil. et Théol.* 2, 1941/2, 415/23 (T. to Joh. ex Aegaeis). Bardy, DTC 15, 299/325. Sellers, JTS 1945, 145/60 *(Expositio rectae fidei).* J. Montalverne, *Theod.i Cyr. Doctrina antiquior de Verbo "inhumato"* (423–35), Ant, R 1948. M. Wagner, DOP 1948, 119/81 (The formal problems of the Letters). Canivet, RSR 1949, 585/93 (la date de la *Curatio*). Brok, RHE 1949, 552/6 (comm. on Pss. written betw. 441 and 449). Brinktrine, Bi 1949, 520/3 (the divine name Aia). Brok, RHE 1950, 487/507 (spurious fragm. of a supposed work against the Jews); JTS 1951, 178/83 (*Expos. rect. fid.* written before 431). F. Rossiter, *Messianic Prophecy acc. to T. of C.,* thesis Greg. R 1950f. Riedmatten in: Grillmeier-Bacht 1, 203/12 (fragms. of Apollinaris in *Eranistes*). On the testimonies of *Eranistes* cf. Richard in: Grillmeier-Bacht 1, 723/5; also Nautin, RHE 1951, 681/3. Brok, StC 1952, 201/12 (value of *Curatio* as an apologetic work). Grillmeier in: Grillmeier-Bacht 1, 183/91 (Christology). Honigmann 1953, 174/80 (d. c. 466). Brok, MSR 1953, 181/94 (fragm. against Manicheans not certainly genuine). Y. Azéma, *T. de C. d'après sa correspondance,* thesis typed P 1952; REG 1954, 82/94 (chronology of 3 letters). McNamara, ITQ 1955, 313/28 (The Unity of Person in Christ). Des Places, REG 1955, 171/84 (citations from Plato). P. Canivet, SCh 57,1958 (Gr. affect. cur.); *Histoire d'une entreprise apol. au Ve s.,* P 1957.

D. The Syriac and Armenian literature

Various other national Christian literatures closely connected with the particularly rich Greek literature gradually developed first on the territory of the Roman Empire and soon also outside it. Nevertheless, a large number of theologically and literarily independent achievements are to be found only among Syrians and Armenians. The literature of other peoples who had been converted to Christianity, namely that of the Copts, Ethiopians, Georgians and Arabs, was in the earliest period mainly confined to translations of Greek works to satisfy the most urgent practical needs. First of all, the books of Holy Scripture were translated into the various national languages, then also liturgical, canonical and exegetical-homiletic writings (cf. the literature given above, § 3).

§ 74. APHRAATES

THE oldest Syrian Church Father Aphraates (or Afrahat), called the Persian sage, was an ascetic and probably also a bishop (in the monastery of St. Matthew near Mossul?). Twenty-three treatises, wrongly called homilies, are extant, which were written in the years 337 (1–10), 344 (11–22) and 345 (23); they give a kind of survey of the whole body of Christian doctrine.

The author writes inter alia on faith (1), charity (2), fasting (3), prayer (4), exhortation to ascetics (6), penance (7), the resurrection of the dead (8), on "Christ, that he is the Son of God" (17). He frequently attacks the Jews and attaches great importance to asceticism. He is as yet hardly influenced by Greek philosophy and Nicene theology. The Gospels are cited according to Tatian's *Diatessaron*. On older Syriac writings v. supra § 10, 6 7; 22, 6; 24, 5.

Edd.: J. Parisot (Patrolog. Syr. 1, 1–2) 1894/1907. Engl. by F. H. Hallock, JSOR 1930, 18/31 (charity), 1932, 43/56 (penitents). Germ. by G. Bert (TU 3, 3–4) 1888. Ital. by G. Ricciotti, Mi 1926. — Treatises: Parisot, DTC 1, 1457/63. —Mgg.: by P. Schwen 1907. I. Ortiz de Urbina, *Die Gottheit Christi bei A.*, R 1933; OCP 1, 1935, 102f. (Mariology). L. Haefeli, *Stilmittel bei A.*, 1932. G. Richter, ZNTW 1936, 101/14 (anti-Jewish polemics). Hausherr, DS 1, 746/52. Maude, ATR 17, 225/33 (Rhythmic Patterns); JTS 1935, 13/21 (*Sons of the Covenant* in Ephraem). N. J. Hommes, *Het Testimoniaboek* 1935, 256/72. E. J. Duncan, *Baptism in the Demonstr. of A.*, W 1945. O. de Urbina, *Stud. Mission.* 1947, 87/105 (Jews). Elderenbosch, NTT 1949, 161/7 (Sacramental teaching). Williams, JTS 1949, 71f. (on Peter). Jargy, OCP 1951, 304/20 (sons and daughters of the covenant); POC 1954, 106/17 (Syr. monastic life in 4th cent.). A. Vööbus, *Celibacy as Requirement for Admission to Baptism in the Early Syr. Church*, Stockh. 1951. Higgins, BZ 1951, 765/71 (dates of Persian persecution).

§ 75. EPHRAEM THE SYRIAN (b. *c.* 306, d. 373)

Ephraem is the great classic writer of the Syrian Church, the "lyre of the Holy Spirit". He was born at Nisibis *c.* 306, very probably of Christian parents, and educated by James, the bishop of his native city.

The story that he accompanied his bishop to the Council of Nicaea and met Basil the Great at Caesarea and the report that he visited the Egyptian monks are probably later legends. Before 338 he became a deacon and remained one throughout his life. After Nisibis had been occupied by the Persians in 363 he left the city, together with many other Christians, and finally settled at Edessa, on Roman territory. The so-called "Persian School" at Edessa is probably connected with his teaching activities there (d. 373). Feast Day: June 18th. Doctor of the Church since 1920.

Ephraem is a brilliant exegete, controversialist, preacher and poet. It is almost impossible to survey the mass of writings he has left, for they have so far been neither critically edited nor have their contents been sufficiently examined and evaluated. The moral and devotional element predominates in them. Very early, many of his writings, which are for the greater part in metrical form were translated into other languages, especially into Armenian and Greek. From these translations other versions were made in Latin and the various oriental languages. Much material bearing his name is spurious, dubious or has been altered.

Edd.: J. S. and S. E. Assemani, 6 vols., R 1732/46 (3 vols. Syr.-Lat., 3 vols. Gr.-Lat.). J. J. Overbeck, O 1865 (new writings, only Syr.). G. Bickel, *Carmina Nisibena,* L 1866. T. J. Lamy, 4 vols. *(Hymni et Sermones),* 1882/1902. C. W. Mitchell, *S. E. Prose Refutations of Mani, Marcion and Bardaisan,* 2 vols., Lo 1912/21. L. Leloir, CSCO 137 and 145, *Comm. de l'évangile concordant (Diatessaron),* 1953 f. R. M. Tonneau, CSCO 152 153, 1955 *(Comm. in Gen. et Ex.).* E. Beck, CSCO 154 155 *(Hymni de fide),* 1955. — Transs.: Armen., 4 vols., Venice 1836. *Comm. on Acts,* ed. N. Akinian, W 1921. F. Murad, ed. 16 hymns on the town of Nicomedia (Armen.); cf. Essabalian, HA 1933, 216/80. Gr.: S. 7. Mercati, I 1, R 1915. Germ.: P. Zingerle, 6 vols., 1830/8 and 3 vols. in BKV 1870/6; S. Euringer and A. Ruecker (BKV[2] 37 and 61), 1919/28. S. Ruiz, *S. Efrém-Endechas* (trans.). Ma 1943. G. Ricciotti, *S. Efr. Inni alla Vergine,* Tu 1940. — Schiwietz 3, 1938, 93/165 (biography and sources); 166/79 (on Abraham of Kidun). Wilmart, RBn 1938, 222/45 (Old Lat. trans. of *Vita Abrahae*). Bardy, RML 1946, 297/300 (E. in Lat. MA). Graf I, 421/33. LTK 3, 715/8. E. Beck, CSCO 186/87, 1959.

1. Only few of his very numerous Scriptural Commentaries have been preserved in full; but many fragments have survived in *catenae*. Commentaries on Genesis and Exodus to 32, 26 are extant in Syriac, those on Tatian's *Diatessaron,* Acts and the Pauline Epistles (here also the so-called *Third Epistle to the Corinthians;* supra § 11, 1) in Armenian. The O.T. commentaries are rather sober and scholarly, the N.T. expositions are partly cast in the form of homilies. Ephraem is principally concerned to emphasize the historical-grammatical sense of the text.

2. Numerous Treatises, Orations and Hymns, frequently in metrical form. The poetic works of Ephraem, who ranks as the greatest Syrian poet, are in the two forms of *memre* and *madrash,* i.e. there is a distinction between metrical speeches and hymns that can be sung. The *memre* are series (of any length) of lines with the same number of syllables, normally seven; the *madrash* consist of lines made into strophes of varying length which alternate with a refrain (EP 703/38).

a. Fifty-six *madrashes* are directed against the heresies of Bardesanes, Marcion and Mani (BKV[2] 61); Ephraem attacks the same opponents also in three prose writings. Other hymns are directed against Gnostics, Arians and Julian Apostata. There are also many homilies in metrical form on verses and passages from the Bible, e.g. fifteen hymns on Gen. 2, 8ff. *(De paradiso),* further many hortatory and penitential sermons and panegyrics on martyrs and feast days, e. g. the hymns on the Nativity and the Epiphany, which are also hymns in praise of the Virgin Mother of the Lord. Fifty-two hymns are collected under the title *De virginitate;* besides we have hymns for public rogation processions as well as for funerals and mourning. The number of liturgical hymns destined to be sung in church is considerable.

b. The seventy-seven *Carmina Nisibena* (8, 22–24 are missing) are important for the history of the times. The collection was probably made by Ephraem himself; the songs are concerned, inter alia, with the distress caused to his native city by the war (338–63) and the fine conduct of the bishops during the repeated sieges to which the city was subjected by the Persians (BKV² 37). Two groups of hymns (15 and 24) are in praise of two hermits personally known to him, Abraham of Kidun and Julian Saba. A *Testament of Ephraem* the nucleus of which is authentic, contains the master's last greetings and wishes for his disciples.

Mgg.: G. Ricciotti, Tu 1925. J. Schaefers, *Ev.-Zitate in E.s Kommentar zu den Paulin. Briefen,* 1917. C. Emereau, *S. E. le Syrien, son œuvre litt. grecque,* 1919; EO 1921, 29/45. J. Molitor, *Der Paulustext des hl. E. aus seinem armen. erhalt. Paulinenkomm.,* 1938. — Treatises: Peradze, OC 1930, 80/5 (Georg.). Polotsky, Or 1933, 269/74 (journey to Egypt). Baumstark, OC 1933, 4/12 (text of Tatian). P. Krueger, OC 1933, 13/62, 144/51 (petitions for rain). Heffenning, OC 1936, 54/79 (against laughter). Doelger, AC 5, 275/81 (against heret. 45, 1). Maude, JTS 1935, 13/21 (Sons of the covenant). Devreesse, RB 1936, 211/3 (fragms. in Gen. and Num.). A. Vööbus, *A Letter of E. to the Mountaineers,* Pi 1947; *Unters. ueb. d. Authentizitaet einiger asket. Traktate,* Pi 1947; OC 39, 1955, 48/55 (on the ascet. writings). C. Bravo, *S. Efrem Siro exegeta dell' AT,* thesis Greg. R 1951; Bi 1950, 390/401 (Comm. al Gen. 1–7). A. Levene, *The Early Syrian Fathers on Gen.* From a Syr. MS on the Pentateuch in the Mingana Coll., Lo 1951. S. G. Mercati, EEBS 1953, 41/4 (the alphabets in the "Greek" Ephr. prob. spurious). Klijn, JTS 1954, 76/8 (on Pauline comm.).

Points of Doctrine

1. On the doctrine of the Trinity and Christology. His eighty hymns on the faith devoted to the struggle against Arianism show how little Ephraem is influenced by the Greek Fathers and their ideas derived from philosophy. Hence no really clear presentation of the philosophical and theological problems of Trinitarian and Christological doctrines is to be expected. Even in theology the Syrian remains a poet using a language rich in images. Ephraem's notions are still vague and his terminology is imperfect. *Physis (Kyânâ),* e.g., may mean individual, but also

approaches the meaning of essence. Naturally the distinction between *hypostasis* and *physis* finally established only by the Cappadocians is as yet non-existent in his theology. There is at the most a beginning to equate the term *quomâ* with *hypostasis* = *persona*. The Holy Spirit is never actually called God, though the baptismal formula and the liturgical doxologies could leave no doubt on his homoousian nature. Ephraem uses the strange expression *ignis et spiritus* for the Holy Spirit, a phrase also applied to the angels; it is also employed in his Christological statements and his teaching on the Eucharist (Beck 1949, 35 ff., 49 ff., 81 ff.).

2. He says about Mary: "You alone (Jesus) and your Mother are more beautiful than all, no stain is in you, Lord, and no blemish in your Mother" (*Carm. Nisib.* 27 f., 44 f.; EP 719). This statement, however, cannot yet be understood in the sense of the immaculate conception; this is ruled out by Ephraem's view of *iustitia originalis* and original sin. Cf., however, Ortiz de Urbina (v. infra).

3. In the eucharist "the living and life-giving Body is consumed" (ibid. 3, 77). In another passage Ephraem puts these words into the mouth of the city of Nisibis: "Be reconciled (O God) by the sacrifice on my altar" (1, 24). In his will he makes the following request: "When thirty days have passed after my death, offer the holy sacrifice for me; for the dead profit by the sacrifices offered by the living" (EP 741).

Mariology: Ginetti, SC 1931, 28/44, 81/90, 177/89. F. S. Mueller, Sch 1934, 165/73. Ortiz de Urbina, OCP 1935, 103/10. De Ceuster, AlgEuchTijd 3, 1931, 160/9 (eucharist). Hausherr, OCR 1933 (30, 3, n. 1; Mary and Martha). I. Armala, *Der roem. Primat i. d. syr. Kirche,* Beyrouth 1933 (Arab.); cf. OC 1934, 143. S. Euringer, Festg. f. A. Ehrhard 1922, 141/99 (Mt. 16, 18 in E.). Michl, TQ 1937, 474/91 (9 choirs of angels). L. Hammersberger, *Die Mariol. der ephrem. Schriften,* 1938. Edsman 1940, 93/133. P. Krueger, ZMissWiss. u. RelWiss 1941, 8/15 (missionary ideas); PJB 1942, 45/57 (bapt. in Syr. lit.). De Urbina, OCP 1940, 60 f. (immaculate conception). Ducros, *Mél. Cavallera* 1948, 163/77 (inspiration). C. Schedl, *Der Herr der Mysterien. Unters. z. Christusbild E.s auf Grund der Epiphanie-Hymnen,* thesis T 1947. E. Beck, OCP 1948, 398/405 (on paradise-virgins); *Die Theol. des hl. E. i. seinen Hymnen ueb. d. Glauben,* R 1949; *Ephr.s Hymnen ueb. d. Paradies* (trans. and comm.), R 1951; *E.s Reden ueb. d. Glauben u. d. geschichtl.*

Rahmen, R 1953; OCP 1953, 5/24 (image of mirror: 1 Cor. 13, 12); OC 38, 1954, 41/67 (doctr. of eucharist). Mariès, RSR 1954, 394/403 (antiphone on Euchar.). De Urbina, EE 1954, 417/22 (Immaculata attested in E.); id., OCP 1955, 457/72 (Le Paradis eschatologique). E. Beck, OrSyr 1, 1956, 111/36 (bapt. in E.); id., OC 40, 1956, 22/39 (Mariology in genuine writings). Mariès-Fromann-Graffin, OrSyr 1959, 73/109 163/92 (Grace). Beck, OrSyr 1958, 273/98 (Ascetics).

§ 76. OTHER SYRIAN POETS AND AUTHORS

1. Cyrillonas, a true poet, left six hymns, among them two on the Last Supper of Christ and a hymn of petition on the occasion of a plague of locusts and a threatening invasion of the Huns (396). Here the sacrificial character of the eucharist and the veneration of saints are also attested.

Syr. text: E. Bickell, ZDtschMorgenlGes 1873, 566/98. Germ. by S. Landersdorfer (BKV² 6) 1913. O. de Urbina, OCP 1935, 110/3 (Mariol.).

2. Balaeus (Syr. Balai), d. *c.* 460, probably as chorepiscopus of Beroea (Aleppo). He was a prolific poet, most of his poems, generally short, are lost. Several hymns were incorporated in the Divine Office. Cf. supra § 70, 2: five panegyrics on Bishop Acacius.

Syr. text in J. J. Overbeck, S. *Ephraemi . . ., Balaei aliorumque op. se .*, O 1865, 251/336. Germ. by S. Landersdorfer (BKV² 6) 1913.

3. Rabbula (d. 436; acc. to Peeters), Bishop of Edessa, became a Christian *c.* 400 and a bishop *c.* 412. Shortly after the Council of Ephesus (431) he went over to Cyril of Alexandria and strongly opposed the followers of Nestorius who where numerous at the school of Edessa. Rabbula has recently been denied to be the author of the Syriac translation of the N.T. (Vööbus). In three short treatises he gives rules of life for priests and monks. Only fragments survive of his forty-six Letters written in Greek; there are also hymns of doubtful authenticity and a sermon against Nestorius. He translated Cyril's treatise *De recta fide* at the author's request. Germ. by G. Bickel (BKV) 1874. On the *Vita R.* v. supra § 46, 13 b.

Syr. texts in J. J. Overbeck, *S. Ephraemi Syri, Rabbulae . . . opera sel.,* O 1865, 159/238. Ziadé, DTC 13, 1620/6. F. C. Burkitt, *The Early Syr. Lectionary System,* 1923. Nau, RHR 103, 1931, 97/135. Van Seelms, *Hervormde Theol. Studies* 4, 1947, 95/117 (Pretoria) (parallel between R. and Augustine). A. Vööbus, *Investigations into the Text of NT used by R. of Ed.,* Pi 1947; *Researches on the Circulation of the Peshitta in the Middle 5th Cent.,* Pi 1948; *La Vie d'Alexandre en grec, un témoin d'une biographie méconnue de R. écrite en syriaque,* Pi 1948; *The Old Syr. Version in a New Light,* and *Urgent Tasks in Text. Criticism of the N.T.,* Stockh. 1949; Mu 1950, 191/204 (oldest traces of the *Pesh.* before 411); CSCO 128, 1951: *Stud. in the Hist. of the Gospel-Text in Syr.;* OC 38, 1954, 1/10 (age of *Pesh.*). Black, BJR 33, 1951, 203/10 (R. and the *Peshitta*); Stud. paul. J. de Zwaan, Haarlem 1953, 20/8 (*Pesh.* and Diatess.). Pericoli-Ridolfini, RivStudOrient 1953, 153/69 (Letter of Andrew of Samosata to R.). Mounayer, OCP 1954, 406/15) (ed. of Syr. text of thirty-four rules for monks).

4. Ibas (d. 457), Bishop of Edessa and successor of Rabbula. He wrote (433/6) a *Christological Letter* to the Persian Bishop Maris, on the strength of which he was deposed at Ephesus in 449. A great part of it is extant in a Greek translation. He was reinstituted at Chalcedon in 451, but his treatise was condemned in 553 as one of the *Three Chapters.* His translations of works of Theodore of Mopsuestia and Aristotle as well as his hymns have perished.

SACO II 1, 3, 32/4 (Christol. letter). Devreesse, RevSR 1931, 543/65. D'Alès, RSR 1932, 5/25.

5. Isaac of Antioch wrote several treatises against the Nestorians and Monophysites and a lament on the destruction of Antioch by an earthquake (459), as is attested by Gennadius (*Vir. ill.* 66). Nothing of these writings has survived. But P. Bedjan was able to edit sixty-seven metrical homilies which had been preserved under this name and which treat dogmatic and ascetical subjects. Only few of these pieces could so far be assigned to Isaac of Antioch or another Isaac. For Bishop Jacob of Edessa (d. 708) mentions three different teachers of the name of Isaac, but no Isaac of Antioch: these are one supposedly Monophysite presbyter Isaac of Amida, who is thought to have visited Rome *c.* 404, an Isaac of Edessa, also a Monophysite, who at the time of Peter Fullo (468–88) wrote at Antioch the still extant poem (2137 lines)

on the parrot who could say the Trisagion with the addition "who was crucified for us", and an orthodox Isaac of Edessa (*c.* 522).

Edd.: G. Bickell, 2 vols., Gie 1873/7. P. Bedjan, P 1903. Germ. by S. Landersdorfer (BKV[2] 6) 1913. C. Moss, ZS 1929, 295/306; 1930, 61/72 (ed. 1 hom.). Furlani, RTr 1923, 257/87 (3 discorsi metrici sulla fede); GiornCritFilosIt 7, no. 4 (psychology). Krueger, OstkStud 1952, 46/54 (trans. of *Sermo de fide*); ibid. 1953, 270/9 (gehenna and Sheol); ibid. 1952, 123/31 (Mariology).

6. Narses, one of the most important representatives of Nestorianism. He became head of the School of Edessa in 437; after his expulsion (457) he founded the School of Nisibis (v. supra § 51) at the invitation of Bishop Bar Sauma. He died shortly after 503, aged 103; he is important as a poet. Metrical homilies and dialogue songs as well as liturgical hymns are among the works that have been preserved. His O.T. Scripture commentaries are lost.

Edd.: A. Mingana, 2 vols., Mossul 1905 (47 homs. and 10 dialogue songs). Tisserant, DTC 11, 26/30. Leclercq, DAL 12, 884/8. R. H. Connolly, *The Liturg. Homilies of N.,* 1909. Krueger, OstkStud 1952, 283/96 (angelology); ibid. 1953, 110/20 (Mariology). Abramowski, ZKG 66, 1954/5, 140/3 (Council of Chalcedon). Guillaumond, OrSyr 1, 1956, 189/207 (poem on baptism). Krueger, OrSyr 1958, 299/316 (Hom. on Martyrs); 1959, 193/210 Steep of dead souls). ZMR 1958, 271/91 (Mission).

7. Jacob of Sarug, Bishop of Batnae near Edessa (d. 521). We are informed about his life and work by no less than three different bio-bibliographical accounts. According to the studies of P. Peeters, P. Krueger and C. Vona the letters betraying his Monophysite outlook have wrongly been foisted upon him; but this does not yet seem to have been conclusively proved. Cf. Leon in Grillmeier-Bacht I, 427 A. 6 and C. Moeller, RHE 1953, 270. He wrote many prose letters and sermons, also funeral orations and edifying biographies; he translated the six *Centuria* of Evagrius Ponticus. There are further long metrical *Homilies* (e.g. 3300 lines on the Passion of our Lord), partly of a high poetical standard, and religious hymns, some of which have been incorporated in the liturgy. Several *Liturgies* or *Anaphora* as

well as an *Order of Baptism and Confirmation* are also attributed to him.

P. Bedjan, *J. S. homiliae selectae,* 5 vols., 1905/10. Germ. by S. Landersdorfer (BKV² 6) 1913. Moss, Mu 1935, 87/112 (ed. hom. on spectacles). F. S. Mueller, Sch 1934, 173/83 (Mariol.). P. Sbath, Cairo 1934; cf. TR 1935, 504f. and OC 1933, 135 (H. Kerio). G. Olinder, *J. S. Epistolae* (CSCO 110, 1952); *The Letters of J. of S. Comments on an Edition,* Lund 1939. Graf I, 444/52. Mouterde, *Mél. de l'Univ.* (Beyrouth) 26, 1944/6, 1/36 (2 ined. homs.). Rinaldi, Aev 22, 1948, 85/93 (Saggi poetici dal siriaco). I. Armala, *J. of S.*, Djounié 1946 (Arabic). Peeters, AB 1948, 134/98 (J. not a Monophysite). H. W. Codrington, *Anaphorae Syriacae,* vol. 2, F. 1, R 1951 (3 *anaphorae* named after J. of S.). Black, JTS 1951, 57/63 (gospel text). Krueger, OstkStud 1953, 199/208 (Jac. a Catholic); ibid. 1952, 187/207 (Immac. Conc. in J. ?). C. Vona, *Omelie Mariologiche di G. di S.,* R 1953. Van Roey, ETL 1955, 46/62 (on Mariology). Krueger, OstkStud 1956, 158/76, 225/42 (Jacob was Catholic).

8. Philoxenus of Mabbug (Hierapolis), since 485 Metropolitan of M., Monophysite; exiled to Thracia in 518/9, d. in exile at Gangra *c.* 523, belongs to the classical Syrian theologians. Of his many writings (*c.* 80) the following have among others so far been printed: thirteen orations on the Christian life, five treatises on the Trinity and Incarnation and several letters. A translation of the Bible into Syriac has been named after him *(Philoxeniana).*

Edd.: E. A. Wallis Budge, *The Discourses of P.,* 2 vols., 1894. A. Vaschalde (CSCO 9/10, 1907. M. Brière (PO 15, 4) 1927. J. Lebon, Mu 1930, 17/84, 149/220 (3 letters). Tisserant, DTC 12, 1509/32. Lebon, RHE 1911, 413/36 *(Version de la Bible).* R. Draguet, *Julien d'Halicarnasse,* 1924, 232/50. Hausherr, RAM 1933, 171/95 (contemplation). Jugie, EO 1934, 185/7 (Papal primacy). G. Olinder, *A Letter of P. of M. sent to a Novice* (ed.), Goeteborg 1941. Graf I, 452f. Lebon in Grillmeier-Bacht I, 425/580 (Christol. of P., Severus Ant. and Timothy Aelurus). De Vries, OCP 1952, 52/88 (Primacy, communion and Church in the early Syr. Monophysites). Vööbus, Misc. K. Kundzins, Eutin 1953, 169/83 (date of *Philoxeniana*). E. Bergstraesser, *Monophysitismus u. Paulus-Tradition b. P. v. M.,* thesis Erlangen 1953. Krueger, OCP 1954, 155/65 (*Sermo de Annunt.* ed. for first time). Bergstraesser, Gedenkschr. W. Elert, 1955. E. Lemoine, SCh 44, 1956 (Homilies).

9. Isaac of Niniveh, d. end of seventh century, an important Nestorian ascetic and mystic. He resigned his episcopal see of Niniveh after five months (661), became a hermit and eventually a monk in a monastery in the mountains of the Persian Susiana.

It is very difficult to sort out his voluminous literary remains on account of his being confused with other authors of the same name (v. supra n. 5). His writings were also widely read by Jacobites and Catholics.

Eighty-two treatises ed. P. Bedjan, I : *De perfectione religiosa,* P 1909, Engl. by A. J. Wensinck, A 1923. Germ. by G. Bickell (BKV) 1874 (6 treatises). Lat. trans. in MG 86, 811/86 (here assigned to I. of Antioch). Arab. texts in P. Sbath, Cairo 1934; cf. OC 1935, 272f.; OCP 1936, 511/3.— Mgg.: J. B. Chabot, Lou 1892. L. Petit, DTC 8, 10/2. H. Laman Trip. de Beaufort, *Uit de geschriften van I. van N.,* Bussum 1931. Hausherr, OCP 1940, 221 (on Gr. text). Van der Ploeg, Mu 1943, 115/27 (*De perfectione relig.;* Lat. trans.).

§ 77. ARMENIAN AUTHORS

IN Armenia, which was already Christianized towards the end of the third century, the creation of an Armenian alphabet by Mesrob (d. 440), a former royal secretary, later a monk and missionary, made it possible for an original Armenian literature to appear. Under the direction of the Patriarch Sahak the Great (390–439) and Mesrob a group of young clerics who had been trained chiefly at Constantinople and Edessa—they were later called the "holy translators"—translated the writings of eminent Greek and Syriac authors. Apart from an Armenian Liturgy, the Bible was the first work to be translated into the vernacular. Though we have no texts of a translation of the Bible made from the Syriac, important reasons favour the view that the Gospels were first read in a translation dependent on a Syriac text of Tatian's *Diatessaron.* In the course of the fifth century the whole Bible was gradually translated from the Greek. A native literature came into being at the same time.

S. Weber, *Die kath. Kirche i. Armenien,* 1903. F. Tournebize, *Hist. politique et relig. de l'Arménie,* 1910. Further lit. v. supra § 3. S. Lyonnet, *Le Parfait en arménien classique* (Évangiles et Eznik), 1933; RSR 1935, 170/87 (Script. trans.), Muyldermans, Mu 1934, 265/92 (Armen. patrist. MSS in Venice). P. Essabalian. *Le Diatessaron de Tatien et la première trad. des Évang. armén.,* W 1937. Akinian,

HA 1935, 550/63 (Script. trans.). Lyonnet, RB 1938, 355/82 *(1e version des Évv.)*; Bi 1938, 121/50 *(Vestiges d'un Diatess. armén.)*. N. Akinian, *Unters. z. Gesch. der armen. Lit.*, 4 vols., W 1932/8 (Armen. with German summary). L. Petit, DTC 1, 1888/1968 *(Arménie)*. Akinian, AP 1949, 74/86 (Armen. bishops in 3th/4th cents.). Hausherr, DS 1, 863/94. Klinge, RACh 1, 678/89. S. Lyonnet, *Les origines de la version armén. de la Bible et le Diatess.*, R 1950. Vööbus, RSR 1950, 581/6 *(première traduction armén. de la Bible)*. H. Thoronian, *Hist. de la littérature armén. des origines jusqu'à nos jours*, P 1951. Inglisian in Grillmeier-Bacht II, 361/417 (Chalcedon and the Armen. Church). Toumanoff, Tr 10, 1954, 109/89 (Church hist. of Armenia and Georgia).

1. Of Mesrob's own writings apparently only the twenty-three orations and circular letters extant under the name of Gregory the Illuminator have been preserved. His life was written by his disciple Koriun.

S. Weber (BKV² 57) 1927. Karst, DTC 10, 789/92. Thorossian, Baz 1931, 446/73; 1932, 5/12, 148/56, 255/63; 1936, 100/8; 1939, 145/52 (Koriun). Akinian, HA 1935, 505/50 (Life of Mesrob). Cowakan, Sion 9, 1935, 181/7 (Koriun and the trans. of the Books of the Macc.). Richard, Mémorial L. Petit 1948, 396/8 (Letter of Sahak).

2. The historical expositions of Faustus of Byzantium are fundamental for our knowledge of the most ancient history of Christian Armenia. His work, written in Greek *c.* 400, treats of the time from 344 to 387 and is extant in an Armenian translation which probably belongs to the fifth century. This work was continued by Lazarus of Pharpi (d. after 491) who gives an account of the years 388 to 458.

Leclercq, DAL 9, 1588/90 (Faustus). Peeters, AB 1921, 65/88. Faustus Germ. by M. Lauer, Cologne 1879. *L. of P.* French by S. Ghesarian in Langlois, *Coll. des hist. anc. et mod. de l'Arménie* 2, 1869, 253/368. Nahabedian, Baz 1930, 367/9, 406/8 (Laz.). Essabalian, HA 1935, 571/90; 1936, 22/39, 185/95, 338/49 (Laz.). Akinian, HA 1938, 9/56 (Faustus).

The history of Gregory the Illuminator and the conversion of Armenia was written under the probably fictitious name Agathangelus, perhaps towards the end of the fifth century. It contains many legendary additions besides historically valuable information.

Armen. Text: Tiflis 1914 and Venice 1930. Gr. trans.: P. de Lagarde, GAG 35, 1888, 3/164. A new unknown Gr. recension ed. G. Garitte, *Documents p. l'étude du livre d'A.* (ST 127) 1946; cf. Garitte, RHE 1941, 190/209; Mu 1943, 35/53; 1946, 413/20; 1948, 89/102. Peeters, AB 1942, 91/130 (Gregory Ill.). Mioni, Baz 1948 *(Inni biz. inediti in on. di S. Gregorio d' Armen.)*. P. Peeters, *Le tréfonds orient. de l'hagiographie byz.*, 1950, 78/82 (on Agathangelus). Garitte, Mu 1950, 231/47 (Arab. trans. of Agathang.). Mu 1952, 51/71 (Arab. *Vita* of Gr. Ill.); *Narratio de rebus Armeniae* (CSCO 132); cf. Honigmann, RHE 1953, 150/68.

The historical work and the other writings of Bishop Moses of Chorene (Chorenaçi; alleged to be fifth century) need not be mentioned here in detail, since they must be dated much later (*c.* 820).

N. Akinian, *Leontius the Priest and M. Khorenatzi,* W 1930 (Armenian); PWK Suppl. 6, 534/41. Hatsumi, Baz 1935, 55/66, 119/30 (for 5th cent.). H. Lewy, Byz 11, 1936, 81/96, 593/6. Adontz, ibid. 97/100. Mlaker, *Wien. Z. f. Kunde d. Morgenl.* 42, 259/94 (2nd half of 9th cent.). Manandjan, VizVrem 1, 1948, 127/43 (written beginning of the 9th cent. at the earliest); cf. BZ 1950, 53.

3. Eznik of Kolb, one of the pupils and collaborators of Sahak and Mesrob wrote *c.* 430 four books *Against the False Doctrines* (against the pagans, Persians, Greek philosophers and Marcionites). The work is distinguished by a particularly elegant style.

Germ. by S. Weber (BKV² 57) 1927. L. Mariès, *Le De Deo d'E. de K.,* 1925. Adontz, ROC 25, 1926, 309/57. Cuendet, REA 1929, 13/40 *(E. et la Bible)*. Karamanlian, HA 1931 and 1932 (Arm. popular rel.). Akinian, HA 1935, 615/7 (Letter to Mastok); id., ib. 1937, 517/32; 1938, 238/58. Williams, JTS 1944, 65/73 (Marcion in Eznik).

4. John Mandakuni, a member of an old noble family, belongs to the circle of "holy translators" and ascended the Patriarchal throne in his old age (d. after 480). Apart from liturgical prayers, twenty-five orations and encyclicals on moral and practical subjects are attributed to him and defended as genuine, though without convincing arguments.

German tr. by S. Weber (BKV² 58) 1927.

5. Three homilies on N.T. pericopes are extant under the name of Mambre Verzanogh who belonged to the same circle.

BKV² 58, 1927.

6. The question of the authenticity of the writings attributed to St. Elishe (Elisaeus) Vardapet (d. *c.* 480) has not yet been settled. The following have been preserved under his name: a cycle of homilies on the life of Christ and others, *Words of Exhortation to the Hermits,* further commentaries on Josue and Judges and an explanation of the Lord's Prayer. His authorship of the historical work on the Vardanian War (449–51) has recently been denied for convincing reasons; it is attributed to an anonymous author of the seventh century.

German by S. Weber (BKV² 58) 1927. N. Akinian, *Elis. V. and his History of the Armen. War,* W 1932/6 (Armen.); cf. AB 1935, 151/4; cont. of study in HA 1932/6; against this Paitschikian, Baz 1931, 193/201. Nahabedian, Baz 1931, 73/5. Irazek, Baz 1931, 265/7.

CHAPTER TWO

The Great Fathers and Ecclesiastical Authors of the West

§ 78. THE POPES OF THE FOURTH AND FIFTH CENTURIES UNTIL LEO THE GREAT

1. No genuine epistles are extant of Pope Silvester (314–35) and his successor Mark (336). Athanasius, who fled from Alexandria to Rome in 339, preserved two Greek Letters of Julius I (337–52) in his *Apologia contra Arianos* 21/35 and 52f. The first letter energetically defends Athanasius and the Nicene faith and reproves the Eusebian and Arian bishops of the East because they did not first "report on the matter of the Alexandrian Church" in order "then to receive a decision from Rome" (35). The second letter addressed to Alexandria is one of recommendation for Athanasius on his return home in 346. On Apollinarian forgeries circulated under the name of Julius I v. supra § 65, 3 c.

See lit. noted supra §§ 25 and 32. Leclercq, DAL 8, 2942/82 *(Lettres des papes)*. P. Batiffol, *Le Siège apostolique 395–451,* 1924. E. M. Pickman, *The Mind of Lat. Christendom,* 1937, 534/655 (Silvester to Gelasius). ML 8, 879/912. Germ. by S. Wenzlowsky, *Briefe der Paepste* (BKV) 2, 1876. F. di Capua, *Il ritmo prosaico nelle lett. dei papi e nei documenti della cancellaria rom. dal IV al XIV sec.,* vols. 1–3, R 1937/48 (from Cornelius to Hormisdas).

2. Liberius (352–66) had to live in exile at Beroea (Thracia) for some time (355–8), because he strenuously defended the Nicene faith. He was allowed to return to Rome only after he had signed the third formula of Sirmium—before that he had probably already accepted the first formula of Sirmium—, abandoned Athanasius and accepted communion with the "oriental" bishops. He manifested his orthodox views by an addition to the third

formula declaring excommunicated any one who did not confess a similarity between Father and Son in essence and in all things (EH 550/69, 853/9).

Of his correspondence thirteen items in all have been preserved either whole or in fragments, among them three *Letters to Bishop Eusebius of Vercelli* and the four hotly contested so-called *Letters from Exile* which compromise the Pope, but the authenticity of which cannot be doubted. The *Address of Liberius* on the occasion of the giving of the virgin's veil to St. Ambrose's sister Marcellina, reproduced in Ambrose, *De Virg.* 3, 1–3, is for the most part the work of Ambrose. — On the *Catalogus Liberianus* v. supra § 50, 5. The so-called *Epitaphium Liberii,* an epitaph on a martyr Pope of fifty-four hexameters, is perhaps to be referred to Pope Martin I (649–53) (EH 570/6).

ML 8, 1345/86. 9 letters in Hilary ed. A. L. Feder (CSEL 65) 1916. Germ. by S. Wenzlowsky (BKV) 1876. Leclercq, DAL 9, 497/530. Amann, DTC 9, 631/59. On the Exile Letters cf. Feder (SbW 162) 1910, 153/83, 325 ff. E. Caspar, *Gesch. des Papsttums* I, 589 f.; Silva-Tarouca, Gr 1931, 357/86. On Marcellina address cf. B. Botte, *Les origines de la Noël et de l'Épiphanie,* Lou 1932, 34/7. RAL 272.

3. Damasus I (366–84), whose reign was troubled by great difficulties within the Church (anti-Pope Ursinus, slanderous accusations of Isaac), obtained nevertheless a higher standing for the jurisdiction of the Bishop of Rome which was recognized by imperial law (Gratian's decree of 378). He worked especially for the reconciliation of East and West, which were torn by the Arian troubles. It was his great merit to have ordered the revision of the Old Latin translation of the Bible by Jerome. Feast day: December 11.

a. The following are among the literary remains of the Pope: ten letters and synodal encyclicals some of which are extant in various recensions, e.g. parts I, 1–3 of the so-called *Decretum Gelasianum* (ed. Dobschuetz 3f.; ES 84) and the twenty-four anathemata against the heresies of the fourth century, which are important for the history of dogma (*Fides* or *tomus Damasi;* ES 58/82).

b. The Pope, who did much for the discovery and adornment of the martyrs' tombs in the catacombs, composed numerous inscriptions *(tituli)* which he had engraved on marble slabs by the skilled calligrapher Philocalus. The latest editor (A. Ferrua) admits fifty-nine epigrams as genuine (EH 585/92).

c. According to Jerome, *Ep.* 22, 22, Damasus composed a *carmen* and a *sermo De virginitate* which are both lost. A poem *De vitiis* attributed to him in several MSS is spurious. In the Middle Ages, from the time of Bede onwards, the Pope was erroneously supposed to be the author of the *Liber Pontificalis* (Ferrua, *Epigrammata* 1942, 9f.).

MP 13, 347/424. M. Ihm, *Damasi Epigrammata,* L 1895. A. Ferrua, *Epigr. Damasiana,* 1942. German by Wenzlowsky (BKV) 2, 1876, 268ff. — Mgg.: by M. Rade 1882; J. Wittig 1902; *Die Friedenspolitik des Papstes Damasus,* 1912; Leclercq, DAL 4, 145/97. Vives, PC 1933, 301/23 (D. born in Catalonia). E. Schaefer, *Die Bedeutung der Epigramme d. Papstes Damasus I. f. d. Gesch. der Heiligenverehrung,* R 1932. Galtier, RSR 1936, 385/418, 563/78 (*Tomus D.* composed in collaboration with Ambrose in 382). On a *Ps.-Damas. Expositio of the Pauline Letters* cf. L. Oliger 1912, 136f. R. Roethe, *Zur Geschichte der roem. Synoden im 3. u. 4. Jh.,* 1936. Silva-Tarouca, *Coll. Thessalonicensis,* R 1937, 16/8. Cochez, ETL 1938, 526/34 *(rythme orat. des lettres pap.).* J. Vives, *S. Dam. papa españo y los Mártires,* Ba 1943; AST 1943, 1/6. Hoepfner, RevEA 1948, 288/304 *(les deux procès du pape D.).* Norton, Folia 4, 1950, 13/31; 5, 1951, 30/55; 6, 1952, 16/39 (Prosography of D.). Richard, AIP 11, 1951, 323/40 (On the D.-letter *Confidimus quidem:* 368 or 372). Vives, *Hispan. Sacra* 5, 1952, 209/26 (D. y Ursicino). Scheidweiler, AIP 13, 1953 (1955), 573/86 (Synodal letter of 371 not extant in Lat.). Kuenzle, RSCI 7, 1953, 1/26 (*Titulus archivorum* di papa D.). Ferrua, RAC 1953, 231/5 *(una dedica Damasiana).* Pricoco, MiscStLChA 1954, 19/40 (lit. value of epigrams). A. de Mendieta, Egl 1, 1954, 261/81 *(Damase, Athan., Pierre, Mélèse et Basile).* — Apocrypha: Blanchard, EL 1949, 376/88 (apocr. correspondence of D. with Jerome). Bignami-Odier, MAH 1951, 187/90 (Apocr. letter of D. to Jerome on Melchisedech).

4. Of Siricius (384–99) seven Letters have been preserved. The most important of these is the *Decretal to Bishop Himerius* of Tarragona (385) which has attracted much attention in the history of the doctrine of the primacy. It answers fifteen questions concerning

Church discipline. In the canonical collections (v. supra § 50, 12ff.) this work is the oldest papal item (EH 657/60; ES 87/90). One encyclical (*c.* 390) is directed against Jovinian and his teaching on the equal value of the married and the virginal life. A letter addressed to Bishop Anysius of Thessalonica condemns Bishop Bonosus of Sardica who denied the permanent virginity of Mary (ES 91).

ML 13, 1131/96. Wenzlowsky (BKV) 2, 1876. H. Getzeny, *Stil u. Form der aeltesten Papstbriefe,* 1922. Goeller, RQ 1931, 93/105 (penance). Bardy, DHG 9, 1096f. (Bonosus).

5. Anastasius I (399–406) wrote three Letters occasioned by the Origenist controversies; they are addressed to the Bishops of Milan Simplicianus and Venerius (EH 713) and to Bishop John of Jerusalem. Anastasius endorses the judgement of Theophilus of Alexandria condemning Origen, but refuses to pronounce a verdict on his translator Rufinus.

ML 20, 68/80; Van den Gheyn, RHL 1899, 1/12 *(Ad Vener.).*

6. Innocent I (402–17) vigorously developed the Roman primacy by his energetic action. He left thirty-six letters, some of which are particularly important as witnesses to the doctrine of the Church (ES 94/100; EP 2014/7).

Ep. 2: validity of heretical baptism, celibacy; *Edd.* 6 and 25; public penance and reconciliation; 6, 7 on the Canon of Scripture and the apocrypha; 25, 3 8: confirmation only by the bishop, anointing by any of the faithful. *Epp.* 29–31 intervene decisively in the Pelagian controversy. 29, 1 contains the following passage on the Papal see; *A quo ipse episcopatus et tota auctoritas nominis huius emersit; Ep.* 30, 5: fate of unbaptized infants in the next world.

ML 20, 463/638. Wurm, *Apollinarius* 12, 1939: Excerptum 7–45: *Ep.* 6 (crit. text). Amann, DTC 7, 1940/50. Connolly, JTS 20, 1918/9, 215/26 *(De nominibus recitandis).* Goeller, RQ 1931, 105/13 (penance). F. Lehr 1934 (supra § 3, 19) 8ff. Ellard, TSW 1948, 3/19 *(Ep. ad Decentium).* Vighetti, *Misc. Francisc.,* R 1951, 39/61; 1952, 92/112 (penance and *Ordo*). Capelle, RTA 1952, 5/16 (Canon of Mass). Griffe, BLE 114/16 (Canon of Mass). Demougeot, RH 212, 1954, 23/38 *(interventions dans la politique séculière).*

7. Of Zosimus (417–18) about sixteen letters are extant. The important *Epistola tractoria* is preserved only in fragments. In the Pelagian controversy the Pope intervened in a rather unfortunate manner. In *Ep.* 12, 1 he says that the papal authority is such that no one can cancel a Roman decision (ES 101/19. ML 20, 639/704). C. H. Turner, 3 (supra § 50, 13).

8. Boniface I (418–22). Nine letters are extant (ES 110). In the controversy on the papal vicariate of Thessalonica (*Epp.* 13–15) he stressed his primacy of jurisdiction, especially in *Ep.* 15.

ML 20, 749/92.

9. Celestine I (422–32). The majority of the sixteen letters of the Pope are concerned with the Nestorian controversy. In *Ep.* 21 Augustine is defended against semi-Pelagian attacks and counted among the *magistri optimi* (ES 128).

ML 50, 417/558 and SACO I, 1, 7, 125/37; 1, 2, 5/101 (15 letters). Portalié, DTC 2, 2051/61. A. M. Bernardini, *S. Cel.,* 1938.

10. Sixtus III (432–40): Seven letters.

ML 50, 583/618. SACO I, 1, 7, 143/5; I, 2, 107/10 (5 letters).

11. Leo I, the Great (440–61). As early as 430, Leo, who came from Toscana, had been an influential personage in the papal curia. As a Pope he guided the destinies of the Church in a time of general catastrophe in the spirit of trust in God. Through his eminent personality and breadth of vision he became not only the guardian of orthodoxy, but also the saviour of Western civilization. By his powerful activity, which embraced the whole Roman Empire, he laid the foundation of the ecclesiastical and political position of the Papacy in the following centuries.

He made world history through his encounter with Attila, the king of the Huns, whom he caused to turn back after meeting him at Mantua (452). With equal courage he met the approaching king of the Vandals, Geiserich, in 455, and obtained at least that when Rome was sacked it was spared torture, murder and fire. His intervention in the Monophysite troubles of the East was no less important for the inner history of the Church. In his famous doctrinal Letter *(Epistola* [28] *dogmatica ad Flavianum)* he gave the hotly disputed Christological doctrine its classical formulation (449). At the Council of Chalcedon (451) which was presided over by his legates this epistle served as the foundation for the Council's dogmatic decision. In Italy he took measures against the Pelagians and Manicheans, and in Spain against the Priscillianists. In order to defend his primacy of jurisdiction, he protested against can. 28 of the Council of Chalcedon and restored order to the hierarchies of Gaul, Illyria and North Africa. Feast day: April 11.

After Damasus I, Leo I is the first Pope of whom other literary works (sermons) have been preserved apart from his letters, the majority of which are probably, also in his case, products of his chancellery (Prosper of Aquitania). His speeches and letters are remarkable for their clarity of thought, precision of expression and purity of language; they betray a good rhetorical training.

a. The ninety-six mostly short *Sermons* were delivered on the feasts of Christ, on June 29, on the anniversary of his own enthronement, on fast days (34) or on days appointed for the collection of alms (6); numbers 52–70 are Passiontide sermons. Controversial theological questions are frequently referred to, especially those of the Christological dogma (EP 2190/214; EA 984/95).

b. The 173 numbers of the Leonine collection of letters contain twenty spurious items and thirty letters addressed to the Pope. In the main the letters are ecclesiastical documents containing the many-sided measures and decisions of Leo's government or epistles intervening in the theological or conciliar questions of the moment.

c. The so-called *Sacramentarium Leonianum,* which should rather be called Sacramentarium Veronense after the probable place of its origin, is the private work of a compiler. On the basis of a Roman *Calendarium* he grouped together the forms of prayer that had originated between *c.* 440 and 550 from various liturgical *Libelli sacramentorum* used in Roman churches. This still unclassified collection of material is but one extant example of several similar attempts and a preliminary step to a fully developed sacramentary (cf. the so-called older *Gelasianum*). The compiler edited the material in the second half of the sixth or at the beginning of the seventh century (Stuiber).

Edd.: P. and H. Ballerini, 3 vols., 1753/57. ML 54/6. 114 Letters in SACO II, 4, 1932. Ed. C. Silva-Tarouca, R 1932 (*Epp.* 28 and 165); R 1934f. *(epistolae contra Eutychis haeresim)*; R 1937 *(Coll. Thessalonicensis)*. — Edd. of the *Ep. ad Flav.* also in SACO II, 2, 1, n. 5; II, 1, 1, pp. 10/20 (Gr.). Wurm, *Apollinaris* 12, 1939, 46/60 (Ed. crit. *Ep.* 4: ML 54, 610/4). — Transs.: S. Wenzlowsky (BKV) 2 vols. Letters, 1878. T. Steeger, BKV² 54/5 = 1927 (Serm.); T. Breme, L 1936 (Serm. 52/70). Leclercq et Dolle, Sermons in SCh 22 49, 1945/57. — Mgg.: Batiffol, DTC 9, 218/301. Lietzmann, PWK 12, 1962/73. A. Wille, *Bischof Julian v. Kios,* 1910. R. Galli, Did 1930, F. 2, 51/235. J. Pschmadt, *L. d. Gr. als Prediger,* 1912. F. di Capua, *Il ritmo prosaico nelle lett. dei papi* I, 1, 1937 *(Leone M.)*. W. J. Halliwell, *The Style of Pope St. L. the Gr.,* W 1939. T. Jalland, *The Life and Times of St. L. the Gr.,* Lo 1941. M. Mueller, *The Vocabulary of Pope St. L. the Gr.,* W 1943. — Treatises: Doelger, AC 2, 252/7 (Inscr.). Silva-Tarouca, Gr 1931, 3/56, 349/425, 547/98 (tradition of letters). Ruiz Goyo, EE 1935, 244/56 (*Ep.* 28); 1936, 367/79 (*Ep.* 15). Silva-Tarouca, StU 151/70 (MSS of the Tomus). Richard, RHE 1937, 794/6 (Testimon. of *Ep.* 165). On *Ep.* 15 (Turribius) cf. De Gaiffier, AB 1941, 34/64; L. A. Luengo, *S. Toribio, ob. de Astorga,* Ma 1939; Alafont 1942 (supra § 50, 14). P. Brezzi, *S. Leone M.,* R 1947. D. Franzes, *P. Leo d. Gr. en S. Hilarius v. Arles,* 1948. Leicht, RivStorDirItal 1949, 181/5 (matters of matrimonial law in a letter). De Gaiffier, Misc. Mohlberg 2, 313/6 (spurious sermon on St. Vincent). Capelle, EL 1953, 201/9 *(une messe pour l'Ascension)*. Carton, VS 1954, 104/14 (*observantia* in the homs.). ClavisPL n. 1655ff. — On the *Sacr. Leon.*: Edd.: ML 55. L. Feltoe, C 1896. Cabrol, DAL 8, 2549/73. A. Baumstark, *Missale Rom.,* N 1930, 23ff. Mohlberg, EL 1933, 3/12 (for Cassiodorus); against this Klauser, JL 13, 1936, 354/6. De Jerphanion, RSR 1936, 364/6. A. Dold, *Das aelteste Liturgiebuch der lat. Kirche,* 1936 (an Old Gall. lectionary [composed *c.* 500]); cf. OC 1936, 114/9. Borella, EL 1946, 93/101 *(Communicantes)*. Capelle, RBn 1945/6, 12/41 (Messes du pape S. Gélase). Callewaert, SE 1, 1948, 35/164 (Léon et les textes du Léonien). Bruylants, *Concordance verbale du Sacr. Léon.,* Abbaye Mont César 1948. Cross, JTS 1949, 191/7 (Pre-Leonic Elements in the Proper of the Rom. Mass). E. Bourque, *Ét. sur les Sacramentaires Romains,* StudiAntChr 20, 1949. Coebergh, Misc. Mohlberg 2, 189/97 *(Sacr. Léon. et liturgie mozarabe)*: ETL 1950, 214/37; EL 1951, 171/81; SE 1952, 46/102 (Gelasius I, the author of several

Masses and *orationes*); SE 1954, 327/42 (Leo, author of the formula *Ad virgines sacras*). Chavasse, EL 1950, 161/213 and conts. (Masses of Pope Vigilius). A. Stuiber, *Libelli Sacramentorum Romani des sog. Sacr. Leon.*, Bonn 1950; cf. Mohlberg, TR 1953, 65/8. Capelle, RBn 1951, 3/14 (Gelasius I and *Sacr. Leon.*). Eizenhoefer, SE 1952, 27/45 (Span. infl. in the Leon.?). A. Schmidt, SE 1952, 103/73 *(De formulis identicis Sacr. Leon., Gelas. et Gregoriani);* against this Capelle, RBn 1954, 157/67. C. Callewaert, *S. Léon le Gr. et les textes du Léonien,* Steenbrugge 1954. ClavisPL 1897. A. P. Lang, *Leo d. Gr. u. die Texte des Alt-Gelasianums,* Steyl 1957. Mohlberg-Eizenhoefer-Siffrin, *Sacram. Veronense (= Sacram. Leon.)* R 1955 f. (crit. text). M. B. de Soos, *Le mystère liturgique de'après S. Léon le Gr.*, M 1958.

Points of Doctrine

1. Christology. On the union of the two natures in Christ Leo writes in his *Ep. dogm. ad Flavianum* following Tertullian and Augustine: Christ is but one Person: *Unus enim idemque est . . . vere Dei filius et vere hominis filius* (4). The two natures continue to exist without any mixture *salva proprietate utriusque naturae et substantiae et in unam coeunte personam* (3). *Agit enim utraque forma cum alterius communione, quod proprium est, Verbo scilicet operante, quod Verbi est, et carne exsequente, quod carnis est* (4). The unity of the Person allows the *communicatio idiomatum:* The Lord is therefore *invisibilis* and *visibilis, incomprehensibilis* and *comprehensibilis, impassibilis* and *passibilis* (4) (ES 143 f.).

2. Baptism. In a Letter addressed to Italic bishops he commands that baptism should be administered only at Easter or at Pentecost, except in case of necessity.

3. Penance. The mediation of the Church is, for those who have committed "mortal sin", the indispensable condition for forgiveness, for, "the one mediator between God and men, the man Jesus Christ" (1 Tim. 2:5) has given the leaders of the Church the power *ut et confitentibus actionem paenitentiae darent et eosdem salubri satisfactione purgatos ad communionem sacramentorum per ianuam reconciliationis admitterent* (*Ep.* 108, 2; ES 146). In *Ep.* 168, 2 the Pope opposes the custom that had gained ground in some dioceses, according to which also those sins of the public penitents that had

remained secret were made public without their consent. The declaration of the Pope is not directed against public penance as such, but only against the publication of those sins that had been confessed in secret *(confessione secreta)* before public *paenitentia* was undertaken (ES 145).

4. Primacy. "Through Peter, the blessed Prince of the Apostles, the holy Roman Church possesses the primacy" *(principatus)* "over all the churches of the whole earth" (*Ep.* 65, 2). The power and authority given to the Apostle Peter continues to be active *in sede sua* (sc. *Romana*), and his dignity is not diminished even in an unworthy heir (*Sermo* 3, 3f.).

5. Church and State. Leo demands the protection of the State in the struggle against heresy and for the preservation of Church discipline (*Epp.* 7. 11. 15). It is true, he considers the convocation of General Councils and the nominations of synodal presidents a right of the Emperor (*Epp.* 29. 33. 34), but he emphasizes that only the ecclesiastical authority is competent in matters of faith.

W. Kissling, *Das Verhaeltnis zwischen Sacerdotium u. Imperium . . .,* 1921. J. Rivière, *Le dogme de la rédemption après S. Augustin,* 1930. Goeller, RQ 1931, 119/53 (penance). Deneffe, Sch 1934, 543/54 (trad. and dogma). Whitney, CambrHist-Journ 1934, 1/24 (primacy). T. Michels, *Das Heilswerk der Kirche,* 1935. K. D. Schmidt, ZKG 1935, 267/75 (primacy). P. Santini, *Il primato e l'infallib. del R. Pont. in S. Leone M. e gli scrittori greco-russi,* Grottaferrata 1936. E. M. Pickman 1937, 589/616 (L. and the Monophysites). Wojtasik, *Nauka sw. L. o Slowie wcielonym,* War 1935. Cavallera, BLE 1937, 67/78, 119/35, 167/79 *(La doctr. sur le prince chrét. dans les letters pontif. du 5ᵉ s.).* Pellegrino, SC 1939, 611/5 *(Corpo mistico).* Burgio, *Studi Francesc.,* 1940, 81/94 (L'incarnazione). A. Hugy, *S. Leo de Gr. Over de Menschwording van Chr.,* 1941 (texts). Willwoll, CC 1942, III 33/9, 152/59 *(La missione di Roma).* U. Gmelin, Auctoritas, St 1937, 111/35 (primacy). V. Gluschke, *Die Unfehlbarkeit des Papstes b. L. d. Gr.,* R 1938. W. Haacke, *Die Glaubensformel des Papstes Hormisdas,* R 1939, 122/31 (primacy). A. Spindeler, *Cur verbum caro factum,* Pa 1938, 136/62. D. Mozeris, *Doctr. S. Leonis M. de Christo restitutore . . .,* Mundelein 1945. E. M. Burke, *The Church in the Works of L. the Gr.,* W 1945.

Latest lit. on Christol. and on L's. relation to the Greek East: Rivera Racio, RET 1949, 31/58 (L. and the heresy of Eutyches). M. Jugie in *Misc. P. Paschini* 1, R 1948, 77/94 (L. and the Eastern Churches). Nicolas, RT 1951, 609/60

(Christology). Du Manoir, AnT 1951, 291/304 (definition of Chalcedon). Galtier in Grillmeier-Bacht I, 345/87 (Christology of Cyril of Al. and Leo). F. Hofmann in Grillmeier-Bacht II, 13/94 (Popes and the dogma of Chalcedon, from Leo to Hormisdas). Emmi, Ang 1952, 3/42 (L. and Eutyches). Richard, RSR 1952, 116/28 (L. and Cyril's scholia *De incarn. Unigeniti*). Monachino, Gr 1952, 531/65 (can. 28 of Chalcedon). Klinkenberg, ZSK 1952, 37/112 (Papacy and Imperial Church). Eizenhoefer in Festschr. J. A. Jungmann 1950, 79/107 (The sacrifice of the faithful in the *Sermones*). C. Fernandes, *La gracia seg. s. L. et Gr.*, Mexico 1951. Oppenheim, EL 1950, 345/8 (L. on the feast of Christmas). A. Guillaume, *Jeûne et charité dans l'Égl. lat. des origines au XIIe s. en particulier chez s. L. le Gr.*, P 1954. Hervé, RTA 1955, 17/55, 193/212 (Doctr. of grace).

§ 79. JULIUS FIRMICUS MATERNUS

PROBABLY *c.* 336, before his conversion to Christianity, the Sicilian rhetor Firmicus Maternus wrote *Matheseos libri VIII,* an astrological work already betraying great moral integrity. As a Christian he wrote (346–8) *De errore profanarum religionum,* an accusation against the dying paganism addressed to the Emperors Constantius and Constans.

Basing himself on the O.T., the author demands that the emperors should destroy paganism by force and effect a compulsory Christianization of the empire. In sometimes violent language and with excessive zeal the treatise attacks particularly the pagan mystery cults, pillorying their absurdity and immorality. The *Cod. Vaticanus Palat. lat. 165* is the only MS of the treatise (nineteenth cent.).

G. Morin has unsuccessfully attempted to prove that the three anonymous books entitled *Consultationes Zacchaei et Apollonii* also belong to Firmicus Maternus. The work is a survey of the Christian truths of faith (2, 19; 1 praef. called *corpus credulitatis*) more adequate than that of Lactantius (v. supra § 37). It is the work of an anonymous author, probably written in Africa after 411.

Book I: Zacchaeus acquaints the pagan philosopher Apollonius with the basic truths of the Christian religion. Book II: On the Trinity and the errors of the Jews and of many Christian heretics.

Book III: Teachings on the Christian life, especially on virginity, the monastic life, the Antichrist and the resurrection.

Edd.: *Math. lib.* 8 ed. W. Kroll, F. Skutsch and K. Ziegler, 2 vols., L 1897/1913. *De errore* ed. K. Ziegler, L 1907 and Mn 1953; trans. M 1953. G. Heuten, *De err.* (text and comm.). Bru 1938. A. Pastorino, ed. *De err.*, Fl 1955. German by A. Mueller (BKV² 14) 1913. *Consult.* ed. G. Morin (FP 39) 1935; cf. Morin, RBn 1934, 456/9 and JL 13, 1936, 185/8; PW 1936, 196/203. — Mgg. and treatises: Boll, PWK 6, 2365/79. F. Groehl, *De syntaxi Firmiciana,* 1918. Van der Leeuw, *Egypt. Religion* 1, 1933, 61/72 (the σύμβολα). P. Henry, *Plotin et l'Occident,* Lou 1934, 25/43 (Math. I, 7); cf. NRT 1936, 126/35. T. Wickstroem, *In Fir. M. studia crit.,* Up 1935 (Math.). Doelger, AC 5, 153/87 (*De error.* 2). J. Coman, *Rev. class.,* Bucharest 1932/3, 73/118 (Essai sur le *De err. prof. rel.*). B. Axelson, *Ein 3. Werk des F. M.?,* Lund 1937 (against Morin). Heuten, Lat 3, 1939, 156/63 (traduct. néerland. de F. M.). Wickstroem, Er 1942, 37/80 (MSS and edd.). B. Botte, *Le canon de la messe rom.* (éd. crit.), Lou 1935. Castiglioni, Acme 1, 1948, 43/5 (on Math. II, 4). — On the *Consultationes:* A. Reatz, *Das theol. System der Cons. Z. et Ap.,* 1920. Cavallera, RAM 1935, 132/46 *(vita monast.).* K. Schwerdt, *Stud. z. Lehre des hl. Ambrosius v. d. Person Christi,* thesis Fr 1937, 122/35. Lawson, RBn 1947, 187/95 (used by Isidore of Seville). Courcelle, RHR 146, 1954, 174/93 (use of August., *Epp.* 135/8 can be proved; first — 484 — cited in Victor de Vita, *Hist. persec.* 2, 77f.). Wickstroem, ER 1955, 172/92 (text. crit. of so-called Apol.).

§ 80. HILARY OF POITIERS (b. *c.* 315, d. 367)

HILARY came from a noble pagan family and was well versed in the philosophical and rhetorical culture of his time. His quest for the meaning of life led him to the study of Scripture and to baptism. Though he was married, the clergy and people of his native city elected him their bishop in 350.

Hilary did not take part in the synods of Arles (353) and Milan (355) which decreed once more the deposition of Athanasius. But he organized (355) the resistance of the Gallic bishops to the metropolitan of Gaul, Saturninus of Arles, who inclined to Arianism. For this reason the Emperor Constantius exiled him to Asia Minor. Here he spent the years 356–9, during which he wrote his principal theological work, the *De Trinitate*. After the Synod of Seleucia (359) which he attended he went to see the Emperor at

Constantinople, but his request to be allowed a public disputation with his opponent Saturninus was not granted. He was sent back to Gaul at the instigation of the Arians to whom he had become a nuisance, being called "the mischief-maker of the East" (*Sulpic. Sev.* 2, 45, 4).

After his return home (360) he obtained the renewed excommunication of Saturninus at a synod of Paris (361). Thus nearly all Gaul had been regained for the Catholic faith. In 364 he presided over a gathering of Italian bishops at Milan, who attempted to have the Arian bishop, Auxentius of Milan, removed by the Emperor, though they did not succeed in this. Hilary died in 367; feast day: January 14.

Hilary was the most important opponent of Arianism in the West and is therefore called the "Athanasius of the West". His character, too, resembled that of St. Athanasius, combining gentleness and strength with the traits of a true ruler. Hilary's pastoral activity coincided with the period of the greatest power of Arianism. It is above all due to him that the Western Church recovered so quickly after the death of Constantius (361) and that the beginning defeat of Arianism soon became apparent.

Hilary was an accomplished stylist who loved literary beauty but disliked empty phrases; his language is vigorous but obscure. He was probably the first to announce the principle that sacred subjects ought to be presented in dignified form. He was distinguished by the depth and boldness of his ideas and by an unusual knowledge of the Scriptures. He is the first dogmatic scholar and the first eminent exegete of the West, to which he introduced important ideas of Eastern theology. He was proclaimed *Doctor Ecclesiae* by Pius IX in 1851.

1. *Exegetical writings*

a. His first literary work composed before his exile is the *Commentary on Matthew,* which is based only on a Latin text of the

Bible. It aims at penetrating to the "deeper", i.e. the allegorical sense *(interior significantia)* (EP 854/6).

b. The *Tractatus super Psalmos* (1, 2, 9, 13, 14, 51/69, 91, 118/50) which have not been preserved completely were written *c.* 365, both the LXX and the Latin text being used. They follow the same hermeneutical principles as the former work. The *Tractatus Mysteriorum,* ed. in fragments as late as 1887 treats of the types *(mysteria)* or prophetical patterns of the O.T. A commentary on Job is lost.

2. *Dogmatic-polemical works*

a. The twelve books *De Trinitate (De fide, Adv. Arianos),* Hilary's principal work, is the best that has been written in defence of the true divinity and consubstantiality of the Son against the Arians.

The treatise which is aflame with enthusiasm for the doctrine it defends contains positive rather than speculative theology. As a controversialist Hilary is forced to do justice to the literal sense of Scripture. Though he uses the intellectual achievements of the Greek theologians, the treatise is nevertheless an important independent work (EP 857/78).

b. Shortly before the meeting of the double synod of Seleucia and Rimini (359) he composed his double encyclical *De synodis seu de fide Orientalium,* an historical appendix to his principal work. In chs. 1–65 he explains several creeds composed after Nicaea (e.g. Antioch 341, Sardica, 1 and 2 Sirmian formulae) for the benefit of the bishops of Gaul and Britain. In chs. 66–91 he addresses the Homoiousian bishops of the East. In an accommodating, open-minded spirit he seeks to show that on the one hand the ὁμοιούσιος can be understood in an orthodox sense, whereas on the other the ὁμοούσιος might be misunderstood; rightly understood, however, the ὁμοούσιος is far more accurate than the ὁμοιούσιος (EP 879/81). He had to defend this point of view against Lucifer of Calaris in his treatise *Apologetica ad reprehensores libri de synodis responsa,* of which only a few fragments are extant. Hilary's attitude prepared the union of the Nicaeans and the Homoiousians.

3. Historical-polemical works

a. The *Opus historicum adversus Valentem et Ursacium* is extant only in fragments and pieces taken out of their original context. It was completed in three sections (published 356, 359–60 and *c.* 367 or after his death). It cannot always be decided with certainty whether the individual documents which are sometimes preserved only here are all genuine, how they were once connected, and whether the connecting text is always by Hilary himself.

The so-called *Liber I ad Constantium* belonged to the first part. Actually it is very probably a letter of the Synod of Sardica (343) to the Emperor, which is followed by an accompanying historical text. The *Exile Letters of Liberius* (supra § 78, 2) belong to the second part. All fragments have now been collected as *Collectanea antiariana Parisina* in CSEL 65, 39/193.

b. After the synod of Seleucia 359 he wrote his *Liber ad Constantium Augustum* in which he asked the Emperor for an audience at Constantinople in order to convict his old opponent Saturnius of lying. Since his request was not granted he wrote a sharp indictment *Contra Constantium imperatorem* (EH 577/9) which was addressed to his fellow-bishops.

c. In the formally exquisite and historically important short treatise *Contra Arianos vel Auxentium Mediolanensem* he gives an account of his unsuccessful efforts to obtain from the Emperor Valentinian I the removal of the Arian bishop, Auxentius, the predecessor of St. Ambrose. The *Libellus contra Dioscorum medicum ad Sallustium praefectum* (Dioscorus shared the opinions of Julian), praised by Jerome, is lost.

4. Hilary was the first Western author to compose hymns. The writing of religious hymns may have been suggested to him by the well-developed church singing he heard in the East. Three incompletely preserved hymns edited by Gamurrini in 1887, two abecedaria on the Trinity and on baptism and a hymn on the struggle of Christ with the devil may probably be considered genuine. A Letter *Ad Abram filiam* (CSEL 65, 237/44) is certainly spurious.

Edd.: S. Maffei, *Verona,* 2 vols., 1730. ML 9/10. A. Zingerle and A. Feder (CSEL 22 and 65) 1891/1916. Wilmart, RBn 1931, 277/83 *(Tract. sup. Ps. 150).* W. N. Myers, *The Hymns of S. H. of P. in the cod. Aretinus,* Phil 1928. Facsimile ed. of the Cod. Archiv. S. Petri in Vatic. D. 182 *(De Trinit.)* by A. Amelli (lib. 1–6), R 1922; by J. L. Perugi, 2 vols., Tu 1932. — Transs.: A. Antweiler (BKV[2] II, 5, 6) 1933/4 *(Trinit.).* J. P. Brisson, *De myst.* (SCh 19), text and trans., 1947. — Mgg.: A. Largent, P 1902. Le Bachelet, DTC 6, 2388/2462. H. Lindemann, *Des hl. H. v. P. Liber mysteriorum,* 1905. A. Feder, *Stud. zu H. v. P.* (SbW 162, 4; 166, 5; 169, 5) 1910/12 and WSt 1920, 51/60, 167/81. H. Jeannotte, *Le psautier de s. H. de P.* (Texts) 1917; on this RB 1917, 61/89. M. F. Buttel, *The Rhetoric of St. H. of P.,* W 1933. M. V. Brown, *The Syntax of the Propositions in the Works of St. H. of P.,* W 1934. M. E. Mann, *The Clausulae of St. H. of P.,* W 1935. R. J. Kinnavey, *The Vocabulary of St. H. of P.,* W 1935. J. H. Gillis, *The Coordinating Particles in St. H., Jerome, Ambr. and Augustine,* W 1938. T. Gimborn, *The Syntax of the Simple Cases in S. H. of P.,* W 1938. Aigrain, *Bull. Soc. des antiquaires de l'Ouest* 17, 1937/8, 691/710 *(Où en est l'étude des œuvres de S. H.?).* Wilmart, *Class. and Mediaev. Stud. in Hon. E. K. Rand,* NY 1938, 293/305 (MS di S. Pietro). Bardy, RHEF 1941, 5/25 *(humaniste chrét. S. H.).* Blatt, Δράγμα *M. P. Nillson,* 1939, 67/95 (crit. text of apocr. Letter in ML 10, 733/50). Glorieux, MSR 1944, 7/34 (Liberius-Letters, forged by Arians?). Pellegrino, VC 1947, 201/26 *(Poesia);* SC 1947, 130/6 (spir. development). Antin, RBn 1947, 82/8 *(H. Gallicano cothurno attollitur).* R. B. Sherlock, *The Syntax of the Nominal Forms of the Verbs . . .,* W 1947. Caruana, *Melita Theol.* (La Valetta) 1, 1947, n. 3, 25/36 (Hil. and Hebr.). J. Fleming, *Comm. on the so-called Op. Hist. of H. of P.,* thesis Durham 1951. Casamassa, StAns 27/8, 231/8 (on *Tract. sup. Pss.*). Klos, MitInstOestGF 1955, 47/52 (new fragm. of Papyr. Cod.). Gusson, VC 1956, 14/24 (text. crit. on Tract. myster. 15/99). A. Gariglio, AttiAccadScTorino 90, 1955/6, 1/15 (Ambrose and H. on Ps. 118).

Points of Doctrine

Christology. Faith in the divinity of Christ is for Hilary the foundation of the Church (*Trin.* 6, 37). He gives it a speculative basis in the eternal generation (*Trin.* 7, 14). In the course of time the Son of God assumed a human nature; however, his body was not an earthly, but a heavenly one (*corpus caeleste; Trin.* 10, 18), and for this reason, that the Lord himself formed his body in the womb of the Virgin without the co-operation of man. The natural state of the Body of Christ was a glorified one even before his resurrection. Hence the Transfiguration and the walking on the water were not miracles, as is usually said, but the mode of being and the activity natural to the Body of Christ. Consequently this was also free from needs and passions (*Trin.* 10, 23) as Clement of Alexandria (*Strom.* 6, 71, 2) had already asserted before him. Nor could Christ really die; if he admitted death and human infirmity, though without pain, this needed each time an act of voluntary self-humiliation (*Trin.* 10, 24ff.).

In the exegesis of Phil. 2:7 he understands by self-emptying (*evacuatio, annihilatio*) not a "depotentiation" (*Depotenzierung*) of the Logos (*Trin.* 9, 14; 11, 14), for he repeatedly emphasizes God's immutability (*Trin.* 9, 72). Hence for Hilary *evacuatio* can only mean that during the time of his life on earth the Logos gave up the glory due to him as God.

A. Beck, *Die Trinitaetslehre des hl. H. v. P.*, 1903. Poxrucker, *Die Lehre des hl. H. v. P. von der Heiligung*, 1922. Mersch 1, 1936, 410/37. Favre, Gr 1936, 481/514; 1937, 318/36 (*communicatio idiomatum*). Limongi, SC 1941, 127/47, 260/73; DTP 1942, 186/201 (peccato orig.). Casel, JL 15, 1941, 156/64 (mystery of the faith). Beumer, BiNJ 1, 1942, 151/67 (unity of man with Christ). B. Lorscheid, *Verhaeltn. der Freiheit des Menschen zur Barmherzigkeit Gottes nach H.*, R 1940. P. Smulders, *La doctr. trinitaire de S. H. de P.*, 1944. J. E. Emmenegger, *The Functions of Faith and Reason in the Theol. of St. H.*, W 1947. J. McMahon, *De Christo mediatore doctrina S. Hilarii*, Mundelein 1947. Giamberardini, DTP 1947, 35/56, 194/205; 1948, 3/18 (*De incarnat. Verbi*); *Misc. Francisc.* 1949, 266/300, 514/33; *De divinitate Verbi sec. s. H.*, Piacenza 1951. A. Verrastro, *Il fundamento ultimo della perfetta consubstanzialità del Figlio al Padre nel De Trin. di s. Il. di P.*, Potenza 1948. Lecuyer, AnT 1949, 302/25 (priesthood of Christians). P. T. Wild, *The Divinization of Man acc. to S. Hil.*, thesis Mundelein 1951. Beumer, TQ 1952, 170/91 (H., Christian Gnostic). Duignon, AL 1953, 123/35 (*Adsumo* and *Adsumptio* in H.).

§ 81. ANTI-ARIAN AND OTHER CONTROVERSIALISTS

1. Bishop Hosius (Ossius) of Cordova was one of the most influential protagonists of orthodoxy against Arianism and played an important part as the ecclesiastical adviser of Constantine the Great (Nicaea) and also later (Sardica 343). Before his death (337–8) he retracted his signature which, at the age of almost a hundred, he had been forced to append to the second Sirmian formula in 357. Various canons of the Synod of Sardica (ML 6, 1317/28) and a letter addressed to Pope Julius I were composed by him. Two treatises which Isidore of Seville (*Vir. ill.* 5) asserts to have been written by him (*De laude Virginitatis* and *De interpretatione vestium sacerdotalium* [of the O.T. high priest]) have not been preserved.

García-Villada 1, 2, 1929, 11/43. F. Sureda Blanes, *La cuestión de Osio y de Liberio*, Ma 1928. Cunill, AST 1926, 285/300. Turner, *Eccl. occid. Monum. Jur. ant.* I, 532 (correct form of name: Ossius) I, 532. H. Yaben, *Osio, ob. de Cord.*, Ba 1945. V. C. de Clercq, *Oss. of Cord.*, W 1954.

2. Eusebius first bishop of Vercelli (d. *c.* 371) was exiled to Scythopolis in Palestine because he courageously opposed the condemnation of St. Athanasius at the Synod of Milan (355). Together with Hilary of Poitiers he later fought against Arianism in Italy (Auxentius of Milan). He left three Letters (ML 12, 947/54). The *Cod. Vercellensis* which has a pre-Jerome text of the Gospels may have been written by him (ML 12, 9/948). The Commentary on the Psalms by Eusebius of Caesarea which he translated into Latin (Jerome, *Ep.* 61, 2) has not been preserved.

Juelicher, PWK 6, 1441/3. Godet, DTC 5, 1553f. Pasté, SC 1932, 142/7 *(Symbolum Quicunque)*, 341/58. Schepens, RHE 1936, 561f. (the 8 books *De Trinit.* of Ps.-Vigilius [ML 62, 237/82] belong to Eusebius); RSR 1950, 295/9 (Ambrosiaster and Euseb.); against this B. Fischer, TLZ 1952, 288. CChL 9.

3. Lucifer of Calaris (Cagliari) in Sardinia (d. 370–1) refused, like Eusebius of Vercelli, to abandon St. Athanasius at the synod of Milan (355) and had to go into exile to Syria, Palestine and the Thebaid. He disturbed the union of Nicenes and Homoiousians

begun at the synod of Alexandria (362) by consecrating the presbyter Paulinus bishop, thus initiating the Antiochene schism. He died separated from the Church by schism. He is venerated as a saint in his native island.

During his exile he wrote five extremely violent pamphlets addressed to the Emperor Constantius: *De non conveniendo cum haereticis, De regibus apostaticis* (of the O.T.), *De s. Athanasio, De non parcendo in Deum delinquentibus, Moriendum esse pro Dei filio.* His writings are linguistically noteworthy because they are written in vulgar Latin; they also have extensive citations which are important for the history of the pre-Jerome text of the Bible.

Edd.: ML 13. W. Hartel (CSEL 14) 1886. — Mgg.: by G. Krueger 1886. Amann, DTC 9, 1032/44. A. M. Coleman, *The Biblical Text of C.* (Acts), Welwyn 1927 (8 pp.). F. Piva, *L. di C. contro l'imperat. Costanzo,* Trent 1928. G. Thoernell, *Studia Luciferiana,* Up 1934. Saba, StU 109/16 (ed. of *Fides s. Luciferi*). G. Cerretti, *L. di C. ed il suo "Mor. esse pro Dei Fil."* (text and comm.), Pisa 1940. C. Zedda, DTP 1949, 276/329 *(Dottrina trinit. di L. di C.).*

4. Faustinus, Roman presbyter of Lucifer's schismatics, defended the Trinitarian doctrine against the objections of the Arians *c.* 380 (ML 13, 37/80) and submitted a Creed to Theodosius I (ibid. 79f.). Together with the presbyter Marcellinus he successfully asked the Emperors Valentinian II, Theodosius I, and Arcadius to protect the followers of Lucifer against the Catholics who oppressed them (ibid. 83/107 and O. Guenther, CSEL 35, 5/44).

5. In 357–8 Phoebadius, Bishop of Agen in Southern France (d. after 392) wrote a *Liber contra Arianos* (ML 20, 13/30; Germ. by J. Draesecke, Progr. Wandsbeck 1910) directed against the second Sirmian formula. A second treatise *De fide orthodoxa* with an appended Creed belongs to Gregory of Elvira (ML 17, 549/68 = 20, 31/50).

Ed.: A. Durengues, *Le livre de s. P. contre les Ar.,* Agen 1927; cf. RPA 1928, 726/36. G. Fritz, DTC 12, 1369/74.

6. C. Marius Victorinus of Africa (d. after 362), a celebrated rhetor under the Emperor Constantius (337–61) in Rome, made

his way to Christianity from neo-Platonic philosophy. "Rome was astonished, and the Church rejoiced" (August., *Conf.* 8, 2, 4) when, *c.* 355, he asked to be baptized. He had to give up his teaching activity under Julian.

In his pagan days he composed grammatical-metrical treatises and commentaries on the rhetorical philosophical writings of Cicero; he also translated Aristotelian treatises, Porphyry's *Isagoge* and very probably parts of the *Enneads* of Plotinus (Aug., *Beata Vita* 1, 4; *Confess.* 7, 9, 13; 8, 2, 3). He also wrote philosophical treatises of his own. As a Christian he sought to reconcile faith and knowledge, but without sufficient theological training. His theology (doctrine of the Trinity) is guided by neo-Platonic metaphysics rather than by Holy Scripture and the *regula fidei*. His metaphysical speculations on the will strongly influenced Augustine's concept of God.

a. Three treatises are directed against Arianism and designed to win an Arian friend of his, Candidus, for the Nicene faith: *De generatione divini Verbi, Adversus Arium* (his principal work) and the short treatise *De* ὁμοουσίῳ *recipiendo* (EP 904/8). Three hymns on the Trinity are in content related to these works; the second of these is a prayer of petition to Christ. The hymns are written in elevated prose without metre, following the law of the parallelism of the Psalms.

b. Commentaries on three Pauline Letters (Gal., Eph. and Phil.) seek to ascertain the text and the literal sense; there are sizable, frequently erroneous dogmatic and philosophical insertions.

ML 8, 999/1310. — Treatises: Wessner, PWK 14, 1840/8. Monceaux (supra § 3) 3, 373/422. J. Woehrer, *Vier Progr. Wilhering,* 1905, 1910/2 (ed. anti-Arian writings). A. Souter 1927, 8/38. E. Benz, *M. V. u. d. Entwicklung der abendl. Willensmetaphysik,* 1932; cf. TR 1933, 345/58. P. Henry, *Plotin et l'Occident,* Lou 1934; partly in RSR 1934, 432/49 *(Adv. Arium).* F. Boemer, *Der lat. Neuplatonismus u. Neupythagoreismus u. Claud. Mamertus in Sprache u. Philosophie,* 1936, 74/96. Citterio, SC 1937, 505/15 (Osesi: azioni sulle opere crist.). W. Karig, *Des C. M. Vict. Komment. z. d. Paul. Briefen,* 1924. De Leusse, RSR 1939, 197/239 (Préexistence des âmes). K. Janssen, *Die Entstehung der Gnadenlehre Aug. s,* 1936, 28/38. —

On the spurious work *De physicis*: Vogels, RBn 1925, 224/38 (the Bible text: African, second half of 4th cent.). M. Michalski, *Nauka teolog. nieznanego autora traktatu De phys.*, Cracow 1937; cf. TR 1938, 272. Courcelle 1948, 196/8 (Porphyry attacked). Travis, HTR 1943, 83/90 (on biogr.). Séjourné, DTC fascs. 146/7, 2887/2954. P. Hadot, *La notion de Dieu "causa sui" chez M. V.*, thesis P 1949; *Typus Stoicisme et Monarchianisme au 4e s. d'après Candide l'Arien et M. V.*: RTA 1951, 177/87. B. Citterio, *C. M. Vittorino*, in Brescia 1948. Henry, JTS 1950, 42/55 (The *Adv. Arium*). G. M. Valveri, *La filosofia teologica di C. M. Vitt.*, Palermo 1950.

7. Zeno, Bishop of Verona from 363 to 371–2, a native of Mauretania, fought zealously against moribund paganism, Arianism and various abuses in his diocese. He left sixteen long and seventy-seven short sermons *(tractatus)*, the latter being for the greater part only drafts. (Here several duplicates: *Tract.* 2, 9 = 2, 20; 39/40 = 41 and 46 = 47). The preacher was a trained rhetor, whose language is strongly influenced by Apulejus of Madaura, Tertullian, Cyprian and Lactantius. He furnishes excellent evidence for the Church's teaching on the Trinity and on Mariology. He speaks especially frequently of baptism and the Easter liturgy.

Text: ML 11, 253/528 and J. B. C. Giuliari, Verona [2]1900. German by A. Bigelmair (BKV[2] II, 10) 1934. — Mg. by A. Bigelmair 1904. Doelger, AC 6, 1/56 (parable of the sun in II 9, 2). Grazioli, SC 1940, 174/99 (S. Zenone), 290/301 (il culto di S. Z.). Pesci, Ant 1948, 33/42 (on hist. of Chr. antiquity). M. Stepanich, *The Christology of Z. of V.*, W 1948. Bardy, DTC 15, 3685/90.

8. Filastrius, Bishop of Brescia (d. *c.* 397), composed a *Liber de haeresibus* (with 156 heresies) between 385 and 391. He probably did not use the *Syntagma* of Hippolytus, but Irenaeus and Epiphanius. Augustine *(De haer.)* drew on this work.

Edd.: ML 12, 1111/1302. F. Marx (CSEL 38) 1898. J. Wittig, *Fil., Gaudentius u. Ambrosiaster*, in KGAbh 8, 1909, 1/56. H. Frank, JL 13, 1936, 10/23 (on ch. 140). E. Schwartz, *2 Predigten Hippolyts*, 1936, 37f. D. Portarena, *Doctrina scripturistica s. Filastrii*, R 1946. CChL 9.

9. Of Gaudentius (d. after 406), Bishop of Brescia and successor of the aforementioned Filastrius, we have twenty-one sermons, the last of which treats of Filastrius. The first of the ten sermons preached in Easter Week treats of the eucharist.

Edd.: ML 20, 827/1002; A. Glueck (CSEL 68) 1936. J. Wittig 1909 (supra n. 8). H. A. Birch, *A Comparison of the Styles of G. of B., the De Sacramentis and the Didascalia Apost. or fragm. Veronensia,* Risca (Monmouth) 1924.

10. Pacian, Bishop of Barcelona (d. before 392), father of the praefectus praetorio Dexter, to whom Jerome dedicated his list of authors (supra § 2). It was he who said: *Christianus mihi nomen est, catholicus cognomen* (*Ep.* 1, 4; EH 627). He wrote three letters against an otherwise unknown Novatianist Sympronian (EP 1243/5) and a short treatise *Paraenesis sive exhortatorius libellus ad paenitentiam,* which are valuable sources for the penitential theory and practice of his time. His sermon *De baptismo* attests the doctrine of original sin.

G. Morin attempted to prove that two anti-Manichean works *Ad Justinum*—formerly wrongly ascribed to Marius Victorinus (ML 8, 999/1010) and claimed without further proof by J. Woehrer for Victorinus of Pettau (v. supra § 35)—and *De similitudine carnis peccati* (ed. Morin, *Études, Textes, Découvertes* I, 1913, 81/150) belong to Pacian. P. Borleffs adduces convincing philological reasons against Morin's thesis, but without suggesting another author (Mn 7, 1939, 180/92); cf. already Mercati, TR 1915, 116f. Borleffs did not know the arguments in favour of Morin's view advanced by L. Tria, *De sim. carn. pecc. Il suo autore e la sua Theologia,* R 1939, which, however, are not convincing. Another view, which is as new as it seems to be well founded, is that recently advanced by J. Madoz, EE 1942, 27/54. According to him *De sim. carn. pecc.* was written in the first half of the fifth century by the probably Spanish presbyter Eutropius mentioned by Gennadius, *Vir. ill.* 50 (ed. Richardson). Two other pseudo-Jeromian ascetica treatises, *De contemnenda hereditate* and *De vera circumcisione* (ML 30, 45/50; 188/210) are for good reasons ascribed to the same author; cf. RHE 1942, 414/7, where Morin agrees with the view of Madoz.

Edd.: ML 13, 1051/94. P. H. Peyrot, Zwolle 1896. — Treatises: Amann, DTC 11, 1718/21. García-Villada 1, 1, 1929, 327/51. Goeller, RQ 1928, 245/61 (doctr.

of penance). B. Poschmann, *Die abendlaend. Kirchenbusse,* 1928, 144/7. J. Vilar Pure, Est. Universitaris Catalans 17, 1932, 1/49 (Bibl. citations). Madoz, EE 1949, 234f. (Ovid). On Eutropius cf. now also: Cavallera, RAM 1948, 60/71. Courcelle, RevEA 1954, 378/90 (the ps.-Jerome Ep. 6: ML 30, 75/104 and an apocryphon of Max. of Turin: ML 57, 933/58 belong to Eutropius, who lived in Aquitania *c.* 400). Domínguez-Del Val, RET 1954, 369/92 (Eutrop. y sus fontes). Crit. ed. of L. R. Fernández, S. Paciano, Ba 1958.

11. Gregory, Bishop of Elvira (Eliberis) near Granada (d. after 392), was greatly esteemed as a defender of Nicene orthodoxy. He later also attacked Priscillianism; after the death of Lucifer of Calaris he became the head of his followers.

Only the most recent research has also restored his claim to literary honours by assigning to him various works that had survived under other names. a. *De fide orthodoxa,* an able defence of the ὁμοούσιος (ML 20, 31/50 under the name of Phoebadius. The work is also printed among those of Gregory of Nazianzus, Ambrose and Vigilius of Tapsus); a brief *Creed* of the faith (ibid. 49f.) belongs to it. b. The so-called twenty *Tractatus Origenis de libris s. Scripturae* (ed. Batiffol-Wilmart, P 1900); all sermons except the last take O.T. texts as their point of departure. c. *Tractatus de epithalamio,* five homilies on the Canticle; the sixth is still unedited (ed. G. Heine, L 1848). For the first time a Western author here applies the bridal imagery to Christ and the Church. d. *De arca Noe* (ed. Wilmart, RBn 1909, 1/12) and *Expositio in Ps. 91* (ed. Wilmart, RBn 1912, 274/93).

A. C. Vega, *Gregorii Elib. Op. Omnia,* E 1944, I (20 *Tract.*). —Juelicher, PWK 7, 1864/7. Clavis PL n. 546ff. H. Jordan, *Die Theologie der neuentdeckten Predigten Novatians,* 1902 (= 20 *Tract.*). H. Rahner, Bi 1941, 389 (for Novatian!). Wilmart, RBn 1912, 56f. (fragm. Gen. homs.). Vaccari, Bi 1922, 188/93 (Ps.-Jerome ep. 34 [ML 30, 245/8] belongs to G. of E.). García-Villada I, 2, 1929, 53/73. H. Koch, ZKG 1932, 238/72 (Sources of the 20 *Tract.*). Z. Cuevas y García Soriano in: BolAcadHist 106, 1935, 389/442, 479/84 (MS containing inter alia the Epithal.). F. Regina, *Il De fide di G. d'E.,* Pompeji 1942. Vega, CD 1944, 205/58 (comprehensive appreciation); 1945, 515/53 (*Comm. in Pr.* 30, 19f. = ML 17, 716/22 and *De fide* = ML 39, 1969/71 belong to G.). De Aldama (v. supra § 54, 20), 89/96 (Creed). S. González Rivas, RevEspir 6, 1947, 178/86 *(Aspecto de su espiritualidad).* A. García Conde, *Cuad. de Estud. Gallegos* 4, 1949, 27/56 (authors of the 20 *Tract.:* the 2 Avitus de Galecia mentioned by Orosius; on these cf. Altaner,

ZKG 1941, 459/62). J. Collantes Lozano, *S. G. di E. Estud. sobre eclesiología*, Granada 1954. A. C. Vega, *España Sagrada* 55, 1957 (contains inter alia the Opera Gregorii: *Epithal., Lib. de fide, 20 Tract. "Origenis"*). MLS1, 358ff.

12. Bachiarius a Spanish monk, not identical with Bishop Peregrinus, had to leave Spain, according to J. Duhr, on account of his Priscillianist sympathies. In 383–4 he wrote in Rome the *Libellus de fide* in order to justify himself, and later (between 394 and 400) the treatise *De lapso* in which he pleads for leniency towards a lapsed deacon. According to Morin, Bachiarius is thought to have taken part in the composition of two ascetical letters by a nun (ed. RBn 1928, 289/310.)

ML 20, 1019/63. Lambert, DHE 6, 58/68. J. Duhr, *Aperçus sur l'Espagne Chrét. du 4e s. ou le De lapso d. B.*, 1934; DS 1, 1187f. D'Alès, RSR 1933, 155ff. (= *Priscillien et l'Esp. chrét.*, 1936, 134ff.). De Aldama, Gr 1934, 589/98 *(B. y Rufino)*. MS of *De lapso* in R. Helssig, *Katalog der Hss der Univ.-Bibl. zu Leipzig*, IV 1, 1935. Cavallera, BLE 1938, 88/97 (Bach., Egeria and Symbol. Tolet. I). J. Madoz, RET 1941, 457/88 *(nueva redacción del Libellus)*; EE 1943, 201/11 (the new version in Ps.-Alcuin). Lawson, JTS 1943, 56/8 (MS). González, EE 1944, 361/73 (B. in Burchard of Worms). Murphy, Folia 5, 1951, 24/9 (Prosopography). J. Duhr, RHE 1952, 530/85 (The ps.-Cyprian letter in CSEL 3, 3, 274/82 prob. belongs to B.; *c.* 385); Text also ML 30, 278/82.

13. Optatus, Bishop of Milevis in Numidia, wrote in 365 against the Donatist bishop, Parmenian. His six books, today called *Contra Parmenianum Donatistam,* written in vigorous, sententious language, were intended to promote a peaceful solution. After 385 he produced a second, improved edition to which he added a seventh book.

Book I.: History of the schism. II.: There is only one true Church, united by the *una cathedra* of Peter, the *apostolorum caput* in Rome (EH 583f.; EP 1242). III.: The Catholics were not responsible for the government's measures against the Donatists. IV.: Against the wrong exegesis of Is. 66:3 and Ps. 140:5. V.: Against re-baptism and on baptism as *opus operatum*. VI.: On the fanaticism of the Donatists: destruction of the altars *(sedes et corporis et sanguinis Christi)* and the chalices *(Christi sanguinis portatores)*. VII.: Appendices: The *traditores* should be judged leniently.

A sermon preserved under the name of Augustine ed. G. Morin, *S. Augustini tract. sive sermones inediti,* 1917, 170/7; on this Wilmart, RevSR 1922, 271/301. Pincherle, RR 1947, 161/4 (author Donatist). P. Courcelle, *Les grandes invasions germaniques,* 1948, 227f. (Author a 5th cent. Optatus). ClavisPL n. 245. — Edd.: ML 11. C. Ziwsa (CSEL 26) 1893. H. V. Soden (KlT 122) 1913. O. R. Vassall-Philipps, *The Work of St. Opt. against the Donatists,* 1917. P. Monceaux (supra § 3), 5th vol., 1920. Amann, DTC 11, 1077/84. E. Altendorf, *Einheit u. Heiligkeit der Kirche,* 1932, 153/8. Blomgren, Er 1939, 85/120 (text crit.). Emonds 1941, 72/82. L. Vischer, *Basilius d. Gr.,* Basel 1953, ch. 4 (digression on *Opt.'s* concept of the Church). MLS1, 288ff.

§ 82. HERETICAL AUTHORS

1. It is not certain that Potamius, Bishop of Lisbon (d. *c.* 360) composed the so-called second Sirmian Formula (357) together with Hosius (ML 10, 482 and 487). His negligible literary remains (two dogmatic letters and two sermons) obviously belong to the time before his defection to Arianism.

PL 8, 1411/8; Wilmart, RBn 1913, 257/85 *(Ep. ad Athan.)*; JTS 19, 1917/8, 289/304 *(De Laz.)*. Madoz, RET 1947, 79/109. MLS1, 202.

2. Ulphilas (d. 383), the famous Arian bishop of the Goths, composed many literary works, but with the exception of a Latin homoean Mass Creed and a baptismal Creed reproduced in the *Epistola* of Auxentius (v. n. 3), only the fragments of his Gothic translation of the Bible have survived. It is not certain whether he also translated the O.T.

W. Streitberg, *Die got. Bibel,* I³ II² 1950. H. van Bakel, *Circa sacra,* Haarlem 1935, 86/113 (Creed of W.). G. W. S. Friedrichsen, *The Gothic Version of the Gospels,* 1926; cf. Wilmart, RB 1927, 46/61. Giesecke 1939, 5/41 (life and doctrine). J. de Vries, *Wulfilae Codices Ambrosiani,* 3 vols., Tu 1936, Bigelmair, LTK 10, 362/4. Bardy, DTC 15, 2084/57. Steubing, ZKT 64, 1952/3, 137/65 (on Goth. trans. of Bible).

3. The Arian Auxentius, Bishop of Dorostorum (Silistria), a pupil of Ulphilas, is the author of an *Epistola de fide, vita et obitu Wulfilae* (in F. Kaufmann, *Aus der Schule des Wulfila,* 1899, 73/6, and Giesecke 1939, 16/22). This important letter has been preserved

because the Arian bishop, Maximinus, included it in a work directed against St. Ambrose (*Dissertatio Maximini contra Ambrosium;* in F. Kaufmann, 65/90) in 383. Later Bishop Maximinus (427–8) opposed St. Augustine in a disputation at Hippo (cf. the minutes of it in MS 42, 709/42). Recently approximately forty sermons and three polemical works have been assigned to him.

Capelle, RBn 1922, 81/108; 1923, 24/6; 1926, 5/15; 1928, 49/86. Spagnolo and Turner, JTS 13, 1911/2, 19/28; 16, 1914/5, 161/76, 314/22; 17, 1915/6, 225/35, 321/37; 20, 1918/9, 89ff. (publ. under the name of Maximus of Turin). Turner, JTS 20, 1918/9, 289/310; 24, 1922/3, 71/9 (essentially agrees with the results of Capelle). Capelle, RBn 1922, 224/33 (letter of Auxentius). Zeiller, RH 1934, 535/40 (Maximin in Africa); RHE 1934, 847/51 (Letter of A. on Montanism). Giesecke 1939, 16/22 (Letter of A.). Klein, ZDADL 83, 1951/2, 239/71 (The dissert. of Max. as a source of the Life of Ulphilas); 84, 1953, 99/154 (A.'s letter on Ulphilas). Beitr. z. Gesch. f. dtsch. Spr. u. Lit. 75, 1953, 165/91 (A. identical with Milan Bishop Aux.). MLS1, 693/764 (Maximinus).

4. The *Opus imperfectum in Matthaeum,* written by an Arian bishop, was preserved anonymously. It is a mutilated Latin commentary full of original ideas which enjoyed a high reputation down to the sixteenth century, being held to be a work of St. John Chrysostom. The work was frequently ascribed to Ulphilas or to the Gothic bishop, Maximinus (supra n. 3). G. Morin dates it *c.* 550. According to him the author, an Arian bishop in N. Italy, is identical with the Latin translator of Origen's commentary on Matthew.

MG 56, 611/946. T. Paas, *Das Opus imp. in Mt.,* 1907. Morin, RBn 1925, 239/62. Wotke, PWK 18, 1, 824/6.

5. We owe the first Latin compendium of Biblical hermeneutics, the *Liber regularum* (*c.* 380) to the Donatist Tyconius; an extract from it has been preserved also in Augustine, *De doctr. christ.* 3, 30/7. His *Commentary on the Apocalypse* exercised a lasting influence; while completely rejecting the historical as well as the chiliastic interpretation, he gained recognition for the spiritual exegesis. A large part of the work has been preserved in the compilation of the Spanish presbyter Beatus of Libana, composed *c.* 786.

Lib. Reg.: ed. F. C. Burkitt, C 1894. ML 18, 15/66. — T. Hahn, Tyconius-Studien, 1900. Monceaux (supra § 3) 5, 165/219. H. A. Sanders, *Beati in Apocalipsin libri XII,* R 1930. Dinkler, PWK II 6, 649/56. H. van Bakel, *Circa sacra,* Haarlem 1935, 114/35. H. J. Vogels, *Unters. z. Gesch. der lat. Apok.-Uebers.,* 1920. Pincherle, RR 1925, 443/56 (T. and August.). Morin, RBn 1933, 43/61 (T. and the sermons on the Apoc. of Caesarius). Bardy, DTC. I. M. Gómez, Misc. Ubach 1935, 387/411 (Comm. on Apoc.). Ratzinger, REAug 2, 1956, 173/86 (Tyc.'s concept of the Church). Forster, MTZ 1956, 173/83 (Tyc.s' *Corpus*-concept). MLS1 621/52.

6. Priscillian, a rich, highly educated layman of great moral integrity, became *c.* 375 the founder of a sect in the South of Spain. It largely revived Gnostic Manichean errors and cultivated prophetic enthusiasm and the reading of apocryphal, partly heretical writings. In 385 Priscillian was condemned at Treves for magic *(maleficium)* by the usurper Emperor Maximus and, despite the opposition of St. Martin of Tours, executed together with six followers.

Eleven treatises have been preserved anonymously and were assigned to Priscillian by their first editor G. Schepss. They are disappointing in that we cannot glean much tangible material for the characterization of this heresy from them, partly, it is true, written with an apologetic tendency. G. Morin assigned these writings to a follower of Priscillian, Bishop Instantius. Despite some opposition this view continues to find much favour. Of the eleven treatises the three most important are: *Liber apologeticus, Liber ad Damasum episcopum* and *De fide (et) de apocryphis.*

We would also mention here an anonymous treatise which originated in Priscillianist circles: *De Trinitate fidei catholicae;* ed. Morin, *Ét., Textes, Découvertes* I, 1913, 159/205; cf. TR 1915, 118.

G. Schepss (CSEL 18) 1899. K. Kuenstle, *Eine Bibliothek der Symbole,* 1900; *Antipriscilliana,* 1905. E. C. Babut, *Priscillien et Priscillianisme,* 1909. Morin, RBn 1913, 153/73 (Instantius author of the 11 Tract.); against this M. Hartberger, TQ 1913, 401/30 and *Priscillianea,* 1922; J. Martin, HJB 1927, 237/51; for it J. A. Davids, *De Orosio et s. Augustino Priscillianistarum adversariis commentatio,* Haag 1930 and D'Alès, RSR 1933, 5/44, 129/75 and *Priscillien et l'Espagne chrét.,* 1936. Bardy, DTC 13, 391/400. J. A. de Aldama, *El símbolo Toledano* I, R 1934. Barnikol, Theol. Jb. 1936/7, 6/18 (Phil. 2, 6f.). Perez de Urbel, RET 1946, 589/606 (Trinit.

doctr.). Bishko, AJP 69, 1948, 377/95 (Spanish *Consensoria monachorum* written in 7th cent., not Priscillianist, against De Bruyne). M. Martin, *Correntes da Filosofia relig. em Braga dos IV a VII,* Porto 1950 (on Priscillianism, Prosius, Martin of Dumio). I. M. Ramos y Losetales, *Acta Salmanticensia,* 1952 (Prisciliano).

7. Pelagius, probably a native of Ireland, arrived in Rome *c.* 384 to obtain a good scholarly (perhaps also juridical) education. He was an ascetic who lived in Rome till 410, at last as a lay monk, held in high esteem because of his moral austerity. His theological thought was mainly influenced by the Ambrosiaster (§ 84, 1), but hardly at all by Greek theologians (Clement of Alex., Chrysostom, Theodore of Mopsuestia). The doctrines on nature and grace, original sin and infant baptism, later to be known by his name, became, very probably, familiar to him through his personal contact with Rufinus the Syrian, who had come to Rome from one of St. Jerome's monasteries at Bethlehem in 399 (§ 82, 8).

In 411 his teaching began to be opposed at Carthage, where he had fled from the Visigoths together with his friend Caelestius. Augustine began his literary feud with him in 412. After the new doctrines had been rejected by several African synods and by the Popes Innocent I and Zosimus, the Council of Ephesus (canon 1 and 4), too, agreed to the judgement of the West in 431.

Of the many writings of Pelagius the following are preserved in full and universally recognized as genuine:

a. *Expositions of the Pauline Letters* (without Hebr.), which was circulated in a revised form under the names of St. Jerome (ML 30, 645/902) and Primasius of Hadrumetum (ML 68, 413/686). The original text, however, is preserved in a Reichenau MS of the ninth century.

b. An *Epistola ad Demetriadem seu liber de institutione virginis* (ML 30, 15/45 and 33, 1099/1120); the recipient is a Roman Patrician lady on whose behalf Jerome (*Ep.* 130) and Augustine (*Ep.* 150) also wrote letters.

c. A short work *Libellus fidei ad Innocentium papam* (ML 48, 488/91).

d. The researches of G. de Plinval have created an entirely new situation. He attributes in all another nineteen minor works to Pelagius on the grounds of internal evidence, the weight of which he emphasizes especially in his last work (1947) which examines the style and language of Pelagius more closely. These are letters and treatises which until then had been attributed either to Jerome, Fastidius and others, or had remained anonymous.

Cf. G. de Plinval, RP 1934, 9/42; RSPT 1936, 429/58; RHE 1939, 5/21; Fliche-Martin, *Hist. générale de L'Église* IV, 1939, 79/128; G. de Plinval, *Pélage. Ses écrits, sa vie et sa réforme,* Lausanne 1943; *Essai sur le style et la langue de P.,* Fri 1947.

According to de Plinval the following twelve works are undoubtedly genuine: 1. *Lib. de vita christ.* (ML 40, 1031/46, also 50, 383/402); 2. *De divitiis* (ed. C. P. Caspari, *Briefe, Abhandl. u. Predigten . . .,* 1890, 25/67); 3. *Ep. de malis doctoribus* (ibid. 67/73); 4. *De divina lege* (ML 30, 55/60); 5. *De virginitate* (ML 30, 163/75, also CSEL 1, 224/50); 6. *Ep. de castitate* (Caspari, l. c. 122/87); 7. *De possibilitate non peccandi* (incomplete, in Caspari, l. c. 114/9); 8. *Consolatio ad virginem* (ML 30, 55/60); 9. *Ep. ad Claudiam* (ML 20, 223/7, also CSEL 1, 219/23); 10. *Ep. ad Oceanum* (ML 30, 282/8); 11. *Ep. ad Marcellam* (ML 30, 50/5, also CSEL 29, 429/36); 12. *Ep. ad Celantiam* (ML 22, 1204/12, also CSEL 29, 436/59 and 56, 329/56).

Seven works regarded as not certainly by Pelagius: 1. *De renuntiatione saeculi* (ML 30, 239/42); 2. *De vera poenitentia* (ML 30, 242/5); *Ep. ad virginem devotam* (ML 17, 579/98); 4. *De contemnenda hereditate* (ML 30, 1145/50); 5. *De vera circumcisione* (ML 30, 188/210); 6. *Lib. de induratione cordis Pharaonis* (1st ed. in De Plinval 1947, 136/203 with trans.); 7. *Ep. ad adulescentem* (in Caspari, l. c. 14/21).

e. The following writings of Pelagius are known to us through citations and separately transmitted fragments: 1. *Lib. Eclogarum* collected in ML 48, 593/6; 2. *De natura* (ML 48, 598/606); 3. *De libero arbitrio* (ML 48, 611/15 and JTS 12, 1910/1, 32/5); 4. On four fragments probably taken from the four books *De trinitate* cf. Martini, Ant 1938, 293/331; 5. On fragments of two works assigned by Morin to the Ambrosiaster, cf. C. Martini, *Ambrosiaster,* R 1944; 6. Acc. to Plinval the texts publ. by Morin, RBn 1922, 265/75 (*Epp. ad Livaniam* etc.) and assigned to Fastidius also belong to Pelagius; 7. Fragm. of a Comm. in Cant. and a treatise *De bono constantiae* in Bede (ML 91, 1066/77).

A. Souter, *P.' Expositions of 13 Epistles of St. Paul,* 2 vols., 1922/6. J. A. Robinson, *P.' Expositions of 13 Epistles of St. P.: Pseudo-Jerome Interpolations,* C 1931. R. Hedde and E. Amann, DTC 12, 675/715; Gaudel, ibid. 12, 382/406. Coméliau, RHE 1935, 77/89 *(Orat. P.i).* H. Koch, RR 1933, 44/62 (*vita aet.* and *regnum cael.* before P.); Rel 1935, 21/30 (P. and Hebr.). On *Ep. ad Demetr.* cf. Consette, NRT 1933, 783/801. Michalski, CT 1936, 143/62 (Christology). Stelzenberger 1933, 178/82. On P. and Ephesinum v. supra § 50, 17. J. J. Dempsey, *P.' Comment. on St. Paul,* R 1937. Dold, RBn 1939, 122/38 (on Bibl. citations of texts in RBn 1922, 265/75). Madoz, EE 1942, 27/39 (v. supra § 81, 10: Eutropius). Rivière, RHE 1946, 5/43 (P. in his doctr. of Redemption not always heret.). Birch, HJ 1947, 56/62 (freedom of the will). Bardy, BLE 1948, 3/20 (beginning of Pelag. controversies). E. Florkowski, *Soteriologia Pelagiusza,* Cracow 1949. Martini, RR 20, 1949, 35/64 (6 fragms. from *De Trinit.*). ClavisPL n. 728/55, 757/66. De Plinval, REL 1951, 284/94 *(Vue d'ensemble de la litt. pélag.).* — De Bruyne, RBn 1931, 142/4 (ed. of anti-Pelag. testimonies). MLS 1, 1101/1570. T. Bohlin, *Die Theol. des Pelag. u. ihre Genesis,* Up — Wiesbaden 1957. J. Ferguson, *Pelagius,* Lo 1957. De Plinval, RSR 1958, 227/36 (Theology of P.).

8. The *Liber de fide,* edited as a spurious work of Rufinus of Aquileia in ML 21, 1123/54 and again ML 48, 451/88, though incomplete, very probably belongs to Rufinus Syrus, mentioned in § 82, 7. The author knew Greek, and his work, which may be called a brief compendium of Pelagian principles, was probably written after 412.

Altaner, TQ 1950, 432/9 (The *Liber de fide,* a work of the Pelagian Rufinus the Syrian). On a Leningrad MS cf. Dobiasche-Rojdestvensky in Sp 5, 1930, 21/48; cf. ClavisPL n. 200 and n. 905.

9. The deacon Anianus of Celeda wrote (before 419) a controversial work against Jerome (Jer., *Ep.* 143, 2) which defended Pelagianism. He is also the only fifth century translator of works of Chrysostom whose name is known to us. He very probably

translated all ninety *Homilies in Mt.* between 419 and 421. Only the first twenty-five homilies are extant or printed, and those only in the older Latin editions of Chrysostom, e.g. *Joh. Chrysostomi Opera omnia latina,* Paris 2, 1581, 1/226. Montfaucon and after him MG 58, 975/1058 only gives the translation of the first eight homilies on Matthew. Chrysostom's seven panegyrics on St. Paul were not translated into Latin before 419–20 (MG 50, 471/514). It cannot be stated with certainty that Anianus translated also other homilies of Chrysostom, as is almost generally believed.

Altaner, HJB 61, 1941, 215/7. Honigmann, ST 173, 54/8 (A. perhaps identical with Greek-writing author of a world chronicle, cf. § 49, 13).

10. Despite much research the writings of the British bishop, Fastidius (first half of fifth century), who is counted among the Pelagians, cannot so far be identified with certainty. According to Gennadius, *Vir. ill.* 56, he composed two treatises *(De vita christiana* and *De viduitate servanda).* Here, too, the studies of De Plinval have created a new situation.

C. P. Caspari, *Briefe, Abhandl. u. Pred. aus den letzten 2 Jahrh. des christl. Altertums . . .,* Christiania 1890, 352/75. J. Kirmer, *Das Eigentum des Fastidius im pelag. Schrifttum,* 1938 (K. assigns 12 works to him); cf. Altaner, TR 1938, 232/5 and esp. De Plinval, RHE 1939, 5/21.

11. Julian, Bishop of Aeclanum near Benevent. Expelled from his see in 418, he lived for a time with Theodore of Mopsuestia and Nestorius in Constantinople; d. *c.* 454. He was the systematic exponent of Pelagianism, in his exegesis he followed the Antiochene school. Very large portions of his treatise *Ad Turbantium* (four books) and *Ad Florum* (eight books) have come down to us through three treatises in which Augustine replied to him. Recently three exegetical writings have been assigned to him: the pseudo-Rufinian commentary on three Minor Prophets (ML 21); a commentary on Job ed. by A. Amelli, *Spicil. Casinense,* 3, I, 1897, 333/417, and also the commentary on the Psalms ed. by G. J. Ascoli, *Archivio glottologico ital.* 5, 1878/89, 8/610 may be

assigned to Julian, following Vaccari. Occasionally Julian has incorporated brief verbatim citations from Theodore of Mopsuestia's commentary on the Psalms. The exegesis of Ps. 16:11 ff. and even more that of Ps. 40:14 ff. may be considered a version of Theodore of Mopsuestia's Commentary on the Psalms (§ 68, 1). Morin stresses that Columbanus, too, influenced the shape of the commentary.

Forget, DTC 8, 1926/31; Hedde et Amann, ibid. 12, 702/7. Mg. by A. Bruckner, 1897; *Die 4 Buecher an Turbantius,* 1910. Devreesse, DBSuppl 1, 1131 f.; RB 1928, 365 f. Bover, EE 1933, 405/14 *(Antioch. theoria).* Morin, RBn 1913, 1/24 (3 Minor Prophets). A. Vaccari, *Un commento a Giobbe di Giul. di Ecl.,* 1915; cf. D'Alès, RSR 1916, 311/24; Stiglmayr, ZKT 1919, 269/88 (against Vaccari). Vaccari, Misc. Amelli 1920, 43/51. — Vaccari, CC 1916, I, 578/96; Bi 1923, 337/51 and AL 1924, 185 (Pss. Comm.). Morin, RBn 1926, 164/77 (J. and Columba). R. I. Best, *The Comm. on the Psalms with Glosses in Old Irish Pres. in the Ambros. Libr.,* 1936; JTS 1938, 188/90; RBn 1940, 162 f. Vaccari, Misc. Mercati I, 175/98. Baxter, AL 21, 1949, 5/54 (J.'s Latin confirms his authorship of the commentaries on Job and Pss.). MLS1, 1573/1679 (comm. on Job). Bourman, *Des Jul. v. Aecl. Komm. zu den Propheten Osee, Joel u. Amos,* R 1858.

§ 83. AMBROSE OF MILAN (339–97)

Ambrose came from a noble Roman family and was probably born at Treves in 339, his father being *praefectus praetorio Galliarum.* After the latter's early death his mother returned to Rome with her three children. Here his sister Marcellina took the veil of consecrated virgins (v. supra § 78, 2); his brother Satyrus, who was a high state official for some time, had already died in 378. About 370 Ambrose, who had received a rhetorical and legal training, became *consularis Liguriae et Aemiliae* with his official residence at Milan.

After the death of the Arian bishop, Auxentius (v. § 80, 3c), the episcopal election led to violent scenes between Catholics and Arians. When Ambrose in his consular capacity attempted to mediate, he was suddenly elected bishop by both parties, as if by higher intervention and despite his energetic resistance, for he was only a catechumen at that time. He was consecrated bishop eight days after his baptism, probably on December 7, 374.

He first devoted himself to theological studies, especially to reading the Greek Fathers, under the direction of the priest Simplicianus who later became his successor. He distributed his considerable fortune among the poor and began to lead a strictly ascetical life. His house was always open to high and lowly alike, and he was constantly besieged by those seeking help. He had extraordinary success as a pulpit orator; cf. Augustine, *Conf.* 6, 4, 6.

He exercised a decisive influence especially on the ecclesiastical and political situation of his time. He fought fearlessly and unrelentingly for the exclusive rights of the Church against paganism, Arianism and other heresies, and not least for its freedom and autonomy in its relations with the secular power ("The Emperor is within the Church, not above the Church"; *Contra Aux.* 35).

It was due to him that the statue of the goddess of victory, which Gratian had removed from the council-room of the senate in 382, was not allowed to be restored, despite the efforts made by the pagan majority of the senate led by the rhetor Symmachus. He also succeeded in frustrating the attempts of the Arian-minded Empress-Mother Justina to give recognition to that heresy by letting the Arians have one of the Milan churches. It is due above all to his energy (Synods of Aquileia 381 and Rome 382) that Arianism was forced back especially in the Illyrian provinces. Ambrose, the friend and adviser of three emperors, was the first bishop to whom princes appealed to support their tottering throne (against the usurper Maximus and the Frank Arbogast). He won respect for the laws of the Church even from the great Theodosius I. When, in consequence of a revolt, the Emperor had ordered the massacre of 7000 people at Thessalonica (in 390), Ambrose wrote him a letter in which he frankly pointed out the greatness of his guilt and the necessity to expiate it. Thereupon the Emperor submitted to public penance (*Ob. Theod.*

34; EH 624 f.). When Theodosius died (395) Ambrose delivered the funeral oration. He himself died in 397; his body rests in the basilica of Milan. Feast day: December 7.

Ambrose was an outstanding personality of perfect purity and utter selflessness, which made a strong impression on all who came into contact with him. Beside Theodosius I, he was the most brilliant man of his time, one of the great minds whose work and thought later furnished essential material for the growing medieval culture.

It is astonishing that despite his extensive pastoral and teaching activity among his flock Ambrose should have found sufficient time to write so many books. It is true, most of them, especially the exegetical writings, grew out of his pastoral work. They are sermons which were made into books after having been but slightly revised; they have an edifying tendency. In his other writings, too, the pastoral and moral interest is uppermost. Ambrose was an authentically Roman, practical personality; though he had received a philosophical education he had neither time nor inclination, nor probably the intellectual equipment, for dogmatic speculation. Hence his moral and ascetical works show independence, whereas he is very dependent on the Greek Fathers in his Biblical and dogmatic writings. His language is frequently of oratorical vigour and poetic beauty, especially in the sermons, and is rich in allusions, especially to Roman classics (Virgil); but it can also be sententiously pithy and polished.

About 422 the cleric Paulinus, his former secretary who had emigrated to Africa, wrote an edifying *Vita s. Ambrosii* (ML 14, 27/46. M. S. *Kaniecka,* W 1928) at the suggestion of St. Augustine.

Ital. trans.: Mi 1930 (anonymous). Criticism of the Vita: G. Gruetzmacher in Festg. A. Hauck 1916, 77/84; J. R. Palanque, *S. Ambroise et l'empire rom.,* 1933, 409/16. Pellegrino, SC 1951, 151/60. On the apocr. *Libellus de benedictionibus patriarch.* cf. Wilmart, RBn 1920, 57/63.

Edd.: J. du Frisch and N. le Nourry, 2 vols., 1686/90. ML 14–17. Exeget. writings ed. C. Schenkl and M. Petschenig (CSEL 32 [3 parts]. 62 64) 1897/1919;

O. Faller, CSEL 73, 1955 *(Explan. Symb., Sacram., Myst., Paenit., Exc. fratris, Ob. Valent., Ob. Theod.)*. Separate edd.: *De virg.* ed. O. Faller (FP 31) 1935, *Ob. Satyri* ed. B. Albers (FP 15) 1921. *Ob. Theod.* ed. M. D. Mannix, W 1925. *Hel. et ieiun.* ed. M. I. A. Buck, W 1929. *De Nabuthe* ed. P. McGuire, W 1927. *De Tobia* ed. L. M. Zucker, W 1933. *De myst.* and *de sacr.* J. Quasten (FP 7) 1936, 113ff. *De consol. Valent.* ed. T. A. Kelly, W 1941. *L'Esamerone* ed. E. Pasteris (with trans.), Tu 1937. *Dei doveri degli Eccles.* (with trans.) ed. A. Cavasin, Tu 1938. Works on virginity ed. M. Salvati (with trans.), Tu 1938. *De virginibus*, ed. crit. I. Cazzaniga, Tu 1948; *De virginitate*, ed. crit., Tu 1954. *De sacram.* with trans. ed. B. Botte, 1949 (SCh 23). *De Spir. Sancto* ed. G. Crone, Mr 1952. *Explan. Symb.* ed. R. H. Connolly - C. Butler, C 1952 (with trans.). *De Nabuthe*, ed. L. Molle, Brescia 1952 (with trans.). — Germ.: J. E. Niederhuber (BKV² 17, 21, 32) 1914/7. J. Huhn, *Ambr., Der Tod — ein Gut* (text and trans.), 1949. T. Thompson-Srawley, *De sacram.* and *De myst.* (SPCK) (trans.), 1950. J. Wytzes, trans. of Letters (Dutch), A 1950. J. Huhn, trans. *De Nabuthe*, Fr 1950. M. Beyenka, trans. of Letters (FathCh), 1954. — Mgg.: A. Baunard, P ³1899. P. de Labriolle, P 1908. A. Largent, DTC 1, 942/51. U. Moricca, Tu 1928. E. K. Rand, *Founders of the Middle Ages*, C (Mass.) 1928, 69/101. H. v. Campenhausen, *A. v. M. als Kirchenpolitiker*, 1929. J. R. Palanque, *S. A. et l'Empire romain*, 1933. F. H. Dudden, 2 vols., O 1935. A. Queirolo, R 1939. I. Card. Schuster, Mi 1940; *S. A. e le più antiche basiliche mil.*, Mi 1940. L. Castano, Tu 1940. A. Paredi, Mi 1941. M.-A. Nagl, Mr 1940. P. Gorla, Mi 1944.

Sant' Ambrogio nel XVI Centenario della Nascita, Mi 1940 (contains 25 contributions, mostly doctrinal and philosophical). *Ambrosiana, Scritti di Storia, Archeologia ed Arte pubbl. nel XVI Centenario della Nascita di S. A.*, Mi 1942; here 45/95: Galbiati (What did the East know of A.?); 97/112: Faller (episc. consecration: 7. XII. 374). — On biogr.: Doelger, AC 3, 62/72 (education of youth). J. Wytzes, *Der Streit um d. Altar der Viktoria* (text and comm.), A 1936. Wilmart, EL 1936, 169/206 *(S. A. et la Légende dorée)*. Van Haeringen, Mn 5, 1937, 28/33, 229/40 (Valentin. II and A. 386). Grazioli, SC 1940, 373/9 *(La giuridiz. di Milano a Verona)*. Cordiglia, SC 1941, 148/54 *(mallatia e morte)*. H. Lietzmann, Sb 1940 n. 11 (Church and state). Saba, *S. Ambrogio nel XVI Cent.*, 1940, 533/69 *(L'opera politica)*. Paribeni, ibid. 17/29 *(Romanità di S. A.)*. Wilbrand, TG 1941, 190/5 (the bishop); *Z. Missionsw. u. Religionsw.* 1941, 97/104 (the missionary bishop). L. Malunowicz, *De ara Victoriae in Curia Rom . . .*, Wilmo 1937. Brok, *Hist. Tydschr.* 1939, 17/35 (Empress Justina). Zavaglio, BollStorCrem 1941, 141/64 (A. and Crema). Schuster, Misc. Mercati V, 48/60 (oldest portrait of A.). Katzenellenbogen, ArtBull, NY 1947, 249/59 (sarcophagus). U. Pestalozza, *La religione di A.*, Mi 1949. Calderini, Misc. G. Galbiati, Mi 3, 1951, 111/16 (first embassy to Treves). Grumel, REB 1951, 154/60 (second embassy to Maximus). A. Alfoeldi, *A Conflict of Ideas in the Late Rom. Empire*. Trans. by H. Mattingly, O 1952. H. Tissot, *Ambr., In Lc. I (lib. 1–6)*, in SCh 45 (with trans.), 1956 and 52, 1958. CChL 14 (Fragm. in Is.). MLS 1, 569/620.

1. In his exegetical writings, which form the greater part of his literary remains, Ambrose follows the Jew Philo and Origen in

assuming the threefold sense of Scripture (v. supra § 40); as a preacher he favours the moralizing and allegorizing interpretation. For contents, too, he depends on these two exegetes more than most other Christian writers. Hence his exegesis is nothing but a sum of allegorical and typological interpretations of the sacred text, even though somewhat moderated by the influence of St. Basil. Ambrose finds profound instructions on faith and life even in the most insignificant facts of Biblical history; for example he understands Noe's ark of the human body, in the various members of which he recognizes the diverse parts of the ark, and compares the animals in the ark with the carnal desires. He has only treated O.T. books or texts, with the single exception of the commentary on Luke.

a. The six books of the Hexaemeron are a literary masterpiece full of brilliant descriptions of nature; it was composed from nine homilies in connexion with Basil's work of the same name after 388 (EP 315/9).

b. Other treatises, nearly all derived from homilies, deal with the following subjects: *De Paradiso, De Cain et Abel, De Noe, De Abraham* (two books), *De Isaac et anima, De Jacob et vita beata* (two books), *De Joseph, De Patriarchis* (Gen. 49), *De Helia et ieiunio, De Nabuthe, De Tobia, De interpellatione Job et David, Apologia prophetae David.* Also *Enarrationes in 12 psalmos* (1, 35–40 43 45 47 48 61) and a very expansive *Expositio in psalmum 118* (EP 1258/63, 1278f., 1312/24; EA 380ff.).

c. The largest of all Ambrose's works is the *Commentary on Luke's Gospel* in ten books, containing about twenty-five sermons and several treatises; books I and II are completely dependent on Origen (EP 1301/10; EA 422/36).

2. *Moral-ascetical writings*

a. The three books *De Officiis ministrorum,* written after 386 and addressed to the clergy of the Milan Church, are the first comprehensive presentation of Christian ethics. It is a companion to Cicero's work of the same title, of Stoic tendency, which Ambrose follows also in the arrangement of his material (EA 444/50).

b. Ambrose praises virginity and especially the order of consecrated virgins in several works: *De virginibus ad Marcellinam sororem* (three books, v. supra § 78, 2), *De viduis, De virginitate, De institutione virginis, Exhortatio virginitatis* and others; on a spurious treatise v. infra and § 84, 2.

3. Dogmatic writings

a. He defends the divinity of the Son against the Arians in five books *De fide ad Gratianum* (381). The three books *De Spiritu Sancto* were also written at the request of the Emperor Gratian to whom they are dedicated. *De incarnationis dominicae sacramento* (EP 1264/74, 1280/9) is also directed against Arianism.

b. *De mysteriis,* destined for the newly baptized, treats baptism, confirmation and the eucharist (EP 1329/34). The author discusses the same questions and, in addition, the Our Father in *De sacramentis libri VI.* These two treatises, written in 390–1, are very important for the history of the Liturgy. According to Morin they are lectures of Ambrose taken down in shorthand and then revised (EP 1336/40). Together with Faller, Frank, Botte and Connolly we may now assert that the treatise is genuine. The authenticity of the brief *Explanatio symboli ad initiandos* is not undisputed, but it is rightly defended as genuine by Connolly (1946) and Faller (ed. 1955).

c. *De paenitentia* (two books), between 387 and the beginning of 390, opposes the rigorism of the Novatianists; only the Catholic Church (not the heretics) has the power to forgive sins. Ecclesiastical penance applies only to the *peccata graviora* and is possible only once: *nam si vere agerent paenitentiam (sc. peccatores), iterandam postea non putarent, quia sicut unum baptisma* (Eph. 4, 5), *ita una paenitentia, quae tamen publice agitur* (II 10, 95; EH 598/603; EP 1292/1300).

d. *Expositio fidei.* Of this work only a fairly long citation is extant in the *Eranistes* of Theodoret of Cyrus (ML 16, 847/50). The authenticity is disputed.

Pertusi, Aev 1944, 184/207 (A. in the Gr. collections of test.: *Expositio* spurious); so also Bardy, Misc. Mercati I, 199/218; against it Richard, Actes VI Congrès InternatÉtByz 1, 1950, 314/6.

4. Orations and Letters, important for the history of the time and of fine literary workmanship. The following have been preserved: *Two funeral orations* on the death of his brother Satyrus (d. 378; EP 1275/7), an oration on the occasion of the funeral of the murdered Emperor Valentinian II (d. 392; EP 621/3), an oration at the obsequies of the Emperor Theodosius I (395; EH 624/6) and a *Sermo contra Auxentium de basilicis tradendis* (396) when Valentinian II had ordered the Milan churches to be given over to the Arians. The letters that were published by Ambrose himself have been preserved only in an incomplete state. Today only ninety-one *Letters* are extant. *Ep.* 23 is spurious. They are for the greater part official letters, records, accounts of synodal proceedings etc.

5. Unlike Hilary's (v. supra § 80, 4) efforts to introduce congregational singing, those of Ambrose were successful. He is the creator of the liturgical hymns in the Western Church. In 386, hymn singing as well as the antiphonal singing of Psalms were firmly established in the Milan Church. From there this kind of chant spread throughout the West.

Ambrose was not only a writer but also a composer of hymns; in his music he was dependent on the Greek church tunes, as is expressly attested by Augustine (*Conf.* 9, 7). From the seventh century church hymns have been called Ambrosian, hence those preserved under his name are not always his work. Augustine attests as Ambrosian the following four hymns in metrically correct iambic dimeters divided into verses of four lines each:

Deus creator omnium (an evening hymn; *Conf.* 9, 12), *Aeterne rerum conditor* (a morning hymn; *Retract.* 1, 21), *Iam surgit hora tertia* (on Christ's death on the Cross; *De nat. et grat.,* c. 63), *Intende qui regis Israel* (a Christmas hymn; *Sermo* 372). At least eight more hymns may be assigned to Ambrose; Dreves considers fourteen, Walpole eighteen to be genuine; Simonetti thinks nine are genuine and four more probably genuine.

Ambrose also composed verse inscriptions, e. g. for the baptistry of the church of St. Thecla in Milan. On the so-called Ambrosian Hymn *Te Deum laudamus* v. infra § 84, 2; on the so-called *Symbolum Athanasianum* v. supra § 54, 20.

6. Spurious writings. *Hegesippus sive de bello Iudaico* is a Latin translation of the *Jewish War* of Flavius Josephus which originated towards the end of the fourth century and appeared anonymously. Morin thinks the *Res gestae Machabaeorum* mentioned in the Prologue of the work can be traced in a *Passio Machabaeorum* which has not yet been published. Dexter, the friend of St. Jerome, may be its author. The *Lex Dei sive Mosaicarum et Romanarum legum collatio* has not been preserved complete; it is important for legal history and presents Roman Law as dependent on the O.T. law (*c.* 394–5); nothing certain can be affirmed about its author.

Mgg.: G. M. Dreves, *Ambr., der Vater des Kirchengesanges,* 1893. A. Steier, *Unters. ueber d. Echtheit der Hymnen des A.,* 1903. Ermoni, DAL 1, 1347/52 (hymns). P. Ramatschi, *Die Quellen von De fide ad Grat.,* thesis Br 1923. G. Mamone, Did 1924, F. 2, 3/164 (Letters). M. F. Barry, *The Vocabulary of the Moral-ascet. Works of St. A.,* W 1926. S. M. Adams, *The Latinity of the Letters of St. A.,* W 1927. M. Klein, *Meletemata Ambros.,* thesis Koenigsberg 1927 *(De Exaemeri fontibus).* M. Martin, *The Use of Indirect Discourse in the Works of St. A.,* W 1930. M. Carpaneto, Did 1930, F. 1, 35/156 *(opere oratorie).* M. D. Diederich, *Vergil in the Works of St. A.,* W 1931. M. T. Springer, *Nature-Imagery in the Works of St. A.,* W 1931. M. R. Delaney, *A Study of the Clausulae in the Works of St. A.,* W 1934. L. T. Phillips, *The . . . Clauses in the Works of St. A.,* W 1937. J. H. Gillis, *The Coordinating Particles . . .* (supr. 318). C. Favez, *La consolation lat. chrét.,* 1937. Muckle, Mediaev. Stud. 1, 1939, 68/80 (*De officiis;* Christianization of Lat.). Bardy, RSR 1940, 274/81 (A. as translator). Riposati, *S. Ambrogio nel XVI centenario,* 1940, 259/305 *(Lingua e stile).* M. Pellegrino, *La poesia crist. lat. dalle origini a S. Ambr.,* Tu 1947. I. Cazzaniga, *Note Ambrosiane. Appunti intorno allo stile delle omelie virginali,* Varese 1948. On the chronology of the works cf. Palanque 1933, 435/79 and Dudden 1935 (supra § 83).

Treatises and Mgg.: Doelger, AC 4, 153/65 (inscr. of Bapt. of Thecla). Lukman, BV 1936, 288/97 (*Off.* 1, 29, 142). Doelger, AC 5, 232/47 (*Ob. Sat.* 1, 43). Lefort, Mu 1935, 62/6 (*De virg.* depend. on Athanas.). Bellini, *Convivium* 1935, 614/24 *(Contenuto polit. dei panegirici).* A. Nohe, *Der Mailaender Psalter,* 1936. Galtier, RSR 1936, 563/78 (A. and the *Tomus Damasi*). G. del Ton, G*li inni di S. A.,* Como 1939. G. Ghedini, *L'innologia ambros.,* Mi 1940. Lazzati, *S. Ambrogio nel XVI Centenario,* 1940, 307/20 *(gli inni).* Bardy, RHE 1944/5, 171/6 (on *De fide ad Grat.* 2, 9); cf. Richard, Actes VIe CongrInternatÉtByz 1, 1950, 371 f. Connolly, JTS 1946, 185/96 (*explanatio symboli* genuine); against Hitchcock, ibid. 58/69.

On *De sacramentis:* Ghedini, *Ambrosius. Boll. liturg.* 1931, 75/80 (genuine). Dudden (supra § 83) 1935, 705/9 (spurious). Birch 1924 (supra § 81, 9). Rivière, RevSR 1934, 550/3 (on 4, 15). Faller, ZKT 1940, 1/14, 81/101 (genuine). Frank, TQ 1940, 67/82 (genuine). H. Connolly, *The De sacram., a work of St. A.,* 1942 and 1946. Srawley, JTS 1943, 199 f. (genuine). Hitchcock, HA 1947, 22/38; 1948, 19/35 (B. Venerius of Milan author of *De sacram.*). Quasten, *Mél. de Ghellinck* 1, 223/34 (Baptismal Creed and Baptismal Act in *De myst.* and *De sacram.*); Misc. Mohlberg 1, 1948, 117/25 (for genuineness of *De sacr.*). Mohrmann, VC 1950, 1/19 (development of style of Canon of Mass); VC 1952, 168/77 (style of *De sacr.*). Birch, JTS 1950, 175 (on *De Sacr.* 3, 2). Perler, RAC 1952, 145/66 (Thecla inscr. at Milan and *De sacr.*). Lazzati, Aev 1955, 17/48 (on genuineness of *De sacr.*). Connolly, DR 1947, 7/20, 121/30 (*Apol. David altera* is genuine). Dressler, Tr 1947, 311 f. *(De Nabuthe).* — On text of Bible: Rolando, Bi 1945, 238/76; 1946, 3/17 (Lc.). Carragliano, Bi 1946, 30/64, 210/40 (Jo.).

Wilbrand, Festschr. f. J. Hessen 1949, 156/61 (relation to Jews). Diederich, CJ 1948, 219/22 (Cicero and A. on friendship). Courcelle, RP 1950, 29/56 (A. and Plotinus); s. § 88. Simonetti, AttiAcadNazLinc., MemClScMorStorFil III 4, F. 6, 1952, 333/485, esp. 376/430 (innologia popolare crist. dei primi sec.); NDid 1953/55, 45/58 (text. crit. on hymns). Deman, RSPT 1953, 409/24 (*De officiis* in the hist. of moral theol.). Marzola, ScrinTheol 1, 1953, 95/123 (text of Acts, Paul. Epp. and Apc.). Cazzaniga, Lat 1954, 569/76 (on *De virginibus* 3, 5, 25 ff.). Coyle, FS 15, 1955, 22/56 (Cic.'s *De off.* and A.'s *De off.*) Courcelle, REL 1956, 220/39 (Platonism in A.).—Spurious Works: Hegesipp. ed. V. Ussani (CSEL 66) 1932. W. F. Dwyer, *The Vocabulary of Heges.,* W 1931. J. P. Mc Cormick, *A Study of the Nominal Syntax and of Indirect Discourse in Heges.,* W 1935. O. Scholz, *Die Heg.-Ambros.-Frage,* 1913. Bareille, DTC 6, 2120/22. On *Lex Dei:* F. Triebs, Studien zur *Lex Dei* 2 F. 1905/7. E. Volterra, MemAcadLincei 3, 1931, 1/123 (author a Jew). Ostersetzer, RevÉt. juives 1934, 65/96. C. Hohenlohe, *Ursprung u. Zweck der Coll. leg.,* W 1935 (Author: Ambrose); StDoctHistJur 5, 486/90. N. Smits, *Mos. et rom. leg. coll.,* thesis Groningen 1935; cf. Kuebler, ZSR 1936, 336/61. F. Schulz, StDoctHistJur 1936, 20/43 (Bibl. texts in *Coll. leg.*). Volterra, RivStorDirIt 1936, 365/80 (Indice delle glosse). v. Hohenlohe, AKK 1939, 352/64 (origin and aim). — On *Passio Machab.*: Morin, RBn 1914, 83/91. H. Doerrie, *Passio SS. Machab.* 1938 (ed. crit.). — *De 42 mans. filio-*

rum Israel: cf. F. Wutz, *Onomastica sacra* 1, 1914, 136, 143 A. 1. *De moribus Brachmanorum* cf. Liénard, RBP 1936, 819/38. Kurfess, Mn 1940, 138/52; PWK 37, 304/6; *Acta S. Sebastiani:* cf. JL 14, 1938, 394. The *Sermo* (ML 17, 671f. belongs to Gregory M., cf. Lambot, RBn 1942, 12/5). — On the treatise *De lapsu virginis,* counting as ps.-Ambr. (ML 16, 367/84) cf. crit. ed. by I. Cazzaniga, Tu 1948, and Id., *La tradizione manoscritta* ad *De lapsu Susannae,* Tu 1950; on this Franceschini, Aev 1952, 467/72; against this Cazzaniga, Acme 6, 1953, 165/71. Cf. § 84, 2. — Vogels, ZNTW 46, 1955, 60/8 (Bibl. text of 3 ps.-Ambr. sermons). Muncey, *The NT text of St. Ambrose,* C 1959.

Points of Doctrine

After his baptism Ambrose worked out a system of Christian truths which was well balanced and essentially complete from the first. Basing himself on sources that were not always innocuous (Philo, Origen), he eliminated their errors with surprising surety of touch, while generously transmitting what was true, so that he became the best witness to the harmony of the Church's faith in East and West.

1. Trinity. Like Hilary he confesses the Nicene faith in Nicene, but also in other orthodox formulae (EP 1269). After Hilary he is the most important champion of orthodoxy against Arianism and Macedonianism. Ambrose teaches and constantly emphasizes the true divinity of the Holy Spirit and his complete equality with the other two Persons in the Trinity (*Spir.* S. 2, 11, 118). If he writes in *Spir.* S. 1, 11, 120: *Spiritus Sanctus procedit a Patre et Filio,* he understands the *procedere* in the sense of a *missio ad extra.* Ambrose did not discuss in detail the inner-Trinitarian procession of the Holy Spirit from the Father and the Son *(operatio ad intra).* Cf. Simonetti, *Maia* 7, 1954, 204/9.

2. Christology. Unlike Hilary (supra § 80), Ambrose teaches quite unequivocally the true humanity of Christ against Docetists, Manicheans and Apollinarians (EP 1267). Once (*Fide* 2, 8, 61) he speaks of the *persona hominis* (Christi), an echo of the Greek notion of πρόσωπον (v. supra § 56, 72), though he confesses that there is One in two natures, complete in both (*Excess. Sat.* 1, 12).

3. The angels are the organs that execute God's plan of salvation. There is a spiritual relationship between angels and men. The angels belong to the *City of God* (*domicilii caelestis habitaculum; Ep.* 76, 12); cf. Augustine's *Civitas Dei.* With Origen, Ambrose believes in guardian angels of individual churches and estates and seems also to assume the existence of guardian angels of individual men (*In Ps.* 37, 43; Ps. 38, 8).

4. Ambrose speaks explicitly of a sinful state inherited by every man which involves him in guilt (*noxiae conditionis hereditas;* Ps. 38, 29), hence children, too, must be baptized (EP 1324). The unbaptized man is organically united with the devil as his *membrum* and *semen.* In some passages, however, the idea of concupiscence and of an inherited inclination to sin is emphasized so strongly as if these were the essence of original sin (*Apol. David* 56). That which man inherited from Adam seems to be a *lubricum delinquendi* rather than a *peccatum,* for which we shall not be punished on the Day of Judgement (Ps. 48, 8). In *De Myst.* 6, 32 Ambrose even says that by baptism only the *propria,* in the footwashing the *hereditaria peccata* are washed away. The *Ob. Val.* 51/3 (EH 621/3) attests the baptism of desire.

5. Mariology. A confession of Mary's freedom from original sin is frequently found in the prayer at the end of Ambrose's exposition of Ps. 118 (*Exp. in Ps.* 118, 22, 30). Here Ambrose prays for a human existence *(suscipe me in carne, quae)* which, after the example of Mary, is to be *incorrupta (sc. caro) ab omni integra labe peccati.* But as the existence here cannot refer to freedom from original sin, Mary cannot here be meant to be the pattern that has not been disfigured by it; Ambrose here thinks only of Mary as the ideal free from all personal sins. He does not know a mariological interpretation of Gen. 3 : 15. The woman is Eve, mankind in general her posterity. Occasionally he also interprets this passage of Christ. Cf. L. Drewniac, *Die mariologische Deutung von Gen. 3 : 15,* Br 1934, 47.

6. The Mass. The word *missa* as a term for the worship of the faithful is first met in Ambrose, *Ep.* 20, 4. Augustine uses the word only once, in *Sermo* 49, 8, where it means the dismissal of the catechumens *(missio = dimissio)*. Ambrose also affirms frequently and unequivocally the sacrificial character of the eucharist, e.g. *Ante agnus offerebatur, offerebatur et vitulus, nunc Christus offertur* (*Offic.* 1, 48, 238).

7. Penance. Ambrose attests the *una paenitentia,* i.e. the sacramental public penance which, according to primitive Christian practice, was permitted only once. He reproaches those who want to undergo penance more often; *quia sicut unum baptisma, ita una paenitentia, quae tamen publice agitur.* In principle he demands public penance also for secret grave sins (*occulta crimina* in the primitive Christian sense), naturally preceded by a secret confession before a priest. The second kind of penance of which Ambrose speaks is the private penance to be practised daily for the *delicta leviora,* which is performed without the mediation of the Church (*Paen.* 1, 16; 2, 10, 95; EH 598/603). Nothing can be deduced for the existence of ecclesiastical private penance from the much discussed information contained in Paulinus, *Vita Ambrosii* 39 (EP 2025).

8. The Roman Primacy. In the interest of Pope Damasus who was endangered by Ursinus, Ambrose writes to the Emperor Gratian: "Do not allow the head of the whole Roman world, the Roman Church and the most holy apostolic faith to be confused; for from there the rights of the venerable communion of the Church pass on to all (churches)" (*Ep.* 11, 4). He reports that before his baptism his brother Satyrus first made sure of the orthodoxy of the bishop whom he asked to give him the sacrament: *Percontatus ex eo (sc. episcopo) est, utrumnam cum episcopis catholicis hoc est cum Romana ecclesia conveniret* (*Exc. Satyr.* 1, 47). It is, however, characteristic for the history of the Biblical basis of the doctrine of the primacy how Ambrose regards Peter's confession at Caesa-

rea Philippi (Mt. 16, 15 ff.). Through his confession of Christ Peter had taken the first place, *primatum egit, primatum confessionis utique, non honoris, primatum fidei, non ordinis* (*Incarnat.* 4, 32).

9. Heaven, purgatory, hell. The souls of all the departed must go through the flames of fire, even though it be John the beloved disciple (*Ps.* 118, *sermo* 20, 12); the just pass through them like Israel through the Red Sea, the infidels like Pharao, and for them the fire becomes *ultor ignis* of eternal duration. In the third category, that of the sinners, two groups are distinguished, according to whether the good or the evil works weigh more heavily in the scales of judgement. The second group suffers the fate of the unbelievers. For the first group the flames become a cleansing fire followed by paradise (*Ps.* 36 26; *Apol. David* 6, 24; *Ep.* 2, 14 16). Yet for the second group, too, Ambrose leaves open the possibility of salvation. He hopes for this; nevertheless he teaches nowhere the Origenistic *apocatastasis* for Christians who die in mortal sin (*Exc. Satyr.* 2, 116; *Ps.* 1, 54).

10. In the history of devotion Ambrose occupies a leading place. He is rightly called the "Patron of the veneration of Mary". He traces an ideal picture of the Virgin Mother of Christ and of her life as a school of virtue (*Lk.* 2, 1 ff.; *Virg.* 2, 2 6 ff.; *Inst. Virg.* 5 ff.); she is the new Eve who brings salvation and has defeated the devil (*Ep.* 63, 32; 49, 2). If he emphasizes Mary's complete sinlessness, this does not mean that he makes any statement about her freedom from original sin (*Inst. Virg.* 33; *Lk.* 10, 42; *Ps.* 118, *sermo* 22, 30). — He has also spoken about the veneration of angels, saints, martyrs and their relics with sometimes actually exuberant enthusiasm. He accords veneration to the cross and nails of Christ for the sake of Christ, to whom alone adoration is given; else it would be pagan superstition (*Ob. Theod.* 46). Ambrose ends his funeral orations with prayers of intercession for the dead for whom he offers the eucharistic sacrifice (*Ep.* 39, 4).

J. E. Niederhuber, *Die Lehre des hl. A. vom Reiche Gottes auf Erden,* 1904; *Die*

Eschatologie des hl. A., 1907. S. Lisiecki, *Quid S. A. de ss. Euch. docuerit,* thesis Br 1910. J. Huhn, *Die Bedeutung d. Wortes Sacramentum bei d. Kirchenvater A.*, 1928; *Ursprung u. Wesen des Boesen u. der Suende nach d. Lehre des A.*, 1933. A. Pagnamenta, *La Mariologia di s. A.*, Mi 1932. Stelzenberger 1933, 234/42, 491/502 and freq. Rivière, RTA 1934, 349/67 (318; alleg. exegesis). Bardy, DS 1, 425/8. K. Schwerdt, *Stud. z. Lehre des hl. A. v. d. Person Christi,* 1937. Wilbrand, Miss.- u. Rel.wiss. 1, 1938, 193/202 (pagan mission). Rivière, RevSR 1939, 1/23 *(rédemption).* Dudden, St. A. 2, 1935, 555/677 (A. as a theologian). K. Janssen, *Die Entstehung der Gnadenlehre Augustins,* 1936, 5/24. M. Drzecnik, *Doctrina S. A.,* de *Christo Deo-homine,* Maribor 1938. J. Gapp, *La doctr. de l'union hypost. chez s. A.*, Issoudun 1938. J. Rinna, *Die Kirche als Corpus Christi, mysticum b. hl. A.*, R 1940. Spedalieri, CC 1940, 321/31 *(il sacerdozio).* Roberti, SC 1940, 140/59 *(il monachismo).* Tosio, *Jus. Pontif.* 1940, 65/74 *(De bello ac pace).* Citterio, SC 1940, 491/5 *(primato di S. Pietro).* G. Odoardi, *La dottr. della penitenza in S. A.*, R 1941. A. G. Rose, *Idee u. Gestalt der Kirche beim hl. A.*, thesis Br 1942. F. Meyer, *Seelsorge des hl. A. durch Formung christl. Bewusstseins* (acc. to the comm. on Lk.), R 1941. *S. Ambrogia nel XVI Centenario della Nascita* (1940) contains also the following contributions: Soranzo 1/15 *(A. e la Chiesa rom.);* Citterio 31/68 *(teologia della Chiesa);* Ceriani 159/207 *(spiritualità);* Franceschini 209/33 *(Verginità);* Rovighi 235/58 *(idee filosofiche);* D'Entrèves 321/35 *(concezione del diritto);* Biondi 337/420 *(influenza sulla legislaz. relig.);* Maschi 421/30 *(lex natur.);* Dossetti 431/83 *(concetto giurd. dello "status religiosus");* Violardo 485/512 *(sul diritto matrimon.);* Giacchi 513/31 *(dott. matrimon. di A. pr. Graziano).*

L. Casaril, *L'attribuzione dei nomi div. al. Figlio in S. A.*, R 1943. A. Madeo, *Le dottr. soteriolog. di S. A.*, Bergamo 1943. C. Fitzgerald, *De sacrificio caelesti set, S. A.*, Mund. 1944. Hitchcock, CQR 1945, 127/53 (Holy Communion). Giet. Science rel. 1944, 95/128 (Basil and A. against taking interest). G. Squitieri, *Ic preteso communismo di S. A.*, 1946. P. J. Couvee, *Vita beata en vita aeterna bij Lactana., A. en Augustinus,* 1947. Perler, Anima 3, 1948, 193/7 (action and contemplation). Quasten, Miscell. Mohlberg I, 1948, 117/25 *(sobria ebrietas).* W. J. Dooley, *Marriage acc. to A.*, W 1948. On hist. of Liturgy: Doelger, AC 4, 271/5 *(missa).* Paredi, SC 1935, 3/14 (bapt. formulae). A. Paredi, *I prefazi ambros.*, Mi 1937. Capelle, RHE 1937, 327/31 *(Ad te Domine).* Morin, RBn 1939, 101/8 *(Canon fixe).* Borella, EL 1939, 60/110 *(missa o dimissio catechum. nelle lit. occident.).* Jungmann, ZKT 1940, 26/77 (hist. of meaning of *missa*). Frank in: *Hl. Ueberlieferung* (Festschr. Herwegen) 1938, 136/73 (reconciliation of penitents in Milan on Maundy Thursday); *Pastor bonus* 1940, 40ff. (Milan eccl. year in A.). Paredi nel: *S. Ambrogio nel XVI Centenario,* 1940, 69/157 *(La liturgia di S. A.);* Ambrosiana 1942, 125/35. Nicodemi, ibid. 273/84 *(arte liturg.).* Capelle, Misc. Mercati I, 219/46 *(L'Exsultet pascal),* against this B. Fischer, *Zeugnis d. Geistes. Gabe zum Benedictus-Jubil.*, Beuron 1947, 234f.; BM 1948, 147f., and Steidle, BM 1948, 147. J. Eger, *Salus gentium. Eine patrist. Studie z. Volkstheol. des A. v. M.,* thesis Mn 1947. S. Stenger, *Das Froemmigkeitsbild des hl. A. nach s. Schriften De Abr., De Isaac u. De bono mortis,* thesis typed T 1948. G. Figuerra, *The Church and the Synagogue in S. A.*, thesis W 1949. Huhn, MTZ 1951, 130/46 (mystery of BMV); ibid. 1951, 377/89 (orig. sin). D. Loepke, *Die Tugendlehre des hl. A.,* Sarnen 1951 (thesis Fr.). Lécuyer,

RUO 1952, 104/26 *(Le Sacerdoce chrét.)*. R. d'Izary, *La virginité sel. s. A.*, thesis Lyons 1952 (2 vols.). C. Morino, *Il ritorno al paradiso di Adamo in s. A.*, thesis Greg. R 1952. Baus, RQ 49, 1954, 21/55 (Origen and A.'s devotion to Christ). Taormina, MiscStLCa 1954, 41/85 (A. and Plotinus). J. Huhn, *Das Geheimnis der Jungfrau Mutter Maria nach A.*, 1954; Anima, 1955, 136/50 (A. and pastoral care); AugMag 1, 221/39 (Mariology in A. and August.). Keseling, ZRGG 5, 1953 (family sense and patriotism in *De off.*). Michiels, QLP 1953, 109/14, 164/9 *(Initiation chrét. sel. s. A.)*. Zonewski, *Annuaire de l'Acad. Théol.*, Sofia 4, 1954/55, 340/83 (views on social matters in A. and Aug.).

§ 84. AMBROSIASTER AND NICETA OF REMESIANA

1. FROM the time of Erasmus a *Commentary on Thirteen Pauline Epistles* (without Hebrews) going under the name of Ambrose has been called *Ambrosiaster* (= Pseudo-Ambrose). The work, which originated in Rome under Pope Damasus (366–84) is generally considered a first-class achievement. It gives a frequently penetrating exegesis which reveals the historical sense and is averse to all allegorical subtleties, without, however, entirely excluding types. It is an important witness to the pre-Jerome Latin Pauline text and to the pre-Augustinian exegesis of Paul.

The much discussed question of the authorship of the work has not yet been solved. One of the candidates is the Jew Isaac, who was converted and later relapsed into Judaism, notorious for his slanderous accusations against Pope Damasus (so Morin [1899], Wittig, Souter). The so-called *Fides Isaatis ex Iudaeo,* a short treatise on the Trinity and Incarnation, is preserved under his name. G. Morin, the author of this thesis, later proposed three other writers: the proconsul Hilarianus Hilarius (1903), Evagrius of Antioch (1914; v. supra § 54, 18) and finally N. Aem. Dexter (1928; v. supra § 2).

The pseudo-Augustinian *Quaestiones Veteris et Novi Testamenti* may also safely be assigned to *Ambrosiaster;* they treat 127 exegetical and dogmatic questions without any systematic arrangement. A second version of 150 *quaestiones* is held by Martini (against

Souter) to be the work of the same author. It is very doubtful whether other works should also be assigned to him (e.g. Hegesippus, *Lex Dei,* v. supra § 83, 6). As regards the doctrinal contents of the Commentary and the *Questiones,* we would point out that the author may in a certain sense be considered a precursor of the Augustinian view of the doctrine of grace and original sin (against Mundle).

Edd.: ML 17, 45/508; *Quaestiones* ed. A. Souter (CSEL 50), 1908. *Fides Isaat.* ed. H. Zeuschner, KGAbh 8, 1909, 101/5, and Turner, JTS 31, 1929/30, 1/9. — Treatises: Morin, RHL 1899, 97/121 (for Isaac). J. Wittig, KGAbh 4, 1906, 1/66 and 8, 1909. Morin, RBn 1903, 113/31; 1914, 1/34; 1928, 251/5. W. Mundle, *Die Exegese der paulin. Briefe im Komm. des A.,* 1919. A. Souter 1927, 39/95. Bareille et Mangenot, DTC 8, 1/8. Gaudel, DTC 12, 367/71 (doctr. of orig. sin). Bardy, DBSuppl 1, 225/41; RB 1932, 343/56. Buonaiuti, RR 1926, 401/27 (doctr. of orig. sin). Jaentsch, Sch 1934, 92/9 (doctr. of grace). C. Martini, *Ambrosiaster,* R 1944; Ant 1947, 23/48 (the 2 collections of *Quaest.*). Schepens, RSR 1950, 295f. (author not a Jew); ibid. 1950, 295/9 (*Ambrosiaster* written by Euseb. of Vercelli, § 81, 2). M. Michalski, *Problem autorstwa tak swanego "Ambroziastra" w swietle jego nauki christolog.,* Cracow 1950. Martini, RST 1, 1954, 40/62 (the 2 edd. of the *Quaest.*). Leeming, DR 1955, 263/75 (Mysterious Ambros.). H. Vogels, *Das Corpus Paulinum des Ambr.,* Bonn 1957. MLS 1, 655/72.

2. Niceta, Bishop of Remesiana, Bela Palanka in Yugoslavia, was a friend of Paulinus of Nola whom he visited twice. According to Paulinus he composed hymns and interested himself in Church singing (d. after 414).

His principal work is *six Libelli instructionis* destined for candidates for baptism. Only the fifth *Libellus* has been preserved in full; it is an explanation of the Apostles' Creed and important for the history of the creeds. The treatise *De ratione fidei* and *De Spiritus sancti potentia* probably belong to the third *Libellus.*

Ad lapsam virginem, mentioned by Gennadius (*Vir. ill.* 22) is probably identical with the pseudo-Ambrosian treatise *De lapsu virginis consecratae* (ML 16, 367/84) (EP 1335), see § 83. Besides, there are two *sermones: De vigiliis* (ed. Turner, JTS 22, 1920/1, 306/20), *De utilitate hymnorum* (ed. Turner, JTS 24, 1922/3, 225/52) and a short treatise *De diversis appellationibus* (Christi).

G. Morin and A. E. Burn believe (without offering convincing evidence) that the hymn of praise, *Te Deum laudamus,* was written by Niceta. He is named author in ten Irish manuscripts, but since the eighth century this hymn has been attributed to Ambrose, Hilary and Augustine.

Edd. and Mgg.: A. E. Burn, C 1905. W. A. Patin, Mn 1909. Amann, DTC 11, 477/9. Turner, JTS 22, 1920/1, 305/20 (ed. *De vigiliis*); 24, 1922/3, 225/52 (ed. *De psalmodiae bono*). Zeiller, CR I, 1942, 356/69. On *Ad laps. virg.* cf. J. Duhr, 1934 (supra § 81, 12) and A. Nohe, *Der Mailaender Psalter,* 1936, 108f. Pippidi, RHSudEstEurope 23, 1946, 99/117 (N. and Christianity in Roumania). Coman, *Biserica ortod. Rom.* 66, 1948, 337/56 (N. in Roumania); on this Pippidi, 1950; cf. BZ 1950, 451. Simonetti, *Maia* 4, 1951, 1/10 (sources of *De Spirit. S.*). ClavisPL n. 646ff. On the *Te Deum* cf. A. E. Burn, *The Hymn Te Deum and its Author,* 1926. Jungmann, ZKT 1937, 105/7. Baumstark, OC 1937, 1/26 (*Te Deum* and Gr. evening hymns). Frost, JTS 1933, 250/7; 1938, 388/91; 1940, 195/8. Simonetti, 1952 (v. § 13, 1), 478/81 (agrees with Morin). E. Kaehler, *Studien zum Te Deum,* Go 1958.

According to Morin, RSPT 1937, 307/17, Laurentius, Bishop of Novae, belongs to the milieu and time of Niceta. Two homilies, *De paenitentia* and *De Eleemosina* (ML 66, 89/116) survive. *De muliere Chananaea* (ML 66, 116/24) is a sermon of Chrysostom which he probably translated into Latin.

See Wilmart, RBn 1926, 157 n. 2. On the history of Novae in Moesia cf. Polaschek, PWK 33, 1125/9.

§ 85. RUFINUS OF AQUILEIA (d. 410)

Tyrannius Rufinus was born of Christian parents at Concordia near Aquileia *c.* 345. He became acquainted with Jerome already during his studies in Rome. For some years he lived as a monk in a monastery at Aquileia, where Jerome, too, stayed for a short time. Here he was baptized. In 371 he went to Egypt, in the suite of the noble Roman lady Melania the Elder. After visiting the monks in the Nitrian and Scetian desert he became the pupil of Didymus the Blind in Alexandria, who imbued him with enthusiasm for Origen. About 378 he followed Melania to Jerusalem, lived as a monk on the Mount of Olives and was ordained priest by Bishop John of Jerusalem.

He continued on a friendly footing with Jerome, who settled near Bethlehem in 386, until Epiphanius started the controversy about Origen in Jerusalem (v. supra § 66). Jerome sided with Epiphanius, Rufinus supported Bishop John. This conflict was at first settled before the return of Rufinus to Italy (397). The latter, however, published a Latin translation of Origen's chief work *De principiis* in Rome, having eliminated as far as possible its heterodox teachings allegedly interpolated by heretics; moreover, in the preface he represented Jerome as an admirer of Origen. This caused the controversy to flare up again, and it was now conducted in extremely violent polemical writings; Rufinus was nearly condemned by the Pope. In 407 the invasion of Italy by the Visigoths caused him to leave Aquileia, where he had been living since 400; he fled to the South and died at Messina in 410.

Rufinus' importance for Christian literature rests chiefly on his activities as a translator. Since the knowledge of Greek continued to decline in the West, he wanted to make important Greek literary works accessible to those interested in theology. There seems to be no definite plan in the selection of the authors he translated.

1. *Translations*

a. His translations of works by Origen are the most numerous: *De principiis,* parts of the *Commentaries* on the Canticle and on Romans; seventeen *Homilies* on Genesis, thirteen on Exodus, sixteen on Leviticus, eighteen on Numbers, twenty-six on Josue, nine on Judges, nine on Psalms. There is also the translation of the first book of Pamphilus' *Apology for Origen;* as an appendix he wrote the treatise *De adulteratione librorum Origenis* (supra § 41, 8).

b. *Pseudo-Clementines: Letter to James* and *Recognitions* (supra

§ 15, 4). *Dialogue on the True Faith* (supra § 42, 4). Basil the Great: two *Rules for Monks* (shortened into one); nine *Homilies*, eight of them edited in MG 31, 1723/84 and *Ep*. 46. Gregory of Nazianzus: nine orations. Several collections of maxims by Evagrius Ponticus and the Christian version of the *Sayings of Sextus* (supra § 13, 3).

c. Eusebius of Caesarea: *Church History* (ten books in nine). Gelasius of Caesarea: *Church History* (as Books X and XI in Rufinus; supra § 49 I, 1). *Historia monachorum* (supra § 46 A, 1).

2. *Writings of his own*

a. Two Apologies in the Origenist controversy: *Apologia ad Anastasium, Romanae urbis episcopum* (400); he excuses his failure to appear before the Roman synod, professes an orthodox creed and justifies his translation of Origen. When Jerome attacked the translation of Origen's *De principiis*, which Rufinus had modified from the doctrinal point of view, and published his own literal translation, Rufinus replied in a very irritated tone in his *Apologia (Invectiva) in Hieronymum* which Jerome refuted with equal harshness and spite in his three books *Apologia adv. libros Rufini*.

b. In his *Commentarius in symbolum Apostolorum* he depends on the *catecheses* of Cyril of Jerusalem. The treatise presents for the first time the Latin text of the Apostles' Creed (supra § 5) and a list of books of Holy Scripture (EP 1344).

De benedictionibus patriarcharum (two books) is an allegorical exegesis of the blessing of Jacob (Gn. 49). All his letters are lost.

Edd.: ML 21. *Reg. Basilii* ed. L. Holstenius, Cod. regul. 1, 1759, 67/108. Nine orations of Gregory ed. A. Engelbrecht (CSEL 46) 1910. *Comm. in symb.* ed. C. A. Heurtley, 2 vols., O 1916 (with trans.). J. N. D. Kelly, *Ruf. A Comm. on the Apostles' Creed* (ACW 20) 1955. — Treatises: J. Brochet, *S. Jérôme et ses ennemis*, 1906. De Aldama, Gr 1934, 589/98 *(Symbol.)*. M. Villain, NRT 1937, 5/33, 139/61 (life and works); RSR 1937, 5/37, 165/95 (Origenist controv.). Hoppe, StU 133/50 (R. as a translator); Glotta 26, 1937, 132/44 (Greek). Bardy, DTC 14, 153/60; RSR 1940, 294/301 (R. as transl.). M. Stenzel, Bi 1942, 43/61 (canon of Script.).

Id., *R. v. A. u. die Bibel,* 1 pt. (Rom.). thesis Fr, 1941. Altaner, HJB 61, 1941, 208/10 (Basil-trans.); on this Huglo, RBn 1954, 129/32. Villain, Science rel. 1944, 129/56 (comm. in symb.). F. X. Murphy, *R. of A.,* W 1945; cf. Peeters, AB 1948, 325/31. M. M. Wagner, *R. the Translator* (on Greg. of Naz., *De fuga*), W 1945. Stenzel, TZ 1953, 81/7 (Lat. trans. of Dodecapropheton). H. Vogels, *Unters. z. Text der paulin. Briefe b. R. u. Ambrosiaster* (§ 84, 1), Bonn 1955. K. H. Schelkle, *Paulus, Lehrer der Vaeter,* 1956, 443/8 (trans. of Origen's comm. on Rom.). Simonetti, *Maia* 8, 1956, 1/28 (on a crit. ed. of *Apologia* against Jerome); T. Rufino, *Apologia,* Alba 1957 (Text and trans.); SE 1957, 5/43 (MSS).

§ 86. JEROME (b. *c.* 347, d. 419 or 420)

Jerome was born of wealthy Catholic parents at Strido in Dalmatia (according to Cavallera and Morin in a place between Aquileia and Emona [Ljubljana], according to Bulič Grahovo Polje in the frontier district between Croatia, Bosnia and Dalmatia) between 340 and 350 (according to Cavallera *c.* 347). Very early (perhaps 354) he came to Rome to receive his grammatical, rhetorical and philosophical education; among his teachers was the famous grammarian Aelius Donatus; Rufinus was one of his fellow pupils. The writings of this Church Father show that he was well read in the Latin classical writers, especially in Virgil, and his *Anti-Ciceronian Dream-Vision* proves that even in later years he was unwilling to give up reading the pagan authors. During his time of studies in Rome he fell a prey to evil influences; however, the grave youthful errors to which he later alludes in sincere sorrow may certainly be interpreted, as Vaccari suggests, "according to the psychology of the Catholic urge for confessing" and thus need not be taken too seriously. In those days he liked to visit the catacombs with his fellow students to be inspired by the examples of Christian heroism. He was baptized in Rome towards the end of his student years.

From Rome he went to Gaul where he gradually decided to consecrate himself to Christ, probably under the influence of the colony of monks at Treves. Afterwards he lived for a time at Aquileia, where he belonged to a circle of friends devoted to the ascetical life, of which Rufinus was a member. He suddenly decided (373–4) to make a pilgrimage to Jerusalem. A severe illness forced him to break his journey at Antioch for a considerable time. Here he attended the exegetical lectures of Bishop Apollinaris of Laodicea and acquired a thorough knowledge of Greek. For about three years (375–8) he lived as a hermit in the desert of Chalcis, east of Antioch; during this time he learned Hebrew. After Pope Damasus had recognized Bishop Paulinus of Antioch (Meletian schism) he was ordained priest by the latter (379) and soon afterwards left Antioch for Constantinople. Here he attended the lectures of Gregory of Nazianzus and became an enthusiastic admirer of the exegesis of Origen. His translations of some of Origen's writings date from this period. At that time (381) he had also friendly relations with Gregory of Nyssa.

At the invitation of Pope Damasus he attended a Roman synod, held in 382, to heal the Antiochene schism, at which Bishop Paulinus and Epiphanius of Salamis were also present. The years of his sojourn in Rome (382–5) greatly influenced his later literary activity, for he became the friend and secretary of the aged Pope—it almost seemed as if he would be his successor—and was charged with the revision of Latin texts of the Bible. From this time he never ceased to be occupied with the study of Scripture. The later so-called Vulgate and many other Biblical studies are the fruit of these labours, which occupied several decades.

In Rome he became the centre of an ascetical circle to which belonged several ladies of the Roman aristocracy (the widows Marcella and Paula and the latter's daughter Eustochium). He mercilessly criticized the abuses rife among the Roman clergy (*Ep*. 22); hence, after the death of his patron Damasus (384) he incurred open hostility and his familiar relations with St. Paula and her family became suspect. When St. Paula's daughter Blesilla died at an early age, the populace was stirred up against him and on the day of her funeral showed their fury against the *detestabile genus monachorum* who had killed the popular girl with their fasts (*Ep*. 39, 6).

Jerome preferred to leave Rome (385) and took the road to Jerusalem for the second time. Paula and Eustochium followed a little later. From Antioch he travelled together with his spiritual friends to the holy places of Palestine; he went to Alexandria, where he stayed for thirty days with Didymus the Blind, and down to the monastic establishments in the Nitrian desert. He eventually settled in Bethlehem.

St. Paula's wealth enabled her to build three convents for women of which she was the superior, and one monastery for men, directed by Jerome. There were also several pilgrim's hostels and a monastic school in which Jerome explained the classic authors. The thirty-four years of his sojourn at Bethlehem were a time of unceasing literary activity. He had at his disposal a considerable library which he had himself collected in the course of years. Yet even the solitude of Bethlehem did not bring him the peace he desired. He became involved in the so-called "first Origenist Controversy" (v. supra § 66) which led to the ugly quarrel with Bishop John of Jerusalem and especially with Rufinus, the friend of his youth. This was followed by controversial writings against Jovinian (393) and Vigilantius (404), and the personal appearance of Pelagius finally brought the "Pelagian Controversy" also to Palestine. In the course of this controversy a band of Pelagians burned his convents (416) and his own life was in danger. The terrors of the great migration of peoples also disturbed the peace of the hermit of Bethlehem, for the hordes of the Huns (402), Isaurian mountain tribes (405) and plundering Saracens (410–12) came threateningly near and made quick flight necessary. Yet he remained young in spirit and ready to fight until the end. He died on September 30, 419 or 420. In the Middle Ages Jerome was venerated as the Patron of schools of learning, theological faculties and asceticism; he was frequently represented in art.

It is not surprising that there are many shadows in Jerome's character, seeing that he had an excitable, hot-tempered nature and that his nervous system had suffered from severe asceticism and grave illness. He was fiery and tempestuous, of biting sarcasm and frequently offensive in controversy; though conscious of his own superiority, he liked to be praised and was extremely sensitive with regard to his own person. Nevertheless, many an offensive invective will be judged more leniently if it be remembered that the Church Father followed famous literary models (Cicero). These faults and weaknesses are balanced by his noble enthusiasm for the Church and for scholarship. Despite his literary and learned ambitions he honestly strove to realize the monk's ideal of perfection.

He was undoubtedly the most learned of all Latin Church Fathers, the greatest polyhistor of his time, and was admired even by his contemporaries as the one *vir trilinguis (latinus, graecus, hebraeus)*.

Edd.: D. Vallarsi, 11 vols., Verona 1734/42. ML 22–30. J. Hilberg and S. Reiter (CSEL 54/6, 59) 1910/18 (Letters, Jer.). *Commentarioli* and *Tract. in Psalmos* and *in evang. Marci* ed. G. Morin, 3 vols., 1895/1903; cf. *Études, textes* etc. 1, 1913, 202/93. Crit. ed.: of N.T. by Wordsworth and White, O 1889/1949. – Rom. ed. of Vulgate: Gn. (1926), Ex. and Lv. (1929), Nm. and Dt. (1936), Jos., Jud., Ruth (1939), Sam. (1943), Kings (1945), *Liber verborum dierum,* 1948; Esra Tob., Judith, 1950; Esth., Job, 1951; *Psalt. Gallic. et Psalt. Roman.*, 1953; *Psalt. iuxta Hebr.,* 1954. Mierow, *Class. Bull.* (St. Louis Univ.) 1946, 31/60 (*Vita Malchi* ed. and trans.). C. Favez, *Hier., Epp. selectae,* Bru 1950. J. M. Harden, *Psalt. iuxta Hebr.,* Lo 1922. Edd. of Chron. v. § 48, I. — Special edd.: *Vir. ill.* (supra § 2). A. Ficarra, *Floril. Hieron.,* Tu 1920; F. A. Wright, Lo 1933 (18 *Epp.* with trans.). J. Schmidt (FP 22) 1930 (corresp. with Aug.). F. Stummer (FP 41) 1935 (*Epp.* 46, 58, 108, 129, 147); cf. OC 1935, 60/74. — Transs.: P. Leipelt (BKV²) 1872/4. L. Schade (BKV² 15, II, 16, 18) 1914, 1936/7 (good bibliogr.). D. Gorce, *Lettres spir.,* 2 vols., 1932/4; *Lectures chrét.* 3, P 1932 (lives of monks). E. Logi, 3 vols., Siena 1935/6 (letters). J. Labouret, *Lettres de s. J.,* 4 vols., 1949/54. J. Czuj, *S. Hier., Listy,* War 1952. — Mgg.: G. Gruetzmacher, 3 vols., 1901/8. F. Cavallera I, 1–2, Lou 1922. A. Vaccari, R 1921. U. Moricca, 2 vols., Mi 1922. A. Ficarra, *La posizione di S. G. nella storia della cultura,* 2 vols., Palermo 1916/30. P. Largent, R 1929. H. Leclercq, Lo 1927 and DAL 7, 2235/304. Forget, DTC 8, 894/983. Lietzmann, PWK 8, 1565/81. A. Queirolo, *Il Leone di Dalmazia,* Rapallo 1937. J. Teix. de Pescoaes, *H., Der Dichter der Freundschaft.* Aus dem Portugies. uebertr.

v. A. V. Thelen 1941. R. Génier, *Ste. Paule,* P 1917. I. d'Ivray, *S. Jér. et les dames de l'Aventin,* 1938. P. Steur, *Het Karakter v. H. bestud. in zijn brieven,* N 1945. M. J. Kelly, *Life and Times as revealed in the Writings of St. J. Exclusive of his Letters,* W 1944. S. Contini, *S. Girolamo,* Albra 1948. A. Penna, *S. G.,* Tu 1949. P. Antin, *Essai sur s. Jér.,* 1951. P. Antin, *S. Jér. Sur Jonas,* in: SCh 43, 1956 (crit. text and trans.). — CChL 72 and 78.

On biogr.: *Miscell. Geronim.,* R 1920. E. K. Rand 1928 (supra § 83), 102/34. C. Favez, *Ét. de lettres,* 1938, 218/32 (Marcella, Fabiola, Paula). Cavallera, BLE 1946, 60/3 *(La patrie).* Morin, *Nova et Vetera* 2, 1941, 159/67 (Italy, J.'s native country?). Gorce, La pensée cath. 12, 1949, 34/66 (J. dans son affreuse demeure). V. Petrillo, *S. Paola Romana e il suo tempo,* Na 1950. J. J. Cuesta, *Archivos Iberoameric. de hist. de la medicina* 1, 1949, 299/366 (J.'s mode of life); *Humanidades* 9, 1950, 89/102 (The dream of J.). Gordini, *Scrinium theol.* 1, 1953, 7/58 *(Vita ascetica a Roma).* C. A. Rapisarda, MiscStLCA 4, 1953, 1/18 (J.'s dream). — Style, linguist. and lit. knowledge: Fonck, Bi 1920, 481/99 (knowl. of nature). Cuendet, REL 1933, 380/400 (Cicero and J. as trans.). Souter, HTR 1935, 1/4 (Gr. and Hebr. in Mt.-comm.). M. C. Herron, *A Study of the Clausulae in the Writings of St. J.,* W 1937. Seliga, CT 16, 1935, 145/81 *(De invectiva Hieron.).* Microw, CJ 1937, 3/17 (Christian Scholar). Suess, Giessener Beitr. dtsch. Philol. 60, 1938, 212/38 (forms of controv.). J. N. Hritzu, *The Style of the Letters of St. J.,* W 1939. Id., *R. v. A. u. die Bibel,* 1. pt. (Rom.), thesis Fr 1941. Altaner, HJB 61, 1941, Bardy, RSR 1940, 281/94 (J. as trans.). Gillis 1938 (supra § 80). Favez 1937 (supra § 34). Coppola, Rend. R. Accad. Bologna Ser. 4, IV 99/122 *(Il latino di S. G.).* Courcelle 1947, 37/115 (ancient class. and patrist. lit.). Pope, Clergy Rev. 1946, 237/52 (St. J. Bird-watcher). Favez, REL 1946, 209/26 (J. as satirist). Antin, RSR 1947, 82/99 *(J. et son lecteur).* J. Kelly, *Life and Times as Revealed in the Writings of St. Jerome Exclusive of his Letters,* W 1944. Gorce, RAM 1949, 117/39 (Comment travaillait s. J.). Tibeletti, Salesianum 11, 1949, 97/117 (Cultura class. e crist.). Basabe, Hel 6, 1951, 161/92 *(J. y los clásicos).* F. X. Murphy, *A Monument to St. J.,* NY 1952 (10 contributions on his personality and culture); here Bardy, 83/112: *J. and the Gr. language;* Quain, *J. as a Humanist:* 201/32; also essays by Burke, Cavallera, Hartmann, Laistner, Palangue. E. P. Arns, RevEcles Brasiliera 12, 1952, 827/58 (diffusion of books in time of J.); *La technique du livre d'après s. J.,* P 1953. Demougeot, RevEA 1952, 83/92 *(J., les oracles sibyll. et Stilicon).* G. d'Anna, RendIstLombScLett 86, 1953, 211/32 (Corn. Nepos as a source). H. M. Werkhahn, *Bibliotheksnachrichten b. H.,* typed, Hei 1953. Bardy, Ir 1953, 337/62 (relation to Gr. theol.). Gilliam, HTR 1953, 103/7 (Cic., *Pro Coelio* in J.). R. Eiswirth, *H.s Stellung zu Lit. u. Kunst,* Wiesbaden 1955.

1. *Works on the Text of the Bible*

Since the Latin Bibles had shown discrepancies for a long time, Pope Damasus was anxious to procure a reliable text. Jerome was charged with a revision (not a new translation) of a text of the Bible in use in Rome.

He first worked on the four Gospels. It is usually assumed that the revision of the other N.T. books followed quickly; against this cf. De Bruyne, RBn 1915, 358/92. This was followed by a superficial revision of the Psalter according to the LXX (384). It is not quite certain whether this revised text of the Psalter is identical with the *Psalterium Romanum* which was used in all churches of the City of Rome till Pius V, and is still in use in St. Peter's.

Soon after his arrival at Bethlehem he began the revision of the text of the whole O.T. according to Origen's *Hexapla* text of the LXX which he had consulted at Caesarea; but he also took account of the Hebrew original. Of these works only the text of the Book of Job and of the Psalms has been preserved in full; the other parts were stolen before he could publish them (*Ep*. 134, 2). This text of the Psalms was first used in the liturgy in Gaul (hence *Psalterium Gallicanum*). It is still in our editions of the Vulgate, and Pius V introduced it into the breviary (1568) and the missal (1570), though individual pieces were left according to the *Psalterium Romanum* (Invitatorium, antiphones, responsories). The *Psalterium iuxta Hebraeos* was not taken into account and remained forgotten.

While still occupied with the revision of the Latin O.T. Jerome decided *c*. 391 to make a new translation of the O.T. on the basis of the Hebrew or Aramaic original. This immense work dragged on till 406. Of the deuterocanonical books, which he considered apocryphal, he only translated Tobias and Judith from the Aramaic. The deuterocanonical parts of Daniel and Esther are translated from Theodotion and the LXX respectively.

The translations are in general faithful and careful, but not slavishly literal. Jerome was guided by the principles of making the text intelligible and considering his readers' feeling for style; he often followed the LXX out of respect for the traditional text. The Greek translations of the Bible then in use served Jerome, so to speak, as Hebrew-Greek lexica. In his work as a translator he is not infrequently influenced by rabbinic traditions, and his knowledge of the history of classical literature and culture was also utilized. The books that were translated later show a better style. In view of the poor resources at his disposal his achievement deserves the highest praise. At first Jerome's translations met almost nothing but violent opposition, but he was soon entrusted with the revision of Old Latin MSS of the Bible. At the time of Gregory the Great (d. 604) his text enjoyed equal rights with the others, and in the eighth and ninth centuries it came fully into its own. The term Vulgate *(vulgata editio)* has been in general use since the thirteenth century.

Mgg.: F. Kaulen, *Sprachliches Handbuch z. bibl. Vulgata,* [2]1904. D. de Bruyne, *Sommaires, Divisions et Rubriques de la Bible lat.,* 1914, and *Préfaces de la Bible lat.,* 1920 (neither of these great works were made available by the booksellers!). W. E. Plater and H. J. White, *A Grammar of the Vulgate,* 1926. F. Stummer, *Einfuehr. i. d. lat. Bibel,* 1928; Bi 1937, 23/50. H. J. Vogels, *Vulgatastudien. Die Evv. der Vulg.,* 1928. A. Allgeier, *Die altlat. Psalterien,* 1928; *Die Ueberlief. der altlat. Psalmenuebers. u. ihre kulturgesch. Bedeutung,* 1931. C. H. Turner, *The Oldest MS of the Vulgate Gospels,* O 1931. De Bruyne et B. Sodar, *Les anciennes traductions lat. des Machabées éditées,* Maredsous 1932. W. Matzkow 1933 (v. supra § 1). Bardy, RBn 1934, 145/64 *(ses maîtres hébreux).* Ginzberg, *Jew. Stud. Cohut* 1935, 279/314 (Haggada in the Church Fathers VI: comm. on Is.). Stummer, Bi 1937, 174/81 (J. and the Targumim); ZATW 17, 1940/1, 251/69 (class. education and Christ. theol. in the Vulg.). A. Allgeier, *Die Psalmen der Vulg.,* 1940. Dold, Bi 1941, 105/46 (new parts of the oldest Vulg. Gospel MSS, 5th cent.). J. Ziegler, *Vorles.-Verzeichnis Braunsberg* WS 1943/4 (predecessors of Vulg. for prophets); on this TLZ 1948, 145/52. Sixdenier, AL 19, 1945/6, 17/22 *(firmamentum* in Vulg.). Perrella, DTP 1945/6, 228/35 (The deuterocan. writings of the O.T.). Sutcliffe, Bi 1948, 112/25 (pronunciation of Hebr.); 195/204 (Hebr. MSS); CBQ 1949, 139/43, 345/52; JTS 1948, 35/42. Allgeier, Bi 1948, 353/90 (Vulgate and Trent). J. H. Gailey, *J.'s Lat. Version of Job from Greek Chs. 1–26,* thesis Princeton 1945. F. Reuschenbach, *H. als Uebers. d. Gen.,* Limburg/L. 1948. Labourt, Bi 1948, 345/52 (The name *Vulgata*). I. O. Smit, *De Vulgaat. Geschiedenis . . .,* Roermond-Maeseyck 1948. Stummer, ZATW 62, 1949/50, 152/67 (on exeg. of Vulg.). Loewe, Hebr. Union Coll. Annual 22, 1949, 265/306 (Rendering of " 'Olam"); VetTestQuart 2, 1952, 261/72 (Treatment of anthropomorphism). Sutcliffe, CBQ 1949, 139/43 (Notes on St. J.'s Hebr. Text). G. Scarpat, *Il Liber Psalmorum e il Psalt. Gallic.,* Arona (It.) 1950. Flasche, EstBibl 10, 1951, 5/49 *(El concepto de cor en la Vulg.).* A. O. Preus, *St. J.'s Translation-Terminology,* thesis typed Minnesota 1951. Vaccari, *Misc. Galbiati* 2, 1951, 157/61 (J. in Gal. 3, 5); Scritti 1, 207/55 *(Salteri di G. di S. Agost.).* Stenzel, VC 1952, 20/7 (vocabulary of N.T. Vulg.); Festschr. Dold 1952, 25/33 (Vulg. text of Cant. Hab.); Bi 1952,

356/62 (Vulg. text of *Cant. Jonae*). Ziegler, Festschr. Dold 1952, 13/24 (LXX of J. in Jerem.). Festschr. Dold contains further contributions on *Vetus Lat.* and *Vulg.* Johannessohn, ZNTW 44, 1952/3, 90/102 (*Vulg.* and later Gr. O.T. transs.); Glotta 33, 1954, 125/65 (*et ecce* in *Vulg.*). Sacchi, GiornItFil 6, 1953, 152/9 (Gr. model of Vulg.). F. Auer, Festschr. Landersdorfer, Passau 1953, 11/24 (J. in his Vulg.). Rehm, Bi 1954, 174/97 (Hebr. words in J.). Gozzo, Ant 1954, 241/54 (H., In Libr. Proverb.). Lo Bue, VC 1955, 21/4 (on Apc.).

2. *Other Translations*

a. Before the outbreak of the Origenist controversy Jerome had looked up to the Alexandrian as the great master of exegesis and translated the following works of his: fourteen homilies on Jeremias, fourteen on Ezechiel (at Constantinople in 381), two homilies on the Canticle for Pope Damasus (383), thirty-nine homilies on Luke for Paula and Eustochium at Bethlehem *c.* 390; after 392, eight homilies on Isaias. As an opponent of Origen he translated the four books *De principiis* in 398 to refute his former friend Rufinus; the translation has not been preserved. His translation of Theophilus of Alexandria's satire on Chrysostom is also lost.

b. In addition to the second part of *The Chronicle of Eusebius* with his own continuation down to 378 he also made a free Latin paraphrase of this author's *Onomasticon* (supra § 48) under the title *De situ et nominibus locorum hebraicorum*. The *Liber de nominibus hebraicis* is a free version of a Greek model of a dictionary of O.T. names wrongly attributed to Philo of Alexandria; according to an equally untenable tradition Origen was supposed to have enriched it by the N.T. names.

c. Jerome's translation (392) saved Didymus' treatise *De Spiritu Sancto* (supra § 55, 2). In 404 he translated the monastic rules of Pachomius, Theodore and Orsisius and their letters (supra § 53, 2f.).

3. *Exegetical works*

His numerous commentaries on the Bible, unique for his time in their knowledge of the older exegetical literature and their historical and archaeological scholarship, have mostly been composed too quickly and superficially; hence they are imperfect in form and often jejune in content.

a. Of the O.T. he explained the Psalms (*Commentarioli;* dependent on Origen), Ecclesiastes and all the Prophets (Jeremiah only 1–32) in works of his own. In 381, moreover, he wrote an allegorical treatise (*Ep.* 18) *De visione Isaiae* (ch. 6) and in *c.* 397 an historical interpretation of the ten visions in Is. 13–23. The *Quaestiones hebraicae in Genesim* were occasioned by the conflict in which his gradually abandoned belief in the inspiration of the LXX had involved him.

b. Of the N.T. he explained four Pauline Epistles (Phil., Gal., Eph., Tit.) in 387–9 and Matthew (superficially) in 398; besides, he revised the commentary on the Apocalypse of Victorinus of Pettau, eliminating chiliastic interpretations (supra § 35) (EP 1362ff.; EA 464/76).

4. *Dogmatic-polemical writings*

In these works Jerome appears as the champion of specifically Catholic ideals (religious state, virginity, devotion to the Blessed Virgin, good works) and opposes the errors of Origen and Pelagius.

a. In the dialogue *Altercatio Luciferiani et orthodoxi* (*c.* 379) he defends, inter alia, the validity of Arian baptism (EP 1358/60).

b. *Adversus Helvidium de perpetua virginitate b. Mariae* (383). Helvidius had alleged that Joseph had had children by Mary after the birth of Jesus. Two books *Adversus Jovinianum* (393), who taught that virginity was not superior to matrimony, that the baptized could no more be induced to fall into sin by the devil, that fasting was worthless and the heavenly rewards the same for all (EP 1378/83; EA 455/63); *Contra Vigilantium* (406) defends the veneration of saints and relics, the monastic ideal and certain liturgical usages.

c. *Contra Ioannem Hierosolymitanum* (396) and the three books *Apologia adv. libros Rufini* (401–2), polemical works composed during the Origenistic controversy, are full of unpleasant personal accusations. His largest and best polemical work is the *Dialogi contra Pelagianos libri III* (415) (EP 1403/6).

5. The historical writings are of comparatively minor importance. Apart from his above-mentioned continuation of *The Chronicle of Eusebius* (supra § 48 I) and his list of authors (supra § 2), he wrote three strongly legendary biographies of monks, the *vitae* of Paul of Thebes, of Malchus of the desert of Chalcis and of Hilarion of Palestine. On the spurious *Martyrologium Hieronymianum* v. supra § 44.

6. *Homilies and Letters*

In 1897 G. Morin published for the first time fifty-nine homilies on the Psalms, ten on Mark and ten on various other Biblical texts; to these were added fourteen further homilies on the Psalms and two homilies on Isaias in 1903. All these are sermons delivered by the saint before his conventual congregation at Bethlehem and taken down by members of the audience.

His letters were highly esteemed already in the Middle Ages. The collection comprises 150 items, of which, however, only 117 are genuine; twenty-six are letters addressed to Jerome or documents.

The letters cover the whole period of his literary activity, thus nearly half a century. They are as important in content as they are excellent in form; they were destined for publication from the beginning. The letters may be divided into those of a personal and family character, ascetical and polemical-apologetic ones, and those of scholarly interest (didactic and exegetical). We would single out *Ep.* 22 *ad Eustochium,* a treatise *De conservanda virginitate, Ep.* 52 to the young priest Nepotian, an instruction on the priestly life. *Epp.* 107 and 128, addressed to two members of the Roman aristocracy, Laeta and Gaudentius, contain thoughts on the education of girls which are important for cultural and educational history.

On individual works: W. Haller, *Jovinianus,* 1897. T. Trzciński, *Die dogmat. Schriften des hl. H.,* 1912 (lit. hist.). N. Pronberger, *Beitr. zur Chronologie der Briefe des hl. H.,* 1914. F. Wutz, *Onomastica sacra,* L 1914/5. G. lo Cascio, *G. da St. Studiato nel suo epistolario,* 1923. G. Bardy, *Rech. sur l'hist. du texte et des versions lat. du "De princ." d'Orig.,* 1923. — Treatises: Van Bakel (supra § 82, 5) 136/56 (Jovinian). Giesser, SM 1935, 241/56 (MS. epp.). Zeiller, CRI 1935, 238/50 (*Ep.* 106, contra De Bruyne). Metlen, *Journ. Engl. Germ. Philol.* 36, 1937, 515/42 (trans. of *Ep.* 106). Schiwietz 3, 1938, 214/20 *(vita Malchi).* Jameson, *Am. Phil. Ass.* 69, 411/22 *(vita Malchi).* Auvray, RSR 1939, 594/610 (controv. with August. on Gal. 2, 11ff.). Simard, RUO 1942, 15/38 (same subj., Gal. 2, 11ff.). Lyonnet, RSR 1939, 344/51 (J. on James the brother of the Lord). Abel, *Vivre et Penser* 1, 1941, 94/119, 212/30 (Cyril of Alex. dependent on J.). On the Pauline commentaries cf. Souter 1927, 96/138. On the Homilies in Pss. cf. Morin, *Études, Textes, Découvertes* I, 1913, 220/93. On the treatise on Is. 6, 1–7 ed. Morin, *Anecd. Maredsol.* III 3, 1903, 103/22 cf. Mercati, OM 2, 1937, 290/7; F. Cavallera, *S. J.* I 2, 1922, 81/6 and W. Dietsche, *Didymus v. Alex. als Verf. der Schrift ueb. d. Seraphenvision,* 1942. With insufficient arguments Dietsche would like to prove Did. to be the author and J. the translator; against this Altaner, TR 1943, 147/51 (prob. author: Theoph. of Alex.). Sofer, WSt 55, 1937, 148/58 (on prologue in Gal. II). On Mt. comment.: Souter, JTS 1941, 171/6 and Lyonnet, Bi 1944, 196/206 (Mt. 2, 23).

Madoz, RET 1944, 211/28; *Epistolario de Alv. de C.,* 1947, 68/80 (J. in Alvaro de Cordoba, who also uses the *Tract. in Pss.*). Quasten, AJP 1942, 207/15 (*Ep.* 64, 19). Chatillon, BullSocÉtHautes-Alpes 62, 1943, 29/151 (on Dardanus, mentioned in *Ep.* 129 and in August., *Ep.* 187). A. Oldfather, *Studies in the Text-Tradition of St. J.'s Vitae patrum,* Urbana 1943. Mierow, Sp 1945, 468/81 (MSS of the *Vita Malchi*). Morin, RBn 1935, 101/13; 1945/6, 5/8 (Eps. Asterius, a pupil of J.). Antin, RML 1947, 53/5 (J. in the *Lib. Pontificalis*). Hulley, HarvStudClassPhil 54, 1943, 83/92 (J. on palaeograph. points); 55, 1945, 87/109 (Principles of text. crit.). Jouassard, Mél. J. Saunier, Lyons 1944, 139/56 *(Adv. Helvid.).* B. Fahl, *Quibus locis . . . attributa ante substantiva collocata sunt,* thesis I 1947. Levy, AJP 1948, 62/8 (on *Ep.* 60, 16: infl. of Claudian). De Blick, RAM 1949, 146/57 (on Ezech: *Syndérèse ou conscience).* Altaner, VC 1950, 246/8 (*Ep.* 106 written betw. 404 and 410). Delahaye, *Mediaev. Stud.* (Toronto) 13, 1951, 65/86 *(L'Adv. Jov. dans quelques écrits lat. du 12e s.)*. F. Valli, *Pubblic. dell'Univ. di Urbino,* ScLettFil 2, 1954 *(Gioviniano. Esame delle fonti e dei frammenti)*. Petzäll, SvenskThKvartalskr 29, 1953, 149/62 (on concept of conscience). Droegereit, *Jb. f. niedersaechs. KG* 1953, 3/15 (Anglo-Saxon fragm. of J.'s *Tract. in Pss.*). Kurfess, SE 1954, 5/12 (Vergil's 4. Ecl. in J. and Aug.). ClavisPL n. 580ff., n. 620: *Epp.* n. 653: spurious *Epp.* Vogels, RBn 1956, 14/9 (*Ambrosiaster* and J.).

On spurious works: De Aldama 1934 (§ 54, 20), 148/50 (*Fides Hieron.* ed.). Griesser, ZKT 1930, 40/87; 1937, 279/321 (MSS of Expos. 4 Evv.). A. Kalff, *Ps.-H., De 7 ordinibus ecclesiae,* thesis Wu 1938 (crit. ed.). *Ep. ad amicum aegrotum* (ML 30, 70/108) cf. L. Drewniak, *Die mariolog. Deutung von Gen. 3, 15,* Br 1934, 57/62; De Orbiso, EstBibl 1942, 1, 187/207, 273/89; on this RHE 1942, 562 and Madoz, EE 1944, 187/200 (Tertull.'s infl.). — Cf. § 81, 10 on 2 ps.-Jer. treatises and § 81, 11 on the ps.-Jer. Ep. 34. M. Pontet, *Rech. crit. sur les comment. des Psaumes attrib. à s. J. et à s. Aug.,* thesis suppl. Lyons 1946 (?). Cavallera, RAM 1949, 158/67 (ML 30, 75/104: *De viro perfecto*). Leclercq, RAM 1949, 140/5 (*J. docteur de l'ascèse* in a Cento from 5 ps.-Jer. letters). Brugnoli, *Benedictina* 9, 1955, 169/73 (*Cod. Farfa* with a ps.-Jer. opusculum). ClavisPL n. 633 and 633a (p. 459): list of spurious letters.

Points of Doctrine

Jerome had neither the inclination nor the gifts to become a speculative theologian. Hence he preferred to avoid purely philosophical trends of thought. His arguments are based almost exclusively on positive material (Scripture, tradition, liturgy, life and practice). In ethical questions he is rigorist in theory, but as a casuist he is more moderate and full of understanding for the demands and difficulties of life.

1. Doctrine of inspiration. In his earlier works he followed the allegorical exegesis of Scripture, but under the influence of his philological activities he increasingly appreciated the historical-grammatical sense of the words of Scripture, without, however, abandoning the Alexandrian method entirely. He held the same axiom as Origen, according to which a Scriptural narrative, if interpreted literally, could contain ridiculous or blasphemous statements. Since he did not work according to consistent hermeneutical principles, his work contains many contradictions and his attitude on fundamental questions is not consistent. He

holds that Scripture is absolutely free from error, even though he does not teach the verbal, but only the real inspiration of the original text. In accordance with contemporary opinion he held at first that the LXX was inspired *(Philem. Prol.)*. Even when commenting on passages such as *Jer.* 28:10; *Helv.* 4 he does not say that the accounts were influenced by erroneous popular views, but only that they were adapted to the prevalent use of language. Owing to Jewish influence he accepted only the protocanonical books of the O.T. (*Prol. Gal.; Praef. Salom.;* EP 1372).

2. Freedom and grace are equally necessary elements in the order of salvation. In some passages he seems not to realize the necessity of prevenient grace: *Nostrum (est) incipere, illius (sc. Dei) perficere* (*Pelag.* 3, 1), and *grandis clementia Dei, ut exspectet nostram poenitentiam et donec nos a vitiis convertamur* (*Is.* 30:18); but in other passages he says that our will, too, is supported by God's help (*Jer.* 24:1 ff.) and that we cannot even do penance unless God converts us (31:18f.). *Velle et nolle nostrum est; ipsumque quod nostrum est, sine Dei miseratione nostrum non est* (*Ep.* 130, 12).

He wants to prove against Pelagius that man cannot be without sin; only God can be without sin, a human being only for some time and with the grace of God (*Pel.* 2, 16; 3, 4). To demand sinlessness from a man would mean to make him God (2, 4). He replies to the objection that if this were so God's commandments would be useless: "God has, indeed, commanded only what is possible, this I too admit; but not each of us can accomplish all these possible things" (1, 23; EP 1404/6).

3. Church and Roman Primacy. No other Church Father before him has expressed his love for the Church so emphatically as Jerome. He fought passionately for the Church and regarded its opponents as his personal enemies (*Pel. Prol.* 2). The doctrinal teaching of the Church is for him the principal source of faith, and he sides decisively with the Roman See. He writes to Pope Damasus: "I follow no one as the first except Christ alone, hence I

want to remain in communion with you, that is, with the see of Peter. I know that the Church is founded on this rock" (*Ep.* 15, 2; EP 1346).

4. Relationship between episcopate and presbyters. In contrast with the conviction of other Fathers of his time, Jerome, basing himself on Phil. 1:1 and Acts 20:17, 28 holds the view that the monarchical episcopate is not *iuris divini* but was instituted by ecclesiastical law especially to prevent the danger of schism within the individual churches. Hence the pre-eminence of the bishops rests *magis consuetudine quam dispositionis dominicae veritate* and *idem est ergo presbyter qui et episcopus* (*Tit.* 1, 5; EH 631/3; EP 1371); however, the bishop alone has the power to ordain *(ordinatio)* (*Ep.* 146, 1) and the bishops are the successors of the apostles (*Ep.* 41, 3).

5. Eschatology. Like Ambrose (supra § 83, 9), Jerome writes that indeed all those who deny God *(negantes et impii)* are subject to the eternal punishment of hell, but not the Christians, even if they are *peccatores;* when they are judged their sentence will be "moderated and mixed with leniency" (*Is.* 66, 24; EP 1402). In *Ep.* 119, 7 he expresses his view even more clearly: *Qui enim tota mente in Christo confidit, etiamsi ut homo lapsus mortuus fuerit in peccato, fide sua vivit in perpetuum.* This merciful attitude of Jerome is due to the attraction of the great Origen which here influenced him even when he had long abandoned his former master of exegesis. Cf. also *Pelag.* 1, 28; *Jov.* 2, 30. The punishments in hell are not, as some think, only interior and spiritual (*Eph.* 3, 5, 6; EP 1370).

L. Schade, *Die Inspirationsl. des hl. H.,* 1910. Encyclical of Benedict XV *Spiritus Paraclitus* of 15th Sept. 1920. J. Niessen, *Die Mariologie des hl. H.,* 1913. L. Hughes, *The Christ. Church in the Epistles of St. J.,* 1923. A. Bardicchia, *Il pensiero morale e pedagogico di S. G.,* Matera 1925. M. S. Weglewicz, *Doctrina S. H. in de ss. Euch.,* R 1931. Ulatowski, *Miscell. theol.,* War 1936, 179/98 (soteriology). G. Violardo, *Il pensiero giuridico di S. G.,* Mi 1937. Waldmann, TQ 1938, 332/71 (doctr. of conscience from Cicero to Jer.). E. Schwarzbauer, *Die Kirche als Corpus Christi Myst. b. hl. H.,* R 1939. J. J. Fahey, *Doctr. S. H.i de gratiae div.*

necessitate, Mund. 1937. Silvestro, SC 1944, 100/10 (Holy Spirit and bapt.). Antin, *Mél. Bénédictines,* S. Wandrille 1947, 69/113 (Le monachisme sel. s. J.). J. P. O'Connel, *The Eschatology of St. J.,* Mund. 1948; cf. TR 1951, 105f. Favez, Mél. Marouzeau, P 1948, 173/81 (J. as educationist). Enrique del S. Corazón y Petro de la Immac., EstJosefinos 3, 1949, 46/80 (St. Josef in J.). A. Penna, *Principi e carattere dell'esegesi di s. G.,* 1950. Baus, TrTZ 1951, 178/88 (prayer to Christ). Nodet, *Mystique et Continence,* Bruges 1952, 308/52 (J. on sexual problems). E. Bruck (v. supra § 3, 28), 76/104 (right of inheritance in J. and August.).

§ 87. CHRISTIAN POETS OF THE FOURTH AND FIFTH CENTURIES

CHRISTIAN poetry, first cultivated in Gnostic circles in the East (supra § 13 and 24, 5), first flourished in the fourth century and in the Latin civilization. Apart from Gregory of Nazianzus the Greek East has produced no important poets. The form of the classic epic was given a new content. The material was furnished by the historical books of Scripture or by the lives and sufferings of the saints and martyrs (Juvencus, Proba, Prudentius, Cyprian). The new lyrical poetry developed in particularly varied ways. To this were added apologetical-polemic poems, poetic letters, epigrams and other forms (Hilary, Ambrose, Niceta, Marius Victorinus, Damasus, Prudentius, Paulinus of Nola, *Carmen adv. Marcionitas*).

H. Lietzmann (KlT 47/9). W. Bulst, *Hymni lat. antiquissimi LXI, psalmi III* ed., 1952 (hymns till 600). — M. Manitius, *Gesch. der christl.-lat. Poesie,* 1891. G. M. Dreves, *Ein Jahrtausend der Hymnendichtung,* 2 vols., 1910. A. S. Walpole, *Early Lat. Hymns,* C 1922. C. Weyman, *Beitr. z. Gesch. d. christl.-lat. Poesie,* 1926. F. J. E. Raby, *A Hist. of Christ. Lat. Poetry,* O ²1953; *A Hist. of Secular Lat. Poetry in the Middle Ages,* 2 vols., 1934. O. J. Kuhnmuench, *Early Christ. Lat. Poets* (4th/6th cents.), Ch 1929. J. Martin, BJ 221, 65/140 (bibliogr. account). Helm, *Natalicium J. Geffcken* 1931, 1/46 (pagan and Christ. elements in late Lat. poets). L. Blume, *Unsere liturg. Lieder,* 1932. Gladysz, CT 1937, 63/98 (Const. the Gr. in the poetry of his time). Mohrmann, *Annal. v. d. Vereeniging . . . de Kathol. in Nederl.* 31, 1939, 197/228 (restraint and freedom in Old Chr. Lat. poetry). Lazzati, SC 1941, 3/15 *(Idee p. una Stor. della Poesia crist.).* Van de Leeuw, Mededeel. Nederl. Ak. Wetensch. N. S. 5, n. 19, 1941 (Galicinium). Raby, *Med. Aevum* 16, 1947, 1/5 (on date). Mohrmann, REL 1947, 28/98 (style and language). Messenger, TP 78, 1947, 208/22 *(Salva festa dies).* Collins, JTS 1949, 68/70 (Corruptions in

Christ. Lat. Poetry). U. Sesini, *Poesia e musica nella latinità crist. dal III al X sec.,* ed. G. Vecchi, Tu 1949. Dohmes, *Gedaechtnisschr. Casel* 1951, 35/53 (pneumatic character of liturg. chant). M. Simonetti (v. § 13, 1) 1952, 339/485 (Hilary. M. Victorinus, Ambrose: 376/430; Irish hymns: 457/77; Te Deum: 478/81). N. K. Chadwick, *Poetry and Letters in Early Christ. Gaul,* 1955.

1. *Laudes Domini.* A miracle that occurred between 316 and 323 is described in 148 hexameters: a dead woman raises her hand in greeting when her husband is being buried beside her. A praise of Christ, the Creator and Redeemer, is appended. In conclusion the poem calls down blessings on the Emperor Constantine and his house. The poet has taken Virgil as his model.

Edd.: ML 61, 1091/4 and W. Brandes, *Progr. Braunschw.* 1887. Bardy, *Mém. de l'Acad. . . . de Dijon* 1933, 36/51 (Reticius of Autun the hero of the miracle?); cf. RSR 1939, 16f.

2. About 330 Juvencus, a Spanish priest, composed a Har mony of the Gospels in 3211 hexameters, entitled *Evangeliorum libri IV.* The Gospel accounts are paraphrased as faithfully as possible in fairly correct verse modelled on Virgil. The poet follows almost exclusively the Itala text of Matthew; scarcely a fifth of the verse is drawn from the other Gospels.

Edd.: J. Huemer (CSEL 24) 1891. Germ. A. Knappitsch, 3 Progr. Graz 1910/2. Mercati, OM 4, 1937, 506/12 (Cod. Vat. lat. 5759). M. Helene, *The class. Bull.* 15, 1939, 57/9 (Vergil). Vega, CD 1945, 209/47 (J. and Prudentius). H. H. Kievits, *Ad J.i Evv. lib. I comment. exegeticus,* thesis Gron. 1940. F. Langaná, *Giovenco,* Catania 1947. J. De Wit, *Ad Juvenci evang. libr. 2 comm. exeget.,* Gron. 1947; VC 1954, 145/8 (text. crit.). Norton, Folia 4, 1950, 36/42 (prosopography of J.). L. Strzelecki, *De Synaloephae apud J. usu:* Rozpravi Wydzialu Filolog. 68 n. 3; cf. REL 1950, 283. N. Hansson, *Textkr. zu J. m. einem vollstaendigen Index verborum,* Lund 1950.

3. About 360 the noble Roman lady Proba treated the Biblical primitive history down to the Flood and the history of the redemption in a cento of 694 hexameters borrowed from Virgil. In this way the historic course of events could, of course, be presented only in indefinite allusions which were often distorted and sometimes actually comic.

Edd.: C. Schenkl (CSEL 16) 1888, 569/609. F. Ermini, *Il Centone di Proba e la poesia centonaria lat.,* 1909.

4. An unknown poet wrote two poems, 167 hexameters *De Sodoma* and 105 hexameters *De Jona* which have been preserved under the names of Tertullian or Cyprian. Though closely following the Biblical account, the poet gives colourful descriptions faithful to nature. The date is uncertain.

Ed.: R. Peiper (CSEL 23) 1891, 212/26.

5. Ausonius, b. *c.* 310 at Bordeaux, was at first teacher of grammar and rhetoric in his native city, where Paulinus of Nola was his pupil. After 365 he was tutor of the princes at Treves, consul in 379[?] he returned to Bordeaux after 393. He was a clever versifier but with few ideas and rather dry. He made an external profession of Christianity only under Valentinian I (364–75). In his poems his religious attitude is not very clear and decided, so that it is a matter of dispute whether he was a pagan or a Christian.

Among his many *Opuscula*—his best-known poem is the *Mosella,* a description of the Moselle region and the city of Treves—there are but few of a Christian character. These are the *Versus paschales* (thirty-one hexameters among his epigrams), a paschal prayer for the Emperor Valentinian I with a Nicene confession of the Trinity (*c.* 370); *Oratio (matutina),* eighty-five hexameters in the *Ephemeris* (poem on the author's daily work); *Oratio versibus rhopalicis* (fourteen strophes of three verses each) so called (*rhopalici* = club-shaped) because the verses begin with words of one syllable followed by others with a regular increase in the number of syllables.

Among his twenty-five versified letters three addressed to Paulinus of Nola after 390 are of special interest. Ausonius wants to dissuade his friend from his intention to leave the world. Paulinus refuses in two letters also metrical (*Carmen* 10 and 11).

Edd.: C. Schenkl (MGAuctAnt 5, 2) 1883. R. Peiper, L 1886. H. G. E. White, 2 vols., Lo 1919/21 (with trans.). M. Jasinski, A. (French trans.), P 1936. *Mosella:* ed. C. Hosius, L [3]1926. W. John, Treves 1932. Trans. H. Besser[2], Marburg 1936. E. H. Blakeney, Lo 1933. — F. Marx, PWK 2, 2562/80. Labriolle, DHGE 5,

773/9; RACh 1, 1020/3. M. J. Pattist, *A. als Christ,* A 1925. On the *Mosella:* Marx, RM 1931, 368/92; Deubner, Phil 1934, 253/8; Thielscher PW 1935, 1102/4; Kurfess, PW 1935, 1295f.; Bieler, RM 1937, 285/7. — V. Crisi, *De re metr. et pros. D. M. Ausonii* I, Udine 1938. Emonds 1941, 82/108. G. Jackmann, Festschr. d. Univ. Koeln 1941, 47/104 (on trad. of A.). John, Her 1943, 92/105. Favez, Lat 6, 1947, 223/33 (school of rhetors at Bordeaux). Kurfess, SE 1953, 141/3 *(In ludum 7 sapientum); Gymnasium* 60, 1953, 262 f. RM 1954, 2 (The 3 Sibyls in A.); *Gymnasium* 1955, 543/6 (trans. of *Epp.* 27 and 30). E. Blanchet, *Humanisme et christianisme A. et S. Paulin* (Conf.), Bordeaux 1954.

6. Aurelius Prudentius Clemens has himself provided information on his life in the foreword to the edition of his works (eight books) which he produced towards the end of it. According to this he was born in 348, probably at Calahorra, received a rhetorical and legal training, was twice consul of a Spanish province and after this held a high official position close to Theodosius I. Eventually he gave up public life in order to live completely for Christ. In 402–3 he made a pilgrimage to Rome and visited the tombs of the martyrs. He died in Spain after 405.

Prudentius is undoubtedly the greatest early Christian poet of the West, who wanted to contribute to the glory of the Church's faith in conscious opposition to paganism and heresy. Being a true poet, he was able to give even the most unpromising material a poetic form, for he had a rich imagination, deep feeling and a figurative language at his disposal. Though influenced by Virgil (especially in the *Psychomachia* and *Contra Symmachum*) he was very versatile and a master of metrical structure. His genius was capable of developing wholly new forms of art. In the *Psychomachia* he created the allegorical epic, and he developed the epigram in an epic-lyrical direction. His hymns are non-liturgical, of purely aesthetical inspiration. Prudentius was the most admired and most widely read poet in the Middle Ages, as is evident, inter alia, from the fact that more than 300 MSS of his works containing about 10,000 lines are extant. For us his work is essentially of historical and aesthetical interest.

The first book is called *Cathemerinon liber* (Book of daily songs).

It contains twelve very long predominantly lyrical poems in various metres. The first six are destined for the different times of day *(ad galli cantum, matutinas, ante cibum, post cibum, ad incensum lucernae, ante somnium)*, whereas the others also contain two Lenten hymns, one hymn for Christmas and one for Epiphany. The hymns of the Roman Breviary for the Feast of the Holy Innocents and the Epiphany (except *Crudelis Herodes,* which is by Sedulius) are taken from the last-named hymn.

The second book *Apotheosis* defends the Church's doctrine of the Trinity against heresy. Gnostic dualism is refuted in the third book *Hamartigenia* (Source of sin), which treats of the origin of sin. The fourth book, *Psychomachia* (Fight for the soul), is the first allegorical poem in Latin; Christian virtues and pagan vices fight for man's soul.

The hard struggle between Christianity and paganism victoriously conducted by Ambrose is cast in poetic form in the next two books (V and VI) *Contra Symmachum* (402–3). The first opposes paganism in general, the second the *Relatio Symmachi,* that is, the petition drawn up by Symmachus (d. 402) as the leader of the pagan faction of the senate in favour of the *Ara Victoriae* (supra § 83). His refutation follows particularly two letters of St. Ambrose (*Epp*. 17f.) which treat of the same subject.

The seventh book *Peristephanon* ("On the crowns of victory" or "martyrdom") is of epic-lyrical, sometimes even dramatic character: fourteen poems in the most diverse metres in praise of Spanish (e.g. Vincent) and Roman (e.g. Hippolytus and Lawrence) martyrs (including also St. Cyprian of Carthage). These martyrs' stories with their graphic, frequently very realistic descriptions, have served as a model for the medieval martyrs' legends and for Christian art, especially in the baroque period.

The eighth book *Dittochaeon* ("Twofold food"), important for the history of art, explains Biblical scenes in forty-nine tetrastichs.

Edd.: ML 59/60. J. Bergman (CSEL 61) 1926. M. Laverenne, 4 vols. (with trans.), 1943 1945 1948 1951. J. Guillén-I. Rodríguez, *Ed. bilingue, vers. y introd.*, Ma 1949. H. J. Thomson, Engl. trans., Lo and C (Mass.) 1949. F. Sciuto, *Lib. cath. with Praefatio and Epilogue* (text and trans.), Ca 1955. R. J. Deferrari and J. M. Campbell, *A Concordance of P.*, C (Mass.) 1932. — Mgg. and Studies: C. Brockhaus 1872. A. Roesler 1886. A. Puech, P 1888. J. Bergman, Dorpat 1922. G. Villada 1, 2, 1929, 155/209. L. Riber, Barcelona 1936. Bardy, DTC 13, 1076/9. E. K. Rand, *P. and Christ. Humanism,* 1920. H. Woodruff, *The Illustr. MSS of P.*, C (Mass.) 1930. M. Lavarenne, *Ét. sur la langue du poète P.*, P 1933 (607/30 full bibliogr.). A. Mahoney, *Vergil in the Works of P.,* W 1934. L. de S. Juan de la Cruz, *Dónde nació P. ?,* Calahorra 1935 (56 pp.). I. Rodríguez-Herrera, *Poeta christ. P.'s Auffass. vom Wesen u. v. d. Aufgabe des christl. Dichters,* thesis Mn 1936. Bardy, RSR 1935, 363 *(Psych.)*. Sanford, CP 1936, 71. Alexander, WSt 1936, 166/73 (Ovid). Vives, AST 1936 (biogr.). Cotogni, RAL 1936, 441/61 *(Psych.)*. Colombo, StU 171/5 (text. crit.). C. Schwen, *Vergil bei P.*, 1937. Rodríguez, Eccl. Rev. (Philad.) 1937, 485/91 (Cath. 11, 61/80). Villoslada, RF 116, 1939, 341/70 (patriot. españ.). G. Meyer, Phil. 93, 1938, 377/403 (text. crit.). Martija, *Palaestra lat. Horatiana,* Cervera 1935, 25/31. Strzelecki, *Commentat. Horatianae,* Cracow 1935, I 36/49. U. Boscaglia, *La Passio S. Laurentii di Pr. e le sue fonti,* Udine 1938. Alamo, RHE 1939, 750/6 (P. born at Calahorra). J. Stam, *Prud.i Hamartigenia,* thesis Ley 1940 (text and comm.). Biener, *Beitr. Gesch. dtsch. Spr. u. Lit.* 64, 1940, 308/34 (Old High Germ. P.-glosses). Waszink, Mn 11, 1942, 68/77 (Cath. 3, 95/100). Blomgren, Er 1940, 109/11. Lavarenne, REL 1941, 76/9. G. Lazzati, *Atti R. Ist. Veneto* 101, P 2, 217/33 (1941/2) *(doppia redazione delle opere)*. M. Liguori Ewald, *Ovid in the C. Symm. of P.,* W 1942. M. J. Bayo, *Perist. de P. Estudio y trad.,* Ma 1943. Bloomfield, Sp 1943, 87/90 *(Psychomachia)*. Gossens, Lat 6, 1947, 197/205 (*Hamart.* 402). Vives, AST 17, 1945, 195/204 (*Peristeph.* 11). Vega (v. supra n. 2) and CD 158, 1946, 193/271 (comprehensive appreciation); CD 159, 1947, 421/67; 160, 1948, 5/34; 185/240 *(Psych.-Peristeph.)*. Lazzati, NDid 1947 *(Transfigurazione della morte)*. Quispel, Lat 6, 1947, 193/5 (on *Hamart.* 905). Manelli, MiscStLCA 1, 1947, 79/126 *(Personalità nel Dittoch.)*. Amatucci, NDid 1, 1947, 35/45 (on *Cathem.*). E. Rapisarda, NDid 2, 1948, 51/61 *(Praefatio)*. VC 1950, 46/60 (infl. of Lucretius); *Introduzione alla lettura di P.,* Ca 1951; Orph. 1, 1954, 1/13 (the 2 *Praefat.* of *C. Symmach.*). E. Rapisarda, MiscStLCA 2, 1948, 21/59 (Gr. language) 1, 1947, 45/65 *(Rappresent. dell'oltre tomba)*. Jannacone, REL 1948, 228/34 (Cod. Par. 8084). P. Parella, *La poesia lat. crist. ant. c. particol. riferimento alle Corone di Prud.,* Na 1952. K. L. Schmidt, TZ 1949, 469 (P. and Erasmus). Madoz, *Hispania sacra* 3, 1950, 131/7 (B. Valerianus in *Peristeph.* 9). Rodríguez, Hel 1, 1950, 85/101 *(Poeta de la Hispanidad)*. Guillén, Hel 1, 273/99 (P. y la mitología). Grasso MiscStLCA 3, 1951, 124/35 (*Testo bibl. in Ham. preaf.* 11/13). B. M. Peebles, *The Poet P.,* NY 1951. Pedraz, *Humanidades* 1951, 22/40 (Filos. de la hist.). S. Cir. Estopañián, *Universidad* (Zaragoza) 28, 1951, 81/144 (home of P.). Madoz 1951, 41/9 (further lit.). Collins, SE 1952, 188/92 (text. crit. of *Cathem.*). W. Schmid, VC 1953, 171/86 (stages of humanity and problems of double redaction). Kurfess, PWK 23, 1039/72.

7. St. Paulinus, Bishop of Nola, b. 353 at Bordeaux, belonged to a very rich senatorial family. He was a pupil and friend of Ausonius, to whom he owed his appointment as governor of Campania in 379. He later led a life of aesthetic leisure on his estates near Bordeaux, where he was baptized *c.* 390.

Soon afterwards, struck by grave misfortunes, he decided to renounce the world. He went to Spain, where he was ordained priest despite his objections, and finally (395) retired to Nola (Campania) together with his wife Therasia, so as to be near the tomb of his patron Saint Felix to whom, as he believed, he owed it that he was not accused of fratricide. Having given up conjugal relations he led a strictly monastic life. He was elected bishop in 409. His contemporaries admired him as a model of Christian austerity and selfless devotion in the service of his neighbours. He died in 431. Feast day: June 22nd.

a. His thirty-five poems composed mostly in hexameters show his cultured taste and his formal skill, but they are lacking in the creative power and the vigour of imagination which mark the works of Prudentius. He dedicated no less than fourteen *Carmina natalicia* of diverse contents to St. Felix, for his feast day on January 14th. *Carmina* 10 and 11, destined for Ausonius, reflect most impressively the opposition and the struggle between pagan and Christian cultural aims.

b. Among the recipients of his prose correspondence which comprises about fifty items we find his most famous Christian contemporaries, e.g. Augustine, Martin of Tours and Sulpicius Severus. The contents offer much instructive information on the religious life, especially with regard to the liturgical and extra-liturgical piety of the time.

Edd.: ML 61. W. Hartel (CSEL 29/30) 1894. — Mgg. and studies: F. Lagrange, P [2]1882. A. Baudrillart, P [2]1905. Leclercq, DAL 8, 2824/6; 12, 1439/65. Amann, DTC 12, 68/71. Helm, PWK 18, 2, 2331/51. P. Reinelt, *Stud. ueb. d. Briefe des hl. P. v. N.*, 1904. P. L. Kraus, *Die poet. Sprache des P. N.*, 1918. V. Iodice, *Profilo stor. et estet. di s. P.*, R 1931 (36 pp.). Wiman, Er 1934.

98/130 (text. crit.). Favez, REL 1935, 266/8 (*Carm.* 32); id. 1937 (v. supra § 34), R. C. Goldschmidt, *P.'s Churches at Nola. Texts, Trans. and Comm.*, A 1940. A. P. Muys, *De briefwiss. van P v. N. en Augustinus*, 1941. Blomgren, Er 1940, 62/7. J. Morelli, *De S. P.i N.i doctr. christol.*, Na 1945. G. Rizza, MiscStLCA 1947, 155/64 *(Imitaz. bibl. e influenza retor.)*. Courcelle, REL 1947, 250/80 *(P. et s. Jér.)*; VC 1947, 101/13 (v. § 87, 13). Boulanger, VC 1947, 183/5 (Christ. friendship). P. Fabre, *Essai sur la chronologie de l'œuvre de s. P. de N.*, 1948 (*Carm.* 32 and 33 and *Passio Genesii* spurious); *S. P. de N. et l'amitié chrét.*, 1949. Hudson-Williams, Er 48, 1950, 70f. (text. crit. of *Carm.* 31, 444). Courcelle, Mél. L. Halphen 1951, 145/53 (P. de N. in Greg. of Tours). — Chierici, RAC 16, 1939, 59/92 and Ambrosiana (Festschr.) (§ 83) 1942, 315/31 (on the excavations of the buildings of P.). Courcelle, RevEA 1951, 253/300 (Correspondence with Aug.).

8. Claudius Claudianus (d. after 404), the greatest pagan poet and representative of Roman mythological poetry. He was a half-Greek Egyptian; according to his own testimony (*Carm. min.* 41, 14), before his emigration from Alexandria to Rome (395) he only wrote in Greek. He lived at the court of the Emperor Honorius as a favourite of the minister Stilicho. Though a pagan at heart, he nevertheless adapted himself to the Christian atmosphere of the imperial court and, as a nominal Christian, also sometimes wrote Christian poems for the sake of the Emperor. The twenty-line *Carmen De Salvatore* (in Birt, *Carm. min.* 32 and ML 53, 788f.) contains a brief Christology. Two other poems, *Laus Christi* and *Miracula Christi* can hardly be considered genuine. Augustine (*Civ.* 5, 26) says of him that he was a *Christi nomine alienus* and Orosius, who certainly exaggerates, calls him *paganus pervicacissimus* (*Hist.* 7, 35), judgements which are understandable in view of his voluminous poetic work entirely devoted to pagan mythology. The certainly genuine hymn to Christ is an impressive document of the syncretistic character of a religious transition period.

Edd.: T. Birt (MGAuctAnt 10) 1892. V. Crépin, 2 vols., P 1933. — Studies: Vollmer, PWK 3, 2652/60. W. Schmid, RACh 3, 152/67. P. Fargues, *C. Ét. sur sa poésie et son temps*, 1933. Turcevic, BZ 1934, 1/9 (home: Paphlagonia). H. Steinbeiss, *Das Geschichtsbild C.s*, 1936. P. Fargues, *C. Panegyricus de 4. consulatu Honorii. Texte et comm.*, Aix-en-Prov. 1936. K. A. Mueller, *C.s Festged. auf d. 6. Konsulat des K. H.*, 1938 (text and comm.). H. L. Lewy, *C. C., The Invect. in Ruf.*, NY 1935 (text and comm.). Fabbri, *Athenaeum* 1939, 27/40 (d. after 410). Nissen,

Her 1940, 298/325 (epic and paneg.). Kurfess, Her 1941, 93/5 (on invectives). A. H. Eaton, *The Influence of Ovid on C.,* W 1943. Levy, AJP 1948, 62/8 (C.'s *In Ruf.* and on *Ep. of St. Jer.*). W. Schmid, SIF 1956, 498/518 (on authenticity of hymn to Christ).

9. Both the place of origin and the date of the pseudo-Tertullian *Carmen adv. Marcionitas* are disputed; it probably belongs to the fourth century.

See BJ 221, 83 f. M. Mueller, *Unters. z. Carm. adv. M.,* 1936 (ed. of text; date before 325). K. Holl, *Ges. Aufsaetze* 3, 1928, 13/53 (date betw. 475 and 525).

10. Cyprian of Gaul. The *Heptateuchos,* imperfectly preserved, is a metrical version of the historical books of the O.T. It was formerly ascribed to Juvencus, being a voluminous counterpart of his work; but its author is an otherwise unknown priest called Cyprian, who lived in Gaul in the first half of the fifth century. He may also have composed the Biblical cento *Caena Cypriani.*

Edd.: R. Peiper (CSEL 23) 1891. ML 4, 925/32 *(Caena).* A. Harnack, TU 19, 3 b, 1899 *(Caena).* Lapôtre, RSR 1912, 497/596 *(Caena).* W. Hass, *Studien z. Heptateuchdichter C.,* thesis B 1912. Kujper, VC 1952, 44/6 (text. crit. on Jud. 547). Krestan, RACh 3, 477/81.

11. Sedulius was a native of Southern Gaul or Italy. According to Isidore of Seville (*Vir. ill.* 20) he was a priest and composed, probably before 431, a *Paschale Carmen* in five books, describing the mighty deeds of God in the O.T. (Book I) and the N.T. (Books II–III) in simple, lively language and an almost classical metric technique. Sedulius treats his material, which is also taken chiefly from St. Matthew's Gospel, far more freely than Juvencus. He later enlarged the work which he published, cast in the form of rhetorical prose, under the title *Paschale opus.*

We also have two hymns of his on Christ. The first, called *Elegy,* gives parallels between the O.T. and the N.T. in fifty-five distichs; the second, a poetically more valuable *Abecedarius,* tells of the life of Christ in twenty-three verses of four lines each; two hymns of the Roman Breviary, *A solis ortus cardine* for Christmas (*Hymn.* 1, 1–28) and the Epiphany hymn *Crudelis*

Herodes, Deum, which begins in Sedulius, *Hostis Herodes impie* (so also in the Dominican rite; *Hymn.* 1, 29–52) are taken from this *Abecedarius.*

Edd.: J. Huemer (CSEL 10) 1885. T. Mayer, *Stud. zu d. Pasch. Carm. des christl. Dichters S.,* 1916. B. Gladysz, *Dogmat. teksty w poet. utworach Seduliusza,* Poznań 1930; *Rym w poezij Sed.,* Lwów 1930. McDonald, Sp 1933, 150/6 (native of S. Gaul or Spain). N. Scheps, *S., P. Carmen 1–2,* Delft 1938 (trans. and comm.): native of S. Gaul or Italy. Manton, JTS 1939, 365/70 (MS of *Pasch. Carm.*). Altaner, ZNTW 39, 1941, 162 168 (S. and Eustathius, the transl. of Basil). F. Corsaro, *La poesia di S.,* Ca 1945; *L'opera poetica di S.,* Ca 1948 (trans. and comm.); *La Lingua di S.,* Ca 1949.

12. Claudius Marius Victor (d. 425–50), rhetor at Marseilles, is the author of a poem *Alethia* in three books. It is written in hexameters and is a paraphrase commenting Genesis material down to the destruction of Sodom. The *Hexaemeron* of St. Ambrose is frequently used.

Edd.: C. Schenkl (CSEL 16) 1888. Mgg.: O. Ferrari, Pavia 1912. Krappe, Sp 17, 1942, 255/60 (Persian myth). A. Staat, *De cultuur beschouwing van Cl. M. Victor. Comment. of Alethia 2,* 1–202, A 1952. P. F. Hovingh, *M. Victor Cl., Alethia. La prière et les vers 1–170 du livre 1* (with introd., trans. and comm.). Groningen 1955; VC 1956, 43/48 (on 2, 219/26).

13. Paulinus of Pella in Macedonia (b. 376, d. after 459) grandson of Ausonius, wrote an autobiography in 616 hexameters in 459, when he was 83 years old. The work has a brief preface in prose called *Eucharisticos (sc. logos).* The description of his sorrowful life gives a vivid idea of the terrible conditions in the moribund Roman Empire.

Text: W. Brandes (CSEL 16, 263/334); not in Migne. L. Rocafort, *Un type gallo–romain, P. de Pella,* 1896 (with prose trans.). G. Misch, *Gesch. der Autobiographie* 1, [2]1931, 445/51. Courcelle, VC 1947, 101/13 (19 lines in *carm. 4* of P. of Nola belong to P. of Pella).

14. Commodian's personality and dates are much disputed. His writings are the only biographical source available; for the information of Gennadius *(Vir. ill.* 15) is taken from them. He was perhaps a layman of ascetical life *(mendicus Christi, Instr.*

2, 39), who probably hailed from Gaza. Even today scholars date his life between the middle of the third and the fifth centuries. According to the traditional view, recently again defended with good arguments especially by J. Martin (1957), Commodian is held to be the oldest Latin Christian poet: he was a countryman of Cyprian, whose works he frequently used. Brisson and Simonetti now also support an early date (against Courcelle). This opinion has frequently been contradicted ever since Brewer (1906ff.) assumed 460 as the date and S. Gaul (Arles) as the home of the poet. The later date is supported especially by linguistic, metrical and prosodical peculiarities; Vogt assigns to him the time after 300, Gasparetti about 400, and Brakman the fifth century in general. Courcelle seeks to prove his dependence on Orosius and Salvian. Even the latest research has not produced any certainty about the date, which can only be deduced from internal evidence capable of different interpretation.

a. *Instructiones,* a collection of eighty poems in acrostic form, is divided into two books. The first of these is apologetic, addressed to pagans and Jews, the second gives exhortations to catechumens and faithful, chiefly instructions for the various Christian estates and vocations (e.g. sick visits, funerals etc.). The end of the world will come to pass 6000 years after its creation.

b. *Carmen apologeticum* has affinities with the contents of the first book of the *Instructiones.* Here, too, the author wants to convince pagans and Jews of the truth of Christianity. The language has a strong admixture of vulgar Latin and is often obscure because of its brevity. The poems *(Instr.)* are only rhythmic prose which is governed by the accent of the words and the number of syllables rather than by quantity. Only the description of the last times shows some poetic inspiration (*Carm.* 791ff.). In his theology the poet shows himself to be a Sabellian and a chiliast. This is probably the reason why the *Decretum Gelasianum* counts his poems among the apocrypha.

Edd.: B. Dombart (CSEL 15) 1887. A. F. van Katwijk, *Lex. Commodianeum,* A 1934. — Mgg.: H. Brewer, *K. v. Gaza,* 1906; *Die Frage um das Zeitalter K.s,* 1910; ZKT 1912, 641/50, 849/63; against this F. Zeller, TQ 1909/10 and J. Martin, TU 39, 4, 1913 and BJ 221, 88/97. J. Durel, *C.,* P 1912. — Studies: E. Rein (Publications of Helsingfors Univ.) 1923, 1/89. Gasparetti, Did 1926, 2, 1/48. Brakman, Mn 1927, 121/44, 269/72. Doelger, AC 4, 271/5 (*Carm.* 76). M. Mueller, *Unters. zum Carmen adv. Marcion.,* 1936, 92f. (C. depends on *Carm. adv. Marc.*). Brisson, RSR 1946, 280/316 (social unrest in Africa in the 3rd cent., acc. to C.). Courcelle, REL 1946, 227/46. Herrmann, ACl 1942, 235/41 (C. supposed to be the hero of the Alexius legend! [§ 46, 13e]). Goodspeed, CP 41, 1946, 46f. N. Papalardo, *C.,* thesis Ca 1947. C. Sessa, *La poesia di C.,* Ca 1947. Schepens, RSR 1949, 603 (on *Instr.* 2, 17 19). E. Castorina, *La poesia di C. nella storia della metrica lat.,* Ca 1950. Simonetti, Aev 1953, 227/39. J. Vogt, ParPass F. 34, 1954, 14. Martin, Tr 1957. Krestan, RACh 3, 248/52.

§ 88. ST. AUGUSTINE (354–430)

ESPECIALLY since 1945 the literature on Augustine has increased so much that it cannot be listed in full. I would refer scholars to two periodicals edited by members of the Augustinian Order, *L'Année théologique* = *L'Année théologique augustinienne* = (since 1955) *Revue des Études augustiniennes,* P, and *Augustiniana* (since 1951) Lou. These have an exhaustive bibliography of all relevant publications. The first-mentioned journal especially, often also contains brief information on the contents of the publications. The Augustinians of the Dutch Province are preparing a *Thesaurus linguae Augustinianae;* cf. VC 1957, 49.

1. *His Life and Importance*

The sources giving an account of Augustine's life and development are of an abundance unique in the history of antiquity. The most illuminating material is to be found in the first nine books of his *Confessions* (till the death of his mother in 387). We can gather further important information and insight into his work from other writings of his, especially from the unfinished *Retractationes* (two books) that give an account of his entire literary production down to 427. Here we are informed on the circumstances in which his works originated. Many statements that seemed erroneous to him or open to misunderstanding are corrected and clarified (EP 1965/74; EH 765/7).

The *Vita,* written by Bishop Possidius of Calama, a disciple and friend of the saint, shortly after the latter's death, gives not always wholly reliable information. An extensive, though not complete list of Augustine's writings *(Indiculus)* is added to it.

Edd. and Studies of the *Retract.:* CSEL 36. G. Bardy, *Les Révisions (=Retract.),* 1950 (text and trans.). P. Montanari (trans.), Fl 1949. M. F. Eller, *The Retract. of St. A.,* thesis Boston 1946; CH 1949, 172/83. Burnaby, AugMag 1, 1954, 85/92. Lagrange, Misc. A 2, 373/95. — *Vita Poss.:* in ML 32. H. T. Weiskotten, Princeton 1919. A. C. Vega, E 1934. F. R. Hoare, *The Western Fathers* (text and trans.), 1954. New crit. ed. by M. Pellegrino, Alba (Cuneo) 1955. — Germ. trans. Romeis, 1930. — Studies and trans.: A. Harnack, AbhB 1930, 1. M. Pellegrino, Aev 1954, 21/44; SC 1954, 249/66. Courcelle, RSR 1951, 428/42 (*Poss.* and *Confess.*). — *Indiculus:* text in ML 46, 5/22. E. Kalinka, SbW 1925, 1; also in Wilmart, MiscA 2, 149/233 and Vega, l. c. — Studies: De Bruyne, MiscA 2, 317/9 (text. crit.) also Jax, WSt 1935, 133/46.

Augustine was born at Thagaste in Numidia in 354. Perhaps neither of his parents was of purely Roman descent.

His father Patricius, who was a municipal official, came to the Church as a catechumen only late in life and was baptized shortly before his death (371). His mother Monica was a devout Christian; her great ambition, however, caused her, like her husband, to think only of a brilliant future for her child; hence she was responsible for many shortcomings in the education of the exceptionally gifted boy. During a grave illness the young Augustine asked for baptism, but as the danger passed quickly, his mother, following the custom of her time, only had him enrolled as a catechumen.

Augustine received his first lessons at Thagaste. As his father wanted him to become a rhetor, he first continued his studies in the neighbouring Madaura but went to Carthage in 371. There the young student was tempted to sensual excesses, and he soon contracted a liaison which lasted till about 384. His son Adeodatus (d. 390) was born in 372. At that time he despised the religion of his mother, as he says himself, as "an old wives' tale". In 373 his curriculum prescribed the reading of Cicero's dialogue *Hortensius,* and this roused in him the desire for a philosophical foundation of his life. Shortly afterwards he joined the Manicheans as an extern *(auditor)*. This sect may have appeared to his intellectual pride as an enlightened religion unfettered by authority and as the true form of Christianity as opposed to ecclesiastical Christianity. When Augustine had finished his studies (374–5) and settled at Thagaste as professor of the liberal arts, Monica did not receive him into her house, because he had forsaken the faith of his parents. A bishop consoled her with the words: "A child of so many tears cannot be lost" (*Conf.* 3, 12). Towards the end of this time his doubts about the truth of the Manichean system increased. Its cosmology seemed incompatible with the teaching of Greek philosophy, and he also recognized the contradictions in its dualism and its conception of God. Moreover, he was greatly disappointed by a conversation with the famous Manichean, Bishop Faustus of Milevis, who, he realized, was actually a not very educated babbler. Nevertheless, he remained in touch with his Manichean friends even in Rome, where he moved in 383 against the will of his mother. During this period of interior instability philosophic scepticism gained a hold over him, even though only for a short time.

At the beginning of 384 he was appointed to the post of professor of rhetoric in Milan advertised by the city, through the good offices of the pagan prefect Symmachus of Rome.

Despite his secure and distinguished position his heart was torn and he was more unhappy than ever, though his mother and some near relations were with him. For he was not only still imprisoned in his sensual passion, but his desire for religious security remained unfulfilled. When, however, he attended the sermons of Bishop Ambrose of Milan, who frequently explained consecutive texts of the O.T. books according to the allegorical method, he realized that this was the way to answer the Manichean objections to the O.T. Here he learned that the concept of God as a pure spirit, the spirituality of the soul and the freedom of the will, could very well be harmonized with the teaching of the Church despite its acceptance of the O.T. If, following P. Courcelle (1950), we might date Ambrose's sermons on the Hexaemeron, on *De Isaac et anima* and *De bono mortis* before August 386, just these homilies, in which Ambrose used especially Plotinus' treatise *On the Beautiful,* would also have acquainted Augustine with neo-Platonic thought. In the decisive year 386 the rhetor in search of a new philosophy had his attention drawn to treatises of Plotinus, already available in a Latin translation, probably by the Christian neo-Platonist Manlius Theodorus (*Conf.* 7, 9, 13; *Beata vita* 4). He was greatly helped intellectually by these writings, in which God was presented to him as a purely spiritual substance, and evil as a negation. Simplicianus, a priest of neo-Platonic leanings, who later succeeded Ambrose as Bishop of Milan showed him how the teaching of Plotinus on the *Nous* was completed by the Logos speculation in the Prologue of St. John's Gospel. Thus philosophy prepared Augustine for faith in the eternal Logos-God (*Civ.* 12, 29, 2). The same Simplicianus also drew his attention to the importance of reading the Letters of St. Paul (*Conf.* 7, 21, 27). As a neo-Platonist he had hoped to achieve union with God through philosophical meditation; now the Apostle taught him that it could be attained only through the grace of God. At a time when his interior struggle was at its height Simplicianus told him how resolutely and without human respect the famous rhetor Marius Victorinus (§ 81, 6) had finally conquered all obstacles barring his reception into the Church, and when one day a friend described to him the austere lives of the hermit Anthony (supra § 52, 1) and other hermits and monks, he felt that the hour of decision had come. Deeply moved, he ran into the garden and there heard the voice of a child repeating the words: *Tolle, lege.* He opened the Pauline Epistles, read Rom. 13:13f. and all the darkness of doubt vanished. A few weeks later, in the autumn of 385, he resigned his office and retired to Cassiciacum, the estate of a friend near the city, to be enrolled for baptism at the beginning of the following Lent.

There are clear indications that even some time before the scene in the garden, Augustine had been firmly resolved to become a Catholic and to submit to the authority of the Church as the representative of the truth he had been seeking so long. From the moving description of his conversion in *Conf.* 8, 6—12, we learn in the first place how the rhetor, who was already willing to believe, came to renounce wealth and honour to choose the more perfect way of complete continence, which he even then held to be more perfect, and to give up marriage. The mind that had been freed from the fetters of sensuality and passion was in future to be wholly devoted to the study of truth and thus to achieve beatitude.

Augustine was baptized by St. Ambrose on Holy Saturday 387, together with his son and his friend Alypius. Several months later he set out on his journey home to Africa via Rome, during which his mother died at Ostia. After Monica's death Augustine stayed in Rome for about a year, occupied with literary works. In the autumn of 388 he arrived at his native city, Thagaste. Here he lived for almost three years together with some friends in monastic seclusion. But his reputation for scholarship and piety was even then very great, thus when, in 391, he entered the church quite unsuspecting, Bishop Valerius of Hippo together with the people asked him to become a priest. He was taken completely by surprise, but eventually agreed to be ordained. With this, his spiritual and intellectual development entered a new stage. His hitherto predominantly philosophical interests and his occupation with the liberal arts gave way to a purely theological orientation and practical activities in the service of the Church. In 395 Valerius had him consecrated his co-adjutor bishop. When soon afterwards the bishop died, Augustine succeeded him.

As a bishop he continued the monastic community life with his clergy, which he had practised already with his friends at Thagaste and later as a priest. He was a zealous preacher and indefatigable in his care for the poor. But he devoted much of his energy to literary activities, especially to the ecclesiastical controversies of the time.

First of all, the literary struggle against Manicheism, with which he had finally broken only when he entered the Church, continued to be at the centre of his activities for over a decade, until 400. This was followed by a period of scholarly work chiefly devoted to the refutation of the Donatist heresy which had paralyzed the African Church almost throughout the fourth century. He fought for the Catholic truth not only in his writings but also in sermons and disputations. In 411 he achieved a brilliant victory in the religious conversations at Carthage, where 286 Catholic and 279 Donatist bishops were present. Already in the following year (412) began the struggle against Pelagianism, which Augustine carried on till the end of his life as the leader of the Catholic party, and which won him the honourable title of *Doctor gratiae*.

Augustine died at Hippo on August 28th, 430, while the city was being besieged by the Vandals.

The great Bishop of Hippo combined the creative power of Tertullian and the intellectual breadth of Origen with the ecclesiastical sense of Cyprian, the dialectical acumen of Aristotle with the idealistic enthusiasm and the profound speculation of Plato, the practical sense of the Latin with the agile intellect of the Greek. Augustine is the greatest philosopher of the patristic age and probably the most important and influential theologian of the Church, whose outstanding achievements had not a few enthusiastic admirers even in his lifetime.

What Origen had been for the scientific theology of the third and fourth centuries, Augustine became in a much purer and more profitable way for the whole life of the Church of the following centuries until modern times. He exercised the strongest influence not only on philosophy, doctrine, moral and mystical theology, but also on the social life of the Church and her charitable activities, on ecclesiastical politics and constitutional law, and became one of the great founders of medieval Western civilization. All his struggles and research were devoted to Catholic truth, which he sought in unconditional dependence on the authority of the Church. If Protestant scholars sometimes have been and still are trying to show that his thought moves partly in opposition to the Church, we must assert against this with K. Holl (*A.' innere Entwicklung,* 1922, 51) that "the Catholic Church has always understood him better than its opponents". The doctrinal magisterium of the Church has probably followed no other theological author so often as it has followed him. This is true also of his doctrine of grace, though this does not mean that the Catholic Church's doctrine of grace is in every way identical with the doctrine of Augustine. Cf. Celestine I, *Ep*. 21, 13; ES 142; supra § 78, 9.

Nothing is more characteristic of him as a scholar and a thinker, as well as of his intense sincerity, than his repeated declarations that he wanted outspoken criticisms of his writings. He did not want men to follow him without examining his views (*Persev*. 21, 55; *Trin*. 3, prooem. 2); he did not wish to be in the company of those who never needed to take back a word of what they had written, or were afraid of doing so (*Ep*. 143, 2f.). His *Retractations* are the unique document of this attitude. In his writings, especially in the *Confessions* and in many of his *Letters* and *Sermons,* we meet not only a pure, serious and deeply religious personality of unique idealism and moral heroism, but also a sensitive psychologist who knew the human heart in its most secret inclinations and impulses. Hence, with his lively temperament, he was capable of achieving extraordinary success in the pastoral and practical sphere as a priest and a kindly guide of souls.

Complete edd.: *Ed. Benedictina,* 11 vols., P 1679/1700. ML 32/47. In CSEL so far 19 vols., 1887/1956. CCL 36 *(Tract. in Jo.)* 1954; 38/40 *(Enarr. Pss.)*; 47/8 *(Civ. Dei)*. Separate edd. v. infra. — Transs.: BKV², 12 vols., 1911/35. *Die fruehen Werke* ed. J. Perl, Pa 1940ff. *Compl. ed. of anti-Pelag. and moral theol. writings* ed. A. Kunzelmann and A. Zumkeller, Wu 1949ff. *Bibl. Augustinienne* ed. F. Cayré; trans. with Maurists' text and comm.; designed to contain 85 vols. in 10 sections, P 1947ff. So far *c.* 20 vols. have appeared. The Spanish *Bibl. de Autores Crist.* ed. by the Papal Univ. of Salamanca will also publish a large part of A.'s works in trans. with Lat. text; so far 12 vols., Ma 1946ff. Many of A.'s works are also publ. in the *Bibl. Agostiniana,* Fl. W. J. Oates, *Basic Writings of St. A.,* NY 1948 (2 large vols.). J. Burnaby, *A., Later Works* (Library of Christ. Class.), Ph 1955. The large number of transs. of individ. works into all languages is listed only in part. Shorter selections: J. Bernhart 1922. A. Harnack 1922. H. Hefele 1923. O. Karrer, 2 small vols., 1925. E. Przywara, *A. Die Gestalt als Gefuege,* 1934. U. v. Balthasar 1942; id., *A. Das Antlitz der Kirche*², 1956. — Bibliogr. surveys: E. Nebreda, *Bibliogr. A.,* R 1928 (incomplete). On the Jubilee lit. of 1930 cf. RC 1931, 461/509 (574 items) and *Intern. Bibliogr. of Hist. Sc.* 5, 1934, 2496/531. Extensive information on text edd. in: *Gesamtkatalog der Preuss. Bibliotheken,* B 1935 (s. voc. *Aug.*), 477/588 and in B. Soto, *Archivio aug.* 39, 1933, 303/20, 456/73; 42, 1934, 115/46 (cont.). Also the periodicals mentioned p. 487 and M. Sciacca, *Bibliogr. der philos. Schriften A.s,* Bern 1948. Bardy, Aug 5, 1955, 441/58 *(Conciles d'Hippone au temps de s. A.)*. — Biogr.: C. Wolfsgruber 1898. G. v. Hertling ²1904. L. Bertrand, P 1913 (popular). P. Guilloux, P 1921. B. Legewie 1925. H. Lesaar 1930 (popular). E. Krebs 1930. G. Papini, Fl 1930. A. Pincherle, Bari 1930. U. Moricca, Tu 1930. E. McDougall, Lo 1930. A. C. de Romanis, R 1931. S. Cassara, Palermo 1931. P. Gorla, Tu 1936. G. Bardy, P ⁶1946. A. Queirolo, Fl 1941. R. Potter, P 1945. Portalié, DTC 1, 2268/472. Labriolle, DHG 5, 440/73. R. v. Kienitz, *A.,* 1947. P. Guilloux - J. Nuñez, *El alma de s. A.,* Ba ²1947. F. v. d. Meer, *A. als Seelsorger,* 1947. J. D. Burger, *S. A.,* Neuchâtel 1948. H. Zimmermann, *Auf d. Wege zu A.,* Mn 1948. M. F. Sciacca, *S. A.* 1, Brescia 1949. T. Philips, *Das Weltbild des hl. A.,* Zu 1949. H. Pope, *St. A.,* Westminster (Maryland) 1949. L. Fabre, *S. A.,* P 1951. E. Hendrikx, Aug 1, 1951, 91/106, 175/91; 2, 1952, 5/18 (cont.): *A. als relig. Persoenlichkeit.* L. Camblor, *S. A.,* Ma 1951. O. Noordmans, *A.,* Haarlem ²1952, P. Simon, Pa 1953. P. P. Gerosa, *S. A.,* Alba 1953. G. de Plinval, P 1954. R. W. Battenhouse, *A Companion of the Study of S. A.,* O 1955. — On his development: H. Becker, *A.,* 1908. W. Thimme, *A.s geist. Entw.,* 1908; ZKG 1910, 172/213. P. Alfaric, *L'évolut. intellect. de s. A.,* 1918. K. Holl, AbhB 1922, 4. J. Noerregaard, *A.s*

Bekehrung, 1923. A. Guzzo, *A. dal Contra academicos al De vera rel.,* Fl 1925. W. J. S. Simpson, *St. A.'s Conversion,* Lo 1930. K. Adam [2]1954. E. Haenchen, *Die Frage nach d. Gewissheit beim jungen A.,* 1932. W. Theiler, *Porphyrius und A.,* 1933; against this P. Henry, *Plotin et l'Occident,* 1934, 63/145; JTS 1937, 1/23 (A. and Plotinus); *La vision d'Ostie,* 1938; cf. Cavallera, RAM 1939, 181/96 and Lebreton, RSR 1938, 457/72. J. Barion, *Plotin u. A.,* 1935. G. Guardini, *Die Bekehrung A.s,* [2]1950. M. P. Garvey, *S. A.: Christian or Neo-Platonist?,* Milwaukee 1933; Muñoz, Gr 1941, 9/24, 325/52; 1942, 35/65, 291/325 (Psicología de la conversión). Moricca, MC 1941, 232/53 *(conversione).* A. Vloemans, *A. Bekeerling . . .,* 1942. Survey of lit. on this question in Mannucci, MiA 2, 23/47. Cilleruello, CD 1946, 55/74; 337/50 (A. as Manichee); Arbor 7, 1947, 29/46 (A. as sceptic). A. Pincherle, *La formazione teolog. di s. A.,* 1947. J. Bourke Vernon, *A.'s Quest of Wisdom,* Milwaukee 1949. O'Meara, DSO 1950, 331/43 (Neo-Platonism). ITQ 1951, 338/46 (Authority and Reason anno 386). S. B. Femiano, *Riflessioni crit. sulla convers. di s. A.,* Na-R 1951. Sejourné, RevSR 1951, 243/64, 333/63 (conversion acc. to *De lib. arb.* I). Van der Lof, NTT 1951, 287/307 (infl. of M. Victorinus). G. Ferretti, *L'infl. di s. Ambr. in s. A.,* Faenza 1951 (thesis Greg. R). C. Boyer, *Christianisme et néo-platonisme dans la formation de s. A.,* R [2]1953; on this Courcelle, Orph. 1, 1954, 83/5. J. O'Meara, *Actes 1 er Congr. de la Fédér. internat. Assoc. d'Ét. class.,* P 1951, 312/7 (on *Conf.* 7, 13, 8, 28f. and *C. Acad.* 2, 5f.); *The Young A. The Growth of St. A.'s Mind up to his Conversion,* 1954. Courcelle, Aug 4, 1954, 225/39 *(Libri Platonicorum);* RStR 1, 1954, 63/71 (on *Conf.* 7, 19, 25). Préaux, RBP 1955, 555/76 (on *Tolle-lege*). Capelle, RACh 1, 981/94. F. Sciacca, *S. A. et le Néoplaton.,* Lou 1956. Further lit. v. under *Confess.* F. Sciacca, *S. Aug. et le Néoplaton.,* Lou 1956.

Questions of biogr. detail: Legewie, MiA 2, 5/21 (illnesses). Meda, ibid. 2, 49/59 (situation of Cassiciacum). Monceaux, ib. 2, 61/89 (A. and monasticism). G. G. Lapeyre, ib. 2, 91/148; *L'anc. Égl. de Carthage,* P 1932 (A. and Carthage). Zarb, Ang 1933, 161/85 (episc. consecr. June/July 395). Sizoo, Stemmen des Tijds, 1934, 503/34 (A.'s working capacity). Brezzi, RFN 1939, 243/62 *(sulla personalità).* Hendrikx, BiNJ 1938, 1/27 (individualism). Pugliese, StU 263/99 *(A. giudice).* Altaner, *Sacramentum Ordinis. Geschichtl. u. syst. Beitr.* ed. Puzik u. Kuss 1942, 139/68 (A. as pastor). Rodríguez, CD 152, 1942, 213/36 *(El humorismo).* Hartke, PWK, Suppl. 6, 520/9 *(Monnica,* this spelling is better establ. by MSS and etym.). H. Karpp, *Monika,* B (Furche-Verlag). Havigan, CHR 1946, 47/58 (Nebridius). Grumel, REL 1946, 76f. (inscription: *Monika*). Sizoo, VC 1948, 106/8 (Alypius, b. 363). Courtois, *Rev. Africaine* 1950, 259/82 (A. and the Punic). Green, in W. Popper Volumen, Berkeley 1951, 179/90 (A.'s Use of Punic). Poulsen, Lat 2, 1949, 271/76 (A. and his disciples). Semple, JEH 1, 1950, 135/50 (St. A.'s secular career in education). Bardy, AnT 1953, 327/46 (A. and the physicians); 1954, 55/79 (Licentius). Koopmans, VC 1954, 149/54 (A.'s first encounter with Pelagius). Perler, REAug 1955, 299/343 (the churches at Hippo). Smulders, BiNJ 1955, 136/55 (The follower of the absolute).

On his Influence: E. Troeltsch, *A.,* 1915. E. Bernheim, *Mittelalterl. Zeitanschauungen etc.,* 1918. J. Geyser, *A. u. d. phaenomenolog. Rel.-Philos. der Gegenwart,* 1923. P. v. Sokolowski, *A. u. d. christl. Zivilisation,* 1927. A. Schultze,

A. u. der Seelteil des german. Erbrechts, 1928; ZSG 1930, 376/85; cf. ibid. 1930, 394/407 and ZSR 1930, 654/71. U. Mariani, *Le teorie polit. di s. A. e il loro influsso nella Scuola agost. del sec. 14,* Fl 1933. H.-X. Arquillière, *L'Augustinisme politique,* [2]1955. A. Hamel, *Der junge Luther u. A.,* 1934. M. Grabmann, *Mittelalterl. Geistesleben,* 1936, 1/34 (his infl. on valuation of antiquity). P. Cherubelli, *Le edizioni volgari delle opere di S. A. nella Rinascita,* 1940. N. Abercrombie, *S. A. and French Class. Thought,* 1938. A. Masnovo, *S. A. e S. Tommaso,* 1942. C. Orth, *Malebranche und A.,* thesis Cologne 1940. Pastore, Atti R. Accad., Tu 75 II 89/106 (Descartes and A.). De Vooght, RTA 1946, 304/36 (A. in J. Huss). Chatillon, RML 3, 1949, 234/7 (A. in Gottschalk and Peter the Ven.). Bardy, RML 1950, 313/6 (A. *Magister Ecclesiarum*). Chroust, *The Modern Schoolman* 27, 1950, 280/96 (A.-citations in Thomas Aq.). Crevola, *Arch. teolog. Granadino* 13, 1950, 5/171; 14, 1951, 41/127 *(A. en las disputas De Auxiliis).* Blumenkranz, RML 1949, 193/6 (A. and the polemics against the Jews in the MA); 1951, 97/110 (A. and Rhabanus Maurus). Altaner, HJB 1952, 37/76 (A. in the Gr. Church till Photius). Landgraf, Sch 1954, 3 (A. and Peter Lombard). Metz, RDC 4, 1954, 405/19 (A. and the Can. Law of 1917). Cranz, Sp 1953, 297/316 (A. and Nic. of Cusa). AugMag 2, 1954, 991/1153 (14 studies). A. Masnovo, *S. A. e s. Tommaso,* Mi [2]1950. H. Paissac, *Théologie du Verbe: S. A. et s. Thomas,* 1951. — Publications for the Aug. Anniversary 1930, the contents of which cannot all be listed in detail; cf. on these RTABull 1931 ff.; partly also Krueger 1933, 292 ff. and TR 1932, 137 ff. M. Grabmann - J. Mausbach, Festschr. der Goerresges. 1930, (439 pp.). *A Monument to St. A.,* Lo 1930 (367 pp.). *Archives Philos.* 7, 2, 1930 (273 pp.). *Miscell. Augustiniana,* N 1930. *Augustiniana,* Tongerloo 1930. *Acta hebdomadae August.-Thomisticae,* R 1931 (344 pp.). RevFilosNeoscol 1931 Suppl. al vol. 23 (510 pp.). RC 1931 n. 43/5. *Miscell. Agostiniana* 2 (= MiA), R 1931 (XXXVI, 1042 pp.). *Augustinus Magister, Congrès Internat. August.,* P 21.–24. September 1954, 2 vols. (110 contributions); 3rd. vol.: Actes (contains comprehensive accounts of the contributions of the first 2 vols. and short information on the discussions; 279/482: 17 further contributions). H. Rondet - C. Morel - M. Jourjon – J. Lebreton, *S. A. parmi nous,* P 1954 (308 pp.): three contributions by Rondet (appreciation of A.'s personality; On Riches and Poverty; Freedom and Grace; also transl. extracts from Possidius' *Vita Aug.; Ep.* 177 and extracts from the *TractJo*); Morel (on prayer; with trans. of *Ep.* 150); Jourjon (A. and his community; *Ep.* 340 and 339 partly trans.). Lebreton (A. in the time of the migration of peoples). Augustiniana. *Napoli a s. Agost. nel XVI centenario della nascita,* Na 1955. AttiCongrItFilosAgost, R 1954.

2. Augustine's works

His prolific literary output and the energy revealed in it can be compared only with the extraordinary achievements of Origen, who is in this respect even greater than he. In the account of his literary work (*Retract.* 2, 67) Augustine himself tells us that by 427 he had already written ninety-three literary works and 232 books; these figures did not include his many sermons and his numerous often very long letters. Only ten of the works he discusses have been lost. Though he was well aware of the importance of his literary theological mission and of his intellectual superiority, nothing was farther from his thought than to put his own person in the limelight. He often said that he owed everything to the goodness of God (*Civ. Dei* 22, 30; *Ep.* 52, 4).

Augustine was not only in full possession of the culture of his time, he was also an accomplished master both of the written and the spoken word, who had all rhetorical artifices (antithesis, metaphor, play on thoughts and words) perfectly at his command. Sometimes his graceful figures of speech can hardly be translated; and his striking antitheses and musical rhymes display the rhetorical art of later antiquity. Hence he is also a master of controversy. Yet for him the laws of rhetoric were not an end in themselves or a means of gaining the vain applause of readers susceptible to aesthetic emotions. This is clearly proved by his capacity to adapt his style to his varying moods, subjects and aims. His words express his ardent soul and convey the spark apt to kindle new flames. He uses his words and his pen only in the service of truth and thus of God and his reign on earth; all personal concerns must give way to this end. Hence in sermons and treatises destined for a wider public he sacrifices rhetorical glamour and adornments and, for the sake of a stronger effect, descends to the common man's way of talk and to vulgar "barbarism" (*Enarr. in Ps.* 36 sermo 3, 6).

Studies of A.'s style, language, literary culture and sources: I. Barry, *A. the Orator,* W 1924. J. Balmus, *Ét. sur le style de s. A.* (*Confess.* and *Civ. Dei*), 1930 (good bibliogr.). N. Comeau, *La rhétorique de s. A. d'après les Tract. in Jo.,* 1930. A. Melardi, *L'arte retor. nelle Confess. di s. A.,* Na 1930/1. Di Capua, MiA 2, 607/64 *(ritmo prosaico)*. Vaccari, ibid. 2, 253/8 (style in *Ep.* 73). M. J. Holman, *Nature-imagery in the works of St. A.,* W 1931. C. L. Hrdlicka, *A Study of the Late Lat. Vocabulary . . . in the Confess. of St. A.,* W 1931. C. Rodríguez, *El alma virgiliana de s. A.,* Ma 1931. C. Mohrmann, *Die altchristl. Sondersprache i. d.*

Sermones des hl. A., N 1932. K. Golebiewski, *Le langage d'après s. A.* (Bull. Soc. Polonaise de Linguistique 1932, 3/37). Schuchter, WSt 52, 1934, 115/38 (style of sermons). M. I. Bogan, *The Vocabulary and Style of the Soliloquies and Dialogues of St. A.,* W 1935. C. Mahoney, *The Rare and Late Lat. Nouns, Adject. and Adverbs in St. A's De civ. Dei,* W 1935. Keenan, CJ 1936, 35/7 (classics in letters). Mohrmann, Mn 3, 1935/6, 33/61 (puns). Sizoo, GTT 1935, 385/98 (Bible study and lit. language). Keenan, TS 1936, 168/90 (med. science). A. B. Paulaszak, *Subjunctive in the Letters of St. A.,* W 1935. M. S. Muldowney, *Word-Order in the Works of St. A.,* W 1937. M. B. Schieman, *The Rare and Late Verbs in St. A.'s De Civ. Dei,* W 1938. M. B. Carroll, *The Clausulae in the Confessions of St. A.,* W 1940. Jenkins, JTS 1938, 59/66 (Class. Quotations). J. Finaert, REL 1938, 3/25, 103/9 *(Un tournant et son style); S. A. rhéteur,* P 1939; *L'évolution litt. de S. A.,* P 1939. G. Combès, *A. et la cult. classique,* 1927. Guignebert, RH 1940, 403/43; RHR 1940, 25/41. K. H. Schelkle, *Virgil i. d. Deutung A.s,* 1939.

Altaner, DP 1939, 19/40 (Gr. lang.); ZKT 1941, 81/90 (A. and Philo); ZRel Geistesgesch. I, 1948 (original Gr. patristic texts in A.). Nailis, Philol. Studien 1939/40, 81/90 (Euhemerus). Keseling, PW 1940, 92f. (Ovid). Courcelle 1947, 137/209. A. Padovani, *S. A. e la patristica,* Como 1944. Bardy, Ir 1948, 249/73 *(A. et la pensée orient.).* Altaner, TR 1948, 73/8 (A.'s library); TSW 1948, 600/3 (A.'s MSS). TQ 1949, 162/72 (A. and Irenaeus); AB 1949, 236/48 (A. and NT *apocrypha, Sibyllines* and *Sayings of Sextus*); RBn 1949, 82/90 (A. and Athanas.); VC 1950, 37/45 (A. and Jul. Africanus); RBn 1950, 17/24 (A. and Basil); Mél. De Ghellinck 1, 1951, 265/75 (A. and Epiphanius); VC 1951, 116/20 (A. and Didymus); RBn 1951, 54/62 (A., Gr. Naz. and Gr. Nyss.); BZ 1951, 1/6 (A. and Euseb. of Caes.); HJB 70, 1951, 15/41 (A. and Origen); ZNTW 44, 1952/3, 76/84 (A. and Jo. Chrys.); RBn 1952, 201/15 (A. and Gr. Patristics. Introduction and gleanings); MTZ 1953, 34/6 (Bibl. onomastica); SE 1952, 5/17 (A.'s method of using sources. His study of Patrist. lit.); Altaner, *In der Studierstube des hl. A.:* Beitr. z. Kenntnis seines schriftstell. Schaffens in: Kleineidam-Kuss-Puzik, Fr 1950, 378/431. H.-I. Marrou, *S. A. et la fin de la culture antique,* 1949; on this 621/711: *Retractatio.*

Mohrmann, *Oudheid en Christendom* ed. Gruytier - Mohrmann 1948, 26/46 (A. en de Eloquentia). Leclercq, RBn 1947, 117/31 (Sermon and rhetoric in an anonymous author *c.* 400). M. Berzius, *A. u. Ciceros De re publ.,* thesis Fr 1950. M. M. Beyenka, *Consolation in St. A.,* W 1950. Kurfess, TQ 1951, 458/63. F. M. Moran, ArchAgust 44, 1950, 413/26 (Virgil in *Civ.*). Bardy, AnT 1953, 145/50 (A. and Tertull.). Courcelle, RevSR 1953, 40/6 (A. and Persius). Sizoo, Aug 1954, 240/47 (A.'s account of his conversion a *narratio*). A. Turienzo, CD 166, 1954, 233/55 (S. A., escritor). Mohrmann, AugMag 1, 111/16 (Christ. Latinity in A.). AugMag 1, 19/239 (25 contributions). Mandouze, BullAssocGBudé 1955, 37/41 (A. ou le rhéteur canonisé). Bardy, REAug 1, 1955, 21/39 (duplicates in A.'s works). García Jiménez, CD 168, 1955, 11/32 (rhetoric and his class. models).

On the MS tradition and the hist. of the ed. of his writings: Lowe, MiA 2, 235/51. Wilmart, ib. 2, 257/319. Souter, JTS 1933, 267/9. De Ghellinck, *Misc. Gessleriana,* Antw. 1948, 530/47 and *Patristique et Moyen Age* 3, 1948, 339/484 (hist. of editions); *Liber floridus. Festschr. P. Lehmann,* 1950, 63/82 (medieval collection of opera omnia). Green, Sp 1954, 531/4 (mediev. recensions of A.). — On the chronol. of the works: Zarb, Ang 1933, 359/96, 478/512; 1934, 78/91; 1935, 52/81, 245/61; 1936, 93/108, 252/82; 1937, 516/37; 1938, 382/408; 1939, 267/95; 1940, 263/94 (chronol. of *Enarr. in Pss.*). Zarb, Ang 1933, 50/110 (chronol. of *Tract. in Jo.*); 1947, 47/69, 265/84; 1948, 37/44 (chronol. of *Enarr. in Pss.*); in book form: S. Zarb, *Chronol. Enarr. s. A. in Pss.,* La Valetta 1948. Le Landais, Ét. August. 1953, 9/95 (chronol. of *Tract. in Jo.*); some of this also in RSR 1948, 226/50; 1949, 517/41. Kunzelmann, MiA 2, 417/520 (chronol. of Sermons).

A. in art: Wilpert, MiA 2, 1/3. K. Smits, *Misc. August.,* N 1930, 197/211. Cabanas, RC 1931, 285/300. García, RC 1934, 53/80. Laurent, *Cahiers de Bysra* 2, 1952, 87/93.

a. The *Confessiones* (thirteen books), written between 397 and 401, are, like the *Retractationes,* something essentially new in the history of Christian literature. He may perhaps have been influenced by Cyprian's work (§ 34, 1) *Ad Donatum.*

Augustine's autobiography allows us to gain an incomparably profound insight into his religious development down to 387 and to take part in his hard struggle for peace in God (1–9). In it he not only accuses himself, frequently too severely, of his own sinful weaknesses, but also, and this especially, confesses his faith and praises and thanks God for having accorded him so much grace and guidance. Book X gives a fine psychological analysis and description of his religious and moral state at the time of writing. Books XI–XIII contain profound meditations on God and the world, time and eternity, evoked by the Biblical account of creation. Here he wants to "praise and glorify" God for the insight he has given him in the religious-intellectual sphere. The work as a whole is one of the great masterpieces of the literature of the world, which reveals Augustine's outstanding capacity for describing the most delicate psychological events and states (EP 1591/6; EA 630/41). Shortly before writing the *Confessions* Augustine had completed his doctrine of divine grace and predestination which had shaken his soul to its foundations; this is probably the reason why he felt impelled at this time to accuse and humble himself before the world with such unsparing frankness, Cf. § 88 3 9.

Recent critics have attempted to prove, though with varying nuances, that the *Confessions* are untrustworthy (A. Harnack, G. Boissier, H. Becker, W. Thimme, P. Alfaric, R. Reitzenstein). They have been particularly at pains to show up a contradiction between this work and the philosophical treatises he wrote immediately after his conversion, especially the philosophical writings composed at Cassiciacum. Usually his acquaintance with the neo-Platonist philosophy has been presented as the only decisive factor that gradually turned his mind to Christianity, while the influence of Ambrose, of the priest Simplicianus, the experience in the garden and the reception of baptism are alleged to be unimportant for his Christianity at that time. On the other hand, contrary criticism as well as the latest research have come to an entirely positive view of the *Confessions* and recognize their historical value. Augustine's conversion was definitely a convinced acceptance of Christianity: J. Mausbach, E. Portalié, C. Boyer, P. Batiffol, K. Holl, J. Noerregaard, P. de Labriolle, K. Adam, G. Krueger, A. Pincherle, P. Courcelle, O'Meara and others.

There is a variant reading given only in the oldest *Cod. Sessorianus* (6th cent.) according to which Augustine had heard the mysterious children's voices *(Tolle—lege)* not *de vicina domo* but *de divina domo* (*Conf.* 8, 12, 29). On the basis of this Courcelle seeks to prove (*Recherches* 1950, 188/202) that this was a purely interior experience of Augustine. He defends his view against various objections in five further studies (RHR 139, 1951, 216/31; AnT 1951, 253/60; Her 1952, 31/46; RHP 1952, 171/200. VC 1953, 194/220). Here he seeks further to support his thesis especially by parallels and analogies from the history of religion. Against Courcelle's interpretation: Mohrmann, VC 1951, 249/54; Cayré, AnT 1951, 144/51, 244/52; RSR 1951, 443/60; Marrou, REL 1951, 400/7; Theiler, Gn 1953, 113/27; esp. 121 f.; De Vos, Aug

1954, 232/44; Fabre, RET 1952, 71f.; Gross, MTZ 1954, 289/95.

Edd.: P. Knoell, W 1898. F. Ramorino, R 1909. C. H. Bruder, L [2]1929. J. Gibb and W. Montgomery, C [2]1927 (with comm.). M. Skutella, L 1934 (best ed.). H. Wagnereck, Tu [3]1939. J. Trabucco, P 1938 (text and trans.). P. de Labriolle, P [3]1944. A. C. Vega, Ma 1946 (with comm. and trans.). J. Capello, Tu 1948. P. de Labriolle, P [6]1955 (with trans.). Loeb, Class. Libr. 26/7, Lo 1950 (with trans.). S. C. Williams, *The Conf. of St. A. Book 8* (with trans.), O 1953. J. Bernhart, Mn 1956 (with trans.). — Transs.: G. v. Hertling (1–10), Fr [23–24]1928. A. Hoffmann (BKV [2]18) 1914. H. Hefele, Jena [2]1922. V. Sánchez, Ma [2]1951. E. Zeballos, Ba 1951. W. Thimme, Zu 1950. Capodicasa, R [2]1951. H. Schiel, Fr [3]1952. C. J. Perl, Pa [4]1955. Mgg.: M. Zepf, *A.'s Confess.,* 1926. F. Billicsich, *Stud. z. d. Bekenntn. A.s,* 1929. W. Thimme, *A.s Selbstbildnis i. d. Konf.,* 1929. P. Schaefer, *Das Schuldbewusstsein i. d. Conf.,* 1930. G. Wunderle, *Einf. in A.s Konf.,* 1930. I. Freyer, *Erlebte u. systemat. Gestaltung i. A.s Konf.,* 1937. M. Heim, *Der Enthusiasmus i. d. Konf. des hl. A.,* 1941. R. Guardini, *Anfang* (*Conf.* I 1–5), [3]1953. — Studies: Geffcken, ARW 1934, 1/13 (*Tolle-lege* exp.); cf. J. Boehmer, BiZ 1935, 58/61. Guardini, *Antike* 1934, 169/94 (on interpretation). Stem, StC 1936, 17/29 (unity). Sizoo, Mn 4, 1936/7, 255 (text. crit.). Eder, TPraktQ 91, 1938, 606/20 (trustworthiness). Dyroff, DP 1939, 86/93 (*Conf.* 7, 9). Manasse, RRel 1943, 361/83 (conversion and liberation). Chatillon, RML 1945, 287/304 (*Conf.* 7, 9, 15). A. Sizoo, *Toelichting op A.' Belijdenissen,* 1948. Caramella, NDid 1, 1947, 49/54 (A. as a neo-Platonist). Pellegrino, EstFilHistLit 5, 1949, 308/21 (new MS). M. Verheijen, *Eloquentia pedisequa,* N 1949 (style in the *Conf.*); *Archivo August.* 45, 1951, 5/9 (theory of rhythm). P. Courcelle, *Recherches sur les Conf. de s. A.,* P 1950. A. Isnenghi, *Progr. Salzburg* 1950, 23/40 (text. crit.). J. M. Le Blond, *Les Conversions de s. A.,* 1950 (theology in the *Conf.*). G. Misch, *Gesch. d. Autobiographie,* [3]1950, 1, 39/79, 693/701. G. Krabbel, *Mutter u. Sohn nach den Conf.,* 1950. Cayré, RSR 1951, 443/60 (myst. and wisdom); AnT 1953, 13/32 (meaning and unity); 1953, 232/59 (Christ); 1953, 347/69 (myst. in *Conf.* and *De Trin.*). T. Suess, *Ciceros Hortensius* in: Jahrb. f. d. Bistum Mainz, 1950, 293/304. Lipgens, MTZ 1951, 164/77 (phlos. of hist.). J. F. Harvey, *Moral Theol. of the Conf.,* W 1951. Riedinger, MTZ 1951, 431/4 (on *Conf.* 7, 21, 27). Courcelle, REL 1951, 295/307 (on *Conf.* 8, 2, 3); RevEA 1951, 273f. (date 397/401). Pepin, RHR 140, 1951, 155/202 (on *Conf.* 9, 10, 24); AL 23, F. 3, 1953, 185/274 (*caelum caeli* in *Conf.* XII). H. Kusch in *Festschr. F. Dornseiff,* L 1953, 124/200 (Trinit. matters in *Conf.* 2–4 and 10–13). Mandouze, AugMag 1, 67/84 (ecstasy at Ostia). F. Bolgiani, PubblFacLett 6, 2, Tu 1954 (oldest Codex of *Conf.*). N. Knauer, *Pss-Zitate i. d. Conf.,* Go 1955. Mathon, REAug 1955, 107/27 (date of conversion). Supplement: M. Pellegrino (trans. and comm.) R 1956.

b. Philosophical works. Augustine's first work *De pulchro et apto,* written in 380–1 when he was a teacher of rhetoric at Carthage has not been preserved (cf. *Conf.* 4, 13ff.). Of the four philosophical treatises written in the solitude of Cassiciacum, the first three reproduce conversations with the friends then living with him and were later formed according to literary and rhetorical rules of composition (ML 32; CSEL 63). Three books *Contra Academicos* oppose the scepticism of the neo-Academics: truth is knowable, beatitude consists not in searching for, but in knowing the truth. These views are elaborated in *De beata vita:* true happiness consists in the knowledge of God. The two books *De ordine* take up for the first time the principal problem of theodicy: Whence comes evil? The *Soliloquia,* a dialogue with his own *ratio* on God and the soul treats especially of the immortality of the soul. The treatise *De immortalitate animae,* which remained unfinished, was written at Milan in 387, before his baptism.

Text edd. and transs.: *De beata vita* ed. M. Schmaus (FP 27) 1931; Germ. by J. Hessen, L 1923; Dutch by J. A. Lieshout, A 1936 (also *Solil.*). *Solil.* trans. by J. Artaud, P 1936. P. de Labriolle, ed. *Solil., De immort., De quant. an.* (with trans.) 1940. *De ord.:* Germ. by C. J. Perl [2]1952; P. Keseling 1940 (with comm.). *Solil.* trans. with comm.: L. Schopp and A. Dyroff 1938. *Obras de s. A.* 3, Ma 1940 (with trans.). R. Jolivet (*Bibl. Aug.* 4), P 1955. W. M. Green, *3 Dialoge,* Ut.-Antw. 1955 (crit. ed. in: *Stromata* 2). H. Fuchs-H. Mueller, *Solil. u. De immort. an.,* Zu 1954 (with trans.). P. Remark, *Solil.,* Mn 1951 (text). M. F. Sciacca, Brescia 1950 (trans. of *Solil.*). J. J. O'Meara, trans. *C. Acad.* (ACW 12), 1950. C. J. Perl, trans. *Der freie Wille,* Pa 1954, and *Solil.* 1955. H. Mueller, *A.s Soliloquien,* thesis Basle 1954; Id., ed. *Solil.,* Zu 1954.—Studies: G. Lazzati, *L'Aristotele perduto,* 1938, 43/54. Bertini, AST 12, 1936, 233/64 (*Solil.* and *Specul. peccatoris* [ps. Aug.] Catalan.). J. Gercken, *Inh. u. Aufg. der Philos. i. d. Jugendschr. A.s,* thesis Mr 1939. Dyroff, RM 1939, 7/16 (*Solil.* 1, 12, 21). F. M. Meijer, *De Sapientia in de erste Geschr. v. S. A.,* 1940. J. Meulenbroek, *Metrik en Rhythm. in A.' Cass.-Dial.,* N 1942. P. M. Garvey, *S. A. against the Acad.* (trans.), Milwaukee 1942. Lekkerkerker, NAKG 1943, 107/37; 1945, 217/57 *(b. vita).* R. A. Brown, *De b. v.,* W 1944 (trans. and comm.). J. Postma, *De b. v.* (with comm.), A 1946. Courcelle, REL 1943/4, 155/74 *(Solil.).* Meulenbroek, Mn 1947, 203/29 (hist. character of dialogues). V. d. Hout, VC 1948, 56 (text. crit.). Diggs, Tr 7, 1949/51, 73/93 (philos. or theol. method of proving the faith in *C. Acad.*). O'Meara, VC 1951, 150/78 (dialogues' literary form). Roberts, JR 1953, 161/81 (earliest writings).

De quantitate animae, a dialogue written in Rome in 388, proves the immateriality of the soul. *De magistro,* written in Africa *c.* 389, is a free reproduction of a conversation with his son Adeodatus, who died soon afterwards. It is important for the psychology of teaching and learning. The *Encyclopedia of the Seven Liberal Arts,* begun in Milan as early as 387, was never finished. Fragments of the section *De grammatica* have been preserved; six books *De musica* treat of rhythm.

De mag. et De vera religione ed. D. Bassi, Fl 1930 (with trans.). *De quant. an.* ed. F. E. Tourscher, Philad. 1933 (with trans.). P. de Labriolle, *Bibl. Aug.* 5, P 1954 *(Immort. an., Quant. an., Solil.).* J. Thonnard, *Bibl. Aug.* 6, P 1954 *(De mag., De lib. arb.).* — J. M. Colleran, trans. of *De mag.* and *De quant. an.* (ACW 9), 1950. M. Casotti e A. Paggi, *De mag.* (trans.), Brescia 1951. — G. Finaert et F. J. Thonnard, *De musica lib. 6* (text and trans.), P 1947. F. J. Knight, *S. A.'s de mus. A Synopsis,* Lo 1949. J. Vecchi, *A. Praecepta artis mus.,* Bologna 1951 (crit. ed.). — Studies: J. Huré, *S. A. musicien,* 1924. Amerio, Did 1929, F. 3, 1/196 *(De mus.).* M. Haesele, *Beitr. zur augustin. Psychologie,* Glarus 1929. W. Hoffmann, Fr 1930 *(De mus.).* Valentini, So 1936, 83/9 *(De mag.).* C. J. Perl, *A.' Musik* (trans.), 1937. Allevi, SC 1937, 545/61 *(De mag.).* A. Wydeveld, *De mag.,* A 1938. H.-I. Marrou, *S. A. et la fin de la cult. ant.,* 1938, 3/327, 570/83. W. L. Wade, *De mag.* (in A. and St. Thomas), NY 1940. H. Edelstein, *Die Musikanschauung A.s,* 1929. H. Davenson - H.-I. Marrou, *Traité de la musique selon l'esprit de s. A.,* Neuchâtel-P 1942. Lind, ClassWeekly 39, 1945/6, 26/9 (on problems of teaching).

c. Apologetic writings. His most important work for the history of the mind *(Geistesgeschichte)* are the twenty-two books of the *De civitate Dei;* they were published in instalments from 413 to 426. Conceived from the historical point of view, the work contains the most valuable early Christian apology of Christianity and gives the first grandiose outline of a theology of history; its basic ideas largely determined the Church's politics in the Middle Ages and are still alive in Christian thought even today.

The work was occasioned by the old reproach, repeated by the pagans with particular vigour after Alaric's conquest of Rome in 410, that Christianity was to blame for all the misfortunes that had befallen the Roman Empire. In the first ten books Augustine proves that the cult of the gods neither guarantees earthly happiness nor is necessary and profitable for eternal life. The following books (11–22) establish the struggle between the *Civitas Dei* and the *Civitas terrena,* i.e. between faith and unbelief, as the principal theme of the history of the world. All good men belong to the City of God, all the wicked to the City of the devil both in this world and the next. During the earthly course of history the two cities are not neatly separated, they penetrate each other. The City of God in particular is not to be equated with the Church, just as the *Civitas terrena* is not co-extensive with any concrete state. The Last separation of the two realms will take place only at the end of time at the Last Judgement (EP 1738/88; EA 659/66). Augustine had explained his view of the *Two cities* already in earlier works, e.g. in *De cat. rud.* and especially frequently and in detail in his Sermons, above all in *Enarr. Pss.* Material for the elucidation of the ideas developed in his principal work can be found there. A. Lauras-H. Rondet in: *Ét. Aug.*, 1953, 99/160.

De civ. Dei is important also for the philologist on account of its many citations from the lost writings of Terentius Varro (*Antiquitates, De gente populi Romani*).

Edd.: E. Hoffmann (CSEL 40, 2 vols.) 1899f. I. E. C. Welldon, 2 vols., Lo 1924. C. Weyman, Mn 1925. B. Dombart-A. Kalb, L [5]1938f. (best ed.). Lambot, RBn 1939, 109/21 (uned. letter of A. on *Civ. Dei*). L. Riber y J. Bastardas (text and trans.) Ba 1953ff., 2 vols., 1955 in CCL 47/8. — Transs.: A. Schroeder (BKV[2]), 3 vols., 1911/6. M. Dods, Lo 1934. J. Fischer, *Der gueltige Gottesstaat* (selection), Hei 1948. R. H. Barrow, *Introd. to St. A.'s City of God* (selection), Lat. and Engl., 1950. B. Zema and G. C. Walsh, FathCh 1950ff. C. J. Perl, 3 vols., Salzbg. 1951ff. W. Thimme, trans. 1, Zu 1955. — Mgg.: S. Angus, *The Source of the First Ten Books of A.'s De Civ. Dei,* Princeton 1906. H. Scholz, *Glaube u. Unglaube i. d. Weltgesch.,* 1911. E. Salin, *Civ. Dei,* 1926. H. Fuchs, *A. u. d. antike Friedensgedanke,* 1926. V. Stegemann, *A.'s Gottesstaat,* 1928. R. Frick, *Gesch. des Reichgottesgedankens . . .,* 1928. Winter, *De doctrinae Neoplat. in Aug.i De civ. Dei vestigiis,* thesis Fr 1928. H. Lindemann, *Die Sondergoetter i. d. Apologetik der Civ. Dei A.s,* 1930. A. Dicker, *Karakter en Cultuur der Romainen in A.s Civ. Dei* 1–5, N 1931. N. Baynes, *The Political Ideas of St. A.'s De Civ. Dei,* L 1936 (19 pp.). F. Ghera, *I problemi del cristian. ant. nella Città di Dio di S. A.,* Palermo 1939. G. Ceriani, *Giustizia e carità nella C. di Dio di S. A.,* Vengono Inf. 1941. W. Ziegenfuss, *A. Christl. Transzendenz i. Ges. u. Gesch.,* B 1948. R. Schneider, *Welt u. Kirche b. A.,* Mn 1949. Marrou, *L'ambivalence du temps de l'hist. chez s. A.,* Montreal 1950. S. Burleigh, *The City of God. A Study of St. A.'s Philosophy,* 1950. G. Cataldo, *La filosofia della stor. . . .,* Bari 1950. G. Ruotolo, *La filosofia della stor. e la Città di Dio,* R [2]1950. G. Amari, *Il concetto di stor. in s. A.*, R 1951. W. Kamlah, *Christentum u. Geschichtlichkeit,* St ²1951. R. T. Marshall, *Studies in the Polit. and Socio-religious Terminol. of the De Civ. Dei,* W 1952. É. Gilson, *Les métamorphoses de la Cité de Dieu,* Lou 1952 (ch. 2 on A.). P. Chiochetta, *Teologia della storia,* R 1953. E. Stakemeier, *Civ. Dei. Die Geschichtstheol. d. hl. A.,* Pa 1955. C. Gallo, *La filosofia della storia nel De Civ. Dei . . .,* Bari 1950. F. G. Maier, *A. u. d. antike Rom,* St 1956. — Studies: G. della Rocca, Modena 1930. Gerosa, MiA 2, 977/1040 *(L'imperialismo rom.).* Vismara, Padovani, Soranzo and Calderini in RivFilosNeosc 1931, 115/66, 220/63, 377/404, 405/21. Lewalter, ZKG 1934, 1/51 (eschatol. and world hist.). A. Kurfess, TQ 1936, 532/42 (Sibyl); 1937, 341/56 (Sallust.). Simard, RUO 7, 1937, 65/72 (lib. 15/8). Brezzi, Riv. Stor. It. 1938, 62/94 *(Città di Dio e le sue interpret. medioev.).* Nygren, Δράγμα M. P. Nillson 1939, 367/73 (XIV 7). Dahlmann, PWK Suppl. 6, 1229/42 (A. and T. Varro). W. v. Loewenich, *A. u. d. christl. Geschichtsdenken,* 1947. Molland, *Serta Eitremiana* 1943, 112/17 (on *Civ.* 8, 11 and *Doctr. Chr.* 2, 43). Rasted, ClassMedievalia 9, 1947, 195/9 (MS of *Civ.* 1, 12/15). Clausen, AJP 1947, 293/301 (Sallust. in *Civ.* 2, 18 and M. Victorinus). Hubaux, *Hommages à J. Bidez et F. Cumont,* Bru 1949, 143/58 (on *Civ.* 8, 53f.). Straub, Historia 1, 1950, 52/81 (hist. apologet. and Rom. Emp.). Cranz, Sp 1950, 215/25 (15, 2: on idea of a Chr. society). Merzbacher, ArchRechts- u. Sozialphilos. 1950, 102/12 (A. and old Rome). Lacroix, VC 1951, 121f. (lib. 11: written 417). Marrou, Mél. De Ghellinck I, 235/49 (chapter headings originally ed. separately). Mommsen, JournHist-Ideas 12, 1951, 346/74 (Christ. idea of progress). A. Adam, TLZ 1952, 385/90 (Manich. origin of "two Cities"). Bardy, AnT 1952, 5/19, 113/29 (idea of *Civ.*). Straub, HJB 1954, 36/60 (A.'s concern for *regeneratio imperii*). Ratzinger, AugMag 2, 965/79 (Kamlah, v. supra). Den Boer, *Tijdschr. vooer Gesch.* 67, 1954, 316/25 (A. and hist.). Spoerl, HJB 1955, 62/78 (A. as creator of a doctr. of the state?). Kinder in: Gedenkschr. f. W. Elert, 1955, 24/42 ("Two cities" in A. and Luther). AugMag 2, 1954, 905/89 (contains 8 studies on *Civ. Dei*). CD 167f., 1955/6 (contains 42 studies on *Civ. Dei*). Further lit. v. supra (on his infl.) and infra (doctr. of state). A. Ehrhardt, *Polit. Metaphysik von Solon bis Augustin,* 2 vols., T 1959.

The work *Adversus Iudaeos,* a sermon dating from the last years of his life (ML 42, 51/64) attempts to show God's justice in rejecting the Jews. *De divinatione daemonum* (CSEL 41) examines the question of the prescience of the demons.

B. Blumenkranz, *Die Judenpredigt A.s,* Basle 1946. Nock, VC 1949, 56 (*De div. daemonum* 1, 1).

d. Dogmatic works (ML 40, CSEL 41).

The *Enchiridion ad Laurentium sive de fide, spe et caritate,* was written *c.* 423 and destined for a Roman layman Laurentius. It gives a brief presentation of the Christian faith in the form of an explanation of the Creed. Despite the title, *de spe et caritate* is treated only summarily at the end (EP 1913/33). Augustine gave another exposition of the Creed in his treatise *De fide et symbolo* and in the probably genuine *Sermo de symbolo ad catechumenos.*

ML 40, 181/96 = CSEL 41; ML 40, 627/36; cf. Sizoo, GTT 1940, 286/301 (*Sermo de symb. ad catech.* genuine).

De Trinitate (fifteen books) is Augustine's chief dogmatic work (ML 42), on which he worked from 399 to 419 and of which he said himself that probably only few readers would be able to follow his discussions (*Ep.* 169, 1). It essentially completes the Patristic speculation on the Trinity. In the first part he gives the proof from Scripture (1–4) and the formulations of the doctrine resulting from it (5–7). In the second part (8–15) he seeks to penetrate the mystery intellectually, especially by showing many analogies in the creatures, above all in the human mind (EP 1649/82).

The following three treatises are all partly occupied also with exegetical questions: *De diversis quaestionibus 83 lib. I* (388/95; EP 1552/6); 396, two books *De diversis quaestionibus ad Simplicianum* (Bishop of Milan) (EP 1569/76); *De octo Dulcitii quaestionibus* (*c.* 425). *De fide rerum quae non videntur,* a sermon preached after 399; *De fide et operibus* (413): faith without works is not sufficient for salvation; two books *De coniugiis adulterinis* (*c.* 420) on the indissolubility of marriage; *De cura gerenda pro mortuis* (*c.* 424), an answer to a question of St. Paulinus of Nola (ML 40).

Edd.: *Enchir.* ed. O. Scheel, T [2]1930; Germ. P. Simon 1923 and S. Mitterer (BKV [3]49) 1925 (also *Fid. et op.*). M. Schmaus (BKV[2] II, 13/4) 1935f. *(De Trin.);* Ital. by P. Montanari, 2 vols., Fl 1932/4. *De cura,* French by A. Landes, P 1930. *Enchirid.:* A. Tonna-Barthet (Ital.), Fl 1951. E. Evans, trans. SPCK 1953. *De Trin.:* Span. by Luis Arias, Ma 1948. M. Schmaus (Germ. selection), Mn 1951. M. Mellet et T. Camelot (*Bibl. Aug.* 15, 1955, with trans.). — P. J. Pegon (*Bibl. Aug.* 8: *De vera rel., Util. cred.* and others). Bardy-Beckaert-Boutet (*Bibl. Aug.* 10: *Quaest. 83, De div. quaest. ad Simpl., Divin. daem., Quaest. 8 Dulcitii*). G. Lombardo, *De fid. et op.,* W 1951. F. McDonald, *De fide rerum quae non vid.,* W 1950 (Crit. ed.). — Studies: Rivière, BLE 1942, 99/115 *(Ench.).* Meyerhoff, *New Scholasti-*

cism 1942, 16/45 (*Div. qu.* 83 n. 46). Hendrikx, AnT 1952, 305/16 *(date de composition du De Trin.).* S. Jannaccone, *La dottr. eresiologica di s. A.,* Ca 1952.

e. Anti-Manichean writings (ML 32, 34, 42; CSEL 25). We would mention at the top of the dogmatic-polemical works the *De haeresibus* (ML 42), written *c.* 428 at the request of the Carthagian deacon Quodvultdeus (§ 89, 2). It is based almost entirely on the catalogues of heresies compiled by Pseudo-Epiphanius and Filastu and enumerates eighty-eight heresies.

S. Jannaccone, *La dottr. eresiologica di s. A.,* Ca 1952.

Against Manicheism Augustine chiefly defends the following theses: Only the good has existed from the beginning, evil is no substance. The O.T. is as much God's work as the N.T. Christ is true Man and did not have a body only in appearance (EP 1538 ff.). *De moribus ecclesiae catholicae et de moribus Manichaeorum* (two books), 387–9; *De libero arbitrio* (three books), 388–95; *De Genesi contra Manichaeos* (two books), 388–9; *De vera religione, c.* 390; *De utilitate credendi, c.* 391; *De duabus animabus, c.* 392; *Acta seu disputatio contra Fortunatum Manichaeum,* 392; *Contra Adimantum,* 394; *Contra epistolam quam vocant fundamenti,* 397; *Contra Faustum Manichaeum* (thirty-three books), 397–400; *De actis cum Felice Manichaeo* (two books), 398; *De natura boni,* 399; *Contra Secundinum Manichaeum,* 399. *Ad Orosium contra Priscillianistas et Origenistas* (§ 49 II 6) is directed against the Priscillianists (415), a sect akin to the Manichaeans. Two Books *Contra adversarium legis et prophetarum* (421) are directed against an unnamed Marcionite heretic.

De vera rel. ed. D. Bassi, Fl 1930. — Transs.: Fl 1938; also by F. M. Bongioanni, Mi 1938, and A. Neno, Fl 1933. *De util. cred.* trans. M. Casacea, Fl [2]1930 and, D. Bassi, Tu 1936 (with text). *De mor. eccl. cath.* trans. A. Neno, Fl 1935. *De lib. arb.* trans. P. Montanari, Fl 1939, and J. Perl, Pa 1947. *De mor. eccl. cath., De ag. christ., De nat. boni* ed. B. Roland-Gosselin (with trans.), P 1936. — Studies: Bardy, MiA 2, 397/416 (sources of *De haer.*). Stroux, Phil 1931, 363/8 (*De ut. cred.* 7, 17); Festschr. R. Reitzenstein, 1931, 106/18 (letter of Secund.). L. Tondelli, *Mani. Rapp. con Bardesane, s. A. e Dante,* Mi 1932. W. Theiler 1933, 7/43 (§ 88, 1; *De vera rel.*). Davids 1930 (§ 49 II 6). C. Terzi, *Il problema del male nella polemica antimanichea di S. A.,* Udine 1937. P. Monceaux, *Le Manichéen Faustus* (CRI 43, 1, 1933); reconstruction of work of Faustus. J. P. Maher, *S. A.'s Defence of the Hexaemeron Against the Manicheans,* R 1946. P. Keseling, *Das Ethos der Christen,* Mr 1948 (= trans. of *De moribus eccl. cath.*). Roche, *Cahiers d'Ét. cathar.* I, 2, 1949, 21/50 (S. A. el les manichéens). Grondijs, NTT 1954/5, 21/42 (Manich. in Numidia). Green, RP 28, 1954, 21/9 (text. crit. of *De lib. arb.*). Chatillon, RML 1954, 191/203 (Adimantus, *Manichaei discipulus*). Aland, AugMag 3, 1955, 339/55 (A. and Montanism). M. Pontifex, *A. The Probl. of Free Choice,* 1955 (ACW 22). — CSEL 74, 1956 (*De lib. arb.,* ed. Green).

f. In his anti-Donatist writings (ML 43, CSEL 51–3) Augustine establishes in detail the Catholic concepts of the Church and the sacraments on a theological basis. The Church is a visible community of saints and non-saints, and the sacraments do not depend for their efficacy on the moral state of the person administering them. The most important of the extant treatises — eight relevant works have been lost — are the following: *Contra epistolam Parmeniani* (three books) *c.* 400; *De baptismo contra Donatistas* (seven books), 400–1; *Contra litteras Petiliani* (three books), 401–5; *De unitate ecclesiae,* 405 (not certainly genuine); *Contra Cresconium grammaticum* (four books) *c.* 406; on the *Breviculus* v. supra § 50, 7; *Contra Gaudentium Donatistarum episcopum* (two books), 421–2; on the *Psalmus contra partem Donati* v. infra n.

Cf. P. Monceaux, vols. 6 and 7 (supra § 3). Mohlberg, RAC 1947/8, 327/49 (MS of *Contra Petil.*). Pincherle, RR 1947, 160/4. W. G. Grimshaw, *St. A. and the Donatist Controv.* (SPCK) 1950; cf. DR 1951, 137/54. H. C. Frend, *The Donatist Church . . .,* O 1952.

g. Against the heresy of Pelagianism, which was concerned with the nature of man, original sin (infant baptism), justification and grace, Augustine published the following works (ML 44/5; CSEL 42, 60; EP 1715 ff.): *De peccatorum meritis et remissione et de baptismo parvulorum* (three books), 412; *De spiritu et littera,* 412; *De gratia Novi Testamenti* (= *Ep.* 140), 412; *De natura et gratia,* 413–5; *De perfectione iustitiae hominis,* 415–6; *De gestis Pelagii,* 417 (v. supra § 50, 8); *De gratia Christi et de peccato originali* (two books), 418; *De nuptiis et concupiscentia* (two books), 419–21; *De anima et eius origine* (four books), 420–1; *Contra duas epistolas Pelagianorum* (four books), 421; *Contra Iulianum* (six books), 422; *Contra secundam Iuliani responsionem imperfectum opus* (six books), 429–30.

Since ecclesiastical circles, too, opposed certain theses of his doctrine of grace and predestination, Augustine wrote the following works to disperse doubts: *De gratia et libero arbitrio* and *De correptione et gratia,* both addressed to the monks of Hadrumetum in 426–7. *De praedestinatione sanctorum* and *De dono perseverantiae,* both addressed to his followers Prosper and Hilary against the monks of Southern Gaul, 428–9.

G. Boyer, *De corrept. et gratia,* R ²1951. J. D. Burger, *De Spir. et litt.,* Neuchâtel 1951 (text and trans.). — A. d'Amato, *Progr. Avellino* 1928/9 (A. and Julian). Morin, RBn 1932, 309/13 *(Opus imperf.).* K. Rahner, ZKT 1938, 171/96 (A. and Semi-Pelag.). Nicotra, SC 1942, 141/7 and cont. (Donatist concept of sacraments and Church). Germ. complete ed. of anti-Pelag. writings ed. A. Kunzelmann and A. Zumkeller, Wu 1949ff. S. Kopp and A. Zumkeller, *A.s Schriften gegen d. Semipelagianer,* Wu 1955 (4 works with Lat. text). Dalmau, EE 1949, 59/65 (on *C. Iul.* 4, 3). Chéné, AnT 1953, 56/109 (beginnings of semi-Pelag. controv.). De Montcheuil, RSR 1956, 162/93 (A.'s polemics against Jul., *Opus imperf.*). M. A. Lesouski, *The De dono perseverantiae* (trans. and comm.), Wa 1956.

h. Anti-Arian writings (ML 42): *Contra sermonem Arianorum,* against an anonymous treatise, 418–19; the minutes of the talks, *Collatio cum Maximino Arianorum episcopo,* give an account of the disputation (427–8) with the Gothic bishop, Maximinus; soon afterwards Augustine wrote a detailed reply: *Contra Maximinum* (two books); v. supra § 82, 3.

i. Works on Biblical exegesis. Augustine did not know Hebrew, but was able to translate Greek texts even though with difficulty. Modern scholars distinguish two Old Latin texts of the Bible, one African and one Western text. Now Augustine (*Doctr. christ.* 2, 15, 22) praises one of the translations circulating in his days, the *Itala,* as the best; hence it must be assumed that the text on which he based his exegesis belonged primarily to the European (Italic) type, a view also corroborated by comparative studies of Biblical quotations. The *Itala,* however, cannot be equated with Jerome's *Vulgate.* In later years Augustine probably also used the *Vulgate,* though it is impossible to make definite statements on the date and extent of its use. Besides, Augustine also seems to have revised for his own use the Latin text of several Biblical books according to the LXX, which he regarded as inspired.

In his learned commentaries and polemical works Augustine often does justice to the literal sense of Scripture; otherwise he prefers the allegorical-mystical sense, especially in his homilies, e.g. on the Psalms and St. John's Gospel.

Bible text: P. Capelle, *Psautier lat.,* 1913. C. H. Milne, *A Reconstruction of the Old-Latin Text of the Gospels used by St. A.,* 1926. De Bruyne, MiA 2, 521/606 (A. revisor of the Bible); against this Lagrange, RB 1932, 161/86; cf. RBn 1932, Bul. n. 336; De Bruyne, RBn 1932, 550/60; RBn 1933, 20/8. Bible in gen.: Allgeier, *Festschr.* 1930 (§ 88, 1) 1/13. Vogels, ibid. 411/21. Sense of Script.: C. J. Costello, *St. A.'s Doctrine on the Inspiration and Canonicity of Scripture,* W 1930; RUO 1932, 125/38 (Canon); ibid. 1934, 81/99 (inspir.). A. Allgeier, *Die Pss. der Vulgata,* 1940, 159/238 (A.'s text of Pss.). Cilleruelo, CD 1943, 455/89; 1944, 259/83 and cont. (A. as exegete). Perella, Bi 1945, 277/302 (lit. sense). Hilmore, HTR 1946, 141/63 (A. and the crit. method). M. Pontet, *L'exégèse de s. A. prédicateur,* 1946. Altaner, ZRGG 1, 1948, 71/9 (use of Gr. Patr. texts); v. supra my studies noted p. 498. Most, CBQ 1951, 284/95 (symbolism of numbers not dependent on Pythagoras, but on Scripture). G. Strauss, *Schriftgedanke, Schriftauslegung u. Schriftbeweise b. A.,* thesis typed Go 1953. Rondet, RSR 1951, 472/7 (on allegor. exegesis). Schildenberger, *Festschr. Dold,* 84/102 (St. A.'s *Itala*). Cilleruelo, CD 165, 1953 (symbolism of number 7 in A.). Sasse, *Festschr. F. Dornseiff,* L 1953, 262/73 (doctr. of inspiration). Payne, Westminster TJ 14, 1953, 46/53 (on allegor. exegesis). Ongaro, Bi 1954, 443/74 (Salterio Veronese e revis. agostin.). Kusch, ForschFortschr 1955, 48 (*Itala* in A.). AugMag 2, 623/701 (7 contributions). P. Brunner, *Kerygma u. Dogma* 1, 1955, 59/69, 85/103 (Script. exegesis acc. to the Prol. of *Doctr. christ.*). Prete, *Sapienza* 8, 1955, 552/94 *(Principi esegetici).*

The treatise *De doctrina christiana* (= On Christian learning; four books) should head his works on Biblical scholarship; it was written for the greater part (1–3, 24) in 396–7, but completed only in 426 (EP 1582/8).

Books I and II treat of the profane and theological training necessary for a successful study of Scripture; III contains hermeneutics and four homiletics. The doctrine of the Church is the supreme rule for the exegesis of Scripture (3, 2, 2ff.). Here Augustine attempted a synthesis between Christianity and ancient learning and traced a Christian programme of culture which profoundly influenced the development of the following centuries.

Edd.: H. J. Vogels (FP 24) 1930. T. Sullivan, 4. book (with comm.), W 1930; Germ. BKV² 49, 1925. A. Sizoo, *A.'werk over de chr. wetenchap,* Delft 1933 (29pp.). Marrou, *S. A. et la fin de la cult. ant.* 1938, 331/540. G. Geelhoud - J. Francke, *A. De Doctr. christ.,* Goes 1952.

α. On the O.T. (ML 34, 36/7; CSEL 28, 1/2). Soon Augustine was no longer satisfied with his allegorical interpretation of the first three chapters of Genesis (supra 2 e) which he had written in his struggle against Manicheism. In 393–4 he therefore attempted an exegesis according to the literal sense: *De Genesi ad litteram imperfectus liber,* which he gave up, however, after interpreting the first chapter. A third voluminous interpretation *De Genesi ad litteram* (twelve books), also treats only the first three chapters (401–15).

Two works of seven books each discuss the Biblical Heptateuch: *Locutiones in Heptateuchum,* on linguistic difficulties of the Latin text; *Quaestiones in Heptateuchum* (419) on difficulties of subject matter. The very long *Enarrationes in Psalmos,* finished *c.* 416, are homilies of predominantly allegorical tendency (EP 1415/19; EA 569/89).

Trans.: U. v. Balthasar, L 1936 (sel. from *Enarr. Pss.*). G. Humeau, *Les plus belles homélies de s. A. sur les Pss.* (1948). — Studies: W. Rueting, *Unters. ueb. A.s Quaest. u. Locut. in Hept.,* 1916. A. V. Billen, *The Old Lat. Texts of the Heptateuch,* 1927. Cavallera, MiA 2, 359/72 (Jerome and A., *Quaest. in Gn.*). De Bruyne, MiA 2, 321/5 *(En. in Pss.)*; 327/40 (Ed. *De 8 quaest. ex Vet. Test.*). Ricciotti, Did 1931, 2nd/3rd F., 23/52 (Gn. comm.). Bardy, RB 1932, 515/37 *(Quaest. in Hept.)*. Inguanez, MiscCasin 1932, 5/13 (MS of *En. in Pss.* and *Tract. in Jo.*). De Blic, Gr 1936, 408/12 (*in Ps.* 31). Wytzes, ZNTW 39, 1940, 137/51 (Neoplaton. in *De Gen. ad litt.*). W. Suess, *Stud. z. lat. Bibel,* I: *A.s Locutiones,* Tartu 1932. H. Taylor, *De Gen. ad litt. XII,* thesis St. Louis Univ. 1948. Delamare, VS 1949, 478/93 (*Enarr. Pss.* 120–34). Taylor, *The Modern Schoolman* 26, 1949, 211/8 (*'spiritus'* in *Gen. ad litt.* 12, 2–4); Sp 1950, 87/93 (on text of *Gen. ad litt.*). Journet, RT 1949, 206/21 (A. on Eph. 5, 27). A. Achilli, *Il Regno di Dio nelle Enarr. Pss. di s. A.,* thesis Greg. R 1950 (not printed). Guttmann, SemiticStudMemory of I. Loew, 1950 (?), 272/6 (Cain and Abel in A.). Lieftinck, Sc 4, 1950, 96/100 (MS questions on *Enarr. Pss.* 63 and *Tract. Jo.* 52). Vaccari, Scritti 1, 1952, 238/55 (St. A.'s Psalter). Michels, FestschrCasel 94/6 (on *Quaest. Num.* 19). Pepin, RHP 1954, 373/400

(*Gen. ad litt.* 12, 10, 21 and Plotinus *Ennead.* 5, 3, 1–9 and 5, 5, 1–2). A. Weber, *A. Die Ausleggn. d. Pss.* (selected and trans.), Pa 1955. Hebgin-Corrigan, ACW 29/30, 1959 (Enarr. in Ps.).-CChL 33 (Quaest.u.Locut.in Hept.; De octo quaest. ex VT).

β. On the N.T. (ML3 4/5). The four books *De consensu evangelistarum* (*c.* 400) have an apologetical aim and are intended to clear up discrepancies in the four Gospels. *Quaestiones evangeliorum* (two books on Matthew and Luke) were finished *c.* 399; the seventeen *Quaestiones in Ev. sec. Mt.* are probably spurious; *De sermone Domini in monte,* 393–4 (two books on Mt. 5–7).

The 124 *Tractatus in Ioannis evangelium* and ten *Tractatus in epistolam Ioannis I* are particularly valuable. According to Zarb sermons 1–54 and the ten sermons in *Ep. I* were preached probably in 413, the others were written only in 418 to be read to the people. Le Landais arrives at a different conclusion (supra p. 498). According to him they are mostly real sermons which Augustine delivered before his congregation at Hippo. They are not sermons dictated to a secretary and then read in church by a priest. This homiletic exposition of St. John's Gospel should be dated between December 414 and August 416.

About 394–5 Augustine wrote an *Expositio quarundam expositionum ex Ep. ad Romanos,* further an *Inchoata expositio* of only a few verses of the same epistle, and finally a complete but very brief *Expositio Ep. ad Galatas.* An *Expositio* on Jas. (411) is lost.

Texts and Transs.: R. Williams, *Tract. Jo.* (CCL 36) 1954. T. Specht (BKV², 3 vols.), *Tract. Jo.* — J. Jepson (ACW 5) 1948 *(De serm. Domini in monte)*. F. Hofmann, *Gott ist d. Liebe* (trans. of *Tract. Ep. Jo.* 1), Fr ²1950. D. J. Kavanagh, *Serm. on the Mount with 17 relat. Sermons* (FathCh) 1951. H. J. Vogels, *A.s Schrift De cons. ev.,* 1908. A. Souter 1927 (supra § 3, 10), 139/204. M. Comeau, *S. A. exégète du 4ᵉ év.,* 1930; REL 1932, 408/22 (MS trad.). E. Logi, *S. A. I vangeli domenicali commentati,* Fl 1933. Dean, JTS 1935, 113/22 (MS of *Tract. Jo.*). Bassi, MiA 2, 915/31 (8 Beatitudes). F. N. Lekkerkerker, *Roem. 7 u. Roem. 9 b. A.,* A 1942. Rétif, RSR 1946, 368/71 (A. on Rom. 7). Mizzi, Aug 4, 1954, 450/94 (Mt. text in *De serm. in monte*). Penna, Bi 1955, 1/19 *(Consenso evang. ed i canoni eusebiani)*. Bonnardière, REAug 1, 1955, 129/48 (on Mt. 6, 12 and 1 Jo. 1, 8).

k. Writings on moral and pastoral theology (ML 34 40; CSEL 12 41). *De agone christiano,* on the struggle with the devil and with sin, 369–7; two treatises on the nature and hideousness of lying, *De mendacio,* 395, and *Contra mendacium, c.* 420. On marriage and virginity: A sermon *De continentia,* 395; *De bono coniugali* (401) shows in what the blessing of the married state consists, while taking into account sayings of St. Jerome (v. § 86, 4b) hostile to marriage. In *De sancta virginitate* (401) he praises the virginal state against Jovinian. *De bono viduitatis,* 414. In *De opere monachorum, c.* 400, Augustine demands that monks should earn their living by the work of their hands. A sermon *De patientia;* the *Speculum* (*c.* 427) gives extracts of moral precepts from the O.T. and N.T. in fifty-one sections. This collection of excerpts (ed. CSEL 12) is very probably spurious and of Pelagian origin. Possidius included it in the catalogue of the Augustian Library. Cf. De Plinval, AugMag 1, 187/92; 3, 49f.

In the *Bibliothèque Aug.,* vols. 1–3: text and trans. by R. Gosselin (3 works) G. Combès (7 works), Saint Martin (4 works). In the Germ. trans. of the moral theol. works (ed. by A. Kunzelmann and A. Zumkeller, Wu 1949ff.) the following took part: I. Dietz (1), J. Schmid (1), A. Maxsein (2) and Keseling (3 works). Span. trans. Cilleruelo and Flórez, *Tratados morales (Obras de s. A. t. 12),* Ma 1954. F. García, *El bien de matr.,* Ma 1954. S. D. Ruegg, *De util. ieiunii,* W 1951 (text, trans. and comm.). J. Perl, *Der christl. Kampf* (trans.), W 1948.

De catechizandis rudibus, written *c.* 400 at the request of the Carthaginian deacon Deogratias, develops for the first time the theory of catechesis. Two model catecheses form the second part of the work (16–27). *Rudes* should not be taken to mean children, but adult catechumens.

Edd.: G. Krueger [3]1934. J. P. Christopher, W 1926 (with comm.); trans. (ACW 2) 1946. A. Sizoo, A 1947 *(Enchirid. and Cat. rud.).* Transs. in BKV[2] 49, 1925 and F. Auer, I 1927. H. Holzapfel, *Die sittl. Wertung der koerperl. Arbeit...,* 1941, 122/36 *(De op. monach.).* Jubani, AST 1942, 9/22 (eloquence in *Doctr. christ.* and *Cat. rud.*). P. L. Huillier, *Le rôle du catéchiste dans la première initiation chrét. d'après s. A.,* thesis Lyons 1947. Touton, POC 1, 1951, 265/85 (comparison with methods followed by Cyr. Jerus. and Theod. Mops.). Capelle, QLP 1952, 55/64 *(Prédication et catéchèse).*

1. Augustine's Sermons (ML 38–9) are reckoned partly with the treatises, partly with the exegetical works. The bulk, how-

ever, is formed by the special group of *Sermones*. The text of the sermons is based almost throughout on shorthand reports taken down by stenographers *(notarii)*.

The Maurist edition recognizes 363 sermons as genuine; thirty-two are considered dubious. As a result of G. Morin's critical examination (1930) of all the 640 sermons published since then under Augustine's name, 138 further *Sermones* could be printed as genuine. During the last few years further finds have come to light. Possidius has listed only 279 *Sermones* in his *Indiculus*.

Edd.: G. Morin, *S. A. Sermones post Maurinos reperti,* R 1930. C. Lambot, *S. A.i sermones selecti 18,* Ut-Bru 1950 (crit. ed.). ClavisPL n. 284/8 (most recent lit. till 1950 on all the *Sermones*). Lambot, RBn 1933, 97/107; 1934, 398/409. Wilmart, RBn 1932, 201/6. Further new sermons ed. Lambot, RBn 1936, 113/6; 1937, 233/78; 1938, 3/25 (7 Ser.), 185/93 (2 Ser.); 1939, 3/30 (Fragm. inédits). — Transs.: G. Humeau, 3 vols., P 1932/4. T. C. Lawler, *St. A.'s Serm. for Christmas and Epiphany* (ACW 15), 1952. T. Michels, *Myst. des neuen Lebens* (20 Homs. on Easter), Salzb. 1952. Amador del Fueyo *(Obras 8 y 10 de s. A.),* Ma 1953; 1952 (171 Serm.); cf. AnT 1953, 376f. — F. Jacobi, *St. A.s Sermones de sanctis. Ein Beitr. z. Gesch. der Predigt,* thesis Mr 1939. Doelger, AC 6, 57/60 (healing magic in Ser. ed. RBn 1938, 8). Pérez, RET 1944, 497/544 (comprehens. appreciation). Lambot, Misc. Mercati I, 247/64 (ed. *Sermo* 254); RBn 1947, 89/108 (MS), 109/16 (ed. *Sermo* 111); 1948, 23/52 (*Sermo* 60 and 389). Charles, NRT 1947, 619/50 (popular lang. in the Sermons). J. Brennan, *A Study of the Clausulae in the Sermons of St. A.,* W 1947. C. Mohrmann, *St. A. Preken voor het volk,* 1948 (trans.; introd. on style and lang.). On 3 or 4 genuine Sermons v. § 89, 2. De Gaiffier, AB 1949, 267/86 (6 Hom. in *hon. s. Vincentii*). Lambot, RBn 1949, 55/81 (3 new sermons, crit. ed.; proofs that *Confessores* were venerated already at that time); AB 1949, 249/66 (on martyr-sermons); RBn 1950, 8/16 (ined. *Sermo* on Ps. 56, 2). Lambot, Mél. De Ghellinck I, 251/63 (MSS of *Sermones* ed. by Maurists); RBn 1952, 95/107 (3 new sermons); Festschr. Dold 1952, 103/12 (Sermo 369 genuine); RBn 1953, 165/210 (*Sermo* 46, crit. ed.); RBn 1954, 3/8 (MS Anglo-Sax. trans. of Serm.); RBn 1955, 208/17 (MSS of Sermo 37; genuine). A. Auer, BM 1954, 137/48 (a newly found *Sermo in Pss.)*. Mizzi, *Melita Theolog.* 7, 1954, 17ff. (on *Sermo* 58, 12). Mohrmann, Maison Dieu 39, 1954, 83/96 *(A. prédicateur)*. Arbesmann, Aug 4, 1954, 305/24 (Idea of Rome in *Sermones*). Simonetti, AugMag 1, 141/49 *(struttura dei Sermones de sanctis)*. Lambot, RB 1956, 20/38, 343 sermones, crit. ed.). Ibid. 1956, 149/56 (crit. ed. of genuine sermons in ML 40, 1127/33).

Sermones apocryphi et anonymi: Wilmart, RBn 1929, 197/203; 1930, 5/18; 1931, 160/4; the same *Sermo* ed. Hauler, WSt 1932, 129/51 (= ML 44, 1144f.). Wilmart, RBn 1935, 3/7. Leclercq, RBn 1952, Bull. n. 1749; 1948, 53/72; 1949, 100/13, 196/201; cf. ClavisPL n. 418/25. De Gaiffier, AB 1949, 267ff. (here also ps.-Aug. Serm.). Van Bawel, Aug 2, 1952, 19/25. Olivar, *Festschr. Dold,* 1952, 113/23 and RBn 1949, 114/36. ClavisPL n. 368, 370/2.

m. The collection of letters edited by the Maurists (ML 33; CSEL 34 44 57/8) contains 270 items, among them forty-seven addressed to Augustine and six to his friends. Later seven further letters were added. Apart from quite personal communications, these letters, which, owing to their length and contents, might sometimes be taken for treatises, deal with questions of philosophy, theology and practical pastoral care; some have an official character (synodal or episcopal collective letters). Of special importance is the correspondence with Jerome.

On *Ep.* 211 and the problem of the *Rule of St. Augustine.* In this letter Augustine settles a dispute that had broken out in the women's convent of Hippo (no. 1–4). In connexion with this (no. 5–16) he gives the convent a religious Rule. From the days of Erasmus the Rule here given has been regarded as the original form of the later so-called *Rule of St. Augustine.* The *regula secunda,* printed in MS 32, 1149/52 and the *regula ad servos Dei,* ibid. 1377/84 which were combined to form the *Rule of St. Augustine* were considered apocryphal. In most recent times both Rules have often been defended as genuine, written by Augustine in 389 and shortly afterwards, before 395, for the monastic communities directed by him at Thagaste and Hippo. The Rule for nuns is supposed to have been composed from the modified Rule for monks perhaps as late as the seventh century, by Fructuosus of Braga. The discussions of this question have not so far led to a final clarification.

Edd.: ML 33. *Ep.* 147 ed. M. Schmaus (FP 23) 1930. *Ep.* 119/20 ed. M. Schmaus (FP 33) 1933. Corresp. with Jerome ed. J. Schmid (FP 22) 1930. — Transs.: A. Hoffmann (BKV² 29/30) 1917. J. H. Baxter, Lo 1930. — MS trad.: H. Lietzmann, SbB 1930, 356/88. De Bruyne, RBn 1931, 284/95. Giesser, SM 1935, 241/56. De Bruyne, ZNTW 1932, 233/48 (corresp. with Jer.); RBn 1932, 303/8 (addressees). Lambot, RBn 1939, 109/21 *(Lett. inéd. relat. au De Civ. Dei).* Auvray, RSR 1939, 594/610 (A. and Jerome on Gal. 2, 11 ff.). A. P. Meys, *De briefwisseling v. Paul. v. Nola en A.,* 1941. A. Allgeier, *Pss. der Vulgata,* 1940, 232f. (*Ep.* 261). Hodgson, CQR 1947, 1/11 (*Ep.* 138). M. Lapper, *De rebus gestis Bonifatii comitis Africae et magistri militum,* Tilburg 1941, 9/17 (on the spurious letters in ML 33, 1093/8). Vallejo, *Emerita 15,* 1947, 149/54 (text. crit. of *Ep.* 137). J. H. Koopmans, *A. Briefwisseling met Dioscurus,* A 1949. Semple, BJR 1950, 111/30 (corresp. with Jerome). Courcelle, RevEA 1951, 253/300 (*lacunae* in the corp. of correspond. with Paulinus of Nola: 38 letters were exchanged).

Text of *Ep.* 211: ML 33, 958/65 and Goldbacher (CSEL 57, 356/71). Text of the Augustinian Rule: Schroeder, ArchUrkundForsch 9, 1926, 281ff. Bruyne, RBn 1930, 316/42. A. C. Vega, Ed. crit., E 1933. — Transs.: W. Huempfner in: H. U. v. Balthasar, *Die grossen Ordensregeln,* Zu-Cologne 1948, 121/33 and in A. Zumkeller, *Das Moenchtum des hl. A.,* 1950, 219/30; here the lit. on the probl. of authenticity 215/8. — For the genuineness of the August. Rule: the above-mentioned Huempfner and Zumkeller; see also Cilleruelo, *El monacato de s. A. y su Regla,* Valladolid 1948. Vega, Misc. Mercati I, 34/56. Merlin, *Anal. Praem.* 1948, 5/19. Verheijen, AnT 1951, 345/8; RML 8, 1952, 97/122; RSR 1953, 231/40; Aug 4, 1954, 258/68; AugMag 1, 255/65. Huempfner, AugMag 1, 242/54. Zumkeller, AugMag 1, 265/76 (convent. obedience). — C. Vaca, *La vida relig. en s. A.,* 2 vols., Ávila 1948f. (meditations on the Rule). — Against the authenticity: Lambot, RBn 1941, 41/58; cf. AugMag 3, 65/8. M. dal Pino, *Studi stor. dell'ord. dei Servi di Maria,* R 5, F. 1/2, 5/36. ClavisPL n. 1939. — Dereine, Sc 2, 1948, 28/36 (MS of the *Reg. tertia*). Bischko, AJP 1948, 377/95 (*Reg. consensoria* betw. 650 and 711 in Spain). ClavisPL n. 262. F. Chatillon, *La règle de s. Aug.,* thesis Str 1955.

n. Poetic Works. In the *Psalmus contra partem Donati* attested by himself (*Retr.* 1, 20) Augustine, whose style often reached poetic heights, intentionally avoided the classical art forms for the sake of the simple people. In twenty verses of twelve lines each he wanted (393/4) to warn people against the danger threatening from Donatism (ML 43; CSEL 51). In addition, a poem *De anima* (fifty-three hexameters) and several epigrams are also ascribed to him. The *Exsultet* of the Roman missal is not by Augustine.

Ermini, MiA 2, 341/52. H. Vroom, *Le psaume abécédaire de s. A. et la poésie lat. rythmique,* N 1933 (crit. text). Lambot, RBn 1935, 312/30 (crit. ed.). Tréhorel, REL 1939, 309/29 (Ps. abéc.). Capelle, Misc. Mercati I, 219/46 (*Exsultet* by Ambrose); cf. ClavisPL n. 162 and Huglo, VC 1953, 79/88 (author a deacon of Gallic. rite). Baxter, SE 1952, 18/26 (text. crit. of ed. of Lambot, RBn 1935). J. Searle, *Verses from St. A.,* Lo 1953. Avery, *Stud. . . . for B. da Costa Greene,* Pr 1954, 374/8 (Ambr. and *Exsultet*).

On Spurious Works: V. § 84, 1. De Bruyne, RBn 1931, 124/41; 1933, 119/41 (*Lib. de div. script.*). Esposito, Ha 1932. Wilmart, RAM 1936, 337/57 (Méditations); RBn 1937, 3/12. Cavallera, DS 1, 1130/5 (list of ascet. apocrypha). On the *Dial. quaest.* (ML 40, 733/7) cf. J. Madoz, *Le symb. du XIe Conc. de Tolède,* 1938 165/77. On *De altercat. Eccl. et Syn. Dial.* (ML 42, 1131/40) cf. G. Segui Vidal

La Carta-Encíclica del ob. Severo, 1937, 67/72 (written by Severus?); cf. Blumenkranz, RML 1954, 5/159 and G. Segui y J. N. Hillgarth, *La Altercatio y la basílica paleocrist. de Son Bou de Menorca,* Palma de Mallorca 1955. B. Fischer, B 1942, 139/64, 241/67 (the Bible text in the ps.-Aug. *Solut. div. quaest.* in Cod. Paris BNL 12 217). Sickenberger, TQ 1946, 373 (on ML 35, 2415/52). Lambot, RBn 1948, 177/222 (ed. fragms. of spur. work *Adv. Fulgentium Donatistam*). Charlier, RBn 1949, 91/9 (MS fragm. of *Ep.* 92A and *Ep.* 173A). G. Quadrio, *Il trattato De Assumpt. BMV dello Ps.-A. e il suo influsso nella teologia assunz. lat.,* R 1951. Dold, RBn 1953, 239/45 (fragm. of a *Sermo de conscientia*). Olivar, SE 1953, 133/40 (on ps.-A. *Sermo* 186, in appendix). Fantini, RStR 1, 1954, 200/9 *(Il tratt. De vera et falsa paenit.)*.

A.'s works as a source of eccl. and cultural hist.: F. D. Morces, *De organisatie van de christl. Kerk van Nord-Afrika . . .,* 1927. Quasten, TG 1933, 318/31 (cult of martyrs). W. Roetzer, *Des hl. A. Schriften als liturgiegesch. Quelle,* 1930. J. Zellinger, *A. u. d. Volksfroemmigkeit,* 1933. Quasten, HTR 1940, 253/66 (against pagan abuses). A. and Monasticism: Moricca, MiA 2, 933/75. Monceaux, ibid. 2, 61/89. F. M. Mellet, *L'itinéraire et l'idéal monastique de s. A.,* 1934. M. M. Getty, *The Life of the North Africans as revealed in the Sermons of St. A.,* W 1931. G. Metzger, *Die afrik. Kirche,* 1934 (from the Letters). Id., *Kirche u. Mission i. d. Briefen A.s,* 1936. M. E. Keenan, *The Life and Times of St. A.,* W 1935 (acc. to the Letters). M. D. Madden, *The Pagan Divinities and their Worship . . .,* W 1930. L. J. Vreese, *A. en de Astrologie,* thesis A 1933. P. de Labriolle 1934 (supra § 19, 3), 437/64 (paganism). M. Pickman, *The Mind of Lat. Christendom,* O 1937, 63/135, 210/28 (hist., nat. science, miracles). Keenan, CP 35, 1940, 294/7 (terminol. of magic). J. Fischer 1947, 32/105. Bardy, Ir 1948, 249/73 *(La pensée orientale);* AnT 1953, 327/46 (A. and the physicians). Diepgen, Centaurus 1, 1951 (Copenhagen): A. and Anatomy in the MA. Mandouze, AnT 1953, 151/71; 201/31 (organization of Christ. life). Hendrikx, Aug 4, 1954, 325/52 (astrology, divination, parapsychology).

3. *Points of Doctrine*

General comprehensive works and treatises on philosophy and theology: P. Batiffol, *Le catholicisme de s. A.,* [5]1929. A. C. Vega, *Introducción a la Filos. de S. A.,* E 1928 (Engl.: Ph 1931). É. Gilson, *Introduction à l'étude de s. A.,* [2]1949. D. Bassi, *Il pensiero di S. A.,* R 1929. J. Hessen, *A.s Metaphysik der Erkenntnis,* 1931. P. Montanari, *Saggio di filos. agost.,* Tu 1931. M. del Rio, *El compuesto humano seg. S. A.,* E 1931. O. Perler, *Der Nus bei Plotin u. das Verbum bei A.,* Frib 1931. C. Boyer, *L'idée de vérité dans la philos. de s. A.,* [2]1940; *Essai sur la doctrine de s. A.,* 1932; S. A. *(Moralistes chrét.)* 1932. J. Morgan, *The Psychological Teaching of St. A.,* 1932. R. Jolivet, *S. A. et le Néoplatonisme chrétien,* 1932; *Dieu, soleil des esprits,* 1934; *Le problème du mal d'après s. A.,* 1936. K. Svoboda, *L'esthétique de s. A.,* 1933. J. Guitton, *Le temps et l'éternité chez Plotin et s. A.,* 1933. W. Verwiebe, *Welt u. Zeit b. A.,* 1933. G. Quadri, *Il pensiero filosof. di S. A. c. part. rig. al probl. dell'errore,* Fl 1934. R. Kuypers, *Der Zeichen- und Wortbegriff im Denken A.s,*

A 1934. J. Goldbrunner, *Das Leib-Seele-Problem bei A.*, 1934. A. Dahl, *Odödlighetsproblemet hos A.*, Lund 1935 (immortality). J. Barion, *Plotin u. A. Unters. zum Gottesproblem*, 1935. K. Delahaye, *Die "memoria interior"-Lehre des hl. A. ...*, 1936. J. Ritter, *Mundus intelligibilis* (in A.), Frankf. a. M. 1936. W. Schulten, *A.s Lehre vom summum esse u. esse creatum*, 1935. B. Switalski, *Neoplaton. a Etyka S. A.*, War 1938. J. Burnaby, *Amor Dei*, Lo [2]1947. J. Cicconradi, *De cognit. sensibili apud S. A.*, R 1939. G. Mancini, *La psicologia di s. A.*, Na 1938. R. Schneider, *Das wandelbare Sein* (b. A.), 1938. M. Simon, *Gewissheit u. Wahrheit b. A.*, 1938. K. Mertens, *Das Verhaeltnis d. Schoenen z. Guten*, thesis Mn 1940. E. Oggioni, *S. A., filosofo e pedagogista*. Saggi, Padua 1940. M. A. Campus, *Il problema gnoseologico ...*, Fl 1943. L. Macali, *Il problema de dolore ...*, R 1943. Muñoz Vega, *Introducción a la síntesis de S. A.*, R 1945. L. Rey Altuna, *Qué es lo bello*, Ma 1945. J. Bourke, *A.'s quest of Wisdom*, Milw. 1945. F. Cayré, *Initiat. à la philos. de s. A.*, 1947. M. Stumpf, *Selbsterkenntnis u. Illuminatio b. A.*, 1945. S. Cuesta, *El equilibrio pasional en la doctrina estoica y en la de s. A.*, 1946. B. Switalski, *Neoplatonism and the Ethics of St. A.*, NY 1946. C. Boyer, *S. Agost.*, Mi 1946. J. Hessen, *Die Philos. des hl. A.*, 1947. J. Couvee, *Vita beata en vita aeterna bij Lactant., Ambros. en A.*, 1947. J. Staindinger, *Das Schoene als Weltanschauung ...*, W 1948. J. F. Callahan, *Four Views of Time in Ancient Philos.* (Plato, Aristotle, Plotinus, A.), C (Mass.) 1948. F. Sciacca, A. in J. M. Bocheński, *Bibliographie. Einfuehrungen i. d. Stud. d. Philosophie*, Berne 1948. F. Cayré et F. Van Steenberghen, *Les directions doctrinales de s. A.*, P 1948. J. Perrodon, *Le dogme cath. à l'école de s. A.*, 1948. R. Schneider, *Welt u. Kirche b. A.*, Mn 1949. W. Falkenhan, *A.s Illuminationstheorie*, thesis Cologne 1949. J. Amstutz, *Zweifel u. Mystik, bes. b. A.*, thesis Berne 1950. O. Perler, *Weisheit u. Liebe nach Texten aus d. Werken des hl. A.*, Fr 1951. J. G. Quevedo, *Ideas innates e illuminación divina*, Comillas 1951. A. Quacquarelli, *La polemica pagano-crist. da Plotino ad A.*, Mi 1952. R. Paciorkowski, *Chrzescijaństwo w apologet. myśli sw. A.*, Poznań 1952. J. Chaiz Ruy, *Les dimensions de l'être et du temps*, Lyons 1953; *S. A., Temps et hist.*, P 1955. H. Marrou - La Bonnardière, *S. A. et l'augustinisme*, 1955. P. Kuenzle, *Das Verhaeltnis der Seele zu ihren Potenzen* (bis Thomas), Fri 1956.

Philosophical Studies. The philos. and theol. contributions contained in the centenary publications mentioned above p. 496 cannot be listed individually. Cayré, RPhilos 1936, 306/28, 477/93 (point of departure of philos.). E. Hoffmann, *Festschr. E. Cassirer*, O 1936, 173/90 (Platonism). Boyer, So 1938, 474/83 *(L'idéalisme)*. Giorgiantonio, So 1941, 34/46 *(il primato della rag. prat.)*. De Vooght, RTA 1938, 317/43; 1939, 5/16, 197/222 *(A. sur le miracle)*. Nicomedi, RFN 23, Suppl. 1931, 500/8 *(A. e l'arte)*). Hausherr, *Philos. Review* (NY) 1937, 503/12 (concept of time). Marrou, *S. A. et la fin de la cult. ant.*, 1938, 561/9 *(scientia et sapientia)*. Prime, JTS 1942, 45/59 (theory of knowl.). Iturrioz, RET 1943, 89/128 *(Trinitarismo en la filos.)*. Solignac, NRT 1948, 3/19 (existentialism). Cilleruelo, RPortugFilos 1948, 51/86 *(Teoría de la sensación)*; RPsicol 4, 1949, 451/74 *(Teoría de la imaginación)*. Pepin, RMetaphysMoral 1950, 128/48; 1951, 316/26 *(Consciences chez Plotin et A.)*. Bachschmidt, PJB 1950, 438/49 (concept of time). Bushman, NewSch 3, 1952, 283/304 (A. and the Stoics). Schmaltz, *Psyche* 6, 1952, 304/19 *(veritatem facere)*. Allers, FranciscStud 12, 1952, 27/46 (Illumination).

Thonnard, AnT 1953, 33/55 *(La vie affective de l'âme)*. Verbecke, Tijdschr. v. Philos. 15, 1953, 195/222, 495/515 (development of human knowledge). Berlinger, AnT 1953, 260/79 (time and man); ZPhilosForsch 7, 1953, 493/510 (time and temporality). Florez, CD 166, 1954, 61/86 (concept of time). Koerner, TQ 1954, 397/447 (*anamnesis* and illumination and the principle of interiority). Hohensee, Folia, suppl. 2, Nov. 1954 (concept of authority). AugMag 1, 335/519 (17 contributions). Muñoz, *Pensamiento* 10, 1954, 455/87 *(Intuicionismo emocional?)*. Vega, RFilos 14, 1955, 55/121 *(Retorno a s. A.)*. González-Quevedo, *Pensamiento* 11, 1955, 5/28 *(La illuminación)*. Armstrong, DR 1955, 47/58 (The doctr. of Plotinus of the infinite in patristic thought). Cf. further studies in: RHE 1955 n. 5055/67 and 1956, n. 1991/6. Poppi, MiscFrancisc (R) 54, 1954, 345/98 (The Holy Spirit and the unity of the Myst. Body). Heijke, BiNJ 1955, 357/77 (*Imago Dei* doctr.). Elorduy, *Pensamiento* 11, 1955, 131/69 (metaphysics). F. Koerner, PJB 64, 1956, 166/217 (subj. of human knowledge). J. Guitton, *Actualité de s. A.*, 1955. J. Heijke, *Imago Dei in the Works of St. A.*, NY 1956. — Texts: L. W. Kecler, *S. A. doctr. de cognitione*, R 1934.

1. Relation between Philosophy and Theology. However great the influence of neo-Platonism on his philosophical and theological thought, Augustine, like the older Fathers, held the same view as the Schoolmen, expressed in Anselm of Canterbury's famous formula: *Credo ut intelligam,* and which he himself expressed in the words: *Intellige, ut credas, crede, ut intelligas* (*Sermo* 43, 7; cf. also *Ep.* 120, 3; *Trin.* I 1, 1). He Christianized neo-Platonism, as later Thomas Aquinas Christianized Aristotelianism. It should, however, be stressed that his terminology is not as clear and notionally fixed as that of Aquinas. His theology is not that of Scholasticism. Only the sensitive mind of a historian is capable of grasping it in its originality. In Augustine's view of the importance of thought in religious matters we find an attitude and a truth which is neither destroyed nor rendered superfluous by later progress of strictly rational thinking. From the point of view of intellectual and cultural history, Augustine's thought does not mark the end of the civilization of antiquity; it is rather the foundation on which later generations built their systems.

2. Proofs of the Existence of God. Augustine has nowhere treated this subject at length and systematically. He knows the proof from man's desire for beatitude *(De beata vita)* as well as

that from history (*Tract. in Jo.* 106 n. 4). He is familiar not only with the theological proof (*sermo* 141 n. 2) but also with the idea that the consideration of the transitoriness of all things in the world leads men to understand that they are created (*Conf.* 11, 4, 6). But his favourite proof is based on the existence in the human mind of the highest objective truths of logic, mathematics, ethics and aesthetics which are immutable and universally valid. The existence of these truths cannot be explained without assuming an essential truth which embraces all partial truths and which is identical with God (*Lib. arb.* 2, n. 7–33).

Apart from the lit. cited supra n. 3, 1 cf. J. Geyser, *A. und die phaenomenol. Religionsphilos. der Gegenwart,* 1923. M. Grabmann, *Der goettl. Grund menschl. Erkennt. n. A. u. Thom. v. A.,* 1924; *Grundgedanken des hl. A. ueb. Seele u. Gott,* [2]1929. G. Philips, *La raison d'être du mal d'après s. A.,* Lou 1927. W. P. Tolley, *The Idea of God in the Philos. of St. A.,* 1930. Despinay, *Le chemin de la foi d'après s. A.,* Vézelay 1930. Sestili, MiA 2, 765/93 (proofs of exist. of God). Wunderle, Arch-Rel.-Psych. 1931 (35 pp.; concept of God). Galli, RFN 23, Suppl. 1931, 182/219 *(atto di fede).* I. Stoszko, *L'apologétique de s. A.,* 1932. L. W. Kaelin, DT 1936, 331/52 (proofs of exist. of God). Rascol, DTC 13, 961/82 *(La providence).* v. Ivánka, Sch 1938, 521/43 (direct knowledge of God). De Samle, Tijdschr. v. Philos. 11, 1949, 589/624 (*Onbepaaldheid* in proofs of existence of God). Cushman, CH 19, 1950, 271/94 (faith and reason). J. Goette, *Jahresber. d. Canisius-Kollegs* 1950/1 (providence in thought and faith); Folia, Suppl. 1 (June 1953): Concept of Provid. Mohrmann, Mél. De Ghellinck I, 1951, 277/85 *(Credere in Deum).* F. Cayré, *Dieu présent dans la vie de l'esprit,* 1951. M. F. Sciacca, *L'existence de Dieu,* trad. R. Jolivet, 1951. Verbecke, Aug 4, 1954, 495/515 (knowl. of God). Huybers, Aug 4, 1954, 269/304 (self-knowledge and knowledge of God). S. Grabowski, *The All-Present God. A Study in St. A.,* St. Louis 1954. M. Loehrer, *Der Glaubensbegriff des hl. A. in seinen ersten Schriften bis z. d. Conf.,* Zu-Cologne 1955.

3. Doctrine of the Trinity. Whereas one school of thought, represented especially by the Greek Fathers, regards above all the Persons, Augustine makes the divine Essence his starting point. The three Persons who exist necessarily within the one essence, are distinguished and subsist by the relations which are the foundations of the inner life of the Godhead. Augustine explains the events of the interior divine life psychologically. Following Tertullian, he regards the generation of the Son as

the act of thought of the Father; the Holy Spirit who proceeds from the Father and the Son is the love between them which has become a Person. All the activity of God *ad extra* proceeds from his essence, hence it is common to all three Persons (*Trin.* 2, 17, 32). Augustine finds images and vestiges of the Trinity especially in the human mind, because of its faculties of memory, intellect and will (*memoria, intelligentia, voluntas-amor*).

M. Schmaus, *Die psychol. Trinitaetsl. des hl. A.,* 1927. L. Legrand, *La notion philos. de la Trinité chez s. A.,* 1931. Lebreton, MiA 2, 821/36 (Theophanies). E. Benz 1932 (supra § 81, 6), 364/412. C. van Lierde, *Doctr. S. A. circa dona Spiritus S. ex textu Is. 11, 2f.,* Wu 1935. I. Chevalier, *S. A. et la pensée grecque. Les relat. trinit.,* Fri 1940. A. Dahl, *A. u. Plotin* (on probl. of Trin.), Lund 1945. Boyer, Gr 1946, 173/99, 333/52 (*L'image de la Trin.).* Grabowski, CBQ 1948, 13/28 (*Spir. Dei* in Gen. 1, 2). F. L. Schmid, *De adumbratione SS. Trin. in VT sec. s. A.,* Mund. 1942. F. Leotta, *La persona dello Spirit. S. nella dottrina di s. A.,* thesis Greg. R 1948. Taylor, *Modern Schoolman* 26, 1949, 211/9 (*Spiritus* in *De Gen.* 12). B. Schultze, OCP 1949, 5/40 (Bulgakow and A.'s Trin. doctr.). H. Paissac, *Théologie du Verbe. S. A. et s. Thomas,* 1951. Cilleruelo, CD 164, 1952, 5/24 (*Memoria* in *Trin.* 10). Huybers, Aug 2, 1952, 88/107, 205/29 (Het beeld van God in de ziel volgens s. A.), Trembley, Ét. et Rech. (Ottawa) 8, 1952, 83/109 (*La théorie psychologique de la Trin.);* RUO 24, 1954, 93*/117* (*Processions du Verbe et de l'amour humaines).* Kusch, *Festschr. F. Dornseiff,* L 1953, 124/83 (Trin. in *Conf.* 2/4 and 10/13); 184/200 (God's title *Dominus* in A. and Thomas). AugMag 1, 569/607 (6 contributions). Camelot, REAug 1956, 2, 163/72 (on *Trin.* 4, 18, 24). G. Mascia, *La Teoria della Relazione nel "De Trin.",* Na 1955. R. Polmann, *Het Woord Gods bij Aug.,* 1955.

4. Doctrine of Creation. His doctrine of the origin of the world is governed by the Scriptural idea of creation (*creatio ex nihilo*). With this he combines Plato's theory of the formation of the world (in *Timaeus*) and the doctrine of the *rationes seminales* which he derived from neo-Platonism. The individual beings in the empirical world have developed from the primeval matter God created from nothing, with the help of seminal powers implanted in it (*Gen. ad litt.* 6, 5, 8; 6, 6, 10). The *Hexaemeron* of Genesis describes visions seen by the angels (ibid. 4, 26–30).

K. Pelz, *Die Engellehre des hl. A.,* 1913. H. Woods, *A. and Evolution,* NY 1924. L. Pera, *La creazione simultanea e virtuale sec. s. A.,* 2 vols., Fl 1928f.; vol. I, [2]1934. K. Staritz, *A.'Schoepfungsglaube,* 1931. A. Darmet, *Les notions de raison séminale et de puissance obéd. chez s. A. et s. Thomas d'A.,* 1935. Capdet, BLE 1936, 3/35 (*La formation des êtres)*. A. Dahl, *Odoedlighetsprobl. hos A.*, Lund 1935. De Blic, RSR 1940, 172/90 (Dieu créateur). Zimara, DT 1941, 269/94 (permissions of God). Perl, TG 1942, 263/8 (the concept of man). Burgieski, Ct 1939, 121/90 *(De immort. animae)*. Rondet, RSR 1939, 163/96 (l'anthropol. rel.). J. Mueller, DT 1942, 237/52 (plurality of subst. forms). De Blic, *Mél. Cavallera* 1948, 179/89 *(processus creationis)*. B. d'Azy, BLE 1948, 100/4 *(Les anges)*. L. A. Krupa, *Obraz Bozy w czlowieku wedlug nauki sw. A.*, Lublin 1948. A. Coccia, *La creazione simult. sec. s. A.*, thesis R 1948. Capdet, BLE 1949, 208/28 *(Les raisons causales)*. Cilleruelo, CD 162, 1950, 445/73 *(Formación del cuerpo)*; ibid. 164, 1952, 5/24 *(memoria en s. A.)*. Arostegui, RFilos 11, 1952, 43/64 *(alma y sus potencias)*. Christian, HTR 1953, 1/25 (A. on creation of world). AugMag 1, 521/67 (5 contributions). Turienzo, CD 166, 1954, 87/125 (probl. of evil). Palmiera, StPat 1, 1954, 370/99 *(La persona umana)*. Dempf, MTZ 1955, 21/31 (doctr. of man). Delehaye, MSR 1955, 121/38 *(les valeurs human.)*. A. Mitterer, *Die Entwicklungsl. A.s....*, 1956.

5. Original Sin. Augustine is the first Father to have clearly established the character of guilt inherent in the sin that has passed from Adam to all mankind. Original sin is a *peccatum* and at the same time also *poena peccati* (*Op. imp. Jul.* 1, 47). He proves original sin chiefly from Rom. 5:12, where he relates the words *in quo (omnes peccaverunt)* to the preceding *per unum hominem*, i.e. to Adam. Through the first sin mankind has become a *massa perditionis* or *damnata* (*Sermo* 26, 12, 13; *Civ. Dei* 21, 12). Original Sin is transmitted from generation to generation by the *concupiscentia carnalis;* for the children are produced by the activity of their parents' concupiscence. Christ was free from original sin, because he came into the world without *concubitus* (*Nupt. Concup.* 1, 24, 27; *Op. Imp. Jul.* 6, 22). The *concupiscentia carnis* belongs to the essence of original sin; this concupiscence is sin and punishment for sin at the same time (*Contra Jul.* 5, 3, 8). Concupiscence is, however, called *peccatum* only *modo quodam loquendi*, because it originates through sin and then, if victorious, leads into sin (*Nupt. Concup.* 1, 23, 25; *Contra duas Epp. Pel.* 1, 13, 27). The *reatus concupiscentiae*, too, belongs to the essence of original sin; it consists in the inherited lack of the living spiritual union with God (*Contra Jul.* 1, 9, 45). This *reatus concupiscentiae* is blotted out in baptism. Augustine says of the effect of baptism: *dimitti*

concupiscentiam carnis in baptismo, non ut non sit, sed ut in peccatum non imputetur (*Nupt. Concup.* 1, 25, 28).

J. Mausbach, *Die Ethik des hl. A.*, 2 vols., ²1929. A. Slomkowski, *L'état primitif de l'homme dans la trad. de l'Égl. avant s. A.*, 1928; *Pierwontny stan czlowieka wedlug sw. A.*, 1933. B. Legewie, *St. A. ueber d. Erbsuende*, 1928. N. Merlin, *S. A. et les dogmes du péché orig. et de la grâce*, 1931. Bardenhewer, MiA 2, 879/83 (Rom. 7, 14ff.). E. Dinkler, *Die Anthropologie A.s*, 1934; against this Ternus, Sch 1935, 82/98. Gaudel, DTC 12, 371/402. A. Pincherle, *La formazione della dottr. ag. del peccato orig.*, Cagliari 1938. Orbe, RET 1941, 313/37 (concupiscencia). E. Anrup, *A.s laera om arosynden*, Lund 1943; cf. TLZ 1948, 156f. Clémence, NRT 1948, 727/54 (orig. sin). G. A. Riggan, *The Idea of Orig. Sin in the Thought of A.*, thesis Yale 1949. Asensio, Gr 1949, 490/520; 1950, 35/62, 163/91, 362/90 (sexual sin in paradise). J. Gross, AugMag 2, 773/87 (nature of or. sin). Strohm, TQ 1955, 184/203 (*natura vitiata*). Further lit. in RAC 343.

6. Christology. Even before the Councils of Ephesus (431) and Chalcedon (451) Augustine had taught: In Christ there are two natures *(substantiae)*; he is God and Man, but one Person, one Christ (*Sermo* 130, 3; *Tract. in Jo.* 78, 3). The two *substantiae* are unconfused and unchanged in the one Person, which is the Person of the Logos (*Trin.* 1, 7, 14; *Corr. Grat.* 11, 30). In his human nature, too, Jesus was the natural, not the adopted Son of God (*Sermo* 183, 5; *Secund.* 5).

7. Mariology. Augustine teaches quite clearly Mary's permanent virginity also *in partu* (*Sermo* 186, 1; 215, 3) and he also attests the belief in her personal sinlessness (*Nat. Grat.* 36, 42; EP 1794); on the other hand, the frequently cited passage in *Op. Imp. Jul.* 4, 122 does not prove that Augustine already taught her immaculate conception.

8. Soteriology. Like Origen and other Fathers Augustine often understands the Redemption in the sense that, through Adam's sin, Satan had obtained a certain legal claim on us, which Christ abolished by his death. By laying hands on him, the innocent one, Satan overstepped and thus lost his "rights"; Christ "set the cross as a trap *(muscipula)*" for him and caught him in it (*Serm.* 181, 5; 263, 1). With regard to this popular way of expression it

should be pointed out that the "rights" the devil has on fallen mankind are integrated in the "law of justice" that God gives himself in his dealings with sinners. Nowhere in Augustine's work does the devil appear as God's equal partner (*Civ. Dei* 10, 22).

O. Scheel, *Die Anschauung A.s ueb. Christi Person u. sein Werk*, 1901. P. Friedrich, *Die Mariologie des hl. A.*, 1907. A. Oddone, *La figura di Cristo nel pensiero di s. A.*, Tu 1930. Schiltz, NRT 1936, 689/713 (Christol.). F. S. Mueller, MiA 2, 885/914 (Immac. concept.); against this Capelle, RTA 1932, 361/70; F. Hofmann, TQ 1932, 299/319 and J. Goetz, TG 1933, 739/44; cf. also RTA 1933 Bull. n. 119; 1934 Bull. n. 573; in addition Dietz, Aug 4, 1954, 362/411 (A. and the Immac. Conc.?). J. Rivière, *Le dogme de la rédemption chez s. A.*, [3]1933; RTA 1932, 308/16 (soteriology before A.); RevSR 1937, 36/41 (*Trin.* 13, 13f.). J. Mohan, *De nominibus Christi doctrinam D. A.i christologicam et soteriologicam exponentibus*, Mund. (Ill.) 1936. Dubarle, RSPT 1940, 244/63 and ETL 1941, 5/25 *(science et connais. hum.)*. A. C. de Romanis, *Gesù Cr. nell'insegnamento di S. A.*, Fl 1940. Trapé, CD 1943, 45/67 (A. against Leporius). É. Gilson, *Philosophie et incarn. sel. S. A.*, 1947. E. Scano, *Il cristocentrismo e i suoi fondamenti dogmat. in s. A.*, Tu 1951. Comeau, RSR 1952, 80/9 *(Le Christ et l'ascens. spirit.)*. F. Hofmann, *Festschr. K. Adam* 1952, 213/24 (BMV in the order of redemption). Cayré, AnT 1953, 232/59 (Christ in the *Conf.*). Gallus, DTP 1953, 265/9 (A., *De morte BMV*); *Verbum Dom.* 32, 1954, 129/41 *(A. ed. Gen. 3, 15)*. J. Van Bavel, *Recherches sur la Christologie de s. A.*, Fri 1954. M. Pellegrino, *Maria santiss. nel pensiero di s. A.*, R 1954. Arbesmann, Tr 1954, 1/28 *(Christus medicus);* in addition AugMag 2, 623/9. — *E. del Segundo Corazón y Pedro,* Est. Josephinos 4, 1950, 150/87 (St. Joseph in A.).

9. Augustine's doctrine of grace and predestination underwent a significant development. Before he became a bishop he held that faith is a work of man, but that, on the other hand, God gives man the power to do good (*Exp. quorund. prop. ep. Rom.* ch. 68). He further taught that man's predestination to heaven or hell was identical with God's foreknowledge of the decisions of the human will and the good or evil works resulting from them (*Lib. arb.* 3, 3, 8).

In the treatise *Ad Simplicianum,* written probably in 396, there appears for the first time his new, very different teaching, which makes the omnipotence and universal causality of God and thus also the irresistibility of divine grace the principle that governs everything. Grace precedes all merits, the human will can do nothing unless God helps us to accomplish the good

(*Simpl.* 1, q. 1, 5. 7. 13. 17; EP 1569ff.). The fact that men are good or bad, faithful or unbelievers, blessed or damned is attributed solely to the divine will. Thus Augustine teaches a limited saving will of God. He bases his point of view on the doctrine of original sin; but it has never been fully accepted within the Catholic Church.

Through Adam's sin all mankind has become *massa damnata.* Yet, through sheer benevolence and to reveal his mercy, God has destined a strictly limited and individually fixed number of men for beatitude, this number corresponding to that of the fallen angels. These elect *(electi, vasa misericordiae)* go infallibly to heaven quite regardless of their later merits, which are only gifts of God's grace; for God's knowledge is certain and his will, which gives grace and finally the *donum perseverantiae,* is insuperable. All other men, whose number is much larger, remain in the *massa perditionis,* i.e., they are without hope eternally lost *(vasa irae),* because they lack the absolutely necessary grace; it has not been given them. They do not thereby suffer injustice, for no one has a legal claim to God's mercy; in their fate God wills to reveal his justice. God's attitude to the non-elect (reprobate) is not active, as it is to the elect, but passive. It is true, Augustine speaks of *praedestinati ad sempiternum interitum* (*Tract. in Jo.* 48, 4 and 6), but never, unlike Calvin, of a *praedestinatio ad peccatum.* To demand an explanation why God saves some and leaves others in perdition is asking for the impossible (*Sermo* 26, 13); we must be content with the conviction that there is no injustice in God (*C. 2 Epp. Pel.* 4, 6, 16).

In his opinion the doctrine of irresistible grace is compatible with human freedom. He sees the solution of the difficulty in the thought that *In electis praeparatur voluntas a Domino* (*Praed. Sanct.* 5, 10). But his theory of God's particular saving will is opposed to St. Paul's saying: "God will have all men to be saved" (1 Tim. 2:4). Augustine seeks to refute this objection by a threefold artificial interpretation: The apostle speaks of all the predestined, meaning that all — but only those — are saved whom God wants to be saved (*Corr. Grat.* 14, 44); or God wants to save men of every class (*reges, privatos, ignobiles, doctos, indoctos . . ., Ench.* 103); or: God makes us want all men to be saved (*Corr. Grat.* 15, 47). From the beginning Augustine's doctrine of grace which is based on a frightening conception of God has roused opposition within the Church, and subsequently has caused grave errors.

Texts: *De corr. et gr.* ed. C. Boyer, R 1932. J. Perredon, *Pages dogmatiques de s. A.* I: *La grâce* 1932 (textes et trad.). M. de Lama, *S. A. doctrina de gr. et praed. (ex op. imp. Jul.),* Tu 1934. — Studies: O. Rottmanner, *Geistesfruechte aus d. Klosterzelle,* 1908, 11/32. T. Selgueiro, *La doctr. de s. A. sur la grâce d'après le traité à Simplicien,* 1925. J. Jauncey, *The Doctr. of Grace up to the End of the Pelag. Controv.,* 1925. H. Jonas, *A. u. das paulin. Freiheitsproblem,* 1930. J. Saint-Martin, *La pensée de s. A. sur la prédestination . . .,* 1930; DTC 12, 2832/96. Leeming, Gr 1930, 58/91 *(massa perd.).* G. Capone-Braga, *La concezione agost. della libertà,* Padua 1931. Jacquin, MiA 2, 853/78 (predest.). Dumont, RevSR 1931, 513/42; 1932, 29/55, 194/219 *(le surnaturel).* E. Mersch 2, 1936, 35/138. V. Capanaga, *La teol. agust. de la gracia y la hist. de las conversiones,* E 1933. A. Guzzo, *A. contro Pelagio,* Tu [2]1934. G. Combés, *La charité d'après s. A.,* 1934. H. Barth, *Die Freiheit der Entscheidung im Denken A.s,* 1935. J. Henninger, *S. A. et doctr. de duplici iustitia,* Moedling 1935. R. Polman, *De praedestinatie van A., Thom. v. A. en Calvijn,* 1936.

K. Janssen, *Die Entstehung der Gnadenlehre A.s,* 1936. T. J. McKugo, *De relatione inter caritatem august. et gratiam actualem,* Mund. 1936. Slomkowski, CT 1937, 32/52 *(Gratia sanctificans et iustitia originalis).* Montanari, RFN 1937, 359/87 (liberty). P. Platz, *Der Roemerbr. i. d. Gnadenl. A.s,* 1938. L. Bovy, *Grâce et liberté chez s. A.,* Montreal 1938. J. Wang Tschang-Tche, *S. A. et les vertus des païens,* 1938. K. Rahner, ZKT 1938, 171/96 (A. and the semi-Pelag.). S. Pedone, *Il probl. della volontà in s. A.,* Lanciano 1940. G. Vranken, *Der goettl. Konkurs z. freien Willensakt des Menschen . . .,* 1943. J. Zameza, *La conversión del mundo infiel,* Burgos 1942. Dalmaú, EE 1943, 5/31 (A.'s doctr. of grace: against Baius, Rottmanner). Canals, CD 1945, 401/62 (justification acc. to A. and the Counc. of Trent). Cayré, AnT 2, 1941, 42/63 (predestin.). F. Brambilla, *La necessità della preghiera . . .,* R 1943. A. Niebergall, *A.s Anschauung v. d. Gnade,* thesis Marbg. 1944. J. Carney, *The Doctrine of St. A. on Sanctity,* W 1945. Léon-Dufour, RSR 1946, 129/63 (grace and free will). N. Lekkerkerker, *Studiën over de rechtvaardiging bij A.,* 1947. J. Schmucker, *Die Gnade des Urstandes u. d. Gnade der Auserwaehlten . . .,* 1940. Liebaert, MSR 1947, 31/48 (trans. of treatise by O. Rottmanner 1908, cited supra). Canals, CD 159, 1947, 488/512 *(iustitia).* Dalmaú, EE 1948, 339/74 (S. A. y Suárez). K. Barth, Festschr. E. Brunner, Zu 1950, 49/64 (freedom in Epictetus and A.). E. Braem, *Het christol. aspect van A.' leer over de heiligmak. genade,* thesis Lou 1951. Aug 1951, 7/20, 77/90; 1952, 201/4; 1953, 5/20, 328/40. A. Stoop, *Die deificatio hominis in die sermones en epist. v. A.,* Ley 1952. J. Plagnieux, *S. Grég. de*

Naz. Théologien, 1952, 413/24 *(La foi purifiante chez A.).* Lenicque, AnT 1953, 110/44 (Liberté des enfants de Dieu). Loewenich, ArchReformG 44, 1953, 52/63 (on doctr. of grace in A. and Luther). Rondet in: *A. parmi nous,* 1954, 199/242 (freedom and grace). AugMag 2, 737/803 (7 contributions on doctr. of grace). Zimara, ZPhilTheol (Fri) 1, 1954, 353/93 (divine foreknowledge). M. Pontifex, *St. A. The Probl. of Choice,* Westm. Md. 1955. Jourjon, VC 1955, 249/51 (the formula *etiam peccata* not coined by A.). L. Arias, *Salmanticensis* 2, 1955, 3/41 (doctor of grace). G. Nygren, *Das Praedestinationsproblem i. d. Theol. A.s,* 1956.

10. Doctrine of the Church (v. supra 2f.). The Church of the Donatists cannot be the true Church, because it is not Catholic, one, holy and apostolic. He who leaves the Church loses his salvation, for *salus extra ecclesiam non est* (*Bapt.* 4, 17, 24). There can never be a just reason for leaving the Church and founding a separate Church (*C. Ep. Par.* 2, 11, 25). The motives of the heretics' actions are earthly considerations, passion and lack of charity (*Sermo* 4, 30, 33). Nevertheless, Augustine distinguishes between a visible and an invisible Church. There are such who are outside the Church through their own fault and others who, without any fault of their own, are not members. Those who are born as Donatists and are in good faith seeking the truth should not be considered heretics (*Ep.* 43, 1). Thus also Catholics who, though excommunicated unjustly do not go over to the enemies of the Church but remain faithful to Catholic truth, continue to belong to the Church's community of grace (*Vera rel.* 6, 11). On the other hand, external membership of the *Catholica* does not in itself guarantee the individual's state of holiness. Here on earth the visible Church will always contain both good and bad, only in heaven will the sanctity of the Church be identical with the sanctity of all its members (*Post coll.* 8, 11).

He considers the Church of Rome as that Church *in qua semper apostolicae cathedrae viguit principatus* (*Ep.* 43, 3 7). He attaches the greatest importance to Rome's judgement in matters of faith: *Iam de hac causa* (of the Pelagians) *duo concilia missa sunt ad sedem apostolicam: inde etiam rescripta venerunt. Causa finita est, utinam aliquando finiatur error* (*Sermo* 131, 10, 10; EP 1507). This is the origin of the adage: *Roma locuta, causa finita.*

C. Romeis, *Das Heil der Christen ausserhalb der wahren Kirche n. A.,* 1908. P. Batiffol, *Le catholicisme de s. A.,* 2 vols., [5]1929. E. Altendorf 1932 (supra § 3, 21), 158/71. F. Hofmann, *Der Kirchenbegr. des hl. A.,* 1933. K. Adam, Festgabe f. A. Ehrhard 1922, 1/23 *(causa finita).* Martil, RET 1941, 279/311, 489/543, 813/44; 1942, 35/61, 357/97, 547/603 (La tradición en S. A.); also sep. Ma 1942. U. v. Balthasar, *A.: Das Antlitz der Kirche,* Einsiedeln 1942 (selected texts). Further lit. supra § 88, 2c. G. Spanedda, *Il mist. della Chiesa nel pens. di S. A.,* Sassari 1945. I. Prina, ... *dottrina del Corpo mist. di Gesù Cr. nelle opere antidonatiste di S. A.,* 1942. Grabowski, TSW 1946, 72/125 (doctr. of the Myst. Body of Christ). 1947, 614/67; 1948, 47/84 (sinners and myst. Body of Christ); Tr 1946, 89/113 (papal primacy). G. Favara, *La necessitd della Chiesa sec. s. A.,* Arcireale 1950; DTP 4, 1952, 375/95 *(Chiesa e grazia).* A. Corticelli, *La dottr. del Corpo Mist. nelle Enarr. Pss.,* thesis Greg. R 1951. Butler, DR 1951, 137/51 (teaching on schism). Ludwig 1952, 73/84 (Papal primacy). Beumer, MTZ 1952, 261/75 (idea of pre-Christ. Church). La Bonnardière, VS 1952, 404/27 (Marthe et Marie, Figures de l'Égl.). Gilson, AHD 28, 1953, 5/23 *(Égl. et Cité de Dieu).* AugMag 2, 805/914 (10 contribs. on Christ and Church). Perler, AugMag 2, 835/58 (Cypr., *De unit.* 4/5 in A.). J. Ratzinger, *Volk u. Haus Gottes in A.s Lehre v. d. Kirche,* Mn 1954. Benz, MainzAkadAbhWissLit 1954, 2 (doctr. of Church). Kinder, *Reich Gottes u. Kirche bei A.,* 1954. Pontet, Egl. 1, 1954, 163/80 (concept of schism). Stud. der Luther-Akad., F. 8, G 1934, 19f. *(causa finita).*

11. General Teaching on the Sacraments. The sacraments of Christ and the Church are not the property of the person who administers them. Hence his personal sanctity or sinfulness is irrelevant to the validity of the sacrament. Unworthy men or heretics can receive the sacraments, but will not receive grace. Those who have been baptized or ordained in schism have received the sacrament validly, even if no grace should have been connected with the reception, for both sacraments imprint a "character" on the recipient, similar to the *character militiae*, the sign branded on the soldier (*C. Ep. Parm.* 2, 13, 28f.).

Hocedez, RSR 1919, 1/29 (concept of Sacr. in *Tract. Jo.* 80). Neveut, DTP 1931, 3/27 *(théol. sacram).* Féret, RSPT 1940, 218/43 *(Sacramentum-res).* Prenter, Studia theol. (Lund) 1, 1948, 5/26. (Metaphys. and eschatol. in sacr. teaching). Van der Meer, *Maison Dieu* 13, 1948, 50/65 *(Sacramentum).* Harding, MedievStud 14, 1952, 79/97 (the word *character*). C. Couturier in *Ét. August.,* 1953, 163/274 *(Sacramentum et mysterium).* P. V. Kornyljak, *S. A.i de efficacitate sacrament. doctr. c. Donatistas,* thesis Prop. Fide, R 1953.

12. Baptism; cf. 7 *libri de baptismo*. He calls infant baptism a *consuetudo nequaquam spernenda ... nec omnino credenda, nisi apostolica esset traditio* (*Gen. Litt.* 10, 23, 39; EP 1705). He ascribes the power to remit sins to the baptism of desire (*Bapt.* 4, 22, 29; EP 1630) in the case of necessity, citing Lk. 23: 43. Martyrdom outside the Church (among the Donatists), however, has no such power, since it is lacking in the *caritas* demanded by St. Paul (1 Cor. 13: 3) (*Bapt.* 4, 17, 24; *Ep.* 108, 3, 9).

Busch, EL 1938, 159/78; 385/483 *(De initiatione christ.)*. A. Bannwarth, *Le bapt. chez s. A.*, thesis Str 1950. Cayré, AnT 1952, 131/43 *(Les enfants morts sans bapt.)*. Hamer, Ir 1952, 268/74 *(Bapt. et l'Égl.)*.

13. When speaking of the eucharist Augustine frequently develops spiritualistic ideas. Christ did not hesitate to say: This is my Body, when giving his disciples *signum corporis sui* (*Adimant.* 12, 3; EP 1566); the eucharist is the Body of Christ *secundum quendam modum* (EP 98, 9); whoever was in the Church, i.e. in the communion of the predestined, could be said to eat the Body of Christ and to have eternal life (*In Jo.* 26, 15; *Civ.* 21, 25, 2). This symbolism, however, which links up with the thought of earlier Fathers, does not exclude the old attested faith in the real presence of Christ in the eucharist. The preacher says to the newly baptized: "The bread you see on the altar is the body of Christ, as soon as it is sanctified by God's word. The chalice, or better what is contained in the chalice, is the blood of Christ, as soon as it is sanctified by God's word" (*Sermo* 277, 1). "Christ bore himself in his hands when he said: This is my body" (*In Pss.* 33, 1, 10; 2, 2; cf. *Sermo* 22, 7; EP 1464, 1519). In the daily sacramental sacrifice of the Church Christ is priest and victim at the same time (*Civ.* 10, 20; EP 1745). The celebration of the eucharist is nothing else but the repetition of Christ's sacrificial death: *Caenam suam dedit, passionem suam dedit* (*Enarr. Pss.* 21, *Sermo* 2, 27). There are no clear statements yet in Augustine on the doctrine of transubstantiation and the constant presence of Christ in the consecrated elements.

Texts: H. Lang (FP 35) 1933. — Studies: K. Adam, *Die Eucharistielehre des hl. A.*, 1908; TQ 1931, 490/536. G. Lecordier, *La doctr. de l'Euch. chez s. A.*, 1930. W. van Dijk, *S. A. en de hl. Euch.*, 1930. P. G. Bracci, *Victima sancta. Pens., dott. e insegn. di S. A. sulla Euc.*, 1931. D. Zaehringer, *Das kirchl. Priestertum n. d. hl. A.*, 1931. P. Bertocchi, *Il simbol. ecclesiol. della Euc. in S. A.*, Bergamo 1937. Brigué, RSR 1939, 335/428 *(La disposiz. per la S. Commun.)*. Camelot, RSPT 1947, 394/410 (realism and symbolism). A. F. Krueger, *Synthesis of Sacrifice acc. to St. A.*, Mund. 1950. Adam, TQ 1951, 490/536 (on doctr. of Euch.). Lekkerkerker, Kerk en Theol. 2, 1951, 154/65. O. Perler, *A. Weisheit u. Liebe*, 1952, 95/105. Mizzi, EL 1953, 210/22 *(formula della consecrazione)*. I. Volpi, *Communione e salvezza in s. A.*, R 1954 (thesis).

14. Penance. Forgiveness of sin can be obtained only in the Church, because it alone possesses the Holy Spirit, who is the principle of all remission of sin. The Holy Spirit effects forgiveness even through an unworthy administrator of the power of the keys, provided only that he is a *minister catholicus* (*Sermo* 71, 20, 33 and 23, 37; *Ench.* 65, 17).

There are three kinds of penance: 1. penance before baptism, 2. penance for venial sins, 3. penance for grave sins *(paenitentia maior, luctuosa, lamentabilis)*. The first two kinds of penance are necessary for all, the third, however, ought to have no place in the normal Christian life (*De symb.* 7, 15, 16; *Ep.* 265, 7, 8; *Sermo* 252, 3, 8; cf. EP 1529/34). The lighter sins *(peccata quotidiana)* include the inevitable sins of weakness (*Sermo* 9, 11, 18; *Ench.* 87, 21), but also the less grave sins, even if they are "mortal" such as adulterous desires (*Sermo* 98, 5; 82, 3, 5). Penance for them consists first of all in prayer (the Our Father, especially the 5th petition), further also in fasting, alms (*Sermo* 17, 5; 131, 7) and in contrite acceptance of fraternal correction (*De fide et op.* 26, 48).

The *peccata gravia*, which result in excommunication, are the object of the *paenitentia maior* (ibid. 26, 48; *De symb.* 7, 15). The lists of vices and the decalogue provide aids for ascertaining what sins belong to this category (*Sermo* 351, 7; *Ench.* 65, 17). Their limitation to the so-called capital sins is rejected *(Spec. Act. Ap.)*. The *paenitentia maior*, the only one that has an ecclesiastical and sacramental character, is permissible only once. Nevertheless, those who relapse into sin may count on God's mercy if they do personal penance (*Ep.* 153, 3 and 7f.). The "loosing" by the Church in the reconciliation results in abolishing the *reatus* of sin (*Sermo* 98, 6) and in the infusion of the Holy Spirit which is connected with the renewed admission as a member of the Church (*Tract. Jo.* 121, 4).

As regards the external form we must distinguish between public and semi-public penance. In the case of public penance which is inflicted for offences causing grave scandal, the excommunication with a corresponding *correptio* is announced publicly, and the reconciliation also takes place in public, while in the case of the semi-public penance for secret sins these acts take place in secret (*Sermo* 82, 7, 10; 351, 4, 9). The semi-public penance, however, is not to be equated with the private ecclesiastical penance in the later sense. It has, on the contrary, all the characteristics of the *paenitentia gravis* (excommunication, belonging to the order of penitents and reconciliation). Augustine does not know a private ecclesiastical penance.

Texts: B. Poschmann (FP 38) 1934. — Studies: K. Adam, *Die kirchl. Suendenvergebg. nach d. hl. A.*, 1917; *Die geheime Kirchenbusse bei A.*, 1921; TQ 1929, 1/66. Against Adam's thesis (A. founder of eccl. private penance) cf. B. Poschmann, *Hat A. die Privatbusse eingefuehrt?*, Braunsberg 1920; ZKT 1921, 208/28, 405/526; B. Poschmann, *Kirchenbusse u. correptio secreta bei A.*, 1923. E. Durkin, *The Theol. Distinction of Sins in the Writings of St. A.*, thesis Mund. 1952. — Mgg. on matrimony in A.: J. Peters, Pa 1918. G. Serrier, P 1928. B. A. Pereira, P 1930. A. Reuter, *S. A.i doctr. de bonis matrimonii*, R 1942. N. Ladomerskij, *S. A., docteur du mariage chrét.*, R 1942. Lochet, NRT 1951, 561/69 (purpose of marriage). M. Mueller, *Die Paradiesehe* . . .. (from A. to Thomas) 1954, 19/32. Meslin in: *Mystique et continence*, 1952, 293/304 *(sainteté et mariage)*.

15. The Doctrine of the State. Augustine rejected the ideal of the state held by antiquity, according to which the state was the highest and essential end of man, and laid the foundations of a Christian concept of the state. The state rests on a psychological quality with which man was endowed by God, which leads him

to associate with other beings of the same nature, i.e. God is mediately the author of the state (*Civ. Dei* 19, 5; 5, 1). It is a mistake to assert that Augustine considered the state to be only a consequence of sin, and that he equated it with the *civitas terrena* (supra 2 c). Changing Cicero's definition of the state he declares: *Populus est coetus multitudinis rationalis, rerum quas diligit concordi communione sociatus* (19, 24). The end of the state is to establish and preserve peace in order, which is done only if *iustitia* sees to a just distribution of things. Where justice is lacking, there can be no peace. Without *pax* the state will perish sooner or later (19, 13). If a state expands through wars of conquest and necessarily violates justice, he calls it *latrocinium* (4, 4). The state is meant also to serve the final end of man and so to enable him to prepare himself for the life to come (19, 17 and 27; *Ep.* 155, 3, 12).

In the course of the Donatist controversy Augustine changed his former view which rejected all compulsion in matters of faith (*Ep.* 23, 7; 93, 5, 17) and finally arrived at the opposite standpoint. Impressed by the good effects and the results obtained by the compulsory measures the state had taken against the Donatists (*Ep.* 185, 7, 29), he defended henceforth the use of force against heretics (*Ep.* 93 and 185). Thus Augustine paved the way for St. Thomas Aquinas who attempted to provide the medieval Inquisition with a theological foundation.

O. Schilling, *Die Staats- u. Soziallehre des hl. A.*, 1910; *Naturrecht u. Staat nach d. Lehre der Alten Kirche,* 1914. J. Bouvet, *S. A. et la répression de l'erreur rel.,* Mâçon 1918. B. Wendorff, *Die Staatsl. des Aur. A. nach De civ. Dei,* 1926. J. Bourgeot, *A.s Philos. des Friedens u. des Krieges,* 1926. G. Combès, *La doctrine politique de s. A.*, 1927. F. X. P. Duijnstee, *S. A. over Kerk en Staat,* Tilburg 1930. De la Brière, RPhilos. 1930, 557/72 (war and peace). Roberti, RFN 23 Suppl. 1931, 305/66 *(diritto Rom. in A.)* A. Brucculeri, *Il pensiero sociale di s. A.*, R 1932, Span. trans., Mexico 1953. Hrabar, *Arch. Philos. du droit* 1932 (droit internat.). Kosters, *Rev. Droit internat.* 1933, 31/61, 282/317, 634/76 (Le "droit des gens"). H.-X. Arquillière, *L'augustinisme politique,* ²1955. R. Regout, *La doctr. de la guerre juste de s. A. à nos jours,* 1935. Wadsworth, *Clergy Rev.* 1936, 22/30 (collective security). Lampe, Th 1938 (theory of kingship). K. Scott, ARW 1938, 121/30 (rel. policy). Chroust, Philos. Rev. 53, 1944, 195/202 (philos. of law). T. Serra, *El Derecho y el Estado en s. A.,* Ma 1944. F. Wiesenthal, *Die Wandlung des Friedensbegriffs v. A. bis Thomas,* thesis Mn 1949. Chroust, Notre Dame Lawyer 1950, 285/315 (philos. theory of law). E. Barker, *Essays on Governmt.,* O [2]1951, 234/70 (A.'s doctr. of state and society). V. Giorgianni, *Il concetto del diritto dello Stato in s. A.,* Padua 1951. H. Eibl, *A. Vom Goetterreich z. Gottesstaat,* 1951, Kilzer, BenedRev 3, 1952, 293/303 (social thought). H.-J. Diesner, *Studien z. Gesellschaftsl. u. soz. Haltung A.s,* Halle 1954. Cranz, HTR 1954, 255/316 (ideas on society). AugMag 2, 915/89 (8 contributions on the theol. of hist. and the doctr. of the state). Joly, RHP 1955, 263/94 *(A. et l'intolérance rel.).*

Studies on Eschatology: C. Hartmann, *Der Tod in seiner Beziehung zum menschl. Dasein b. A.,* 1932; cf. *Catholica* 1, 1932, 159/90. H. Eger, *Die Eschat. A.s,* 1933. Lewalter, ZKG 1934, 1/51. J. Leahy, *S. A. on Eternal Life,* 1939. J. Hubaux, BullAcadBelgClLett 40, 1954, 658/73 (A. et la crise eschatol.). — On Moral Theology: J. Mausbach, *Die Ethik A.s,* 2 vols., [2]1929. B. Roland - Gosselin, *La morale de s. A.,* 1925. A. Reul, *Die sittl. Ideale des hl. A.,* 1928. H. Arendt, *Der Liebesbegr. bei A.,* 1929. Oddone, RFN 23 Suppl. 1931, 264/85 *(dottr. sulla menzogna).* C. Boyer, S. A., 1932 *(moralistes chrét.).* V. Talija, *Eticki sistem s. A.,* Beograd 1934. L. Cecchini, *Il probl. morale in s. A.,* Reggio (Em.) 1934. G. Combès, *La charité d'après s. A.,* 1934. A. Petzaell 1935; cf. RHE 1936, 307*, n. 5533. V. Nolte, *A.s Freundschaftsideal in s. Briefen,* 1939. J. Rohner, *La finalité mor. chez les théolog. de s. A. à Duns Scot,* 1939. G. Hultgren, *Le commandement d'amour chez s. A. (d'après les écrits de 386–400)* 1939. C. A. Oberstar, *S. A.i doctr. de vitio capit. superbiae,* Ljubl. 1940. Pascher, *Festschr. E. Eichmann,* 1941 *(servitus religiosus* since A.). A. Kis Gyuerki, *Gedanken A.s ueb. d. Sklaverei,* thesis W 1942. W. M. Green, *Univers. Californ. Publ. in ClassPhil* 13, n. 13, 1949, 407/32 *(Initium omnis peccati superbia).* M. Arattukulan, *Doctr. S. A.i de vulnere ignorantiae,* Cochin-S. India 1950. J. F. Harvey, *Moral Theol. of the Confess.,* W 1951. J. Hubaux, BullAcadBelgClLett 40, 1954, 658/73 *(A. et la crise eschatol.).* H. Vandenberghe, *S. A. et le sens du péché,* Bru 1954. AugMag 2, 703/36 (3 contributions). Rondet, *Aug. parmi nous,* 1954, 111/48 (riches and poverty). E. Bruck (v. supra § 3, 28) 84/104 (right of inherit. in A.). On Mysticism and Spir. Life: Boyer, DS I, 1101/30. F. Cayré, *La contemplation aug.,* [2]1954; *La divine présence d'après s. A.,* 1933; *La méditation selon l'esprit de s. A.,* 1935. E. Hendrikx, *A.s Verhaeltn. zur Mystik,* 1936. J. Ziegler, *Dulcedo Dei* 1937, 88/98. Morel, RAM 1947, 222/58 (A.'s life of prayer). De Bovis, RAM 1949, 180/93 *(Le Christ et la prière).* Galtier, RAM 1949, 169/79 *(De quoi s'accusent les saints?).* G. della Volpe, *La mistica da Plotino a s. A.,* Messina 1949/50. J. Amstutz, *Zweifel u. Mystik bes. b. A.,* Berne 1950. Lorenz, ZKG 63, 1950/1, 75/132; 64, 1952/3, 34/60 *(fruitio Dei).* C. Butler, *Western Mysticism,* new ed. Lo 1951. I. Berrachina Vicedo, *El mundo como enemigo del alma en los Tract. in Jo. de s. A.,* thesis Greg. R 1951. Delamare, VS 1952, 477/93 *(La prière à l'école de s. A.).* Connolly, IER 1952, 44/53; 1953, 28/36 (The Platonism of A.'s "Ascent" to God). Adnès, RAM 1952, 208/23 (humility). Comeau, RSR 1952, 80/9 *(l'ascension spirit.).* Cayré, AnT 1953, 349/65 *(mysticisme de la sagesse).* Sage, REB 1953, 252/65 (*Supplices te rogamus* in the Canon in A.). Baus, TrTZ 1954, 321/39 (Christ in the prayer of A.). Morel in: *A. parmi nous,* 1954, 57/110 (prayer life). F. Cayré, *La contempl. aug.,* 1954. Courcelle,

AugMag 1, 53/7 *(expérience aug. de l'extase)*. H. Meyer, AugMag 3, 429/37 (A. not a mystic). Olphe-Galliard, DS 2, 1912/21 (Contemplation). — On education: F. X. Eggersdorfer, *Der hl. A. als Paedagoge,* 1907. F. Zillmann, *La Scuola dei sordomuti,* 1933 (education of the deaf and dumb, 48 pp.). J. Hogger, *Die Kinderpsychol. A.s,* 1937. A. M. Vellico, *S. A. e la pedagogia crist.,* R 1934. W. v. d. Sluis, *A. in de praktijk van zyn ondervijs,* A 1937. J. Wessel, *Bedeutung u. Wesen d. sexuellen Erziehung* (b. A.), 1938. Bennefoy, RET 1953, 25/54 (Le docteur chrét. sel. s. A.). Jourjon in *Aug. parmi nous,* 1954, 149/97 (pastoral activity). *Contribución españ. a una misionología Agust.,* Burgos 1955.

§ 89. PUPILS AND FRIENDS OF AUGUSTINE

1. Paulus Orosius (supra § 49 II 6).

2. St. Quodvultdeus, a pupil and friend of Augustine, became Bishop of Carthage *c.* 437. In 439 he had to flee from Geiserich and went to Campania, where he died *c.* 453.

Franses assigned twelve pseudo-Augustinian sermons (of the years 437–9), to Quodvultdeus. Of these Kappelmacher, Nock and Simonetti recognized for good reasons three or four as genuine sermons of Augustine. The others are assigned to two unknown authors. Cassiodorus assigned *De promissionibus et praedicationibus Dei* (ML 51, 733/858) to Prosper of Aquitaine *(Inst.* I 1); this work cannot be considered a definitely genuine work of Quodvultdeus. The only certainly authentic writings of his are two letters contained in the Augustinian corpus (*Epp.* 221 and 223).

Mgg.: D. Franses, Mn 1920; Katholiek 132, 1922, 93/104. Schepens, RSR 1919, 230/43; 1923, 76/8. Wilmart, RBn 1930, 5/18 (ps.-Aug. *Sermo*). On Franses 1920, 18/21 cf. Kappelmacher, WSt 49, 1931, 89ff. On ML 40, 677/86 cf. K. Strecker, *Studi medievali* 5, 1932, 167/86 (Virgil, *Ecl.* 4, 7). Nock, VC 1949, 48/55 (*Lib de promiss.* 3, 38: Asclepius). Simonetti, IstLombRendClLett 83, 1950, 6/18.

3. Marius Mercator was probably an African by birth. In 418 he wrote two treatises, now lost, against the Pelagians, which he sent to Augustine. In 429, when he was probably living in a Latin monastery in Thracia, he published another anti-Pelagian treatise

which was destined for ecclesiastical circles at Constantinople and the court. All his later, generally not very voluminous writings and translations opposing Pelagianism and Nestorianism were composed for the benefit of the religious of his monastery and finished shortly after 431. As a theologian he completely depends on Augustine and Cyril of Alexandria. We have no further information on his life. Later, probably only after 533, a Scythian monk combined his writings with other documents which he published in the so-called *Collectio Palatina* (supra § 50, 17).

a. Two memoranda are directed against Pelagianism: The *Commonitorium super nomine Caelestii* (Greek 429, Latin 431) and the *Commonitorium against Pelagius, Caelestius and Julian;* he also translated four anti-Pelagian sermons of Nestorius and a letter of the same to Caelestius.

b. The following are anti-Nestorian: *Refutatio symboli Theodori Mopsuesteni* and *Comparatio dogmatum Pauli Samosateni et Nestorii;* he translated five sermons of Nestorius on the Theotokos, a correspondence between Cyril and Nestorius, and excerpts made by Cyril from writings of Nestorius.

ML 48, SACO I, 5, 5/70. Eltester, PWK 14, 1831/5. Lepka, RHE 1931 572/9 (2nd *Commonit.*).

4. St. Prosper Tiro of Aquitaine (d. after 455), a lay theologian, who, as a friend of Augustine, at first eagerly defended his genuine doctrine on grace and predestination against the attacks of the Semi-Pelagians (Cassian, Vincent of Lerins).

About 428 Prosper and his friend Hilary informed St. Augustine of the opposition to his doctrine of grace which began to stir in the monasteries of Southern Gaul, where Prosper himself was living as a monk (Marseilles). Thereupon Augustine wrote his two treatises *De praedestinatione sanctorum* and *De dono perseverantiae*. After Augustine's death Prosper and his friend went to Rome to ask Celestine I for the condemnation of Augustine's opponents. But he only obtained a letter in which Augustine was generally defended, but which gave no theological decision. From 432 onwards Prosper gradually moved ever farther away from strict Augustinianism. Under Leo I (440) he joined the staff of the Papal chancellery as theological assistant and, according to the testimony of Gennadius (ch. 84) drafted the Papal Epistles against Monophysitism *(Ep. 28 ad Flavianum)*.

a. His *Poema ad uxorem* dates from the time before he entered the monastery; it is an invitation to his wife to dedicate herself entirely to God. He followed up his Letter to Augustine (Aug., *Ep*. 225) by a series of writings in verse and prose which are nearly all directed against Pelagianism and depend on writings of Augustine. In his *Carmen de ingratis* (i.e. of the ungrateful or graceless ones) he elaborates in 1002 hexameters ideas which he had already expressed before in a letter addressed to a certain Rufinus. Four controversial writings (431–4): *Liber contra collatorem* (i.e. Cassian), *Pro Augustino responsiones* (three individual works; addressed to two priests at Genoa "against the objections of the Gallic slanderers" and against Vincent of Lerins).

b. The following belong to the later period: The so-called *Capitula Caelestini* (between 435 and 442), a collection of *testimonia* only recently assigned to him (ES 129/42), *Expositio psalmorum* (Pss. 100–150), a compilation from Augustine's great commentary on the Psalms. The anonymous work *De vocatione omnium gentium* (*c*. 450) can also very probably be attributed to him. The *Liber* (392) *sententiarum ex operibus s. Augustini delibatarum* (*c*. 450) is a survey of Augustinian theology without systematic arrangement. This work is the basis of his *Liber* (106) *epigrammatum ex sententiis s. Augustini.* On the Chronicle, v. supra § 49 II 7; on a spurious work v. supra n. 2. The poem *De divina providentia* (ML 51, 617/38) in 876 hexameters frequently attributed to him is also spurious. Pelagianizing views can clearly be discerned in it. Cf. G. de Plinval, *Pélage,* 1943, 241, 404. Fischer 1947, 177f.

On Prosper's doctrine of predestination. He remained faithful to strict Augustinianism only till 432. He gave up the Augustinian doctrines of the limited saving will of God and of predestination *ad poenam ante praevisa demerita* under the influence of the objections raised by the Semi-Pelagians, and finally became the energetic protagonist of the universal saving will of God in his work *De vocatione omnium gentium*. All men are called to be saved by a general grace offered to all, but only those reach the goal who are given a particular grace, to which no one has a right. Since he wants to gain the *defensores liberi arbitrii* he emphasizes not only the freedom of the will for the beginning and for perseverance in the good, but also the divine prescience in fixing for ever the *numerus electorum*. Grace and nature work together in harmony (EP 2024/7).

ML 51. *Carm. de ingr.* Germ. by O. Hagenbuechle 1920. P. Deletter, trans. of *De vocat. omn. gent.* (ACW 14) 1952. Bardy, DTC 13, 846/50. Franses, StC 1927, 145/55 (P. and Cassian). Cappuyns, RBn 1927, 198/226 *(voc. omn. gent.)*; 1929, 156/70 *(Capitula)*. P. Alfonso, *Riv. liturg.* 1930, 199/203 *(Orat. solemn.)*. Silva-Tarouca, Gr 1931, 159f. (author of Papal letters). Morin, RBn 1934, 36/40 (Pss. comm.) — F. Woerter, *Beitr. z. DG des Semipel.*, 1898; *Zur DG des Semipel.*, 1899. Cappuyns, RTA 1929, 309/37. L. Pelland, *S. P. Aqu. doctrina de praedestinatione et vol. Dei salvif.*, Montreal 1936. Pickman, *The Mind of Lat. Christendom*, 1937, 418/36. Fischer 1947, 127ff., 168f. Eguiluz, *Verdad y Vida* 1948, 45/67 *(Lex orandi, lex credendi)*. Gaidioz, RevSR 1949, 270/301 (P. and the *Tom. ad Flav.*). K. Federer, *Liturgie u. Glaube. Legem credendi lex statuit supplicandi,* Fri 1950. J. J. Young, *Studies on the Style of the "De vocat. omn. gent." ascribed to P. of Aqu.,* W 1952. Chéné, RSR 1948, 566/88 (Semi-Pelagianism acc. to the letters of P. to August.).

§ 90. GALLIC WRITERS

1. John Cassian, very probably a native of the Roman province Scythia Minor (Dobrudcha), was born *c.* 360 and received his religious training in a monastery at Bethlehem; later he lived for ten years with the monks of Egypt. In Constantinople he was ordained deacon by St. Chrysostom, whose cause he defended before Pope Innocent I in Rome (404). He was ordained priest

probably in Rome, and *c.* 415 founded at Marseilles two religious houses, one for men and one for women. He promoted the spread of monasticism in the West by his writings, written in classic Latin, and thus became one of the great religious educators of the West. He is venerated as a saint at Marseilles and elsewhere (d. 430–5).

a. *De institutis coenobiorum et de octo principalium vitiorum remediis* (419–26), in twelve books. Books I–IV treat of the customs and rules of the monasteries in Egypt and Palestine, e.g. of the clothes of the monks, of the prayers and psalmody, and the conditions for being accepted as a novice; books V–XII of the eight vices against which the monk has to struggle and of the means by which he is to conquer them (EA 775/85).

b. The twenty-four *Collationes Patrum* are conversations, for the greater part probably fictitious, with the most distinguished solitaries of Egypt. They were published in three sections after 420; they frequently refer to the *De institutis.* They were greatly esteemed for their edifying contents. They were recommended by St. Benedict, Cassiodorus, Gregory the Great, John Climacus and other spiritual authors.

c. At the request of the then Roman deacon, later Pope Leo I, he wrote (429–30) seven books *De incarnatione Domini contra Nestorium* (EP 2054/7).

Points of Doctrine

1. Nature and Grace. Through *Collatio* 13 Cassian has become the Father of Semi-Pelagianism, which for 100 years had many enthusiastic followers in the monasteries of S. Gaul, until it was condemned by the second Synod of Orange (529). Grace and freedom must co-operate in the work of salvation. Grace accompanies good-will and assures its success; but the inclination to faith *(initium fidei)* and the good will are normally due to man (*Coll.*

13, 8f.; EP 2052f.). The denial of God's universal saving will is an *ingens sacrilegium;* predestination to beatitude is not absolute, but rests on the prescience of God, since the beginning of faith depends on man (*praevisis meritis; Coll.* 13, 7. 17. 18).

2. The perfection of the monk does not consist in renouncing the world and living in his solitary cell, but in the virtues of the inner man. In *Coll.* 11, 7ff. perfection is identified with perfect love, which is a gift of God and assimilates man to God. Perfect love and purity of heart are the conditions of contemplation which is an anticipation of the heavenly beatitude (*Coll.* 1, 8ff.). The eight capital sins (gluttony, impurity, avarice, wrath, accidie, sloth, vainglory, pride) are for him the worst enemies of the monk. With Evagrius Ponticus and Augustine, Cassian marks the beginning of the time when theologians began to develop the teaching on sin according to its nature and degrees even to the subtlest casuistry.

In his teaching on perfection Cassian is also influenced by the Messalian writings *(Liber graduum)* and by Gregory of Nyssa (Kemmer 1938 and 1955).

Edd.: ML 49–50. M. Petschenig (CSEL 13. 17) 1886/8.—Transs.: A. Abt and K. Kohlhund (BKV), 2 vols., 1879. A. Kemmer, *J. K., Weisheit der Wueste,* Einsiedeln 1948 (selected texts). D. Pichery, *The first* 7 *Coll.* (SCh 42), 1955. — Mgg.: Godet, DTC 2, 1823/9. Cabrol, DAL 2, 2348/57. Olphe-Galliard, DS 2, 214/76. Cappuyns, DHG 1949 II, 1319/48. A. Hoch, *Lehre des J. C. von Natur u. Gnade,* 1895. J. Laugier, *J. C. et sa doctrine sur la grâce,* 1908. S. Marsili 1936 (§ 52, 6). — Studies: Oliger 1912, 155 (Gr. trans.). Stelzenberger 1933, 385/8, 395/7 and freq. Marsili, RAM 1934, 241/5 (§ 71, 4). Doelger, AC 4, 122/9 (home of C.). Olphe-Galliard, RAM 1935, 252/88; 1936, 28/60, 181/91; 1937, 141/60 (spir. life); 1935, 289/98 (sources of *Coll.* 11). Ménager, VS 1936, Supp. 73/106 (against Olphe-Galliard). Golinski, CT 1936, 491/502 (white lie). Balanos, Ἐπιστ. ἐπετηρίας 1936, 60/9 (his doctr. of grace orthodox), Engl. trans.: D. Lolis, Emory Univ. 1949. Pickman 1937 (§ 89, 4) 468/83 (monasticism). Kraus, ZAM 1938, 165/83 (Holy Spirit). A. Kemmer, *Charisma maximum . . .,* Lou 1938; cf. TR 1939, 320/2. Capelle, RTA 1939, 110/8 (C. and Benedict). Schwartz, ZNTW 38, 1939, 1/11 (dates of life). Voegtle, RACh 1, 74/9 (8 vices doctr.). Marrou, RML 1945, 5/26 *(C. à Marseille).* Solé, Manresa 17, 1945, 22/43 *(motivación espirit.).* L. Christiani, *C. ou la spirit. du désert,* 2 vols., 1946. Bloomfield, HTR 1941, 124/8 (7 deadly sins). Masai, AL 1945/6, 23/37 (Divine office). Marrou, OCP 1947, 588/96 (home: Dobrudcha). D. Gorce, *Un spécialiste de l'interview* (C.), Str 1947. Madoz, *Principe de Viana* 7, 1947, 1/12 (Cass., *De incar.* 7, 6). Chéné, RSR 1948, 566/88 *(Initium fidei)*; AnT 1953, 56/109 (Origines de la controverse semipél.). O. Chadwick, *J. Cass. Study in Primitive Monasticism,* C 1950. Corbett-Masai, Sc 1951, 60/74 (Ed. Plantin de Cass.). Froger, ALW 2, 1952, 96/102 (on *Inst.* 3, 4; 6). O. Looritz, *Der hl. K. u. d. Schaltjahrlegende,* Hel 1954. Griffe, BLE 1954, 240/4 *(Cass. prêtre d'Antioche?)*. Courcelle, RecTrav. off. à C. Brurel, 1955, 316/9 (MS fragm. of *Contra Nest.*). Kemmer, OCP 1955, 451/66 (C. uses Gr. *of* Nyss., not Ps.-Macarius).

2. Vincent of Lerins (d. before 450), priest monk in the monastery of Lerins on an island near Nice. He was a semi-Pelagian and an opponent of St. Augustine. In 434 he wrote two *Commonitoria* (Notebooks) on the Catholic principle of tradition (cf. Tertullian's *De praescr. haer.*) under the pseudonym of Peregrinus; only the first *Commonitorium* has been preserved with an extract from both made by Vincent himself. The work is a valuable document of ancient Christian doctrine.

Without mentioning his opponent's name he rejects in this work Augustine's doctrine of grace as a novelty. Another work, the *Obiectiones* (supra § 89, 4) written somewhat earlier and attacked by Prosper, has been lost.

A florilegium of citations from Augustine compiled with an anti-Nestorian tendency became known as late as 1940. It contains Trinitarian and especially Christological texts. These *Excerpta* are perhaps the source of several terms used in the symbolum *Quicunque*.

Points of Doctrine

1. Holy Scripture alone is no sufficient norm and source of the faith, since, owing to its depth, it can be interpreted in quite different ways *(paene quot homines sunt, tot illinc sententiae erui posse videntur)*; hence the exegesis must be performed "in the ecclesiastical and Catholic sense" (*Comm.* 2; EP 2168; EH 812/4).

2. He gave the Catholic principle of tradition the formulation that has come to be regarded as classical: *Magnopere curandum est, ut id teneamus, quod ubique, quod semper, quod ab omnibus creditum est, hoc est etenim vere proprieque catholicum* (2, 5); but he did not yet understand it in the sense in which it was held later, in the light of a deeper insight into the dogmatic developments. In connexion with his anti-Augustinian polemics he takes it in the sense: only that is to be believed that has been believed explicitly *(fide manifesta, i.e. explicita)* either everywhere or always or by all men. If he writes (ch. 23, 4): *Crescat igitur oportet et multum vehementerque proficiat tam singulorum quam omnium, tam unius hominis quam totius ecclesiae, aetatum ac saeculorum gradibus intelligentia, scientia, sapientia,* he does not yet teach a dogmatic progress from *fides implicita* to *fides explicita,* but only a more precise grasp of what had already been known before both in content and form.

Edd.: ML 50. A. Juelicher [2]1925. G. Rauschen (FP 5) 1906. Germ. (BKV[2] 20) 1914; J. Madoz 1935 (Span. with comm.); also 1944. — Mgg.: F. Brunetière et P. Labriolle, P 1906. H. Koch, *V. von L. u. Gennadius,* 1907. J. Madoz, *El concepto de la tradición en s. V. de L.,* R 1933; partly in Gr 1932, 32/74; EE 1931, 305/38; 1932, 484/502. D'Alès, RSR 1936, 334/56 (anti-August.). J. Madoz, Gr 1940, 75/94 and *Excerpta Vincentii Lir.,* Ma 1940; RET 1944, 475/83 (*Excerpta* in 8th cent.); RSR 1951, 461/71 *(Cultura humanistica).* Sciuto, MiscStLCA 1954, 127/38 (Tertull. in V.).

3. Bishop Eucherius of Lyons (d. 450–5) left two exegetical treatises, *Formulae spiritalis intelligentiae* (containing examples of allegorical exegesis) and *Instructiones ad Salonium libri duo* (in Book 2 Hebrew and Greek words are explained according to Jerome); also two short ascetical treatises *De laude heremi* and *De contemptu mundi,* as well as a *Passio Agaunensium martyrum* (Legion of the Thebaid).

Edd.: ML 50. C. Wotke (CSEL 31) 1894. — Studies: Bardy, RB 1933, 14/20. Monaci, RAC 1933, 19/26 *(Passio).* Altaner, *Miscell. Isidor.* 1936, 11f. and Anspach, ibid. 1936, 340/3 (on spurious Script. comms.). Bellet, EstBibl 1950, 209/23 (Claudius of Turin, author of comm. *In Gen. et Reg.* of Ps.-Euch.).

4. Hilary (d. 449), monk of the monastery of Lerins, founded by St. Honoratus (d. 428–9) and his successor as metropolitan of Arles. He wrote a *Sermo de vita s. Honorati* (ML 50, 1249/72). S. Cavallin, *Vitae SS. Honorati et Hilarii*, Lund 1952 (crit. ed.); on this VC 1954, 116f. Acc. to Cavallin, Honoratus, Bishop of Marseilles, not Reverentius, is the author of the *Vita s. Hilarii Arelat.* (ML 50, 1219/46).

See Waszink, VC 1954, 116f. and RHE 1956, 806f. B. Kolon, *Die Vita s. H. Arel.,* Pa 1925. Corti, Rendic. R. Ist. Lomb. 73, 202/12 *(Vita Hil.).* D. Franses, *Paus Leo de Gr. en S. H. v. Arles,* Bois-le-Duc 1948. Cavallin, Er 1948, 133/76 (on *Vita Caesarii, Hilarii and Honorati*); and in *Festschr. P. Lehmann* 1950, 83/93 (text. crit. of *V. Honorati*). F. R. Hoare, *Western Fathers,* Lo 1954 (here also trans. of *V. Honorati*).

5. About 430 the priest Evagrius wrote the *Altercatio Simonis Iudaei et Theophili Christiani,* one of the last early Christian pamphlets against the Jews.

Edd.: ML 20. E. Bratke (CSEL 45) 1904. A. L. Williams 1935 (supra § 3, 4).

6. Salvian of Marseilles, b. *c.* 400, entered the monastery of Lerins (425) after a short marriage, soon became a priest and moved to Marseilles before 439, where he died soon after 480.

His principal work, written in 440, is the eight books entitled *De gubernatione Dei.* It is a first class source for the history of culture, giving a vivid impression of the frightful misery of the period of the migration of peoples. Salvian wanted to meet the objection, understandable in view of the misfortunes of the present, that God had no care for earthly things and that this was the only explanation of the torments of the Roman (i.e. Catholic) population. According to him, God had not reserved his punishing justice for the future Judgement, but was already exercising it in the present. Hence, having in the first two books proved Providence from reason, history and Scripture, he paints a frightening picture of moral conditions among the Romanic Catholics in Gaul, Spain and Africa, especially of their domestic and public immorality in the theatres and circus, of their callousness towards the needy and their injustice in social life. The barbarians were excused more easily since, being pagans (Saxons, Franks, Huns), they did not know the divine law, or, if they were heretics (Goths and Vandals), they knew it only in a corrupt form; yet they were modest and sympathetic towards the poor and feared and trusted God more. Thus the political downfall of the Roman Empire was a well-deserved judgement of God and a striking proof of the divine government of the world. Free from denominational and national prejudice, the author senses the historical importance of the Germanic world (EH 903/14).

Apart from nine letters we also possess a treatise of his, *Ad ecclesiam libri quatuor* which appeared in 435 under the pseudonym Timothy. Here Salvian makes the radical demand that all owners of property, especially the clerics, should leave their possessions to the Church and thus to the poor at least at their death. By introducing a kind of compulsory communism he wanted to alleviate the immense social misery of his time.

His presentation, especially in *De gub. Dei,* is not without a certain enthusiastic élan, even though it is diffuse and at times wearies the reader by repetition. Style and language show the author's rhetorical training. Though his Latin is frequently classically correct, a certain looseness of style foreshadows the transition to vulgar Latin.

Edd.: ML 53. F. Pauly (CSEL 8) 1883. C. Halm (MGAuctAnt 1, 1), 1877. Germ. by A. Mayer (BKV² II, 11) 1935. Engl. E. M. Sandford, NY 1930 and F. O'Sullivan, NY 1947. — Mgg.: A. Schaefer, *Roemer u. Germanen bei S.,* 1930. L. Rochus, *La Latinité de S.,* BullAcadBelgClLett 30, 1934. O. Jansen, *L'expressivité chez S. de M.,* I: *Les adverbes,* N 1937. Pickman, O 1937, 353/76 (justice and virtue; supra § 89, 4). M. Pellegrino, *S. di M. Stud. crit.,* 1939. Fischer 1947, 179/95. P. Courcelle, *Hist. littér. des grandes invasions germaniques,* 1948, 119ff. M. Lanelli, *La caduta d'un impero nel capolavoro di S.,* Na 1948. G. Vecchi, *Studi salvianei* I, Bologna 1951 (MS trad.). Bardy, DTC 14, 1056/8. — Studies: Sternberg, TSK 1909, 29/78, 163/205 (Christianity in the 5th cent.). K. Richter, Opusc. philol. 4, 1929, 39/60 (scheme of *Gub. Dei*). Morin, RBn 1931, 194/206 (MS of *Ad eccl.*). Rochus, RBP 1932, 107/21 (*concinnitas* in S.). Haefer, ATR

1934, 8/15 (*Ep.* 9). Bordone, StU 315/44 *(La società Romana)*. Pellegrino, SC 1940, 302/18 *(S. Ilario di Poit. e S.)*; VC 1952, 99/108 (MSS). Vecchi, VC 1950, 190/2 (on *Gub.* II, 8, 37). E. Bruck (v. supra § 3, 28), 105/17 *(iusta patrimonii portio)*.

§ 91. ITALIC AUTHORS

1. Aponius, the mysterious author of a voluminous allegorical exposition of the Canticle of Canticles. It is generally supposed that he wrote his work in Italy, probably in Rome, between 405 and 415. The pre-eminence of the Roman Church is repeatedly emphasized very strongly.

Text: H. Battino et J. Martini, R 1843 (not printed in ML). J. Witte, *Der Kommentar des A. z. Hohenlied,* thesis Erlangen 1903. Harnack, *Festschr. Delbrueck,* 1908, 37/46 and SbB 1927, 433ff. (on doctr. of primacy). Courcelle 1948, 128. Welsersheimb, ZKT 1948, 44/6 (on picture of Church). Bellet, EstBibl 12, 1953, 28/38 (on the extant MS of an extract in homilet. form). On 7th cent. date cf. ClavisPL n. 194. Mommsen, StHonFriend, 1955, 96/111 (A. and Orosius: transference of the Epiphany to 25th Dec.).

2. Peter Chrysologus (d. *c.* 450) became Archbishop of Ravenna under Pope Sixtus II (432–40). Reliable information on his life is lacking, since the oldest legendary biography was written as late as *c.* 830 by Abbot Agnellus. Since 1792 his feast has been kept on 4th December. In the Missale Romanum *(Rubr. gener. tit. XI)* he is listed among the Doctors of the Church.

He was in close contact with Pope Leo I. When Eutyches (449) appealed to Peter for help and asked for his judgement, the latter referred him to the Pope in a reply (*Leon. Ep.* 25) that has been preserved: "In the interests of peace and the faith we cannot listen to matters of faith without the consent of the Bishop of Rome" (EP 2178).

The 176 sermons that have so far been accepted as genuine contain explanations of Scriptural passages of a mostly moral and practical tendency. Numbers 56–62 explain the creed, numbers 67–72 the Our Father. The research carried out by A. Olivar for the critical edition of the *Sermones* in CCL will reveal a greater number of apocrypha than has hitherto been supposed.

Edd.: ML 52. Germ. by G. Boehmer (BKV² 43) 1923. A. Pasini, Ital. trans., Siena 1953. — Mgg.: G. Boehmer, *P. C. als Prediger,* 1919. F. J. Peters 1919. D. L. Baldisserri, *Imola* 1921. De Bruyne, JTS 29, 1927/8, 362/8 (9 new *Sermones*). H. Koch, PWK 19, 1361/72. K. D. Schmidt, ZKG 1935, 269. So far Olivar has publ. the following contributions on questions of authenticity: RBn 1949, 114/36; EL 63, 1949, 236/48; *Festschr. Dold* 1952, 113/23; EL 1953, 129/37; MiscBibl B. Ubach, 1953 (1954), 413/37. On the state of the relevant research: ClavisPL n. 227/37 and Olivar, SE 1954, 327/42. E. Bruck (v. supra § 3, 28) 117/9. R. H. McGlynn, *The Incarnation in the sermons of St. P. Chrys.,* thesis Mund. 1956.

3. Bishop Maximus of Turin, on whose life we have no further information, died between 408 and 423, according to the clear testimony of Gennadius (*Vir. ill.* 40). He must not be identified with a later Bishop Maximus of Turin who is attested to have attended the Synods of 451 and 465. There are still many spurious items among the 240 Sermons which, after a first examination, were considered genuine by Bishop Bruni (1784). About forty of them belong to the Arian bishop of the Goths Maximinus (v. supra § 82, 3).

On the basis of Gennadius' information twenty-four *Sermones* can be identified at once and thus be proved genuine. All other sermons assigned to him in reliable old MSS will have to be proved genuine mainly on stylistic evidence. The new critical edition of the *Sermones* prepared by A. Mutzenberger should clarify the position with regard to the number of genuine works.

Hence we can give a description of his sermons only with reservations. They are short and to the point and show Maximus as a true popular preacher; they contain much information on the paganism that was still prevalent in Northern Italy and are important for the history of the liturgy, e.g. the twenty-two Lenten homilies (EP 2217/9).

The views expressed in the literature cited below will also have to be considerably corrected.

Edd.: ML 57. Moricca, Bilychnis 1929, 1/22, 81/93; Did 1929 F. 1, 3/6 (25 ined. homs.). — Studies: Callewaert, RBn 1920, 132/44 *(Le carême à Turin).*

Capelle, RBn 1933, 108/18 (3 treatises on baptism, spurious). Opitz, PWK Suppl. 6, 289f.; cf. RTA 1936, 314. Gallesio, SC 1936, 617/39 (Christol.), thesis R 1937. Hitchcock, JTS 1946, 58/69 (M., author of Ambros. *Explanat. symb.*); against this Connolly, ibid. 185/96. O. Heggelbacher, *M. v. T. u. s. Bibeltext,* thesis Fr 1945. Kalinka, WSt 61/2, 1943/7, 118ff. (here also on the homilies). P. Bongiovanni, *S. M., vesc. di Torino e il pensiero teol.,* Tu 1952. Mutzenberger, SE 1954, 343/72 (on trad. of Sermons). Provisional survey of results from research into authenticity in ClavisPL n. 220/6; cf. Laurentin 1953, 132/5. M. Pellegrino, AttiAccadScTurin 90, 1955 (on authenticity of sermons, also published separately).

4. Arnobius the Younger, a monk who had probably fled from Africa due to the Vandals, lived in Rome from *c.* 432. He opposed the Augustinian doctrine of grace (Semi-Pelagian, d. after 451).

He wrote: a. an allegorical exposition of the Psalms *(Commentarii); Expositiunculae in evangelium,* scholia on texts from Matthew, Luke, John; *Conflictus Arnobii catholici cum Serapione Aegyptio,* the account of a dispute with a Monophysite opponent held in Rome *c.* 455.

b. The *Praedestinatus* (three books), preserved anonymously, was written under Sixtus III (432–40). It is akin to the commentary on Psalms both in style and subject matter. Book I gives a survey of ninety heresies based on Augustine's *De haeresibus,* except for the last and greatest, that of the Predestinatianists; Book II is a presentation of the doctrine of grace and predestination wrongly circulated under Augustine's name; III refutes the ideas developed in Book II.

c. *Liber ad Gregoriam,* first edition by Morin, is an ascetical treatise of consolation for a lady of the Roman nobility who was unhappily married. Arnobius seems also to have written hagiographical legends.

Edd.: ML 53. G. Morin, *Anecdota Maredsol.* 3, 3, 1903, 129/51 *(Exposit.); Ét., textes, découvertes* 1, 1913, 383/439 *(Ad Greg.).* — Mgg.: H. v. Schubert, *Der sog. Praedestinatus,* 1903. H. Kayser, *Die Schr. d. sog. A. Jun.,* 1912. Labriolle, DHG 4, 547/9. Amann, DTC 12, 2775/80 *(Praedest.).* Monachesi, *Boll. di studi stor.-relig.* 2, 1922, 66/125 *(Passio Sebastiani, Thomae, Caeciliae etc.);* cf. RBn 1924 Bull. n. 209. W. Levison, ST 38, 1924, 159/247 *(Acta Silvestri).* Doelger, AC 3, 225/30 (Ps. 44, 6). Plinval, RP 1934, 38f. *(Ad Greg.).* Morin, RevSR 1936, 177/84 (African; hagiographer). Levison, ZSK 1926, 501/11 *(Acta Silvestri).* Bardy, RBn 1928, 256/61 *(Praedest.).* ClavisPL n. 239/43.

PART THREE

THE END OF THE PATRISTIC PERIOD OF LITERATURE

§ 92. GENERAL CHARACTERISTICS

From the middle of the fifth century great intellectual and at the same time political and cultural changes were taking place, which gradually also affected Christian literature. The central problems of the Christian faith (Trinity, Christology, doctrine of grace) had in many cases been finally and authoritatively clarified (four General Councils); hence no further scientific treatment of theology seemed necessary. The exegetical-historical and dogmatic-speculative interest flagged and was almost entirely ousted by liturgical and ascetical requirements. The iconoclastic controversy which broke out in the eighth century clearly revealed that the situation of theology had long been changed.

Another important factor contributed to the change of outlook. In the first half of the sixth century Leontius of Byzantium and John Philoponus in the East and Boethius in the West placed Aristotelian philosophy, especially its logic, at the service of theological thought. This was to become the formal foundation for the later development of medieval scholasticism. As theologians were lacking in originality and creative power they came to depend more and more on the authority of the Church Fathers of the fourth and fifth centuries, until finally traditionalism, which was only concerned to hand on the teaching of the Fathers and renounced new achievements, was elevated into a principle.

Many writers were only interested in collecting and arranging the products of the intellectual labours of the past for easier use. Thus the *catenae* (chain commentaries) and *florilegia* (collections of maxims) came into being, though only in the Greek East; the former contained excerpts from the exegetical works of the past, the latter *testimonia* on questions of doctrine and moral theology.

Thus the treasures of philosophical and theological knowledge were saved for the future (the same holds good for various spheres of profane culture), later to be used to build up scholastic theology. The great encyclopedist and "last Church Father" of the West, St. Isidore of Seville, exercised a decisive influence on early medieval culture.

The general decline in literary productivity is partly explained also by the circumstances of the time; for in the West the Roman civilization was then succumbing to the attacks of the barbarians, whereas in the East the dominant Caesaropapism was strengthened even further by the struggle with the fanatic Monophysites. With the constantly decreasing knowledge of Greek in the West and of Latin in the East the vital relationship between the two halves of the Empire was being lost. Large districts where Greek culture had held sway became a desert under the onslaughts of Islam, which eventually developed its own brilliant civilization on the ruins of the forcibly expelled Christian one.

The Germanic tribes showed themselves receptive to the influences of the Roman Church culture, and thus intellectual life could continue in some measure in Gaul, Italy and in the sixth century especially in Spain. Indeed, the cultural decline in the West was less catastrophic than in the East. Nevertheless here, too, the Christian rhetorical school of Gaza had its greatest period and the Greek Church produced a great mystic in Pseudo-Dionysius and important theologians in Maximus Confessor and John of Damascus.

CHAPTER ONE

Latin Authors

§ 93. THE POPES FROM HILARY TO PELAGIUS II

General lit. supra § 78, 1. E. Caspar, *Gesch. des Papsttums* 2, 1933. A. Neunkirchen, *Das Papsttum u. d. german. Landeskirchen,* thesis Bonn 1944. F. di Capua, *Il ritmo prosaico nelle lettere dei papi* . . . III 2: *Da Ilaro a Ormisda (461–523),* R 1946. F. Hofmann in: Grillmeier-Bacht II, 13/94 (Popes from 451 to 519 and the dogma of Chalcedon). R. Haacke, ibid. 95/177 (Imperial policy and Chalcedon).

1. The eleven letters of Pope Hilary (461–8) are mostly concerned with questions of ecclesiastical discipline in Gaul and Spain.

ML 58, 11/32. A. Thiel, *Ep. Rom. Pontificum,* 1868, 126/74.

2. Simplicius (468–83). His twenty letters were occasioned by the Monophysite troubles of the East. In *Ep.* 3, 5 Simplicius emphasizes the permanent validity of papal decisions on matters concerning the Faith (ES 160).

ML 58, 35/62. A. Thiel 1868. 14 Letters in O. Guenther (CSEL 35) 1895. 4 Letters in E. Schwartz, *Publizist. Sammlungen zum Akac. Schisma,* 1934; AbhMn 32, 6, 1927, 118, 130f. (7 anathematisms prob. spurious).

3. Felix II (III) (483–92): Eighteen letters which are also almost exclusively concerned with affairs of the East.

ML 58, 893/973. A. Thiel 1868. 14 Letters in E. Schwartz 1934 (supra n. 2).

4. Gelasius I (492–6) is, after Leo I, the most important Pope of the fifth century, also as a writer. He came probably from Africa and had already decisively influenced papal policy under his predecessor as the author of official Letters.

He conducted the struggle against the Acacian schism with

great vigour and sharply emphasized the *primatus iurisdictionis* which belonged to the Bishop of Rome; decrees of episcopal synods acquire legal force only if confirmed by the Pope. As regards the relation between Church and State he taught that both powers are of divine origin, and are autonomous and equal in their respective spheres.

a. We possess sixty letters or decrees of his as well as many fragments; further, six theological treatises, four of which are directed against Monophysitism and one against Pelagianism, e.g. *Gesta de nomine Acacii* (original version Thiel 510/9 = Guenther, CSEL 35, n. 99), a survey of the history of the controversy between Rome and Byzantium; *De duabus naturis in Christo.*

Edd.: ML 59. A. Thiel (supra n. 1) 285/613. S. Loewenfeld, *Ep. Pontif. Rom. ineditae,* 1885; in E. Schwartz 1934 (supra n. 2) 8 letters and tract. 2–4; cf. AB 1936, 151/9. — Studies: Kissling (supra § 78, 11. 5) 1921. W. Grzelak, *Nauka pap. Gel. I o autorytecie Stolicy apost.,* 1922; *Nauka christol. pap. Gel.,* 1925; CT 1932, 261/97 (orig. sin, grace). Caspar, *Gesch. des Papsttums* 2, 749/52. H. Koch, *G. im kirchenpolit. Dienste seiner Vorgaenger,* 1935. L. Knabe, *Die gelas. Zweigewalten-theorie bis z. Ende des Investiturstreits,* 1936. Brezzi, Nuova Riv. stor. 1936 (eccl. politics; 28 pp.). Cavallera, BLE 1937, 67/78 (the "Christ. prince" in the papal letters of the 5th cent.). Ertl, ArchUrkundenf 1937, 56/112 (G. dictator of Papal letters under Felix II, not under Simplicius). U. Gmelin, *Auctoritas,* St 1937, 135/49. Brinktrine, RQ 45, 1937, 67/9 (against Geiselmann). P. Charanis, *Church and State in the Later Rom. Empire (491–518),* Madison 1939. Doelger, AC 6, 133/46 (on *Ep.* 14, 19: epilepsy as obstacle to ordination). Ziegler, CHR 1942, 412/37 (state and Church). V. Bagan, *The Syntax of the Letters of P. G. I,* W 1945. F. Illwitzer, *Die Theologie der Gnade des P. G. I.,* thesis R 1940. Soranzo, RSCI 1, 1947, 3/21 (precursors of the so-called "Gelasian" Theory). F. Hofmann in: Grillmeier-Bacht II, 52/66. Ensslin, HJB 1955, 661/8 (*auctoritas* and *potestas*). Dvornik, BZ 1951, 111/6 (G. and the Emp. Anast. I). Jonkers, TijdschriftRechtsgesch 20, 1952, 335/49 (G. and Civil Law). Merkelbach, VC 1955, 176f. (text. crit. of *Ep.* 99 [CSEL]).

b. The so-called *Decretum Gelasianum de libris recipiendis et non recipiendis* is spurious; it is the private work of a cleric, produced probably in Southern Gaul in the sixth century, reflecting, however, Roman views and conditions. The Damasan nucleus (parts 1–3; supra § 78, 3) contains: 1. decisions of a Roman Council (381) on the Holy Spirit and the names of Christ; 2. a list of books of

Holy Scripture; 3. a declaration on the Roman primacy and the patriarchal sees. Part 4 treats of General Councils and Church Fathers. Part 5 gives a list of apocryphal and otherwise theologically suspect writings (ES 162/6).

Edd.: E. v. Dobschuetz 1912. — E. Schwartz, ZNTW 1930, 161/8. Goeller, RQ 1931, 190/3 (penance).

c. The so-called *Sacramentarium Gelasianum* is a pseudonymous Roman missal, the nucleus of which was probably composed even before 600. It was used in Gaul at a very early date, hence its further development took place on Gallic soil. Its earliest form available today is the *Cod. Vat. Reg.* 316, written after 750.

Edd.: ML 74. H. A. Wilson, O 1894. K. Mohlberg, *Das fraenk. Sakrament. Gel.*, [2]1939. G. Manz, *Ein St. Galler Sacrament.-Fragm.*, 1939. — Studies: Cabrol, DAL 6, 747/777. Brinktrine, EL 1935, 46ff. *(Praefat.)*. De Puniet, EL 1935/6 (sacram. de Gellone). Wilmart, RBn 1938, 324/8 *(une messe fourvoyée)*. Manz, EL 1938, 192/6 *(missa de invent. S. Crucis)*. V. L. Kennedy, *The Saints of the Canon of the Mass*, R 1938. Capelle, RHE 1939, 22/34 (Gel. et la messe rom.). Callewaert, RHE 1942, 20/45 (hist. of the *Kyrie*). Quasten, Tr 1, 1943, 55/73 (Oriental Infl. in the Gallican Liturgy). Chavasse, *Mél. L. Vaganey*, Lyons 1948, 79/98 (deux rituels de l'admission au catéchumenat in Sacr. Gel.); EL 1949, 257/75 (Lenten Masses in the *Sacr. Gel.*). Brinktrine, Misc. Mohlberg 2, 61/9 (on Ep. to Bishop Elpidius of Volaterra). Capelle, JTS 1951, 129/44 *(L'œuvre liturg. de s. G.)*. Ashworth, EL 1953, 9/23 (Greg. Elements in the *Gel. Sacr.*). ClavisPL n. 1899. A. P. Lang, *Leo d. Gr. u. die Texte des Altgelasianums*, Steyl 1957. A. Chavasse, *Le sacram. Gélasien*, P 1958. L. C. Mohlberg, *Liber sacram. . . .*, R 1960 (new ed.).

5. Anastasius II (496–8): Four letters (in Thiel, 615ff.). In a letter to the Emperor Anastasius he declared heretical ordinations valid: in a letter to the bishops of Gaul he condemned Generatianism as heretical and declared himself in favour of Creatianism (ES 169f.).

L. Broel-Plater, *De primatu Rom. Pont. (496-590)*, R 1930. H. Rahner, *Die gefaelschten Papstbriefe aus d. Nachlass von J. Vignier*, 1935 (1 to Hilary, 1 by Gelas., 1 by Anast. II, 1 by Sym.).

6. Symmachus (498–514): Nine letters and synodal writings were occasioned by the Laurentian and Acacian schisms and the quarrels of jurisdiction between Arles and Vienne (in Theil 639 to 738).

Townsend, JR 1935, 165/74 (Sym. forgeries); cf. RHE 1936, 81/8. Poma, SC 1935, 559/81 *(L'ingiudicabilità del Rom. Pontef.).* E. Caspar (KlT 162) 1931. Townsend, CQR 1938, 201/15. v. Poelnitz, RHE 1936, 81/8 *(synodes apocryphes).* G. Westenburger, *Der Sym.-Prozess v. 501,* thesis T 1940. Alessandrini, Arch-RomStorPatria 67, 1944, 153/207 (Theoderic and S.).

7. Hormisdas (514–23): some ninety letters and documents dealing mostly with the Acacian schism which was healed in 519. The *Libellus professionis fidei* signed by the Emperor and by all the bishops both of East und West contains the following statement: *In Sede Apostolica citra maculam semper est catholica servata religio . . . in qua est integra et verax christianae religionis et perfecta soliditas* (ES 171).

Edd.: ML 63. O. Guenther (CSEL 35) 1895.—W. Haacke, *Die Glaubensformel des P. H. . . .,* 1939. S. Martin, RET 1941, 767/812 *(La prima salus del papa H.).* Morin, RBn 1940, 3/14 *(Les papes du 6ᵉ s. et la liturgie).*

8. John I (523–6) is probably identical with the John the Deacon who wrote the *Epistola ad Senarium* (ML 59, 399/408) which is important for the history of the liturgy of baptism and who is also supposed to be the author of the treatise *De fide catholica* preserved among the theological works of Boethius.

On *Ep. ad Sen.:* Wilmart (ST 59) 1933, 158/79 (new ed.). Alfonso, Riv. lit. 1930, 54/7. Dondeyne, RHE 1932, 751/9; cf. RBn 1933, 108/18. Ensslin, BZ 1951, 127/34 (J. I as legate at Constant.). Loewe, HJB 1953, 83/100 (Theod. the Gr. and John I). Goubert, OCP 1958, 339/52 (Journey to Kopel).

9. Felix III (IV) (526–30): Four letters and a decree by which the Pope appointed the deacon Boniface his successor.

ML 65, 11/6; vide no. 10.

10. Boniface II (530–32) was by birth a Romanized Goth. His only extant work is a document addressed to Caesarius of Arles, in which he confirms the decrees of the second Synod of Orange (529) which had condemned Semi-Pelagianism.

ML 65, 31/4; ES 174/200. C. Silva-Tarouca, *Coll. Thessalon.,* R 1937. E. Schwartz, *Festschr. R. Reitzenstein* 1931, 137/59 *(Coll. Thessalon.).*

11. John II (533–5): Five letters.

ML 66, 11/26.

12. Agapitus I (535–6): Seven letters.

ML 66, 35/80. Marrou, MAH 1931, 124/69 (Library of the Pope).

13. Vigilius (537–55): Twenty-six letters and documents connected with the Three Chapters controversy. ML 69, 15/328. — His nephew, the Roman deacon Rusticus, was a decided opponent of the condemnation of the Three Chapters which was finally also pronounced by Vigilius. Rusticus continued in his opposition despite being deposed and excommunicated. Together with the African Abbot Felix in Constantinople, he composed a treatise, now lost, against the decree of the Council of 553. Later he wrote a *Disputatio contra Acephalos*: ML 67, 1167/1254. Here (l. c. 1238 B) a *Sermo de definitionibus* is mentioned, a work against the doctrine of the Monophysites and the Nestorians which has not so far been listed in any Patrology: it is also lost. Rusticus' Latin redaction and translation of the Acts of the Councils of Ephesus and Chalcedon (§ 50, 17 f.) is of great historical value. We can see even from his *Disputatio* that he used with great skill the method of argumentation, introduced into the West by Boethius, which employs not only the Biblical and patristic sources but especially the *ratio theologica.*

Capelle, RBn 1938, 306/8 (*Ep. ad Profuturum;* ML 69, 18 f.). E. Schwartz, *Vigiliusbriefe. Zur Kirchenpolitik Justinians* (BAS 1940, 2). — Bardy, DTC 14, 371 f. (Rusticus). Amann, DTC (Vigile), 15, 2994/3005. Chavasse, EL 1950, 161/213 (Masses of Vigil. in *Sacr. Leon.*). Grillmeier-Bacht II, 816/22 (Rusticus).

14. Pelagius I (555–61) was a Roman deacon and papal apocrisiarius in Constantinople where he opposed the condemnation of the Three Chapters and thus also the attitude finally adopted by Pope Vigilius.

He gave the reasons for his point of view in his treatise *In defensione Trium Capitulorum,* written in 554 and preserved in a mutilated form. In this he made use especially of Facundus of Hermiane (§ 97, 4). As Pope he agreed with the decrees of the Council of Constantinople (553) and in many of his approximately

100 letters sought, though without much success, to overcome the violent opposition to the condemnation of the Three Chapters which had shown itself in Africa, N. Italy and Gaul. Cf. also supra § 46, 5 on the *Verba seniorum.*

Edd.: ML 69, 393/422 and S. Loewenfeld (supra n. 4). — *In defens. tr. cap.* ed. R. Devreesse (ST 57) 1932; cf. RevSR 1933, 250/8; DTC 12, 660/9. E. Sloots, *De diaken Pel. en de verdediging du Drie Kap.,* N 1936. Nagl, PWK Suppl. 7, 836/47. L. Abramowski, VC 1956, 160/93 (quotations from the treatise *In defens. Trium Capit.*). C. M. Bastie-P. M. Gasso, *Pelag. I papa Epp. quae supersunt,* Ab. de Montserrat 1956 (crit. ed.).

Two letters are addressed to Bishop Agnellus of Ravenna. A treatise against Arianism, *De ratione fidei ad Armenium,* written by the latter has been preserved (ML 68, 381/6). Critical text of this with commentary by J. Huhn in *St. Bonifatius. Gedenkgabe zum 1200. Todestag,* Fulda 1954, 102/38.

15. When still a Roman subdeacon, John III (561–74) produced a Latin version (supra § 46, 5) of the second part of the *Verba seniorum* (ML 75, 991/1022) and perhaps compiled also an *Expositum in Heptateuchum.*

Pitra, Spicil. Solesm. 1, 1852, 278/301. RBn 1937, 236 A. 4.

16. Pelagius II (579–90): Seven letters.

ML 72, 703/90. Amann, DTC 12, 669/75.

17. No genuine letters are extant of John I (supra n. 8), Silverius (536–7), John III (supra n. 15) and Benedict I (575–9).

§ 94. POPE GREGORY THE GREAT (590–604)

Gregory, b. *c.* 540, living in the period between antiquity and the Middle Ages, was destined to lay the foundations of the new structure of the medieval Papacy that was to govern the Western world after the catastrophes Italy had suffered through the wars and invasions of the sixth century.

Apart from his own writings and contemporary information in Gregory of Tours, the *Liber Pontificalis* and Isidore of Seville, we owe our knowledge of his life and work to the three, though frequently legendary, *Vitae* written by an unnamed English monk (*c.* 713; ed. A. F. Gasquet, Lo 1904), Paul the Deacon (ed. H. Grisar, ZKT 1887, 158/73) and John the Deacon (872/82; ML 75, 59/242).

Gregory who came from a family of the high senatorial nobility became prefect of the city of Rome in 572–3. In this position and later in Constantinople he acquired the business ability which distinguished him as Pope. After the death of his father Gordianus he decided to renounce the world (*c.* 575) and changed his parental palace on the *Clivus Scauri* into a monastery (of St. Andrew), besides founding six further monasteries on his family estate in Sicily. At this time he practised such austerities that he probably weakened his health for the rest of his life.

The happy time of peaceful contemplation did not last long. Pope Pelagius II sent the deacon Gregory as his apocrisiarius to Constantinople (579), where he administered his office under the most difficult conditions till 585. After his return to Rome he once more lived in his monastery, though remaining the adviser of the Pope.

When, in 590, Pelagius II died of the plague, Gregory was elected his successor despite his genuine resistance. The fourteen years of his government were decisive for the history of the world.

He took many measures that gave the Papacy a leading position such as had not been known before; he organized with great skill the enormous estates of the Roman Church *(Patrimonium Petri)* and increased their profits, which he used to mitigate social misery. He protected Rome from the Langobards and cultivated friendly relations with the Franks and closer ties with the Visigoths in Spain. Finally he prepared the conversion of the Langobards to Catholicism, sent missionaries to the Anglo-Saxons and healed the schism of the Milan province of the Church that had existed since the Three Chapters controversy. All these actions prepared the ground for the secular rule of the Papacy in the States of the Church.

The opposition between Rome and Constantinople continued to increase. Like his predecessor, Gregory, too, objected to the Patriarch John Jejunator's title οἰκουμενικός, which had been in use for some time. For himself, too, he refused the similar designation *universalis papa*, calling himself *Servus servorum Dei*. Feast day: March 12.

Edd.: ML 75–9. *Reg. epist.* ed. P. Ewald et L. M. Hartmann, 2 vols., 1891/9 (MGEp 1–2). *Dialog. lib. 4* ed. U. Moricca, R 1924. *Reg. past.* ed. H. Hurter 1872. — Transs.: T. Kranzfelder (BKV) 1874 (Letters). J. Funk (BKV² II, 3, 4) 1933 *(Past. Dial.)*. EvHom, 2 vols., Klosterneuburg 1931/2. E. Logi, 2 vols. Siena 1933/4 *(Dial.)*. F. Bouchage, *S. G. le Gr.*, 1930 (anthol.). C. Pera, *S. G. M Lettere scelte,* Tu 1948. H. Davis, trans. of *Reg. past.* (ACW 11) 1950. R. Gillet-De Gaudemaris, *Morales sur Job I/II* (SCh 32), 1952. — Mgg.: C. Wolfsgruber ²1897. F. H. Dudden, 2 vols., Lo 1905. F. Tarducci, R 1909. H. H. Howorth, Lo 1912. A. Snow, Lo ²1924. H. Grisar, R ²1928. P. Batiffol, P ²1928. Leclercq, DAL 6, 1753/76; 8, 2861/7. — On biogr.: W. Stuhlfath, *G.s Leben bis zur Wahl zum Papst,* 1913. E. Spearing, *The Patrimony of the Roman Church in the Time of G. the Gt.,* 1918. W. J. Boast, *The Relations of Pope G. the Gt. with the Churches of the Rom. Emp. of the East,* B'ham 1930. Haggerty-Krappe, *Le Moyen Age,* 1936, 161/77 (G.-legend). G. Ferroni, *S. G. M. e la difesa di Roma,* 1939. Ortmayr, RAC 1941, 97/111 (G. M. and the *Ecce Homo* in S. Croce in Rome). S. Brechter, SM 1939, 209/24 (Was G. the Gt. an Abbot?); *Die Quellen zur Angelsachsenmission Gr.s d. Gr.,* 1941. Schuster, SC 1945, 137f. *(servus Dei)*. H. Goll, *Die Vita Gr.i des Joh. Diac.,* Fri 1940. E. H. Fischer, ZSK 1950, 15/144 (G. and Byzantium). E. M. Marian, *S. G. I, papa della carità,* thesis Anton. R 1951. Bertolini, RSCI 1952, 1/46 (G. and Spoleto and Benevent.). R. Wasselynck, *Les Moralia in Job de s. G. et leur influence sur la morale du Haut Moyen Age Lat.,* thesis Lille 1952. Halkin, OCP 1955, 109/14 (G. dans l'hagiographie byz.). A. Valori, *G. M.,* Tu 1955. Hallinger, StAns 42, 1957, 231/319 (G.'s monasticism belongs to the pre-Benedictine tradition).

1. The Letters. 854 letters in all have been preserved, which were handed on for the greater part (848) in three collections extracted from the original register of the Lateran. To these should be added several letters of Pope Pelagius II which were probably written by Gregory when he was a deacon. The letters give an overwhelming impression of the official activities of the Pope; the majority reveal his personal manner, even though a sub-

stantial number are of purely business character. Hence they are not only of historical but also of literary importance (EP 2291/301).

2. His writings are mostly devoted to questions of pastoral practice. a. The *Liber regulae pastoralis* (four books) is a programmatical treatise as well as an examination of conscience, written on the occasion of his accession, in which Gregory outlines his ideal of a shepherd of souls. The book deals with four main questions: i. the character and motives of the man who wants to undertake the office of spiritual direction, the "art of arts" (I 1) (11 chs.); ii. the virtues necessary for the pastor (11 chs.); iii. his doctrinal task and the pastoral and pedagogical care of those entrusted to him (40 chs.); iv. the necessity of daily recollection and examination of conscience (1 ch.).

Even in Gregory's lifetime the Emperor Mauritius had a Greek translation made by the Patriarch Anastasius II of Antioch. King Alfred translated the book into Anglo-Saxon. In the Middle Ages it was for the secular clergy what the Rule of St. Benedict was for the Religious Orders.

b. *Moralia in Job*, an unusually voluminous commentary on Job in thirty-five books. It was begun at Constantinople at the request of Bishop Leander of Seville, who was there at the same time, and was finished *c.* 595. Gregory provides an historical, allegorical and moral exegesis. By far the greater part of the work is taken up with discussions of moral theology and practical applications and admonitions which bear eloquent witness to his profound knowledge of human nature and his serene wisdom; hence it may almost be considered a manual of moral theology and ascetics (EP 2302/17; EA 1131/214).

The following may serve as an example of his exegetical method: Job is a type of the Saviour, his wife of the carnal life, the friends symbolize the heretics. The seven sons of Job are interpreted morally as the seven principal virtues and allegorically as the twelve apostles, since $7 = 3 + 4$, $12 = 3 \times 4$.

c. Collections of homilies: forty mostly short homilies on pericopes from the Gospels and twenty-two longer sermons of the year 593 which contain a running explanation of Ezechiel 1–3 and 40. The Gospel homilies were probably delivered in the course of one ecclesiastical year (590–91) and published in 592; the first twenty were dictated by the Pope and delivered in his presence by an ecclesiastical notary, the other twenty were preached by himself (EP 2324/36; EA 1221/76). Of other homilies attributed to Gregory 2 *Hom. in Cant.* 1, 1–8 may be considered genuine.

d. The four books *Dialogi de vita et miraculis patrum Italicorum* (593–4) are composed in the form of an antique dialogue. They contain accounts of miracles, prophecies and visions which exercised a profound influence on the mentality of medieval men and fostered especially their craving for miracles.

Gregory converses with an old friend of his youth, a deacon called Peter. At the beginning the latter expresses the view that Italy, in contrast with the East, had produced scarcely any holy ascetics who distinguished themselves by miracles. Thereupon Gregory begins to narrate the miracles told him by trustworthy informants. Apart from Paulinus of Nola and Benedict of Nursia, to whom the whole second book is devoted, the saints of whom Gregory writes are otherwise hardly known at all. Book IV gives accounts of apparitions of the dead which are supposed to prove the immortality of the soul; IV, 55 mentions "Gregorian Masses".

Mgg.: W. M. Peitz, *Das Register Gregors I.*, 1917. M. B. Dunn, *The Style o, the Letters of St. G.*, W 1931. J. F. O'Donnell, *The Vocabulary of the Letters of St. G.*. W 1934. V. S. Martié, *De genere dicendi s. G. in 40 hom. in evang.*, thesis Fri 1934. H. Schwank, *G. d. Gr. als Prediger*, 1934. Wilmart, RBn 1935, 3/7 (*in Ez.* 2, 8), On the *Dial.:* v. d. Steinen, H. Z. 143, 1931, 229/56 (G. as hagiogr.). Cénnamen AR 1932, 51/95 (Ital. trans.). S. Santangelo, *Libru de lu Dialogu de S. G. i*). *R. Accad. . . . di Palermo*, Suppl. n. 2, 1933. Lambot, RLM 1934, 137/65 (2nd bk.*h* Harting, *Neophilologus* 1937, 281/302 (Old Engl. trans.). G. Traina, *Su i dialog5i di S. G. . . .*, Palermo (on Ital. trans.). Haggerty-Krappe, *Moyen Age*, 1937, 272/t. Dold, ZBW 1938, 235/9 (MS). J. Seitz, *Die Verwendungsweise der Abstrakta* (in efh

Dial.), 1938. A. J. Kinnerey, *The Late Lat. Vocab. of the Dial.,* W 1935. J. McCann, *St. Bened. by St. G. the Gt.,* Rugby 1941. J. Zimmermann and R. Avery, *Life and Miracles of St. Bened. by Pope St. G. the Gt.,* Collegeville 1949. Auer, *Misc. G. Galbiati* 3, Mi 1951, 117/22 (MS fragm. *Dial.* 2, 8). Deschamps, Neuphil. Mitteil. (Hel.) 53, 1952, 466/70 (middle-Dutch trans. of *Dial.*). Jaatinen, Neuphil. Mitteil. (Hel.) 53, 1952, 82/115 (Lubeck MS of *Dial.*). A. Fiorini-I. B. Boccolini, *S. G. M., Vita e miracoli di s. Bened....,* R 1954. Proja, RivStorBened 1954, 94/109 (S. Gallo in the *Dial.*).

D. Norberg, *In Registrum G.i M. stud. crit. I e II,* Up 1937/9. R. M. Hauber, *The Late Lat. Vocab. of the Mor. of St. G. the Gt.,* W 1938. K. Brazzel, *The Clausulae in the W. of St. G. the Gt.,* W 1939. W. Schroeder, BGDS 1941, 1/105 (Old-Germ. gloss. on Hom.). Aimes, Rev. de la Corse 1937, 133/6 (on Corsica). — Vaccari, VD 9, 1929, 304/17 and Capelle, RBn 1929, 204/17 *(HomCant)*. F. Wasner, Jus Pontif. 1938, 774/85; 1939, 293/9 (*Respons. ad August.* genuine); against this Brechter, 1941 (supra § 94). Bauerreiss, SM 1938, 202/4 (spur. prayer). Lambot, RBn 1942, 12/5 (ML 17, 671 f. Ps.-Ambros., prob. by G.). Vega, CD 1943, 145/7 (*Excerpta S. G.i* of Tajon). D. M. Wertz, *The Infl. of the Reg. Past. to the Year 900,* thesis Cornell Univ, Ithaca 1936. A. W. Ziegler, MTZ 1, 1950, 35/44 (on 35th Gosp. hom.). F. L. Battles, *A Trans. and Crit. Study of the 1st Book of the Hom. on Ezech.,* thesis Hartford Seminary 1950. P. Salmon, StAns 27/8, 1951, 187/94 (Le texte de Job utilisé par s. G. dans les *Moralia*). Brechter, Bonifatius-Festschr., Fulda 1954, 22/33 (G.'s instruction for mission of Bonif.). Verbraken, RBn 1956, 39/62 (text of ps.-Greg. *Expositio in Reg. I* [ML 79, 17/468]); 1956, 151/217 (this *expositio* is genuine). ClavisPL n. 1708 ff. Kahl, ZMR 1956, 93/111, 190/200 (Greg. the Gr. and the Christ. terminology of the Anglo-Saxons).

e. Liturgical Activities. Gregory reformed the Mass, and, among other things, gave the canon its present form and generally re-edited the Missal *(Sacramentarium Gregorianum)*.

The missal which Pope Hadrian I sent to Charlemagne *c.* 790 was already an enlarged *Sacramentarium Gregorianum,* which gradually replaced the so-called *Sacramentarium Gelasianum* (supra § 93, 4 c) which had been in use in the Frankish kingdom until then. The original copy which Charlemagne had kept in the court library at Aix-la-Chapelle could be reconstructed by H. Lietzmann. A sacramentary which is preserved in the Chapter library of Padua (Cod. D 47), however, is even nearer to the originally Gregorian form of the Roman Missal. It was copied in the ninth century from a Roman missal probably in use towards the end of the sixth century. Gregory probably also revised the texts of the liturgical chant and produced a new edition of the *Antiphonarium missae*. It has long been a matter of dispute (which is not settled yet) whether he also composed new chant tunes and may be regarded as the creator of the so-called *Cantus Gregorianus*. The view, wide-spread in the Middle Ages, that Gregory had even written a treatise on the theory of music and composed hymns should not be credited.

Sacram. Greg. ed. H. A. Wilson, C 1915; H. Lietzmann 1921; cf. *Misc. Ehrle* 1, 1924, 141/58. K. Mohlberg and A. Baumstark, *Die aelteste erreichb. Gestalt des Lib. Sacramentorum anni circuli der roem. Kirche,* 1927. A. Baumstark, *Missale Rom.,* N 1929. Cabrol, DAL 6, 1776/96. Capelle, RBn 1937, 13/28. B. Botte, *Le canon de la Messe rom.,* Lou 1935. Michels, JL 13, 1936, 188/90 (canon of the Mass). Callewaert, RHE 1937, 306/26 (Alleluja); EL 1938, 189/91; 1939, 191/203 *(messes quadragés.)*; RHE 1942, 35/40 (Kyrie). Verbeke, EL 1938, 67/76 *(la messe de S. Agathe)*. Capelle, RHE 1938, 556/9 *(Lection de la messe avant s. Grég.)*. Klauser, HJB 1933, 169/89 (Rom. and Franco-Germ. Church). Beran, EL 1941, 81/7 (St. Andrew in Embolism). — On Greg. Chant: P. Wagner, *Ursprung u. Entw. der liturg. Gesangsformen,* ³1910. Leclercq, DAL 1, 2443/61; 3, 286/311. K. Wachsmann, *Unters. zum vorgreg. Gesang,* Fri 1935. Eidenschink, *The Jurist* 3, 23/58; 4, 1945, 181/215 (Dedication of Sacred Places). Froger, EL 1948, 6/48 (Alleluja). B. Fischer, Festschr. Dold 1952, 144/59 (Lessons of Easter Vigil). Chavasse, RBn 1952, 3/94 *(Types du lectionnaire et de l'antiphonaire)*; EL 1953, 108/11 (date of *Sacr. Greg.*). Hucke, RQ 48, 1953, 147/94 (Christ. liturg. chant. to Greg. Chant). Ashworth, BJR 1954, 305/24 (Lombard invasion and *Greg. Sacr.*). Griffe, BLE 1954, 164/6 (*Pater noster* in the Mass). K. Gamber, *Wege z. Urgregorianum,* Beuron 1956. ClavisPL n. 1902f. *(Sacr. Greg.)*.

Points of Doctrine

Gregory's importance for the history of doctrine is negligible. We do not find in him original ideas of lasting influence on the great questions of the faith; he consistently follows tradition, especially St. Augustine, whose uncompromising teaching on the divine will of salvation and on predestination he mitigated in the sense of the post-Augustinian development (Prosper, Synod of Orange 529).

1. He enriched Christology by his discussions of the knowledge

of Christ which were directed against the Agnoeti (*Ep.* X 35. 39; ES 248).

2. He took over from Augustine the view, based on Ecclus. 18, 1, that God created the angels simultaneously with the material world, and from the Areopagite the doctrine that the angels are divided into nine choirs, and that only the inferior choirs are destined for the service of man. For this reason he reckoned the archangels with the inferior choirs (*Hom. Ev.* 34, 7f.; EP 2335). This idea became important for the angelology of the West.

3. Baptism and ordinations of heretics are valid (*Ep.* XI 67; ES 249). He reprimanded the bishops of Southern Gaul who wanted to compel the Jews to be baptized (*Ep.* I 47).

4. The doctrine and practice of penance are essentially no further developed by Gregory than they had been by Augustine and Leo the Great (supra § 78; § 88, 14). The existence of ecclesiastical private penance beside public penance is not yet attested by him. In the spurious commentary on 1 Kings, 6, 2, 33 (ML 79, 439) the following view is expressed: *Tria quippe in unoquoque consideranda sunt veraciter paenitente videlicet conversio mentis, confessio oris et vindicta peccati;* but if this should include private penance it probably presupposes a slightly later stage of the development of penitential practice.

5. Following Innocent I (*Ep.* 6, 12) and Leo I (*Ep.* 159, 1–4) Gregory teaches the indissolubility of marriage (*Ep.* XI 45).

6. *Cura totius ecclesiae et principatus committitur* to the apostle Peter (*Ep.* V 20). The Bishop of Rome is *caput fidei* (*Ep.* XIII 37); the Roman See *universali ecclesiae iura sua transmittit* (*Ep.* III 57). Gregory esteems the first four General Councils as highly as the four gospels (*Ep.* I 25; EP 2291). The same valuation of the first four great Councils is to be found as early as 516 in Cyril of Scythopolis, *Vita Sabae* 56 (ed. E. Schwartz, TU 49, 2, 152). Justinian, *Corp. iur. civ.*, receives the *dogmata* of these Councils as *sanctas scripturas:* in Anastos, DOP 6, 1951, 158 A. 132; cf. also

Ep. 16, 12 of the Scythian monks of the year 519 (ML 65, 467) and E. Caspar, *Gesch. des Papsttums* 2, 1933, 771–4, who produces further evidence for the high esteem in which the four Councils were held.

7. He proves belief in purgatory *(purgatorius ignis)* from Mt. 12: 32 (*Dial.* 4, 39. 57; EP 2321).

8. Not only the saints themselves, but also their relics and images may be venerated (*Ep.* IV 30; XI 13; *Hist. E.* 1053/6).

C. Butler, *Western Mysticism,* Lo 1951. J. Rivière, *Le dogme de la rédemption après s. Augustin,* 1930. Goeller, RQ 1931, 195/267 (doctr. of penance). J. Geiselmann, *Die Abendmahlslehre an d. Wende d. christl. Spaetantike,* 1933, 209/17 (*Ep.* IX 12; *epiclesis*). F. Lieblang, *Grundfr. der myst. Theol. nach G.s Moralia u. EzHom.,* 1934. J. Spoerl, Festschr. R. Guardini 1935, 198/211 (G. and antiquity). Laistner, History 20, 1935, 49/54 (attitude to pagan lit.). A. Boros, *Doctrina de haereticis ad mentem s. G.,* R 1935. Fischer, ZKT 1938, 37/75 (lower clergy). L. Kurz, *G.s d. Gr. Lehre v. d. Engeln,* 1938. L. Bauer, *De Christo vivificatore S. Gi. doctr.,* Mund. 1938. F. Westhoff, *D. Lehre G.s d. Gr. ueb. d. Gaben des Hl. Geistes,* 1940. M. Walther, *Pondus, dispensatio, dispositio,* Kriens (Switz.) 1941. Ménager, VS 1939, 39/56 *(contemplatio).* N. Hill, *Die Eschatologie G.s d. Gr.,* thesis Fr 1942. L. Weber, *Hauptfragen der Moraltheol. G.s d. Gr.,* Fri 1947. P. Benkert, *Die Missionsidee G.s d. Gr.,* thesis L 1946. Rush, Tr 1945, 369/80 (death and devil). J. Voss, *De fundamentis actionis cath. ad mentem s. G.,* Mund 1943. A. Eidenschink, *The Election of Bishops in the Letters of G.,* W 1945. G. Damizia, *Benedictina* 2, 1948, 195/239 *(Registrum Epp.* e il *Corp. iur. civ.); Lineamenti di diritto can. nel. Registrum Epp.,* R 1949. G. G. Carluccio, *The Seven Steps to Spir. Perf. acc. to St. G. the Gt.,* Ottawa 1949. O. M. Porcel, *La doctr. monastica de s. G. y la Reg. monachorum,* Ma 1950 and W 1951. Manselli, RStR 1, 1954, 72/88 *(L'eschatologia).* M. Frickel, *Deus totus ubique simul,* thesis Anselm. Fr 1956.

Appendix. The *Liber pontificalis* is a collection of lives of Popes all composed according to the same pattern. It begins with Peter and continues down to Hadrian II (d. 872) and Stephen V (d. 891) respectively; later continuations to 1431. The oldest part which continues to Felix III (526–30) *(Catalogus Felicianus)* was probably compiled by a Roman cleric under Boniface II (530–2) and is based on the *Catalogus Liberianus* (supra § 50, 5). It contains material of genuine value for the time from Anastasius II (496–8) onwards (*Hist. E.* 1002/10).

Edd.: L. Duchesne, 2 vols., 1886/92 (with the *Vitae* to Martin V, d. 1431); 2 vols., Siena 1934/5 (from Constantine to John IX). T. Mommsen (MG *Gesta pontif. Rom.* I, 1898, to 715). D. L. R. Loomis, *The Book of the Popes* I (to Gregory I), NY 1916. — Studies: Leclercq, DAL 9, 354/460. Vieillard, RAL 1928, 89/103 (les titres rom.). E. Caspar, *Gesch. des Papsttums* 2, 314/20. Jungmann, ZKT 1932, 599/604 (December ordinations); cf. JL 12, 1932, 380. Antin, RML 1947, 53/5 (Jerome).

The *Liber Diurnus Romanorum Pontificum* as we have it today was probably not, as hitherto assumed, the official book of formulae of the papal chancellery in use from end of the sixth to the second half of the eleventh century. According to the researches of L. Santifaller we probably have only the book of exercises used for the training of the staff of the chancellery till the tenth century. The real book of the chancellery can be at least partly reconstructed from it. Nevertheless, the work is an important source for ecclesiastical and legal history, containing much valuable material also for doctrinal and liturgical history. It can be taken as an established result of modern research that some of its parts go back to the time before Gregory the Great. Mohlberg, too, denies the official character of the collection against Peitz, who holds the *Liber Diurnus* to be the official book of formularies actually in use from the third to the eleventh centuries. M. thinks it is a private work compiled in Northern Italy in the sixth century.

Edd.: T. Sickel, W 1889. L. Gramatica e G. Galbiati, *Il Codice Ambrosiano del Lib. D. Rom. Pont.,* R 1921 (80 tables). — W. M. Peitz, *Lib. Diurnus* (SbW 185), 1918. H. Steinacker, *Misc. Ehrle* 4, 1924, 105/76. Santifaller, MittOest-InstG 1936, 225/66 (Use of the L. D. in the Privileges of the Popes). Di Capua, StU 345/61 *(Analisi ritmica delle formole)*. E. Stein, CHR 1935, 148f. W. Peitz, *Das vorephesin. Symbol der Papstkanzlei,* R 1939; against this Mohlberg - Altaner, TR 1939, 297/306; Santifaller, HZ 161, 1940, 533/8. W. Peitz, *Liber Diurnus,* R 1940 (against Mohlberg). Rodao, *Misc. Comillas.* 2, 1943, 337/65 *(Symbola)*. Huyben, Misc. Hist. A. de Meyer 1, 1946, 255/65 (MS). Santifaller, *Anzeiger Ph.-hist. Kl. Ak. Wiss.* W 17, 1946, 172/212 (Vatic. MS). New ed.; H. Foerster, Bern 1958.

§ 95. GALLIC AUTHORS

1. Faustus of Riez (Reji), a Briton by birth, became abbot of Lerins *c.* 433 and Bishop of Riez in Provence about 458. He was a zealous preacher and fought Arianism and Macedonianism. Beside Cassian he was the best-known representative of Semi-Pelagianism and an opponent of the Gallic priest Lucidus, who defended strict Augustinianism (Predestinarianism) and was therefore condemned at the Gallic synods of Arles and Lyons (473–4). From 477 to 485 Faustus lived in exile, having been expelled by Euric, the Arian king of the Visigoths. He died 490–500. He is venerated as a saint in the South of France.

The following works belong to his literary remains: two books *De Spiritu Sancto,* directed against the Macedonians; two books *De gratia Dei,* written against Lucidus at the demand of the synods of 473–4.

There are also ten Letters; five of these are addressed to Bishop Ruricius of Limoges (d. after 507) of whom eighty-two letters have been preserved (CSEL 21). The Sermons of Faustus have not so far been completely collected and examined. Engelbrecht included thirty-one in his edition. According to Morin he is the author of seventy-five other homilies which the MSS ascribe to Eusebius of Emesa (supra § 48). These Sermons were revised and edited by a compiler on the basis of materials from the literary remains of Faustus.

Doctrine of Grace. Like Cassian, Faustus teaches that grace is preceded by the will that tends towards salvation (*Grat.* 2, 10). He understands the grace by which "the Father draws" (Jo. 6, 44) only in the sense of an external grace (revelation, sermons, Holy Scripture; *Grat.* 1, 16). He defends the universal saving will of God with great energy and combats St. Augustine's doctrine of predestination, which jeopardizes God's justice and mercy (2, 4), leaving no place for true morality because it denies the freedom of the will (1, 3. 9). According to him the predestination to beatitude or damnation is founded solely on the divine prescience (2, 2. 3).

2. Faustus was a traducianist like Tertullian and Gregory of Nyssa; he attributed a certain corporeity to the human soul like Justin, Tertullian and Cassian (*Ep.* 3). The priest Claudianus Mamertus (d. *c.* 474) opposed this view in his treatise *De statu animae* (ML 53; CSEL 11), in which the author depends chiefly on neo-Platonist and Augustinian views.

Edd.: ML 58. A. Engelbrecht (CSEL 21) 1891. Huhn, TQ 1950, 176/83 (ed. *De ratione fidei*); TQ 1953, 408/26 (*Fides s. Ambrosii* ed.; an excerpt from Ambr., *De Spir. S.* — Mgg.: A. Koch 1895. F. Woerter 1899 (supra § 89, 4). Morin, ZNTW 1935, 92/115 (75 homs. of Ps.-Euseb.). Souter, JTS 1940, 47/57 (Ps.-Eus.); v. supra § 49, 2 (Eus. of Emesa). Pickman (supra § 90, 6) 1937, 436/42 (free will). A. G. Elg, *In Faustum R. studia,* Up 1937. Bardy, RHEF 1938, 23/46 *(controverses théol.)*. G. Weigel, *F. of Riez,* Ph 1938; cf. ZKT 1939, 259f. Weigel, *Ann. Facultad Teol. Santiago* 1940, 35/53 *(concepto de la fe)*. A. G. Elg, *In Ep. Fausti R. tertiam adnotationes,* Lund 1945; Er 45, 1947, 78/80. Fischer 1947, 105ff. (From Sulpicius Sev. to Venant. Fortun.). — H. Hagendahl, *La correspondance de Rur.,* Goeteborg 1952. Bardy, DTC 14, 205f. (Ruricius). — Claud. Mamert.: F. Boemer, *Der lat. Neuplaton. u. Neupythagoreismus u. Cl. M.,* 1936; cf. Gn 1937, 552/8 and PW 1938, 1033/41. A. Haerleman, *De Cl. M. Gall. latinitatis scriptore quaest.,* Up 1938; Er 1939, 64/8 (Cl. M. I 26). J. Madoz, *Liciniano da Cartagena* 1948, 35/53 (Cl. M. in Licinianus and Alvarus of Córdoba). Courcelle 1948, 223/35. W. Schmid, RACh 3, 169/79. N. K. Chadwick, *Poetry and Letters in Early Christ. Gaul,* Lo 1955, 207/10.

3. Gennadius, the much discussed historian of ancient Christian literature (supra § 2) was a priest at Marseilles (d. 492–505) of semi-Pelagian leanings. He wrote many works against Nestorius, Pelagius and Eutyches which have all been lost, and also eight books *Adversus omnes haereses,* the final section of which has perhaps been preserved in the *Liber ecclesiasticorum dogmatum*. A pseudo-Augustinian commentary on the Apocalypse (ML 35, 2417/52) and a Creed (C. P. Caspari, *Kirchenhist. Anecdota* 1, 1883, 301/4) are also assigned to him.

Edd.: ML 58. *Lib. eccl. dog.* ed. Turner, JTS 7, 1906, 78/99; 8, 1907, 103/14 (original version). — On *Vir. ill.:* Feder, Sch 1927, 481/514 (Semi-Pelag.);

1928, 238/43; 1933, 217/32, 380/99. B. Kolon, *Die Vita S. Hilarii Arelat.*, 1925, 171/23 (c. 100). Madoz, RF 1941, 237/9 (genuineness of *Lib. eccl. dogm.*). — On the comm. on the Apoc. cf. Sanders 1930 (supra § 82, 5). Bardy in Grillmeier-Bacht II, 771/89 (Christol. controversies in Gennadius, Arnobius Jun., Avitus, Vigilius of Thapsus).

4. The priest Julian Pomerius (d. after 498), a native of Mauretania, lived in Southern Gaul, where he was the teacher of St. Caesarius of Arles and wrote an excellent spiritual book for clerics, *De vita contemplativa* (ML 59, 415/520).

Fritz, DTC 12, 2537/43. Trans. M. J. Suelzer, ACW 4, 1947. A. C. Prendergast, *The Latinity of the De v. cont.*, W 1938. Plumpe, VC 1947, 227/39 (terminological matters).

5. Alcimus Ecdicius Avitus, *c.* 494–518 Bishop of Vienne, was the soul of Catholic Church life in the Kingdom of the Arian Burgundians. The conversion of Sigismund, the heir to the throne, to the Catholic Church was his work.

He tried to establish the closest possible relations between the Burgundian Church and Rome. With a view to the Laurentian and Acacian schisms he expressed the much quoted opinion: *Si papa urbis vocatur in dubium, episcopatus iam videbitur, non episcopus, vacillare* (*Ep.* 34). Feast day: February 5.

a. Among the eighty-six historically valuable letters are some theological treatises in epistolary form; *Ep.* 2 and 3, addressed to King Gundobad, are directed against the heresy of Eutyches and *Ep.* 4 against the Semi-Pelagianism of Faustus of Riez.

b. Only three of his *c.* 34 homilies have been preserved intact; two of them are sermons he delivered *in Rogationibus*, i.e. on the Rogation days before the Ascension which had been introduced by Bishop Mamertus of Vienne *c.* 470.

c. Books I–III of his five *Libelli de spiritalis historiae gestis*, a Biblical epic in 2552 hexameters, treat for the first time the theme of paradise lost (creation and fall) which later became so popular; Books IV–V: Deluge and passing through the Red Sea as types of baptism. *De consolatoria castitatis laude* (666 hexameters) is destined to be a poem of comfort for his sister, the nun Fuscina.

Edd.: ML 59. R. Peiper (MGAuctAnt 6, 2) 1883. U. Chevalier, Lyons 1890. — Mgg.: A. Charaux, P 1876. P. N. Frantz, thesis Greifsw. 1908. Vernet, DTC 1, 2639/44. G. Krueger, *Die Bibeldichtung zu Ausg. des Altertums,* 1919. Martin, BJ 221, 76f. Morin, RBn 1935, 207/10 (*Ep*. 12). H. Goelzer, *Le Latin de S. A.*, 1909. M. Burckhardt, *Die Briefsamml. des B. A.*, 1938. Vinay, Convivium 1937, 431/56 *(La poesia di S. A.)*. Giesecke 1939, 143/67 (fight against Arianism). Norberg, Er 1938, 129f. (*Ep*. 9). A. Schippers, *Avitus, De Mundi initio,* A 1945. Kuijper, VC 1955, 50/60 (on *Carm*. 1, 110). V. supra § 95, 3: Bardy in: Grillmeier - Bacht II. Chadwick 1955 (supra § 95, 2, Claud. Mamert.).

6. The life of St. Caesarius of Arles (d. 542), the most prominent Gallic bishop of his time, is described in a *Vita* composed by Cyprian of Toulon and other friends and disciples (542–9). Caesarius was a monk of the monastery of Lerins; he was trained in rhetoric by Julian Pomerius (supra n. 4) and was archbishop of Arles, the "Gallic Rome", from 502 to 542, at a time of political and spiritual revolution and ferment.

Several of the synods over which he presided were concerned with the reform of ecclesiastical discipline. Of special importance was the second Synod of Orange (529) which condemned Semi-Pelagianism and upheld a moderate Augustinianism, though abandoning the doctrine of the particular saving will of God and the irresistibility of grace. It was confirmed by Pope Boniface II soon afterwards (ES 174/200). Caesarius was a zealous pastor and perhaps the greatest popular preacher of the old Latin Church after St. Augustine.

a. Among his literary remains the first place is due to his 238 Sermons which have at last been critically examined in a good edition. The collection contains not only homilies on Scriptural passages and sermons for feasts of the Church, but also many speeches of interest for the history of customs and morality which, inter alia, combat surviving pagan usages.

b. Two treatises are directed against Semi-Pelagianism and one treats *De mysterio s. Trinitatis*. Here he shows himself particularly dependent on Augustine and Faustus of Riez, but also on Hilary of Poitiers, Ambrose and Fulgentius. The following are also extant: three pastoral and admonitory epistles; one of these, an *Admonitio* addressed to his suffragan bishops (in Malnory 1894, 294/307) stresses especially the duty to preach. Two religious Rules, one *Regula ad monachos* and one *Regula ad virgines,* with several letters concerned with the monastic life. In *Reg. ad virg.* 18 (ed. Morin) we read: *Omnes litteras discant;* chapter 32 mentions a woman librarian. The *Testamentum Caesarii* is genuine. The Symbol *Quicumque* (§ 54, 20) cannot be assigned to him (cf. Derenkemper 1953, 127/39). Morin, *Op. omnia II* assigns to Caesarius also a *Breviarium adv. haeret.* which was formerly attributed to Leo the Great, Faustus of Riez and others.

Edd.: G. Morin, *S. Caes. Op. omnia* 1/2, 1937/42. Id., *Reg. ad virg. and Letters* (FP 34), 1933. ML 67. MGLL 3, Conc. 1, 1893, 35/61. MGEp 3, 1892, 35/58, new impress. in CCL, *Op. omnia,* t. 103/4. Ibid. C. Lambot will edit further *Sermones.* — Mgg.: C. F. Arnold, L 1894. A. Malnory, ²1934. J. Fassy, P 1909. M. Chaillan, P 1921. Lejay, DTC 2, 2168/85. — Studies: Morin, RBn 1934, 178/89 (Symbol), 190/205, 410/3; AL 1937, 5/14 *(raretés philol.);* RHE 1938, 35/53 (ML 13, 653/72: *Brev. fidei*); RSR 1938, 257/63 (Teridius). D'Alès, RSR 1938, 290/9 (C. and Hermas); 315/84 (ed. of Morin). Vaccari, AL 1943, 135/48 *(volgarismi).* Bardy, RHEF 1943, 201/36; DS 2. Millmann, ZMW 1933, 12/27 (mission sermons). On Penance: Goeller, AKK 1929, 3/126 and Poschmann, ZKT 1930, 239/47. Hoppmann, *Die christl. Froemmigkeit b. C.,* thesis Br 1942. Rivière, BLE 1943, 3/20 *(rédemption).* Benoît, *Bull. monumental* 1938, 137/43 *(la tombe).* Schroebler, BGDS 1939, 287/94 (Old German glosses). Bardy, RHEF 1947, 241/56 (polit. position). Blumenkranz, VC 1948, 102/5 (C. and Augustine). K. Berg, *C. v. A. als liturgiegesch. Quelle,* thesis R 1946, Kalinka, WSt 61/2, 1943/7, 118/49 (inter alia also on *Op. de gratia*). Cavallin, Er 1948, 133/57 (supra § 90, 4). Rahlfs, StudNeophilol. Up 21, 1949, 42/6 *(anniculae).* G. J. Beck, *The Pastoral Care of Souls in S.-E. France during the 6th Cent.,* R 1950 (from Caes. to Greg. of Tours). B. Fischer, VC 1951, 84/7 (citation from *Visio s. Pauli*). M. Dorenkemper, *The Trinitarian Doctr. and Sources of St. C. of Arles,* Fri 1953, E. F. Bruck, *Ueb. Roem. Recht im Rahmen der Kulturgesch.,* B 1954, 146/63 (C. and the *Lex Rom. Visigothorum*). E. Lio, *Studia Gratiana* 3, 1955, 51/81 (C. in Gratian). Fransen, RBn 1955, 262/6 (C. in Bede and Florus). E. F. Bruck (v. supra § 3, 28) 163/7.

Vita S. Caesarii: ML 67; MGSSrer. Merov. 3, 1896, 433/501 and in Morin 2, 1942. S. Cavallin, *Stud. z. Vita C.i,* Lund 1934; Id., *Eine neue Hs der Vita C.i,*

Lund 1936. — On the Canons of Orange: Fritz, DTC 11, 1087/1103. Cappuyns, RTA 1934, 121/42 (chs. 1–8 perh. go back to John Maxentius).

7. Gregory of Tours (538–94) came from a senatorial family of Clermont-Ferrand. In 573 he became Bishop of Tours, the city of St. Martin, which was then the religious centre of Gaul. He was one of the ecclesiastically and politically most influential men of the Merovingian Empire.

All his writings were composed while he was a bishop. Despite the author's defective grammatical and rhetorical training they have an altogether unique value as sources for the religious life and for the political and ecclesiastical history of the sixth century. Gregory's language clearly shows the change of Latin to Romance.

a. The *Historia Francorum* (ten books) is his principal work, which was finished in 591. It is the first Christian work on national history.

The first four books give an account of the time down to 575. From the fifth book Gregory's presentation of the history of his time is based on his own notes. The whole work is governed by a religious and moralizing tendency; accounts of uncritically accepted miracles and virtues are given pride of place.

b. In his great hagiographical collection *(Miraculorum libri VIII)* his credulity and lack of criticism with regard to accounts of miracles are even more evident.

Book I, *In gloria martyrum,* tells of miracles of the Lord, the apostles and especially of the Gallic martyrs; book II, *De virtutibus s. Iuliani,* gives an account of the miracles that took place at the tomb of the martyr who died near Clermont-Ferrand in 304; four books *De virtutibus s. Martini* of miracles at the tomb of St. Martin of Tours; the seventh book, *De vita Patrum,* contains twenty-three *vitae* of Gallic saints, mostly from the districts of Clermont-Ferrand and Tours; the eighth book, *In gloria confessorum* narrates miracles of Gallic saints who were not martyrs. Besides, Gregory produced the oldest Latin version of the legend of the so-called

Seven Holy Sleepers *(Passio septem dormientium)*. The miracle books *De miraculis beati Andreae apostoli* and *De miraculis beati Thomae* are of doubtful authenticity.

c. *De cursu stellarum ratio,* a manual for determining the time of the night offices by the position of the stars. Of a commentary on the Psalms only negligible fragments have been preserved.

Edd.: ML 71. W. Arndt, B. Krusch and M. Bonnet, MGSS rer. Merov. 1, 1884/5; 7, 1919/20, 757/69; [2]1937 (Hist.). R. Pourpardin, P 1913. H. Morf, Hei 1922 (selection). — Transs. of *Hist. Franc.* Engl. by O. M. Dalton, 2 vols., 1927; Germ. S. Hellmann, 3 vols., [4]1911/3. — Mgg.: J. W. Loebell [2]1869. Leclercq, DAL 6, 1711/53. M. Bonnet, *Le Latin de G. de T.,* 1890. G. Kurth, *Études francques* 1, 1919, 1/29 (Class. stud.); 2, 117/206 *(L'autorité de G.),* 207/73 (G.'s sources). Blomgren, Er 1936, 25/40 (text. crit.). Waszink, Mn 11, 1942, 68ff. *(HFranc.* 4, 16). Graviers, RHE 1946, 103/6 (date of beginning of year). Tomassia, *Atti R. Ist. Veneto* 88, 1029/36 (Homer). Stroheker, Klio 1942, 293/305 (senators). G. Vinay, *G. di T.,* 1940. Fournier, CRI 1947, 496/501 (*HFranc.* 1, 32). R. - A. Meunier, *G. de T. et l'hist. morale du centreouest de la France,* 1946. Levillain, BiblÉcChartes 107, 1947/8, 62/8 (on *Hist. Fr.* 2, 27). Herrmann, Lat 1948, 197/209 (on *Hist. Fr.* 4, 9). W. C. McDermott, *G. of T. Selections from Minor Works* (text and trans.), Ph 1949. Chadwick, JTS 1949, 38/49 (on *Hist. Fr.* 10, 1). Silvestre, Lat 1950, 437 (G. and Boethius). Courcelle, *Mél. de Ghellinck* 1, 1951, 311/9 *(Philostrate et G.);* cf. VC 1954, 187. Wallace-Hadrill, Transact. of the R. H. S 1951, 5th ser. 1, 25/45 (G. and modern research). Lambrechts, Lat 1954, 207/17 *(De pass. s. Juliani).* R. Buchner, *Hist. Fr.* I, lib. 1–5, B 1956 (with trans.).

§ 96. ITALIC WRITERS

1. Magnus Felix Ennodius, b. 473–4 probably at Arles, was the descendant of a noble family. After the early death of his parents he was brought up by an aunt at Pavia. Having broken off an engagement, he became deacon at Pavia *c.* 493; *c.* 496 he moved to Milan where he distinguished himself as a writer and also as a rhetor. In 514 he became Bishop of Pavia. Twice, in 515 and 517, he headed a papal legation to Constantinople to prepare a reconciliation between Rome and the Greek Church (Acacian schism), but his efforts were unsuccessful (d. 521).

His poetic and prose works, which show an extensive knowledge of classical literature, are a strange mixture of pagan and Christian elements. They prove most strikingly that even at that time the influence of the antique rhetorical schools on Christian circles was extremely strong. His works, poor in content but abounding in bombastic phrases, are clearly the products of a period of decline.

a. 297 letters, nearly half of his literary remains. They are private communications frequently addressed to eminent personages; their tone is personal and they are without interest for the history and culture of the time.

b. Since the publication of J. Sirmond's edition (1611) the following are included in the group of the ten *Opuscula miscella:* (α) The panegyrical *Vita* of his (last but one) predecessor Bishop Epiphanius (d. 496) and the *Vita* of the monk Anthony of Lerins. (β) In a *Libellus adversus eos, qui contra synodum scribere praesumpserunt*, he defends the Roman synod of 502 which sided with Pope Symmachus against a pamphlet of the opposing party. (γ) The intervention of Theodoric the Great on behalf of Pope Symmachus (506–7) was the occasion of the historically important panegyric on the Emperor. (δ) The *Paraenesis didascalica*, a guide to higher education, praises rhetoric as the most important branch of learning. (ε) The so-called *Eucharisticum de vita sua* (after 511) is an autobiography modelled on Augustine's Confessions. (ζ) 2 *Benedictiones cerei*, blessings of the paschal candle.

c. Twenty-eight *Dictiones* are speeches on diverse questions and subjects: six among them are on spiritual subjects, seven are school speeches, five take their subjects from pagan mythology.

d. *Carmina* in two books: Book I contains twenty-one rather long poems, among them twelve hymns, Book II consists of 151 epigrams. Ennodius is rhetorically clever but lacking in authentic poetic inspiration. Beside Christian themes he also treats quite profane subjects; there are even obscenities among them.

Papal Primacy. In his *libellus* for Pope Symmachus (22, 3–5),

Ennodius, following an idea of Pope Gelasius I, clearly defends the thesis: *Papa a nemine iudicatur* (EH 961 f.). He was the first to restrict the title of *papa* almost exclusively to the Bishop of Rome.

Edd.: ML 63. W. Hartel (CSEL 6) 1882. F. Vogel (MGAuctAnt 7) 1885. — Studies: F. Magani, 3 vols., Pavia 1886. A. Dubois, *La latinité d'E.,* 1903. P. Plattner, Progr. Brixen 1910. E. Cesareo, *Il carme natal. nella poesia lat.,* Palermo 1928. Townsend-Wyatt, *Festschr. E. K. Rand* 1938, 277/91 (*Ep.* 11. 14; Hartel 54 f.). Poma, SC 1936, 3/23 *(errata sentenza circa la santità pontif.)*. Cauvreur, Philo. Studien 5, 1933/4, 122/33, 215/26 (*Paraen. didascal. Opusc.* 6). G. M. Cook, *The Life of St. Epiph. by E.,* W 1942 (trans. and comm.). Courcelle, RevEA 1947, 169/77 (on *Vita Epiph.*). Anastasi, MiscStLCA 1947, 145/62 *(Dati biogr. su Aratore)*. A. Fougnies, RBP 26, 1948, 1044/53 and in: Verhandel. AcadKlassLett. 13, 12, Bru 1951 (Clausula studies).

2. Eugippius, a pupil of St. Severinus (d. 482), wrote *c.* 511 the *Vita s. Severini,* the great apostle of Noricum, which is an important source for the time of the migration of peoples. He also compiled the sizable *Excerpta ex operibus s. Augustini* which were much used in the Middle Ages. He died after 533 as abbot of a monastery at Castellum Lucullanum near Naples.

Edd.: ML 62. P. Knoell (CSEL 9, 1 f.) 1885 f. *Vita s. S.* ed. H. Sauppe (MG-AuctAnt I) 1877. T. Mommsen *(SS rer. Germ.)* 1898. P. Becker, Mr 1935. — Transs. of *Vita* by E. Rodenberg ^{3}1912; N. Hovorka, W 1925. E. K. Rand, *The Earliest Book of Tours,* C (Mass.) 1934. F. Kaphahn, *Zwischen Antike u. MA,* 1947. M. Schuster, *Eug., Vita S.i* (Lat. and Germ.), W 1946. *Vita s. Sev.* ed. W. Bulst, Hei 1948; Welt als Gesch. 10, 1950, 18/27 (E. and the legend of St. Sev.) A. R. Natale, *Il codice di Eug. . . . Note paleografiche,* Mi 1950. G. Capovilla in: *Misc. G. Galbiati* 1, 1951, 213/401 (also on *Vita Sev.*). Courcelle, *Recueil off. à. M. C. Brunel,* P 1955, 313/6 (MS fragms. of *Excerpta*).

3. Dionysius Exiguus, as he humbly called himself, was a native of the Latinized province of Scythia Minor (Dobruja). From *c.* 500 to 545 he lived as a monk in Rome; he was a friend of Cassiodorus (*Inst.* 23). He did important work in propagating Greek education and may be considered one of the fathers of medieval civilization. He made translations, collected documents relating to Canon Law and worked on chronological subjects.

a. Through his chronological writings *(Liber de paschate, Argumenta paschalia, Epistolae duae de ratione paschae)* he was responsible for the victory of the Alexandrian over the Roman calculation of Easter (cycle of nineteen years); for in 525 he continued the Easter tables of Cyril of Alexandria (supra § 56 d) for another ninety-five years. In doing so he counted for the first time the years from the birth of Christ, which, however, he wrongly dated in the year 754 (A.U.C.), i.e. at least four years too late. His error has not been rectified even now.

b. Collections of Canon Law (v. supra § 50, 13).

c. Dionysius translated inter alia a *Vita* of St. Pachomius, the *Historia inventionis capitis s. Ioannis Baptistae,* and Gregory of Nyssa's treatise *De hominis opificio*. To support his countrymen, the so-called Scythian (= Gothic) monks who were in Rome in 519–20 to obtain the approval of the theopaschite formula, he further translated Cyril's letters 17, 45 and 46 and the *Tomus ad Armenos* of Proclus of Constantinople. It cannot be proved, however, that he produced the *Exempla patrum* (SACO IV, 2, 74/96), a doctrinal florilegium of the Fathers compiled in the cause of Theopaschitism.

Edd.: ML 67. SACO I 5, 2, 233/44 (*Cyrilli ep.* 17); I 4, 2, 196/205 *(Procli tom. ad Arm.);* IV 2, XVII f. (list of all works trans. by D. with 11 numbers). V. Schurr, *Die Trinitaetslehre des Boëthius,* 1935, 168/97 (trans.). Rops, Sp 1934, 408/21 (Easter table). B. Krusch, *Stud. z. ma. Chronologie* (AbhB 1937, 8) 1938. Frankl, CT 1934, 2/23 (*Exempla patrum* compiled by D.); against this Altaner, HJB 72, 1953, 568 ff. Peitz, Schweizer Rundschau 45, 1945/6 prob. = RevEspañDerechoCan 2, 1947, 9/32 (D. as a canonist; produces bold new theses which, however, are untenable). Foerster, Schweizer Beitr. z. allgem. Gesch. 4, 1946, 282/8 (canons). Peitz, *Studia Gratiana,* Bologna 1, 1953, 53/79 (Gratian and D.). Rambaud-Buhot, DictDroit-Can F. 23/4, 1949, 1134/52.

4. John Maxentius, the leader of the Scythian (= Gothic) monks who supported the theopaschite formula *Unus ex Trinitate carne passus est* at Constantinople and Rome (519–20). He is the author of a *Libellus fidei,* a dialogue *Contra Nestorianos* and several other short *libelli,* among them the *Ad epistolam Hormisdae responsio* which sharply attacks Pope Hormisdas. The *canones* 1–8 of the Synod of Orange in 529 are perhaps also derived from formulae found in his

writings. Until most recent times it was wrongly believed that this monk, who belonged to the Latin civilization, wrote his works in Greek and that we had only a Latin translation.

Edd.: MG 86, 1, 75/158. SACO IV 2, 3/62. — Studies: Cappuyns, RTA 1934, 121/42 (*can.* 1–8 of Orange). Altaner, HJB 1953, 572/5; TQ 1947, 147ff. (on J. M.'s biogr.). On hist. of Scyth. monks and their theol. cf. SACO IV 2, V/XII and V. Schurr, *Die Trinitaetslehre des Boëthius,* 1935, 127/97. R. Devreesse, *Essai sur Théodore de Mopsv.,* 1948, 176/93. Grillmeier in: Grillmeier-Bacht II, 797/805. Amann, DTC 15, 505/12. On Barks' hypothesis v. supra § 50, 17.

5. Direct information on Benedict of Nursia (d. prob. 547), the reformer and patriarch of Western monasticism, was written down only two generations later by Gregory the Great (second book of the *Dialogi*).

Born *c.* 480 at Nursia (Umbria), he belonged to a noble family and studied in Rome which he left, however, prematurely on account of the immorality of his fellow students. He fled to Enfide in the Sabinian mountains and from there to a cave in the Anio valley near Subiaco, where he lived at first as a hermit, practising the strictest asceticism. He gradually founded twelve monasteries in the neighbourhood and wrote his *Regula monasteriorum* between 523 and 526. Intrigues forced him to leave, and he finally founded the monastery of Monte Cassino, which became the cradle and centre of the Benedictine Order. Feast day: March 21.

The *Regula S. Benedicti,* a monastic rule still in force after 1400 years, is the fruit of the orderly Roman spirit. Benedict's practical sense and organizing ability gave to monasticism a form suited to Western conditions. In his Rule the traditions of pre-Benedictine monasticism, not always clearly distinguishable, are welded into an harmonious whole. Benedictine spirituality and asceticism have been formed by the spirit of a Martin of Tours, Augustine, Cassian, and last but not least by the asceticism of the monks of Lerins. But elements of Eastern monasticism (Anthony, Pachomius, Basil), too, gained entrance into the new rule of

Western religious life by direct or even more by indirect influence.

The internal and external life of the monastic community is regulated in seventy-three chapters: 1–3: constitution; 4–7: life of virtue; 8–20: choir office; 21–30: faults; 31–57: administration of houses; 58–66: reception of new members; 67–73: appendices. The Rule sets the monastic community a double aim: prayer and work, founded on the faithful observance of stability *(stabilitas loci)*, of pure moral conduct *(conversatio = conversio morum)*, and of obedience under the patriarchal government of the abbot (*c.* 58). The Rule soon became the only one to be observed in the West (until the twelfth century) and the basis of the powerful medieval monastic culture (EH 975/1001). It is a much discussed question whether the devotion of the Order to study and scholarship is due to Benedict himself or only to the influence of Cassiodorus (§ 96, 6). We would reply that the founder himself created the conditions for the flowering of learned pursuits. For ch. 48 of the Rule assigns more than 1200 hours a year to the *lectio* (study of the Bible, the Fathers and the manuals). The establishment of a library and hence also of a scriptorium was provided for from the beginning; and at the same time a school was to combat illiteracy. The Rule contains not a few prescriptions urging the monks to devote themselves to serious intellectual activity. Thus the foundation was laid for a gradually extending pursuit of the various branches of scholarship (*Reg.* chs. 9, 33, 38, 57). Cf. Christ, ZBW 1943, 33/59; Assche, SE 1948, 13/34; Mundó, RBn 1950, 65/92.

The shorter text of the MSS of St. Gall, Vienna and Munich (ninth cent.) gives the text of the original copy, the longer text of the older MSS is interpolated and the result of a gradual development. Cf. Mohrmann, VC 1952, 108/39 against Paringer, RBn 1951, 81/140.

Edd. and Transs.: C. Butler, Fr [3]1935. B. Linderbauer 1922 (FP 17) 1928. Card. I. Schuster, Tu 1942. C. Koessler, Graz 1931 (with trans. and explan.). *Règle de s. B.*, Maredsous 1945 (with trans.). A. Lentini, Montecassino 1947. G. Arroyo, Silos 1947. H. Koenders, *Concordantiae s. Regulae*, Westmalle 1947. — P. Bihlmeyer (BKV² 20) 1914, also sep. ⁴1934. B. Linderbauer 1928. C. Selmer, *Middle-High-German Transs. of the Reg. s. B.,* C (Mass.) 1933. J. McCann, Lo 1952 (text with trans.). P. Schmitz, Maredsous ²1954. P. Delatte, Comm. and French trans., 1949; Engl. Lo 1950; Ital. Bergamo 1951. Colombas-Sanscqundo-Cunill, *S. B., su vida y su regla,* Ma 1954 (2 vols.). G. Penco, *S. Benedicti regula,* Fi 1958 (Text, trans., comm.).

In view of the extraordinarily numerous publications on the life and Rule of St. Benedict, we can here only list the most important literature. Moreover, a reliable survey of contemporary research is given by the various periodicals ed. by members of the Order. The *Bull. d'Hist. Bénéd.* of the RBn gives what is probably the most complete information on the multitude of new publications.

Bibliographies: A. M. Albareda, *Bibliografía de la Regla Bened.,* Montserrat 1933 (902 items). Most recent information in RBnBull 1952 n. 2204/19; ibid. 1954, 3094/137; on the *Vita:* ibid. 1952, n. 2192/200.

P. Schmitz, DS 1, 1371/88. De Puniet, ibid. 1388/1409 *(doctr. spir.).* Brechter, SM 1937, 157/229; RBn 1938, 89/135 (hist. of text of *Reg.*). I. Herwegen, *Vaeterspruch u. Moenchsregel,* 1937. Casel, *Festschr. Herwegen,* 1938, 96/123 *(B. als Pneumatiker)*; ibid. 1938, 21/50 (*Militia spirit.* in philos. of antiquity). Wuermser, SM 1939, 99/112 *(convers. morum).* H. Gruenewald, *Die paedagog. Grundsaetze der Ben.-Reg.,* 1939. Card. I. Schuster, *Note stor. sulla Reg. mon. di S. B.,* Tu 1940; SC 1942, 265/70 *(Didache); La vie monastique . . .,* P 1953. Friedrich, SM 1941, 200/26 *(convers. morum).* A. Lentini, *Ritmo prosaico . . .,* 1942. I. Herwegen, *Sinn u. Geist der Ben.-Reg.,* 1944. V. Stebler, *Die Reg. als Norm beschaul. Lebens,* thesis Fri 1947. Hausherr, OCP 1947, 195/218 *(opus Dei).* W. Betz, *Deutsch u. Lateinisch. Die Lehnbildungen der althochdeutschen Ben.-Reg.,* Bonn 1949. G. Aulinger, *Das Humanum i. d. Regel des hl. B.,* St. Ottilien 1950. B. Steidle, *Die Reg. d. hl. B.,* Beuron 1952. E. v. Hippel, *Der Krieger Gottes. Die Regel d. B. als Ausdruck fruehchristl. Gemeinschaftsbildung,* Pa ²1953. Harrison, RBn 1953, 833/9 (1 Clem., Ign. of Ant., Cyprian in the *Regula*). Penco, *Benedictina* 8, 1954, 25/42 (on ch. 73). ClavisPL n. 1852ff.

On the Hist. of St. B.: I. Herwegen ⁴1951. S. du Fresnel, P 1926. J. Chapman, Lo 1929. L. Salvatorelli, Bari 1929; Germ. G. Kuehl-Claasen 1937. F. Cabrol, P 1933. P. Schmitz, DHG 8, 225/41; *Hist. de l'Ordre de s. B.* 1, 1942. Germ. Zu 1947. Emonds, RACh 2, 130/6. G. Salvi, Subiaco 1948. I. Schuster, *Storia di S. B.,* ³1953; French trans. P 1950. E. Dubler, St. Ottilien 1953. I. Cabitza, Fl 1954. — Studies: *Casinensia,* 2 vols., Monte Cassino 1929. T. P. McLaughlin, *Le très ancien droit monast. de l'Occid. de S. B. de N. à S. B. d'Aniane,* 1935. Card. I. Schuster, *Appunti sulla stor. di S. B.,* Tu 1937. Frank, SM 1938, 77/88; 1939, 51/4 and Emonds, SM 1938, 89/103 (year of death). Brechter, SM 1938, 109/50 (1st destruction of Monte Cassino). Schuster, SC 1942, 97/108 (S. B. fu sacerdote?). Bauerreiss, SM 1947, 12/9 (B.'s day of death). — The following centenary publications appeared in 1947: *Benedictus, der Vater des Abendlandes* (St. Ottilien), ed. by S. Brechter 1947. *Vir Dei Benedictus,* ed. R. Molitor 1947. *Zeugnis des Geistes,* ed. Erzabtei Beuron 1947. *Studia Anselmiana* F. 18/9, R 1947. *Mélanges Bénédictines,* S.-Wandrille 1947. *Horae monasticae* 1. vol., Thielt 1948. The contributions in these are not here listed individually.

On the *Regula Magistri*. Until 1937 it had been the undisputed view that the *Regula Magistri* was a later version or paraphrase of the *Regula Benedicti*. At the Congress of Abbots in Rome (S. Anselmo) A. Génestout voiced for the first time the opinion that the Rule of Benedict depends on the *Regula Magistri*. So far the questions of the relation of the two documents, of the personality of the author, the date and the sources of the *Regula Magistri* could not be definitely solved despite all the acumen lavished on them. The discussions will probably continue for a long time. Neither the defenders of the priority of the *Regula Magistri* nor their opponents are agreed on the various questions of detail that have to be solved. It seems clear that the methods used so far will not produce a solution. Perhaps we may hope with C. Mohrmann that detailed philological and linguistic research will produce a more satisfying result.

Here we would only mention some accounts on the progress of the discussions that have come to hand. Cf. A. Nuiy in: *Horae Monasticae* I, Thielt 1948, 95/111; Cavallera, RAM 1948, 72/9; Franceschini, Aev 1949, 52/72; McCann, Ampleforth Journal 55, 1950, 75/89 and Mohrmann, VC 1954, 239/51.

Edd.: ML 88, 943/1052. Vanderhoven-Masai-Corbett, *Reg. Mag. Ét. diplomatique,* Bru 1953. ClavisPL n. 1858. Penco, StAns 1956, 283/306.

6. Anicius Manlius Severinus Boethius, b. *c.* 480, belonged to the old noble Roman gens Anicia. He received an excellent education, being also introduced to Greek philosophy and literature at Alexandria. He took up a career in the East-Gothic empire as a youth and became consul as early as 510; in 522 his two sons received the same honour while still only boys. Soon afterwards, however, owing to the political tension with East Rome, he was wrongly suspected of having been involved in treasonable relations with Constantinople. In 524 he was executed at the order of King Theodoric the Great, who had become hard and suspicious in his old age.

Though Boethius did not die for his Catholic faith, he was

venerated as a martyr in several dioceses of N. Italy from the eighth century. Leo XIII confirmed his cult for Pavia in 1883.

Through his writings Boethius has exercised a decisive influence on the development of medieval scholarship. His greatest merit is probably that he communicated the knowledge of Aristotelian logic to subsequent generations by translating Aristotle's treatises on logic and several relevant Greek commentaries, as well as through his own logical writings. He opened new lines of approach through his theological works, using Aristotelian philosophy for the intellectual penetration of the doctrines of the Church. His philosophical treatise on consolation belonged to the most widely read books of the Middle Ages. He also wrote works that became fundamental for the medieval theory of music and arithmetics.

a. Philosophical works.

α) Boethius wrote his version of the four subjects of the *Quadrivium,* regarded as an introduction to philosophy, in close dependence on Greek manuals; only the *Institutio arithmetica* (two books) and five books *De institutione musica* have been preserved in full.

β) Translations and interpretations of philosophical works. Owing to his early death his grandiose plan of translating all the works of Aristotle and all Plato's dialogues was never executed in its entirety. The following are extant: a translation of Aristotle's *Categories* with commentary (four books), a translation of *De interpretatione* (with two commentaries for beginners and advanced students), a translation of the *Isagoge* of the neo-Platonist Porphyry with two commentaries, the first of which is based on the translation of the *Isagoge* made by Marius Victorinus; his commentary on Cicero's *Topica* is preserved incomplete.

γ) Boethius treated problems of logic in several writings of his own. The following are extant: *Introductio ad syllogismos categoricos, De syllogismo hypothetico, De differentiis topicis.*

b. Four minor theological treatises. The first and second treatises deal with the doctrine of the Trinity, the third with the relation of being and being good in things; in the fourth Boethius opposes Nestorianism and Monophysitism. A fifth treatise, *De fide catholica,* a summary of Catholic doctrine (v. supra § 93, 8) is also considered genuine by Rand (Sp 1936, 153/6) and Cappuyns (DHG 9, 359, 371 f. and RTA 1931, 237/72). Cf. also Bark, HTR 1946, 55/69.

c. *De consolatione philosophiae* (five books), his principal work, was written in the solitude of his prison before his execution.

The work is an exquisitely constructed dialogue between the author and philosophy, which appears to him as a noble lady. In beautiful language he develops the consoling thoughts which philosophy offers to the severely tried prisoner. Deeply felt poems of perfect form (thirty-nine in all) are inserted in the serious philosophical considerations which are inspired not only by reason but also by the feelings and the imagination. There is nothing specifically Christian in the whole work; Christ is never named, and there is no reference to the Christian belief in the next world. This is to be explained by the fact that Boethius was mostly influenced by contemporary pagan neo-Platonism, especially by the philosopher Ammonius who had been teaching at Alexandria since 485. Nevertheless, there is no real opposition to the Christian point of view in his work, since even the *theologia naturalis* of Ammonius had already a Christian tendency. The view that Boethius, the last of the philosophers of antiquity, had been a Christian only in name could be maintained for so long only because the genuineness of his *Opuscula theologica* had formerly been disputed, and only because he had neglected to produce, or even to attempt, a synthesis between his Christian conviction and its philosophical presuppositions. Moreover, it was a custom of the time to borrow the thoughts of the old philosophy except for actually theological works. Cf. SCh

13, 1947, 61/85 (John Chrysostom in his letters). The purity and certainty of his moral principles presuppose the Christian faith (Courcelle 1948, 278/304).

Contents. In the first book philosophy appears to him asking him to tell her his sorrow so that she might share his burden with him. He then tells her why he is in prison. The second book shows that instability belongs to the nature of good fortune and that true happiness is to be found only in man's heart. The third proves that supreme bliss is only in God, the final goal of all things. The fourth book treats of divine providence and supplies a theodicy: there is no such thing as chance; the good fortune of the wicked is only apparent, and the good are purified by their visitations. The fifth book answers the question of the relation between human freedom and divine foreknowledge: divine knowledge which is above the limitations of time sees everything past, present and future as present and does not destroy the freedom of man's will.

This book of consolation was extremely popular in the Middle Ages and was frequently commented, imitated and translated; among others King Alfred (d. 901) translated it into Anglo-Saxon and Notker Labeo (d. 1022) into German.

Edd.: ML 63/4. C. Meiser, 2 vols., L 1877/80 (Aristotle). S. Brandt (CSEL 48) 1906 (Porphyry). H. F. Stewart - E. K. Rand, Lo 1918/26 (*Opusc. theol.* with trans.). *Consol.* ed. R. Peiper, L 1871. A. a Forti Scuto, Lo 1925. E. Gothein, B 1931 (with trans.). G. Weinberger (CSEL 67) 1934; cf. Bieler, WSt 1936, 128/41; Klinger, Gn 1940, 26/32; Buechner, Her 1940, 279/97; Marigo, R. Accad. (Palermo), Atti ser. 3, III, 2, 1942 (text. crit.). K. Buechner, Hei 1947 and Mn 1952, trans. K. B. - F. Klinger, 1939, and S. J. Suys-Reitsma, A 1953. L. Cooper, *A concordance of B.,* C (Mass.) 1928. Biogr., importance and doctr.: Cappuyns, DHG 9, 348/80. Vernet, DS 1, 1739/45. Wotke, RACh 2, 482/8. Rand 1928 (supra § 83), 135/80; RCC 1936, 450/63. A. Guzzo, *L'Isag. di Porf. e i commenti di B.,* Tu 1934. Schuster, SC 1943, 369/72 (place of execution). Bark, AmHistRev 1944, 410/26 (B. and Theoderic). Courcelle 1948, 257/312 (Greek education). K. Bruder, *Die philos. Elemente der Opusc. sacra des B.,* 1928; cf. Gn 1930, 165/8. G. Pietzsch, *Die Klassifikation der Musik von B. bis Ugol. v. Orvieto,* 1929; *Die Musik im Erzieh.- u. Bildungsideal des ausgehenden Altertums u. d. fruehen MA,*

1932. Carton, RPhilos. 1930, 573/659 (Christianisme et Augustinisme). H. J. Brosch, *Der Seinsbegriff bei B.,* I 1931. Schrade, AGP 1932, 363/400 (music). Courcelle, MAH 1935, 185/223 (B. and the Alex. school). V. Schurr, *Die Trinitaetsl. des B. im Lichte der skyth. Kontroversen,* 1935; cf. Sp 1936, 153/6. A. Bekker - Freyseng, *Die Vorgesch. des philos. Terminus "contingens",* 1938. M. Galdi, *Saggi Boeziani,* Pisa 1938. McKinlay, *Festschr. E. K. Rand* 1938, 209/19 *(De syllogismis categor.).* Duchateau, *Tijdschr. Philos.* 1939, 134/60; 1941, 329/37 *(De disciplina scholarium).* Silk, HTR 1939, 19/39 (*Consol. phil.* dependent on Aug.'s *Dial.* and *Soliloq.*). Degl'Innocenti, DTP 1939, 397/9 *(De hebdomadibus).* H. M. Barett, *B. Some Aspects of His Times and Work,* C 1940. Dienelt, Glotta 1941, 98/128; 1942, 129/38 (linguistic matters of *Consol.*).

On legend of martyrdom: Bark, Sp 1946, 312/7 and A. Patch, Sp 1947, 443/5; against this Coster, Sp 1948, 284/7. Anastasi, MiscStLCA 1, 1947, 21/39 (trial). Schooneman, StC 1950, 286/306 (not a martyr). E. de Bruyne, *Études d'esthétique médiév.* I, Bruges 1946 (B., Cassiodore, Isidore). E. Rapisarda, *La crisi spirituale di B.,* Fl 1947 e Ca 1953; Ital. trans. of *Opusc. theol.,* 1947. L. Alfonsi, AttiIstVenetoScLett 102, p. 2, 1942/3, 723/7; RFN 1943, 223ff.; *Studi di lingua e di lett. ital.,* Como 1944; *Atti della Riunione costit. della Sodalitas Erasmiana,* Na 1950, 166/80; Aev 1951, 132/46, 210/29; Antiquitas 9, 1954, 3ff.; Orph. 1955, 10/6; *Convivium* 1955 *(Stor. interiore e stor. cosmica nella Consol. boez.).* Merone, GiorItFilol 1, 1948, 337/52 (on biogr. of Maximianus). Buechner, HJB 62/9, 1949, 31/42 (on bk. 3 of *Consol.*). Boano, RFC 1949, 198/216 (Elegies of Maximianus and B.). Daly, Sc 1950, 205/19 (MS of B.). Pfligersdorffer, VC 1953, 98/115 (Andronicus of Rhodes in B.). Coster, Mél. H. Grégoire 4, 1953, 45/81 (B.'s character). K. Reichenberger, *Unters. z. literar. Stellung d. Consol.,* Cologne 1954. K. Duerr, *The Proportional Logic of B.,* A 1951. Anastasi, MiscStLCA 3, 1951, 93/109 (genuineness of *Opusc. theol.*). Grillmeier in: Grillmeier - Bacht II, 792/96 (on Christol.). Nedoncelle, RevSR 1955, 201/38 (concept of person). W. Schmid, *Festschr. B. Snell,* Mn 1956, 113/44 (philos. and medic. matters in *Consol.,* esp. on importance of description of lethargy); abridged Engl. ed. in: *Studia Patristica* (TU) B 2, 1957, 368/75.

Later influence: W. Jansen, *D. Kommentar des Clarenbaldus v. Arras zu B.s De Trinit.,* 1926. A. Auer, *Joh. v. Dambach u. d. Trostbuecher vom 11. bis 16. Jh.,* 1928. G. P. Knapp, *The Paris Psalter and the Meters of B.* ed., NY 1932. Wilmart, ST 59, 1933, 259/62 (MS of a comm. on *Consol.*). Burbach, *Dtsch. Vierteljahrschr.* 11, 1933, 530/8 *(Consol.).* W. Bach, *Die althochdeutschen B.-glossen u. Notkers Uebers. der Consol.,* 1934. E. T. Silk, *Saeculi IX auctoris in B.i Cons. phil. comm.* ed., R 1935. H. R. Patch, *The Tradition of B.,* Lo 1935. K. H. Schmidt, *Koenig Alfreds B.-Bearbeitg.,* thesis Go 1934. A. Brandl, SbB 1937, N. 16 (early Anglo-Sax. proverb from the MS Tiberius B. 13). Courcelle, AHD 14, 1939, 5/140 *(commentaires de la Consol. de B., 9e—14e s.).* Van de Vyver, *Hum. Renaiss.* 6, 1939, 247/73 *(Traduct. du De consol. en litt. comparée).* Dedeck - Héry, Sp 1940, 432/43 (trans. of *Consol.* of J. de Meung). De Vooys, TNederlTaal 1940, 1/25 (B.-Vertaling v. J. Vilt). Solmsen, AJP 1944, 69/74 (B. and the hist. of the *Organon*). Marshall, Sp 1950, 471/82 (B.'s definitions of *persona* in the M. A.). Silvestre, RHE 1952, 44/122 *(Scot. Érigène et lib. 3 du De Consol.).* I. Schroebler, *Notker III. v. St. Gallen als*

Uebers. u. Kommentator von B.s De Consol., T 1953. K. Isaac, *Le Peri Hermeneias en Occident de B. à s. Thomas,* P 1953.

7. Flavius Magnus Aurelius Cassiodorus Senator (b. *c.* 490) came from a famous old family of distinguished state officials in Calabria. As early as 507 he became a *quaestor* and thus private secretary of Theodoric the Great. In 514 he was appointed consul and in 533 *praefectus praetorio.* As a leading statesman he aimed at reconciling Rome and the Germanic nations. Soon after 540 he retired to the monastery of Vivarium which he had founded on his family estates near Squillace in Calabria to devote himself completely to scholarship, religion and the education of his monks. Whether Cassiodorus himself became a monk in his monastery is a disputed question (d. *c.* 583).

Unlike Boethius, who was an idealist and theoretician, Cassiodorus was an altogether practical man. All his writings were occasioned by outside suggestions and destined to serve special needs of his time and milieu. He did not develop essentially new ideas; he was a collector and encyclopedist who wanted to prepare the material he gathered for practical use. During his career as a statesman he was almost exclusively occupied with historic-political questions, and when he was living in his monastery he aimed at introducing his brethren to theological and profane learning. By imposing intellectual work (studying and copying books) on his monks (*Inst.* 1, 30) he strongly underlined the obligation of intellectual activity imposed on the monks by the Rule of St. Benedict. Hence it is due to him that in the following centuries of barbarism learning was preserved in the monasteries and the treasures of the old Roman culture were saved from destruction.

a. Works of the statesman. Apart from two historical works that have already been mentioned (*Chronicle of the World* and *History of the Goths,* supra § 49 I 16) the following works belong to the same period: *Variae* (sc. *epistolae*), a collection of 468 documents (in twelve books) of great historical value, which became a pattern for the style of medieval chancelleries; they were composed by Cassiodorus in the name of the kings whom he served. He enlivened the dry subjects and showed his own comprehensive knowledge by various learned explanations and by giving juridical, political and moral reasons for the decrees he issued. The treatise *De anima* (12 chs.) counts as the thirteenth book of the *Variae;* it makes use of Augustine and provides the transition to Cassiodorus' religious writings.

Only fragments are extant of his panegyrics on members of the royal house and of his treatise on his family history entitled *Ordo generis Cassiodororum.*

b. Works of the monk. (α) Beside the Church history mentioned above (supra § 49 I 16) his most important work is the *Institutiones divinarum et humanarum lectionum.* Since the wars of the Goths had prevented the realization of his great plan of founding a theological college in Rome with the help of Pope Agapitus (535–536), Cassiodorus sought to further his educational programme of transmitting Latin culture especially through this treatise, which was destined for his monks. The first book provides an introduction to the study of theology, especially of Holy Scripture, giving an account of the literary aids and the individual authors required for a deeper study. The second book (7 chs.) is a jejune summary designed to introduce the student to the "seven liberal arts".

(β) A commentary on the Psalms of allegorical tendency which depends on Augustine; also *Complexiones in epistolas et acta apostolorum et apocalypsin* which single out for interpretation only some important passages, mostly from the Pauline Epistles. The orthodox version of the *Pauline Commentary* of Pelagius (ML 68) preserved under the name of *Primasius* is the work of Cassiodorus and his disciples. At the great age of 92 he wrote an instruction *De orthographia* for his monks. The spurious commentary on the Canticle (ML 70, 1055/1106) which Vega, CD 1942, 143/55, would assign to Isidore of Seville, belongs to Haymo of Halberstadt or to Haymo of Auxerre; while the commentary printed among the works of Isidore (ML 83, 1119/32) is but an excerpt from this commentary of Ps.-Cassiodorus; cf. ClavisPL n. 910. 1220.

Edd.: ML 69/70. T. Mommsen (MGAuctAnt 11 12) 1894. *Instit.* ed. R. A. B. Mynors, O 1937; also Rand, Sp 1938, 433/47.— Mgg.: Cappuyns, DHG 11, 1349/1408. Helm, RACh 3, 915/25. ClavisPL n. 896ff. Leclercq, DAL 2, 2357/65. Van de Vyver, Sp 1931, 244/92. — On biogr.: Bischoff, SM 1937, 100f. (4 alleged friends of C.). G. Vetter, *Die Ostgoten u. Theodorich,* 1938, 64/79, 116/8 (C.'s influence). — *Variae:* A. T. Heerklotz, *Die V. des C. als kulturgesch. Quelle,* 1926. G. A. Punzi, *L'Italia del sec. 6 nelle V. di C.,* Aquila 1927. B. H. Skahill, *The Syntax of the V. of C.,* W 1934. A. Souter I, 1922 (supra § 82, 7) 60/3 (Ps.-Primasius). G. Pietzsch 1929 and 1932 (supra § 96, 5). Gladysz, CT 1936, 51/69 (Influence on medieval schools). E. Schwartz, AbhMn 1939, N. 2 *(Var.).* Courcelle, RevEA 1942, 65/86 (hist. of origin of *Inst.*). Courcelle 1948, 313/48 (Gr. education). Janne, Byz 11, 1936, 225/7 (on *C. Apionem*).

On *Vivarium,* its history and library: Baehrens, TU 42, 1, 1916, 186/99 (MSS). Weinberger, Misc. Ehrle 4, 1924, 75/88 (MSS). Morin, RBn 1931, 145/52 *(Heures canon.).* Thiele, SM 1932, 378/419 (foundation, infl. in Middle Ages). Gomoll, ZBW 1936, 186/9 (MSS). Courcelle, CRI 1937, 212/5 (library); MAH 1938, 259/307 *(Le site du monastère);* 1948 (cf. Index). Blatt, *Class. et Mediaev.* 1, 1938, 217/42 (also on transl. activities at *Viv.*). Souter, JTS 1940, 46 (library). Van de Vyver, RBn 1941, 59/89 (*Instit.* and *Viv.*). Schuster, SC 1942, 409/14 (library). Blum, ZBW 64, 1950, 52/7 (*Cod. Amiatinus* at *Viv.*). Courcelle, RevEA 1954, 424/8 *(Corpus vivarien des Chroniques).*

G. Euis, *The Vocabulary of the Inst. of C.,* W 1939. O. Zimmermann, *The Vocab. of the Var. of C.,* W 1944. M. J. Suelzer, *The Clausulae in C.,* W 1944. J. v. d. Besselaar, *C. senator en zijn Variae,* N 1945; *C. Leven en werken,* Antw. 1950. G. I. Paschali, *Unters. z. C.s Institutiones,* thesis Marbg. 1947. Jones, Sp 1945, 433/42; 1947, 254/6, 275/7 (infl. of *Inst.* in the Middle Ages); trans. of *Inst.,* NY 1946. Bardy, AnT 1945, 383/425 *(C. et la fin du monde ancien).* Loewe, RomanForsch 60, 1948, 420/46. G. Mercati, Bi 1948, 282f. (on *Comm. in Pss.* ch. 15: *fastucium*). Morison, CQR 1949, 121/32 (Cass.). A. J. Fridh, *Ét. critiques et syntax. sur les Var. de C.,* Goeteborg 1950. Mundó in: *Misc. Bibl. D. Ubach* 1953 (1954), 161/76 *(El colofo a Ester de la Pandectes minutiore manu de C.).*

§ 97. AFRICAN WRITERS

THE relatively lively literary activities of the Africans were mainly devoted to combating Arianism, which the intolerant Vandals had propagated. Later, from the middle of the sixth century the *Three Chapters* were almost the only, hotly disputed, subject of theological literature.

Leclercq, RBn 1948, 53/72 (Afric. inedita from the *Homiliarium* of Fleury).

1. Bishop Maximus is known from a letter addressed to Theophilus of Alexandria (§ 55, 3) in which he pleads for nuns fleeing to Egypt; he lived in Africa, not in Gaul (against Morin, RevCharlemagne 2, 192, 89/104); cf. Courcelle, RBP 1953, 24/9.

2. Bishop Victor of Vita was the author of an *Historia persecutionis Africanae provinciae,* published 488/9, which gives an account of the terrible sufferings of the Catholics under the Vandal kings Geiseric (428–77) and Huneric (477–84). A *Passio septem monachorum* was later added by another author.

Edd.: C. Halm (MGAuctAnt 3, 1) 1879. M. Petschenig (CSEL 7) 1881. Germ. by A. Zink, Progr. Bamberg 1883. — Studies: Schepens, RSR 1916, 139/48; 1919, 369f. *(Notitia)*. G. G. Lappeyre, *L'anc. égl. de Carthage,* 2nd vol., 1932. M. Schwartz, *D. Kampf d. arian. Vandalen geg. d. Kirchenpol. Roms u. Byzanz',* 1938. Marrou, RevEA 1943, 225/32 (V. and Diadochus of Phot.). Déjardins, BullTrimSocGéogrArch d'Oran 65, 1944, 77/81 (on *Hist.* 1, 13). C. Courtois, *V. de V. et son œuvre. Ét. crit.,* Algier 1954.

3. Vigilius of Thapsus belongs to the group of Catholic bishops who attended a religious conversation at Carthage ordered by Huneric in 484. Otherwise nothing is known about his life. Two works are extant: a *Dialogus contra Arianos, Sabellianos et Photinianos* and five books *Against Eutyches.* Two further anti-Arian writings are lost. Other works, e.g. twelve books *De Trinitate* (ML 62, 237/334) are spurious (v. supra § 54, I, 4 and 81, 2).

Edd.: ML 62. — Mg.: Ficker 1897. On the use of *C. Eutychen* and *De Trin.* in *Sententiae SS. Patrum* ed. K. Kuenstle, *Eine Bibl. der Symbole,* 1900, 149/73; cf. ibid. 100/15 and J. Madoz, *Le symbole du XI Conc. de Tolède,* 1938, 178/84. On Ps.- August., *Ep.* 20 (ML 33, 1156/62) cf. Giesecke 1939, 185f.; cf. 220/2. J. Humensky, *Christologia Vig.i, T.,* R 1935; Bardy, DTC 15, 3005/8. D. Baldino, *La dottrina trinitaria di V. di T.,* Na 1949. Simonetti, IstLombScLett 83, 1950, 1/3 (*V.* dependent on Ps.-Athanas., *Trin.* 12; supra § 54, I 4).

4. Fulgentius of Ruspe (b. 467, d. 1 Jan. 533) was probably the greatest theologian of his time, a vigorous opponent of Arianism

and a defender of the Augustinian doctrine of grace against the attacks of the semi-Pelagians of Gaul.

We are informed about his life by the fine *Vita* written by his disciple, the Carthaginian deacon Ferrandus soon after his death. Ferrandus also gives an account of the Canon Law then in force in his *Breviatio canonum* (ML 67). His seven letters are of doctrinal and historical importance.

Edd.: ML 65, 117/50. ML 67, 887/962. — G. F. Lapeyre, *Vita F.i,* P 1929 (with trans.). Germ. in BKV² II 9. G. Krueger, *Harnack-Ehrung* 1921, 219/23 *(Vita)*. W. Pewesin, *Imperium, Eccl. univ., Roma,* St 1937, 18/42 (letters). Giesecke 1939, 189 A. 79 (F. not the author of the *Vita*).

The descendant of a noble family, he received a sound scholarly training including Greek language and literature. He was first a *procurator* (tax collector) in his native town of Telepte, then became a monk. He was elected Bishop of Ruspe *c.* 507. Soon afterwards (508) he was exiled to Sardinia, together with over sixty Catholic bishops, where he had to live till 515 and again from *c.* 517 to 523. The idea that he is identical with the mythographer of the same name is untenable.

a. Anti-Arian writings (EP 2248 ff.): *Contra Arianos,* a reply to ten questions of King Thrasamund; *Ad Thrasamundum regem* (three books) continues the polemical discussion. Other controversial writings are: *Contra sermonem Festidiosi Ariani, Contra Fabianum* (thirty-nine large fragments are extant), *De Trinitate ad Felicem, De incarnatione ad Scarilam.* The following are not directly polemical: *De fide ad Petrum* (EP 2260/75), a compendium of dogmatics in the Middle Ages attributed to St. Augustine and widely used; *De remissione peccatorum ad Euthymium* (two books). The treatise *Adversus Pintam,* an Arian bishop, is lost. The work *Adversus Pintam* printed in ML 65, 707/20 is perhaps identical with the lost *Commonitorium de Spiritu S.* (D'Alès). Recently an anti-Arian *Psalmus abecedarius* has come to light.

b. Fulgentius wrote three treatises against Semi-Pelagianism:

Ad Monimum (three books), *De veritate praedestinationis et gratiae Dei* (three books) and the lost seven books *Contra Faustum Reiensem*.

c. Among the eighteen letters printed in the editions there are five that are addressed to Fulgentius. Some letters are fairly long dogmatic treatises; two of them (*Epp*. 15 and 17) are formal collective letters of the bishops in exile in Sardinia; *Ep*. 17, a reply to the Scythian monks on the doctrine of grace, agrees with the formula: "One of the Trinity has suffered in the flesh" (supra § 72, 3). *Epp*. 1–7 treat predominantly questions of moral theology (virginity, marriage problems, penance). About seven sermons may be considered genuine.

Points of Doctrine

In his doctrine of grace Fulgentius holds the same views as Augustine. He teaches the particular saving will of God and the unconditional predestination to beatitude or damnation; he believes unbaptized infants to be excluded from beatitude and attributes the transmission of original sin to the concupiscence of the parents (*Verit. praed.* 3, 14/23). He explicitly denies the immaculate conception of the BVM (*Ep*. 17, 6, 13).

Edd.: ML 65. Germ. by L. Kozelka (BKV² II 9) 1934. — Mgg.: O. Friebel 1911 (for identity with mythographer). G. G. Lapeyre, P 1929; *L'anc. Égl. de Carthage,* 2 vols., 1932. — Studies: Stiglmayr, ZKT 1925, 341/57 (author of the *Quicunque*). B. Nisters, *Die Christologie des F. v. R.,* 1930. D'Alès, RSR 1932, 304/16 *(Commonit. de Sp. S.)*. Dold, BM 1932, 467/71 (Epiph.-sermon). Delehaye, AB 1934, 103/5 (d. 533). Lambot, RBn 1936, 221/34 (ined. *psalmus abeced.*). Jugie, EO 1936, 324/30 *(epiclesis)*. Giesecke 1939, 189/95 *(Ad Thrasam)*. F. d. Sciascio, *F. di R. Un grande discepolo di Agost.,* R 1941; cf. ZKT 1942, 57f. Altaner, HJB 1953, 578/81 (*Ep*. 16). Beumer, Gr 1942, 326/47 *(De fid. ad P.)*. Gavigan, Tr 1947, 313/22 (on bapt.). J. v. d. Besselaar, *Preken* (trans. from Fulg., Mart. of Braga and Leander of Sev.), Bussum 1946. Leclercq, RBn 56, 1945/6, 93ff. (on 2 spurious *Sermones* in: ML 65, 833/42). ClavisPL n. 814/46. Grillmeier in: Grillmeier - Bacht II, 807/14 (Christol. of Ferrandus and Facundus).

5. In the Three Chapters controversy the learned Bishop Facundus of Hermiane opposed the ecclesiastical policy of

Justinian I in his large work *Pro defensione trium capitulorum,* written *c.* 550. He persisted in his point of view even after the Council of Constantinople (553) and Pope Vigilius had approved the condemnation of the Three Chapters. In the same sense he wrote two smaller treatises *Contra Moncianum* (550–2) and the *Epistola fidei catholicae* (568–9).

W. Pewesin, *Imperium, Eccl. universalis, Roma,* St 1937; cf. TR 1938, 335/8.

6. Bishop Verecundus of Junca (d. 552 at Chalcedon) was an opponent of the *Three Chapters* and left the *Excerptiones de gestis Chalcedonensis concilii,* excerpts of the acts of the council. Besides, he wrote after 534 a *Commentary on nine O.T. Canticles* (e.g. Ex. 15, Dt. 32) and composed in profound contrition a penitential hymn *De satisfactione paenitentiae* (212 hexameters).

Edd.: Not in ML. J. B. Pitra, *Spicil. Solesmense* 4, 1858, 1/191. E. Kulendorff, *Textkr. Beitr. zu V. J.,* Lund 1943 (ed. *De satisf.*); cf. TLZ 1947, 33f. Bardy, DTC 15, 2672/4. Hudson-Williams, VC 1952, 47/51 (text. crit. on *De satisfact.*). Brou, SE 1954, 73/95 (Collectes du Psautier et V.).

7. The Carthaginian deacon Liberatus was an opponent of the *Three Chapters* (560–6). Basing himself on good sources he wrote the valuable *Breviarium causae Nestorianorum et Eutychianorum,* a brief history of the heresies till 553.

Edd.: ML 68. SACO 2, 5 (v. supra § 50, 18 e). — Studies: Hildebrand, HJB 1922, 223/32. Bardy, RSR 1931, 201/4 and Puech, *Annuaire de l'école prat. des Hautes Ét.* 1930/1, 3/39 (L. and the date of the ps.-Dionys. writings).

8. Primasius, Bishop of Hadrumetum (d. soon after 552), agreed to the condemnation of the *Three Chapters.* Apart from a lost history of heresies, he wrote a commentary on the Apocalypse which is important because of its many borrowings from the lost work of Tyconius (supra § 82, 5). On the spurious commentary of the Pauline Epistles v. supra § 96, 6 β.

ML 68. — On a MS of the comm. on the Apc. cf. RHE 1936, 214. Amann, DTC 13, 245/7. H. J. Vogels, *Zur Gesch. der lat. Apok.-Uebers.,* 1920. W. Kamlah, *Apokal. u. Geschichtstheol.,* 1935. Devreesse, MAH 1940, 143/66 (Byzantium in Africa).

9. At the suggestion of the just mentioned Primasius Junilius (Junillus?) Africanus, *quaestor sacri palatii* at the court of Justinian, translated and edited *c.* 542 the Greek work of a Persian, Paul of Nisibe, under the title *Instituta regularia divinae legis;* it is an introduction to the study of the Bible which faithfully reflects the views of Theodore of Mopsuestia.

Edd.: ML 68 and in H. Kihn, *Theod. von Mops. u. Jun. als Exegeten,* 1880. E. Stein, BullAcadBelgClLett 5, 23, 1937, 265/90.

§ 98. SPANISH AUTHORS

On the authors of the patristic period not discussed in this work cf. J. Pérez de Urbel, "Las letras en la época visigoda" in: *España visigoda* (441/711), Ma 1940, 379/413 *(*in *Historia de España III dir. p. P.-M. Pidal).* Madoz, RF 1941, 228/40 *(ecos del saber antiguo).* B. Altaner, *Patrología. Trad. por E. Cuevas y U. Domínguez-Del Val. Con un resumen de patrología española,* Ma [4]1956. Also J. Madoz in: *Hist. General de las Literaturas Hisp.* I, Ba 1950, 85/140, 259/74; and further the bibliographical works cited supra § 4, 7 by J. Madoz and id., SE 1953, 105/32 (on Span. authors and their knowledge of the classic writers of antiquity) and U. Domínguez-Del Val, RET 1955, 399/444 (new publications of the years 1951/4). J. Alonso, *La cura pastoral en la España romanovisigoda,* R 1955.

1. Bishop Justus of Urgel (Isid., *Vir. ill.* 34) was a member of the Synod of Valencia in 546. He left an allegorical explanation of the Canticle *(Mystica explicatio)* dedicated to his metropolitan Sergius of Tarragona and the deacon Justus. As had long been the custom, the Bridegroom is identified with Christ, the Bride with the Church.

Text: ML 67, 961/94. The Prologue and the *Ep. dedicatoria* to the deacon Justus not in ML, but in García-Villada II 2, 265 f.; cf. also ibid. 120/2 and freq. On MSS cf. id., EE 1924, 432/4 and RHE 1935, 768; 1936, 214. On his *Sermo de s. Vincentino:* De Gaiffier, AB 1949, 278/80. ClavisPL n. 1091/2.

2. Apringius, Bishop of Beja (Portugal), wrote soon after 551 a commentary on the Apocalypse preserved incomplete in a single MS (on 1, 1 to 5, 7 and 18, 6 to 22, 21). The lacunae between the extant pieces of the commentary are filled up with excerpts from the commentary of Victorinus in the version of Jerome (§ 35).

Vega's attempt to ascribe these excerpts to Apringius himself was a failure.

Edd.: M. Ferotin, *A. de B.,* P 1900. A. C. Vega. *A. i Pacensis Ep. i Tract. in Apoc.,* E 1941 (with first ed. of Excerpts); cf. CD 153, 1941, 399/406; TR 1942, 119f. and Bull RTA 5, 1946, 15f.

3. Martin of Bracara (Braga), Bishop in Pannonia *c.* 515, became a monk in Palestine and came to Gallaecia in N. W. Spain *c.* 550. There he was first abbot, then Bishop of Dumio, and finally metropolitan of the Suevian royal city Bracara (before 572). He worked with great success for the conversion of the Arian Suevians. His literary works show him not only as a trained theologian and competent translator, but especially also as a practical pastor and shepherd of his flock who had both his feet on the ground. Besides Seneca, Augustine, Cassian and Caesarius of Arles were the authors he read and used most assiduously (d. 580).

a. Writings on moral theology and asceticism: *Formula vitae honestae,* dedicated to King Miro (570/83), a treatise on the four cardinal virtues based on Seneca's lost work *De officiis; De ira,* an excerpt from Seneca's work of the same title; three treatises, also destined for King Miro: *Pro repellenda iactantia, De superbia, Exhortatio humilitatis,* which originally formed one whole (ML 72, 21/52).

The sermon *De correctione rusticorum,* written for Bishop Polemius of Astorga, contains descriptions of superstitions rife in peasant milieu that are of great interest for the history of culture. In some respects this work is a counterpart of Augustine's *De catechizandis rudibus.* Later the Sermon was used by Eligius of Noyon and Pirminus of Reichenau. (Ed. C. P. Caspari 1883).

b. Writings on canon law and liturgical subjects: *Capitula Martini,* a collection of canons of Eastern, African and Spanish synods (ML 84, 574/86); *Epistola de trina mersione,* important for the baptismal liturgy (Flórez, *España sagrada* 15, 1769, 422/5); *De pascha,* on fixing the date of Easter, is not certainly genuine (in A. E. Burn [supra § 84, 2], 1905, 93/107); three metrical inscriptions (in R. Peiper [supra § 95, 5], 194/6).

c. The translation of a Greek collection of apophthegmata *Aegyptiorum patrum (110) sententiae* (ML 74, 381/94). He had a second collection translated by the monk Paschasius of Dumio (supra § 46, 5).

Madoz, EE 1945, 335/53 (new recens. of *De corr. rust.*). C. W. Barlow, *Mart. Ep. Brac., Opera omnia,* New Haven 1950 (1st compl. crit. ed.). Amann, DTC 10, 203/7. Stelzenberger 1933, 502/6. Lambert, RevMabillon 1935, 1/27 (M. and the Officium S. Martini Turon.). Bickel, RM 1905, 505/51 (Formula). S. McKenna, *Paganism and Pagan Survivals in Spain . . .,* W 1938 (ch. 4). Alafont 1942 (supra § 50, 14) ed. an *Excerptum de canonibus.* Besselaar 1947 (supra § 97, 4). P. David, *Ét. hist. sur la Galice et le Portugal,* 1947; cf. Brou, EL 1949, 66/70. P. Francœur, *The Relationship in Thought and Language betw. L. Aen. Seneca and M. of Braga,* thesis Univ. of Michigan 1944. Fontan and Bover, Emerita 18, 1950, 377/85 (text. crit. on *De ira*). Tavares and De Sousa, RevPortugFilos 6, 1950, 381/87 (Seneca). P. David, BullÉtPortugInstitFrançPortug 14, 1950, 283/99 (*De pascha* spurious); id., *Un traité priscillianiste de comput pascal,* Coimbra 1951 (author of *De pascha* a Priscillianist of the end of the 6th cent.). Coelho, Bracara Augusta, 2, 1951, 414/45 (centenary articles). Madoz, EE 1951, 219/42 (appreciation). Barlow, Folia 6, 1952, 5/15 (life and work). Liefvoghe, MSR 1954, 133/46 *(Idées morales).* Text. crit. by Kurfess in: *Athenaeum* (Pavia), 1954, 250/8; 404/09; 1955, 55/63; Aev 1955, 181/6. ClavisPL n. 997 1080f. 1163 1787f.; on spuria n. 1089 and 2302. Further publications listed in Madoz, Seg. decenio 1951, 86/92 and Domínguez-Del Val, RET 1955, 412f.

4. Licinian, Bishop of the then Byzantine Cartagena. Only three letters, written *c.* 590–600, survive of his voluminous correspondence. In the first of these he thanks Pope Gregory the Great for sending him his *Regula pastoralis.* The second letter is a rather long treatise, written in collaboration with Bishop Severus in which the spirituality and incorporality of angels and human souls is defended against an unnamed bishop. The letter is addressed to Epiphanius, the deacon of the bishop attacked. In the third letter Bishop Vincent of the Isle of Ibiza is sharply rebuked because he believed in the authenticity of a letter of Christ said to have dropped from heaven in Rome.

Text: ML 72, 689/700. J. Madoz, *L. de Cart. y sus cartas,* Ma 1948 (crit. ed. and comm.); on this Vega, CD 155, 156/67. J. A. Platero, *L. de C. y su doctr. espirit.,*

Oña 1946. Madoz, RET 1948, 203/30 (on 2nd Letter). Vallejo, *Emerita* 15, 1947, 149/54 (text. crit. on 2nd Letter). Brunel, AB 1950, 383/96 (on 3rd Letter).

5. Eutropius, abbot of the monastery Servitanum (near Cartagena?), became Bishop of Valencia after 589 (third Synod of Toledo). He corresponded with Licinian of Cartagena (Isid., *Vir. ill.* 45). Only two treatises addressed to Bishop of Arcavica are extant today: *De districtione monachorum,* in which he demands strict monastic discipline, and *De octo vitiis,* chiefly an excerpt from Cassian, Coll. 5.

Text: ML 80, 9/20. U. Domínguez-Del Val, RET 1954, 367/92 (sources of E.).

6. Leander of Seville, b. before 549 at Cartagena which was then Byzantine, came from a distinguished Romanic family. From *c.* 580 he was a friend of Gregory the Great (in Constantinople). In 589 he presided over the Synod of Toledo and there received Recared, the King of the Visigoths, into the Church (d. 600–1).

Two anti-Arian treatises as well as his letters are lost. There is extant a religious rule for women, *De institutione virginum* (twenty-one chapters) destined for his sister Florentina, and an oration *In laudem Ecclesiae* delivered on the occasion of the synod mentioned above.

Edd.: ML 72, 873/98; oration Germ. trans. BM 1927, 372/6. — Amann, DTC 9, 96/8. Porter, Laudate 10, 1932, 7/14 (Rule). Madoz, Misc. Mercati I, 265/95 (sources of Rule). Vega, CD 1947, 277/94 ed. a version of the Rule containing 10 more chs., again ed. E 1948; here also the speech delivered at the Synod of Toledo in 589 together with a hitherto unknown sermon for the feast of St. Vincent. The text ed. by Madoz, AB 1949, 407/24 is closely related to the longer Rule. J. Besselaar, 1947 (supra § 97, 3).

7. Isidore of Seville (b. *c.* 560, d. 636) is generally called the last Church Father of the West. In 600–1 he succeeded his elder brother Leander (v. supra) as Archbishop of Seville. In 633 he presided over the fourth National Synod of Toledo. Feast day: April 4.

Isidore, who was an extraordinarily industrious author, exercized a very great influence on the cultural development of the following centuries. Together with Boethius and Cassiodorus he is one of the great teachers of the Middle Ages. His learned works, mostly only mosaic-like compilations from other authors, did not only serve his own time, but preserved many treasures of antiquity for the future. Their lack of originality together with their clarity of expression and their encyclopedic character made them widely popular; thus his *Etymologies,* for example, are extant even today in about 950 manuscripts. Not a few of his many works (especially the exegetical ones) remain still to be printed.

a. His most influential work are the twenty books of *Etymologiae,* also called *Origines,* an encyclopedia of the entire secular and religious knowledge of his time.

The voluminous work was written for King Sisebut, but was given its final form only after Isidore's death by his friend Bishop Braulio of Saragossa and other editors. The strange title is due to the fact that the scholarly notions and objects treated in the work generally begin with an explanation of the etymology of the term in question. Since his etymological explanations, like those of the ancient grammarians and rhetors, are often based only on the sound of the word, he frequently gives the most astonishing interpretations. Thus *apis* is explained as *sine pedibus* and *amicus* is derived from *hamus* (hook), *sagitta* from *sagaci iactu, pharetra* from *a ferendo iacula.*

The titles of the individual books characterize in a way the contents of the work: 1. *De grammatica,* 2. *De rhetorica et dialectica,* 3. *De quatuor disciplinis mathematicis* (arithmetic, geometry, music, astronomy), 4. *De medicina,* 5. *De legibus et temporibus* (at the end an extract from the *Chronicle of the World*), 6. *De libris et officiis ecclesiasticis,* 7. *De Deo, angelis et fidelium ordinibus,* 8. *De ecclesia et sectis diversis,* 9. *De linguis, gentibus, regnis, militia, civibus, affinitatibus,* 10. *Vocum certarum alphabetum* (only etymologies), 11. *De homine et portentis,* 12. *De animalibus,* 13. *De mundo et partibus,* 14. *De terra et partibus,* 15. *De aedificiis et agris,* 16. *De lapidibus et metallis* (also on weights and measures), 17. *De rebus rusticis*, 18. *De bello et ludis*, 19. *De navibus, aedificiis et vestibus*, 20. *De penu* (food) *et instrumentis domesticis et rusticis.*

Isidore's main sources were the works of the Church Fathers, scholia on authors of antiquity and manuals of diverse departments of knowledge. His quotations from older classical authors are nearly always taken from secondary sources.

b. Writings of profane learning: *Differentiarum libri II* and *Synonymorum libri II* treat of grammatical questions; chiefly scientific matters are contained in *De natura rerum* and *De ordine creaturarum;* on the historical works v. supra § 2, 2 and § 49 II 12. The twenty-seven *tituli Isidori,* inscriptions on the walls and library cupboards of his house in Seville, are of interest for the history of culture.

c. Biblical scholarship: *Quaestiones in Vetus Testamentum. De ortu et obitu patrum,* biographical notes on eighty-six Biblical personages.

d. Dogmatic and polemical works: *Sententiarum libri III,* a manual of dogmatics and morals in the form of theses. It is based mainly on the *Moralia* of Gregory the Great; *Contra Iudaeos ad Florentinam sororem* was translated into Old German as early as the eighth century. *Liber de variis quaestionibus adversus Iudaeos et ceteros infideles* (hitherto regarded as a work of Rhabanus Maurus). Ed. A. E. Anspach et A. C. Vega, E 1940 (for Isidore); against this Madoz, EE 1949, 147/68; author Felix of Urgel; against this Vega, CD 161, 1949, 217/68 (for Isidore); against this Madoz, EE 1950, 435/58 (for Felix). *De haeresibus,* a history of the heresies (ed. Vega ²1940; cf. TR 1937, 59, 1942, 117/9).

e. *De ecclesiasticis officiis,* on the Mass, liturgical prayers, Church festivals and feast days (book I), ecclesiastical offices and states (book II). Isidore also wrote a *Regula monachorum.* According to Vaccari, *Mél. Cavallera,* Toulouse 1948, 147/62 the *Commonitiuncula ad sororem,* an ascetical treatise (ed. A. E. Anspach, E

1935; cf. TR 1938, 58) belongs to an anonymous author of the second half of the seventh century — On the *Collectio Isidoriana* v. supra § 50, 14.

Edd.: F. Arevalo, 7 vols., R 1797/1803. ML 81/4. Hist. works v. supra § 49 II 12. *Origines* ed. W. M. Lindsay, 2 vols., O 1911. *Institutionum disciplinae* ed. Anspach, RM 1912, 557/63. *De Trinitate* ed. G. Villada 2, 2, 1933, 282/9. *De divinis scripturis* ed. de Bruyne, RBn 1933, 119/41. E. Anspach, *Taionis et Isidori nova fragmenta et opera,* Ma 1930, 57/64 (ed. enlarged Vita of I. by Braulio - ML 82, 53/6), 159/65 (2 prayers and 1 hom.). — Transs.: of *Allegoriae* by Molinero, Buenos Aires 1936; *Synonyma* by Valdès Solis, Ma 1946, L. Cortes y Góngora y M. Díaz, Complete trans. of *Etymologiae,* Ma 1951; other Span. transs. of I.'s works cf. RHE 1951, 869f. and Gracía Rives, RevArchBibliotMus 56, 1950, 279/320. — On Bibliogr.: R. B. Brown, *The Printed Works of I. of S.,* Lexington 1949 (Kentucky Univ.); also Madoz, Seg. dec. 1951, 115/22 and U. Domínguez-Del Val, RET 1955, 429/34. — Mgg.: Schenk-Schmekel-Philipp, PWK 9, 2069/80. Bareille, DTC 8, 98/111. C. H. Beeson, *Isidorstudien,* 1913 (157/66 ed. *tituli*). A. Schmekel, *I. v. S., Sein System u. seine Quellen,* 1914; cf. Wessner, Her 1917, 201/92. N. P. Salmerón, *S. I. Estudio bio-bibliográfico,* Ma 1915. P. Séjourné, *Le dernier Père de l'Égl. S. I. de S. Son rôle dans l'hist. du droit can.,* 1929. J. Sofer, *Lat. u. Romanisches aus den Etym. des I. v. S.,* 1930. A. v. Fragstein, *I. v. S. u. die sog. Germanicusscholien,* 1931. J. R. Geiselmann, *Die Abendmahlslehre ... (des) I. v. S.,* 1933. M. Kordel, *Liturgja mozarabska w dziele De eccl. off. sw. I. ze. S.,* Cracow 1935. E. Ulrich, *Die althochdtsch. Glossen zu I.s Buechern ueb. d. Pflichten,* 1938. J. Mullins, *The Spir. Life Acc. to S. I.,* W 1940. L. Aranjo-Costa, *I., arzob. de S.,* 1942. J. Pérez de Urbel-T. Ortega, *Breviarios del pensamiento españ. s. I.,* Ma 1940. I. Quiles, *S. I. Biografia, escritos, doctrinas,* Buenos Aires 1945. L. W. Nelson, *Etymol. v. I. van S.* (lecture, 39 pp.), Ley 1954. J. Fontane *I. de S. et la culture classique,* 2 vols., P 1959.

Studies: *Miscellanea Isidoriana,* R 1936, 386 pp.; I have there *(Der Stand der Isidorforschung)* given a crit. account of all relevant publications that had appeared 1910–35; hence, apart from the most recent publications, I give here only a selection. *Misc. Isid.* contain the following contributions: G. Villada 33/8 (la obra de S.I.); Llamazares 39/55 (I. not monk but canon regular); De Aldama 57/89 (chronol. of works); Zarb 91/134 *(I.i cultus erga Sacras Litt.);* Ogara 135/50 *(tipol. bibl.);* Morin 151/63 (I. and the text of the Mozarabic Psalter); Vaccari 165/75 *(una fonte del De ortu et ob. patr.);* Madoz 177/220 *(el floril. patríst. del segundo Conc. de Sevilla 619);* Séjourné 221/51 *(I. et la liturgie wisigoth.);* Bidagor 253/85 (nature of marriage); Zeiller 287/92 *(I. et les orig. chrét. des Goths et des Suèves);* Elorduy 293/322 (pedagogics); Anspach 323/56 (infl. in 7/9th cents.); Silva-Tarouca 357/63 (MS of Ps.-I.); Ruiz 364/84 (F. Arevalo). — García-Pelajo, RCienc-JurSoc 17, 1934, 375/90 (legal conceptions). Yaben, RevEcles 10, 1936, 561/74; 11, 3/18 *(Ideas jurid.).* Uhden, Mn 1936, 1/28 (map of world). De la Fuente, CD 152, 1936, 128/31, 274/90 *(De eccl. off.).* Anspach-Vega, CD 153, 1936, 33/48 *(Quaest. adv. Iud.).* Vega, CD 152, 1936, 145/63 *(Un tratado inéd.).* Ramos, RevEcles 10,

1936, 587/601 (so-called Braulio-Vita of I.). Ortiz, *Cruz y Raya* 1936, 6/63 (I. legend in Middle Ages). Porzig, Her 1937, 129/70 (recens. of *Etym.*). Champeaux, RHistDroitFranc 1937, 1/19 *(La parenté fraternelle et la prima stemma d'I.)*. Madoz, RHE 1938, 5/20 (I. author of Symbol of Toledo 633). Lawson, RBn 1938, 26/36 (sources of *De eccl. off.*). Havet, ETL 1939, 22/93 *(sacrements et l'Esprit S.)*. Madoz, RF 1939, 247/57; 1941, 229/31 *(De laude Spaniae)*. Duran, Atenas 11, 1938, 41/51 *(De nat. ver.)*. Basulto, *Ciencia Tom.* 1939, 364/88 (canon escriturist.). Delgado, AST 1941, 59/74 *(Formación clás.)*. On Vega, CD 1942, 143/55 cf. § 96, 7 β. Tabera, StudDocumHistJur 1942, 23/47 *(furtum)*. Madoz, RET 1942, 229/55 (Rom. primacy); EE 1947, 217/23 *(Versus I.i)*. Saguès, EE 1943, 227/57, 517/46 and cont. *(doctr. del Cuerpo míst.)*. Stach, *Antike* 1943, 63/76 (King Sisebut). On I., *De musica* cf. RHE 1947, 540. Levy, Sp 1947, 81f. (*Etym.* 8, 9, 9). Lawson, RBn 1947, 187/95 (*Consulat. Zachaei* . . . in I.). Guarino, StudDocumHistJur 10, 1944, 317/32 *(I. et l'origine dei codicilli)*. Rodríguez-Alvarez, ArchLeonenses 1, 1947, 125/67 (I. fragm. in the cathedral library of León). Romero, QuadHistEsp 8, 1947, 6/71 (polit. views). Beltran, AnalUnivMurcia 1947/8, 605/8 (birth place). Donati, AcadLinRendClScMorStor 3, 1948, 370/80 (I. and mediev. aesthetics). Vallejo, Emerita 17, 1949, 263f. *(striges)*. Silvestre, *Le moyen-âge* 55, 1949, 247/51 (on *Etym.*). Madoz, RET 1952, 189/204 (I. and Counc. of Chalc.). Diaz y Diaz, SE 1953, 147/66 (*Lib. de ord. creaturarum* spurious, of Irish origin). Fontaine, REL 1953, 271/300 (astrology). ClavisPL n. 1186ff.

On I.'s most important disciple and friend Braulio cf. C. H. Lynch, *S. B. . . . His Life and Writings,* W 1938; Span. trans. by P. Galindo, Ma 1950. J. Madoz, *Epistolario de S. B. de Z.,* 1941; cf. Alamo, RHE 1942, 417/22 (Letters are spurious); successfully defended as genuine by Madoz, EE 1943, 433/85; cf. RHE 1946, 549. P. de Urbel, DHG 10, 441/53. Cazzaniga, AnnFacFilosLett (Milan) 7, 1954, 533/49 (text. crit. of B.'s Vita s. Aemiliani).

§ 99. POETS

1. Paulinus of Périgueux is the author of an epic *De vita s. Martini* (*c.* 470); it is a metrical version (3622 hexameters) chiefly of the relevant writings of Sulpicius Severus (v. supra § 49 II f.). Two minor poems (80 and 25 hexameters) treat of the same saint.

Edd.: M. Petschenig (CSEL 16) 1888. — Weyman 1926 (v. supra § 87 before 1) 140f. Chase 1932 (supra § 49 II 4).

2. Sidonius Apollinaris, b. in 432, was the descendant of a noble family of Lyons and the son-in-law of the Roman Emperor Avitus. He wrote twenty-four *Carmina* modelled on Virgil and Claudius Claudianus, among them three panegyrics on Roman emperors; they are all carefully polished works according to the

taste of the times, without any Christian ideas but full of mythological imagery.

Having reluctantly become Bishop of Arverna (Clermont-Ferrand) in 469, he turned to epistolography. Following in the footsteps of Pliny the Younger and Symmachus, he left nine books of 147 epistles which, though rich in words and poor in thought, are yet important for the history of culture and frequently adorned with poems, epitaphs and Church inscriptions (d. 480–90).

Edd.: C. Luetjohann (MGAuctAnt 8) 1887. P. Mohr, L 1895. Trans. by O. M Dalton, 2 vols., O 1915. W. B. Anderson 1: Poems and Letters. Book 1/2 (text and trans.), Lo 1936. — Mgg.: P. Allard, P 1910. E. C. Stevens, NY 1933. Klotz, PWK II, 2, 2230/8. — Studies: Martin, BJ 221, 133/6. A. Coville, *Rech. sur l'hist. de Lyon du 5ᵉ s. au 9ᵉ*, 1928, 33/75 (episc. consecr.: 471/2). Cesareo 1928 (v. supra § 96, 1). Helm 1931 (supra § 87 before 1). P. Henry 1934 (supra § 81, 6), 199/202. K. A. Moosberg, *Stud. Sidon. crit. et semasiol.*, Up 1934. J. Champomier, *Esquisse pour un portrait de S. A.*, 1938. H. Rutherford, *S. A.*, Clerm.-Ferr. 1938. A. Loyen, *Rech. hist. s. les panégyr. de S. A.*, 1942; *S. A. et l'esprit précieux en Gaule . . .*, 1943. Faral, Misc. Mercati I, 567/80 (techn. litt.). Bardy, DTC 14, 2, 2033/5. N. K. Chadwick, *Poetry and Letters in Early Christ. Gaul*, Lund 1955.

3. Dracontius, Blossius Aemilius, a lawyer in Carthage, is one of the bestknown, truly lyrical poets of the later age. He was imprisoned by King Guntamund (484–86) because of a poem that was probably dedicated to the Byzantine Emperor. During the time of these sufferings he composed the following: *Satisfactio* (158 distichs), a confession of guilt before God and the king with the request for pardon, and three books *De laudibus Dei* (2327 hexameters), his most mature work, a praise of God, the Creator of the world which he keeps in being. The third book exhorts to love God in return and to trust in him.

In the ten poems of the collection *Romulea (= Carmina Romana)* he treats pagan subjects. The *Orestis tragoedia* which also belongs to him has been preserved anonymously.

Edd.: F. Vollmer (MGAuctAnt 14) 1905 and L 1914. St. Margaret, *D.i Satisfactio*, Philad. 1936 (text, trans., comm.). — Vollmer, PWK 5, 1635/44. Weyman 1926 (supra § 87 before 1), 142/60. Hudson-Williams, CQ 1947, 95/108. G. Vittorio, *D., Orestis tragoed.* (Ital. trans.), Ca 1948. S. Gennaro, *D., Satisfactio* (Ital.

trans.), Ca 1948. E. Rapisarda, *D., Orest. trag.* (trans. and comm.), Ca 1948; Orph. 2, 1955, 1/9 *(D., Poeta della misericordia divina)*. Arena, MiscStLCA 3, 1951, 110/23 *(Reposiano e D.)*. Collins, SE 1952, 185/8 (text. crit. on *Satisfactio*). Stern, REG 1952, 372/82 (D. infl. by *De mensibus* in *Anthologia Palatina*). Corsaro, MiscSTLCA 1954, 110/26 (D. and Milton). Bailey, VC 1955, 178/83 (text. crit. on *Romulea*). Langlois, RACh 4 (1958) 250/69.

4. An anonymous author probably living in Africa wrote *c.* 500 a *Carmen ad Flavium Felicem de resurrectione mortuorum et de iudicio Domini* (406 hexameters), is extant under the name of Cyprian.

Edd.: G. Hartel (CSEL 3, 3, 308/25) 1871. J. H. Waszink (FP, Suppl. 1) 1937. — Miltner - Zurunic, WSt 1930, 82/97. A. Eizenhoefer, *Die Prosodie des Carm. ad Flav.*, thesis Hei 1942.

5. Following Cavallin, we may identify the controversial personality of one Rusticus Helpidius most probably with Rusticus Helpidius Domnulus who lived in the second half of the fifth century and belonged to the circle of the poet Sidonius Apollinaris (supra n. 2). He probably died in 501–2 as Bishop of Lyons. The following are preserved under his name: A *Carmen de Christi Jesu beneficiis* (149 hexameters) showing unusual poetic ability and twenty-four three line *Epigrammata* (tristichs) on O.T. and N.T. subjects meant to serve the explanation of pictures (cf. the *Dittochaeon* of Prudentius, supra § 87, 6).

Text: ML 62, 543/8. *Carmen* ed. W. Brandes, Progr. Bruns. 1890, and D. H. Groen (with trans. and comm.), Groningen 1942. — F. Corsaro, MiscStLCA 3, 1951, 7/44 and Elpidio Rustico, Ca 1955 (R. identified with the deacon and physician at the court of Theoderic the Gt.). Cavallin, SE 1955, 49/66 (Prosopographic matters). Alfonsi, VC 1956, 33/42 (H. infl. by Boeth. *Consol.*); RFC 1956, 173/8 (H. dependent on Claudianus, *De salvatore*). Waszinsk, VC 1956, 243/6 (in support of thesis by C.).

6. Arator, a protégé of Ennodius (supra § 96, 1), was a Roman subdeacon who dedicated to Pope Vigilius (544) an *Epos de actibus apostolorum* (2336 hexameters) full of the most far-fetched interpretations of Acts. The author was allowed to read his work to an audience in the Roman church of S. Petri ad vincula. He also wrote three epistles in distichs addressed to benefactors (one to Pope Vigilius).

Edd.: ML 68, 63/252. P. McKinley, *De Act. Apost.* (CSEL 72, 1951). — A. Ansorge, *De A. vet. poetarum lat. imitatore,* 1914. Cuzzi, RendIstLomb 69, 1936, 241/7 (3 cod. Ambrosiani). McKinley, *A., Codices Cantab.,* 1942; HarvStClassPhil 54, 1943, 93/115 (Studies in A. II). Lowe - McKinley, Sp 1944, 351/9 (New fragm.). Anastasi, MiscStLCA 1, 1947, 145/52 (on biogr.). McKinley, Sc 6, 1952, 151/6 (Lat. comm. on A.). Hudson - Williams, VC 1953, 89/97 (text and interpret. of A.). Eizenhoefer, RBn 1953, 329/33 (A. I 338/69 cited in the *Contestatio* I of the Mone-Masses). Waszink, VC 1954, 87/92 (on ed. of McKinley).

7. Venantius Fortunatus, b. *c.* 530 near Treviso in Venetia, died soon after 600, studied at Ravenna. In 567 he went to Tours on a pilgrimage to the tomb of St. Martin whom he wanted to thank for a cure of an eye disease. Shortly afterwards he settled at Poitiers, where he came to know two nuns, St. Radegundis and her foster daughter Agnes. The two pious women persuaded him to have himself ordained priest, and he became the chaplain of their convent. Towards the end of the sixth century he was elected Bishop of Poitiers. His fame as a poet and his pleasantly cheerful disposition brought him into contact with all the intellectually and spiritually important men of Gaul. He was a particular friend of Bishop Gregory of Tours.

Fortunatus was a very gifted poet of exceptional formal skill, trained in the school of the classical Latin poets, especially Virgil. He displayed his many-sided talent in more than 300 poems. Though these belong to antiquity as regards form, his emotional and cultural make-up bears a medieval imprint. Most of the products of his smooth-flowing Muse are occasional poems in elegiac distichs. Places and districts he visited, spiritual and secular celebrities who favoured him, his hosts and the meals he enjoyed, in short all his experiences were turned into poetry. Besides much that is second-hand, his verse shows nevertheless a true lyrical talent: ecstatic dreams and enjoyment, vivid descriptions of nature are its subjects. We find in his poems the first poetic view of nature penetrated by religious Christian feeling; cf. e.g. the Easter hymn (III 9) where the awakening of nature in spring is interpreted as the joy of the resurrection; cf. also IX 3.

a. His *Carmina miscellanea* in eleven books contain hymns, elegies, panegyrics, epigrams, epitaphs and diverse occasional poems. We would single out the following: (α) his hymns in praise of the holy Cross, written on the occasion of the Byzantine Emperor Justinus II's gift to Radegundis of a particle of the Cross; among them are the famous Passion hymns *Pange lingua* and *Vexilla regis* used in the Roman Breviary. (β) *De navigio suo* (10, 9), an attractive description (82 lines) of a trip on the Moselle from Metz to Andernach; it is a companion piece of the *Mosella* of Ausonius (supra § 87, 5). The collection of poems also contains several letters and two short treatises in prose: an *Expositio orationis dominicae* (10, 1) and an *Expositio symboli* (11, 1), which are dependent on Rufinus (supra § 85, 2b).

b. The following have been preserved outside the collection of hymns: a Marian hymn *Quem terra, pontus, aethera* which has also been included in the Breviary and a fairly long poem *In laudem s. Mariae*. *De excidio Thoringiae* (172 lines) is a touching lament on the extinction of the royal house of Thuringia and at the same time a monument of his friendship with Radegundis. The epic poem *De vita s. Martini* divided into four books (2244 hexameters) follows closely the writings of Sulpicius Severus and Paulinus of Périgueux (supra § 49, II 4, § 99, 1). Apart from these Venantius wrote seven saints' lives in prose, among them a *Vita s. Hilarii* (of Poitiers), *s. Germani* (Paris) and *s. Radegundis*.

Edd.: ML 88. F. Leo et B. Krusch (MGAuctAnt 4) 1881/5. W. Levison and B. Krusch, MGSS rer. Merov. 7, 1919/20, 205/24, 337/428. — Mgg. and Studies: C. Nisard, P 1890. W. Meyer, GAG 1901, n. 5. R. Koebner, L 1915. D. Tardi, P 1927. Leclercq, DAL 5, 1882/97. Martin, BJ 221, 136/40. G. M. Dreves, *Hymnol. Studien zu V. F. u. Rab. Maurus,* 1908. Ganzenmueller, ArchKulturgesch 12, 1916, 200/3 (feeling for nature). Radò, EL 1928, 58/65 (the 1st metrical Mass [ed. F. J. Mone] composed by V. F.; v. supra n. 6: Eizenhoefer). F. Dagianti, *Studio sintattico della opera poetica di V. F.,* Veroli 1921. Gougaud, La vie et les arts liturg. 11, 1924/5, 252/62 *(Salve festa dies)*. Chase 1932 (supra § 49 II 4). S. Blomgren, *Studia Fortunatiana,* Up 1, 1933 (text. crit.); 2, 1934 (*In laudem s. Mariae* is genuine). Amatucci, StU 360/71 (criteria of authenticity). F. S. Kopp, *Ein neues Elogium v. V. F.,* 1938. Messenger, TP 1947, 208/22 (50 different transs. of *Salve festa dies*). Agrain, REL 1948, 99/101 (text. crit.). M. Laso, QuadEstGallegos 1949, n. 14, 349/66 (on *Lib. s. Jacobi*). Blomgren, Er 1950, 150/56 (Statius, Lucan. and Claudian in V. F.). A. F. Memoli, *Il ritmo prosaico in V. F.,* Morinello 1952. Gaiffier, AB 1952, 262/84 (cult). *Ét. mérovingiennes. Actes des Journées de Poitiers 1952,* 1953 (also on F. and Radegundis). Chadwick 1955 (supra n. 2).

CHAPTER TWO

Greek Authors

§ 100. PSEUDO-DIONYSIUS THE AREOPAGITE

FOUR Works. Four long treatises, all dedicated to his disciple Timothy, and eleven short letters are extant under the name of Dionysius the Areopagite.

1. *De divinis nominibus* (13 chs.) treats of the divine names occurring in the Bible and explains from these the nature and properties of God (EP 2280/5; EA 1039/43).

2. *De mystica theologia* (5 chs.), on the mystic union of the soul with God, which takes place in a state of complete passivity; the soul apprehends God directly in ecstatic visions (EA 1054/9).

3. *De caelesti hierarchia* (15 chs.), on the realm of the heavenly spirits, their nature, properties and division into three triads of three choirs each (EA 1044f.).

4. *De ecclesiastica hierarchia* (7 chs.) treats of the Church as an image of the works of spirits. It, too, contains three triads: three holy sacraments: baptism, eucharist, confirmation; three priestly orders: bishops, priests, deacons; three orders subject to these: monks, lay Christians, imperfect members (catechumens, energumeni, penitents). As an appendix a description of the funeral rites follows in ch. 7 (EP 2286f.; EA 1046/53).

5. The following figure, among others, as recipients of the eleven letters: a monk Caius four times, the apostle John (ten), the bishops Titus (nine) and Polycarp (seven) once each. The letters supplement the teaching of the main writings and give practical pastoral precepts (EA 1060/5).

The author wants to be taken for St. Paul's convert, the Areopagite Dionysius (Acts 17: 34) (*Ep*. 7: 3; *Div. Nom*. 2, 11).

Hence he addresses his writings to apostles and disciples of apostles and asserts that he watched at Heliopolis the eclipse of the sun that took place at the death of Christ (*Ep*. 7, 2). He also alleges to have been present with Peter and James at the funeral of the Blessed Virgin Mary (*Div. Nom*. 3, 2). In fact the writings originated as late as the end of the fifth century. The author's thought is essentially influenced by neo-Platonism, the fundamental ideas of which he wanted to integrate with the Christian doctrines. His style is very strange and obscure; he indulged in neologisms and artificial constructions.

The first traces of these writings are to be found in the works of the Monophysite-minded Patriarch Severus of Antioch (512–18). When the Monophysites appealed to them at the religious colloquy of Constantinople in 532, they were rejected as spurious by Hypatius of Ephesus, the leader of the Catholic bishops. They were, however, already accepted as authentic by Leontius of Byzantium, Pope Gregory the Great and Sophronius of Jerusalem. All opposition quickly ceased after Maximus Confessor (d. 662) had allayed all misgivings by his orthodox interpretation of heretically-sounding passages. Abbot Hilduin of St. Denis (d. *c*. 844) circulated the legend that St. Paul's disciple was identical with the author of the Areopagitica and the martyr Dionysius of Paris (3rd cent.). The Middle Ages knew Pseudo-Dionysius through the Latin translation made by Scotus Erigena *c*. 850; his ideas had a profound influence on the philosophical and theological thought of the great Schoolmen.

The humanist Laurentius Valla (d. 1457) was the first to express doubts about the authenticity of the writings; he was soon followed by Erasmus and the Reformers. In the nineteenth century the authenticity was being increasingly denied; until, in 1895, J. Stiglmayr (HJB 1895, 253/73, 721/48) and H. Koch (TQ 1895, 353/420;

Phil 1895, 438/54; *Ps.-D. in seinen Beziehungen zum Neuplatonismus und Mysterienwesen*, 1900) though working independently, arrived at the same result: the Areopagitic writings cannot have originated before the end of the fifth century, because their author did not only use Plotinus (d. 270), but also reproduced, sometimes even verbatim, the neo-Platonist Proclus (d. 485). The investigations of Stiglmayr and Koch were later amplified by further research. The home of Pseudo-Dionysius can probably be taken to have been Syria, since in his liturgical comments he explains a Syriac rite (Hanssens, EL 1924, 283/92).

Stiglmayr contends that Severus of Antioch is the great unknown (Sch 1928, 1/27, 161/89) and he upholds his thesis (Sch 1932, 52, 67; BKV² II, 2, 169/72) despite the objections of J. Lebon (RHE 1930, 880/915; 1932, 296/313). R. Devreesse (AHD 1929, 159/67) wanted to date the writings before 450; G. Bardy and A. Puech (v. supra § 97, 7) adduced decisive reasons against him, Athenagoras, Ὁ γνήσιος συγγραφεὺς τῶν εἰς Διονύσιον τὸν Ἀ. ἀποδιδομένων συγγραμμάτων, At 1932; EPh 1933, 9/51; 1934, 161/93, 443/62, 521/40 (offprint Alex. 1934); Θ 1936, opposing Lebon, held the wholly unacceptable view that the Pseudo-Areopagite is to be identified with Dionysius the Great of Alexandria; cf. EO 1932, 458/65; BNJ 9, 1933, 380/4. The idea that Ps.-D. should be sought in the milieu of Basil the Great will be found equally unacceptable; thus C. Pera, RSPT 1936, 5/75, and Mazzantini, RFN 1937, 411/21; against this Cavallera, RAM 1936, 90/5. v. Ivánka, Sch 1940, 386/99 (cf. also BZ 19) suggests the second half of the fourth century as the date because of similarities with the thought of Gregory of Nyssa. Id. in: *Actes VIe Congr. Intern. d'Ét. Byz.* (P 1948), 1, 1950, 239f. (directed against neo-Plat. propaganda of Emp. Julian). Elorduy, EE 1944, 501/57 even asserts that the *Corpus Dionysiacum,* to which should be added several other writings, should be assigned to Ammonius Saccas. Tavar, *Emerita* 16, 1948, 277/81 (against Elorduy); Elorduy,

Pensamiento 9, 1953, 481/9 (The probl. of evil in Proclus and Ps.-A.). G. Della Volpe, *La dottr. del Areop. e i suoi presuppositi neoplatonici,* R 1941. Peter the Iberian is proposed as an author by Honigmann 1952 (v. § 46, 13d), as before him by a Russian scholar in 1942 and 1944 (cf. BZ 1952, 453); cf. against this Hausherr, OCP 1953, 247/60 (Dion. lived in the milieu suggested by Honigmann). Roques, RHR 49, 1954, 69/98; Engberding, OC 38, 1954, 68/95 and Grumel, REB 1955, 21/49. Engberding, PhJB 1956, 218/27.

Edd.: MG 3/4. Quasten (FP 7) 1937, 275/328 (*Eccl. H.* 2/4). — Transs.: J. Stiglmayr (BKV² 2, II, 2) 1911, 1933. P. Chevallier, *Dionysiaca. Recueil donnant l'ensemble des traductions lat. des ouvrages attr. au D. de l'A.,* 2 vols., 1937/50; cf. RHE, 1950, 234/40. A. v. d. Daele, *Indices Ps.-Dionysiani,* Lou 1941. Siegmund 1948, 182/9. Engl., W. Watts (*Theol. myst.; Epp.* 1 and 5) 1944; French, M. de Gandillac, P 1943; Germ., Trisch, *Cael. and eccl. hier.,* Mn 1955. J. Wytzes, *Hier. eccl.* (Dutch), A 1953. Graf I, 268/71. E. Bulhak, *Authenticité des œuvres de s. D. l'A.* (a curiosity!). Peradze, E 1937, 3/35 *(Ep. ad Timoth.)*. Cumont, Isis 26, 1936/7, 8/12 (*Ep.* 11; MG 3, 1119/22). — Stephanou, EO 1932, 446/69 (lit. since 1914). Roques, DS 2, 1952, 1885/1911 *(contempl., extase et ténèbre);* DS 3, 1954, 245/429 (state of the probl., writings and doctrine; infl. in E. and W.). Hornus, RHP 1955, 404/48 *(recherches récentes)*. Turolla, So 1956, 46/65 (introduction to D. A.). Roques, RAC 3, 1075/1121. Heil-Roques-de Gandillac, SCh 58, 1958 *(cael. hier.)*.

Influence: J. Durantel, *St. Thomas et le Ps.-D.,* 1919. Drexl, BJ 230, 266/70. K. Hansmann, *Ein neuentdeckter Kommentar zum Jo.-Ev.,* 1930. G. Théry, AL 1931, 185/280 (Scotus Eriug.); *Ét. Dionysiennes. Hilduin traducteur de D.,* P 1932. Thomson, JTS 1936, 137/40 (MS of Hilduin's trans.). Hausherr, OCP 1936, 484/90 (doubts in Middle Ages). Woroniecki, CT 1936, 25/40 (D. in Thomism). Buchner, HJB 1936, 441/80; 1937, 31/60; 1938, 55/96, 361/409 (Areopag. of Hilduin). G. Théry, *Ét. Dionys.,* II: *éd. de la trad. de Hilduin,* 1938; AHD 11, 1938, 87/132 (MSS in Austria). Thomson, RBn 1938, 246/53 (Lat. trans. of *Eccl. Hier.*). L. Baur, *N. Cusanus u. Ps.-D.* (SbHei 1940/1 n. 4), 1941. Gamba, Aev 1942, 251/71 (Lat. comm. on *Myst. Theol.*); ed. of Grosseteste's comm. on *Myst. Theol.,* Mi 1942. Vos de Wael, *De myst. Theol.* (in Dion. the Carthus.), N 1942. A. Combes, *Jean Gerson, commentateur dionysien;* cf. RHR 127, 1944, 145/50. J. Overbeck, *Der Einfl. des Ps.-D. auf d. Sakramenten- u. Kirchenl. des hl. Albert d. Gr.,* thesis Bonn 1948. v. Ivánka, RSR 1949, 5/24 *(La signification du Corp. Aréop.)*. Loenertz, AB 1950, 94/107 (Dion. in Mich. Syncellus); AB 1951, 217/37 (the Paris legend). Sherwood, SE 1952, 174/84 (Syr. transs.). Weisweiler, RTA 1952, 26/47 (D. in Scotus Erig. and Hugh of St. Victor); Sch 1952, 321/43 (D. in Hugh of St. Victor). H. F. Dondaine, RTA, 311/5 (MS of a comm. on the first 5 letters by Thomas Gallus); *Corp. Dion. de l'Univ. de Paris au 13ᵉ s.,* R 1953. E. Turolla, *Dion. Areop. Le opere. Versione e interpretazione,* Padua 1956.

Points of Doctrine

1. God and the world. The essence of God, who is the cause of all things, can be defined neither by affirmative nor by negative predicates. God is the one (ἕν) from which all things proceed (πρόδρομος) in order later to return to it (ἐπιστροφή). The whole universe appears to the Areopagite as an organic whole; it is a ladder reaching to heaven, the highest rung of which, the angelic choir of the three highest orders, still penetrates into the darkness surrounding God, while the lowest steps reach down into the realm of irrational and lifeless being. The fullness of the divine light steadily decreases in passing through all the intermediary steps.

2. Christology. Dionysius speaks of a unique divine-human activity (μία θεανδρικὴ ἐνέργεια) in Christ (*Ep.* 4; EP 2279). The followers of Severus of Antioch and the Monothelites appealed to this formula, which was later (649 and 680–1) rejected by the Church. *Div. Nom.* 2, 9 speaks of a "formation of God" (θεοπλαστία) in Jesus that sounds Monophysite.

3. Angelology. While most of the older Fathers, especially in the West, were of the opinion that the angels have an ethereal body, the Areopagite held them to be pure, immaterial spirits, and the later Fathers such as Pope Gregory the Great and John of Damascus followed his view. Cyril of Jerusalem (*Cat.* 23, 6; EP 849) and the Apostolic Constitutions (8, 12, 8) already name nine choirs of angels, though not yet divided into three triads. The earlier Fathers were still uncertain whether the various terms used in the Bible expressed differences among the angels or not. The Areopagite taught that the highest triad of angels serves only God and has no relations with men. Later this was also asserted by Thomas Aquinas and Suarez, who therefore placed the angels Michael, Gabriel and Raphael, who had been sent to men, in the second lowest order of the archangels; the majority of theologians, how-

ever, continued to hold the opinion that all the angelic choirs can be sent to serve men.

4. Penance. *Ep.* 8, addressed to a monk Demophilus, attests the old opposition between pneumatic monasticism and hierarchical priesthood. The monk had claimed for himself the administration of the sacrament of penance. For this he is sharply rebuked: according to the order instituted by God the power of absolution belongs only to the priests. Dionysius thought, however, like Origen and many later theologians down to Abelard in the twelfth century (8, 2), that a sinful priest could not "give light", i.e. mediate the grace of God.

5. The Sacrament of confirmation (μύρον) is, according to Dionysius, on a par with the eucharist (*Eccl. Hier.* 4, 1). It is meant to give the baptized the Holy Spirit (4, 3, 11). It follows from the words of the Areopagite that the consecration of the holy oils, the altars and the priests is reserved to the bishop (5, 5).

H. Fuchs, *Augustin u. d. antike Friedensgedanke,* 1926, 126/38 *(Div. nom.* 11). Sartori, Did 1927 F. 2, 35/125; 3, 1/53 (Doctr. of God). Maric, SoS 1932, 105/73 (Christol.); RevSR 1933, 258/63. Quadri, RivInternFilosDir 1937, 430/76 *(L'ontologia del molteplice).* Lossky, RSPT 1939, 204/21 (neg. theol.). A. v. d. Daele, BiNJ 1940, 17/72, 331/94 (philos. contents). Roques, RAM 1947, 142/70 (purification of intelligence). Oppenheim, Misc. Mohlberg 1, 259/82 (monastic consecration and baptismal rite). Schepens, EL 1949, 357/75 (liturgy). V. Lossky, *Essai sur la théol. myst. de l'Égl. de l'Orient,* P 1944. Hornus, RHP 1947, 37/63 *(Ps.-D. l'A. et la myst. chrét.).* O. Semmelroth, *Das ausstrahlende u. emporziehende Licht. Die Theol. des Ps.-D. Ar.,* thesis Bonn 1947; Sch 1949, 367/79 (redemption); ibid. 1950, 209/34 (God's super-essential unity); Sch 1950, 389/403 (God's united multiplicity); ibid. 1952, 1/11 (symbol. theol.); Sch 1953, 481/503 (God's emanating light); ibid. 1953, 24/52 (ascent of creatures). S. Scimé, *L'assoluto nello Ps.-Dion.,* Messina 1950; *Studi sul Neoplat. Filos. e Teologia nello ps.-Dion.,* Messina 1950; *Studi sul Neoplat. Filos. e Teologia nello ps.-D.,* ibid. 1953. J. Gross, ZRGG 1952, 32/42 (original sin). Roques, RAM 1949, 200/12 (Notion de théol.); AHD 1949, 183/222; 18, 1950/1, 5/44 (notion of hierarchy); BLE 1951, 44/56 (conditions of contempl.); RAM 1954, 268/74 (theol. methods); *L'univers dion. Structure hiérarch. du monde sel. le Ps.-D.,* 1954. DHG 14, 266/90. W. Voelker, *Kontempl. u. Ekstase bei Ps.-D. Areop.,* Wiesbaden 1958. A. Vanneste, *Le mystère de dieu,* Bruges 1959 (Mysticism). Riedinger, BZ 1959, 276/96 (Ps. Dion. = Petrus Fullo, Patriarch of Antioch., d. 488).

§ 101. MONOPHYSITE THEOLOGIANS OF THE SIXTH CENTURY

1. Severus, 512–18 Patriarch of Antioch, was deposed by the Emperor Justin I for his monophysitism and henceforth lived at Alexandria (d. 538). On his relation to Pseudo-Dionysius v. supra § 100. Since 522 he opposed Bishop Julian of Halicarnassus who, like himself, had been living in exile at Alexandria since 518, for teaching the incorruptibility (ἀφθαρσία) of the body of Christ. It can be gathered, especially from his large work *Against the Godless Grammarian*, that, in contrast to Eutyches and Julian, Severus was much nearer to the teaching of the Council of Chalcedon than his violent polemics against the Council and the Tome of Leo the Great would lead one to think. He confesses with the Council that Christ is one, perfect in his Godhead and perfect in his Manhood, and that the difference of the natures is not abolished by their union. Severus opposes solely the formulation of the Council that Christ is one and the same in two natures; this he holds to be Nestorianism, for in Christology "in two natures" means the same as "in two persons". In opposition to this he confesses that "out of two natures, the Godhead and the Manhood, there shows itself one Emmanuel and one incarnate nature of the God-Logos" (II 6). It may be affirmed with Lebon, that Severus of Antioch and the theologians near to him intended to teach nothing other than what Cyril of Alexandria had expressed imperfectly in his formula of μία φύσις and in his twelve anathematisms before the symbol of union in 433.

The voluminous literary remains of Severus are preserved almost solely in a Syriac translation only a small part of which has so far been printed.

a. Dogmatic-polemical treatises: *Philalethes,* a polemical treatise written between 509 and 511 against an anonymous work which defended the doctrine of Chalcedon: ed. A. Sanda, Beyrouth 1928; a better ed. by R. Hespel (CSCO 133 134), 1952. His principal work, containing about 1250 citations from the Fathers, is the *Liber contra impium Grammaticum* ed. J. Lebon (CSCO 93/94 101/02 111/12, 1929/38; new impress. 1952; cf. TLZ 1940, 130/6). J. Lebon, ibid. 119/20 (*Orat. ad Nephalium, Severi ac Sergii Grammatici epp. mutuae*), 1949. R. Hespel, *Le florilège cyrillien réfuté par S. d.'A.,* Lou 1955. A. Sanda edited part of the controversial writings against Julian of Halicarnassus: *Severi Antiiulianistica,* Beyrouth 1931. An epistle against Julian, ed. Draguet, Mu 1927, 75/92; two short treatises against Julian written by disciples of Severus, ibid. 1931, 255/317. Garitte, Mu 1952, 185/98 (*Severi ep. ad Soterichum;* Copt. fragm.).

b. Of 125 homilies, delivered between 512–18 the following have so far been edited in the Syriac translation of Jacob of Edessa (*c.* 700): n. 1 in OC 2, 1902, 265ff.; n. 109 and 123 in I. E. Rahmani, *Stud. syriaca* 4, 1909; n. 52–125 in PO 4, 1; 8, 2; 12, 1; 16, 5; 20, 2; 22, 2; 23, 1; 25, 1, 4; 26, 3 (1906/56). F. Nau, ROC 7, 1929/30, 3/30 (hom. 89 and 94, partly Greek). Hom. 77 in PO 16, 5 (Gr.). Fragm. graeca in A. Mai, *SS vet. nova Coll.* 9, 725/41 and *Spicil. Roman.* 10, 202/5. Lat. trans.: n. 86 100 110 114 in Mai, *Coll.* 9, 742/58 and n. 67 in Mai, *Spicil. Roman.* 10, 212/20.

c. Of the approximately 4000 letters divided into twenty-three books E. W. Brooks ed. *The Sixth Book of the Select Letters of Severus,* 2 vols., Lo 1902/4 (123 letters), 118 more letters in PO 12, 2 and 14, 1 (1915/9).

d. Liturgical Writings. The *Octoechos,* still in use in the Greek Church, contains many hymns written by Severus; he wrote the oldest Marian prayer common to East and West, *Sub tuum praesidium.* Hymns ed. in PO 6, 1; 7, 5 (1910/11). An *Anaphora,* too, bears his name.

H. W. Codrington, *Ed. S.i Anaphora,* R 1939; cf. JTS 1938, 141/50. M.-A.

Kugener, PO 2, 1 and 3 (1902/4): *Vitae Severi,* Syr. — J. Lebon, *Le monophysitisme Sévérien,* Lou 1909. J. Maspéro, *Hist. des patriarches d'Alexandrie (518–616),* 1923. Jugie, *Theol. dogm.* 1935 (supra § 72, 1), 422ff., 433/7 and freq. Opitz, 1935, 168/79 (Athanasius). K. Weber, *Oktoechos-Forsch.,* L 1937. E. Schwartz, *Publizist. Sammlgn. z. acacian. Schisma,* 1934, 238/48 (*Vita* till 512). Graf I, 418/20. Bardy, DCT 14, 1988/2000, and Mémorial L. Petit 1948, 15/31 *(textes patrist.).* Lantschoot, Mu 1946, 469/77 *(Lettre à Théognoste).* Lebon, Mu 1946, 513/28 (letter to Dioscurus of Antioch). Lebon in: Grillmeier-Bacht I, 581/602 (Counc. of Chalc. acc. to Monophys. historians). O'Leary, Aegyptus 32, 1952 (1953), 425/36 (S. in Egypt). Engberding, OC 37, 1953, 132/4 (on chronol. of his *Vita*).

2. Bishop Julian of Halicarnassus, the opponent of Severus (v. n. 1), the chief of the Julianists (*Aphthartodocetae* or Phantasiasts). During the controversy with Severus he wrote four treatises, of which only the 154 fragments collected by Draguet have been preserved. Three new letters have been edited by A. Šanda, *Severi Antiiulianistica,* in 1931. — On a commentary on Job wrongly attributed to Julian v. supra § 53, 2.

R. Draguet, DTC 8, 1931/40; *J. d'H. et sa controverse avec Sévère d'A.,* Lou 1924. Against Draguet's milder interpretation of Julian's teaching: M. Jugie, EO 1925, 129/62, 256/85 and *Theol. dogmatica* 1935 (supra § 72, 1) 435/7; against this Draguet, RHE 1937, 92/5. On a Creed cf. Akinian-Casey, HTR 1931, 143ff.; BZ 1932, 183f. Draguet, Mu 1941, 59/89 (ed. an anti-Julian. work of the 2nd half of the 6th cent.), and ibid. 1941, 91/106 (on hist. of later Julianites). H. Grondijs, *L'iconographie byz. du crucifié mort sur la croix,* 1941 (J.'s Christology).

3. John Philoponus (= lover of work), who lived in Alexandria and was probably a Christian from his youth (not converted as late as *c.* 520, cf. E. Evrard) wrote several grammatical works and a number of commentaries on Aristotle as well as theological treatises. He was anxious to reconcile the teaching of the Church with Aristotelianism (d. soon after 565).

The following theological writings have been preserved: *De aeternitate mundi* opposes the teaching of the neo-Platonist Proclus (ed. H. Rabe, L 1899); *De opificio mundi* (ed. G. Reinhardt, L 1897) is a commentary on the Biblical account of creation; *De paschate* (ed. C. Walter, L 1899).

His principal dogmatic work, *The Umpire* (Διαιτητής, ed. A. Šanda, *Opuscula monophysitica J. Philoponi,* Beyrouth 1930), which is preserved complete only in a Syriac translation, represents tritheism, admitting only a notional unity, not a unity of nature of the three Persons. In his Christology he follows Severus of Antioch. Six antitritheistic works were ed. by G. Furlani in PO 14, 4, 1920.

Studies: W. Kroll, PWK 9, 1764/95. Bardy, DTC 8, 831/9. T. Hermann, ZNTW 1930, 209/64 (monophys.). Jugie, EO 1934, 187/9 (against Papal primacy). M. de Corte, Liège 1934; cf. RTABull 2 n. 800. Koster, Mn 1931, 132/64 (accent). Devreesse, RB 1936, 364/73 (Patristic texts in *De op. mundi*). P. Henry, *États du Texte de Plotin,* 1938, 271/7 *(aet. mundi)*. Mansion, *Mél. A. Pelzer,* 1947, 525/46 *(Le texte du De intellectu)*. E. Evrard, BullAcadBelgClLett 5th Ser. 39, 1953 *(Les convictions rel. de J. P. et la date de son comm. aux Météoroliques.)* Reiner, Her 82, 1954, 480/2 (Gr. MS of comm. on Metaphys.). Saffrey, REG 1954, 396/410 (The Christ. J. P. and the Alex. school).

4. Stephen Gobarus, who wrote in Egypt or Syria, probably under Justin II (565–78), was another tritheist. According to Photius, Bibl. cod. 232, he treated diverse theological questions in fifty-two chapters and an appendix, according to the method of *Sic et non,* as was later done also by Abelard.

Harnack, HTR 1923, 205/34. Bardy, REB 1947, 5/30 (Florileg.); cf. REB 7, 1949/50, 51f.

§ 102. ANTI-MONOPHYSITE THEOLOGIANS OF THE SIXTH CENTURY

1. The grammarian John of Caesarea wrote an Apology of the Chalcedonense between 514 and 518. In 519 Severus of Antioch (§ 101, 1a) attacked this work in a large treatise, in which the indefatigable opponent of the decision of Chalcedon included forty-four long passages from John's Apology. Since J. Lebon edited this controversial work *Contra impium Grammaticum,* John's Christology can be clearly understood. He may be called the first important representative of the so-called neo-Chalcedonian Christology. His work aimed at a further clarification of the differences that still existed between the terminology of Cyril and that of the Antioch-

enes, though these had been authoritatively settled by the Council of 451. He wanted especially to emphasize certain elements of Cyril's theology. Thus he defended the formula *Unus ex Trinitate* (§ 72, 3) and even Cyril's Anathematisms. At the same time, however, he also wanted to show that the formula of union of 433 (§ 56) signed by Cyril, as well as the Tome of Leo the Great and the doctrine of Chalcedon, if rightly synthesized, will safeguard the whole truth. He is the first to use in his Christology the terminology the Cappadocians applied to the Trinity, which clearly distinguishes οὐσία from ὑπόστασις, and he emphasized hat the humanity of Christ had never for a moment existed alone and independent of the divinity. Another improvement was the formula coined by him of the two natures united by an hypostatic union in one *hypostasis.*

Forty-four fragms. in Lebon, *C. imp. Grammaticum,* 3 vols., 1929/38 CSCO 93 101 111 (Syriac); also 3 Greek fragms. in Eulogius of Alex. (580/604) ed. C. Moeller, RHE 1951, 683/8. — R. Draguet, *Julien d'Halicarnasse,* Lou 1924, 62/73 (J. of C. is not the anonymous opponent attacked by Sev. of Ant. in his *Philalethes*). Moeller, RHE 40, 1944/5, 122/7 and in Grillmeier - Bacht I, 672/4. Richard, MSR 1946, 156/61 *(Le néochalcédonisme)* and in Grillmeier - Bacht I, 736.

2. John of Scythopolis in Galilee, a contemporary of the John discussed in n. 1, belongs to the increasingly influential group of neo-Chalcedonian theologians. Only fragments of his rather extensive literary output are extant. He published his treatise against the Aposchites (i.e. against Eutyches, Dioscurus and his followers) already before 512. About the same time he, like his namesake of Caesarea, wrote a detailed Apologia of the Council of Chalcedon, with which Severus of Antioch also intended to deal in his work *Contra impium Grammaticum;* but he did not succeed in securing a copy of it. John also distinguished himself as a discerning critic of the forgeries circulated by the followers of Apollinaris of Laodicea (§ 65). Finally he wrote, after 532, the first commentary on the writings of Ps.-Dionysius, the greater part of which Maximus Confessor incorporated in his Scholia on

the Areopagitica. Beside Severus of Antioch he was probably the greatest expert on the literature and culture of antiquity in his time.

Citations from the eighth book against Severus in the Acts of the Council of 533 (Mansi 10, 1107; 11, 737/40) and in the *Doctrina Patrum* ed. F. Diekamp, 1907, 85f. The Scholia on the *Areopagitica* by Max. Conf. in MG 4; cf. U. v. Balthasar, Sch 1940, 16/38. Moeller in Grillmeier – Bacht I, 644, 674/6 and frequently.

3. Leontius of Byzantium. Nothing definite is known about the life of this author who has so far been wrongly considered the probably most important theologian in the first half of the sixth century. The problems connected with his literary remains, too, are by no means completely cleared up even today. We know from his own testimony *(C. Nest. et Eut. III prooem.)* that he lived in the company of Nestorians in his youth and was brought back to orthodoxy only by a gracious act of providence.

F. Loofs (1887) attempted to give more body and colour to the *Vita* of this elusive personality by identifying him with other bearers of the same name. Today, however, this attempt must be held to have failed, even though until now Loofs' assumptions had been almost universally accepted. Above all, it is not true that the theologian Leontius is identical with the Scythian monk Leontius known through the Theopaschite controversy (cf. § 96, 4). Nor was he, as has usually been assumed, the theological adviser of the Emperor Justinian who, through Theodore Ascidas, incited the theologically-minded monarch to attack the *Three Chapters*. Following Richard, he is to be identified with the Origenist Leontius Eremita, known from the *Vita Sabae* of Cyril of Scythopolis. Leontius was a skilled controversialist equally well grounded in Aristotelian logic and neo-Platonist psychology. He was a successful opponent especially of contemporary Monophysitism (Severians, Julianites). In Christology he was a strict adherent of the definition of Chalcedon (Moeller in: Grillmeier-Bacht I, 662).

a. His principal work is the *Libri III adversus Nestorianos et Eutychianos*, a fine testimony to his acumen and patristic learning. It was written shortly before his death (543–4) by way of a cautious objection to the anti-Origenist edict (543).

Book I shows that despite their mutually opposed teaching Nestorius and Eutyches start from the same false premises. Book II reproduces a disputation between an orthodox Christian and an aphthartodocetist. Book III is directed against the Nestorian heresy, especially against the errors he ascribes to Theodore of Mopsuestia. Each of these three books was written on a different occasion.

b. Two shorter works against Severus of Antioch: *Solutio argumentorum Severi* and *Triginta capita adv. Severum*. The probably spurious little treatise *Adversus fraudes Apollinistarum* (MG 86, 2, 1947/76) exposes as forgeries several patristic citations manufactured in heretical circles. It is an achievement of source criticism as praiseworthy as it was rare in those days. The treatise *De sectis* (MG 86, 1, 1193/1268), also published under Leontius' name, was written only between 581 and 607. It is not certain if Theodore of Raithu (§ 102, 5) was its author (Diekamp, AP 176/8). Two further works which, according to Loofs, are extant in later versions, do not belong to him but to Leontius of Jerusalem, an author who has so far been neglected. He probably attended the religious discussion with the Severians (probably 532) and the Synod of Constantinople (536). (*Adv. Nestorianos:* MG 86, 1399/1769; *Contra Monophysitas:* ibid. 1769/1901). This Leontius was a neo-Chalcedonian, i.e. he treated the Christological question in close relation to the terminology of Cyril and of the Monophysites. He wrote a treatise before 433. Cf. *Adv. Nest.* 1, 20 (MG 86, 1, 1485).

Christology. The Monophysites alleged that a nature could only subsist as its own hypostasis, hence if there were two natures in Christ, there would have to be also two hypostases or persons in him. Against them Leontius showed that the human nature of Christ is not itself an hypostasis, because the notion of hypostasis includes not only individuality but also subsistence, i.e. independent existence. Now a nature can have its subsistence in another hypostasis without thereby becoming an accident; it would then be ἐνυπόστατος, but not ἀνυπόστατος. Thus the human body is enhypostatized into the soul, and it is the same also with the human nature of Christ, which is ἐν τῷ λόγῳ ὑποστᾶσα. Even before Leontius the term ἐνυπόστατον had had its history in Christian theology. The notion (not the term) enhypostasis is taken from neo-Platonic philosophy. Leontius was the first to have given the mystery of the ἕνωσις καθ' ὑπόστασιν a short and pertinent formula in the term ἐνυπόστατος. On defects and obscurities in his notion of hypostasis cf. Moeller in: Grillmeier-Bacht I, 700f.

Edd.: MG 86, 1–2. — Mgg.: F. Loofs (TU 3, 1–2) 1887. W. Ruegamer 1994. V. Ermoni, P 1895. J. P. Junglas 1908. Grumel, DTC 9, 400/26. — Studies: Grumel, EO 1926, 393/406 and *Mél. P. Mandonnet* 2, 1930, 15/22 (Christol.). Devreesse, RevSR 1930, 545/76 *(Florilège de L.)*. Rees, HTR 1931, 111/9 (Christol.). Jugie, EO 1936, 257ff. *(Spir. S.)*. On *De sectis:* Cf. Diekamp, AP 1938, 176/8; Rees, JTS 1939, 346/60; Richard, RHE 1939, 695/723. On question of identifications cf. against Loofs: Altaner, TQ 1947, 147/65 (L. of B. and L. the Scyth. monk). Richard, RSPT 1938, 27/52 (L. et Pamphile); MSR 1944, 35/88 (L. de Jérus. et L. de Byz.); REB 1947, 31/66 (L. de B. Origenist). Rees, JTS 1940, 263/80 (Life of L. of B.). — Grumel, EO 1937, 385/97 *(Sotériol.)*. C. Martin, Byz 12, 1937, 361 (MG 59, 715/20 belongs to L.). — On L. of Jer. cf. Ehrhard, TU 51, 1938, 148 149 A. 1. Moeller, ETL 1951, 467/82 *(Textes monophys. de Léonce de Jér.)* and in: Grillmeier - Bacht I, 686f., 701/2 and freq. (Christol.). A. Theodoru, Θ 1955, 211/22, 421/35 and cont. (Christol.). Hammerschmidt, OstkSt 1955, 147/57 (Philos.-theol. concepts in L. of B., John Damasc. and Theod. Abu Qurra).

4. Hypatius, Bishop of Ephesus, was the trusted adviser of the Emperor Justinian during the eventful years 531–6. He was the spokesman of the Catholic bishops (SACO IV 2, 169/84) at the *Collatio cum Severianis* at Constantinople (probably 532). In 533

he travelled to Pope John II on behalf of the Emperor and obtained the papal recognition of the Theopaschite formula (*Coll. Avell., Ep.* 84; ed. Guenther 320/8). At the Synod of Constantinople (536) he was the spokesman of the bishops present (SACO III 178/80; d. after 537–8 and before 552).

Only small fragments have been preserved of his Συμμικτὰ ζητήματα (at least two books) in which he answers questions of Bishop Julian of Atramytion (Diekamp 127/9; On the veneration of images; perhaps also 151/3). 8 (or 94 respectively) fragments from *catenae* collected by Diekamp (129/51) allow us to assume that Hypatius wrote a Commentary on the Psalms and one on the twelve Minor Prophets. It is doubtful whether he also wrote a commentary on Luke. An inscription of thirty-five lines found during excavations at Ephesus in 1904 gives a decree of the bishop on the Christian duty of burial.

F. Diekamp, *Anal. Patrist.* 1938, 109/53 (biogr. matters and ed. of texts). On question of solution of the *catenae lemma* ὑπ cf. ibid. 249 and M. Richard, RHE 1939, 790. J. N. Bakhuizen van den Brink, *De oudchrist. monum. v. Ephesus,* 1923, 129/48 and ZNTW 1927, 213/9 (inscr.). Moeller in: Grillm.-Bacht I, 661f. (Christol.). Baynes, HTR 1951, 93/106 (on image veneration). Alexander, HTR 1952, 177/84 (images).

5. Theodore of Raithu, a priest monk in a monastery near Raithu on the S. W. coast of the Sinai peninsula, wrote, probably between 537 and 553, his *Praeparatio* (Προπαρασκευή), usually cited inexactly as *De incarnatione*. The eight chapters of the first part describe various heresies, from Manes to Severus of Antioch. The second part contains philosophical definitions important for Christology. On the treatise *De sectis* extant under the name of Leontius of Byzantium cf. § 102, 3b.

First. ed. of compl. *Praepar.* in F. Diekamp, *Anal. Patrist.* 1938, 173/222. MG 91, 1483/1504 (1st part). Grumel, EO 1928, 259/65 (Theodore of Pharan). Richard, DTC 15, 282/4. Moeller in: Grillm.-Bacht I, 685f. Elert, TLZ 1951, 671/6 (T. of Pharan = T. of Raithu); against this Moeller in Grillm.-Bacht I, 685f., 695 A 167. W. Elert, *Der Ausgang der altkirchl. Christologie,* B 1957 (Th. of Pharan).

6. Pamphilus. Under the wrong title *Panoplia dogmatica* A.

Mai published the treatise Κεφαλαίων διαφόρων ἤτοι ἐπαπορήσεων λύσις περὶ τῆς εἰς Χριστὸν εὐσεβείας as the work of an anonymous author. It examines Christological questions and opposes the view of Severus of Antioch and of Monophysite tritheism. The author is an otherwise unknown Pamphilus who is not identical with Pamphilus, the friend of Cosmas Indicopleustes (§ 104, 6). He depends inter alia on Leontius of Byzantium (*C. Nestor. et Monophys.; Epilysis* and thirty chapters against Severus) and on the Emperor Justinian's treatise *Confessio rectae fidei.* He wrote probably soon after 560, but certainly before 630.

A. Mai, *Nova Patr. Bibl.* 2, 1844, 597/653. J. P. Junglas, *Leontius v. Byzanz,* 1908, 57/65. M. Richard, RSPT 1938, 27/52 *(Léonce et P.).*

7. Anastasius I (559–99), Patriarch of Antioch, opposed the Aphthartodocetism of the Emperor Justinian and was therefore exiled in 570. He was allowed to return only in 593, at the request of Gregory the Great. His many dogmatic-polemical works including one *Against the Umpire* of John Philoponus are lost. Three of the four Sermons printed in MG 89, 1361/98 are not certainly genuine. The "Sermon" (actually it is a canonistic treatise) printed in the fourth place was written after 787 (seventh General Council), cf. 1397 A, and is therefore spurious. The sermon delivered on his return from exile edited by Pitra is genuine. Five dogmatic treatises on the nature and infinity of God, the Incarnation, passibility and resurrection of Christ are as yet accessible only in the Latin translation of F. Turianus (MG 89, 1309/62). Feast day: April 21.

Edd.: MG 89, 1293/1408. J. B. Pitra, *Juris eccl. Graec. hist. et mon.* 2, 1868, 251/7. — Studies: Rivière 1931, 230/3. Jugie, EO 1936, 257ff. *(Spir. S.).* Vailhé, DTC 1, 1166. Janin, DHG 2, 1460.

8. Anastasius II, Patriarch of Antioch 599–609, translated the *Regula Pastoralis* of Gregory the Great into Greek. The translation, however, is no longer extant.

J. B. Kumpfmueller, *De Anastasio Sinaita,* Wu 1865, 12/5.

9. Eulogius, Patriarch of Alexandria 580–607, a friend of Gregory the Great, attacked the Novatianists and especially the Monophysites in many writings which are now lost; only a few fragments have been preserved (MG 86, 2, 1937/64). According to S. L. Epifanovic, *Festschr. N. I. Karajev*, St. Petersb. 1917, 130/41, the excerpts from a treatise *De Trinitate* (ed. O. Bardenhewer, TQ 1896, 353/401) and also the fully preserved homily on Palm Sunday (MG 86, 2, 2913/38) are spurious. The latter belongs to Sophronius of Jerusalem. Cf. RHE 1928, 802; BNJ 8, 1931, 424f. Moeller, RHE 1951, 683/8 (3 fragms. of John of Caesarea [§ 102, 1] in E.).

§ 103. THE EMPEROR JUSTINIAN I (527–65)

Justinian, a man of outstanding intellectual gifts and comprehensive education, was indefatigable as a statesman, lawgiver, patron of architecture and poet. He also considered himself the supreme authority in the Church, hence he not only intervened in the inner life of the Church with incisive measures relentlessly carried through, which not infrequently concerned even the doctrine of the Church, but he also had the ambition to gain renown as a theological author. It may, however, be surmised that the theological treatises, epistles and decrees published under his name were partly composed by Bishop Theodore Ascidas who had great influence at the court.

a. Against Monophysitism: an edict against the Severians addressed to Bishop Menas of Constantinople (536); a *Tractatus contra Monophysitas* addressed to Egyptian monks (542–3) who had returned from Monophysitism to the Church.

b. Against Origenism: Edict of 543; a *Letter to the Holy Synod* (553).

c. Against Nestorianism (= Three Chapters, i.e.: 1. Person and writings of Theodore of Mopsuestia, 2. writings of Theodoret of Cyrus against Cyril and the Council of Ephesus, 3. Letter of Ibas of Edessa): *Exposition of the True Faith,* 543–4, lost; *Confession of the True Faith* (between 551 and 553); a *Letter* (τύπος) *to the Holy Synod* (553) and a treatise vehemently attacking a lost work in defence of the Three Chapters (550 or 553).

d. Various writings: thirteen letters to several Popes; *Novellae,* laws concerning Church affairs (v. supra § 50, 21 b); an edict in favour of the *Aphthartodocetae* (shortly before 565) is lost; *Troparium* (antiphonal hymn) Ὁ μονογενὴς υἱὸς τοῦ θεοῦ (*c.* 535).

Edd.: MG 86, 1. ML 69, 177/328. Letters in ML 63. 66. 69 (among the letters of the Popes). Laws in ML 72, 921/1110 (v. supra § 50, 21 b). E. Schwartz, AbhMn 1939, 18 (ed. *C. Monophys., Epp.* against the 3 Chs., *Conf. rectae fid.*); cf. BZ 1940, 472/4. — Mgg.: E. Grupe 1923. G. P. Baker, Lo 1932. W. G. Holmes, *The Age of J. and Theodora,* 2 vols., [2]1912. N. Jorga, *Hist. de la vie byz.* 1, 1933. Jugie, DTC 8, 2277/90. Fritz, DTC 11, 1565/87 *(Origénisme).* Leclercq, DAL 8, 507/603. Amann, DTC 15, 1868/1924 (Three Chapters). De Clercq, DictDroitCan 644/80 *(Législation relig. Collections canon.).* H. S. Alivisatos, *Die kirchl. Gesetzgebung J.s,* 1913. J. Pargoire, *L'Égl. byz. 527–847,* [3]1923. L. Duchesne, *L'Égl. au 6e s.,* 1925. Biondi 1936 (supra § 50, 21 b). — Studies: Grumel, EO 1923, 398/418 (hymn). Collinet 1931 (supra § 96, 4). Jugie, EO 1932, 399/402 (J. an Aphthartodocetist). Popescu, *Studii teologice* 4, 1933, 17/66 (anti-Orig. decrees). P. Browe, AnnalGreg 8, 1935, 109/46 (legisl. on Jews). W. Pewesin, *Imper. Eccl. universalis, Roma,* St 1937, 139/41, 150/8 (19 fragms.). C. Diehl, *Théodora, impér. de Byz.,* 1937 and Fl 1939. E. Schwartz, *Kyrillos v. Skythopolis,* 1939, 386/408 and SbMn 1940, 2, 32/81 (eccl. policy). Altaner, ZRGG 1948, 170 f. (Augustin.-Testim. in J.). R. Devreesse, *Essai sur Théodore de Mops.,* 1948, 194/258. G. A. Kinsella, *The Two Phases of the Eccl. Policy of J. I,* thesis W 1948. E. Stein, *Hist. du Bas-Empire,* II: *De la disparition de l'Empire d'Occident à la mort de J.,* p. p. J.-R. Palanque, 1949. Anastos, DOP 1951, 125/60 (Theod. of Mops. justly condemned). Kaden, MémFacultéDroitGenève 9, 1952, 109/44 (Church and State).

Agapetus, deacon at the Hagia Sophia in Constantinople, who is said to have been Justinian's teacher, wrote, probably about the time of the Emperor's accession, an exposition (Ἔκθεσις) of the duties of a Christian prince in the form of seventy-two proverbs. In later times this "Mirror of princes" was used as a schoolbook.

Edd.: MG 86, 1, 1163/86. — K. Emminger, *Stud. zu den griech. Fuerstenspiegeln,* 1913.

Timothy, priest at the Hagia Sophia in Constantinople, gives an instructive enumeration and characterization of the schisms and heresies of the sixth century. The work was written *c.* 600. MG 86, 1, 11/68.

§ 104. BIBLICAL AND EXEGETICAL LITERATURE

NOTHING shows more clearly the decline of patristic literature and the gradual slackening of the productive power of the later age than the development of exegetical literature. Now scholars no longer write their own commentaries on the Biblical books, but work existing patristic commentaries into *catenae* (*catena* = σειρα), i.e. expositions of earlier exegetes on the respective Biblical passages are strung together without any personal opinion being offered. In the Latin West this form of literature was not developed in the patristic age.

H. Lietzmann, *Catenen,* 1897. G. Karo u. J. Lietzmann, GN 1902, F. 1, 3, 5. Devreesse, DBSuppl 1, 1083/1234. M. Faulhaber, LTK 5, 888f. A. Zanolli, *Di una vet. cat. sul Lev.... in armeno,* Venice 1938. Reuss 1941. Sickenberger, ZNTW 39, 151/61 (Nicetas). Reuss, ZNTW 42, 1949, 217/28 and Bi 1954, 207/16 (on Gospel *catenae*). G. Mercati, *Alla ricerca dei nomi degli "altri" traduttori nelle omelie sui salmi di Giov. Crisost. e variazioni su alcune catene del salterio* (ST 158), 1952. Cf. the works cited supra § 3, 10 by K. Staab, 1933 and R. Devreesse, RB 1935. 1936 and p. xiv in DBSuppl I and J. Reuss 1941 supra p. xvii. M. Richard, BullInformatInstRechHistTextes n. 3, 1954, 87/106 (MSS peu connus des chaînes exégét. et des comment. grecs sur le Psautier).

1. In the second half of the fifth century the otherwise unknown exegete Symmachus, who cultivated almost exclusively the allegorical and moral exegesis, composed an *Explanation of the Book of Proverbs* in the interest of ascetic theology. 357 fragments have been preserved in the *catena* of the Cod. Vat. Gr. 1802. Besides, he is very probably the author of a commentary on the Canticle of Canticles, of which the explanation of 6, 9 to 18, 14 is extant.

M. Faulhaber, *Hohelied-, Proverbien- u. Prediger-Catenen,* 1902, 90/4; cf.

J. Sickenberger, TR 1904, 135 and 216. O. Hopmann, *Die Catene des Vatic. gr.*, 1802, 1912, p. VII. C. van den Eynde, *La version syr. du comment. de Grég. de Nysse sur le cant. des cant.*, Lou 1939, 77/89, 104/16 (Syr. with trans.). G. Mercati, ST 95, 91/3; Vivre et Penser 1, 5ff. n. 3.

2. Scholia under the name of an otherwise unknown Victor appear in *catenae* of several books of the O.T. and N.T. Seventeen MSS name a presbyter Victor of Antioch as the author of a completely preserved commentary on Mark. Actually this is not a commentary but a *catena* compiled after 500, of which Chrysostom's Homilies on Matthew are the main source, besides Origen (on Mt.), Cyril of Alexandria (on Lk.) and Titus of Bostra (on Lk.). Victor is probably the name of the compiler.

Edd.: C. F. Mathaei, Moscow 1775 (best ed.). I. A. Cramer, *Cat. in Ev. Matth. et Marci,* O 1840, 259/447. — H. Smith, JTS 19, 1917/8, 350/70. E. Klostermann, TU 47, 2, 1932, 2/6. Devreesse, DBSuppl 1, 1175/81. Reuss 1941, 118/41. Bardy, DTC 15, 2872/4.

While the rhetorical schools of the Greek East were about to disappear, the School of Gaza flourished for a short time in the fifth and sixth centuries. All the "sophists" there, were already Christians, and the most eminent among them, Procopius and Aeneas, also published theological works.

3. Procopius of Gaza (d. *c.* 538), probably the brother of Zacharias Rhetor (§ 49, 12), was the first author to compile extensive *catena* commentaries: one *catena* of the *Octateuch* in a double version; the shorter one, printed in full only in a Latin translation, is extant in direct tradition. Besides, the *catenae* in 1–4 Kings, 1–2 Para., Is. and Cant. are also available in print. The *catena* of Proverbs (MG 87, 1, 1221/1544) is spurious.

His 163 letters (ed. R. Hercher, *Epistolographi graeci,* P 1873, 533/98) are as important for his biography as the funeral oration of his disciple Choricius (ed. Foerster - E. Richtsteig, L 1929, 109/28), but without theological interest. Of his speeches only a panegyric on the Emperor Anastasius has been preserved (d. 518; ed. C. Kempen 1918).

Edd.: MG 87, 1–2. K. Seitz, *Die Schule von Gaza,* 1892. Mg. by L. Eisenhofer 1897. E. Lindl, *Die Oktateuchkatene des P. v. G.,* 1902. Devreesse, DBSuppl 1, 1087/9 and freq. Valdenberg, StudiBiz 1935, 67ff. (polit. ideas). Baz 93, 1936, 413/8 *(catenae)*. P. Friedlaender, ST 89, 1939 (ed. Ἔκφρασις εἰκόνος). Abel, RB 40, 19/31, 5ff. (Gaza). Honigmann, ST 173, 201/4 (Procopius, brother of Zacharias Rhetor). Géraud, *Journ. of Egypt., Archeology* 40, 1954, 63/7 (Origen, Περὶ Πάσχα in P. of G.).

4. Aeneas of Gaza (d. shortly after 518), the slightly older contemporary of Procopius, is the author of a dialogue *Theophrastus or On the Immortality of the Soul and the Resurrection of the Body*. The work is directed against neo-Platonism and was much read in the Middle Ages. Besides, we possess twenty-five short letters in the rhetorical style (ed. Hercher [v. supra n. 3] 24/32).

Edd.: MG 85, 871/1004. — Mgg. by G. Schalkhausser 1898. S. Sikorski 1909. Valdenberg, Byz 4, 1927/8, 262/8. L. Massa in: *Collana di studi greci dir. da V. de Falco,* Na 1950 (Ed. crit. of Letters) and GiornItalFilol 5, 1952, 205/7 (MS).

5. Olympiodorus, from *c.* 510 deacon in Alexandria, wrote commentaries on Eccl., Job and Jer.-Bar., which have only partly been printed (MG 89, 13/780). A commentary on Esdras and a treatise against Severus of Antioch have perished.

Cf. Devreesse, DBSuppl 1, 1137. 1141. 1164 and frequently.

6. Cosmas Indicopleustes, a probably Nestorian merchant from Alexandria, travelled to E. Africa and as far as Ceylon; he later became a hermit. In the twelve books of his Χριστιανικὴ τοπογραφία (*c.* 550) which contain much valuable geographical, scientific and cultural information, he gives a presentation of the Biblical system of the universe and opposes the Ptolemaic system. Book V treats of questions of Biblical propaedeutics.

Edd.: MG 88, 51/470. E. O. Winstedt, C 1909. Wecker, PWK 11, 1487/90. Leclercq, DAL 8, 820/49. Peterson, EL 1932, 66/74 (Alex. liturgy). G. Ricciotti, *L'apoc. di Paolo sir.,* 1932, 46/61 *(cosmologia)*. BNJ 8, 1931, 395 (Rjedin). Anastos, DOP 1946, 73/80 (written in Alexandria); and id. in Προσφορὰ εἰς Στ. Κυριακίδην, 1953, 35/50 (Cosmas and the *Physics* of Aristotle). Bengtson, *Historia* 4, 1955, 151/6 (Cosmas and the Ptolemaeans). H. Winter, *Die Erde,* B 1955, 63/8 (C. I.'s map of the world, 535/47). B. Schleissheimer, *Kosm. Ind.,* Diss, Mn 1959.

7. Oecumenius, philosopher and rhetor, not identical with the Bishop Oecumenius of Tricca in Thessalia who lived in the tenth century, was a follower of Severus of Antioch. In the first half of the sixth century he wrote a commentary on the Apocalypse in twelve books. Other commentaries on Acts and the Pauline and Catholic epistles (MG 118/9) published under his name are spurious; they only contain citations from his *scholia* on the Pauline homilies of St. Chrysostom.

Edd.: E. Hoskier, *Ann Arbor* 1928. K. Staab 1933, 423/69 *(glossae)*. — Studies: Devreesse, DB Suppl 1, 1211/4. J. Schmid-Spitaler, OC 1934, 208/18; cf. Bees, BNJ 12, 1936, 317/9. J. Schmid, BNJ 14, 1938, 322/30 (O. the exegete and O. the bish.). Bees, ibid. 330 (O. the bish.).

8. Approximately between 563 and 614 Archbishop Andrew of Caesarea wrote a commentary on the Apocalypse which gives a spiritual exegesis and at the same time constantly discusses Oecumenius. It is important chiefly from the point of view of textual criticism, for it supplies information on one of the two later recensions of the Greek text of the Apocalypse. The commentary on the Apocalypse by Arethas of Caesarea (*c.* 895) is for the most part a free version of this work. Of a second work called Θεραπευτική only fragments have been preserved.

Edd.: MG 106, 207/486, 1387/1412. J. Schmid, *Studien z. Gesch. des griech. Apok.-Textes* I, 1956 (crit. text of comm. on Apoc.). On the Armen. version of Nerses Lamprion cf. TR 1904, 260. On a Georg. trans. by Euthymius (d. 1028) cf. HTR 1928, 287. — Diekamp, HJB 1897, 1/36; SbB 1901, 1054/6; AP 1938. 161/72 (Fragm. of *Therap.*). J. Schmid, BiZ 1931, 233/5.

9. Of Gregory, Bishop of Agrigentum in Sicily (*c.* 592) we have a commentary on Ecclesiasticus in ten books which also tries to do justice to the literal sense (MG 98, 741/1182). There is a *Vita Gregorii* by a certain Leontius in MG 98, 549/716).

Gennaro, MiscStLCA 3, 1951, 162/84 (Gr. authors in comment.); StBizNeoell 7, 1953, 145 f. Mannelli, MiscStLCA 3, 1951, 185/94 (probl. of freedom of will). I. C., Bull. Badia di Grottaferrata 5, 1951, 77/91 (chronol. in *Vita G.*). Stramondo, MiscStLCA 4, 1952 (hist. errors in *Vita G.*).

10. An otherwise unknown Peter of Laodicea is wrongly mentioned as a commentator of Matthew, Luke and John in late MSS. In fact it is a case of *catenae* from which the *lemmata* are absent. It is even doubtful whether this Peter may be taken to be the author of a *catena* on the Gospels. Heinrici attempted to prove that Peter is a commentator, but more recent research has discounted this theory.

Mt. comm. ed. by C. F. G. Heinrici, L 1908. Mg. on the Lk. comm. by M. Rauer, Mr 1920. Fritz, DTC 12, 1939f. Manson, ZNTW 1936, 307. Devreesse, DBSuppl 1, 1165/7. Klostermann, TU 47, 2, 1931, 13f. Reuss 1941, 72/8, 182f. Fruechtel, ZNTW 36, 1938, 81/5 (Clem. Alex.-citations in Mt. comm.).

11. Timothy of Jerusalem, presbyter. Five sermons treating of Biblical subjects belong to an author who lived between the sixth and eighth centuries and who cannot be identified with certainty. Number one (MG 86, 1, 237/52) on the presentation of Christ in the Temple is preserved under the name of Timothy of Jerusalem; number two (MG 86, 1, 256/65) on the transfiguration is said to be by one Timothy of Antioch. The other three texts are Ps.-Athan.: MG 28, 905/14 (on the annunciation of the birth of the Baptist and of Jesus); MG 28, 943/58 (on the journey of Mary and Joseph to Bethlehem and on the birth of our Lord); MG 28, 1001/24 (on the healing of the man born blind, John 9:1ff.). M. Jugie and O. Faller tried to assign the presbyter Timothy of Jerusalem to the time about 400, but without success.

B. Capelle, EL 1949, 5/26. M. Jugie, *La mort et l'assomption de la sainte Vierge,* R 1944, 70/6. O. Faller, *De priorum saeculorum silentio circa assumptionem B. M. V.,* R 1946, 27/34. Altaner, TR 1948, 130f. M. Pellegrino, EnciclopCathol. 12, 1954, 111. M. Jugie, *L'immaculée Conception,* R 1952, 74 A. 3 (now dates Tim 4th–6th cents.).

§ 105. ASCETICAL AUTHORS

1. Of Barsanuphius (d. *c.* 540) and John (d. *c.* 530), monks of a monastery near Gaza, 396 and 446 letters respectively have been preserved, which were combined in one collection. They concern

ascetical and pastoral matters; 100 are addressed to the ascetic Dorotheus (EA 1068/75).

Edd.: Nicodemus Hagiorita, Venice 1816. Fragms. in MG 86, 1, 891/902; 88, 1811/22. Vailhé, EO 1904, 268/76; 1905, 14/25, 154/60.

2. Dorotheus, abbot of a monastery near Gaza, a disciple of Barsanuphius and St. John (n. 1). He left twenty-three Spiritual Colloquies which were later highly esteemed and eight short letters addressed to religious brothers (EA 1079/92). *Doctrina XXIV* is spurious; it belongs to the Nestorian mystic John Saba the Elder (eighth cent.).

Edd.: MG 88, 1611/1844; Germ. by B. Hermann, Kevelaer 1928. Vailhé, DTC 4, 1785f. Phokylides, EPh 1918, 319/36, 449/64; 1925, 245/321. Vari, EgyetPhilolKoezloeny 1927, 110/5 (MS). Hausherr, OCP 1940, 220/2 *(Doctr. XXIV)*. Strung, StHonFriend 1955, 82/7 (D. explains a paschal hymn by a passage from a serm. of Greg. of Naz.); cf. BZ 1955, 449. J. Sajdak, *Hist. crit. scholiastarum et commentar. Greg. Naz.*, Cracow 1914, 22f., 30/2 (MSS of *Doctrinae* explaining texts of Greg.). T. Sinko, *De trad. orationum Greg. Naz.*, Cracow 1923, 14/9 (Greg. of Naz. in the *Doctr.*).

3. Antiochus, monk of the Saba monastery near Jerusalem. Apart from an account of the capture of Jerusalem by the Persians (614) we have of his the voluminous Πανδέκτης τῆς ἁγίας γραφῆς (130 chs.), a collection of moral sayings taken from the Scriptures and works of the Fathers (620).

Edd.: MG 89, 1421/1850. Conybeare, EngHistRev 1910, 502/17 (trans. of hist. account). Graf, *Das Heilige Land* 67, 1923, 19/29. Bardy, DS 1, 701f. Graf I, 411f.; II, 497. Acc. to P. Peeters, AB 1912, 304f.; 1920, 137/47; *Mél. Univ. Beyrouth* 9, 1, 1923, 3/42 the author of the hist. account is not identical with the author of the *Pand.*

4. John Climacus (b. before 579, d. *c.* 649), monk on Mt. Sinai, owes his surname to his work Κλῖμαξ τοῦ παραδείσου *(Ladder of Paradise)*. In thirty chapters or steps the vices threatening the monk (1–23) and the virtues that should adorn him (24–30) are discussed in a popular manner. The work was very widely read and translated into many languages. An appendix was added to it, entitled a *Word to the Shepherd* (i.e. the monastic

superior), which is addressed to Abbot John of Raithu (EA 1093/1130).

Edd.: MG 88, 631/1210. *Vita* in MG 88, 596/608 and Nau, OC 1902, 58/87. P. Trevisan, 2 vols. (with trans;), Tu 1941.—Trans. by Father Robert, Lo 1858. — Studies: Petit, DTC 8, 690/3. L. Oliger 1912, XLIff. (Lat. and Old Ital. trans.). H. Ball, *Byz. Christent.*, ²1931, 1/60. Saudreau, VS 1924, 353/70 *(Doctr. spir.)*. Osieczkowska, Byz 9, 1934, 261ff. (MS). Altaner, ZKG 1934, 484f. (Lat. trans.). G. Hofmann, OCP 1941, 461/79 (*Clim.* in Photius). Graf I, 409f. A. Bontschev, *Die Aesthetik u. Mystik des J. Klim.*, thesis Marbg. 1948. J. R. Martin, *The Illustration of the Heavenly Ladder of J. C.*, Pr 1954; also Downey, Sp 1955, 484/93.

5. Thalassius, abbot of a monastery in the Libyan desert (*c.* 650) and a friend of Maximus Confessor, left a collection of sayings (in 4 *centuria*) on the life of virtue and the desire for perfection (MG 91, 1427/70; EA 1314/28).

Disdier, ÉtByz 2, 1944, 79/118 (analysis of 4 centuria).

6. Of John, Bishop of Carpathus, an island between Crete and Rhodus (*c.* 680), two collections of ninety-seven and eighty-two items each have been printed. They contain teachings and exhortations destined for monks.

Edd.: MG 85, 791/826, 1837/60; Petit, DTC 8, 753f.; against this Disdier, EO 1932, 17/43, 284/303; id., EO 39, 1941/2, 290/311 *(l'homme, l'œuvre, la doctr. spir.)*.

§ 106. ANTI-HERETICAL WRITERS OF THE SEVENTH CENTURY

1. St. Sophronius was a native of Damascus. He was probably first a teacher of rhetoric, then a monk in the monastery of Theodosius near Jerusalem. Accompanied by his older friend John Moschus (d. 619; v. supra § 46, 9) he travelled to Egypt and Rome. In 633 he defended the doctrine of Chalcedon against Carus, the Monothelite Patriarch of Alexandria, and soon afterwards he did the same at Constantinople against Sergius, the Patriarch of the capital. After he had been raised to the patriarchal see of Jerusalem (634) he at once published a synodal letter against Mono-

thelitism in which he exhaustively explained the doctrine of the two energies in Christ (EP 2289 f.). He died in 638, one year after the capture of Jerusalem by the Caliph Omar.

Besides the synodal letter Sophronius wrote another work against Monothelitism which is lost, a *Florilegium* with 600 testimonies from the Fathers in favour of the doctrine of the two energies. He is also author of the above-mentioned (supra § 46, 10) hagiographical writings and left about eleven sermons (supra § 102, 9) and twenty-three anacreontic odes on feasts of the Church. The imperfectly preserved *Commentarius liturgicus* is spurious (twelfth cent.).

Edd.: MG 87, 3, 3147/4014. Hippolytos, NS 1922, 178/86 (Epitome of synod. letter). — Studies: Phokylides, EPh 1918, 319/36 (Christmas sermon). Mg. Zuretti, Did 1926, 1, 19/68. Grumel, EO 1929, 19/32 (against Monergism). Opitz, ZNTW 1934, 24 (Syr. letter to Arcadius of Cyprus). Eustratiades, NS 1934, 188/93 and 4 conts. (esp. poems). — On hist. of Monothelitism cf. Grumel, EO 1928, 6/10, 257/77 and cont. Nissen, BZ 39, 1939, 89/115 (text. crit.; *Or. in s. Crucem* spur.); 349/81 (medicine and magic). G. Cosmas, *De oeconomia incarnat. sec. S. S.*, R 1940; cf. OCP 1940, 535 f. Bardy, DTC. Graf I, 371 f. Wellesz, JournRomStud 37, 1947, 145/51 (12 trop. for Christmas). Solowij, Anal. Ord. S. Basil. 1, 1950, 372/84 *(De comm. liturg.)*. Bonis, Θ 19, 1951 (2 anacreont. odes on St. Paul: MG 87, 3, 3776/84) (also off-print). Gigante, ParPass 1954, 303/11 (ode 14: capture of Jerus., ed.).

2. Maximus Confessor, b. *c.* 580, came of a noble family from Constantinople. At first he was first secretary of the Emperor Heraclius, but entered a monastery at Chrysopolis (Scutari) in 613–14. In 626 he had to flee from the Persians; in 632 he was in Alexandria together with Sophronius (v. supra n. 1) and after that probably resided in N. Africa (Carthage). He first combated Monophysitism and only from 642 also Monothelitism, with whose representatives (Sergius, Pyrrhus I) he had entertained friendly relations for a considerable time. In 645 he defeated the former Patriarch Pyrrhus of Constantinople in a disputation at Carthage (cf. the minutes in MG 91, 287/354), caused Monothelitism to be rejected by several African synods and finally obtained

the solemn condemnation of the heresy *(Ekthesis, Typus)* at the Lateran Synod in Rome (649).

Maximus was taken to Constantinople as a prisoner probably as early as 653. The trial ended with his banishment to Thracia (655). In 662 he had again to appear before a synod at Constantinople. There he and his fellow sufferers, his disciple Anastasius and the Roman Anastasius Apocrisiarius were exiled to Lazia in Colchis, after the steadfast confessors had had their tongues cut out and their right hands cut off. In the same year Maximus succumbed to his sufferings and died in exile. Feast day: August 13. See the accounts of the trial and an anonymous *Vita* in MG 90, 67/172: here 90. 120B also an accusation of Origenism. Devreesse, AB 1955, 5/16 (Anastas. Apocris.: first ed. of the Greek account of the death of Max. C.).

Maximus is the greatest Greek theologian of the seventh century, and his learning defeated Monothelitism. His writings show him to have been an ingenious theologian and a profound mystic, who also interested himself in exegetical and liturgical questions. His orthodox interpretation of the pseudo-Dionysian writings (v. supra § 100) was of far-reaching importance. As a philosopher he was an eclectic who was influenced especially by Aristotle and neo-Platonism. His works (EA 1296/1313) are written in a turgid style which is often difficult to understand.

a. In his exegetical writings which mostly give explanations of difficult passages he shows himself a follower of the allegorical and moral exegesis: *Quaestiones ad Thalassium; Quaestiones et dubia;* exegesis of Ps. 59 and of the Lord's Prayer.

b. Commentaries on several *Orationes* of Greg. of Naz. *(Ambigua)*. In his explanation of Ps.-Dion. he depends almost entirely on John of Scyth. (§ 102, 2).

c. Eleven dogmatic-polemical treatises and letters oppose Monophysitism and twenty-three Monothelitism. Three treat of anthropological questions (*De anima;* cf. supra § 41, 4).

d. Ascetic-mystical writings: the most important are the highly praised dialogue *Liber asceticus,* also the 400 *Capita de caritate* and the 200 *Capita gnostica* (MG 90, 1084/1176). To this should be added the 100 *Capita gnostica* which came to light through Epifanovic in 1917. The following have lately been proved to be spurious: 500 *diversa capita theologica et oeconomica* (cf. W. Soppa, thesis Br 1922; Disdier, EO 1931, 160/78) which were compiled from genuine works *c.* 1100, and the 243 *Capita alia* (MG 90, 1401/62) which belong to the monk Elias Ecdicus who lived in the eleventh-twelfth centuries (Disdier, EO 1932, 17/43; cf. MG 127, 1128/76).

e. Liturgical writings: *Mystagogia,* a symbolic interpretation of the liturgy; *Computus ecclesiasticus* on the calculation of the festive seasons of the Church and other chronological questions. Three hymns are spurious (v. Maximus Margunius).

Edd.: MG 90/1; 4, 15/432, 527/76; 19, 1217/80. New texts in S. L. Epifanovic, Kiew 1917; cf. BNJ 8, 1931, 374/6. R. Cantarella, *S. M. Conf. La mistagogia ed altri scritti,* Fl 1931 (with trans.). — Transs.: M. Garbas, Br 1925 *(Lib. ascet.).* Irénikon 1936, 466/72 (cont. *Mystag.*). B. Hermann, *Weisheit, die betet,* 1941 (selected texts). J. Pegon, SCh 9, 1945 *(Carit.).* Peradze, OC 1933, 181 f. (Georg. trans.). Franceschini, JTS 1933, 355/63 (trans. of Grosseteste). Dalmais, VS 1948, 294/303 (*Ep.* 2: MG 91, 391/408). B. Terebessy, ed. Lat. trans. of *Carit.,* 12th cent. (MG 90, 959/1080), Budapest 1944. P. Sherwood, ACW 21, 1955 *(Lib. ascet.* and *Carit.).* — On *Vita:* Devreesse, AB 1928, 5/49; 1935, 49/80 (*Hypomnest.* de Théod. Spoudée). Grumel, DTC, 448/59. Starr, BNJ 16, 1940, 192/6 (*Ep.* 8: compulsory baptism of Jews 632). — Writings: J. Sajdak, *Hist. crit. Scholiastarum et Comment. Greg. Naz.* 1, 1914, 32/7 and BZ 30, 1929/30, 270 (Schol. in Gr. Naz.). T. Sinko, *De tradit. orat. G.i Naz.* 2, 1923, 8 f., 19/31. Viller, RAM 1930, 154/84, 239/68 (*Cap. de carit.* depend on Evagrius); cf. also Hausherr, OCP 1936, 351/62. Messerschmidt, RQ 1931, 68 f. *(Comm. in Apc.).* Bardy, RB 1933, 332/9 *(Quaest.).* Devreesse, RevSR 1937, 25/35 *(la fin inéd. de l'Ép. 8).* J. Pierres, thesis R 1940 (John Dam. dependent on M.; *Florileg. synodi Lateran.* 649 by Max.); cf. TR 1942, 50 f. U. v. Balthasar, *Die "Gnost. Centurien" des M. C.,* 1941 (MG 90, 1084/1176); cf. TR 1942, 51/3. *Propylaeum ad ASS Deç., Martyrolog. Roman.* 1940, 470/3 (Max. Conf.). P. Sherwood, *Amer. Ben. Rev.* 1, 1950, 347/56 (Notes on M. C.); *An Annotated Date-List of the Works of M. the C.,* R 1952 (only 4 of 91 works cannot be dated exactly); S. M. the C., Lo 1955. A. Ceresa-Gastaldo (oldest *Cod. of. Cap. de carit.;* cf. BZ 1955, 454). G. Giannelli, on an ed. maior of the *Quaestiones et Dubia* in MG 90, 785/856; cf. Bz 1956, 180. Spurious works: cf. S. H. Mercati, Mél. Bidez 1933/34, 619/25 (3 hymns); BZ 1934, 48/51 (MG 90, 1461 f.).

1. Christology. The Logos is at the centre of world history. The time before Christ is the age of preparation for the incarnation of God (σάρκωσις), the age after Christ is the time of the deification of man (θέωσις) which is inaugurated by the incarnation of the Logos.

Being a new principle of man's life, Christ must necessarily be true God and perfect man. But from the duality of the integral natures follows the duality of the wills and the modes of actions (ἐνέργειαι). Now, only the willing and the faculty of the will belong to the nature; the choosing and the willing-thus, on the other hand, are the concern of the person. Maximus calls the willing-thus or the direction of the will the gnomic will (ἡ γνώμη). The human nature of Christ has only a physical will, not the gnomic will; for the direction of the will is determined only by the Logos, whose divine will directs also the human will and thus excludes all error and sin from it.

2. Eschatology. Maximus struggles with the difficult problem of the ἀποκατάστασις ἁπάντων and clearly betrays his sympathy with the view that was earlier expounded by Origen and Gregory of Nyssa. Nevertheless he would not have this opinion presented openly and without restraint. Beginners and imperfect Christians should not be led to the abyss of God's mercy by friendly smiles alone; they must also be guided by fear (*Cap*. 200 [2, 99]; MG 90, 1172 D). This doctrine is reserved to those possessing a profoundly mystical understanding: "We will honour it by silence" (*Quaest. Thal. Prol.;* MG 90, 260 A). An echo of the classical-Origenistic view can be discovered in that Maximus regards the crucifixion and resurrection also as generally cosmic events (MG 90, 1108 A, B). Cf. BZ 1951, 303.

H. Straubinger, *Die Christologie des hl. M. C.,* 1906. G. Schoenfeld, *Die Psychol. des M. C.,* 1918. Saudreau, VS 1919, 255/64 and Disdier, EO 1930, 296/313 *(Spiritualité)*. Lampen, StC 1926, 373/83 (Eucharist). Stephanou, EO 1932, 398/414 (doctr. of soul). Heintjes, StC 1935, 175/200; BiNJ 1942, 260/307; 1943, 64/123 (ascet. and myst.). J. Loosen, *Logos u. Pneuma im begnadeten Menschen b. M. C.*, 1941; cf. ZKG 61, 386f. U. v. Balthasar, *Kosmische Liturgie. M. C.*, 1941; French trans. 1947. Unger, FrancStud NY 9, 1949, 50/62 (Christ centre and meaning of creation). I. Hausherr, *Philautie. De la tendresse p. soi à la charité sel. s. M. C.*, R 1952. Dalmais, VS 21, 1952, 216/26 *(L'œuvre spir.)*; RSPT 1952, 244/9 *(Logoi des créatures)*; Ir 1953, 17/39 *(Doctr. ascét.)*; RAM 1953, 123/59 (infl. of the Comm. on Our Father on John Dam. and Thomas Aquinas). Parente, REB 1953, 241/59 (the term *Theotokos*). Gauthier, RTA 1954, 51/100 *(Psychologie de l'acte humain)*. P. Sherwood, *The Earlier Ambigua of St. M. C. and his Refutation of Origenism*, R 1955.

3. Anastasius Monachus and Anastasius Apocrisiarius, the two fellow sufferers of St. Maximus (v. supra § 106, 2). The monk (d. 662) is the author of a letter, extant in Latin, on the two wills in Christ (MG 90, 131/6). The Apocrisiarius (d. 666) wrote the above-mentioned (§ 106, 2) accounts of the trial (ibid. 90, 109/70) and a letter with patristic testimonies against Monothelitism (MG 90, 173/94). According to Stiglmayr (BZ 1909, 14/40) he is also the compiler of a doctrinal florilegium, the *Doctrina patrum* (ed. F. Diekamp 1907), which is directed chiefly against the Monophysite and Monothelite heresies and is important as a mine of citations from lost writings. Diekamp is inclined to think that Anastasius Sinaita is its author.

4. Abbot Anastasius Sinaita (d. shortly after 700), an ardent defender of the teaching of the Church against Nestorians, Monophysites, Monothelites and Jews. His works have so far been little investigated and are printed incompletely.

The *Viae Dux* instructs on how to oppose heretics; an allegorical exegesis of the *Hexaemeron* in twelve books; the 154 questions and answers which mostly treat exegetical subjects have later additions (EH 1108); a short history of the heresies and synods (ed. Pitra); several sermons; v. infra § 108, 3.

Edd.: MG 89. J. B. Pitra, *Iuris eccl. Graecorum hist. et monum.* 2, 1868, 238/94. Nau, OC 1903, 56/90. — Studies: Spacil, *La teol. di s. A. S.*, R 1923 (from *Bessarione*). Juelicher, ZNTW 1925, 20/8 (*Viae dux* betw. 690 and 700). Cumont, BZ 30, 1929/30, 31/5; Mél. Thomas, Bruges 1930, 152/60 (John Lydus in A.). Bardy, RB 1933, 339/43 *(Quaest.)*; DS 1, 546f. H. Doerries, *Symeon v. Mesopotamien*, 1941, 465/70 *(Quaest.)*. Mercati, OM 2, 1937, 437f., 440/4 *(Opusc. circa la bestemmia e la dignità sacerd.)*. Diekamp, AP 1938, 223/9 (ed. a florileg.

from *Doctr. Patr.*). Graf I, 375f. Hulshoff, Sc 1952, 33/8 (Anast. and Hippol. fragms.). On fragms. MG 89, 1143/50 (compl. in MG 44, 1327/44); cf. H. Merki, Ὁμοίωσις Θεῷ, Frib 1952, 174f. Caranicolas, Θ 1955, 259/62 (on 2 MSS with uned. texts); cf. BZ 1955, 430. Giannelli, EEBS 1955, 159/67 (Cod. Vat. 1702 has, among others, a *recensio brevior* of the *Viae Dux*). Guillou, MAH 1955, 237/58 (first ed. of a Hom. *De Transfiguratione*); cf. BZ 1956, 180, 221 and AB 1956, 245 (6 further MSS not used).

§ 107. ANTI-HERETICAL WRITERS OF THE EIGHTH CENTURY

1. GERMANUS of Constantinople (d. 733). Under pressure from the Emperor he professed Monothelitism when he was Bishop of Cyzicus (712); but after he had become Patriarch of Constantinople he already had the heresy condemned by a synod in 715. He was deposed in 730 because he was in favour of images. Feast day: May 12.

Of his four dogmatic letters, three are important for the early history of the iconoclastic controversy, the fourth *(Ep. ad Armenos)* is a defence of the doctrine of Chalcedon. *De vitae termino* discusses the meaning and end of man's life and justifies divine Providence. *De haeresibus et synodis* is an historical treatise (*c.* 727). Of nine homilies six treat of the Blessed Virgin, three *De Dormitione B. M. V.* (EP 3236 c). Many hymns have been attributed to him. An important liturgical treatise has been preserved under the misleading title *Hist. Eccl. et mystica contemplatio* (MG 98, 383/454); though it is spurious, it deserves to be more closely examined.

Edd.: MG 98, 39/454. — Cayré, DTC 6, 1300/9. N. Borgia, *Il comm. liturg. d. s. G. e la versione lat. di Anastasio Bibl.,* Grottaferrata 1912. Jerphanion, Bess 1919, 146/54 (on the spurious *Hist. eccl.*). Chevalier, Gr 1937, 372/7 (Marian sermons). Eustratiades, NS 1938, 370ff. (hymns). J. List, *Stud. zur Homiletik G. I. v. K. u. seiner Zeit,* At 1939. Carli, *Marianum* 3, 1941, 47/63 *(Assunz. B. M. V.).* Fecioru, *Biserica Ortod. Rom.* 64, 1946, 60/92, 180/93 (G. as a preacher); ibid. 386/97 (text of *Hom. in Annunt. B. M. V.,* missing in MG). M. Jugie, *La mort et l'assomption BMV,* R 1946, 226/33; *L'immaculée Conception,* R

1952, 114/9 (Mariol.). Papescu-Tierbinti, *Biserica Ortod. Rom.* 1948, 113/53 (on *Hist. eccl.*.). Duobuniotos, Θ 1950, 258/68 (on Epitome of the explanation of the Liturgy). Melchior, Mar 15, 1953, 195/230 *(Assumpt. B. M. V.)*. E. Perniola, *La mariologia de s. G.*, R 1954.

On the beginnings of the Iconoclastic Controversy: E. J. Martin, *A Hist. of the Iconocl. Controv.*, 1930. Caspar, ZKG 1933, 29ff. Bréhier, EO 1939, 17/22. Florovsky, CH 19, 1950, 77/96 (Origen, Eusebius and the Icon. Contr.). Ladner, DOP 1953, 1/34 (The concept of the image). Kitzinger, DOP 1955, 83/150 (Cult of Images before Iconocl.).

2. Four sermons of Cosmas Vestitor (before 740) are preserved only in Latin. They treat of the death and assumption of the BVM. and contain sometimes verbatim reminiscences of Germanus of Constantinople.

Cf. A. Wenger, REB 1953, 284/300.

3. John of Damascus (b. *c.* 675, d. 749?). We have only little reliable information on his life, since the *Vitae* (Greek and Arabic) which belong to the tenth and eleventh centuries are legendary. He came from a noble Christian family. He was born *c.* 675 at Damascus, which was then governed by the Caliph. He succeeded his father in the office of a *logothetes* or civil chief of the Christian population. He resigned his office for the sake of the faith and entered the Saba monastery near Jerusalem between 718 and 720, together with his adoptive brother Cosmas, who became Bishop of Majuma near Gaza in 743. John was ordained priest and devoted himself entirely to the spiritual life and his literary work.

He and St. Germanus were anathematized by the iconoclastic synod of 754; the Second (Seventh General) Council of Nicaea in 787 gave much praise to the two defenders of the veneration of images. Feast day: March 27, *Doctor ecclesiae* since 1890.

John was the last theologian of the early Greek Church whose outlook was universal. He was devoted to tradition and carried out his programme expressed in the words that he did not want to say anything of his own. Hence he cannot be numbered among the creative theologians who open up new ways of thought. Never-

theless he had an astonishingly versatile and constructive minc
capable of building up a coherent system from the most divers
materials. Though belonging to the late period, he mastered th
language and literary form to a remarkable degree. He wa
occupied not only with questions of dogmatic, moral anc
ascetic theology, but also with those of exegesis and history
Besides, he left excellent homilies and composed liturgica
hymns of lasting value (EP 2337/90; EA 1329/36).

a. He is most famous as the author of the *Source of Knowledg*
(Πηγὴ γνώσεως).

The work was written after 742 and is dedicated to Cosmas. I
is divided into three parts: 1. *Dialectica,* a philosophical introductio
to dogmatics which discusses especially the philosophical concept
which are taken from Aristotle and the Church Fathers. 2
A History of the Heresies which depends entirely on Ephiphanius
Theodoret and other sources known to us; only the presentatio
of the last three heresies (ch. 101/3: Islam, Iconoclasm, mysticism o
the Aposchites) is original, but probably added by another author
3. *De fide orthodoxa* (100 chs.) gives an independent summary c
the teaching of the Greek Fathers on the principal Christia
doctrines. This third part of the work was not, however, used a
the classical textbook of dogmatics by the Greek and Sla
orthodox Churches during the Middle Ages and until moder
times, though this has constantly been asserted. True, its influenc
on important medieval theologians was great, even though it i
only rarely cited. This third part is extant in two versions (the bette
one in MG) both of which probably go back to John of Damascu
himself.

In the West the third part was divided into four books, modelle
on the Sentences of Peter Lombard; I. On God, II. On Creatio
and Providence, III. On Christ, IV. Continuation of Christolog
on baptism and the eucharist, the veneration of saints and image
on the canon of Holy Scripture, on evil and the last things. I

the doctrine of God John follows above all Pseudo-Dionysius, for the Trinitarian theology he prefers Gregory of Nazianzus, for Christology Leontius of Byzantium, Maximus Confessor and Anastasius Sinaita, for the doctrine of creation Nemesius of Emesa.

b. Minor dogmatic writings. The following four treatises may be regarded as something like drafts for his principal work: *Institutio elementaris ad dogmata,* similar to the *Dialectica; Libellus de recta doctrina,* probably compiled for a converted Monothelite bishop (MG 94, 1421/32); a catechism *De sancta Trinitate;* a Creed preserved in Arabic translation. The last two works are not certainly genuine (MG 95, 9/18 and 417/38).

c. The following belong to the group of mostly short controversial writings: three *Orationes pro sacris imaginibus* (MG 96, 699/762), written between 726 and 730 may be regarded as a threefold version of the same theme occasioned by the changing political situation of the Church. They became the foundation for all later discussions on the veneration of images and relics.

Two treatises oppose Nestorianism, two Monophysitism, to which must be added as a third the letter on the Trisagion addressed to the Archimandrite Jordanes (v. supra § 72, 3, § 76, 5), one against Monothelitism, two against Manicheism and fragments of a treatise on dragons and sorceresses which combats superstitious ideas.

d. His exegetical work, a commentary on the Pauline Letters, is a compilation from Chrysostom, Theodoret and Cyril of Alexandria.

e. His principal work on moral and ascetical theology is the three books of *Sacra Parallela,* a very large collection of maxims and devotional texts on the Christian life from the Holy Scriptures and the Fathers of the Church. Recent scholars, however, do not consider its authenticity to be beyond doubt. It cites about 5–6000 patristic testimonia of which scarcely a quarter has so far been identified. The first two books have been preserved, even though in drastically abridged form (1. God and his action; 2. Man and his life), and besides two shorter versions of the work in which, however, the original elaborate structure of the whole has been abandoned. The following three short ascetical treatises belong to the same group of writings: *De octo spiritibus nequitiae,* i.e. on the eight capital sins; *De virtutibus et vitiis, De sacris jejuniis,* on the duration of the Lenten fast in the various Churches.

f. Of the thirteen homilies printed in MG 96, 545/816, to which must be added certain other texts extant only in MS, the following can be provisionally considered as genuine. Hom. 1 *In Nativ. B.M.V.* (MG 96, 661/80); *In ficum arefactum* (96, 575/88); *In Sabb. Sanctum* (601/44); *In Transfig. Dni.* (545/76); further three sermons Εἰς τὴν κοίμησιν, i.e. on Mary's assumption into heaven (699/762); cf. supra § 22, 6; § 107, 1. The second of these sermons contains an account from the so-called *Hist. Euthymiaca* (ch. 18), which has long been recognized as an interpolation; cf. Hoeck, OCP 1951, 44f. Also three further genuine sermons (two of these not yet edited): *Hom. in Dominica Palmarum, In Nativ. Dni.* and *In Hypapanten Dni.*

g. John is also the author of hagiographical writings and liturgical encomia. The following have now been recognized as certainly genuine: one *Encomium in s. Anastasiam* (ined.), a *Passio s. Artemii,* an *Encomium in s. Barbaram,* a *Passio s. Catharinae* (lost) and an *Encomium in s. Joannem Chrysostomum.*

h. John continues to be famous in the Greek Church also for his partly metrical, partly rhythmic hymns. They are full of vigour and warm feeling and celebrate mostly feasts of the Lord. His *canones* are particularly famous; they are poems consisting of nine odes that differ in their metrical structure as well as in their tunes. The *Octoechos* (v. supra § 101, 1 d), too, which as a whole is of later origin, contains not a few hymns composed by him.

However, the examination of the authenticity of the hymns attributed to John will not be concluded for a long time. The views on the number of his genuine poetic works vary from hardly a dozen to more than 1200 (Hoeck, OCP 1951, 53).

i. The *Vita Barlaam et Joasaph,* a romance written in picturesque language, using and cleverly transforming Indian legends glorifying Buddha. In the Middle Ages it became a widely read Christian book of popular devotion. The hero of the legend is an Indian prince Joasaph whom a hermit Barlaam converts to Christianity despite the intrigues of his father and who finally, having become king, converts his whole kingdom to the faith; he dies a hermit.

The most recent view, that the author of the legend was a Greek monk of the end of the tenth century who incorporated in his work, among other material, the *Apologia* of Aristides (§ 20, 2), must be abandoned. According to this view the monk used as his model which he developed a story translated by Euthymius of Iviron from the Georgian or the Greek. F. Doelger has proved, in a discussion with H. Zotenberg (1886) and P. Peeters (1931), that the authorship of John of Damascus can be recognized in the identity of the theological and polemical points of view as well as in the agreement with his theological formulae and the characteristic elements of his composition and style.

On the criticism of this well-founded result cf. Halkin, AB 1953, 475/80; Laurdas, EEBS 1954, 383f.; Tarchnisvili, OC 38, 1954, 113/24; D. M. Lang, BullSchoolOrAfricanStud 17, Lo 1955, 306/25; Downey, Sp 1956, 165/70; cf. Doelger, BZ 1955, 215; 1956, 181, who will reply in detail.

k. Spurious writings. *On the Faithful Departed* shows how the dead can be assisted by prayer, Mass and almsgiving. The *Epistola de confessione* which attributes the power to give absolution also to monks who are not priests (supra § 100, 4) is the work of Simeon the "New Theologian" (d. 1022). On numerous other spurious or dubious writings cf. Hoeck, OCP 1951, 18ff.

Edd.: M. le Quien, 2 vols., P 1712. MG 94/6. Dyobuniotes, EPh 1914, 53/69,

119/49. Diekamp, TQ 1901, 555/95 (against Nestor.). *Barlaam and Joasaph,* ed. with trans. G. R. Woodward and H. Mattingley, Lo 1014. A crit. ed. of all the works is being prepared by the Byzant. Instit. of Scheyern - Ettal (J. Hoeck and F. Doelger). — Transs.: D. Stiefenhofer (BKV² 44) 1923 *(Fid. orth.).* L. Burchard, Mn 1924 *(Baarl. and Joas.).* R. I. Szigeti, *Trans. lat. J. Damii* (*Fid. orth.* 3, 1–8), Budapest 1940, cf. Haring, MedievStud 12, 1950, 214f. Peradze, OC 1931, 240/2 (Georg. trans.). Calari, Atti R. Ist. Ven. 100 II, 1940/1, 197/240 *(Burgundio Pis.).* Graf I, 377/9, 546f. — Mgg.: V. Ermoni, P 1904. Phokylides, EPh 1922, 357/440. D. Fecioru, Bucharest 1935 (Greek). Leclercq, DAL 7, 2186/90. Jugie, DTC 8, 693/751; EO 1924, 137/61; LTK 5, 488/91. — Studies: K. Holl (TU 16, 1) 1896; (20, 2) 1899 *(Sacra Parall.).* Chevalier, Gr 1937, 361/88 (Marian serm.). J. Nasrallah, *S. J. de D. Son époque—sa vie—son œuvre,* Harissa 1950; cf. TR 1952, 153. Merrill, *The Muslim World* 51, 1951, 88/97 (no detailed knowledge of Koran). Garitte, Mu 1954, 71/92 (Georg. vita of Stephen Sabbaita; 749 not year of J. D.'s death). Doelger, Byz. 1950, 303/14 and Hoeck, OCP 1951, 5/60 (on research). Eustratiades, NS 1931/3; Θ 1938, 60/3 (hymns). Baumstark, OC 36, 1941, 205/23 (Pentecost canon in Syr. trans.). Hussey, JTS 1946, 200/3 (6 hymns in MG 96 belong to John Mauropus). Hoeg-Tillyard-Wellesz, *Monumenta musicae byz.: The Hymns of the Octoechus Pars I and II,* Copenhagen 1940/9. T. Hydes, *Die jambischen Kanones des J. v. D.,* At 1948; *Ueber die J. v. D. zugeschriebenen Idiomela der Totenliturgie,* At 1950; cf. BZ 1950, 418. A. Laily, *L'infl. liturg. et musicale de J. de D.,* Harissa 1950. B. Studer, *Die theol. Arbeitsweise des J. D.,* Ettal 1956. B. Kotter, *Die hsl. Ueberlieferung der Pege gnoseos des hl. J. D.,* thesis typed Mn 1956. Rozemond, *La christologie de S. Jean Dam.,* Ettal 1959.

On *Barl. and Joas.:* Van den Gheyn DTC 2, 410/6. Bardy, DHG 6, 813/5. H. Haas, *Buddha i. d. abendl. Legende?* 1923, 31ff. Peeters, AB 1931, 276/312 (The Georg. monk Euthymius [978] author of the Gr. model); cf. Wolff, HTR 1939, 131/9. Jullian, MAH 1931, 170/84 (sculpture). Stefanescu, Byz 7, 1932, 347/69 (paintings). H. Zotenberg, *Notice sur le livre de B. et J. . . .,* P 1935 (new impress.). D. Nersessian, *L'illustration du roman de B. et J.,* 1937. J. Sonet, *Le roman de B. et J.,* I: *Recherches sur la trad. manuscrite lat. et franc.,* Lou 1949; II: *La Version anonyme franc. Texte crit.,* Namur 1950. Bacht, RACh 1, 1193/1200. F. Doelger, *Der griech. Barlaam-Roman. Ein Werk des hl. J. v. D.,* 1953. Tarchnisvili, OC 38, 1954, 113/24 (Euthymius of Iviron). Spurious writings: I. Hausherr et G. Horn, OC 12, 1928 (Symeon the New Theol.); EO 1928, 163/7; 1933, 231. H. Biedermann, *Symeon der Neue Theol.,* Wu 1950. Pfister-Riedinger, BZ 1955, 86/8 (on spur. *Ep. ad Theophilum:* MG 95, 368).

On Influence: Dausend, TQ 1937, 173/92 (J. in Salimbene). De Ghellinck, *Mouvement* 1948, 374/415 (in the W.). G. Hofmann, OCP 1950, 177/90 (in E. and W. 1054–1500). Trypanis, *Medium Aevum* 19, 1950, 43/9 (Dante and a Byzant. Treatise on Virtues and Vices. MG 95, 85/98). Buytaert, FrancisStud 1951, 49/67 (*De orth. fid.* 3, 1/8); 1953, 17/70 (MSS of Burgundio). O. A. Colligan, *St. J. D.* (*Dialectica* in the trans. of R. Grosseteste) ed. NY-Lou-Pa 1953. E. M. Buytaert, *St. John Dam., De fide orth. Versions of Burgundio and Cerbanus,* Lou 1955.

Points of Doctrine

1. Scripture and Tradition. John does not include the deutero-canonical writings of the O.T. in his canon; he includes also the Apostolic Canons in the N.T. (v. supra § 7, 5; *Fid. orth.* 4, 17; EP 2373). Besides Holy Scripture he also admits the unwritten tradition. Thus the threefold immersion in baptism, the prayer facing the East, and the veneration of the Holy Cross and the images are consecrated by tradition. He also considers the unanimous teaching of the Fathers as binding (*Imag.* 1, 23; 2, 16; 1, 1; 2, 4).

2. In Christology he differentiates like Leontius (supra § 102, 3), between ἐνυπόστατον and ἀνυπόστατον *(accidens)* teaching that the human nature of Christ subsists in the Logos (*Fid. orth.* 3, 9). Because of the hypostatic union, the soul of Christ possessed all wisdom from the beginning; hence there was no real progress in its knowledge, and therefore Lk. 2:52 is to be understood only from the manifestation of the wisdom dwelling in Christ (ibid. 3, 22; EP 2368).

3. The Holy Spirit proceeds from the Father and "rests in the Son". John does not object to him being called the Spirit of the Son as well as of the Father; not because he proceeds from the Son, but because he proceeds through the Son from the Father (*Fid. orth.* 1, 8 12).

4. The angels are incorporeal, and, before their temptation, could be moved to evil only with difficulty. Now they are immovable, not, however, by nature but by grace. They are divided into nine choirs or three triads; they protect the continents, preside over nations and places, and help us in our concerns (*Fid. orth.* 2, 3; EP 2350/6).

5. Veneration of Mary and the Saints. *Latria* and *proskynesis* are due only to God, the Creator. Since Mary is *Theotokos,* in whose bodily assumption John believes *(Fid. orth)*, she is venerated by *proskynesis,* as are also the saints because they are God's chosen friends (*Imag.* 3 41; EP 2378).

6. Veneration of Images. John restricts the O.T. prohibition of images to the presentation of the invisible God as such, for which contemporary Greek art had only symbols, not pictures in human form, and to the adoration *(latria)* of images; Christ, however, might be represented by images. The veneration given to the images is not absolute, but refers to the person represented (*Imag.* 1, 21). The images are useful, because they present the facts of the redemption and the virtues of the saints and thus serve as books for the illiterate (1, 17).

7. Eschatology. Like Ambrose (*Lk.* 7, 205) he does not think that the fire of hell is material fire (οὐχ ὑλικόν, *Fid. orth.* 4, 27). Jerome, too, testified that this was the view of many (*Eph.* 3, 5, 6; EP 1370. 2376; supra § 86, 5).

Jugie, DTC 8, 708/48. J. Bilz, *Die Trinitaetslehre des hl. J. v. D.*, 1909. J. Graef, *Die Psychol. des J. D.*, 1923. V. A. Mitchel, *The Mariology of St. J. D.*, Kirkwood 1930. Lottin, RT 1931, 631/61 *(La psychol. de l'acte humain)*. C. Chevalier, *La mariologie de s. J. D.* (OC n. 109) 1936; cf. Grumel, EO 1937, 318/46. H. Menges, *Die Bilderlehre des hl. J. v. D.*, 1937. Bonfiglioli, SC 1939, 423/50, 554/73 *(peccato originale)*. M. Francesconi, *La dottr. del D. sulla predestinaz.*, R 1945. Nersessian, Byz 17, 1944/5, 58/87 (question of images in 7th cent.). Gross, ZRGG 1935, 118/53 (J. knows no orig. sin but only consequences of the first sin). Ladner, DOP 1953, 3/34 (images to J. D.). J. Meany, *The Image of God in Man acc. to the Doctr. of J. D.*, Manila 1954. Grondijs, *Actes du VIe Congr. Intern. Ét. Byz.* (P 1948) 2 1951, 145/70 (veneration of images in J. D., Nicephorus and Theod. Stud.). Ferroni, Mar 17, 1955, 1/36 *(Maria cooperatrice e mediatrice)*.

8. In the MS tradition there occurs a Bishop John of Euboea also called John, μοναχὸς καὶ πρεσβύτερος Εὐβοίας, a younger contemporary of John of Damascus. Doelger thinks that he came from a place near Damascus. So far three homilies (MG 96, 1459, 1508 and AB 1949, 19/26) and two as yet inedited panegyrics on St. Paraskeue and St. Anastasia may be assigned to him. A dubious Christmas sermon (ed. Eustradiades Νέος ποιμήν 3, 1921, 23/42) belongs probably to John of Damascus. John of Euboea shows himself as a popular, lively preacher who frequently sharply attacks the Jews.

F. Doelger, AB 1949, 5/26.

§ 108. POETS

On the History of the Greek Church hymns in general. Edd.: W. Christ and M. Paranikas, *Anthologia graeca carminum christ.*, L 1871. J. B. Pitra, *Analecta sacra*, P 1, 1876. P. Maas (KlT 52/3) [2]1931. N. Borgia, *Frammenti eucaristici antichissimi*, Grottaferrata 1932; cf. Pantelakis, At 1933 (RHE 1933, 1077); BZ 1936, 208. — Studies: E. Bouvy, *Poètes et mélodes*, Nîmes 1886. Maas, BZ 1910, 285/306 *(Kontakion)*. C. Emerau, *Hymnographi byz.* in EO 1921/6. Wellesz, BZ 1933, 33/66 (rhythm. in Byz. tunes). Pantelakis, Θ 1937, 223/39 and cont. cf. BZ 1938, 220f. W. Tillyard, *Handbook of the Middle Byz. Music Notation*, Copenhagen 1935; *The Hymns of the Sticher for Nov.*, 1938; cf. Georgiades, BZ 1939, 67/88. E. Wellesz, *Die Hymnen des Stich. f. Sept.*, 1936. T. Nissen, *Die byz. Anakreonteen* (SbMn 1940, 3). Kunz, BZ 1941, 40/4 (The 3 oldest Epiph.-trop.). Tillyard, *Monum. mus. byz.* (Hymns of the Octoechus, 2 vols., 1940/9. R. Cantarella, *Poeti Bizant.*, 2 vols. (comm. and trans.), Mi 1948. Smothers, *Mél. de Ghellinck* 1951, 1, 321/44 (date of 4 unknown hymns).

1. Romanus Melodus (ὁ μελῳδός), the greatest early Byzantine poet, born at Emesa (Syria) *c.* 490. He was a deacon at the church of the Anastasis in Constantinople; d. *c.* 560. He is said to have composed about 1000 hymns. Of the eighty-five hymns *(kontakia)* assigned to him in the MSS sixty-one have so far been edited; about twenty of these are judged to be spurious (BZ 1953, 139).

His hymns which also came to be used in the liturgy have mostly twenty-four or more strophes. They take account only of the free rhythm of the accent of the words, no longer of the quantity of the syllables which is used only in poetry destined for a public trained in aesthetics and literature (e.g. in the poems of Sophronius, Ps.-Maximus, George Pisidas). His hymns for Christmas and Easter are especially beautiful. Since the tenth century Romanus has been recognized as the classical poet of the Church.

Edd.: J. B. Pitra (v. supra) 1876 (29 hymns). Maas, BZ 24, 1923/4, 1/13 (Christmas hymns). G. Camelli, *R. il melode*, Fl 1930 (8 hymns with trans.). On the ed. of Eustratiades cf. BZ 1933, 426f.; 1936, 476; 1940, 264f.; 1950, 104. Kadri, Al-M 1948, 66/80, 199/214, 413/33 (3 hymns). N. B. Tomadakes, 2 vols., At 1952/4; cf. BZ 1952, 454f.; 1953, 139f.; 1954, 212 (ed. Komines), 1955, 142/54 (Joannou against ed. of Tomadakes); BZ 1955, 114 (on ed. Tomadakes); BZ 1955, 453 (Tomad. against Joannou); cf. BZ 1956, 179. — Studies: K. Krumbacher, SbMn 1898/9, 1901, 1903; AbhMn 1907. On the work of P. Blastos 1934/5 cf. BNJ 12,

1936, 202. Amann, DTC 13, 2895/8. M. Carpenter, *R. and the Mystery Play of the East,* Univ. of Missouri (Col.) 1936. E. Mioni, *Atti R. Ist. Veneto* 96, 1936/7, 2, 23/87 (hymn on Archangel Michael); *R. il Melode, Saggio critico e 10 inni inediti,* Tu 1937. Chevalier, RSR 1938, 48/71 (Mariology). Baud-Bovy, Byz 13, 1938, 217/26 *(prélude),* 321/34 *(sacrifice d'Abraham).* On 2 notices of Maas and Kunz cf. BZ 1940, 511. Sophronios, EEBS 1939, 182/255 (comprehensive appreciation). Mioni, StBizNeoell 5, 1939, 507/13 (MSS). Peters, OCP 1942, 468/76 (R. depends on Greek *Diatessaron*). E. Bickersteth, *Actes du VIe Congr. Intern. Ét. Byz.* (P 1948) 1, 1950, 375/81 (sources of *kontakion* on *Hypapante*). BZ 1950, 417 (T. Hydes). BZ 1953, 222 (Nicopoulos). Eustratiades, EEBS 1955, 211/83; cf. BZ 1956, 476.

2. The 'Ακάθιστος hymn, which was sung standing, like the *Te Deum* of the West, is perhaps the most famous liturgical hymn of the Greek Church, a song of joy in praise of Mary (twenty-four strophes). The author has not so far been established with certainty. Several names have been suggested, George Pisidas, the two Patriarchs of Constantinople, Sergius (610–38), the father of Monothelitism, and Germanus (715–30). At present Romanus is fairly unanimously recognized as the author.

Edd.: MG 92, 1335/48. Pitra 1 (v. supra). — Recent lit. in BZ 1928, 420; 1936, 476; 1940, 265. F. Doelger, BZ 1933, 380 (for Rom.). Germ.: BM 1939, 262/5. Peeters, Mu 1940, 89/104 (Arab. trans.). McNabb, O 1947 (Engl. trans.). BZ 1950, 417 (Hydes 1947). C. del Grande, *D'Inno Acatisto,* Fl 1948 (Rom.). A. Pertozzi, *Der Akathistos,* thesis Greg. R 1948 (Rom.). E. Mercenier, *La prière des Églises de rite byz.* II 2, 1949 (ch. 2 on *Akath.*); cf. Doelger, TR 1951, 24 (Rom.). BZ 1950, 417 and 1956, 179 (Hydes). Huglo, Mu 1951, 27/61 (Lat. trans. of *Akath.*: 9th cent.). Wellesz, DOP 9/10, 1956, 141/74 (structure and music of Ak.; author probably Rom.).

3. It remains uncertain whether Anastasius, the author of a beautiful funeral hymn (ed. Pitra 1, 242/9) is to be identified with Anastasius Sinaita (Petrides, ROC 1901, 444/52).

4. George of Pisidia, deacon at Constantinople in the time of the Emperor Heraclius (610–41) treats mostly profane subjects (Persian wars of Heraclius, his victory over Chosroes II, the recovery of the Holy Cross, the attack on Constantinople by the Avari) in his poems, which are of great literary value. The following are, among others, concerned with theological subjects: his *Hexaemeron* (1894 lines) on the creation of the world,

De vanitate vitae (262 lines), *Contra Severum* (726 lines), against Monophysitism, and Epigrams.

Edd.: MG 92, 1197/1754. — Stephanou, DTC 12, 2130/4. Nissen, Her 1940, 298/325 (hist., epic and paneg.). Gigante, BollBadiaGrottaferrata 7, 1953, 44/6 (*Hexaem.* 380/97). Pertusi, Aev 1956, 395/427 (lost poems of G. of Pis.).

5. Andrew of Crete, Bishop at Damascus *c.* 660, monk in Jerusalem in 678, deacon in Constantinople 685. He became Archbishop of Gortina in Crete *c.* 692 and defended the veneration of images (d. 740). He left twenty-three sermons (among them three on the assumption of Mary) which establish him as a first-class orator, also many *idiomela* (short songs with their own tunes), and as the author of the so-called *canones* (v. supra § 107 g) became the inventor of a new kind of hymn. His *Great Canon* is particularly famous; it is a penitential hymn of 250 strophes which still retains its place in the Eastern liturgy.

Ed.: MG 97, 805/1444. — Studies: Petit, DAL 1, 2034/41. Emereau, EO 1922, 267/71. Mg. by S. Eustratiades, NS 1934, 673/88; 1935, 3/10 and cont. Further items in BNJ 10, 1933, 433. Chevalier, Gr 1937, 68/372 (Marian sermons). O. Bardenhewer, *Marienpredigten aus d. Vaeterzeit,* 1934, 118/30. Nissen, Phil 1937, 177/98 (serm. *De vita hum.*); 382/5 (text. crit.). BZ 1950, 105 (Laurdas: first ed. of an *Encomium*). BZ 1951, 418 (Hydes: on the *Great Canon*). P. K. Chrestos, thesis Th 1952 (on the *Great Can.*); cf. BZ 1953, 447. BZ 1952, 456 (V. Iljine: *Great Can.* 711/3). BZ 1953, 447 (Mercenier: new impress. of parts of some canons). Sanz, JahrbOesterreichByzGes 4, 1955 (fragm. of a new canon).

6. Cosmas Melodus wrote, like his adoptive brother John of Damascus, *idiomela* and at least fourteen canons after the example of Andrew of Crete, which were later highly esteemed despite the very artificial structure of their verses. It is difficult to distinguish between genuine and spurious works, because the teacher of the two, Cosmas the Elder, is also said to have composed religious hymns. A commentary on the poems of Gregory of Nazianzus is also attributed to Cosmas Melodus.

Edd.: MG 98, 459/624. Christ-Paranikas (v. supra) 161/204. — Studies: T. Sinko, *De tradit. Orationum G.i Naz.* 2, 1923, 31/6 (comm. in Gr. of Naz.). Tillyard, BZ 1928, 25/37 (Can. on Exaltation of Cross). Lauriotes, 1931, 340/9 and cont. (ined.). Eustratiades, NZ 1933, 83/99 and cont. BZ 1950, 418 (Hydes on seven canons on feasts of Christ).

Index

ALFRED WIKENHAUSER

Pauline Mysticism

Christ in the Mystical Teaching of St. Paul

"This is an important book. No serious study of Pauline theology is possible without a grasp of its principles. The analysis of pertinent texts is thorough and clear. Contrary opinions are stated fairly and evaluated honestly. The sections on comparative religions are handled with skill. Here are insights of rare beauty and passages of unforgettable power."

Mother Kathryn Sullivan, Purchase, N.Y.

"This little book on *Pauline Mysticism* is spirituality on a high scholarly level, and a rewarding experience for serious readers who have more than a passing acquaintance with St. Paul." *Cross and Crown*, St. Louis, Mo.

LUCIEN CERFAUX

Christ in the Theology of St. Paul

The purpose of this book is to show the gradual evolution of St. Paul's Christological thought. Mgr. Cerfaux provides a true picture of St. Paul's work by dividing it into three parts, following the chronological order of the Epistles, and sees each part as distinct attempt by St. Paul to form a synthesis.

"The approach is so refreshingly different that even veteran students of St. Paul will find this work excitingly thought-provoking."

Catholic Biblical Quarterly, Denver, Col.

LUCIEN CERFAUX

The Church in the Theology of St. Paul

The author distinguishes three phases in St. Paul's thought, the first depending on concepts inherited from Judaism with which is linked the formula of the primitive Jerusalem community; the second on his Christian experience and the life of the churches he had founded; the third assimilating and transforming the foregoing in the light of his maturest theology.

"There is no doubt that Cerfaux's book marks an epoch in the theology of the Church." *Theological Studies*, Woodstock, Md.

"Profound, lucid and scholarly." *Blackfriars*, Oxford